Travel Rule #1:
When kids smile,
you relax.

Holiday Inn®
LOOK AGAIN.™

At Holiday Inn®, we know it's easy to make kids happy when you travel: a sparkling pool, a comfy bed, and room to explore. That's why our hotels offer even more to please tiny travelers and grown-up adventurers.

www.holidayinn.com/aaa

- Kids Eat & Stay Free*
- Swimming pools
- Free high-speed Internet access
- Fresh, cooked to order breakfast available

PRIORITYCLUB. REWARDS Earn points or miles. | **BOOK WITH CONFIDENCE**® 1-800-734-4275

*Kids Eat Free is available for kids age 12 and under. Call hotel or see www.holidayinn.com for details. For complete Priority Club® Rewards terms & conditions, visit priorityclub.com or call 1-888-211-9874. ©2006 InterContinental® Hotels Group. All rights reserved. Most hotels are independently owned and/or operated.

I ♥ NY®

turns 30 this year.

Get your official **2007 New York State Travel Guide,** with hundreds of ideas to help you plan your celebration.

For your free guide,

call 800/I LOVE NY or go to aaa.iloveny.com

Where will *you* celebrate?

I ♥ NY® 1977 - 2007

New York

Are we meeting your travel·needs?
Send written comments to:

AAA Member Comments
1000 AAA Drive, Box 61
Heathrow, FL 32746-5063

Published by AAA Publishing
1000 AAA Drive
Heathrow, FL 32746-5063
Copyright AAA 2007

**Advertising Rate and Circulation
Information: (407) 444-8280**

**Printed in the USA by
Quebecor World, Buffalo, NY**

*Photo Credit: (Cover & Title Page)
Adirondack Mountains,
near Lake Placid
© James Randklev Photography*

Printed on recyclable paper.
Please recycle whenever possible.

Mixed Sources
Product group from well-managed
forests and other controlled sources
www.fsc.org Cert no. SW-COC-1610
© 1996 Forest Stewardship Council
FSC

Stock #4618

New York

Featured Information

4

Find Hotels As Easy As 1-2-3-4-5!

For reliable hotel stays matched to your needs, every time, use AAA's valuable two-part rating system:

- First, rest assured that *every* hotel designated **AAA Approved** upholds qualities important to members – cleanliness, service, and value.

- Focus your selection using the descriptive one-to-five **AAA Diamond Ratings** assigned exclusively to Approved properties to help you match your expectations.

Find AAA Approved and Diamond rated properties in the TourBook®, in print and on aaa.com. Look for the AAA logo on signage and billboards.

Read about **AAA Diamond Ratings** on page 20-21 or visit aaa.com/Diamonds.

Show Your Card
Approved Lodging

For hotel reservations and vacation planning, get right to the point on *aaa*•*com*. Reserve AAA approved and Diamond rated hotels at the lowest online prices. Plus, enjoy these additional tools and benefits:

AAA.com TourBook® – Find thousands of AAA Approved and Diamond rated hotels and restaurants, plus destinations, attractions, & events.

AAA.com TripTik® – Get complete trip routings with hotel reservations, sightseeing stops, member discount locations, and more.

AAA Drive Trips – Enjoy nearly 100 flexible, preplanned driving itineraries for popular destinations.

Vacation Getaways – Get exclusive benefits on flights, tours, cruises, and Disney vacation packages from AAA's Preferred Travel Partners.

Hertz – Save up to 20% on car rental.

Show Your Card & Save® – Search for exclusive member savings at 150,000 locations worldwide at AAA.com/save.

AAA Travel Money – Get no-fee travelers cheques, foreign currency, and prepaid cards.

Books – Save 5% on AAA travel publications at aaa.com/barnesandnoble.

AAA Credit Card – Get up to 5% gas rebate.

AAA Approved Auto Repair – Find reliable service facilities at home and away.

Plan your next trip on *aaa*•*com* — the only travel Web site backed by thousands of highly trained travel professionals at more than 1,000 AAA/CAA offices!

aaa•com
Plan to go.

Products and services available through participating AAA and CAA clubs.

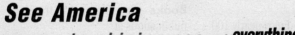

Attractions, lodgings and restaurants are listed on the basis of merit alone after careful evaluation and approval by one of AAA/CAA's full-time, professionally trained Tourism Editors. Evaluations are unannounced to ensure that we see an establishment just as you would see it.

An establishment's decision to advertise in the TourBook guide has no bearing on its evaluation or rating. Advertising for services or products does not imply AAA endorsement.

All information in this guide was reviewed for accuracy before publication. However, since changes inevitably occur between annual editions, we suggest you work with your AAA travel professional or check on AAA.com to confirm prices and schedules.

How the TourBook Guide is Organized

The TourBook guide is organized into three distinct sections.

The **Points of Interest** section helps you plan daily activities and sightseeing excursions and provides details about the city or attraction you are visiting.

The **Lodgings and Restaurants** section helps you select AAA Approved accommodations and dining facilities meeting your specific needs and expectations.

The **Reference** section provides indexes for locating information within this guide and items to aid the trip planning process.

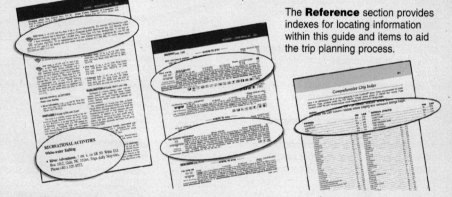

Locating the Attractions, Lodgings and Restaurants

Attractions, lodgings and restaurants are listed under the city in which they physically are located - or in some cases under the nearest recognized city. Most listings are alphabetically organized by state, province, region or island, then by city and establishment name.

A color is assigned to each state or province so that you can match the color bars at the top of the page to switch from the **Points of Interest** section to the **Lodgings and Restaurants** section.

Spotting maps help you physically locate points of interest, lodgings and restaurants in the major destinations.

The Comprehensive City Index located in the **Reference** section contains an A-to-Z list of cities.

Destination Cities and Destination Areas

Destination cities, established based on government models and local expertise, include metropolitan areas plus nearby vicinity cities. **Destination areas** are regions with broad tourist appeal; several cities will comprise the area.

If a city falls within a destination's vicinity, the city name will appear at its alphabetical location in the book, and a cross reference will give you the exact page on which listings for that city begin.

An orientation map appears at the beginning of each destination section to orient you to that destination.

Understanding the Points of Interest Listing

GEM Designation

A ⬥ indicates the attraction has been rated a AAA GEM, a "must see" point of interest that offers a *Great Experience for Members®*. These attractions have been judged to be of exceptional interest and quality by AAA Tourism Editors.

A GEM listing page with a brief description of individual GEM attractions follows the Orientation map near the beginning of each state or province Points of Interest section. Cross-references guide the reader to the attraction's listing page.

Discount Savings

The SAVE icon denotes those attractions offering AAA/CAA, AAA MasterCard, AAA VISA or international Show Your Card & Save discount cardholders a discount off the attraction's standard admission. Present your card at the attraction's admission desk.

A list of participating points of interest appears in the Reference section of this guide.

Shopping establishments preceded by a SAVE icon also provide to AAA/CAA members a discount and/or gift with purchase; present your card at the mall's customer service center to receive your benefit.

Exceptions

- Members should inquire in advance concerning the validity of the discount for special rates.
- The SAVE discount may not be used in conjunction with other discounts.
- Attractions that already provide a reduced senior or child rate may not honor the SAVE discount for those age groups.
- All offers are subject to change and may not apply during special events, particular days or seasons or for the entire validity period of the TourBook guide.

Shopping areas: Mast General Store, 630 W. King St., operates out of a 1913 building, stocked with a variety of goods ... Swain Box 5

⬥ SAVE **RED OAK,** is off I-95 exit 4A, just n. to Dogwood restored 1812 house has eight 60-foot columns and Allow 1 hour minimum. Daily 9-5, Apr. 1-Labor Da Labor Day-Nov. 30; by appointment rest of year. Cl 6-12, $5; ages 2-5, $4; family rate (two adults and two child 5555 or (800) 555-5555.

⬥ SAVE **RED OAK,** is off I-95 exit 4A, just n. to Dogwood Dr., then 2 mi. e. to 610 Magnolia St. The restored 1812 house has eight 60-foot columns and is furnished in period. Costumed guides demonstrate the 1812 lifestyle. Allow 1 hour minimum. Daily 9-5, Apr. 1-Labor Day; Thurs.-Sun. 9-5, Feb.-Mar. 31 and day after Labor Day-Nov. 30; by appointment rest of year. Closed holidays. Admission $8; over 65 and ages 6-12, $5; ages 2-5, $4; family rate (two adults and two children) $12. DS, MC, VI. ($10). Phone (828) 555-5555 or (800) 555-5555.

RECREATIONAL ACTIVITIES
White-water Rafting

- **River Adventures,** 1 mi. s. on SR 50. Write P.O. Box 1012, Gale, NC 35244. Trips daily May-Oct. Phone (828) 555-5555.

BREVARD (F-3) pop. 6,789, elev. 2,229'

The town is a popular summer resort at the entrance to Pisgah National Forest (*see place listing* p. 165). Brevard is in an area known as the "Land of Waterfalls," sporting more than 250 named waterfalls such as Laughing Falls and Courthouse Falls. Brevard Music Center offers concerts nightly last weekend in June to mid-August.

Brevard is ...

RECREATIONAL ACTIVIT
White-water Rafting

- **River Adventures,** 1 mi. s. Box 1012, Gale, NC 35244. Phone (828) 555-5555.

Directions

Unless otherwise specified, directions are given from the center of town, using the following highway designations:

I=interstate highway	**US**=federal highway
SR=state route	**CR**=county road
FM=farm to market	**FR**=forest road
Mex.=Mexican highway	**Hwy.**=Canadian or Caribbean highway

Prices and Dates of Operations

Admission prices are quoted without sales tax. Children under the lowest age specified are admitted free when accompanied by an adult. Days, months and age groups written with a hyphen are inclusive.

Prices pertaining to points of interest in the United States are quoted in U.S. dollars; points of interest in Canada are quoted in Canadian dollars; prices for points of interest in Mexico and the Caribbean are quoted as an approximate U.S. dollar equivalent.

Credit Cards Accepted

AX=American Express	**JC**=Japan Credit Bureau
CB=Carte Blanche	**MC**=MasterCard
DC=Diners Club	**VI**=VISA
DS=Discover	

Bulleted Listings

Casino gambling establishments are visited by AAA personnel to ensure safety; casinos within hotels are presented for member information regardless of whether the lodging is AAA Approved.

Recreational activities of a participatory nature (requiring physical exertion or special skills) are not inspected.

Wineries are inspected by AAA Tourism Editors to ensure they meet listing requirements and offer tours.

All are presented in an abbreviated bulleted format for informational purposes.

NE — BURLINGTON, NC   125

Chamber of Commerce: P.O.
on City, NC 28713; phone (828)

hen 2 mi. e. to 610 Magnolia St. The
shed in period. Costumed guided tours.
s.-Sun. 9-5, Feb.-Mar. 31 and day after
lidays. Admission $8, over 65 and ages
2. DS, MC, VI. ($10). Phone (828) 555-

19W. Write
y. 19W, Bryson City, NC 28713. Trips
y-Sept. Phone (828) 488-9366 or (800)

ft, 12 mi. s. on US 19W. Write 11044
W, Bryson City, NC 28713. Trips daily
pt. Phone (828) 488-3316 or (800)
8.

ater Ltd., 12 mi. s.w. on US 19/74W.
P.O. Box 309, Long Creek, SC 29658.
daily Apr.-Oct. Phone (828) 488-2384 or
51-9972. *See color ads starting on p. 146.*

NGTON (B-5) pop. 44,917, elev. 656'
ngton is a textile industry center with nu-
factory outlet shops that attract bargain
from nearby states. Clothing, leather goods,
blankets, sheets, carpets and furniture are
products.

centerpiece of 76-acre City Park, at South
Street and Overbrook Road, is a 1910 Dent-
enagerie Carousel. Known for their detail and
te carvings, only 14 such carousels still exist
wide. In addition to 26 horses, the hand-
d animals include a lion, tiger, giraffe and re-
r, four pigs, rabbits, ostriches and cats. The
sel operates seasonally and hours vary; phone
222-5030.

ngton/Alamance County Convention and
eau: 610 S. Lexington Ave., P.O.
ington, NC 27216-0519; phone
637-3804.

ington Manufacturer's
r 145, houses more

TATE HISTORIC
5 mi. s.w. on SR
e between Royal-
tia and an inexpe-
ners known as the
xes, corrupt officials
John Allen house, a log

50. Write P.O.
daily May-Oct.

Understanding the Lodging Listing

Official Appointment

AAA or **CAA** indicates our Official Appointment (OA) lodgings. These properties guarantee members the lowest public rate available at the time of booking for the dates of stay or a minimum 10% discount off the standard room rates published in TourBook guides. We highlight these properties with red and a SAVE icon to help you quickly identify them.

Diamond Rating

The number of diamonds informs you of the overall complexity of a lodging's amenities and service. Red indicates an Official Appointment lodging. An **fyi** in place of diamonds indicates the property has not been rated but is included as an "information only" service. A detailed description of each rating level appears on page 20.

Classification

All diamond rated lodgings are classified using three key elements: style of operation, overall concept and service level. See pages 22-23 for details on our classifications.

Online Reservations

This notation indicates AAA/CAA members can conveniently check room availability, validate room rates and make reservations for this property in a secure online environment at AAA.com.

Rates

Shown from left to right: dates the rates are effective; any meal plan included in the rates (see below); standard room rates for 1 person (1P) or 2 persons (2P); extra person charge (XP); and any applicable family plan indicator (see below).

Rates are provided to AAA by each lodging and represent the regular (rack) rate ranges for a standard room. Rates are rounded to the nearest dollar and do not include taxes. U.S., Mexican and Caribbean rates are in U.S. dollars; rates for Canadian lodgings are in Canadian dollars.

Meal Plan Indicators

AP = American Plan of three meals daily
BP = Breakfast Plan of full hot breakfast
CP = Continental Plan of pastry, juice and another beverage
ECP = Expanded Continental Plan, which offers a wider variety of breakfast items
MAP = Modified American Plan of two meals daily

See individual listing "Terms" for additional meal plans not included in the room rate.

Family Plan Indicators

F = Children stay free
D = Discounts for children
F17 = Children 17 and under stay free
D17 = Discount for children 17 or under

The number displayed will reflect the property's age policy.

MURPHY pop. 1,568

BEST WESTERN OF MURPHY
5/24-11/30
4/1-5/23
12/1-3/31

VISTA SUITES
Book great rates at AAA.com
12/24-9/1 [BP]
12/1-12/22 & 9/2-11/30 [BP]
1P: $139-$169
1P: $109-$129
Location: I-4, exit 16A, 1.8 mi e. 1222 Center Way D
Facility: A well-maintained, mature property. 24 rior corridors. **Bath:** combo or shower only. **Pari**
Classic Resort — **Dining:** 6:30 am-9 pm, cocktails. **Pool(s):** heat
Small-scale Hotel plan available. **Amenities:** video games, voice courts, exercise room. **Fee:** game room. **Guest Services:** wireless in major attractions. **Business Services:** meeting rooms, PC, fax (fee). ties: full breakfast, newspaper and high-speed internet. (See co

Bed & Breakfast Fax: ... at this homey, in-town property rating units. 2 stories (no elevator), interior corridors. **Bath:** combo or s no pets allowed (owner's dog on premises). **Amenities:** video lib

DOYLE'S CEDAR HILL RESTAURANT — WHERE T
Lunch: $
Location: US 19/79/129, 0.5 mi w on Bulldog Dr, pm, Sat 5 pm-9 pm, Sun 11 am-3 pm an hou Continental **Features:** Guests can kick back and enjoy the porch seating that affords a view of the mounta Among favorites are spicy Thai green curry scallops and choppe family-owned. Casual dress; wine only. **Parking:** on-site. **Cards:** A

SHOE BOOTIES CAFE
Lunch: $3-$7
Location: Center. 25 Peachtree St 28906. Hour American **Reservations:** accepted. **Features:** One exam salmon, totally unexpected in this area. Lun weekends for the live music. Casual dress; cook

NAGS HEAD —See Outer Banks p. 672.

NEW BERN pop. 23,128

THE AERIE INN — WHERE TO S
All Year
1P: $69-$129
Location: Just e of Tryon Palace; downtown. Located in **Facility:** Built in the 1880s, this Victorian-style ho Historic Sites and Gardens. Smoke free premises. Bed & Breakfast terior corridors. **Bath:** combo or shower only. Ameni [BP] meal plan available. **Cards:** AX, DS, MC, VI. **Free Special Amenities** evening beverages. **Cards:** AX, DS, MC, VI. **Free Special Amenities** ability with advanced reservations).

BRIDGEPOINTE HOTEL & MARINA Book great rates at AAA.co
All Year [CP]
1P: $60-$67
Location: Just n of US 70 Bypass, on US 70 Business corridors. **Parking:** on-site. **Amenities:** voice mail, in Small-scale Hotel tails. **Pool(s):** outdoor. **Leisure Activities:** Fee: meeting rooms, business center. **Cards:** nental breakfast and newspaper.

Credit Cards Accepted

AX=American Express
CB=Carte Blanche
DC=Diners Club
DS=Discover
JC=Japan Credit Bureau
MC=MasterCard
VI=VISA

Spotting Symbol

Black ovals with white numbers are used to locate, or "spot," lodgings on maps we provide for larger cities.

Service Availability

Unit types, amenities and room features preceded by the word "Some" indicate the item is available on a limited basis, potentially within only one unit.

Free Special Amenities

Some OA properties offer special amenities such as Continental breakfast; expanded Continental breakfast or full breakfast; early check-in and late check-out; room upgrade or preferred room; local phone calls; or daily newspaper. This does not imply that only these properties offer these amenities.

Icons

Lodging icons represent some of the member values, services and facilities offered.

Discounts

(ASK) May offer discount

(S/D) Offers minimum 10% senior discount to members over 59

Member Services

(+) Airport transportation
(pets) Pets allowed
(restaurant) Restaurant on premises
(restaurant off) Restaurant off premises (walking distance)
(24t) 24-hour room service
(Y) Cocktail lounge
(child) Child care

Accessibility Features

(&M) Accessible features
(ear) Hearing-impaired equipment available
(&) Roll-in showers

In-Room Amenities

(X) Designated non-smoking rooms
(VCR) VCR
(movies) Movies
(refrig) Refrigerator
(microwave) Microwave
(coffee) Coffee maker
(AC) No air conditioning
(TV) No TV
(CTV) No cable TV
(phone) No telephones

Leisure Activities

(casino) Full-service casino
(pool) Pool
(health) Health club on premises
(health off) Health club off premises
(rec) Recreational activities

Safety Features (see page 24)
(Mexico and Caribbean only)

(S) Sprinklers
(D) Smoke detectors

SOME UNITS printed above the icons indicates the amenity is available on a limited basis, potentially in only one unit. **FEE** appearing below an icon indicates that an extra charge applies.

Understanding the Restaurant Listing

Official Appointment

(AAA) or (CAA) indicates our Official Appointment (OA) restaurants. The OA program permits properties to display and advertise the AAA or CAA emblem. We highlight these properties in red to help you quickly identify them. The AAA or CAA Approved sign helps traveling members find restaurants that want member business.

Diamond Rating

The number of diamonds informs you of the overall complexity of food, presentation, service and ambience. Red indicates an Official Appointment restaurant. A detailed description of each diamond level appears on page 21.

Cuisine Type

The cuisine type helps you select a dining facility that caters to your individual taste. AAA currently recognizes more than 90 different cuisine types.

Menus

This notation indicates AAA/CAA members can conveniently view the restaurant's menu in a secure online environment at AAA.com.

Credit Cards Accepted

AX=American Express
CB=Carte Blanche
DC=Diners Club
DS=Discover
JC=Japan Credit Bureau
MC=MasterCard
VI=VISA

SLEEP INN *Book at AAA.com*
3/1-7/31 [ECP]
12/1-2/29 & 8/1-11/30 [ECP]
Small-scale Hotel **Location:** I-40, exit 210 westt
ries, interior corridors. **Bath:** combo or shower e
lines, voice mail, irons, hair dryers. **Pool(s):** sr
(fee). **Cards:** AX, CB, DC, DS, JC, MC, VI.

THE SEASONS RESTAURANT *Menu on AAA.com*
(AAA) **Location:** On I-459, exit 13 (US 31); 0.3
Mon, also Tues 5/1-11/18. **Reservatic**
Regional establishment. Dining is an all-arou
American service approach to the tranquil, ocea
The chef transforms ingredients, base
dishes. Decadent desserts put an
entertainment. **Parking:** valet. **Cards:**

ANTON'S RESTAURANT Lun
Location: 1.3 mi nw on Battleground
Italian pm, Fri-10:30 pm, Sat 4:30 pm-10:
has served a loyal local following a
signature broiled flounder. Casual dress; cocktails. wooden beams is carried downsta

ARIGATO JAPANESE STEAKHOUSE
Location: I-40/85, exit Coliseum; at jct
Ethnic pm, Fri & Sat 4 pm-10:30 pm. Sun 4
weekends with flair by Japanese chefs. Watch
served with delicious sauces for dipping. Casual dress; c **Features:** Hear the sizzle

BASIL'S TRATTORIA AND WINE BAR
Location: 2.5 mi n on US 220, just n
Italian **Hours:** 5:30 pm-10 pm, Fri & Sat-11
Features: Aromas of Northern Italian
taste for which the bistro is known. Homemade is the only enter the quaint eatery. Warm, freshly b
Cards: AX, DC, MC, VI.

BISTRO SOFIA Dinner: $
Location: I-40, exit 213, 2 mi n, just e on Fr
Nouvelle American pm. Closed major holidays; also Mon. R
the place for an intimate dining experie
to create a cozy, warm setting. Dressy casual; cocktails. Park knowledgeable staff will satisfy all your ex

DI VALLETTA Lunch: $9-$15
Location: I-85, exit 120 (Groometown Rd), jus
Regional Center. 1000 Club Rd 27407. **Hours:** 6 a
Continental **Reservations:** suggested. **Features:** The
castle, affords excellent views of manicure
cocktails. **Parking:** on-site and valet. **Cards**

GATE CITY CHOP HOUSE Lunch: $9-$1
Location: I-40, exit 214B, 1.8 mi n to Holden Rd
American Fri & Sat 4:30 pm-10:30 pm. Closed:
Features: Visit the beautifully landscaped g
housemade chocolate cake. Casual dress; cocktails. **Parking:** room complete with a fireplace. Dine outside

GRAPEVINE CAFE & JUICE BAR Lunch: $4-$
Location: Just s of W Friendly Ave; located behin
Vegetarian pm. Closed major holidays; also Sun. **Featur**
veggie chili and lasagna popular; internatio
on-site. **Cards:** MC, VI.

GREENSBORO, NC 625

699   2P: $64-$104   **Phone:** (236)931-1272
579   2P: $54-$84   **XP:** $5   F18
rd), just n; exit 210 eastbound, just e on Albert Pick Rd, then just n on   **XP:** $5   F18
336/931-1496. **Facility:** 116 one-bedroom standard units. 7 sto-
n-site. **Terms:** cancellation fee imposed. **Amenities:** dual phone
uest **Services:** valet and coin laundry. **Business Services:** fax

SOME UNITS

Dinner: $16-$36   **Phone:** 336/555-5555 ⑤
802. 1000 Ocean Blvd 35244. **Hours:** 6 pm-10 pm. Closed:
ed. **Features:** Guests are in for a treat at this top-notch
ble experience—from the wait staff's casually elegant
to the striking grounds views from the cozy dining area.
seasonally and regionally available, into mouthwatering
mark on the meal. Dressy casual attire; cocktails;
DS, MC, VI. **Classic**

DINE

Dinner: $8-$19
ndover Ave. 1628 Battleground Ave 27408. **Phone:** 336/273-1386
major holidays; also 12/24 & Sun. **Hours:** 11 am-10
ustic Italian theme with black and white table cloths and **Features:** This eatery
dining area. Famous for its lasagna, it also features a
ards: AX, MC, VI.

$18-$30
d Patterson St. 1200 S Holden Rd 27407. **Phone:** 336/299-1003
Closed: 11/25, 12/24, 12/25. **Hours:** 5 pm-10
eak, chicken, shrimp and sauteed vegetables **Reservations:** suggested;
g cooked right at your table and enjoy huge portions prepared
g: on-site. **Cards:** AX, MC, VI.

9-$30
ve; in Irving Park Plaza. 1720 Battleground Ave 27408. **Phone:** 336/333-9833
major holidays; also Sun. **Reservations:** suggested.
m the wood-burning oven and reach diners as they
pped in olive oil is one small example of the delicious
ual dress; cocktails; entertainment. **Parking:** on-site.

just s. 616 Dolley Madison Rd 27410. **Phone:** 336/855-1313
suggested. **Features:** Elegant but not stuffy, this is **Hours:** 5 pm-10
. The Bistro was a house that has been converted French cuisine served by extremely helpful and
ards: AX, DC, MC, VI.

er: $19-$30
1 Grandover Pkwy; in Grandover Resort & Conference **Phone:** 336/294-1800
30 pm, Sun 6-11 am, 11:30-2:30 & 6-10 pm.
g, which reflects the ambience of a European
the 18th hole of the east course. Casual dress;
DS, MC, VI.

ner: $19-$30
06 S Holden Rd 27407. **Phone:** 336/294-9977
12/25; also Sun. **Hours:** 11:30 am-10 pm.
upscale bistro, which features a private dining **Reservations:** suggested.
and end your meal with the creamy, mile-high
.X, DC, DS, MC, VI.

nner: $4-$10
435B Dolley Madison Rd 27410. **Phone:** 336/856-0070
an entrees, fresh fruits and vegetable juices; **Hours:** 11 am-8
dishes. Casual dress; beer only. **Parking:**

Prices

Rates shown represent the minimum and maximum entree cost per person. Exceptions may include one-of-a-kind or special market priced items. Rates are rounded to the nearest dollar and do not include taxes. U.S., Mexican and Caribbean rates are in U.S. dollars; rates for Canadian restaurants are in Canadian dollars.

Spotting Symbol

White ovals with black numbers serve as restaurant locators and are used to locate, or "spot," restaurants on maps we provide for larger cities.

Icons

Icons provide additional information about services and facilities.

- 🏠 No air-conditioning
- 🔥M Accessible features
- 🍸 Cocktail lounge
- 🚭 Designated smoking section available

Classifications

If applicable, a restaurant may be defined as:

Classic - renowned and/or landmark restaurant in business longer than 25 years, known for unique style and ambience.

Historic - properties must meet one of the following criteria:

- Listed on the U.S. National Register of Historic Places
- Designated a U.S. National Historic Landmark
- Located in a U.S. National Register Historic District

Separate criteria designate historic properties in Canada, Mexico and the Caribbean.

Lodging Rates Guaranteed

AAA/CAA members are guaranteed they will not be charged more than the maximum regular rate printed in the TourBook guide in each rate range for a standard room. Rates may vary within the range, depending on season and room type. Listed rates are based on last standard room availability. Obtain current AAA/CAA member rates and make reservations at AAA.com.

Discounts

Member discounts will apply to rates quoted within the rate range and are applicable at the time of booking. Special rates used in advertising, as well as special short-term promotional rates lower than the lowest listed rate in the range, are not subject to additional member discounts.

Exceptions

Rates for properties operating as concessionaires for the U.S. National Park Service are not guaranteed due to governing regulations. Rates in the Mexico TourBook are not guaranteed and may fluctuate based on the exchange rate of the peso.

Lodgings may temporarily increase room rates, not recognize discounts or modify pricing policies during special events. Examples of special events range from Mardi Gras and the Kentucky Derby (including pre-Derby events) to college football games, holidays, holiday periods and state fairs. Although some special events are listed in AAA/CAA TourBook guides and on AAA.com, it is always wise to check in advance with AAA travel professionals for specific dates.

Get the Room You Reserved

When making your reservation, identify yourself as a AAA or CAA member and request written confirmation to guarantee: type of room, rate, dates of stay, and cancellation and refund policies. At registration, show your membership card.

When you find your room is not as specified, and you have written confirmation of reservations for a certain type of accommodation, you should be given the option of choosing a different room or finding one elsewhere. Should you choose to go elsewhere and a refund is refused or resisted, submit the matter to AAA/CAA within 30 days, along with complete documentation, including your reasons for refusing the room and copies of your written confirmation and any receipts or canceled checks associated with this problem.

If you are charged more than the maximum rate listed in the TourBook guide for a standard

room, question the additional charge. If management refuses to adhere to the published rate, pay for the room and submit your receipt and membership number to AAA/CAA within 30 days. Include all pertinent information: dates of stay, rate paid, itemized paid receipts, number of persons in your party and the room number you occupied, and list any extra room equipment used. A refund of the amount paid in excess of the stated maximum will be made if our investigation indicates that unjustified charging occurred.

Deposit, Refund and Cancellation Policies

Most establishments give full deposit refunds if they have been notified at least 48 hours before the normal check-in time. Listing prose will note if more than 48 hours' notice is required for cancellation. Some properties may charge a cancellation or handling fee. When this applies, "cancellation fee imposed" will appear in the listing. If you cancel too late, you have little recourse if a refund is denied.

When an establishment requires full or partial payment in advance and your trip is cut short, a refund may not be given.

When canceling a reservation, phone the lodging immediately. Make a note of the date and time you called, the cancellation number if there is one, and the name of the person who handled the cancellation. If your AAA/CAA club made your reservation, allow them to make the cancellation for you as well, so you will have proof of cancellation.

Check-in and Check-out Times

Check-in and check-out times are shown in the lodging listings, under Terms, only if they are before 10 a.m. or after 3 p.m. respectively.

Members Save With Our Partners

Show Your Card & Save®

These National Show Your Card & Save® partners provide the listed member benefits. Admission tickets that offer greater discounts may be available for purchase at the local AAA/CAA club. A maximum of six tickets is available at the discount price at the gate. Visit AAA.com to discover all the great Show Your Card & Save® discounts in your area.

SeaWorld/Busch Gardens   AAA.com/SeaWorld

- Save $5 on 1-day gate admission at SeaWorld, Busch Gardens, and Sesame Place
- Save $3 on 1-day admission at Water Country USA and Adventure Island

SeaWorld
ADVENTURE PARKS
Orlando, San Antonio & San Diego

- Save 10% on select up-close dining. Reservations are required; visit Guest Relations for details   AAA.com/BuschGardens

Busch **GARDENS**
WILLIAMSBURG   TAMPA BAY

Six Flags Theme Parks

- 10% OFF Brunch with Bugs
- 10% OFF merchandise purchases of $15 or more at all Six Flags operated locations.

SixFlags

Universal Orlando   AAA.com/Universal

- Save $4 on a 2-day/2-park pass at Universal Orlando's theme parks (savings apply to tickets purchased at the gate)

UNIVERSAL *Orlando*

- Save 10% on select dining and souvenirs at both Universal Orlando theme parks and at select Universal CityWalk Orlando restaurants (excludes Emeril's)

Universal Studios Hollywood

- Save $3 on a 1-day Universal Studios Hollywood pass (savings applies to tickets purchased at the gate)   AAA.com/Universal

UNIVERSAL STUDIOS HOLLYWOOD

- Save 10% on select dining and souvenirs at Universal Studios Hollywood and Universal CityWalk

Gray Line
AAA.com/GrayLine

- Save 10% on sightseeing tours of 1 day or less

Landry's Seafood House, The Crab House, Chart House, Muer Seafood Restaurants, Joe's Crab Shack and Aquarium and Downtown Aquarium Restaurants

- 10% discount on food and non-alcoholic beverages at all of the above restaurants.

- 10% discount on novelty merchandise at Joe's Crab Shacks and Aquarium and Downtown Aquarium Restaurants.

Hard Rock Cafe

- Save 10% on food, beverage and merchandise at all U.S. and select Canadian and international locations

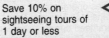

Restaurant Partner Savings applies to AAA/CAA members and up to five guests.

Tanger Outlet Centers   www.tangeroutlet.com

- Save up to 20% on total purchase at select merchants with AAA/CAA coupon booklet
- Member BONUS: FREE $5 gift card for each additional Tanger Outlet Center visited after first within same calendar year

- Show membership card and register at the AAA customer service desk when you visit

Lodging Partners

SAVINGS. SELECTION. SATISFACTION.—When contacting one of these lodging partners, you will be given AAA/CAA's best rates for your dates of stay. Your valid membership card must be presented at check-in. Select the chain you want and have your membership card available when making a reservation and checking in. Let the property know if you are dissatisfied with any part of your stay. If the matter cannot be resolved, you are entitled to recompense (see page 17).

Offer good at time of publication; chains and offers may change without notice. Lodging partners offering discounts to AAA/CAA members may vary in Mexico and the Caribbean.

Understanding the Diamond Ratings

AAA/CAA Tourism Editors have evaluated and rated each of the 60,000 lodging and restaurant establishments in the TourBook series to ensure quality travel information for our members. All properties must meet AAA's 27 minimum requirements (for lodgings) concerning cleanliness, comfort and security - or - AAA's 12 minimum requirements (for restaurants) pertaining to cleanliness, food preparation and service.

Eligible applicants receive an unannounced evaluation by a AAA/CAA Tourism Editor that includes two distinct components:

- AAA Approval: The Tourism Editor first must determine whether the property meets the criteria required to be AAA Approved. Every establishment that meets these strict guidelines offers AAA members the assurance that, regardless of the diamond rating, it provides acceptable quality, cleanliness, service and value.
- AAA Diamond Rating: Once an establishment becomes AAA Approved, it is then assigned a rating of one to five diamonds, indicating the extensiveness of its facilities, amenities and services, from basic to moderate to luxury. These diamond ratings guide members in selecting establishments appropriately matched to their needs and expectations.

LODGINGS

1 Diamond

One diamond lodgings typically appeal to the budget-minded traveler. They provide essential, no-frills accommodations and basic comfort and hospitality.

2 Diamond

Two diamond lodgings appeal to family travelers seeking affordable yet more than the basic accommodations. Facilities, decor and amenities are modestly enhanced.

3 Diamond

Three diamond lodgings offer a distinguished style. Properties are multi-faceted, with marked upgrades in physical attributes, amenities and guest comforts.

4 Diamond

Four diamond lodgings are refined and stylish. Physical attributes are upscale. The fundamental hallmarks at this level include an extensive array of amenities combined with a high degree of hospitality, service and attention to detail.

5 Diamond

Five diamond lodgings provide the ultimate in luxury and sophistication. Physical attributes are extraordinary in every manner. Service is meticulous, exceeding guest expectations and maintaining impeccable standards of excellence. Extensive personalized services and amenities provide first-class comfort.

fyi The lodging listings with **fyi** in place of diamonds are included as an *information only* service for members. The icon indicates that a property has not been rated for one or more of the following reasons: too new to rate, under construction, under major renovation, not evaluated, may not meet all AAA requirements.

A property not meeting all AAA requirements is included for either its member value or because it may be the only accommodation available in the area. Listing prose will give insight as to why the **fyi** designation was assigned.

4 Diamond

Four diamond restaurants provide a distinctive fine-dining experience that is typically expensive. Surroundings are highly refined with upscale enhancements throughout. Highly creative chefs use imaginative presentations to augment fresh, top-quality ingredients. A proficient service staff meets or exceeds guest expectations. A wine steward may offer menu-specific knowledge to guide selection.

5 Diamond

Five diamond restaurants are luxurious and renowned for consistently providing a world-class experience. Highly acclaimed chefs offer artistic menu selections that are imaginative and unique, using only the finest ingredients available. A maitre d' leads an expert service staff in exceeding guest expectations, attending to every detail in an effortless and unobtrusive manner.

RESTAURANTS

1 Diamond

One diamond restaurants provide simple, familiar specialty food (such as burgers, chicken, pizza or tacos) at an economical price. Often self-service, basic surroundings complement a no-nonsense approach.

2 Diamond

Two diamond restaurants offer a familiar, family-oriented experience. Menu selection includes home-style foods and family favorites, often cooked to order, modestly enhanced and reasonably priced. Service is accommodating yet relaxed, a perfect complement to casual surroundings.

 The restaurants with **fyi** in place of diamonds are included as an *information only* service for members. These listings provide additional dining choices but have not yet been evaluated.

3 Diamond

Three diamond restaurants convey an entry into fine dining and are often positioned as adult-oriented experiences. The atypical menu may feature the latest cooking trends and/or traditional cuisine. Expanded beverage offerings complement the menu. The ambience is well coordinated, comfortable and enhanced by a professional service staff.

Understanding the Lodging Classifications

To ensure that your lodging needs and preferences are met, we recommend that you consider an establishment's classification when making your travel choices. While the quality and comfort at properties with the same diamond rating should be consistent (regardless of the classification), there are differences in typical decor/theme elements, range of facilities and service levels.

Large-scale Hotel

A multistory establishment with interior room entrances. A variety of guest unit styles is offered. Public areas are spacious and include a variety of facilities such as a restaurant, fitness center, spa, business center, shops or meeting rooms.

Hotel Royal Plaza, Lake Buena Vista, FL

Small-scale Hotel

A multistory establishment typically with interior room entrances. A variety of guest unit styles is offered. Public areas are limited in size and/or the variety of facilities available.

Baymont Inn, Dallas Ft. Worth-Airport N, TX

Motel

A 1- to 3-story establishment typically with exterior room entrances facilitating convenient access to parking. The standard guest units have one bedroom with a bathroom and are typically similar in decor and design throughout. Public areas are limited in size and/or the variety of facilities available.

Best Western Deltona Inn, Deltona, FL

Country Inn

Similar in definition to a bed and breakfast but usually larger in scale, with spacious public areas offering a dining facility that serves at least breakfast and dinner.

Greenville Inn, Greenville, ME

Bed & Breakfast

Small-scale properties emphasizing a high degree of personal touches that provide guests an "at home" feeling. Guest units tend to be individually decorated. Rooms may not include some modern amenities such as televisions and telephones, and may have a shared bathroom. Usually owner-operated with a common room or parlor separate from the innkeeper's living quarters, where guests and operators can interact during evening and breakfast hours. Evening office closures are normal. A Continental or full, hot breakfast is served and is included in the room rate.

1884 Paxton House Inn, Thomasville, GA

Condominium

Vacation-oriented or extended-stay, apartment-style accommodations that are routinely available for rent through a management company. Units vary in design and decor and often contain one or more bedrooms, a living room, full kitchen and an eating area. Studio-type models combine the sleeping and living areas into one room. Typically, basic cleaning supplies, kitchen utensils and complete bed and bath linens are supplied. The guest registration area may be located off-site.

Sands of Kahana, Kahana, Maui, HI

Cabin/Cottage

Vacation-oriented, small-scale, freestanding houses or cabins. Units vary in design and decor and often contain one or more bedrooms, a living room, kitchen, dining area and bathroom. Studio-type models combine the sleeping and living areas into one room. Typically, basic cleaning supplies, kitchen utensils, and complete bed and bath linens are supplied. The guest registration area may be located off-site.

Desert Rose Inn, Bluff, UT

Ranch

Typically a working ranch with an obvious rustic, Western theme. In general, equestrian-related activities are featured, but ranches may

Lost Valley Ranch, Deckers, CO

include other animals and activities as well. A variety of guest unit styles is offered in a family-oriented atmosphere.

Vacation Home

Vacation-oriented or extended-stay, large-scale, freestanding houses that are routinely available for rent through a

ResortQuest, Hilton Head Island, SC

management company. Houses vary in design and decor and often contain two or more bedrooms, a living room, full kitchen, dining room and multiple bathrooms. Typically, basic cleaning supplies, kitchen utensils, and complete bed and bath linens are supplied. The guest registration area may be located off-site.

Lodging Subclassifications

The following are subclassifications that may appear along with the classifications listed previously to provide a more specific description of the lodging.

Casino

Extensive gaming facilities are available such as blackjack, craps, keno and slot machines. Note: This subclassification will not appear beneath its diamond rating in the listing. It will be indicated by a 🎰 icon and will be included in the row of icons immediately below the lodging listing.

Classic

Renowned and landmark properties, older than 50 years, well-known for their unique style and ambience.

Historic

These properties are typically over 75 years of age and exhibit many features of a historic nature with respect to architecture, design, furnishings, public record or acclaim. Properties must meet one of the following criteria:

- Maintained the integrity of the historical aspect
- Listed on the U.S. National Register of Historic Places
- Designated a U.S. National Historic Landmark
- Located in a U.S. National Register Historic District

Separate criteria designate historic properties in Canada, Mexico and the Caribbean.

Vacation Rental

Typically houses, condos, cottages or cabins; these properties are a "home away from home" offering more room and greater value for the money and generally provide the conveniences of home, such as full kitchens and washers/dryers. They are located in resort or popular destination areas within close proximity to major points of interest, attractions, or recreation areas. These properties may require a pre-arranged reservation and check-in at an off-site location. Housekeeping services may be limited or not included.

Resort

Recreation-oriented, geared to vacation travelers seeking a specific destination experience. Travel packages, meal plans, themed entertainment, and social and recreational programs are typically available. Recreational facilities are extensive and may include spa treatments, golf, tennis, skiing, fishing, water sports, etc. Larger resorts may offer a variety of guest accommodations.

Guest Safety

Room Security

In order to be approved for listing in AAA/CAA TourBook guides for the United States and Canada, accommodations must have dead-bolt locks on all guest room entry doors and connecting room doors.

If the area outside the guest room door is not visible from inside the room through a window or door panel, viewports must be installed on all guest room entry doors. Bed and breakfast properties and country inns are not required to have viewports. Ground floor and easily accessible sliding doors must be equipped with some type of secondary security locks.

Even with those approval requirements, AAA cannot guarantee guest safety. Tourism Editors view a percentage of rooms at each property since it is not feasible to evaluate every room in every lodging establishment. Therefore, AAA cannot guarantee that there are working locks on all doors and windows in all guest rooms.

Fire Safety

Because of the highly specialized skills needed to conduct professional fire safety inspections, AAA/CAA Tourism Editors cannot assess fire safety.

Properties must meet all federal, state and local fire codes. Each guest unit in all U.S. and Canadian lodging properties must be equipped with an operational, single-station smoke detector. A AAA/CAA Tourism Editor has evaluated a sampling of the rooms to verify this equipment is in place.

Mexico and the Caribbean

Requirements for some features, such as door locks and smoke detectors/sprinkler systems, differ in Mexico and the Caribbean. If a property met AAA's security requirements at the time of the evaluation, the phrase "Meets AAA guest room security requirements" appears in the listing.

Service Animals

The Americans with Disabilities Act (ADA) prohibits U.S. businesses that serve the public from discriminating against persons with disabilities. Some businesses have mistakenly denied access to persons who use service animals. Businesses must permit entry to guests and their service animals, as well as allow service animals to accompany guests to all public areas of a property.

A property is permitted to ask whether the animal is a service animal or a pet, and whether the guest has a disability. The property may not, however, ask questions about the nature of the disability, the service provided by the animal or require proof of a disability or certification that the animal is a service animal. These regulations may not apply in Canada, Mexico or the Caribbean.

No fees or deposits, even those normally charged for pets, may be charged for service animals. Service animals fulfill a critical need for their owners—they are not pets.

Frank Frand with his seeing eye dog, Cardinal.
Todd Masinter © 2006

Savings for all Seasons

Hertz rents Fords and other fine cars. ® REG. U.S. PAT. OFF. © HERTZ SYSTEM INC., 1999/2006/99.

No matter the season, Hertz offers AAA members exclusive discounts and benefits.

Operating in 150 countries at over 8,100 locations, Hertz makes traveling more convenient and efficient wherever and whenever you go. Hertz offers AAA members discounts up to 20% on car rentals worldwide.

To receive your exclusive AAA member discounts and benefits, mention your AAA membership card at time of reservation and present it at time of rental. **In addition**, to receive a free one car class upgrade on daily, weekly or weekend rental in the United States and Canada, mention PC# 969194, and in Puerto Rico mention PC# 969183 at the time of reservation. Offer available through 12/15/07.

For reservations and program details, visit aaa.com/hertz, call your AAA Travel office or the Hertz/AAA Desk at **1-800-654-3080.**

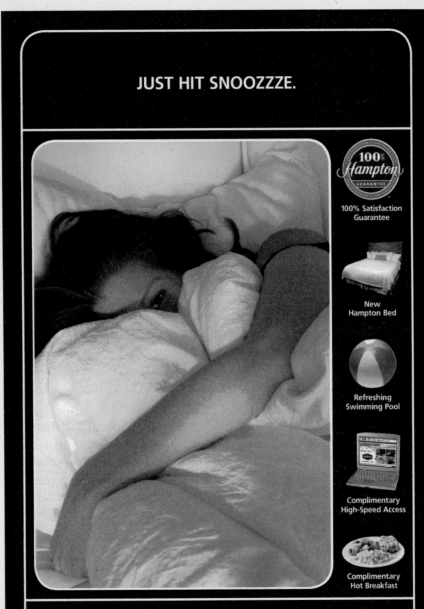

New York

The Big Apple

Skyscrapers, theaters, museums, shopping, bustling crowds— New York City

Take a Sip

New York state's wines compare with the world's finest

Niagara Falls

The power of Mother Nature is awesome

Historic Canals

When the Great Lakes met the Hudson River, commerce flowed

Explore the Outdoors

Raft, hike, boat, fish, bike, canoe, ski—you can do it all in New York

Cochecton Center
© Dennis Hallinan / Alamy

an intriguing collage

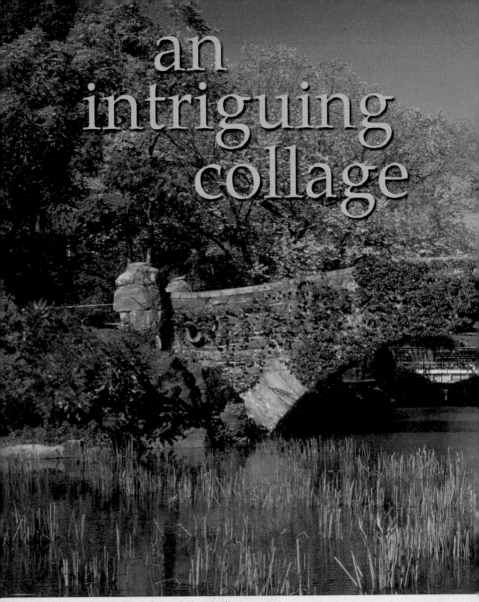

Central Park, Manhattan / © age fotostock / SuperStock

Take an escalator to an observation floor in Manhattan's towering Empire State Building, and you'll view a busy panorama of asphalt and skyscrapers.

As spectacular as that sight may be, it's a one-dimensional snapshot of the state of New York. The broader picture encompasses much more.

A rich maritime and farming heritage characterizes Long Island, a resort playground with pristine beaches, breathtaking mansions and quaint lighthouses.

The Catskills and the Adirondacks give you adventure—by water, by land and by air.

The past is the draw in the Hudson Valley, in which Franklin D. Roosevelt's ancestral home is counted among the many historic sites.

Albany, the state capital, is noted for its art and architecture, while vineyards are the trademark in the fertile Finger Lakes region.

You'll find romance at Niagara Falls and in the Thousand Islands, an area with scenic trails and warm beaches.

History and sports are the focus in the Leatherstocking region where the Erie Canal system and baseball and soccer legends are celebrated.

And varied cultures—American Indian and Amish—in Chautauqua-Allegheny grant you the opportunity to expand your horizons.

Its many images and varied attractions make New York an intriguing collage.

Brazilian. Chinese. German. Irish. Italian. Korean. Mexican. Polish. Russian. South African. Vietnamese.

These nationalities represent a mere handful of the full shelf of ethnic spices that add zest to the New York City melting pot. The city's cultural stew is an epicurean *piéce de résistance.*

Similarly, the tantalizing attractions of the state as a whole combine in a recipe equally appetizing.

Among the most savory ingredients is history, and you'll find it in several flavors.

One traces the turmoil and strife of the Revolutionary War. Nearly a third of the war's battles were fought on New York soil—at such places as Johnstown, Saratoga, Schuylerville and White Plains. Weapons, uniforms, paintings and documents relating to the struggle for independence fill a museum at Fort Ticonderoga.

The story of the Underground Railroad is another. Many slaves found freedom taking cover in the safe houses along the route. Among those preserved sites are the Harriet Tubman Home in Auburn; the H. Lee White

Marine Museum in Oswego; and the John Brown Farm State Historic Site in Lake Placid. Displays in Fenton History Center in Jamestown provide a wealth of information about the abolitionist network.

Yet a third recounts America's love of sports. In addition to being the home of numerous professional teams, the Empire State boasts halls of fame for several sports, including boxing, horse racing and soccer. Most notable, though, is Cooperstown's National Baseball Hall of Fame and Museum, which pays homage to the national pastime.

Architectural Smorgasbord

Add to this historical stock samples of diverse styles of architecture.

Albany's Capitol, one of few such buildings without a dome, bears intricate carvings that give it a decidedly French feel. The Beaux-Arts style characterizes the Vanderbilt Mansion National Historic Site in Hyde Park. A Greek Revival flair marks the Rose Hill Mansion in Geneva.

Fold in a rich dollop of art. Renowned museums in Albany, Buffalo and New York show off the talents of such artists as Willem de Kooning, Pablo Picasso, Auguste Rodin and

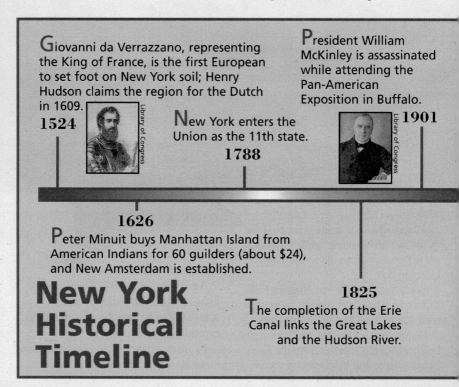

Giovanni da Verrazzano, representing the King of France, is the first European to set foot on New York soil; Henry Hudson claims the region for the Dutch in 1609.
1524

Library of Congress

New York enters the Union as the 11th state.
1788

President William McKinley is assassinated while attending the Pan-American Exposition in Buffalo.

Library of Congress
1901

1626
Peter Minuit buys Manhattan Island from American Indians for 60 guilders (about $24), and New Amsterdam is established.

New York Historical Timeline

1825
The completion of the Erie Canal links the Great Lakes and the Hudson River.

Andy Warhol. Exquisite glass is the centerpiece at Corning Museum of Glass.

The Statue of Liberty, equal parts architecture and art, rises up from Liberty Island as a 151-foot-tall symbol of freedom on a 154-foot-high pedestal.

Sprinkle in a pinch of nature's architectural treasures. Brick walkways weave through the stalactites and stalagmites in Howe Caverns in Howes Cave. Huge outcroppings comprise the Panama Rocks in Panama.

Top it all off with a heaping spoonful of something home-grown—presidential homesteads. Millard Fillmore, Franklin D. Roosevelt, Theodore Roosevelt and Martin Van Buren all were New York natives.

Liquid Assets

Pour in plenty of water. Hugging varied borders are the Atlantic Ocean, Long Island Sound, lakes Champlain, Erie and Ontario, and the Delaware and St. Lawrence rivers. The aptly named Finger Lakes, 11 glacial lakes, gash vertical blue streaks in the landscape south of the stretch of I-90 linking Rochester and Syracuse.

Breathtaking waterfalls—including 215-foot Taughannock Falls near Ithaca, Rainbow Falls in Watkins Glen and the honeymooner's paradise of Niagara Falls—cascade and plummet all over the state.

Tour Goat Island, which separates the Niagara River to form Horseshoe and American falls, then venture onto nearby Three Sisters Islands to view the thundering rapids up close and personal.

Constructed to link major waterways and thereby open trade west of the Appalachians, the famed Cayuga-Seneca, Champlain, Erie and Oswego canals occupy their own niche in New York lore.

Accompany each course with a glass of premium wine from one of six major viticultural regions: Cayuga Lake, the Finger Lakes, Hudson River, Lake Erie, the Long Island Hamptons and the Long Island North Fork. More than 100 vineyards produce upwards of 20 million gallons of such varieties as chardonnay, pinot noir and cabernet sauvignon each year.

Bon appetit!

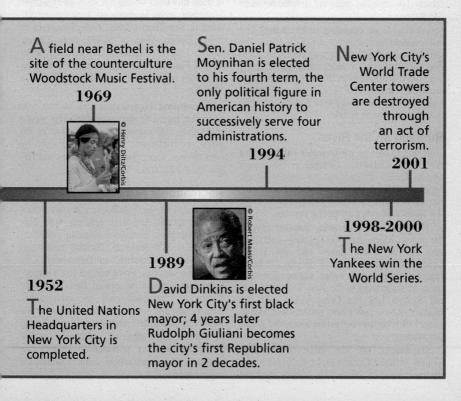

A field near Bethel is the site of the counterculture Woodstock Music Festival.

1969

© Henry Diltz/Corbis

Sen. Daniel Patrick Moynihan is elected to his fourth term, the only political figure in American history to successively serve four administrations.

1994

New York City's World Trade Center towers are destroyed through an act of terrorism.

2001

1989

© Robert Maass/Corbis

David Dinkins is elected New York City's first black mayor; 4 years later Rudolph Giuliani becomes the city's first Republican mayor in 2 decades.

1998-2000

The New York Yankees win the World Series.

1952

The United Nations Headquarters in New York City is completed.

Recreation

Forests. Mountains. Valleys. Waterways. If you're looking for fun in the great outdoors, New York has it all.

From the heights of the rugged Adirondacks to the pine barrens of Long Island, New York entices explorers of all stripes with miles upon miles of **hiking** trails. Notable among them are the Appalachian, Erie Canal, Finger Lakes and Northville-Lake Placid trails; the Long Island Greenbelt; and the Long Path, which links New York City with the Adirondacks. In winter many of these routes are popular for cross-country skiing.

Get a different perspective while **spelunking** alongside the subterranean river in Howe Caverns, in Howes Cave.

Steady yourself on two wheels and go **bicycling** along the 35-mile Mohawk-Hudson Bikeway, near Albany; through the 32 miles of trails in Old Erie Canal State Park, east of Syracuse; and on the 60-mile Barge Canal Recreationway, which traverses Monroe and Orleans counties.

If **horseback riding** is your thing, visit Allegany State Park, Connetquot State Park Preserve or Rockefeller State Park Preserve. Nearly 100 miles of trails are divided between the three.

Looking to go **canoeing** or **kayaking?** The Adirondacks are a good place to start. The range boasts 2,800 lakes and ponds in addition to thousands of miles of rivers. Explore the scenic wilderness in the Saint Regis canoe area—57 lakes and ponds near Saranac Lake—or head for Old Forge and navigate the Adirondack Canoe Route.

Running on the River

If you're new to **white-water rafting,** try a run on the Delaware, Genesee or Sacandaga rivers. Thrills abound on the feistier Black, Moose and Salmon rivers. Combine spectacular scenery and turbulent waters and you get the Hudson River, a perennial favorite.

There are plenty of other ways to play in the water. More than 4,000 lakes—including two of the Great Lakes and the Finger Lakes—add up to scores of options for **boating, swimming** and **water skiing.** The 524 miles of waterways in the New York State Canal System link the Great Lakes with the Hudson River and other northeastern inland waters to form another prime locale for pleasure boating.

Shipwrecks off the coast of Oswego County in Lake Ontario make for great **scuba diving.** Also of interest to divers is Lake George, where the well-preserved _Land Tortoise_ sank; Lake Champlain, home of a legendary beast akin to the Loch Ness Monster; Long Island Sound; and the crystal-clear waters of the Thousand Islands-Seaway region.

Cast a line in one of New York's bodies of water, and you're in for a **fishing** adventure. Fresh waters yield bass, trout, perch, muskie, salmon and panfish. Bluefish, fluke, striper and weakfish swim in the surf. Long Island is noted for its cod, blackfish and flounder.

Three outstanding fishing streams—Beaver Kill, Neversink and Willowemoc—are within Catskill Forest Preserve in Catskill.

Playing on the Edge

For a rush of adrenaline, try **rock climbing** in the Adirondack, Catskill, Shawangunk or Taconic mountains; **parasailing** over Lake George; or **hang gliding** over the Rondout River near Ellenville. You'll also feel that excitement while **surfing** in the ocean off Long Island, **windsurfing** on the Finger Lakes or **snowmobiling** through Finger Lakes National Forest.

Exhilaration also is the name of the game at such **downhill skiing** hot spots as Belleayre Mountain, near Highmount; Big Tupper Ski Area in Big Tupper Lake; Gore Mountain in North Creek; Holiday Valley, near Ellicottville; Hunter Mountain in Hunter; Lake Placid/Whiteface in Wilmington; Windham Mountain in Windham; and Titus Mountain in Malone.

A **camping** excursion is sure to free you from the rigors of everyday life. The state's more than 500 campgrounds are all over the place: in backwoods spots reached only by boat or foot, along the shores of lakes and rivers, on the beautiful Atlantic coast.

Recreational Activities

Throughout the TourBook, you may notice a Recreational Activities heading with bulleted listings of recreation-oriented establishments listed underneath. Similar operations also may be mentioned in Destination City recreation sections. Since normal AAA inspection criteria cannot be applied, these establishments are presented only for information. Age, height and weight restrictions may apply. Reservations often are recommended and sometimes are required. Addresses and/or phone numbers are provided so visitors can contact the attraction for additional information.

Fast Facts

POPULATION: 18,976,457.

AREA: 49,576 square miles; ranks 30th.

CAPITAL: Albany.

HIGHEST POINT: 5,344 ft., Mount Marcy.

LOWEST POINT: Sea level, Atlantic Ocean.

TIME ZONE(S): Eastern. DST.

MINIMUM AGE FOR UNRESTRICTED DRIVER'S LICENSE: 18.

MINIMUM AGE FOR GAMBLING: 18.

SEAT BELT/CHILD RESTRAINT LAWS: Seat belts required for driver and front-seat passengers 16 and older. Children ages 7-16, are required to be in a seat belt; child restraints required for under age 7.

HELMETS FOR MOTORCYCLISTS: Required for all riders.

RADAR DETECTORS: Permitted.

FIREARMS LAWS: Vary by state and/or county. Contact the New York State Police Headquarters, Building 22, State Campus, Albany, NY 12226; phone (518) 457-6811.

HOLIDAYS: Jan. 1; Martin Luther King Jr. Day, Jan. (3rd Mon.); Lincoln's Birthday, Feb. (1st Mon.); Washington's Birthday, Feb. (3rd Mon.); Memorial Day, May (last Mon.); July 4; Labor Day, Sept. (1st Mon.); Columbus Day, Oct. (2nd Mon.); Election Day, Nov.; Veterans Day, Nov. 11; Thanksgiving; Christmas, Dec. 25.

TAXES: New York's statewide sales tax is 4 percent, with local options for additional increments of up to 4.5 percent. Localities may impose taxes on lodgings, admissions or restaurant meals. New York City imposes a 13.38 percent plus $1.50 room tax as well as additional sums depending on the room rate.

INFORMATION CENTERS: State welcome centers on/near the New York State Thruway (I-87) open daily year-round: Sloatsburg N.;

Harriman exit 16; Catskill exit 21; New Baltimore N. and S.; Utica exit 31; Seneca W.; and Grand Island Blvd. exit 18A N. Centers open daily, May-Oct.: Newburgh exit 17; Plattekill N.; westbound Pattersonville, Warners, Schuyler and Clarence; Angola E. and W.; Westfield exit 60; and Pembroke E. State Gateway Information Centers open daily year-round: Binghamton rest area (I-81) N.; Thousand Island International Bridge S. and Beekmantown rest area (Adirondack Northway) S.

FURTHER INFORMATION FOR VISITORS:

Empire State Department of Tourism
30 S. Pearl St.
Albany, NY 12245
(518) 474-4116
(800) 225-5697 (50 states and territories)

RECREATION INFORMATION:

New York State Office of Parks, Recreation and Historic Preservation
Agency Building #1
Empire State Plaza
Albany, NY 12238
(518) 474-0456
(800) 456-2267 (camping reservations)

FISHING AND HUNTING REGULATIONS:

Division of Fish, Wildlife and Marine Resources
State Environmental Conservation Department
625 Broadway, 5th Floor
Albany, NY 12233-4750
(518) 402-8920

NATIONAL FOREST INFORMATION:

Forest Supervisor
Finger Lakes National Forest
5218 State Route 414
Hector, NY 14841
(607) 546-4470
(877) 444-6777 (reservations)

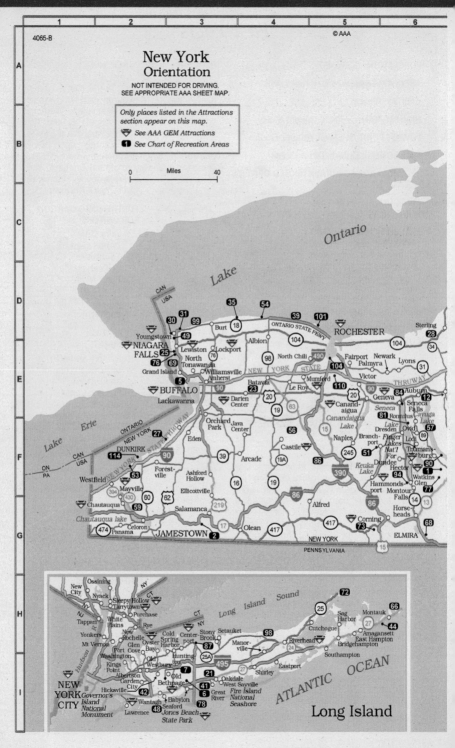

4065-B

© AAA

New York
Orientation

NOT INTENDED FOR DRIVING.
SEE APPROPRIATE AAA SHEET MAP.

Only places listed in the Attractions
section appear on this map.

⬇ See AAA GEM Attractions

1 See Chart of Recreation Areas

Miles
0 ――――― 40

Lake Ontario

ROCHESTER

NIAGARA FALLS

BUFFALO

Lackawanna

Lake Erie

DUNKIRK

Westfield

Mayville

Chautauqua

Chautauqua lake

Panama

JAMESTOWN

Youngstown

Lewiston

North Tonawanda

Grand Island

Williamsville

Amherst

Burt

Albion

North Chili

Fairport

Palmyra

Lyons

Newark

Victor

Geneva

Seneca Falls

Romulus

Auburn

Cayuga Lake

Canandaigua

Canandaigua Lake

Naples

Branch-port

Flower Lakes Nat'l For

Dundee

Keuka Lake

Hammonds-port

Montour Falls

Watkins Glen

Horse-heads

Trumansburg

Lodi

Ovid

Dresden

Hector

Batavia

Le Roy

Mumford

Darien Center

Orchard Park

Java Center

Eden

Forest-ville

Ashford Hollow

Ellicottville

Salamanca

Coleron

Arcade

Castile

Alfred

Olean

Corning

ELMIRA

Sterling

ONTARIO STATE PKWY

NEW YORK STATE THRUWAY

ONTARIO NEW YORK

CAN USA

ON PA

NEW YORK
PENNSYLVANIA

Long Island

Long Island Sound

New City

Ossining

Nyack

Sleepy Hollow

Tarrytown

Purchase

White Plains

Rye

Tappan

Yonkers

Mt Vernon

New Rochelle

Glen Cove

Oyster Bay

Cold Spring Harbor

Center-port

Stony Brook

Setauket

Manor-ville

Riverhead

Cutchogue

Sag Harbor

Montauk

Amagansett

East Hampton

Bridgehampton

Southampton

Eastport

Shirley

Oakdale

West Sayville

Great River

Fire Island National Seashore

Huntington

Old Westbury

Bethpage

Seaford

Jones Beach State Park

Babylon

Wantagh

Lawrence

Hicksville

Garden City

Albertson

Kings Point

Port Washington

Governor's Island National Monument

NEW YORK CITY

ATLANTIC OCEAN

Hudson

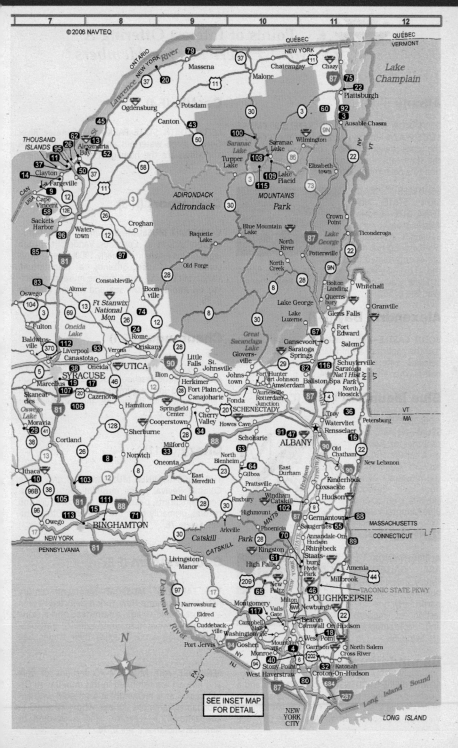

© 2006 NAVTEQ

SEE INSET MAP FOR DETAIL

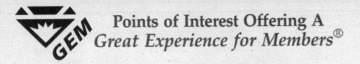

Points of Interest Offering A
Great Experience for Members®

Albany (F-10)

GOVERNOR NELSON A. ROCKEFELLER EMPIRE STATE PLAZA—In the heart of New York's capital, the plaza is a government complex consisting of the state capitol and the state museum in addition to a performing arts center. See p. 55.

SCHUYLER MANSION STATE HISTORIC SITE—George Washington and Benjamin Franklin were among the notables entertained in this 1761 Georgian home; its owner Phillip Schuyler was a general during the Revolutionary War. See p. 56.

Alexandria Bay (B-7)

BOLDT CASTLE—Hotel magnate George C. Boldt had this replica of a Rhineland castle built for his beloved wife; construction was immediately halted when she died in 1904. See p. 56.

Blue Mountain Lake (C-10)

ADIRONDACK MUSEUM—Nearly two centuries of Adirondack culture and history are explored in this museum's 23 indoor and outdoor exhibits overlooking Blue Mountain Lake. See p. 61.

Buffalo (E-2)

ALBRIGHT-KNOX ART GALLERY—A stately Greek Revival building houses a particularly fine collection of modern and contemporary art. See p. 66.

Canandaigua (E-5)

SONNENBERG GARDENS—Elegant gardens and a Queen Anne-style mansion reflect the summertime lakeside lifestyle experienced by an affluent Victorian-era couple from New York City. See p. 74.

Castile (F-4)

LETCHWORTH STATE PARK—The Genesee River Gorge, three waterfalls and scenic roads, trails and views are the highlights of this state park. See p. 74.

Centerport (H-3)

VANDERBILT MUSEUM—William K. Vanderbilt II, great-grandson of Cornelius Vanderbilt, began work on his estate in the early 1900s; the 43 acres contain landscaped grounds, a planetarium, Vanderbilt's home and a marine museum reflecting his interest in the sea and marine life. See p. 75.

Chautauqua (G-1)

CHAUTAUQUA INSTITUTION—Begun in 1874 as a center for Sunday-school teachers, the institution has evolved into a summer arts and education center known for its lectures and entertainment offerings. See p. 75.

Chazy (A-11)

THE ALICE T. MINER MUSEUM—This gray stone Colonial Revival house museum contains glass, porcelain, prints, paintings, carpets, furniture and textiles, primarily from the 18th and 19th centuries. See p. 76.

Cooperstown (F-8)

THE FARMERS' MUSEUM—Nineteenth-century rural life in upstate New York is depicted here in a restored 1845 village, a farmstead and a stone dairy barn now used to house exhibits; craftspeople in period attire practice their trades. See p. 77.

FENIMORE ART MUSEUM—Collections of folk and fine art are exhibited in this museum on Otsego Lake, as is memorabilia associated with author James Fenimore Cooper, who was raised in Cooperstown; a separate wing is devoted to American Indian art. See p. 78.

NATIONAL BASEBALL HALL OF FAME AND MUSEUM— You won't strike out by visiting this museum where baseball legends are enshrined; the museum traces the history of the nation's pastime from its 19th-century beginnings to the present. See p. 78.

Corning (G-5)

CORNING MUSEUM OF GLASS—The artistry and history of glass, its uses and its manufacturing process are explained through museum exhibits and glassblowing demonstrations. See p. 79.

ROCKWELL MUSEUM OF WESTERN ART—Western and Native American art is the focus here, pardner. See p. 79.

Darien Center (E-4)

SIX FLAGS DARIEN LAKE—You will definitely be entertained at this complex where roller coasters, water parks, stage shows and thrill rides are all part of the fun. See p. 81.

Fort Stanwix National Monument (D-8)

FORT STANWIX NATIONAL MONUMENT—Built in 1758, the original fort protected the Mohawk Valley during the French and Indian and Revolutionary wars; its reconstruction contains archeological exhibits and living-history demonstrations. See p. 86.

Fort Ticonderoga National Historic Landmark (C-11)

FORT TICONDEROGA NATIONAL HISTORIC LANDMARK—The fort's strategic position on Lake Champlain led to its constant changes in ownership—from the French to the British to the Americans and back to the British; now restored, it has a museum with period artifacts. See p. 86.

Garrison (H-11)

BOSCOBEL—Saved from destruction in the mid-1900s, this restored 1804 Federal-style mansion is on a bluff overlooking the Hudson River. See p. 152.

Geneva (E-5)

ROSE HILL MANSION—The 1839 Greek Revival mansion overlooking Seneca Lake has 21 rooms furnished in period that can be seen on guided tours. See p. 87.

Glens Falls (D-11)

THE HYDE COLLECTION—The Hyde mansion and four galleries provide the setting for an extensive collection of art that includes European antiques and works by European old masters and American artists. See p. 88.

Hammondsport (F-5)

GLENN H. CURTISS MUSEUM—The achievements of a speed enthusiast and aviation entrepreneur who held the first pilot's license issued in the United States are chronicled. See p. 89.

PLEASANT VALLEY WINE CO.—The cellars carved into the hillside and the wooden and stone structures of this winery date to its 1860 founding, adding to its Old World feeling; the Great Western Winery Visitor Center features tours, tastings and exhibits. See p. 90.

Howes Cave (F-9)

HOWE CAVERNS—Tours of the prehistoric cave proceed through chambers of stalagmites and stalactites and end with a quarter-mile boat ride on underground Lake of Venus. See p. 91.

Hudson (G-11)

FASNY MUSEUM OF FIREFIGHTING—The history of firefighting, from its early 18th-century origins to the present, is examined by the Firemen's Association of the State of New York (FASNY). See p. 91.

OLANA STATE HISTORIC SITE—Landscape painter Frederic Church's attention to the design details of his Moorish villa and landscaped grounds 1870-91 resulted in a singular work of art. See p. 91.

Hyde Park (G-11)

FRANKLIN D. ROOSEVELT PRESIDENTIAL LIBRARY AND MUSEUM —Home of the first presidential library, the museum includes family possessions as well as photographs, speeches and gifts from heads of state; a section is devoted to FDR's wife Eleanor. See p. 92.

HOME OF FRANKLIN D. ROOSEVELT NATIONAL HISTORIC SITE—FDR's home has been maintained as it was when he died in 1945; the graves of the president and his wife are in a rose garden. See p. 92.

VANDERBILT MANSION NATIONAL HISTORIC SITE—Frederic Vanderbilt's elegant mansion, built during the "Gilded Age" of the late 19th-century, contains original furnishings; the grounds afford scenic views of the Hudson River and the Catskill Mountains. See p. 92.

Ithaca (F-7)

MUSEUM OF THE EARTH—Specimens from this natural history museum's impressive collection of more than 3 million fossils treat visitors to a timeline of Earth's development. See p. 93.

Kingston (G-10)

SENATE HOUSE STATE HISTORIC SITE—This stone house belonging to Abraham Van Gaasbeek was where the governmental system of New York state was adopted in 1777; a museum contains works by area artists. See p. 96.

Lewiston (E-3)

POWER VISTA—The electrifying story of the harnessing of Niagara Falls' power is explained at the Niagara Power Project's visitor center. See p. 167.

Lockport (E-3)

LOCKPORT LOCKS AND ERIE CANAL CRUISES—Passengers experience "locking up" and "locking down" as the boat makes its way through double working locks during a narrated tour of the historic Erie Canal. See p. 168.

Mumford (E-4)

GENESEE COUNTRY VILLAGE & MUSEUM—Craftspeople and guides in period costume portray life in a typical 19th-century country village; nature trails and a gallery of sporting and wildlife art complete the complex. See p. 102.

Newburgh (H-10)

WASHINGTON'S HEADQUARTERS STATE HISTORIC SITE—The general had his headquarters in this house 1782-83 as he directed troops during the Revolutionary War; a museum contains exhibits about the Continental Army. See p. 103.

New Paltz (H-10)

HISTORIC HUGUENOT STREET TOURS—Houses built by the original settlers still stand in the historic district. See p. 103.

New York (I-1)

AMERICAN MUSEUM OF NATURAL HISTORY—A freestanding dinosaur greets visitors in the rotunda; his relatives and other fossil displays are the highlights of this natural history museum. See p. 123.

BROADWAY THEATER DISTRICT—Dubbed the Great White Way as early as 1901 for its profusion of dazzling lights, Broadway is the most famous theater district in the world. See p. 126.

BRONX ZOO—The animals in this 265-acre park, a landmark since 1899, reside in natural habitats. See p. 136.

BROOKLYN BOTANIC GARDEN—A 52-acre garden grows in Brooklyn; formal and informal gardens include a fragrance garden for the blind, a Japanese garden, a conservatory and a bonsai museum. See p. 136.

BROOKLYN MUSEUM—With a collection of more than 1 million objects representing everything from ancient Egyptian to contemporary art, this museum establishes itself as the second-largest in Greater New York City. See p. 137.

CENTRAL PARK—An 840-acre oasis in the middle of bustling Manhattan, the park contains lakes, skating rinks, an Egyptian obelisk, a wildlife conservation center, gardens and a theater; see it all by buggy ride, horse-drawn hansom cab or a walking tour conducted by a park ranger. See p. 126.

CHINATOWN—This little bit of China in New York City's Lower East Side is an exotic ethnic neighborhood of Asian restaurants, street vendors and shops stocked with everything Oriental. See p. 115.

THE CLOISTERS—A branch of the Metropolitan Museum of Art, The Cloisters is known for medieval art; five French cloisters, gardens, 15th-century tapestries and illuminated manuscripts carry out the theme. See p. 132.

DAHESH MUSEUM OF ART—Works by artists trained in European academies embody classical ideals. See p. 127.

ELLIS ISLAND—Audiotapes guide visitors around the processing station where millions of hopeful immigrants entered the country to begin a new life. See p. 121.

EMPIRE STATE BUILDING—This 1931 art deco building has long symbolized New York City; its two observatories afford panoramic views, one from the 86th floor, the other from the 102nd. See p. 127.

FEDERAL HALL NATIONAL MEMORIAL—This historic site was where our fledgling nation protested "taxation without representation," where the first Congress met and where George Washington was inaugurated; a museum contains exhibits pertaining to these events. See p. 115.

FRICK COLLECTION—Philanthropist Henry Clay Frick's collections of paintings, Oriental rugs, Limoges enamels and other art treasures are displayed. See p. 127.

LINCOLN CENTER FOR THE PERFORMING ARTS—This 14-acre complex encompasses the halls and theater where the New York Philharmonic, the Metropolitan Opera, the New York Ballet and the New York City Opera perform. See p. 128.

METROPOLITAN MUSEUM OF ART—One of the world's great museums, the Metropolitan's collections span 5,000 years of art history. See p. 128.

MUSEUM OF JEWISH HERITAGE—A LIVING MEMORIAL TO THE HOLOCAUST—Personal narratives, photographs and artifacts guide visitors through the 20th-century Jewish experience. See p. 118.

THE MUSEUM OF MODERN ART (MOMA)—More than 100,000 pieces of modern art, including paintings, sculptures, drawings, prints and photographs, comprise MoMA's comprehensive collection of 20th-century works. See p. 130.

NEW YORK BOTANICAL GARDEN—Stop and smell the roses here, and also visit a glass palacelike conservatory and specialty gardens featuring mountain flowers, plants native to the eastern United States, day lilies, perennials and herbs. See p. 136.

RIVERSIDE CHURCH—The 74 bronze bells of its carillon ring out three times each Sunday at this interdenominational church. See p. 135.

ROCKEFELLER CENTER—A city within a city, Rockefeller Center is well-known as the home of Radio City Music Hall and the "Today" show. See p. 130.

ROSE CENTER FOR EARTH AND SPACE—The secrets of the cosmos are revealed through multifaceted exhibits, interactive stations, high-definition images and the Hayden Planetarium's spectacular space show. See p. 123.

RUBIN MUSEUM OF ART—Feast your eyes on more than two millennia of transcendent Himalayan art presented in this stunning space. See p. 119.

ST. PATRICK'S CATHEDRAL—Surrounded by skyscrapers, the twin spires of St. Patrick's have been a Manhattan landmark since 1879. See p. 131.

SOLOMON R. GUGGENHEIM MUSEUM—Frank Lloyd Wright's circular design for the museum is a perfect complement for the modern  art collection hung along its sloping walkway. See p. 135.

STATUE OF LIBERTY NATIONAL MONUMENT AND ELLIS ISLAND—Lady Liberty, a gift from France, has welcomed millions of immigrants to America's shores; nearby Ellis Island was the entry point. See p. 120.

TIMES SQUARE—Crowds have gathered in Times Square to celebrate New Year's Eve ever since the lowering of the first lighted ball atop One Times Square in 1907. See p. 132.

UNITED NATIONS HEADQUARTERS—Flags of all member nations mark this complex of buildings where the countries of the world meet to discuss global problems. See p. 132.

Niagara Falls, New York (D-3)

CAVE OF THE WINDS TRIP—Get a topsy-turvy view of the American Falls from wooden walkways at its base. See p. 162.

GOAT ISLAND—Skirt the edges of both the Canadian and American falls from mid-stream. See p. 164.

MAID OF THE MIST—Rides on these boats take visitors directly in front of the powerful falls. See p. 164.

NIAGARA AEROSPACE MUSEUM—Find out about western New York's contributions to aviation history. See p. 164.

NIAGARA FALLS—Visit Niagara Falls State Park to get splendid views. See p. 164.

Niagara Falls, Ontario (E-2)

JOURNEY BEHIND THE FALLS—Get a behind and bottom-up view of Horseshoe Falls from this unusual vantage point. See p. 169.

MAID OF THE MIST—You'll be grateful for the waterproof clothing provided on this boat trip in front of the falls. See p. 174.

MARINELAND—After you've seen the spectacular shows, make a spectacle of yourself on the roller coaster. See p. 174.

NIAGARA FALLS—A favorite of honeymooners, daredevils and millions of tourists, the majestic falls are a true natural wonder. See p. 174.

OH CANADA EH? DINNER SHOW—Performing characters and a family-style meal give visitors a "taste" of Canadian culture and traditions. See p. 175.

QUEEN VICTORIA PARK—If the falls have dampened your spirit, let these fine floral displays perk you up. See p. 175.

RIPLEY'S BELIEVE IT OR NOT! MUSEUM—Explore the outer limits of reality at this museum of the unusual. See p. 178.

WHIRLPOOL AERO CAR—Get a bird's-eye view of the Niagara Gorge and the whirlpool from this cable car. See p. 178.

WHITE WATER WALK—You'll be swept away by this close-up view of the rolling Niagara River rapids. See p. 178.

Ogdensburg (A-8)

FREDERIC REMINGTON ART MUSEUM—Paintings, bronzes, watercolors and drawings by the great artist of the American West are  exhibited in this museum near his birthplace. See p. 180.

Old Bethpage (I-3)

OLD BETHPAGE VILLAGE RESTORATION—Long Island's pre-Civil War history is documented through a collection of buildings moved here from various locations. See p. 180.

Oyster Bay (H-2)

PLANTING FIELDS ARBORETUM STATE HISTORIC PARK—In addition to 409 acres of greenhouses, gardens and natural habitats, the historic site's grounds are graced with a 65-room Tudor Revival mansion with 16th- and 17th-century furnishings. See p. 183.

Queensbury (D-11)

THE GREAT ESCAPE & SPLASHWATER KINGDOM—One of New York's largest theme parks keeps visitors active with thrill rides, live shows, a water park, roller coasters and attractions just for children. See p. 186.

Riverhead (H-4)

ATLANTIS MARINE WORLD—The Lost City of Atlantis holds the secrets of deep blue sealife, from eels to octopi and stingrays to sharks. See p. 187.

Rochester (D-5)

GEORGE EASTMAN HOUSE INTERNATIONAL MUSEUM OF PHOTOGRAPHY AND FILM—The estate of the founder of Eastman Kodak Co., re-  stored to its early 20th-century appearance, contains gardens and the Dryden Theater See p. 188.

MEMORIAL ART GALLERY—A diverse 11,000-piece collection includes artifacts from ancient Greece, two ornate Egyptian coffins and contemporary art glass. See p. 190.

ROCHESTER MUSEUM & SCIENCE CENTER—This museum, which specializes in science, technology and the environment, also presents star and laser sound-and-light shows in its planetarium. See p. 190.

STRONG NATIONAL MUSEUM OF PLAY— The story of everyday life in America is related through col-  lections of items dating from 1820—toys, housewares and home furnishings, clothing and advertising materials. See p. 191.

Saratoga Springs (E-10)

LAKE GEORGE OPERA FESTIVAL—Operas are presented by a regional repertory company in June and July; the company strives to develop young American artists and provide a combination of new and traditional works. See p. 194.

Sleepy Hollow (H-2)

KYKUIT, THE ROCKEFELLER ESTATE—Four generations of Rockefellers have occupied the Hudson River estate built for Standard Oil mogul John D. Rockefeller. See p. 154.

Springfield Center (E-9)

GLIMMERGLASS OPERA—Opera is performed in repertory on the shores of Otsego Lake in a theater whose walls open to reveal views of the countryside. See p. 198.

Staatsburg (G-10)

STAATSBURGH STATE HISTORIC SITE—A 65-room mansion, built in 1832 and enlarged in 1895, sits on a 900-acre site; elaborately decorated, the house has marble fireplaces, ornate furniture and artifacts from around the world. See p. 198.

Tarrytown (H-2)

WASHINGTON IRVING'S SUNNYSIDE—On the banks of the Hudson River, Washington Irving's estate includes a charming stone mansion that still has the  wisteria he planted at its entranceway; interpreters in period costume conduct tours. See p. 156.

Trumansburg (F-6)

TAUGHANNOCK FALLS STATE PARK—The waterfall for which the park is named cascades 215 feet between 400-foot-tall rocky cliffs; trails offer a choice of views from either above or below the falls. See p. 201.

Utica (E-8)

MUNSON-WILLIAMS-PROCTOR ARTS INSTITUTE— The institute, which consists of an art museum, a performing arts program and an art school, has fine collections of American and Euro-  pean art. See p. 203.

Wantagh (I-3)

JONES BEACH STATE PARK—The attraction here is swimming—at oceanfront and bay beaches or in two pools; a 2-mile-long boardwalk follows part of the shoreline. See p. 203.

Watkins Glen (F-6)

WATKINS GLEN STATE PARK—Scenic gorges sculpted by nature, waterfalls, rocky cliffs and a bridge over the chasm are high points at this popular state park. See p. 205.

West Point (H-11)

UNITED STATES MILITARY ACADEMY—Many of America's military heroes were trained at this venerable academy overlooking the Hudson River. See p. 206.

WEST POINT MUSEUM—This museum at the military academy contains exhibits about military and academy history and extensive collections of artifacts from Revolutionary War days to the present. See p. 207.

Wilmington (B-11)

WHITEFACE MOUNTAIN VETERANS' MEMORIAL HIGHWAY—Constructed 1929-35 as a tribute to New Yorkers killed in World War I, the 6-mile road provides numerous scenic mountain and lake viewpoints. See p. 208.

Youngstown (D-2)

OLD FORT NIAGARA STATE HISTORIC SITE—On the grounds of Fort Niagara State Park, the fort was constructed by the French and has served under the flags of three nations. See p. 168.

RECREATION AREAS

	MAP LOCATION	CAMPING	PICNICKING	HIKING TRAILS	BOATING	BOAT RAMP	BOAT RENTAL	FISHING	SWIMMING	PETS ON LEASH	BICYCLE TRAILS	WINTER SPORTS	VISITOR CENTER	LODGE/CABINS	FOOD SERVICE
NATIONAL FORESTS (See place listings)															
Finger Lakes (F-6) 16,000 acres in north-central New York on a ridge between Seneca and Cayuga lakes, via I-90, I-81, I-86 and SR 17.		•	•	•				•		•		•			
NATIONAL RECREATION AREAS (See place listings)															
Gateway															
Breezy Point District (I-2)			•	•				•	•		•		•		•
Jamaica Bay District (I-2) Horse rental.			•	•	•	•		•		•		•	•		•
Staten Island Unit (I-2)			•	•	•	•		•		•		•	•		•
NATIONAL SEASHORES (See place listings)															
Fire Island (I-3) 6,220 acres on Fire Island, off the s. shore of Long Island.		•	•	•	•			•	•	•					
STATE															
Allan H. Treman Marine (F-6) 1 mi. n. of Ithaca on SR 89.	❶		•		•	•		•		•					
Allegany (G-3) 60,398 acres (two areas) s. of Salamanca on State Park Rd. 1. Cross-country skiing; horse rental.	❷	•	•	•	•	•	•	•	•	•	•	•	•	•	•
Ausable Point (B-11) 500 acres 12 mi. s. of Plattsburgh on US 9.	❸	•	•		•			•	•						•
Bear Mountain (H-10) 5,067 acres 5 mi. s. of West Point off US 9W. Museum, nature trails, zoo. (See West Point p. 206)	❹	•	•	•	•	•	•	•	•	•	•	•	•	•	•
Beaver Island (E-3) 1,081 acres 8 mi. w. of Buffalo on southern tip of Grand Island. Snowmobiling.	❺		•	•	•			•	•	•		•			•
Belmont Lake (I-3) 459 acres 4 mi. n. of Babylon off Southern State Pkwy. exit 38. Bridle paths.	❻		•	•	•		•	•	•	•		•			
Bethpage (I-3) 1,475 acres 1 mi. n. of Farmingdale. Cross-country skiing, golf, tennis, tobogganing; bridle paths.	❼		•	•						•	•	•	•		•
Bowman Lake (F-8) 653 acres 8 mi. n.w. of Oxford off SR 220. Nature trails.	❽	•	•	•	•		•	•	•	•		•	•		
Burnham Point (C-7) 12 acres 3 mi. e. of Cape Vincent on SR 12E.	❾	•	•		•			•		•					
Buttermilk Falls (F-7) 751 acres s. of Ithaca on SR 13. Cross-country skiing.	❿	•	•	•					•	•	•	•		•	•
Canoe-Picnic Point (B-7) 70 acres on southern tip of Grindstone Island; access is by boat only.	⓫	•	•		•			•		•					
Cayuga Lake (E-6) 141 acres 3 mi. e. of Seneca Falls on SR 89. Sledding; recreation building.	⓬	•	•		•	•		•	•	•		•			
Cedar Island (B-8) 10 acres on Cedar Island w. of Chippewa Bay; access is by boat only.	⓭	•	•		•			•		•					
Cedar Point (B-7) 48 acres 6 mi. w. of Clayton on SR 12E.	⓮	•	•		•	•	•	•		•					
Chenango Valley (G-8) 1,071 acres 13 mi. n.e. of Binghamton on SR 369. Nature trails.	⓯	•	•	•	•		•	•	•	•	•	•	•	•	•
Cherry Plain (F-11) 175 acres 2 mi. n. of Stephentown on Miller Rd.	⓰		•	•	•		•	•	•	•					
Chittenango Falls (E-8) 192 acres 4 mi. n. of Cazenovia on SR 13.	⓱	•	•	•					•		•				
Clarence Fahnestock Memorial (H-11) 6,800 acres 11 mi. w. of Carmel on SR 301. Cross-country skiing.	⓲	•	•	•	•		•	•	•	•		•	•		•
Clark Reservation (E-7) 310 acres 3 mi. s.e. of Syracuse on SR 173. Playground.	⓳		•	•						•		•			
Coles Creek (A-9) 1,800 acres 5 mi. e. of Waddington on SR 37.	⓴	•	•		•	•		•	•	•					•
Connetquot Preserve (I-3) 3,473 acres near Oakdale/Bohemia on SR 27. Historic. Cross-country skiing; bridle paths.	㉑		•					•				•			
Cumberland Bay (A-11) 350 acres 1 mi. n. of Plattsburgh off US 9.	㉒	•	•					•	•	•		•			

RECREATION AREAS

	MAP LOCATION	CAMPING	PICNICKING	HIKING TRAILS	BOATING	BOAT RAMP	BOAT RENTAL	FISHING	SWIMMING	PETS ON LEASH	BICYCLE TRAILS	WINTER SPORTS	VISITOR CENTER	LODGE/CABINS	FOOD SERVICE
Darien Lakes (E-4) 1,845 acres 2 mi. w. of Darien Center on US 20. Cross-country skiing, snowmobiling.	23	•	•	•	•			•	•			•			•
Delta Lake (D-8) 400 acres 6 mi. n.e. of Rome on SR 46. Snow-mobiling.	24	•	•	•	•	•	•	•	•	•	•	•			•
Devil's Hole (E-2) 42 acres 4.5 mi. n. of Niagara Falls. Scenic. Nature trails.	25		•	•				•	•						
DeWolf Point (B-7) 13 acres on Wellesley Island in the St. Lawrence River.	26	•		•	•			•	•						
Evangola (F-2) 733 acres 5 mi. s.w. of Angola on SR 5.	27	•	•	•				•	•	•					•
Fair Haven Beach (D-6) 865 acres 1 mi. n. of Fair Haven off SR 104A. Cross-country skiing, snowmobiling; nature trails.	28	•	•	•	•	•	•	•	•	•		•			•
Fillmore Glen (F-7) 939 acres 1 mi. s. of Moravia on SR 38.	29	•	•	•								•	•		•
Fort Niagara (D-3) 504 acres at the mouth of the Niagara River off SR 18F. Snowmobiling, tobogganing. (See Youngstown p. 168)	30		•	•	•			•				•	•		•
Four Mile Creek (D-3) 248 acres 4 mi. e. of Youngstown on SR 18.	31	•		•				•	•						
Franklin Delano Roosevelt (I-11) 952 acres w. of Yorktown Heights off the Taconic State Pkwy. Snowmobiling.	32		•	•	•			•	•	•		•			•
Gilbert Lake (F-9) 1,569 acres 12 mi. n.w. of Oneonta off SR 205. Cross-country skiing.	33	•	•	•	•			•	•	•		•		•	•
Glimmerglass (F-9) 593 acres 4 mi. s. of East Springfield. Snow-mobiling.	34	•	•	•	•			•	•	•		•			•
Golden Hill (D-3) 510 acres 5 mi. n.e. of Barker off SR 148. Snowmobiling.	35	•		•	•	•		•		•		•			•
Grafton Lakes (E-11) 2,357 acres .5 mi. s. of Grafton off SR 2. Cross-country skiing; nature trails.	36		•	•	•			•	•	•		•			•
Grass Point (B-7) 66 acres 5 mi. s. of Alexandria Bay off SR 12.	37	•	•	•	•			•	•						
Green Lakes (E-7) 1,700 acres 4 mi. n.e. of Fayetteville on SR 290. Cross-country skiing.	38	•	•	•	•			•	•	•		•		•	•
Hamlin Beach (D-4) 1,243 acres 5 mi. n. of Hamlin on Lake Ontario. Cross-country skiing; nature trails.	39	•	•	•	•			•	•	•		•	•		•
Harriman (I-10) 46,613 acres 5 mi. w. of Stony Point on SR 210. Cross-country skiing; nature trails.	40		•	•	•	•	•	•	•	•		•			•
Heckscher (I-3) 1,657 acres 1 mi. s. of East Islip off Southern State Pkwy. Cross-country skiing; bridle paths.	41	•	•	•	•	•		•		•		•			•
Hempstead Lake (I-2) 775 acres 2 mi. s. of Hempstead. Tennis; bridle paths, nature trails.	42		•	•				•			•				•
Higley Flow (B-9) 1,200 acres 2 mi. w. of South Colton off SR 56. Cross-country skiing; nature trails.	43	•	•	•	•			•	•	•		•		•	•
Hither Hills (H-6) 1,755 acres 8 mi. w. of Montauk on SR 27.	44	•	•	•				•	•						•
Jacques Cartier (B-8) 461 acres 2 mi. w. of Morristown off SR 12. Cross-country skiing.	45	•	•		•			•	•				•		•
James Baird (H-11) 590 acres 11 mi. e. of Poughkeepsie on Taconic State Pkwy. Cross-country skiing, golf.	46		•	•									•		•
John Boyd Thacher (F-10) 2,000 acres 4 mi. n. of New Salem on SR 157. Nature trails.	47		•	•						•	•	•			•
Jones Beach (I-2) 2,413 acres on the ocean shore of Long Island off Meadowbrook or Wantagh Pkwy. Golf. (See Wantagh p. 203)	48		•					•	•				•		•
Joseph Davis (D-3) 388 acres 2.5 mi. s. of Youngstown off Robert Moses Pkwy.	49		•	•				•	•	•	•				•
Keewaydin (B-7) 180 acres 1 mi. w. of Alexandria Bay on SR 12.	50	•	•		•	•	•	•	•	•					•
Keuka Lake (F-5) 621 acres 6 mi. s.w. of Penn Yan off SR 54A. Snowmobiling.	51	•	•		•	•		•	•	•			•		•
Kring Point (B-8) 51 acres 10 mi. n.e. of Alexandria Bay.	52	•	•		•	•		•	•					•	•

RECREATION AREAS

	MAP LOCATION	CAMPING	PICNICKING	HIKING TRAILS	BOATING	BOAT RAMP	BOAT RENTAL	FISHING	SWIMMING	PETS ON LEASH	BICYCLE TRAILS	WINTER SPORTS	VISITOR CENTER	LODGE/CABINS	FOOD SERVICE
Lake Erie (F-2) 355 acres 2 mi. n. of Brocton on SR 380. Snowmobiling, tobogganing.	53	•	•	•				•	•	•		•	•		
Lakeside Beach (D-4) 734 acres 1.5 mi. e. of Kuckville on SR 18. Cross-country skiing.	54	•	•						•	•	•	•			•
Lake Taghkanic (G-11) 1,568 acres 12 mi. s.e. of Hudson on SR 82. Cross-country skiing, snowmobiling.	55	•	•	•	•	•	•	•	•	•		•	•	•	
Letchworth (F-4) 14,336 acres 2 mi. n. on SR 19A to Denton's Corners, then 2 mi. e. Scenic. Cross-country skiing; nature trails. *(See Castile p. 74)*	56	•	•	•				•	•	•	•	•	•	•	•
Long Point (C-7) 108 acres 4 mi. s. of Aurora off SR 90 to Lake Rd.	57		•		•	•	•		•						
Long Point (C-7) 23 acres 11 mi. s.w. of Three Mile Bay off SR 12E.	58	•	•		•	•	•	•							
Long Point on Lake Chautauqua (G-2) 360 acres 1 mi. s. of Maple Springs off I-86/SR 17. Snowmobiling.	59		•	•	•	•	•	•	•	•		•			•
Macomb Reservation (B-11) 600 acres 3 mi. w. of Schuyler Falls off SR 22B. Cross-country skiing.	60	•	•	•	•	•	•	•	•	•					
Margaret Lewis Norrie (G-10) 329 acres 3 mi. n. of Hyde Park on US 9.	61	•	•	•	•	•	•	•		•			•	•	
Mary Island (B-7) 13 acres at n.e. end of Wellesley Island; access is by boat only.	62	•	•		•			•							
Max V. Shaul (F-10) 15 acres 5 mi. s. of Middleburgh on SR 30.	63	•	•	•					•	•	•				
Mine Kill (F-10) 15 mi. s. of Middleburgh via SR 30.	64		•	•	•	•		•	•	•		•			
Minnewaska (H-10) 10 mi. w. of New Paltz via US 44/SR 55. Cross-country skiing.	65			•				•	•	•	•	•			
Montauk Point (H-6) 724 acres 4 mi. e. of Montauk on SR 27. Nature Trails.	66		•	•				•							•
Moreau Lake (D-11) 645 acres 4 mi. s. of Glens Falls off US 9. Cross-country skiing; nature trails.	67	•	•	•	•	•	•	•	•	•		•			
Newton Battlefield Reservation (G-6) 330 acres 5 mi. e. of Elmira via SR 7.	68	•	•	•						•			•	•	
Niagara Falls (E-3) 433 acres at foot of Falls St. in Niagara Falls. Scenic. Nature trails, recreation programs. *(See Niagara Falls p. 164)*	69		•	•					•	•	•	•			•
Ogden and Ruth Livingston Mills Memorial (G-10) 575 acres 5 mi. n. on US 9 to Old Post Rd. Cross-country skiing, golf.	70		•	•				•		•	•	•			
Oquaga Creek (G-8) 1,482 acres 9 mi. s. of Sidney off SR 206.	71	•	•	•	•	•	•	•	•	•		•			
Orient Beach (H-5) 357 acres 3.5 mi. e. of Orient off SR 25.	72		•	•				•	•	•					•
Pinnacle (G-5) 2 mi. s. of Addison off Ackerson Rd. Golf.	73		•	•						•		•			•
Pixley Falls (D-8) 375 acres 6 mi. s. of Boonville off SR 46.	74	•	•	•				•		•					
Point Au Roche (A-11) 850 acres 4 mi. n. of Plattsburgh e. of SR 9. Cross-country skiing; nature center.	75		•	•	•	•		•	•	•	•	•	•		•
Reservoir (E-2) 132 acres 2 mi. n. of Niagara Falls at jct. SRs 265 and 31.	76		•	•				•		•		•			
Robert H. Treman (F-6) 1,025 acres 5 mi. s.w. of Ithaca off SR 327.	77	•	•	•				•	•	•		•		•	
Robert Moses/Fire Island (I-3) 1,000 acres on the w. end of Fire Island on the Atlantic Ocean, accessible via the Robert Moses Causeway from Captree State Park. *(See Fire Island National Seashore p. 85)*	78		•	•				•	•						•
Robert Moses/Massena (A-9) 4,122 acres 2 mi. n.e. of SR 37 on Barnhart Island. Scenic. Downhill skiing; nature trails. *(See Massena p. 100)*	79	•	•	•	•	•	•	•	•	•	•	•	•	•	•
Rockland Lake (I-11) 1,079 acres 3 mi. n. of Nyack on US 9W. Cross-country skiing; nature trails.	80		•	•	•	•	•	•	•	•		•	•		

RECREATION AREAS

RECREATION AREAS	MAP LOCATION	CAMPING	PICNICKING	HIKING TRAILS	BOATING	BOAT RAMP	BOAT RENTAL	FISHING	SWIMMING	PETS ON LEASH	BICYCLE TRAILS	WINTER SPORTS	VISITOR CENTER	LODGE/CABINS	FOOD SERVICE
Sampson (E-6) 1,853 acres 5 mi. n. of Ovid on SR 96A. Recreation building.	81	●	●	●	●	●		●	●	●	●				●
Saratoga Spa (E-11) 2,002 acres n. of I-87 exit 13N in Saratoga Springs. Cross-country skiing, snowmobiling. *(See Saratoga Springs p. 194)*	82		●	●				●	●	●	●	●			●
Selkirk Shores (D-7) 980 acres 5 mi. w. of Pulaski on SR 3. Snowmobiling.	83	●	●	●	●	●		●	●	●		●		●	●
Seneca Lake (E-6) 141 acres 1 mi. e. of Geneva off US 20. *(See Geneva p. 87)*	84		●		●	●		●	●	●					
Southwick Beach (C-7) 313 acres 32 mi. s.w. of Watertown off SR 3. Nature trails.	85	●	●	●				●	●	●					
Stony Brook (F-5) 577 acres 3 mi. s. of Dansville on SR 36. Snowmobiling.	86	●	●	●					●	●		●			
Sunken Meadow/Governor Alfred E. Smith (H-3) 1,266 acres 1 mi. n. of Kings Park. Cross-country skiing, golf, sledding; bridle paths.	87		●	●					●	●		●	●		
Taconic-Copake Falls (G-11) 4,647 acres 1 mi. e. of Copake Falls on SR 344. Nature trail.	88	●	●	●				●	●					●	
Taconic-Rudd Pond (G-11) 210 acres 3 mi. n. of Millerton.	89	●	●	●	●	●	●	●	●						●
Taughannock Falls (F-6) 783 acres 4 mi. s. of Trumansburg on SR 89. *(See Trumansburg p. 201)*	90	●	●	●	●	●		●	●	●		●		●	●
Thompson's Lake (F-10) 50 acres 3 mi. s.w. of East Berne on SR 157A.	91	●	●	●					●	●		●			
Valcour Landing (B-11) 4 mi. s. of Plattsburgh off US 9.	92	●	●		●			●							
Verona Beach (E-8) 1,735 acres 1 mi. s. of Sylvan Beach off SR 13. Cross-country skiing, snowmobiling.	93	●	●	●				●	●	●		●			
Watkins Glen (F-6) 1,000 acres adjoining Watkins Glen at the s. end of Seneca Lake. Recreation building. *(See Watkins Glen p. 205)*	94								●	●		●	●		●
Wellesley Island (B-7) 2,636 acres 2 mi. n. of Alexandria Bay via the Thousand Islands Bridge.	95	●	●	●	●	●	●	●	●	●			●	●	●
Westcott Beach (C-7) 319 acres 4 mi. s.w. of Sackets Harbor off SR 3.	96	●	●		●			●	●	●					
Whetstone Gulf (C-8) 1,902 acres 3 mi. s. of Martinsburg off SR 26. Nature trails.	97	●	●	●					●	●		●			
Wildwood (H-4) 769 acres 3 mi. e. of Wading River off SR 25A. Cross-country skiing.	98	●	●	●					●	●		●	●	●		●
Wilson-Tuscarora (D-3) 390 acres 1 mi. w. of Wilson on SR 18.	99		●	●	●	●		●	●	●					
OTHER															
Adirondack (B-10) 6,000,000 acres in upstate New York. Horse rental. *(See place listing p. 53)*	100	●	●	●	●	●	●	●	●	●	●	●	●	●	●
Braddock Bay (D-5) 2,295 acres 10 mi. w. of Rochester on Lake Ontario. Nature trails.	101		●	●	●	●		●				●	●		●
Catskill Forest Preserve (G-10) 287,989 acres in the Catskill Mountains. *(See Catskill p. 75)*	102	●	●	●	●	●		●	●			●			
Dorchester (F-7) 1,242 acres 2 mi. n. of Whitney Point on SR 26.	103	●	●	●	●	●		●							
Genesee Valley (E-5) 2.5 mi. s.w. of Rochester on Elmwood Ave. Golf (18-hole), ice skating, tennis.	104		●	●					●						
Greenwood (G-7) 440 acres 13 mi. n. of Endicott on SR 26.	105	●	●	●	●	●		●							●
Highland Forest (E-7) 2,700 acres 4 mi. e. of Fabius on SR 80.	106		●	●								●	●	●	●
Jamesville Beach (E-7) 250 acres off SR 173 on Apulia Rd. in Jamesville.	107		●	●					●	●					●
Lake Colby (B-10) 1 mi. n. of Saranac Lake Village on SR 86.	108		●		●	●		●	●				●		
Lake Flower (B-10) in Saranac Lake Village on SR 86. Canoeing, tennis.	109		●		●	●	●	●						●	●

RECREATION AREAS

	MAP LOCATION	CAMPING	PICNICKING	HIKING TRAILS	BOATING	BOAT RAMP	BOAT RENTAL	FISHING	SWIMMING	PETS ON LEASH	BICYCLE TRAILS	WINTER SPORTS	VISITOR CENTER	LODGE/CABINS	FOOD SERVICE
Mendon Ponds (E-5) 2,462 acres 12 mi. s.e. of Rochester on SR 65. Nature trails.	110		•	•	•			•	•	•		•	•	•	
Nathaniel Cole (G-8) 370 acres 5 mi. e. of Kirkwood on Colesville Rd.	111		•	•	•		•	•	•	•			•		•
Oneida Shores (E-7) 390 acres on Bartell Rd. off I-81 exit 31 in Brewerton.	112	•	•		•	•		•	•	•			•		
Otsiningo (G-7) 84 acres 1 mi. n. of Binghamton on US 11.	113		•	•						•	•	•	•		
Point Gratiot (F-2) 75 acres on Lake Shore Dr. W. in Dunkirk.	114							•	•	•			•		
Saranac Lakes (C-10) Three lakes.	115														
Lower Saranac Lake .5 mi. w. of Saranac Lake off SR 3W. Horse rental.		•	•	•	•	•	•	•	•	•			•	•	
Middle Saranac Lake 3 mi. w. of Saranac Lake off SR 3W.		•	•	•	•			•	•				•		
Upper Saranac Lake 11 mi. w. of Saranac Lake off SR 3W. Horse rental.		•	•	•	•	•		•	•	•			•	•	
Saratoga Lake (E-11) 3 mi. e. of Saratoga Springs via SR 9P.	116	•	•		•	•	•	•	•				•		•
Thomas Bull Memorial (H-10) 652 acres s.w. of Montgomery on SR 416. Golf, tennis.	117		•		•			•	•		•		•		•

New York Temperature Averages
Maximum/Minimum
From the records of The Weather Channel Interactive, Inc.

	JAN	FEB	MAR	APR	MAY	JUNE	JULY	AUG	SEPT	OCT	NOV	DEC
Albany	31/14	33/15	42/24	57/36	70/46	79/56	84/61	81/59	73/50	62/40	48/31	35/19
Bear Mountain	33/19	33/19	43/28	55/38	67/48	75/56	79/63	78/61	71/54	60/44	47/33	36/22
Binghamton	30/15	31/15	39/23	53/34	65/45	74/55	79/60	77/58	70/50	59/40	45/30	33/19
Buffalo	30/17	30/16	38/23	52/34	65/44	75/55	80/59	79/58	72/51	60/44	46/32	33/21
New York	40/28	40/27	48/34	59/43	71/53	80/63	85/69	83/68	76/61	66/51	54/41	42/30
Oswego	32/18	32/18	40/26	51/36	62/45	72/55	79/62	76/61	70/54	59/44	47/34	35/22
Rochester	33/18	33/17	40/24	55/36	67/46	78/56	83/61	80/59	73/52	62/42	48/33	36/22
Syracuse	32/17	32/17	40/25	55/37	68/47	78/57	82/62	81/60	72/52	61/42	47/33	35/21

Exploring New York

For descriptions of places in bold type, see individual listings.

Adirondack Mountains

Stretching over 6 million acres and consisting of 46 peaks more than 4,000 feet tall, the Adirondack Mountains encompass thousands of miles of rivers and streams and more than 2,000 lakes and ponds. Low winter temperatures and heavy snowfall create excellent conditions for winter sports.

Lakes Champlain and George form the region's eastern border, while the Mohawk and St. Lawrence river valleys define its southern and northern limits.

Providing access to the region's mountainous interior are SRs 9N/86 and 73 from I-87; and SRs 30 and 12/28 from I-90.

A popular spot for hot-air balloonists between the Hudson River and Lake George, **Glens Falls** features the Hyde Collection of fine arts in a Florentine-style mansion. Cruise boats depart from the village of **Lake George** to explore the 365 islands of 32-mile-long Lake George.

The village also serves as a base for exploring lakeshore recreational facilities and historical sites. Scenic Lake Shore Drive links the village to **Fort Ticonderoga,** which controlled the narrow isthmus between lakes Champlain and George during Colonial times.

Extending southward 120 miles from Canada, Lake Champlain varies in width from one-quarter of a mile to 12 miles. From **Plattsburgh,** Port Kent and Essex, ferries reach Vermont.

Off I-87, **Ausable Chasm** has a series of waterfalls and rapids. Plattsburgh, near the Canadian border, played a strategic role in the War of 1812.

SRs 9N/86 and 73 wind through about 50 miles of small farms, resort communities and rugged mountains before joining near **Lake Placid.** East of town is **Wilmington,** where 4,867-foot Whiteface Mountain ranks as the highest skiing peak in the East. West of Lake Placid is the town

Statue of Liberty National Monument and Ellis Island, Lower Manhattan / © Catherine Gehm / Danita Delimont Agency

Escape to the Empire State

of **Saranac Lake,** where author Robert Louis Stevenson sought relief from tuberculosis and wrote extensively.

Blue Mountain Lake, at the junction of SRs 30 and 28, features the Adirondack Museum, which provides a thorough background on the region. Along Raquette Lake near the town of **Tupper Lake** lie the extravagant "Great Camps" of the Victorian-era industrialists.

Catskill Mountains

American Indians called this heavily forested section of the Appalachian escarpment *Onteora,* or "land in the sky." With its trout-filled streams and established resorts, the Catskill region is popular among artists and entertainers.

Four routes reach the Catskills from the Hudson River Valley. From the town of **Catskill,** scenic SRs 23 and 23A climb the steep 1,000-foot wall of the Catskills' eastern edge. SR 23 reaches the ski resort of **Windham** and continues on to **Oneonta.**

Before joining SR 23 at **Prattsville,** SR 23A winds upward through scenic Kaaterskill Clove to the mountain ski resort of Hunter. From **Kingston,** SR 28 passes Ashokan Reservoir and heads into the heart of the 278,000-acre Catskill Forest Preserve. From there, SR 28 crosses one of the least developed sections of the Catskills.

SR 17 between Harriman State Park/I-87 and **Binghamton** allows access to resort towns. Monticello serves as a base for exploring the headwaters of the Delaware River.

Winter recreational opportunities in the Catskills include hiking and snowshoeing. For ski enthusiasts, the Catskills offer snowmaking capacity for more than 1,100 acres, a combined vertical drop in excess of 8,890 feet and more than 200 trails. Cross-country skiing is available in state parks, the Catskill

Forest Preserve and at area ski centers.

Mohawk Valley

The Mohawk Valley Heritage Corridor is a mosaic of picturesque landscapes and legendary places where great events shaped the history of America. Homeland to the Iroquois Confederacy, the region stretches 130 miles from the Hudson River to Oneida Lake and includes Albany, Fulton, Herkimer, Montgomery, Oneida, Saratoga, Schenectady and Schoharie counties as well as the Oneida Indian Nation.

Heroic battles fought and won in the area became the turning point in the Revolutionary War. Once one of the busiest thoroughfares from the Atlantic seaboard, waves of settlers traversed the area heading westward through the Adirondack and Appalachian mountains. Many settled along the Erie Canal, creating a vibrant 19th century center of industrial innovation and commerce.

The primary east-west route is the I-90/NYS Thruway toll road from **Albany** to **Utica.** Albany was the site of the first general congress of all the Colonies in 1754. Northwest of Albany, **Schenectady** displays its Dutch heritage in the restored Stockade District. With the opening of the Erie Canal in 1825, **Amsterdam,** just west of Schenectady, became an important industrial town.

Nearby **Johnstown** remains a glove-making center and contains the site of one of the last battles of the Revolution. Utica, 60 miles west, developed with the canal. **Rome,** a portage station that connected the Hudson River to the Great Lakes before the Erie Canal, grew up around the site of **Fort Stanwix,** which played an important role in the Revolutionary War.

Central

Pivotal in the growth of water-powered industry and the opening of the West via the Erie Canal, central New York consists of rolling hills, dense forests and ample rivers. The region is demarcated by the Hudson River to the east; the Adirondacks, Mohawk River and Oneida Lake to the north; the Finger Lakes to the west; and the Catskills to the south.

James Fenimore Cooper's novels chronicled the area's pioneer days and gave the region its nickname, Leatherstocking Country. As the Erie Canal system became obsolete, many of the towns declined; except for scattered dairy farms, much of the countryside has reverted to its natural state.

From Schenectady, I-88 heads southwest across rolling farmland to Binghamton. Two scenic routes offer access to the southern portion of the region: SR 12 runs from Binghamton to Utica, and SR 28 runs from Oneonta to **Cooperstown.**

Beginning with the collection of salt from Onondaga Lake, **Syracuse** blossomed into a leading industrial and university city. Chittanango Falls State Park to the southeast contains one of the state's most beautiful waterfalls.

Binghamton developed after the opening of the Chenango Canal, which created a direct route between Pennsylvania coal fields and the Erie Canal. At the turn of the 20th century Eastern European immigrants sought work in shoe factories, leaving their mark in golden, onion-domed churches.

From Oneonta, home of the National Soccer Hall of Fame, SR 28 heads to Cooperstown, the home of the National Baseball Hall of Fame and the setting for James Fenimore Cooper's novels. Near the town of **Howes Cave** are

Lake George, Adirondack Park / © Linda Burton / Robertstock

caverns that contain a river, a lake and the floor of an ancient ocean.

Finger Lakes

Glaciers carved 11 deep, narrow, finger-shaped lakes and the distinctive drumlin ridges and left a landscape bearing names reminiscent of the Iroquois Indian civilization. Artistic retreats, wineries and parkland are a few of the region's attractions. The **Finger Lakes** lie south of I-90 between Syracuse and **Rochester,** northeast of SR 17/I-86/I-390 between Binghamton and Rochester, and west of I-81 between Syracuse and Binghamton.

The following routes allow access to the shorelines of the principal lakes: SR 13 between **Cortland, Ithaca** and **Elmira;** scenic SR 89 along Cayuga Lake between Ithaca and the Montezuma National Wildlife Refuge; and SR 14 along Seneca Lake from **Geneva** via **Watkins Glen** to Elmira. The region's most popular wineries line SRs 89, 14 and 54 at Keuka Lake.

At the northern end of Owasco Lake, **Auburn** is an agricultural center with fine Victorian houses. **Seneca Falls,** at the head of Cayuga Lake, was the birthplace of the women's rights movement. At the southern end of the lake, Ithaca boasts Cornell University. Nearby Taughannock Falls plunges 215 feet.

In Geneva, at the northern tip of Seneca Lake, is the Greek Revival-style Rose Hill estate. Watkins Glen, at the southern end of the lake, is known for auto racing and a state park where a stream has cut unusual patterns in the rocks as it drops 700 feet in a series of 18 waterfalls.

South of Seneca and Keuka lakes is Elmira, where Mark Twain spent his summers. **Corning,** synonymous with glass manufacturing, displays its products at the Corning Museum of Glass. Northwest of Corning via SR 54 is **Hammondsport,** associated with the state's grape and wine industry. **Canandaigua,** at the north end of Canandaigua Lake, serves as a performing arts and grape-growing center.

Freeport / KKM Photos / Long Island Convention & Visitors Bureau

Home of the Eastman Kodak Co., Rochester is known for its parks, gardens and estates. South off I-390, Mount Morris provides access to Letchworth State Park's "Grand Canyon of the East."

The Hamptons

When city streets begin to bake in the summer sun—an event that occurs with increasing regularity after Memorial Day—thousands of New Yorkers head for the cooler retreats of Long Island Sound and the Atlantic Ocean. Poshness seems to increase as one travels eastward on **Long Island.**

Generally speaking, the working class heads for such closer spots as Coney Island and **Jones Beach State Park.** Free spirits trek to **Fire Island National Seashore.** Young professionals splurging on group house rentals migrate to Westhampton. The truly rich and famous, however, congregate in multimillion-dollar beach houses in an area of summer colonies known as the Hamptons.

SR 27 winds through this area of vineyards, marinas, farmlands and sandy beaches. Luxurious resort communities dot the landscape. At the junction of SRs 114 and 27 are the magnificent estates of **East Hampton.**

In **Montauk,** Montauk Lighthouse, commissioned by President George Washington in 1796, stands at the easternmost tip of Long Island. From Montauk a ferry departs for Block Island, R.I., during the summer. The season also is enlivened by numerous fishing tournaments.

Perhaps the best-known and most exclusive Hampton is **Southampton,** east on SR 80 from SR 27. Settled in 1640 and named after the aristocratic Earl of Southampton, the town's social distinctions and conservative politics are firmly rooted.

According to one story, satires printed in a neighboring village's newspaper stating that the town council had voted to ban cars more than 3 years old and to reserve parking for vehicles worth more than $30,000 were reputedly accepted at face value by some Southamptonites. Twelve-foot hedges acting as green sentries shield the huge mansions on Gin Lane from the roadway.

Culture manages to maintain a foothold in Southampton even amid the rusticity of sand and salt spray. In the summer there is some sort of festival—wine, antique, art, theater—held almost every week.

Contrary to popular belief, the Hamptons region is not all high society glitter. Tucked among the fashionable enclaves is **Sag Harbor,** once one of the world's largest whaling centers. Other communities on Long Island Sound's south fork include **Amagansett, Bridgehampton** and Quogue.

Hudson River Valley

The size of the Hudson River estuary led explorer Henry Hudson to believe he had discovered a passage to the Orient. Because of its navigability, the river developed into a strategic waterway that attracted invading armies, facilitated exploration and trade westward, sustained the Industrial Revolution and guaranteed the growth of New York City as an international port.

Breathtaking bridges span 400-foot cliffs; farms and estates line the valley; and recreational possibilities abound in the Catskills and Taconic mountains to the west and east.

Primary routes paralleling the Hudson from **New York City** include the spectacular Palisades Interstate Parkway and US 9W on the west bank via the George Washington toll bridge; the faster New York Thruway toll road (I-87), via the Tappan Zee toll bridge; the scenic Henry Hudson Parkway/US 9/SR 9D/SR 9G route on the east bank; and the faster Saw Mill River Parkway/Taconic State Parkway road farther east.

Just north of New York City on the east bank off SR 9A is **Yonkers**, a major industrial town containing the Georgian-style Philipse Manor Hall. **Tarrytown** occupies a cove under the Tappan Zee Bridge on SR 9. Washington Irving's "Legend of Sleepy Hollow" described the town; Sunnyside was the author's home.

Sleepy Hollow, formerly North Tarrytown, contains the 18th-century Dutch-style Philipsburg Manor as well as John D. Rockefeller's Kykuit and the Union

Church of Pocantico Hills. **Ossining's** claim to fame is the infamous maximum-security prison Sing Sing. Nearby **Croton-on-Hudson** contains Van Cortlandt Manor, the estate of a Colonial Dutch patroon.

At the Bear Mountain Bridge north of Peekskill, scenic SR 9D follows the Hudson River, which narrows at the rugged cliffs of the Hudson Highlands. In the shadow of 1,000-foot Storm King Mountain, **Garrison** features the Boscobel mansion, an example of Federal architecture. **Poughkeepsie** is built on rocky terraces rising 250 feet above the Hudson and is home to Vassar College.

Just north, **Hyde Park** has the Home of Franklin D. Roosevelt National Historic Site, Eleanor Roosevelt's Val-Kill retreat and the FDR Presidential Library. Nearby **Rhinebeck** contains Beekman Arms, said to be the oldest hotel in the United States, and the Old Rhinebeck Aerodrome, known for vintage aircraft and summer air shows.

Finally, the former whaling town of **Hudson**, the northernmost point of interest along the river's east bank, features unusual Olana, a blend of castle and mosque designed by painter Frederick Church.

On the Hudson's west bank about 41 miles north of New York City is Bear Mountain State Park, where the river begins slicing through the Appalachian mountain chain. An observation deck provides views of four states—New York, New Jersey, Connecticut and Massachusetts. Guarding this narrow stretch is **West Point**, home of

the vast United States Military Academy. **Newburgh** served as Gen. George Washington's headquarters during the Revolutionary War from April 1792 until August 1783.

New Paltz, established by French Huguenots in the 17th century, boasts some of the oldest neighborhoods in America. **Kingston**, a Dutch trading post, lies at the mouth of the Delaware and Hudson Canal, which transported Pennsylvania coal and the Catskill Mountain bluestone that was destined to be the curbing and sidewalks of Manhattan.

Rip Van Winkle's legendary nap took place in the town of **Catskill**, which also is the beginning of scenic SR 23 northwest over East Windham Mountain.

As home to the United States' second largest state government, Albany provides diverse architecture ranging from the original Dutch settlement of Quackenbush and the Schuyler Mansion State Historic Site to the sleek high-rises of the Empire State Plaza complex of government buildings.

At the nearby confluence of the Mohawk and Hudson rivers lies industrial **Troy**. Along with neighboring communities, Troy forms the Hudson-Mohawk Urban Cultural Park, which commemorates the area's crucial role in 19th-century commerce and industry.

The northern end of the Hudson Valley is celebrated for horse racing and the health-giving properties of its springs. **Saratoga Springs** developed into a premier Victorian horse racing resort. It also is the summer home of the New York City Ballet and the Philadelphia Orchestra. Although summer activities center on Thoroughbred races and the arts, the town also is becoming a year-round sports and convention center.

Southeast via SR 29 and US 4 is **Saratoga National Historical Park**, which commemorates the Battles of Saratoga, fought on Sept. 19 and Oct. 7, 1777 and considered the turning point of the American Revolution.

Saratoga National Historical Park / National Park Service

Long Island

A bedroom community of Manhattan, the westernmost portion of Long Island is truly an extension of New York City, since it contains Brooklyn and Queens, two of the city's boroughs.

As Long Island extends eastward about 125 miles, the most densely populated areas give way to farms, vineyards, posh resorts and old whaling ports.

Glaciers scraped this low-lying extension of the New England coastal plain to produce the low bluffs of the North Shore along Long Island Sound and the moraines in the center of the island. The Atlantic Ocean continues to shape the dune-covered barrier islands of the South Shore.

Most of Long Island is less than a 2-hour drive from Midtown Manhattan. The Long Island Expressway, I-495, runs east-west through the center of the island, allowing convenient access to most points of interest. Highlights of the island include 20th-century mansions and 17th-century saltbox houses.

SR 25A offers a more leisurely, scenic route along the North Shore, while the Southern State Parkway and Sunrise Highway, SR 27, provide access to the South Shore.

As an alternative to driving, the Long Island Railroad links Manhattan to most major towns on Long Island.

The elegant estates that inspired F. Scott Fitzgerald's novel "The Great Gatsby" line the western half of the North Shore, also called the Gold Coast. Old Westbury Gardens, in the town of **Old Westbury,** once served as the estate of industrialist John S. Phipps.

Sagamore Hill National Historic Site, near **Oyster Bay,** was Theodore Roosevelt's summer White House. The 1885 house displays his family memorabilia. From this point SR 25A leads to **Centerport,** where the Vanderbilt mansion stands overlooking Northport Harbor. The Spanish Revival home is furnished with period pieces.

Cape Vincent / © Andre Jenny

The eastern terminus of I-495 is at **Riverhead,** where Long Island separates into two peninsulas, the North and South Forks. SR 25 skirts the farms of the North Fork to Orient Point, where the Cross Sound Ferry sails to New London, Conn. From Riverhead, SR 24 merges with scenic SR 27 to follow the South Fork to its eastern terminus, also called The Hamptons.

Along the South Shore of Long Island heading west, SR 27 parallels undeveloped Fire Island National Seashore and the more commercialized Jones Beach State Park, both popular recreation spots for New York City residents.

New York City

New York City is indebted to the tough bedrock that anchors the lofty skyscrapers of **Manhattan,** heart of the culturally rich, energetic "Big Apple."

With one of the highest traffic densities in the nation, as well as scarce and expensive parking, Manhattan poses problems for the motorist. For those driving between Upper, Midtown and Lower Manhattan, take the route consisting of controlled-access sections of FDR Drive, East River Drive, Harlem River Drive, I-95, the West Side Elevated Highway and the Henry Hudson Parkway (SR 9A).

The outlying boroughs of New York City also have much to offer. From Upper Manhattan, the Cross-Bronx Expressway (I-95) and the Major Deegan Expressway (I-87) reach **The Bronx.** Highlights here include the New York Botanical Garden, covering some 250 acres and featuring 28 specialty gardens, and the Bronx Zoo, one of the country's largest urban zoos.

From Midtown Manhattan the Long Island Expressway (I-495) via the Queens Midtown tunnel reaches **Queens,** which has Flushing Meadows-Corona Park, site of the 1939-40 and 1964-65 New York World's Fairs.

From Lower Manhattan, **Brooklyn** is reached via the Brooklyn Battery toll tunnel and the Prospect Expressway; the Brooklyn and Manhattan bridges also link Manhattan to the borough. Brooklyn contains the Brooklyn Botanic Garden, Brighton Beach and the vintage Coney Island Boardwalk.

Staten Island, reached from Brooklyn via the Verrazano-Narrows toll bridge or by the Staten Island Ferry, is home to Historic Richmond Town, a restored 100-acre village re-creating 3 centuries of local history.

Thousand Islands-St. Lawrence River

Called the "jewels in the crown of the Empire State," the **Thousand Islands** range in size from 2 square feet to 20 square miles and are a paradise for anglers, boaters and swimmers. Although the region was the scene of some of the bloodiest battles of the War of 1812, Canada and the United States now cooperate along their "Fourth Seacoast" in operating the **Great Lakes-St. Lawrence Seaway System** and in generating electricity.

A principal route through the region is I-81, between Syracuse and the Thousand Islands International Bridge. A scenic combination of SRs 12E and 12 then follows the St. Lawrence southwest to Lake Ontario. In the opposite direction SRs 12 and 37 lead to **Massena.**

Along I-81 in wooded, gently rolling farmland is **Watertown,** the birthplace of the Woolworth five-and-dime store chain. **Sackets Harbor,** a nearby lakeside resort, saw a U.S. victory against British warships during the War of 1812. From Fishers Landing the Thousand Islands International Bridge to Ontario offers a perspective of some of the rocky, pine-covered islands.

Boat tours from **Alexandria Bay** offer a closer perspective of Boldt Castle on Heart Island, a 1900 turreted stone castle.

SR 12/37 crosses semiwooded farmland to **Ogdensburg,** the oldest settlement in upstate New York and the boyhood home of artist Frederic Remington. A museum displays some of his American West-themed paintings.

Farther northeast, an 80-foot drop in the river marks the location of Massena, the U.S. end of the Moses-Saunders Power Dam, which generates 2 million kilowatts for Ontario and New York state. The town lies on the St. Lawrence Seaway, a series of connecting locks, lakes and rivers that compensate for rapids and the 602-foot change in altitude from the mouth of the St. Lawrence to the Great Lakes.

Western

Thundering Niagara Falls and the Allegheny Mountains draw visitors to New York's western region, which is bordered by the Niagara River and Lake Erie to the west, the Pennsylvania border to the south, Lake Ontario to the north and the Finger Lakes to the east.

The principal routes include I-90 between Rochester via **Buffalo** and the Pennsylvania border and I-290/190 around Buffalo to **Niagara Falls** and Lake Ontario. From its junction with I-390, I-86/SR 17 traverses the Allegheny Mountains and crosses Chautauqua Lake.

New York's second largest city, Buffalo serves as a major international port and manufacturing center. It also has strong ethnic neighborhoods and such architectural treasures as the Albright-Knox Art Gallery and the Guaranty Building skyscraper. The Peace toll bridge provides access to Canada. Just east off US 20 amid rolling farm country is **Darien Center,** where there is a Six Flags amusement park.

From Buffalo I-190 leads to Niagara Falls via **Grand Island,** a residential community in the middle of the Niagara River.

For a spray-catching close-up of the falls themselves, which consist of the massive American Falls, tiny Bridal Veil Falls and the magnificent Canadian Horseshoe Falls, ride the *Maid of the Mist* around the base of the falls, or hike near the Cave of the Winds on Goat Island, where walkways bring you to within 25 feet of the American Falls.

The falls power one of North America's largest hydroelectric projects, which is the focus of Power Vista, the Niagara Power Project's visitor center. An observation building affords wonderful views of the falls, while working models and displays explain how the generators operate. The Rainbow and Whirlpool Rapids toll bridges lead into Canada.

Lockport, 17 miles east of Niagara Falls on SR 31, preserves the history of the Erie Canal. Visitors can see the original locks, no longer active, and ride a boat through working locks.

From Niagara Falls, follow the Robert Moses Parkway or SR 18F north along the Niagara River, which churns through the breathtaking Niagara Escarpment. Fort Niagara, outside of **Youngstown,** guards the strategic mouth of the Niagara River on Lake Ontario. Built by the French in 1726, the fort played an important role during Colonial times.

Between Buffalo and the Pennsylvania border, southbound I-90 parallels a section of the old Underground Railroad through rolling vineyards and fruit orchards within sight of Lake Erie. **Chautauqua,** a Victorian-style summer resort and center of a wine-producing region on the shores of Chautauqua Lake off SR 394, offers a variety of arts- and education-related activities.

Near the southeastern end of the lake is **Jamestown,** known for its furniture and wood products. From Jamestown, I-86/SR 17 heads eastward through forested mountains to 60,398-acre Allegany State Park, New York's largest state park.

Farther east, **Salamanca** is the home of the Seneca-Iroquois National Museum. The collection portrays the life and culture of the Iroquois.

Rock City Park in nearby **Olean** allows hikers to examine 500-million-year-old quartz boulders that project from the edge of the Allegheny Mountains.

Prospect Point Observation Tower, Niagara Falls / © Byron Jorjorian / Alamy

Points of Interest

ADIRONDACK PARK (C-9)

Encompassing about two-thirds of upstate New York, Adirondack Park embraces some 6 million acres of both private and state land. Nearly half of it is wilderness. Physical features range from rugged mountains and sheer cliffs to low rolling uplands, beaver meadows, swamps and a grassy plain.

Among the 42 mountains that exceed 4,000 feet in elevation is 5,344-foot Mount Marcy, the highest in the state. Some 2,800 lakes and ponds, 1,200 miles of rivers and more than 30,000 miles of brooks and streams cover the landscape, allowing a mere 1,100 miles of highway and 120 miles of railroad to squeeze between the park's southwest border at Remsen and the northeast border at Lake Placid.

The park's geologic base reveals the contrasts of eons of change. Part of the main mountain chain is an outcropping of the Laurentian, or Canadian, Shield, a rare surfacing of some of the oldest and hardest known rock forged in the Earth's interior. Other areas contain fossil-rich strata formed millions of years later at the bottom of prehistoric seas.

Ecosystems, which range from alpine and subalpine to boreal and lowland lake to wetland, present an overlapping of northern and southern forest types with an occasional stand of virgin timber. With the exception of small areas near lakes George and Champlain, the park harbors no poisonous snakes.

The area was named after the Algonquin Indians. The Iroquois Indians called Algonquin *Ha-De-Ron-Dah* or "bark eaters" because they ate certain kinds of tree bark. The domain of hunters and loggers during the 18th and early 19th centuries, the Adirondacks were not "discovered" until after the Civil War. They evolved into a woodland retreat for the wealthy, who built luxurious resorts, private camps *(see Raquette Lake p. 187)* and summer homes on the lakes.

The wild and peaceful setting is being preserved for recreation. There are scenic views at every turn, some still bearing the vestiges of logging activity and the stubborn scars left by the forest fires of 1899, 1903 and 1908, and the hurricane of 1950.

Recreational possibilities span the seasons; boating, bird-watching, camping, canoeing, fishing, horseback riding, downhill and cross-country skiing, snowmobiling and snowshoeing are available. Areas with major development include Blue Mountain Lake, Lake George and Lake Placid *(see place listings pp. 61, 96 and 97).*

Two interpretive visitor centers provide indoor and outdoor exhibits and programming about the park. Both centers offer a surfaced trail system with interpretive signage.

The visitor center at Paul Smiths, 1 mile north of SR 86 on SR 30, provides information about the history, people and ecology of the Adirondack Park region. Features of the Newcomb Center, 14 miles east of Long Lake on SR 28N, include an exhibit about the birth and development of the conservation and preservation movements and the 20-minute multi-image presentation "Adirondack Passages." Comprehensive information about the park and its outdoor recreation opportunities can be obtained by contacting the Department of Environmental Conservation, P.O. Box 296, SR 86, Ray Brook, NY 12977; phone (518) 897-1200.

The visitor centers are open daily 9-5; closed Thanksgiving and Dec. 25. Free. Phone (518) 327-3000. *See Recreation Chart the AAA Northeastern CampBook.*

ALBANY (F-10) pop. 95,658, elev. 30'

See map page 54.

Albany is the state capital. The city's modern governmental complex, construction of which began in 1962, contrasts with its pastoral surroundings along the Hudson River.

Although French trappers were in the area in the mid-1500s, it was not until 1609 that Dutch fur traders arrived and established a trading center and fort. The first permanent settlement was founded in 1624 by 18 Walloon families, French Protestants who left the Spanish Netherlands seeking religious freedom. The settlement was called Beverwyck until it was transferred to England and renamed in honor of the Duke of York and Albany.

Albany was chartered in 1686 with Pieter Schuyler as the first mayor. By 1750 it had become an important trading center. Robert Fulton's *North River Steamboat* made the first successful steamboat run from New York to Albany in 1807. The opening of the Erie Canal between Buffalo and Albany in 1825 and the city's growth as a major railroad terminus greatly increased its importance.

Albany's notable citizens have included U.S. presidents Martin Van Buren, Millard Fillmore and Theodore and Franklin Roosevelt as well as authors Herman Melville and Henry James.

Albany is an expanding cultural center with museums, theaters and historic buildings. Governor Nelson A. Rockefeller Empire State Plaza *(see attraction listing)*, a 98.5-acre, 11-building complex that comprises state government offices and cultural and convention facilities, commands downtown Albany.

Other cultural showcases include the Palace Theatre, home of the Albany Symphony Orchestra, and Park Playhouse, one of the larger outdoor theaters on the East Coast. The Capital Repertory Theatre, the area's resident professional equity theater, presents a variety of plays year-round.

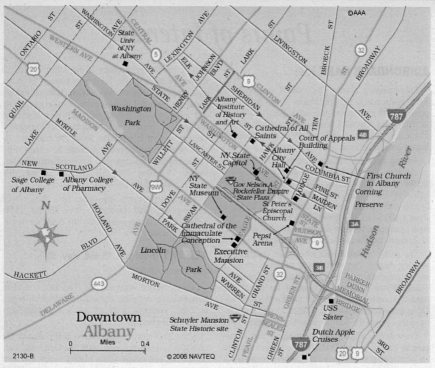

©AAA

Downtown
Albany

0   Miles   0.4

2130-B   ©2006 NAVTEQ

The Albany Heritage Area Visitor Center, at the intersection of Broadway and Clinton avenues at 25 Quackenbush Sq., has hands-on exhibits tracing the history of Albany; phone (518) 434-0405. The Henry Hudson Planetarium within the visitor center presents shows Saturdays.

Nestled along the Hudson River waterfront in downtown Albany is the Corning Preserve, a narrow strip of land several miles long that has nature trails popular for jogging, walking, bicycling and inline skating. The site also beckons picnickers and is frequently used for concerts and festivals.

Albany County Convention and Visitors Bureau: 25 Quackenbush Sq., Albany, NY 12207; phone (518) 434-1217 or (800) 258-3582.

Self-guiding tours: The Albany Heritage Area Visitor Center has self-guiding walking tour information.

Shopping areas: Colonie Center, Wolf Road and Central Avenue, has Macy's and Sears as its anchor stores, while Crossgates Mall, on Crossgates Mall Road, counts JCPenney and Macy's among its more than 230 stores.

SAVE **ALBANY INSTITUTE OF HISTORY AND ART,** 125 Washington Ave., presents permanent and changing exhibits about the art, culture and history of Albany and the Hudson Valley region. Collections include Hudson River School landscapes, early Dutch limner portraits, Albany silver, and 18th- and 19th-century New York furniture, sculpture, pewter, ceramics and decorative arts. The museum also houses an Egyptian collection and a library.

Allow 1 hour minimum. Wed.-Sat. 10-5, Sun. noon-5; closed holidays. Admission $8; senior citizens and students with ID $6; ages 6-12, $4. Phone (518) 463-4478.

CATHEDRAL OF ALL SAINTS is at 62 S. Swan St. This 1884 Gothic Revival Episcopal church has stained glass, mosaics, stone carvings, 17th-century choir stalls carved in Belgium, and historic and artistic objects. Allow 30 minutes minimum. Daily 9-3. Donations. Phone (518) 465-1342.

CATHEDRAL OF THE IMMACULATE CONCEPTION is at 125 Eagle St. This 1852 neo-Gothic Revival Catholic cathedral has a carved pulpit, stained glass and historic and artistic objects. Open Mon.-Fri. 7-5:30, Sat.-Sun. 8-6. Guided tours are given Wed. at 1, Memorial Day-Labor Day; by appointment rest of year. Free. Phone (518) 463-4447.

COURT OF APPEALS BUILDING, 20 Eagle St. at Pine St., opposite Academy Park, dates from 1842. This Greek Revival structure houses New York's highest court and features a courtroom designed by Henry Hobson Richardson. Mon.-Fri. 9-5, or by appointment. Free. Phone (518) 455-7711.

DUTCH APPLE CRUISES, 141 Broadway at Madison Ave., offers 2-hour narrated sightseeing cruises on the Hudson River. Cruises with meals are available. Departures daily at 10-6, May-Oct. Schedule may vary; phone ahead. Fare $28.95-$32.95; ages 4-12, $18.95-$22.95. Departures require a minimum of 20 persons. MC, VI. Phone (518) 463-0220.

FIRST CHURCH IN ALBANY (Reformed), 110 N. Pearl St., was founded in 1642. Its pulpit and weather vane both date from 1656. Mon.-Fri. 8:30-3. Donations. Phone (518) 463-4449.

GOVERNOR NELSON A. ROCKEFELLER EMPIRE STATE PLAZA, downtown between Madison Ave. and State St., houses a governmental center, a performing arts center, a meeting center, the New York State Museum and a collection of modern American art. A free tour of the art collection is available by reservation. The 42-story Corning Tower Building features an observation deck. Allow 1 hour minimum. Observation deck daily 10-2:30; closed Jan. 1, Easter, Thanksgiving and Dec. 25. Free. Phone (518) 474-2418 for general information or (518) 473-7521 to arrange a tour of the art collection.

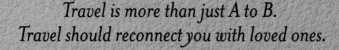

New York State Capitol, bounded by Washington Ave. and Swan, State and Eagle sts., was built in the late 1800s and houses the governor's office and the New York State Senate and Assembly. Carvings on the Million Dollar Staircase depict famous people in American history as well as friends and relatives of the sculptors. Guided 1-hour tours are given Mon.-Fri. at 10, noon, 2 and 3, Sat.-Sun. at 11, 1 and 3; closed Jan. 1, Easter, Thanksgiving and Dec. 25. Free. Phone (518) 474-2418.

New York State Museum is in the Empire State Plaza. Multimedia exhibits focus on the Adirondack wilderness, the New York City metropolis and American Indians of the state. The latter exhibit includes a full-size replica of an Iroquois longhouse. Participatory programs about art, history, science and technology are offered. Carousel rides are available. Allow 1 hour, 30 minutes minimum. Daily 9:30-5; closed Jan. 1, Thanksgiving and Dec. 25. Donations. Phone (518) 474-5877.

HISTORIC CHERRY HILL is between First and McCarty aves. at 523½ S. Pearl St. The 1787 Georgian-style house, once the center of a Colonial farm, contains furniture, silver, china, glass, letters and clothing from five generations. Allow 1 hour minimum. Guided tours on the hour Tues.-Sat. 10-3, Sun. 1-3, July-Sept.; Tues.-Fri. noon-3, Sat. 10-3, Sun. 1-3, Apr.-June and Oct.-Dec. Closed major holidays. Fee $4; over 62, $3; college students with ID $2; ages 6-17, $1. Phone (518) 434-4791.

ST. PETER'S EPISCOPAL CHURCH is 1 blk. e. of the Capitol at State and Lodge sts. The 1859 French Gothic church contains stained-glass windows, elaborate floor mosaics, a replica of the Queen Anne silver presented in 1712 and a British general's grave beneath the vestibule. Open Mon.-Fri. 8-4. Organ recitals are given Fri. at 12:30, Sept.-June. Donations. Phone (518) 434-3502.

SCHUYLER MANSION STATE HISTORIC SITE, 32 Catherine St., was the residence of Philip Schuyler, a noted Revolutionary War general and U.S. senator from New York. His daughter Betsy married Alexander Hamilton in the house. Guided tours on the hour Tues.-Sun. 11-5, June-Aug.; Wed.-Sun. 11-5, Apr.-May and Sept.-Oct.; by appointment rest of year. Closed Columbus Day. Last tour begins 1 hour before closing. Fee $4, senior citizens and students with ID $3, under 13 free. Phone (518) 434-0834.

SHAKER HERITAGE SOCIETY, off I-87 exit 4, then 1.5 mi. w. on Albany-Shaker Rd. (CR 151), is on the site of what is said to be the country's first Shaker settlement, established in 1776. The complex includes the 1848 Shaker Meeting House, with displays of furniture, tools and handicrafts; the cemetery where sect founder Mother Ann Lee is buried; and a nature preserve with trails. Picnicking is permitted. Allow 1 hour minimum. Tues.-Sat. 9:30-4, Feb.-Dec. Guided tours are given Sat. at 11:30 and 1:30, June-Oct. Donations. Tour fee $3.50, under 18 free. Phone (518) 456-7890.

SAVE **USS *SLATER*** is off I-787N exit 2, then n. on Broadway to the Snow Dock, or e. off I-787S exit 3B. This restored World War II destroyer escort offers a look at the floating environment for 216 men. Highlights include the crew's quarters, officers' country, radio room, galley and bridge with combat information center. Guided tours are available. Some steep stair climbing is required. Allow 30 minutes minimum. Wed.-Sun. 10-4, Apr.-Nov. Admission $7; over 65, $6; ages 6-14, $5. Rates may vary; phone ahead. Phone (518) 431-1943.

ALBERTSON (I-2) pop. 5,200, elev. 140′

CLARK BOTANIC GARDEN, 193 I.U. Willetts Rd., is reached from the Northern State Pkwy. and Long Island Expwy. via Willis Ave. S. exits. Rose, wildflower, vegetable and herb gardens as well as woodlands are available. Allow 1 hour minimum. Daily 10-4; closed Jan. 1, Thanksgiving and Dec. 25. Donations. Phone (516) 484-8600.

ALBION (D-4) pop. 7,438

COBBLESTONE SOCIETY MUSEUM is at jct. SRs 104 and 98 at 14393 Ridge Rd. This collection of seven historic buildings includes three cobblestone structures: an 1834 church, an 1840 parsonage once owned by Horace Greeley and a one-room schoolhouse built in 1849. Four frame buildings house blacksmith, harness and print shops as well as 19th- and 20th-century farming tools and implements.

Guided tours are available. Allow 1 hour, 30 minutes minimum. Tues.-Sat. 11-5, Sun. 1-5, June 23-Labor Day; Sun. 1-5, day after Labor Day-Oct. 31. Admission $3.50; over 54, $3; ages 5-17, $2. Phone (585) 589-9013.

ALEXANDRIA BAY (B-7)
pop. 1,088, elev. 274′

SAVE **1000 ISLANDS SKYDECK** is between the spans of the Thousand Islands International Bridge. A 400-foot observation tower offers excellent views of the Thousand Islands through three observation decks, one of which is glass-enclosed. On a clear day visibility is more than 40 miles. A photo ID and proof of citizenship or a passport are required. Daily 9-8, July-Aug.; 9-6, Apr.-June and in Oct.; 9-7 in Sept. (weather permitting). Admission $8.95; ages 6-12, $4.95. Bridge toll $2 per private vehicle. AX, MC, VI. Phone (613) 659-2335.

AQUA ZOO is off I-81 exit 50 n. to 43681 SR 12. The aquarium offers more than 80 exhibits of fish, coral and invertebrates from around the world. Allow 30 minutes minimum. Daily 10-7, Memorial Day-Labor Day; otherwise varies. Admission $5.50; ages 3-12, $5. DS, MC, VI. Phone (315) 482-5771.

BOLDT CASTLE, on Heart Island, is accessible by ferry service or boat tours (*see attraction listings*). The turreted, stone, 120-room, six-story castle was begun in 1900 by George C. Boldt, the proprietor of New York's Waldorf-Astoria hotel and Philadelphia's Bellevue-Stratford. Intended as a summer home for his wife, it was abandoned when she died in 1904, never to be furnished or occupied.

For more than 70 years the estate deteriorated to a state of almost complete disrepair. Restoration of the castle, yacht house, towers, service buildings and gardens has been ongoing since 1977. Exhibits, including artifacts from the era and a videotape presentation, depict the lives of the Boldts and the development of the 1000 Islands. The grounds and formal Italian garden are well-maintained.

Picnicking is permitted. Food is available. Allow 1 hour, 30 minutes minimum. Daily 10-7:30, July 1-Labor Day; 10-6:30, early May-June 30 and day after Labor Day to mid-Oct. Admission $5.75; ages 6-12, $3.50. Ferry or tour fares are not included in castle admission. Phone (315) 482-9724, (315) 482-2501 in the off-season, or (800) 847-5263.

Boldt Yacht House, reached via ferry from the castle, is on Wellesley Island. The restored yacht house features a collection of antique wooden boats. Allow 30 minutes minimum. Ferry departs every 30 minutes from the castle. Yacht house open daily 10:30-6:30, late May-late Sept. Fare $3; ages 6-12, $2.

SAVE *UNCLE SAM* BOAT TOURS is off I-81 exit 50N to foot of James St. Offered are a variety of sightseeing cruises of the 1000 Islands region aboard double- and triple-deck vessels. The 2.5-hour Two Nation Tour stops at Boldt Castle *(see attraction listing)*; the 4-hour Two Castle Tour visits Boldt and Singer castles; and the 1-hour Millionaire's Row Tour cruises a section of the St. Lawrence Seaway where millionaires built palatial estates, including Boldt Castle. Lunch, dinner and twilight cruises are offered in summer. Ferry service to Boldt Castle also is available.

Two Nation Tour departs daily at 10-4:30, July 1-Labor Day; 10-3, Apr. 29-June 30 and day after Labor Day-Oct. 8. Two Castle Tour departs daily at 10 and 2, July 1-Labor Day; Sat.-Sun. at 10 and 2, May 27-June 30 and day after Labor Day-Oct. 8. Millionaire's Row Tour departs daily 10-4, July 1-Labor Day; daily at 4:30, May 13-June 30 and day after Labor day-Oct. 8. Ferry departs daily every 30 minutes 10-6, July 1-Labor Day; 10-5, May

13-June 30 and day after Labor Day-Oct. 8. Phone ahead to verify schedules. Two Nation Tour $14.50; ages 4-12, $7.25. Two Castle Tour $26; ages 4-12, $13. Millionaire's Row Tour $10; ages 4-12, $5. Ferry $7; ages 4-12, $4.50. Fares do not include admission to Boldt Castle. DS, MC, VI. Phone (315) 482-2611 or (800) 253-9229. *See color ad.*

ALFRED (G-5) pop. 3,954, elev. 1,671'

THE SCHEIN-JOSEPH INTERNATIONAL MUSEUM OF CERAMIC ART AT ALFRED, in Binns-Merrill Hall at Alfred University, houses contemporary American ceramics and ceramic technology, pottery of the ancient Americas, and ceramics from Africa, Asia and Europe. The Fosdick-Nelson Gallery, located in Harder Hall, presents changing exhibits.

Allow 30 minutes minimum. Museum open Wed.-Fri. 10-4 and by appointment; closed holidays. Gallery open Mon.-Fri. 11-4, Sat. 1-3, Sept.-May; by appointment rest of year. Free. Phone (607) 871-2777 for the museum or (607) 871-2149 for the Fosdick-Nelson Gallery.

ALTMAR (D-7) pop. 351

SALMON RIVER FISH HATCHERY, 7 mi. e. of Pulaski off SR 13 following signs, has fish tanks and videotape monitors that explain hatchery operations. Allow 30 minutes minimum. Daily 9-4, Apr.-Nov. Free. Phone (315) 298-5051.

AMAGANSETT (H-5) pop. 1,067, elev. 64'

Despite its lack of a natural harbor, Amagansett has been a fishing village since it was settled in 1690. In the 18th and early 19th centuries the whaling industry was one of the town's most important sources of commerce and employment as well as the basis for an enduring folklore immortalizing old salts and the big ones that got away. *Also see Long Island p. 99.*

SAVE **EAST HAMPTON TOWN MARINE MUSEUM** is .5 mi. s. of jct. SR 27 and Atlantic Ave. on Bluff Rd. Dioramas and exhibits depict early whaling and modern fishing industries. A gunning shanty display with bird decoys, a children's

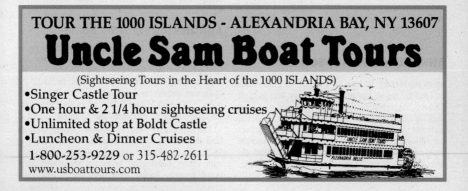

discovery room and a garden also are on the grounds. Allow 1 hour minimum. Tues.-Sat. 10-5, July-Aug.; Sat. 10-5, Sun. noon-5, Memorial Day-June and Sept. 1-Columbus Day. Admission $3, over 64, $2; children $1. Phone (631) 267-6544 or (631) 324-6850.

AMENIA (G-11) pop. 1,115

WINERIES

- Cascade Mountain Winery is 3 mi. n. on SR 22, then 3.5 mi. w. on Webutuck School Rd. to 835 Cascade Rd., following signs. Thurs.-Sun. 11-5, Apr.-Oct.; by appointment, rest of year. Closed Thanksgiving and Dec. 25. Phone (845) 373-9021.

AMHERST—*see Buffalo p. 71.*

AMSTERDAM (E-10) pop. 18,355, elev. 275'

Amsterdam, settled in 1783, became an important industrial center with the opening of the Erie Canal in 1825. After the Utica & Schenectady Railroad came through 11 years later, the town entered its commercial heyday with more than 100 industrial plants manufacturing such goods as carpets, brooms, buttons, clothing and linseed oil.

Montgomery County Chamber of Commerce: 366 W. Main St., P.O. Box 309, Amsterdam, NY 12010; phone (518) 842-8200 or (800) 743-7337.

NOTEWORTHY INDIAN MUSEUM, 100 Church St., houses American Indian artifacts and exhibits that trace Mohawk habitation in central New York. Displays include beadwork, baskets, pottery and a scaled-down replica of a Mohawk longhouse. Guided tours are available. Allow 1 hour minimum. Tues.-Fri. 11-4, Sat. 11-2, July-Aug.; by appointment rest of year. Donations. Phone (518) 843-4761.

OLD FORT JOHNSON—*see place listing p. 86.*

WALTER ELWOOD MUSEUM is reached via I-90 exit 27, w. on SR 5, 3 blks. n. on Evelyn St., then w. to 300 Guy Park Ave. The museum contains four permanent exhibits about natural history, Native American history, Victorian times, and factory life and community. A gallery features changing exhibits by local artists. Allow 1 hour minimum. Mon.-Fri. 10-3; closed holidays. Donations. Phone (518) 843-5151.

ANNANDALE-ON-HUDSON (G-11)

MONTGOMERY PLACE is .2 mi. off SR 9G. Built in 1805 by the widow of Revolutionary War general Richard Montgomery, the Federal mansion was later transformed to the Classical Revival style by noted architect Alexander Jackson Davis. Gardens reflect the influence of 19th-century horticulturist Andrew Jackson Downing. The 434-acre Hudson River estate includes a coach house, chalet-style cottage, greenhouse and nature trails.

Note: The house is closed for renovations; reopening is scheduled for spring 2007; phone for schedule. Picnicking is permitted on the grounds. Grounds open Sat.-Sun. 10-5, May-Oct. Admission to grounds $5, children $3. Audiotape grounds tour free. AX, MC, VI. Phone (845) 758-5461.

ARCADE (F-4) pop. 2,026, elev. 1,455'

ARCADE AND ATTICA RAILROAD, on SR 39 at 278 Main St., offers a historical and educational 15-mile steam locomotive train ride. Various themed excursions are held throughout the year, including a Civil War trip the third weekend in August and Santa runs in December.

Allow 3 hours minimum. Departures Wed. and Sat.-Sun. at noon and 2, Fri. at 2, July-Aug.; Fri. at 2, Sun. at noon, 2 and 4, Columbus Day at noon and 2, early Oct. to mid-Oct.; Sat.-Sun. and Labor Day at noon and 2, Memorial Day weekend-June 30 and in Sept. Fare $12; senior citizens $10; ages 3-11, $7; under 3 on lap free. Reservations are recommended for themed tours. MC, VI. Phone (585) 496-9877 or (585) 492-3100.

ARKVILLE (G-9) elev. 1,373'

[SAVE] **DELAWARE AND ULSTER RAILROAD,** 43510 SR 28, offers 1- and 1.75-hour round-trip train rides through the scenic Catskill Mountains to Roxbury and Arkville. The depot displays railroad memorabilia. Twilight and train robbery rides also are offered. Departures Thurs.-Sun., July-Aug.; Sat.-Sun., Memorial Day weekend-June 30 and Sept.-Oct. Phone for departure schedule. Fare $11; over 63, $9; ages 3-12, $7. MC, VI. To verify schedule and fares phone (845) 586-3877, or (800) 225-4132 in New York.

ASHFORD HOLLOW (F-3)

GRIFFIS SCULPTURE PARK, 2.7 mi. w. on Ahrens Rd., then 1.5 mi. s. on Mill Valley Rd., following signs, displays 200 steel, aluminum and bronze sculptures in meadows overlooking the rolling countryside. The park, which is in a 400-acre nature preserve, offers 10 miles of hiking trails. Picnicking is permitted. Daily 9-dusk, May-Oct.; by appointment rest of year. Admission $5, senior citizens and students with ID $3, under 13 free. Phone (716) 677-2808.

AUBURN (E-6) pop. 28,574, elev. 694'

In 1793 Auburn's location at the northern tip of Owasco Lake attracted its first settler, surveyor and Revolutionary War hero Col. John Hardenbergh. He built a cabin and a mill on the site. In 1805 the town was named for a locale in Oliver Goldsmith's poem "Deserted Village." Five years later the community boasted 90 dwellings and 17 mills.

The opening in 1817 of the state prison, built on land donated by citizens, and the establishment in 1829 of a theological seminary, which is affiliated with Union Theological Seminary, stimulated additional growth. Prison labor was cheap and, until

1882, legal. By the early 1920s the town was firmly entrenched as an industrial center and market for the region's agricultural products.

Fort Hill Cemetery, 19 Fort St., contains part of a hill thought to have been erected by Moundbuilders as well as the graves of William Seward, secretary of state under Presidents Lincoln and Andrew Johnson; former slave and Underground Railroad champion Harriet Tubman; and Logan, a Mingo Indian orator who led a war party in 1774 in retaliation for the murder of his family. *Also see Finger Lakes p. 84.*

Cayuga County Office of Tourism: 131 Genesee St., Auburn, NY 13021; phone (315) 255-1658 or (800) 499-9615.

CAYUGA MUSEUM/CASE RESEARCH LAB MUSEUM, 203 Genesee St., has changing and permanent Cayuga County history displays and 19th-century furnishings. The Case Research Laboratory, site of the invention of early sound motion pictures, is on the grounds. Tues.-Sun. noon-5, Feb.-Dec.; closed all major holidays. Donations. Phone (315) 253-8051.

EMERSON PARK, 2.5 mi. s. via SR 38A on Owasco Lake, covers 133 acres. Boating, fishing, picnicking and swimming are permitted. Daily dawn-dusk, Memorial Day-Labor Day. Parking $2 per private vehicle. Phone (315) 253-5611.

HARRIETT TUBMAN HOME, 1.5 mi. s. on SR 34 at 180 South St., features a 25-minute videotape about the life of the former slave who delivered dozens of slaves from the South on the Underground Railroad. During the Civil War Tubman rendered invaluable service to the Union Army as a nurse, scout and spy. A guided tour includes the home for the aged built and run in her honor.

Allow 1 hour minimum. Tues.-Fri. 10-4, Sat. 10-3, Feb.-Oct.; by appointment, rest of year. Admission $3. Phone (315) 252-2081.

HOOPES MEMORIAL PARK, 1.2 mi. e. on US 20 at E. Genesee St., contains a pond and gardens. Ice skating is available in the winter. Daily 7 a.m.-9 p.m. Free. Phone (315) 252-9300.

SCHWEINFURTH MEMORIAL ART CENTER, 205 Genesee St., houses changing exhibitions featuring works by area children, senior citizens and contemporary New York artists as well as an annual quilt exhibit. Tours, lectures, art classes, workshops and videotapes supplement the exhibits. Allow 1 hour minimum. Tues.-Sat. 10-5, Sun. 1-5; closed major holidays. Admission $3, under 12 free. An additional fee may be charged during special exhibits. Phone (315) 255-1553.

SEWARD HOUSE, 33 South St., was the home of the secretary of state under Presidents Abraham Lincoln and Andrew Johnson. It contains original family furnishings, clothing, antique toys and mementos of William H. Seward's career. A painting by Emanuel Leutze depicts Seward's negotiations for the purchase of Alaska. Allow 1 hour minimum. Tues.-Sat. 10-4, Sun. 1-4, July 1 to mid-Oct.; Tues.-Sat. 11-4, mid-Oct. through Dec. 31 and Feb.-June. Closed major holidays. Admission $6; over 59, $5; students with ID $2; under 12 free. Phone (315) 252-1283.

WARD W. O'HARA AGRICULTURAL MUSEUM, 2.5 mi. s. on SR 38A, across from Emerson Park, contains farm and household implements recalling rural life 1800-1930. Settings include a general store, creamery, blacksmith shop, veterinarian's office and kitchen. A large collection of farming equipment features locally manufactured tractors, wagons and agricultural machinery. Picnicking is permitted. Allow 1 hour minimum. Daily 11-4, mid-May to mid-Sept.; otherwise by appointment. Donations. Phone (315) 252-7644.

WILLARD MEMORIAL CHAPEL, 2 blks. e. of SR 34 at 17 Nelson St., is an example of the interior design work of Louis Comfort Tiffany and the Tiffany Decorating and Glass Co. The 1892 Romanesque Revival chapel has carved wooden pews, stained-glass windows, leaded-glass chandeliers, mosaic floors, and oak wainscoting and furnishings. Guided tours are available. Allow 1 hour minimum. Tues.-Fri. 10-4, Sun. 1-4, July-Aug; by appointment, rest of year. Closed holidays. Admission $3. Phone (315) 252-0339.

AURIESVILLE (E-10) elev. 304′

NATIONAL SHRINE OF NORTH AMERICAN MARTYRS, off I-90 exits 27 or 28, on SR 5S, marks the site of the Mohawk village of Ossernenon, where Father Isaac Jogues and his companions were killed in the 1640s. They were later canonized as martyrs. It also is the birthplace of the Blessed Kateri Tekakwitha, a Mohawk Indian recommended for canonization.

The site includes an American Indian museum and the Big Round Church, which seats 6,500. Picnicking is permitted. Food is available. Allow 2 hours minimum. Mon.-Sat. 10-4, Sun. 9:30-5, May-Oct. Donations. Phone (518) 853-3033.

AURORA (F-6) pop. 720

MACKENZIE-CHILDS TOURS is 1.5 mi. n. on SR 90. The design and production studios are on a 75-acre former dairy farm overlooking Cayuga Lake. A video tour of the studios offers a behind-the-scenes glimpse of artisans creating decorative clay dinnerware and one-of-a-kind pieces of furniture. A Victorian farmhouse shows the products in various interior design settings. Gardens and live animals grace the grounds. Artisans give demonstrations in the visitor center.

Allow 1 hour minimum. Farmhouse Mon.-Fri. at 10:30, Sat.-Sun. at 2, Oct. 16-May 14; Mon.-Fri. at 11 and 3, rest of year. Closed Jan. 1, Easter, July 4, Thanksgiving and Dec. 25. Farmhouse tour $10; senior citizens, students with ID and under 12, $6. AX, DS, MC, VI. Phone (800) 640-0546.

AUSABLE CHASM (B-11)

AUSABLE CHASM is reached via I-87 exit 34. The steep chasm formed by the Ausable River has perpendicular sandstone walls that rise as high as 200 feet above the river. Waterfalls, rapids and rock formations are highlights. A 2-mile, self-guiding trail walk to the chasm involves descending a series of gradual stairs. Shuttle buses and a trolley are available for the return trip. Optional participatory tubing or rafting trips are offered.

Comfortable shoes are recommended. Picnicking is permitted. Allow 2 hours minimum. Daily 9:30-5, July 1-Labor Day; 9:30-4, Memorial Day-June 30 and day after Labor Day-Columbus Day. Trail $16; ages 5-11, $9. Tube or raft trip $9. AX, DS, MC, VI. Phone (518) 834-7454.

RECREATIONAL ACTIVITIES

White-water Rafting

- **Hudson River Rafting Co.**, off I-87 exit 34 or 35 to SR 9. Write P.O. Box 47, North Creek, NY 12853. Trips depart daily, mid-May to mid-Oct. Phone (518) 834-7454 or (800) 888-7238.

BALDWINSVILLE (E-7) pop. 7,053, elev. 389′

BEAVER LAKE NATURE CENTER, 8477 E. Mud Lake Rd., covers 675 acres, including 238-acre Beaver Glacier Lake. Up to 10,000 geese stop in the area during spring migration, and many return in the fall. Eight trails traverse forest, meadows, lakeshore and wetlands. Trail highlights include boardwalks, an observation tower, interpretive signs, telescopes and a bog with orchids and insect-eating plants. Guided canoe trips are offered in summer. Daily 7:30-dusk; closed Thanksgiving and Dec. 25. Admission $2 per private vehicle. Phone (315) 638-2519.

BALLSTON SPA (E-11) pop. 5,556, elev. 288′

NATIONAL BOTTLE MUSEUM, 76 Milton Ave., promotes the study, appreciation and preservation of the American mouth-blown bottle industry. Exhibits include permanent and changing displays of bottles, containers and glass-blowing tools. A videotape describes glassblowing and mold blowing techniques. The museum also has a research library. Allow 30 minutes minimum. Daily 10-4, June-Sept.; Mon.-Fri. 10-4, rest of year. Donations. MC, VI. Phone (518) 885-7589.

BATAVIA (E-4) pop. 16,256, elev. 956′

Batavia was only a junction of the old Genesee Road and Tonawanda Creek Indian trails when Robert Morris bought more than 3 million acres in western New York from Massachusetts in 1797. Having obtained the Indian title to the land by the Big Tree Treaty, Morris sold most of his holdings to the Dutch Holland Land Co. The town is named for the Netherlands republic from which the owners originated.

Genesee County Chamber of Commerce: 210 E. Main St., Batavia, NY 14020; phone (585) 343-7440 or (800) 622-2686.

HOLLAND LAND OFFICE MUSEUM, 131 W. Main St., is in the original 1815 Holland Land Co. office. Exhibits deal with the early history of Genesee County, with emphasis on the Holland Purchase. Allow 30 minutes minimum. Mon.-Sat. 10-4, Memorial Day-Labor Day; Tues.-Sat. 10-4, rest of year. Closed county holidays. Donations. Phone (585) 343-4727.

BINGHAMTON (G-8) pop. 47,380, elev. 866′

The site of Binghamton was bought by Philadelphia merchant William Bingham in 1786 and settled by Joseph Leonard and other pioneers the following year. Originally called Chenango for the river it bordered, the settlement was renamed Binghamton in honor of the man whose donations of land allowed it to grow into a village and later into a full-fledged town.

Railroads, photography equipment and cigar making were the town's major industries before 1900, but shoe manufacturing became the dominant enterprise in the early 20th century. Such high-tech corporations as Universal Instruments and Link Flight Simulation, which manufactures aerospace equipment, later came to the forefront. IBM established its first plant in nearby Endicott.

Gold- and onion-domed churches of various Eastern European cultures are found throughout Broome County. Binghamton also includes among its cultural assets a branch of the State University of New York. The Anderson Center for the Performing Arts at Binghamton University presents performing artists of national and international acclaim. The Forum on Washington Street hosts cultural productions.

The Binghamton area has six antique, woodcarved carousels that visitors can ride from Memorial Day through Labor Day (weather permitting). George F. Johnson, who donated the carousels to local parks, stipulated that the municipalities never charge a fee for a ride. The carousels are at C. Fred Johnson Park in Johnson City; George W. Johnson Park in Endicott; Highland Park in Endwell; Recreation Park in Binghamton; Binghamton Zoo at Ross Park (*see attraction listing*); and West Endicott Park in Endicott.

Greater Binghamton Chamber of Commerce: Metro Center, 49 Court St., P.O. Box 995, Binghamton, NY 13902; phone (607) 772-8860 or (800) 836-6740.

Self-guiding tours: Brochures outlining walking tours of scenic and historic attractions in the Triple Cities—Binghamton, Endicott and Johnson City—are available at the chamber of commerce.

Shopping areas: Oakdale Mall, 3 miles west on Reynolds Road (SR 17 exit 70N), has JCPenney, Macy's and Sears among its 126 stores. Kohl's anchors Parkway Plaza, on SR 434 at SR 17 exit 70S.

Clinton Street's Antique Row, off SR 17 exit 72, attracts antique enthusiasts.

BINGHAMTON ZOO AT ROSS PARK, 60 Morgan Rd., is a 25-acre facility. Animals include lions, tigers, spectacled bears, endangered red wolves, otters, blackfooted penguins and golden lion tamarins. Signs explain each animal's habitat, diet and social structure. A 1919 carousel operates daily Memorial Day through Labor Day. Picnicking is permitted. Allow 1 hour, 30 minutes minimum. Daily 10-5, Apr.-Oct. Admission $5.50; senior citizens and ages 3-11, $4. Carousel free. Phone (607) 724-5461.

Discovery Center of the Southern Tier is at 60 Morgan Rd., in Binghamton Zoo at Ross Park. Hands-on activity stations invite children to fly a jet plane, ride a fire engine, shop in a grocery store or present the news on television. Allow 1 hour minimum. Tues.-Fri. 10-4, Sat. 10-5, Sun. noon-5; closed Jan. 1, Easter, Memorial Day, July 4, Labor Day and Dec. 24-25. Admission $5.50; over 16, $4.50; under 1 free; family rate $25. Phone (607) 773-8661.

ROBERSON MUSEUM AND SCIENCE CENTER, 30 Front St., is a regional museum of 19th- and 20th-century art, history, folk life, science and natural history. It is composed of the historic 1907 Roberson Mansion and a museum, planetarium and science gallery. Also on site is the Binghamton Visitor Center, which features permanent and changing heritage displays and a slide presentation. Planetarium shows are offered.

Allow 2 hours minimum. Tues.-Sat. 10:30-4:30 (also Thurs. 4:30-8); closed major holidays. Planetarium show schedule varies; phone ahead. Admission $6, over 61 and students with ID $4, family rate $20. Planetarium shows $1 with museum admission. Phone (607) 772-0660.

BLUE MOUNTAIN LAKE (C-10)
elev. 1,789′

To the north of Blue Mountain Lake, Blue Mountain rises 3,759 feet. Splendid views of the region are available from the summit, reached by a 3-mile trail. *Also see Adirondack Park p. 53.*

Blue Mountain Lake Association: Main Street, Blue Mountain Lake, NY 12812; phone (518) 352-7659.

ADIRONDACK MUSEUM, on SR 30, explores the culture, environment and history of the Adirondack region from the early 1800s to the present. The museum, on 32 acres overlooking Blue Mountain Lake, has 23 indoor and outdoor exhibits about logging, boating, recreation and mining. Visitors also can enjoy an elegant private railroad car, a collection of freshwater boats, a schoolhouse and a cottage with rustic furniture.

The crowd-pleasing Photobelt exhibit features selections from an extensive collection of historic Adirondacks photographs. Special displays are introduced each season.

Food is available. Allow 3 hours minimum. Daily 10-5, Memorial Day weekend-Oct. 16; Sat.-Sun. 10-5, Oct. 17-31. Admission $15; ages 6-12, $8. A family rate is available for up to two adults and all children ages 6-17. AX, DS, MC, VI. Phone (518) 352-7311.

BOLTON LANDING (D-11)

A resort area on the west shore of Lake George, Bolton Landing originated as an American Indian encampment on a wilderness trail. It later became the Bolton Landing stage stop on the Great Road. Wealthy families made the area their summer home. Scenic SR 9N runs north and south and is part of a lake shore route through the Adirondack Mountains.

Bolton Chamber of Commerce: 4928 Lakeshore Dr., P.O. Box 368, Bolton Landing, NY 12814; phone (518) 644-3831.

MARCELLA SEMBRICH OPERA MUSEUM, .5 mi. s. on SR 9N to 4800 Lakeshore Dr., contains mementos of the early 20th-century opera star's career. Lakeside walking paths on the grounds lead to vistas. Allow 30 minutes minimum. Daily 10-12:30 and 2-5:30, June 15-Sept. 15. Donations. Phone (518) 644-9839.

BOONVILLE (D-8) pop. 2,138, elev. 1,135′

Boonville was named for Garret Boon, an agent of the Holland Land Co., which owned property in the region at the end of the 18th century. The Black River Canal and the Black River Railroad brought prosperity to the town in the mid-1800s. Many of the grand houses of that period are on Schuyler Street. Hulbert House, a Georgian coach inn, was built in 1812.

Boonville Area Chamber of Commerce: 122 Main St., P.O. Box 163, Boonville, NY 13309; phone (315) 942-5112.

BRANCHPORT (F-5) elev. 736′

WINERIES

• **Hunt Country Vineyards** is off SR 54A at 4021 Italy Hill Rd. Mon.-Sat. 10-6, Sun. noon-6, Nov.-June; Mon.-Sat. 10-5, Sun. noon-5, rest of year. Phone (315) 595-2812 or (800) 946-3289.

BRIDGEHAMPTON (H-5)
pop. 1,381, elev. 50′

BRIDGEHAMPTON HISTORICAL MUSEUM is at 2368 Montauk Hwy. The early 19th-century Greek Revival Corwith House displays local artifacts and is furnished in various periods dating from the late 18th century. Working antique engines and farm machines can be found in the Hildreth-Simons Machine Shop; the George W. Strong Wheelwright Shop displays tools used in wagon repair. Guided tours Tues.-Sat. 10-3, June 1-Sept. 15; Mon.-Fri. 10-3, rest of year. Donations. Phone (631) 537-1088.

Buffalo

City Population: 292,648   Elevation: 680 ft.

Editor's Picks:

© James Schwabel / Panoramic Images

How Buffalo was named remains a mystery, although the site has never been called anything else. Ironically there have never been buffalo in Buffalo; even the shaggy beasts at the Buffalo Zoological Gardens are technically North American bison. One theory blames the misnomer on a mispronunciation of the French *beau fleuve*, or "beautiful river." The river in question is the Niagara.

The French explorer Robert La Salle paddled his canoe down the Niagara in 1628. A small French settlement was established in 1758. It was burned by the British the following year, but the settlers held fast. Joseph Ellicott informed them in 1800 that the Holland Land Co. had bought the land. Ellicott mapped out plans for a town to be called New Amsterdam and patterned after Washington, D.C.

The town was built, but residents insisted on calling it Buffalo. Put to the torch again by the British during the War of 1812, the town was quickly reconstructed. In 1818 the first Great Lakes steamboat, *Walk-on-the-Water*, was built, the first of two major events that turned a small village into a major city in only 16 years.

The second event was the opening of the Erie Canal in 1825. By connecting numerous trade and transportation routes, the canal made Buffalo the nucleus of the shipping trade between the Great Lakes region, Canada and the eastern United States. Ten years later the addition of railroads to Buffalo's transportation network boosted the city's growth potential even higher.

Buffalo's major industries include glass, rubber, plastics, electronics, and airplane and automobile manufacturing. High technology has emerged as a viable successor to the city's imperiled heavy industries. Agriculture also plays an important economic role, particularly the growing of fruits and vegetables. Grain distribution and flour and feed production have been part of the local economy since the 1950s. The city also is the home of the only player piano roll manufacturer in the world.

Buffalo has produced important people as well. Two of its residents, Millard Fillmore and Grover Cleveland, became president. Fillmore is buried in Forest Lawn Cemetery. Theodore Roosevelt was sworn in at the Wilcox Mansion on Delaware Avenue after President William McKinley's assassination at the city's Pan-American Exposition in 1901.

Other former Buffalo residents include William G. Fargo of the Wells Fargo stagecoach line, as well as the inventors of the windshield wiper, the pacemaker and the electric chair. Ellsworth Statler opened the first Hotel Statler on Delaware Avenue in 1908 with the slogan "A room with a bath for a dollar and a half."

Samuel Clemens, a resident in the 1870s, was editor of the *Buffalo Express*. Author Taylor Caldwell also called Buffalo home. Such musical classics as "When Irish Eyes Are Smiling," "My Wild Irish Rose" and "Over the Rainbow" were penned by Buffalo composers. Edwin P. (Ned) Christy launched the Christy Minstrels show in Buffalo.

Frank Lloyd Wright left his mark on Buffalo with the Darwin D. Martin House *(see attraction listing p. 68)*, on Jewett Parkway. Some say it is one of his

---

best examples of prairie architecture. Wright also designed Martin's summer retreat, Graycliff Estate *(see attraction listing p. 71)*, in nearby Derby.

Buffalo can aptly be called a college town; its 18 higher educational facilities range in curriculum from liberal arts to business to vocational training. The State University of New York at Buffalo is the largest university in the state.

The Albright-Knox Art Gallery *(see attraction listing p. 66)*, Kleinhans Music Hall and other cultural centers balance industrial practicality with aesthetic appreciation. At the stadiums and arenas, cheering the local teams is almost a prerequisite for citizenship in a town known for its high attendance at sporting events.

Downtown / © Lawrence Worcester
Lonely Planet Images

Getting There

By Car

From Rochester and other points east I-90 approaches Buffalo's northeast corner. It then joins I-190 and travels south, paralleling the city's eastern boundary before continuing west along the Lake Erie shoreline. The segment of I-290 that connects I-90 from the east and I-290 going north to Niagara Falls is called the Youngmann Expressway.

I-190 approaches the city from the northwest, passing through the west side before cutting across town and joining I-90 to the east. Toll barriers along I-190 are inbound only and are found between the Scajaquada Expressway (SR 198) and the Peace Bridge and between I-90 and Ogden Street. Travelers using I-90 from the west can go either northwest through the city via I-190 or northeast via I-90. Both I-90 and I-190 are part of the New York State Thruway.

Entering the area from the south are US 219 (Southern Expressway) from Springville and SR 400 (Aurora Expressway) from South Wales. Both join I-90 headed northeast. SR 5 from Dunkirk joins I-190 just below Seneca Street; SR 5 then becomes Main Street, cutting northeast. US 62 (Bailey Avenue), going north and south, bisects Buffalo.

The Kensington Expressway (SR 33) comes in from the east; the Scajaquada Expressway (SR 198) enters from the west off I-190. At the intersection of these two expressways, the Scajaquada ends; the Kensington Expressway continues south to downtown and east to Buffalo-Niagara Falls International Airport on Genesee Street.

Getting Around

Street System

Buffalo's major streets branch off from its central business district in a radial pattern. Because Lake Erie borders the city's southwest side, most roads

Destination Buffalo

*T*he "Queen City" has something for everyone. Travel back in time to the days of the dinosaurs at the Buffalo Museum of Science or watch history come alive at the Naval and Military Park.

Buffalo Niagara CVB & Angel Art, Ltd.

*C*heer on football's Bills or watch hockey's Sabres slice the ice. For a taste of Buffalo, sample its spicy chicken wings or visit the Buffalo and Erie County Historical Society, where more than 700 Buffalo-made products include Cheerios.

Graycliff Estate, Derby.
One of the area's two fine prairie-style homes designed by Frank Lloyd Wright overlooks Lake Erie. (See listing page 71)

Buffalo and Erie County Historical Society.
Keepers of the past, both the society and the building constructed for the 1901 Pan-American Exposition have lots of stories to tell. (See listing page 68)

© Gibson Stock Photography

Buffalo Transportation Pierce-Arrow Museum

Buffalo Transportation Pierce-Arrow Museum.
If it has wheels and history, you just might see it on display at this museum. (See listing page 67)

Buffalo

North Tonawanda

Grand Island

Amherst

CANADA
USA

See Vicinity map p. 67

Derby

Orchard Park

East Aurora

Eden

© Lawrence Worcester Lonely Planet Images

Delaware Park, Buffalo.
Look for a zoo and this Lincoln statue in Buffalo's Olmsted-designed park. (See listing page 68)

The Informed Traveler

Sales Tax: The sales tax in Buffalo is 8.25 percent. There also is a 7 percent tax levied on lodgings and a 5 percent tax on rental cars.

WHOM TO CALL

Emergency: 911

Police (non-emergency): (716) 853-2222

Time: (716) 844-1717

Weather: (716) 844-4444

Hospitals: Buffalo General, (716) 859-5600; Mercy Hospital, (716) 826-7000.

WHERE TO LOOK

Newspapers

The *Buffalo News* is the local daily newspaper. Also available are more than 40 weekly and special-interest publications.

Radio

Buffalo radio station WEBR (970 AM) is an all-news/weather station; WBFO (88.7 FM) is a member of National Public Radio.

Visitor Information

Buffalo Niagara Convention and Visitors Bureau: 617 Main St., Buffalo, NY 14203; phone (716) 852-0511 or (800) 283-3256.

For parks information phone (716) 851-5806.

TRANSPORTATION

Air Travel

Airport Taxi Service provides limousine transportation to the airport from major hotels and the Ellicott Street Bus Terminal daily 6 a.m.-11 p.m.; phone (716) 633-8294.

The Niagara Shuttle runs to major hotels in Niagara Falls daily; phone (800) 551-9369.

Rental Cars

Hertz, (716) 632-4772 or (800) 654-3080, offers discounts to AAA members. For listings of other agencies check the telephone directory.

Rail Service

Amtrak has two connecting stations: one at Exchange Street near the junction of Main and Seneca streets and another on Dick Road, in the Cheektowaga area.

Buses

Greyhound Lines Inc. operates out of the Ellicott Street Bus Terminal downtown; phone (800) 231-2222. For Empire Trailways information phone (800) 295-5555.

Taxis

Cab companies include Airport Taxi Service, (716) 633-8294; Broadway, (716) 896-4600; and City Service, (716) 852-4000. The rate is $1.80 per mile. For a complete list of taxi services check the telephone directory.

Public Transport

The major Metro bus routes operate daily 5 a.m. to midnight. Service varies by route, but buses generally run every 20 minutes on weekdays. The base fare is $1.25; exact fare is required. Zone charges apply in the suburbs; transfers are 25c. Tokens can be purchased at Metro offices and local banks.

A light rail rapid transit system runs from HSBC Arena at the base of Main Street through Buffalo Place and the theater district, ending at the State University of New York at Buffalo campus. Rail fares are the same as bus fares, with free transfers available between the two systems. Route maps are available at the Transportation Center at 181 Ellicott St.; phone (716) 855-7211.

begin downtown and branch out to the north and east. Niagara Square is the primary downtown intersection. From the square Delaware Avenue runs north and south; Niagara Street goes diagonally northwest to the Black Rock Canal and then heads north. Genesee Street extends northeast from Niagara Square to the airport.

Main Street, 2 blocks east of Delaware Avenue, runs north and south downtown but branches off to the northeast at Ferry Street. Main Street downtown and to the northeast is SR 5; however, to the south SR 5 is known as Fuhrmann Boulevard and then Hamburg Turnpike as it goes farther south down the Lake Erie shoreline.

Because of the creation of Buffalo Place, a pedestrian mall downtown, Main Street has been permanently closed to traffic from the theater district to the foot of Main Street.

Seneca Street and Abbott Road are two main east-west routes connecting downtown and the southeast suburbs. Clinton Street begins 4 blocks east of Niagara Square at Lafayette Square and heads alternately south and east, detouring around the two-block section from Michigan Avenue to Pine Street.

The downtown speed limit is 30 mph. Unless otherwise posted, right turns at red lights are permitted after a complete stop; left turns at red lights from a one-way street to another one-way street are permitted after a complete stop. Rush hours, 7-9 a.m. and 4-6 p.m., should be avoided.

Parking

Metered parking is available downtown, but spaces fill quickly. With patience, unmetered spaces also can be found. Many parking garages are available at $4-$5 per day. Underground parking is offered at Main Place, One M&T Plaza and One HSBC Center.

What To See

ALBRIGHT-KNOX ART GALLERY, just s. of jct. SR 198 on Elmwood Ave., is a Greek Revival building housing paintings and sculptures dating from 3000 B.C. to the present. The contemporary collection of American and European art is especially notable and includes works by Willem de Kooning, Henri Matisse, Pablo Picasso and Jackson Pollock.

Food is available. Allow 2 hours minimum. Wed.-Thurs. 10-5, Fri. 3-10, Sat.-Sun. 10-5; closed Jan. 1, July 4, Thanksgiving and Dec. 25. Admission $10, over 62 and students with ID $8, under 13 free, family rate (two adults and two children) $12. Parking $5. Phone (716) 882-8700.

BUFFALO AND ERIE COUNTY BOTANICAL GARDENS is at 2655 South Park Ave. (US 62). The gardens are in South Park, which was designed by Frederick Law Olmsted in the late 1890s. A restored, triple-domed glass conservatory patterned after England's Crystal Palace houses tropical and subtropical plants grouped by region, in the Victorian style. Other features include an arboretum, an

Albright-Knox Art Gallery / © Andre Jenny

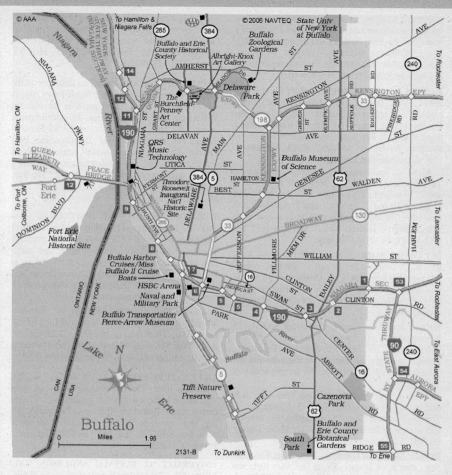

evergreen collection, flowering annuals, a bog garden, a lake, dinosaur topiaries and an extensive ivy collection.

Allow 1 hour minimum. Daily 10-5 (also Thurs. 5-6). Admission $5, students with ID and senior citizens $4, under 4 free; family rate $11. Phone (716) 827-1584.

[SAVE] **BUFFALO MUSEUM OF SCIENCE,** 1020 Humboldt Pkwy. at Northampton St. (Best St. exit from SR 33), has exhibits about Egyptians, dinosaurs, insects, space and endangered species as well as a children's discovery room. Interactive exhibits allow visitors to experiment with science. The Kellogg Observatory offers sun shows in the summer.

Allow 2 hours minimum. Mon.-Sat. 10-5, July-Aug.; Wed.-Sat. 10-5, Sun. noon-5, rest of year. Closed Jan. 1, July 4, Thanksgiving and Dec. 25. Admission $7; over 61, $6; ages 3-18, $5. AX, MC, VI. Phone (716) 896-5200.

[SAVE] **BUFFALO TRANSPORTATION PIERCE-ARROW MUSEUM** is at 263 Michigan Ave. at Seneca St. The development of transportation in the Buffalo area is chronicled through exhibits of automobiles, motorcycles, bicycles and such related motoring memorabilia as signs, parts and accessories. Of particular interest is a collection of Pierce-Arrow automobiles and hood ornaments. Muscle cars also are displayed.

Note: The museum will remain open in 2007 while undergoing construction of the Buffalo Filling Station by Frank Lloyd Wright; it is scheduled to open in fall 2008. Allow 1 hour minimum. Wed.-Sun. noon-5, Apr.-Sept.; Fri.-Sun. noon-5, rest of year. Hours may vary during construction periods; phone ahead. Admission $7; over 60, $6; ages 6-17, $3. MC, VI. Phone (716) 853-0084.

THE BURCHFIELD-PENNEY ART CENTER, in Rockwell Hall on Elmwood Ave. on the Buffalo State College campus, has a variety of changing exhibits and presentations. Featured is a collection of watercolor paintings by Charles E. Burchfield. Permanent exhibits include a re-creation of Burchfield's studio and Roycroft furniture and decorative objects. Allow 30 minutes minimum. Tues.-Sat. 10-5, Sun. 1-5. Admission $5; over 65, $4; students with ID and ages 8-18, $3. Phone (716) 878-6011.

DARWIN D. MARTIN HOUSE COMPLEX is at 125 Jewett Pkwy. One of Frank Lloyd Wright's finest examples of prairie architecture was built for the Darwin Martin family 1903-06. It was integrated along with a smaller house into Wright's only multi-structure residential complex, which harmonizes with the surrounding landscape.

Allow 1 hour minimum. Guided tours depart Tues.-Fri. at 11 and 3, Sat. at 10 and 1, Sun. at 1 and 2, June-Sept.; Tues.-Thurs. at 3, Fri. at 11 and 3, Sat. at 10 and 1, Sun. at 1 and 2; Apr.-May and Oct.-Nov.; Sat. at 10 and 1, Sun. at 1, rest of year. Admission $10; students with ID and ages 6-12, $8. MC, VI. Phone (716) 856-3858.

DELAWARE PARK, 2 mi. n. on Elmwood Ave., then e. on Iroquois Dr., is part of the park system designed by Frederick Law Olmsted in 1870 and was later the primary site of the 1901 Pan American Exposition. Recreational offerings include tennis, bicycling and golf.

Buffalo and Erie County Historical Society, 25 Nottingham Ct., is housed in the only remaining building from the 1901 Pan-American Exposition. Exhibits highlight the commercial and industrial development of the Buffalo area. An archive library is available.

Allow 1 hour minimum. Exhibits Tues.-Sat. 10-5, Sun. noon-5. Library Wed.-Sat. 1-5. Closed Jan. 1, Thanksgiving and Dec. 25. Admission $6; over 59 and students with ID $4; ages 7-12, $2.50. Library $6. MC, VI. Phone (716) 873-9644.

Buffalo Zoological Gardens, 2 mi. n. on Elmwood Ave., then e. on Iroquois Dr. to Delaware Park, has indoor and outdoor displays of more than 1,000 animals and birds on 23.5 acres. A highlight is the one-horned rhinoceros. Special exhibits include a wildlife building, lion and tiger outdoor habitat, gorilla rain forest and children's zoo. Carousel and train rides are available in season.

Food is available. Allow 1 hour, 30 minutes minimum. Gates open daily 10-5, June 1-Labor Day; daily 10-4, rest of year. Admission $8.50; over 62 and ages 2-14, $5. Parking $3.25. DS, MC, VI. Phone (716) 837-3900.

NAVAL AND MILITARY PARK, on Lake Erie at the foot of Pearl and Main sts. at 1 Naval Park Cove, is one of the few inland naval parks in the country. Visitors can board fighting ships, the guided-missile cruiser USS *Little Rock,* the destroyer USS *The Sullivans* and the World War II submarine USS *Croaker.* Displays include aircraft, scale models of ships and airplanes, and a videotape about the park's features and history. Daily 10-5, Apr.-Oct.; Sat.-Sun. 10-4, in Nov. Admission $8; over 59 and ages 6-16, $5. Phone (716) 847-1773.

THEODORE ROOSEVELT INAUGURAL NATIONAL HISTORIC SITE (Wilcox Mansion), 641 Delaware Ave., is an 1838 Greek Revival structure. Theodore Roosevelt was sworn in as the 26th president in the library. Displays include items relating to President William McKinley's assassination and President Roosevelt's inauguration, a slide presentation and changing art exhibits.

Allow 1 hour minimum. Mon.-Fri. 9-5, Sat.-Sun. noon-5; closed Jan. 1, Easter, Memorial Day, July 4, Labor Day, Thanksgiving and Dec. 24-25 and 31. Admission $5; over 62 and high school students with ID $3; ages 6-14, $1. Phone (716) 884-0095.

TIFFT NATURE PRESERVE is w. on SR 5 to 1200 Fuhrmann Blvd. The park encompasses 264 acres with nature trails, a wildflower garden and a 75-acre cattail marsh. Picnicking, fishing, cross-country skiing and snowshoeing are permitted. Park open Mon.-Fri. 8:30-7:30, Sat.-Sun. 10-5:30. Donations. Phone (716) 825-6397.

UNIVERSITY AT BUFFALO ANDERSON GALLERY, SR 33W (Main St. exit), then n. on Englewood Ave. to Martha Jackson Pl., offers changing exhibits of post-World War II art, many with a regional theme. Display media range from paintings and photographs to sculpture. Wed.-Sat. 11-5, Sun. 1-5. Free. Phone (716) 829-3754.

What To Do

Sightseeing

Those unfamiliar with Buffalo may wish to begin their sightseeing with an aerial view of the city from the observation deck of City Hall at Niagara Square downtown; phone (716) 851-5891. The deck is open Mon.-Fri. 9-4; closed holidays.

Many of Buffalo's historic structures have been renovated or restored; Allentown, a historic preservation district just south of North Street between Elmwood Avenue and Main Street, has Victorian buildings, ethnic restaurants, art galleries and boutiques. Information about tours of Allentown is available from the Allentown Association, 14 Allen St., Buffalo, NY 14202; phone (716) 881-1024.

Boat Tours

[SAVE] **BUFFALO HARBOR CRUISES/MISS BUFFALO II CRUISE BOATS** depart from the Erie Basin Marina at Marine Dr. and Erie St. Offered is a variety of 2-hour, narrated sightseeing tours of the Buffalo River and area waterways. Meal cruises with entertainment also are available. Sightseeing cruises depart Tues.-Sun., July 1-Labor Day; departure days and times vary according to type of cruise. Fare $13.50; ages 6-12, $9. AX, DS, MC, VI. Phone (716) 856-6696 or (800) 244-8684.

Bus Tours

Bus tours of Buffalo are offered by Bedore Tours Inc., (716) 285-7550; [SAVE] Gray Line of Buffalo & Niagara Falls, (716) 694-3600, (716) 695-1603 or (800) 695-1603; and Motherland Connextions Inc., (716) 282-1028.

Industrial Tours

QRS MUSIC TECHNOLOGY, .5 mi. n. of the Peace Bridge at 1026 Niagara St., offers guided tours of the world's only manufacturer of player piano rolls. Tours are limited to 12 persons and are not recommended for small children. Mon.-Fri. at 10 and 2; closed Jan. 1, Good Friday, Memorial Day, July 4, Labor Day, Thanksgiving and Dec. 24-25 and 31. Fee $2; under 12, $1. Phone (716) 885-4600.

Walking Tours

A variety of guided walking tours of historic Buffalo can be arranged through Campaign for Buffalo History, Architecture and Culture, (716) 884-3138, or Preservation Coalition of Erie County, (716) 885-3897.

Brochures for self-guiding walking tours are available from the Buffalo Visitor Centers at 617 Market St. and in Walden Galleria Mall. For more information contact the Buffalo Niagara Convention and Visitors Bureau (see The Informed Traveler).

Sports and Recreation

Buffalo has an extensive municipal park system where sports enthusiasts can find ample playing space. More than 100 **baseball** and **softball** diamonds are available, as are 84 **tennis** courts and three **soccer** fields. Sports such as **lawn bowling** and **cricket** also are offered. **Swimming** can be enjoyed at local pools and beaches.

Running tracks are available for walkers, joggers and runners. **Basketball** courts and **football** fields are scattered throughout town; six indoor ice rinks offer year-round **ice skating.**

Skiing is very popular in the region. Nine major areas with chair lifts, T-bars and other facilities are within close driving distance of the city; Kissing Bridge and Holiday Valley are less than an hour away. Other winter sports such as **tobogganing**, **sledding** and **snowmobiling** are permitted in public parks.

Those who consider spectating a sport in its own right will find plenty of company in Buffalo, where stadiums and arenas are filled with professional fans. Football lovers can see the Buffalo Bills at Ralph Wilson Stadium; phone (716) 649-0015. The Buffalo Bisons play baseball at Dunn Tire Park; phone (716) 843-4373. Slicing the ice in the HSBC Arena every winter is the Buffalo Sabres **hockey** team; phone (716) 855-4100. Buffalo's numerous colleges and universities also offer a wide variety of sporting events.

Four-legged athletes offer their share of excitement to **horse racing** buffs as well. **Harness racing** is held at the Buffalo Raceway in Hamburg; phone (716) 649-1280 for schedule.

Note: Policies concerning admittance of children to pari-mutuel betting facilities vary. Phone for information.

Shopping

The variety of stores offering fashions, fads and foods for every taste and budget make shopping in Buffalo an adventure. The eclectic mix of options on Elmwood Avenue ranges from funky boutiques to chic shops and eateries.

Antique and specialty gift shops are found in the Allentown area, Buffalo's version of Greenwich Village. Bargain hunters will appreciate tax-free shopping for brand-name merchandise at [SAVE] Duty Free America's, at The Peace Bridge.

Broadway Market at Broadway and Fillmore streets is an indoor marketplace in an Old World setting offering fresh produce, baked goods, crafts and specialty items. The Hertel and North Main Street commercial areas also offer a wide range of shops.

Walden Galleria, at I-90 and Walden Avenue, offers more than 200 stores including JCPenney, Macy's, Lord & Taylor and Sears.

Performing Arts

Shea's Performing Arts Center, an ornate 1926 theater at 646 Main St., presents performances year-round. For information about schedules and tickets phone (716) 847-0850. The Theatre of Youth (TOY) Company performs children's shows in the Allendale Theatre; phone (716) 884-4400.

The rejuvenated theater district also includes The New Phoenix Theatre at 95 Johnson Pkwy., phone (716) 855-2225; Studio Arena Theater at 710 Main St., phone (716) 856-5650; and Ujima Theatre at 545 Elmwood Ave., phone (716) 883-0380. Plays and musicals are presented September through early June. Shakespeare in Delaware Park gives free outdoor performances June through August; phone (716) 856-4533.

The Alleyway Theatre, One Curtain Up Alley, is a professional theater company dedicated to performing new plays in off-Broadway style; phone (716) 852-2600. The Irish Classical Theatre Co. performs international classics and plays from Irish literature at 625 Main St.; phone (716) 853-4282. Just outside of downtown at 320 Porter Ave. is the Kavinoky Theatre-D'Youville College; phone (716) 881-7668.

In addition to a theater and opera series, Shea's Performing Arts Center offers concerts. Other musical entertainment venues include HSBC Arena, One Seymour H. Knox III Plaza, and Kleinhans Music Hall, 3 Symphony Cir., performance home of the Buffalo Philharmonic Orchestra; phone (716) 855-4100 and (716) 885-5000, respectively. The Buffalo Chamber Music Society also presents a series of concerts at Kleinhans Music Hall; phone (716) 838-2383.

Special Events

In May the city is enlivened by the Hellenic Festival, offering cultural displays, folk dancing and Greek food. During the second weekend in June the Allentown Art Festival in the historic Allentown district displays the works of local artisans.

July 1-4, Buffalo and Fort Erie, Ontario, celebrate brotherhood during the Friendship Festival. Festivities include arts and crafts exhibits, a cultural parade, equestrian jumping, concerts and fireworks. Buffalo's best restaurants prepare epicurean delights from chicken wings to cheesecakes for the second weekend of July's Taste of Buffalo festival.

At the Erie County Fairgrounds, 12 miles south off I-90 exit 56 in Hamburg, one of the nation's oldest and largest county fairs takes place in mid-August. Over Labor Day weekend the National Buffalo Wing Festival draws cooks and tasters from across the nation. Buffalo's Winterfest, celebrated from December to January, is highlighted by ice skating, snow sculpture competitions and other activities.

The Buffalo Vicinity

AMHERST (E-3) pop. 116,510, elev. 260'

Amherst borders Buffalo-Niagara Falls International Airport, which is the focus of major air service to the Buffalo-Niagara Falls area. In the center of town is one of two campuses belonging to the State University of New York at Buffalo.

Amherst Chamber of Commerce: 350 Essjay Rd., Suite 200, Amherst, NY 14221; phone (716) 632-6905.

Shopping areas: Boulevard Mall, near Niagara Falls Boulevard at Maple Road, features more than 100 stores and is anchored by JCPenney, Macy's and Sears.

[SAVE] **AMHERST MUSEUM** is reached from I-990 to SR 263, then n. on New Rd. to 3755 Tonawanda Creek Rd. Featured are 12 restored 19th-century buildings. Highlighting local history are a costume collection, a children's discovery room and a hands-on Erie Canal exhibit. Allow 2 hours minimum. Museum open Tues.-Fri. 9:30-4:30, Sat.-Sun. 12:30-4:30, Apr.-Oct.; Tues.-Fri. 9:30-4:30, rest of year. Buildings open May 15-Oct. 15. Closed holidays. Admission $5; ages 5-12, $1.50; family rate (two adults and two children) $12. DS, MC, VI. Phone (716) 689-1440.

DERBY (E-3) pop. 1,200, elev. 707'

GRAYCLIFF ESTATE is at 6472 Old Lake Shore Dr. Frank Lloyd Wright designed this summer estate in 1927 for Darwin and Isabelle Martin. The manor house on a cliff overlooking Lake Erie incorporates Wright's vision of "organic architecture," blending with the natural landscape. Allow 1 hour minimum. Guided tours depart Tues.-Fri. at 11 and 2, Sat. at 11, noon, 1, 2 and 3, Sun. at noon, 1, 2, 3 and 4, Apr.-Nov.; closed Easter and Thanksgiving. Twilight tours are available some Fri., July-Aug. Reservations are required. Admission $10, students with ID $8. MC, VI. Phone (716) 947-9217.

EAST AURORA (E-4) pop. 6,673

East Aurora is home to Roycroft Campus, an art community founded in 1895 by Elbert Hubbard, a former salesman and marketing genius turned artist, writer, publisher and craftsman. Hubbard, a leader in the American Arts and Crafts movement, went on to design a simple, straight-line style of furniture that remains popular. The Elbert Hubbard Museum, 363 Oakwood Ave., features a collection of Roycroft arts and crafts.

A restored 1826 cottage built by Millard Fillmore before he became president is on Shearer Ave. and includes some of Fillmore's furnishings and presidential memorabilia.

Explore and More Children's Museum, 300 Gleed Ave., has interactive learning and play stations for children up to age 10; phone (716) 655-5131.

Greater East Aurora Chamber of Commerce: 431 Main St., East Aurora, NY 14052; phone (716) 652-8444.

Self-guiding tours: A brochure about 14 historic buildings, including the Roycroft Inn, on Roycroft Campus is available from the chamber.

Shopping areas: Antique and art shops line Main Street; a five-and-dime store adds old-fashioned charm to this quaint shopping district.

TOY TOWN MUSEUM, 1.1 mi. e. of SR 16/78 to 636 Girard Ave., is dedicated to preserving the heritage of toys from the early 1900s to the present. Toy Works, designed for children over 7, is the museum's interactive learning lab. Allow 30 minutes minimum. Mon.-Sat. 10-4. Free. Phone (716) 687-5151.

EDEN (F-3) pop. 3,579, elev. 797'

THE ORIGINAL AMERICAN KAZOO CO., 8703 S. Main St., is a factory that produces metal kazoos. The factory floor is closed to visitors, but there is a special area for viewing the production process. Exhibits depict the musical toy's West African origins as well as modern production methods. Guided tours are available by reservation. Allow 30 minutes minimum. Tues.-Wed. and Fri.-Sat. 10-5, Thurs. 10-8, Sun. noon-5; closed holidays. Free. Phone (716) 992-3960.

GRAND ISLAND (E-2) pop. 18,621

MARTIN'S FANTASY ISLAND, off I-190 exit 19, is a theme park with rides, shows and attractions. A water park, miniature golf course and canoes are available. Picnicking is permitted. Allow 4 hours minimum. Tues.-Sun. 11:30-8:30, mid-June through Labor Day; Sat.-Sun. 11:30-8:30, mid-May to mid-June. Admission $25; under 48 inches tall $20; over age 65, $13.95; under age 2 free. DS, MC, VI. Phone (716) 773-7591.

NORTH TONAWANDA (E-3) pop. 33,262

The Erie Canal spurred the development of North Tonawanda and its neighbor Tonawanda with a flourishing lumber industry. Today, the canal provides numerous recreational opportunities, including walking and biking along the Canalway Trail.

Chamber of Commerce of the Tonawandas: 15 Webster St., North Tonawanda, NY 14120; phone (716) 692-5120.

SAVE **THE HERSCHELL CARROUSEL FACTORY MUSEUM,** 180 Thompson St., preserves one of several local factories that produced carousels and band organs. Exhibits detail the process of hand-carving the various carousel animals and other objects. Of special note is a restored and working 1916 carousel. A children's carousel also is available. Mon.-Sat. 10-4, Sun. noon-4, July-Aug.; Wed.-Sun. noon-4, Apr.-June and Sept.-Dec. Admission $5; over 60, $4; ages 2-12, $2.50. Phone (716) 693-1885.

ORCHARD PARK (F-3) pop. 3,294, elev. 886'

Founded by Quakers in the early 1800s, Orchard Park now is home to the NFL's Buffalo Bills, who play in Ralph Wilson Stadium. An outdoor lovers dream, the area offers 1,500-acre Chestnut Ridge Park, complete with hiking trails and picnicking areas. Winter brings snow to the hills, perfect for tobogganing and sledding.

Orchard Park Chamber of Commerce: 4211 N. Buffalo Rd., Suite 14, Orchard Park, NY 14127; phone (716) 662-3366.

SAVE **PEDALING HISTORY BICYCLE MUSEUM** is at 3943 N. Buffalo Rd. With more than 300 antique and reproduction bicycles, this museum is said to be the country's largest of its kind. Displays include a collection of children's wheeled vehicles dating from the 1890s; boneshakers, built during the 1860s and so named because of the jarring riders experienced; wooden highwheels; and folding paratrooper bicycles used during World War II.

Allow 1 hour minimum. Mon.-Sat. 11-5, Sun. 1:30-5, Apr. 2-Jan. 14; Fri.-Sat. and Mon. 11-5, Sun. 1:30-5, rest of year. Closed Jan. 1, Thanksgiving and Dec. 25. Admission $7.50; over 62, $6.75; ages 7-15, $4.65; family rate $22. AX, DS, MC, VI. Phone (716) 662-3853.

Naval and Military Park / © Andre Jenny

This ends listings for the Buffalo Vicinity.
The following page resumes the alphabetical listings of cities in New York.

BURKE (A-10) pop. 213

WILDER HOMESTEAD—BOYHOOD HOME OF ALMANZO WILDER is 2.5 mi. e. of SR 30 on US 11, 1 mi. s. on CR 23, 1 mi. s. on Donahue Rd, then .5 mi. on Stacy Rd., following signs. The boyhood home of Laura Ingalls Wilder's husband Almanzo was the setting for her novel "Farmer Boy." It is furnished in period. A visitor center museum displays family photographs and a model of the farm as described in the book. On the grounds are three barns constructed from drawings of the original barns built by James Wilder in the 1840s.

Picnicking is permitted. Guided tours are given Mon.-Sat. 11-4, Sun. 1-4, and by appointment, Memorial Day weekend-Sept. 30. Last tour begins 1 hour before closing. Admission $6; ages 6-16, $3. Phone (518) 483-1207.

BURT—*see Niagara Falls p. 167*

CANAJOHARIE (E-9) pop. 2,257, elev. 317'

In an area settled by Dutch and Germans in the early 1700s, Canajoharie gets its name from an American Indian expression meaning "the pot that washes itself." The pot is a large pothole in the gorge of Canajoharie Creek. A 45-foot waterfall can be seen at the gorge from Wintergreen Park.

The first paper bag was invented in Canajoharie by James Arkell in 1859. In 1891 his son started a packing company that later became Beech-Nut Nutrition, a baby food manufacturer since 1931.

The village is part of the historic Mohawk Valley Heritage Corridor (*see Exploring New York p. 48*); phone (518) 673-1045 for information.

Canajoharie-Palatine Bridge Chamber of Commerce: P.O. Box 38, Canajoharie, NY 13317; phone (518) 673-4434.

CANAJOHARIE LIBRARY AND ART GALLERY, s.w. off New York Thruway exit 29 at Church St. and Erie Blvd., contains works by such American painters as John Singleton Copley, George Inness, John Singer Sargent and Gilbert Stuart along with a collection of watercolors by Winslow Homer. Other displays feature local history; industry, including the Beech-Nut and Life Savers companies; and genealogy.

Note: The art gallery is closed for renovations; reopening is scheduled for late June 2007. Guided tours are available by appointment. Allow 30 minutes minimum. Mon.-Thurs. 10-7:30, Fri. 10-4:30, Sat. 10-1:30; closed holidays. Donations. Phone (518) 673-2314.

CANANDAIGUA (E-5) pop. 11,264, elev. 685'

Canandaigua stands on the shore of the lake that shares its name. The town is on the site of the Seneca Indian village *Kan-an-dar-gue*, destroyed by Gen. John Sullivan in 1779. One of the most beautiful of the Finger Lakes, Canandaigua Lake is 17 miles long and averages about a mile wide. It harbors bass, pickerel, pike and trout. Around the lake are thousands of acres of vineyards. New York Wine & Culinary Center , 800 S. Main St., is a hub for information about wine production in Finger Lakes Wine Country and throughout the state. Tours, wine tastings, culinary demonstrations, displays and wine courses are offered; phone (585) 394-7070. *Also see Finger Lakes p. 84.*

Thoroughbred horse racing takes place Friday through Tuesday, early April through late November, at Finger Lakes Race Track, 8 miles north on SR 96 just east of its junction with SR 332; for information phone (585) 924-3232.

Note: Policies concerning admittance of children to pari-mutuel betting facilities vary. Phone for information.

Canandaigua Chamber of Commerce: 113 S. Main St., Canandaigua, NY 14424; phone (585) 394-4400.

CAPTAIN GRAY'S BOAT TOURS, 770 S. Main St., offers 1-, 2- and 3-hour narrated cruises on Canandaigua Lake. One-hour cruises depart Mon.-Fri. at 9:30, 11, 1, 3, 5 and 7, June 1-Labor Day. Fare for 1-hour cruise $12; under 12, $6. Phone (585) 394-5270.

SAVE **GRANGER HOMESTEAD AND CARRIAGE MUSEUM** is at 295 N. Main St. This restored 1816 Federal-style homestead was built by Gideon Granger, U.S. postmaster general under Presidents Thomas Jefferson and James Madison. The Carriage Museum has more than 44 horse-drawn vehicles made or used in the region 1810-1920.

Guided tours of the house and museum are given on the hour Tues.-Wed. 1-5, Thurs.-Fri. 11-5, mid-May through May 31 and Sept. 1 to mid-Oct.; Sat.-Sun. 1-5, June-Aug. Admission $5; over 61, $4; ages 7-16, $1. Phone (585) 394-1472.

DID YOU KNOW

European settlers introduced the apple to New York in the 1600s.

ONTARIO COUNTY HISTORICAL SOCIETY MUSEUM, 55 N. Main St., features exhibits about local and regional history. Archives and a genealogy research room also are available. Allow 1 hour minimum. Tues.-Sat. 10-4:30 (also Wed. 4:30-9); closed major holidays. Museum admission $3. Research room $7.50. Phone (585) 394-4975.

ROSELAND WATERPARK is at 250 Eastern Blvd. (US 20). The park includes a giant wave pool, body flume, raft ride, tube slide and children's splash pool. Kayaks and paddleboats are available to rent. Allow 1 hour minimum. Daily 10-7:30, mid-June to early Sept. Admission $17.99; children under 48 inches tall, $13.99; over age 60, $5; under age 2 free with paid adult. Additional fee for lockers, paddleboats and kayaks. MC, VI. Phone (585) 396-2000.

SONNENBERG GARDENS is n. off SR 21 (Gibson St.) at 151 Charlotte St., near New York State Thruway (US 90) exits 43 and 44. The 1887 Queen Anne-style mansion served as the summer retreat of Frederick Ferris, founder of the First National Bank of the City of New York, and his wife Mary Thompson, the daughter of a former New York governor. A variety of colors and textures accent the mansion's rustic facade. The interior reflects the Victorian-era penchant for mixing architectural styles, as seen in the English Tudor entry hall, medieval great hall, Colonial dining room, and Arts and Crafts trophy room.

Sonnenberg is a German word meaning "sunny hill." The 50-acre estate overlooking Canandaigua Lake consists of more than a dozen elegant theme gardens with fountains, streams, ponds, statues and greenhouses.

Tram rides, guided tours and food are available. Allow 2 hours minimum. Daily 9:30-5:30, Memorial Day-Labor Day; 9:30-4, early May-day before Memorial Day and day after Labor Day to mid-Oct. Guided tours are given Mon.-Fri. at 1, Sat.-Sun. at 10 and 1, Memorial Day-Sept. 30. Admission $10; over 59, $9; under 12 free. Admission prices may vary during special events. MC, VI. Phone (585) 394-4922.

CANASTOTA (E-7) pop. 4,425, elev. 436′

CANASTOTA CANAL TOWN MUSEUM, 122 Canal St., is in an 1874 house. Displayed are antiques, Erie Canal historical items and local memorabilia including photographs, maps, dolls, a water pump at an old-fashioned kitchen sink and examples of the handmade crystal for which Canastota was well-known in the early 1900s. Allow 30 minutes minimum. Mon.-Fri. 10-4, Sat. 10-1, June-Aug.; Tues.-Fri. 11-3, Apr.-May and Sept.-Oct. Closed holidays. Admission $3, under 12 free. Phone (315) 697-3451.

INTERNATIONAL BOXING HALL OF FAME, off New York State Thruway (I-90) exit 34 at 1 Hall of Fame Dr., offers videotapes and displays of such boxing memorabilia as robes, gloves and ticket stubs. Allow 30 minutes minimum.

Mon.-Fri. 9-5, Sat.-Sun. 10-4; closed holidays. Admission $7; over 65, $6.50; ages 7-15, $5.50. AX, DS, MC, VI. Phone (315) 697-7095.

CANTON (B-9) pop. 5,882, elev. 375′

Canton was settled by Vermonters in the early 1800s. The names for this town and nine others in the county were chosen from the world atlas in the hope that familiar names would help the land sell more easily. In 1861 Frederic Remington, sculptor and painter of the American West, was born in Canton, where his father was editor of the newspaper. Canton is home to St. Lawrence University, a liberal arts institution of about 2,000 students, which was founded in 1856.

Canton Chamber of Commerce: P.O. Box 369, Canton, NY 13617; phone (315) 386-8255.

ST. LAWRENCE COUNTY MUSEUM, 3 E. Main St., was the home of Silas Wright Jr., U.S. senator 1833-34 and New York governor 1844-46. The exterior and first-floor interior have been restored to the period of Wright's occupation. Permanent and changing exhibits relate to St. Lawrence County history; a research library with family history archives is available. Allow 1 hour minimum. Museum and library open Tues.-Sat. noon-4 (also Fri. 4-8); closed holidays. Museum free. Archives fee $5. Phone (315) 386-8133.

CAPE VINCENT (C-7) pop. 760, elev. 253′

CAPE VINCENT HISTORICAL MUSEUM, next to Horns Ferry Dock on lower James St., features area history displays. A genealogy room is available by appointment. Allow 30 minutes minimum. Daily 10-4, July-Aug.; by appointment rest of year. Donations. Phone (315) 654-4400.

CASTILE (F-4) pop. 1,051, elev. 1,397′

LETCHWORTH STATE PARK, 2 mi. n. on SR 19A to Denton's Corners, then 2 mi. e., is noted for the three waterfalls of the Genesee River Gorge. Middle Falls, a 107-foot cascade, is lighted nightly until 11. The walls of the 17-mile gorge reach heights up to 600 feet, offering views of the river and surrounding area. Scenic roads and trails pass through the park.

Food is available. Allow 4 hours minimum. Daily 6 a.m.-11 p.m. Admission $5 per private vehicle daily, Apr.-Oct. and Sat.-Sun. and holidays Dec.-Feb.; free rest of year. Phone (585) 493-3600. *See Recreation Chart.*

William Pryor Letchworth Pioneer and Indian Museum, in Letchworth State Park, has a varied display of artifacts. Allow 3 hours minimum. Daily 10-5, mid-May to mid-Oct. Free. Phone (585) 493-2760.

CATSKILL (G-10) pop. 4,392, elev. 67′

Near Catskill is the scene of Rip Van Winkle's legendary nap. The area affords a number of scenic drives, such as the section of SR 23 northwest over East Windham Mountain and SR 23B over Hunter Mountain.

Greene County Promotional Department: P.O. Box 527, Catskill, NY 12414; phone (518) 943-3223 or (800) 355-2287.

CATSKILL FOREST PRESERVE, comprising 287,989 acres in the Catskill Mountains, is particularly beautiful in June when the laurel blooms and in October when the leaves turn. Slide Mountain, with a height of 4,180 feet, is the highest point in the preserve. The preserve also is the location of Beaver Kill, Neversink and Willowemoc, three of the best fishing streams in the state. Daily 24 hours. Free. Phone (845) 256-3000. *See Recreation Chart.*

CAZENOVIA (E-8) pop. 2,614, elev. 1,205′

Cazenovia embraces the end of Cazenovia Lake, originally called *Ho-wah-ge-neh* (lake where the yellow perch swim) by American Indians. In 1793 John Lincklaen, a land agent for the Holland Land Co., settled in this area and renamed the site for Theophile Cazenove, the general agent for the company. The village first prospered as the economic crossroads of the region.

The invention of the modern game of football is credited to Cazenovia native Gerrit Smith Miller, who adapted it from a form of rugby around 1860.

Greater Cazenovia Area Chamber of Commerce: 59 Albany St., Cazenovia, NY 13035; phone (315) 655-9243 or (888) 218-6305.

LORENZO STATE HISTORIC SITE is off SR 13, .2 mi. s. of US 20 at 17 Rippleton Rd. The 1807 mansion overlooking Cazenovia Lake contains original furnishings. The grounds include a formal garden and a carriage collection. Allow 1 hour minimum. Tues.-Sun. 10-4:30. Guided tours are available May-Oct. Admission $5; over 61 and students with ID $4; ages 5-11, $1. Phone (315) 655-3200.

CELORON (G-2) pop. 1,295

SUMMER WIND CHAUTAUQUA LAKE CRUISES depart from the dock in Lucille Ball Memorial Park, 1 mi. n. of SR 394. Two-hour sightseeing cruises on Chautauqua Lake are given. Cruises with meals also are offered. Sightseeing cruises depart Mon.-Fri. at 12:30 and 2:30, Sat. at noon, Sun. at 10 and 1, July-Aug.; departure times vary May-June and Sept.-Oct. Fare $14.75; over 64, $13.75; ages 4-11, $9.75. Reservations are recommended. AX, DS, MC, VI. Phone (716) 763-7447.

CENTERPORT (H-3) pop. 5,446, elev. 50′

VANDERBILT MUSEUM is 1.5 mi. n. of SR 25A to 180 Little Neck Rd. Overlooking Northport Harbor, the 43-acre estate of William K. Vanderbilt II contains a Spanish Revival-style mansion, boathouse, seaplane hangar, marine and natural history museum, planetarium and gardens with water and architectural features. The

house is filled with original furnishings, family memorabilia, decorative arts, firearms, ethnic objects and natural history specimens. A highlight is a 3,000-year-old mummy purchased in 1931.

The marine museum has one of the largest privately owned collections of marine specimens in the world. Also on the grounds is the Dino-Stars exhibition, with life-size dinosaur replicas and interactive touch screens.

Guided tours are available. Mansion open Tues.-Sat. 10-5, Sun. and holidays noon-5, late June-Labor Day; Tues.-Sun. noon-5, May 1-late June and day after Labor Day-Oct. 31; Tues.-Fri. noon-4, Sat.-Sun. noon-5, rest of year. Closed Jan. 1, Easter, Thanksgiving and Dec. 24-25 and 31. Last admission 1 hour before closing. Grounds $7; senior citizens and students with ID $6; under 12, $3. Mansion tour $3. Phone (631) 854-5555 or (631) 854-5579.

Planetarium, on Little Neck Rd., contains astronomy and science exhibits, telescopes, an observatory and a sky theater with a 60-foot-diameter dome. The Goto projector creates special effects with multiple projections of stars, the moon, and planets. Children's programs also are offered. Sky shows Fri. at 8:30, Sat. at 11, noon, 1 and 3, Sun. at noon, 1 and 3. Laser shows Sat.-Sun. at 2 and 4. Show schedules vary; phone ahead. Sky shows $3. Laser shows $8. Phone (631) 854-5555 or (631) 854-5579.

CHATEAUGAY (A-10) pop. 798, elev. 1,010′

HIGH FALLS PARK, 1 mi. w. on SR 11 to Cemetery Rd., following signs, features a 120-foot waterfall, which is reached by nature trails through a wooded area. Signs identify trees and plants; picnic facilities adjoin a playground. Daily 9-9, May 1-Oct. 15. Admission $2; over 55, students with ID and ages 6-11, $1. Phone (518) 497-3156.

CHAUTAUQUA (G-1) pop. 4,666, elev. 1,427′

A summer arts and education center bordering Chautauqua Lake, Chautauqua Institution is a secluded community whose population reaches as high as 7,500 during the summer. Victorian cottages line narrow wooded streets that slope down to the water. Boating, fishing and swimming are among the activities available at the lake.

Chautauqua County Visitors Bureau: P.O. Box 1441, Chautauqua, NY 14722; phone (800) 242-4569.

CHAUTAUQUA INSTITUTION is on SR 394. Founded in 1874 as an educational center for Sunday-school teachers, the institution has become known for its concept of presenting lectures and entertainment to large groups. Chautauqua Institution offers activities for all ages in the arts, education, religion and recreation, including symphony, opera, theater and dance. For further information contact Chautauqua Institution, Box 28, Chautauqua, NY 14722.

Lectures and popular entertainment are presented in the amphitheater June 23-Aug. 26. Daily gate ticket prices range between $11 and $36. AX, MC, VI. Phone (800) 836-2787.

CHAZY (A-11) pop. 4,181, elev. 151'

Chazy was founded in 1763 by Jean Fromboise. During the Revolution the British forces of Gen. John Burgoyne overran the area, and Fromboise was forced to flee. After the war Fromboise returned to Chazy, where he planted the region's first apple orchard. The McIntosh orchards in Chazy are some of the largest in the world.

Another notable area resident was William H. Miner, a railroad industrialist and philanthropist. One of his gifts to the town is the Miner Institute, an agricultural research center.

THE ALICE T. MINER MUSEUM is reached via I-87 exit 41, 1 mi. e. on US 191, then .5 mi. s. on US 9 to 9618 Main St. The Colonial Revival limestone house museum contains collections primarily from the 18th and 19th centuries. Included are prints, paintings, porcelain, glass, carpets, furniture and textiles. Allow 1 hour, 30 minutes minimum. Guided tours are given Tues.-Sat. at 10, 11:30, 1 and 2:30, Feb. 1-Dec. 22; closed holidays. Fee $3; over 61, $2; students with ID $1; under 5 free. Phone (518) 846-7336.

CHERRY VALLEY (E-9)
pop. 592, elev. 1,326'

Settled in 1740, Cherry Valley was an important stagecoach stop on the Cherry Valley Turnpike, now US 20. A large stone monument in the village cemetery commemorates the victims of the Massacre of 1778, when 700 American Indians and Tories killed or captured most of the residents.

CHERRY VALLEY MUSEUM, 49 Main St., exhibits household articles, Civil War and Revolutionary War memorabilia, books and documents, pumpers, clothing and farm implements. Allow 1 hour minimum. Daily 10-5, Memorial Day weekend-Oct. 15; by appointment rest of year. Admission $3; over 59, $2.50; under 11 free with an adult. Phone (607) 264-3303 or (607) 264-3098.

CLAYTON (B-7) pop. 1,821, elev. 276'

The Thousand Islands extend more than 10 miles above and below the village of Clayton on the St. Lawrence River. The Handweaving and Arts Center offers workshops in folk arts and crafts.

Clayton Area Chamber of Commerce: 517 Riverside Dr., Clayton, NY 13624; phone (315) 686-3771 or (800) 252-9806.

ANTIQUE BOAT MUSEUM is 6 mi. s.w. of 1000 Islands Bridge (I-81) on SR 12N at 750 Mary St. This collection of freshwater wooden boats includes American Indian dugout and birch bark canoes, St. Lawrence skiffs and early 20th-century speedboats, launches and pleasure craft. Featured are the *Dixie II*, the *Miss Canada III* and other Gold Cup boats along with the personal boats of Presidents Ulysses S. Grant and James Garfield. Boat rides are available.

Allow 1 hour, 30 minutes minimum. Daily 9-5, mid-May to Columbus Day. Admission $12; over 54 and military with ID $11; ages 13-17, $10; ages 6-12, $6. MC, VI. Phone (315) 686-4104.

THE THOUSAND ISLANDS MUSEUM is at 312 James St. Life along the St. Lawrence River is depicted through historical artifacts, antiques and exhibits about hunting, fishing and commerce. Among the displays are record muskies and award-winning decoys. A research library is available and history programs are offered. Daily 9-5, July-Aug.; Mon.-Sat. 9-5, May-June and Sept.-Oct. Donations. Phone (315) 686-5794.

COLD SPRING HARBOR (H-2)
pop. 4,975, elev. 100'

COLD SPRING HARBOR WHALING MUSEUM, on Main St. (SR 25A), offers self-guiding tours and audio cassette tapes that tell the story of the whaling industry and its impact on the area. Displays include a fully equipped whaleboat, whaling implements, marine paintings, ship models and a diorama depicting 1850 Cold Spring Harbor. Changing exhibits

and a family activity room also are offered. Daily 11-5, Memorial Day-Labor Day; Tues.-Sun. 11-5, rest of year. Admission $4; over 64 and ages 5-18, $3. Phone (631) 367-3418.

CONSTABLEVILLE (D-8) pop. 305

CONSTABLE HALL, .5 mi. e. of SR 26, is an 1819 Georgian mansion. The house contains original furnishings, artifacts and a library. The grounds include a garden. Allow 1 hour minimum. Guided tours Wed.-Sat. 10-4, Sun. 1-4, June 1-Oct. 15. Admission $5; ages 6-13, $3. Phone (315) 397-2323.

COOPERSTOWN (F-8)
pop. 2,032, elev. 1,270'

Cooperstown was founded in 1786 by Judge William Cooper, father of James Fenimore Cooper, who wrote "The Last of the Mohicans" and other tales. Nine-mile-long Otsego Lake, set among hills and forests, is the "Glimmerglass" of Cooper's stories. The original appearances of many of the town's picturesque buildings and houses have been carefully maintained.

Another renowned Cooperstown resident was Gen. Abner Doubleday, who, by official decree of the National Baseball Commission in 1908, was credited with founding the game of baseball in 1839 while a student at a military academy. However, more recent research indicates that credit also is due to the man who devised the playing field and many of the rules, New York City resident Alexander Joy Cartwright.

Cooperstown Chamber of Commerce: 31 Chestnut St., Cooperstown, NY 13326; phone (607) 547-9983.

BREWERY OMMEGANG is at 656 CR 33. In the 19th century, 80 percent of all hops grown in America came from Otsego County. Tours of this farmstead brewery cover the history of hops and the process of making traditional Belgian beers, from recipes to fermentation to cellaring. Tastings are offered. Allow 1 hour minimum. Daily 11-6, Memorial Day-Labor Day; noon-5, rest of year. Closed Jan. 1, Thanksgiving and Dec. 25. Free. MC, VI. Phone (607) 544-1800 or (800) 544-1809.

COOPERSTOWN & CHARLOTTE VALLEY RAIL-ROAD—*see Milford p. 101.*

THE FARMERS' MUSEUM, 1 mi. n. on Lake Rd. (SR 80), is one of the oldest rural-life museums in the country, providing visitors with an opportunity to experience 19th-century rural and village life firsthand through demonstrations and interpretive exhibits. Founded in 1944, the museum comprises a Colonial Revival stone barn listed on the National Register of Historic Places, a recreated historic village circa 1845, and a working farmstead.

The museum preserves examples of upstate New York architecture, early agricultural tools and equipment, and heritage livestock. A collection of more than 23,000 items encompasses historic objects ranging from butter molds to carriages and hand planes to plows. A range of interactive educational programs that explore and preserve the region's rich agricultural history are presented.

Food is available. Allow 2 hours minimum. Daily 10-5, mid-May through Columbus Day; Tues.-Fri. for guided tours only at 10:30, 12:30 and 2, Sat-Sun. 10-4 (self-guiding), day after Columbus Day-Oct. 31; Tues.-Fri. for guided tours only at 10:30, 12:30 and 2, Sat. 10-4 (self-guiding), Apr. 1 to mid-May; Fri.-Sat. after Thanksgiving 10-4. Closed Thanksgiving.

Combination Tickets

Individual admission and combination tickets are available for The Farmers' Museum, Fenimore Art Museum and the National Baseball Hall of Fame and Museum *(see attraction listings)*.

Combination admission for all attractions $29; ages 7-12, $12. National Baseball Hall of Fame and Museum and either The Farmers' Museum or Fenimore Art Museum $20.50; ages 7-12, $8. Fenimore Art Museum and The Farmers' Museum $17.50; ages 7-12, $8. Phone (607) 547-1400.

Admission $11; over 64, $9.50; ages 7-12, $5. Combination tickets with Fenimore Art Museum and/or National Baseball Hall of Fame and Museum are available. AX, DS, MC, VI. Phone (607) 547-1450, or (607) 547-1500 for recorded information, or (888) 547-1450.

 FENIMORE ART MUSEUM is 1 mi. n. on Lake Rd. (SR 80). This museum features collections of American fine art, folk art and American Indian art in a neo-Georgian structure with terraced gardens overlooking Otsego Lake. James Fenimore Cooper memorabilia, 19th-century American paintings, decorative art, historic photographs and changing exhibitions are presented. Of particular interest are the Thaw Collection of North American Indian Art in the American Indian wing and the Mohawk Bark House, a reproduction of a late 18th-century Iroquois hunting and fishing camp.

Food is available. Daily 10-5, mid May through Columbus Day; Tues.-Sun. 10-4, Apr. 1 to mid-May and day after Columbus Day-Dec. 31. Closed Thanksgiving and Dec. 25. Admission $11; over 64, $9.50; ages 7-12, $5. Combination tickets with The Farmers' Museum and/or National Baseball Hall of Fame and Museum are available. AX, DS, MC, VI. Phone (607) 547-1400, or (607) 547-1500 for recorded information, or (888) 547-1450.

NATIONAL BASEBALL HALL OF FAME AND MUSEUM, 25 Main St., chronicles the history of baseball through photographs, artifacts, player memorabilia, sports ephemera and interactive terminals. Exhibits cover such topics as women in baseball and the World Series. The museum's centerpiece is a gallery with plaques representing Hall of Fame inductees.

Daily 9-9, Memorial Day weekend-Labor Day; 9-5, rest of year. Closed Jan. 1, Thanksgiving and Dec. 25. Admission $14.50; over 65, $9.50; ages 7-12, $5; military with ID free. A combination ticket with The Farmers' Museum and Fenimore Art Museum is available. AX, MC, VI. Phone (607) 547-7200 or (888) 425-5633.

CORNING (G-5) pop. 10,842, elev. 938'

Corning, on a plateau divided by the Chemung River, traces its economic origins to the manufacture of glass. After the completion of the Chemung Canal in 1833, Erastus Corning of Albany bought real estate in the area and built a railroad from Pennsylvania to the canal. In 1868 the Flint Glass Co. of Brooklyn relocated to Corning and reorganized, selling two-fifths of the company to local residents. Home to the Corning Museum of Glass *(see attraction listing)*, Corning is recognized as one of the world's glass centers.

Historic Market Street, the main commercial district, has been restored to its late 19th-century appearance and features tree-lined brick sidewalks, shops and restaurants. Visitors can watch glass making in progress at several galleries along Market Street. A shuttle bus provides transportation from

Market Street to the Corning Museum of Glass and the Rockwell Museum of Western Art *(see attraction listing)* every 15 minutes. *Also see Finger Lakes p. 84.*

The Spencer Crest Nature Center, off Denison Pkwy. on Powderhouse Rd., is situated on 200 acres of rolling wooded grounds and includes 7 miles of nature trails and interpretative displays. Opportunities for hiking, fishing, picnicking, cross-country skiing and snowshoeing are available; phone (607) 962-9012.

Greater Corning Area Chamber of Commerce: 1 W. Market St., Suite 302, Corning, NY 14830; phone (607) 936-4686.

SAVE **THE BENJAMIN PATTERSON INN MUSEUM,** 59 W. Pulteney St., is home to various restored buildings representing the area's history as well as the Corning-Painted Post Historical Society. The Benjamin Patterson Inn is a restored 1796 inn containing 19th-century furniture and crafts. The Browntown Schoolhouse retains the flavor of the late 19th century, and the 1860s Starr Barn contains an agricultural exhibit. The complex also features a blacksmith shop and an 1860 log cabin.

Allow 1 hour minimum. Mon.-Fri. 10-4, mid-Mar. to mid-Dec.; closed major holidays. Admission $4; over 59, $3.50; students with ID, $2; family rate (up to six persons) $12. Phone (607) 937-5281.

GEM SAVE **CORNING MUSEUM OF GLASS,** off I-86 exit 46 following signs to 1 Museum Way, is home to one of the world's most comprehensive glass collections, which spans 35 centuries of glassmaking. Galleries showcase pieces from around the world, while interactive exhibits tell of glass inventions and technology.

The Hot Glass Show, in a theater-style setting in the working glass factory, presents narrated glassblowing demonstrations by master glassblowers; shows run continuously throughout the day. Visitors can also watch artisans create miniature glass animals. Hands-on glassmaking experiences are offered for a fee at the walk-in workshop.

Food is available. Allow 3 hours minimum. Daily 9-8, Memorial Day weekend-Labor Day; 9-5, rest of year. Closed Jan. 1, Thanksgiving and Dec. 24-25. Admission $12.50, under 18 free. AX, DS, MC, VI. Phone (800) 732-6845. *See color ad.*

GEM SAVE **ROCKWELL MUSEUM OF WESTERN ART** is at 111 Cedar St. in downtown's Gaffer District. The museum displays a comprehensive collection of traditional and contemporary Western and Native American paintings and sculpture. Also included is a children's art trail. Until the 1970s, the Romanesque revival-style brick building served as Corning's city hall, fire station and jail.

Guided tours are available. Allow 1 hour minimum. Daily 9-8, Sun. 11-8, July 1-Labor Day; 9-5, rest of year. Closed Jan. 1, Thanksgiving and Dec. 24-25. Admission $6.50; over 59, $5.50; under 18 free. AX, DC, DS, MC, VI. Phone (607) 937-5386.

WEST END GALLERY, 12 W. Market St., show-cases original oils and watercolors by regional artists. Exhibits change every 6 to 8 weeks. Allow 30 minutes minimum. Mon.-Fri. 10-5:30 (also Fri. 5:30-8), Sat. 10-5, Sun. noon-5. Free. Phone (607) 936-2011.

CORNWALL-ON-HUDSON (H-11)
pop. 3,058, elev. 12'

MUSEUM OF THE HUDSON HIGHLANDS, .7 mi. s.w. off SR 218 on The Boulevard, is devoted to the natural and cultural history of the Hudson Valley and features changing art exhibits in the Ogden Gallery, hands-on natural history exhibits and live animals, including frogs, turtles, snakes, chipmunks and birds. Thurs.-Sat. 10-4, Sun. noon-4; closed Jan. 1, Easter, July 4, Thanksgiving and Dec. 24-25 and 31. Admission $2. MC, VI. Phone (845) 534-5506.

CORTLAND (F-7) pop. 18,740, elev. 1,130'

Established in 1808, Cortland was named for Gen. Pierre Van Cortlandt, New York's first lieutenant governor. The Cortland Repertory Theatre presents five main-stage productions mid-June through August in the turn-of-the-20th-century Pavilion Theatre. The theater is in Dwyer Memorial Park on Little York Lake, 8 miles north on SR 281. Further information is available from the Cortland Repertory Theatre Business Office, 37 Franklin St., Cortland, NY 13045; phone (607) 756-2627.

Cortland County Convention and Visitors Bureau: 50 Union Ave., Cortland, NY 13045; phone (607) 753-8463, or (800) 859-2227 in New York.

THE 1890 HOUSE MUSEUM, 1 blk. s.w. on SR 13 at 37 Tompkins St., is a Victorian mansion with period furnishings, cherry and oak woodwork, elaborate wall stenciling and stained glass. Tues.-Sun. 1-4; closed major holidays. Admission $5, senior citizens and students with ID $3, under 12 free. Phone (607) 756-7551.

COXSACKIE (F-11) pop. 2,895, elev. 139'

Named for an American Indian word meaning "hoot of an owl," Coxsackie was an exclusively Dutch settlement from the late 1600s until 1790, when other settlers arrived. In 1775, 225 of the villagers wrote and signed a declaration of independence protesting "arbitrary and oppressive acts of the British Parliament"—a year before their counterparts farther south drafted their own declaration.

The village, situated along the banks of the Hudson River, features Colonial and Victorian houses. Riverside Park offers a panorama of the Hudson River and the Berkshire Mountains.

SAVE BRONCK MUSEUM is off US 9W to Pieter Bronck Rd. Dutch Hudson Valley history is reflected in the main houses of stone and brick, the oldest dating from 1663. Buildings include a New World Dutch barn and a 13-sided barn. Allow 1 hour minimum. Wed.-Fri. noon-4, Sat. and Mon.

holidays 10-4, Sun. 1-4, Memorial Day-Oct. 15. Last admission is at 3:30. Admission $5; ages 6-11, $2. Phone (518) 731-6490.

CROGHAN (C-8) pop. 665, elev. 847'

SAVE AMERICAN MAPLE MUSEUM, 9756 Main St. (SR 812), illustrates the history of maple production through displays of lumbering and syrup-making equipment. The museum also contains the Maple Industry Hall of Fame. Mon.-Sat. 11-4, July 1-Labor Day; Fri.-Sat. and Mon. 11-4, mid-May through June 30 and day after Labor Day-early Oct. Phone to verify schedule. Admission $4; ages 5-14, $1; family rate $10. Phone (315) 346-1107.

CROSS RIVER—*see New York p. 152.*

CROTON-ON-HUDSON—
see New York p. 152.

CROWN POINT (C-11) pop. 2,119, elev. 126'

CHAMPLAIN MEMORIAL LIGHTHOUSE is 7.5 mi. n.e. following SR 9N/22, then e. on CR 903 to the New York end of the Lake Champlain Bridge. The original light station was constructed in 1858. A new light and memorial were erected by Vermont and New York in 1912 to honor Samuel de Champlain, who discovered the lake in 1609. The bas-relief "La Belle France" by Auguste Rodin was a gift from France.

Picnicking and camping are permitted. Allow 30 minutes minimum. Mon.-Fri. 10-4, Memorial Day-Columbus Day (weather permitting). Admission $4. Phone (518) 597-3603.

CROWN POINT STATE HISTORIC SITE is 7.5 mi. n.e. at the New York end of the Lake Champlain Bridge. The site contains the preserved ruins of fortifications used during the French and Indian and Revolutionary wars. A museum has history and archeology exhibits that focus on the 1734 French Fort St. Frederic and the 1759 British fort at Crown Point.

Allow 2 hours minimum. Grounds open daily 9:30-5, May-Oct. Museum open Wed.-Mon. 9:30-5. Grounds admission Sat.-Sun. and holidays $5. Museum admission $3, senior citizens $2, under 13 free. Phone (518) 597-4666.

PENFIELD HOMESTEAD MUSEUM, off I-87 exit 28, 12 mi. e. on SR 74, then 3 mi. n. on Corduroy Rd. (CR 2), is a complex of 19th-century buildings in the Ironville Historic District. Structures include the 1827 home of Allen Penfield and ruins of the Crown Point Iron Co. works, reputedly the first industrial operation to use electricity. The house museum has displays about iron mining, the Civil War and 19th-century residents. A research center is available.

Allow 2 hours minimum. Sat.-Sun. 11-4, early June-second Sun in Oct. Research center Wed.-Sun. 9-noon, year-round. Admission $4; under 6, $2. Phone (518) 597-3804.

CUDDEBACKVILLE (H-9)

SAVE **NEVERSINK VALLEY AREA MUSEUM** is at 26 Hoag Rd. in the D&H Canal Park. Within a 300-acre historical park that includes a 1-mile portion of the D&H Canal, the museum contains exhibits and photographs as well as miniature replicas and artifacts pertaining to area history and the canal's importance to community development. A self-guiding canal walking tour is available. Allow 1 hour, 30 minutes minimum. Thurs.-Sun. noon-4, Apr.-Nov. Admission $3; ages 6-17, $1.50. Phone (845) 754-8870.

CUTCHOGUE (H-5) pop. 2,849, elev. 40′

The Corchaug Indian word Cutchogue means "it splits off land." The Old House, built in 1649, was moved to Cutchogue's Village Green in 1661 from nearby Southold. Exposed sections inside show construction features. Also on the Village Green are the 1700 Wickham Farmhouse and the 1840 Old Schoolhouse. *Also see Long Island p. 99.*

Cutchogue-New Suffolk Chamber of Commerce: P.O. Box 610, Cutchogue, NY 11935; phone (631) 734-2335.

WINERIES

- **Castello di Borghese/Hargrave Vineyard**, on Sound Ave. (CR 48) at Alwah's Ln. Daily 11-5. Hours may vary; phone ahead. Phone (631) 734-5111 or (800) 734-5158.

DARIEN CENTER (E-3) elev. 931′

GEM **SAVE** **SIX FLAGS DARIEN LAKE** is 6 mi. s. of I-90 exit 48A on SR 77 at 9993 Allegheny Rd. This entertainment complex features more than 100 rides, live shows and attractions with five roller coasters, including Superman-Ride of Steel, one of the Northeast's tallest coasters. Highlights also include The Big Kahuna, an extreme tubing experience where passengers twist and splash along a triple-dip, spiraling slide and speed through a section of closed, dark track before bursting into the sunshine in a cool catch pool. The Tornado, a six-story giant funnel water attraction; Looney Tunes Seaport kids area; and Hook's Lagoon water park. Also on the grounds are camping facilities.

Food is available. Park opens at 10:30, May-Sept. Days of operation and closing times vary; phone ahead. Admission $34.99, under 48 inches tall $24.99, under age 3 free. Parking $10. AAA members save on select services and merchandise. See guest relations for details. AX, DS, MC, VI. Phone (585) 599-4641.

DELHI (G-9) pop. 2,583, elev. 1,360′

DELAWARE COUNTY HISTORICAL ASSOCIATION, 2.5 mi. n.e. on SR 10, features seven historic buildings. Included are the 1797 Frisbee House and a barn, schoolhouse, blacksmith shop, 19th-century gun shop and turnpike tollhouse as well as the Christian Church at Fitch's Bridge. Changing art and history exhibits are shown in two galleries. The complex also houses a research library. A half-mile nature trail is available.

Picnicking is permitted. Allow 1 hour minimum. Galleries open Mon.-Fri. 10-4. Library open Mon.-Tues. 11-3. Buildings open Tues.-Sun. 11-4, Memorial Day-Oct. 15. Admission $4; under 12, $1.50. Phone (607) 746-3849.

DERBY—*see Buffalo p. 71.*

DUNDEE (F-6) pop. 1,690, elev. 994′

WINERIES

- **Glenora Wine Cellars**, on SR 14. Daily 9-9, July-Aug.; daily 10-6, May-June and Sept.-Oct.; Mon.-Sat. 10-5, Sun. noon-5, rest of year. Closed Jan. 1, Easter, Thanksgiving and Dec. 25. Phone (800) 243-5513.

DUNKIRK (F-2) pop. 13,131, elev. 613′

Founded as Chadwick's Bay in 1805, Dunkirk was renamed in 1817 because its harbor was said to resemble that of Dunkerque, France. On Thanksgiving 1946 the citizens of Dunkirk aided their war-impoverished namesake with a shipment of more than $100,000 worth of emergency supplies.

Dunkirk's harbor, which has been a key factor in the town's commercial growth, offers numerous recreational opportunities, including fishing, boating, swimming and water skiing. Lake Erie State Park is 7 miles west *(see Recreation Chart)*. The Lily Dale Assembly, 8 miles south of US 90 exit 59, offers a diversified summer program of lectures and workshops about spiritualism.

Northern Chautauqua Chamber of Commerce: 10785 Bennett Rd., Dunkirk, NY 14048; phone (716) 366-6200.

DUNKIRK HISTORICAL LIGHTHOUSE AND VETERANS PARK MUSEUM is n. on Lighthouse Point Dr. off SR 5. The lighthouse was built in 1875 on the site of the first Point Gratiot lighthouse, established in 1826. The museum, housed in the keeper's quarters, displays armed services and war memorabilia as well as exhibits related to the lighthouse and its keepers. Also on the grounds is a Coast Guard and submarine exhibit room.

Allow 1 hour minimum. Mon.-Tues. and Thurs.-Sat. 10-4, July-Aug.; Mon.-Tues. and Thurs.-Sat. 10-2, late Apr.-June 30 and Sept.-Oct. Hours may vary; phone ahead. Museum and grounds $5; ages 4-12, $2. Grounds $1. Phone (716) 366-5050.

DUNKIRK HISTORICAL MUSEUM, .5 mi. s. of SR 5 at 513 Washington Ave., contains permanent and changing exhibits about local businesses, schools and veterans as well as paintings by local artists. In addition to the displays, the museum offers a small library and information about local attractions. Allow 30 minutes minimum. Mon.-Fri. noon-4 and by appointment; closed holidays. Donations. Phone (716) 366-3797.

WINERIES

- **Woodbury Vineyards Winery**, .5 mi. s. off I-90 exit 59, 1 mi. e. on US 20, then 1 mi. s. on Roberts Rd. Daily 9-7, June 15-Sept. 15; Mon.-Sat. 9-5, Sun. noon-5, rest of year. Closed major holidays. Phone (716) 679-9463.

EAST AURORA—*see Buffalo p. 71.*

EAST DURHAM (F-10)

IRISH AMERICAN HERITAGE MUSEUM, on SR 145, has changing exhibits about Irish-American culture and history. A 7-minute film providing background information about the museum and an audiovisual reading library for research purposes also are available. Allow 1 hour minimum. Wed.-Sun. noon-4, Memorial Day-Labor Day. Admission $3.50; over 64, students with ID and under 12, $2; family rate $9. Phone (518) 634-7497 June-Sept. or (518) 432-6598 rest of year.

EAST HAMPTON (H-5) pop. 1,334, elev. 55'

This section of Long Island's south shore has many fashionable summer colonies and estates. The Clinton Academy, the first chartered academy in the state, has changing local history exhibits; phone (631) 324-6850. *Also see Long Island p. 99.*

East Hampton Chamber of Commerce: 79A Main St., East Hampton, NY 11937; phone (631) 324-0362.

EAST HAMPTON TOWN MARINE MUSEUM— *see Amagansett p. 57.*

GUILD HALL OF EAST HAMPTON, 158 Main St., is a cultural center with changing art exhibits, theater presentations and educational programs. Mon.-Sat. 11-5, Sun. noon-5, Memorial Day-Labor Day; Thurs.-Sat. 11-5, Sun. noon-5, rest of year. Admission $7; over 61, $5. Phone (631) 324-0806.

"HOME SWEET HOME" is across the village green from SR 27 at 14 James Ln. Dedicated to the memory of playwright, actor and diplomat John Howard Payne, who wrote the song "Home Sweet Home," the house contains 17th- and 18th-century furniture and a collection of English ceramics and lusterware. An herb garden and the 1804 Pantigo Windmill also are on the grounds. A garden with period plantings surrounds the house. Allow 30 minutes minimum. Mon.-Sat. 10-4, Sun. 2-4, May-Sept.; Fri.-Sat. 10-4, Sun. 2-4, Oct.-Nov. Closed Thanksgiving. Admission $4; ages 2-12, $2. Phone (631) 324-0713.

[SAVE] **THE MULFORD FARMHOUSE,** across the village green from SR 27 at 10 James Ln., is a 4-acre site that preserves the original 17th-century settlement of Maidstone. Highlights include decorative arts exhibits, information about East Hampton's architectural styles and tours by costumed interpreters. Thurs.-Sat. 10-5, Sun. noon-5, July-Aug.; Sat 10-5, Sun noon-5, Memorial Day-June 30 and Sept. 1-Columbus Day. Admission $3, senior citizens $2, children $1. Phone (631) 324-6869.

EAST MEREDITH (F-9) elev. 1,353'

HANFORD MILLS MUSEUM, 73 CR 12, is a restored 19th-century water- and steam-powered milling and industrial complex. Exhibits and demonstrations are featured at the sawmill and gristmill. Other buildings include a feed mill, barn, hardware store, wagon and lumber shed and restored farmhouse. Guided tours are available. Allow 1 hour minimum. Tues.-Sun. 10-5, mid-May to mid-Oct. Admission $7; ages 6-12, $3.50. DS, MC, VI. Phone (607) 278-5744 or (800) 295-4992.

EASTPORT (I-4) pop. 1,454, elev. 25'

SHRINE OF OUR LADY OF THE ISLAND is midway between Long Island Expwy. (I-495) exit 70 and Sunrise Hwy. (SR 27) exit 61 on Eastport Manor Rd. The 70-acre site includes wooded walkways, the stations of the cross, gardens, statues and chapels. Picnicking is permitted. Grounds open daily dawn-dusk. Chapels open daily 9:30-4. Free. Phone (631) 325-0661.

EDEN—*see Buffalo p. 71.*

ELIZABETHTOWN (B-11)
pop. 1,315, elev. 550'

One of the most picturesque drives in northern New York is US 9, which extends south through the Boquet River Valley.

[SAVE] **ADIRONDACK HISTORY CENTER,** 7590 Court St., offers displays covering such topics as pioneer settlement, wilderness exploration, transportation and the local community. The center also has a forest-fire observation tower and a formal garden. Allow 1 hour minimum. Mon.-Sat. 9-5, Sun. 1-5, Memorial Day weekend-Columbus Day. Admission $5; over 59, $4; ages 6-18, $2. Phone (518) 873-6466.

ELLICOTTVILLE (F-3) pop. 472, elev. 1,549'

In winter Ellicottville's snow-festooned evergreens lure skiing enthusiasts. The 60,398 acres of nearby Allegany State Park *(see Recreation Chart and the AAA Northeastern CampBook)* provide cold-weather devotees with opportunities for cross-country skiing, snowmobiling and ice fishing, while those who prefer the summer sunshine can hike, bike, fish, swim, camp and ride horseback.

For an unusual site, view a herd of buffaloes on the hill adjacent to the ski slopes at the B&B Buffalo Ranch on Horn Hill Road.

Ellicottville Chamber of Commerce: P.O. Box 456, Ellicottville, NY 14731; phone (716) 699-5046 or (800) 349-9099.

Shopping areas: Washington Street is home to various antiques and specialty shops.

RECREATIONAL ACTIVITIES
Skiing

• **Holiday Valley Resort,** s. on US 219. Write P.O. Box 370, Ellicottville, NY 14731. Other activities are available. Mon.-Thurs. 9 a.m.-10 p.m., Fri.-Sun. 8:30 a.m.-10:30 p.m., late Nov.-Easter (weather permitting). Phone (716) 699-2345.

ELMIRA (G-6) pop. 30,940, elev. 854'

Nine years after the decisive 1779 battle of Newtown, the first permanent settlers built their cabins on the site that is now Elmira. According to local tradition, the city was named after a neighborhood child who wandered into an 1808 meeting where local politicians were trying to decide on a town name.

Samuel Clemens, better known as Mark Twain, married Elmira native Olivia Langdon in 1870; thereafter the Clemens family spent its summers at Olivia's sister's farm. It was in Elmira that Twain wrote "The Adventures of Huckleberry Finn" and other classic works.

From early July through late August the Trolley Into Mark Twain Country travels past historic and architectural points of interest; phone the chamber of commerce for more information. Year-round entertainment is available at the Clemens Performing Arts Center at Clemens Center Parkway and Gray Street.

Woodlawn National Cemetery contains more than 3,000 graves of Confederate soldiers who died in the local prisoner of war camp.

Soaring has been a popular activity in the area since 1930, when the first national soaring contest was held. Sailplane rides are available from Schweizer Soaring School at the Elmira-Corning Regional Airport and from Harris Hill Soaring Corporation *(see attraction listing)* and the National Soaring Museum *(see attraction listing). Also see Finger Lakes p. 84.*

Chemung County Chamber of Commerce: 400 E. Church St., Elmira, NY 14901; phone (607) 734-5137 or (800) 627-5892.

Self-guiding tours: Maps and brochures outlining a self-guiding tour of the Near Westside historic neighborhood are available from the chamber of commerce; phone (607) 733-4924.

Shopping areas: Arnot Mall, exit 51 off SR 17 between Elmira and Corning, has 117 stores, including The Bon-Ton, JCPenney, Macy's and Sears.

ARNOT ART MUSEUM is at 235 Lake St. Housed in an 1833 Greek Revival mansion, the museum's collections include 17th-, 18- and 19th-century Dutch, Flemish, French and German paintings as well as 19th- and 20th-century American art and sculpture. Noteworthy is the museum's collection of contemporary works. Allow 30 minutes minimum. Tues.-Sat. 10-5, Sun. 1-5; closed holidays. Admission $5; over 60 and students with ID $4.50; ages 6-12, $2.50; family rate $12.50; free to all Sat.-Sun. Phone (607) 734-3697.

DID YOU KNOW

Approximately one-third of all battles fought during the Revolutionary War were fought on New York soil.

CHEMUNG VALLEY HISTORY MUSEUM, [SAVE] 415 E. Water St., contains regional historical artifacts and information about Mark Twain and the Elmira Prison Camp. Allow 1 hour minimum. Museum Tues.-Sat. 10-5, Sun. 1-5; closed holidays. Admission $3, senior citizens $2, students with ID $1, under 5 free. Phone (607) 734-4167.

GRAVE OF MARK TWAIN, facing East Hill in Woodlawn Cemetery at the n. end of Walnut St., is identified by a monument that is 12 feet high or "mark twain." The expression, which Samuel Clemens adopted as his byline, refers to the 2-fathom (12-foot) water depth necessary for riverboats to pass through a river.

Clemens' son-in-law, the distinguished musician Ossip Gabrilowitsch, is buried at his request at Clemens' feet. Grave markers bear quotes from the author's works. Daily dawn-dusk. Free.

HARRIS HILL SOARING CORPORATION, I-86/SR 17 exit 51S, then w. on CR 64 in Harris Hill Park, features flights in training and modern, high-performance sailplanes above the scenic Chemung Valley. Allow 1 hour minimum. Daily 10-6, late June-late Aug.; Sat.-Sun. 10-6, early Apr.-late June and late Aug.-late Oct. Fare $65-$75. MC, VI. Phone (607) 734-0641.

MARK TWAIN STUDY, on the Elmira College campus, is an octagonal study built in the form of a Mississippi riverboat pilothouse. A gift from Clemens' sister-in-law, the study once overlooked the city from atop East Hill and still contains some of its original furniture. Guided tours of the study and Hamilton Hall's Mark Twain exhibit are available. Mon.-Sat. 9-5, Sun. noon-5, May 1-Labor Day; Sat. 9-5, Sun. noon-5, day after Labor Day to mid-Oct.; by appointment rest of year. Free. Phone (607) 735-1941.

NATIONAL SOARING MUSEUM is off [SAVE] I-86/SR 17 exit 51A following signs to Harris Hill Park. Featured is a collection of gliders and sailplanes. Interactive exhibits include a computerized flight simulator lab and a full-size glider simulator. Visitors will see replicas of the 1902 and 1911 Wright Brothers' gliders. Sailplane rides are available seasonally.

Allow 1 hour minimum. Daily 10-5; closed Jan. 1, Thanksgiving and Dec. 24-25. Admission $6.50; over 59, $5.50; college students with ID and ages 5-17, $4; family rate (two adults and two children) $18. AX, DS, MC, VI. Phone (607) 734-3128.

SULLIVAN'S MONUMENT AT NEWTOWN BATTLEFIELD, 3 mi. e. on I-86/SR 17, was the site of a Revolutionary War campaign staged by Gen. John Sullivan and Brig. Gen. James Clinton. Occasional battle re-enactments are presented throughout the year. Hiking and biking trails are available as well as campsites, cabins, playgrounds and picnic areas. Allow 30 minutes minimum. Daily 10-dusk, Fri. before Memorial Day-Columbus Day. Free. Phone (607) 732-6067.

FAIRPORT (E-5) pop. 5,740, elev. 492'

WINERIES

- **Casa Larga,** off I-90 exit 45, 1 mi. n. on SR 96, then 1.4 mi. n. on Turk Hill Rd. Tours daily at 1, 2, 3 and 4, Memorial Day-Thanksgiving; Sat.-Sun. at 1 and 3, rest of year. Closed Jan. 1, Easter, Thanksgiving and Dec. 25. Phone (585) 223-4210.

FINGER LAKES

American Indian folklore holds that the Finger Lakes were formed when God placed his handprint on some of the most beautiful land ever created. There are actually 11 finger-shaped lakes beginning just east of I-390 and extending east almost to I-81 south of Syracuse; the northern boundary straddles I-90, with I-86 and SR 17 defining the southern edge.

The lakes are named for the tribes of the Six Nations of the Iroquois: the Cayugas, Mohawks, Onondagas, Oneidas, Senecas and Tuscaroras. SRs 14 and 89, which parallel the western shores of Seneca and Cayuga lakes, respectively, are major north-south routes cutting through the center of the region. Seneca and Cayuga are the largest lakes. Boating, fishing and swimming are popular area recreational pastimes.

Finger Lakes is one of the largest wine producing regions in the eastern United States. Dozens of wineries offering tours and tastings surround the larger lakes and are identified on wine trail driving brochures available in most towns. For additional winery information phone Finger Lakes Wine Country, (607) 936-0706.

Information about regional attractions can be found in place listings for Auburn, Branchport, Canandaigua, Corning, Elmira, Geneva, Hammondsport, Horseheads, Ithaca, Lodi, Montour Falls, Moravia, Naples, Palmyra, Seneca Falls, Skaneateles, Trumansburg and Watkins Glen.

FINGER LAKES NATIONAL FOREST (F-6)

Elevations in the forest range from 1,400 ft. at the southeast corner near Reynoldsville to 1,860 ft. at Hector Backbone. Refer to AAA maps for additional elevation information.

Finger Lakes National Forest lies on a ridge between Seneca and Cayuga lakes, via I-90, I-81 and SR 17. New York's only national forest was officially designated as such in October 1985. The forest comprises just 16,000 acres and is one of the country's smallest national forests.

More than one-third of the land provides pasture for beef and dairy cattle. The remaining area is used for camping, hiking on the 33-mile trail system, horseback riding, fishing and hunting. Midsummer draws blueberry pickers, and winter attracts cross-country skiers and snowmobilers to the gently rolling hillsides. The Forest Service office is about 9 miles north of Watkins Glen on SR 414; the office is open weekdays 8-4:30. Free.

For further information contact the District Ranger, Finger Lakes National Forest, 5218 SR 414, Hector, NY 14841. Phone (607) 546-4470. *See Recreation Chart.*

FINEVIEW (B-7)

MINNA ANTHONY COMMON NATURE CENTER, off I-81 exit 51 in Wellesley Island State Park *(see Recreation Chart and the AAA Northeastern CampBook),* is a 600-acre wildlife sanctuary with 8 miles of trails. The visitor center has nature exhibits and a butterfly house. Trails are available for cross-country skiing.

Allow 30 minutes minimum. Center open daily 8:30-4, June-Aug.; 10-4, rest of year. Butterfly house open daily 8:30-4, June-Aug. Trails open daily dawn-dusk. Admission $7 per private vehicle, July-Aug.; free rest of year. Phone (315) 482-2479.

FIRE ISLAND NATIONAL SEASHORE (I-4)

Fire Island National Seashore encompasses most of the lands between Robert Moses State Park *(see attraction listing)* and Smith Point County Park off the south shore of Long Island. Low shrubs and beach grass along the Atlantic shore protect sand from erosion; in sheltered portions, high thickets and groves of pitch pine are common.

Wildlife is abundant along the seashore. Anglers can find bass, blowfish, bluefish, fluke, mackerel, weakfish and winter flounder. Waterfowl are numerous October through March; white-tailed deer, red foxes and rabbits also can be seen.

The seashore is accessible by car near its eastern end at Smith Point County Park, via the Robert Moses Causeway from the west or by mainland ferry service that leaves Bay Shore, Sayville and Patchogue in summer. A visitor center at Smith Point West next to Smith Point County Park has exhibits and visitor information; a ranger is on duty year-round. A national wilderness area extends west for 7 miles.

The lightkeeper's quarters of the mid-19th-century Fire Island Lighthouse is a visitor center with exhibits about the history of the site. To reach the lighthouse, park at the east end of Robert Moses State Park and walk about a quarter-mile over a dirt trail. Physically impaired persons can park at the lighthouse; phone (631) 321-7028.

Sailors Haven, 1 mile west of the private community of Cherry Grove, offers a marina, beach and picnic areas. A self-guiding nature trail leads through the Sunken Forest. Access to Sailors Haven is by boat or walk-on ferry from Sayville; phone (631) 589-0810. Round-trip fare is $10; ages 2-11, $6. Visitor services are offered during the summer.

The William Floyd Estate is at 245 Park Dr. in Mastic Beach. The preserved house of one of the signers of the Declaration of Independence reflects the changes in styles during the 250 years of Floyd family ownership. Guided house tours and self-guiding grounds tours are available; phone (631) 399-2030.

For further information contact the Superintendent, Fire Island National Seashore, 120 Laurel St., Patchogue, Long Island, NY 11772. Phone (631) 289-4810. *See Recreation Chart and the AAA Northeastern CampBook. Also see Long Island p. 99.*

ROBERT MOSES STATE PARK is on the w. end of Fire Island. On the Atlantic Ocean, the park is accessible via the Robert Moses Cswy. from the Long Island Expwy. or Southern State Pkwy. Recreational facilities include a pitch-and-putt golf course, boat anchorages, a fishing pier and bathhouses. Picnicking is permitted. Daily dawn-dusk, Memorial Day-Labor Day; Sat.-Sun. dawn-dusk, day after Labor Day-Oct. 31; 7-5:30, rest of year. Free. Parking $8, Memorial Day to mid-Sept.; $6, rest of year. Phone (631) 669-0449. *See Recreation Chart.*

FONDA (E-10) pop. 810, elev. 291'

THE NATIONAL SHRINE OF BLESSED KATERI TEKAKWITHA AND NATIVE AMERICAN EXHIBIT is .5 mi. w. on SR 5. The shrine honors the place where this American Indian girl was baptized and lived almost half her life. Also included is the 1663 Caughnawaga Indian village, an excavated and staked-out Iroquois village, and American Indian artifacts. Picnicking is permitted. Allow 2 hours minimum. Daily 9-7, May-Oct. Donations. Phone (518) 853-3646.

FORESTVILLE (F-2) pop. 770, elev. 928'

WINERIES

- **Merritt Estate Winery** is at 2264 King Rd. Mon.-Sat. 10-5, Sun. noon-5. Phone (888) 965-4800.

FORT EDWARD (D-11) pop. 3,141, elev. 144'

On the portage trail between the Hudson River and Lake Champlain, Fort Edward was fortified throughout the French and Indian and Revolutionary wars. During the Revolutionary War, local citizen Jane McCrea was murdered on the way to see her fiancé in the British Army. Her grave can be seen at Union Cemetery on Broadway.

Fort Edward Chamber of Commerce: P.O. Box 267, Fort Edward, NY 12828; phone (518) 747-3000.

[SAVE] **OLD FORT HOUSE MUSEUM,** .5 mi. s. on US 4 to 22-29 Lower Broadway, was built in 1772. A tavern and courthouse under British rule, it was the Revolutionary War headquarters for Gens. Philip Schuyler, John Burgoyne and John Stark. On the grounds are a 19th-century tollhouse and schoolhouse, the 1870 Washington County Fair building, a turn-of-the-20th-century water works building, a law office and a research center.

Allow 1 hour, 30 minutes minimum. Daily 1-5, June 1-Labor Day; Tues.-Sun. 1-5, day after Labor Day-Columbus Day. Closed July 4. Admission $5, under 18 free. Phone (518) 747-9600.

FORT HUNTER (E-10)

Alongside the Erie Canal in Fort Hunter is Schoharie Crossing, a 3-mile nature trail with interpretive signage and picnic facilities.

Vestiges of the original Erie Canal locks, as well as structures from two other phases of canal construction, can be seen at Schoharie Crossing State Historic Site on Schoharie Street. The site preserves the six remaining arches from the Schoharie Aqueduct, built in 1842 to carry the Erie Canal over Schoharie Creek, as well as a restored 1850 canal store. A visitor center is open Wednesday through Sunday, the first Wednesday in May through the last weekend in October. The site also offers nature and bike trails and a boat launch; phone (518) 829-7516.

FORT JOHNSON (E-10) pop. 491

OLD FORT JOHNSON is on SR 5 w. of SR 67. Sir William Johnson's 1749 fieldstone house was fortified during the French and Indian War and remains virtually unchanged. It contains original family furnishings, a rare 18th-century privy and artifacts reflecting Mohawk Valley history. Wed.-Sun. 1-5, May 15-Oct. 15. Admission $2, under 12 free. Phone (518) 843-0300.

▼ FORT STANWIX NATIONAL MONUMENT (D-8)

Off SR 26 in Rome, Fort Stanwix was built during the French and Indian War. In 1776, at the outbreak of the Revolution, the fort was repaired and restored by American rebels. Attacked by a force of British, Tories and American Indians in 1777, it withstood a 3-week siege. The fort contains exhibits. Costumed interpreters re-enact 18th-century life in a military outpost. Open daily 10-4, Apr.-Dec.; closed Thanksgiving and Dec. 25. Free. Phone (315) 338-7730.

▼ FORT TICONDEROGA NATIONAL HISTORIC SAVE LANDMARK (C-11)

Approximately 1 mile east of Ticonderoga on SR 74, Fort Ticonderoga was built in 1755 by the French, who named it Fort Carillon. Bordering Lake Champlain, the fort controlled the connecting waterway between Canada and the American Colonies. In 1758 the French successfully defended Fort Carillon against the British, but in 1759 British general Jeffery Amherst captured, rebuilt and renamed the fort.

Ethan Allen and his Green Mountain Boys, along with Benedict Arnold, took the fort in a bloodless surprise attack in 1775; the next year Arnold assembled the first American fleet and fought the Battle of Valcour Island on Lake Champlain. In 1777 Gen. John Burgoyne captured the fort for the British. It remained under British control for the remainder of the American Revolution.

Fort Ticonderoga has been restored on the original foundations according to the French plans. The museum contains collections of weapons, military artifacts, paintings and papers dealing with the Colonial and Revolutionary periods. A well-marked battleground surrounding the fort was the site of the British and Colonial defeat in 1758 by the French under the Marquis de Montcalm. Costumed interpreters give guided tours.

Fort open daily 9-5, early May-late Oct. Cannon firings and fife-and-drum corps performances are offered July-Aug. Admission $12; over 64, $10.80; ages 7-12, $6. AX, MC, VI. Phone (518) 585-2821.

MOUNT DEFIANCE is 1 mi. s.e. off SR 22/74 via a blacktop road. British cannon mounted at this point forced Gen. Arthur St. Clair to surrender American-held Fort Ticonderoga in 1777. At an elevation of 853 feet, the overlook provides a panorama of Lake Champlain, the valley and the Green Mountains. Daily 9-5, early May to mid-Oct. Free. Phone (518) 585-2821.

FULTON (D-7) pop. 11,855, elev. 393'

Fulton lies along the Oswego River about 11 miles south of Lake Ontario. The town was founded in the late 18th century by Dutch settlers from the Hudson and Mohawk valleys.

In the 1820s the Oswego Canal opened, linking the Erie Canal and Lake Ontario and boosting Fulton's economy. Locks enabled boats to negotiate the falls of the Oswego River, which drop 14 feet, and a series of rapids to the north, which drop another 30 feet. An observation area in Canal Park overlooks the lower locks. Recreation Park, on Lake Neahtahwanta at the west end of town, offers sports facilities.

Exhibits related to Fulton's history can be seen at the Pratt House, 177 S. First St.; phone (315) 598-4616.

Oswego County Chamber of Commerce: 41 S. 2nd St., P.O. Box 148, Fulton, NY 13069; phone (315) 598-4231.

GANSEVOORT (D-11)

GRANT COTTAGE STATE HISTORIC SITE is off I-87 exit 16 on the grounds of the Mount McGregor Correctional Facility, following signs. This summer cottage is where Gen. Ulysses S. Grant spent his last days and completed his memoirs in 1885. The cottage has been left largely as it was the day he died.

Note: Visitors must check in at the access post and present a valid driver's license. Pets are not permitted. Wed.-Sun. 10-4, Memorial Day-Labor Day; Sat.-Sun. 10-4, day after Labor Day-Columbus Day. Admission $4; senior citizens and students with ID $3; ages 6-12, $2. Phone (518) 587-8277.

GARDEN CITY (I-2) pop. 21,672, elev. 88′

Near Garden City is Roosevelt Field, where Charles A. Lindbergh began his historic transatlantic flight in 1927. *Also see Long Island p. 99.*

Garden City Chamber of Commerce: 230 7th St., Garden City, NY 11530; phone (516) 746-7724.

Shopping areas: Roosevelt Field Shopping Center, off Meadowbrook Parkway exit M2W, is near Garden City. Among its 185 stores are JCPenney and Macy's.

CATHEDRAL OF THE INCARNATION (Episcopal), Cathedral Ave. at 6th St., is of 13th-century Gothic style. The 1885 church is noted for its hand-carved mahogany woodwork and rare marble. Tues.-Fri. 9:30-4, Sat.-Sun. 8-2. Hours may vary; phone ahead. Free. Phone (516) 746-2955.

CRADLE OF AVIATION MUSEUM, on Charles Lindbergh Blvd., features exhibits and more than 75 aircraft chronicling Long Island's role in civilian and military aviation history, from the first official air mail flight in 1911 to the Grumman plant's production of Apollo lunar modules in the 1960s. Charles Lindbergh flew from Roosevelt Field to Paris in 1927. IMAX films feature aviation themes; the theater is said to be Long Island's only domed theater.

Allow 1 hour, 30 minutes minimum. Tues.-Sun. and Mon. holidays 9:30-5; closed Thanksgiving and Dec. 25. Admission $9; ages 2-12, $8. AX, MC, VI. Phone (516) 572-4111.

(SAVE) **LONG ISLAND CHILDREN'S MUSEUM** is at 11 Davis Ave. Through multimedia exhibits children are challenged to be creative while learning about a variety of topics including communications, music and the environment. Allow 2 hours minimum. Tues.-Sun. 10-5, July-Aug.; Wed.-Sun. and Mon. holidays 10-5, rest of year. Closed Jan. 1, Easter, Memorial Day, Labor Day, Thanksgiving and Dec. 24-25. Admission $9; over 65, $8. AX, MC, VI. Phone (516) 224-5800.

GARRISON—*see New York p. 152.*

GATEWAY NATIONAL RECREATION AREA (I-2)

Comprising the Sandy Hook Unit in New Jersey and three units in New York City, Gateway National Recreation Area offers urban residents and visitors a chance to enjoy nature and the sea.

The Breezy Point Unit, on Rockaway Peninsula, includes Jacob Riis Beach, historic Fort Tilden and the westernmost point of the peninsula. The Jamaica Bay Unit includes Jamaica Bay Wildlife Refuge in Queens (*see New York p. 138*), Canarsie Pier, Plumb Beach and Floyd Bennett Field in Brooklyn. The Staten Island Unit consists of Great Kills Park and Miller Field. The Sandy Hook Unit in Highlands, N.J., includes a beach, a lighthouse and Fort Hancock.

Historical, educational, cultural and recreational events are presented throughout the year. The beaches are open daily, Memorial Day weekend-Labor Day. For further information contact the Public Affairs Office, Gateway National Recreation Area, Headquarters, Bldg. 69, Floyd Bennett Field, Brooklyn, NY 11234. Phone (718) 354-4606. *See Recreation Chart.*

GENEVA (E-5) pop. 13,617, elev. 671′

On Seneca Lake, largest of the Finger Lakes, Geneva is the center of a rich agricultural and nursery region. Nearby Seneca Lake State Park (*see Recreation Chart*) offers numerous types of aquatic recreation.

A local wine research and development center explores new ways of growing grapes and making wine. Numerous vineyards can be found in the area via a wine trail off I-90 exit 42.

The Geneva Historical Society Museum, 543 S. Main St. (SR 14) in the Prouty-Chew House, has permanent and changing exhibits about local history; phone (315) 789-5151. *Also see Finger Lakes p. 84.*

Geneva Area Chamber of Commerce: 35 Lakefront Dr., P.O. Box 587, Geneva, NY 14456; phone (315) 789-1776.

Self-guiding tours: A brochure outlining a self-guiding walking tour of Geneva's historic S. Main Street is available from the Geneva Historical Society.

Self-guiding walking tours of the Hobart and William Smith College campus are detailed in a brochure available at the Alumni House, 615 S. Main St.; phone (315) 781-3700.

THE MIKE WEAVER DRAIN TILE MUSEUM is on SR 96A at East Lake Rd., 1.5 mi. s. of jct. US 20/SR 5; visitors should go to Rose Hill Mansion (*see attraction listing*) for admission. The museum displays 350 styles of drain tile dating from 100 B.C. to the present. Mon.-Sat. 10-4, Sun. 1-5, May-Oct. Admission $3. Phone (315) 789-3848 or (315) 789-5151.

ROSE HILL MANSION is 3 mi. e. on SR 96A, 1 mi. s. of jct. US 20/SR 5. This beautifully restored 1839 mansion on 30 acres of land overlooks Seneca Lake. Furnished in the Empire style of the period, the house is one of America's finest examples of Greek Revival architecture. Many furnishings are original to the Swan family, who occupied the mansion 1850-90. Twenty-one rooms are open to the public.

Guides provide detailed explanations of furnishings and demonstrations of how items of that period were used in daily life. Paint colors, wallpaper and textiles in the house are typical of the period, as is the extensive use of wall-to-wall carpeting. Allow 1 hour, 30 minutes minimum. Mon.-Sat. 10-4, Sun. 1-5, May-Oct. Admission $6; over 62 and ages 10-18, $4; family rate (two adults and all children ages 10-18) $15. Phone (315) 789-3848.

GERMANTOWN (G-11) pop. 862, elev. 11'

CLERMONT STATE HISTORIC SITE, 4 mi. s. on SR 9G, then 1 mi. w. on CR 6 following signs, comprises the 500-acre Hudson River estate of Chancellor Robert R. Livingston, delegate to the second Continental Congress and member of the committee to draft the Declaration of Independence. The original circa 1730 mansion was burned by the British in 1777 and rebuilt 1779-82. The grounds contain historical nature trails and restored formal gardens.

Grounds open daily 8:30-dusk. Visitor center open Tues.-Sun. and Mon. holidays 10:30-5, Apr.-Oct.; Sat.-Sun. 11-4, rest of year. Guided mansion tours are given every 30 minutes Tues.-Sun. and Mon. holidays 11-5, Apr.-Oct.; Sat.-Sun. 11-4, rest of year. Last tour begins 30 minutes before closing. Grounds admission (includes mansion tour) Sat.-Sun. and Mon. holidays $5, Mon.-Fri. free, Apr.-Oct.; free rest of year. Mansion tour $5, senior citizens and students with ID $4, under 13 free. Phone (518) 537-4240.

GILBOA (F-10) pop. 1,215, elev. 960'

Off SR 342 just west of the Schoharie Creek bridge is a group of fossil tree stumps that represent the oldest known species of trees on Earth. Known as *eospermatopteris*, they were seed-bearing tree ferns that grew in the shore muds of an ancient Devonian sea west of the present Catskill Mountains. The fossils are identified by a historical marker.

GLEN COVE (H-2) pop. 26,622, elev. 115'

GARVIES POINT MUSEUM AND PRESERVE is n. on Glen Cove Rd. to the fire station, then following signs to 50 Barry Dr. This 62-acre preserve overlooking Hempstead Harbor has 5 miles of nature trails and a museum with regional archeology and geology exhibits as well as changing displays. Tues.-Sun. 10-4; closed Jan. 1 and Dec. 25. Admission $2; ages 4-14, $1. Phone (516) 571-8010.

GLENS FALLS (D-11) pop. 14,354, elev. 376'

Part of a land grant settled in 1763, Glens Falls grew up around the 40-foot falls on the Hudson River, a site known to the indigenous population as *Chepontuo*, "a difficult place to get around." The village was destroyed by the British in 1780 and resettled in 1788 by Col. Johannes Glen. Paper and lumber milling along with lime and granite production and banking established the town as an industrial and commercial center.

Adirondack Regional Chamber of Commerce: 5 Warren St., P.O. Box 158, Glens Falls, NY 12801; phone (518) 798-1761.

Shopping Areas: Aviation Mall, a quarter-mile east of I-87 exit 19 in Queensbury, is a major local shopping center. Among its 80 stores are JCPenney and Sears. Million Dollar Half-Mile, a series of factory outlet stores, is located off I-87 exit 20 on US 9.

CHAPMAN HISTORICAL MUSEUM, 348 Glen St., includes the restored, Victorian-era DeLong House. Two exhibition galleries contain changing area history exhibits and Seneca Ray Stoddard's photographs of the Adirondacks. Tues.-Sat. 10-4, Sun. noon-4; closed major holidays. Guided tours are offered on the hour. Donations. Phone (518) 793-2826.

THE HYDE COLLECTION is at 161 Warren St. The museum encompasses a historic house and four art galleries. The art collection includes paintings, watercolors and sculpture by European masters and American artists. Textiles, antique furnishings and decorative arts also are displayed. Hyde House, an example of American Renaissance architecture, was built 1910-12 for Louis and Charlotte Hyde. Guided tours are available.

Allow 1 hour, 30 minutes minimum. Tues.-Sat. 10-5, Sun. noon-5; closed holidays. Guided tours are given 1-4. Donations. Phone (518) 792-1761.

RECREATIONAL ACTIVITIES

Hot Air Ballooning

- **Adirondack Balloon Flights** depart near I-87 (Adirondack Northway) exit 19. Write P.O. Box 65, Glens Falls, NY 12801. Departures daily Apr.-Nov. Reservations are required. Phone (518) 793-6342.

GLOVERSVILLE (E-10)
pop. 15,413, elev. 796'

FULTON COUNTY MUSEUM, 2.5 mi. w. of SR 30A at 237 Kingsboro Ave., offers historical displays with emphasis on the manufacture of leather and gloves, for which the city was named. Also exhibited are Victorian clothing, regional 19th-century folk art and memorabilia of the Sacandaga Amusement Park, which was flooded when the dam that created Great Sacandaga Lake was built. Allow 1 hour minimum. Tues.-Sat. 10-4, July-Aug.; Tues.-Sat. noon-4, May-June and in Sept. Donations. Phone (518) 725-2203.

GOSHEN (H-10) pop. 5,676, elev. 431'

The Goshen Public Library, 203 Main St., contains the signatures of Alexander Hamilton and Benedict Arnold among its historical artifacts. The collection and a genealogical library are available by appointment; phone (845) 294-6606.

The Historic Goshen Track is one of the oldest harness racetracks in the United States and the sporting world's first national historic landmark. Self-guiding walking tours of the barn and blacksmith shop are available; phone (845) 294-5357.

Note: Policies concerning admittance of children to pari-mutuel betting facilities vary. Phone for information.

Orange County Tourism: 124 Main St., Goshen, NY 10924; phone (845) 291-2136 or (800) 762-8687. *See color ad p. 206.*

SAVE **HARNESS RACING MUSEUM & HALL OF FAME,** 240 Main St., honors the sport of harness racing. The Tudor-style building, originally a stable, houses a collection of Currier & Ives trotting prints, a timeline tracing the sport's history, and trotting memorabilia and interactive exhibits. A 3-D simulator takes visitor for a ride. The Hall of Fame showcases the people and horses that have contributed to the sport. Allow 1 hour minimum. Daily 10-6, Apr.-Oct.; 10-5, rest of year. Closed Jan. 1, Thanksgiving and Dec. 25. Admission $7.50; over 61, $5.50; ages 6-15, $3.50. AX, DS, MC, VI. Phone (845) 294-6330.

GRAND ISLAND—see *Buffalo p. 71.*

GRANVILLE (D-12) pop. 2,644, elev. 403′

THE PEMBER MUSEUM OF NATURAL HISTORY, 33 W. Main St., is a Victorian-period museum housing specimens of birds and mammals, rocks and minerals, shells, eggs and other objects related to natural history. Hiking trails are open year-round at the Pember Nature Preserve; trail maps are available at the museum. Programs and guided nature hikes are available by appointment. Allow 1 hour minimum. Tues.-Fri. 1-5, Sat. 10-3. Admission $3; senior citizens and under 18, $1. Phone (518) 642-1515.

GREAT LAKES-ST. LAWRENCE SEAWAY SYSTEM

Extending from the Atlantic Ocean to the headwaters of the Great Lakes, the Great Lakes-St. Lawrence Seaway System is a 2,342-mile marine highway. It was completed in 1959 as a joint venture between the United States and Canada. The United States dredged the Thousand Islands section and constructed the Wiley-Dondero Ship Channel and two locks with auxiliary facilities near Massena.

Canada built canals and four locks in territorial waters between Cornwall, Ontario, and Montréal, Québec; built a canal and lock at Iroquois, Ontario; and deepened channels of the Welland Canal. *For information about points of interest in the St. Lawrence Seaway area, see Alexandria Bay, Clayton, Massena, Ogdensburg and Thousand Islands pp. 56, 76, 100, 180 and 201.*

GREAT RIVER (I-3) pop. 1,546, elev. 21′

BAYARD CUTTING ARBORETUM, on SR 27A (Montauk Hwy.), covers 697 acres, more than 140 acres of which are open to the public. Plantings include azaleas, evergreens, hollies, rhododendrons and wildflowers. A 68-room Tudor-style house, the former Cutting residence features lavish woodwork, stained-glass windows and large fireplaces as well as a collection of American Indian artifacts.

Food is available. Allow 2 hours, 30 minutes minimum. Arboretum open Tues.-Sun. 10-5, mid-Mar. to early Nov.; 10-4, rest of year. Cutting House Tues.-Sun. 10-5. Admission $6 per private vehicle Tues.-Sun., early Apr.-Labor Day, and Sat.-Sun., day

after Labor Day-Oct. 31; free rest of year. Phone (631) 581-1002.

HAMILTON (E-8) pop. 3,509, elev. 1,109′

Colgate University is on SR 12B. The Case Library houses exhibits and rare books; Alumni Hall displays archeological and ethnological materials; and the Dana Arts Center contains the Picker Art Gallery and the University Theater. Free guided campus tours can be arranged through the admissions office; phone (315) 228-7401.

HAMMONDSPORT (F-5) pop. 731, elev. 740′

The Keuka Lake community of Hammondsport is the center of the state's grape and wine industry as well as the home of aviation pioneer Glenn H. Curtiss. *Also see Finger Lakes p. 84.*

GEM SAVE **GLENN H. CURTISS MUSEUM,** .5 mi. s. on SR 54, displays early motorcycles, engines and aircraft, many of which were developed for military use by Glenn H. Curtiss in his Hammondsport manufacturing plant.

A skilled mechanic, speed enthusiast and aviation pioneer, Curtiss won the title "fastest man in the world" for a motorcycle speed record set in 1907; the next year he piloted the first documented public flight in the United States. After the U.S. Navy purchased its first airplane—a Curtiss design—in 1911, Curtiss became known as the Father of Naval Aviation.

In addition to a tribute to the first female aviators, galleries feature Curtiss family art objects, early automobiles and turn-of-the-20th-century furnishings and memorabilia.

Allow 1 hour, 30 minutes minimum. Mon.-Sat. 9-5, Sun. 10-5, May-Oct.; Mon.-Sat. 10-4, Sun. 11-5, rest of year. Closed Jan. 1, Easter, Thanksgiving and Dec. 24-25. Admission $7; over 65, $5; ages 7-18, $4; family rate (two adults and two children or more) $20. AX, DS, MC, VI. Phone (607) 569-2160.

KEUKA MAID **DINNER BOAT** departs from the Hammondsport town dock on SR 54, .2 mi. n. of SR 54A. The ship is a 500-passenger, three-deck vessel that operates on Keuka Lake. Day, evening and teen cruises are available. Allow 2 hours, 30 minutes minimum. Trips depart Tues.-Sat. at 12:30 and 6:30, Sun. at noon and 6:30, May-Oct. Phone ahead for special event cruise schedule. Boarding begins 30-60 minutes before departure. Fare (without meals) $15. Reservations are required 1 day in advance. AX, DS, MC, VI. Phone (607) 569-2628 or (888) 372-2628.

THE WINE AND GRAPE MUSEUM OF GREYTON H. TAYLOR is off SR 54A, 1 mi. n. on Greyton H. Taylor Memorial Dr., next to Bully Hill Vineyards. Displays trace the process of wine production. The wood and stone building dates from the late 19th century and houses antique equipment used for tending the vineyards and producing wines and brandy; coopers' tools and local historical memorabilia also are displayed. Mon.-Sat. 9-5, Sun. noon-5, May-Oct. Donations. Phone (607) 868-3610.

WINERIES

- **Bully Hill Vineyards**, off SR 54A, then 2 mi. to 8843 Greyton H. Taylor Memorial Dr. Tours are offered on the hour; Mon.-Sat.10-4, Sun. noon-4, Nov. 1 to mid-May; Mon.-Sat. 9-5, rest of year. Phone (607) 868-3610 or (607) 868-3210.

- ◢◣ **Pleasant Valley Wine Co.**, off SR 54 GEM and CR 88 following signs. Daily 10-5, Apr.-Dec.; Tues.-Sat. 10-4, rest of year. Closed Jan. 1, Easter, Thanksgiving and Dec. 25. Phone (607) 569-6111.

HECTOR (F-6) elev. 853'

WINERIES

- **Chateau Lafayette Reneau** is 7 mi. n. on SR 414. Mon.-Sat. 10-6, Sun. 11-6, Apr.-Oct.; Mon.-Sat. 10-5, Sun. 11-5, rest of year. Phone (607) 546-2062.

HERKIMER (E-9) pop. 7,498, elev. 398'

Settled in 1725 by German Palatines, Herkimer began as a dairying center, then became a focus of state politics and conventions during the early 1800s. In 1865 Warner Miller perfected the process of making paper from wood pulp, which cut the cost of newsprint and caused a huge increase in newspaper, magazine and book publishing.

A trial at the Herkimer County Courthouse inspired Theodore Dreiser's novel "An American Tragedy." More recent local activities include digging for "Herkimer diamonds," which are actually rare, exceptionally clear, double-terminated quartz crystals. An open-pit mine and museum can be found on SR 28; phone (315) 891-7355.

Herkimer County Chamber of Commerce: 28 W. Main St., Mohawk, NY 13407; phone (315) 866-7820 or (877) 984-4636.

HERKIMER COUNTY HISTORICAL SOCIETY, 400 N. Main St., provides an overview of agriculture, industry and domestic life in Herkimer County from the 1700s to the 1990s. Allow 1 hour minimum. Mon.-Fri. 10-4, Sat. 10-3, July-Aug.; Mon.-Fri. 10-4, rest of year. Closed holidays. Museum free. Phone (315) 866-6413.

LIL' DIAMOND CRUISES is off I-90 exit 30 at 800 Mohawk St. at Herkimer Marina. A narrated tour on the historic Erie Canal includes a trip through Lock 18 to the Mohawk River. During the "lock-thru" experience, water levels raise and then lower the boat 20 feet. Allow 2 hours minimum. Departures daily at 1 and 4, late May to mid-Oct. Fare $18; ages 3-10, $12. AX, CB, DS, MC, VI. Phone (315) 717-0350.

HICKSVILLE (I-2) pop. 41,260, elev. 149'

SAVE **HICKSVILLE GREGORY MUSEUM,** at Heitz Pl. and Bay Ave., is in the 1895 Heitz Place Courthouse. The museum's mineral collection features specimens from throughout the world. A butterfly and moth collection emphasizes species native to Long Island. Visitors can see the 1915 jail, where inmates were supervised by a constable who resided in quarters above the courtroom. Audiovisual programs and changing exhibits also are offered.

Allow 1 hour minimum. Tues.-Fri. 9:30-4:30, Sat.-Sun. 1-5; closed major holidays. Admission $5; over 59 and ages 5-16, $3; family rate $15. Phone (516) 822-7505.

HIGH FALLS (G-10) pop. 627, elev. 256'

DELAWARE & HUDSON CANAL MUSEUM, .5 mi. s. of SR 213 on Mohonk Rd., is devoted to the history of a 108-mile canal that linked the company's coal fields to the Hudson River at Kingston 1828-98. Exhibits depict 19th-century canal life and canal boat activities. Also included are photographs, artifacts, dioramas and working models of a lock and a gravity railroad car. A self-guiding tour of the nearby "Five Locks" also is available. Allow 1 hour minimum. Thurs.-Sat. and Mon. 11-5, Sun. 1-5, May-Oct. Admission $4; under 12, $2. Phone (845) 687-9311.

HIGHMOUNT (G-10) elev. 795'

A winter sports center, Highmount is near Belleayre Mountain, said to have the highest base elevation in the Northeast. Downhill and cross-country skiing are popular.

HORSEHEADS (G-6) pop. 6,452, elev. 915'

Horseheads is named for the remains of the pack horses Gen. John Sullivan used to transport his men from Pennsylvania to western New York to fight the Six Nations of the Iroquois. On the return trip the horses collapsed, and Sullivan destroyed an estimated 300 of them at this site. Their sun-bleached skulls were all that remained when the first European settlers arrived in 1789. The Horseheads Historical Society Museum houses local historical artifacts in addition to works by early 20th-century political cartoonist Eugene "Zim" Zimmerman. *Also see Finger Lakes p. 84.*

SAVE **WINGS OF EAGLES DISCOVERY CENTER** is off SR 17 exit 51 following signs to Elmira-Corning Regional Airport. Military aviation history is highlighted through exhibits and a collection of 34 vintage aircraft.

Guided tours are available. Allow 1 hour minimum. Mon.-Fri. 10-4, Sat. 9-5, Sun. 11-5; closed Jan. 1, Thanksgiving and Dec. 25. Admission $7; over 62, $5.50; ages 6-17, $4; family rate (two adults and three children) $18. AX, DS, MC, VI. Phone (607) 739-8200.

HOWES CAVE (F-9) elev. 795'

 HOWE CAVERNS is off I-88 exit 22, 1.7 mi. e. on SR 7, then 1.5 mi. n. following signs. The 80-minute guided tour begins as elevators descend into the prehistoric caverns, 160 to 200 feet underground. Brick walkways follow the subterranean river through chambers with stalactites and stalagmites to the departure point for a boat ride on the underground Lake of Venus. The caverns have a constant temperature of 52 degrees Fahrenheit (12 C).

Visitors can take a self-guiding, above-ground cave walk. Geode cutting and gemstone mining are available all year. Pony rides are offered July 1-Labor Day (weather permitting).

Food is available. Allow 2 hours minimum. Tours daily 8-8, July 1-Labor Day; 9-6, rest of year. Closed Thanksgiving and Dec. 25. Fee $18; over 65 and ages 12-15, $15; ages 5-11, $10. AX, DS, MC, VI. Phone (518) 296-8900. *See color ad p. 278.*

IROQUOIS INDIAN MUSEUM, off I-88 exit 22, 1.7 mi. e. on SR 7, then 1 mi. n. on Caverns Rd., is devoted to the Iroquois people, their culture and the preservation of their heritage. The museum houses a collection of contemporary Iroquois artwork as well as archeological and historical exhibits. A children's museum contains hands-on exhibits. Nature trails through a 45-acre park are available.

Allow 1 hour minimum. Tues.-Sat. 10-5, Sun. noon-5, Apr.-Dec.; closed Easter, Thanksgiving and Dec. 24-25. Admission $8; senior citizens and ages 13-17, $6.50; ages 5-12, $5. MC, VI. Phone (518) 296-8949.

HUDSON (G-11) pop. 7,524, elev. 67'

Named after Henry Hudson, who landed at this site in 1609, Hudson was chartered in 1785 and missed being the state capital by just one vote. This once booming whaling port and port of entry has one of the country's largest assortments of 19th-century architecture.

The 1811 Robert Jenkins House and Museum contains Hudson River School paintings, local artifacts, whaling lore and a genealogical library. Several antique shops line Warren Street in the business district. Promenade Hill overlooks the Hudson River and the Catskills.

Columbia County Tourism Department: 401 State St., Hudson, NY 12534; phone (518) 828-3375 or (800) 724-1846.

FASNY MUSEUM OF FIREFIGHTING, at the Volunteer Firemen's Home at 117 Harry Howard Ave., was founded in 1925. One of the country's oldest museums of its type, it contains more than 95 fire engines dating 1725-1974 and 3,500 pieces of equipment, gear and memorabilia depicting the evolution of firefighting. Allow 1 hour minimum. Daily 9-4:30; closed major holidays. Free. Phone (518) 822-1875 or (877) 347-3687.

OLANA STATE HISTORIC SITE is off New York State Thruway (I-87) exit 21 to SR 23E, then 1 mi. s. to 5720 SR 9G. The Victorian estate was the home of Frederic Edwin Church, landscape painter of the Hudson River School. The mansion, built 1870-76 in the Persian style, commands a view of the Hudson River Valley and the Catskills. The visitor center offers a film and exhibit about Church. Recreational opportunities include hiking and cross-country skiing.

Guided tours are available. Picnicking is permitted. Allow 2 hours minimum. Grounds daily 8-dusk. Visitor center daily 9:30-5, early Apr.-late Oct. Guided tours Tues.-Sun. 10-5. Last tour begins at 5. Guided tours $3; under 12 free. Tours are limited to 12 persons; reservations are recommended. Phone (518) 828-0135.

HUNTINGTON (I-3) pop. 18,403, elev. 205'

Huntington is the birthplace of poet Walt Whitman and the place where patriot Nathan Hale was arrested. Situated on Long Island's North Shore, Huntington is characterized by rolling hills, bluffs and picturesque harbors. The John Lloyd Manor House, built 1766-67, is a restored local historic site. The Lloyd Neck Black Oak, north from SR 25A on West Neck Road, measures 19 feet, 7 inches in circumference and is the largest known black oak in the United States.

Huntington Township Chamber of Commerce: 164 Main St., Huntington, NY 11743; phone (631) 423-6100.

Shopping areas: Walt Whitman Mall, 2 miles north of I-495 exit 49N on the east side of SR 110, serves the Huntington area. Bloomingdale's, Macy's and Saks Fifth Avenue are among its 100 stores.

HECKSCHER MUSEUM, in Heckscher Park at 2 Prime Ave., contains a permanent collection of nearly 1,900 pieces of European and American art ranging from works by Renaissance masters to contemporary local artists. Also offered are changing exhibits, educational programs and lectures. Allow 30 minutes minimum. Tues.-Fri. 10-5 (also first Fri. of the month 5-8:30), Sat.-Sun. 1-5; closed Thanksgiving and Dec. 25. Admission $5; over 62 and students with ID $3; ages 5-12, $1. Phone (631) 351-3250.

HUNTINGTON HISTORICAL SOCIETY HOUSE MUSEUMS are at 2 High St. and 434 Park Ave. The David Conklin Farm House, on High Street, was built in 1750 and contains period furnishings, including a chair used by George Washington on a 1790 visit to Long Island. The Dr. Daniel W. Kissam House, built in 1795, reflects the lifestyle of an affluent local physician and is restored to its 1840s appearance. Allow 30 minutes minimum. Conklin House open Tues.-Fri. and Sun. 1-4. Hours may vary; phone ahead. Kissam House open by appointment. Admission (each house) $2.50, children $1. Rates may vary; phone ahead. Phone (631) 427-7045.

NATHAN HALE MEMORIAL MONUMENT, 1 mi. n. of SR 25A on SR 110 and Mill Dam Rd., marks the spot where the patriot spy was captured. Daily 24 hours. Free.

[SAVE] **WALT WHITMAN BIRTHPLACE STATE HISTORIC SITE** is off SR 110 at 246 Old Walt Whitman Rd. The 1819 farmhouse is where Walt Whitman spent his early childhood years. Visitors can delve into Whitman's life and poetry through a series of exhibits that trace the poet's development from his boyhood on Long Island to his international prominence as one of the country's visionaries. Available are more than 130 portraits of Whitman as well as original letters, manuscripts and artifacts.

Picnicking is permitted. Allow 30 minutes minimum. Mon.-Fri. 11-4, Sat.-Sun. noon-5, last week in June-Labor Day; Wed.-Fri. 1-4, Sat.-Sun. 11-4, rest of year. Closed major holidays. Admission $4; over 62 and students with ID $3; ages 7-12, $2. Phone (631) 427-5240.

HYDE PARK (G-11) pop. 20,851, elev. 8′

Hyde Park is the home of the Culinary Institute of America, a vocational training school for aspiring chefs. The school was founded in 1946 with 16 students; its most recent enrollment is about 1,800. The institute occupies a former Jesuit seminary on US 9 overlooking the Hudson River. The institute's four restaurants are open to the public by reservation.

Hyde Park Chamber of Commerce: 4389 Albany Post Rd., P.O. Box 17, Hyde Park, NY 12538; phone (845) 229-8612.

ELEANOR ROOSEVELT NATIONAL HISTORIC SITE is off SR 9G, .5 mi. n. of St. Andrews Rd. to 4077 Albany Post Rd. Val-Kill, the main cottage, was Mrs. Roosevelt's weekend and holiday retreat during her husband's presidency. After President Franklin D. Roosevelt died in 1945, she lived in the cottage until her death in 1962. The grounds include gardens, outbuildings, woodland trails and a pond. The site's access road is unpaved and narrow; check locally for road conditions.

Allow 1 hour minimum. Daily 9-5, May-Oct.; Thurs.-Mon. 9-5, rest of year. Closed Jan. 1, Thanksgiving and Dec. 25. Last tour of Val-Kill begins 30 minutes before closing. Admission $8, under 15 free. DS, MC, VI. Phone (845) 229-9115, or (845) 229-2501 Sat.-Sun.

▼GEM **FRANKLIN D. ROOSEVELT PRESIDENTIAL LIBRARY AND MUSEUM,** next to the Home of Franklin D. Roosevelt National Historic Site, was the first presidential library. The museum's displays of photographs, artworks, official documents and speeches, gifts from admirers and heads of state, and family possessions and letters chronicle the lives and careers of President and Mrs. Roosevelt.

Allow 1 hour, 30 minutes minimum. Daily 9-6, May-Oct.; 9-5, rest of year. Closed Jan. 1, Thanksgiving and Dec. 25. Admission $14, under 15 free. DS, MC, VI. Phone (800) 337-8474.

▼GEM **HOME OF FRANKLIN D. ROOSEVELT NATIONAL HISTORIC SITE,** 2 mi. s. on US 9, consists of more than 200 acres and includes the home and graves of President and Mrs. Roosevelt. The 1826 house remains almost exactly as it was at the time of the president's death in 1945. The estate includes stables, icehouses, a walking trail and a tourist information center. The graves, marked by a plain white marble monument, are in the Rose Garden, northeast of the house.

Allow 1 hour, 30 minutes minimum. Daily 9-5; closed Jan. 1, Thanksgiving and Dec. 25. Admission $14, under 17 free. DS, MC, VI. Phone (845) 229-9115, or (845) 229-5320 Sat.-Sun.

▼GEM **VANDERBILT MANSION NATIONAL HISTORIC SITE** is 2 mi. n. on US 9. This 1898 mansion exemplifies the Beaux-Arts architecture of the late 19th-century "Gilded Age." The French and Italian furnishings are original pieces. Also exhibited are Flemish and French tapestries and Oriental rugs. The grounds afford views of the Hudson River. Allow 1 hour minimum. Daily 9-5; closed Jan. 1, Thanksgiving and Dec. 25. Admission $8, under 15 free. DS, MC, VI. Phone (845) 229-9115.

ILION (E-9) pop. 8,610, elev. 392′

REMINGTON ARMS CO. PLANT TOUR departs from the museum entrance on Catherine St. Visitors walk 1.5 miles through the plant to view the gunmaking process. No cameras, backpacks or strollers are allowed on the tour. Allow 1 hour minimum. Tours depart Mon.-Fri. at 10 and 1, Memorial Day-Labor Day. Free. Phone (315) 895-3200.

Remington Museum, on Catherine St., offers a display of firearms ranging from flintlock rifles to rare pistols and revolvers. Other Remington products from the past include a 19th-century typewriter and a 1900s bicycle. A videotape presentation is offered. Allow 30 minutes minimum. Mon.-Fri. 8-5, Sat. 10-4; closed holidays. Phone (315) 895-3200.

ITHACA (F-7) pop. 29,287, elev. 836′

Ithaca is at the southern tip of Cayuga Lake. Buttermilk Falls, Taughannock Falls *(see Trumansburg p. 201)* and Robert H. Treman state parks offer recreational opportunities *(see Recreation Chart)*. The Cayuga Wine Trail begins at this point and continues north on scenic SR 89, passing several wineries along the western shore of the lake.

Founded in 1892 as a conservatory of music, Ithaca College, atop South Hill off SR 96B, offers drama and music presentations and a public art gallery. Campus tours are available through the admissions office; phone (800) 429-4274. *Also see Finger Lakes p. 84.*

Ithaca/Tompkins County Convention and Visitors Bureau: 904 E. Shore Dr., Ithaca, NY 14850; phone (607) 272-1313 or (800) 284-8422.

Shopping areas: Ithaca Commons, downtown between Green and Seneca streets, is an outdoor shopping enclave with one-of-a-kind boutiques offering such items as local handicrafts, imports, camping gear and clothing along with art galleries and gourmet restaurants.

CORNELL UNIVERSITY is on the n.e. side of town. The Herbert F. Johnson Museum of Art is open Tues.-Sun. 10-5. Chimes at the University Clock Tower are played regularly when school is in session. Other places of interest on the campus include Triphammer Bridge, with its view of Fall Creek Gorge, Triphammer Falls and Beebe Lake; the Olin Library; Anabel Taylor Hall; and the Lua A. Minns Memorial Gardens.

Central campus tours depart from the main lobby of Day Hall Mon.-Fri. at 9, 11, 1 and 3, Sat. at 9, 10:30 and 1, Sun. at 1, Apr.-Nov.; daily at 1, rest of year. Closed Jan. 1, Nov. 24-27, and Dec. 24-25. Phone (607) 254-4636 for campus tours or (607) 255-6464 for museum information.

Cornell Plantations, 2.5 mi. n. on SRs 79 and 366 at One Plantation Rd., lie along the Cascadilla and Fall Creek gorges. The plantations contain trails, botanical gardens, ponds, streams, woodlands, swamps, a lake and an arboretum. Picnicking is permitted. Allow 1 hour minimum. Daily dawn-dusk. Free. Phone (607) 255-3020.

Sapsucker Woods, 3 mi. n.e. of the main campus at 159 Sapsucker Woods Rd., is the home of the Cornell Laboratory of Ornithology research center. Four miles of sanctuary trails wind through woodlands and swamps filled with nesting and migrating birds. The Limogene Powers Johnson Center overlooks a bird-feeding garden and a 10-acre pond. Displayed is a collection of paintings by ornithological painter Louis Agassiz Fuertes.

Allow 1 hour minimum. Observatory open Mon.-Thurs. 8-5, Fri. 8-4, Sat. 9:30-4, Sun. 11-4; closed Jan. 1 and Dec. 25. Trails open daily 24 hours. Donations. Phone (607) 254-2473.

HISTORY CENTER IN TOMPKINS COUNTY, 401 E. State St., presents seasonal exhibits focusing on local industries, arts and ethnic groups. A reference room is available Tuesdays, Thursdays and Saturdays. Museum open Tues.-Sat. 11-5; closed Jan. 1, July 4, Thanksgiving and Dec. 25. Donations. Phone (607) 273-8284.

 MUSEUM OF THE EARTH is 3 mi. n. at 1259 Trumansburg Rd. (SR 96). Geological records along with fossils, skeletons and other specimens from the northeastern United States present a timeline of Earth's development through a variety of exhibits. Beneath an Ancient Sea, Where Dinosaurs Walked and A World Carved by Ice explore three stages of paleontological science. The Fossil Preparation Lab allows visitors to observe fossil research and preservation, while discovery stations encourage hands-on examination of fossils.

Full skeletons of the Hyde Park Mastodon and Right Whale #2030 are displayed along with a 500-foot mural tracing the growth of fossils from macroscopic size. Another exhibit demonstrates how geothermal heat is used to control the building's temperature. Film presentations on large plasma screens help transition visitors between the major exhibits.

Allow 2 hours minimum. Mon. and Wed.-Sat. 10-5 (also Thurs. 5-7), Sun. noon-4. Admission $8; over 62 and students with ID $5; ages 3-17, $3. MC, VI. Phone (607) 273-6623.

SCIENCENTER is at 601 First St. This interactive science museum features numerous hands-on displays that allow visitors to explore scientific principles while having fun. Exhibits include "whisper dishes"(long-range voice projectors) and a hydraulic raceway, two-story ball machine and giant walk-in camera. Allow 2 hours minimum. Mon.-Sat. 10-5, Sun. noon-5, July-Aug.; Tues.-Sat. 10-5, Sun. noon-5, rest of year. Admission $6; over 64, $5; ages 3-17, $4. Phone (607) 272-0600.

STEWART PARK, on Cayuga Lake, .5 mi. n. on Meadow St., has a carousel, a goldfish pond and a rose garden. Adjoining the park are the Fuertes Wild Fowl Preserve and the Renwick Bird Sanctuary. Picnicking is permitted. Allow 30 minutes minimum. Daily 8 a.m.-10 p.m. Free.

JAMESTOWN (G-2) pop. 31,730, elev. 1,323′

Jamestown's founder, James Prendergast, built the town's first dam and sawmill in 1811, taking advantage of the vast white pine forests on the hills overlooking the southeast tip of Chautauqua Lake. By the mid-1800s Jamestown was one of the state's leading producers of furniture and wood products. Locally produced "pearl ash" was used to make glass, and the town was nicknamed Pearl City.

Old-fashioned family fun can be found at Midway Park, on SR 430 in nearby Maple Springs. Highlights include picnic areas, a roller skating rink and several amusement rides, including bumper boats and go-carts; phone (716) 386-3165.

Jamestown Area Chamber of Commerce: 101 W. 5th St., Jamestown, NY 14701; phone (716) 484-1101.

Self-guiding tours: Jamestown is the site of many 19th-century commercial and industrial buildings, churches and private houses. Brochures detailing self-guiding walking tours are available from the Fenton History Center Museum & Library *(see attraction listing).*

Shopping areas: Chautauqua Mall, 3 miles west on SR 394, includes The Bon-Ton, JCPenney and Sears among its 60 stores.

ART GALLERY, in the James Prendergast Library at 509 Cherry St., contains 19th- and 20th-century French, German and American paintings as well as changing exhibits. Allow 30 minutes minimum.

Mon.-Fri. 9-8:30, Sat. 9-5, Sun. 1-3:30, Nov.-Apr.; Mon.-Fri. 9-8:30, Sat. 9-4:30, rest of year. Free. Phone (716) 484-7135.

AUDUBON CENTER & SANCTUARY, 2 mi. s. on SR 60, 3 mi. s. on US 62, then .5 mi. e. to 1600 Riverside Rd., is a 600-acre wildlife sanctuary with 5 miles of nature trails through wetlands, fields and pine forests. Also featured are an arboretum, a bald eagle enclosure, an herb and butterfly garden, and towers and overlooks for viewing wildlife habitats. A nature center has hands-on exhibits and more than 200 mounted bird specimens.

Allow 1 hour minimum. Sanctuary daily dawn-dusk. Interpretive building Mon.-Sat. 10-4:30, Sun. 1-4:30, Mar.-Oct.; Sat.-Sun. by appointment, rest of year. Closed holidays. Admission $4, under 18 free. Phone (716) 569-2345.

SAVE **DESILU PLAYHOUSE** is at 2 W. Third St. The center includes full-size replicas of three television studio sets from the "I Love Lucy" shows as well as memorabilia related to the series. Ongoing showings of popular episodes also are featured. Allow 45 minutes minimum. Mon.-Sat. 10-5:30, Sun. 1-5; closed Jan. 1, Easter, Thanksgiving and Dec. 24-25 and 31. Admission $10; over 59, $9; ages 6-18, $7. AX, DS, MC, VI. Phone (716) 484-0800 or (877) 582-9326.

FENTON HISTORY CENTER MUSEUM & LIBRARY is at 67 Washington St. (SR 60), just s. of Washington St. bridge. The 1863 Italianate mansion of former New York Gov. Reuben E. Fenton features a restored Renaissance Revival drawing room, rooms depicting the Victorian and settlement periods, changing topical exhibits and a reference/genealogy library. An annual holiday exhibit highlights historic and ethnic observances and celebrations.

Guided tours are available by appointment. Allow 1 hour minimum. Mon.-Sat. 10-4 (library also open Mon. 4-9), year-round (also Sun. 1-4, Thanksgiving-Jan. 31); closed Jan. 1, Memorial Day, July 4, Thanksgiving and Christmas. Admission $5; ages 4-12, $4; family rate (two adults and three children) $20. Phone (716) 664-6256.

SAVE **LUCY-DESI MUSEUM,** 212 Pine St., celebrates the lives and entertainment careers of Jamestown-native Lucille Ball and her co-star husband Desi Arnaz through interactive displays, personal belongings and video screenings. Mon.-Sat. 10-5:30, Sun. 1-5; closed Jan. 1, Easter, Thanksgiving, and Dec. 24-25 and 31. Admission $6; over 59, $5; ages 6-18, $4. AX, DS, MC, VI. Phone (716) 484-0800 or (877) 582-9326.

ROBERT H. JACKSON CENTER is at 305 E. Fourth St. The center preserves documents, artifacts and historical memorabilia related to the life and works of United States Supreme Court Justice Robert H. Jackson, who served as the lead American prosecutor during the Nuremberg trials of Nazi war criminals. Exhibits are housed in an elegant 1858 Italianate mansion furnished with antiques. Allow 1

hour minimum. Mon.-Sat. 10-2; closed major holidays. Admission $4, under 12 free. Phone (716) 483-6646.

ROGER TORY PETERSON INSTITUTE OF NATURAL HISTORY, 311 Curtis St., is a national center for nature education named for the award-winning naturalist and author of a popular series of natural history field guides. Featured are nature exhibits as well as wildlife art and photography. Trails and a butterfly garden are on the 27 wooded acres. A natural history library is available. Tues.-Sat. 10-4, Sun. 1-5. Admission $5, students with ID $3, family rate (two adults and three children) $12. Phone (716) 665-2473.

JAVA CENTER (F-3)

BEAVER MEADOW AUDUBON CENTER, 1610 Welch Rd., features several nature trails, including one that passes near a couple of old farmsteads and others that follow the edge of Beaver Pond. Free nature walks are offered. A visitor center contains exhibits. Allow 1 hour minimum. Tues.-Sat. 10-5, Sun. 1-5; closed Jan. 1, July 4, Thanksgiving and Dec. 25. Nature walks Sun. at 2. Donations. Phone (585) 457-3228.

JOHNSTOWN (E-10) pop. 8,511, elev. 650'

Johnstown was founded by and named for Sir William Johnson, a British general and Superintendent of Indian Affairs during the mid-1700s. Johnstown has been a center of the glove-making industry since its earliest days, as has the adjoining city of Gloversville *(see place listing p. 88)*. Elizabeth Cady Stanton, a pioneer of women's rights, was born in Johnstown in 1815.

Johnstown Battlefield preserves the site of what was probably the Revolutionary War's last battle, fought Oct. 25, 1781, 6 days after Gen. Charles Cornwallis surrendered at Yorktown.

The Fulton County Court House, on W. Main Street between N. William and N. Melcher streets, was erected in 1772 and is the only Colonial courthouse standing in the state. The courthouse and five other historic sites are highlighted on a free guided walking tour departing from the corner of Main and Market streets. For a tour schedule and to make reservations contact Historic Johnstown Walking Tour; phone (518) 762-8309.

JOHNSON HALL STATE HISTORIC SITE, .2 mi. w. off SR 29 on Hall Ave., is a 1763 Georgian mansion. The house was a center for American Indian trade and negotiations prior to the Revolution. Picnicking is permitted. Allow 1 hour minimum. Guided tours Wed.-Mon. 10-5, May-Oct. Fee $4; over 65, $3; under 12 free. Phone (518) 762-8712.

KATONAH—see New York p. 152.

KINDERHOOK (F-11) pop. 1,275, elev. 288'

COLUMBIA COUNTY MUSEUM, 5 Albany Ave., has a genealogical library, a regional art gallery and changing exhibits of historical artifacts. Allow 30 minutes minimum. Mon., Wed. and Fri.-Sat. 10-4; closed holidays. Donations. Phone (518) 758-9265.

JAMES VANDERPOEL HOUSE, 16 Broad St., is an 1820 Federal-style house containing period furniture and decorative arts. Guided tours are available. Allow 1 hour minimum. Thurs.-Sat. 10-4, Sun. noon-4, Memorial Day weekend-Labor Day weekend; closed federal holidays. Admission $3; over 64, college students with ID and ages 12-18, $2. Combination admission with the Luykas Van Alen House $5; over 64 and ages 12-18, $3. Phone (518) 758-9265.

LUYKAS VAN ALEN HOUSE AND ICHABOD CRANE SCHOOLHOUSE are 1 mi. s. on SR 9H. The 1737 farmhouse is furnished with period furniture and 18th-century decorative arts. The 1850 one-room schoolhouse has been restored to its 1920s appearance and displays Columbia County school artifacts.

Allow 1 hour minimum. Guided tours Thurs.-Sat. 10-4, Sun. noon-4, Memorial Day weekend-Labor Day weekend; closed federal holidays. Grounds open year-round 7-dusk. Admission $3; over 64, college students with ID and ages 12-18, $2. Combination admission with the James Vanderpoel House $5; over 64 and ages 12-18, $3. Grounds free. Phone (518) 758-9265.

MARTIN VAN BUREN NATIONAL HISTORIC SITE, 2 mi. s. on SR 9H to 1013 Old Post Rd., is the estate of the eighth U.S. president. The 1797 mansion was remodeled in the Italianate style. Guided tours are available. Allow 1 hour, 30 minutes minimum. Daily 9-4, mid-May to late Oct. Admission $4, under 17 free. Phone (518) 758-9689.

KINGS POINT (I-2) pop. 5,076

U.S. MERCHANT MARINE ACADEMY, on Steamboat Rd. facing Long Island Sound, trains and educates officers for the Merchant Marine and Naval Reserve. The grounds include the estate of automobile manufacturer Walter Chrysler, the American Merchant Marine Museum and the U.S. Merchant Marine Memorial Chapel. Allow 1 hour minimum. Campus open daily 9-5. Museum open Tues.-Fri. 10-3, Sat.-Sun. 1-4:30. Closed federal holidays. A photo ID is required for admission. Hours may vary; phone ahead. Campus free. Museum admission by donations. Phone (516) 773-5000.

KINGSTON (G-10) pop. 23,456, elev. 295'

Established as a Dutch trading post in 1614, Kingston became a permanent settlement in 1652. The first state constitution was drafted and adopted in Kingston in 1777, when the city became the first capital. Several Colonial houses are in the Kingston area; one of the most notable is the Bevier House, which serves as the Ulster County Historical Society Headquarters and Museum.

Ulster County Tourism: 10 Westbrook Ln., Kingston, NY 12401; phone (800) 342-5826.

Self-guiding tours: Brochures outlining a walking tour of the historic Uptown Stockade area, Midtown and Rondout Creek corridor are available at the Heritage Area Visitor Center, 20 Broadway; phone (845) 331-7517 or (800) 331-1518. Brochures also are available May through October from the visitor center at 308 Clinton Ave., and at city hall, 420 Broadway; phone (845) 331-9506 or (845) 331-0080, respectively.

ASHOKAN RESERVOIR is w. off SRs 28 and 28A. The reservoir provides New York City with more than 500 million gallons of water daily when full. A scenic 40-mile route encircles the impoundment. Phone (845) 657-2304.

SAVE **HUDSON RIVER CRUISES** depart from Rondout Landing on Broadway aboard the MV *Rip Van Winkle*. The 2-hour narrated sightseeing cruise passes several lighthouses and magnificent Hudson River mansions. Music, dinner and sunset cruises also are available. Allow 2 hours minimum. Two-hour cruise departs Tues.-Sun. at 11:30 and 2:30, July-Aug.; at 2:30, May-June and Sept.-Oct. Fare $17; over 60, $16; ages 4-11, $10. DS, MC, VI. Phone (845) 340-4700 or (800) 843-7472.

OLD DUTCH CHURCH AND CEMETERY is on Main St. between Wall and Fair sts. The church was established in 1659; the cemetery dates from 1661 and contains the grave of George Clinton, first governor of the state. Mon.-Fri. 10-4 and by appointment. Free. Phone (845) 338-6759.

GEM **SENATE HOUSE STATE HISTORIC SITE,** 296 Fair St., was the meeting site of the first New York State Senate. A museum features Hudson Valley furnishings and art exhibits relating to John Vanderlyn and other Hudson Valley artists. Rooms in the Senate House are furnished as they would have appeared in 1777 when the New York State Senate met in the home of Abraham Van Gaasbeek. Allow 30 minutes minimum. Guided tours Wed.-Sat. and Mon. 10-5, Sun. 11-5, mid-Apr. to Oct. 31. Fee $4; over 62, $3; ages 5-12, $1. Phone (845) 338-2786.

VOLUNTEER FIREMEN'S HALL AND MUSEUM OF KINGSTON, 265 Fair St., houses a parade carriage, a display of 1800s fire convention badges and a collection of souvenir mugs. The museum has a functioning fire alarm system and a fire company parlor, complete with a working player piano and ornately carved furniture with the fire company's initials on each piece. Wed.-Fri. 11-3, Sat. 10-4, June-Aug.; Fri. 11-3, Sat. 10-4, Apr.-May and Sept.-Oct. Donations. Phone (845) 331-0866 or (845) 331-1247.

LA FARGEVILLE (B-7) pop. 588, elev. 375′

NORTHERN NEW YORK AGRICULTURAL HISTORICAL SOCIETY MUSEUM, 6 mi. s. on SR 180, illustrates the development of agriculture in the region. The complex includes a one-room schoolhouse, a church/meetinghouse and a cheese factory.

Guided tours daily 9-4, June 1-Sept. 25; by appointment in May. Admission $5; ages 6-12, $1. Phone (315) 658-2353.

LAKE CHAMPLAIN (A-12)

Extending from Canada southward for 120 miles, Lake Champlain varies from a quarter-mile to 12 miles wide. Two-thirds of its cubic area lies in Vermont; the rest, except for a small Canadian portion, is in New York. Lake Champlain accommodates large vessels and, with its Hudson River connector, the Champlain Canal, makes navigation possible from New York City to Montréal and the Great Lakes.

Legends of Lake Champlain's own version of the Loch Ness Monster have persisted since Samuel de Champlain sighted what he described as a serpentine creature 20 feet long, as thick as a barrel and with a head like a horse. Occasional sightings of the elusive creature, affectionately named "Champ," still occur, but whether or not a distant cousin of the Scottish sea serpent really resides in the lake remains a matter of speculation.

LAKE CHAMPLAIN FERRIES depart from Plattsburgh, Essex and Port Kent. Offered are scenic links between New York and Vermont via three separate crossings: Plattsburgh to Grand Isle, Vt. (crossing time 12 minutes); Essex to Charlotte, Vt. (crossing time 20 minutes); and Port Kent to Burlington, Vt. (crossing time 1 hour). Plattsburgh ferry operates daily 24-hours year-round. Essex ferry operates year-round, ice conditions permitting. Port Kent ferry runs mid-May to mid-Oct. AAA clubs have complete schedules and fare information. Phone (802) 864-9804.

LAKE GEORGE (D-10) pop. 985, elev. 353′

The village of Lake George is at the southern end of the 32-mile-long lake. Of the 365 islands dotting the lake, 92 have been developed for camping *(see Adirondack Park p. 53 and the AAA Northeastern CampBook)*. On the southern shore along Beach Road are a public beach, departure points for steamboat and cruise boat rides and areas where speedboats, parasails and horse-drawn carriages may be rented.

Million Dollar Beach, east of US 9 on Beach Road, is a popular swimming beach with a bathhouse, lifeguard, lockers, picnic facilities and volleyball courts. It is open Memorial Day through Labor Day; phone (518) 668-3352 to verify hours and prices. Scenic Lake Shore Drive (SR 9N) follows the west shore between the towns of Lake George and Ticonderoga *(see place listing p. 201).*

Lake George Chamber of Commerce: P.O. Box 272, Lake George, NY 12845; phone (518) 668-5755 or (800) 705-0059.

Shopping areas: Several factory outlet centers including Adirondack Factory, French Mountain Commons and Lake George Plaza are located along "Million-Dollar-Half-A-Mile" on SR 9 off I-87 exit 20.

FORT WILLIAM HENRY MUSEUM is on US 9 (Canada St.) in the center of town. This 1755-57 British fort was the subject of James Fenimore Cooper's "The Last of the Mohicans." The replica contains barracks, stockades, dungeons and fort artifacts. Living-history demonstrations include canon and musket firing, a bomb toss and musket ball molding. The Archeological Hall contains an exhibit about the 1997 archeological dig. Allow 2 hours minimum. Daily 9-6, May-Oct. Tours are given on the hour 9-5. Tour $11.95; over 59, $10.55; ages 5-11, $7.25. AX, DS, MC, VI. Phone (518) 668-5471.

THE GREAT ESCAPE & SPLASHWATER KINGDOM—see Queensbury p. 186.

LAKE GEORGE BATTLEFIELD PARK, .5 mi. s. off US 9, contains the ruins of Fort George, an American Indian monument and a memorial to Jesuit missionary Father Jogues. Picnicking is permitted. Daily 10-6:30, late June-Columbus Day; Sat.-Sun. 10-6:30, early May-late June. Park free. Parking $6 per private vehicle. Phone (518) 668-3352. See the AAA Northeastern CampBook.

LAKE GEORGE OPERA FESTIVAL— see Saratoga Springs p. 194.

LAKE GEORGE STEAMBOAT CO., with cruises departing from Steel Pier in Lake George Village, offers a narrated 4.5-hour Discovery Tour, with a complete tour of Lake George, and a 2.25-hour Paradise Bay cruise aboard the *Mohican*. One-hour paddle wheeler cruises are available aboard the *Minne-ha-ha*. Two-hour excursions aboard the *Lac du Saint Sacrement* are available with or without a meal. Two-hour moonlight cruises also are offered. A fireworks cruise is available each Thursday.

Discovery Tour departs daily at 9, June 21-Labor Day. Paradise Bay cruise departs daily at 2:30, Memorial Day weekend-Columbus Day. Paddle wheeler cruise departs daily 10-7:30, June 21-Columbus Day. Cruises on the *Lac du Saint Sacrement* depart daily at noon and 6:30, May-Oct.

Round-trip Discovery Tour $21.50; ages 3-11, $10.75. Paradise Bay cruise $16.75; ages 3-11, $7.50. Paddle wheeler cruise $10.50; ages 3-11, $5.75. *Lac du Saint Sacrement* cruise (excludes meal) $16.50; ages 3-11, $7.25. Reservations are recommended for lunch and dinner cruises. AX, DS, MC, VI. Phone (518) 668-5777 or (800) 553-2628, ext. 4.

PROSPECT MOUNTAIN VETERANS MEMORIAL HIGHWAY, I-87 exit 21, then 1 mi. n. on US 9, provides a scenic 5.5-mile drive to a crest overlooking Lake George. The summit is reached via bus or a hiking trail. Picnicking is permitted. Allow 1 hour minimum. Daily 10-6, Memorial Day-Oct. 21. Admission $6 per private vehicle. Phone (518) 668-3352.

SHORELINE CRUISES OF LAKE GEORGE leave from the lakefront at 2 Kurosaka Ln. Narrated 1- to 2-hour tours explain the scenic and historic sites along the shore. Lunch, dinner, sunset and entertainment cruises also are available. Sightseeing cruises depart Wed.-Sun. 10-6, May-Oct. Cruises $10.95-$38.95, under 3 free. MC, VI. Phone (518) 668-4644 or (888) 542-6287.

LAKE LUZERNE (D-10)
pop. 2,240, elev. 624'

RECREATIONAL ACTIVITIES

White-water Rafting

• **Hudson River Rafting Co.**, off I-87 exit 21, 11 mi. s. on SR 9N to Church St., then w. to 11 Main St. Write P.O. Box 47, North Creek, NY 12853. Trips daily July-Aug.; Sat.-Sun. in spring and fall. Reservations are recommended. Phone (518) 696-2964 or (800) 888-7238.

LAKE PLACID (B-10) pop. 2,638, elev. 1,864'

The village of Lake Placid lies on the shores of Mirror Lake and Lake Placid; the former provides a backdrop for the Main Street commercial district. Host of the 1932 and 1980 Winter Olympics, the area boasts downhill skiing at Whiteface Mountain, 8 miles north, as well as other competitive and recreational sports activities at both state-operated and private facilities.

Summer recreational facilities include foot and bicycle paths, private and public beaches, tennis courts, six golf courses, hiking trails and the indoor Olympic Arena for summer ice skating. Boats can be rented at either lake. Whiteface Mountain provides gondola rides over grassy ski slopes, and the Whiteface Mountain Veterans' Memorial Highway *(see Wilmington p. 208)* runs almost to the summit.

The United States Olympic Training Center, 421 Old Military Rd., offers self-guiding tours of its facilities; phone (518) 523-2600. The Uihlein Sugar Maple Field Station on Bear Cub Lane contains maple sugar exhibits and demonstrations.

Lake Placid/Essex County Visitors Bureau: Olympic Center, 2610 Main St., Suite 2, Lake Placid, NY 12946; phone (518) 523-2445 or (800) 447-5224.

HIGH FALLS GORGE—see Wilmington p. 208.

THE HISTORY MUSEUM, LAKE PLACID/NORTH ELBA HISTORICAL SOCIETY, 242 Station St., chronicles Lake Placid's history over the last 200 years. The waiting and baggage rooms of this former train depot house displays of primitive farm implements, musical instruments, period photographs and memorabilia. Allow 30 minutes minimum. Wed.-Sun. 10-4, Memorial Day-Columbus Day. Admission $2. Phone (518) 523-1608.

JOHN BROWN FARM STATE HISTORIC SITE is .5 mi. s. on SR 73, then .7 mi. s. on John Brown Rd. A monument and restored farmhouse mark the burial spot of abolitionist John Brown. A self-guiding trail passes through the grounds, which are accessible year-round. Cross-country skiing is permitted in winter. Guided farmhouse tours are available. Allow 30 minutes minimum. House open Wed.-Mon. 10-5, May 1-Oct. 3. Admission $2; senior citizens and ages 13-18, $1. Phone (518) 523-3900.

LAKE PLACID BOAT RIDES, 1 mi. n. on Mirror Lake Dr. at Lake Placid Marina, offers narrated 1-hour cruises. Departures daily at 10:30, 1, 2:30 and 4, late June-early Sept.; Mon.-Sun. at 10:30 and 2:30, Sat.-Sun. at 10:30, 2:30 and 4, late May-late June; daily at 10:30, 1:30 and 3, early Sept.-early Oct. Fare $8.50; over 62, $7.50; ages 3-12, $6.50. Phone (518) 523-9704 to verify schedule and fares.

OLYMPIC CENTER, 2634 Main St. off SR 86, is a multipurpose facility hosting numerous world- and national-class sports events. Originally built for the ice events of the 1932 Winter Olympic Games, the center received an additional wing to host the 1980 Winter Olympic Games, providing a total of four indoor ice rinks. Other sites include the Whiteface Mountain facilities, MacKenzie-Intervale Ski Jumping Complex and Olympic Sports Complex at Mt. Van Hoevenberg.

Allow 4 hours minimum. Center open daily 9-5. Summer Olympic Site Passport (includes admission to all venues) offered daily 9-5, mid-June to mid-Oct. Winter Passport available late Dec. to mid-Mar. Passport $25. Phone (518) 523-1655.

1932 & 1980 Lake Placid Winter Olympic Museum, within the Olympic Center at 2634 Main St., explores the legacy of the 1932 and 1980 Olympic Games. Video booths feature athletes' uniforms and equipment as well as changing exhibits. Allow 30 minutes minimum. Daily 10-5; closed Jan. 1, Easter, Thanksgiving and Dec. 25. Admission $5; over 62, $4; ages 7-12, $3. Phone (518) 523-1655.

MacKenzie-Intervale Ski Jumping Complex, 2 mi. s.e. of the village on SR 73, is a year-round training and event facility. The Sports Park is a freestyle skiing training center. In the winter the site is home to international competition and training; in summer plastic matting is used to simulate snow. Featured is a 26-story tower with a glass-enclosed elevator and a view of Mount Marcy and surrounding peaks.

Daily 9-4. Admission $12; with chairlift pass and elevator to top of ski jump; over 61 and ages 5-12, $7. Phone (518) 523-1655 or (518) 523-2202.

Olympic Sports Complex at Mt. Van Hoevenberg, 7 mi. s.e. on SR 73, offers more than 50 miles of groomed cross-country ski trails and a combined bobsled/luge/skeleton track. Bobsled rides are offered year-round.

Open daily 9-4. Bobsled rides daily 10-4 (weather permitting). Day-use fees (special events excluded) $5. Cross-country ski area $14; senior citizens and under 12, $12. Bobsled rides $40. Phone (518) 523-4436 or (800) 462-6236.

SANTA'S WORKSHOP—see Wilmington p. 208.

LAWRENCE (I-2) pop. 6,522, elev. 30'

ROCK HALL MUSEUM, 199 Broadway, is a restored 1767 Georgian Colonial mansion furnished in the style of the late 18th century. A garden and picnic area are on the grounds. Wed.-Sat. 10-4, Sun. noon-4; closed holidays. Free. Phone (516) 239-1157.

LE ROY (E-4) pop. 4,462, elev. 863'

[SAVE] **LE ROY HOUSE MUSEUM AND JELL-O GALLERY,** I-90 exit 47, then s. on SR 19 to 23 E. Main St., was built in the early 19th century. Seven rooms are furnished in period, including a basement kitchen and a children's playroom. An exhibit about Jell-O, the dessert food invented in Le Roy in 1897, is presented in another building on the property.

Allow 30 minutes minimum. Jell-O Gallery Mon.-Sat. 10-4, Sun. 1-4, Apr.-Dec.; Mon.-Fri. 10-4, rest of year. Le Roy House Mon.-Fri. 10-4, Sun. 1-4, May-Oct.; Closed Jan. 1, Easter, Thanksgiving and Dec. 25. Admission $4; ages 6-11, $2.50. MC, VI. Phone (585) 768-7433.

LEWISTON—see Niagara Falls p. 167.

LITTLE FALLS (E-9) pop. 5,188, elev. 370'

Water has always been a factor in the development of the city of Little Falls. Although in the city's earliest days the falls may have created a navigational problem, they soon became a natural blessing; their presence spurred the onset of settlement in the gorge and became a source of water power. Lock #17, with a drop of 40 feet, is the largest lock on the Barge Canal. As transportation improved, trade increased, and Little Falls soon became a stopping point between New York City and the western part of the state.

Historic Canal Place is a revitalized industrial area that includes two refurbished 19th-century stone mill buildings set amidst two parks along the Mohawk River. The area includes antique and art galleries as well as other shops and restaurants and a visual and performing arts center. An underground walkway connects Historic Canal Place with Main Street.

Of interest is the Little Falls Historical Society Museum at 319 S. Ann St. Exhibits housed in the restored 1833 bank building include local memorabilia, genealogical files, a bank vault and Victorian clothing; phone (315) 823-0643.

Self-guiding tours: Brochures detailing self-guiding tours of the city's landmarks, historic areas and natural wonders are available at the Little Falls

Historical Society Museum or at the Urban Renewal Office, 45 W. Main St.; phone (315) 823-3560.

Shopping areas: Little Falls Antique Center, 25 W. Mill St. in Historic Canal Place, offers two floors of antiques and decorative arts displayed in an 1855 stone mill building. Several art galleries also call this area home.

HERKIMER HOME STATE HISTORIC SITE, 3 mi. e. on SR 169 at I-90 exit 29A, was the home of American Revolutionary War general Nicholas Herkimer. The 1764 house contains historic furnishings, artifacts and memorabilia. The site includes a Colonial herb and vegetable garden. A visitor center presents an orientation film about the history of the home.

Allow 1 hour minimum. Daily 9-5, mid-May to Oct. 31. Guided tours begin on the half-hour Tues.-Sat. 10-5, Sun. 1-5, July-Aug.; Wed.-Sat. 10-5, Sun. 1-5, mid-May through June 30 and Sept.-Oct. Tour $4; over 62 and ages 13-17, $3; ages 5-12, $1. Phone (315) 823-0398.

LIVERPOOL (E-7) pop. 2,505, elev. 420'

ONONDAGA LAKE PARK, off I-81 Liverpool exit 24, then 1.5 mi. w. on SR 370W to Ononadaga Pkwy., extends 6 mi. along the eastern shore of Onondaga Lake. Features include a visitor center, dog park, skate park, marina, boat launch and athletic fields as well as the original Salt Spring and the Jesuit Well. The Salt Museum contains a replica of a 19th-century salt boiling block and other artifacts. Tram rides and inline skate and bicycle rentals are available mid-May through Columbus Day.

Picnicking is permitted. Food is available. Park open daily dawn-dusk. Museum open daily 1-6, May 1-Columbus Day. Free. Skate park $3 per 2.5 hours. Phone (315) 453-6712 or (315) 451-7275.

SAINTE MARIE AMONG THE IROQUOIS is off I-81 Liverpool exit 24A, then 1.5 mi. w. on SR 370W to Onondaga Lake Pkwy. This re-creation of a 17th-century Jesuit mission features costumed interpreters who demonstrate daily activities of the French missionaries, including cooking, spinning yarn, quilting, woodworking, blacksmithing and singing. An orientation center has exhibits about the cultural differences between the Iroquois and French peoples. The winter holidays are celebrated during Christmas Around the World.

Allow 1 hour minimum. Mon.-Fri. 9-4, Sat.-Sun. noon-5, May-Oct.; Fri.-Sat. 5-9 p.m. late Nov.-Dec. 23 Admission $3; over 62, $2.50; ages 6-17, $2; family rate $10. MC, VI. Phone (315) 453-6768.

LIVINGSTON MANOR (G-9)
pop. 1,355, elev. 1,400'

Livingston Manor is at the southern edge of Catskill Forest Preserve in the Catskill Mountains. Camping, hiking and fly fishing in the Willowemoc and Beaver Kill trout streams are popular recreational pursuits.

Sullivan County Visitor's Association-Livingston Manor: 100 North St., P.O. Box 5012, Monticello, NY 12701; phone (845) 794-3000.

CATSKILL FLY FISHING CENTER AND MUSEUM is off SR 17 exit 96, then 2 mi. w. to 1031 Old SR 17. Exhibits interpret the history, science and art of fly fishing. The center's 55 acres feature nature trails and trout streams. Picnicking is permitted. Allow 30 minutes minimum. Daily 10-4, Apr.-Oct.; Tues.-Fri. 10-1, Sat. 10-4, rest of year. Admission $3; under 12, $1. MC, VI. Phone (845) 439-4810.

LOCKPORT—*see Niagara Falls p. 168.*

LODI (F-6) pop. 338

WINERIES

- **Wagner Vineyards and Micro Brewery** is just s. of SR 96A on SR 414. Daily 10-5. Brewery open Mon.-Sat. 10-5, Sun. noon-5. Closed Jan. 1, Thanksgiving and Dec. 25. Phone (607) 582-6450.

LONG ISLAND

Ask both a New Yorker and a geography student to define Long Island, and you will get two different answers. Geographically speaking, the island encompasses 1,723 square miles within its boundaries, which extend 125 miles to the east of Manhattan.

A New Yorker pictures the island a bit differently, however. Because two counties—Queens and Kings (Brooklyn)—of the island's four are boroughs of New York City, only the remaining Nassau and Suffolk counties form Long Island in the minds of many city dwellers. Queens and Brooklyn account for the majority of the island's total population.

The northern side of Nassau county forms the island's Gold Coast, whose beautiful gardens and elegant estates were the aspirations of Jay Gatsby in F. Scott Fitzgerald's novel "The Great Gatsby." Some of New York's most well-known beaches extend from western Nassau County along the southern shore through Suffolk County. These include Jones Beach State Park *(see Wantagh p. 203)* and Fire Island National Seashore *(see place listing p. 85).*

At the eastern end of Suffolk County are the North and South Forks, site of some of New York's most productive farmland. The more urban South Fork also is known as the Hamptons. The populations of these quiet towns swell each summer with the wealthy, the famous and others who wish to escape the hectic and humid city.

From such 20th-century mansions as Old Westbury House in Nassau County to the 17th-century saltboxes of Sag Harbor in Suffolk County, carefully preserved buildings and houses dot Long Island.

Places and towns on Long Island with individual place listings are (clockwise around the island from the northwest) King's Point, Glen Cove, Oyster Bay,

Cold Spring Harbor, Centerport, Stony Brook, Setauket, Riverhead, Cutchogue, Bridgehampton, Sag Harbor, Montauk, Amagansett, East Hampton, Southampton, Eastport, Manorville, Shirley, Fire Island National Seashore, West Sayville, Oakdale, Great River, Wantagh, Old Bethpage, Old Westbury, Albertson, Lawrence and Garden City.

Long Island Convention and Visitors Bureau and Sports Commission: 330 Motor Pkwy., Hauppauge, NY 11788; phone (631) 951-3440 or (877) 386-6654.

The Suffolk County branch office is on the Long Island Expressway between exits 51 and 52 eastbound, and the Nassau County branch office is off the Southern State Parkway between exits 12 and 13 eastbound.

LYONS (E-6) pop. 5,831, elev. 406'

WAYNE COUNTY HISTORICAL SOCIETY MUSEUM, 2 blks. w. of the County Court House at Butternut and Church sts., is housed in a brick mansion and an attached stone jail built in 1854. Displays include antiques, farm implements, ship artifacts and exhibits depicting the area's early judicial system. The restored horse barn contains transportation artifacts and agricultural and domestic equipment.

Guided tours are available by appointment. Allow 1 hour minimum. Mon.-Fri. 10-4, Sat.-Sun. by appointment, July 4-Labor Day; Tues.-Sat. 10-4, rest of year. Closed holidays. Donations. Phone (315) 946-4943.

MALONE (A-10) pop. 6,075, elev. 756'

FRANKLIN COUNTY HISTORICAL & MUSEUM SOCIETY HOUSE OF HISTORY, 51 Milwaukee St., features guided tours of an 1864 home complete with period furniture, photographs and household items. There also are displays about weaving, spinning and broommaking. A staffed genealogical library is available for on-site research. Allow 30 minutes minimum. Tues.-Sat. 1-4, June 1-Sept. 4; Sat. 1-4, Sept. 5-Oct. 31; by appointment, rest of year. Closed holidays. Donations. Phone (518) 483-2750.

MANORVILLE (H-4) pop. 11,131

THE ANIMAL FARM, .2 mi. n. off SR 27 exit 59 or 3 mi. s. of I-495 (Long Island Expwy.) exit 69 to 296 Wading River Rd., is a 10-acre refuge for neglected and unwanted animals. The petting zoo is designed so children may touch, feed and have close contact with farm and exotic animals. Pony rides are available. Picnicking is permitted. Food is available. Mon.-Fri. 10-5, Sat.-Sun. 10-6, Apr.-Oct. Admission $12; over 65 and ages 2-16, $10. AX, MC, VI. Phone (631) 878-1785.

LONG ISLAND GAME FARM WILDLIFE PARK, off I-495 (Long Island Expwy.) exit 70, then 2.2 mi. s. on Chapman Blvd. following signs, has a wildlife collection, a petting zoo and performing animal shows. Themed nature trails and several rides also are available.

Picnicking is permitted. Allow 2 hours, 30 minutes minimum. Mon.-Fri. 10-5, Sat.-Sun. 10-6, Apr.-Oct. Admission Memorial Day-Labor Day $16.95; over 60 and ages 3-11, $14.95. Admission prices vary rest of season; phone ahead. DS, MC, VI. Phone (631) 878-6644.

MARCELLUS (E-7) pop. 1,826, elev. 492'

CENTERS FOR NATURE EDUCATION/BALTIMORE WOODS is off SR 175, then .4 mi. n. on Bishop Hill Rd. Seven trails wind around a re-created pioneer homestead, herb garden, open fields, two spring-fed streams and undisturbed hillside forests of mixed hardwood and old-growth timber. Interpreted programs about the ecology of the area are offered. Allow 2 hours minimum. Daily dawn-dusk. Free. Phone (315) 673-1350.

MASSENA (A-9) pop. 11,209, elev. 24'

An 80-foot drop in the St. Lawrence River along the Great Lakes-St. Lawrence Seaway System (see place listing p. 89) has been a two-fold boon to Massena. Two locks, the Bertrand Snell and Dwight D. Eisenhower, were built to overcome the descent, while the Moses-Saunders Power Dam was constructed to take advantage of it. Approximately 3,000 ships from international ports carry passengers and cargo through the locks each year.

Viewing decks and parking are available at the Dwight D. Eisenhower Visitor Center off SR 37, open Memorial Day through Labor Day. Recorded information about upbound and downbound shipping traffic is available; phone (315) 769-2422.

Greater Massena Chamber of Commerce: 50 Main St., P.O. Box 387, Massena, NY 13662; phone (315) 769-3525

Shopping areas: St. Lawrence Centre Mall on SR 37 features more than 55 stores, including JCPenney and Sears, as well as specialty shops. [SAVE] Duty Free America's, a tax and duty free shop, is at the American Bridge Plaza in Rooseveltown, northeast off SR 37.

MASSENA MUSEUM, 200 E. Orvis, contains items of local interest, including an 1882 hotel book signed by President Chester A. Arthur, a carved Victorian hearse adapted for winter with sled runners, Victorian furnishings and an exhibit of aluminum artifacts from area manufacturers. A town historian is available mornings. Allow 30 minutes minimum. Mon.-Fri. 10-4; closed major holidays. Free. Phone (315) 769-8571.

ROBERT MOSES STATE PARK is 2 mi. n.e. of SR 37 on Barnhart Island. This 4,122-acre park overlooks lock operations. An information center offers seaway brochures and a marina provides a boat ramp and boat rentals. Park open daily dawn-dusk, mid-May through Columbus Day. Information center open daily 8-10, Memorial Day-Labor Day; daily 9-5, day after Labor Day-Columbus Day. Beach open daily June 1-Labor Day. Park free. Beach $7, reduced admission after 4. Phone (315) 769-8663. *See Recreation Chart and the AAA Northeastern CampBook.*

MAYVILLE (F-2) pop. 1,756, elev. 1,303′

Located on the northwest shore of Chautauqua Lake, Mayville began as a portage point between Lake Erie and the Allegheny and Ohio rivers. Boating, hiking, bicycling, fishing, snowmobiling and cross-country skiing are among the recreational opportunities available nearby.

Mayville/Chautauqua Chamber of Commerce: P.O. Box 22, Mayville, NY 14757; phone (716) 753-3113.

MILFORD (F-9) pop. 511

SAVE **COOPERSTOWN & CHARLOTTE VALLEY RAILROAD**, .3 mi. e. on SR 166 to Milford Depot at 136 E. Main St., offers scenic 8-mile sightseeing trips to Cooperstown *(see place listing p. 77)* in 1928 passenger coaches and an open-air gondola. A museum is in the restored 1869 depot. Round trips also originate in Cooperstown.

Departures Sat.-Thurs., mid-June through Labor Day, Sat.-Sun. and holidays, Memorial Day to mid-June and day after Labor Day to mid-Oct. Evening, special-event and holiday excursions also are offered. Departure days and times may vary; phone for schedule. Round-trip fare $10; over 62, $9; ages 4-12, $7. AX, MC, VI. Phone (607) 432-2429.

MILLBROOK (H-11) pop. 1,429, elev. 567′

WINERIES

- **Millbrook Vineyards & Winery**, 3.5 mi. n. on SR 82 to Shunpike Rd. (CR 57), then 3 mi. e. following signs to 26 Wing Rd. Daily 11-6, Memorial Day-Labor Day; noon-5, rest of year. Closed major holidays. Phone (845) 677-8383 or (800) 662-9463.

MILTON (H-10) pop. 1,251

WINERIES

- **Royal Kedem Winery**, 1519 SR 9W. Sun.-Thurs. 9-5:30; closed Jewish holidays. Phone (845) 236-4281.

MONROE (I-10) pop. 7,780, elev. 607′

MUSEUM VILLAGE is 1.2 mi. w. on SR 17M or s. off SR 17 exit 129. This 17-acre outdoor museum has exhibit buildings with collections of 19th-century Americana. Included are a drugstore, schoolhouse and natural history museum. Demonstrations of 19th-century crafts, family workshops and farm animals also are featured. Food is available. Open Mon.-Fri. 10-2, Sat.-Sun. 11-4, Sept.-Nov. and in June; Wed.-Sun. 11-4, July-Aug. Admission $10; over 59, $8; ages 4-15, $5. MC, VI. Phone (845) 782-8247.

MONTAUK (H-5) pop. 3,851, elev. 9′

Once inhabited by the Montaukett Indians, Montauk is a resort on a peninsula along the south shore of extreme eastern Long Island. The "cod ledge" off the banks of Montauk is one of the most renowned fishing areas in the world.

Hither Hills State Park *(see Recreation Chart and the AAA Northeastern CampBook)* and Montauk Point State Park *(see Recreation Chart)* has various recreational facilities. Montauk County Park also offers recreational facilities as well as the 1799 Third House Museum. *Also see Long Island p. 99.*

A passenger ferry to Block Island, R.I., departs from Viking Landing daily at 9, late May to mid-Oct.; Fri.-Sun. at 9, mid- to late May. The ferry returns at 4:30; phone (631) 668-5700.

MONTAUK POINT LIGHTHOUSE MUSEUM, 6 mi. e. on SR 27, is in one of the oldest active lighthouses in the country. The 1796 lighthouse was commissioned by George Washington in 1792. Visitors may climb the 137 steps to the top of the tower. Exhibits about maritime history and a videotape are available.

Allow 1 hour minimum. Open daily at 10:30, Memorial Day-Columbus Day; closing times vary. Phone for winter schedule. Admission $7; senior citizens $6; under 13, $3. Parking $6. Under 41 inches tall are not permitted in the tower. Phone (631) 668-2544 or (888) 685-7646.

SECOND HOUSE MUSEUM is .5 mi. w. at e. jct. of Old Montauk Hwy. and SR 27. This late 18th-century house, said to be the oldest house in Montauk, contains period artifacts and a one-room school. A rose garden tour also is available. Allow 1 hour minimum. Thurs.-Tues. 10-4, July 4-Columbus Day; Sat.-Sun. 10-4, Memorial Day-July 1. Admission $4; ages 6-12, $1. Phone (631) 668-5340.

MONTGOMERY (H-10) pop. 3,636, elev. 388′

HILL-HOLD MUSEUM, n.e. on SR 416, re-creates life on an 1830s Hudson Valley farm. The grounds contain an herb garden, a one-room schoolhouse and barnyards with livestock. Original furnishings include pieces that were crafted on the farm. Allow 1 hour minimum. Wed.-Sun. 10-4:30, early May-early Oct.; phone for December holiday schedule. Admission $3; under 16, $2; family rate (two adults and up to three children under 16) $7. Phone (845) 291-2404 or (845) 457-4905.

MONTOUR FALLS (F-6)
pop. 1,797, elev. 456′

Montour Falls occupies the site of Catharines Town, a village ruled by and named for Queen Catharine Montour of the Iroquois Nation. A score of waterfalls flow through the seven glens that surround the town.

Havana Glen has hiking trails past numerous waterfalls, pools and cascades as well as camping facilities. Picnicking is permitted. Chequa-gua Falls,

156 feet high, is at the head of Main Street; the falls are illuminated at night. Seneca Lake is immediately north of the village; a marina is open daily from mid-April to mid-October. Recreational opportunities include boating, camping and fishing. Picnicking is permitted.

Nearby Catharine Creek is known for its rainbow and brown trout fishing, which is at its best April through December. *Also see Finger Lakes p. 84.*

SCHUYLER COUNTY HISTORICAL SOCIETY MUSEUM, 108 N. Catharine St., is housed in the 1830 Old Brick Tavern, the county's oldest brick building. The Georgian-style building displays period artifacts that characterize 19th-century life in rural upstate New York. Among the exhibits are antique farm implements and tools of various trades, American Indian relics, women's fashions, antique toys and medical memorabilia. The bedrooms are furnished in period.

Allow 1 hour minimum. Tues.-Fri. 10-4, Sat. noon-4, Memorial Day-Labor Day; closed major holidays. Donations. Phone (607) 535-9741.

MORAVIA (F-7) pop. 4,040, elev. 802′

MILLARD FILLMORE CABIN is 1 mi. s. on SR 38 in Fillmore Glen State Park. The cabin is a replica of the one in which the 13th president was born. The Fillmore birthplace, designated by markers within Fillmore Glen State Park *(see Recreation Chart and the AAA Northeastern CampBook),* is 4 miles east via Skinner Hill Road. Park open daily dawn-dusk. Cabin open daily 8 a.m.-dusk, early May-early Oct. Admission $6 per private vehicle, late June-Labor Day; $7 per private vehicle, rest of year. Phone (315) 497-0130.

DID YOU KNOW

Forty million gallons of water spill over Niagara Falls every minute.

MOUNTAINVILLE (H-10)

STORM KING ART CENTER, off SR 32 on Old Pleasant Hill Rd., is a 500-acre outdoor sculpture park and museum with more than 120 sculptures. The permanent collection contains pieces by Magdalena Abakanowicz, Siah Armajani, Alexander Calder, Mark di Suvero, Louise Nevelson, Isamu Noguchi and David Smith; exhibitions change annually. Tram rides and audiotapes are available.

Allow 2 hours minimum. Wed.-Sun. 11-5:30, Apr. 1-late Oct. (also Sat. 5:30-8, July-Aug.); 11-5, late Oct. to mid-Nov. Admission $10, over 64 and college students with ID $9, students K-12 with ID $7, under 5 free. Tram fare included with admission. Audio tour $5. Phone (845) 534-3115.

MOUNT VERNON—*see New York p. 152.*

MUMFORD (E-4) elev. 617′

GENESEE COUNTRY VILLAGE & MUSEUM, 1.2 mi. w. of SR 36 on Flint Hill Rd., occupies 600 acres and has some 70 19th-century structures that have been moved from their original sites, restored and authentically furnished. Costumed villagers portray 19th-century daily life, while craftspeople demonstrate spinning, weaving, cooking and other skills and crafts.

An art gallery displays some 700 works of wildlife and sporting art by nationally-acclaimed artists including John James Audubon and Frederic Remington. A nature center features more than 5 miles of interpretive trails crossing 175 acres of woodlands and meadows. Trolley transportation throughout the village is available.

Guided tours are available. Picnicking is permitted (cans and bottles not allowed). Food is available. Allow 4 hours minimum. Village and art gallery Tues.-Sun. and holidays 10-5, July 1-Labor Day; Tues.-Fri. 10-4, Sat.-Sun. and holidays 10-5, May-June and day after Labor Day-Oct 31. Last admission is 1 hour before closing. Nature center Tues.-Fri. 10-4, Sat.-Sun. 10-5, Jan.-Oct.; Sat.-Sun. 10-5, rest of year.

Combined admission to village, museum, nature center and art gallery $14; over 62 and college students with ID $11; ages 4-16, $8. Gallery of Sporting Art admission $5.50; over 61 and college students with ID $4.50; ages 4-16, $3.50. Nature center admission $3.50; over 61 and college students with ID $3; ages 4-16, $2.50. AX, MC, VI. Phone (585) 538-6822.

NAPLES (F-5) pop. 1,072, elev. 818′

Near the southern end of Canandaigua Lake, Naples is in the vicinity of three scenic glens—Parrish, Tannery and Grimes—with many waterfalls. Rainbow trout fishing is popular. *Also see Finger Lakes p. 84.*

CUMMING NATURE CENTER is 1.2 mi. w. on Clark St., then 7 mi. n. to 6472 Gulick Rd. Part of the Rochester Museum & Science Center *(see Rochester p. 190)*, this 900-acre environmental center in Bristol Hills has 6 miles of themed trails for nature walks and cross-country skiing and snowshoeing; equipment rentals are available. Featured are natural history programs, exhibits and seasonal events. Trails open Mon.-Fri. 9-4:30, Sat.-Sun. 9-5. Visitor center open Sat.-Sun. 9-5. Closed for seasonal maintenance mid-Nov. to late Dec. Admission $3; family rate $10. Phone (585) 374-6160.

WINERIES

- **Widmer's Wine Cellars Inc.**, 1 Lake Niagara Ln. Mon.-Sat. noon-5, Sun. noon-5, May-Dec.; daily 1-4, rest of year. Closed Jan. 1, Easter, Thanksgiving and Dec. 25. Phone (800) 836-5253.

NARROWSBURG (H-9) pop. 414, elev. 716′

Narrowsburg is sandwiched between Sullivan County's lake region and the Upper Delaware Scenic and Recreational River *(see place listing p. 202)*, which forms a meandering boundary between New York and Pennsylvania. A public boat launch is nearby. Visitors can obtain information about river recreation at an information center on Main Street.

Sullivan County Visitor's Association-Narrowsburg: 100 North St., P.O. Box 5012, Monticello, NY 12701; phone (845) 794-3000, ext. 5010.

FORT DELAWARE MUSEUM OF COLONIAL HISTORY, .7 mi. n. on SR 97, is an 18th-century stockade with blockhouses, three log cabins, a gun platform, storehouses, a blacksmith shop, an armory, an animal yard and an herb garden. The fort is patterned after the mid-1700s Cushetunk settlement. Guides in period dress present lectures, demonstrations and slide and videotape shows about Colonial arts and crafts.

Allow 1 hour minimum. Wed.-Sun. 10-5:30, June 30-Labor Day; Sat.-Sun. and holidays 10-5:30, Memorial Day weekend-June 27. Admission $4.50; over 64, $3.50; ages 6-16, $2.50; family rate (two adults and three children) $13. Phone (845) 252-6660.

NEWARK (E-5) pop. 9,682, elev. 457′

HOFFMAN CLOCK MUSEUM, 2 blks. s. of SR 31 in the Newark Public Library at 121 High St., displays antique clocks. Allow 1 hour minimum. Mon.-Thurs. 9:30-9, Fri. 9:30-6, Sat. 9:30-5. Free. Phone (315) 331-4370.

NEWBURGH (H-11) pop. 28,259, elev. 164′

The site of George Washington's headquarters for more than a year during the Revolutionary War, Newburgh later based its economy on a thriving whaling industry. With the demise of whaling the town successfully turned its ships to other trade in the late 1800s; its seafaring tradition is still evident. Downtown Newburgh's 455-acre historic district contains 18th- and 19th-century structures.

Orange County Chamber of Commerce, Inc.: 11 Racquet Rd., Newburgh, NY 12550; phone (845) 567-6229.

Self-guiding tours: Brochures for self-guiding tours of the historic district are available from the Newburgh Historical Society, 189 Montgomery St.; phone (845) 561-2585.

WASHINGTON'S HEADQUARTERS STATE HISTORIC SITE, Liberty and Washington sts., was Gen. George Washington's headquarters from April 1782 until August 1783 and the place from which Washington issued orders for the cessation of the Revolutionary War. The 1750 Hasbrouck House is furnished as a military headquarters. A museum contains exhibits relating to the Continental Army and a 6-acre park includes the 1887 Tower of Victory monument. Wed.-Sat. and Mon. 10-5, Sun. 1-5, mid-Apr. to late Oct.; by appointment, rest of year. Admission $4; over 61, $3; ages 5-11, $1. Phone (845) 562-1195.

NEW CITY—*see New York p. 153.*

NEW LEBANON (F-12) pop. 2,454

MOUNT LEBANON SHAKER VILLAGE, s. of US 20 on Shaker Rd., was the home of the Shakers 1785-1947. Known for their celibate lifestyle and community living, the Shakers designated this village the "Center of Union," a site of spiritual importance equivalent to that of the Vatican for Catholics or Mecca for Muslims. Visitors can learn about the traditions, architecture and handmade furniture unique to the sect. The village has 26 buildings.

Guided tours are available by appointment. Allow 1 hour, 30 minutes minimum. Wed.-Mon. 10-5, Memorial Day-Oct. 31; by appointment rest of year. Admission $8; ages 8-17, $4; family rate (two adults and two children) $18. MC, VI. Phone (518) 794-9500.

NEW PALTZ (H-10) pop. 6,034, elev. 252′

New Paltz was established by French Huguenots on land purchased from the Esopus Indians. Stone houses built 1692-1894 stand on Huguenot Street as reminders of the original settlement.

New Paltz Chamber of Commerce: 124 Main St., New Paltz, NY 12561; phone (845) 255-0243.

HISTORIC HUGUENOT STREET TOURS, departing from DuBois Fort on Huguenot St., visits a selection of buildings in a 300-year-old Huguenot village comprising six houses, the fort and a reconstructed 18th-century stone church. Established in 1677, New Paltz was home to 12 French Huguenot refugee families whose descendents lived in the houses well into the 20th century. Many of the houses contain family furnishings reflecting various periods of ownership. Architectural styles range from Colonial to Victorian.

Tours depart Tues.-Sun. 10-4, May-Oct. Fee $10; over 62 and college students with ID $9; ages 6-17, $5. Children must be with an adult. MC, VI. Phone (845) 255-1660 or (845) 255-1889.

NEW ROCHELLE—*see New York p. 153.*

New York

City Population: 8,008,278   **Elevation:** 54 ft.

Editor's Picks

East River / Lester Lefkowitz / Getty Images

New York is a city of such extremes that any visitor would be hard pressed to describe it without resorting to superlatives. Words like biggest and best come to mind when referring to America's most populated city. The superlatives are not always positive though. The enormous number of people, pace of life and stark urban landscape contribute to an often grim and sometimes frustrating experience when walking along its streets. Despite problems common to any major city, New York attracts 34 million visitors each year to its man-made canyons.

A true archipelago, the 314 square miles that make up New York City are a series of islands that embrace five boroughs, or administrative districts: Manhattan, Brooklyn, Queens, Staten Island and the Bronx. More than 8 million people live in the city's metropolitan area, which includes Long Island and parts of southern New York State, northeastern New Jersey and southwestern Connecticut.

The city's early history laid the foundation for that "New York state of mind"—a powerfully independent, rambunctious outlook on life. Both the Dutch and English spent years quarreling over the rights to Manhattan after its official discovery in 1609 by Englishman Henry Hudson (the Hudson River's namesake), who navigated the area's waterways.

Fifteen years later it was the Dutch who claimed the area by forming a settlement called New Amsterdam, a principal colony of New Netherland. Two years later Peter Minuit, sailing with the Dutch West India Company, finagled the purchase of Manhattan from the local Indians for trinkets worth about 60 guilders, or $24.

The English returned in 1664 and, angered by their trade rivalries with the Dutch in Europe, seized New Amsterdam. A more autocratic form of government was instituted, and the area was renamed New York after King Charles II's brother, the Duke of York. Just 9 years later the Netherlands launched a surprise attack on New York, reclaiming the area and christening it New Orange. In 1674 New York changed hands for the last time, the result of the Treaty of Westminster between England and the Netherlands. In 1686 New York became the first city in the colonies to be granted a royal charter.

The 1825 opening of the Erie Canal furthered development by connecting the city with Buffalo, the Great Lakes and parts of the West. Overseas trade burgeoned. The increase in international stature had another important effect: Those in other parts of the world, victims of failed revolutions or poverty or motivated by an adventurous spirit, bid farewell to their homelands and set sail for a haven promising greater opportunities.

From the mid-19th to the mid-20th centuries New York was the official port of entry for millions of immigrants. From 1855 to 1890 newcomers first landed at Castle Garden in Lower Manhattan, near what is now Battery Park. As the numbers swelled, the federal government was forced to find a larger facility, and an island in the New York Bay seemed the logical choice. Ellis Island, southwest of the tip of Lower Manhattan, was first used as a dump site for ships' ballast and later as a fort. Named after its

owner, Samuel Ellis, the 27.5-acre island was transformed into a processing station.

Waves of immigrants swept onto the shores of Ellis Island. German, Irish, Scandinavian and central European families clutched sacks filled with personal items. Frightened, anxious and weary from their arduous passage, Italians, Poles, Czechs and Russians waited for entrance into the United States.

The red-brick buildings were cramped and drafty, containing scowling immigration inspectors standing between a fresh start and heartbreaking deportation. Many of those permitted to stay began new lives not far from where they had disembarked. It was these immigrants, mostly skilled laborers and those willing to work cheaply, who built the city's bridges, tunnels, roads and elevated transportation systems—infrastructure that helped New York make the leap from city to metropolis.

With this sudden surge in population came a boom in economic enterprises, from manufacturing to entertainment. New citizens worked furiously not only to improve their island home but also to make New York one of the most influential cities in the world.

Increasing interdependence of the five boroughs roused city leaders to discuss merging. Although Brooklyn initially resisted, Manhattan, the Bronx, Queens, Staten Island and Brooklyn consolidated to form Greater New York on Jan. 1, 1898.

This proverbial melting pot fostered a strong sense of ethnic pride within neighborhoods, and newcomers' craftsmanship lent a striking beauty to the city streetscape. Embellishments on many of New York's older buildings stand as a testament to painstaking Old World artistry.

Central Park, Midtown Manhattan
© Paul Barton / Corbis

Considered the city's first skyscraper, the 285-foot-tall brick and limestone Flatiron Building was built in 1902 on the south side of Madison Square. This impressive Italian Renaissance structure was shaped like a wedge of pie to fit into the triangular area between Broadway and Fifth Avenue. Two years later the IRT, the city's first subway line, began operations, running from City Hall to 145th Street. Today subways in New York City are much more extensive: They move 1.2 billion people a year over 656 miles of track.

In 1931 the Empire State Building became a distinctive Art Deco-style landmark in the city's skyline. Rising some 1,454 feet above Manhattan, construction of the 102-story office building sped along at almost a floor a day. Forty years later this impressive architectural feat was topped by the World Trade Center, each of its two towers 110 stories tall. The buildings were destroyed by terrorists in 2001.

In New York bridges and tunnels are themselves attractions. They include the Verrazano-Narrows

Destination New York City

*F*rom classic opera at Lincoln Center to a walk on the wild side at the Bronx Zoo, the Big Apple has something for everyone.

*Y*ou say you like museums? Well, there are some 150 with exhibits ranging from dinosaurs to Degas. Do you have the theater bug? Stop on Broadway to catch a show. Got your head in the clouds? Check out the diverse architecture of the city's skyscrapers. And if things are moving too swiftly, hop in a buggy for a quiet ride through the city's backyard—Central Park.

South Street Seaport Museum, Lower Manhattan.
A revitalized section of the historic international seaport district looks much as it did in the 18th century. (See listing page 120)

New York Botanical Garden, The Bronx.
The crystalline Enid A. Haupt Conservatory shows off a collection of plants from around the world. (See listing page 136)

*P*laces included in this AAA Destination City:

American Museum of Natural History, Midtown Manhattan.
Occupying several blocks along Central Park West, this museum holds the wonders of the natural world. (See listing page 123)

© NYC & Company

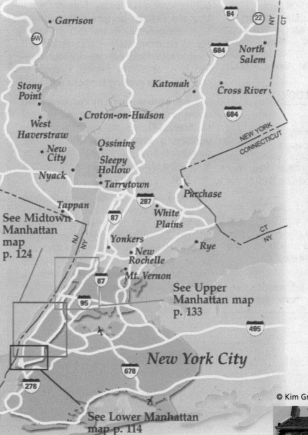

· Garrison

North Salem

Katonah

Cross River

Stony Point

Croton-on-Hudson

West Haverstraw

New City

Ossining

Nyack

Sleepy Hollow

Tarrytown

Purchase

Tappan

See Midtown Manhattan map p. 124

White Plains

Yonkers

New Rochelle

Rye

Mt. Vernon

See Upper Manhattan map p. 133

New York City

NEW YORK
CONNECTICUT

© Black Star / Alamy

Central Park Zoo, Midtown Manhattan.
Sea lions, polar bears, penguins and rain forest birds, just to name a few occupants, thrive in natural habitats in this lovely urban zoo. (See listing page 126)

See Lower Manhattan map p. 114

© Kim Grant / Lonely Planet Images

Museum of the City of New York, Upper Manhattan.
A treasure trove of documents, photographs, costumes, textiles, paintings, prints and toys illuminates the city's colorful past. (See listing page 135)

The Informed Traveler

Sales Tax: The sales tax in New York City is 8.375 percent. The tax on hotel rooms is 13.38 percent plus $1.50 per room, per day occupancy fee. Car rental tax is 13.62 percent.

WHOM TO CALL

Emergency: 911

Police (non-emergency): Use local precinct phone number.

Hospitals: Beth Israel Medical Center, (718) 252-3000; Elmhurst Hospital Center, in Flushing, (718) 334-4000; Mount Sinai Hospital, (212) 241-6500; New York-Presbyterian Hospital, (212) 746-5454; New York University Medical Center, (212) 263-7300.

WHERE TO LOOK

Newspapers

New York City has numerous English and foreign language newspapers. The most popular English language papers are *Newsday, New York Daily News, New York Post, New York Times* and *The Wall Street Journal.*

Radio

New York radio stations WCBS (880 AM) and WINS (1010 AM) are all news/weather stations; WNYC (93.9 FM or 820 AM) is a member of National Public Radio.

Visitor Information

NYC & Company Visitor Information Center: 810 Seventh Ave., New York, NY 10019; phone (212) 484-1222, (212) 397-8222, or (800) 692-8474 for visitors' literature.

WHAT TO PACK

The best times to visit New York are spring and fall. Not only is the weather more comfortable than in summer and winter, but the scenery is downright breathtaking. May and October daytime high temperatures are generally in the mid- to upper 60s. Dress moderately—slacks, jacket and comfortable footwear are appropriate—and bring a slightly heavier sweater or coat for cooler evening temperatures.

Summer in New York City can be stifling unless you are near the coast, where cool sea breezes temper the heat. For summer sightseeing bring lightweight clothing, sunglasses, and comfortable sneakers or thick-soled sandals (the pavement can get very hot).

New York winters can be trying. Daytime temperatures average in the upper 30s or low 40s; at night temperatures can drop into the 20s. Although most of your sightseeing will be indoors, winter gear should be layered in order to acclimate to warm restaurants and crowded theaters. *For additional information see temperature chart on p. 46.*

Bridge, the second longest single span bridge in the world, and the Holland Tunnel, a marvel of engineering skill at the time of its completion in 1927. The Brooklyn Battery Tunnel is one of the world's longest, and the Bayonne Bridge is one of the longest steel arch bridges in the world. But the Brooklyn Bridge is undoubtedly the world's best known—and most purchased—bridge. The ability to sell the Brooklyn Bridge to gullible visitors was long a standard of a con man's worth.

In 1948 what is now the 4,930-acre John F. Kennedy International Airport opened in Queens. Kennedy and La Guardia, also in Queens, along with Newark Liberty International, in nearby New Jersey, combine to service some 86.5 million passengers annually.

New York's population explosion fueled a building boom and job growth and generated worldwide recognition. Unfortunately its ethnic diversity gave rise to racial tensions. Harlem, in Upper Manhattan, was considered the most notable African-American community in the United States in the 1920s—a haven for intellectuals, artists and writers. But as overcrowding and racial discrimination began to eat away at the city, several destructive blows were dealt.

In 1963, Dr. Martin Luther King Jr. delivered his stirring "I Have a Dream" speech during the March on Washington; racial tensions in New York continued to escalate. And activist Malcolm X was killed in 1965 at a Harlem rally. In 1966 a race riot broke out in East Brooklyn; the following year more violence erupted in East Harlem. African-Americans and other minority groups gathered together for a cause—social and economic justice and improvements to their neighborhoods.

If the '60s were socially volatile, the '70s were financially bereft. In 1978, after more than 10 years of spending and borrowing, the city narrowly avoided bankruptcy. New Yorkers blamed their failing economy on spendthrift politicians and sought a mayor who could reverse the city's downward fiscal slide; they chose Democrat Edward Koch, the son of Polish Jewish immigrants. Mayor Koch, who reigned for 12 years, was revered for his brazen outspokenness and his dedication to the middle class.

As New York finally emerged from its financial doldrums, its beloved 151-foot-tall Lady of the Harbor re-emerged from a cocoon of scaffolding after a much-needed makeover. During an $85 million restoration project, American and French workers replaced worn sheets of copper to enhance the statue's blue-green patina. Elevators and stairs leading to the crown also were replaced. The torch, having long since fallen into disrepair because of the strain of visitors seeking an unobstructed view of the city, was restored as well.

In 1986 the centennial of the Statue of Liberty was observed after completion of the restoration. Americans celebrated the beauty of Lady Liberty in grand style with fireworks, marching bands and tall ships on parade in the harbor. The festivity was a fitting tribute to the lady who offered solace to those millions following the light from her torch in search of refuge from poverty and strife.

Battery Park, Lower Manhattan / © Kim Grant / Lonely Planet Images

Eighth Avenue / © PCL / Alamy

Getting There

By Car

Entering the city from the north, the New York Thruway (I-87) connects with the Major Deegan Expressway, following the east side of the Harlem River through the Bronx and connecting with the Bruckner Expressway (I-278) at the Triborough Bridge. This route bypasses Manhattan and allows easy access to Brooklyn, Queens and other points on Long Island.

Also from the north, the New England Thruway (I-95) leads through the eastern part of the Bronx to either the Bronx-Whitestone Bridge or to the Throgs Neck Bridge, again bypassing Manhattan and allowing easy access to Long Island. Both routes also connect with various points in Manhattan, including the Cross Bronx Expressway (I-95), heading east-west, which leads to the Henry Hudson Parkway (SR 9A), running north-south along the Hudson River.

I-80 from the west in New Jersey runs congruently with I-95 as it approaches the George Washington Bridge. Once across the bridge it continues east to connect with roads leading to Long Island or swings south on Henry Hudson Parkway or Harlem River Drive to Franklin D. Roosevelt Drive (East River Drive) and downtown Manhattan.

The New Jersey Turnpike (I-95) is the major southern access road to the city. Motorists traveling to Brooklyn and points east should take New Jersey exit 10 to SR 440E (the West Shore Expressway on Staten Island) to I-278E, which crosses Staten Island. Then use the Verrazano-Narrows Bridge to Brooklyn and Long Island.

Lower Manhattan is best approached from the New Jersey Turnpike via the Holland Tunnel. Motorists heading for mid-Manhattan should continue on the turnpike to exit 16E and the Lincoln Tunnel approach.

Air Travel

The New York City area has three airports. John F. Kennedy and La Guardia, two of the world's busiest airports, are in Queens; Newark Liberty International is in New Jersey.

John F. Kennedy Airport, the area's largest, is located in Queens off the Van Wyck Expressway (I-678) about 15 miles east of Manhattan.

From JFK to Manhattan, take the Van Wyck Expressway to Grand Central Parkway, then head west on the Long Island Expressway. To reach Lower Manhattan, take the Brooklyn Queens Expressway and access either the Brooklyn, Manhattan or Williamsburg bridges leading into the city. To reach Midtown Manhattan, stay on the Long Island Expressway, which feeds directly into the Queens Midtown Tunnel. Drive time is about 1 hour.

Or take the subway: Take the A train directly from the Howard Beach JFK Airport station. The Q10 bus also connects JFK airport to Union Turnpike (E or F train), 121st Street (J or Z train) and Lefferts Boulevard (A train) stations; phone (718) 995-4700 for schedules.

AirTrain, the Port Authority of New York and New Jersey's airport rail system, ushers airline passengers from the airport to the Howard Beach terminal for subway connections to Manhattan or to Jamaica Station to catch a subway or the Long Island Rail Road. For AirTrain schedules and information about connections and transfers, phone (718) 244-4444.

Just 8 miles east of Midtown in northwest Queens, La Guardia Airport handles many domestic flights. The airport was named after the city's former mayor, Fiorello La Guardia (1934-45), who is credited with helping develop the metropolitan area's accessibility for the aviation age.

Upon leaving La Guardia Airport, take Grand Central Parkway west to the Triborough Bridge, then to Franklin D. Roosevelt Drive. Going north on FDR Drive takes you into Harlem; traveling south on FDR Drive takes you to Midtown Manhattan. Drive time is about 40 minutes.

New York Airport Service provides bus service from La Guardia and JFK airports to Manhattan and to the Jamaica, Queens, Long Island Rail Road station. The bus stops in Manhattan at the Port Authority bus terminal, 41st Street and Park Avenue, Grand Central Terminal and most midtown hotels. Fares are: from La Guardia to Manhattan $12; from JFK to Manhattan $15; between La Guardia and JFK $13; from La Guardia to hotels $12; and from JFK to hotels $15. Buses run frequently; for schedules and other information phone New York Airport Service at (718) 875-8200.

SuperShuttle departs from all La Guardia terminals and drops off passengers at Manhattan hotels. Fares range $13-$22 and the schedule varies according to passenger demand; phone (212) 315-3006 for information or (212) 258-3826 to make reservations. SuperShuttle also offers shuttle service from all three airports in vans designed to handle wheelchairs; reservations are required. Fares are $15-$19 from Kennedy or Newark.

The Q48 bus provides service from La Guardia to the 111th Street or Main Street stations (both via the 7 train). On the subway, take the Q33 bus from La Guardia to Roosevelt Avenue station (via the E, F, G or R train) or the 74th Street/Broadway station (via the 7 train). For additional information, phone MTA, (718) 330-1234.

New Jersey's Newark Liberty International Airport handles domestic and transatlantic flights. Located on Newark Bay about 16 miles southwest of Manhattan, Newark is an ideal fly-in point for those proceeding to Lower Manhattan or points along the borough's western side. Take the New Jersey Turnpike to the Holland Tunnel for access to Lower Manhattan, and follow the signs to the Lincoln Tunnel if you are headed for Midtown Manhattan. It will take you about 40 minutes to reach the city.

Express buses from Newark Liberty stop at the Port Authority Bus Terminal at W. 42nd Street and Eighth Avenue in Midtown Manhattan; Olympia Trails Bus Service buses depart every 20 minutes from 6 a.m. to midnight. One-way fare is $13; phone (908) 354-3330.

New Jersey Transit bus #62 runs between Newark Liberty and selected points in Newark, including Newark's Penn Station, where PATH subways depart for Broadway at 33rd Street. Buses leave Mon.-Fri. and Sun. every 20-30 minutes from 6 a.m. to 2 a.m., and Sat. every 30 minutes from 6:30 a.m. to 2 a.m. The fare is $1.10.

AirTrain's rail system links Newark Liberty International Airport with Newark Liberty International Airport Station, where passengers can transfer to Amtrak or New Jersey Transit trains to continue on to New York City; phone (888) 397-4636.

Taxis are plentiful at all airports; a taxi ride from Kennedy, La Guardia or Newark Liberty to Midtown Manhattan costs $45 plus tolls and tip.

Hertz, 310 E. 48th St., offers discounts to AAA members; phone (800) 654-3080. All major car rental agencies have offices in New York City and at each airport.

Rail Service

If you enter the city by rail, you will arrive at either Grand Central Terminal or Pennsylvania Station, both in the heart of Manhattan. Built in 1913, Grand Central, at Park Avenue and E. 42nd to 44th streets, is an architectural delight. It supports Metro-North commuter trains, including the New Haven, Harlem and Hudson lines traveling to the northern suburbs and suburban Connecticut. This commuter railroad serves Westchester, Putnam, Rockland and Dutchess counties in New York as well as Fairfield and New Haven counties in Connecticut. For information phone (212) 532-4900 or (800) 638-7646.

Amtrak departs from Sixth Avenue and 33rd Street. Penn Station supports Long Island Railroad trains and New Jersey Transit trains. For schedules, fares and reservations phone (800) 872-7245.

PATH trains, also originating from Penn Station, run 24 hours a day to stops in Lower Manhattan. The fare is $1.50. For more information phone (800) 234-7284.

The Staten Island Railway limits its service to Staten Island, from the St. George terminal to the Tottenville terminal. The fare is $2. Phone (718) 966-7478 for information or schedules.

Buses

The Port Authority Bus Terminal, Eighth to Ninth avenues between W. 40th and 42nd streets, is the main terminal for the city; phone (212) 564-8484.

Getting Around

Street System

Manhattan streets were laid out in an easy-to-follow grid pattern back in the early 1800s. Unfortunately, maneuvering within the city is not as simple nowadays. For those unfamiliar with Manhattan traffic, the best driving advice is: DON'T. If you absolutely must drive, timing doesn't really mean much. Although rush hours are 7-9:30 a.m. and 4:30-6:30 p.m., city streets are always busy.

Be alert at all times. The traffic density of streets in Manhattan is probably the highest in the country. A good street map is helpful. When driving in the other boroughs a street index and map are necessities. **Note:** Drivers should keep car doors locked at all times.

In Manhattan consecutively numbered streets run east/west, and avenues cross north/south. Fifth Avenue is the dividing line between east and west streets. Most avenues are one-way and are alternately northbound and southbound. In general, even-numbered streets are eastbound and odd-numbered streets are westbound. Most downtown streets are one-way. Exceptions are Canal, Houston, 14th, 23rd, 34th, 42nd, 57th and 125th streets, which run both east and west.

As you make your way into Lower Manhattan, the city's efficient grid pattern system falls apart in the Greenwich Village and SoHo areas. From Houston Street south, both the numbered streets and Fifth Avenue come to an abrupt end.

Crosstown traffic usually moves faster on 14th, 23rd, 34th, 42nd and 57th streets, because these streets are wide. Northbound and southbound traffic moves faster, at least during non-rush hours, on one-way avenues: These northbound avenues are First, Third, Madison, Avenue of the Americas (Sixth Avenue) and Eighth, while the southbound avenues include Second, Lexington, Fifth, Seventh and Ninth. Gridlock is a particular hazard of driving in the city; it is illegal to stand or stop in the middle of an intersection or to make left turns, except where otherwise indicated.

For those who do not wish to use surface streets to travel, East River Drive and West Side Highway provide elevated, controlled-access roads around the city. **Note:** Avoid the parkways and expressways during rush hours.

The speed limit on downtown streets is 30 mph, or as posted. **No one under 17 is allowed to drive in New York City,** even with a valid driver's license from another state.

Parking

Finding a parking space may be the most difficult aspect of your visit to New York City. Parking is prohibited on most downtown Manhattan streets and is next to impossible in entertainment districts. If you do find a space, read the curbside signs to avoid having the car towed and paying a $185 towing fee plus a fine and storage fee.

Very few accommodations have free parking, and Midtown Manhattan parking lots and garages average about $13 an hour. Guests staying at a hotel with parking facilities often find it is easiest to leave the car in the lot or garage and use public transportation or taxis.

The best strategy available for those wishing to avoid the heavy traffic and exorbitant parking fees in Manhattan is to "park and ride" with the daily commuters. From Queens, parking is available near the #7 Flushing line at Shea Stadium, 126th Street and Roosevelt Avenue, from 5-5: fee before 11, $5; after 11 and after 5 p.m. for Mets games $8.

Another garage is located at Queens Plaza and Jackson Avenue above the Queens Plaza IND subway line and one block from the Queensboro Plaza IRT subway line. Fee $1.50 per half-hour; $8 maximum per 12 hours.

Commuters and visitors from New Jersey have the option to park at NY Waterway's Weehawken, Hoboken and Jersey City terminals and ride a ferry to Lower or Midtown Manhattan. Connecting bus transportation from the Manhattan ferry terminals into the city is available. For schedules, fares and parking fees phone (800) 533-3779.

Taxis

With more than 12,000 licensed yellow medallion cabs roaming the streets, the taxi is one of the most frequently used modes of transportation by visitors. Yellow medallion taxis are the only vehicles authorized to pick up street hails. To avoid being "taken for a ride" and paying more than you should, always give the driver the intersection nearest to your destination as well as the full street address.

Once the meter starts, it continues running. Even at a standstill in traffic, you pay. Taxi fares begin at

Statue of Liberty, Lower Manhattan / © NYC & Company

$2.50, then increase 40c each additional fifth of a mile, or 40 cents for each 60 seconds waiting in traffic. A 10 to 20 percent tip is customary. A 50c per fare surcharge applies between 8 p.m. and 6 a.m., plus any bridge and tunnel tolls. One fare generally covers all passengers—taxis can carry four people maximum (three in the back seat, and one in the front).

Complaints or lost articles can be reported to the Taxi and Limousine Commission; phone (212) 692-8294. When calling, passengers must provide the taxicab identification number.

Public Transportation

Compared to some cities, public transportation in New York is a good bargain. A $2 fare buys you an unlimited-mileage ride as long as you do not get off. In Manhattan subways traverse the length of Avenue of the Americas (Sixth Avenue), Broadway, Seventh and Eighth avenues and several portions of both Lexington and Park avenues.

Crosstown subways operate on 14th, 42nd, 53rd and 60th streets. In addition there is a shuttle train from Grand Central Terminal to Times Square (intersection of Seventh Avenue and Broadway from 42nd to 43rd streets), where passengers can transfer free of charge to other lines.

Subways also are fast. The New York City subway system accommodates some 1.2 billion riders annually because it is fast, efficient and one of the cheapest ways of getting around. Although New York City subways can be intimidating, directional signs and maps are posted at each station.

Using them is a snap if you heed these four pearls of wisdom: Avoid using the system during weekday rush hours (usually 8-9:30 a.m. and 5-6:30 p.m.) and late at night; ride in the conductor's car if possible (located in the middle of the train); try to avoid using the subway restrooms; and avoid the express and take the local trains (although not as fast as the express, the local trains stop at each station, so missing the correct stop is less likely).

MetroCard, a thin plastic fare card, replaced the familiar tokens for subway admission. You can purchase individual cards at subway station vending machines, neighborhood merchants and tourist information centers. The Pay-Per-Ride MetroCard is good for 11 rides and costs $15. Unlimited ride cards for 1, 7 or 30 days range $7-$70. The card can be used on all New York City buses and at all subway stations.

Maps for both subway and bus routes are available at the Grand Central, Pennsylvania and Columbus Circle stations and the New York Convention and Visitors Bureau.

Note: In the *What To See* section attraction listings will often include the nearest subway (S) station or stations. Consult a subway map to determine which train line is nearest and most direct; not every train runs from each station.

Riding the aboveground rails is another option. The Metro North Railroad serves Westchester, Putnam and Dutchess counties. For schedules phone

Solomon R. Guggenheim Museum, Upper Manhattan
© R. Kord / Robertstock

(212) 532-4900 in New York City, or (800) 638-7646 elsewhere in New York. The Long Island Rail Road serves Nassau and Suffolk counties; for schedule information phone (516) 822-5477.

From New Jersey, the NJ Transit stops every hour at Harmon Meadow Boulevard; phone (973) 762-5100.

More than 200 bus routes serve New York City. Buses run uptown on Tenth, Eighth, Sixth, Madison, Third and First avenues and downtown on Ninth, Seventh, Fifth and Second avenues. Some of the major east-west crosstown bus routes are 14th, 23rd, 34th, 42nd, 57th, 65th and 79th streets. Upon boarding, ask the bus driver for a free transfer from an uptown or downtown bus to a crosstown bus, or vice versa.

Most bus stops have Guide-A-Ride signs, showing bus stops and transfer points along that route. Fare on the Manhattan and Bronx lines is $2; exact change (no bills) is required. For information concerning the subway and city-operated buses phone the New York Transit Authority at (718) 330-1234.

What To See

LOWER MANHATTAN

AFRICAN BURIAL GROUND is between Duane and Elk sts., behind the Federal Building at 290 Broadway. The 18th-century cemetery was discovered in 1991 during the construction of an office building. Although much of the 5-acre tract lies beneath existing buildings, it is believed to hold more than 20,000 bodies of African slaves and free

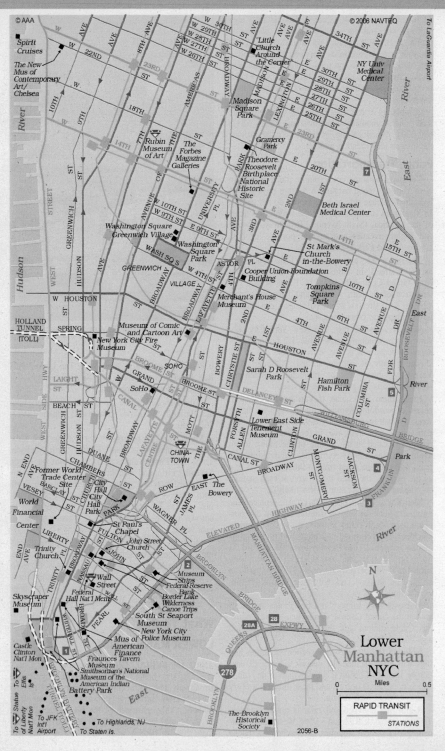

© AAA   © 2006 NAVTEQ

To LaGuardia Airport

Lower
Manhattan
NYC

0   Miles   0.5

RAPID TRANSIT
◼ STATIONS

2056-B

people; more than 400 bodies were recovered and ceremoniously reinterred. The Federal Building contains displays. Allow 30 minutes minimum. Mon.-Fri. 9-4. Free. Phone (212) 637-2019.

AMERICAN NUMISMATIC SOCIETY, 96 Fulton St. at William St., has more than 600,000 coins and medals; a selection is displayed. A research library also is available. **Note:** Exhibition space is closed until completion of the new exhibition hall in 2007 or 2008. Until then, an exhibit about the history of money may be seen at the Federal Reserve Bank *(see attraction listing).* Mon.-Fri. 9-5; closed holidays. Library Tues.-Fri. 9:30-noon and 1-4:30; phone for an appointment. Free. Phone (212) 571-4470.

New York Botanical Garden, the Bronx / © NYC & Company

BATTERY PARK, at the s. tip of Manhattan Island (S: South Ferry), was the site of a fort established by the first Dutch settlers in 1624. The park affords views of New York Harbor and the Statue of Liberty. The East Coast War Memorial is inscribed with the names of American servicemen who died on the seas during World War II. "The Sphere" a sculpture representing world peace, was salvaged from the World Trade Center debris. Daily 24 hours. Free.

Castle Clinton National Monument in Battery Park at the s. tip of Manhattan Island (S: South Ferry, Bowling Green) commemorates the 1811 West Battery Fort built to defend New York Harbor. The fort was U.S. Army headquarters during the War of 1812. Tickets to the Statue of Liberty *(see attraction listing p. 120)* are available. Daily 8:30-5; closed Dec. 25. Hours may vary; phone ahead. Free. Phone (212) 344-7220.

THE BOWERY, extending from Chatham Sq. n. to E. 4th St., was once the city's liveliest district and later the habitat of the homeless.

CHELSEA ART MUSEUM is at 556 W. 22nd St. at Eleventh Ave. (S: 23rd St.). The permanent collection includes postwar abstract paintings by European and American artists, anchored by significant works by Jean Miotte. Temporary exhibits are presented on a regular basis. Allow 1 hour, 30 minutes minimum. Tues.-Sat. noon-6 (also Thurs. 6-8 p.m.). Admission $6, senior citizens and students with ID $3, under 18 free. Admission Thurs. after 6 p.m. $3. AX, DS, MC, VI. Phone (212) 255-0719.

 CHINATOWN, near Chatham Sq., w. of the Bowery (S: Canal St.), includes Mott, Pell and Doyers streets. Chinese restaurants and shops line these streets, and vendors crowd the busy sidewalks. Mott Street is home to Church of the Transfiguration, one of the oldest churches in Lower Manhattan. Fish and vegetable markets near Mott and Grand streets sell the freshest ingredients available, while Asian grocery stores stock imported cooking condiments. Chinese tea houses and the area's first dim sum restaurant can be found along Doyers Street.

Locals congregate daily for conversation, relaxation and recreational activities in Columbus Park, which borders legendary Five Points. Memorials in Chatham Square honor Chinese-Americans who participated in World War II as well as Chinese notable Lin Ze Xu. New York's Chinatown is one of the largest Chinese-American communities in the United States.

CITY HALL faces City Hall Park at Chambers St. and Broadway (S: City Hall). Near this spot, in the presence of Gen. George Washington, the Declaration of Independence was read to the Army on July 9, 1776. Mon.-Fri. 10-3:30. Guided tours are available. Reservations are required. The last tour begins at 2. Free. Phone (212) 788-2170 or (212) 639-9675.

COOPER UNION FOUNDATION BUILDING is at E. 7th St. and Third Ave. When constructed in 1859 to house industrialist and inventor Peter Cooper's free college, this Italianate brownstone was the tallest building in New York City. Of interest is the Great Hall, which served as a public forum and a platform for speeches by Abraham Lincoln, Frederick Douglass, Sioux Chief Red Cloud, Mark Twain, P.T. Barnum and Theodore Roosevelt. Allow 30 minutes minimum. Mon.-Sat. noon-5. Free. Phone (212) 353-4195.

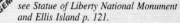 **ELLIS ISLAND—** *see Statue of Liberty National Monument and Ellis Island p. 121.*

FEDERAL HALL NATIONAL MEMORIAL, Wall and Nassau sts. (S: Wall St., Rector St.), was built in 1842 and is on the site of the first U.S. Capitol. The museum contains material pertaining to George Washington's inauguration, the Bill of Rights and old Federal Hall. Special events and programs also are available. Mon.-Fri. 10-4; closed major holidays. Free. Phone (212) 825-6888.

The Lincoln Highway

The horseless carriage rolled onto the American landscape in the 1890s. By 1910 there were more than 450,000 registered automobiles, yet the country still lacked a public road system.

Organized movements for better roads brought issues to the attention of the federal government, which had not participated in major road construction since it funded the National Road project in 1806.

But one particular initiative captured the public's support with a unique idea. In 1913 Carl Fisher—the man who built the Indianapolis Motor Speedway in 1909—and automobile industry leaders chartered the Lincoln Highway Association for the purpose of defining a direct coast-to-coast automobile route.

The LHA's first official act was to delineate a 3,389-mile, 12-state continuous route from New York to California—one that would be passable before the opening of the 1915 Panama-Pacific International Exposition in San Francisco. Although not perfect, the throughway was ready as promised, and a motion picture of America's transcontinental highway was shown at the exposition. Over time, the association improved surfaces by using better materials, shortened the driving distance with realignments and published guidebooks about the Lincoln Highway. Automobile touring had never been so good.

Through example, the LHA educated the public as well as state and federal governments about the value of good roads for almost 15 years. The 1919 moving of a military convoy over the "Lincolnway" foretold the utility of an integrated highway system for national defense and interstate commerce.

With the 1921 Federal Highway Act came the funds for states to construct and maintain connecting arteries. Four years later the United States adopted a highway numbering system, and most of the Lincoln route became US 30, 40

FEDERAL RESERVE BANK, 33 Liberty St. (S: Fulton St., Wall St.), offers tours by appointment that include a brief explanation of the Federal Reserve System. The history and significance of money is chronicled through the American Numismatic Society's exhibit of more than 800 coins, medals and currency used worldwide. **Note:** A photo ID is required for admittance. Allow 1 hour minimum. Exhibit open Mon.-Fri. 10-4. Bank tours are given Mon.-Fri. at 9:30, 10:30, 11:30, 1:30 and 2:30. Reservations should be made at least 1 week in advance. Free. Phone (212) 720-6130.

THE FORBES MAGAZINE GALLERIES is at 62 Fifth Ave. at 12th St. (S: 14th St./Broadway, 14th St./Sixth Ave.). Among the eclectic array of items collected by magazine founder Malcolm Forbes are toy boats, miniature toy soldiers, presidential papers, trophies and loving cups, and various versions of the Monopoly board game. A fine art gallery displays 19th-century paintings. Photography is not permitted. Allow 30 minutes minimum. Tues.-Wed. and Fri.-Sat. 10-4; closed holidays. Free. Under 16 must be with an adult. Phone (212) 206-5548.

FRAUNCES TAVERN MUSEUM, on the second and third floors of 54 Pearl St. at Broad (S: Whitehall St./South Ferry), was built in 1719 and became a tavern in 1762. In 1783 Gen. George Washington bade farewell to the officers of the Continental Army at the site. It housed the first American War Department. Tues.-Fri. noon-5, Sat. 10-5; closed major holidays except Washington's Birthday and July 4. Admission $4; over 64 and ages 7-18, $3. Phone (212) 425-1778.

GOVERNORS ISLAND NATIONAL MONUMENT lies 800 yards off the southern tip of Manhattan and is accessible only by a 7-minute ferry ride, departing from the Battery Maritime Building, 10 South St., adjacent to the Staten Island ferry.

In 1624, the island was settled by the Dutch West India Company. Governors Island was fortified by George Washington in 1776 and remained a U.S. military reservation for various branches of service until 1997. The 172-acre island features pre-Civil War arsenal buildings, architecturally interesting houses and two early 19th-century fortifications said to be the best remaining examples of their kind.

A 1.5-hour guided tour of the 90-acre National Historic Landmark District features the fortifications, the area's landscape and the 200-year history of the island. An exhibit hall displays historical photographs and details the history of the island. A 1-mile esplanade affords amazing views of the harbor, the Brooklyn Bridge, Manhattan, the Statue of Liberty and Ellis Island.

No food or water is available; visitors are advised to bring their own. Visitors may only enter buildings marked with a flag; buildings not marked are unsafe to enter. Comfortable walking shoes are recommended for the guided tour. Open early June-early Sept. Exhibit hall Fri.-Sat. 10-4:45. Guided 1.5-hour walking tours are given at 10 and 1, Tues.-Thurs., early June to late Aug. Recreational access to the island's 1-mile esplanade is available Sat., early June-late Sept., by reservation; the ferry departs 10-3. The island closes at 5. Phone ahead to confirm 2007 ferry and tour schedules as they may vary.

Monument and tour free. Tours are limited to 40 people on a first-come, first-served basis and tickets are required. Ferry fare Sun.-Thurs. $5; ages 5-12, $3. Ferry free Fri.-Sat. Rates may vary; phone ahead. Phone (212) 514-8296 or (212) 825-3045.

GRAMERCY PARK, E. 20th St. between Third Ave. and Park Ave. S., is a private park surrounded by a high iron fence. The gates are locked at all times. Since 1831 only persons living in the immediate vicinity have had keys to the grounds. In this section of the city are the National Arts Club, The Players Club, a statue of Edwin Booth and a synagogue.

GREENWICH VILLAGE extends from 14th St. s. to Houston St. and Washington Sq. w. to the Hudson River (S: W. 4th St., 8th St., Christopher St., Astor Pl.). Known for many years as the city's Bohemian center, "the Village"' is famed for its restaurants, curio shops, bookstores, art shows, coffeehouses and nightclubs. *For a walking tour description, see What To Do, Sightseeing p. 140.*

HARBOR EXCURSIONS—
see What to Do, Sightseeing p. 140.

JOHN STREET CHURCH (United Methodist), 44 John St. (S: Fulton St., Broadway-Nassau St.), was dedicated as Wesley Chapel in 1768 and is said to be the oldest Methodist society in the United States. The church was torn down and rebuilt in 1817 and 1841. It contains many Methodist relics. Mon., Wed. and Fri. 11-5 and by appointment. Free. Phone (212) 269-0014.

LITTLE ITALY is 4 blks. e. of Broadway on Grand St. to Mulberry St. The aroma of Italian food and the ambience of old Italy permeate the narrow streets of this neighborhood settled by Italian immigrants. Nineteenth-century tenements and architecturally interesting buildings lend to the flavor of the historic district. Activities center on Mulberry Street on weekends and during the popular 10-day Feast of San Gennaro in mid-September.

LOWER EAST SIDE TENEMENT MUSEUM, 108 Orchard St., between Delancey and Broome sts. (S: Essex St., Delancey St.), recognizes the nation's urban, working class immigrants through exhibits based on the lives of tenement residents. Some 7,000 people from 20 countries occupied apartments in the 97 Orchard St. building 1863-1935.

Guided tours depart from the visitor center. Neighborhood walking tours also are offered. Parking is available at a lot on Broome St. between Norfolk and Suffolk streets. Allow 1 hour minimum.

The Lincoln Highway (continued)

and 50. The association disbanded in 1928, but not before it engaged Boy Scout troops across the country to place some 3,000 concrete Lincoln Highway markers along the route in all 12 states: New York, New Jersey, Pennsylvania, Ohio, Indiana, Illinois, Iowa, Nebraska, Wyoming, Utah, Nevada and California. Many of these markers still exist.

Times Square in **New York City** was the official eastern terminus of the Lincoln Highway, which consisted of only 1 mile of road in New York state. From Broadway, motorists departed what Lincoln Highway guidebooks called "one of the most congested thoroughfare points in the world" and drove west on 42nd Street to the Hudson River, then caught a ferry to Weehawken, N.J. The Holland Tunnel, from Canal Street in Lower Manhattan to Jersey City, N.J., was completed about 1927; however, the Weehawken ferry served motorists crossing from Midtown Manhattan until the Lincoln Tunnel was built at 39th Street in the late 1930s. **Look for these New York Lincoln Highway landmark towns in this Tour-Book guide.**

For more information about the old Lincoln Highway, contact the new Lincoln Highway Association, P.O. Box 308, Franklin Grove, IL 61031; phone (815) 456-3030.

NEW YORK

New York City

Digital Archives

CityPass

CityPass offers savings to those who plan visits to five New York City attractions. The pass covers admission with no waiting in ticket lines to American Museum of Natural History, Empire State Building and Observatory (includes an audio tour), The Museum of Modern Art (MoMA), Solomon R. Guggenheim Museum and either a 2-hour Circle Line Sightseeing Cruise or an evening Harbor Lights Cruise. Additional savings are available at shopping venues, including Bloomingdale's, and 12 restaurants.

CityPass tickets are valid for 9 days from the first date of use and cost $53; ages 6-17, $46. CityPass booklets can be purchased at any of the participating attractions. Passes also are available at the New York City Visitors Center, 810 Seventh Ave. at 53rd St.; phone (707) 256-0490. *See color ad p. 121.*

· Digital Archives

Visitor center Mon. 11-5:30, Tues.-Fri. 11-6, Sat.-Sun. 10:45-6 (also Thurs. 6-6:30). Guided tours are given every 40 minutes Tues.-Fri. 1:20-4:45, every 30 minutes Sat.-Sun. 11:15-4:45; closed Jan. 1, Thanksgiving and Dec. 25. Admission $15, over 65 and students with ID $11, under 5 free. Purchasing tickets in advance is recommended. Parking for 3 hours is free with validated museum ticket. AX, MC, VI. Phone (212) 431-0233.

MERCHANT'S HOUSE MUSEUM is at 29 E. 4th St., between Lafayette St. and The Bowery (S: 8th St, Astor Pl., Broadway/Lafayette St.). This elegant 1832 Greek Revival town house was occupied continuously by hardware merchant Seabury Tredwell's family 1835-1933. Marble mantelpieces, mahogany pocket doors, furniture by local cabinetmakers, decorative accessories and intact personal possessions such as clothing, needlework and photographs present a composite of a prosperous 19th-century lifestyle.

Allow 1 hour minimum. Thurs.-Mon. noon-5; closed holidays. Guided tours are given Sat.-Sun. Admission $8, over 65 and students with ID $5, under 12 free. AX, DC, MC, VI. Phone (212) 777-1089.

SAVE **MUSEUM OF AMERICAN FINANCE,** 28 Broadway (S: Whitehall, Bowling Green), is in the heart of the financial district. Exhibits explain the history of American capital and finance in the stock market, politics, business, industry and entrepreneurship. **Note:** The museum is scheduled to move to 48 Wall St. in April 2007; phone ahead. Allow 30 minutes minimum. Tues.-Sat. 10-4; closed major holidays. Admission $8, over 62 and students with ID $5, under 6 free. Phone (212) 908-4110.

MUSEUM OF COMIC AND CARTOON ART is at 594 Broadway (between Houston and Prince sts.). Exhibits examine every genre of comic and cartoon art, including comic strips and books, gag cartoons, computer-generated art and animation. Allow 45 minutes minimum. Fri.-Mon. noon-5; closed holidays. Admission $3, under 13 free. MC, VI. Phone (212) 254-3511.

MUSEUM OF JEWISH HERITAGE—A LIVING MEMORIAL TO THE HOLOCAUST, 36 Battery Pl. in Battery Park City (S: Bowling Green, South Ferry, Whitehall), chronicles the 20th-century Jewish experience through artifacts, photographs and videotaped personal narratives in three exhibits: Jewish Life a Century Ago introduces the Jewish culture; the Holocaust is remembered by survivors in The War Against the Jews; and Jewish Renewal highlights the post-World War II achievements of the Jewish people. A Torah recovered from the Nazis is displayed in a hexagon-shaped room.

The six-sided building, itself a monument to Jewish heritage, symbolizes the points of the Star of David and the 6 million Jews who died in the Holocaust. An audiotape tour narrated ·by actress Meryl

Streep and violinist Itzhak Perlman highlights the museum's artifacts.

Allow 2 hours minimum. Sun.-Tues. and Thurs. 10-5:45, Wed. 10-8, Fri. and eve of Jewish holidays 10-5, Apr.-Oct.; Sun.-Tues. 10-5:45, Wed. 10-8, Fri. and eve of Jewish holidays 10-3, rest of year. Closed Thanksgiving and Jewish holidays. Last admission is 1 hour before closing. Admission $10; over 54, $7; students with ID $5; under 12 free. Audiotape tour $5. Advance purchase tickets are available. MC, VI. Phone (646) 437-4200.

THE NEW MUSEUM OF CONTEMPORARY ART/ CHELSEA is closed during the construction of a new facility scheduled to open at 235 Bowery in late 2007; phone for information. The museum displays works focusing on experimental ideas as well as exhibits portraying the development of emerging artists. Tues.-Sat. noon-6 (also Thurs. 6-8 p.m.); closed holidays. Admission $6, senior citizens and students with ID $3, under 18 free. Admission by donations Thurs. after 6. Phone (212) 219-1222.

NEW YORK CITY FIRE MUSEUM, 1 blk. n. of the Holland Tunnel at 278 Spring St. between Hudson & Varick sts. (S: Spring St.), displays the combined collection of fire memorabilia from the New York City Fire Department and The Home Insurance Co. The 1904 Beaux Arts-style firehouse has firefighting vehicles and tools from Colonial days to the present as well as displays about infamous fires, the firefighter and the history of fire insurance. A memorial exhibit honors firefighters who died Sept. 11, 2001.

Allow 1 hour minimum. Tues.-Sat. 10-5, Sun. 10-4; closed major holidays. Admission $5; over 64 and students with ID $2; under 12, $1. Phone (212) 691-1303.

NEW YORK CITY POLICE MUSEUM, 100 Old Slip between Water and South sts. (S: South Ferry, Wall St.), houses police vehicles, weapons, uniforms, shields and memorabilia. An exhibit details the story of how the NYPD reacted to the 2001 terrorist attack of the World Trade Center. Interactive exhibits allow visitors to explore a crime scene or experience a day in the life of emergency service personnel. Allow 1 hour minimum. Mon.-Sat. 10-5; closed major holidays. Admission $6; over 64, $4; ages 6-18, $2. Phone (212) 480-3100.

RUBIN MUSEUM OF ART is at 150 W. 17th St. at Seventh Ave. (S; Eighth Ave.).

A comprehensive collection of Himalayan art treasures includes paintings, sculpture, textiles and prints dating from the 12th century forward. Audiotapes help visitors understand the religious symbolism incorporated in many of the pieces.

Guided tours are available. Allow 1 hour minimum. Wed.-Mon. 11-5 (also Wed. 5-7, Fri. 5-10, Sat.-Sun. 5-6); closed Jan. 1, Thanksgiving and Dec. 25. Guided tours Wed.-Mon. at 3. Admission $10, senior citizens and students with ID $7, under 12 free; free to all Fri. 7-10 p.m. AX, MC, VI. Phone (212) 620-5000.

New York Pass

New York Pass is valid for full admission at more than 40 New York City attractions, including the Empire State Building, Madame Tussaud's New York, Solomon R. Guggenheim Museum and Circle Line Harbor Cruises. The purchase price includes a 140-page guidebook, admission to selected attractions without waiting in line and discounts or special offers at 25 restaurants, shops, theaters and helicopter rides. Passes for 1, 2, 3 or 7 days range $49-$139, children $39-$99. New York Pass is available at Madame Tussaud's New York, NY SKYRIDE, Planet Hollywood and the Port Authority of New York, at Eighth Avenue and 42nd St.; phone (877) 714-1999.

Digital Archives

Yankee Stadium, the Bronx / © NYC & Company

ST. MARK'S CHURCH IN-THE-BOWERY (Episcopal), Second Ave. at 10th St. (S: Astor Place, Broadway, 8th St.), was built in 1795. Peter Stuyvesant, the last Dutch governor of New Netherland, is buried in the church. Mon.-Fri. 10-3. Donations. Phone (212) 674-6377.

ST. PAUL'S CHAPEL (Episcopal), Trinity Parish, is at Broadway and Fulton St. (S: Fulton St., Chambers St.). Dedicated in 1766, the church is purported to be the oldest public building in continuous use now standing in Manhattan. George Washington and Gov. George Clinton had designated pews. An interactive exhibit honors volunteerism and the church's participation in relief efforts after the destruction of the World Trade Center. Mon.-Sat. 10-6, Sun. 8-4; closed holidays. Free concerts are given Mon. at 1, Sept.-June. Admission $2. Phone (212) 602-0874.

SKYSCRAPER MUSEUM is at 39 Battery Pl. (S: Bowling St., Whitehall St., Rector St.). Through artifacts, photographs, timelines and documents, the museum examines the history, architecture, construction, aesthetic and significance of the high-rise building. The core exhibit centers on the development of the New York skyline. Allow 30 minutes minimum. Wed.-Sun. noon-6; closed Dec. 25. Admission $5, over 60 and students with ID $2.50, under 10 free. AX, DS, MC, VI. Phone (212) 968-1961.

SMITHSONIAN'S NATIONAL MUSEUM OF THE AMERICAN INDIAN is next to Battery Park in the Alexander Hamilton U.S. Custom House at One Bowling Green (S: South Ferry). Artifacts depict the art, culture and lifestyles of North, Central and South American Indians since prehistoric times. Collections include tools, weapons, ornaments, clothing, utensils, containers, toys and means of transport. The Beaux Arts-style building was constructed at the turn of the 20th century and features exterior sculpture and a large rotunda with elaborate murals. Allow 1 hour minimum. Daily 10-5 (also Thurs. 5-8); closed Dec. 25. Free. Phone (212) 514-3700.

SOHO, an acronym for "south of Houston Street," is 3 blks. s. of Washington Square Park. Avant-garde galleries, shops and eateries line the streets between West Broadway, Houston, Lafayette and Canal streets. SoHo's trademark cast-iron buildings appealed to poor artists, who transformed the area into one of the city's hot spots.

SAVE **SOUTH STREET SEAPORT MUSEUM** is bounded by South, John, Pearl and Dover sts. (S: Broadway-Nassau St., Fulton St.). This 12-block historic district was a flourishing 17th- and 18th-century port. The museum is comprised of landmark buildings, refurbished warehouses and the "Street of Ships." Of interest are art galleries, a print shop with antique presses, a 1923 tugboat pilothouse and a lighthouse memorial to the victims of the 1912 *Titanic* disaster.

Food is available. Allow 2 hours minimum. Tues.-Sun. 10-6, Apr.-Oct.; Fri.-Mon. 10-6, rest of year. Admission $8; over 61 and students with ID $6; ages 5-12, $4; under 12 free. AX, MC, VI. Phone (212) 748-8600.

Museum Ships are docked at Pier 16 in the East River. Vessels along the "Street of Ships" include the *Pioneer*, an 1885 schooner; the 1908 *Ambrose*, a floating lighthouse used to guide ships through lower New York Bay; and the *Peking*, a restored, four-masted German merchant vessel launched in 1911. Guided tours are available.

GEM **STATUE OF LIBERTY NATIONAL MONUMENT AND ELLIS ISLAND** is in Upper New York Bay on Liberty Island. The statue was presented to the United States by France and dedicated in 1886 in commemoration of the two countries' alliance during the American Revolution. Measuring 151 feet high on a 154-foot-high pedestal, it is the tallest statue of modern times. Ellis Island *(see attraction listing)* is nearby.

Visitors can take self-guiding or ranger-led tours of Liberty Island. Audiotape tours that can be used on both Liberty and Ellis islands also are available. Free timed passes for guided tours inside the statue are available but must be reserved prior to arrival on Liberty Island.

Liberty Island is only accessible by ferry service, available daily from Battery Park in Lower Manhattan and from Liberty State Park in Jersey City, N.J. A round-trip ticket includes stops at both Liberty and Ellis islands. Food is available. Allow 3 hours minimum. Boats depart from Battery Park and Liberty State Park daily 9:30-3:30 (weather permitting), Apr.-Sept.; 8:30-3:30, rest of year. Closed Dec. 25. Hours may vary; phone ahead. Ferry $11.50; over 61, $9.50; ages 4-12, $4.50. Audiotape tour $6. Phone (212) 363-3200 for the National Park Service, (212) 269-5755 for ferry departures from N.Y., (201) 435-9499 for ferry departures from N.J., or (866) 782-8834 to reserve timed passes for guided tours.

Ellis Island, in New York Harbor north of the Statue of Liberty (S: South Ferry, Bowling Green), was the nation's main point of entry for millions of immigrants 1892-1954. Some 30 galleries and exhibits chronicle the history of immigration into the United States.

Highlights include the baggage, registry and hearing rooms; the American Family Immigration History Center, a computerized genealogy center with the names of immigrants processed during the peak years, 1892-1924; and the American Immigrant Wall of Honor, containing the names of more than 400,000 immigrants. Ranger-led and audiotape tours are available.

The 28-minute film, "Island of Hope, Island of Tears," tells the story of immigrants traveling via steerage to the United States. An immigration-themed play is offered during spring and summer months.

Ellis Island is only accessible by ferry service, available daily from Battery Park in Lower Manhattan and from Liberty State Park in Jersey City, N.J. A round-trip ticket includes stops at both Liberty and Ellis islands. Allow 3 hours minimum. Boats depart from Battery Park and Liberty State Park daily 9:30-3:30 (weather permitting); closed Dec. 25. Hours may vary; phone ahead. Museum open daily 9:30-5. Hours vary in summer; phone ahead. Film runs continuously throughout the day. Seasonal play schedule varies. Ferry $11.50; over 61, $9.50; ages 4-12, $4.50. Museum and film free. Cost of play tickets varies; reservations are recommended. Audiotape tour $6. Phone (212) 363-3200 for the National Park Service, (212) 269-5755 for N.Y. ferry departures, (201) 435-9499 for N.J. ferry departures, or (212) 561-4539 for play information.

THEODORE ROOSEVELT BIRTHPLACE NATIONAL HISTORIC SITE, 28 E. 20th St. between Park Ave. S. and Broadway (S: 23rd St., Park Ave. S.), is the reconstructed boyhood home of the only United States president born in New York City. It was his home 1858-72. Galleries and 1865-period rooms relate the story of young Teddy. The four floors contain items pertaining to Roosevelt's youth, ranch life, presidency and exploring days. Guided tours on the hour Tues.-Sat. 9-5; closed federal holidays. Last tour begins 1 hour before closing. Admission $3, under 16 free. Phone (212) 260-1616.

TRINITY CHURCH (Episcopal), Broadway at Wall St. (S: Rector St., Wall St.), was originally built 1696-97. In 1754 it was the first site of King's College (now Columbia University). The present edifice was completed in 1846. Alexander Hamilton and Robert Fulton are buried in the church. Church museum open Mon.-Fri. 9-11:45 and 1-3:45, Sat. 10-3:45, Sun. 9:30-11 and 12:45-4. Guided tours Mon.-Sat. at 2, Sun. at 12:45. Free. Phone (212) 602-0800.

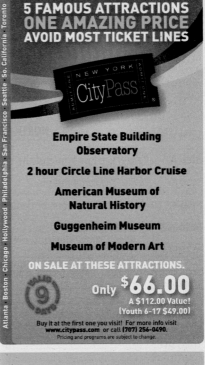

Key to Manhattan Street Numbers

Correct use of this formula will locate the cross-street of virtually any address in Manhattan.

NORTH-SOUTH AVENUES

Step A: Cancel the last figure of the house number.

Step B: Divide the remainder by 2.

Step C: Add the key number, or deduct as indicated.

Example: 1165 Third Ave. A: Cancel the last figure—result 116. B: Divide by 2—result 58. C: Add 10 (key number for Third Ave.)—result 68th St.

*On streets or address numbers preceded by an asterisk, omit Step B from the computation.
**On streets or address numbers preceded by two asterisks, omit Steps A and B from the computation and divide the house number by 10.

Ave. A, B, C, D	3	Tenth Ave.	13
First Ave.	3	Eleventh Ave.	15
Second Ave.	3	Amsterdam	59
Third Ave.	10	Columbus	59
Fourth Ave.	8	Lexington	22
Fifth Ave.:		Madison	27
1-200	13	Park	34
201-400	16	West End	59
401-600	18	Central Park West**	60
601-775	20	Riverside Dr.**:	
776-1286*	Deduct 18	1-567*	73
		Above 567*	78
Avenue of the Americas	Deduct 12		
		Broadway: 1-753 are below 8th St.	
Seventh Ave.:		754-858	Deduct 29
1-1800	12	858-958	Deduct 25
Above 1800	20	Above 1000	Deduct 31
Eighth Ave.	9		
Ninth Ave.	13		

EAST-WEST NUMBERED STREETS

Addresses begin at the streets listed below.

East Side		West Side	
1	Fifth Ave.	1	Fifth Ave.
101	Park Ave.	101	Avenue of the Americas
201	Third Ave.	201	Seventh Ave.
301	Second Ave.	301	Eighth Ave.
401	First Ave.	401	Ninth Ave.
501	York or Ave. A	501	Tenth Ave.
601	Ave. B	601	Eleventh Ave.

WALL STREET (S: Wall St.) is between Broadway and South St. The financial keystone of the country, it takes its name from the wooden wall erected by the Dutch burghers in 1653 to protect the colony from attack. The New York Stock Exchange is at 11 Wall St.

WASHINGTON SQUARE, foot of Fifth Ave., is the scene of art shows in the spring and fall. Washington Arch, designed by Stanford White, stands at the head of the square.

WORLD FINANCIAL CENTER is off West St. between Vesey and Liberty sts. (S: Cortlandt St.). The center is the business and commercial hub of Battery City Park. It comprises four major towers integrating office, retail, restaurant and public space. Free art exhibits, cultural programs and special events are staged in a European-style courtyard, an outdoor plaza and the glass-enclosed Winter Garden. Allow 1 hour minimum. Free. Phone (212) 945-2600 for event information.

Brooklyn Bridge / © NYC & Company

WORLD TRADE CENTER SITE is bounded by Liberty, Vesey, Church and West sts. A viewing wall surrounding the former site of the World Trade Center Twin Towers features see-through grids and history panels with the names of individuals who died when the buildings were destroyed by terrorists on Sept. 11, 2001. Rebuilding plans include construction of a symbolic 1,776-foot-tall skyscraper to be known as Freedom Tower; "Reflecting Absence," a below-grade, 6-acre memorial consisting of reflecting pools embedded in the footprints of the two towers; and a 100,000-square-foot underground museum with an interpretive center.

The NYC Heritage Tourism Center kiosk in City Hall Park (Broadway between Vesey and Barclay streets) and the Skyscraper Museum *(see attraction listing)* are good places to get information about the history and future of this site during redevelopment. Allow 30 minutes minimum. Daily dawn-dusk. Free.

MIDTOWN MANHATTAN

AMERICAN FOLK ART MUSEUM, 45 W. 53rd St. (S: Fifth Ave./53rd St.), celebrates American creativity through exhibits of folk art dating from the 18th century to the present day. Allow 1 hour, 30 minutes minimum. Tues.-Sun. 10:30-5:30 (also Fri. 5:30-7:30); closed Jan. 1, July 4, Thanksgiving and Dec. 25. Admission $9, over 62 and students with ID $7, under 12 free; free to all Fri. 5:30-7:30. AX, MC, VI. Phone (212) 265-1040.

AMERICAN MUSEUM OF NATURAL HISTORY, Central Park W. at 79th St. (S: 79th St./Broadway, 81st St./Central Park W.), explores American Indian, Asian, Pacific Island, South American, Aztec and Mayan cultures through changing and permanent exhibits.

Six fossil halls with more than 600 specimens trace the development of vertebrates and feature interactive exhibits. In the Hall of Biodiversity visitors can experience the sounds and smells of a rain forest and learn how the world's species and ecosystems are being preserved.

The Hall of Human Biology and Evolution educates visitors on the marvels of the human body through the use of models, dioramas, animation and holograms. An IMAX theater shows films about natural, scientific and anthropological subjects.

Guided tours and food are available. Allow 3 hours minimum. Daily 10-5:45; closed Thanksgiving and Dec. 25. IMAX films are shown daily; phone ahead for schedule. Admission (includes Rose Center) $14; over 59 and students with ID $10.50; ages 2-12, $8. Combination ticket for museum, Rose Center and Hayden Planetarium space show $22; over 59 and students with ID $16.50; ages 2-12, $13. Theater and special exhibition prices vary. AX, CB, DC, DS, JC, MC, VI. Phone (212) 769-5100. *See color ad p. 121.*

Rose Center for Earth and Space is on 81st St. at Central Park West or entered through the American Museum of Natural History (S: 81st St./Central Park W., 79th St./Broadway). Exhibits explore Earth's origins, geology, climate, habitats and relationship to the universe.

Visitors will find answers to frequently asked questions about the cosmos in the Hall of the Universe, which features images taken from satellites and through telescopes. Rocks and minerals are displayed in the Hall of Planet Earth.

The 360-foot-long Cosmic Pathway traces 13 billion years of cosmic evolution, equating each human step on the walkway to 75 million years of celestial development. In the Scales of the Universe exhibit, models of man-made and cosmic objects are juxtaposed to show their relative size.

The Hayden Planetarium's space show "Passport to the Universe" takes viewers on a virtual trip through the Milky Way to the edge of the universe.

Allow 2 hours minimum. Daily 10-5:45 (also Fri.-Sat. 5:45-8:45); closed Thanksgiving and Dec.

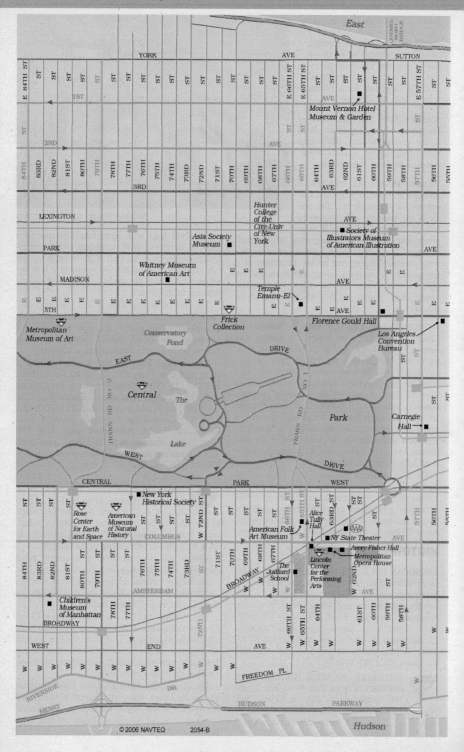

East

SUTTON

YORK   AVE

1ST

Mount Vernon Hotel
Museum & Garden

2ND   AVE

E 84TH ST
ST ST ST ST ST ST ST ST ST ST ST ST ST ST ST E 66TH ST E 65TH ST ST ST ST E 57TH ST

84TH 83RD 82ND 81ST 80TH 79TH 78TH 77TH 76TH 75TH 74TH 73RD 72ND 71ST 70TH 69TH 68TH 67TH 66TH 65TH 64TH 63RD 62ND 61ST 60TH 59TH 58TH 57TH 56TH 55TH

3RD   AVE

LEXINGTON

Hunter
College
of the
City Univ
of New
York

AVE

PARK

Asia Society
Museum ■

■ Society of
Illustrators Museum
of American Illustration

AVE

Whitney Museum
of American Art ■

MADISON

AVE

E E E E E E E E E E E E E E E E E E E E

5TH

Temple
Emanu-El ■

E E AVE

Frick
Collection

Florence Gould Hall

Metropolitan
Museum of Art ▽

Conservatory
Pond

Los Angeles
Convention
Bureau ■

DRIVE

EAST

TRANS RD NO 2

Central ▽

The

Park

Carnegie
Hall → ■

Lake

TRANS RD NO 1

WEST

DRIVE

CENTRAL   PARK   WEST

■ New York
Historical Society

ST ST ST
ST ST ST

Rose
Center ▽
for Earth
and Space

American
Museum ▽
of Natural
History

W 72ND ST

ST ST ST ST ST

COLUMBUS

American Folk
Art Museum ■

W 66TH ST
W 65TH ST

Alice
Tully
Hall ■

ST ST
ST ST

ST ST

57TH

56TH

84TH 83RD 82ND 81ST 80TH 79TH 76TH 75TH 74TH 73RD ST 71ST 70TH 69TH 68TH 67TH

NY State Theater ■
AAA

AVE

W 64TH ST
W 63RD ST

The
Juilliard
School

Lincoln
Center
for the
Performing
Arts

■ ■ Avery Fisher Hall
Metropolitan
Opera House

62ND
ST

61ST 60TH 59TH 58TH

AMSTERDAM

Children's
Museum ■
of Manhattan

BROADWAY

78TH 77TH

72ND

BROADWAY

W 66TH ST
W 65TH ST
W 64TH ST

W 61ST
W 60TH
W 59TH
W 58TH

WEST   END   AVE

W W W W W W W W W W W

W W

W W W W W W W W W

FREEDOM PL.

RIVERSIDE   DR

HENRY

HUDSON   PARKWAY

© 2006 NAVTEQ   2054-B

Hudson

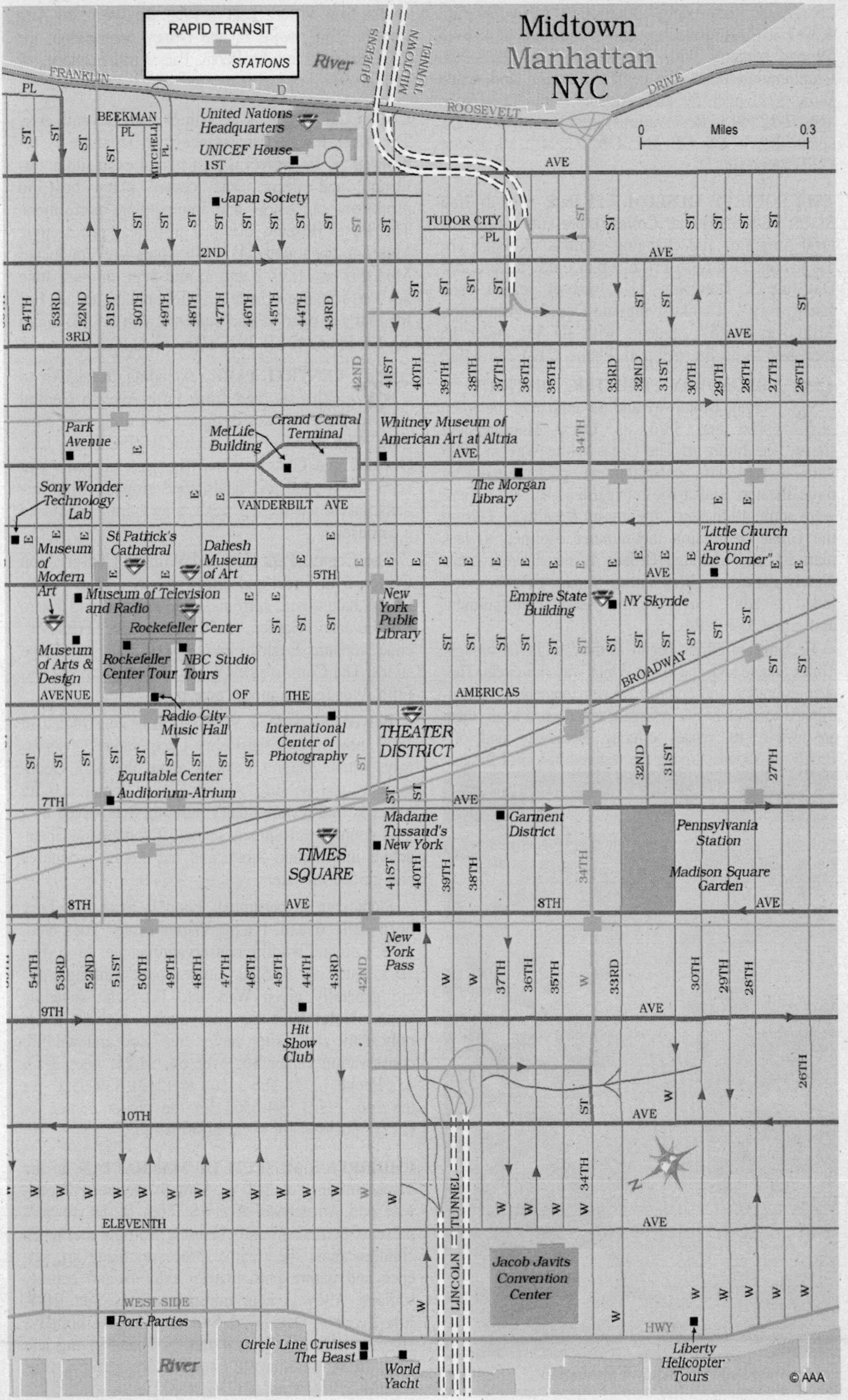

Midtown
Manhattan
NYC

RAPID TRANSIT
STATIONS

River

FRANKLIN
PL

QUEENS MIDTOWN TUNNEL

ROOSEVELT

DRIVE

Miles

0   0.3

BEEKMAN
PL

MITCHELL PL

ST
ST
ST
ST

United Nations
Headquarters

UNICEF House
1ST

AVE

ST

Japan Society

ST
ST
ST
ST
ST
ST
ST

2ND

TUDOR CITY
PL

ST
ST

AVE

54TH
53RD
52ND
51ST
50TH
49TH
48TH
47TH
46TH
45TH
44TH
43RD

3RD

42ND
41ST
40TH
39TH
38TH
37TH
36TH
35TH

33RD
32ND
31ST
30TH
29TH
28TH
27TH
26TH

ST
ST
ST

ST
ST

ST

AVE

Park
Avenue

MetLife
Building

Grand Central
Terminal

Whitney Museum of
American Art at Altria

AVE

34TH

Sony Wonder
Technology Lab

VANDERBILT AVE

The Morgan
Library

Museum
of
Modern
Art

St Patrick's
Cathedral

Dahesh
Museum
of Art

5TH

New
York
Public
Library

Empire State
Building

NY Skyride

"Little Church
Around
the Corner"

AVE

Museum of Television
and Radio

Rockefeller Center

Museum
of Arts &
Design

Rockefeller
Center Tour

NBC Studio
Tours

AVENUE   OF   THE

AMERICAS

BROADWAY

ST
ST

Radio City
Music Hall

International
Center of
Photography

THEATER
DISTRICT

32ND
31ST

27TH

ST
ST
ST
ST
ST
ST

Equitable Center
Auditorium-Atrium

7TH

ST
ST

AVE

TIMES
SQUARE

Madame
Tussaud's
New York

Garment
District

Pennsylvania
Station

8TH

AVE

41ST
40TH
39TH
38TH

34TH

8TH

Madison Square
Garden

AVE

54TH
53RD
52ND
51ST
50TH
49TH
48TH
47TH
46TH
45TH
44TH
43RD
42ND

9TH

New
York
Pass

37TH
36TH
35TH

33RD

AVE

30TH
29TH
28TH

26TH

Hit
Show
Club

ST

10TH

AVE

34TH

ELEVENTH

AVE

Jacob Javits
Convention
Center

34TH

HWY

WEST SIDE

Port Parties

Circle Line Cruises
The Beast

World
Yacht

Liberty
Helicopter
Tours

River

LINCOLN TUNNEL

© AAA

25. Space show daily 10:30-4:30 (also Fri.-Sat. 4:30-7:30). Admission (includes museum) $14; over 59 and students with ID, $10.50; ages 2-12, $8. Combination ticket for center, museum and space show $22; over 59 and students with ID $16.50; ages 2-12, $13. Reservations are recommended for space shows. AX, CB, DC, DS, JC, MC, VI. Phone (212) 769-5100.

ASIA SOCIETY MUSEUM, 725 Park Ave. at 70th St. (S: 68th St.-Hunter College), presents Asian cultural programs and changing exhibits of Asian art. Tues.-Sun. 11-6 (also Fri. 6-9 p.m.), day after Labor Day-July 3; Tues.-Sun. 11-6, rest of year. Closed Jan. 1, July 4, Thanksgiving and Dec. 25. Admission $10; over 64, $7; students with ID $5; under 16 free; free to all Fri. 6-9 p.m. Phone (212) 288-6400.

BROADWAY THEATER DISTRICT is along Broadway and Seventh Ave. between 41st and 53rd sts. Oscar Hammerstein shaped the future of The Great White Way in 1895 with a first-class entertainment palace featuring three theaters and a rooftop garden. By 1915 there were some 40 theaters lighting up Broadway. During the Great Depression the number declined to less than 10, and although Broadway never went completely dark, the glitzy Times Square neighborhood faded as adult movie houses, seedy entertainment and crime took hold.

Reclamation efforts begun in the late 1970s brought Times Square and The Great White Way full circle. Theater restoration and commercial development have contributed to Broadway's resurgence, and once again there are nearly 40 venues offering Broadway and off-Broadway shows. Among the restored historical theaters

Empire State Building, Midtown Manhattan
© NYC & Company

are the New Victory, built in 1900; the 1902 New Amsterdam, now owned by the Disney organization; the 1907 Belasco; and the Booth, Palace and Schubert, all built in 1913.

CARNEGIE HALL is at 57th St. and Seventh Ave. The 1891 Italian Renaissance-style structure is renowned for its perfect acoustics and exquisite architecture and decor. The center plays host to prominent orchestras and international performers. The Rose Museum offers a historical perspective. Museum open daily 11-4:30. Tours are conducted Mon.-Fri. at 11:30, 2 and 3, mid-Sept. through June 30. Performance schedule varies; phone ahead. Fee for tour $9; over 61 and students with ID $6; under 12, $3. Phone (212) 247-7800.

CENTRAL PARK, extending from 59th to 110th sts. and from Fifth Ave. to Central Park W., was designed as a refuge for New York City residents by architects Frederick Law Olmsted and Calvert Vaux. The park contains 843 acres of wooded and landscaped grounds with gardens, lakes, ice-skating rinks, a swimming pool and a carousel.

The Central Park Zoo and Wildlife Conservation Center, 64th Street and Fifth Avenue, displays wildlife in naturalistic surroundings. The formal, 6-acre Conservatory Garden, 105th Street and Fifth Avenue, contains English, French and Italian landscape styles. The Conservatory Water, near 74th Street and Fifth Avenue, is a model boat pond.

Belvedere Castle, a Victorian folly constructed in 1872, now houses the Henry Luce Nature Observatory, which features exhibits about the park's ecosystems and wildlife. A park visitor center at 65th Street is in a restored dairy building that served as a 19th-century refreshment center; it contains an interactive information kiosk and has maps, brochures and guides for sale.

Picnicking is permitted. Food is available. Park open daily 6 a.m.-1 a.m. Visitor center Tues.-Sun. 10-5. Zoo and wildlife conservation center Mon.-Fri. 10-5, Sat.-Sun. 10-5:30. Guided park walking tours are generally given Wed. and Fri.-Sun.; schedule varies. **Note:** Visit the park during daylight hours only. Park and visitor center free. Zoo and wildlife conservation center $6; over 64, $1.25; ages 3-12, $1. Phone (212) 360-3456, or (212) 439-6500 for the zoo, (212) 794-6564 for the visitor center, or (212) 360-3444 for event information.

CHILDREN'S MUSEUM OF MANHATTAN, in the Tisch Building at 212 W. 83rd St. between Broadway and Amsterdam Ave. (S: 86th St./Broadway), presents permanent and changing exhibits that teach children about the creative processes using art, science and nature participatory exhibits and activity stations. Allow 1 hour minimum. Tues.-Sun. 10-5, July 1-Labor Day; Wed.-Sun. and school holidays 10-5, rest of year. Closed Jan. 1, Thanksgiving and Dec. 25. Admission $9; over 64, $6; under 1 free. AX, MC, VI. Phone (212) 721-1223.

DAHESH MUSEUM OF ART, 580 Madison Ave. between 56th and 57th sts., exhibits and interprets 19th- and early 20th-century **SAVE** works by academically trained European artists whose art embraced classical ideals of beauty, humanism and skill. The collection includes paintings, drawings, watercolors, sculptures and prints representing the main academic categories: history paintings, landscapes, portraiture, still lifes, genre scenes, animal depictions and orientalism. **Note:** The museum has plans to relocate in 2007; phone ahead. Tues.-Sun. 11-6; closed holidays. Admission $10; over 61, $8; students with ID $6, under 12 free. Phone (212) 759-0606.

EMPIRE STATE BUILDING, 350 Fifth Ave. at 34th St. (S: 33rd St., 34th St. Herald Sq.), is one of the world's tallest office buildings. The Art Deco building, soaring 1,454 feet, has 2 million square feet of office space. Elevators run to the observatory on the 86th floor (1,050 feet), where visitors can see approximately 50 miles. Another elevator rises to the circular glass-enclosed observation tower on the 102nd floor (1,250 feet).

Completed in 1931, the building is made of Indiana limestone and granite trimmed with sparkling stainless steel. The lobby features marble imported from Belgium, France, Germany and Italy as well as eight original art works depicting the Seven Wonders of the Ancient World and the Eighth Wonder of the Modern World—the Empire State Building. The top 30 floors of the building are lit year-round from dusk to midnight with changing colors throughout the year.

Observation tower open daily 8 a.m.-midnight. Last ticket sold 45 minutes before closing. **Note:** Visitors may encounter long lines and can expect to wait up to 3 hours. Tower admission $18; over 61 and ages 12-17, $15; ages 6-11, $10. Admission to 102nd floor additional $14. Express tickets $40. Audiotapes (available in 6 languages, and for nighttime and low visibility) $7. Lobby exhibits free. Phone (212) 736-3100. *See color ad p. 121.*

FRICK COLLECTION is at 1 E. 70th St. between Fifth and Madison aves. (S: 68th St.-Hunter College). Housed in the Henry Clay Frick mansion erected 1913-14, the collection features the paintings, antiques, decorative art and furnishings owned by the industrialist and philanthropist. Paintings include works by Thomas Gainsborough, Frans Hals, Claude Monet, Johannes Vermeer and James McNeill Whistler. Also displayed are Limoges enamels, Oriental rugs, porcelains and sculpture.

Allow 1 hour minimum. Tues.-Sat. 10-6, Sun. 11-5; closed holidays. Admission $15; over 62, $10; students with ID $5. Donations Sun. 11-1. Under 10 are not admitted; ages 10-16 must be with an adult. Phone (212) 288-0700.

GARMENT DISTRICT, bounded by Sixth and Eighth aves. and 34th and 40th sts., accounts for one-third of the clothes manufactured in this country. During working hours this is one of the busiest areas of the city, with workers pushing racks of clothes down the street and transporting bolts of cloth between factories.

GRAND CENTRAL TERMINAL, 42nd St. between Lexington and Vanderbilt aves. (S: Grand Central), is the city entrance through which half a million commuters pass every day. The 1913 Beaux Arts terminal serves the MTA Metro-North Railroad and has a subway stop connecting the station to city destinations. Shops and restaurants are on the premises. Be sure to gaze up at the constellation mural on the 120-foot-high ceiling of the main concourse. Tours are given Wed. and Fri. at 12:30. Free. Phone (212) 697-1245.

MetLife Building, next to the Grand Central Terminal, rises 59 stories and is one of the world's largest office buildings.

INSIDE CNN STUDIO TOUR is at 10 Columbus Cir., in the Time Warner Center between W. 58th and W. 60th sts. The tour visits various departments including television sets of such media celebrities as Larry King, Paula Zahn and Anderson Cooper. Through overhead observation windows guests view the newsroom and other production areas. Guides demonstrate special effects using a weather map and show how a TelePromTer works.

Allow 1 hour minimum. Tours depart every 20 minutes Mon.-Sun. 9:30-5; closed Thanksgiving and Dec. 25. Last tour begins 1 hour before closing. Admission $15; over 64, $13; ages 4-12, $11. Reservations are recommended. AX, MC, VI. Phone (212) 275-8687 or (866) 426-6692.

INTERNATIONAL CENTER OF PHOTOGRAPHY is at 1133 Avenue of the Americas at 43rd St. (S: 42nd St.). Established in 1974, the gallery is devoted to the exhibition, preservation and study of all

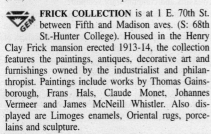

DID YOU KNOW

The nickname Empire State is derived from a comment about the seat of empire made by George Washington in 1784.

aspects of photography—from master photographers to newly emerging talent, from photo journalism to the avant-garde, and from photograph aesthetics to technique. Exhibits change every 3 months. Allow 30 minutes minimum. Tues.-Sun. 10-6 (also Fri. 6-8 p.m.); closed Jan. 1, July 4, Thanksgiving and Dec. 25. Admission $12, over 64 and students with ID $8, under 12 free. AX, DS, MC, VI. Phone (212) 857-0000.

JAPAN SOCIETY, 333 E. 47th st. between First and Second aves. (S: Grand Central Station/42nd St.), presents exhibits of traditional and contemporary Japanese art. Films, performing arts and topical lectures are offered. Tues.-Fri. 11-6, Sat.-Sun. 11-5, during exhibits. Hours may vary; phone ahead. Admission $10, over 64 and students with ID $8, under 16 free. Ticket prices may vary with each event. Phone (212) 752-0824 for current exhibits.

LINCOLN CENTER FOR THE PERFORMING ARTS, 62nd to 66th sts. between Columbus and Amsterdam aves. (S: 66th St./Broadway), is a 14-acre complex of educational and artistic institutions. The buildings were designed by some of the nation's finest architects.

Tours leave the center concourse daily at 10:30, 12:30, 2:30 and 4:30; closed Jan. 1, July 4, Thanksgiving and Dec. 25. Tour fee $13.50; over 64 and students with ID $10; under 12, $6. Guided 1-hour tours are limited to 19 persons per tour. Reservations are recommended. Phone (212) 875-5350.

Alice Tully Hall, Broadway at 65th St., is the home of the Chamber Music Society of Lincoln Center.

Avery Fisher Hall, Broadway at 65th St., is the home of the New York Philharmonic Orchestra.

The Juilliard School, Broadway at W. 65th St., contains four auditoriums and classrooms for music students.

Metropolitan Opera House, Tenth Ave. & 65th St., is the home of the renowned Metropolitan Opera.

New York Public Library for the Performing Arts (Library and Museum of the Performing Arts), 40 Lincoln Center Plaza, has extensive archives covering music, theater and dance. The Bruno Walter Auditorium presents chamber concerts, dance recitals, poetry readings and other events. Exhibition areas are devoted to displays about the performing arts. Library open Tues.-Sat. noon-6 (also Thurs. 6-8 p.m.); closed holidays. Phone (212) 870-1630.

New York State Theater, Columbus Ave. and 63rd St., houses the New York City Ballet and the New York City Opera.

"LITTLE CHURCH AROUND THE CORNER" is at 1 E. 29th St. near Fifth Ave. (S: 28th St.). It is also known as the Church of the Transfiguration (Episcopal). Daily 8-5:30. Donations. Phone (212) 684-6770 or (212) 684-6771.

MADAME TUSSAUD'S NEW YORK is at 234 W. 42nd St. between Seventh and Eighth aves.

(S: 42nd St./Times Square). Realistic wax figures representing icons of popular culture, entertainment, sports, politics and New York history are staged in interactive vignettes. Visitors can mix music with Usher, perform on an "American Idol" stage, hang out with the Osbourne family, or train with Lance Armstrong.

The Opening Night Party exhibit depicts a glitzy, after-theater gathering of luminaries. Likenesses of John F. Kennedy, the Dalai Lama and Diana, Princess of Wales are featured in an exhibit centered on world notables.

Hope, an exhibit about Sept. 11, 2001, portrays scenes of bravery and patriotism. Other exhibits include the multisensory Chamber of Horrors and a behind-the-scenes look at how wax portraiture is created.

Allow 1 hour, 30 minutes minimum. Opens daily at 10. Closing times vary; phone ahead. Admission $29; over 55, $26; ages 4-12, $ 23. AX, DS, MC, VI. Phone (212) 512-9600 or (800) 246-8872. *See color ad p. 129 & ad p. 441, and coupons in Savings Section.*

MADISON SQUARE GARDEN is at 4 Pennsylvania Plaza, between Seventh and Eighth aves. and 31st and 33rd sts. (S: 34th St.). The Garden has facilities for simultaneous major events and is the home of the city's basketball and hockey teams. Behind-the-scenes guided tours visit the 20,000-seat main arena, the theater, restaurants, a luxury suite and locker rooms. Allow 1 hour minimum. Tours are given daily 11-3 except during performances and games; phone ahead. Fee $17; under 12, $12. Phone (212) 465-5800.

METROPOLITAN MUSEUM OF ART, 1000 Fifth Ave. at 82nd St. (S: 86th St./Lexington Ave.), is one of the great museums of the world. Among the collections are Egyptian, Greek and Roman art; Near Eastern art and antiquities; European and Asian paintings and sculpture; arms and armor; musical instruments; arts from Africa, Oceania and the Americas; modern art; ancient glass; and European and American decorative arts and contemporary sculpture.

The Iris and B. Gerald Cantor Roof Garden provides a vantage point overlooking Central Park and features modern sculpture such as "The Burghers of Calais" by Auguste Rodin.

Allow 3 hours minimum. Tues.-Sun. 9:30-5:30 (also Fri.-Sat. 5:30-9), closed Jan. 1, Thanksgiving and Dec. 25. Admission $20; over 65, $10; students with ID $10, under 12 free. Admission includes The Cloisters in Upper Manhattan (*see attraction listing p. 132*). Phone (212) 535-7710.

THE MORGAN LIBRARY, 29 E. 36th St. at Madison Ave. (S: 34th St.), a palazzo-style building of Renaissance architecture, was the private library of J. Pierpont Morgan. Rare editions and illuminated manuscripts are featured as well as art objects, paintings, sculpture and a glass-enclosed garden court. Changing art and literature exhibits also are presented.

Food is available. Tues.-Thurs. 10:30-5, Fri. 10:30-9, Sat. 10-6, Sun. 11-6; free to all Fri. 7-9 p.m. Closed Jan. 1, Thanksgiving and Dec. 25. Admission $12, over 64 and students with ID $8, under 13 free. Phone (212) 685-0008.

MOUNT VERNON HOTEL MUSEUM & GARDEN is at 421 E. 61st. St. between First and York aves. During its early 19th-century heyday the Mount Vernon Hotel was a fashionable country retreat lying just 4 miles outside the city limits. Nine rooms furnished in period contain decorative arts, textiles, costumes and ephemera. A reproduction garden features plantings in configurations reminiscent of the era. Allow 1 hour minimum. Tues.-Sun. 11-4, Sept.-July; closed Jan. 1, July 4, Thanksgiving and Dec. 25. Last tour is at 3:15. Admission $8, over 61 and students with ID $7, under 12 free. AX, DS, MC, VI. Phone (212) 838-6878.

MUSEUM OF ARTS & DESIGN, 40 W. 53rd St. (S: 5th Ave., 53rd St.), exhibits 20th-century pieces created by artists in the forms of arts, craft and design and includes works in such media as clay, glass, wood, metal and fiber. Allow 1 hour, 30 minutes minimum. Daily 10-6 (also Thurs. 6-8 p.m.); closed Jan. 1, July 4, Thanksgiving and Dec. 25. Admission $9, over 64 and students with ID $7, under 12 free. Phone (212) 956-3535.

MUSEUM OF BIBLICAL ART is at 1865 Broadway at 61st St. In addition to religiously inspired artwork, the museum displays one of the world's most important collections of rare Scripture publications and manuscripts, which document the history of the Bible. Allow 30 minutes minimum. Tues.-Sun. 10-6 (also Thurs. 6-8 p.m.); closed Jan. 1, July 4, Thanksgiving and Dec. 25. Free. Phone (212) 408-1500.

THE MUSEUM OF MODERN ART (MOMA), 11 W. 53rd St. (S: Fifth Ave./ 53rd St.), offers a survey of 20th-century paintings, sculptures, drawings, prints, photographs, architectural models and plans, design objects, films and videotapes. Classic, artistic or documentary movies are shown.

Food is available. Allow 2 hours, 30 minutes minimum. Wed.-Mon. 10:30-5:30 (also Fri. 5:30-8); closed Thanksgiving and Dec. 25. Film schedule varies. Admission $20; over 64, $16; students with ID $12; under 16 free with an adult; free to all Fri. 4-8. Phone (212) 708-9400. *See color ad p. 121.*

MUSEUM OF TELEVISION AND RADIO, 25 W. 52nd St. (S: 5th Ave.), maintains a collection of some 120,000 radio and television program tapes. Visitors can select material from the museum's library, then watch or listen to it at one of 96 radio and television consoles. Tues.-Sun. noon-6 (also Thurs. 6-8 p.m.); closed Jan. 1, July 4, Thanksgiving and Dec. 25. Admission $10; over 64 and students with ID $8; under 14, $5. Phone (212) 621-6800.

NEW YORK HISTORICAL SOCIETY, 170 Central Park W. at W. 77th St. (S: 81st St.), houses a museum, print room and reference library. Allow 1 hour, 30 minutes minimum. Museum open Tues.-Sun. 10-6. Library open Tues.-Sat. 10-5 (also Fri. 6-8 p.m.). Closed Jan. 1, Thanksgiving and Dec. 25. Admission $10; over 64 and students with ID $5; under 12 free when accompanied by an adult; free to all Fri. 6-8 p.m. Phone (212) 873-3400.

NEW YORK PUBLIC LIBRARY, 42nd St. and Fifth Ave. (S: 42nd St./Ave. of Americas, Fifth Ave.), houses a research library that contains more than 5 million volumes, including 21 specialized collections of American history, art, periodicals and Slavic, Jewish and Oriental literature. Main room open Tues.-Wed. 11-7:30, Thurs.-Sun. 10-6; closed federal holidays. Free. Phone (212) 930-0800.

SAVE **NY SKYRIDE** is on the 2nd floor of the Empire State Building, Fifth Ave. and 34th St. (S: 33rd St., 34th St. Herald Sq.). Two 40-seat, big-screen, flight-simulator theaters feature a ride over various city landmarks, including the Statue of Liberty and Times Square. Motion simulators synchronized to the film's action move and tilt the seats, giving passengers the feel of soaring over Manhattan, gliding through Wall St., and riding Coney Island's Cyclone roller coaster. The experience includes two pre-shows.

Allow 30 minutes minimum. Daily 10-10. Admission $25.50; over 61 and ages 12-17, $18.50; ages 6-11, $17.50. AX, MC, VI. Phone (212) 279-9777.

PARK AVENUE, between 46th and 60th sts., is the site of major office buildings that incorporate innovative architectural features. Among the most impressive structures are the Seagram Building, 375 Park Ave.; the Lever House, 390 Park Ave.; and the corporate headquarters of Manufacturer's Hanover Bank, 270 Park Ave.

ROCKEFELLER CENTER, Fifth Ave. to Avenue of the Americas (Sixth Ave.) and 48th to 51st sts. (S: 47th St./50th St., 49th St., 50th St., 51st St.), is a model of urban planning and design, housing 24 acres of underground shops and restaurants. A self-guiding tour brochure is available at the information desk. Phone (212) 632-3975.

NBC Studio Tours, departing from the NBC Experience Store at 30 Rockefeller Plaza, gives 70-minute behind-the-scenes tours of the production areas of several television shows. Tours depart every 15 minutes Mon.-Sat. 8:30-5:30, Sun. 9:30-4:30. Ticket sales begin at 8. Fee $17.95; senior citizens and ages 6-16, $15.50. Under 6 are not permitted. A combination ticket with Rockefeller Center Tour is available. AX, DS, MC, VI. Phone (212) 664-3700 or (212) 664-7174.

SAVE **Radio City Music Hall Stage Door Tour** is on Avenue of the Americas (Sixth Ave.) between W. 50th and W. 51st sts. This 1932 Art Deco theater presents musical stage spectaculars with the Rockettes as well as theatrical productions and live concerts. Guided 1-hour tours departing from the lobby are available. Daily 11-3. Tour $17; senior citizens $14; under 12, $10. AX, DS, MC, VI. Phone (212) 247-4777.

Rockefeller Center Tour departs from the NBC Experience Store at 30 Rockefeller Plaza. Guided outdoor walking tours explore the art, architecture and history of the "city within a city." Highlights include more than 100 works of art, the Channel Gardens, the ice skating rink and the spot where "Today" show onlookers hang out. Allow 1 hour minimum. Tours are given on the hour Mon.-Sat. 8:30-5:30, Sun. 9:30-4:30; closed Thanksgiving and Dec. 25. Fee $17.95; senior citizens and ages 6-16, $15.50. Under 6 are not permitted. Reservations are recommended. A combination ticket with NBC Studio Tours is available. AX, DS, MC, VI. Phone (212) 664-3700.

Top of the Rock is atop 30 Rockefeller Plaza in Rockefeller Center. The entrance is on W. 50th St., between Fifth and Sixth aves. The glass-enclosed, 70th-floor observation deck reopened in 2005 after a 20-year closure and offers unparalleled views of the city. High-speed elevators feature glass ceilings that flash images from the past and highlight the illuminated elevator shaft. There are interactive exhibits on the mezzanine.

Allow 1 hour minimum. Daily 8:30 a.m.-midnight. Last elevator goes up at 11 p.m. Admission $17.50; over 61, $16; ages 6-12, $11.25. AX, MC, VI. Phone (212) 698-2000 or (877) 692-7625. *See color ad p. 443 and coupon in Savings Section.*

ST. PATRICK'S CATHEDRAL (Roman Catholic), Fifth Ave. at 50th St. (S: 47th St./50th St., 49th St., 50th St., 51st St.), is one of the largest churches in the United States, with a seating capacity of 2,400. The rose window is 26 feet across, and the pipe organ has more than 7,380 pipes. Twin spires 330 feet high grace the 14th-century Gothic-style structure.

The foundations of the church were laid before the Civil War, but the church was not open until 14 years after the war ended. Guided tours are available by appointment. Daily 6:30 a.m.-8:45 p.m. Phone (212) 753-2261.

SOCIETY OF ILLUSTRATORS MUSEUM OF AMERICAN ILLUSTRATION, 128 E. 63rd St. (S: 59th St./Lexington Ave.), displays changing exhibits by noted illustrators of the past and present. Lectures and special demonstrations also are held. Allow 1 hour minimum. Tues.-Fri. 10-5 (also Tues. 5-8), Sat. noon-4. Free. Phone (212) 838-2560.

SONY WONDER TECHNOLOGY LAB, between 55th and 56th sts. at 550 Madison Ave. (S: 53rd St./5th Ave.), is an interactive science and technology museum that emphasizes hands-on state-of-the-art communications technology. Allow 1 hour minimum. Tues.-Sat. 10-5, Sun. noon-5. Last admission 1 hour before closing. Free. Phone (212) 833-8100.

TEMPLE EMANU-EL, Fifth Ave. and 65th St. (S: 68th St.), was founded in 1845 and is one of the world's largest reform synagogues. Completed in 1929, the building features striking architecture, mosaics and stained-glass windows. Visitors are welcome to the festivals and a community service offered on high holy days. Sun.-Thurs. 10-4:30, Fri. 10-3; closed to visitors prior to Jewish festivals and on high holy days. Free. Phone (212) 744-1400.

TIMES SQUARE is at the crossroads of Broadway and Seventh Ave. On December 31, 1904 *The New York Times* celebrated the opening of its new building on the traffic triangle between 42nd and 43rd streets with a public fireworks display; four months later, the three-sided Longacre Square was officially renamed Times Square. With the commencement of the annual New Year's Eve ball drop in 1907 and the installation of the "zipper" news bulletin board in 1928, Times Square became America's gathering place during significant events of the 20th century.

Home to Broadway theaters, television studios, financial institutions, museums and shops ranging from a five-floor Toys "R" Us with an indoor Ferris wheel to Virgin Megastore (promoted as the world's largest entertainment store), the Times Square district is the only place in the city where businesses are required to advertise in bright lights.

The Times Square Visitors Center, in the restored Embassy Theater at 1560 Broadway, offers tourist information and a wide variety of services, including theater ticket and MetroCard sales. Visitor center open daily 8-8. A free walking tour departs Fridays at noon. Free. Phone (212) 869-1890.

UNICEF HOUSE, 3 United Nations Plaza at 44th St. between 1st and 2nd Ave. (S: 42nd St.), offers multimedia presentations about world peace, global development and the future of the world. Allow 1 hour minimum. Mon.-Fri. 9-5:30. Donations. Phone (212) 326-7000.

UNITED NATIONS HEADQUARTERS, on First Ave. between 42nd and 48th sts. (S: Grand Central/42nd St.), is along the East River. The visitors entrance is at First Ave. and 46th St. The complex consists of the majestic Secretariat Building, the domed General Assembly Building, the Conference Building and the Hammarskjold Library. Each building was designed and decorated by celebrated architects and artisans.

Tours lasting 45-60 minutes depart from the public lobby every 30 minutes Mon.-Fri. 9:30-4:45, Sat.-Sun. 10-4:30, Mar.-Dec.; Mon.-Fri. 9:30-4:45, rest of year. Closed major holidays and the last week in Dec. Tour $11.50; over 61, $8.50; students with ID $7.50; ages 5-14, $6.50. Under 5 are not permitted on tour. Phone (212) 963-8687 for tour information.

WHITNEY MUSEUM OF AMERICAN ART, 945 Madison Ave. at 75th St. (S: 77th St.), presents modern sculptures, paintings, photographs, drawings, films and videotapes. An inverted pyramid construction allows 30,000 square feet of exhibition space in a building only 97 feet tall.

Allow 1 hour, 30 minutes minimum. Wed.-Thurs. and Sat.-Sun. 11-6, Fri. 1-9; closed Jan. 1, Thanksgiving and Dec. 25. Admission $15, over 62 and college students with ID $10, under 12 free with an adult; by donations Fri. 6-9 p.m. Phone (212) 570-3676.

WHITNEY MUSEUM OF AMERICAN ART AT ALTRIA, 120 Park Ave. at 42nd St. (S: 42nd St./Grand Central Station), presents changing exhibits on the ground floor and in the sculpture court. Museum talks are held Wednesday at 1. Gallery open Mon.-Fri. 11-6 (also Thurs. 6-7:30 p.m.). Sculpture court open Mon.-Sat. 7:30 a.m.-9:30 p.m., Sun. 11-7. Free. Phone (917) 663-2453.

UPPER MANHATTAN

AMERICAN ACADEMY OF ARTS AND LETTERS, 633 W. 155th St., with gallery entrance on Audubon Terr., offers two exhibits a year. Allow 30 minutes minimum. Thurs.-Sun. 1-4, in Mar. and mid-May to mid-June; closed major holidays. Free. Phone (212) 368-5900.

APOLLO THEATER BACKSTAGE TOUR is at 253 W. 125th St. between Seventh and Eighth aves. On a 1-hour tour visitors learn about the history of the theater and the African-American and Latino performers whose careers were launched onstage at the Apollo's legendary Amateur Night. Allow 1 hour minimum. Guided tours are given Mon.-Tues. and Thurs.-Fri. at 11, 1 and 3, Wed. at 11, Sat.-Sun. at 11 and 1. Fee Mon.-Fri. $16, Sat.-Sun. $18. Reservations are required. Phone (212) 531-5337.

CATHEDRAL OF ST. JOHN THE DIVINE (Episcopal), 112th and Amsterdam Ave. (S: 110th St. Cathedral Pkwy.), was begun in 1892. Built entirely of stone, including Maine granite and Indiana limestone, St. John's is two football fields long and 17 stories high. The Biblical Garden contains more than 100 plants mentioned in Scripture; the Peace Fountain is by Greg Wyatt.

Allow 1 hour minimum. Daily 9-5. Guided tours Tues.-Sat. at 11, Sun. at 1. Guided tour $5, senior citizens and students with ID $4. Phone (212) 316-7490.

THE CLOISTERS is in Fort Tryon Park, first exit n. of George Washington Bridge off Henry Hudson Pkwy. (S: 190th St. or M4 bus "Cloisters" on Madison Ave. to end). Devoted to medieval art, this branch of the Metropolitan Museum of Art includes parts of five French cloisters, a Romanesque chapel and extensive gardens. Collections include statues, paintings, stained-glass windows and tapestries.

Tues.-Sun. 9:30-5:15, Mar.-Oct.; 9:30-4:45, rest of year. Closed Jan. 1, Thanksgiving and Dec. 25. Admission $20, over 64 and students with ID $10, under 12 free. Admission includes the Metropolitan Museum of Art in Midtown Manhattan *(see attraction listing p. 128)* when visited on the same day. Phone (212) 923-3700.

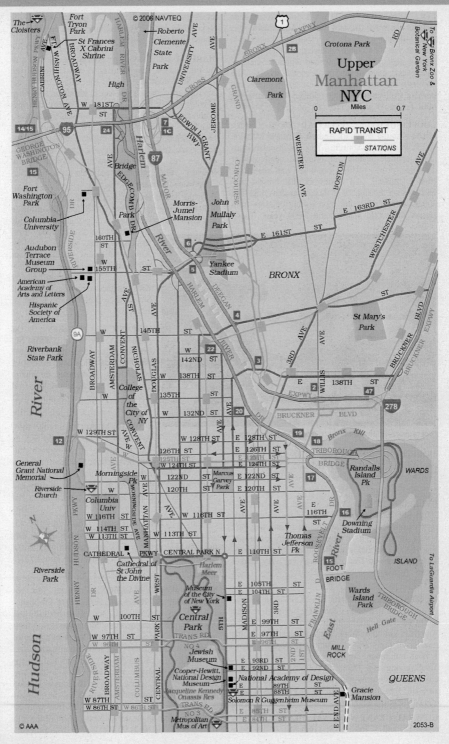

The Cloisters

Fort Tryon Park

© 2006 NAVTEQ

Roberto Clemente State Park

St Frances X Cabrini Shrine

BROADWAY

FT WASHINGTON AVE

CABRINI

HENRY HUDSON PKWY

High

UNIVERSITY AVE

AVE

CROSS

BRONX EXPWY

Crotona Park

RIVER

HARLEM RIVER DR

Upper Manhattan NYC

Miles

0   0.7

RAPID TRANSIT

STATIONS

2B

Claremont Park

GRAND

WEBSTER AVE

BOSTON

JEROME

AVE

W 181ST ST

14/15

95

GEORGE WASHINGTON BRIDGE

15

24

EDWIN L GRANT HWY

7

1C

87

Bridge

Harlem

EDGECOMB AVE

Park

Morris-Jumel Mansion

John Mullaly Park

E 163RD ST

WESTCHESTER AVE

Fort Washington Park

Columbia University

160TH ST

Audubon Terrace Museum Group

American Academy of Arts and Letters

Hispanic Society of America

RIVERSIDE DR

MAJOR

River

6

E 161ST ST

155TH

AVE

ST

Yankee Stadium

5

DEEGAN

HARLEM RIVER

BRONX

St Mary's Park

BRUCKNER BLVD

BRUCKNER EXPWY

9A

Riverbank State Park

145TH

BROADWAY

AMSTERDAM

CONVENT

NICHOLAS

DOUGLAS

W 142ND ST

22

W 138TH ST

3RD AVE

AVE

E 138TH ST

4

River

College of the City of NY

135TH ST

W 132ND ST

AVE

20

3

WILLIS

47

278

General Grant National Memorial

12

W 129TH ST

CONVENT

AVE

W 128TH AVE ST

E 128TH ST

19

18

Bronx Kill

WARDS

Morningside Pk

W 126TH ST

125TH

W 124TH ST

E 126TH ST

E 124TH ST

TRIBOROUGH BRIDGE

Randalls Island Pk

Riverside Church

Columbia Univ

MORNINGSIDE AVE

122ND ST

Marcus Garvey Park

E 122ND ST

17

Riverside Park

W 116TH ST

120TH ST

MANHATTAN AVE

W 116TH ST

AVE

E 120TH ST

E 116TH ST

16

Downing Stadium

W 114TH ST

W 113TH ST

113TH ST

AVE

AVE

Thomas Jefferson Pk

ROOSEVELT

River

ISLAND

To LaGuardia Airport

CATHEDRAL PKWY

CENTRAL PARK N

E 110TH ST

15

FOOT BRIDGE

Wards Island Park

TRIBOROUGH BRIDGE

Cathedral of St John the Divine

Harlem Meer

E 105TH ST

East

Hudson

Riverside Park

HENRY HUDSON PKWY

Museum of the City of New York

WEST

CENTRAL PARK

Central Park

W 100TH ST

E 104TH ST

MADISON

E 99TH ST

3RD

E 97TH ST

E 96TH ST

2ND

Hell Gate

MILL ROCK

QUEENS

RIVERSIDE

BROADWAY

AMSTERDAM

COLUMBUS

CENTRAL

5TH

TRANS RD

NO 4

Jewish Museum

Cooper-Hewitt, National Design Museum

Jacqueline Kennedy Onassis Res

W 87TH ST

W 86TH ST

W 86TH ST

TRANS RD

NO 3

Metropolitan Mus of Art

E 93RD ST

E 92ND ST

National Academy of Design

89TH ST

88TH ST

Solomon R Guggenheim Museum

E 85TH ST

E 84TH ST

E END AVE

Gracie Mansion

© AAA

2053-B

COLUMBIA UNIVERSITY is in Morningside Heights, between Broadway and Amsterdam Ave. and 114th and 120th sts. (S: 116th St.). Founded in 1754 as King's College, it includes Columbia College, School of Engineering and Applied Sciences, and several graduate and professional schools. The university is affiliated with Teachers College and Barnard College for women. Guided tours are given Mon.-Fri. at 11 and 2. Free. Phone (212) 854-4900.

COOPER-HEWITT, NATIONAL DESIGN MUSEUM is in the landmark Andrew Carnegie Mansion at 2 E. 91st St. (S: 86th St.). This Smithsonian Institution affiliate features historic and contemporary drawings, prints, textiles, ceramics, wall coverings, glass, metalwork and woodwork that present perspectives on the impact of design on daily life. The 250,000-piece collection representing cultures from around the world spans some 3,000 years. Tues.-

Times Square, Midtown Manhattan / © NYC & Company

Thurs. 10-5, Fri. 10-9, Sat. 10-6, Sun. noon-6; closed Jan. 1, Thanksgiving and Dec. 25. Admission $12, senior citizens and students with ID $7, under 12 free. Phone (212) 849-8400.

DYCKMAN HOUSE, 204th St. and Broadway (S: 207th St.), dates from 1784 and is the only Dutch farmhouse remaining on Manhattan Island. It is furnished in the style typical of wealthy colonists. Wed.-Sat. 11-4, Sun. noon-4; closed Jan. 1, July 4, Thanksgiving and Dec. 25. Hours may vary; phone ahead. Admission $1; under 10 free. Phone (212) 304-9422.

EL MUSEO DEL BARRIO is at 1230 Fifth Ave. at 104th St. (S: 103rd St., Central Park N.). More than 8,000 pieces of art highlight Caribbean and Latin American cultures. Works include paintings, sculpture installations and pre-Columbian objects. Allow 1 hour minimum. Wed.-Sun. 11-5; closed Jan 1., Thanksgiving and Dec. 25. Admission $6, senior citizens and students with ID $4, under 12 free with an adult; free to senior citizens on Thurs. AX, MC, VI. Phone (212) 831-7272.

GENERAL GRANT NATIONAL MEMORIAL, Riverside Dr. and 122nd St. (S: 116th St.), is the tomb

of President Ulysses S. Grant and his wife. Daily 9-5; closed Jan. 1, Thanksgiving and Dec. 25. Free. Phone (212) 666-1640.

HARLEM is bounded s. by 96th St., n. by 155th, w. by the Hudson River and e. by the Harlem River. Peter Stuyvesant established the village of Harlem in 1658. By the 1870s, open farmland and large country estates had given way to residential neighborhoods studded with row houses, multifamily dwellings and luxury apartments. Overbuilding led to a housing glut and the eventual collapse of the real estate market. Property abandoned during this decline was later transformed into affordable rental housing that attracted middle-class African-Americans to the area.

In the 1920s resident writers such as Zora Neale Hurston, Langston Hughes and Ralph Ellison fueled Harlem's literary renaissance, bringing worldwide attention to the district. Today, Harlem is regarded as a center for African-American culture. Visitor information is available at the Harlem Visitor Information Center Kiosk in the Adam Clayton Powell State Office Building Plaza, 163 W. 125th Ave.

HISPANIC SOCIETY OF AMERICA, Broadway at 155th St., exhibits Spanish and Portuguese sculpture, paintings and decorative arts. Allow 30 minutes minimum. Tues.-Sat. 10-4:30, Sun. 1-4; closed holidays. Free. Phone (212) 926-2234.

JEWISH MUSEUM, 1109 Fifth Ave. at 92nd St. (S: 86th St.), is said to be the largest Jewish museum in the Western hemisphere. Culture and Continuity: The Jewish Journey is a permanent exhibition that traverses 4,000 years of Jewish art, history and culture. Also available are changing art exhibits and a family interactive exhibit.

Allow 1 hour minimum. Sun.-Wed. 11-5:45, Thurs. 11-8; closed major and Jewish holidays. Admission $12, over 64, $10; students with ID $7.50, under 12 free, by donation Thurs. 5-8. Phone (212) 423-3200.

MORRIS-JUMEL MANSION, 65 Jumel Terr. between 160th and 162nd sts., .5 blk. e. of St. Nicholas Ave. (S: 163rd St.), served as British and American army headquarters during the Revolutionary War. Built around 1765, the mansion is one of Manhattan's oldest surviving residential structures; it houses Colonial, Revolutionary, Federal and American Empire furniture. Wed.-Sun. 10-4, Mon.-Tues. by appointment; closed major holidays. Guided tours are given Sat. at noon. Admission $4, over 64 and students with ID $3, under 12 free with an adult. Tour fee $5, senior citizens and students with ID $3.50. Phone (212) 923-8008.

MUSEUM OF THE CITY OF NEW YORK, Fifth Ave. and 103rd to 104th sts. (S: 103rd St./Lexington Ave.), is devoted to the life and history of the city. Weekend educational and entertainment programs are held in the auditorium. The museum also offers seasonal walking tours of various parts of the city (see What To Do, Sightseeing p. 144). Tues.-Sun. 10-5; closed holidays. Admission $9, over 64 and students with ID $5, family rate $20; free to all Sun. 10-noon. Phone (212) 534-1672.

NATIONAL ACADEMY OF DESIGN, 1083 Fifth Ave. at 89th St. (S: 86th St.), displays a permanent collection of artworks as well as changing drawing, painting, sculpture and architectural exhibits. Allow 30 minutes minimum. Fri.-Sun. 11-6, Wed.-Thurs. noon-5; closed major holidays. Admission $10; over 64 and students with ID $5, under 12 free. AX, MC, VI. Phone (212) 369-4880.

NATIONAL TRACK & FIELD HALL OF FAME is at 216 Fort Washington Ave. between 168th and 169th sts. in The Armory. Three floors of exhibits commemorate U.S. track and field athletes. Through interactive stations visitors can learn about nutrition, fitness, training and what it takes to be a champion. An exhibit about marathons in the United States features a large floor map illustrating the 26-mile route of the New York City Marathon. The Armory is the home venue of the U.S. Indoor National Track and Field Championships. Allow 1 hour minimum. Tues.-Sat. 10:30-6, Dec.-Mar.; Tues.-Fri. 10:30-6, rest of year. Closed holidays. Free. Phone (212) 923-1803.

NEUE GALERIE MUSEUM FOR GERMAN AND AUSTRIAN ART is at 1048 Fifth Ave. at 86th St. (S: 86th St.). Examples of early 20th-century fine and decorative art from Germany and Austria are displayed in a restored, opulent Beau Arts building once occupied by Mrs. Cornelius Vanderbilt III. Collections include jewelry, paintings, photographs and furniture. Allow 1 hour minimum. Fri.-Mon. 11-6 (also Fri. 6-9 p.m.); closed Jan. 1, July 4, Labor Day, Thanksgiving and Dec. 25. Admission $15, senior citizens and students with ID $10. Under 16 must be with an adult; under 12 are not permitted. Phone (212) 628-6200.

RIVERSIDE CHURCH is at 490 Riverside Dr. between 120th and 122nd sts. (S: 116th St.). The design of this Gothic-style church was inspired by a 13th-century cathedral in Chartres, France. The cornerstone was laid in 1927 and the congregation held its first service in 1930. A 392-foot-high tower with an open-air observation platform houses the 74-bronze-bell carillon donated by John D. Rockefeller Jr. and said to be the heaviest and second-largest carillon in the world. Stained glass windows and several religious paintings and tapestries adorn the interior of the sanctuary.

Note: The bell tower is temporarily closed for restoration; phone ahead for information. Church open daily 9-5. Bell tower open Tues. and Sun. 11-4. Guided church tours are given Sun. at 12:30.

The carillon is played Sunday at 10:30, 12:30 and 3. Admission $2; college students with ID and ages 11-18, $1. Under 6 are not permitted in the bell tower. Phone (212) 870-6700.

ST. FRANCES X. CABRINI SHRINE, 701 Fort Washington Ave. (S: 190th St. or M4 bus to 190th St.), is dedicated to the first American saint, who is the patron saint of immigrants. Displayed are objects and clothes that belonged to her. Allow 30 minutes minimum. Daily 9-4:30; closed Memorial Day, July 4, Labor Day and Thanksgiving. Free. Phone (212) 923-3536.

SCHOMBURG CENTER FOR RESEARCH IN BLACK CULTURE is at 515 Malcolm X Blvd. at 135th St. (S: 135th St.). The center presents changing exhibits depicting the African-American experience and has research and reference divisions with photographs and prints; art and artifacts; manuscripts, archives and rare books; and film and recordings.

Note: Exhibition area closes between exhibits; phone ahead to confirm exhibit status. Due to construction, visitors must enter through the Landmark Building at 103 W. 135th St. The entrance for the physically impaired is on 136th Street. Guided tours are available. Allow 30 minutes minimum. Tues.-Sat. 10-6, Sun. 1-5; closed holidays. Hours vary by exhibition; phone ahead. Free. Phone (212) 491-2200.

SOLOMON R. GUGGENHEIM MUSEUM, 1071 Fifth Ave. at 89th St. (S: 86th St./Lexington Ave.), was designed by Frank Lloyd Wright. The domed circular section of the building creates an interesting visual effect; paintings are hung along the spiraled walkway. In addition to the permanent collection, the museum exhibits late 19th- and early 20th-century and contemporary paintings and sculpture.

Food is available. Allow 2 hours minimum. Sat.-Wed. 10-5:45, Fri. 10-7:45; closed Thanksgiving and Dec. 25. Admission $18, over 64 and students with ID $15, under 12 free with an adult, by donations Fri. 6-8. AX, MC, VI. Phone (212) 423-3500. See color ad p. 121.

STUDIO MUSEUM IN HARLEM is at 144 W. 125th St. between Lenox Ave. and Adam Clayton Powell Jr. Blvd. (7th Ave.) (S: 125th St.). The museum showcases works by African-American artists in changing exhibits drawn from a permanent collection of more than 1,600 paintings, drawings, prints, photographs and mixed-media compositions. Archives contain James VanDerZee's photographs chronicling life in Harlem 1906-84. Performance arts and traveling exhibitions also are offered.

Allow 1 hour minimum. Wed.-Fri. and Sun. noon-6, Sat. 10-6; closed holidays. Admission $7, senior citizens and students with ID $3, under 12 free. VI. Phone (212) 864-4500.

The Bronx pop. 1,332,650

BARTOW-PELL MANSION MUSEUM, e. of the Orchard Beach exit of the Hutchinson River Pkwy., then .5 mi. n. to 895 Shore Rd. (S: Pelham Bay Park), occupies a site bought from the Siwanoy Indians in 1654. The first house was destroyed during the Revolutionary War; the existing mansion was built 1836-42. Furnished in period, it is the only home of its era in this region. Gardens adorn the grounds.

Gardens open daily 8:30-dusk. Mansion open Wed. and Sat.-Sun. noon-4, first Fri. of the month 5:30-9:30, otherwise by appointment; closed Jan. 1, Easter, July 4, Thanksgiving weekend and Dec. 25. Mansion admission $5, senior citizens and students with ID $3, under 6 free, free to all Wed. Phone (718) 885-1461.

BRONX COMMUNITY COLLEGE is in University Heights on University Ave. and W. 181st St. (S: 183rd St.). On campus is the Hall of Fame for Great Americans, open daily 10-5. Free. Phone (718) 289-5100.

BRONX ZOO, off the Bronx River Pkwy. at exit 6/Fordham Rd. (S: Pelham Pkwy., E. Tremont Ave.), displays more than 4,000 animals in naturalistic indoor and outdoor habitats on 265 wooded acres. Congo Gorilla Forest, a 6.5-acre simulated African rain forest, is home to one of the largest gorilla troops in a North American zoo plus such endangered or threatened species as Wolf's monkeys, mandrills, okapis and hornbills.

At Tiger Mountain visitors can learn about Siberian tigers through demonstrations given by animal keepers. JungleWorld is an indoor tropical Asian setting with gibbons, langurs, bats and other wildlife. The Butterfly Garden is home to 32 species of North American butterflies and features interactive exhibits, meandering paths and a flowering meadow.

Food is available. Mon.-Fri. 10-5, Sat.-Sun. and holidays 10-5:30, Apr.-Oct.; daily 10-4:30, rest of year. Admission Apr.-Oct. $12; over 64 and ages 2-12, $9. Admission rest of year $8; over 64 and ages 2-12, $6. Parking $8. Hours and prices may vary; phone ahead. Phone (718) 367-1010.

FORDHAM UNIVERSITY, Third Ave. at E. Fordham Rd., near n.w. Bronx Park (S: Fordham Rd.), was founded in 1841 as an independent Jesuit university. Fordham's 10 schools have three campuses: Rose Hill, Lincoln Center and Tarrytown. Guided tours of Rose Hill and Lincoln Center are available. Rose Hill tours are given Mon.-Fri. at 10, noon and 2:30. Lincoln Center tours are given at Mon.-Fri. at noon. Tour schedules may vary; phone ahead. Free. Phone (718) 817-1000.

NEW YORK BOTANICAL GARDEN, 200th St. and Kazimiroff Blvd. (S: Bedford Park Blvd.), was founded in 1891 and is one of the world's largest botanical gardens, covering 250 acres. The grounds have 28 specialty gardens and plant collections. The palacelike, glass-enclosed Enid A. Haupt Conservatory contains plants displayed in settings similar to their tropical, subtropical and desert habitats.

Outdoor gardens feature rocks, native plants, herbs, roses and perennials as well as 50 acres of original forest that once covered the city. The 12-acre, indoor/outdoor Everett Children's Adventure Garden has 40 hands-on activities for discovering plants and nature, plus mazes and topiaries. Other features include narrated tram rides, children's activities and guided walking tours.

Picnicking is permitted. Food is available. Grounds open Tues.-Sun. 10-6, Apr.-Oct.; 10-5, rest of year. Hours vary for conservatory and children's, rock and native plant gardens; phone ahead. Closed Thanksgiving and Dec. 25.

Grounds $6; senior citizens and students with ID $3; ages 2-12, $2; free to all Wed. and Sat. 10-noon, Apr.-Oct. Conservatory rates vary; phone ahead. Parking $10. Phone (718) 817-8700.

VAN CORTLANDT HOUSE MUSEUM is at Broadway and W. 246th St. in Van Cortlandt Park. This 1748 mansion features 17th- and 18th-century Dutch, English and American furnishings. Tues.-Fri. 10-3, Sat.-Sun. 11-4; closed holidays. Admission $5, over 59 and students with ID $3, under 12 free; free to all Wed. Phone (718) 543-3344.

WAVE HILL, off the Henry Hudson Pkwy. at W. 249 St. and Independence Ave., was built in 1843 and features a 28-acre garden and cultural center overlooking the Hudson River. The Glyndor House presents changing horticultural exhibits. Guided walks among the herb, wildflower and aquatic gardens are held Sunday at 2:15; special events are held periodically.

Allow 1 hour minimum. Tues. and Thurs.-Sun. 9-5:30, Wed. 9-9, June-July; Tues.-Sun. 9-5:30, Apr. 15-May 31 and Aug. 1-Oct. 14; Tues.-Sun. 9-4:30, rest of year. Closed Jan. 1, Thanksgiving and Dec. 25. Admission Mar.-Nov., $4, over 64 and students with ID $2, under 6 free; free to all Tues. all day and Sat. 9-noon. Free rest of year. Phone (718) 549-3200.

WOODLAWN CEMETERY, Webster Ave. at E. 233rd St. (S: Jerome Ave.), was established in 1863 and contains more than 250,000 graves, including those of Duke Ellington, Herman Melville, Joseph Pulitzer and Elizabeth Cady Stanton. Sculpture adorns the landscaped grounds. Musical programs, tours and special events are held regularly. Open daily 8:30-5 (weather permitting). Free. Phone (718) 920-0500.

Brooklyn pop. 2,465,326

BROOKLYN BOTANIC GARDEN has entrances at Flatbush Ave. and Empire Blvd. and at Washington Ave. and Eastern Pkwy. (S: Eastern Pkwy., Prospect Park). Its 52 acres include the Garden of Fragrance for the visually impaired; the Japanese Hill-and-Pond Garden; and a conservatory housing tropical plants and a bonsai museum under three glass pavilions.

Allow 1 hour minimum. Garden open Tues.-Fri. 8-6, Sat.-Sun. and Mon. holidays (except Labor Day) 10-6, Apr.-Sept.; Tues.-Fri. 8-4:30, Sat.-Sun. and Mon. holidays 10-4:30, rest of year. Conservatory open Tues.-Sun. and Mon. holidays (except Labor Day) 10-5:30, Apr.-Sept.; Tues.-Sun. 10-4, rest of year. Closed Jan. 1, Thanksgiving and Dec. 25. Admission $5, over 64 and students with ID $3, under 16 free, free to all Tues. all day and Sat. 10-noon, free to over age 64 Fri. Phone (718) 623-7200.

BROOKLYN CHILDREN'S MUSEUM, 145 Brooklyn Ave. (S: St. Mark), contains more than 77,000 artifacts. Children learn through touching, entering or interacting with exhibits. Arrive early on weekends to avoid crowds. Tues.-Fri. 1-6, Sat.-Sun. and Mon. holidays 11-6 (also Fri. 6-6:30), July-Aug.; Wed.-Fri. 1-6, Sat.-Sun. and Mon. holidays 11-6; closed Jan. 1, July 4, Thanksgiving and Dec. 25. Admission $5. Phone (718) 735-4400.

[SAVE] **THE BROOKLYN HISTORICAL SOCIETY,** 128 Pierrepont St. at Clinton St. (S: Borough Hall/Court St./Jay St.), is in the restored 1881 Queen Anne-style building designed by George B. Post, architect of the New York Stock Exchange building. The museum's central exhibit chronicles the daily life of Brooklyn's working class over 400 years through re-created living and working environments, displays of locally manufactured products and recorded stories. Allow 1 hour minimum. Wed.-Sun. noon-5. Admission $6, over 64 and students with ID $4, under 12 free. Phone (718) 222-4111.

[GEM] **BROOKLYN MUSEUM,** Eastern Pkwy. and Washington Ave. at Prospect Park (S: Eastern Pkwy./Brooklyn Museum), houses collections of Egyptian, African, Asian, Oceanic, classical, New World and ancient Middle Eastern art as well as American paintings and an outdoor sculpture garden.

The Egyptian galleries display mummies, statuary, reliefs and pottery from various dynasties. Artifacts from ancient civilizations such as Assyria and Sumeria are featured in the Ancient Middle Eastern Art Gallery. An extensive decorative arts collection highlights some 23 period rooms representing the 17th through 20th centuries. Visitors can view more than 1,500 objects including pewter, pressed glass, silver, ceramics and furniture in the Luce Center for American Art. Feminist art, including Judy Chicago's The Dinner Party, is shown in the Elizabeth A. Sackler Center for Feminist Art.

Note: Period rooms are undergoing renovations and may be closed to the public. Guided museum tours and audiotape rentals are available. Allow 3 hours minimum. Wed.-Fri. 10-5, Sat.-Sun. 11-6 (also first Sat. of each month 6-11 p.m.); closed Jan. 1, Thanksgiving and Dec. 25. Guided tours are given Wed.-Fri. at 1:30, Sat.-Sun. at 1, 2 and 3. Admission $8, over 64 and students with ID $4, under 12 free with an adult. Audiotape tour $3. Parking $3-$12. AX, MC, VI. Phone (718) 638-5000, or TTY (718) 399-8440.

CYPRESS HILLS NATIONAL CEMETERY is on Jamaica and Hale aves. (S: Cypress Hills). The original 3,170 graves are casualties received from Civil War hospitals in the New York City vicinity. Daily 9-4:30. Free. Phone (718) 277-2900.

FORT GREENE PARK, at Myrtle and DeKalb aves., and St. Edwards and Cumberland sts. (S: Fulton St./Lafayette Ave.), contains Martyrs' Monument, designed by Stanford White and dedicated to the Continental soldiers who died on British prison ships in Wallabout Bay. Daily dawn-dusk. Free.

NEW YORK AQUARIUM, on the Coney Island Boardwalk (S: West 8th St. N.Y. Aquarium, Coney Island Stillwell Ave.), exhibits marine life in outdoor pools and indoor tanks. The Oceanic tank features a Beluga whale. Local species are featured in the Hudson River exhibit. The Gulf Stream Habitat examines the various fish that are swept up the river by the stream during the summer. The Sea Cliffs exhibit is a replica of the rocky Pacific Coast and features walruses, sea otters, seals and penguins.

Mon.-Fri. 10-6, Sat.-Sun. 10-7, Memorial Day weekend-Labor Day; Mon.-Fri. 10-5, Sat.-Sun. 10-5:30, early Apr.-day before Memorial Day weekend and day after Labor Day-late Oct.; daily 10-4:30, rest of year. Admission $12; over 64 and ages 2-12, $8. Parking $8. Phone (718) 265-3474.

NEW YORK TRANSIT MUSEUM, jct. of Boerum Pl. and Schermerhorn St. (S: Borough Hall, Court St., Jay St./Borough Hall), is in a decommissioned subway station and traces the history of New York City public transportation through photographs, equipment, artifacts and memorabilia. Numerous trains and vehicles are displayed, some of which can be entered. Allow 1 hour minimum. Tues.-Fri. 10-4, Sat.-Sun. noon-5; closed major holidays. Admission $5; over 61 and ages 3-17, $3. Phone (718) 694-1600.

DID YOU KNOW

Colin Powell, the nation's first African-American secretary of state, hails from South Bronx.

PROSPECT PARK, between Prospect Park W. and Prospect Park S.W. and Flatbush and Parkside aves. (S: 7th Ave./Grand Army Plaza), contains a Quaker graveyard, gardens, woodlands, waterfalls, nature trails, a zoo, a restored vintage carousel, boating facilities, pools, and Lefferts Historic House, an 18th-century homestead museum with furnishings and relics. Grand Army Plaza has an arch commemorating Civil War heroes and a memorial to John F. Kennedy. Prospect Park Audubon Center at the Boathouse features nature exhibits in a restored 1905 Beaux Arts boathouse. Carousel rides and electric boat tours are available for a fee.

Food is available. Park open daily dawn-dusk. Visitor center open Thurs.-Sun. noon-6, July 1-Labor Day; Thurs.-Sun. noon-5, Apr.-June and day after Labor Day-Dec. 31. Lefferts Historic House open Thurs.-Sun. 1-4, Apr.-Nov. Free. Phone (718) 965-8951, or (718) 287-3400 for the nature center, or (718) 965-8999 for recorded information, or (718) 789-2822 for Lefferts Historic House.

ST. JOHN'S EPISCOPAL CHURCH, 9818 Fort Hamilton Pkwy. (S: 95th St.), was founded in 1834. Generals Robert E. Lee and Thomas "Stonewall" Jackson were members of the congregation while at Fort Hamilton. Mon.-Fri. 9-1. Free. Phone (718) 745-2377.

Queens pop. 2,229,379

FLUSHING MEADOWS CORONA PARK is bounded by Roosevelt Ave., Van Wyck Expwy., Union Tpke. and 111th St. (S: Willets Point/Shea Stadium). Site of New York's World Fairs 1939-40 and 1964-65, the park has bicycle paths, the Queens Wildlife Conservation Center, a carousel, freshwater fishing, pitch-and-putt golf, an indoor ice-skating rink and a marina. Baseball, cricket, football and softball fields are available, as are boccie courts. Picnicking is permitted. Daily 9-dusk. Free. Phone (718) 760-6565.

JAMAICA BAY WILDLIFE REFUGE is 3 mi. s. on Crossbay Blvd. off Belt Pkwy. exit 17. The 9,155-acre refuge contains varied habitats, including freshwater ponds, marshes, bays, fields, wooded areas and islands. It is a major stopover for migrating birds; some 329 species have been recorded since the mid-1950s. A 1.75-mile walking trail allows visitors to see the early stages of forest development. Allow 2 hours minimum. Refuge daily dawn-dusk. Visitor center daily 9-5. Free. Phone (718) 318-4340.

KING MANOR MUSEUM is at 150-03 Jamaica Ave. (S: Jamaica Center). The 18th-century Dutch-style house was home to Rufus King, a signer of the U.S. Constitution, New York statesman and anti-slavery stalwart. Exhibits in period rooms chronicle King's life and village history. Allow 30 minutes minimum. Thurs.-Fri. noon-2, Sat.-Sun. 1-5, Feb.-Dec. Admission $5, over 65 and students with ID $3, under 17 free. Phone (718) 206-0545.

LOUIS ARMSTRONG HOUSE is at 34-56 107th St. (S: 103rd St.-Corona Plaza). The preserved two-story house of Louis "Satchmo" and Lucille Armstrong contains original furniture, fixtures and decorative pieces as well as personal memorabilia. Decorated in a 1960s contemporary style with Oriental influences, it features a high-tech kitchen with aqua appliances and an ornate bathroom with gold faucets. Allow 1 hour minimum. Tues.-Fri. 10-5, Sat.-Sun. noon-5; closed holidays. Admission $8; senior citizens, students with ID and ages 4-11, $6. AX, MC, VI. Phone (718) 478-8274.

[SAVE] **MUSEUM OF THE MOVING IMAGE,** 35th Ave. and 36th St. in Astoria (S: Steinway St.), chronicles the art, history, technique and technology of motion pictures, television, video and digital media. The museum occupies a renovated building on the site of the former Astoria Studio, a 1920s facility used by Paramount Pictures. Interpretive programs, changing exhibitions and screenings are offered. Strollers are not permitted. Wed.-Thurs. 11-5, Fri. 11-8, Sat.-Sun. 11-6:30; closed Memorial Day, Thanksgiving and Dec. 25. Admission $10; over 65 and students with ID $7.50; ages 5-18, $5; free to all Fri. after 4. Phone (718) 784-0077 or (718) 784-4777.

NEW YORK HALL OF SCIENCE, 111th St. and 46th Ave. in Flushing Meadows Corona Park (S: 111 St.), is a hands-on science and technology center. Many of the exhibits are geared toward making scientific processes understandable for children. The center also has a multimedia library.

Allow 2 hours minimum. Mon.-Fri. 9:30-5, Sat.-Sun. 10-6, July-Aug.; Tues.-Thurs. 9:30-2, Fri. 9:30-5, Sat.-Sun. 10-6, rest of year. Closed Jan. 1, Labor Day, Thanksgiving and Dec. 25. Admission $11; over 61 and ages 5-17, $8; free to all Fri. 2-5 and Sun. 10-noon, Sept.-June. Parking $10. AX, MC, VI. Phone (718) 699-0005.

THE NOGUCHI MUSEUM, 32-37 Vernon Blvd. (S: Broadway), displays the noted 20th-century artist's sculpture in galleries within a renovated photoengraving plant and in an outdoor garden. Works in clay, metal, stone and wood are featured along with Noguchi's Akari Light Sculptures and interior designs. Food is available. Allow 30 minutes minimum. Wed.-Fri. 10-5, Sat.-Sun. 11-6. Guided tours are given at 2. Admission $10, senior citizens and students with ID $5. Shuttle service to and from Manhattan is available Sat.-Sun. for a fee. MC, VI. Phone (718) 204-7088.

QUEENS BOTANICAL GARDEN is at 43-50 Main St.; take I-495 (Long Island Expwy.) exit 23 to Main St., then 1 mi. n. to Dahlia Ave. (S: Main St.). Trails and paths wind through rose, rock and formal gardens, and a live beehive is the focal point in a wildflower meadow. Special programs, educational tours and projects are offered throughout the year. Tues.-Fri. and Mon. holidays 8-6, Sat.-Sun. 8-7, Apr.-Oct.; Tues.-Sun. and Mon. holidays 8-4:30, rest of year. Free. Parking $5. Phone (718) 886-3800.

QUEENS COUNTY FARM MUSEUM is off Cross Island Pkwy. exit 27, .4 mi. e. on Jericho Tpke., then 1.7 mi. n. on Little Neck Pkwy. This 7-acre historical farm is said to be the largest remaining plot of agricultural land within the New York City limits. The complex includes a shingled 1772 farmhouse restored to its 1856 appearance; a wagon shed, two barns and three greenhouses built after 1927; animal pens with cows, goats, pigs and sheep; and productive fruit orchards and vegetable gardens.

Allow 1 hour minimum. Grounds Mon.-Fri. 9-5, Sat.-Sun. 10-5; closed Jan. 1, Easter, Memorial Day, July 4, Thanksgiving and Dec. 25. House tours are given Sat.-Sun. 10-5. Hayrides are offered Apr.-Nov. Grounds free. Admission is charged during special events. Hayrides $2. Phone (718) 347-3276.

QUEENS MUSEUM OF ART, in the New York City Building at Flushing Meadows Corona Park (S: Willets Point/Shea Stadium) *(see attraction listing),* offers changing art exhibitions. Allow 1 hour minimum. Wed.-Sun. noon-6 (also Fri. 6-8 p.m.), late June-early Sept.; Wed.-Fri. 10-5, Sat.-Sun. noon-5, rest of year. Closed holidays. Admission $5, senior citizens and students with ID $2.50, under 5 free. Phone (718) 592-9700.

Staten Island pop. 443,728

ALICE AUSTEN HOUSE is off I-278 Bay St. Exit, n. 1 mi. to Hylan Blvd. then e. to 2 Hylan Blvd. This Victorian house, carefully restored to its 1890s appearance, displays photographs taken from the late 1800s through the first half of the 20th century by Alice Austen, who lived here 1866-1929. Allow 1 hour minimum. Thurs.-Sun. noon-5, Mar.-Dec.; closed major holidays. Admission $2. Phone (718) 816-4506.

SAVE **HISTORIC RICHMOND TOWN** is s. of I-278 via Richmond Rd./Clove Rd. exit. This living history village and museum complex interprets 3 centuries of daily life and culture on Staten Island. Restored houses, shops and public buildings from the 1690s to the 1900s feature furnished interiors and exhibits. Guides in period dress lead tours and conduct participatory programs.

Allow 2 hours minimum. Wed.-Fri. 10-5, Sat.-Sun. 1-5, July-Aug.; Wed.-Sun. 1-5, Mar.-June and Sept.-Dec. Closed Easter, Thanksgiving and Dec. 25. Tours are given Mon.-Fri. at 2:30, Sat.-Sun. at 2 and 3:30. Admission $5; over 61 and college students with ID $4; ages 5-17, $3.50. Phone (718) 351-1611.

SAVE **JACQUES MARCHAIS MUSEUM OF TIBETAN ART** is at 338 Lighthouse Ave.; take I-278W to Richmond Rd., then 5 mi. s. to Lighthouse Ave. Designed like a small Tibetan mountain temple, the museum collects, preserves and displays Tibetan, Tibeto-Chinese, Nepalese and Mongolian art objects and paintings. Terraced sculpture gardens, a lily and fish pond and a view of the Lower Bay provide a serene atmosphere. Lectures, demonstrations and performances are offered on selected Sunday afternoons.

Allow 1 hour minimum. Wed.-Sun. 1-5; closed Thanksgiving, day after Thanksgiving, Dec. 24-25 and 31, and Jan. 1. Admission $5, over 64 and students with ID $3, under 6 free. Phone (718) 987-3500.

SNUG HARBOR CULTURAL CENTER, Clove Rd. exit off I-278, then 3 mi. n. to 1000 Richmond Terr., was founded in 1801 as the nation's first maritime hospital and home for retired sailors. Restored buildings include Main Hall, with its Newhouse Center for Contemporary Art, and Veterans Memorial Hall, a concert venue.

The 83-acre Staten Island Botanical Garden includes formal displays of annuals, a variety of themed gardens, a Chinese garden, sculpture and fountains. Newhouse Center and Chinese Garden open Tues.-Sun. 10-5. Botanical garden open daily dawn-dusk. Center $2, senior citizens $1, under 10 free. Chinese garden $6; senior citizens and students with ID $5; under 12, $3. Grounds free. Prices may vary; phone ahead. Phone (718) 448-2500.

SAVE **Staten Island Children's Museum,** in the Snug Harbor Cultural Center, contains exhibits about art, science and humanities. Hands-on workshops, performances and special events designed for preschool through eighth grade children are presented throughout the year. Allow 1 hour, 30 minutes minimum. Tues.-Sun. 10-5 (also Wed. 5-8), July 1-Labor Day; Tues.-Fri. noon-5, Sat.-Sun. 10-5, rest of year. Closed Jan. 1, July 4, Thanksgiving and Dec. 25. Admission $5, under 1 free. Phone (718) 273-2060.

SAVE **STATEN ISLAND MUSEUM,** 75 Stuyvesant Pl. near the St. George ferry terminal, displays art, natural science and history collections as well as exhibits about Staten Island and its people. The archives and library have documents dating from the early 1700s. Allow 1 hour minimum. Tues.-Fri. 9-5, Sat. 10-5, Sun. noon-5; closed major holidays. Admission $2, over 64 and students with ID $1. Phone (718) 727-1135.

SAVE **STATEN ISLAND ZOO,** in Barrett Park at 614 Broadway, is an educational zoo with mammals, birds, reptiles and tropical fish. Exhibits include a representation of a tropical rain forest, a re-creation of an African savannah, an aquarium, a serpentarium and a children's center emphasizing domestic animals that help man. Allow 1 hour minimum. Daily 10-4:45; closed Jan. 1, Thanksgiving and Dec. 25. Admission $7; over 60, $5; ages 3-14, $4; by donation Wed. 2-4:45. Phone (718) 442-3100.

What To Do

Sightseeing

Boat Tours

Boat tours can make sightseeing even more exciting. One of the best sightseeing bargains in the city is a ride on the Staten Island Ferry. Leaving South Ferry in Battery Park every day at least once an hour, the free ride provides views of the Lower Manhattan skyline and the Statue of Liberty. Avoid the ferry during peak commuter hours, Mon.-Fri. 8-10 and 4-6; phone (718) 390-5253.

The 1885 schooner *Pioneer* offers 2-hour excursions of New York Harbor Tues.-Sun., June-Sept.; Sat.-Sun., Apr.-May. Tickets are sold at the Pier 16 ticket booth; phone (212) 748-8786.

THE BEAST departs from Pier 83 at W. 42nd St. and Twelfth Ave. A high-speed powerboat takes up to 145 passengers on a 30-minute thrill ride around New York Harbor and stops briefly at the Statue of Liberty for photographs. Allow 30 minutes minimum. Departures daily noon-dusk, May-Sept., Sat.-Sun. noon-dusk in Oct. Fare $17; under 13, $11. Under 40 inches tall are not permitted. AX, DS, MC, VI. Phone (212) 563-3200.

[SAVE] **CIRCLE LINE CRUISES** departs from Pier 83, W. 42nd St. at the Hudson River. Two-hour narrated sightseeing trips off Lower Manhattan afford views of the Statue of Liberty *(see attraction listing)* and the Manhattan skyline. Highlights of a 3-hour cruise around the island include three rivers, docks, seven bridges and more than 25 landmarks. Trips of varying lengths as well as evening cruises and combination trips also are available. Cruises daily Apr.-Dec.; Wed.-Mon., in Mar.; Thurs.-Mon., rest of year. Departure times vary. Closed Dec. 25. Fare for 2-hour cruise $23; over 64, $19; under 13, $12. Fare for 3-hour cruise $29; over 64, $24; under 13, $16. AX, DC, DS, MC, VI. Phone (212) 563-3200. *See color ad p. 121.*

NY WATERWAY HARBOR SIGHTSEEING CRUISES departs from Pier 78 at W. 38th St. and 12th Ave. Offered are a 2-hour sightseeing cruise around the island of Manhattan and a 90-minute tour of New York Harbor. Twilight, entertainment, dinner and holiday cruises also are available. Bus transportation is available from local hotels.

Manhattan and harbor cruises depart daily, mid-May to early Nov.; schedule varies rest of year. Departure times vary according to type of cruise; phone for schedule. Two-hour cruise $27; over 61, $22; ages 3-12, $16. Ninety-minute cruise $22; over 61, $18; ages 3-12, $12. AX, DS, MC, VI. Phone (201) 902-8711 or (800) 533-3779.

SPIRIT CRUISES departs from Pier 61, Chelsea Piers, off W. 23rd St., and from Weehawken, NJ. Offered are narrated 2-hour lunch cruises on the East and Hudson rivers. Music and entertainment are provided. Dinner cruises with entertainment also

are available. Cruises depart daily; phone for departure times. Lunch cruises $32-$45; fares may vary. Reservations are required. AX, DC, DS, MC, VI. Phone (212) 727-2789 or (866) 211-3805.

WORLD YACHT, Pier 81 and W. 41st St. on the Hudson River, offers 2-hour brunch and 3-hour dinner cruises in New York harbor. Cruises include dazzling views of the Statue of Liberty and the New York city skyline, a four-course dinner, music and dancing. Allow 3 hours minimum. Dinner cruises board daily at 6 and depart at 7, brunch cruises board Sun. at 11:30 and depart at 12:30; closed Jan. 1 and Dec. 25.

Dinner cruise (jacket required) Sun.-Thurs. $80.21, Fri.-Sat. $88.83. Brunch cruise $49.32. Parking fee. Schedule may vary; phone ahead. Reservations are required. AX, MC, VI. Phone (212) 630-8100.

Bus Tours

To see the most in the least amount of time, take a bus tour. There are numerous bus tours that cover all parts of the city; information is available either from your local AAA club or by phoning the bus lines directly.

[SAVE] Gray Line New York offers a variety of sightseeing tours in double-deck buses. The All Loops Tour includes the Uptown, Downtown and Night Loop/Holiday Lights Tour. The all-day Show-Biz Insiders Tour offers behind-the-scenes looks at a Broadway theater and other performance venues. A motor coach tour of Manhattan includes lunch. Tickets can be purchased at the Gray Line Visitors Center, 777 Eighth Ave. (between 47th and 48th streets); phone (212) 445-0848 or (800) 669-0051. *See color ad p. 111.*

CitySights NY double-deck bus tours visit historic sites and popular points of interest throughout Manhattan; phone (212) 812-2700. *See color ad p. 426.* On Location Tours takes passengers to sites featured on well-known television shows. Various theme tours are available; phone (212) 209-3370.

Helicopter Tours

LIBERTY HELICOPTER TOURS departs from the VIP Heliport at W. 30th St. at 12th Ave. A helicopter sightseeing tour of the Big Apple includes views of the Statue of Liberty, the Manhattan skyline, Central Park and the George Washington Bridge. Photo identification is required. Allow 1 hour minimum. Daily 9:30-8:30. Fee for 5-7 min. tour $62; 10-12 min. $112; 15-17 min. $179. AX, MC, VI. Phone (212) 967-6464.

Walking Tours

(AAA) Walking Tour: Greenwich Village

See map following. The tour takes 3-5 hours, depending on your pace and the number of listed sites you visit along the way. Those that appear in bold type have detailed listings in the What to See section. Even if you decide not to visit a listed site, reading the listing when you reach that point should make the tour more interesting.

Although just a short subway ride from the scurrying throngs and imposing skyscrapers of Midtown, Greenwich Village seems a world apart. Characterized by quiet side streets, secluded courtyards, tree-shaded parks and brick townhouses, the Village is about as pedestrian-friendly a place as you are likely to find in a huge city like New York. A stroll along its relatively peaceful sidewalks offers a break from the frenetic bustle that characterizes much of Manhattan. Walking also happens to be the best way to experience the funky ambience of this famously unconventional neighborhood.

Not only do Village residents have a long history of defying convention, the streets themselves defy the ordered grid that makes navigation so easy in other areas of Manhattan. Fortunately there are plenty of street signs, and contrary to popular stereotype, New Yorkers are often very willing to assist with directions.

The walking tour begins and ends in Greenwich Village's leafy heart: **Washington Square,** at the southern end of Fifth Avenue. To get there, take the A, C, E, F or S train to the West 4th Street Subway Station; the park is a block east. You might be disappointed to learn that New York City's subway tokens have gone the way of the pterodactyl, but the fare cards (called MetroCards) that have replaced those distinctive little coins are easy to use, easy to obtain and much lighter in your pocket. A 1-Day Fun Pass good for unlimited rides for 1 day on city subway trains and buses is available for $7 at MetroCard vending machines.

Originally a marsh, the area that is now Washington Square Park was used as a cemetery in the late 1700s. Excavations a century later uncovered numerous skeletons and headstones, much to the dismay of the well-heeled residents who lived along the park's borders at the time. Today you would have a hard time envisioning Washington Square's funereal past, particularly on summer weekends when the park fills with children, chess players, joggers, skaters, couples with baby strollers, people walking their dogs, food vendors, street entertainers, musicians rehearsing and tourists sitting on benches and resting their weary feet. Adding a youthful air to this already vibrant environment are the students of New York University. One of America's largest private universities, N.Y.U. owns many of the buildings surrounding the park, making Washington Square a de facto part of the school campus.

Presiding over this crazy quilt of humanity is the square's majestic ❶ Washington Memorial Arch. Dedicated in 1895, the 77-foot-high, white-marble monument at the end of Fifth Avenue was designed by Stamford White to commemorate the centennial of George Washington's inauguration. It replaced an earlier wooden arch temporarily constructed less than a block north on Fifth Avenue. "Washington in War," a statue of the first president wearing military attire, was added to one side of the arch in 1916 and a second, called appropriately enough "Washington in Peace," was installed in 1918. Other park monuments include a statue of Giuseppe Garibaldi, known as the Father of Modern Italy, and a bust of Alexander Lyman Holley, who perfected the Bessemer process of manufacturing steel, giving rise to the U.S. steel industry.

Walk over to the park's central fountain and proceed from there to Washington Square South. The bell tower to your right is part of Italian Renaissance-style ❷ Judson Memorial Church, built in 1896. The church is noted for its stained-glass windows, which were designed at the turn of the 20th century by eminent artist John La Farge.

Turn left and head over to Washington Square East. The massive red stone building to your right with fluted walls is N.Y.U.'s ❸ Elmer Bobst Library. Set on a pedestal adjacent to the library is a piece of ornate stonework from the university's original Gothic building, which was demolished in the late 1800s. Founded in 1831, N.Y.U. occupies buildings throughout the Village. You'll recognize them by the large violet banners emblazoned with the school's symbol: a flaming torch.

Turn left again and follow Washington Square East to Washington Square North. The building at the corner of Washington Square East and Waverly Place is the university's ❹ Main Building, which stands on the site of the original Gothic structure mentioned earlier. Famous occupants of that first building include painter Winslow Homer, poet Walt Whitman, author Henry James and electric telegraph developer Samuel Morse, who, interestingly enough, taught painting and sculpture and is credited with establishing America's first

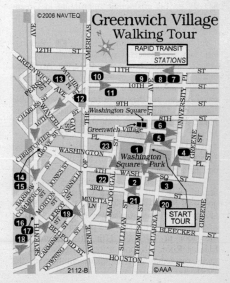

Broadway / © Prisma / SuperStock

academic fine arts department. Within the current Main Building is the Grey Art Gallery, where you can see an array of visual arts on display.

Now walk west along Washington Square North. The **5** Greek Revival townhouses here were built in 1833 for wealthy New Yorkers, but most now belong to the university. Henry James grew up around the corner, and his grandmother lived in a townhouse on this very block. James drew heavily on his aristocratic upbringing in Greenwich Village when he wrote his novel, "Washington Square."

Proceed north on Fifth Avenue to **6** Washington Mews, a peaceful pedestrian-only alley on your right. You'll notice a towering Art Deco building, built in 1926, on the other side of the mews. Stables once lined this narrow brick-paved street, but they were replaced by desirable apartments long ago. As you exit onto University Place, the buildings on your right and left are the French and German departments of N.Y.U.

Walk 4 blocks north on University Place to East 11th Street and turn left. Half way down the block on the north side is a small 19th-century building tucked in between two larger buildings and hidden behind trees. This is the **7** Conservative Synagogue of Fifth Avenue, which, like the residences along Washington Mews, was originally used as a stable. Across the street, a plaque to the left of the door at 20 East 11th St. indicates that Eleanor Roosevelt, one of the Village's many famous residents, kept an apartment here in the 1930s and '40s.

Continue west and turn right at Fifth Avenue to the broad stairway of the **8** Salmagundi Club, an artist's organization founded in 1871 as the New York Sketch Club. Members have included Childe Hassam, Louis Comfort Tiffany and N.C. Wyeth. The club took its current name from "The Salmagundi Papers," Washington Irving's satirical take on social life in early 19th-century New York. Incidentally, it is within "The Salmagundi Papers" that Irving first referred to New York as Gotham, which has been a nickname for the city ever since. The club has occupied the 1853 Italianate mansion—the last of its kind remaining on this stretch of Fifth Avenue—since 1917.

Across Fifth Avenue from the club is the Gothic Revival-style **9** First Presbyterian Church. Completed in 1846, the church was modeled after the Church of St. Saviour in Bath, England. Just a bit farther south on Fifth Avenue, at the corner of 10th Street, looms another example of Gothic Revival architecture: the 1841 Church of the Ascension.

North of the First Presbyterian Church, between 12th and 13th, you'll find the **FORBES Magazine Galleries.** Inside, countless toy soldiers of every description are displayed marching or engaged in battle. Toy boats, historical documents, collectible trophies and Monopoly board games round out this eclectic hodgepodge amassed by the late Malcolm Forbes.

Return to 11th Street and head west. A wall and wrought iron fence on the south side of 11th near Sixth Avenue protects a small corner of a once-larger cemetery. **10** The Second Cemetery of the Spanish and Portuguese Synagogue dates back to 1805. Take a peek through the bars into the dim, well-tended space beyond, which is filled with tombstones of various shapes and sizes beneath sheltering evergreen trees.

Continue to Sixth Avenue, turn right and turn right again on West 10th Street. On the south side of 10th is a row of **11** Anglo-Italianate townhouses connected by a single shallow terrace with an ornate iron railing. These residences were built in the 1850s and designed by James Renwick, Jr., who also designed historic Grace Church at 802 Broadway; St. Patrick's Cathedral on Fifth Avenue between 50th and 51st streets; and the Smithsonian Castle in Washington, D.C.

Retrace your steps back to Sixth Avenue and cross the street. The building with the pyramid-topped clock tower to your left is **12** Jefferson Market Courthouse, completed in 1887. In the hearts of Villagers this Victorian Gothic landmark ranks second only to the Washington Memorial Arch, although in the early 1960s "Old Jeff" came perilously close to demolition. Angered Villagers came to the rescue, and after a 1967 restoration, it reopened as a branch of the New York Public Library. Behind the courthouse, where a women's prison once stood, is a volunteer-maintained viewing garden.

Across West 10th Street from the courthouse you'll find ⓭ Patchin Place, a quiet, dead-end street lined with three-story residences. These were built in 1848 as boardinghouses for waiters at a nearby hotel, but in the 20th century Patchin Place counted several renowned writers among its residents, including poets e.e. cummings and John Masefield, authors Theodore Dreiser and John Reed and playwright Eugene O'Neill. Just around the corner on Sixth Avenue is Milligan Place, another picturesque courtyard lined with former boardinghouses, these built in 1852.

Proceed west on 10th Street to Seventh Avenue and turn left. The intersection ahead where seven streets come together is ⓮ Sheridan Square, roughly the geographical center of Greenwich Village. With so many streets meeting in one spot, the square has earned a reputation for disorienting visitors. Just try to remember your position relative to Seventh Avenue, the main thoroughfare.

A statue of Civil War general Philip Henry Sheridan, for whom the square was named, stands in Christopher Park, which is the triangular park to your left created by the intersection of Seventh Avenue and Christopher and Grove streets. For such a small area, Christopher Park seems crowded with statues. Opposite the general is a grouping of four whitewashed bronze figures known as the Gay Liberation Monument, evidence of the Village's tolerant live-and-let-live ethos. Nearby, a second triangular park created by the intersection of Washington Place, 4th Street and Barrow Street features a viewing garden.

Go back to Seventh Avenue and continue south to where Seventh intersects with Bleeker and Barrow streets. Turn right on Barrow and follow it for one block to Bedford. Another right will bring you to 86 Bedford St., better known as ⓯ Chumley's, a restaurant opened in 1922 that served as a speakeasy during Prohibition. A veritable Who's Who list of literary greats have frequented Chumley's over the years, including James Agee, e.e. cummings, Theodore Dreiser, F. Scott Fitzgerald, Lillian Hellman, Edna St. Vincent Millay, John Dos Passos, Upton Sinclair and John Steinbeck.

Return to Bedford and Barrow, turn right and then make a left on Commerce Street. Where the street curves to the left stands the ⓰ Cherry Lane Theater, founded by Edna St. Vincent Millay in 1924. One of the city's first off-Broadway venues, the theater has showcased challenging, experimental plays by the likes of Eugene Ionesco, David Mamet, Harold Pinter and Sam Shepard for more than 75 years.

Follow the bend in Commerce Street until you're back on Bedford, then make a right, after which you will immediately be confronted by two Greenwich Village superlatives. On the corner at 77 Bedford St. is the ⓱ Isaacs-Hendricks House, which was built in 1799 and is recognized as the oldest in the Village. By comparison, the house next door

at 75½ Bedford, built in 1873, is a relative newcomer. With just one glance, however, you can guess what its claim to fame is. At under 10 feet wide, 75½ Bedford has earned the reputation as the narrowest house in the Village. Edna St. Vincent Millay lived there briefly during the 1920s.

Walk south on Bedford to Seventh Avenue and turn right. Turn right again on Leroy Street, which for a short stretch is known as ⓲ St. Luke's Place. The impressive row of Italianate townhouses along the street's north side was constructed in the 1850s for New York's mercantile elite. Ornate facades, grand entryways, tall windows, shade trees and a park across the street make these some of the most sought after addresses in the Village. Number 6 was the home of Jimmy Walker, mayor of the city 1926-32. Two lamps, which traditionally identify the mayor's house in New York, still frame the entrance.

Retrace your steps back to Seventh Avenue and cross it, following Leroy Street east to Bleeker. Make a right onto Bleeker in front of ⓳ Our Lady of Pompeii, a large Roman Catholic Church built in 1928 for the Italian immigrant community. Continue on Bleeker, but when you reach Sixth Avenue be careful: Four streets intersect here making it somewhat tricky to find where Bleeker resumes. Follow Bleeker to MacDougal Street and stop. If your energy levels are beginning to dip, you're in luck. With a café at every turn, this intersection is known as café corner, a perfect spot to sit, relax and enjoy a cup of coffee.

After you've revived, proceed east on Bleeker to La Guardia Place. This area of the Village is thick with second-hand clothing and record stores, cafés and intimate nightspots offering live jazz and rock music. The Bitter End at the corner of Bleeker and La Guardia features live entertainment and even sports a plaque honoring the establishment for its "contribution to the artistic life of New York."

Turn left on La Guardia. Halfway up the block on the east side of the street you'll spy a bronze ⓴ statue of Fiorello La Guardia, New York City mayor 1934-45. The statue shows the diminutive 5'2" La Guardia, known as "the little flower," stepping forward, mouth open and hands poised as if clapping. While far from the dignified posture one might expect of an honored statesman, the statue captures the enthusiasm and energy of one of the city's most popular mayors, who served three consecutive terms during a difficult period in the city's history and is remembered for his sweeping reforms and efforts to curb corruption.

Continue north on La Guardia to West 3rd Street and turn left. On your left will be a bright red Victorian building housing the ㉑ Number 2 Fire Engine Co. Notice the painted carving of a woman's face over the arched main door. From 3rd Street turn right onto MacDougal, which is one block after Sullivan. The historic ㉒ Provincetown Playhouse, which opened in 1916, is on the left side of the street. The theater has played a pivotal role in fostering the early careers of many playwrights including Edna St. Vincent Millay and Eugene O'Neill as well as numerous actors, directors and set designers, and it continues to produce innovative plays to this day.

Just a few steps north and you're back at Washington Square Park. Before you finish your tour, however, walk farther north, crossing West 4th Street and Washington Place. The building at the corner of Waverly Place with the elaborate marquee was the ㉓ home of Eleanor Roosevelt 1942-49. A plaque to the left of the entrance pays tribute to the first lady. To return to the West 4th Street Subway Station, backtrack to West 4th Street and turn right. The station is one block ahead of you.

Guided Walking Tours

Various guided walking tours are offered daily by the Municipal Art Society, based in the Urban Center at 457 Madison Ave. and 51st Street. Of interest is an in-depth look at Grand Central Terminal (see attraction listing p. 127); phone (212) 935-3960.

The Museum of the City of New York (see attraction listing p. 135) periodically conducts guided walking tours of Manhattan throughout the year. Fees vary according to tour and reservations are required; phone (212) 534-1672, ext. 3393.

Theme tours of Harlem, including jazz, soul food and art galleries, are available from Harlem, Your Way! Tours; phone (800) 382-9363. New York City Cultural Walking Tours, (212) 979-2388, offers guided tours that emphasize Manhattan's architecture and history.

Ethnic neighborhoods and historic districts are highlighted by Big Onion Walking Tours, departing from various locations; phone (212) 439-1090.

Weaving history and architecture with insight into people and events that shaped the heart of Lower Manhattan, the Downtown Alliance's free, 90-minute Wall Street Walking Tour departs from the steps of the U.S. Custom House, which houses the Smithsonian's National Museum of the American Indian (see attraction listing p. 120), every Thursday and Saturday at noon; phone (212) 606-4064.

The Times Square Business Improvement District offers tours highlighting landmarks, hotels and famous theaters in Times Square (see attraction listing p. 132). Tours depart from the Times Square Visitors Center on Broadway Fridays at noon; phone (212) 768-1560 or (212) 869-1890.

Self-guiding Walking Tours

An inexpensive way to see the city is by self-guiding walking tours. Various ethnic neighborhoods offer intriguing shops, restaurants and sidewalk fairs best sampled on foot.

Some of the best known communities include Little Italy, centering on Mulberry Street; the Jewish sector, on Essex and Orchard streets; the Middle Eastern enclave, along Atlantic Avenue; and the East Indian neighborhood, on Lexington Avenue. Check with a local AAA club for more information about what other areas would lend themselves to walking tours.

Talk-A-Walk offers audiotape tours of various Lower Manhattan attractions and the Brooklyn Bridge. The audiotapes can be obtained through the mail for $9.95 each (plus $2.90 for postage and shipping for up to six cassettes) by writing Talk-A-Walk, 30 Waterside Plaza, 10D, New York, NY 10010; phone (212) 686-0356.

Spectator Sports

No one takes sports quite as seriously as New Yorkers. Seven professional sports teams dominate the sports scene, including two football, baseball

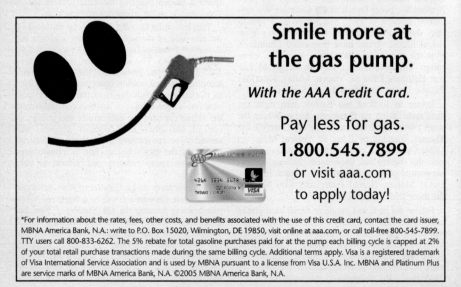

and ice hockey teams. Being a fan here involves unfeigned loyalty: Just ask Yankees and Mets fans what happens when they share a baseball stadium, or how Dodgers fans felt when their team moved to Los Angeles.

Baseball

New Yorkers are especially passionate about the national pastime. The **New York Yankees**, who produced such legendary "Bronx Bombers" as Joe DiMaggio, Lou Gehrig, Mickey Mantle and Babe Ruth, play at **Yankee Stadium** in the Bronx. This American League club won the World Series in 1996, 1998, 1999 and 2000. The season runs from April to October; phone (718) 293-4300.

The **Mets**, New York City's National League team, stole the World Series from the Boston Red Sox in 1986. They play at **Shea Stadium** in Queens. The season runs from April to October; phone (718) 507-6387 or (718) 507-8499.

The majors have several Minor League baseball counterparts. The **Staten Island Yankees** kick off the season in June at **Richmond County Bank Ballpark at St. George**. For ticket information phone (718) 720-9265. The Mets-affiliated **Brooklyn Cyclones** play at **Keyspan Stadium** on Surf Avenue in Coney Island; phone (718) 449-8497. **EAB Park** in Central Islip is where the Atlantic League's **Long Island Ducks** swing into action; phone (888) 332-5600.

Basketball

When the **New York Knicks** hit the court at **Madison Square Garden** (see attraction listing p. 128), fans are assured of an exciting game. The season runs from November to June; phone (212) 465-5867 for Knicks information, or (212) 465-6741 for the Garden.

New York loves its college hoopsters, too. The beloved **St. John's University Red Storm** occasionally play at Madison Square Garden; phone (718) 990-6211 for ticket information. The **Long Island University Blackbirds** and **St. Francis College Terriers** both hoop it up in Brooklyn; phone (718) 488-1030 for the Blackbirds and (718) 489-5490 for the Terriers. The **Fordham University Rams**, (718) 817-4300, play in the Bronx, while the **Wagner College Seahawks** take to the court at **Frederik Sutter Gymnasium** in Staten Island; phone (718) 420-4039.

Football

From September to December, Super Bowl III winners the **New York Jets** and two-time NFL champions the **New York Giants** scramble on the gridiron in **Giants Stadium** in East Rutherford, N.J., at the **Meadowlands** complex; phone (201) 935-8222 (Giants) or (516) 560-8200 (Jets). Tickets are scarce, so unless you know someone with a season pass, your plans may be sidelined.

Hockey

After a 54-year dry spell the **New York Rangers** brought home the coveted Stanley Cup in 1994 to the cheers of die-hard fans at Madison Square Garden; phone (212) 465-6741. The **New York Islanders**, Stanley Cup winners 1980-83, play out of **Nassau Coliseum** on Long Island. The season runs from November to April; phone (800) 882-4753.

Horse Racing

If you enjoy the ponies, try **Aqueduct Race Track** in Queens, (718) 641-4700; **Belmont Park Race Track** on Long Island, (718) 641-4700 or (516) 488-6000; and the Meadowlands in East Rutherford, N.J., (201) 935-3900. Harness racing can be seen at **Yonkers Raceway** in Yonkers; phone (914) 968-4200.

Note: Policies on admitting children to parimutuel facilities vary. Phone for specific information.

Recreation

When the hustle and bustle of the city streets is too much to handle, shift into a slower gear. New York's parks and beaches offer peaceful respite. The lush lawns, trees, shrubs and meadows as well as lakes, fountains, sculptures and bridges make **Central Park** (see attraction listing p. 126) a favorite spot with visitors and New Yorkers alike.

Bicycling

Roadways in Central Park are closed to motorized traffic year-round from Fri. 7 p.m.-Mon. 6 a.m. (also Mon.-Thurs. 10 a.m.-3 p.m. and 7-10 p.m., Fri. 10 a.m.-3 p.m., Apr.-Oct.). However, the transverse roads are always open to traffic. Access to three bicycle routes—6.1 miles, 5.2 miles or 1.7 miles in length—is possible by following the park drives, which encircle the park. Another option is to enter at 72nd Street and Central Park West Drive and pedal south to 59th Street, east to East Drive, then north on East Drive to 72nd Street. Exit at Fifth Avenue, or continue north along East Drive until your legs are tired.

For a scenic ride along the Hudson River, pedal around **Riverside Park**, off Riverside Drive on the Upper West Side.

Golf

Obviously you will not find a golf course in Manhattan, but the Department of Parks does operate 12 18-hole public courses in the other boroughs. On weekends golfers might have to wait as long as 8 hours before they are able to tee off; to learn of the waiting times, try the weekend news broadcasts over WNYC (93.9 FM or 820 AM).

Most fees are Mon.-Fri. $29, $25 after 1, $15 for twilight golf; Sat.-Sun. and holidays $35-$42, $26 after 1, $16 for twilight golf. Cart fees are $29, and those under 18 must have a golf permit.

Courses listed under each borough are open all year. Phone the individual courses or (718) 225-4653 for citywide reservations. The following courses accept reservations, but not for same-day playing: Clearview, Douglaston, Dyker Beach, Kissena, La Tourette, Silver Lake, South Shore and Split Rock.

The Bronx: Pelham and Split Rock courses, 870 Shore Rd., Pelham Bay Park, (718) 885-1258; and Van Cortlandt, Van Cortlandt Park South and Bailey Avenue, (718) 543-4595.

Brooklyn: Dyker Beach, Seventh Avenue and 86th Street, (718) 836-9722; and Marine Park, Flatbush Avenue between Avenue U and the Belt Parkway, (718) 338-7113.

Queens: Clearview, 23rd Avenue and Willets Point Boulevard, (718) 229-2570; Douglaston Park, Commonwealth Boulevard and Marathon Parkway, (718) 224-6566; Forest Park, Forest Park Drive and Jackie Robinson, (718) 296-0999; and Kissena, 164-15 Booth Memorial Rd., (718) 939-4594.

Staten Island: La Tourette, 1001 Richmond Hill Rd., (718) 351-1889; Silver Lake, 915 Victory Blvd., (718) 447-5686; and South Shore, Hugenot Avenue and Arthur Kill Road, (718) 984-0101.

Horseback Riding

Equestrian activity in Manhattan is confined to trails in Central Park. The **Claremont Riding Academy**, 175 W. 89th St. between Amsterdam and Columbus avenues, rents horses for $50 an hour and also offers lessons; phone (212) 724-5100. Riders must be experienced in English riding, and reservations are required.

Jogging and Walking

These are the sports of necessity in New York City, particularly if you want to get from here to there in reasonable time. For those with only the sport in mind, the hottest spot is in Central Park on the 2-mile path surrounding the Reservoir. There also are designated jogger's lanes throughout the park.

Picturesque Riverside Park, between the Hudson River and Riverside Drive, also is a popular spot. Upper Manhattan's **Riverbank State Park** attracts joggers. Other patches of greenery include **Battery Park**, at the tip of Lower Manhattan (*see attraction listing p. 115*); **Gramercy Park**, between E. 20th and 21st streets at Lexington Avenue (*see attraction listing p. 117*); and **Washington Square Park**, in Greenwich Village.

Tennis

Eight Manhattan locations have courts: Central Park, 93rd Street and West Drive; **East River Park**, at Broome Street; **Fort Washington Park**, at 172nd Street; **Fred Johnson Park**, at W. 151st Street east of Seventh Avenue; **Inwood Hill Park**, 207th Street and Seaman Avenue; Riverside Park (two sections), at 96th and at 119th streets; and **Sunken Meadow Randalls Island**. The Department of Parks issues permits; phone (212) 360-8131.

Several courts are open to the public at the site of the U.S. Open, the **U.S.T.A. National Tennis Center** in Flushing Meadows, Queens. Your best bet is to phone (718) 760-6200 2 days in advance to make a reservation; the center is busy on weekends.

Water Sports

Since New York City is surrounded by water, a great way to escape the summertime heat is to visit one of its many beaches. **Jones Beach State Park** (*see Wantagh p. 203*) is your best bet: With 6 miles of beaches, a boardwalk and a theater playing host to outdoor concerts, you'll forget all about hot blacktop. Beaches listed below can be reached by either bus or subway.

Head to **Coney Island Beach and Boardwalk** in Brooklyn to ride the wooden roller coaster or Ferris wheel; don't pass up a famous Nathan's hotdog for lunch. **Manhattan Beach**, Oriental Boulevard from Ocean Avenue to Mackenzie Street, also is in Brooklyn.

Pelham Bay Park and **Orchard Beach** are in the Bronx. **Jacob Riis Park** and **Jamaica Bay**, Beach 149th to Beach 169th streets, and **Rockaway Beach and Boardwalk**, Beach 9th to Beach 149th streets, are in Queens.

The following beaches are in Richmond (Staten Island): **Great Kills Park**, Hylan Boulevard, Great Kills; **South Beach and Boardwalk**, Fort Wadsworth to Miller Field, Midland Beach; and **Wolfe's Pond Park**, Holten and Cornelia avenues, Prince's Bay.

Few people would believe you if you claimed to have gone boating in the middle of Manhattan, but it is possible. Rowboats are for rent in Central Park at **Loeb Boathouse**, 72nd Street and Fifth Avenue, for $10 an hour and a $20 deposit; phone (212) 517-2233, ext. 3. As for swimming, only a few municipal pools are still open: **Lasker Pool** on the north end of Central Park is one. Phone the New York City Parks and Recreation Swimming Information hotline at (718) 699-4219 for the latest on pool locations and openings.

Looking for one-stop recreation? Visit **Chelsea Piers**, a 30-acre sports village along the Hudson River between 17th and 23rd streets. Highlights of the four renovated shipping piers include heated hitting stalls for golfers, a 25-yard swimming pool, an indoor running track, a hockey rink open to ice skaters and an outdoor roller rink. Sailing, kayaking and speedboat tours of the harbor also are offered. Various shops and eateries call the historic piers home; phone (212) 336-6666.

Winter Sports

When there is a chill in the air, New Yorkers head to the nearest ice skating rink to participate in a living portrait by Currier and Ives. The rink at **Rockefeller Center** (*see attraction listing p. 130*) has more glitz, especially when the giant Christmas tree is lit in December. Every year nearly 100,000 skaters are enticed to take a turn on the ice beneath a fabulous golden sculpture of Prometheus.

In 1986 real-estate tycoon Donald Trump paid to have **Wollman Memorial Rink** in Central Park refurbished, to the delight of fellow New Yorkers. Skating is from October to March. There also is a smaller venue on the north end of Central Park, **Lasker Rink**, and the **World's Fair Ice Skating Rink** in Flushing Meadows Corona Park is open all year and has rentals (*see attraction listing p. 138*).

Shopping

New York is a shopping mecca for whatever your heart desires. You will have no trouble hunting down the basics or the extravagances in the stores lining block after enticing block.

While Peter Minuit got the best trade in the city's history—in 1626 he paid $24 for Manhattan Island, currently worth more than $50 billion—Manhattan is still a borough of bargains. The saying "I can get it for you wholesale" is nowhere more applicable.

Antiques

There are plenty of places in the city for antique lovers to indulge their whims. Good hunting grounds for antiques are along Madison Avenue; on Second and Third avenues from the upper 40s to the 80s; on E. 55th Street; and on 57th Street.

Manhattan Art and Antiques Center, 1050 Second Ave. between 55th and 56th streets in Midtown Manhattan, has nearly 100 shops with furniture, glassware, jewelry, pottery and other period pieces sold by a number of independent vendors.

For those looking for something a bit more down to earth, flea markets set up almost every weekend. Try the **Outdoors Annex Antiques Fair and Flea Market**, Sixth Avenue between W. 24th and 27th streets, or the **SoHo Antiques Fair, Collectibles and Crafts**, Broadway and Grand streets.

Malls

Typical American malls do not exist in New York City. Such a compact urban area lacks the luxury of unlimited space and miles of parking; expect something a little different and quite a bit more extravagant here.

Stern's department store anchors the **Manhattan Mall**, W. 33rd Street at Sixth Avenue in Midtown Manhattan, and its collage of 60 shops. The eight-floor mall boasts four glass elevators, marble flooring and free entertainment.

Large malls are mostly found outside Manhattan. **Kings Plaza Shopping Center** is an enclosed mall 1 mile north of Belt Parkway exit 11N in Brooklyn. Elmhurst, in Queens County, has **Queens Center**, 2 blocks west of the Long Island Expressway (I-495) on Queens Boulevard. **Staten Island Mall**, 2 miles south of I-278 on Richmond Avenue, has 170 stores, including Macy's and Sears.

The Market at Citicorp Center, on Lexington at 54th Street, is a seven-story building housing international restaurants and shops. The atrium contains an indoor garden cafe with skylights; free entertainment is offered daily.

From designer originals to sweet treats, one of the 200 stores at **Rockefeller Center** (see attraction listing p. 130) is bound to carry what you crave. **Trump Tower**, 725 Fifth Ave. at E. 56th Street, has an elegant collection of fashion, food and gift shops within its glass, marble and bronze atrium. The building, reputedly the tallest concrete structure in New York, includes walkways, hanging gardens and an 80-foot waterfall.

Shoppers make a day of it at the **South Street Seaport Museum** (see attraction listing p. 120) complex on the East River. Here, **Fulton Market** sells a variety of goods at what was once a fish market. Fresh produce is still available, and there are trendy retailers like **Ann Taylor** and **Abercrombie & Fitch**.

While one-stop shopping in suburbia means the mall, in Midtown Manhattan it means the department store. Among New York's leading department stores are **Bloomingdale's**, 1000 Third Ave. at 59th Street; **Lord & Taylor**, Fifth Avenue at 38th Street; and **Saks Fifth Avenue**, 611 Fifth Ave. at 50th Street. And let's not forget **Macy's**, known as the world's largest store, 151 W. 34th St. at Herald Square.

Takashimaya, 693 Fifth Ave. near 54th Street, is a popular Japanese store, and **Alfred Dunhill Ltd.**, 450 Park Ave. at 57th Street, is a haven for gifts.

Women's clothing is the specialty of **Bergdorf Goodman**, Fifth Avenue at 57th Street; and **Wallach's**, 4123 13th Ave. in Brooklyn. **Bolton's**, with several locations including 57th Street between Fifth and Sixth avenues, and **Loehmann's**, on Seventh Avenue at W. 16th Street, are renowned for their discounted women's apparel.

For men's clothing, try **A. Sulka & Co.**, Park Avenue at 56th Street; **Barney's**, 660 Madison Ave. at 61st Street; **British American House**, 488 Madison Ave.; **Brooks Brothers**, Madison Avenue at 44th Street; and **Paul Stuart**, Madison Avenue at 45th Street.

In Midtown Manhattan at 1540 Broadway in Times Square is **Planet Hollywood**, where the fascination with all that is Hollywood is captured in souvenirs ranging from designer T-shirts to key chains to leather jackets.

Outlets

Despite the emphasis on high-priced merchandise, New York also has plenty of bargains. The city prides itself on its discount clothing houses. Buying from exporters and wholesalers on **Seventh Avenue** can be rewarding, but there are some restrictions: usually cash-only transactions and no returns.

Clothing outlets are found all along Madison and Fifth avenues and along side streets between the Garment District (see attraction listing p. 127) and 85th Street.

Burlington Coat Factory, 707 6th Ave., is said to be the largest coat retailer in the country. It sells designer merchandise at a hefty discount. Go to **Syms**, 42 Trinity Pl. in the financial district, to buy bargain-priced men's and women's apparel. Do not expect doting salesclerks, and be ready to pay in cash.

In addition, you may find discounts of up to 80 percent on shoes, handbags and clothing at **Daffy's**, 111 Fifth Ave. at E. 18th Street in Lower Manhattan.

Specialty Districts

Often many shops of the same specialty are found within a radius of several blocks. These informal groupings are a boon for shoppers, who reap the benefits of convenience and competitive prices.

Art galleries are grouped between Fifth and Madison avenues from 45th to 85th streets; bookstores cluster between Madison and Fifth avenues, 46th to 57th streets, and 57th Street between Seventh and Third avenues. Flower markets adorn the 28th Street and Sixth Avenue area. And rumor has it that the **Diamond District**, W. 47th Street between Fifth and Sixth avenues near Rockefeller Center, is where most of the big deals on big rocks are made.

Macy's anchors the **34th Street Shopping District**, Midtowns Manhattan's 31-block retail, dining and entertainment hub bounded by Park and Tenth avenues and 31st and 36th streets.

Rows and rows of small retail shops sell shoes, suits, linens and more are at the **Historic Orchard Street Shopping District** on the Lower East Side.

Let it be known: **Fifth Avenue** is to shoppers what Baskin Robbins is to most ice cream lovers. For a seemingly limitless selection of goods visit the area from 54th to 59th streets, give or take a block in either direction. Here you can find **Tiffany & Co.** and **F.A.O. Schwarz**. Simply window shopping is quite a treat. Scoot down 57th Street, east or west, for more browsing at **Rizzoli Bookstore**, **Ann Taylor** and **Hermes**.

Shops that rival those on Fifth Avenue can be found on Manhattan's Upper East and West sides. Lots of glitter and plenty of funky threads can be found along **Columbus Avenue** (West Side) between 70th and 83rd streets. **Madison Avenue** (East Side) from 59th to 79th streets is another shoppers' playground, with dozens of retailers and restaurants galore. The **Crystal District** features the luxury boutiques of Daum, Baccarat, Lalique, Steuben and Swarovski on Madison Avenue between 58th and 63rd street.

For gourmet and specialty food items, follow your nose to Lower Manhattan's **Chelsea Market**, occupying a full block on Ninth Avenue between 15th and 16th streets. Built by Nabisco in 1890, this former commercial building is where the first Oreo cookie was baked.

Jewelry and handicraft items can be found in stores at **Greenwich Village** (see attraction listing p. 117). If you do not see what you want, describe it to the shopkeeper—who often also is the artisan—and he or she will either be able to make it for you or tell you where to obtain it.

Performing Arts

The soul of New York City—its unique vibrance and urban beat—bears witness to a love of the arts and a willingness to share this fascination with everyone. The choices are endless—theater, music, opera, dance, film; traditional or experimental; indoors or outdoors; free or ticketed. There is no escaping the delightful barrage of offerings.

Most types of performances take place at **Lincoln Center for the Performing Arts** (see attraction listing p. 128) at Broadway and 65th Street. Its plaza includes **Alice Tully Hall**, (212) 875-5050, the only public concert hall of orchestral size to be constructed in the city since 1891; **Avery Fisher Hall**, (212) 875-5030; **Juilliard School of Music**, (212) 769-7406; **Metropolitan Opera House**, (212) 362-6000; the **New York State Theater**, (212) 870-5570; **Vivian Beaumont and Mitzi E. Newhouse theaters**, (212) 239-6200; and the **Walter Reade Theater**, (212) 875-5600.

Dance

As the nation's cultural mecca, New York City invests a great deal of time and money into its expressive nature, including dance. The greats have all danced here, and Mikhail Baryshnikov, Gregory Hines and Rudolf Nureyev even embraced the city as their home turf.

In a class by itself, the **New York City Ballet** garners rave reviews for its performances of contemporary works under the guidance of well-respected, inventive choreographers. The troupe performs November through February at the New York State Theater at Lincoln Center. The **American Ballet Theatre** presents the classics and some newer ballets to a global audience at the nearby Metropolitan Opera House from April through June.

Modern dance enthusiasts flock to several distinguished venues, such as the **Joyce Theater** in Lower Manhattan. This dance emporium caters to all forms, from its ballet company in residence, the **Ballet Tech** to more contemporary, avant-garde works.

In seasons past, Midtown Manhattan's **City Center**, the city's largest concert hall, has played host to such great modern troupes as the **Alvin Ailey Dance Company**, the **Dance Theater of Harlem**, the **Joffrey Ballet** and the **Paul Taylor Dance Company**. The venue is on 55th Street between Sixth and Seventh avenues; phone (212) 581-1212.

Film

Moviegoing is an event in New York City. You can see the latest blockbusters, an oldie but goodie and everything in between. Foreign and domestic art films are abundant, with both small and large houses catering to those in the mood for an offbeat documentary or underground film.

The Walter Reade Theater at the Lincoln Center schedules repertory showings, sometimes by genre or director. It's an ideal setting for studying film. The **Florence Gould Hall**, 55 E. 59th St., Midtown Manhattan, also shows films; phone (212) 355-6160.

Several museums and art societies hold their own film revivals. In Queens, head to the **Museum of the Moving Image** for an American film series. In Midtown Manhattan **Asia Society Museum, The Museum of Modern Art** (rare classics) and **Museum of Television and Radio** have showings. See attraction listings under What To See.

Foreign and independent films are shown throughout the city. Try the **Film Forum**, 209 W. Houston St.,(212) 627-2035; **The Joseph Papp Public Theater**, 425 Lafayette St., (212) 260-2400; or **Millennium**, 66 E. Fourth St., (212) 673-0090.

Music

Musical director Kurt Masur conducts the illustrious **New York Philharmonic Orchestra**, the oldest symphony in the United States, in Avery Fisher Hall at the Lincoln Center for Performing Arts September through June. In July and August the Philharmonic performs free concerts under the stars in various city parks. The innovative **American Symphony Orchestra** also performs in Avery Fisher Hall.

The **Chamber Music Society** of Lincoln Center performs in Alice Tully Hall at the Lincoln Center from September through May, often in conjunction with visiting ensembles and famous soloists. Don't forget to check out the **Brooklyn Academy of Music (BAM)**, 30 Lafayette Ave., which boasts an active opera performance schedule as well as its orchestra in residence, the Brooklyn Philharmonic. Phone (718) 636-4100.

The famed **Carnegie Hall**, 57th Street and Seventh Avenue, plays host to celebrated orchestras, noted conductors and a variety of performers *(see attraction listing p. 126)*. **Town Hall**, noted for its fine acoustics and excellent seating layout, is between Sixth and Seventh avenues on 43rd Street; phone (212) 840-2824.

There are dozens of classical music locales throughout the city and plenty of performances to choose from, even concerts for children put on by the **Little Orchestra Society**; phone (212) 971-9500 for current offerings. The group normally appears at Florence Gould Hall, 55 E. 59th St., the **Sylvia and Danny Kaye Playhouse**, 695 Park Ave., and Lincoln Center.

For complete, current information about outdoor concerts, phone the City Parks Events Hotline at (212) 360-3456.

Opera

Tenor Luciano Pavarotti brings the house down every time he performs with the **Metropolitan Opera Company** in the elegant surroundings of the Metropolitan Opera House at Lincoln Center. The Met's season runs from September to April and normally includes crowd pleasers like "La Boheme," "Rigoletto" and "Figaro." Founded in the late 1880s, the Met continues to captivate audiences.

The **New York City Opera**, which performs September to April, assembles at the Lincoln Center's New York State Theater. This younger company also is known for fine performances, including "Carmen" and "Madame Butterfly." The **Amato Opera Theatre** offers a classic repertoire at its Lower Manhattan location; phone (212) 228-8200 for performance dates and times.

Theater

New York is the theater capital of the world. Whether on Broadway, off-Broadway or off-off-Broadway, the glitzy bright lights of New York's theater district beckon showgoers from around the world. Simply put, theater *flourishes* in New York City.

Theater Ticket Bargains

Theater tickets for Broadway and off-Broadway shows are sold at a discount on performance day at two TKTS booths. The Times Square booth, in Midtown Manhattan, is at Broadway and 47th Street. Ticket purchase hours are 3-8 for Mon.-Sat. evening tickets; 10-2 for Wed. and Sat. matinee tickets. For Sun. matinee and evening tickets purchase hours begin at 11.

In Lower Manhattan tickets can be purchased at the South Street Seaport booth, on Front Street, Mon.-Sat. 11-6 for evening performances and 11-3:30 for Sun. evening shows. Matinee tickets must be purchased a day in advance.

© NYC & Company

A $3 surcharge is added to the ticket price. Only cash or travelers checks are accepted. Caution: lines form early. For more information phone (212) 221-0013.

Free coupons for a 30 to 50 percent discount off the box-office purchase price of tickets for some shows are available at many newsstands, coffee shops and drugstores, and from the New York Convention and Visitors Bureau *(see The Informed Traveler)*. The coupons are seldom valid on weekends.

Television Show Tickets

If available, tickets to attend the major television shows can be obtained from the networks. Contact the networks' respective Guest Relations Offices: American Broadcasting Co., 38 W. 66th St., New York, NY 10023, (212) 456-3537; Columbia Broadcasting System, 524 W. 57th St., New York, NY 10019, (212) 975-2476; and National Broadcasting Co., 30 Rockefeller Plaza, New York, NY 10012, (212) 664-3056.

Centered on the Times Square area between 41st and 53rd streets from Eighth to Sixth avenues are the theaters that have perpetuated the magic of Broadway—only two of these theaters are actually on Broadway. Glittering marquees announce the latest productions.

The categories of Broadway and off-Broadway indicate the size of the theater—all off-Broadway houses have fewer than 465 seats. This size distinction allows apparent contradictions in that some of the theaters in the Times Square area are classified as off-Broadway; other houses almost next door are described as Broadway theaters.

While the Broadway shows stick to the formula of name stars, writers and directors, the off-Broadway productions are noted for their experimental presentations and revivals. These sometimes equal or surpass the artistry of Broadway and are usually the offerings of young hopefuls, although it is not uncommon for a Broadway "name" to appear in them.

Some Broadway theaters have become as well-known as the mainstream blockbuster plays they have supported, like "*Les Miserables*" at the **Imperial** and "The Phantom of the Opera" at the **Majestic. The Ford Center for the Performing Arts** on 42nd Street is home to the revival production of one of Broadway's longest running musicals, "42nd Street". The **Lunt-Fontanne Theatre** on W. 46th Street presents the long-running Disney musical classic "Beauty and the Beast"; phone (212) 827-5451. *See color ad p. 428.*

Off-Broadway has its share of fine productions and performers, many along W. 42nd Street in places like the **Playwright's Horizons.**

Cherry Lane Theatre, 38 Commerce in Greenwich Village, is where many young actors got their start.

Queens Theatre in the Park, in the New York State Pavilion at Flushing Meadows Corona Park, presents a year-round schedule of plays, children's theater and dance; phone (718) 760-0064.

Off-off-Broadway is a free-for-all of experimental performances, usually by unknowns with something to say. Performances are staged at smaller venues and in out-of-the-way cafes.

Current theater listings appear in *New York* and *The New Yorker* magazines, in the newspapers and in *Variety*, a weekly newspaper devoted to the entertainment world, including off-Broadway theaters in Greenwich Village.

Tickets to Broadway shows are hard to come by but not impossible. Advance planning is the key to obtaining the best tickets for the best prices. Seats to Broadway shows are on sale anywhere from 3 months to 1 year in advance. Otherwise, TKTS booths at Times Square in Midtown Manhattan and near the South Street Seaport in Lower Manhattan sell discounted tickets on the day of the performance *(see Theater Ticket Bargains)*. Seating varies and there is a service charge, but the effort may be well worth your while. In addition, tickets generally are available at theater box offices a few hours before show time (usually 8 p.m.).

Hit Show Club offers discounts of up to 50 percent off Broadway theater tickets. For a complete listing of services phone (800) 222-7469. *See color ad p. 433.*

© AAA

Theater Map Key

❶ Al Hirschfeld	⑲ Longacre
❷ Ambassador	⑳ Lunt-Fontanne
❸ American Airlines	㉑ Lyceum
❹ Belasco	㉒ Majestic
❺ Booth	㉓ Marquis
❻ Broadhurst	㉔ Minskoff
❼ Broadway	㉕ Music Box
❽ Brooks Atkinson	㉖ Neil Simon
❾ Cadillac Winter Garden	㉗ New Amsterdam
❿ Circle in the Square	㉘ New Victory
⓫ Cort	㉙ Palace
⓬ Ethel Barrymore	㉚ Plymouth
⓭ Eugene O'Neill	㉛ Richard Rodgers
⓮ Ford Center	㉜ Royale
⓯ Gershwin	㉝ St. James
⓰ Helen Hayes	㉞ Shubert
⓱ Imperial	㉟ Virginia
⓲ John Golden	㊱ Walter Kerr

© 2006 NAVTEQ

Or contact a ticket agency. Agencies charge a fee in addition to the price printed on the ticket; they also may charge a service fee for delivery of tickets to the hotel or box office.

Special Events

Most ethnic groups in New York City observe at least some of their native holidays with parades, festivals or celebrations. When dates vary for events listed below, only the month in which the event occurs is given. For a comprehensive listing of special events, contact the New York Convention and Visitors Bureau *(see The Informed Traveler).*

It is said that everyone loves a parade, and New Yorkers may love them more than most. Spring parades include **St. Patrick's Day** and **Greek Independence Day** in March; **Easter** in March or April; **American Ethnic** in April; **Solidarity Day, Armed Forces Day, Norwegian Constitution Day** and **Memorial Day** in May; and **Israeli Day**, held in the spring (the month varies).

Parades spanning the rest of the year include **Puerto Rican Day** in June; **Labor Day, Steuben Day, African-American Day** and **West Indian-American Day**, in September; **Pulaski Day, Desfile de la Hispanidad: Columbus Day** and **Columbus Day** in October; **Greenwich Village Halloween** on Oct. 31; and **Veterans Day** and **Macy's Thanksgiving Day Parade** in November.

When not parading, New Yorkers attend festivals: **Ukrainian** and the **Ninth Avenue International Food** in May; **Saint Anthony** in June; **Shakespeare**, held June through August; **Festa Italiana** and **Fourth of July Fireworks** in July; **Greenwich Village Jazz** in August and September; and the **Feast of San Gennaro**, which occurs in mid-September.

Then there are celebrations that cannot be classified as either parades or festivals: **Chinese New Year** in late January; **Museum Mile** in June; **Harlem Week** and **Lincoln Center Out-of-Doors** in August; and the **New York is Book Country Day** in September.

Other seasonal events include the beginning of the circus engagement in March or April; the annual **Egg Rolling** contest in Central Park, held the Saturday before Easter; **Washington Square Outdoor Art Show** from late May through June and August to mid-September; the opening of the **Metropolitan Opera season** in September; the **Tree Lighting Ceremony and Christmas Carols** at Rockefeller Center in December; Christmas services throughout the month of December; and the famous **New Year's Eve Celebration** in Times Square.

Take note of such musical events as **Juilliard's Focus! Festival** in January; the **Rockettes' Easter Show** at Radio City Music Hall; and the **Mostly Mozart Festival** at Lincoln Center in July or August. The **New York Film Festival** presents an international menu of movies from late September to mid-October.

Sporting events include the **U.S. Open Tennis Championships**; since 1978 such greats as Andre Agassi, Steffi Graf and Pete Sampras have played at the **Arthur Ashe Stadium** in Flushing. The tournament takes place annually in late August and early September. Following in November are the **Chase Championships of the Janex Women's Tennis Association Tour** and the **New York City Marathon**, which begins in Staten Island and ends in Central Park.

The New York City Vicinity

CROSS RIVER (I-11)

WARD POUND RIDGE RESERVATION, jct. SRs 35 and 121, is a 4,700-acre park and wildlife sanctuary. Camping shelters and picnic areas are available, as are hiking and skiing trails and a wildflower garden. Plant, animal and American Indian artifacts displays are in the Delaware Indian Resource Center in the Trailside Nature Museum. Park open daily 8-dusk. Museum open Tues.-Sun. 9-4; closed Jan. 1, Thanksgiving and Dec. 25. Admission $8 per private vehicle. Phone (914) 864-7317.

CROTON-ON-HUDSON (I-11)
pop. 7,606, elev. 8'

Croton-on-Hudson, once part of the estate of Van Cortlandt Manor *(see attraction listing),* was founded by Irish and Italian laborers working on the Croton Reservoir dam in the 1840s. During the 1920s the town became a fashionable haven for intellectuals, including poet Edna St. Vincent Millay, feminist Doris Stevens, journalist John Reed and economist Stuart Chase.

Croton Point Park is a retreat for recreation seekers. Surrounded on three sides by the Hudson River, the 504-acre park offers swimming, fishing, camping, cross-country skiing and hiking; a nature center also is available. At the southern tip of the peninsula is Teller's Point, where a small group of Revolutionary War patriots repelled HMS *Vulture* while British Maj. John Andre met secretly onshore with Benedict Arnold to plot the takeover of West Point. Unable to return to his ship, Andre fled but was captured later near Tarrytown; the conspiracy was exposed.

VAN CORTLANDT MANOR is off US 9 at 525 S. Riverside Ave. This restored 18th-century Dutch-English manor house on 20 acres of what was originally an 86,000-acre estate shows the lifestyle of a patriotic family just after the American Revolution. Family portraits, furniture, silver and porcelains are exhibited. Costumed interpreters demonstrate 18th-century craft skills. The restored Ferry House and Ferry House Kitchen at the east end supplied food and lodging to travelers on the Albany Post Road.

Guided tours are available. Allow 1 hour minimum. Wed.-Mon. 10-5, Apr.-Oct.; Sat.-Sun. 10-4, Nov.-Dec. Closed Thanksgiving and Dec. 25. Last tour begins 1 hour before closing. Grounds $5. Grounds and guided tour $10; over 61, $9; ages 5-17, $6. AX, DS, MC, VI. Phone (914) 631-8200 or (914) 271-8981.

GARRISON (H-11)

BOSCOBEL is 8 mi. n. of Bear Mountain Bridge on SR 9D in the Hudson River Valley. The facade of the restored 1804 New York Federal-style mansion has three unusual draperies of carved wood. Other features include *trompe*

l'oeil wallpaper, period furniture, china and silver. The grounds offer a panorama of the Hudson Valley and contain a gatehouse, springhouse, orangery, herb garden and woodland walk.

Guided tours are available. Grounds Wed.-Mon. 9:30-5, Apr.-Oct.; Wed.-Mon. 9:30-4, Nov.-Dec. Closed Thanksgiving and Dec. 25. Last tour begins 45 minutes before closing. Grounds $7; ages 6-14, $5. Tour $10; over 62, $9; ages 6-14, $7. MC, DS, VI. Phone (845) 265-3638.

GRAYMOOR SPIRITUAL LIFE CENTER, US 9 just s. of SR 403, is on a mountaintop overlooking the Hudson River Valley. Home of the Franciscan Friars of the Atonement, the center contains many shrines and chapels. Picnicking is permitted. Grounds open daily dawn-dusk. Free. Phone (845) 424-3671.

KATONAH (I-11) elev. 226'

CARAMOOR HOUSE MUSEUM is off I-684 exit 6, just e. on SR 35, then 1.8 mi. s. on SR 22 to 149 Girdle Ridge Rd. This house museum is one of only five in the country whose original owners collected entire rooms, usually from European estates, to create their homes. Walter and Lucie Rosen built the Mediterranean-style house 1929-39 and filled it with Eastern, Medieval and Renaissance art and artifacts. The home sits on 100 acres with elaborate gardens.

Allow 1 hour minimum. Wed.-Sun. 1-4, May-Oct; Tues.-Fri. by appointment, rest of year. Last tour begins 1 hour before closing. Admission $10, under 16 free. Phone (914) 232-8076.

JOHN JAY HOMESTEAD STATE HISTORIC SITE, 400 Jay St. (SR 22), was the retirement home of the first chief justice of the United States and second governor of New York. The house has restored period rooms with family memorabilia and portraits by American artists. The grounds include landscape plantings and 19th- and 20th-century farm outbuildings.

Guided tours are available. Allow 1 hour minimum. Tues.-Sat. 10-4, Sun. 11-4, Apr.-Oct.; hours vary rest of year. Guided tours are given on the hour. Admission $7; over 62, $5; under 12 free. Phone (914) 232-5651.

[SAVE] **KATONAH MUSEUM OF ART,** SR 22 and Jay St., presents changing exhibits from major museums, artists and private collectors. Allow 30 minutes minimum. Tues.-Sat. 10-5, Sun. noon-5; closed major holidays and during the installation of new exhibits. Guided tours are offered Tues.-Sun. at 2:30. Admission $5, under 12 free. Free to all before noon. Phone (914) 232-9555.

MOUNT VERNON (H-1)
pop. 68,381, elev. 100'

In 1850, a merchant tailor named John Stevens founded the Industrial Home Association with the goal of helping working-class New Yorkers buy their own homes. More than 1,000 people joined, and the association collected enough dues to purchase 369 acres of farmland. In a vote to select the town name, Monticello was the original winner. With that name already taken, Mount Vernon won in the second round.

ST. PAUL'S CHURCH NATIONAL HISTORIC SITE is at 897 S. Columbus Ave. (SR 22). The 6-acre site includes a museum, a historic church and cemetery, and the remnants of a town village green. The church was used as a hospital during the Revolutionary War Battle of Pell's Point; Aaron Burr argued law in the church's makeshift courtroom after the war. Guided tours are available. Mon.-Fri. 9-5. Donations. Phone (914) 667-4116.

NEW CITY (H-1) pop. 34,038, elev. 163′

Several farms and orchards in the New City area allow visitors to pick their own strawberries and apples during harvest time.

Rockland County Office of Tourism: 18 New Hempstead Rd., New City, NY 10956; phone (845) 708-7300 or (800) 295-5723.

HISTORICAL SOCIETY OF ROCKLAND COUNTY is off Palisades Pkwy. exit 11, e. onto New Hempstead Rd., then n. at Main St. to 20 Zukor Rd. The museum presents changing exhibits, including a holiday miniature dollhouse display in December. Guided tours of an 1832 restored Dutch farmhouse are offered some Sundays; phone for dates. Allow 30 minutes minimum. Tues.-Sun. 1-5; closed federal holidays and briefly between exhibits. Hours may vary; phone ahead. Admission $5; ages 6-12, $3. Rates may vary during holiday season. Phone (845) 634-9629.

NEW ROCHELLE (H-2) pop. 72,182, elev. 72′

The New Rochelle area was settled in 1688 by Huguenot refugees who named their community after their old home, La Rochelle, in France. New Rochelle grew quickly due to its healthy shipbuilding industry, its location as a key port of trade with New York City and other nearby harbors and its position on the strategic Boston Post Road, the major route to cities farther north.

In the 1890s the town became a popular retreat for noted actors, artists and authors, including Eddie Foy, Agnes Booth and Frederic Remington. The town still is known as a wealthy suburb of commuters who work in New York City.

The Thomas Paine Cottage, 20 Sicard Ave., was the home of the American political theorist and writer. A museum 100 yards north houses Thomas Paine artifacts. Both are open to the public. Phone (914) 633-1776 for Friday through Sunday hours and fees.

New Rochelle Chamber of Commerce: 459 Main St., New Rochelle, NY 10801; phone (914) 632-5700.

NORTH SALEM (H-11) pop. 5,137

[SAVE] HAMMOND MUSEUM AND JAPANESE STROLL GARDEN is off I-684 exit 7, 4.3 mi. e. on SR 116, then n. on SR 124 to Deveau Rd., following signs. The museum's collections include decorative arts, Asian art and photographs by Carl Van Vechten. The grounds feature indigenous plantings mixed with Japanese and Chinese specimens, waterfalls, ponds, a bamboo grove and meandering paths. Wed.-Sat. noon-4, Apr. to mid-Nov. Admission $5; over 61, $4; under 12 free. Phone (914) 669-5033.

NYACK (H-1) pop. 6,737, elev. 100′

Nyack's way of life has always been tied to the Hudson River: The Nyack Indians gathered oysters on its banks, European settlers established a prosperous river landing and today pleasure craft abound. Artist Edward Hopper was born in Nyack in 1882; his boyhood home is now a public art gallery.

The Nyacks Chamber of Commerce: P.O. Box 677, Nyack, NY 10960; phone (845) 353-2221.

Self-guiding tours: Brochures outlining several walking tours through historic and scenic areas in Nyack are available for a nominal fee from Friends of the Nyacks, P.O. Box 120, Nyack, NY 10960. Phone (845) 358-4973.

OSSINING (H-2) pop. 24,010, elev. 8′

TEATOWN LAKE RESERVATION, w. off Taconic Pkwy. to SR 134, then 1 mi. n. to 1600 Spring Valley Rd., is an 834-acre environmental education center and nature preserve with 15 miles of nature trails. Changing exhibits relating to mammals, birds, plants and geology are presented in a museum; live native birds of prey also are on view.

Guided tours of Wildflower Island, including a display of rare orchids, are available by appointment May 1 through Sept. 15. Nature center open Tues.-Sun. 9-5; closed major holidays. Grounds open daily dawn-dusk. Donations. Phone (914) 762-2912.

PURCHASE (H-2) elev. 355′

DONALD KENDALL SCULPTURE GARDENS, off Anderson Hill Rd. at PepsiCo, is a 114-acre garden with modern sculpture. Highlights include exotic trees and shrubs, a water lily pool and works by such artists as Henry Moore, Alexander Caulder and Auguste Rodin. A self-guiding tour brochure is available. Daily dawn-dusk. Free. Phone (914) 253-2000.

NEUBERGER MUSEUM OF ART is at 735 Anderson Hill Rd. on the campus of Purchase College, State University of New York (SUNY). The museum features 10-12 changing exhibitions of modern, contemporary and emerging American and European artists annually, as well as a permanent exhibition of African art. The museum offers lectures, workshops, gallery tours, performances and special events throughout the year.

Allow 1 hour minimum. Tues.-Fri. 10-4, Sat.-Sun. 11-5; closed major holidays. Guided gallery talks are conducted Tues.-Fri. at 1, Sun. at 2 and 3, mid-Sept. through June 30. Admission $5, over 61 and students with ID $3, under 12 free, free to all first Sat. of the month. Parking Mon.-Fri. $6. Phone (914) 251-6100.

RYE (H-2) pop. 14,955, elev. 49′

PLAYLAND, off I-95 exit 19 following signs to Playland Pkwy., is a recreational complex offering rides, a beach and boardwalk, a saltwater lake, riverboat excursions, an 18-hole miniature golf and a children's park. Playland was among the earliest totally planned amusement parks in the country. Features include original Art Deco buildings, a long grass mall, the Dragon Coaster and a vintage carousel. Free entertainment is provided daily.

Allow 3 hours, 30 minutes minimum. Park opens Wed.-Sun. at noon, Tues. at 11, closing times vary, late June-Labor Day; Wed.-Fri. at 10, Sat.-Sun. and Memorial Day at noon, closing times vary, late May to late June; Sat.-Sun. at noon, closing times vary, early to late May and day after Labor Day-Sept. 30. Hours may vary; phone ahead. Six-hour unlimited rides wristband $35; 36-ticket book $28; 24-ticket book $21; individual ride tickets $1. Additional admission is charged for the beach, pool and miniature golf course. Parking Sat.-Sun. $7, Tues.-Fri. $5, holidays $10. MC, VI. Phone (914) 813-7000.

SLEEPY HOLLOW (H-2) pop. 9,212

Sleepy Hollow, North Tarrytown until 1996 when the residents voted to change the town's name, is on the east bank of the Hudson, where the river widens to form the Tappan Zee. In 1680, near where the Pocantico River flows into the Hudson, Frederick Philipse built a stone house, a church and other buildings. The church was popularized by Washington Irving in "The Legend of Sleepy Hollow."

HEADLESS HORSEMAN BRIDGE carries US 9 across the Pocantico River where the old bridge once stood from which, in Irving's story, the headless horseman hurled his pumpkin head at Ichabod Crane.

 KYKUIT, THE ROCKEFELLER ESTATE is off SR 119; tours depart from Philipsburg Manor on US 9 (see attraction listing). Home to four generations of the Rockefeller family, Kykuit, meaning lookout, is on a hilltop overlooking the Hudson River. Built in 1913 under the supervision of John D. Rockefeller's son Junior, the stone mansion is appointed with antiques, fine art and family memorabilia. The fine art collection includes paintings from the mid-20th century.

Fountains and a collection of 20th-century sculpture assembled by Nelson A. Rockefeller accent the terraced and formal gardens. The coach barn contains vintage automobiles and carriages.

Food is available. Allow 2 hours, 30 minutes minimum. House and Inner Garden Tour departs every 15 minutes Wed.-Mon. 10-3, late Apr.-early Nov. Other tours are available; phone ahead for schedule. Note: Tours are not recommended for under age 10. House and Inner Garden Tour $22; over 61, $20; under 18, $18. Fees for other tours vary. AX, DC, DS, MC, VI. Phone (914) 631-9491.

PHILIPSBURG MANOR, on US 9, is an early 18th-century commercial complex that consists of a stone manor house, an operating gristmill, an oak-timbered dam and a barn. Farming, trading and milling operations were carried out by slaves owned by the Philipse family, wealthy Anglo-Dutch merchants. The house is furnished with period artifacts. Costumed guides lead tours, and a reception center offers exhibits.

Food is available. Allow 2 hours minimum. Wed.-Mon. 10-5, Apr.-Oct.; Wed.-Mon. 10-4, Nov.-Dec.; Sat.-Sun. 10-4, in Mar. Closed Thanksgiving and Dec. 25. Last tour begins 1 hour before closing. Admission $10; over 61, $9; ages 5-17, $6. AX, DS, MC, VI. Phone (914) 631-8200.

SLEEPY HOLLOW CEMETERY, on US 9, includes the graves of Washington Irving, Andrew Carnegie, William Rockefeller and Whitelaw Reid. Daily 8:30-4:30. Free. Phone (914) 631-0081.

UNION CHURCH OF POCANTICO HILLS is at 555 Bedford Rd. John D. Rockefeller, Jr. donated the land and funds for the construction of the nondenominational church in 1921. It contains stained glass windows by Henry Matisse and Marc Chagall. Allow 30 minutes minimum. Wed.-Fri. and Mon. 11-5, Sat. 10-5, Sun. 2-5, Apr.-Dec. Admission $5, under 6 free. Phone (914) 332-6659.

STONY POINT (I-10) pop. 11,744, elev. 32′

STONY POINT BATTLEFIELD STATE HISTORIC SITE is 8 mi. s. of the Bear Mountain bridge off US 9W on Park Rd. This was the location of a successful midnight assault by the American Corps of Light Infantry, commanded by Brig. Gen. Anthony Wayne, against a British garrison in July 1779. A museum presents exhibits. Interpreters in period dress offer demonstrations with muskets and artillery; cooking and the daily tasks of camp life also are portrayed.

Picnicking is permitted. Allow 1 hour minimum. Grounds Mon.-Sat. 10-5, Sun. noon-5, Apr.-Oct. Museum Wed.-Sat. and Mon. holidays 10-4:30, Sun. noon-4:30. Admission Sat.-Sun. $5 per private vehicle; otherwise free. Increased admission may be charged during special events. Phone (845) 786-2521.

TAPPAN (H-1) pop. 6,757, elev. 50′

Historically, Tappan is best noted for being the setting for the prologue and denouement of the Benedict Arnold-Maj. John Andre conspiracy. At his DeWint House headquarters, Gen. George Washington gave the command of West Point to Arnold, who arranged to betray the garrison to the British.

However, Arnold's contact, Andre, was captured, and the plans were uncovered. Andre was jailed in the old Seventy-Six House and executed by hanging on what is known as Andre Hill. His body was later traded for that of Gen. Richard Montgomery, who was killed in the Siege of Quebec in 1775. Andre was interred in Westminster Abbey in 1821.

GEORGE WASHINGTON'S HEADQUARTERS AT TAPPAN (The DeWint House), 20 Livingston St. at Oak Tree Rd., was built in 1700 and was used on occasion by Gen. George Washington as an army headquarters during the Revolutionary War. This restored house features furnished period rooms. The Carriage House Museum contains Washington artifacts and various memorabilia. Daily 10-4; closed Jan. 1, Thanksgiving and Dec. 25. Donations. Phone (845) 359-1359.

TARRYTOWN (H-2) pop. 11,090, elev. 14′

"In the bosom of one of those spacious coves which indent the eastern shore of the Hudson, at that broad expansion of the river denominated by the Tappan Zee there lies a small market town or rural port, which by some is called Greenburgh, but which is more generally and properly known as Tarry Town."

So Washington Irving described the town nearest the bucolic little glen that figures in "The Legend of Sleepy Hollow." Tarrytown is joined on the south by Irvington and on the north by Sleepy Hollow, formerly North Tarrytown. These three communities form the well-known Sleepy Hollow country.

According to Irving the name of Tarrytown was given by housewives "from the inveterate propensity of their husbands to linger about the village tavern on market days."

Near the boundary of Sleepy Hollow and Tarrytown British spy Maj. John Andre was captured, exposing Benedict Arnold's treachery.

Sleepy Hollow Chamber of Commerce: 54 Main St., Tarrytown, NY 10591; phone (914) 631-1705.

LYNDHURST, .2 mi. e. of jct. US 9 and I-287 at 635 S. Broadway (US 9), overlooks the Hudson River and is one of the nation's finest examples of Gothic Revival architecture. The house is furnished in Gothic, Beaux Arts and French 19th-century styles. The interior has ribbed and vaulted ceilings, figured bosses, stained-glass windows and panels, and walls painted to resemble dressed stone. Landscaped grounds surround the mansion.

Allow 1 hour minimum. Tues.-Sun. and Mon. holidays 10-5, mid-Apr. through Oct. 31; Sat.-Sun. and Mon. holidays 10-4, rest of year. Closed Jan. 1, Thanksgiving and Dec. 25. Last tour begins 45 minutes before closing. Grounds $4. Grounds and house tour $10; over 61, $9; ages 12-17, $4. Phone (914) 631-4481.

DID YOU KNOW

New York was named for the Duke of York, who later became James II of England.

PATRIOTS' PARK, on Broadway (US 9), contains Andre Brook, the dividing line between the Tarrytowns. Captors' Monument is topped by a bronze figure of John Paulding, one of the captors of British spy Maj. John Andre. Daily dawn-dusk. Free. Phone (914) 631-8347.

WASHINGTON IRVING MEMORIAL, W. Sunnyside Ln. at Broadway (US 9), is by Daniel Chester French, sculptor of the seated figure in the Lincoln Memorial in Washington, D.C. The memorial consists of a bust of the author with figures of characters from his stories. Daily 24 hours. Free. Phone (914) 631-1705.

WASHINGTON IRVING'S SUNNYSIDE, .5 mi. s. of Tappan Zee Bridge on US 9 to W. Sunnyside Ln., was the home of Washington Irving 1835-59. Set at the bottom of a hill next to the Hudson River, this is the home the romantic Irving called his "little snuggery." The house was built in the late 17th century as a tenant farmer's cottage and was occupied in the 18th century by a branch of the Van Tassel family that figures in "The Legend of Sleepy Hollow."

Irving modified the house, planned the grounds and planted wisteria and ivy vines. The interior has features that were far advanced for their day, such as a bathtub with running water and a hot water tank in the kitchen fed by pipes from the pond that Irving called the "Little Mediterranean." Costumed guides explain the house and its furnishings, which include the author's library.

Picnicking is permitted. Allow 1 hour minimum. Wed.-Mon. 10-5, Apr.-Oct.; Wed.-Mon. 10-4, Nov.-Dec.; Sat.-Sun. 10-4 in Mar. Closed Thanksgiving and Dec. 25. Last tour begins 1 hour before closing. Grounds $5. Grounds and tour $10; over 61, $9; ages 5-17, $6. AX, DS, MC, VI. Phone (914) 631-8200.

WEST HAVERSTRAW (I-10)
pop. 10,295, elev. 100'

The village of West Haverstraw is in the area 17th-century Dutch landholders called Haverstraw, meaning oat straw. Merchant trade out of Haverstraw Bay shored the community in the early years,

giving way to textile milling and a lucrative brick-making industry that grew to include 42 plants by 1885. Helen Hayes Hospital, founded in 1900 and later named in honor of the First Lady of the American Theater for her 49 years of service on its visitors' board, is one of the village's major employers.

The Ramapo Mountains, to the west, and Lake Sebago, off Seven Lakes Parkway, offer year-round recreational opportunities.

From its home port at Haverstraw Marina, Hudson Highlands Cruises offers narrated Hudson River sightseeing excursions between West Haverstraw and West Point aboard the MV *Commander*, a 1917 ferry boat commissioned by the U.S. Navy during World War I; phone (845) 534-7245.

MARIAN SHRINE, 2 mi. e. of Palisades Pkwy. exit 14 off Filors Ln., includes among its 200 acres an Italian marble rosary way, a replica of the St. John Bosco birthplace and a 48-foot bronze statue of the Rosary Madonna. Daily 9-5. Donations. Phone (845) 947-2200.

WHITE PLAINS (H-2) pop. 53,077, elev. 201'

Seat of Westchester County, White Plains was the birthplace of the state; the first Provincial Congress met at this site on July 10, 1776. Gen. George Washington headquartered here during the last phase of the Battle of White Plains.

Westchester County Office of Tourism: 222 Mamaroneck Ave., White Plains, NY 10605; phone (914) 995-8500.

Shopping areas: Galleria Mall is 2 blocks east of Bronx River Parkway exit 21 at 100 Main St. Among its 149 stores are JCPenney and Sterns.

WHITE PLAINS NATIONAL BATTLEFIELD SITE consists of three monuments, one at Chatterton Hill and two on Battle Avenue. The monuments mark Washington's position during the Battle of White Plains, fought Oct. 28, 1776. Daily 24 hours. Free.

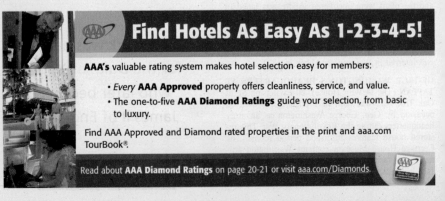

YONKERS (H-1) pop. 196,086, elev. 300'

Once a village of the Manhattes Indians, the site of Yonkers was part of a parcel of land granted to Adriaen Cornelissen van der Donck by the Dutch West India Co. in 1646. His title, De Jonkheer, became the city's name.

Today the city is a major industrial center, supported by more than 100 different industries. Despite its nearness to New York City, the city is not a bedroom community—most of its breadwinners are employed in Yonkers.

Yonkers Chamber of Commerce: 20 S. Broadway, Suite 1207, Yonkers, NY 10701; phone (914) 963-0332.

Shopping areas: Cross County Shopping Center, south of Cross County Parkway exit 5, has 108 stores, including Sterns and Wanamakers.

THE HUDSON RIVER MUSEUM OF WESTCHESTER, 511 Warburton Ave., overlooks the Hudson River and includes changing exhibitions of 19th- and 20th-century American art from its permanent collection. The elements of art, history and science are combined in a given subject. Within the museum complex are the 19th-century Glenview Mansion and the Andrus Planetarium. Programs for senior citizens and children are offered regularly.

Food is available. Allow 1 hour, 30 minutes minimum. Museum open Wed.-Sun. noon-5 (also Fri. 5-8); closed major holidays. Planetarium shows Fri. at 7, Sat.-Sun. at 12:30, 1:30, 2:30 and 3:30. Museum $5; over 62 and ages 5-16, $3; free to all Fri. 5-8. Planetarium $2; over 62 and ages 5-16, $1; free to all Fri. Phone (914) 963-4550.

PHILIPSE MANOR HALL STATE HISTORIC SITE is at 29 Warburton Ave. This 17th-century residence of wealthy gristmill owner Frederick Philipse was the nucleus of a vast estate that eventually became the town of Yonkers. At one time it served as the city hall; today it is a museum of history, art and architecture. Guided tours are available. Allow 1 hour minimum. Tues.-Fri. noon-5, Sat.-Sun. 11-5, Apr.-Oct.; Sat.-Sun. noon-4, rest of year. Closed holidays. Admission $4; over 62 and students with ID $3; ages 5-12, $1. Phone (914) 965-4027.

Central Park, Midtown Manhattan / © age fotostock / SuperStock

This ends listings for the New York City Vicinity.
The following page resumes the alphabetical listings of cities in New York.

Niagara Falls

(including Niagara Falls, Ontario)

Maid of the Mist / © Steve Vidler / eStock Photo

City Population: 55,593   **Elevation:** 571 ft.

Editor's Picks:

Cave of the Winds Trip............ *(see p. 162)*

Maid of the Mist................... *(see p. 164)*

Niagara Falls........................*(see p. 164)*

Young in geologic time, Niagara Falls were created by the recession and melting of a mammoth ice sheet. As the ice retreated some 50,000 years ago the land rose behind it, forming such ridges as the Niagara Escarpment. The melting ice formed a vast lake in what is now Lake Erie and its surrounding lowlands; the lake overflowed about 12,000 years ago, creating Niagara Falls.

The falls originally formed 7 miles north in what is now Lewiston. Due to erosion they are currently about midway between lakes Erie and Ontario on the Niagara River, a 37-mile-long strait that is bisected by the international boundary. The cities of Niagara Falls, N.Y., and Niagara Falls, Ontario, are connected by bridges across the river.

The Canadian, or Horseshoe, Falls are 177 feet high with a deeply curving crest of about 2,200 feet. The American Falls, higher at 184 feet, have a shorter, fairly straight crest of about 1,075 feet. The third and smallest of Niagara's falls, Bridal Veil, is separated from the other falls by Luna and Goat islands.

Untouched, the combined flow of the water over the falls would be about 1.5 million gallons per second; however, one-half to three-quarters of the river is diverted for the generation of electricity before it reaches the falls. Most of the siphoning is done at night. The water flow is reduced to about 700,000 gallons per second during the tourist season and to less at other times.

The first people to gaze upon this natural spectacle were ancestors of the Seneca Indians. They were the area's first inhabitants some 2,000 years ago. One of the earliest Europeans to view the falls was French priest Father Louis Hennepin in 1678. History recounts that upon seeing the spectacle Hennepin fell to his knees in prayer, saying of the falls that "the universe does not afford its parallel."

In the next few years the French built and rebuilt several forts at the mouth of the river. Old Fort Niagara *(see Youngstown p. 168)* was to play key roles in the major wars of the next 90 years. In 1759, during the French and Indian War, the British captured the fort. They held it until 1796 when they withdrew to Fort George in Canada.

The War of 1812 was the most devastating to hit Niagara Falls. Many small settlements on both sides of the river were looted and burned. Niagara Falls witnessed the Battle of Lundy's Lane, the war's bloodiest, on July 25, 1814. Neither side could claim victory in that fierce conflict. Five months later the Treaty of Ghent ended 2.5 years of fighting and reinstated the boundary line.

After the war Niagara Falls entered a new era of peace and prosperity. Settlement began in earnest, and by 1892 Niagara Falls was incorporated as a city. With the arrival of steamships in 1820, the Erie

Getting There — *starting on p. 159*

Getting Around — *starting on p. 159*

What To See — *starting on p. 162*

What To Do — *starting on p. 166*

Where To Stay — *starting on p. 516*

Where To Dine — *starting on p. 525*

Canal in 1825 and the railroad in 1840, the town became accessible to tourists. An old saw predicts that "the love of those who honeymoon here will last as long as the falls themselves."

A different type of romance lured daredevils to the falls in the 1800s and early 1900s. The first stuntster was Sam Patch. He survived two dives into the waters below the falls. The first person to go over the falls in a barrel was Annie Taylor in 1901. William Fitzgerald took the plunge in 1961. He was arrested as soon as he surfaced, because stunts on the river and falls had by then been outlawed.

In 1895 the world's first commercial hydroelectric plant was built at the falls. The Niagara Power Project opened in 1961 with 13 generators and a total installed power of 2,190,000 kilowatts, one of the largest hydroelectric facilities in the world. But the power won't last forever; the falls are eroding about an inch per year. For the next 2,500 years, however, the falls will look much the same as they have since Father Hennepin's visit.

Getting There

By Car

Traffic arriving from the south can connect with a part of the New York State Thruway (I-90), which interchanges with both I-290 and I-190. I-190, an expressway spur, leads across Grand Island to Niagara Falls, connecting with the major arteries to downtown. For the most direct and scenic route to the falls from I-190 take the Robert Moses Parkway and follow the signs to Niagara Falls State Park (see attraction listing p. 164).

From points east, access is primarily via I-90, which collects traffic from across the state. From the

© Andre Jenny

Rochester area, however, SRs 31 and 104 each offer an alternate route to the city.

Approaches from the west are via any of several highways in Canada, with three bridges funneling traffic stateside: the Rainbow Bridge in the southwest part of the city near Prospect Park; the Whirlpool Rapids Bridge in the northwest just below Whirlpool State Park (see attraction listing p. 165); and the Lewiston-Queenston Bridge in Lewiston, which connects the northern end of I-190 with Canada's Hwy. 405.

Getting Around

Street System

In Niagara Falls the streets are laid out in the traditional grid pattern. Numbered streets run north to south, from First Street on the western edge of the city to 102nd Street on the eastern boundary. Named streets generally run east to west. Avenues run east to west, and roads and boulevards run north to south or diagonally.

Destination Niagara Falls

While the falls are Niagara's primary diversion, the area offers more than meets the eye.

See how the river's power is harnessed at Power Vista, the Niagara Power Project's visitor center. Cross a footbridge and hike wooded Goat Island. Say hello to a colony of Peruvian penguins at the Aquarium of Niagara. Or view some contemporary art at the Castellani Art Museum.

Maid of the Mist, Niagara Falls. Put this exhilarating boat ride on your list of things to do while visiting. (See listing page 164)

© Tom Carroll Index Stock Imagery

© Byron Jorjorian / Alamy

Prospect Point Observation Tower, Niagara Falls. Elevators inside this 260-foot tower whisk visitors up to the observation deck or down to the *Maid of the Mist* boarding dock. (See listing page 165)

Power Vista, Lewiston Falls. Interactive exhibits reveal how the Niagara Power Project transforms the power of the falls into electricity. (See listing page 167)

Niagara Falls

CANADA U.S.A.

•Burt

•Youngstown

Lewiston•

•Lockport

Niagara Falls

See Vicinity map page 163

ONT. N.Y.

© Gibson Stock Photography

Places included in this AAA Destination City:

The Informed Traveler

Sales Tax: The sales tax in Niagara Falls is 8 percent. An additional 12 percent is levied for hotel/motel rooms, and 12 percent is added for rental cars.

WHOM TO CALL

Emergency: 911

Police (non-emergency): (716) 286-4711

Time and Temperature: (716) 844-1717

Hospitals: Mount St. Mary's, in Lewiston, (716) 297-4800; Niagara Falls Memorial Medical Center, (716) 278-4000.

WHERE TO LOOK

Newspapers

Niagara Falls has one daily paper, the morning *Niagara Gazette*. The *Buffalo News*, as well as such metropolitan dailies as the *New York Times* and the *New York Daily News* also are available.

Radio

Radio station WEBR (970 AM) is an all-news/weather station; WBFO (88.7 FM) is a member of National Public Radio.

Visitor Information

Niagara Tourism and Convention Corp.: 345 Third St., Suite 605, Niagara Falls, NY 14303; phone (716) 282-8992 or (800) 338-7890. *See color ad p. 521 and coupon in Savings Section.*

For parks information contact the New York State Parks Commission in Prospect Park at (716) 278-1770.

TRANSPORTATION

Air Travel

The nearest airport offering major domestic and international flight service is the Buffalo-Niagara Falls International Airport at Genesee Street and Cayuga Road. Shuttle buses run between the airport and major hotels; phone (800) 551-9369. Taxi service is available with fares averaging $35. Short- and long-term parking is available at SunPark at 4099 Genesee St.; phone (716) 633-6040.

The Niagara Falls International Airport on Porter Road serves charter and private flights.

Rental Cars

Hertz, (716) 297-1800 or (800) 654-3080, offers discounts to AAA members. For listings of other agencies check the telephone directory.

Rail Service

Passenger rail service is available at the Amtrak station at Hyde Park Boulevard and Lockport Road; phone (716) 285-4224.

Buses

Connections by bus may be made at Portage and Ashland roads; phone (716) 285-9319.

Taxis

Cab companies include LaSalle Cab Co., (716) 284-8833, and United Cab Co., (716) 285-9331. Rates are $1.50 for the first half-mile, then 75c for each additional sixth of a mile. For a complete list of taxi services check the telephone directory.

Public Transport

The Niagara Frontier Transportation Authority (Metro) offers bus service within the city and outlying areas, including connections to Lockport and Buffalo. Service is generally from 5 a.m. to 10:30 p.m. Fares are $1.50 plus 25c for each additional zone; over 64, ages 5-11 and the physically impaired 65c plus 10c for each additional zone; phone (716) 285-9319.

Robert Moses Parkway parallels the river as it runs along the extreme western and southern edges of Niagara Falls, while Niagara Expressway (I-190) bypasses downtown traffic as it hugs the eastern edge before crossing into Canada.

Parking

Parking is plentiful on the U.S. side of the river and ranges from on-street parking to free or pay lots. State-owned lots are in Prospect Park and on the east and west ends of Goat Island. Pay lots average a minimum of $3 per day.

What To See

[SAVE] **AQUARIUM OF NIAGARA,** 701 Whirlpool St. at Pine Ave. (US 62), has more than 1,500 aquatic animals ranging from the Great Lakes to the coral reefs and is home to a large collection of Great Lakes fish. Visitors can see California sea lions, piranhas and more. Highlights include a colony of endangered Peruvian penguins, a shark exhibit and an outdoor harbor seal pool. The aquarium is the site of the 81st "Whaling Wall" by marinelife artist Wyland.

Open daily at 9. Closing hours vary; phone ahead. Closed Thanksgiving and Dec. 25. Penguins are fed daily at 9:30 and 2:30; seals are fed daily at 11 and 3:45; and sharks are fed on alternate days at 11:30. Admission $8; over 59, $6.50; ages 4-12, $5.50. AX, DS, MC, VI. Phone (716) 285-3575 or (800) 500-4609.

BEDORE TOURS departs from the Howard Johnson at the Falls at 454 Main St., near the Rainbow Bridge, and from area hotels. The U.S./Canadian Deluxe Combo Tour, the All-American Adventure Tour and the All-Canadian Adventure Tour are among the excursions offered. Each tour visits the American, Horseshoe and Bridal Veil falls. The day tours also include sightseeing aboard the *Maid of the Mist* tour boats, the Cave of the Winds Trip and Skylon Tower *(see attraction listings).*

Departures daily Apr.-Oct. During peak season there are three tours daily. Fare for All-American Adventure Tour or All-Canadian Adventure Tour $69.95; ages 6-12, $39.95. U.S./Canadian Deluxe Combo Tour $129.90; ages 6-12, $69.90. Reservations are required. AX, DS, MC, VI. Phone (716) 696-3200 or (800) 538-8433.

[GEM] **CAVE OF THE WINDS TRIP,** on Goat Island *(see attraction listing),* follows wooden walkways to within 25 feet of the base of the falls. An elevator takes visitors 175 feet through the Niagara rock escarpment into the Niagara Gorge to view the falls from the bottom. After donning a souvenir raincoat and footwear, visitors are guided to the Hurricane Deck, just 20 feet from the roaring Bridal Veil Falls, where a good dousing can be expected. Rainbows are generally visible day and night.

The Gorge Trip, which operates seasonally, takes guests by elevator down into the Niagara Gorge to an observation deck at the base of Bridal Veil Falls.

Lockport / © Lockport Locks and Erie Canal Cruises

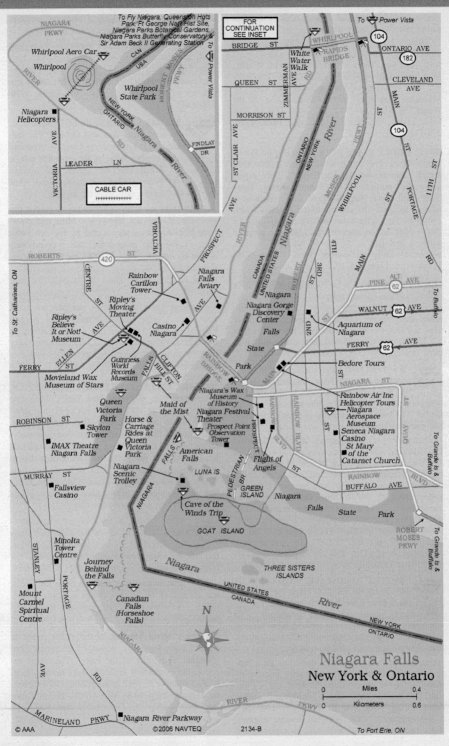

To Fly Niagara, Queenston Hgts
Park, Ft George Nat'l Hist Site,
Niagara Parks Botanical Gardens,
Niagara Parks Butterfly Conservatory &
Sir Adam Beck II Generating Station

FOR
CONTINUATION
SEE INSET

NIAGARA
PKWY

Whirlpool Aero Car

Whirlpool

Niagara
Helicopters

LEADER LN

CABLE CAR

CAN
USA

Whirlpool
State Park

FINDLAY
DR

WHIRLPOOL

BRIDGE ST

QUEEN ST

MORRISON ST

White
Water
Walk

RAPIDS
BRIDGE

104

ONTARIO AVE

182

CLEVELAND
AVE

104

ROBERTS ST

420

Rainbow
Carillon
Tower

Ripley's
Moving
Theater

Ripley's
Believe
It or Not!
Museum

Movieland Wax
Museum of Stars

FERRY ST

Niagara
Falls
Aviary

Casino
Niagara

Guinness
World
Records
Museum

Queen
Victoria
Park

Skylon
Tower

IMAX Theatre
Niagara Falls

ROBINSON ST

MURRAY ST

Fallsview
Casino

Minolta
Tower
Centre

Journey
Behind
the Falls

Mount
Carmel
Spiritual
Centre

Maid of
the Mist

Horse &
Carriage
Rides at
Queen
Victoria
Park

Niagara
Scenic
Trolley

Canadian
Falls
(Horseshoe
Falls)

Niagara
Niagara Gorge
Discovery
Center

Falls

State

Park

Niagara's Wax
Museum
of History

Niagara Festival
Theater

Prospect Point
Observation
Tower

American
Falls

LUNA IS

Cave of the
Winds Trip

GOAT ISLAND

Flight of
Angels

GREEN
ISLAND

Aquarium of
Niagara

FERRY AVE 62

Bedore Tours

Rainbow Air Inc
Helicopter Tours
Niagara
Aerospace
Museum
Seneca Niagara
Casino
St Mary
of the
Cataract Church

RAINBOW

BUFFALO AVE

Niagara

Falls State Park

ROBERT
MOSES
PKWY

THREE SISTERS
ISLANDS

UNITED STATES
CANADA

Niagara

River

NEW YORK
ONTARIO

N

Niagara Falls
New York & Ontario

Miles
0   0.4
Kilometers
0   0.6

Niagara River Parkway

© AAA   ©2006 NAVTEQ   2134-B   To Fort Erie, ON

To Power Vista

To St. Catharines, ON

To Buffalo

To Grande Is &
Buffalo

To Grande Is &
Buffalo

MARINELAND PKWY

Also available is a special viewing deck for children and physically impaired persons.

Allow 1 hour minimum. Cave of the Winds Trip Sun.-Thurs. 9 a.m.-10 p.m., Fri.-Sat. 9 a.m.-11 p.m., July-Aug.; Sun.-Thurs. 9-9, Fri.-Sat. 9 a.m.-10 p.m., May-June; daily 9-8, Sept.-Oct. Gorge Trip daily 9-5, late Mar. to mid-May and late Oct.-Dec. 31. Schedules may vary; phone ahead. Cave of the Winds Trip $10; ages 6-12, $7. Gorge Trip $3; ages 6-12, $1.50. AX, DC, DS, MC, VI. Phone (716) 278-1730.

DEVIL'S HOLE STATE PARK is 7 mi. n. on Robert Moses Pkwy. This small wooded park offers wonderful views of the Niagara Gorge and the rapids along this portion of the Niagara River. Three trails—part of the Niagara Gorge Trail System—run through the park and connect to trails within Whirlpool State Park a mile upriver. One path follows the bluff's edge and another descends into the gorge to within a few feet of the rapids. Allow 30 minutes minimum. Daily dawn-dusk. Free. Phone (716) 284-4691, or (716) 278-1070 for trail information.

FLIGHT OF ANGELS is at 310 Rainbow Blvd. S. A tethered helium balloon rises 400 feet in the air and offers views of the falls. Allow 30 minutes minimum. Daily 9 a.m.-midnight, June-Sept.; 10-10 in May and Oct. (weather permitting). Fare $20; under 12, $10; family rate $55-$60 (two adults and up to three children). MC, VI. Phone (716) 278-0824.

MAID OF THE MIST boats depart from the dock at Prospect Point Observation Tower on the American side and is also listed in Niagara Falls, Ontario, where this information is included. The boats pass directly in front of the falls and enter the Horseshoe Basin.

Trips depart daily beginning at 9:15, Memorial Day weekend and mid-June through Labor Day; at 10, mid-Apr. through day before Memorial Day weekend (depending on ice conditions in the river), day after Memorial Day to mid-June and day after Labor Day-Oct. 24. Closing times vary; phone ahead. **Note:** These hours reflect the American side; the Canadian side runs 15 minutes earlier. Fare (waterproof clothing included) $11.50; ages 6-12, $6.75. Elevator cost included. MC, VI. To confirm daily schedules phone (716) 284-8897 in N.Y. or (905) 358-5781 in Ontario.

NIAGARA AEROSPACE MUSEUM is at 345 Third St. Exhibits trace the development of aviation from its beginnings to recent space exploration programs, with emphasis on achievements in western New York. A hall of fame highlights contributing scientists, inventors, entrepreneurs and aviators.

Among the full-size aircraft displayed are a replica of a 1910 Curtiss bamboo and wire airframe biplane; a GA-36 experimental airplane and a Piper Cub, both built in the 1930s; a Schweitser Sailplane flown during World War II; and a rare 1947 Bell 47B-3 helicopter. Other exhibits feature engines, flight simulators, model airplanes, photographs and

aviation paraphernalia. Films of historical moments in aviation are shown in three small theaters.

Allow 1 hour, 30 minutes minimum. Tues.-Sun. 10-4, Memorial Day to mid-Sept.; Tues.-Sat. 10-3, rest of year. Admission $7; senior citizens and college students with ID $6; ages 5-18, $4; family rate (up to 6 persons) $25. MC, VI. Phone (716) 278-0060.

NIAGARA FALLS is in the Niagara River between New York and Ontario. The falls are divided into three cataracts separated by islands. Horseshoe Falls, on the Canadian side, is the widest. Bridal Veil, the middle and smallest falls, surges between Goat and Luna islands. And the 184-foot American Falls is the highest.

While there are many opportunities to gaze at this spectacle, it was not always so. Mills and plants once blocked public access, and by the late 1860s most of the land around the falls was privately owned by entrepreneurs. In 1885 the falls were reclaimed for public enjoyment through the creation of the Niagara Reservation, the nation's first state park.

Excellent views of the river and falls are available from several vantage points within Niagara Falls State Park (see attraction listing). Each night the falls are illuminated for 2.5 to 3.5 hours after dusk. A variety of guided sightseeing tours also is available (see What to Do/Sightseeing).

NIAGARA FALLS STATE PARK, at Prospect Point, covers more than 400 acres. New York's oldest state park, it opened in 1885. The visitor center has information about area attractions. The Rainbow Cubs, Rainbow and Droplet, greet visitors and offer storytelling and interactive shows for children at various sites throughout the park. Park open daily dawn-dusk. Visitor center open daily at 7; closing time varies. Rainbow Cub performances are given Tues.-Sun. 9:30-4, Memorial Day-Labor Day. Free. Phone (716) 278-1796. See Recreation Chart.

Goat Island, in the Niagara River, separates the Canadian and American falls. Easily accessible by foot or vehicular bridge, this wooded island has paved drives and walks that offer spectacular views from the edges of both falls.

The Three Sisters Islands, which lie in the rapids, are accessible by footbridge, as is Luna Island, which lies between the American and Bridal Veil falls.

Niagara Festival Theater, in the visitor center at Niagara Falls State Park, presents a 23-minute film, "Niagara: A History of the Falls." The movie recounts the events that made the falls famous, from its first sighting in 1697 to the present. Shows every 60 minutes daily 10-8; May 16-day before Labor Day; 10-6, Labor Day-Oct. 1; 9-5, Apr. 1-May 15 and Oct. 2-Dec. 31. Admission $2; ages 6-12, $1. Phone (716) 278-1792.

NIAGARA GORGE DISCOVERY CENTER, .5 mi. n. of the Rainbow Bridge, is accessible from Robert Moses Pkwy. following signs. This center offers interactive displays and a multiscreen theater presentation about the natural history of the Niagara Gorge and the falls. A geological garden, scenic overlook, climbing wall and gorge trailhead are on the grounds. Guided hikes are available for a fee.

Allow 1 hour minimum. Daily 9-7, Memorial Day-Labor Day; 9-5, late Mar.-day before Memorial Day and day after Labor Day-late Nov. Last theater presentation begins 30 minutes before closing. Admission $3; ages 6-12, $1.50. Climbing wall $5 for 1 climb, $10 for 3 climbs (weather permitting). AX, DS, MC, VI. Phone (716) 278-1070, or (716) 278-0337 for information about the climbing wall.

SAVE NIAGARA'S WAX MUSEUM OF HISTORY, 303 Prospect St., exhibits figures such as Princess Diana and Mother Theresa as well as famous explorers and statesmen prominent in area history. Barrels and other implements used by daredevils who attempted a tumble over the falls and a hall of presidents also are displayed. Daily 9:30 a.m.-11 p.m., May 15-Sept. 15; 10-5, rest of year. Closed Dec. 25. Admission $7; over 64 and ages 6-12, $6. AX, MC, VI. Phone (716) 285-1271.

SAVE OVER THE FALLS TOURS, offers pick-up service at area accommodations. A variety of sightseeing tours cover highlights of Niagara Falls, N.Y., and Niagara Falls, Ontario, including opportunities to ride the *Maid of the Mist* and visit Journey Behind the Falls, Cave of the Winds, Table Rock, Goat Island, Konica Minolta Tower Centre, Skylon Tower and other key viewing areas. Other tours are available.

Allow 4 hours, 30 minutes minimum. Tours depart daily 8-7. Hours may vary; phone ahead. Fare $68.95; ages 5-12, $42.95; under 5 on lap free. Reservations are required. AX, DS, MC, VI. Phone (716) 283-8900 or (877) 783-8900.

PROSPECT POINT OBSERVATION TOWER, next to the American Falls in Prospect Park, is a 260-foot structure that rises above the cliffs. Stairs lead from the tower to the Crow's Nest, an observation area beside the falls. Four elevators descend into the gorge, permitting access to the base of the falls and *Maid of the Mist* boats *(see attraction listing),* which board near the landing. Open daily at 9:30, early Apr.-late Oct.; closing time varies. Admission $1, under 6 free. Phone (716) 284-8897.

SAVE RAINBOW TOURS OF NIAGARA offers pick-up service at local lodgings. The 4- to 5-hour bus tours visit either the Canadian or American sides of the falls and include a ride on the *Maid of the Mist* boat. The American tour goes to Cave of the Winds, the Whirlpool, and Goat, Luna and Three Sisters islands. Canadian tour highlights include Dufferin Island, Konica Minolta Tower Centre, Niagara Parks Floral Showhouse and the Floral Clock. Other tours are available.

Daily 8:30-5:30. Hours may vary; phone ahead. Fare $71.99; ages 5-12, $44.95; under 5 on lap free. AX, DC, DS, MC, VI. Phone (716) 773-7087.

ST. MARY OF THE CATARACT CHURCH, 259 Fourth St., was built in 1847. Highlights of this renovated church include 19th-century stained glass windows and a steeple as tall as the American Falls. Open daily 8-5. Free. Phone (716) 282-0059.

SAVE THUNDER THEATER is at 21 Michael O'Laughlin Dr. Through a 4-D sensory film, viewers go on a Niagara Falls discovery journey. The film is preceded by a quiz show with audience participation. Allow 30 minutes minimum. Shows daily on the half-hour 9:30 a.m.-10 p.m., May-Oct. Hours may vary; phone ahead. Admission $9.95; ages 3-10, $7.95. AX, DS, MC, VI. Phone (716) 205-0770.

WHIRLPOOL STATE PARK, on the Robert Moses Pkwy. n. of the Whirlpool Bridge, is on a bluff overlooking the whirlpool that results from the Niagara River's 90-degree turn. Gorge and rim trails are available. Ramps and steps wind along the gorge. Daily dawn-dusk. Free. Phone (716) 284-5778.

CASINOS

- **Seneca Niagara Casino** is at 310 Fourth St. Daily 24 hours. Phone (716) 299-1100.

What To Do

Sightseeing

Sightseeing is what Niagara Falls is all about, and there is an amazing array of ways to view the falls. Many of the attractions listed in the What To See section are basically different forms of sightseeing.

Information about guide services and sightseeing companies is available from your local AAA club or from the Niagara Falls Tourism and Convention Corp. (see The Informed Traveler). The New York State Parks Commission, (716) 285-3892, also has area sightseeing information.

Bus and Van Tours

Major tour bus companies include Coach USA, (716) 372-5500; Gavin Travel Service Inc., (716) 282-3715; Grand Island Transit, (716) 433-6777; SAVE Gray Line of Niagara Falls, (716) 695-1603; and SAVE Niagara Majestic Tours, (716) 285-2113.

NIAGARA SCENIC TROLLEY can be boarded at several locations on Goat Island and near Prospect Point Observation Tower (see attraction listings). Thirty-minute tours follow a 3-mile route and take visitors close to the falls and other points of interest as guides provide historical narration. Stopovers are made at six sites, and passengers have the option of getting on and off the trolley as they choose.

Sun.-Thurs. 9 a.m.-10:30 p.m., Fri.-Sat. 9 a.m.-11:30 p.m., July 1-Labor Day; daily 9 a.m.-9:30 p.m., mid-May through June 30 and in Sept.; daily 9-9, Apr. 1 to mid-May; daily 9-6:30, Oct.-Dec.; daily 9-5, rest of year. Fare $2; ages 6-12, $1. MC, VI. Phone (716) 278-1796.

Helicopter Tours

RAINBOW AIR INC. HELICOPTER TOURS, departing from 454 Main St., offer views of both the American and Canadian falls. Daily 9-dusk. Fare for 10-12 minutes $75. MC, VI. Phone (716) 284-2800.

Sports and Recreation

Niagara Falls has several city and state parks that offer recreational opportunities, as do nearby lakes Erie and Ontario. Most parks offer picnicking, scenic views and nature trails; several have fishing, swimming, tennis courts, bike trails and playgrounds. Boating and fishing are available at many sites on lakes Erie and Ontario, which also have sandy beaches for swimming.

In the southeast are Griffon, Hennepin, Jayne and LaSalle parks; in the southwest, Niagara Falls State Park (see attraction listing p. 164 and Recreation Chart) comprises Prospect Park, Upper Rapids Park and Goat Island. In the northwest are Devil's Hole and Whirlpool state parks and Centre Court and Unity city parks.

In the center of Niagara Falls at Hyde Park Boulevard and Pine Avenue is Hyde Park, the largest of the city parks. Hyde Park has two nine-hole public golf courses and a swimming pool.

During winter several of the nature trails in the area's parks convert to cross-country skiing and snowmobile trails. Downhill skiing is available within an hour's drive at Kissing Bridge, the Alpine Recreation Area or Tamarack Ridge, all southeast on SR 240.

For further information about recreational facilities phone the state parks commission at (716) 278-1770, or the city parks service at (716) 286-4943.

Shopping

Souvenirs of the falls can be found downtown on Main Street, just a few minutes from the Rainbow Bridge. Three Sisters Trading Post offers gifts, souvenirs and American Indian crafts. Nearby Artisans Alley at 10 Rainbow Blvd. is a shop and gallery featuring the works of more than 600 artisans. A 1-mile strip of Pine Avenue/Niagara Falls Boulevard known as Little Italy is lined with unique shops, Italian eateries and an open-air market. Summit Park Mall, on Williams Road between SR 384 and US 62, is anchored by The Bon-Ton and Sears.

For those on a budget or just looking for a good deal, Prime Outlets at 1900 Military Rd. offers savings on such items as clothing, glassware, jewelry, shoes, accessories and toys; stores include Bass, Liz Claiborne, Ralph Lauren and Mikasa.

Visitors to the Canadian side can shop for discounted merchandise at the Niagara Duty Free Shop.

Note: Visitors to Niagara Falls, Ontario, should be aware that currency exchange rates vary by merchant and are sometimes lower than the official rate offered by banks. U.S. Customs regulations limit or prohibit the importation of certain goods (such as sealskin products) from Canada; further information is available at customs offices or in the Border Regulations section of the Canadian TourBooks.

Performing Arts

Theatrical and musical performances can be found in nearby Buffalo and at Earl W. Brydges ArtPark, 7 miles north on Robert Moses Parkway in Lewiston (see place listing p. 167).

Special Events

Re-enactors from the United States and Canada create a 1759 historical battle during the French and Indian War Encampment held at Old Fort Niagara State Historic Site in Youngstown (see place listing p. 168) in early July. Winterfest Niagara lights up the city throughout the holiday season, late November through December, with a parade, musical performances and a fair.

The Niagara Falls Vicinity

BURT (D-3) pop. 400

SAVE **MURPHY ORCHARDS** is off Wilson-Burt Rd. at 2402 McClew Rd. Offered is a variety of narrated 30- and 90-minute theme tours of a working farm. Agricultural, wildlife or historical tours may include a tractor-drawn wagon ride through orchards, planting and cider pressing demonstrations, a visit to a petting zoo or information about the farm's role as a stop on the Underground Railroad. Visitors may also take a self-guiding tour and pick fruit.

Picnicking is permitted. Food is available. Daily 8:30-6:30. Guided tours require a minimum of 10 persons for departure. Grounds free. Thirty-minute tour fee $1.95. Ninety-minute tour fee $3.50. Reservations are required for guided tours. AX, DS, MC, VI. Phone (716) 778-7926.

LEWISTON (E-3) pop. 2,781, elev. 363'

The site of Niagara Falls some 12,000 years ago, the Lewiston area later was home to various tribes, including the Attawandaronk, Hopewell and Seneca, who landed their canoes here to portage around the deadly rapids and falls of the Niagara River. Though also the site of portages by explorers in the late 1600s, the area was not settled until 1796, when the British surrendered nearby Fort Niagara.

Named for Gov. Morgan Lewis, Lewiston quickly grew into a center of trade and transportation; a tramway built by the British is said to have become America's first railroad. Another of Lewiston's innovations is the cocktail, which was invented by a local tavern proprietress who mixed some gin and herb wine in a tankard and stirred the drink with the tail feather of a stuffed cock pheasant.

CASTELLANI ART MUSEUM is on Senior Dr. on the Niagara University campus. The museum's permanent collection emphasizes 20th-century and contemporary art and includes works by Charles Burchfield, Louise Nevelson, Pablo Picasso and Andy Warhol. In addition there are collections of paintings, drawings, photographs and prints. Changing exhibits also are presented. Tues.-Sat. 11-5, Sun. 1-5; closed major holidays. Free. Phone (716) 286-8200.

SAVE **EARL W. BRYDGES ARTPARK** is on S. Fourth St. along the Niagara River gorge. This state park blends visual and performing arts with recreation and nature. The main theater presents Broadway musicals, big-band concerts and celebrity performances. A variety of family-oriented festivals and events is offered in an outdoor amphitheater.

Sculpture installations, working artists-in-residence and hands-on art activities round out the cultural offerings. Historic and geological sites and such recreational facilities as nature areas, fishing docks, and hiking and cross-country skiing trails make up the 150-acre complex.

Picnicking is permitted. Park open daily dawn-dusk. Theater performances are presented June-Sept.; phone for schedule and ticket prices. Parking $6, June-Aug. Phone (716) 754-9000 or (800) 659-7275.

NATIONAL SHRINE BASILICA OF OUR LADY OF FATIMA, 1.5 mi. e. on US 104, 2 mi. n. on SR 18, then .5 mi. e. on Swan Rd., is an outdoor cathedral with more than 100 life-size statues, a giant rosary and a translucent domed chapel that has an observation deck on top. Picnicking is permitted. Food is available. Daily 9-5, early Jan. to mid-Nov.; 9-9, mid-Nov. to late Dec. Closed Thanksgiving and Dec. 25. Free. Phone (716) 754-7489.

GEM **POWER VISTA** is 4.5 mi. n. of the falls on US 104, or reached from Robert Moses Pkwy. N. following signs. The Niagara Power Project's visitor center features more than 50 interactive exhibits explaining the development of hydroelectricity in the Niagara area. The Electric Lab features an operating model of a hydropower turbine. Modern energy efficiency is demonstrated in a Victorian house setting.

A large-scale terrain map provides a geographic overview of the Niagara Project, the source of one-seventh of the state's power. Just steps away, an outdoor observation deck 350 feet above the Niagara River affords views of the gorge and power plant.

Other exhibits highlight solar power, electric vehicles and local history. A mural by Thomas Hart Benton depicts Father Louis Hennepin viewing the falls for the first time. Daily 9-5; closed Jan. 1, Thanksgiving and Dec. 24-25 and 31. Free. Phone (716) 286-6661 or (866) 697-2386.

WHIRLPOOL JET BOAT TOURS, departing from 115 S. Water St., offers 45-minute trips on the lower Niagara River on 48- to 54-seat jet boats. The river can be experienced on either "wet jet" trips, where a good soaking can be expected, or a "dry" version of the trip in a domed jet boat. Features of the tours, which are half historic/scenic and half white-water adventure, include historic forts, the Niagara Gorge, white-water rapids and the whirlpool. A complete rain suit and wet boots are provided for the "wet" trip.

Allow 2 hours minimum for preparation, tour and clothing changes. **Note:** A change of clothes is recommended for the "wet jet" trip. Participants should be in good health; a signed release is required. Trips are not recommended for those with heart, back or neck problems, and pregnant women may not take the tours. Trips depart daily 10-7, May-June and Sept.-Oct; at 7, July-Aug. Schedule may vary; phone ahead. Arrive 30 minutes early to prepare for the trip. "Wet jet" or jet dome fare $50; ages 6-13, $42. Under age 6 or under 44 inches tall are not permitted. Reservations are recommended. Inquire about refund policy. MC, VI. Phone (905) 468-4800 or (888) 438-4444.

LOCKPORT (E-3) pop. 22,279, elev. 544'

Lockport derived its name from the Erie Canal locks that overcome the difference in elevation along the Niagara Escarpment. The historic five flights of locks, built in 1825, can be seen from Pine Street Bridge or from the boats that offer narrated cruises along the canal and through working locks.

The town also boasts one of the widest bridges in the world, located downtown within walking distance from the locks, and an upside-down railroad bridge, built with its supporting structures facing downward to hinder competing canal shipping. Part of the original canal towpath is used today for hiking and walking.

Niagara Tourism and Convention Corp.: 345 Third St., Suite 605, Niagara Falls, NY 14303; phone (716) 282-8992 or (800) 338-7890. *See color ad p. 521 and coupon in Savings Section.*

Self-guiding tours: Brochures for a walking tour of the canal district are available at the municipal building on Main Street.

ERIE CANAL DISCOVERY CENTER is at 24 Church St. This center interprets Eric Canal and Lockport history through multimedia stations, interactive murals and exhibits. Allow 30 minutes minimum. Daily 9-5, May-Oct.; closed holidays. Admission $6; ages 5-12, $3. DS, MC, VI. Phone (716) 439-0431.

KENAN CENTER, 433 Locust St., is a regional arts, educational and recreational campus on 25 acres. Kenan House, the 1800s Victorian mansion of William R. Keenan Jr., features a ladies' parlor and an art gallery. Taylor Theater is in a restored carriage house. The campus also includes formal gardens, a sports arena and playground. Allow 1 hour minimum. Art gallery Mon.-Fri. noon-5, Sat.-Sun. 2-5, day after Labor Day-Memorial Day; Mon.-Fri. noon-5, Sun. 2-5, rest of year. Closed holidays. Free. Admission may be charged during special events. Phone (716) 433-2617.

SAVE **LOCKPORT CAVE AND UNDERGROUND BOAT RIDE** departs from the ticket office at 2 Pine St., near Main St. Tour activities include exploring the Erie Canal locks, viewing industrial ruins, walking through a 1,600-foot tunnel blasted out of solid rock in the mid-1800s, and riding a boat on an underground waterway. Tunnel features include stalactites, flowstone, geological formations and workmen's artifacts.

Allow 1 hour, 30 minutes minimum. Tours depart daily on the hour 10-5, June 23-Labor Day; daily on the hour noon-4, May 26-June 22; Mon.-Fri. at noon, 1:30 and 3, Sat.-Sun. and Columbus Day on the hour noon-4, day after Labor Day-Columbus Day. Fare $9; ages 4-12, $6. AX, MC, VI. Phone (716) 438-0174.

LOCKPORT LOCKS AND ERIE CANAL CRUISES depart from a restored 1840s stone warehouse at 210 Market St. off SR 31. Two-hour narrated Erie Canal cruises take passengers past the original 1800s locks, under an inverted trestle bridge and lift bridges, alongside the original towpath and through a rock cut. The boat passes through working locks, where it is locked up (raised) 50 feet to overcome the difference in elevation of the Niagara Escarpment; locking down is experienced on the return trip. The Erie Canal Heritage Museum has exhibits, photographs and artifacts.

Food is available. Picnicking is permitted. Trips depart daily at 10, 12:30, 3 and 5:30, June 20-Labor Day; Sun.-Fri. at 12:30 and 3, Sat. at 10, 12:30, 3 and 5:30, May 9-June 19 and day after Labor Day-Oct. 16. Fare $13.75; ages 4-10, $8. DS, MC, VI. Phone (716) 433-6155 or (800) 378-0352.

THE HISTORY CENTER OF NIAGARA COUNTY HISTORICAL SOCIETY, 215 Niagara St., is a complex devoted to county history. Exhibits include business and medical memorabilia, farm tools, Civil War items and Indian artifacts. Also displayed are the one-of-a-kind 1923 Junior R, a locally produced aluminum automobile, and a 1954 Pontiac, reputedly the first General Motors car with air conditioning. Allow 1 hour, 30 minutes minimum. Mon.-Sat. 9-5; closed holidays. Admission $2. Phone (716) 434-7433.

Col. William M. Bond House, 143 Ontario St., is an 1824 brick house featuring 12 period rooms used as backdrops for changing exhibits. Allow 1 hour minimum. Mon., Wed. and Sat. 1-5, June-Dec. Donations. Phone (716) 434-7433.

YOUNGSTOWN (D-2) pop. 1,957, elev. 301'

FORT NIAGARA STATE PARK is at the mouth of the Niagara River off SR 18F, following signs to Robert Moses Pkwy. Basketball, boating, fishing and swimming facilities are available Memorial Day through Labor Day at this 504-acre park. Daily dawn-dusk. Free. Parking $6 daily, last weekend in June-Labor Day; free, rest of year. Swimming $3; ages 6-12, $1.50. Boat launch $6. Phone (716) 745-7273. *See Recreation Chart.*

Old Fort Niagara State Historic Site, adjacent to the Fort Niagara State Park grounds, was begun by the French in 1726. Active under three flags, the fort contains many mounted cannons, a hot shot furnace, a drawbridge and pre-revolution buildings. The site includes the only fortified French castle in the United States; it has been restored and furnished to recreate its stark 18th-century atmosphere. Drills and ceremonies are presented daily July through Labor Day. Re-enactments are held throughout the year.

The museum contains exhibits related to the fort's involvement in World Wars I and II, including weapons, military clothing and furniture. A visitors center displays a rare American flag captured by the British at the fort in 1813. Allow 1 hour minimum. Daily 9-7:30, July-Aug.; Mon.-Fri. 9-6:30, Sat.-Sun. 9-7:30, in June; daily 9-5:30, Apr.-May and Sept.-Oct.; daily 9-4:30, rest of year. Closed Jan. 1, Thanksgiving and Dec. 25. Admission $10; over 64, $9; ages 6-12, $6. AX, DS, MC, VI. Phone (716) 745-7611.

Nearby Ontario

NIAGARA FALLS pop. 78,815

BIRD KINGDOM AT THE NIAGARA FALLS AVIARY, next to the Rainbow Bridge at 5651 River Rd., is a journey through a rain forest filled with more than 500 free-flying tropical birds representing close to 80 species from around the world as well as tropical foliage, palm trees, ponds, streams and 40-foot-high waterfall. The conservatory has a lost kingdom theme and features an indoor aviary, said to be the world's largest, where visitors can interact with the birds.

Food is available. Allow 30 minutes minimum. Daily 9-9, July 1-day before Labour Day; 9-6, rest of year. Last admission 1 hour before closing. Admission $14.95; over 65, $13.95; ages 5-12, $9.95. AX, DS, MC, VI. Phone (905) 356-8888 or (866) 994-0090.

CLASSIC IRON MOTORCYCLE MUSEUM is at 5743 Victoria Ave. in the Clifton Hill District. This museum displays more than 60 motorcycles representing such brands as Harley-Davidson, Triumph, Indian, Sunbeam, Ariel, Matchless and B.S.A. Visitors can see motorcycles dating back to the 1920s and '30s, motorcycle-themed artwork and replicas of the choppers ridden by Peter Fonda and Dennis Hopper in "Easy Rider." Allow 30 minutes minimum. Daily 10 a.m.-11 p.m. Admission $8.55; ages 7-17, $6.84. Phone (905) 374-8211.

FALLS INCLINE RAILWAY, next to Table Rock Point, operates twin cable-rail cars between the Fallsview tourist area and Table Rock Point areas. The historic railway transports visitors up and down the Niagara Escarpment. Rail cars operate daily, late Mar.-late Oct. (weather permitting). Phone ahead to confirm schedule. One-way fare $2. Phone (905) 357-9340. *See color ad p. 172.*

SAVE **GUINNESS WORLD RECORDS MUSEUM,** 4943 Clifton Hill, displays exhibits demonstrating world records in sports, science and nature. Videotapes depict accomplishments in outer space and high-speed travel. Daily 9 a.m.-2 a.m., June-Sept.; daily 10-10, Oct.-Mar.; otherwise varies rest of year. Admission $11.99; over 59 and students with ID $9.50; ages 4-12, $6.99. AX, MC, VI. Phone (905) 356-2299.

IMAX THEATRE NIAGARA FALLS, next to the Skylon Tower at 6170 Fallsview Blvd., presents "Niagara: Miracles, Myths & Magic," an exciting view of the falls on a screen six stories tall. The 40-minute film tells the story of legends, explorers and daredevils, including a dramatic re-enactment of a steamship ride down the rapids and a true story of a boy who survived plunging over the falls. Artifacts from daredevils who have challenged the falls and rapids in the past are displayed.

Food is available. Films shown daily on the hour 9-9, May-Oct.; Sun.-Thurs. 10-4, Fri.-Sat. 10-9, rest of year. Admission $12; over 64, $9.50; ages 4-12, $8.50. MC, VI. Phone (905) 358-3611 or (905) 374-4629. *See color ad.*

GEM **JOURNEY BEHIND THE FALLS,** 1.6 km (1 mi.) s. of Rainbow Bridge on the Niagara River Pkwy. at Table Rock Point, contains elevators that descend to the base of the Horseshoe Falls. Three tunnels lead from the elevators and provide excellent vantage points for

NIAGARA'S PREMIER HOTELS OVERLOOKING THE FALLS

Embassy Suites - Fallsview
1-800-420-6980

Hilton Niagara - Fallsview
1-888-370-0700

Marriott Fallsview & Spa
1-888-501-8916

Oakes Hotel Overlooking the Falls
1-877-843-6253

Radisson Hotel & Suites Fallsview
1-877-Fallsview

Ramada Plaza Hotel Fallsview
1-800-461-2492

Renaissance Fallsview Hotel & Conference Centre
1-800-363-3255

Sheraton Fallsview Hotel & Conference Centre
1-877-35-Falls

The Excitement in Fallsview is Reaching New Heights!

NIAGARA'S GREAT VALUE ACCOMMODATIONS

Best Western Fallsview
1-800-263-2580

Comfort Inn Fallsview
1-800-463-1938

Days Inn Fallsview Casino
1-800-461-1251

Fallsview Inn
1-800-263-2565

Holiday Inn by the Falls
1-800-263-9393

Knight's Inn by the Falls
1-800-843-5644

Old Stone Inn
1-800-263-6208

President Motor Inn
905-358-7272

Rodeway Inn Fallsview
1-866-633-4526

Stanley Motor Inn
905-358-9238

The World Comes to Fallsview

NIAGARA FALLS... ONE WONDER AFTER ANOTHER

THE **AUTHENTIC** FALLS EXPERIENCE

4 GREAT ATTRACTIONS
1 LOW PRICE

- ◆ Journey Behind the Falls
- ◆ Maid of the Mist
- ◆ White Water Walk
- ◆ Butterfly Conservatory

The Niagara Falls & Great Gorge Adventure Pass includes all-day transportation on the People Mover and Incline Railway. PLUS valuable coupons for discounts at other Niagara Parks Attractions. Pass will be valid during the time the Maid of the Mist is sailing (approx. May to October 2007).

AUDIO TOURS!

Purchase a Niagara Falls & Great Gorge Adventure Pass and enjoy Audio Tours at Journey Behind the Falls and the Butterfly Conservatory. ITEC enhanced tours are available in English, French, Spanish, German, Mandarin or Japanese at no extra cost.

Ask your local AAA office about the
Niagara Falls & Great Gorge Adventure Pass

Niagara
Parks

An agency of the Government of
Ontario since 1885

close-up views of the thundering falls and the Niagara River. The observation plaza is about 38 metres (125 ft.) below the gorge embankment and 8 metres (26 ft.) above the river's edge. Disposable raincoats are provided.

Saturdays and Sundays in July and August a Royal Canadian Mounted Police officer in ceremonial uniform is posted near the brink of the falls to pose with visitors for photographs. Complex opens daily at 9; closing times vary. Tunnels close 30 minutes before complex closing; phone ahead for closing times. Closed Dec. 25. Tunnel $11; ages 6-12, $6.50. AX, DC, JC, MC, VI. Phone (905) 354-1551. *See color ad p. 172.*

KONICA MINOLTA TOWER CENTRE overlooks the falls at 6732 Fallsview Blvd. The center rises 99 metres (325 ft.) above the base of the falls. An indoor observation deck at the top of the center provides a magnificent view of the falls and the surrounding area.

Food is available. Allow 1 hour minimum. Daily 7 a.m.-10 p.m., with extended hours during the summer. Admission $6.95, over 64 and students with ID $4.95, under 6 free with an adult. AX, DS, MC, VI. Phone (905) 356-1501 or (800) 461-2492.

LOUIS TUSSAUD'S WAXWORKS is at 5907 Victoria Ave. in the Clifton Hill District. Lifelike wax replicas of celebrities, politicians, historical figures and fictional characters occupy two floors of this museum. Because the sculptures are not roped off, visitors can have their photos taken next to such personages as Nicole Kidman, Brad Pitt, Hillary Clinton, Hannibal Lecter, Harry Potter and the crew from the original "Star Trek" television series. Celebrity life masks adorn the walls between exhibits.

Allow 30 minutes minimum. Daily 9 a.m.-1:30 a.m., mid-June to mid-Sept.; 10-10, mid-Mar. to mid-June and mid-Sept. through Dec. 31; 11-7, rest of year. Admission $13.99; over 60, $10.99. A combination ticket with Ripley's Believe It or Not! Museum and Ripley's Moving Theater is available. Phone (905) 374-6601.

LUNDY'S LANE HISTORICAL MUSEUM, 1.6 km (1 mi.) from the falls off Hwy. 420 at 5810 Ferry St., is on the site of one of the fiercest battles of the War of 1812, the Battle of Lundy's Lane, fought here July 25, 1814. The museum, in the 1874 former Stamford Township Hall, has exhibits about the city's history. Highlights include Indian artifacts and displays about the early settlers and black history as well as a prime collection of items from the War of 1812.

Allow 30 minutes minimum. Daily 10-5, May-Oct.; daily noon-4, Jan.-Apr.; Wed.-Sun. noon-4, rest of year. Admission $3; over 64 and students with ID $2.50; ages 6-12, $2. Phone (905) 358-5082.

MAID OF THE MIST boats depart from the dock at Clifton Hill and River Rd. on the Canadian side. Since 1846 visitors have experienced the majesty and power of the falls from a series of boats, all named *Maid of the Mist*. Today's steel, double-deck, diesel-powered vessels enter the Horseshoe Basin, fight the mighty current and pass directly in front of the American and Horseshoe falls. Raincoat-clad passengers on the tossing, heaving ship are guaranteed a generous soaking from the spray of the cataract.

Trips depart daily beginning at 9, Memorial Day weekend and mid- June through Labour Day; at 9:45, mid-Apr. through day before Memorial Day weekend (depending on ice conditions in the river), June 1 to mid-June and day after Labour Day-Oct. 24. Closing times vary; phone ahead. **Note:** These hours reflect the Canadian side; the American side runs 15 minutes later. Fare (waterproof clothing included) $14; ages 6-12, $8.60. Elevator cost included. MC, VI. To confirm daily schedules phone (905) 358-5781 in Ontario or (716) 284-8897 in N.Y. *See color ad p. 172.*

MARINELAND, 7657 Portage Rd., is known for its marine shows, which feature dolphins, walruses and sea lions. There also are a freshwater aquarium and wildlife displays with bears, elk and buffalo and a deer petting park. At the interactive whale habitat and Arctic Cove, visitors can touch and feed beluga whales. Friendship Cove features killer whales.

Several rides are available, including Dragon Mountain, a large steel roller coaster, and Sky Screamer, a triple tower ride. A few children's rides also are available. Show times vary according to the season.

Food is available. Daily 9-6, late June-Labour Day; 10-5, Victoria Day weekend-late June and day after Labour Day-early Oct. Admission $38.95; ages 5-9, $31.95. Parents should ask about height restrictions before paying admission. Phone to verify schedule and prices. AX, MC, VI. Phone (905) 356-9565.

MOUNT CARMEL SPIRITUAL CENTRE, n. of McLeod Rd. at 7021 Stanley Ave., just above the falls, was founded in 1894; it is now used for religious retreats. The main altar has woodcarvings and paneling in American white oak. The center contains Our Lady of Peace Church, built in 1827. Daily 9-4. Free. Phone (905) 356-4113.

MOVIELAND WAX MUSEUM OF THE STARS, 4950 Clifton Hill, displays figures of film and television personalities in scenes that made them famous. Visitors can make replicas of their own hand in the Wax Hands Emporium. Daily 9 a.m.-1 a.m., May-Sept.; 10-10, rest of year. Admission $9.99; under 11, $5.99. AX, MC, VI. Phone (905) 358-3061.

NIAGARA FALLS is on the Niagara River at the international border between Canada and the United States. The thundering falls, consisting of the Horseshoe Falls on the Canadian side and American and Bridal Veil falls in the U.S.,

were formed by a retreating glacier 12,000 years ago. The Canadian falls, 54 metres (177 ft.) high and 675 metres (2,215 ft.) wide, derives its name from its crescent shape.

Often heard before they can be seen, the falls have long been a favorite of honeymooners, making the city of Niagara Falls a favorite of newlyweds. In addition to scenic overlooks in Queen Victoria Park, the grandeur of the falls also can be appreciated by boat, helicopter, observation towers and bridges. The falls are illuminated at night year-round.

NIAGARA FALLS ART GALLERY/KURELEK COLLECTION AND NIAGARA CHILDREN'S MUSEUM, 1.5 km (.9 mi.) s.e. of QEW exit 27 (McLeod Rd.) at 8058 Oakwood Dr., has an outstanding collection of works by Canadian artist William Kurelek, including the series known as "The Passion of Christ."

Also noteworthy are a collection of more than 400 works of art depicting Niagara Falls and the surrounding area and "Stepova Baba" (Grandmother of the Steppes), a work at least 2,500 years old. The gallery also houses the Niagara Children's Museum. Art gallery open Mon.-Fri. 11-5, Sat.-Sun. 1-5, June-Sept.; daily 1-5, rest of year. Children's museum open Mon.-Fri. 11:30-5, Sat. 1-5, June-Sept.; Mon.-Fri. 3-5, Sat.-Sun. 11-5, rest of year. Donations. Phone (905) 356-1514.

NIAGARA HELICOPTERS, 3731 Victoria Ave., near the Whirlpool Rapids on the Niagara River Pkwy., provides an aerial perspective of the falls and river during 9-minute flights. Headsets provide a taped narration. Daily 9-dusk (weather permitting); closed Dec. 25. Fare $110; ages 2-11, $65; couples $210; a family rate is available. AX, DC, MC, VI. For reservations phone (905) 357-5672. *See color ad p. 175.*

THE NIAGARA PARKS BOTANICAL GARDENS, 8 km (5 mi.) n. of the falls on Niagara River Pkwy., is the home of The Niagara Parks School of Horticulture, said to be the only residential school in Canada for apprentice gardeners. Floral displays and both formal and informal gardens, including 2,300 varieties of roses, are on the 40-hectare (99-acre) site.

Other gardens include rock, herb, annual, perennial and vegetable. The best viewing time is April through October, when the blooms are at their peak. Daily dawn-dusk. Guided 30-minute tours are available. Free. Phone (905) 356-8554.

Horse & Carriage Rides at The Niagara Parks Botanical Gardens depart from the gardens; timed tickets can be purchased at the Niagara Parks Butterfly Conservatory ticket booth. Forty-minute narrated tours conducted in covered, horse-drawn carriages provide an overview of the botanical gardens and a chance to see the horticulture students at work. Departures every 15 minutes daily 10-4, May-Oct. Hours may vary; phone ahead. Fare $15, children on lap free. MC, VI. Phone (905) 358-0025.

Niagara Parks Butterfly Conservatory, 2405 Niagara River Pkwy. on the grounds of the Botanical Gardens, is home to some 2,000 free-flying butterflies. Waterfalls and various tropical flora line the pathways throughout the glass-enclosed conservatory, said to be North America's largest, where more than 40 butterfly species can be observed. There also is a native butterfly garden outside the conservatory.

Allow 1 hour minimum. Daily 9-5 (closing times are extended Mar. 1-second Mon. in Oct.); closed Dec. 25. Timed-tickets are available. Admission $11; ages 6-12, $6.50. MC, VI. Phone (905) 358-0025. *See color ad p. 172.*

NIAGARA PARKS FLORAL SHOWHOUSE, .8 km (.5 mi.) s. of the Canadian Horseshoe Falls, has seasonal displays of local flowers and foliage, palm trees, more than 75 tropical birds and other tropical plants and aquatic life, all set in the midst of waterfalls and pools. There also is an outdoor fragrance garden for the visually impaired. Daily 9:30-5 (closing hours are extended mid-June through Labour Day); closed Dec. 25. Free. Phone (905) 354-1721.

NIAGARA SKYWHEEL is at 4960 Clifton Hill. The 53-metre (175-ft.) Ferris wheel offers impressive views of the falls and surrounding area. Glass-enclosed gondolas are equipped with heating and air-conditioning for year-round comfort. Allow 15 minutes minimum. Daily 9 a.m.-1 a.m. Admission $9.99, children $5.99. AX, MC, VI. Phone (905) 358-4793 or (800) 801-8557. *See color ad p. 177.*

OAKES GARDEN THEATRE, 1 km (.6 mi.) n. of the Horseshoe Falls on the Niagara River Pkwy. at the foot of Clifton Hill, is a Greco-Roman style amphitheater in a setting of rock gardens, lily ponds, terraces and promenades overlooking the American Falls. Daily dawn-dusk. Free. Phone (905) 354-5141.

 OH CANADA EH? DINNER SHOW is at 8585 Lundy's Lane. A taste of Canada's culture and traditions can be experienced at this production staged in a rustic log cabin decorated with Canadiana. A five-course family-style Canadian meal is served during the show by such Canadians as Anne of Green Gables, singing Mounties, lumberjacks, a hockey player and other performing characters.

Allow 2 hours, 30 minutes minimum. Shows are presented daily at 6:30 p.m., late Apr.-late Oct.; schedule and shows vary rest of year. Admission $52; ages 6-12, $25. Rates may vary; phone ahead. Reservations are required. MC, VI. Phone (905) 374-1995 or (800) 467-2071.

 QUEEN VICTORIA PARK, on the Niagara River Pkwy. at the falls, originated in 1887. It is a 62-hectare (154-acre) landscaped park offering fine views of the falls and beautiful seasonal floral displays. The park is illuminated at night and is the site of daily summer entertainment and many special events. Daily dawn-dusk. Free.

Horse & Carriage Rides at Queen Victoria Park depart from the Queen Victoria Place Gift Shop on Niagara River Pkwy. at the falls. Fifteen-, 45- and 80-minute narrated tours in a horse-drawn carriage provide scenic views of the cataract as well as commentary about the falls and the Niagara area.

Niagara Parks Commission Passes

The Niagara Parks Commission Passes provide savings for guests interested in visiting several Niagara Falls attractions.

The *Niagara Falls and Great Gorge Adventure Pass* includes admission to four attractions—*Maid of the Mist*, Journey Behind the Falls, the Niagara Parks Butterfly Conservatory and White Water Walk—as well as an all-day transportation pass for the People Mover and Falls Incline Railway. The pass also includes coupons, including a discount for the Whirlpool Aero Car. The passport is available May through October. Fee $37.95; ages 6-12, $23.95.

The pass can be purchased at all Niagara Parks attractions and information centers and many hotels. *See color ad p. 172.*

Departures daily 4-11, mid-May through Labour Day (weather permitting). Hours may vary; phone ahead. Fare $40 per carriage for 15-minute tour; $100 per carriage for 45-minute tour; $170 per carriage for 80-minute tour. DS, MC, VI. Phone (905) 358-5935.

RAINBOW CARILLON TOWER, at the terminus of the Rainbow Bridge, presents 1-hour concerts on its 55 tuned bells. Concerts are given daily at noon, 3 and 6. Free.

RIPLEY'S BELIEVE IT OR NOT! MUSEUM, 4960 Clifton Hill, displays world-traveler Robert Ripley's collection of strange, odd and unusual items. Hundreds of exhibits feature curiosities and illusions such as interactive puzzles, an eight-legged buffalo and a shrunken human head. Daily 9 a.m.-2 a.m., mid-June to mid-Sept.; 10-10, mid-Mar. to mid-June and mid-Sept. through Dec. 31; 11-7, rest of year. Admission $12.95; over 60, $10.50; ages 6-12, $6.99. A combination ticket with Ripley's Moving Theater is available. AX, MC, VI. Phone (905) 356-2238.

Ripley's Moving Theater, 4983 Clifton Hill, offers two adventure rides in a motion simulator complete with wind, mist and laser effects. **Note:** The rides are not recommended for persons with back or neck problems. Daily 9 a.m.-2 a.m., mid-June to mid-Sept.; 10-10, mid-Mar. to mid-June and mid-Sept. through Dec. 31; 11-7, rest of year. Admission $12.95; over 60, $10.50; under 12, $6.99. Under 43 inches tall are not permitted. A combination ticket with Ripley's Believe It or Not! Museum is available. AX, MC, VI. Phone (905) 356-2261.

SKYLON TOWER, overlooking the falls at 5200 Robinson St., rises 160 metres (525 ft.) above the ground and 236 metres (774 ft.) above the base of the falls, providing a magnificent view of the surrounding area. Three levels at the top include two dining rooms and an indoor/outdoor observation deck. The interactive entertainment area Skylon Fun Centre and a theater showing 3-D films are at the base of the tower. Observation deck daily 8 a.m.-midnight, May 1 through mid-Oct.; otherwise varies. Observation deck $10.95; over 64, $9.95; ages 6-12, $6.45. AX, DC, DS, JC, MC, VI. Phone (905) 356-2651 to verify prices or (888) 673-7343. *See color ad p. 177.*

WHIRLPOOL AERO CAR, on the Niagara River Pkwy. 3.25 km (2 mi.) n. of Horseshoe Falls, is a cable car carrying passengers 76.2 metres (250 ft.) above the Niagara Gorge and back on a 529-metre-long (1,800-ft.) cableway, affording views of the rapids and nearby hydroelectric plants. Below the suspended aero car the churning river backs up into the 24-hectare (60-acre) Whirlpool Basin.

Allow 30 minutes minimum. Car operates daily 9-5, mid-Mar. to mid-Nov. (weather permitting); closed periodically for maintenance. Closing hours are extended mid-June through Labour Day. Last car departs 30 minutes before closing. Phone ahead to confirm schedule. Timed tickets are available. Round trip $11; ages 6-12, $6.50. AX, JC, MC, VI. Phone (905) 354-5711.

WHITE WATER WALK is n. of the Whirlpool Rapids Bridge on the Niagara River Pkwy. After taking an elevator to the river level, visitors can stroll along a boardwalk beside the rapids of the lower Niagara River. The scenic 305-metre (1,000 ft.) pathway along the edge of the river provides a close-up view of the rapids as they rush from the falls.

Daily 9-5 (closing times are extended Sat.-Sun.), mid-Mar. to mid-Nov. Last admission 30 minutes before closing. Phone ahead to confirm hours. Admission $8.50; ages 6-12, $5. AX, DC, MC, VI. Phone (905) 374-1221. *See color ad p. 172.*

CASINOS

• **Casino Niagara** is at 5705 Falls Ave. Daily 24 hours. Phone (905) 374-3598 or (888) 946-3255.

• **Fallsview Casino** is at 6380 Fallsview Blvd. Daily 24 hours. Phone (888) 325-5788.

**The previous listings were for the Niagara Falls Vicinity.
This page resumes the alphabetical listings of cities in New York.**

NORTH BLENHEIM (F-9) elev. 791'

BLENHEIM-GILBOA PUMPED STORAGE POWER PROJECT, 3 mi. s. on SR 30, has two reservoirs. During the day water is released from the upper reservoir to create electricity, and at night electricity is used to pump water from the lower to the upper reservoir to repeat the process the next day. A 19th-century dairy barn houses the New York Power Authority's visitor center, which features interactive energy displays. Daily 10-5; closed Jan. 1, Thanksgiving and Dec. 25. Free. Phone (518) 287-6380 or (800) 724-0309.

Historic Lansing Manor Museum adjoins the power project's visitor center. The 1819 house was part of an 840-acre estate owned by John T. Lansing Jr., an aide to Revolutionary War general Philip Schuyler. The restored manor is furnished in period. Wed.-Mon. 10-5, May-Oct. Free. Phone (518) 287-6380 or (800) 724-0309.

OLD BLENHEIM BRIDGE, on SR 30 across Schoharie Creek, was built in 1854 and is said to be the world's longest single-span wooden covered bridge. It is 232 feet long, 26 feet wide and has two driveways. The bridge is open only to pedestrians. Free. Phone (518) 827-6344.

NORTH CHILI (E-4) elev. 582'

VICTORIAN DOLL MUSEUM AND CHILI DOLL HOSPITAL, 4.5 mi. w. off I-490 exit 7B at 4332 Buffalo Rd. (SR 33), has more than 2,000 identified dolls made of bisque, china, wax, tin and vinyl. Also displayed are toys, Victorian memorabilia, a puppet theater, a circus and a Noah's Ark. A doll hospital also is featured. Allow 1 hour minimum. Tues.-Sat. 10-4:30, Feb.-Dec.; closed holidays. Admission $2.50; under 12, $1.50. Phone (585) 247-0130.

NORTH CREEK (C-10) elev. 1,013'

North Creek is a popular access point for recreation in the surrounding Adirondack Park. Downhill and cross-country skiing are available 5 miles northwest off SR 28 at Gore Mountain, (518) 251-2411, and at Garnet Hill, (518) 251-2821. White-water rafting expeditions depart from downtown.

Gore Mountain Region Chamber of Commerce: Tannery Pon Community Center, SR 28N and Main Street, P.O. Box 84, North Creek, NY 12853; phone (518) 251-2612.

RECREATIONAL ACTIVITIES
White-water Rafting

- **Hudson River Rafting Co.** is off I-87 exit 23, n. on SR 9 to SR 28, then 16 mi. w. to departure point at Cunningham's Ski Barn. Write P.O. Box 47, North Creek, NY 12853. Daily, in spring; Tues., Thurs. and Sat.-Sun., in summer and fall. Reservations are recommended. Phone (518) 251-3215 or (800) 888-7238.

- **Mountains Unlimited Adventures** departs from Main St., off I-87 exit 23. Write 336 Lakewood Rd., Waterbury, CT 06704. Departures daily at 9, Apr. 1-Columbus Day. Phone (888) 240-6976.

NORTH HOOSICK (E-11)

BENNINGTON BATTLEFIELD STATE HISTORIC SITE, 3 mi. e. on SR 67, is the site of one of the earliest decisive Colonial victories of the Revolutionary War. In 1777 Gen. John Stark and his New Hampshire, Vermont and Massachusetts militia captured a British expeditionary force. An interpretive sign explains the course of the battle. A hilltop picnic area overlooks the battlefield.

Allow 1 hour minimum. Daily 10-7, May 1-Labor Day; Sat.-Sun. 10-7, day after Labor Day-Columbus Day (weather permitting). Free. Phone (518) 279-1155.

NORTH RIVER (C-10) elev. 1,073'

BARTON MINES GARNET MINE TOUR is 4.5 mi. n. on SR 28, then w. 5 mi. on Barton Mines Rd. One of the largest garnet mines in the world, it was begun in 1878. In 1983, the main mining operation moved to nearby Ruby Mountain. One-hour guided tours feature the original site and include a walk through an open-pit mine 800 feet below the summit of Gore Mountain.

Tours depart on the hour Mon.-Sat. 10-4, Sun. 11-4, late June-Labor Day; Sat. on the hour 10-4, Sun. 11-4, day after Labor Day-Columbus Day. Admission (season pass) $10; ages 60-90, $8.50; ages 7-14, $6.50. Rocks collected cost $1 per pound. Phone (518) 251-2706 to verify schedule and prices.

NORTH SALEM —*see New York p. 153.*

NORTH TONAWANDA —*see Buffalo p. 71.*

NORWICH (F-8) pop. 7,355, elev. 1,015'

⟦SAVE⟧ **NORTHEAST CLASSIC CAR MUSEUM,** 24 Rexford St. (SR 23), has more than 100 restored automobiles dating from the turn of the 20th century to the 1960s. Included are Auburns, Cords, Duesenbergs, Packards and models by Chalmers Detroit, Holmes, Stutz and Pierce Arrow. An extensive collection of Franklin luxury cars also is featured. Mannequins in period clothing are displayed next to cars of the day.

Allow 1 hour minimum. Daily 10-5; closed Jan. 1, Thanksgiving and Dec. 25. Admission $9; ages 6-18, $4. AX, DS, MC, VI. Phone (607) 334-2886.

NYACK—*see New York p. 153.*

OAKDALE (I-3) pop. 8,075, elev. 17'

CONNETQUOT RIVER STATE PARK PRESERVE, entered off SR 27, is a 3,473-acre nature preserve with hiking, equestrian and skiing trails. Guided nature walks and interpretive tours are conducted Tuesday through Sunday; reservations are required. Fly-fishing is permitted with a state fishing license. Equestrian permits are available. Tues.-Sun. 7-dusk, Apr.-Sept.; Wed.-Sun. 8-4, rest of year. Parking $6. A fee is charged for some permits. Phone (631) 581-1005.

OGDENSBURG (B-8) pop. 12,364, elev. 276'

Situated on the banks of the St. Lawrence River, Ogdensburg was founded as the French Fort La Presentation in 1749 by the Sulpician missionary Abbé François Picquet. The fort, which also served as a mission, trading post and school, was damaged by the French before the British could capture it in 1760. On the ruins of La Presentation the British built Fort Oswegatchie, which was an important military stronghold during the Revolution.

In 1796 Oswegatchie was turned over to Col. Samuel Ogden, and in 1817 it was incorporated as the village of Ogdensburgh. The village dropped its "h" when incorporated as a city in 1868.

The Custom House, 127 Water St., designated the oldest federal government building in the United States, was built 1809-10. The building offered protection to both American and British soldiers during a battle on Feb. 23, 1813. Battle scars are visible near the roof peak on the north side of the building. It has served as the customhouse since 1928.

The New York State Armory, a massive castellated-style edifice, 225 Elizabeth St., was constructed 1897-98 by architect Isaac Perry. Built for the Fortieth Separate Co., the building has been historically significant due to its association with American military history.

Twin-towered St. Mary's Cathedral, at Hamilton and Greene streets, features a series of stained glass windows depicting prominent religious figures.

Greater Ogdensburg Chamber of Commerce: 1020 Park St., Ogdensburg, NY 13669; phone (315) 393-3620.

Shopping areas: A [SAVE] Duty Free America's, is at Bridge Plaza off SR 37. Gateway Centre also is off SR 37, and Seaway Shopping Center is on Canton Street.

FREDERIC REMINGTON ART MUSEUM, 303 Washington St., displays bronzes, oil paintings, watercolors and pen-and-ink illustrations by Frederic Remington, known for his depictions of the American West. The artist's tools, library, personal notes and furnishings from his home are on display. In addition the museum presents traveling exhibitions that relate to the artist's style, theme and time period.

Allow 1 hour minimum. Mon.-Sat. 10-5, Sun. 1-5, May-Oct.; Wed.-Sat. 11-5, Sun. 1-5, rest of year. Closed Jan. 1, Easter, Thanksgiving and Dec. 25. Admission $8; over 65 and students age 6-22, $7. Phone (315) 393-2425.

OLD BETHPAGE (I-3) pop. 5,400

OLD BETHPAGE VILLAGE RESTORATION, 1 mi. s. of Long Island Expwy. exit 48S on Round Swamp Rd., is a reconstructed pre-Civil War working farm village on 209 acres. Buildings moved from locations throughout Long Island reflect architectural styles dating from the early 1700s. Included are a blacksmith shop, a church, homes, a store, a hat shop, a school and an inn.

The 165-acre Powell farmstead, with the original family house and carriage shed, includes an English-style barn, a smokehouse and live animals. The Schenck farmhouse is one of the area's oldest Dutch structures. The Layton Store doubled as a family home in the 1860s and today contains period merchandise. Costumed guides explain each building and the activities of its former inhabitants.

A highlight is Old Time Baseball, a series of games played seasonally according to early 19th-century rules.

Picnicking is permitted. Allow 2 hours minimum. Wed.-Sun. 10-5, Mar. 1 to mid-Oct.; Wed.-Fri. 10-4, Sat.-Sun. 10-5, mid-Oct. to Oct. 31; Wed.-Sun. 10-4, Nov. 1-Dec. 23. Closed Election Day, Nov. 11 and Thanksgiving. Last admission is 1 hour before closing. Admission $7; over 59 and ages 4-14, $5. Phone (516) 572-8400.

OLD CHATHAM (F-11) elev. 551'

[SAVE] **THE SHAKER MUSEUM AND LIBRARY** is 1 mi. w. on CR 13 following signs to 88 Shaker Museum Rd. Twenty-six exhibit areas include painted shaker furniture, baskets, poplarware, domestic items and pre-1900 tools. Displays span more than 200 years of Shaker history. Museum Wed.-Mon. 10-5, May 27-Oct. 16. Library open year-round by appointment. Admission $8; ages 8-17, $4. Phone (518) 794-9100, ext. 100.

OLD FORGE (D-9) elev. 1,706'

Originating in Old Forge is a canoe trip through the eight lakes of the Fulton Chain as well as Raquette, Forked, Long and Saranac lakes. McCauley Mountain offers summer and winter recreation.

Central Adirondack Association: P.O. Box 68, Old Forge, NY 13420; phone (315) 369-6983.

ADIRONDACK SCENIC RAILROAD is 1 mi. s. on SR 28 at Old Forge/Thendara Station. A 20-mile round-trip excursion to Otter Lake provides views of the Moose River region. Other excursions are available. Moose River 75-minute trip departs Wed.-Sun. and some holidays at 10, 12:30 and 2:45, Memorial Day weekend-Oct. 31. Schedule may vary; phone ahead. Fare $14; over 61, $13; ages 3-12, $6. Reservations are recommended. MC, VI. Phone (315) 369-6290 or (877) 508-6728.

ARTS CENTER/OLD FORGE, .3 mi. n. at 3260 SR 28, exhibits paintings, pottery, photography and other media as well as works from the permanent collection. Special month-long exhibitions are offered year-round. Workshops and performances also are offered. Allow 30 minutes minimum. Mon.-Sat. 10-4, Sun. noon-4; closed major holidays. Donations. Admission is charged during special exhibits. Phone (315) 369-6411.

ENCHANTED FOREST/WATER SAFARI, 3183 SR 28, is a 60-acre family-oriented water theme park with 44 rides, including 31 heated water rides and attractions. Featured are five themed areas and The Shadow, a double-flume slide. Circus shows are offered twice daily. Food is available. Daily 9:30-7, late June to mid-Aug.; schedule varies mid- to late June and mid-Aug. through Labor Day. Admission $24.95; ages 3-11, $21.95. DS, MC, VI. Phone (315) 369-6145.

GOODSELL MEMORIAL MUSEUM is at 2993 Main St. Adirondack history is explained through photographs, memorabilia, North American Indian lithographs, a birch bark canoe, handmade baskets and snowshoes, and other regional artifacts. A research library is available. Town walking tours are offered in July and August. Allow 30 minutes minimum. Tues.-Sat. 10-3. Free. Phone (315) 369-3838.

SAVE **OLD FORGE LAKE CRUISES** depart from the SR 28 dock on Old Forge Pond. Narrated cruises on the first four lakes of the scenic Fulton Chain of Lakes follow historic steamboat and mailboat routes, affording views of Adirondack camps, the Shoal Point Lighthouse, the Bald Mountain Fire Tower and wildlife. Trips include the 2-hour Sightseeing Cruise, 1.5-hour Kids' Cruise and 3-hour Mailboat Cruise. Fireworks cruises also are available.

Cruises depart daily Memorial Day-Columbus Day. Departure days and times vary according to cruise type; phone ahead for schedule. Sightseeing cruise $14; over 64, $13; ages 3-12, $10. Kids' cruise $12; over 64, $11; ages 3-12, $8. Mailboat cruise $16.50; over 64, $15.50; ages 3-12, $12.50. MC, VI. Phone (315) 369-6473.

OLD WESTBURY (I-2) pop. 4,228

OLD WESTBURY GARDENS is at 71 Old Westbury Rd. between Long Island Expwy. (I-495) and Jericho Tpke. (SR 25). The 1906 Westbury House is furnished with antique furniture and art, including paintings by Henry Raeburn, Sir Joshua Reynolds, John Singer Sargent and Richard Wilson. The grounds feature landscaping and formal gardens patterned after the English "great parks" of the 18th century.

Picnicking is permitted. Food is available. Allow 2 hours minimum. Guided tours are given Wed.-Mon. 10-5, late Apr.-Oct. 31. Holiday tour schedule varies Nov.-Dec. Admission $10; over 62, $8; ages 7-12, $5. Reduced admission Mon. for over 62. Holiday tour fees may vary; phone ahead. Phone (516) 333-0048.

OLEAN (G-4) pop. 15,347, elev. 1,435′

Olean was founded at the headwaters of the Allegheny River in 1804 by Revolutionary War hero Maj. Adam Hoops. The settlement flourished as a supply depot and departure point for pioneers heading west on makeshift rafts and flatboats. With the completion of the Buffalo and Washington Railroad in the 1870s and a subsequent oil boom, Olean emerged as a major petroleum shipping center at the turn of the 20th century. The name Hoops gave his land 100 years earlier is derived from the Latin word *oleum,* meaning oil.

Olean Point Museum, 302 Laurens St., contains town memorabilia; phone (716) 376-5642. The restored Fannie E. Bartlett Historical House on Laurens Street is furnished in the Victorian style, recalling Olean's heyday; phone (716) 376-5642.

Greater Olean Area Chamber of Commerce: 120 N. Union St., Olean, NY 14760; phone (716) 372-4433.

ROCK CITY PARK, 5 mi. s. on SR 16, has paths and stairways that wind through 320-million-year-old quartz boulders projecting from the edge of the Allegheny Mountains. The site reputedly has the world's largest exposure of quartz conglomerate, also known as pudding stone. One stairway is believed to have been built by the Seneca Indians, who used the area as a fortress.

Picnicking is permitted. Allow 1 hour minimum. Daily 9-6, May-Oct. (weather permitting). Admission $4.50; over 62, $3.75; ages 6-12, $2.50. Phone (716) 372-7790.

DID YOU KNOW

America's first railroad consisted of the 11-mile stretch between Albany and Schenectady.

ONEIDA (E-8) pop. 10,987, elev. 427'

The Oneida Community was founded nearby in 1848 by John Noyes. A religious and social commune who called themselves Perfectionists, they shared all property and looked for ways of improving their self. The communal way of life was abandoned in 1881. However a joint stock corporation was formed to carry on the manufacturing activities. The present corporation has retained some cooperative features; Oneida Ltd. has factories and home offices in the area as well as in Sherrill, where silverware is made.

Of interest is the Oneida Community Mansion House at 170 Kenwood Ave. Begun in 1860, the home contains some 300 rooms that reflect the needs of the society that lived as one family. Guided tours present family portraits, Empire and Victorian furniture, costumes and historical photographs; phone (315) 363-0745.

Greater Oneida Chamber of Commerce: 136 Lenox Ave., Oneida, NY 13421-1745; phone (315) 363-4300. *See color ad p. 77.*

MADISON COUNTY HISTORICAL SOCIETY HEADQUARTERS, 435 Main St., occupies the Gothic Revival mansion Cottage Lawn. The house offers changing exhibits about local history, a genealogical library and seven period rooms. The carriage barn has an agricultural museum with a display about hops. Guided tours are given Mon.-Fri. 9-4; closed major holidays. Tour $2; under 12, $1. Phone (315) 363-4136.

ONEONTA (F-9) pop. 13,292, elev. 1,083'

Oneonta is the Oneida Indian word for "cliffs abound" or "exposed rock in side of hills." The town is on the western edge of the Catskills, surrounded by hills.

Oneonta became the site of a major railroad car-building shop for the Albany & Susquehanna line in 1863. Twenty years later a handful of train yard workers formed the Brotherhood of Railroad Brakemen, the embryo of today's Brotherhood of Railroad Trainmen. When first built, the Delaware and Hudson roundhouse was one of the largest turntables in the world.

Otsego County Chamber of Commerce: 12 Carbon St., Oneonta, NY 13820; phone (877) 568-7346.

NATIONAL SOCCER HALL OF FAME, I-88 exit 13 to 18 Stadium Cir., tells the story of soccer in America through interactive exhibits, videotape footage and artifacts, including the world's oldest soccer ball and the Women's World Cup trophy. Soccer buffs can test their skills in the Kick's Game Zone with 11 different games.

Allow 1 hour minimum. Daily 9-7, Memorial Day-Labor Day; 10-5, rest of year. Closed Jan. 1, Thanksgiving and Dec. 25. Phone ahead to verify schedule. Admission $12; students with ID $9; over 54, $8; ages 6-12, $7.50. AX, DC, MC, VI. Phone (607) 432-3351.

SCIENCE DISCOVERY CENTER OF ONEONTA is in the Physical Science Building at State University College on Ravine Pkwy. This center promotes the enjoyment and understanding of science by children and adults through direct, hands-on experiences and educational fun. Allow 1 hour minimum. Mon.-Sat. noon-4, July-Aug.; Thurs.-Sat. noon-4, rest of year. Closed Good Friday, July 4, Thanksgiving and Dec. 25. Free. Phone (607) 436-2011.

YAGER MUSEUM OF ART & CULTURE, on the Hartwick College campus, includes holdings of Upper Susquehanna American Indian, South American pre-Columbian and Mesoamerican artifacts along with Southwestern pottery, baskets and rugs and a small collection of objects from Micronesia. Works in the fine arts collection range from European Renaissance through contemporary American paintings, sculpture and prints. Open Tues.-Sun. noon-4:30, Sept.-May; Wed.-Sun. noon-4:30, July-Aug. Closed holidays. Free. Phone (607) 431-4480.

ORCHARD PARK—*see Buffalo p. 72.*

ORISKANY (E-8) pop. 1,459, elev. 423'

ORISKANY BATTLEFIELD STATE HISTORIC SITE, 6 mi. e. on SR 69, is marked by a granite shaft. On Aug. 6, 1777, in the "bloodiest battle of the Revolution," Mohawk Valley militiamen en route to relieve Fort Stanwix were ambushed by a large force of Tories and Indians. The Colonists and Oneida Indian allies led by Gen. Nicholas Herkimer were victorious, though badly mauled, in the 6-hour battle. Guided tours are available. Allow 30 minutes minimum. Wed.-Sat. and Mon. holidays 9-5, Sun. 1-5, mid-May to mid-Oct. Hours may vary; phone ahead. Free. Phone (315) 768-7224.

ORISKANY MUSEUM, 420 Utica St., exhibits items commemorating the Battle of Oriskany, fought during the Revolutionary War, as well as other military contributions from the area. An airplane and an anchor from the aircraft carrier USS *Oriskany*, which served during the Korean and Vietnam wars, also are displayed. Guided tours are available. Allow 30 minutes minimum. Wed.-Sat. 1-5; closed Dec. 25. Free. Phone (315) 736-7529.

OSSINING—*see New York p. 153.*

OSWEGO (D-7) pop. 17,954, elev. 298'

On Lake Ontario at the mouth of the Oswego River, Oswego was fought over by the French, English and Americans during most of the 1700s because of its strategic position at the end of the inland water route. By 1796 Oswego was firmly in U.S. hands, and the town soon became a booming port. Oswego is the largest U.S. port on Lake Ontario and the home of the State University of New York at Oswego.

Greater Oswego Chamber of Commerce: 44 E. Bridge St., Oswego, NY 13126; phone (315) 343-7681.

FORT ONTARIO STATE HISTORIC SITE, 5 blks. n. of SR 104 on E. Fourth St., overlooks Oswego Harbor and Lake Ontario. The site was first fortified during the French and Indian War and remained in use through World War II, when it was the only American site to house Jewish refugees. Barracks, guard houses, a powder magazine, two officers' quarters, underground stone casements and the grounds have been restored to the 1868-72 time period.

Picnicking is permitted. Allow 1 hour minimum. Tues.-Sun. 10-4:30, May-Oct. Admission $4, over 62 and students with ID $3, under 13 free. Phone (315) 343-4711.

SAVE **H. LEE WHITE MARINE MUSEUM,** SR 104 to W. First St., then .5 mi. n. to pier, houses exhibits covering 300 years of Oswego and Great Lakes history. Included are displays about local American Indians, early settlement, navigation on Lake Ontario and the activities of the Underground Railroad in the area. A World War II tugboat and an Erie Canal barge can be toured. Allow 1 hour minimum. Daily 10-5, July-Aug.; 1-5, rest of year. Admission $4; ages 5-11, $2. AX, MC, VI. Phone (315) 342-0480.

RICHARDSON-BATES HOUSE MUSEUM, 135 E. Third St., contains period rooms dating from around 1890 with original Victorian pieces, an exhibit about county history and changing exhibits. Allow 1 hour minimum. Tues.-Fri. 10-5, Sat. 1-5, Apr.-Dec.; Tues.-Fri. 10-5, rest of year. Closed holidays. Admission $4, over 64 and students (to age 25) with ID $2, under 5 free; family rate $10. Phone (315) 343-1342.

SAFE HAVEN MUSEUM AND EDUCATION CENTER is at 2 E. Seventh St. The museum preserves the stories of 982 European Holocaust refugees who were sheltered at Fort Ontario during World War II by order of President Franklin D. Roosevelt. Exhibits show how they lived, interacted with the community during an 18-month stay, and relocated after the war. This was the only camp in the United States established for Holocaust survivors. Allow 1 hour minimum. Tues.-Sun. 11-5; closed Thanksgiving and Dec. 25. Admission $4; over $65, $2; students with ID $1; under 5 free; family rate (two adults and three children) $10. MC, VI. Phone (315) 342-3003.

OVID (F-6) pop. 612, elev. 816'

WINERIES
- **Cayuga Ridge Estate Winery** is 4 mi. e. via SR 96A and CR 138, then .5 mi. n. on SR 89. Mon.-Sat. 11-5, Sun. noon-5, mid-May through Dec. 31; Fri.-Sun. noon-5, rest of year. Guided tours are offered daily at 2:30, mid-May to mid-Nov. Phone (607) 869-5158.

OWEGO (G-7) pop. 20,365

THE TIOGA COUNTY HISTORICAL SOCIETY MUSEUM, 110 Front St., offers permanent and changing interpretive exhibits about local and regional history. Displays include American Indian artifacts, folk art portraiture and 19th-century tools,

toys, fashions and transportation artifacts. Area genealogical information dating from 1800 also is available. Allow 30 minutes minimum. Museum open Tues.-Sat. 10-4. Research library open Tues.-Fri. 1-4, Sat. 10-4. Closed holidays. Museum free. Library $5. Phone (607) 687-2460.

OYSTER BAY (H-2) pop. 6,826, elev. 8'

Oyster Bay, discovered in 1653 by settlers from Massachusetts, found itself in the middle of a tug of war: The Dutch Government in New Amsterdam and the English Colonial government in Hartford were unable to agree on who had jurisdiction over Oyster Bay. The settlers made appeals to both governments for protection.

During the Revolutionary War the village was headquarters for British lieutenant colonel John Graves Simcoe, a close friend of Maj. John Andre, adjutant general of the British Army in North America. As Benedict Arnold's British contact, Andre played an instrumental role in the ensuing scandal and was executed as a British spy in 1780. From 1901 to 1909 Oyster Bay was the site of President Theodore Roosevelt's summer White House. *Also see Long Island p. 99.*

Oyster Bay Chamber of Commerce: 34 Audrey Ave., P.O. Box 21, Oyster Bay, NY 11771; phone (516) 922-6464.

Self-guiding tours: Brochures detailing self-guiding tours of Oyster Bay are available from the chamber of commerce.

EARLE-WIGHTMAN HOUSE MUSEUM, 20 Summit St., was built in 1720 as a one-room home, with additional rooms added over the following 150 years by successive owners. One room has been renovated to reflect the 18th century, and a second room depicts a 19th-century parlor. Other rooms feature changing exhibits. An 18th-century garden is on the grounds.

Allow 30 minutes minimum. Tues.-Fri. 10-2, Sat. 9-1, Sun. 1-4; closed Jan. 1, July 4, Thanksgiving and Dec. 25. Donations. Phone (516) 922-5032.

GEM **PLANTING FIELDS ARBORETUM STATE HISTORIC PARK,** w. via Mill River and Oyster Bay rds., covers 409 landscaped acres of greenhouses, gardens and natural habitat. Collections include rhododendrons, azaleas, camellias, orchids, ferns and bromeliads. The Synoptic Garden's ornamental shrubs and small trees are arranged alphabetically and are identified by botanical and common name and by family and country of origin.

Allow 1 hour, 30 minutes minimum. Arboretum daily 9-5; closed Dec. 25. Greenhouses daily 10-4:30. Camellia house daily 10-4. Admission free. Parking $6 daily, May-Oct., Sat.-Sun. and holidays, rest of year. Phone (516) 922-9200.

SAVE **Coe Hall**, on the arboretum grounds, is a 65-room Tudor Revival mansion furnished with 16th- and 17th-century pieces. Carpets, paintings and tapestries were imported from Europe. Examples of stained glass from the 13th through 19th centuries are found throughout the house. The Buffalo Room contains murals of buffalo and American Indians set against a Western landscape. Allow 1 hour minimum. Guided tours are given daily noon-3:30, Apr.-Sept.; closed holidays. Admission $5; over 62 and students with ID $3.50; ages 7-12, $1; under 6 free. Parking $6. Phone (516) 922-9210.

RAYNHAM HALL MUSEUM, 20 W. Main St., British headquarters during the Revolutionary War, was the home of Samuel Townsend, who was partially responsible for the capture of Maj. John Andre and the exposure of Benedict Arnold's plan to betray West Point. Allow 30 minutes minimum. Tues.-Sun. noon-5, July 1-Labor Day; Tues.-Sun. 1-5, rest of year. Closed holidays. Admission $4; over 65 and ages 6-18, $3. Phone (516) 922-6808.

SAGAMORE HILL NATIONAL HISTORIC SITE, 3 mi. e. via E. Main St. and Cove Neck Rd. to 20 Sagamore Hill Rd., was the home of President Theodore Roosevelt until his death in 1919. The house served as the "summer White House" during his administration. The 1885 house displays trophies, furniture and other memorabilia. The nearby Old Orchard Museum offers audiovisual programs and exhibits relating to the political career and family life of President Roosevelt.

Grounds daily dawn-dusk. Visitor center daily 9-5, Memorial Day-Labor Day; Wed.-Sun. 9-5, rest of year. Guided tours of the house are given daily on the hour 10-4, Memorial Day-Labor Day; Wed.-Sun. 10-4, rest of year. Closed holidays. Admission $5, under 15 free. Grounds free. Tour tickets go on sale at 9. AX, DS, MC, VI. Phone (516) 922-4788.

THEODORE ROOSEVELT SANCTUARY AND AUDUBON CENTER is 2 mi. e. on E. Main St. to 134 Cove Rd. Features include three trails lined with oak trees and a variety of songbird species. Young Memorial Cemetery, next to the sanctuary, contains President Roosevelt's grave. Allow 30 minutes minimum. Daily 9-4:30; closed Jan. 1, Thanksgiving and Dec. 25. Donations. Phone (516) 922-3200.

PALMYRA (E-5) pop. 3,490, elev. 442'

Palmyra was the birthplace of Mormonism and the early home of Joseph Smith. The Church of Jesus Christ of Latter-day Saints was organized and the "Book of Mormon" was published nearby in 1830. A visitor center on the Peter Whitmer Farm, where the church was founded, is 5 miles south of Waterloo on SR 96. *Also see Finger Lakes p. 84.*

ALLING COVERLET MUSEUM, 122 William St., has changing 19th-century coverlet and quilt displays. Daily 1-4, June 1-Sept. 15. Free. Phone (315) 597-6737.

BOOK OF MORMON HISTORIC PUBLICATION SITE, 217 E. Main St., is the site where the first 5,000 copies of the "Book of Mormon" were printed by E.B. Grandin. The restored site includes a bindery and the print shop. Allow 1 hour minimum. Forty-minute guided tours are given Mon.-Sat. 9-7, Sun. 12:30-7, June-Aug.; Mon.-Sat. 9-6, Sun. 12:30-6, Apr.-May and Sept.-Oct.; Mon.-Sat. 9-5, Sun. 12:30-5, rest of year. Visitor center Mon.-Sat. 9-9, Sun. 12:30-9, June-Aug.; Mon.-Sat. 9-8, Sun. 12:30-8, Apr.-May and Sept.-Oct.; Mon.-Sat. 9-7, Sun. 12:30-7, rest of year. Free. Phone (315) 597-5982.

HILL CUMORAH, 2 mi. n. of I-90 exit 43, is where Joseph Smith is said to have received from the angel Moroni the golden plates inscribed with the history of ancient Americans, from which he translated the "Book of Mormon." A 40-foot monument crowns the hill. The visitor center has an audiovisual tour centering on the life of Jesus Christ. Twenty-five minute guided tours are given Mon.-Sat. 9-9, Sun. 11-9, June-Aug.; Mon.-Sat. 9-6, Sun. 1-6, Apr.-May and Sept.-Oct.; hours vary rest of year and on holidays. Free. Phone (315) 597-5851.

JOSEPH SMITH HOME, 4 mi. s. on SR 21 to Stafford Rd., includes the Smith frame home, a reconstructed log home and the Sacred Grove. Guided tours of the homes are given Mon.-Sat. 9-7, Sun. 11-7, June-Aug.; Mon.-Sat. 9-6, Sun. 11-6, Apr.-May and Sept.-Oct.; hours vary rest of year. Free. Phone (315) 597-5851.

PANAMA (G-2) pop. 491, elev. 1,548'

PANAMA ROCKS, .2 mi. w. of jct. SR 474 and CR 33, then w. on CR 10 (Rock Hill Rd.), is an outcrop of Paleozoic sea islands compressed into quartz-conglomerate rock fractured by earthquakes and unearthed by glaciers. The huge rocks, some more than 60 feet high, extend along a half-mile ridge. Geologic features include cavernous dens, small caves, passageways and crevices. A 1-mile hiking trail is available. Visitors can also enjoy off-trail exploration and rock climbing.

Pets are not permitted. Picnicking is permitted. Daily 10-5, May 12-Oct. 21. Admission $6; over 59 and ages 13-17, $5; ages 6-12, $4. Under 18 must be with an adult. Phone (716) 782-2845.

PETERSBURG (F-11) pop. 1,563, elev. 684'

BERKSHIRE BIRD PARADISE SANCTUARY, 2 mi. n. on CR 87 from jct. SR 2 and CR 87, then 1 mi. e. to 43 Red Pond Rd., is dedicated to the conservation of wild birds. The site is home to more than 1,000 birds, including raptors, tropical birds and birds of prey. Allow 1 hour minimum. Daily 9-5, mid-May through Oct. 31 Admission $8; under 12, $5. Phone (518) 279-3801.

PHOENICIA (G-10) pop. 381, elev. 795′

RECREATIONAL ACTIVITIES

Tubing

- [SAVE] **The Town Tinker Tube Rental** is at 10 Bridge St. Write P.O. Box 404, Phoenicia, NY 12464. Daily 9-6 (last rental is at 4), May 15-Sept. 30. Phone (845) 688-5553.

PLATTSBURGH (A-11)
pop. 18,816, elev. 109′

On Lake Champlain, Plattsburgh was the site of the Battle of Plattsburgh on Sept. 11, 1814. While Gen. Alexander Macomb restrained a superior British land force, the Americans, under Cmdr. Thomas Macdonough, scored a decisive naval victory in Plattsburgh Bay.

Plattsburgh North Country Chamber of Commerce: 7061 SR 9, P.O. Box 310, Plattsburgh, NY 12901; phone (518) 563-1000.

Shopping areas: Two major malls serve the Plattsburgh area. Champlain Centers Mall, a quarter-mile east on SR 3 from exit 37, and Consumer Square, farther east on SR 3, include JCPenney and Sears.

[SAVE] **CLINTON COUNTY HISTORICAL MUSEUM,** 3 Cumberland Ave., contains a diorama of the 1814 Battle of Plattsburgh and the 1776 Battle of Valcour. Also displayed are domestic and historical artifacts and memorabilia, including a collection of Redford glass. **Note:** The museum plans to move to Ohio Avenue in 2007; phone ahead to confirm location. Tues.-Fri. 9-2. Admission $4; over 64, $3; students with ID $2. Phone (518) 561-0340.

KENT-DELORD HOUSE MUSEUM, 17 Cumberland Ave., overlooks Lake Champlain at the mouth of the Saranac River. The Federal-style structure was commandeered by the British in 1814. They left behind an oak tea chest when they fled. American decorative arts and period furniture also are displayed. Exhibits interpret daily life 1800-1913, with emphasis on the War of 1812, the Civil War and women's issues of the late 19th century. Tues.-Sat. noon-3:15, May-Dec.; closed major holidays. Admission $5; students with ID $3; under 12, $2. Phone (518) 561-1035.

LAKE CHAMPLAIN FERRIES—
see Lake Champlain p. 96.

PLATTSBURGH STATE ART MUSEUM is at 101 Broad St., on the campus of the State University of New York. Displays include a collection of paintings, drawings and books by illustrator Rockwell Kent. The gallery also houses photographs by Ansel Adams, German expressionist prints and prints by Paul Cézanne, Albrecht Dürer and Peter Paul Rubens. Changing historical and contemporary exhibitions of mixed media and an outdoor sculpture garden also are available. Allow 30 minutes minimum. Daily noon-4; closed holidays. Donations. Phone (518) 564-2813 or (518) 564-2474.

PORT JERVIS (H-9) pop. 8,860, elev. 442′

An important 19th-century railroad and river transportation hub, Port Jervis was named for John B. Jervis, chief engineer of the Delaware and Hudson Canal. One of two railroad turntables built around the turn of the 20th century is still in operation.

Stephen Crane reputedly drew inspiration for "The Red Badge of Courage" while interviewing veterans of New York's 124th Regiment at the 1886 dedication of a Civil War monument in Veteran's Memorial Park.

GILLINDER GLASS FACTORY, corner Erie and Liberty sts., uses century-old techniques to produce commercial and decorative glass. Visitors to the factory floor can watch the pouring, pressing and cooling of molten glass. A museum chronicles the history of local glass making. Allow 1 hour minimum. Guided tours Mon.-Fri. at 10:15, 12:30 and 1:30. Tours $4; over 55 and under 16, $3.50. MC, VI. Phone (845) 856-5375.

PORT WASHINGTON (H-2)
pop. 15,215, elev. 140′

Port Washington Chamber of Commerce: 329 Main St., P.O. Box 121, Port Washington, NY 11050; phone (516) 883-6566.

SANDS POINT PRESERVE, 6 mi. n. of I-495 exit 36 on Searingtown Rd./Port Washington Blvd., was the early 19th-century estate of Howard Gould, and later of Harry F. Guggenheim. The grounds include a 216-acre forest and shoreline preserve, two castle-like structures built by Gould and a manor house built in the 1920s by Harry F. Guggenheim. The restored homes display artifacts and antiques. Nature and science exhibits are on the grounds. Allow 2 hours, 30 minutes minimum. Grounds open daily 9-5. Grounds admission Sat.-Sun. and holidays $2, free otherwise. Special events may incur an additional charge. Phone (516) 571-7900.

Castle Gould, in Sands Point Preserve, is a huge 1902 stone castle that once served as a stable. It houses a visitor reception center and a main exhibit hall. Allow 1 hour minimum. Tues.-Sun. 10-5, Feb.-Oct. Last admission is at 4. Visitor center free. Main exhibit hall $7; over 59 and ages 3-12, $4. Hours and prices may vary; phone ahead.

Falaise, in Sands Point Preserve, was built by Capt. Harry F. Guggenheim in 1923. The elegant Normandy-style manor house contains original furnishings and historic memorabilia relating to Guggenheim's support of aeronautical technology. Allow 1 hour minimum. Guided tours Thurs.-Sun. noon-3, May-Oct. Last tour begins 1 hour before closing. Tour $6; over 59, $5. Under 10 are not permitted.

POTSDAM (B-9) pop. 9,425, elev. 397′

Potsdam was settled in 1803 by land agent Benjamin Raymond. Five years later a post office opened to serve a thriving community of more than 900. The Clarkson family ran a farm and a variety of businesses, built Trinity Church and founded the Thomas Clarkson Memorial College of Technology, now known as Clarkson University. Raymond built a schoolhouse, which became part of the state university system in 1949. Sandstone quarried in the area has been used for structures in Ottawa, Syracuse, and New York City.

Potsdam Chamber of Commerce: Potsdam Civic Center, 1 Market St., P.O. Box 717, Potsdam, NY 13676; phone (315) 265-5440.

GIBSON GALLERY, on SR 56 in Brainerd Hall on the State University of New York campus, presents changing exhibitions featuring student and regional, national and international artists throughout the year and houses a permanent collection and a sculpture park. Allow 1 hour minimum. Mon.-Fri. noon-5 (also Tues.-Thurs. 7-9 p.m.), Sat.-Sun. noon-4 and by appointment; closed during school breaks. Free. Phone (315) 267-2245 or (315) 267-2481.

POTSDAM PUBLIC MUSEUM, on SR 11 in the Civic Center, houses the Burnap Collection of English pottery, dating 1700-1870. The collection includes Delft chargers, Wedgwood, lusterware, transfer prints and relief wares. Also displayed are American decorative glassware, furniture and changing exhibits pertaining to local history. Tues.-Sat. noon-4, Sept.-May; Tues.-Fri. noon-4, rest of year. Closed holidays. Free. Phone (315) 265-6910.

POTTERSVILLE (C-11)

NATURAL STONE BRIDGE AND CAVES PARK is 1 mi. n. of I-87 exit 26 on US 9, then 2.5 mi. w. following signs. A well-marked path leads through a series of caves, rock formations and underground waterways. Natural paths cover some uneven terrain. Rental shoes are available.

Picnicking is permitted. Allow 1 hour minimum. Daily 9-7, Memorial Day weekend-Labor Day; 10-5, day after Labor Day-Columbus Day. Admission $12; ages 5-12, $6. AX, DC, MC, VI. Phone (518) 494-2283.

POUGHKEEPSIE (H-11)
pop. 29,871, elev. 168′

Originally settled by the Dutch, Poughkeepsie became the state capital in 1777. Eleven years later the state ratified the U.S. Constitution. The city is built on the rocky terraces rising 250 feet above the Hudson River and the level plateau above. The Home of Franklin D. Roosevelt and the Vanderbilt Mansion national historic sites are nearby (see Hyde Park p. 92).

Dutchess County Tourism Promotion Agency: 3 Neptune Rd., Poughkeepsie, NY 12601; phone (845) 463-4000 or (800) 445-3131.

THE FRANCES LEHMAN LOEB ART CENTER, on the campus of Vassar College at 124 Raymond Ave., contains more than 12,500 art objects. Exhibits include works from the permanent collection displayed chronologically in the Main Gallery and selections from the college's significant holdings in Asian art. Among the displays are works by Pieter Brueghel the Younger, Alexander Calder, Paul Cézanne, Georgia O'Keeffe and Jackson Pollock. Allow 1 hour minimum. Tues.-Sat. 10-5, Sun. 1-5; closed major holidays. Free. Phone (845) 437-5632.

LOCUST GROVE, THE SAMUEL MORSE HISTORIC SITE, 2 mi. s. of Mid-Hudson Bridge at 2683 South Rd. (US 9), was the home of artist, educator and telegraph inventor Samuel F.B. Morse 1847-72. Designed by A.J. Davis, the house contains period furnishings, china, art, original telegraph equipment and other Hudson Valley memorabilia. The 150-acre site includes hiking trails and historic formal gardens, carriage and ice houses, a picnic grove and a visitor center.

Allow 1 hour, 30 minutes minimum. Grounds daily 8 a.m.-dusk. House daily 10-3 and by appointment, May-Nov.; closed Thanksgiving. Fee $9; ages 6-18, $5. AX, MC, VI. Phone (845) 454-4500.

PRATTSVILLE (F-10) pop. 2,064, elev. 1,165′

[SAVE] **ZADOCK PRATT MUSEUM,** on SR 23 (Main St.), was the home of Prattsville's founder and U.S. representative Zadock Pratt. The 1828 house contains original and period furnishings; exhibits pertain to Pratt's lively and varied occupations, as well as to town and regional history. Thurs.-Sun. 1-4, Memorial Day-Columbus Day. Tours lasting 45 minutes are given on the hour. Last tour begins 1 hour before closing. Admission $5; under 12 free. Phone (518) 299-3395 to verify schedule.

PURCHASE—see New York p. 153.

QUEENSBURY (D-11) pop. 25,441, elev. 293′

THE GREAT ESCAPE & SPLASHWATER KINGDOM is 3.7 mi. n. on US 9, just e. of I-87 Northway via exits 19 or 20. With 140 [SAVE] acres, this is one of the state's larger theme parks. More than 135 rides, shows and attractions include the classic wooden coaster The Comet, and Canyon Blaster, a steel coaster almost 2,000 feet long that simulates a ride on a runaway mine train. In addition to seven roller coasters, features include a full water park, Storytown USA and a variety of shows for children. Looney Tunes National Park with is a children's area with 10 rides and attractions.

Allow 6 hours minimum. Park opens daily at 10, the Fri. of Memorial Day weekend-Labor Day; opens Sat.-Sun. (also Columbus Day Mon.) at noon, day after Labor Day-Oct. 31. Closing times vary. Admission $39.99, and 48 inches tall and under $24.99, under age 3 free. Parking $10. AX, DS, MC, VI. Phone (518) 792-3500.

LAKE GEORGE OPERA FESTIVAL—
see Saratoga Springs p. 194.

RAQUETTE LAKE (C-9) elev. 1,810′

GREAT CAMP SAGAMORE, 4 mi. s. of SR 28 following signs, via a dirt road, was a rustic summer retreat of the Vanderbilts built in 1897 and expanded in 1901. Exemplifying the 19th century's Great Camps, the lakeside main lodge features log and bark siding. Other buildings include the caretakers' quarters, a bowling alley and a dining hall.

A 2-hour guided tour is offered daily at 10 and 1:30, late June-Labor Day; daily at 1:30, day after Labor Day-Columbus Day; Sat. at 1:30, Memorial Day-late June. Admission $12, senior citizens and college students with ID $11, children $6. Reservations are recommended. MC, VI. Phone (315) 354-5311.

RENSSELAER (F-11) pop. 7,761, elev. 21′

Across the Hudson from Albany, Rensselaer was founded in 1631 by Dutch settlers sent by wealthy patron Killean Van Rensselaer. Fort Crailo was built in 1704 for protection against the indigenous inhabitants. It is said that "Yankee Doodle" was composed in Rensselaer in 1758 as a satire of the Provincial troops.

CRAILO STATE HISTORIC SITE is 1.5 blks. s. of jct. US 9 and US 20 at 9 ½ Riverside Ave. The museum houses exhibits that explain the history, development, culture and influence of Dutch settlements in the Upper Hudson Valley area. Allow 1 hour minimum. Grounds open dawn-dusk. Guided tours are given every 30 minutes Wed.-Sat. 10-5, Sun. 1-5, Apr. 15-Oct. 31; closed Easter. Tour $3; ages 5-12, $1. Phone (518) 463-8738.

RHINEBECK (G-11) pop. 3,077, elev. 203′

OLD RHINEBECK AERODROME, .5 mi. n. on US 9 off SR 9G, then 1.5 mi. e. to 42 Stone Church Rd., presents antique airplanes from 1908-37. Fifteen-minute barnstorming rides in a 1929 open cockpit airplane are available. Daily 10-5, mid-May to late Oct. Air shows Sat.-Sun. at 2, mid-June to mid-Oct. Barnstorming rides Sat.-Sun., June-Oct. Museum $6; senior citizens $5; ages 6-10, $2. Air shows $15; over 64, $10; ages 6-10, $5. Plane rides $50. Phone (845) 752-3200.

RIVERHEAD (H-4) pop. 10,513, elev. 25′

 ATLANTIS MARINE WORLD is at 431 E. Main St. Indoor and outdoor areas simulating the ruins of the Lost City of Atlantis feature eel, piranha, shark, octopus and tortoise exhibits along with one of the largest live coral reefs in North America. Towering trees and large river creatures are highlights of the Amazon Rain Forest exhibit.

A stingray touch tank and an interactive salt marsh provide hands-on experiences. Sea lion shows, shark feedings and educational programs are presented daily. Naturalist-led environmental boat tours of the Peconic River and Flanders Bay also are offered and last 2 hours.

Guided behind-the-scenes tours are available. Allow 1 hour, 30 minutes minimum. Daily 10-5; closed Dec. 25. Boat trips daily at 11:30 and 2, May-Oct. (weather permitting). Admission $18.50; over 61 and ages 3-11, $15.50. Guided tours $5. Boat trip $18.50; over 61 and under 12, $16.50. Reservations are recommended for boat trips. AX, DS, MC, VI. Phone (631) 208-9200.

SPLISH SPLASH WATER PARK is .5 mi. w. of jct. I-495 and SR 25 at 2549 Splish Splash Dr. The 96-acre park contains such water rides as Splash Landing, Lazy River and Giant Twisters. Children's areas and tropical bird shows also are featured.

Food is available. Allow a full day. Daily 9:30-7, mid-June to mid-Aug.; Sat.-Sun. 9:30-5, Memorial Day to mid-June. Over 48 inches tall $30.99, over age 62 and children under 48 inches tall $22.99, under age 3 free. Parking $9. Prices may vary; phone ahead. AX, DS, MC, VI. Phone (631) 727-3600.

SUFFOLK COUNTY HISTORICAL SOCIETY, on SR 25 at 300 W. Main St., has permanent and changing exhibits about the history of Suffolk County, including early crafts, textiles, china, whaling and American Indian artifacts and a research library. Allow 1 hour minimum. Tues.-Sat. 12:30-4:30; closed holidays. Library open Wed.-Thurs. and Sat. 12:30-4:30. Donations. Library $2. Phone (631) 727-2881.

DID YOU KNOW

The Stars and Stripes was flown in battle for the first time at Fort Stanwix in Rome.

ROCHESTER (D-5) pop. 219,773, elev. 660'

Originally called the "Flour City" because of its milling industries, Rochester also became known as the "Flower City" because of its nurseries, parks and fruit and garden areas. Rochester leads in the manufacture of optical, surgical, dental, check-protecting and gear-cutting goods.

Some of the local parks preserve historical sites; others were created especially for recreation. Cobb's Hill Park between Highland Avenue and Culver Road contains Lake Riley, the old Erie Canal turning basin; phone (585) 428-6909. The city can be viewed from the hilltop. Upper Falls Park, on the Genesee River off St. Paul Street, has a 100-foot waterfall; phone (585) 325-2030. Originally used to power the city's flour mills, the falls continue to generate electricity. Monroe County Park at Clover Street and Pond Road is a 2,500-acre park with a natural preserve and self-guiding trails; phone (585) 256-4950.

City Hall at Church and Fitzhugh streets presents exhibits in its Link Gallery; phone (585) 428-6690. Another landmark is Mount Hope Cemetery on Mount Hope Avenue. One of the oldest Victorian-era cemeteries in the nation, it contains the graves of Susan B. Anthony and Frederick Douglass; phone (585) 428-7999.

Rochester's contribution to education and technology is evident at the University of Rochester's Laboratory of Laser Energetics, where nuclear fusion research takes place. The Rochester Institute of Technology has the School for American Craftsmen and the National Technical Institute for the Deaf.

The Rochester Philharmonic Orchestra performs at the Eastman Theater; phone (585) 454-2100. The GEVA Theatre Centre, 75 Woodbury Blvd., offers performances throughout the year; phone (585) 232-4382. Local theater and musical companies and touring Broadway troupes also offer productions. The Eastman School of Music is said to produce more professional musicians than any other conservatory in the country.

One of the most popular recreational pursuits is fishing. Lake Ontario and its tributaries offer ice fishing in winter and warm-water angling in summer. Abundant species include coho and giant chinook salmon, smelt, bass, pike and steelhead, rainbow and brown trout. Hiking and biking are popular along the Erie Canal Trail.

Greater Rochester Visitors Association, Inc.: 45 East Ave., Rochester, NY 14604; phone (585) 546-3070 or (800) 677-7282.

Self-guiding tours: Brochures detailing self-guiding walking tours of the downtown historic district and other areas are available from the visitors association.

Shopping areas: Several major enclosed malls serve the Rochester area. Near Greece in Rochester's northwest suburbs is Greece Ridge Mall, with 100 stores 1 mile west of I-390 at West Ridge Road; anchor stores are JCPenney, Macy's and Sears.

Eastview Mall, on SR 96 near I-490 in Victor, counts Macy's and Sears among its 106 stores. Marketplace Mall, at W. Henrietta and Jefferson roads in Henrietta, has a Macy's and 147 other stores.

Discounted merchandise can be found at the Southtown Plaza, 3333 W. Henrietta Rd. at Jefferson Road, and the 27 stores at the Panorama Mall and Plaza, 3 miles east of I-490 on Penfield Road in Penfield.

Tree-lined Park Avenue has jewelry, art, wine, candy, flower and other specialty shops tucked in a quaint neighborhood. Village Gate Square, housed in a renovated 1800s printing factory at 274 N. Goodman St., offers antique shopping. Fine handicrafts are the specialty at Craft Company No. 6, 785 University Ave.

DURAND-EASTMAN PARK, 7 mi. n. off I-590, has a 2-mile frontage on Lake Ontario. Part of the Monroe County Arboretum, the park contains an 18-hole golf course and a large collection of flowering wild crab apples. Daily 10 a.m.-11 p.m. Free. Phone (585) 266-1372.

GENESEE COUNTRY VILLAGE & MUSEUM—*see Mumford p. 102.*

GEORGE EASTMAN HOUSE INTERNATIONAL MUSEUM OF PHOTOGRAPHY AND FILM is at 900 East Ave. This 50-room mansion, once occupied by George Eastman, founder of Eastman Kodak Co., has been restored to its early 1900s appearance. Formal gardens grace the 12.5-acre estate. The International Museum of Photography and Film houses changing displays of photography, film, technology and related literature.

The Dryden Theater presents evening film programs Tuesday through Sunday. Guided garden tours are offered May through September. A research library is available.

Allow 2 hours minimum. Tues.-Sat. 10-5 (also Thurs. 5-8), Sun. 1-5; closed Thanksgiving and Dec. 25. Museum tours are given Tues.-Sat. at 10:30 and 2, Sun. at 2. Admission $8; over 60 and students with ID $6; ages 5-12, $3. Film programs $6. AX, MC, VI. Phone (585) 271-3361, or TTY (585) 271-3362.

HIGHLAND PARK, off I-490 exit 12 or 14 following signs, contains botanic gardens, a conservatory and a collection of more than 1,200 lilac bushes. A Vietnam veteran's memorial, AIDs memorial, victim's rights memorial, Warner Castle, sunken garden and Highland Park Bowl amphitheater are on the grounds. Allow 1 hour, 30 minutes minimum. Park open daily 7 a.m.-11 p.m. Conservatory open daily 10-4. Admission $1, senior citizens 50c, under 13 free. Phone (585) 256-5878.

LANDMARK SOCIETY OF WESTERN NEW YORK is at 133 S. Fitzhugh St. The historical society's exhibit gallery and research library are in the

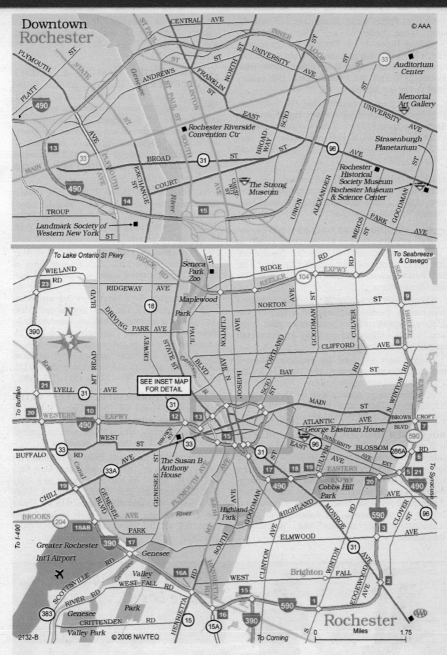

Downtown
Rochester

© AAA

PLYMOUTH ST
STATE ST
Genesee ST
ANDREWS ST
CENTRAL AVE
ST PAUL ST
FRANKLIN ST
NORTH ST
CLINTON ST
UNIVERSITY AVE
INNER LOOP
33
Auditorium Center
Memorial Art Gallery
UNIVERSITY AVE
PLATT
490
13
33
MAIN
PLYMOUTH AVE
EXCHANGE ST
BROAD
COURT
490
14
TROUP
Landmark Society of Western New York ST
EAST AVE
SOUTH AVE
Rochester Riverside Convention Ctr
BROAD WAY
ST
31
CHESTNUT ST
River
15
The Strong Museum
96 AVE
Strasenburgh Planetarium
Rochester Historical Society Museum
Rochester Museum & Science Center
UNION ST
ALEXANDER ST
MEIGS ST
PARK AVE
GOODMAN ST

To Lake Ontario St Pkwy
WIELAND RD
23
RIDGE RD
RIDGEWAY AVE
N
390
21
LYELL AVE
31
20
To Buffalo
WESTERN EXPWY
10
490
WEST ST
BUFFALO RD
33
33A
19
CHILI AVE
BROOKS AVE
204
18AB
Greater Rochester Int'l Airport
390
17
Genesee
383
Genesee Valley Park
CRITTENDEN RD
SCOTTSVILLE RD
RIVER RD
Valley WEST FALL RD
16A
HENRIETTA RD
15
15A
390
To Corning
RIDGE RD
Seneca Park Zoo
MAPLEWOOD Park
18
DRIVING PARK AVE
DEWEY AVE
STATE ST
Genesee
PAUL BLVD
CLINTON AVE N
JOSEPH AVE
SEE INSET MAP FOR DETAIL
31
12
13
BROWN ST
33
15
The Susan B. Anthony House
GENESEE ST
PLYMOUTH AVE
River
PARK
MT READ BLVD
ST
RIDGE AVE
KEELER ST
104
NORTON ST
PORTLAND AVE
SCIO ST
BAY ST
MAIN ST
ATLANTIC AVE
George Eastman House
EAST AVE
96
CULVER RD
UNIVERSITY
BLOSSOM
31
17
18 19
490
Cobbs Hill Park
EASTERN EXPWY
20
HIGHLAND AVE
Highland Park
GOODMAN ST
MT HOPE AVE
SOUTH AVE
ELMWOOD AVE
CLINTON AVE
WINTON RD
MONROE AVE
Brighton
FALL
31
590
15
1
To Corning
GOODMAN ST
SEA BREEZE EXPWY
9
BREEZE RD
CULVER RD
CLIFFORD AVE
8
N WINTON RD
BROWN CROFT
BLVD
7
590
286A
5
21
6
490
To Syracuse
5
EDGEWOOD AVE
CLOVER ST
96
590
3
2
Rochester
To Seabreeze & Oswego
To Buffalo
To I-490

2132-B
© 2006 NAVTEQ

Miles
0   1.75

1840 Hoyt-Potter House. Guided tours of two historic house museums are offered. Campbell-Whittlesey House, 123 S. Fitzhugh St., is a restored Greek Revival house furnished to illustrate the lifestyle of a 19th-century flour miller. Stone-Tolan House, 2370 East Ave., was an early 19th-century rural tavern and farmhouse.

Allow 2 hours minimum. Mon.-Fri. 9-4, Mar.-Dec. Tours of Campbell-Whittlesey House are given Thurs.-Fri. noon-3. Tours of Stone-Tolan House are given Fri.-Sat. noon-3. Fee (one house) $3; ages 8-18, $1. Two houses $5; ages 8-18, $1.50. Phone (585) 546-7029.

MAPLEWOOD PARK, 100 Maplewood Ave., contains one of the nation's largest municipal rose gardens. Allow 1 hour minimum. Daily 8-dusk. Free. Phone (585) 428-6444.

MEMORIAL ART GALLERY, 500 University Ave., features a collection of 11,000 art works spanning 50 centuries. Notable artists whose works are displayed include Mary Cassatt, Paul Cézanne, Winslow Homer, Henri Matisse and Claude Monet.

The museum's collection of antiquities includes a 16th-century Flemish painting and a pair of 4th-century Egyptian coffins. Contemporary glass sculpture by Dale Chihuly and works by American craft masters also are displayed.

Guided tours and food are available. Allow 2 hours, 30 minutes minimum. Wed.-Sun. 11-5 (also Thurs. 5-9); closed major holidays. Admission $7; over 61 and college students with ID $5; ages 6-18, $3; $2 to all Thurs. after 5. DS, MC, VI. Phone (585) 473-7720, or TTY (585) 473-6152.

ROCHESTER HISTORICAL SOCIETY MUSEUM is at 485 East Ave. The museum is housed in Woodside, an 1840 Greek Revival mansion. A distinctive feature is the house's round, glazed cupola set on a square pedestal surrounded by balustrades. Rooms display portraits, period furnishings and costumes. An enclosed perennial garden laid out in parterres is beyond the rear veranda. The collections include a reference library, archives and genealogical information.

Allow 1 hour minimum. Mon.-Fri. 10-3; closed holidays. Admission $3; over 60 and college students with ID $2; ages 6-18, $1. Phone (585) 271-2705.

ROCHESTER MUSEUM & SCIENCE CENTER, 657 East Ave., provides visitors the opportunity to explore science and technology, the natural environment and the cultural heritage of the region. The museum has family-oriented activities and permanent and changing exhibits. Highlights include a collection of Haudenosaunee (Iroquois) artifacts. The museum also operates the Cumming Nature Center in Naples (see Naples p. 102).

Food is available. Allow 2 hours, 30 minutes minimum. Mon.-Sat. 9-5, Sun. noon-5; closed Thanksgiving and Dec. 25. Admission $8; senior citizens and college students with ID $7; ages 3-18, $6. DS, MC, VI. Phone (585) 271-1880.

Strasenburgh Planetarium, 657 East Ave., presents large-format science/nature films in the Star Theater. Current events star shows and laser sound-light shows also are presented. "I See the Sky" is designed for children ages 3-5 and is offered Saturdays at 10. The observatory is open May-Oct.; phone for schedule. Shows are presented daily; phone for times. Closed Thanksgiving and Dec. 25. Admission $8; over 59 and college students with ID $7; ages 3-18, $6. Prices vary with type of show. Under 5 are not admitted to evening shows. DS, MC, VI. Phone (585) 697-1945 or (585) 271-1880.

SEABREEZE PARK/RAGING RIVERS WATER PARK, off I-590 and SR 104 at Culver Rd., is an amusement and water park with roller coasters, water slides, children's rides, a classic wooden carousel and a log flume. Live shows are presented.

Allow 4 hours minimum. Daily 11-10 (also Fri.-Sat. 10-11 p.m.), mid-June through Labor Day; Sat.-Sun. 11-10, May 1 to mid-June. Water park daily 11-8. Ride and slide pass $20.95, under 48 inches tall $16.95. Admission after 5 p.m. $13.95. Under age 2 free. Phone ahead to verify schedule and prices. DS, MC, VI. Phone (585) 323-1900 or (800) 395-2500.

SENECA PARK ZOO, 2222 St. Paul St., along the Genesee River Gorge, features a Rocky Coasts Exhibit that offers underwater viewing of polar bears, sea lions and penguins. The zoo also houses African elephants, cougars, primates, Eurasian arctic wolves, white rhinos and Bornean orangutans. Allow 1 hour minimum. Zoo open daily 10-5, Memorial Day-Labor Day; 10-4, rest of year. The grounds are open 1 hour later. Admission $6; over 63, $5; ages 3-11, $3. Phone (585) 336-7200 or (585) 467-9453.

 STRONG NATIONAL MUSEUM OF PLAY, One Manhattan Sq., features a variety of interactive learning environments, including a "Sesame Street" exhibit where visitors can appear on a television screen with characters from the show. Children can scan groceries in a child-size supermarket, produce their own TV show, or visit an old-fashioned ice-cream fountain.

Collections include dolls, dollhouses, miniatures and home furnishings as well as a toy hall of fame. A glass atrium features a historic street scene, vintage operating diner and 1918 carousel. More than 800 butterflies inhabit the butterfly garden's rainforest environment. A 1,000-gallon indoor aquarium displays tropical fish, anemones and other tropical creatures that live in coral reefs.

Allow 3 hours minimum. Mon.-Sat. 10-5 (also Fri. 5-8), Sun. noon-5; closed Thanksgiving and Dec. 25. Admission $9; over 62, $8; college students with ID and ages 2-17, $7. Butterfly house $3; advance purchase is recommended. DS, MC, VI. Phone (585) 263-2700, or TTY (585) 712-2702.

THE SUSAN B. ANTHONY HOUSE, 17 Madison St., was the home of the well-known civil rights leader during the most politically active period of her life. It also was the site of her famous arrest for voting in 1872. Guided tours of the red brick Victorian house feature personal items and a collection of suffrage material. A visitor center provides additional exhibits. Tues.-Sun. 11-5, Memorial Day-Labor Day; Wed.-Sun. 11-4, rest of year. Last tour begins 1 hour before closing. Admission $6; over 65, $5; students with ID and under 13, $3. DS, MC, VI. Phone (585) 235-6124.

VICTORIAN DOLL MUSEUM AND CHILI DOLL HOSPITAL—*see North Chili p. 179.*

ROME (D-8) pop. 34,950, elev. 435′

Long before the Europeans discovered Rome, it was called *De-O-Wain-Sta,* an American Indian term meaning "the carrying place." In the city's center is a portage on the only practical water route south of the St. Lawrence River, which connected the Great Lakes with the Hudson River.

Francis Bellamy, author of the "Pledge of Allegiance to the Flag," is buried in the Rome cemetery. The Tomb of the Unknown Soldiers of the American Revolution is next to the city hall at 207 N. James St. It was designed by Lirimer Rich, who also planned the Tomb of the Unknown Soldier in Arlington National Cemetery in Virginia.

The Tug Hill plateau north of Rome receives up to 200 inches of snow a year. This region is renowned for its skiing, snowmobiling and year-round hunting and fishing.

Rome Chamber of Commerce: 139 W. Dominick St., Rome, NY 13440; phone (315) 337-1700.

[SAVE] **ERIE CANAL VILLAGE,** 3 mi. w. on SR 49 at 5789 Rome-New London Rd., is a re-creation of an 1840 community with museums and restored buildings. Demonstrations, audiovisual programs and farm, canal and Americana exhibits are featured. A 30-minute horse-drawn packet boat ride along a restored part of the canal and a 4.5-mile train ride also are offered. Halloween and Christmas programs are available.

Allow 1 hour, 30 minutes minimum. Wed.-Sat. 10-5, Sun., noon-5, Memorial Day weekend-Labor Day; Sat.-Sun. noon-5, day after Labor Day-Sept. 30. Admission $15; over 62 and ages 13-17, $12; ages 5-12, $10. AX, MC, VI. Phone (315) 337-3999 or (888) 374-3226.

FORT RICKEY CHILDREN'S DISCOVERY ZOO is 3 mi. w. on SR 39. Such exotic and native animals and reptiles as bobcats, deer, spider monkeys, mountain lions, porcupines and owls are on display. A petting area allows children to interact with animals. Children also can enjoy pony rides, animal shows and a playground.

Picnicking is permitted. Food is available. Allow 1 hour, 30 minutes minimum. Daily 10-5, late June-Labor Day; daily 10-4, mid-May to late June; Sat.-Sun. 10-4, in Sept. Admission $9.50; over 64 and ages 2-15, $7.50. MC, VI. Phone (315) 336-1930.

FORT STANWIX NATIONAL MONUMENT—*see place listing p. 86.*

ROME-BOONVILLE GORGE, traversed by SR 46, is a narrow valley from Rome to North Western and a gorge from North Western to Boonville. Portions of the Black River Canal can be seen along the drive.

ROMULUS (E-6) pop. 2,036, elev. 717′

WINERIES

• **Swedish Hill Vineyard and Winery** is .5 mi. s. of jct. SR 336 at 4565 SR 414. Tours are given Mon.-Fri. at 1 and 3, Sat.-Sun. at noon, 2 and 4, May-Oct. Phone (315) 549-8326.

ROTTERDAM JUNCTION (E-10)

MABEE FARM HISTORIC SITE is at 1080 Main St. (SR 5S). The 9-acre preserved farmstead contains a 300-year-old Dutch Colonial house; a brick building that served as a trading post, slave quarters and auxiliary housing; an old inn; two barns; and the Mabee family cemetery. Farming methods, domestic chores, social habits and daily life of a typical Mohawk Valley farming family are interpreted. The site is owned by the Schenectady County

Historical Society. Allow 1 hour minimum. Tues.-Sat. 10-4, mid-May to late Sept. Admission $3. Phone (518) 887-5073.

ROXBURY (G-10) pop. 2,509, elev. 1,495'

RECREATIONAL ACTIVITIES
Skiing

- SAVE **Plattekill Mountain** is on Plattekill Mountain Rd. Other activities are available. Daily Dec.-Apr. Phone (607) 326-3500 or (800) 633-3275.

RYE—see New York p. 154.

SACKETS HARBOR (C-7)
pop. 1,386, elev. 255'

A resort on eastern Lake Ontario, Sackets Harbor saw one of the first battles in the War of 1812, when five British battleships were repelled by one U.S. ship and a group of farmers on shore with a single cannon. The only British shot to land near the farmers was loaded into the cannon and returned; it took down the mast of the British flagship.

The Old Military Cemetery on Dodge Avenue has graves of soldiers from the War of 1812, including that of Gen. Zebulon Pike, discoverer of Pikes Peak.

SAVE Seaway Trail Discovery Center, in an 1871 limestone building at Ray and W. Main sts., serves as an orientation center for the scenic 500-mile Seaway Trail, which stretches from New York to Pennsylvania along Lake Erie, the Niagara River, Lake Ontario and the St. Lawrence River. The center has exhibits, a mural and driving maps; the trail is marked with interpretive signs; phone (800) 732-9298.

Sackets Harbor Visitor Center: 301 W. Main St., Sackets Harbor, NY 13685; phone (315) 646-2321.

Self-guiding tours: A pamphlet describing a combination walking and driving tour past the historic buildings and sites of Sackets Harbor is available for a fee at the visitors center in the Sacket Mansion on W. Main Street.

SACKETS HARBOR BATTLEFIELD STATE HISTORIC SITE, 504 W. Main St., was the site of two battles in the War of 1812, during which Sackets Harbor served as headquarters for the Army of the Northern Frontier and the Navy of the Great Lakes. The restored commandant's house dates from 1850. Behind the house the 1812 Navy Exhibit depicts a sailor's life aboard the *Jefferson* during the war. A visitors center is at the west end of Main Street.

Guided tours are available. Allow 1 hour minimum. Grounds and trails open daily 8-dusk. Historic buildings open Mon.-Sat. 10-5, Sun. 1-5, July to mid-Aug.; Wed.-Sun. 10-5, mid-May to June, mid-Aug. through day before Labor Day and day after Columbus Day-Oct. 31; Sat. 10-5, Sun. 1-5, Dec. 1-9. Hours may vary; phone ahead. Living-history camp Wed.-Sat. 10-4:30, June-Aug. Admission $3;

senior citizens and students with ID $2; ages 6-12, $1. Phone (315) 646-3634.

SAG HARBOR (H-5) pop. 2,313, elev. 10'

Sag Harbor's sheltered position between the North and South Forks of Long Island made it important from its earliest days. As early as 1707 it had assumed such stature as a port that the British Crown appointed an officer to stop the "running of illicit cargos into Sagg Harbour, the principal port of Long Island." The town was one of the first two ports of entry created by Congress in 1789.

The whaling industry was of primary importance to Sag Harbor's development. During this period the town was the source of many real and imagined heroes, including those of the sea stories of James Fenimore Cooper, who began his first novel in this area in 1824. Sag Harbor ranked as one of the largest whaling ports in the world before the industry died in 1871.

Antique hunters have long since replaced whale hunters. The streets of the town's historic district contain interesting buildings ranging from simple weathered saltbox cottages to the more ornate houses of its wealthy past. *Also see Long Island p. 99.*

Sag Harbor Chamber of Commerce: 459 Main St., P.O. Box 2810, Sag Harbor, NY 11963; phone (631) 725-0011.

CUSTOM HOUSE, Main and Garden sts., is the restored home of a customs officer and postmaster of Sag Harbor in the late 1700s and early 1800s. Original and restored furnishings and artifacts are displayed. Allow 30 minutes minimum. Tues.-Sun. 10-5, July-Aug.; Sat.-Sun. 10-5, May-June and Sept.-Oct. Admission $3; senior citizens and ages 7-14, $1.50. Phone (631) 692-4664.

SAG HARBOR WHALING MUSEUM is on Main St. opposite the library. Exhibits include whaling equipment, scrimshaw, oil paintings, ships models, fishing gear, logbooks and other objects connected with Colonial eastern Long Island. Allow 30 minutes minimum. Mon.-Sat. 10-5, Sun. 1-5, mid-May through Nov. 30; by appointment rest of year. Admission $5; over 64, $3; under 12 free. Phone (631) 725-0770.

ST. JOHNSVILLE (E-9) pop. 1,685

Situated in the Mohawk Valley, St. Johnsville was first home to the Dutch in the mid-1600s, followed by the Palatine who were driven from their home along the Rhine River in Germany. They called the area "the Promised Land" because it resembled their homeland.

Hunting for "Herkimer diamonds"—extremely clear, double-terminated quartz crystals found only in central New York—is a favorite pastime at Crystal Grove Diamond Mine, 5 miles north on CR 114; phone (518) 568-2914 or (800) 579-3426.

FORT KLOCK HISTORIC RESTORATION, 2 mi. e. on SR 5, is a fortified 1750 farmhouse built for defense purposes as well as a fur trading post. Partially furnished with antiques, the main house contains exhibits relating to rural 18th-century life. A 19th-century schoolhouse, Dutch barn and blacksmith shop are on the premises. Picnicking is permitted. Allow 1 hour minimum. Tues.-Sun. 9-5, Memorial Day to mid-Oct. Admission $2; ages 10-15, $1. Phone (518) 568-7779.

MARGARET REANEY MEMORIAL LIBRARY AND MUSEUM, 3 blks. e. of Main St. at 19 Kingsbury Ave., was built in 1909. Among the many historical displays are Civil War items, period rooms and farm and trade tools. The library contains approximately 25,000 volumes, including genealogy records and local history reference books. Allow 1 hour minimum. Mon. and Fri. 9:30-5 and 6:30-8:30, Tues.-Wed. 9:30-5, Thurs. 1-5, Sat. 9:30-noon. Free. Phone (518) 568-7822.

SALAMANCA (G-3) pop. 6,097, elev. 1,389'

Salamanca's Iroquois heritage is evident in the abundance of local artisans who create traditional arts and crafts.

Salamanca Area Chamber of Commerce: 26 Main St., Salamanca, NY 14779; phone (716) 945-2034.

SALAMANCA RAIL MUSEUM, 170 Main St., is a restored 1912 Buffalo, Rochester and Pittsburgh Railway passenger depot. Artifacts, photographs and videotapes depict the role railroads played in area history. **Note:** The museum is closed temporarily due to a fire. Phone ahead for information. Mon.-Sat. 10-5, Sun. noon-5, May-Sept.; Tues.-Sat. 10-5, Sun. noon-5, in Apr. and Oct.-Dec. Closed Thanksgiving and Dec. 25. Donations. Phone (716) 945-3133.

[SAVE] **SENECA-IROQUOIS NATIONAL MUSEUM** is off US 17 exit 20 on the Allegany Indian Reservation, Broad St. extension. The museum's collection portrays the life and culture of the Iroquois Indians, with emphasis on the Seneca Nation. Guided tours are available by reservation 2 weeks in advance.

Allow 30 minutes minimum. Mon.-Sat. 9-5, Sun. noon-5, May-Nov.; Mon.-Fri. 9-5, Feb.-Apr. and in Dec. Closed major holidays. Admission $5; senior citizens and students with ID $3.50; ages 7-16, $3. Phone (716) 945-1760.

SARANAC LAKE (B-10)
pop. 5,041, elev. 1,535'

First settled in 1819, Saranac Lake was a major tuberculosis treatment center during the late 1800s and early 1900s. The area's mountains and lakes make it a popular vacation site. Many cottages, inns and treatment centers from the late 1800s and early 1900s still stand along Saranac Lake's winding streets.

Saranac Lake Area Chamber of Commerce: 39 Main St., Saranac Lake, NY 12983; phone (518) 891-1990 or (800) 347-1992.

CHARLES DICKERT WILDLIFE COLLECTION, 109 Main St. in the Saranac Lake Free Library, exhibits mounted specimens of many animal species native to the Adirondacks. Mon.-Sat. 10-5:30 (also Thurs. 5:30-8), Sept.-June; Mon.-Fri. 10-5:30, Sat. 10-1, rest of year. Free. Phone (518) 891-4190.

ROBERT LOUIS STEVENSON COTTAGE, off jct. SRs 3 and 86 on Stevenson Ln. via Church and Main sts., was the author's home during the winter of 1887-88. The cottage and original furniture have been preserved. The museum reputedly holds the world's largest collection of Stevenson memorabilia. Tues.-Sun. 9:30-noon and 1-4:30, July 1-Columbus Day; by appointment rest of year. Admission $5, under 12 free. Phone (518) 891-1462.

▼GEM SARATOGA NATIONAL HISTORICAL PARK (E-11)

Eight miles south of Schuylerville on US 4, the Battlefield of Saratoga National Historical Park embraces partially wooded country along the west side of the Hudson River. In addition to the 3,200-acre battlefield, the park is made up of two other areas: the Schuyler House in Schuylerville and the Saratoga Monument in Victory. The park commemorates the Battles of Saratoga, fought on Sept. 19 and Oct. 7, 1777, in which Gen. Horatio Gates' American forces defeated Gen. John Burgoyne's British forces.

On Oct. 17, 1777, Burgoyne surrendered to the Americans near Schuylerville (Old Saratoga), thus preventing British control of the Hudson and the east-west split of the Colonies that would have ensued. This victory is generally accepted as the turning point of the Revolutionary War. Eight miles north of the battlefield stands the Saratoga Monument commemorating Burgoyne's surrender *(see Schuylerville p. 196).* A 155-foot stone obelisk marks the approximate location where part of the British army was encamped the week before their surrender.

Benedict Arnold, second in command during the Sept. 19 battle, led the October attack on the Balcarres Redoubt then galloped through cross fire to join the assault on the Breymann Redoubt, where he was wounded for a second time in the left leg. Ironically, just 3 years later he would attempt to turn West Point over to the British. The Boot Monument at Breymann Redoubt documents Arnold's heroics on the day of his injury.

A visitor center on Fraser Hill, the highest point in the park, affords a view of the battlefield and surrounding area and offers an orientation film. A museum contains battleground artifacts, including surrender cannons.

A self-guiding, 10-mile driving tour road through the battlefield has 10 designated historical points of interest. The trail starts at the visitor center. Costumed interpreters present living-history programs at the Nielsen House, the generals' headquarters during the battles, from late May to late August as staffing permits. There are more than 10 miles of hiking trails in the park. Trail maps and information about trail conditions are available at the visitor center.

Picnicking is permitted. Allow a full day. Visitor center daily 9-5; closed Jan. 1, Thanksgiving and Dec. 25. Tour road open Apr.-Nov. (weather permitting). Park admission and visitor center free. Tour road $5 fee per private vehicle; $3 on foot, bicycle or horseback; under 16 free. Tour road and trail charges are good for 7 days. An annual pass is available for $10. Phone (518) 664-9821, ext. 224.

THE PHILIP SCHUYLER HOUSE, 8 mi. n. of the visitor center on US 4 in Schuylerville, is the restored country home of Revolutionary War general Philip Schuyler. The two-story wooden house is furnished in period. Guided tours are available. Allow 1 hour minimum. Wed.-Sun. 9:30-4:30, Memorial Day weekend through Labor Day. Free. Phone (518) 664-9821, ext. 224.

SARATOGA SPRINGS (D-10)
pop. 26,186, elev. 312'

Saratoga Springs is renowned for the beauty of its setting, the reputed health-giving properties of its waters and the gaiety of its summer life. The city boasts more than 1,000 examples of Victorian architecture in its eight historic districts.

The resort also is gaining popularity as a year-round sports and convention center. Equestrian events are popular year-round. Harness races are held spring through fall and polo is played during the summer at Saratoga Gaming & Raceway off Nelson Avenue; phone (518) 584-2110. In August spectators can watch the Thoroughbred races at Saratoga Race Course on Union Avenue, said to be the oldest course in the country; phone (518) 584-6200.

Note: Policies concerning admittance of children to pari-mutuel betting facilities vary. Phone for information.

Winter events focus on Saratoga Springs' many alpine and cross-country skiing facilities and ice skating and snowshoeing areas. The Saratoga Springs Heritage Area and Visitor Center, across from Congress Park, shows an orientation videotape and is open all year; phone (518) 587-3241.

Saratoga County Chamber of Commerce: 28 Clinton St., Saratoga Springs, NY 12866; phone (518) 584-3255.

Self-guiding tours: Brochures with maps detailing the points of interest downtown and in the surrounding area are available from the chamber of commerce and the visitor center.

Shopping areas: On SR 50 is the Wilton Mall, which includes JCPenney and Sears. Downtown Saratoga's Broadway Street features specialty stores with fine art, decorative crafts and antique books.

LAKE GEORGE OPERA FESTIVAL presents performances at the Spa Little Theatre in Saratoga Spa State Park. This regional professional repertory company offers two to four main stage performances each season. The company is committed to the development of young American performers through an apprentice artist program.

The main stage season runs June-July. Admission $40-$75, with reduced rates for senior citizens and students. Reservations are recommended. MC, VI. Phone (518) 584-6018 for general information or main stage tickets.

NATIONAL MUSEUM OF DANCE & HALL OF FAME, 1 mi. s. at 99 S. Broadway (US 9), presents changing exhibits about professional dance. The museum also includes the Dance Hall of Fame. Dance classes can be observed in the Lewis A. Sawyer Studio. Allow 1 hour minimum. Tues.-Sun. 10-5. Admission $6.50; senior citizens and students with ID $5; under 12, $3. Phone (518) 584-2225.

NATIONAL MUSEUM OF RACING AND HALL OF FAME, 191 Union Ave. at Ludlow St., contains exhibits about the past, present and future of Thoroughbred racing in America. Displays include paintings and sculptures. The Hall of Fame honors horses, jockeys and trainers. Photographs, videotapes and a skeleton illustrate selective breeding and anatomy. In a simulated racetrack, videotapes of well-known trainers and jockeys explain training and racing techniques.

Allow 1 hour minimum. Daily 9-5, late July-Labor Day; Mon.-Sat. 10-4, Sun. noon-4, rest of year. Closed Jan. 1, Easter, Thanksgiving and Dec. 25. Admission $7, senior citizens and students with ID $5, under 6 free. Phone (518) 584-0400.

SARATOGA AUTOMOBILE MUSEUM is at 110 Avenue of the Pines. Automobiles are displayed in an Art Deco-inspired setting in a restored 1935 water bottling plant. Highlights include models built in New York and an assortment of vehicles tracing the development of motorized transportation. Plaques describe the history of each car. Exhibits in the main gallery change several times each year and feature race cars, classic cars and cars from around the globe.

Allow 30 minutes minimum. Daily 10-5, May-Oct.; Tues.-Fri. 10-5, rest of year. Closed Jan. 1, Thanksgiving and Dec. 25. Admission $7; over 65 and active military with ID $5; students ages 6-16, $3.50. MC, VI. Phone (518) 587-1935.

SARATOGA SPA STATE PARK, n. of I-87 exit 13N, features bathhouses, mineral springs and geyserlike spouters, three swimming pools, walking and hiking trails, two outdoor ice skating rinks, golf courses and picnic pavilions on 2,500 acres. The park also includes the Saratoga Performing Arts Center and the Spa Little Theatre.

Allow 4 hours minimum. Park open daily 8 a.m.-dusk. Pool open Mon.-Fri. 10-6, Sat.-Sun. 10-7, late June-Labor Day. Parking daily $6, Memorial Day-Labor Day, Sat.-Sun. in May and day after Labor Day-Columbus Day; free, rest of year. Phone (518) 584-2535, or (518) 587-3330 for program and ticket information. *See Recreation Chart.*

SARATOGA SPRINGS HISTORY MUSEUM, off Broadway (US 9) in Congress Park, is housed in the 1870 Canfield Casino and features exhibits that trace Saratoga Springs' growth from a rural village to a flamboyant resort. Topics of interest include gambling paraphernalia, lake houses and notable residents. The park contains Italian sculpture gardens and works by Daniel Chester French, who created the seated Lincoln in the Washington, D.C., memorial.

Allow 30 minutes minimum. Daily 10-4, Memorial Day-Labor Day; Wed.-Sun. 10-4, rest of year. Admission $5, over 59 and students with ID $4, under 12 free. Phone (518) 584-6920.

YADDO, just w. of I-87 Northway exit 14 on Union Ave., is a private estate made available as a working community for visual artists, writers, filmmakers, choreographers and composers. Although the estate is private, the rose gardens are open to visitors daily 8-dusk. Free. Phone (518) 584-0746.

SAUGERTIES (G-11) pop. 4,955, elev. 159′

Saugerties has changed little since the days when riverboats stopped at its port on the Hudson. Victorian houses and small shops help to maintain the town's rural atmosphere.

OPUS 40 AND QUARRYMAN'S MUSEUM is 6 mi. w. on SR 212 from I-87 exit 20 to Glasco Tpke. following signs. Opus 40 consists of curvilinear pathways, pools and fountains of bluestone fitted to the contour of the land and surrounding a 9-ton monolith. The Quarryman's Museum houses 19th-century tools and household furnishings of the quarryman and other tradesmen.

Allow 1 hour minimum. Fri.- Sun. and Mon. holidays noon-5, Memorial Day-Columbus Day. Admission $10; over 61 and students with ID $7; ages 6-12, $3. Phone (845) 246-3400.

SCHENECTADY (E-10)
pop. 61,821, elev. 246′

On the Mohawk River at the eastern side of the scenic Mohawk Valley, Schenectady was founded in 1661 by Dutch settlers under the leadership of Arendt Van Curler. The Dutch influence is visible in much of the architecture of the Stockade Historic District, site of the original settlement that was burned in 1690; the area includes private homes and buildings built 1690-1930.

The G.E. Realty Plot, bounded by Lenox Road, Nott Street, West Alley and Union Avenue, has some 130 homes dating from the early 1900s, when the neighborhood was created as an exclusive residential community for corporate executives of the General Electric Co. Queen Anne, Federal, Greek Revival, and Arts and Crafts are among the many architectural styles represented. The world's first all-electric house was built in the G.E. Realty Plot in 1903.

Schenectady's downtown renaissance is apparent in the Arts and Entertainment District, which includes Proctor's Theatre, a restored 1926 vaudeville house presenting touring Broadway shows, dance performances, music events and films; phone (518) 346-6204.

Scenic Central Park includes a rose garden, nature trails and an outdoor theater offering free concerts. Jackson's Garden, 8 acres of formal gardens and woodland, is on the 100-acre, architecturally-designed campus of Union College, which was founded in 1795; phone (518) 388-6000. The Mohawk-Hudson Bikeway provides views of the Mohawk River.

The Chamber of Schenectady County: 306 State St., Schenectady, NY 12305; phone (800) 962-8007.

Self-guiding tours: Brochures detailing self-guiding tours of the city's historic areas are available at the chamber or at Schenectady Heritage Area Visitors Center in the Schenectady Museum *(see attraction listing).*

Shopping areas: Rotterdam Square Mall, off I-890 exit 2A on Campbell Road, has Macy's and Sears. Specialty stores can be found along Upper Union Street and the Jay Street Pedestrian Walkway.

SCHENECTADY COUNTY HISTORICAL SOCIETY MUSEUM OF SCHENECTADY HISTORY, 32 Washington Ave., is housed in the 1895 Dora Jackson house. The museum contains 18th- and 19th-century furnishings, artifacts of Dutch heritage, an 1834 dollhouse and the Grems-Doolittle genealogy library. Allow 1 hour minimum. Museum Mon.-Fri. 1-5. Library Mon.-Fri. 1-5, Sat. 9-noon; closed major holidays. Admission $4, under 12 free. Library $5. Phone (518) 374-0263.

SCHENECTADY MUSEUM & PLANETARIUM AND SCHENECTADY HERITAGE AREA VISITORS CENTER, on Nott Terrace Heights between SR 5 and Union St., features a planetarium, a theater, a children's discovery area and exhibits about art, regional history and the history of the electrical industry.

Allow 2 hours minimum. Tues.-Sun. 10-5; closed major holidays. Planetarium show schedule Tues.-Fri. at 2, Sat.-Sun. at 1, 2 and 3. Museum $5; senior citizens $4; ages 4-12, $3. Museum and planetarium $7.50; senior citizens $6.50; ages 4-12, $5.50. Phone (518) 382-7890.

SCHOHARIE (F-10) pop. 1,030, elev. 611′

Schoharie, one of the oldest villages in upstate New York, was called Brunnen Dorf when it was settled in 1712. Many of the town's original buildings remain, including the 1770 George Mann

House, the 1772 Swartz Tavern, the 1795 Lasell Hall and the Old Stone Fort *(see attraction listing)*. One of the oldest buildings in Schoharie County, the restored 1743 Palatine House on Spring Street, is known as the Old Lutheran Parsonage; the house serves as a museum.

The old Middleburgh-Schoharie Railroad Complex on Depot Lane has been restored and is a historic cultural center open weekends. It has original buildings and an 1890 passenger/baggage train car that houses a small museum.

Schoharie County Chamber of Commerce: P.O. Box 400, Schoharie, NY 12157; phone (518) 295-7033 or (800) 418-4748.

[SAVE] OLD STONE FORT MUSEUM COMPLEX, 1 mi. n. on N. Main St. to 145 Fort Rd., is a 1772 Dutch Reformed church, stockaded as a fort during the American Revolution. Other buildings include a 1760 Palatine house, an 18th-century Dutch barn, an 1830 law office, an 1890 schoolhouse and a library. Furnishings, weaponry, automobiles, tools and farm implements are displayed.

Mon.-Sat. 10-5, Sun. noon-5, July-Aug.; Tues.-Sat. 10-5, Sun. noon-5, May-June and Sept.-Oct. Admission $5; over 62, $4.50; ages 5-17, $1.50. MC, VI. Phone (518) 295-7192.

SCHUYLERVILLE (E-11)
pop. 1,197, elev. 146′

Schuylerville, originally a Native American camping ground, was settled by French refugees in 1688 and named Saratoga. In 1831 it was renamed Schuylerville after Revolutionary War general Philip Schuyler.

The turning point of the Revolutionary War took place in Schuylerville in 1777; the British army was trapped after retreating from the Battle of Saratoga *(see Saratoga National Historical Park p. 193)*. The field of grounded arms is in the area. The Saratoga Monument commemorates British general John Burgoyne's surrender.

SEAFORD (I-2) pop. 15,791, elev. 9′

TACKAPAUSHA MUSEUM AND PRESERVE, off Seaford-Oyster Bay Expwy. exit 2E, .5 mi. e. on Sunrise Hwy., then .5 mi. s. on Washington Ave., occupies an 80-acre glacial outwash plain. Museum exhibits focus on the habitats and the life cycles of Long Island animals and plants. Changing videotapes and programs cover a variety of natural history topics. Nature trails traverse the wildlife sanctuary. Tues.-Sat. 10-4, Sun. 1-4; closed major holidays. Admission $2; ages 4-14, $1; under 4 free with an adult. Phone (516) 571-7443.

SENECA FALLS (E-6) pop. 6,861, elev. 473′

Seneca Falls is known as the birthplace of the women's rights movement. Notable former residents include Amelia Bloomer, who popularized the undergarments that bore her name, and Elizabeth Cady Stanton, organizer of the first Women's Rights Convention and an early feminist leader. The nation's first women's rights convention was held in Seneca Falls in 1848.

Several wineries lie within a 20-mile area of scenic SR 89, known as the Cayuga Wine Trail, which skirts the western shore of Cayuga Lake. As its name suggests, the Cayuga-Seneca Canal connects Cayuga and Seneca lakes and passes through diverse landscapes. The double locks at Seneca Falls create a 49-foot change in elevation. Houseboat rentals by the week are available locally; contact the chamber of commerce. *Also see Finger Lakes p. 84.*

Seneca County Chamber of Commerce: P.O. Box 70, Seneca Falls, NY 13148; phone (315) 568-2906.

MONTEZUMA NATIONAL WILDLIFE REFUGE, with its headquarters 5 mi. e. on US 20/SR 5, covers more than 7,000 acres. A link in the Atlantic flyway, the refuge is a nesting and resting spot for migratory waterfowl and other birds including geese, ducks and shorebirds. The refuge also has a resident population of bald eagles. Facilities include a visitor center, nature trail, boat launch, public fishing site and two observation towers. A self-guiding automobile tour is available. Bicycling is not permitted. Daily dawn-dusk. Visitor center open daily 10-3, Apr.-Dec. Free. Phone (315) 568-5987.

NATIONAL WOMEN'S HALL OF FAME, 76 Fall St., honors and celebrates the achievements of distinguished American women who have made contributions to the arts, athletics, business, government, philanthropy, humanities, science and education. Among the women enshrined in the hall are Susan B. Anthony, Amelia Earhart, Sandra Day O'Connor, Georgia O'Keeffe, Rosa Parks and Eleanor Roosevelt.

Allow 30 minutes minimum. Mon.-Sat. 10-5, Sun. noon-5, May-Oct.; Wed.-Sat. 11-5, Feb.-Apr. and Nov.-Dec. Closed major holidays. Admission $3, senior citizens and students with ID $1.50, family rate $7. Phone (315) 568-8060.

SENECA FALLS HISTORICAL SOCIETY, 55 Cayuga St., was founded in 1896 and occupies an imposing 1880 Queen Anne style mansion. It features Victorian period rooms, exhibits of local history and an extensive research library. The society also owns a collection of glass plate negatives relating to the Women's Rights Movement, which many historians consider to have begun in the town.

Guided tours are available. Allow 1 hour minimum. Tours are given on the hour Mon.-Fri. 9-4, (also Sat.-Sun. 1-4, July-Aug.); closed major holidays. Admission $3, over 49, $2.50, students with ID $1.50, under 5 free; family rate $7.50. Phone (315) 568-8412.

WOMEN'S RIGHTS NATIONAL HISTORICAL PARK, 136 Fall St., chronicles the development of the women's rights movement. Highlights include changing exhibits, films and summer interpretive talks. Guided tours of the restored 1846 Elizabeth

Cady Stanton Home at 32 Washington St. are offered on a varying schedule.

Allow 1 hour minimum. Park and visitor center open daily 9-5; closed Jan. 1, Martin Luther King Jr. Day, Presidents Day, Thanksgiving and Dec. 25. Admission $3, under 15 free. House tour $1. Phone (315) 568-0024.

SETAUKET (H-3) elev. 189′

Setauket is part of a region called The Three Villages, which encompasses Setauket, Stony Brook and Old Field. Revolutionary War spies used the town as a headquarters; the town later became known for shipbuilding. William Sidney Mount captured the area's post-Revolutionary lifestyle on canvas in the mid-1800s from his mobile art studio.

The 1729 Caroline Church of Brookhaven is open on request; phone (631) 941-4245. Open by appointment, the Sherwood-Jayne House contains a varied furniture collection and hand-painted wall frescoes; phone (631) 692-4664. Three Village Historical Society, 93 North Country Rd., offers walking tours every other week on Saturday and Sunday; phone (631) 751-3730. *Also see Long Island p. 99.*

THOMPSON HOUSE, 1 mi. n.e. of Stony Brook Station to 91 N. Country Rd., is a typical 17th-century saltbox house ·with period furnishings. Guided tours are available. Allow 30 minutes minimum. Fri.-Sun. 1-5, July-Aug.; Sat.-Sun. 1-5, Memorial Day-June 30 and Sept. 1-Columbus Day. Last tour begins 30 minutes before closing. Admission $3; over 64 and ages 7-14, $2. Phone (631) 692-4664.

SHERBURNE (F-8) pop. 1,455, elev. 1,048′

ROGERS ENVIRONMENTAL EDUCATION CENTER, 1 mi. w. on SR 80 off SR 12, provides 600 acres of habitat for plants and animals in a variety of aquatic, woodland and field environments. Short nature trails begin at the visitor center. Mounted North American birds are displayed. More than 6 miles of trails are open year-round for hiking, cross-country skiing and snowshoeing. Educational programs are offered on Saturday.

Picnicking is permitted. Allow 1 hour minimum. Visitor center open Mon.-Fri. 8:30-4:45, Sat.-Sun. 1-4:45, June-Aug.; Mon.-Fri. 8:30-4:45; Sat. 1-4:45, rest of year. Grounds and trails open daily dawn-dusk. Free. Phone (607) 674-4017.

SHIRLEY (I-4) pop. 25,395

LONG ISLAND NATIONAL WILDLIFE REFUGE COMPLEX, .5 mi. s. on Smith Rd. off Montauk Hwy., has its headquarters in Wertheim National Wildlife Refuge. Wertheim offers boating, crabbing, fishing and a nature trail.

Morton National Wildlife Refuge is on Noyack Road *(see Southampton p. 197).* Target Rock National Wildlife Refuge, 4.5 miles north on W. Neck Road off SR 25A in Huntington village, then 3 miles east on Lloyd Harbor Road, has walking trails.

Wertheim open daily 8-4:30. Morton and Target Rock refuges open daily 30 minutes before dawn-30 minutes before dusk. Admission to Target Rock and Morton refuges $4 per private vehicle, $2 each for persons on bicycles or on foot, over 62 free. Admission to Wertheim free. Phone (631) 286-0485.

MANOR OF ST. GEORGE is off SR 27 (Sunrise Hwy.) and 3.2 mi. s. on William Floyd Pkwy. On a 127-acre site overlooking Great South Bay, the three-story manor house displays furnishings from the early 1800s and paintings and documents concerning the estate, which was granted to Col. William Tangier Smith by the British Crown in 1693. Allow 30 minutes minimum. Wed.-Sun. 10-4, May-Oct. Free. Phone (631) 281-5034.

SKANEATELES (E-7) pop. 2,616, elev. 903′

MID-LAKES NAVIGATION CO., 1 blk. w. of jct. SRs 321 and 20 at 11 Jordan St., offers 1-hour sightseeing and 3-hour mailboat cruises. Dinner, brunch and lunch cruises also are available. Cruises depart Tues.-Sun., early July-late Aug. Sightseeing cruise departs at 1:30. Mailboat cruise departs Mon.-Sat. at 10, July 1-day after Labor Day. One-hour cruise $10; under 13, $6; family rate $30. Mailboat cruise $19; under 13, $13. Rates may vary; phone ahead. AX, DS, MC, VI. Phone (315) 685-8500 or (800) 545-4318 for sightseeing schedule.

SLEEPY HOLLOW—see New York p. 154.

SOUTHAMPTON (H-5) pop. 3,965, elev. 45′

Settled in 1640 by English colonists from Massachusetts, Southampton is one of the oldest English settlements in New York. In the mid-19th century the proximity of its scenery and beaches to New York City began to draw summer visitors, who boarded with farmers and fishermen. The coming of the railroad to Southampton in 1870 brought thousands more persons, who began to buy · land and build estates.

Soon the "Hamptons" gained the reputation as one of the East Coast's principal resorts for the wealthy and famous. The residents of the luxurious beachfront homes along Gin and Meadow lanes rub elbows with tourists and young professionals from the city as they shop at the boutiques and local branches of New York City stores along Job's Lane and Main Street.

In spite of the modern lines of some of the luxurious beach "cottages," Southampton Village has managed to retain much of its past. Roads with names like Ox Pasture and Meeting House Lane are lined with pleasant houses ranging in style from Colonial cedar shake to Victorian gingerbread.

The descendants of the Shinnecock Indians, who welcomed the first settlers, have a reservation next to the town off SR 27A. *Also see Long Island p. 99.*

Southampton Chamber of Commerce: 76 Main St., Southampton, NY 11968; phone (631) 283-0402.

Self-guiding tours: Information about self-guiding tours of Southampton by car, bicycle or foot is available from the chamber of commerce. Information also is available from the Southampton Historical Museum *(see attraction listing).*

MORTON NATIONAL WILDLIFE REFUGE, e. on SR 27 to exit 9, 2.5 mi. n. on N. Sea Rd. (SR 38), then 5 mi. e. on Noyack Rd., is a feeding, resting and nesting area for migratory birds on the Atlantic flyway, particularly for endangered piping plovers, least terns and ospreys. The refuge offers birdwatching, fishing and hiking. A nature trail traverses a forest and field, past wetlands and onto a bay beach.

Daily 30 minutes before dawn-30 minutes after dusk; public access is sometimes restricted. Admission $4 per private vehicle, $2 each for persons on bicycles or on foot, over 61 free. Phone (631) 286-0485. *See also Long Island National Wildlife Refuge Complex attraction listing in Shirley p. 197.*

PARRISH ART MUSEUM AND ARBORETUM, 25 Job's Ln., displays 19th- and 20th-century American art, including a collection of William Merritt Chase and Fairfield Porter. The grounds include an arboretum and statuary. Allow 1 hour minimum. Mon.-Sat. 11-5, Sun. 1-5 (also Mon. 5-8 p.m.), early June to mid-Sept.; Thurs.-Sat. and Mon. 11-5, Sun. 1-5, rest of year. Admission $5, senior citizens and college students with ID $3, under 18 free. Phone (631) 283-2118.

SOUTHAMPTON HISTORICAL MUSEUM, off Main St. at 17 Meeting House Ln., consists of an 1843 whaling captain's home and 11 other buildings, including blacksmith, carpentry, cobbler, paint and harness shops, a carriage house and a country store housed in a pre-Revolutionary barn. A one-room schoolhouse and two original outhouses also are displayed.

Allow 1 hour minimum. Tues.-Sat. 11-5, Sun. 1-5, June 12-Dec. 31; Thurs.-Sat. noon-5, Jan.-Apr. Admission $4; over 64, $3; under 12, $2. Phone (631) 283-2494.

THE THOMAS HALSEY HOUSE, .5 mi. s. on Main St., is a restored two-story 1648 house that is deemed one of the oldest frame houses in the state. Built by one of the original settlers, Thomas Halsey, it contains 17th- and 18th-century furnishings. Behind the house is a Colonial herb garden. Allow 30 minutes minimum. Fri.-Sat. noon-5, Sun. 1-5, early July to mid-Oct. Admission $3; over 64, $2; under 12, $1. Phone (631) 283-2494.

SPRINGFIELD CENTER (E-9)

GLIMMERGLASS OPERA, on Otsego Lake, 2 mi. s.w. on SR 80, features four operas performed in repertory at the Alice Busch Opera Theater. The theater has side walls that open to the landscape. Guided backstage tours are available. Opera previews are given 1 hour before performances.

Allow 1 hour minimum for tour; 2 hours, 30 minutes to 3 hours for performances. Performances July-Aug. Guided tours are given Sat. at 11 in Aug.; by appointment rest of year. Tickets $37-$110; previews and tours are free. AX, DS, MC, VI. Phone (607) 547-2255.

STAATSBURG (G-11) pop. 911, elev. 30'

STAATSBURGH STATE HISTORIC SITE is 5 mi. n. on US 9 to Old Post Rd. The 65-room mansion was built in 1832 and remodeled and enlarged in 1895 by architect Stanford White for Ogden and Ruth Livingston Mills. It contains marble fireplaces, wood paneling, gilded plaster work, ornate furniture and art objects from around the world. The Ogden and Ruth Livingston Mills Memorial Park has recreational facilities *(see Recreation Chart).*

Allow 1 hour minimum for tour. Mansion open Tues.-Sat. 10-5, Sun. 11-5, Apr.-Oct.; Wed.-Sun. noon-5, day after Thanksgiving-Dec. 31; Sun. 11-4, Jan.-Mar. Guided house tours are conducted every half-hour. Last tour begins 30 minutes before closing. Grounds open daily 8-dusk. Admission $5, over 62 and students with ID $4, under 12 free. Phone (845) 889-8851.

STERLING (D-6) pop. 3,432, elev. 320'

STERLING RENAISSANCE FESTIVAL is held off SR 104A at 15385 Farden Rd., following signs. The festival presents costumed minstrels and players, jousting, street theater, plays, games, madrigals, food and puppet shows, and crafts reminiscent of Renaissance England. Allow 3 hours minimum. Sat.-Sun. 10-7, July 1-Aug. 13. Admission $19.99; ages 6-12, $6.99. AX, MC, VI. Phone (315) 947-5783.

STONY BROOK (H-3) pop. 13,727

Settled by New Englanders in 1665, Stony Brook developed into a prosperous farming community whose economy was supplemented in the early 1800s by shipping and shipbuilding.

In 1940 Ward Melville sponsored the rehabilitation of Stony Brook's Main Street. The crescent-shaped shopping center was designed around a Federal-style post office overlooking a 2-acre village green on Stony Brook Harbor. Atop the building a mechanical, carved wooden eagle flaps its wings on the hour. *Also see Long Island p. 99.*

Self-guiding tours: Free brochures outlining a walking tour of Stony Brook's historic district are available in the shops at the Stony Brook Village

Center on Main Street (on the harbor) or by contacting the Ward Melville Heritage Organization, Box 572, Stony Brook, NY 11790; phone (631) 751-2244.

[SAVE] **DISCOVERY WETLANDS CRUISE,** departing from the dock on Shore Rd., offers a 90-minute pontoon boat cruise through the wetlands off the historic village of Stony Brook. Highlights include views of area estates, birds and waterfowl in addition to insights into the area's history, geology and ecology. Trips depart daily at high tide, May-Oct. Fare $20; over 64, $18; under 12, $10. AX, MC, VI. Phone (631) 751-2244.

THE LONG ISLAND MUSEUM OF AMERICAN ART, HISTORY AND CARRIAGES, Main St. and SR 25A, is a 9-acre complex with exhibits of 19th- and 20th-century American art and history. In addition to museums and historic buildings, the complex also encompasses gardens and a family burial ground dating from 1796.

Allow 2 hours, 30 minutes minimum. Wed.-Sat. and Mon. holidays 10-5, Sun. noon-5. Closed Jan. 1, Thanksgiving and Dec. 24-25. Admission $7; over 62, $6; college students with ID and ages 6-17, $3. Phone (631) 751-0066.

Art Museum, 1200 SR 25A, presents changing exhibits of works by 19th- and 20th-century American artists.

Carriage Museum, 1200 SR 25A, has 10 galleries displaying more than 100 horse-drawn wagons and sleighs, including European royal coaches, firefighting equipment and gypsy wagons.

History Museum, 1200 SR 25A, in a renovated lumber mill, has the Antique Decoy and Miniature Room galleries, and changing exhibits about American history.

Historic Buildings, in the museum complex, include the blacksmith shop, one-room schoolhouse, a 1794 barn and an 1867 carriage shed.

STONY BROOK GRIST MILL, on Harbor Rd. off Main St., is a working 1751 grist mill. A rare example of Dutch framing, the site is run by a miller as it was in the 18th and 19th centuries. Allow 30 minutes minimum. Fri.-Sun. noon-4:30; July-Labor Day; Sat.-Sun. noon-4:30, May-June and day after Labor Day-Dec. 31. Hours may vary; phone ahead. Admission $2; under 12, $1. Phone (631) 751-2244.

STONY POINT—see New York p. 155.

SYRACUSE (E-7) pop. 147,306, elev. 522′

The growth of Syracuse as a prominent city is due to its geographic location and geologic wealth. In 1570 Onondaga leader Hiawatha chose the site as the location of the capital of the Iroquois Confederacy. The Jesuits founded a mission and fort called Ste. Marie de Gannentaha in the area in 1656. The fort was abandoned after 2 years.

Salt first brought the Indians and the French to the shores of Onondaga Lake; the first Anglo-American settlers came to boil the brine in 1788. The city of Syracuse was founded in 1805 and for many years supplied the bulk of the salt used in the world.

Syracuse's American Indian population is concentrated south of the city in Nedrow at the Onondaga Indian Reservation, which is the seat of the Iroquois Confederacy.

Syracuse University, founded in 1870, occupies a 640-acre campus; its most outstanding feature is the Carrier Dome.

Basilica of the Sacred Heart of Jesus, 927 Park Ave., is one of the oldest in central New York and features Gothic architecture, stained glass windows by the Keck studio, a Papal chair and fixtures of oak, marble and bronze; phone (315) 422-2343.

Syracuse Convention and Visitors Bureau: 572 S. Salina St., Syracuse, NY 13202; phone (315) 470-1910 or (800) 234-4797.

Self-guiding tours: Brochures detailing a walking tour of the downtown area are available from the Syracuse Heritage Area Visitor Center at the Erie Canal Museum *(see attraction listing).* Interpretive signs are located throughout the downtown area, describing the history of the city and the people who built it.

Shopping areas: Downtown Syracuse offers the historic Armory Square District, with quaint shops and restaurants. Carousel Center, off I-81 exit 23, features more than 170 stores and shops including JCPenney, Macy's and Lord & Taylor as well as cinemas and restaurants.

Two major shopping malls serve Syracuse's outlying suburbs. Great Northern Mall, at the intersection of SRs 481 and 31 in Clay, has The Bon-Ton, Dick's Clothing and Sporting Goods, Macy's, Sears, specialty shops, cinemas and a food court. Shoppingtown Mall, on E. Erie Boulevard in De Witt, has more than 100 stores including The Bon-Ton, JCPenney, Macy's and Sears. Towne Center at Fayetteville, at the intersection of SR 5, E. Genesee and N. Burdick streets in Fayetteville, features Kohl's and a variety of specialty stores and eateries.

ERIE CANAL MUSEUM, 318 Erie Blvd. E., is in the 1850 Syracuse Weighlock Building. Designed to weigh canal boats for assessing a toll, this building is reputedly the only surviving structure of its kind in the country. The museum features a full-size canal boat replica; artifacts, maps and images detailing Erie Canal construction and early canal life; a penny-postcard arcade; changing exhibits; and the Syracuse Heritage Area Visitor Center *(see Self-guiding tours).*

Flash photography is not permitted. Allow 1 hour minimum. Tues.-Sat. 10-5, Sun. 10-3; closed major holidays. Donations. Phone (315) 471-0593.

EVERSON MUSEUM OF ART, 401 Harrison St., displays American paintings and sculpture from Colonial times to the present, and a large ceramics collection. The museum also displays changing exhibits. Food is available. Tues.-Fri. and Sun. noon-5, Sat. 10-5. Donations. Phone (315) 474-6064.

MID-LAKES NAVIGATION CO. LTD. cruises depart from Dutchman's Landing, 3 mi. w. of Liverpool; take I-90 exit 38 (SR 57N) to John Glen Blvd., w. to SR 370, then w. on River Road to Hillside Rd. Erie Canal cruises offer good views of the city along the tree-lined Onondaga Lake portion of the canal. Jazz, brunch, lunch, dinner and sightseeing cruises also are available.

Cruises depart Tues.-Sun., early July-late Aug. Sightseeing cruise departs at 1:30. All-day cruise $48. One-hour cruise $9. Reservations are required. AX, DS, MC, VI. Phone (315) 685-8500 or (800) 545-4318.

MILTON J. RUBENSTEIN MUSEUM OF SCIENCE AND TECHNOLOGY, Franklin St. at W. Jefferson St., is a hands-on science museum with exhibits that explain scientific and technological phenomena. Displays address topics such as animals, chemistry, color, computers, gravity, light, sound and the stars.

Demonstrations are offered. The Bristol Omnitheater offers showings on a six-story IMAX domed screen.

Museum open Wed.-Sun. 10-5. Omnitheater films are shown Wed.-Fri. and Sun. 11-5, Sat. 11-9. Museum admission $4; over 61 and ages 2-11, $3.50. Museum and Omnitheater $8; over 61 and under 12, $6. DS, MC, VI. Phone (315) 425-9068.

ONONDAGA HISTORICAL ASSOCIATION MUSEUM, 321 Montgomery St., features a permanent collection of items, paintings, photographs and memorabilia documenting 300 years of Onondaga history. The museum also has changing exhibits. Allow 1 hour minimum. Wed.-Fri. noon-4, Sat.-Sun. 11-4; closed holidays. Donations. Phone (315) 428-1864.

SAVE **ROSAMOND GIFFORD ZOO AT BURNET PARK** is off I-81 exit 22, following signs. The zoo displays domestic and exotic animals in simulated natural settings. Elephants are exhibited daily (weather permitting) and there is a Siberian tiger exhibit. The veterinary clinic and kitchen can be viewed through windows.

Allow 2 hours minimum. Daily 10-4:30; closed Jan. 1, Thanksgiving and Dec. 25. Admission $6.50; over 62 and students with ID, $4.50; ages 3-15, $4. Phone (315) 435-8511.

TAPPAN—*see New York p. 155.*

TARRYTOWN—*see New York p. 155.*

THOUSAND ISLANDS (B-7)

A French explorer called this region "Thousand Islands," although the islands number more than 1,700. Some of these islands in the St. Lawrence River are mere points of rocks and others are village size, but most can accommodate only a home or summer camp. Numerous stone castles and summer homes dot the islands, and many historical markers commemorate the arrival of the Loyalists to British North America.

The best way to see the islands is to take a boat tour offered by the boat lines described under Alexandria Bay and Clayton *(see place listings pp. 56 and 76)*. Between the spans of the Thousand Islands Bridge is the 1000 Islands Skydeck *(see Alexandria Bay p. 56)*.

The Thousand Islands embrace the St. Lawrence Islands National Park, which consists of 21 widely scattered units in the St. Lawrence River between Kingston and Brockville, Ontario, and a 96-acre (39-hectare) area at Mallorytown Landing on the mainland. Mallorytown Landing contains the park headquarters, picnic areas, a children's play area and a beach. A visitor center has displays about the natural and cultural history and settlement of the Thousand Islands region.

Access to the park by private vehicle is available only at the Mallorytown Landing entrance. Day use facilities are open Victoria Day weekend through the second Monday in October. For additional information write the Superintendent's Office, St. Lawrence Islands National Park, 2 CR 5, RR 3, Mallorytown, ON, Canada K0E 1R0; phone (613) 923-5261.

TICONDEROGA (C-11) pop. 5,167, elev. 277′

FORT TICONDEROGA NATIONAL HISTORIC LANDMARK— *see place listing p. 86.*

TICONDEROGA HISTORICAL SOCIETY LIBRARY AND MUSEUM, 6 Moses Cir. at Montcalm St., is in a reproduction of John Hancock's Boston home. Displays include original and reproduction American furniture, Redford glass and historic town memorabilia. Facing the house is the bronze Liberty Monument by Charles Keck. Wed.-Sat. 10-4. Donations. Phone (518) 585-7868.

TROY (E-11) pop. 49,170, elev. 35′

Troy, an industrial city at the head of Hudson River navigation, was home to the man who inspired the national symbol of Uncle Sam. In the early 1800s meatpacker Sam Wilson's "U.S. Beef" meat stamp was jokingly interpreted as "Uncle Sam's Beef." Life became legend, and the character of Uncle Sam was born.

Troy's Rensselaer Polytechnic Institute is one of the nation's foremost technological institutions of higher learning and one of the oldest engineering schools in the English-speaking world. The school owns and operates Rensselaer Technology Park, the site of a growing number of Troy's high-tech companies.

Troy and neighboring communities form the Hudson-Mohawk Urban Cultural Park, which preserves the historical features at the confluence of the Hudson and Mohawk rivers. Included in the park are waterfalls, 19th-century mill districts and workers' houses, river fronts, canals, warehouses, music halls, churches and merchants' mansions. A 26-mile heritage trail links the park's various features, and 2nd Street offers many fine examples of 19th-century architecture.

An audiovisual program, exhibits and computerized area information kiosks are available Tuesday through Saturday at the RiverSpark Visitor Center, 251 River St., Troy, NY 12180; phone (518) 270-8667.

Rensselaer County Regional Chamber of Commerce: 31 2nd St., Troy, NY 12180; phone (518) 274-7020.

Self-guiding tours: A brochure detailing a self-guiding tour of the Hudson-Mohawk Urban Cultural Park and a brochure detailing a self-guiding walking tour through downtown historic districts and neighborhoods can be obtained at the RiverSpark Visitor Center.

JUNIOR MUSEUM is at 250 Jordan Rd. This hands-on children's museum has exhibits relating to science, history and the arts. A planetarium also is available. Dome and animal shows are offered. Allow 1 hour minimum. Daily 10-5, in summer; Thurs.-Sun. 10-5, rest of year. Closed major holidays. Hours may vary; phone ahead for schedule and days and times of dome and animal shows. Admission $5 Thurs.-Sun., under 2 free. Admission $3 Mon.-Wed., under 2 free. Shows $1. Phone (518) 235-2120.

RENSSELAER COUNTY HISTORICAL SOCIETY MUSEUM, 57 Second St., features changing art and history exhibits and a research library with historical information about Rensselaer County. Allow 1 hour minimum. Tues.-Sat. noon-5, Feb. 1-Dec. 23; closed holidays. Museum admission by donations. Research library $4, senior citizens $3, students with ID free. Phone (518) 272-7232.

UNCLE SAM TABLET, in Oakwood Cemetery, marks the grave of Samuel Wilson, the original "Uncle Sam." He was an Army beef contractor in the War of 1812; his trademark and caricature eventually became a national symbol. Daily 9-4:30. Free. Phone (518) 272-7520.

TRUMANSBURG (F-6) pop. 1,581, elev. 960′

TAUGHANNOCK FALLS STATE PARK is 4 mi. s. on SR 89. The 215-foot Taughannock Falls is in a .75-mile-long glen with sides rising from 350 to 400 feet. Trails follow the edge of the gorge. The park offers a weekly schedule of guided tours and nature programs. Camping and swimming are permitted in season.

Park open daily 8 a.m.-dusk. Trails open mid-May to mid-Oct. Admission $7 per private vehicle, June 1-Labor Day; $6, day after Labor Day-Columbus Day; free rest of year. Phone (607) 387-6739. *See Recreation Chart and the AAA Northeastern CampBook.*

TUPPER LAKE (B-9) pop. 3,935, elev. 1,556'

Tupper Lake, which began as a lumber and sawmill village in the 1890s, is a resort in the Adirondacks. As the logging industry diminished, the town shifted its commercial interests to its other natural resources.

Fishing, swimming and boating opportunities abound at Tupper Lake, Lake Simond, Raquette River and Raquette Pond, easily reached from Tupper Lake.

The resort also boasts a municipal park with a beach, campground, tennis courts, 18-hole golf course and boat-launching sites. The nearby mountains are suited to skiing, climbing and hiking. Other recreation areas can be found in Adirondack Park *(see Recreation Chart and the AAA Northeastern CampBook).*

Tupper Lake Chamber of Commerce: 60 Park St., Tupper Lake, NY 12986; phone (518) 359-3328.

THE WILD CENTER is off SR 3 at 45 Museum Dr. The natural, historical and cultural resources of the Adirondacks are told in rich media journeys. Features include a glacier ice wall; an indoor trail exhibit simulating wetlands, a waterfall, a forest and other environments which include live animals such as river otters, birds, fish and amphibians; and outdoor trails and observation towers. High-definition films are shown in a widescreen theater.

Allow 1 hour minimum. Daily 10-6, Memorial Day-Columbus Day; Fri.-Mon. 10-5, rest of year. Closed Jan. 1, Thanksgiving and Dec. 25. Admission $14; over 64, $12; ages 4-14, $9. Phone (518) 359-7800.

UPPER DELAWARE SCENIC AND RECREATIONAL RIVER

The Upper Delaware Scenic and Recreational River comprises 73 miles of the Upper Delaware River from just north of Port Jervis, Pa., to Hancock. Along this stretch the river changes from long, placid eddies to swift water and challenging rapids. It is paralleled on the New York side by SR 97, which has several scenic overlooks.

Almost all land along the river is privately owned; public river access areas are located on both the Pennsylvania and New York shores. Private campgrounds and canoe liveries are available near the river.

The Upper Delaware was an important transportation route for American Indians and early settlers. In 1828 the Delaware and Hudson Canal opened, bringing coal-laden boats from the Pennsylvania interior to the port of New York. However, problems soon developed at the point where the canal crossed the river: Slow-moving boats being towed across the river were constantly colliding with the huge log and timber rafts that were coursing down the river to sawmills and shipyards in Trenton, N.J., and Philadelphia. To solve the problem the canal company approved a plan to "build the canal above the water."

John Roebling, who later designed the Brooklyn Bridge, built the Delaware Aqueduct. The aqueduct is considered to be the oldest wire suspension bridge in America. The adjacent tollhouse contains exhibits interpreting the history of the Delaware and Hudson Canal, John Roebling and the Delaware Aqueduct. It is open Saturdays and Sundays, Memorial Day to mid-October.

Area wildlife includes bears, white-tail deer, beavers, otters, muskrats, minks, squirrels and rabbits. Birds include bald eagles, ospreys, great egrets, great blue herons, turkey vultures, Canada geese and several varieties of hawks and ducks.

Recreational opportunities include rafting, canoeing, boating and fishing. National Park Service programs are offered in the summer. Included are cultural and natural history walks, canoeing demonstrations and guided canoe tours.

Information stations are located at the public boating access sites in Ten Mile River and at Skinner's Falls, as well as in Lackawaxen, Pa. An information center on Main Street in Narrowsburg *(see place listing p. 103)* generally is open Fri.-Sun. 9:30-4:30 Memorial Day weekend through Labor Day. Phone (845) 252-3947 or (570) 729-7134.

UTICA (E-8) pop. 60,651, elev. 452'

Built on land granted to William Crosby in 1734, Utica was the site of Old Fort Schuyler, erected in 1758. Sparsely settled for many years, Utica did not begin to develop until after the Revolution; its real growth as a commercial and industrial center dates from the completion of the Erie Canal in 1825.

Mohawk Valley Chamber of Commerce: 200 Genesee St., Utica, NY 13502; phone (315) 724-3151.

SAVE **THE CHILDREN'S MUSEUM** is at 311 Main St. Interactive exhibits inspire children to learn about varied topics, including space exploration, local history, archaeology, weather, transportation and technology. Allow 1 hour minimum. Mon.-Tues. and Thurs.-Sat. 9:45-3:45; closed Jan. 1, Easter, Thanksgiving and Dec. 25. Admission $8, under 1 free. MC, VI. Phone (315) 724-6129.

SAVE **THE MATT BREWING CO.,** Court and Varick sts., demonstrates the process of beer manufacturing and offers trolley rides June through August to the 1888 Tavern, where samples are served. Allow 1 hour minimum. Guided tours are given on the hour Mon.-Sat. 1-4, June-Aug.; Fri.-Sat. at 1 and

3, rest of year. Closed major holidays. Tour $5, under 13 free. Reservations are recommended Sept.-May. Phone (315) 624-2434 or (800) 765-6288.

 MUNSON-WILLIAMS-PROCTOR ARTS INSTITUTE, 310 Genesee St., is a fine arts center with programs in the visual and performing arts and an art museum. The museum's collections include American art from the Colonial period to the present, with an emphasis on 19th- and 20th-century paintings and sculpture. Works by European artists are displayed, as are examples of graphic and decorative arts. Fountain Elms, an 1850 Victorian house museum, adjoins the center. Allow 1 hour, 30 minutes minimum. Tues.-Sat. 10-5, Sun. 1-5. Free. Phone (315) 797-0000.

ONEIDA COUNTY HISTORICAL SOCIETY, 1608 Genesee St., has exhibits about Utica, Oneida County and Mohawk Valley history. A reference library also is available. Allow 1 hour minimum. Tues.-Fri. 10-4:30, Sat. 11-3. Exhibits free. Library $5 per day. Phone (315) 735-3642.

SAVE **UTICA ZOO,** 99 Steele Hill Rd., has more than 200 animals from around the world. Included are North American grizzly bears, Asian tigers, Australian emus and wallabies, and California sea lions. Sea lion demonstrations are held Wed.-Mon. at noon and 3. Food is available. Allow 1 hour, 30 minutes minimum. Daily 10-5; closed Jan. 1, Thanksgiving and Dec. 25. Admission $5; over 65, $4.50; ages 4-12, $3; free to all Nov.-Mar. Phone (315) 738-0472.

VAILS GATE (H-10) pop. 3,319

KNOX'S HEADQUARTERS STATE HISTORIC SITE is at jct. SR 94 and Forge Hill Rd. The Georgian-style home of prominent businessman John Ellison served as Maj. Gen. Henry Knox's military headquarters during the Revolutionary War and housed Maj. Gen. Horatio Gates during the last months of the war. The site includes the house, mill ruins, a garden and hiking trails. Exhibits explore Hudson Valley life during the 18th and 19th centuries. Allow 1 hour minimum. Wed.-Sat. 10-5, Sun. 1-5, Memorial Day-Labor Day. Admission $3; over 64, $2; ages 5-12, $1. Phone (845) 561-5498.

NEW WINDSOR CANTONMENT STATE HISTORIC SITE, 1 mi. s. of I-84 on Temple Hill Rd. (SR 300), is the site of the last winter encampment of Gen. George Washington's Continental Army. Costumed interpreters demonstrate 18th-century military life, including musket and artillery drills, woodworking and blacksmithing. A visitor center has exhibits about the Revolutionary War in the Hudson Highlands and on the cantonment. The National Purple Heart Hall of Honor pays tribute to military heroes.

Picnicking is permitted. Wed.-Sat. 10-5, Sun. 1-5, Apr. 15-Oct. 31. Admission $4; over 61, $3; ages 5-12, $1. Phone (845) 561-1765.

VERONA (E-8) pop. 6,425

CASINOS

• **Turning Stone Casino** is .5 mi s. on I-90 exit 33 at 5218 Patrick Rd. Daily 24 hours. Phone (315) 361-7711. *See color ad p. 418.*

VICTOR (E-5) pop. 2,433

GANONDAGAN STATE HISTORIC SITE is w. on CR 41 (Boughton Hill Rd.) to SR 444. On the site of a 17th-century Seneca village are interpretive trails, a bark longhouse and a visitor center with displays and a half-hour videotape. An exhibit by Seneca artist Carson Waterman focuses on the Iroquois clan system. Allow 1 hour minimum. Trails open daily 8 a.m.-dusk (weather permitting). Visitor center open Tues.-Sun. 9-5, May 15-Oct. 31. Longhouse open Tues.-Sun. 10-4. Admission $3, senior citizens and students with ID $2. Phone (585) 924-5848.

WANTAGH (I-2) pop. 18,971

JONES BEACH STATE PARK, approximately 7 mi. s. on Wantagh Pkwy., covers 2,413 acres on the ocean shore of Long Island and offers supervised swimming in Zach's Bay, oceanfront beaches and two pools. Bathhouses are available; a boardwalk follows part of the shoreline. Facilities at Field 4 include a pitch-and-putt golf course and court games. Free events include softball games and outdoor dancing. Planned programs are presented weekends.

Park open daily dawn-midnight, second weekend in June-Labor Day; dawn-dusk, rest of year. Parking daily $8, mid-May to mid-Sept; $6, rest of year. Phone (516) 785-1600. *See Recreation Chart.*

WASHINGTONVILLE (H-10)
pop. 5,851, elev. 310'

WINERIES

• **Brotherhood Winery** is 2 blks. e. on SR 94 to 100 Brotherhood Plaza Dr. Daily 11-5, Apr.-Oct.; Sat.-Sun. 11-5, rest of year. Closed Jan. 1, Thanksgiving and Dec. 25. Hours may vary; phone ahead to verify schedule. Phone (845) 496-3661.

WATERTOWN (C-7) pop. 26,705, elev. 454'

During an 1878 county fair F.W. Woolworth tested the idea of selling a fixed-price line of merchandise in a department store. The result of his experiment was the Woolworth store chain. Watertown also is noted as the home of Fort Drum.

Greater Watertown North Country Chamber of Commerce: 1241 Coffeen St., Watertown, NY 13601; phone (315) 788-4400.

JEFFERSON COUNTY HISTORICAL SOCIETY, 228 Washington St., is in the 1878 Paddock Mansion, which contains high-Victorian furnishings and decorative art, American Indian artifacts from Jefferson County, historic water turbines, Civil War memorabilia and coverlets. A re-created Victorian garden, a reconstructed 19th-century log cabin and a carriage barn with antique automobiles and farm implements also are on the premises. Guided tours area available by appointment. Allow 30 minutes minimum. Tues.-Fri. 10-5, Sat. noon-5, May-Nov.; Tues.-Fri. 10-5, rest of year. Closed major holidays. Donations. Phone (315) 782-3491.

[SAVE] **THE SCI-TECH CENTER OF NORTHERN NEW YORK,** 154 Stone St., is a hands-on science museum. Exhibits focus on light, sound and electricity. Guided tours are available by appointment. Allow 1 hour minimum. Wed. noon-4, Thurs. 9-2, Fri. noon-6, Sat. 10-2; closed Jan. 1, July 4, Thanksgiving and Dec. 25. Admission $3; over 54, $2; under 3 free; family rate $10. Phone (315) 788-1340.

THOMPSON PARK, just e. off SR 12, has playground, swimming, tennis and golf facilities. Designed by the Olmsted firm at the turn of the 20th century, the 200-acre park has an adjoining 35-acre zoo with more than 90 North American animal species including wolverines, bears and mountain lions. Picnicking is permitted. Daily 10-5, Apr.-Oct.; 10-4, rest of year. Closed Jan. 1, Thanksgiving and Dec. 25. Park free. Zoo $6, senior citizens $4, children $3, under 3 free. MC, VI. Phone (315) 782-6180.

RECREATIONAL ACTIVITIES

White-water Rafting

- [SAVE] **ARO Adventures** depart from various locations. Write P.O. Box 649, Old Forge, NY 13420. Trips depart Wed.-Mon. in Aug. and Wed.-Sun. in July; weekend trips are available May-June and Sept.-Oct. Phone (315) 369-3536 for reservations or (800) 525-7238 for information.

- **Hudson River Rafting Co.** is e. off I-81 exit 46, 1.5 mi. e. on Coffeen St., w. on City Center Dr., n. on Whitewater Way. Write P.O. Box 47, Watertown, NY 13801. Trips depart Wed.-Mon. in Aug.; Fri.-Sun., Apr.-June and Sept.-Oct.; Wed.-Sun. in July. Phone (315) 782-7881 or (800) 888-7238.

WATERVLIET (F-11) pop. 10,207, elev. 50′

WATERVLIET ARSENAL MUSEUM, off I-787 exit 8, then 1 mi. s. on Broadway (SR 32), is the nation's oldest continuously active arsenal. Built in 1813, the arsenal is owned by the government and continues to produce large-caliber weapons. Housed in the 1859 cast-iron storehouse, the museum chronicles the history of big guns and displays cannon and other military equipment from the 16th century through the present. A restored 1900s machine shop demonstrates early artillery production. Sun.-Thurs. 10-3; closed holidays. A photo ID is required for admittance. Donations. Phone (518) 266-5805.

WATKINS GLEN (F-6)
pop. 2,149, elev. 1,008′

At the southern tip of Seneca Lake, Watkins Glen is renowned for its summer auto racing at Watkins Glen International. Long before the roar of cars, this small town's most notable features were the nearby salt wells, which made this region one of the state's major salt producers.

Watkins Glen is in the Finger Lakes Wine Country. Several wineries can be found on either side of Seneca Lake, off SRs 14 and 414. *Also see Finger Lakes p. 84.*

Schuyler County Chamber of Commerce: 100 N. Franklin St., Watkins Glen, NY 14891; phone (607) 535-4300.

CAPTAIN BILL'S SENECA LAKE CRUISES depart from the foot of Franklin St. Scenic 10-mile trips are offered; lunch, dinner and other cruises also are available. Sightseeing departures daily on the hour 10-8, July 1-early Sept.; daily on the hour 11-4, early Sept.-Oct. 15; Mon.-Fri. on the hour 11-4, Sat.-Sun. and holidays on the hour 10-8, May 15-June 30. Sightseeing fare $10; under 13, $5. AX, DS, MC, VI. Phone (607) 535-4680.

FARM SANCTUARY is 1.5 mi. w. on 4th St. (CR 409), then 8 mi. n.w. on SR 23 following signs. This 175-acre working farm is home to hundreds of cows, pigs, turkeys and goats rescued from slaughterhouses and stockyards and nursed back to health. Visitors can pet the animals on 1-hour guided tours. Some uphill walking is necessary; comfortable shoes are recommended.

Note: Videotapes and photographs promote responsibility toward animals; some content might not be suitable for children. Tours are given on the hour Wed.-Sun. 11-3, June-Aug.; Sat.-Sun. 11-3, in May and Sept.-Oct. Tour $2; ages 4-12, $1. Phone (607) 583-2225.

INTERNATIONAL MOTOR RACING RESEARCH CENTER AND MUSEUM is at 610 S. Decatur St. Films, photographs, memorabilia and ephemera document the history of motorsports. The collection includes fine art and rare posters depicting racing topics. A research library and archives are available. Allow 1 hour minimum. Mon.-Sat. 9-5; closed Jan. 1, Thanksgiving and Dec. 25. Free. Phone (607) 535-9044.

MALABAR X SIGHTSEEING CRUISES depart from the fishing pier at the foot of Franklin St. The vintage wooden schooner *Malabar X* was built in 1930 and won the Bermuda Race the same year and again in 1932. Sightseeing cruises on Seneca Lake provide passengers with opportunities to trim the sails and man the helm. Allow 2 hours, 30 minutes minimum. Departures daily at 1 and 5:30, May-Oct. Fare $39. Reservations are recommended. A minimum of six passengers is required for sailing. MC, VI. Phone (607) 535-5253.

WATKINS GLEN INTERNATIONAL, 2790 CR 16, plays host to NASCAR, sports car and Indy racing events April through September. Highlights include the Watkins Glen Indy Grand Prix in June, the SCCA Glen Nationals in July, the NASCAR NEXTEL Cup Series in August and the Zippo U.S. Vintage Grand Prix in September. Thunder Road Tours allow guests to ride three paced laps around the track in their own car. Allow 1 hour minimum. Thunder Road Tours are offered May-Oct.; dates and times are subject to track availability. Tour fee $25. Phone (607) 535-2338 for track tour information or (866) 461-7223 for race tickets.

© International Speedway Corporation
AAA is the Official Auto Club of Watkins Glen International.

WATKINS GLEN STATE PARK adjoins the village at the s. end of Seneca Lake. The scenic glen, which drops about 400 feet in 2 miles, is highlighted by rock formations and 19 waterfalls; Rainbow Falls is especially lovely. Cliffs rise 300 feet above the stream; a bridge 165 feet above the water spans the glen.

Shuttle buses to the head of the glen run every 15 minutes for those who wish to avoid climbing the 832 steps. The park offers a weekly schedule of guided tours and nature programs.

Allow 1 hour, 30 minutes minimum. Park open daily 8 a.m.-dusk. Gorge trail open daily 8 a.m.-dusk, mid-May through Nov. 10. Buses depart daily 9-6, late June-Labor Day; Sat.-Sun. 9-5, day after Labor Day-Columbus Day. Park admission $7 per vehicle, mid-June through Labor Day; $6, rest of season. Bus fare $3. Phone (607) 535-4511. *See Recreation Chart and the AAA Northeastern Camp-Book.*

WESTFIELD (F-2) pop. 3,481, elev. 728′

Those who like to walk will find plenty of room in which to travel in Westfield. The Chautauqua Gorge extends 7 miles along a 100-foot-deep gorge between Westfield and Mayville. Barcelona Harbor offers fishing and a boat launch. It is the site of a historical lighthouse. Westfield is part of Chautauqua wine country, and several small wineries west of the city off US 20 offer wine tastings and guided tours in season.

Shopping areas: The Westfield streets are lined with various antiques shops, including Landmark Acres and Priscilla Nixon Antiques on W. Main Rd.; Militello Antiques at 31 Jefferson St.; and Antique

AAA and Motorsports

AAA, a pioneer in the development and growth of auto racing during the first half of the 20th century, has returned to the racetrack. Today the association is the "Official Auto Club" and "Official Roadside Assistance Provider" of 11 tracks owned and operated by the International Speedway Corporation (ISC), which hosts the NASCAR NEXTEL Cup Series and Indy Racing League (IRL) events.

As part of an agreement with ISC, AAA's widely recognized logo appears on track safety and recovery vehicles as well as on track signs, in racing programs and at other promotional venues. ISC, a leading promoter of motorsports activities in the United States, conducts more than 100 events annually. ISC/AAA facilities include California Speedway in Fontana, Calif.; Darlington Raceway in Darlington, S.C.; Daytona International Speedway in Daytona Beach, Fla.; Homestead-Miami Speedway in Homestead, Fla.; Kansas Speedway in Kansas City, Kan.; Martinsville Speedway in Martinsville, Va.; Michigan International Speedway in Cambridge Junction, Mich.; Phoenix International Raceway in Phoenix, Ariz.; Richmond International Raceway in Richmond, Va.; Talladega Superspeedway in Talladega, Ala.; and Watkins Glen International in Watkins Glen, N.Y.

© International Speedway Corporation

Marketplace, Eley Place, Monroe's Mini Mall, Saraf's Emporium and W.B. Mollard Antiques, all on E. Main St.

THE McCLURG MANSION, jct. US 20 and US 394, was built in 1820 and contains period furniture, a pioneer kitchen, Colonial farm implements, American Indian artifacts and an exhibit exploring county history during the presidency of Abraham Lincoln. Tues.-Sat. 10-4; closed most holidays. Hours may vary; phone ahead. Admission $3. Phone (716) 326-2977.

WINERIES

• **Johnson Estate Winery** is 2 mi. w. on US 20 (E. Main Rd.). Daily 10-6, July-Aug. Reservations are recommended for tours. Phone (716) 326-2191 or (800) 374-6569.

WEST HAVERSTRAW—*see New York p. 156.*

WEST POINT (H-11) pop. 7,138, elev. 10′

BEAR MOUNTAIN STATE PARK is 5 mi. s. off US 9W. The George W. Perkins Memorial Drive winds to the 1,305-foot summit of Bear Mountain, where a tower and observation deck provide views of four states and the Hudson River Valley. Picnicking is permitted. Food is available. Park open daily dawn-dusk. Drive open daily 8-dusk (weather permitting), Apr.-Nov. Tower daily 9-4. Park admission free.

Parking $6. Phone (845) 786-2701. *See Recreation Chart.*

Trailside Museum and Zoo is s. on US 9W near the park entrance. A nature trail leads to animal enclosures, museums, trailside exhibits, the outer breastworks of Fort Clinton and a statue of Walt Whitman. The museums feature animal habitat displays as well as geological, historical and natural exhibits. Allow 3 hours minimum. Daily 10-4:30. Admission $1; ages 6-12, 50c.

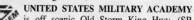 **UNITED STATES MILITARY ACADEMY** is off scenic Old Storm King Hwy. (SR 218). A visitor center just outside Thayer Gate (South Post) offers orientation films, exhibits, a replica of a cadet barracks room, and maps and brochures while serving as the departure point for narrated, 1-hour bus tours of the campus. The academy grounds and buildings are not open to the public.

Tour highlights include Cadet Chapel, which features stained-glass windows and one of the largest church organs in the world, and Trophy Point, a repository of war relics dating from the American Revolution.

Other campus buildings include Chapel of the Most Holy Trinity, Norman Gothic in style and patterned after the St. Ethelred's Carthusian abbey church in England; Jewish Chapel, which reflects the Gothic architecture of West Point; and Old Cadet Chapel, built in 1836.

Visitor center daily 9-4:45; closed Jan. 1, Thanksgiving and Dec. 25. One-hour bus tours depart Mon.-Sat. 9:45-3:30, Sun. 11-3:30, Apr.-Oct.; Mon.-Fri. 10-2:30, Sat. and Fri. after Thanksgiving 10-3:30, Sun. 11-3:30, in Nov.; daily at 11:15 and 1:15, rest of year. Two-hour tours depart daily at 11:15 and 1:45, June-Oct; Sat.-Sun. and Fri. after Thanksgiving at 1:45, in Nov. Extended tours are available daily May-Oct. No tours are given on home football Saturdays and during graduation week. Visitor center free. One-hour bus tour $9; under 12, $6. Two-hour tour $11; under 12, $9. Reservations are recommended for the 2-hour tour and a photo ID is required for all tours. Phone (845) 938-2638 for the visitor center or (845) 446-4724 for bus tour information.

West Point Museum is in Olmsted Hall at Pershing Center. West Point was declared the permanent depository of war trophies by Executive Order after the 1846-48 Mexican War. Exhibits chronicle the garrisoning of West Point and the subsequent establishment of the United States Military Academy in 1802. Military warfare from antiquity to modern times is surveyed through displays of hand-held weapons, heavy artillery and battle dioramas. Allow 1 hour minimum. Daily 10:30-4:15; closed Jan. 1, Thanksgiving and Dec. 25. Free. Phone (845) 938-2203.

WEST SAYVILLE (I-3) pop. 5,003, elev. 28′

LONG ISLAND MARITIME MUSEUM, e. on Montauk Hwy. on the grounds of the West Sayville Golf Course at 86 West Ave., displays ships models, paintings and artifacts as well as floating historic vessels. Allow 1 hour minimum. Mon.-Sat. 10-4, Sun. noon-4; closed Jan. 1, Easter, Thanksgiving and Dec. 25. Admission $4; over 64 and under 18, $2. Phone (631) 854-4974.

WHITEHALL (D-11) pop. 2,667, elev. 123′

Settled by Capt. Philip Skene and about 30 other British families in 1759, Whitehall was originally named Skenesborough in the captain's honor. After the Revolutionary War, during which Skene supported the British, the town changed its name.

Whitehall Chamber of Commerce: P.O. Box 97, Whitehall, NY 12887; phone (518) 499-2292.

Self-guiding tours: Historic buildings dating from 1824 are in a downtown area bounded by Broadway, Williams, Saunders and Clinton streets. A brochure detailing self-guiding walking and driving tours of Whitehall's historic areas is available at the Skenesborough Museum.

SKENESBOROUGH MUSEUM, just n. of US 4 to SR 22, then e. on Skenesborough Drive, includes a Navy room with models of 1776 and 1812 shipyards

and ships models, a doll room, a military room and local historical artifacts. The D&H Railroad caboose is open for viewing. Mon.-Sat. 10-4, Sun. noon-4, mid-June through Labor Day; Sat. 10-3, Sun. noon-3, day after Labor Day to mid-Oct. Admission $2, senior citizens $1, students with ID $1, family rate (two adults and one child) $5. Phone (518) 499-0716.

WHITE PLAINS—*see New York p. 156.*

WILMINGTON (B-11) pop. 1,131, elev. 1,019′

With the Ausable River and Whiteface Mountain nearby, the village of Wilmington offers scenic diversions as well as many opportunities for summer and winter recreation.

Whiteface Mountain Regional Visitors Bureau: P.O. Box 277, Wilmington, NY 12997; phone (518) 946-2255 or (888) 944-8332.

HIGH FALLS GORGE, 4.5 mi. s.w. on SR 86, is a deep ravine cut into the base of Whiteface Mountain by the Ausable River. A colorful variety of strata, rapids, falls and potholes can be seen from a network of well-constructed bridges and paths. The center of the gorge can be reached without climbing stairs. The main building features mineral displays. In July and August, visitors may mine for gems at the Ausable River Mining Company.

Picnicking is permitted. Food is available. Allow 1 hour minimum. Daily 9-5:30, first Sat. in May-last Sun. in Oct.; 8:30-4:30, Fri. after Thanksgiving-last Sun. in Mar; 8-5:30, President's Day week and Christmas week. Hours may vary; phone ahead. Last admission is 30 minutes before closing. Downhill ski, snowboard and snowshoe rentals are available in winter; phone for trail hours and rates. Admission $10.25; ages 4-12, $7.25. DS, MC, VI. Phone (518) 946-2278 to verify schedule and prices.

SANTA'S WORKSHOP, 1.5 mi. w. on SR 431 at North Pole, has Santa Claus, live reindeer, craft shops, live entertainment, children's rides and storybook characters. Rides are available late June through August and on fall weekends.

Allow 3 hours, 30 minutes minimum. Daily 9:30-4:30, late June-Labor Day; Sat.-Sun. and Columbus Day 10-3:30, day after Labor Day to mid-Oct.; Sat.-Sun. 10-3, late Nov.-late Dec. Admission $17.95; ages 2-16, $15.95. AX, DS, MC, VI. Phone (518) 946-2211 or (518) 946-2212 to verify schedule and prices.

WHITEFACE MOUNTAIN VETERANS' MEMORIAL HIGHWAY, 3.5 mi. w. via SR 431, is a 6-mile macadam road leading to a parking area near the summit of Whiteface Mountain. The 4,867-foot summit is reached by a .2-mile hiking trail or by an unusual electric elevator set in the cone of the peak. Wear proper footwear and warm clothing. On a clear day the summit house affords a view across more than 100 miles, including the St. Lawrence River and lakes Champlain and Placid.

Allow 1 hour minimum. Daily 8:30-5, late June-Labor Day; 9-4, mid-May to late June and day after Labor Day to mid-Oct. (weather permitting). Admission per private vehicle (including driver) $9, each passenger $5; motorcycle (including driver) $9, passenger $5. Phone (518) 523-1655 or (518) 946-2223, ext. 319.

RECREATIONAL ACTIVITIES
Skiing

• **Whiteface Mountain Ski Center** is 3 mi. s. on SR 86. Write P.O. Box 1980, Wilmington, NY 12997. Other activities are offered. Lifts operate daily 8:30-4, mid-Nov. to mid-Apr. (weather permitting). Phone (518) 946-2223.

WINDHAM (G-10) pop. 359

RECREATIONAL ACTIVITIES
Skiing

• **Windham Mountain,** off SR 23W following signs. Write P.O. Box 459, Windham, NY 12496. Other activities are offered. Mon.-Fri. 9-4 (also Thurs.-Fri. 4-10 p.m.), Sat. 8-10, Sun. 8-4, Nov.-Mar. Phone (518) 734-4300.

YONKERS—*see New York p. 157.*

YOUNGSTOWN—*see Niagara Falls p. 168.*

With the AAA Visa TravelMoney® card, worry-free travel is here. Like travelers cheques, this card has replacement and refund options, emergency assistance service, zero liability, purchase security, and even luggage protection.

You don't have to worry about unauthorized spending because the funds are not linked to a bank account.

By keeping a pre-paid amount on your card, you can track what you spend and not go over your budget.

The next time you travel, don't forget to pack the AAA Visa TravelMoney card.

Honey,
I lost my wallet.

Without the AAA Visa TravelMoney® card, their money problems would be monumental.

* Terms and conditions apply, see detailed terms and conditions provided with your card fulfillment kit. Information correct at time of printing, subject to change.

Visit Participating AAA offices **Click** aaa.com/travelmoney **Call** 866-339-3378

New York

Cochecton Center
© Dennis Hallinan / Alamy

New York Orientation
Map to destinations

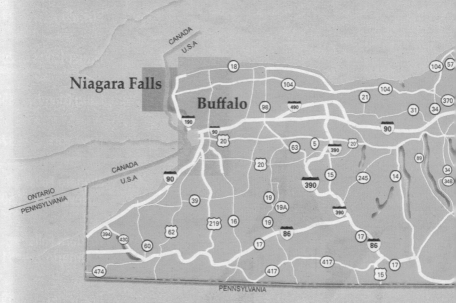

Niagara Falls

Buffalo

CANADA / U.S.A
ONTARIO / PENNSYLVANIA
CANADA / U.S.A
PENNSYLVANIA

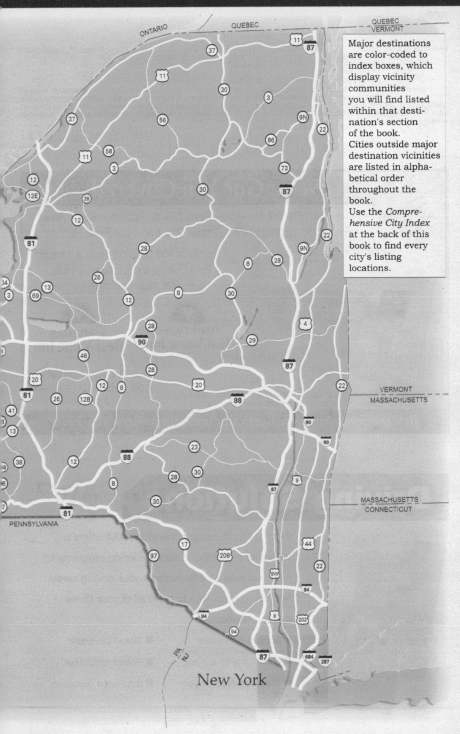

Major destinations
are color-coded to
index boxes, which
display vicinity
communities
you will find listed
within that desti-
nation's section
of the book.
Cities outside major
destination vicinities
are listed in alpha-
betical order
throughout the
book.
Use the *Compre-
hensive City Index*
at the back of this
book to find every
city's listing
locations.

New York

ACRA

──── **WHERE TO STAY** ────

LANGE'S GROVE SIDE

Phone: (518)622-3393

11/18-4/30 [BP]	1P: $75-$80	2P: $85-$95	XP: $25
6/25-9/2 [BP]	1P: $60-$65	2P: $80-$90	XP: $10
5/1-6/24 [BP]	1P: $55-$65	2P: $75-$85	XP: $10
9/3-11/17 [BP]	1P: $50-$65	2P: $75-$85	XP: $10

Motel   **Location:** Jct SR 145, 4.5 mi w. 6047 SR 23 12405. Fax: 518/622-3393. **Facility:** 23 one-bedroom standard units. 1 story, exterior corridors. **Parking:** on-site. **Terms:** 2-3 night minimum stay, 3 day cancellation notice, package plans. **Dining:** 8:30 am-10 & 5:30-7 pm, cocktails. **Pool(s):** heated outdoor. **Leisure Activities:** whirlpool, tennis court, table tennis, playground, shuffleboard. **Cards:** AX, DS, MC, VI. **Free Special Amenities:** full breakfast and local telephone calls.

SOME UNITS

Driving Solutions

From teens to mature operators, AAA offers a variety of in-depth, powerful learning programs to help you stay safe throughout your driving career. You can rely on AAA to meet all of your driver training needs:

- Mature operators
- Online traffic school
- Teaching teen drivers
- Ticket dismissal
- Points reduction
- Insurance discounts

*For more information about **AAA**'s driver training programs, contact a participating **AAA** office or visit www.aaa.com.*

Adirondacks Area

ADIRONDACK MOUNTAINS —*See BOLTON LANDING, CHESTERTOWN, DIAMOND POINT, ELIZABETHTOWN, GLENS FALLS, INLET, KEESEVILLE, LAKE GEORGE, LAKE LUZERNE, LAKE PLACID, LONG LAKE, NORTH CREEK, OLD FORGE, QUEENSBURY, SARANAC LAKE, SCHROON LAKE, SPECULATOR, TICONDEROGA, TUPPER LAKE, WARRENSBURG & WILMINGTON.*

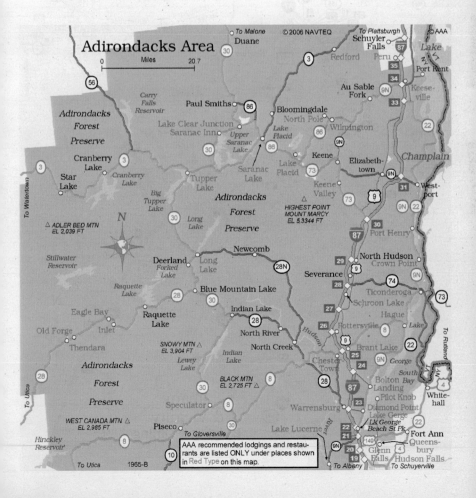

AAA recommended lodgings and restaurants are listed ONLY under places shown in Red Type on this map.

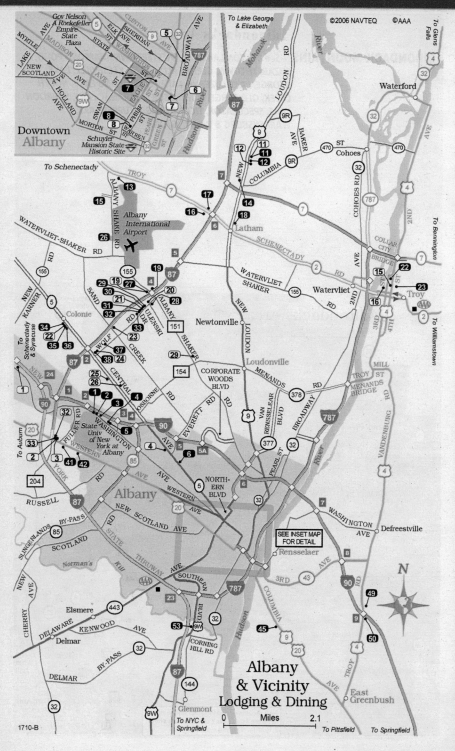

Albany
& Vicinity
Lodging & Dining

✈ Airport Accommodations

Spotter/Map Page Number	OA	ALBANY INTERNATIONAL AIRPORT	Diamond Rating	Rate Range High Season	Listing Page
32 / p. 218		Albany Marriott, 2 mi se of terminal	▽▽▽	$149-$229	273
30 / p. 218	AAA	Best Western Albany Airport Inn, 2 mi se of terminal	▽▽	$99-$159 SAVE	274
33 / p. 218		Courtyard by Marriott, 2 mi se of terminal	▽▽▽	$104-$179	274
27 / p. 218	AAA	The Desmond Hotel, 1.5 mi e of terminal	▽▽▽	$189-$199 SAVE	274
28 / p. 218	AAA	Hampton Inn Wolf Road, 2 mi se of airport	▽▽▽	$135-$159 SAVE	274
26 / p. 218	AAA	Hilton Garden Inn-Albany Airport, just w of terminal	▽▽▽	$99-$199 SAVE	275
29 / p. 218		Holiday Inn Turf on Wolf Road, 2 mi se of terminal	▽▽▽	$149-$189	275
31 / p. 218		Red Roof Inn #7112, 2 mi se of terminal	▽▽	$93-$112	275
15 / p. 218	AAA	Comfort Inn Albany Airport & Conference Center, 0.5 mi w of terminal	▽▽▽	$109-$149 SAVE	352

Albany and Vicinity

This index helps you "spot" where approved accommodations and restaurants are located on the corresponding detailed maps. Lodging rate ranges are for comparison only and show the property's high season; rates are per night, unless only weekly (W) rates are available. Restaurant rate range is for dinner, unless only lunch (L) is served. Turn to the listing page for more detailed rate information and consult display ads for special promotions.

Spotter/Map Page Number	OA	ALBANY - Lodgings	Diamond Rating	Rate Range High Season	Listing Page
1 / p. 218		The Albany Thruway Courtyard	▽▽▽	$99-$204	222
2 / p. 218		CrestHill Suites	▽▽▽	$116-$129	222
3 / p. 218		Extended StayAmerica	▽▽	Failed to provide	223
4 / p. 218		Fairfield Inn by Marriott	▽▽▽	$140-$165	223
5 / p. 218		TownePlace Suites by Marriott	▽▽▽	$160-$185	224
6 / p. 218	AAA	Albany Clarion Hotel	▽▽▽	$99-$219 SAVE	222
7 / p. 218	AAA	Crowne Plaza Hotel and Resort Albany	▽▽▽	$204 SAVE	222
8 / p. 218	AAA	Albany Mansion Hill Inn & Restaurant	▽▽▽	$175 SAVE	222
		ALBANY - Restaurants			
1 / p. 218		Mallozzi's Restaurant	▽▽▽	$16-$20	224
2 / p. 218		Bountiful Bread	▽	$5-$8	224
3 / p. 218		Mangia	▽▽	$7-$20	224
4 / p. 218		Carmine's Restaurant	▽▽▽	$15-$22	224
5 / p. 218		Nicole's Bistro At Quackenbush House	▽▽▽	$17-$26	225
6 / p. 218	AAA	Jack's Oyster House	▽▽▽	$12-$20	224
7 / p. 218		La Serre Restaurant	▽▽▽	$14-$24	224
8 / p. 218		Albany Mansion Hill Inn & Restaurant	▽▽▽	$15-$24	224
		LATHAM - Lodgings			
11 / p. 218	AAA	The Century House, a Clarion Hotel	▽▽▽	$140-$230 SAVE	352
12 / p. 218		Hampton Inn-Latham	▽▽▽	Failed to provide	353

Spotter/Map Page Number	OA	LATHAM - Lodgings (continued)	Diamond Rating	Rate Range High Season	Listing Page
13 / p. 218		Residence Inn by Marriott Albany Airport	◆◆◆	$149-$269	353
14 / p. 218	AAA	Holiday Inn Express-Airport	◆◆◆	$130 SAVE	353
15 / p. 218	AAA	Comfort Inn Albany Airport & Conference Center	◆◆◆	$109-$149 SAVE	352
16 / p. 218	AAA	Microtel Inn, Albany Airport	◆◆	$45-$169 SAVE	353
17 / p. 218	AAA	Quality Inn & Suites	◆◆	$107-$140 SAVE	353
18 / p. 218		La Quinta Inn & Suites - Albany Airport - see color ad p 360	◆◆◆	$119-$149	353
19 / p. 218		Wingate Inn	◆◆◆	$144-$156	353
		LATHAM - Restaurants			
11 / p. 218	AAA	Century House	◆◆◆	$16-$27	354
12 / p. 218		Kirker's Steak & Seafood	◆◆	$12-$22	354
		TROY - Lodgings			
22 / p. 218	AAA	Franklin Square Inn & Suites	◆◆	$106-$189 SAVE	637
23 / p. 218	AAA	Best Western-Rensselaer Inn	◆◆	$84-$99 SAVE	637
		TROY - Restaurants			
15 / p. 218		Holmes & Watson Ltd	◆	$11-$15	637
16 / p. 218		Daisy Bakers	◆◆	$15-$35	637
		COLONIE - Lodgings			
26 / p. 218	AAA	Hilton Garden Inn-Albany Airport	◆◆◆	$99-$199 SAVE	275
27 / p. 218	AAA	The Desmond Hotel	◆◆◆	$189-$199 SAVE	274
28 / p. 218	AAA	Hampton Inn Wolf Road - see color ad p 223	◆◆◆	$135-$159 SAVE	274
29 / p. 218		Holiday Inn Turf on Wolf Road	◆◆◆	$149-$189	275
30 / p. 218	AAA	Best Western Albany Airport Inn	◆◆	$99-$159 SAVE	274
31 / p. 218		Red Roof Inn #7112	◆◆	$93-$112	275
32 / p. 218		Albany Marriott	◆◆◆	$149-$229	273
33 / p. 218		Courtyard by Marriott	◆◆◆	$104-$179	274
34 / p. 218	AAA	Quality Inn-Albany Airport	◆◆	$79-$149 SAVE	275
35 / p. 218	AAA	Comfort Inn & Suites	◆◆◆	$99-$129 SAVE	274
36 / p. 218		America's Best Value Inn	◆	$69-$99	273
37 / p. 218	AAA	Econo Lodge	◆◆	$89-$99 SAVE	274
38 / p. 218	AAA	Cocca's Inn & Suites, Wolf Rd - see color ad p 223	◆◆	$89-$149 SAVE	274
		COLONIE - Restaurants			
19 / p. 218		Scrimshaw	◆◆◆	$18-$30	276
20 / p. 218		Wolf Road Diner	◆	$8-$11	276
21 / p. 218		Real Seafood Co	◆◆◆	$14-$28	276
22 / p. 218		Garcia's Mexican Restaurant	◆◆	$7-$14	276
23 / p. 218		The Barnsider	◆◆	$18-$25	275
24 / p. 218		Bangkok Thai Restaurant	◆◆	$10-$17	275
25 / p. 218		Ralph's Tavern	◆	$5-$13	276

Spotter/Map Page Number	OA	COLONIE - Restaurants (continued)	Diamond Rating	Rate Range High Season	Listing Page
26 / p. 218	AAA	Grandma's Country Restaurant	▽▽	$8-$15	276
		GUILDERLAND - Lodgings			
41 / p. 218		Holiday Inn Express Turf on Western Ave	▽▽▽	$129-$199	311
42 / p. 218	AAA	Best Western Sovereign Hotel Albany	▽▽	$89-$159 SAVE	310
		GUILDERLAND - Restaurants			
32 / p. 218		Londonderry Cafe	▽▽	$8-$17	311
33 / p. 218		Provence	▽▽▽	$12-$26	311
		RENSSELAER - Lodgings			
45 / p. 218	AAA	Econo Lodge	▽▽	$59-$139 SAVE	597
		EAST GREENBUSH - Lodgings			
49 / p. 218		Residence Inn by Marriott	▽▽▽	$169-$259	288
50 / p. 218		Fairfield Inn by Marriott-Albany/East Greenbush	▽▽▽	$119-$129	288
		GLENMONT - Lodgings			
53 / p. 218	AAA	Comfort Inn	▽▽▽	$99-$169 SAVE	307
		LOUDONVILLE - Restaurant			
29 / p. 218		Pearl of the Orient	▽▽	$7-$17	361

ALBANY pop. 95,658 (See map and index starting on p. 218)

—— WHERE TO STAY ——

ALBANY CLARION HOTEL — *Book great rates at AAA.com*
Phone: (518)438-8431 **6**

AAA SAVE — All Year — 1P: $99-$219 — 2P: $99-$219 — XP: $10 — F16
Location: I-90, exit 5 (Everett Rd), just s, then e. 3 Watervliet Ave Ext 12206. Fax: 518/438-8356. **Facility:** 216 units. 215 one-bedroom standard units, some with efficiencies. 1 one-bedroom suite. 2-9 stories, interior corridors. **Parking:** on-site. **Terms:** weekly rates available, package plans, pets ($25 fee, in designated
Small-scale Hotel units). **Amenities:** voice mail, safes, irons, hair dryers. **Dining:** 6:30 am-10 pm, Sun 7 am-11 & 5-9:30 pm, cocktails. **Pool(s):** small outdoor, small heated indoor. **Leisure Activities:** exercise room. **Guest Services:** valet and coin laundry, area transportation-bus & train station, wireless Internet. **Business Services:** conference facilities, business center. **Cards:** AX, CB, DC, DS, JC, MC, VI. **Free Special Amenities: expanded continental breakfast and high-speed Internet.**

SOME UNITS

ALBANY MANSION HILL INN & RESTAURANT
Phone: 518/465-2038 **8**

AAA SAVE — All Year — 1P: $175 — 2P: $175 — XP: $10 — F
Location: I-787, exit 3B (Madison Ave/US 20 W) to Philip St, 0.4 mi s. 115 Philip St at Park Ave 12202 (45 Park Ave). Fax: 518/434-2313. **Facility:** In an older neighborhood, the property features a rustic courtyard and is renovated with modern amenities; original buildings date to 1860 and 1913. 8 one-bedroom standard units.
Historic Bed 2 stories (no elevator), interior/exterior corridors. **Parking:** on-site and street. **Terms:** office hours 9 am-5
& Breakfast pm, check-in 4 pm, 5 day cancellation notice, [BP] meal plan available, package plans. **Amenities:** dual phone lines, voice mail, irons, hair dryers. **Dining:** restaurant, see separate listing. **Guest Services:** valet laundry, area transportation-bus & train station. **Business Services:** meeting rooms. **Cards:** AX, CB, DC, DS, JC, MC, VI. **Free Special Amenities: full breakfast and high-speed Internet.**

SOME UNITS

THE ALBANY THRUWAY COURTYARD — *Book great rates at AAA.com*
Phone: (518)435-1600 **1**

All Year — 1P: $99-$204 — 2P: $99-$204
Location: I-90, exit 2 westbound, just s on Fuller Rd, then just e; exit eastbound, just e. 1455 Washington Ave 12206.
Small-scale Hotel Fax: 518/435-1616. **Facility:** Smoke free premises. 78 units. 70 one-bedroom standard units. 8 one-bedroom suites. 3 stories, interior corridors. **Bath:** combo or shower only. **Parking:** on-site. **Terms:** [BP] meal plan available, package plans. **Amenities:** high-speed Internet, dual phone lines, voice mail, irons, hair dryers. **Pool(s):** small heated indoor. **Leisure Activities:** whirlpool, exercise room. **Guest Services:** valet and coin laundry. **Business Services:** meeting rooms. **Cards:** AX, DC, DS, JC, MC, VI.

SOME UNITS

CRESTHILL SUITES — *Book at AAA.com*
Phone: (518)454-0007 **2**

5/1-10/31 — 1P: $116-$129 — 2P: $116-$129
11/1-4/30 — 1P: $98-$109 — 2P: $98-$109
Small-scale Hotel **Location:** I-90, exit 2 westbound, just s on Fuller Rd, then just e; exit eastbound, just e. 1415 Washington Ave 12206. Fax: 518/454-0003. **Facility:** 95 units. 42 one-bedroom standard units with kitchens. 33 one- and 20 two-bedroom suites ($159-$189) with kitchens. 3 stories, interior corridors. **Bath:** combo or shower only. **Parking:** on-site. **Terms:** pets ($150 deposit). **Amenities:** video library, high-speed Internet, dual phone lines, voice mail, irons, hair dryers. **Pool(s):** heated outdoor. **Leisure Activities:** exercise room. **Guest Services:** sundries, complimentary and valet laundry, area transportation, wireless Internet. **Business Services:** meeting rooms, business center. **Cards:** AX, DC, DS, MC, VI.

SOME UNITS

CROWNE PLAZA HOTEL AND RESORT ALBANY — *Book great rates at AAA.com*
Phone: (518)462-6611 **7**

AAA SAVE — 5/1-5/31 & 9/8-4/30 — 1P: $204 — 2P: $204
6/1-9/7 — 1P: $184 — 2P: $184
Location: At Lodge and State St; downtown. Located at Ten Eyck Plaza. 89 State St 12207. Fax: 518/462-2901.
Facility: 384 units. 380 one-bedroom standard units. 4 one-bedroom suites ($325-$500). 15 stories, interior
Large-scale Hotel corridors. **Bath:** combo or shower only. **Parking:** on-site (fee) and valet. **Terms:** check-in 4 pm, [AP] meal plan available. **Amenities:** CD players, dual phone lines, voice mail, irons, hair dryers. **Dining:** 6 am-10 pm, Sat & Sun from 7 am, cocktails. **Pool(s):** small heated indoor. **Leisure Activities:** whirlpool. **Guest Services:** gift shop, valet laundry, area transportation-bus & train station, wireless Internet. **Business Services:** conference facilities, business center. **Cards:** AX, CB, DC, DS, MC, VI.

SOME UNITS

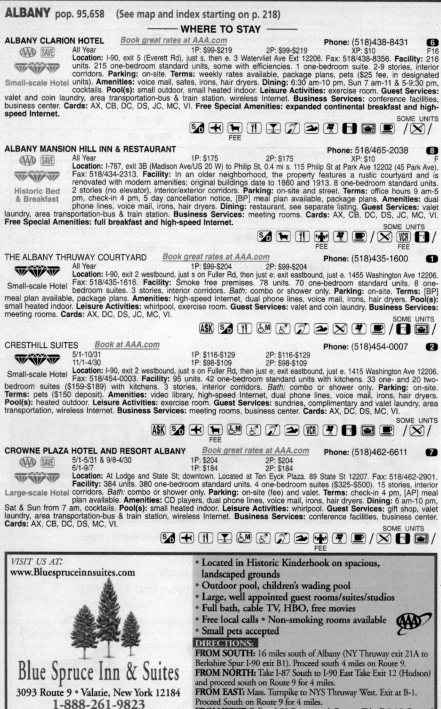

(See map and index starting on p. 218)

EXTENDED STAYAMERICA   *Book at AAA.com*   **Phone:** 518/446-0680   **3**
Property failed to provide current rates
Location: I-90, exit 2 westbound, just s on Fuller Rd, then 0.5 mi e; exit eastbound, just e. 1395 Washington Ave 12206.
Small-scale Hotel   Fax: 518/446-0779. **Facility:** 134 one-bedroom standard units with efficiencies. 2 stories, interior corridors. *Bath:* combo or shower only. **Parking:** on-site. **Amenities:** high-speed Internet (fee), voice mail, irons.
Guest Services: coin laundry.

SOME UNITS

FAIRFIELD INN BY MARRIOTT   *Book great rates at AAA.com*   **Phone:** (518)435-1800   **4**
All Year   1P: $140-$160   2P: $145-$165   XP: $5   F18
Location: I-90, exit 2 westbound, just s on Fuller Rd, then 0.6 mi e; exit eastbound, just e. 1383 Washington Ave 12206.
Small-scale Hotel   corridors. *Bath:* combo or shower only. **Parking:** on-site. **Amenities:** voice mail, irons, hair dryers. **Pool(s):**
small heated indoor. **Leisure Activities:** whirlpool. **Guest Services:** valet laundry, wireless Internet. **Business Services:** fax.
Cards: AX, DC, DS, MC, VI.

SOME UNITS

(See map and index starting on p. 218)

TOWNEPLACE SUITES BY MARRIOTT

Book great rates at AAA.com   Phone: (518)435-1900   **5**

All Year   1P: $160-$180   2P: $165-$185   XP: $5   F18

Small-scale Hotel

Location: I-90, exit 2 westbound, just s on Fuller Rd, then 0.6 mi e; exit eastbound, just e. 1379 Washington Ave 12206. **Fax:** 518/446-8170. **Facility:** Smoke free premises. 100 units. 74 one-bedroom standard units with kitchens. 4 one- and 22 two-bedroom suites with kitchens. 3 stories, interior corridors. *Bath:* combo or shower only. **Parking:** on-site. **Terms:** pets ($75 fee). **Amenities:** voice mail, irons, hair dryers. **Pool(s):** small heated outdoor. **Leisure Activities:** exercise room. **Guest Services:** valet and coin laundry, wireless Internet. **Business Services:** PC, fax (fee). **Cards:** AX, DC, DS, MC, VI.

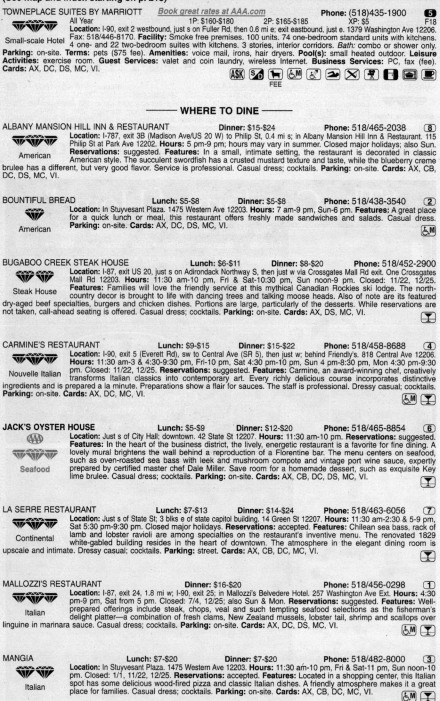

———— WHERE TO DINE ————

ALBANY MANSION HILL INN & RESTAURANT
Dinner: $15-$24   Phone: 518/465-2038   **8**

American

Location: I-787, exit 3B (Madison Ave/US 20 W) to Philip St, 0.4 mi s; in Albany Mansion Hill Inn & Restaurant. 115 Philip St at Park Ave 12202. **Hours:** 5 pm-9 pm; hours may vary in summer. Closed major holidays; also Sun. **Reservations:** suggested. **Features:** In a small, intimate setting, the restaurant is decorated in classic American style. The succulent swordfish has a crusted mustard texture and taste, while the blueberry creme brulee has a different, but very good flavor. Service is professional. Casual dress; cocktails. **Parking:** on-site. **Cards:** AX, CB, DC, DS, MC, VI.

BOUNTIFUL BREAD
Lunch: $5-$8   Dinner: $5-$8   Phone: 518/438-3540   **2**

American

Location: In Stuyvesant Plaza. 1475 Western Ave 12203. **Hours:** 7 am-9 pm, Sun-6 pm. **Features:** A great place for a quick lunch or meal, this restaurant offers freshly made sandwiches and salads. Casual dress. **Parking:** on-site. **Cards:** AX, DC, DS, MC, VI.

BUGABOO CREEK STEAK HOUSE
Lunch: $6-$11   Dinner: $8-$20   Phone: 518/452-2900

Steak House

Location: I-87, exit US 20, just s on Adirondack Northway S, then just w via Crossgates Mall Rd exit. One Crossgates Mall Rd 12203. **Hours:** 11:30 am-10 pm, Fri & Sat-10:30 pm, Sun noon-9 pm. Closed: 11/22, 12/25. **Features:** Families will love the friendly service at this mythical Canadian Rockies ski lodge. The north-country decor is brought to life with dancing trees and talking moose heads. Also of note are its featured dry-aged beef specialties, burgers and chicken dishes. Portions are large, particularly of the desserts. While reservations are not taken, call-ahead seating is offered. Casual dress; cocktails. **Parking:** on-site. **Cards:** AX, DS, MC, VI.

CARMINE'S RESTAURANT
Lunch: $9-$15   Dinner: $15-$22   Phone: 518/458-8688   **4**

Nouvelle Italian

Location: I-90, exit 5 (Everett Rd), sw to Central Ave (SR 5), then just w; behind Friendly's. 818 Central Ave 12206. **Hours:** 11:30 am-3 & 4:30-9:30 pm, Fri-10 pm, Sat 4:30 pm-10 pm, Sun 4 pm-8:30 pm, Mon 4:30 pm-9:30 pm. Closed: 11/22, 12/25. **Reservations:** suggested. **Features:** Carmine, an award-winning chef, creatively transforms Italian classics into contemporary art. Every richly delicious course incorporates distinctive ingredients and is prepared a la minute. Preparations show a flair for sauces. The staff is professional. Dressy casual; cocktails. **Parking:** on-site. **Cards:** AX, DC, MC, VI.

JACK'S OYSTER HOUSE
Lunch: $5-$9   Dinner: $12-$20   Phone: 518/465-8854   **6**

Seafood

Location: Just s of City Hall; downtown. 42 State St 12207. **Hours:** 11:30 am-10 pm. **Reservations:** suggested. **Features:** In the heart of the business district, the lively, energetic restaurant is a favorite for fine dining. A lovely mural brightens the wall behind a reproduction of a Florentine bar. The menu centers on seafood, such as oven-roasted sea bass with leek and mushroom compote and vintage port wine sauce, expertly prepared by certified master chef Dale Miller. Save room for a homemade dessert, such as exquisite Key lime brulee. Casual dress; cocktails. **Parking:** on-site. **Cards:** AX, CB, DC, DS, MC, VI.

LA SERRE RESTAURANT
Lunch: $7-$13   Dinner: $14-$24   Phone: 518/463-6056   **7**

Continental

Location: Just s of State St; 3 blks e of state capitol building. 14 Green St 12207. **Hours:** 11:30 am-2:30 & 5-9 pm, Sat 5:30 pm-9:30 pm. Closed major holidays. **Reservations:** accepted. **Features:** Chilean sea bass, rack of lamb and lobster ravioli are among specialties on the restaurant's inventive menu. The renovated 1829 white-gabled building resides in the heart of downtown. The atmosphere in the elegant dining room is upscale and intimate. Dressy casual; cocktails. **Parking:** street. **Cards:** AX, CB, DC, MC, VI.

MALLOZZI'S RESTAURANT
Dinner: $16-$20   Phone: 518/456-0298   **1**

Italian

Location: I-87, exit 24, 1.8 mi w; I-90, exit 25; in Mallozzi's Belvedere Hotel. 257 Washington Ave Ext. **Hours:** 4:30 pm-9 pm, Sat from 5 pm. Closed: 7/4, 12/25; also Sun & Mon. **Reservations:** suggested. **Features:** Well-prepared offerings include steak, chops, veal and such tempting seafood selections as the fisherman's delight platter—a combination of fresh clams, New Zealand mussels, lobster tail, shrimp and scallops over linguine in marinara sauce. Casual dress; cocktails. **Parking:** on-site. **Cards:** AX, DC, DS, MC, VI.

MANGIA
Lunch: $7-$20   Dinner: $7-$20   Phone: 518/482-8000   **3**

Italian

Location: In Stuyvesant Plaza. 1475 Western Ave 12203. **Hours:** 11:30 am-10 pm, Fri & Sat-11 pm, Sun noon-10 pm. Closed: 1/1, 11/22, 12/25. **Reservations:** accepted. **Features:** Located in a shopping center, this Italian spot has some delicious wood-fired pizza and classic Italian dishes. A friendly atmosphere makes it a great place for families. Casual dress; cocktails. **Parking:** on-site. **Cards:** AX, CB, DC, MC, VI.

(See map and index starting on p. 218)

NICOLE'S BISTRO AT QUACKENBUSH HOUSE   **Lunch:** $6-$12   **Dinner:** $17-$26   **Phone:** 518/465-1111   ⑤
▼▼▼▼   **Location:** Just off Clinton Ave exit; downtown. 25 Quackenbush Square 12207. **Hours:** 11:30 am-2:30 & 5-10 pm,
Nouvelle American   Sat from 5 pm. Closed major holidays; also Sun. **Reservations:** suggested. **Features:** The converted 17th-
century home is decorated in soft tones and charcoal sketches. Flavorful dishes, such as steak au poivre
and onion soup gratinee, are prepared with obvious thought to color and texture. The light, sweet chocolate
mousse is exquisite. Dressy casual; cocktails. **Parking:** on-site. **Cards:** AX, CB, DC, DS, MC, VI. **Historic**   ⛾

ALBION pop. 7,438

——— WHERE TO STAY ———

FAIRHAVEN INN   **Phone:** 585/589-9151
ⒶⒶⒶ 〔SAVE〕   All Year   1P: $55   2P: $60   XP: $10   F10
▼▼▼▼   **Location:** Jct SR 104 and 98. 14369 Ridge Rd 14411. Fax: 585/589-7341. **Facility:** Smoke free premises. 8 one-
Motel   bedroom standard units. 1-2 stories (no elevator), exterior corridors. Bath: combo or shower only. **Parking:**
on-site. **Dining:** Tillman's Village Inn, see separate listing. **Guest Services:** gift shop. **Business Services:**
meeting rooms. **Cards:** AX, CB, DC, DS, JC, MC, VI. **Free Special Amenities: local telephone calls and
early check-in/late check-out.**

〔🍴〕〔✕〕〔📷〕〔🖥〕

LAMONT'S ORCHARD VIEW BED & BREAKFAST   **Phone:** 585/589-7702
▼▼▼▼   All Year   1P: $75-$95   2P: $75-$95   XP: $15
Bed & Breakfast   **Location:** Jct SR 104, 1.4 mi s. 3027 Densmore Rd 14411. Fax: 585/589-7023. **Facility:** Featuring casual
elegance in apple country with Victorian-era style, this homestead is situated in a fruit orchard offering
peace and tranquility. Smoke free premises. 4 one-bedroom standard units, some with whirlpools. 2 stories
(no elevator), interior corridors. Bath: some shared or private, combo or shower only. **Parking:** on-site. **Terms:** age restrictions
may apply, 14 day cancellation notice-fee imposed. **Amenities:** hair dryers. Some: DVD players. **Cards:** AX, DS, MC, VI.

SOME UNITS
〔A$K〕〔✕〕〔☎〕 / 〔AC〕〔VCR〕 /

——— WHERE TO DINE ———

TILLMAN'S VILLAGE INN   **Lunch:** $4-$8   **Dinner:** $9-$18   **Phone:** 585/589-9151
▼▼ ▼▼   **Location:** Jct SR 104 and 98; in Fairhaven Inn. 14369 Ridge Rd 14411. **Hours:** 11:30 am-9 pm. Closed: 12/25;
American   also Mon 1/1-3/3. **Reservations:** accepted. **Features:** The former stagecoach stop offers prime rib, steaks,
seafood and home-style comfort foods, including barbecue ribs and roast turkey with stuffing. Casual dress;
cocktails. **Parking:** on-site. **Cards:** AX, DC, DS, MC, VI.   ⛾

ALEXANDRIA BAY pop. 1,088

——— WHERE TO STAY ———

OTTER CREEK INN   **Phone:** 315/482-5248
ⒶⒶⒶ 〔SAVE〕   6/17-9/3   1P: $80-$105   2P: $80-$105   XP: $10   F12
▼▼ ▼▼   5/1-6/16 & 9/4-10/13   1P: $60-$80   2P: $60-$80   XP: $10   F12
Motel   **Location:** Jct Crossmon and Church sts, follow signs. Located at the St. Laurence River Upper Bay. 2 Crossmon St
Extension 13607. Fax: 315/482-5542. **Facility:** 32 one-bedroom standard units. 2 stories (no elevator),
interior/exterior corridors. **Parking:** on-site. **Terms:** open 5/1-10/13, office hours 8 am-10 pm, 2-3 night
minimum stay - seasonal and/or weekends, 3 day cancellation notice. **Leisure Activities:** fishing, picnic
tables. Fee: boat dock. **Cards:** DS, MC, VI.

SOME UNITS
〔S/D〕〔✕〕 / 〔✕〕〔📠〕 /

——— **WHERE TO DINE** ———

CAPT'S LANDING
Lunch: $5-$10   **Dinner:** $13-$22   **Phone:** 315/482-7777
American
Location: On Bayfront; center. 49 James St 13607. **Hours:** Open 5/18-10/31; 7 am-9 pm. **Reservations:** suggested. **Features:** Guests that step aboard the "barge made into a restaurant" at dockside actually are floating on Alexandria Bay. The friendly, casual staff serves seafood, pasta, beef and chicken as diners enjoy the view across the bay toward Boldt Castle. The barge does move on waves from passing boats. Casual dress; cocktails. **Parking:** on-site. **Cards:** AX, DS, MC, VI.

CAVALLARIO'S STEAK & SEAFOOD HOUSE
Dinner: $14-$23   **Phone:** 315/482-9867
Steak & Seafood
Location: Center. 24 Church St 13607. **Hours:** Open 5/1-10/16; 5 pm-9 pm, Fri & Sat-10 pm. **Reservations:** accepted. **Features:** Steak, seafood, veal, live Maine lobster and Italian fare make this restaurant one of Alex Bay's favorite casual dining choices. Casual dress; cocktails. **Parking:** on-site. **Cards:** AX, DS, MC, VI.

JACQUES CARTIER DINING ROOM
Dinner: $24-$32   **Phone:** 315/482-9917
Continental
Location: I-81, exit 50, 4.9 mi n on SR 12, 0.6 mi e on Walton, then just ne; in Riveredge Resort-Hotel. 17 Holland St 13607. **Hours:** Open 5/12-10/31; 6 pm-10 pm. **Reservations:** suggested. **Features:** The dining room affords wonderful views of the St. Lawrence River and historic Boldt Castle. A harpist adds to the decidedly romantic atmosphere. Such dishes as Chilean sea bass and rack of lamb are carefully prepared and flavorful. Service is attentive, accomplished and unpretentious. Dressy casual; cocktails; entertainment. **Parking:** on-site and valet. **Cards:** AX, CB, DC, DS, MC, VI.

——— *The following restaurant has not been evaluated by AAA* ———
but is listed for your information only.

COLEMANS SMOKEHOUSE
Phone: 315/482-7427
[fyi]
Not evaluated. **Location:** Center. 5 Market St 13607. **Features:** The real Southern barbecue joint serves beef, chicken, ribs and pork with tasty sides.

ALFRED pop. 3,954

——— **WHERE TO STAY** ———

SAXON INN
Phone: (607)871-2600
Small-scale Hotel
5/1-12/20 & 1/3-4/30   1P: $93-$149   2P: $103-$149   XP: $10   F12
Location: I-86, exit 33, 3.8 mi s on SR 21, 1.7 mi w on SR 244, through to campus, then just s; on Alfred University campus. 1 Park St 14802 (Saxon Dr). Fax: 607/871-2650. **Facility:** 25 one-bedroom standard units. 2 stories, interior corridors. **Parking:** on-site, winter plug-ins. **Terms:** open 5/1-12/20 & 1/3-4/30, cancellation fee imposed, [CP] meal plan available. **Amenities:** high-speed Internet, voice mail, hair dryers. *Some:* irons. **Guest Services:** valet laundry, wireless Internet. **Business Services:** meeting rooms. **Cards:** AX, DC, DS, MC, VI.
SOME UNITS

ALLEGANY pop. 1,883

——— **WHERE TO STAY** ———

BEST WESTERN UNIVERSITY INN
Book great rates at AAA.com
Phone: (716)372-1300
Small-scale Hotel
All Year [BP]   1P: $64-$149   2P: $74-$159   XP: $10   F12
Location: I-86, exit 24, 2 mi e on SR 417 (State St). 3051 W State St 14706. Fax: 716/372-0212. **Facility:** 60 one-bedroom standard units, some with kitchens and/or whirlpools. 2 stories, interior corridors. **Bath:** combo or shower only. **Parking:** on-site. **Terms:** cancellation fee imposed. **Amenities:** video library, DVD players, high-speed Internet, voice mail, irons, hair dryers. **Pool(s):** small heated indoor. **Leisure Activities:** exercise room. **Guest Services:** valet and coin laundry, wireless Internet. **Business Services:** PC. **Cards:** AX, CB, DC, DS, MC, VI.

COUNTRY INN & SUITES, OLEAN
Book at AAA.com
Phone: 716/372-7500
Small-scale Hotel
Property failed to provide current rates
Location: I-86, exit 25 westbound; exit 24 eastbound. 2 mi e. Located across from St. Bonaventure University. 3270 NYS Rt 417 W 14706. Fax: 716/372-7525. **Facility:** 77 units. 53 one-bedroom standard units, some with whirlpools. 24 one-bedroom suites. 3 stories, interior corridors. **Bath:** combo or shower only. **Parking:** on-site. **Amenities:** dual phone lines, voice mail, irons, hair dryers. **Pool(s):** heated indoor. **Leisure Activities:** whirlpool, exercise room. **Guest Services:** valet and coin laundry, wireless Internet. **Business Services:** meeting rooms.
SOME UNITS

MICROTEL INN & SUITES-OLEAN/ALLEGANY
Book at AAA.com
Phone: 716/373-5333
Small-scale Hotel
All Year   1P: $55-$69   2P: $55-$69   XP: $5   F18
Location: I-86, exit 24, 2.1 mi e on SR 417 (State St). Located across from St. Bonaventure University. 3234 NYS Rt 417 14760. Fax: 716/373-2559. **Facility:** 50 one-bedroom standard units. 2 stories, interior corridors. **Bath:** combo or shower only. **Parking:** on-site. **Terms:** cancellation fee imposed, [CP] meal plan available, pets ($10 fee). **Amenities:** voice mail. *Some:* hair dryers. **Leisure Activities:** exercise room. **Guest Services:** coin laundry. **Business Services:** PC. **Cards:** AX, DC, DS, MC, VI.
SOME UNITS
FEE

AMAGANSETT pop. 1,067

——— WHERE TO DINE ———

LOBSTER ROLL

Seafood

Lunch: $8-$13   **Dinner:** $6-$18   **Phone:** 631/267-3740
Location: 4 mi e on SR 27. 1980 Montauk Hwy E 11930. **Hours:** Open 5/1-10/17 & 4/15-4/30; 11:30 am-9:30 pm, Fri-Sun to 10 pm. **Features:** A seasonal institution, the local favorite is lovingly called "lunch" by those in the know. It may not look like much more than an old roadside seafood stand, but it's charming. Sit in the plastic-enclosed porch with flower baskets, hanging plants and red and white checkered tablecloths. The lobster roll is good, as are the fried oyster, clam roll, fish and chips, blue-claw crab cakes, marinated charbroiled fish and the puffers, tempura blow fish, fins and all. The pie is worth the splurge. Casual dress; cocktails. **Parking:** on-site. **Cards:** MC, VI.

AMHERST —See Buffalo p. 253.

AMITYVILLE pop. 9,441

——— WHERE TO DINE ———

ROSE COTTAGE

Continental

Lunch: $10-$15   **Dinner:** $15-$26   **Phone:** 631/691-6881
Location: SR 27A, 0.5 mi e of SR 110. 348 Merrick Rd 11701. **Hours:** 5 pm-9 pm, Fri & Sat-10 pm, Sun 3 pm-8 pm. **Closed:** 1/1, 7/4, 12/25; also Mon. **Reservations:** suggested, weekends. **Features:** Enhancing the restaurant's French chalet decor are knotty pine walls, beamed ceilings, dried-flower wreaths and intimate lighting. An extensive wine list complements a menu that centers on steak and pasta. Casual dress; cocktails. **Parking:** on-site. **Cards:** AX, DC, DS, MC, VI.

AMSTERDAM pop. 18,355

——— WHERE TO STAY ———

HALCYON FARM BED & BREAKFAST

Bed & Breakfast

Phone: 518/842-7718
5/1-10/31	1P: $110-$150	2P: $110-$150	XP: $30
11/1-4/30	1P: $90-$130	2P: $90-$130	XP: $25

Location: I-90, exit 27, 2 mi s on SR 30, then 3 mi s on SR 161. 157 Lang Rd 12010. Fax: 518/842-5562. **Facility:** 5 one-bedroom standard units. 2 stories, interior corridors. *Bath:* combo or shower only. **Parking:** on-site. **Terms:** 14 day cancellation notice. **Amenities:** hair dryers. *Some:* DVD players. **Leisure Activities:** hiking trails. **Business Services:** fax. **Cards:** DS, MC, VI.

SOME UNITS

SUPER 8 MOTEL   *Book at AAA.com*

Small-scale Hotel

Phone: (518)843-5888
All Year	1P: $59-$199	2P: $59-$199	XP: $4 F16

Location: I-90, exit 27 (SR 30 S). 5502 Rt 30 S 12010. Fax: 518/843-5888. **Facility:** 67 one-bedroom standard units. 2 stories (no elevator), interior corridors. **Parking:** on-site, winter plug-ins. **Terms:** 20 day cancellation notice. **Cards:** AX, CB, DC, DS, MC, VI.

SOME UNITS

ANGELICA pop. 903

——— WHERE TO STAY ———

ANGELICA INN B&B

Historic Bed & Breakfast

Phone: 585/466-3063
All Year [BP]	1P: $64-$119	2P: $64-$119	XP: $20 D16

Location: I-86, exit 31, 0.5 mi w. 64 W Main St 14709. Fax: 585/466-3063. **Facility:** Located on the Main Street of this historic village, the recently restored Victorian manor has period decor and striking woodwork throughout. Smoke free premises. 6 units. 3 one-bedroom standard units, some with whirlpools. 3 two-bedroom suites, some with kitchens. 3 stories (no elevator), interior/exterior corridors. *Bath:* combo or shower only. **Parking:** on-site. **Terms:** 14 day cancellation notice-fee imposed, small pets only (in designated units). **Amenities:** video library, hair dryers. **Leisure Activities:** limited exercise equipment. **Guest Services:** wireless Internet. **Cards:** AX, DS, MC, VI.

SOME UNITS

APALACHIN pop. 1,126

——— WHERE TO STAY ———

QUALITY INN   *Book great rates at AAA.com*

Small-scale Hotel

Phone: (607)625-4441
5/1-8/31 [CP]	1P: $90-$190	2P: $90-$190	XP: $10 F18
9/1-4/30 [CP]	1P: $80-$190	2P: $80-$190	XP: $10 F18

Location: SR 17, exit 66, just e. 7666 SR 434 13732 (PO Box 473). Fax: 607/625-4631. **Facility:** 51 units. 50 one-bedroom standard units. 1 one-bedroom suite with efficiency. 2 stories, interior corridors. *Bath:* combo or shower only. **Parking:** on-site. **Terms:** pets ($10 fee). **Amenities:** voice mail, irons, hair dryers. **Leisure Activities:** exercise room. **Guest Services:** valet laundry, wireless Internet. **Business Services:** meeting rooms, PC. **Cards:** AX, CB, DC, DS, JC, MC, VI. **Free Special Amenities:** expanded continental breakfast and high-speed Internet.

SOME UNITS

——— WHERE TO DINE ———

BLUE DOLPHIN DINER

American

Lunch: $4-$7   **Dinner:** $6-$19   **Phone:** 607/625-5029
Location: SR 17, exit 66, just e. 7670 SR 434 13732. **Hours:** 7 am-9 pm. Closed: 12/25. **Reservations:** accepted. **Features:** Easy on/off the highway for a delicious quick bite at this old-fashioned diner, offering traditional American fare served by friendly staff. Casual dress; beer & wine only. **Parking:** on-site. **Cards:** DS, MC, VI.

ARMONK —See New York p. 498.

AUBURN pop. 28,574—See also FINGER LAKES.

———— WHERE TO STAY ————

HOLIDAY INN-AUBURN/FINGER LAKES *Book great rates at AAA.com*
Phone: (315)253-4531

(AAA) (SAVE)

7/1-9/3	1P: $99-$179	2P: $99-$179	XP: $10 F18
5/1-6/30 & 9/4-4/30	1P: $79-$159	2P: $79-$159	XP: $10 F18

Small-scale Hotel
Location: SR 34, just n of US 20/SR 5. 75 North St 13021. Fax: 315/252-5843. **Facility:** 165 one-bedroom standard units, some with whirlpools. 5 stories, interior corridors. **Parking:** on-site, winter plug-ins. **Terms:** package plans, small pets only ($10 extra charge). **Amenities:** dual phone lines, voice mail, irons, hair dryers. **Dining:** 6:30 am-10 pm; hours vary in winter, cocktails. **Pool(s):** heated indoor. **Leisure Activities:** exercise room. *Fee:* game room. **Guest Services:** valet and coin laundry, beauty salon, wireless Internet. **Business Services:** meeting rooms. **Cards:** AX, CB, DC, DS, JC, MC, VI. **Free Special Amenities: newspaper and high-speed Internet.**

SOME UNITS

INN AT THE FINGER LAKES *Book at AAA.com*
Phone: (315)253-5000

6/29-9/3 [CP]	1P: $110-$160	2P: $110-$160	XP: $10 F18
5/1-6/28 & 9/4-4/30 [CP]	1P: $100-$160	2P: $100-$160	XP: $10 F18

Small-scale Hotel
Location: Jct SR 34/38, just e on US 20/SR 5; center. 12 Seminary Ave 13021. Fax: 315/253-9090. **Facility:** 77 one-bedroom standard units. 3 stories, interior corridors. *Bath:* combo or shower only. **Parking:** on-site, winter plug-ins. **Terms:** small pets only ($15 fee, in designated units). **Amenities:** dual phone lines, voice mail, irons, hair dryers. **Leisure Activities:** exercise room. **Guest Services:** complimentary evening beverages: Mon-Fri, valet and coin laundry, wireless Internet. **Business Services:** meeting rooms. **Cards:** AX, CB, DC, DS, MC, VI.

SOME UNITS

SPRINGSIDE INN
Phone: (315)252-7247

5/1-10/31	1P: $100-$200	2P: $100-$200	XP: $20 F
11/1-4/30	1P: $85-$150	2P: $85-$150	XP: $20 F

Historic
Country Inn
Location: Jct SR 34, 2.3 mi s on SR 38. Located across from Owasco Lake. 6141 W Lake Rd 13021 (PO Box 327). Fax: 315/252-8096. **Facility:** Attractively renovated rooms offer modern conveniences at this 1851 inn with Old World charm. A well-landscaped lawn includes a gazebo and duck pond. Smoke free premises. 7 units. 6 one-bedroom standard units, some with whirlpools. 1 one-bedroom suite ($150-$200) with whirlpool. 3 stories (no elevator), interior corridors. *Bath:* combo or shower only. **Parking:** on-site. **Terms:** office hours 7 am-10 pm, 10 day cancellation notice-fee imposed, package plans. **Amenities:** video library, CD players, voice mail, hair dryers. *Some:* DVD players, irons. **Dining:** restaurant, see separate listing. **Leisure Activities:** boat dock, fishing. **Business Services:** meeting rooms. **Cards:** AX, MC, VI.

SOME UNITS

———— WHERE TO DINE ————

PARKER'S GRILLE & TAP HOUSE
Lunch: $5-$7 **Dinner:** $6-$10 Phone: 315/252-6884

American
Location: Center. 129 Genesee St 13021. **Hours:** 11 am-midnight, Sun from noon. Closed major holidays. **Features:** Guests can partake of a casual meal amid brick walls, stained-glass lights and bright beer brand lights that reflect the 20 draft and 50 bottled beer choices. New York state wines are featured. Grilled mesquite chicken, French onion soup and hot and cold sandwiches are representative of items served by the friendly staff. Casual dress; cocktails. **Parking:** street. **Cards:** AX, MC, VI.

SPRINGSIDE INN
Dinner: $11-$23 Phone: 315/252-7247

(AAA)

American
Location: Jct SR 34, 2.3 mi s on SR 38; in Springside Inn. 6141 W Lake Rd 13021. **Hours:** 5 pm-9 pm, Sun 10:30 am-1 pm; seasonal hours may vary. Closed major holidays; also Tues & Wed 10/1-5/1 & Mon. **Reservations:** suggested. **Features:** Diners can sit on the porch overlooking Owasco Lake in summer or by the large fireplace in cooler weather. Friendly service in the restored 1850s inn ensures a pleasant meal any time of the year. Hot popovers, served immediately, are a treat. Dishes such as veal sauteed in wine sauce with portobello mushroom will satisfy the heartiest appetite. Dessert is displayed on a tempting tray; consider the "house sundae," served with three homemade sauces. Casual dress; cocktails. **Parking:** on-site. **Cards:** AX, MC, VI. **Historic**

AURORA pop. 720

———— WHERE TO STAY ————

AURORA INN
Phone: 315/364-8888

(AAA) (SAVE)

6/1-8/31 [BP]	1P: $225-$350	2P: $225-$350	
9/1-10/31 [BP]	1P: $125-$350	2P: $125-$350	
5/1-5/31 & 11/1-4/30 [BP]	1P: $125-$275	2P: $125-$275	

Historic
Country Inn
Location: On SR 90; center. Located on Cayuga Lake. 391 Main St 13026. Fax: 315/364-8887. **Facility:** Elegant, luxurious guest rooms at this 1833 Federal-style country inn have marble baths and Frette linens; some have a fireplace and whirlpool bath. Smoke free premises. 10 units. 8 one-bedroom standard units, some with whirlpools. 2 one-bedroom suites ($225-$350) with whirlpools. 3 stories, interior corridors. *Bath:* combo or shower only. **Parking:** on-site. **Terms:** 7 day cancellation notice-fee imposed, package plans. **Amenities:** video library, DVD players, CD players, high-speed Internet, voice mail, safes, irons, hair dryers. **Dining:** restaurant, see separate listing. **Leisure Activities:** boating, canoeing, boat dock, kayaks, bicycles. *Fee:* evening pontoon boat cruise. **Guest Services:** wireless Internet. **Business Services:** meeting rooms. **Cards:** AX, DS, MC, VI. **Free Special Amenities: full breakfast and high-speed Internet.**

SOME UNITS

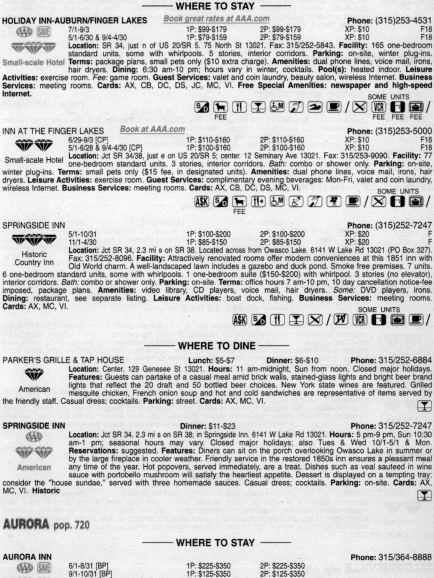

——— WHERE TO DINE ———

AURORA INN
AAA
American

Menu on AAA.com   **Lunch:** $7-$15   **Dinner:** $18-$35   **Phone:** 315/364-8888
Location: On SR 90; center; in Aurora Inn. 391 Main St 13026. **Hours:** 7-10 am, 11:30-2:30 & 5-8:30 pm. Closed: 5/28, 9/3, 12/25; also Mon & Tues. **Reservations:** suggested. **Features:** Diners appreciate beautiful views of Cayuga Lake from the terrace and elegantly casual dining room. Creative seasonal entrees, such as blue crab-stuffed shrimp and grilled duck breast, are excellent choices, as are a few country comfort food options, including traditional pot roast and roasted chicken with feather dumplings. Dressy casual; cocktails. **Parking:** on-site. **Cards:** AX, DC, DS, MC, VI.

AVERILL PARK pop. 1,517

——— WHERE TO STAY ———

LA PERLA AT THE GREGORY HOUSE COUNTRY INN & RESTAURANT   *Book at AAA.com*   **Phone:** 518/674-3774
Historic Country Inn

All Year   1P: $90-$130   2P: $110-$150   XP: $20
Location: Center. 3016 SR 43 12018 (PO Box 401). Fax: 518/674-8916. **Facility:** This 1830s inn offers modern conveniences in a country-style, homey atmosphere; some guest rooms have balconies and all have coordinated decor themes. Smoke free premises. 12 one-bedroom standard units. 2 stories (no elevator), interior corridors. **Parking:** on-site. **Terms:** 8 day cancellation notice, small pets only. **Pool(s):** small outdoor. **Cards:** DS, MC, VI.

AVON pop. 2,977—See also FINGER LAKES.

——— WHERE TO DINE ———

TOM WAHL'S
American

Lunch: $4-$7   **Dinner:** $4-$7   **Phone:** 585/226-2420
Location: On US 20/SR 5; center. 283 E Main St 14414. **Hours:** 10:30 am-10 pm; earlier closing hours off season. Closed: 11/22, 12/25. **Features:** Good comfort food is ordered at the counter and prepared quickly. Among choices are roast beef on kimmelwick, barbecue beef and pulled pork sandwiches and children's fun meals. Casual dress. **Parking:** on-site. **Cards:** AX, MC, VI.

BABYLON pop. 12,615

——— WHERE TO DINE ———

DON RICARDO'S MEXICAN RESTAURANT
Mexican

Lunch: $8-$12   **Dinner:** $12-$19   **Phone:** 631/587-0122
Location: Between Deer Park Ave and SR 231. 94 E Main St 11702. **Hours:** noon-10 pm, Fri-11 pm, Sat & Sun 1 pm-11 pm. Closed: 7/4, 11/22, 12/25. **Reservations:** suggested. **Features:** The first two dining rooms have the feel of a Mexican tavern, while the back room, made up of a brick courtyard with skylights and a stone fountain, exudes a friendly warmth. Menu offerings center on hearty and tasty Mexican and Spanish fare. Casual dress; cocktails. **Parking:** street. **Cards:** AX, MC, VI.

POST OFFICE CAFE
American

Lunch: $8-$11   **Dinner:** $13-$24   **Phone:** 631/669-9224
Location: 0.3 mi w of jct SR 231, on SR 27A. 130 W Main St 11702. **Hours:** noon-midnight, Fri & Sat-1 am, Sun-11 pm. **Features:** This popular nightspot is also a great place to enjoy burgers, wraps and dinner specials consisting of mostly chicken, pasta and steaks. The place gets busy at night as the bar crowd starts to appear. Large carousel figurines hang from the high ceilings reminding guests this is a playful and fun spot. Casual dress; cocktails. **Parking:** street. **Cards:** AX, DC, DS, MC, VI.

BAINBRIDGE pop. 1,365

——— WHERE TO DINE ———

OLDE JERICHO TAVERN
American

Lunch: $5-$10   **Dinner:** $10-$25   **Phone:** 607/967-5893
Location: Center. 4 N Main St 13733. **Hours:** noon-9 pm, Sat from 8 am, Sun 8 am-7 pm. **Reservations:** accepted. **Features:** In business since 1793, the stately, Colonial tavern has a storied history which is brought to life in pictures and postcards. Such tempting choices as ribs, peel-and-eat shrimp and black bean soup line the buffet. Fresh blueberry muffins are delicious. Casual dress; cocktails. **Parking:** on-site. **Cards:** AX, DS, MC, VI.

BALDWINSVILLE pop. 7,053

——— WHERE TO STAY ———

MICROTEL INN & SUITES   *Book at AAA.com*   **Phone:** (315)635-9556
Small-scale Hotel

	1P	2P	XP	
5/1-10/31 [ECP]	1P: $55-$85	2P: $65-$120	XP: $5	F18
1/1-4/30 [ECP]	1P: $50-$60	2P: $60-$75	XP: $5	F18
11/1-12/31 [ECP]	1P: $50-$55	2P: $60-$75	XP: $5	F18

Location: SR 690, exit SR 31 W, 0.4 mi e. 131 Downer St 13027. Fax: 315/635-1972. **Facility:** 61 one-bedroom standard units. 2 stories, interior corridors. **Bath:** combo or shower only. **Parking:** on-site. **Terms:** small pets only ($5 extra charge). **Guest Services:** wireless Internet. **Cards:** AX, DS, MC, VI.

SOME UNITS
FEE

—— WHERE TO DINE ——

BLUEWATER GRILL **Dinner:** $6-$22 Phone: 315/638-3342

American
Location: Downtown; on Seneca River waterfront. 2 Oswego St 13027. **Hours:** 4:30 pm-9:30 pm, Fri & Sat-10:30 pm; hours vary in winter. Closed: 1/1, 11/22, 12/25. **Reservations:** accepted. **Features:** On the riverside, the contemporary setting is fitting for casual, upbeat dining. On the menu are fresh seafood, entree salads, wraps, nachos, steaks, pasta and even Yankee pot roast. Casual dress; cocktails. **Parking:** on-site.
Cards: AX, MC, VI.

TASSONE'S WINE GARDEN **Lunch:** $6-$11 **Dinner:** $9-$25 Phone: 315/635-5133

Italian
Location: Jct SR 370, 31 and Dexter St. Rt 370 13027. **Hours:** 11 am-9:30 pm, Fri & Sat-10:30 pm, Sun noon-9:30 pm; hours vary in winter. Closed major holidays. **Features:** Daily specials include the popular 1.5-pound Cornish game hen stuffed with mushroom dressing and all-you-can-eat crab legs. Friendly hometown service can be expected in the casual wine-garden atmosphere. Casual dress; cocktails. **Parking:** on-site.
Cards: AX, MC, VI.

BALLSTON SPA pop. 5,556

—— WHERE TO DINE ——

GREAT BAY CLAM CO **Lunch:** $5-$9 **Dinner:** $10-$20 Phone: 518/885-0583

Seafood
Location: 1.5 mi n of jct SR 50 (Double Day Ave) and 67. 2149 Double Day Ave (Rt 50) 12020. **Hours:** 11:30 am-9 pm, Sat from 4 pm, Sun 12:30 pm-8:30 pm. Closed: 11/22, 12/25; also Mon. **Reservations:** accepted. **Features:** Family owned for 30 years, the popular restaurant prepares the freshest seafood available. Casual dress; cocktails. **Parking:** on-site. **Cards:** AX, DC, DS, MC, VI.

JT'S SHRIMP SHACK **Lunch:** $4-$18 **Dinner:** $4-$18 Phone: 518/285-2511

Seafood
Location: 0.4 mi n of SR 67 and SR 50. 2007 Double Day Ave (SR 50) 12020. **Hours:** 11 am-9 pm, Thurs-Sat to 10 pm. Closed major holidays. **Features:** JT's does fresh seafood just about anyway you like it — from Buffalo fried shrimp to blackened catfish and tuna skewers. Burgers and sandwiches are also offered. Take out is available. Casual dress. **Parking:** on-site. **Cards:** MC, VI.

SPA BRAUHAUS **Dinner:** $10-$20 Phone: 518/885-4311

German
Location: I-87, exit 12, 1.5 mi w on SR 67 to E Line Rd, 2 mi n, then 0.3 mi e. 200 E High St 12020. **Hours:** 4 pm-10 pm, Sun noon-9 pm. Closed: 12/24, 12/25; also Mon except 4/1-8/31. **Reservations:** suggested. **Features:** A cozy atmosphere, warmed by a lighted fireplace on chilly evenings, welcomes families and diners. The traditional tureen of homemade soup brought to the table by a friendly waiter starts off a hearty dining experience. Among choices are three ways of serving crispy Wiener schnitzel, which comes with red cabbage and spaetzle noodles. Dessert is made in-house. Casual dress; cocktails. **Parking:** on-site. **Cards:** CB, DC, MC, VI.

BANGALL

—— WHERE TO DINE ——

BULLIS HALL **Dinner:** $68 Phone: 845/868-1665

American
Location: Center; in Bullis Hall. 88 Hunns Lake Rd 12506. **Hours:** 6:30 pm-8 pm. Closed: Sun & Mon. **Reservations:** suggested. **Features:** The fully restored Greek revival has an amazing library for your dining experience. It's quaint and feels rich with history. The service is personalized and the chef is wonderful. Dressy casual; cocktails. **Parking:** on-site. **Cards:** AX, MC, VI.

BARNEVELD pop. 332

—— WHERE TO STAY ——

SUGARBUSH BED AND BREAKFAST *Book at AAA.com* Phone: (315)896-6860
All Year [BP] 1P: $75-$85 2P: $105-$115 XP: $20

Historic Bed & Breakfast
Location: Jct SR 12, 0.3 mi se. 8451 Old Poland Rd 13304. Fax: 315/896-8828. **Facility:** Eight acres of grounds surround this restored 1800s Colonial home. Smoke free premises. 5 units. 3 one-bedroom standard units. 2 one-bedroom suites ($155-$170). 2 stories (no elevator); interior corridors. *Bath:* combo or shower only. **Parking:** on-site. **Terms:** 8 day cancellation notice-fee imposed. **Amenities:** hair dryers. **Leisure Activities:** cross country skiing, playground, volleyball. **Business Services:** fax. **Cards:** AX, DS, MC, VI.

SOME UNITS

BATAVIA pop. 16,256

—— WHERE TO STAY ——

BEST WESTERN CROWN INN & SUITES *Book great rates at AAA.com* Phone: (585)344-8882

Small-scale Hotel

6/16-9/9	1P: $94-$169	2P: $94-$179	XP: $6 F17
5/1-6/15 & 9/10-4/30	1P: $74-$134	2P: $74-$144	XP: $6 F17

Location: I-90, exit 48, just w. 8210 Park Rd 14020. Fax: 585/344-7187. **Facility:** 71 one-bedroom standard units, some with whirlpools. 2 stories (no elevator). *Bath:* combo or shower only. **Parking:** on-site. **Terms:** package plans. **Amenities:** high-speed Internet, voice mail, safes (fee), irons, hair dryers. **Pool(s):** small heated indoor. **Leisure Activities:** whirlpool, exercise room. **Guest Services:** valet and coin laundry, wireless Internet. **Business Services:** PC. **Cards:** AX, DC, DS, MC, VI. **Free Special Amenities:** early check-in/late check-out and room upgrade (subject to availability with advance reservations).

SOME UNITS

BUDGET INN

Phone: (585)343-7921

6/24-9/7	1P: $70-$80	2P: $75-$110	XP: $6	F12
5/17-6/23	1P: $55-$80	2P: $60-$80	XP: $6	F12
9/8-4/30	1P: $40-$60	2P: $45-$70	XP: $6	F12
5/1-5/16	1P: $40-$60	2P: $45-$65	XP: $6	F12

Motel **Location:** I-90, exit 48, just n. 301 Oak St 14020. **Fax:** 585/343-6701. **Facility:** 20 one-bedroom standard units. 2 stories (no elevator), interior corridors. **Parking:** on-site. **Terms:** 5 night minimum stay - seasonal, cancellation fee imposed, [CP] meal plan available, package plans, small pets only ($4 extra charge). **Amenities:** high-speed Internet. **Guest Services:** wireless Internet. **Cards:** AX, DS, MC, VI. **Free Special Amenities: continental breakfast and local telephone calls.**

SOME UNITS

COMFORT INN   *Book great rates at AAA.com*

Phone: (585)344-9999

6/1-9/8	1P: $89-$149	2P: $89-$149	XP: $10	F
5/1-5/31	1P: $79-$129	2P: $79-$129	XP: $10	F
9/9-10/31	1P: $79-$119	2P: $79-$119	XP: $10	F
11/1-4/30	1P: $59-$109	2P: $59-$109	XP: $10	F

Small-scale Hotel **Location:** I-90, exit 48, just n on SR 98. 4371 Federal Dr 14020. **Fax:** 585/345-7400. **Facility:** 60 one-bedroom standard units, some with whirlpools. 2 stories (no elevator), interior corridors. **Bath:** combo or shower only. **Parking:** on-site. **Terms:** pets ($10 fee). **Amenities:** high-speed Internet, safes (fee), irons, hair dryers. **Pool(s):** outdoor. **Leisure Activities:** exercise room. **Guest Services:** valet laundry, wireless Internet. **Business Services:** meeting rooms, PC. **Cards:** AX, DC, DS, MC, VI. **Free Special Amenities: expanded continental breakfast and early check-in/late check-out.**

SOME UNITS

DAYS INN   *Book great rates at AAA.com*

Phone: (585)343-6000

5/1-9/4	1P: $59-$129	2P: $59-$129	XP: $10	F12
9/5-12/31	1P: $55-$69	2P: $55-$69	XP: $10	F12
1/1-4/30	1P: $49-$69	2P: $49-$69	XP: $10	F12

Small-scale Hotel **Location:** I-90, exit 48, just s. 200 Oak St 14020. **Fax:** 585/343-5322. **Facility:** 119 one-bedroom standard units. 2 stories (no elevator), interior/exterior corridors. **Parking:** on-site. **Terms:** pets ($10 extra charge). **Amenities:** hair dryers. *Some:* irons. **Pool(s):** outdoor. **Guest Services:** coin laundry, wireless Internet. **Business Services:** meeting rooms, PC. **Cards:** AX, DC, DS, MC, VI.

SOME UNITS

HAMPTON INN   *Book great rates at AAA.com*

Phone: (585)815-0475

6/1-9/8	1P: $134-$159	2P: $134-$159	XP: $10	F
9/9-4/30	1P: $79-$139	2P: $79-$139	XP: $10	F
5/1-5/31	1P: $74-$134	2P: $74-$134	XP: $10	F

Small-scale Hotel **Location:** I-90, exit 48, just n on SR 98. 4360 Commerce Dr 14020. **Fax:** 585/815-0284. **Facility:** 59 one-bedroom standard units. 3 stories, interior corridors. **Bath:** combo or shower only. **Terms:** cancellation fee imposed, [ECP] meal plan available. **Amenities:** high-speed Internet, dual phone lines, voice mail, irons, hair dryers. **Pool(s):** small heated indoor. **Leisure Activities:** whirlpool, exercise room. **Guest Services:** valet and coin laundry, wireless Internet. **Business Services:** business center. **Cards:** AX, DC, DS, MC, VI. **Free Special Amenities: expanded continental breakfast and high-speed Internet.**

SOME UNITS

HOLIDAY INN-DARIEN LAKE   *Book great rates at AAA.com*

Phone: (585)344-2100

6/22-9/4	1P: $69-$129	2P: $69-$129	XP: $10	F
5/1-6/21 & 9/5-10/31	1P: $59-$99	2P: $59-$99	XP: $10	F
11/1-4/30	1P: $54-$89	2P: $54-$89	XP: $10	F

Small-scale Hotel **Location:** I-90, exit 48, just w. 8250 Park Rd 14020. **Fax:** 585/344-0238. **Facility:** 195 units. 147 one-bedroom standard units. 48 one-bedroom suites ($99-$179). 5 stories, interior corridors. **Parking:** on-site. **Terms:** [AP], [BP], [CP], [ECP] & [MAP] meal plans available, package plans, small pets only ($15 extra charge). **Amenities:** voice mail, irons, hair dryers. **Dining:** 6:30 am-2 & 5-10 pm; hours vary in winter, cocktails. **Pool(s):** outdoor, heated indoor. **Leisure Activities:** saunas, steamrooms, exercise room. *Fee:* game room. **Guest Services:** valet and coin laundry. **Business Services:** conference facilities, PC. **Cards:** AX, DC, DS, MC, VI. **Free Special Amenities: newspaper and high-speed Internet.**

SOME UNITS

QUALITY INN & SUITES   *Book great rates at AAA.com*

Phone: (585)344-7000

6/25-9/3 [ECP]	1P: $89-$189	2P: $89-$189	XP: $10	F
5/1-6/24 & 9/4-10/31 [ECP]	1P: $79-$179	2P: $79-$179	XP: $10	F
11/1-4/30 [ECP]	1P: $69-$169	2P: $69-$169	XP: $10	F

Small-scale Hotel **Location:** I-90, exit 48, just w. 8200 Park Rd 14020. **Fax:** 585/343-4787. **Facility:** 52 one-bedroom standard units, some with whirlpools. 3 stories, interior corridors. **Bath:** combo or shower only. **Parking:** on-site. **Terms:** pets ($10 extra charge). **Amenities:** voice mail, irons, hair dryers. **Pool(s):** small heated indoor. **Leisure Activities:** exercise room. **Guest Services:** wireless Internet. **Business Services:** meeting rooms, PC. **Cards:** AX, DC, DS, MC, VI. **Free Special Amenities: expanded continental breakfast and high-speed Internet.**

SOME UNITS

RAMADA LIMITED *Book great rates at AAA.com* — Phone: (585)343-1000

	6/25-9/3 [CP]	1P: $69-$119	2P: $69-$119	XP: $10 F
	5/1-6/24 & 9/4-10/31 [CP]	1P: $59-$99	2P: $59-$99	XP: $10 F
	11/1-4/30 [CP]	1P: $49-$89	2P: $49-$89	XP: $10 F

AAA **SAVE**

Small-scale Hotel **Location:** I-90, exit 48, just w. 8204 Park Rd 14020. Fax: 585/343-8608. **Facility:** 74 one-bedroom standard units. 2 stories, interior corridors. **Parking:** on-site. **Terms:** pets (must be attended). **Amenities:** voice mail, irons, hair dryers. **Leisure Activities:** pool privileges, exercise room privileges. **Guest Services:** valet laundry, wireless Internet. **Business Services:** meeting rooms. **Cards:** AX, DC, DS, MC, VI. **Free Special Amenities: newspaper and high-speed Internet.**

SOME UNITS

SUPER 8 *Book at AAA.com* — Phone: (585)345-0800

5/1-9/4	1P: $59-$119	2P: $59-$119	XP: $10 F12
9/5-12/31	1P: $55-$69	2P: $55-$69	XP: $10 F12
1/1-4/30	1P: $49-$69	2P: $49-$69	XP: $10 F12

Small-scale Hotel **Location:** I-90, exit 48, just s. 200A Oak St 14020. Fax: 585/344-1983. **Facility:** 54 one-bedroom standard units. 2 stories (no elevator), interior corridors. **Parking:** on-site. **Amenities:** hair dryers. **Guest Services:** wireless Internet. **Cards:** AX, DS, MC, VI.

SOME UNITS

———— WHERE TO DINE ————

ALEX'S PLACE — Lunch: $3-$9 — Dinner: $7-$22 — Phone: 585/344-2999

AAA

American **Location:** I-90, exit 48, just w. 8322 Park Rd 14020. **Hours:** 11 am-10 pm, Fri & Sat-midnight, Sun noon-9 pm. Closed: 12/25. **Features:** Family-owned for more than 15 years, the cozy restaurant serves popular American fare, with a focus on steaks and seafood. Next to Batavia horse race track, this place is convenient for pre- or post-racing dining. Casual dress; cocktails. **Parking:** on-site. **Cards:** AX, DS, MC, VI.

MISS BATAVIA FAMILY RESTAURANT *Menu on AAA.com* — Lunch: $3-$5 — Dinner: $6-$8 — Phone: 585/343-9786

AAA

American **Location:** I-90, exit 48, s on SR 98 to SR 5, then 1.3 mi e. 566 E Main St 14020. **Hours:** 6 am-9 pm. Closed: 1/1, 11/22, 12/25; also closes early 12/24 & 12/31. **Features:** Friendly hometown waitresses serve affordable, home-cooked meals. Built in 1933, the newly renovated diner offers pleasant surroundings. Casual dress. **Parking:** on-site. **Cards:** AX, DC, DS, MC, VI.

PONTILLO'S PIZZA & PASTA — Lunch: $4-$7 — Dinner: $4-$7 — Phone: 585/343-3303

Italian **Location:** I-90, exit 48, 1 mi s on SR 98, then 1 mi e on SR 5. 500 E Main St 14020. **Hours:** 11 am-11 pm, Fri & Sat-1 am, Sun noon-11 pm; hours may vary in winter. Closed: 3/23, 11/22, 12/25. **Features:** Established in 1947, the casual family restaurant delivers traditional Italian and American dishes, such as chicken wings, homemade pasta and tasty pizza baked in stone-hearth ovens. Diners can watch food being prepared in the open kitchen. Outdoor patio seating is available. Casual dress; beer & wine only. **Parking:** on-site. **Cards:** AX, DS, MC, VI.

BATH pop. 5,641—See also FINGER LAKES.

———— WHERE TO STAY ————

BATH SUPER 8 *Book at AAA.com* — Phone: (607)776-2187

5/1-10/31	1P: $63-$83	2P: $73-$98	XP: $10 F
11/1-4/30	1P: $53-$63	2P: $63-$73	XP: $10 F

Small-scale Hotel **Location:** I-86, exit 38, just n. 333 W Morris St 14810. Fax: 607/776-3206. **Facility:** 50 one-bedroom standard units. 3 stories (no elevator), interior corridors. **Parking:** on-site. **Amenities:** high-speed Internet, hair dryers. **Guest Services:** valet laundry. **Cards:** AX, CB, DC, DS, MC, VI.

SOME UNITS

BUDGET INN *Book great rates at AAA.com* — Phone: (607)776-7536

All Year	1P: $40-$60	2P: $50-$100	XP: $5 F12

AAA **SAVE**

Small-scale Hotel **Location:** I-86, exit 38, just n. 332 W Morris St 14810. Fax: 607/776-4898. **Facility:** 21 one-bedroom standard units. 2 stories (no elevator), interior corridors. **Parking:** on-site. **Terms:** [CP] meal plan available. **Amenities:** hair dryers. **Cards:** AX, DS, MC, VI. **Free Special Amenities: continental breakfast and local telephone calls.**

SOME UNITS

DAYS INN *Book great rates at AAA.com* — Phone: (607)776-7644

5/1-12/1	1P: $70-$115	2P: $70-$115	XP: $5 F18
12/2-4/30	1P: $60-$115	2P: $60-$115	XP: $5 F18

Small-scale Hotel **Location:** I-86, exit 38, just n. 330 W Morris St 14810. Fax: 607/776-7650. **Facility:** 104 one-bedroom standard units, some with whirlpools. 5 stories, interior corridors. **Parking:** on-site, winter plug-ins. **Terms:** [ECP] meal plan available. **Amenities:** high-speed Internet, voice mail, safes. *Some:* hair dryers. **Pool(s):** heated indoor. **Guest Services:** coin laundry. **Business Services:** meeting rooms. **Cards:** AX, DC, DS, MC, VI.

SOME UNITS

—————— **WHERE TO DINE** ——————

CHAT-A-WHYLE

American

Lunch: $4-$5   **Dinner:** $5-$9   **Phone:** 607/776-8040
Location: Center. 28 Liberty St 14810. **Hours:** 5:30 am-8 pm. Closed major holidays. **Reservations:** accepted. **Features:** Centrally located in the main shopping district, the neat little restaurant always seems busy with hungry diners who come for the generous portions of homemade comfort food and personable service. Casual dress. **Parking:** on-site (fee) and street. **Cards:** AX, DS, MC, VI.

CIELITO LINDO

Mexican

Lunch: $4-$7   **Dinner:** $6-$18   **Phone:** 607/776-8458
Location: 4 mi s. 7500 SR 54 14810. **Hours:** 11:30 am-9 pm; to 8 pm in winter. Closed: 11/22, 12/24, 12/25; also Sun in winter. **Features:** Mexican and American specialties are made from fresh ingredients at this family-style restaurant decorated in festive colors. Casual dress; cocktails. **Parking:** on-site. **Cards:** AX, DS, MC, VI.

PUDGIE'S PIZZA & SUBS

Pizza

Lunch: $4-$8   **Dinner:** $4-$8   **Phone:** 607/776-7676
Location: SR 17, exit 38, just w. 121 Geneva St 14810. **Hours:** 11 am-10 pm, Fri & Sat-midnight. Closed: 3/23, 11/22, 12/25. **Features:** This basic eatery serves up their pizza, subs and pasta dishes for hungry diners to eat-in or take-out. Party packs and delivery available. Casual dress. **Parking:** on-site. **Cards:** AX, DS, MC, VI.

BAY SHORE pop. 23,852

—————— **WHERE TO DINE** ——————

MILK AND SUGAR CAFE

American

Lunch: $6-$10   **Dinner:** $14-$25   **Phone:** 631/969-3655
Location: On SR 27A, just ne of jct CR 10. 49 W Main St (SR 27A) 11706. **Hours:** 9 am-10 pm, Fri & Sat-11 pm; Sunday brunch. Closed: 7/4, 11/22, 12/25. **Features:** Known as "the place to be" in town, the casually elegant cafe has comfortable upholstered antique sofas and chairs. In the dining room are a beautiful pressed-tin ceiling, gold-framed mirrors, faux topiaries and dark wood floors. Among creative American dishes are Alaskan crab cakes, pistachio-encrusted chicken with honey Dijon sauce, homemade meatloaf and chicken pot pie. A cappuccino bar in the back lets guests savor house-blended coffee drinks and homemade pies and muffins on the go. Casual dress; wine only. **Parking:** street. **Cards:** AX, DC, MC, VI.

BELLMORE pop. 16,441

—————— **WHERE TO DINE** ——————

OAK CHALET

Continental

Lunch: $9-$16   **Dinner:** $15-$28   **Phone:** 516/826-1700
Location: Southern State Pkwy, exit 25S, 0.6 mi s on Newbridge Rd, then 0.8 mi se. 1940 Bellmore Ave 11710. **Hours:** noon-3 & 5-9:30 pm, Sat from 5 pm, Sun 2 pm-8:30 pm. Closed: Mon & 12/24. **Reservations:** not accepted. **Features:** Evocative of a quaint chalet, the dining room has a vaulted wood-paneled ceiling, a floor-to-ceiling brick fireplace and bay windows filled with numerous types of green plants. Specialties of German and Continental fare include Wiener schnitzel Holstein, kassler rippchen, goulash with spaetzle, and bratwurst or knockwurst with sauerkraut. Casual dress; cocktails. **Parking:** on-site. **Cards:** AX, MC, VI.

BEMUS POINT pop. 340

—————— **WHERE TO STAY** ——————

MORNING GLORY BED & BREAKFAST COUNTRY INN

Bed & Breakfast

Phone: 716/386-5938
5/1-9/30   1P: $115-$135   2P: $115-$135   XP: $10   F
Location: SR 17, exit 10, 0.5 mi on SR 430 w, 1.5 mi n on Mahanna, then just e. 4766 Maple Springs Ellery Rd 14712. Fax: 716/386-2267. **Facility:** The extravagantly renovated farmhouse has a driving range, ceramic studio, large public areas and rooms with king-size beds and a decorator's touch. Smoke free premises. 5 units. 4 one-bedroom standard units, some with whirlpools. 1 one-bedroom suite. 2 stories (no elevator), interior/exterior corridors. *Bath:* combo or shower only. **Parking:** on-site. **Terms:** open 5/1-9/30, age restrictions may apply, 7 day cancellation notice, package plans. **Amenities:** video library, DVD players, CD players, irons, hair dryers. *Some:* high-speed Internet. **Leisure Activities:** driving range. **Cards:** AX, DS, MC, VI.

SOME UNITS

—————— **WHERE TO DINE** ——————

ITALIAN FISHERMAN

American

Lunch: $6-$12   **Dinner:** $13-$26   **Phone:** 716/386-7000
Location: SR 17, exit 10, 0.7 mi w on SR 430. 61 Lakeside Dr 14712. **Hours:** Open 5/1-10/31; 11:30 am-10 pm, Fri & Sat-midnight. **Reservations:** suggested. **Features:** The restaurant's outdoor decks, casual gathering places for families, overlook Lake Chautauqua. The eclectic menu satisfies a wide range of appetites, such as steak, lemon-pepper tuna or pasta. Service is attentive and inquisitive. Casual dress; cocktails; entertainment. **Parking:** on-site and street. **Cards:** AX, DC, DS, MC, VI.

YE HARE N' HOUNDS INN

American

Dinner: $17-$27   **Phone:** 716/386-2181
Location: SR 17, exit 10, 1 mi s on SR 430 E. 64 Lakeside Dr 14712. **Hours:** 5 pm-9 pm, Fri & Sat-10 pm, Sun 4 pm-9 pm; hours may vary in winter. Closed: 12/24, 12/25. **Reservations:** suggested. **Features:** Patrons can enjoy lovely views of Lake Chautauqua from the informal, rustic dining room of the English-style inn. Preparations of seafood, chicken, veal and steak are flavorful. The restaurant is host to the Bemus Bay Pops free open-air concert, as well as specialty theme party nights. Casual dress; cocktails. **Parking:** on-site. **Cards:** AX, MC, VI.

BINGHAMTON pop. 47,380

──────── WHERE TO STAY ────────

BEST WESTERN BINGHAMTON REGENCY HOTEL
AND CONFERENCE CENTER   *Book great rates at AAA.com*   **Phone:** (607)722-7575

▼▼ ▼▼   All Year   1P: $98-$350   2P: $98-$350   XP: $10   F
Location: SR 17, exit 72 to US 11 (Front St), 1 mi s, just e on E Clinton St, then just s; downtown. 225 Water St 13901.
Large-scale Hotel   Fax: 607/724-7263. **Facility:** 205 units. 196 one-bedroom standard units. 9 one-bedroom suites ($145-$395), some with whirlpools. 10 stories, interior corridors. **Parking:** on-site. **Terms:** check-in 4 pm, package plans. **Amenities:** video games (fee), high-speed Internet, voice mail, irons, hair dryers. **Pool(s):** heated indoor. **Leisure Activities:** saunas, exercise room. **Guest Services:** sundries, valet laundry. **Business Services:** conference facilities. **Cards:** AX, DC, DS, MC, VI. *(See color ad below)*

(A$K) (S/D) (🍴) (Y) (⛪M) (🐕) (🏊) (🎥) (💻) / (✕) (VCR) (🔌) /
SOME UNITS
FEE

COMFORT INN OF BINGHAMTON   *Book great rates at AAA.com*   **Phone:** (607)724-3297

(AAA) (SAVE)   5/18-5/20 [ECP]   1P: $140-$200   2P: $140-$200   XP: $10   F17
5/1-5/17 [ECP]   1P: $90-$120   2P: $90-$120   XP: $10   F17
▼▼ ▼▼   5/21-4/30 [ECP]   1P: $85-$120   2P: $85-$120   XP: $10   F17
Location: I-81, exit 5, 1 mi n on US 11 (Front St). 1000 Front St 13905. Fax: 607/771-0206. **Facility:** 104 units.
Small-scale Hotel   103 one-bedroom standard units. 1 one-bedroom suite ($140-$250). 4 stories, interior corridors. **Parking:** on-site. **Terms:** pets ($5 extra charge, in smoking units). **Amenities:** irons, hair dryers. *Some:* high-speed Internet. **Pool(s):** outdoor. **Leisure Activities:** grill and picnic area, exercise room, basketball. **Guest Services:** valet and coin laundry, wireless Internet. **Business Services:** meeting rooms, PC. **Cards:** AX, CB, DC, DS, JC, MC, VI. **Free Special Amenities:** expanded continental breakfast and high-speed Internet.

(S/D) (🛒) (🍴+) (⛪M) (🏊) (✕) (🎥) (💻) / (✕) (VCR) (🔌) (🖥) /
SOME UNITS
FEE   FEE FEE

ECONO LODGE INN & SUITES   *Book great rates at AAA.com*   **Phone:** (607)724-1341

▼▼ ▼▼   5/1-10/31   1P: $55-$149   2P: $55-$149
11/1-4/30   1P: $55-$75   2P: $55-$75
Small-scale Hotel   **Location:** I-81, exit 5, just n, then w. 690 Front St 13905. Fax: 607/773-8387. **Facility:** 107 one-bedroom standard units, some with whirlpools. 2 stories (no elevator), interior/exterior corridors. **Parking:** on-site. **Terms:** cancellation fee imposed, [CP] meal plan available. **Amenities:** *Some:* hair dryers. **Pool(s):** outdoor. **Guest Services:** wireless Internet. **Business Services:** meeting rooms. **Cards:** AX, CB, DC, DS, JC, MC, VI.

(A$K) (S/D) (🏊) / (✕) (🔌) (🖥) /
SOME UNITS

FAIRFIELD INN BY MARRIOTT-BINGHAMTON   *Book great rates at AAA.com*   **Phone:** 607/651-1000
▼▼▼▼   All Year [ECP]   1P: $99-$134
    Location: I-81, exit 5, just n on US 11 (Front St). Located across from Broome Community College. 864 Front St 13905.
Small-scale Hotel   Fax: 607/651-1022. **Facility:** Smoke free premises. 82 one-bedroom standard units. 4 stories, interior
corridors. *Bath:* combo or shower only. **Parking:** on-site. **Terms:** cancellation fee imposed.
Amenities: video games (fee), high-speed Internet, dual phone lines, voice mail, irons, hair dryers. **Pool(s):** small heated
indoor. **Leisure Activities:** whirlpool, exercise room. **Guest Services:** valet laundry, wireless Internet. **Business Services:**
meeting rooms. **Cards:** AX, CB, DC, DS, JC, MC, VI.

SOME UNITS

(ASK) ⊞ &M 🛢 🐾 ✕ 🎦 🖥 / ⬛ /
FEE

GRAND ROYALE HOTEL-A CLARION COLLECTION
HOTEL   *Book great rates at AAA.com*   **Phone:** (607)722-0000
▼▼▼ ▼▼   All Year   1P: $73-$250   2P: $73-$250   XP: $10   F
    Location: Just n of jct Hawley St; downtown. 80 State St 13901. Fax: 607/722-7912. **Facility:** 61 units. 57 one-
Large-scale Hotel   bedroom standard units. 4 one-bedroom suites ($150-$205), some with efficiencies and/or whirlpools. 6
stories, interior corridors. *Bath:* combo or shower only. **Parking:** on-site. **Terms:** pets ($10 extra charge).
Amenities: high-speed Internet, voice mail, safes, irons, hair dryers. *Some:* DVD players (fee). **Guest Services:** complimentary
evening beverages: Mon-Thurs, valet laundry. **Business Services:** meeting rooms, PC. **Cards:** AX, DC, DS, MC, VI.

SOME UNITS

(ASK) S☎ 🐾 ⊞ 🏊 🎦 🛢 🖥 / ✕ VCR
FEE   FEE

HOLIDAY INN ARENA   *Book at AAA.com*   **Phone:** (607)722-1212
▼▼▼▼   5/18-5/19   1P: $239-$300   2P: $239-$300
    5/1-5/17 & 5/20-4/30   1P: $99-$159   2P: $99-$159
Large-scale Hotel   **Location:** Downtown. 2-8 Hawley St 13901. Fax: 607/722-6063. **Facility:** 237 units. 225 one-bedroom standard
units. 12 one-bedroom suites ($159-$350), some with whirlpools. 9 stories, interior corridors. *Bath:* combo or
shower only. **Parking:** on-site. **Terms:** check-in 4 pm, [BP] meal plan available, package plans, small pets only ($35 fee).
Amenities: voice mail, irons, hair dryers. *Fee:* video library, video games. **Pool(s):** heated indoor. **Leisure Activities:** exercise
room. **Guest Services:** valet and coin laundry, beauty salon, wireless Internet. **Business Services:** conference facilities, PC.
Cards: AX, CB, DC, DS, JC, MC, VI.

SOME UNITS

(ASK) S☎ 🐾 ⊞ 🍸 &M 🛢 🐾 🎦 🖥 / ✕ 🛢 🖥 /
FEE   FEE FEE

MOTEL 6 - 1222   *Book at AAA.com*   **Phone:** 607/771-0400
▼▼▼   6/30-9/3   1P: $43-$53   2P: $49-$59   XP: $3   F17
    5/1-6/29 & 9/4-4/30   1P: $39-$49   2P: $45-$55   XP: $3   F17
Small-scale Hotel   **Location:** I-81, exit 6 southbound, 2 mi s on US 11 (Front St); exit 5 northbound, 1 mi n on US 11 (Front St). Located in
a light-commercial area. 1012 Front St 13905. Fax: 607/773-4781. **Facility:** 99 one-bedroom standard units. 2
stories (no elevator), interior corridors. *Bath:* combo or shower only. **Parking:** on-site. **Terms:** small pets only. **Guest Services:**
coin laundry. **Cards:** AX, CB, DC, DS, MC, VI.

SOME UNITS

S☎ 🐾 ⊞ &M 🛢 🎦 / ✕ /

------ **WHERE TO DINE** ------

THE COPPER CRICKET CAFE   **Lunch:** $6-$8   **Dinner:** $9-$19   **Phone:** 607/729-5620
▼▼ ▼▼   **Location:** I-81, exit 5, 1 mi s on US 11 (Front St), then 1 mi w; SR 17, exit 71, 0.5 mi s on Airport Rd, 0.5 mi s on
    Glenwood Ave, then w. 266 Main St 13905. **Hours:** 11:30 am-2 & 5-9 pm, Fri & Sat-10 pm. Closed: 1/1, 7/4,
Continental   12/25; also Sun. **Reservations:** suggested. **Features:** Old hats hang along the walls and wine bottles line
    the sills of crank windows in the dining room. Representative of menu selections are baked brie with
almonds, pork barbecue and cream of mushroom and amaretto soup. Service is informal but attentive. Casual dress; beer &
wine only. **Parking:** on-site. **Cards:** AX, DS, MC, VI.

CORTESE RESTAURANT   **Lunch:** $3-$13   **Dinner:** $3-$25   **Phone:** 607/723-6477
◆◆◆   **Location:** SR 17/I-81, exit 4, s to Robinson St exit, then e. 117 Robinson St 13904. **Hours:** 11 am-10 pm, Fri & Sat-
▼▼ ▼▼   midnight. Closed: 4/8, 11/22, 12/24, 12/25. **Reservations:** suggested, weekends. **Features:** Family-
    operated since 1947, the family-oriented restaurant boasts a convivial, upbeat atmosphere. The tempting
Italian   scents of aromatic steak, chops and pizza hang in the air of the dining room. Italian desserts are
    homemade. Casual dress; cocktails. **Parking:** on-site. **Cards:** AX, CB, DC, DS, MC, VI.
🍸

LITTLE VENICE   **Lunch:** $5-$10   **Dinner:** $8-$20   **Phone:** 607/724-2513
▼▼ ▼▼   **Location:** Downtown. 111 Chenango St 13901. **Hours:** 11:30 am-11 pm. Closed: 7/4, 11/22, 12/24, 12/25; also
    Mon. **Reservations:** suggested. **Features:** An area institution since 1946, the restaurant is known for tasty
Italian   Italian and American cuisine, particularly pasta and spaghetti sauce. Dining room walls are covered with
    original artwork, some of which date back to the 1800s. Casual dress; cocktails. **Parking:** on-site.
Cards: AX, DS, MC, VI.
🍸

LOST DOG CAFE/COFFEEHOUSE   **Lunch:** $7-$15   **Dinner:** $13-$18   **Phone:** 607/771-6063
▼▼ ▼▼   **Location:** Downtown. 222 Water St 13901. **Hours:** 11:30 am-10 pm, Fri & Sat-11 pm. Closed major holidays;
    also Sun. **Reservations:** not accepted. **Features:** Appointed in a mix of Americana furnishings, the trendy
American   bistro has a cafe-style ambience. Health-conscious diners appreciate the creative menu, which focuses on
    nouvelle cuisine and features many vegetarian dishes. Creative salads, pasta, sandwiches and homemade
desserts are complemented by freshly-brewed specialty coffees, lattes, cappuccinos and herbal teas. Casual dress; beer & wine
only. **Parking:** street. **Cards:** AX, DS, MC, VI.

NUMBER 5   **Dinner:** $16-$35   **Phone:** 607/723-0555
American
Location: I-81, exit 4S to SR 434, just over bridge. 33 S Washington St 13903. **Hours:** 5 pm-10 pm, Fri & Sat-11 pm, Sun-9 pm. Closed: 7/4, 9/3, 12/25. **Reservations:** suggested. **Features:** An extensive wine list complements traditional preparations of steak, fish, veal, pasta and chicken, as well as many Greek entrees. Many antiques and old photographs decorate the restored fire station. The atmosphere is warm and comfortable. Dressy casual; cocktails. **Parking:** on-site. **Cards:** AX, CB, DC, DS, JC, MC. **Historic**

SPOT DINER RESTAURANT   **Lunch:** $3-$13   **Dinner:** $8-$33   **Phone:** 607/723-8149
American
Location: I-81, exit 5 and 6, on US 11 (Front St) and 12. 1062 Front St 13905. **Hours:** 24 hours. **Reservations:** accepted. **Features:** Greek and Italian dishes, such as gyros and lasagna, are among selections on the casual restaurant's extensive menu. As diners enter, they're tempted by an appealing display of freshly-baked pastries, fluffy cheesecake and luscious Greek desserts. Casual dress; cocktails. **Parking:** on-site. **Cards:** AX, CB, DC, DS, MC, VI.

WHOLE IN THE WALL RESTAURANT   **Lunch:** $5-$7   **Dinner:** $8-$17   **Phone:** 607/722-5138
Vegetarian
Location: I-81, exit 4S to SR 434, just over bridge. 43 S Washington St 13903. **Hours:** 11:30 am-9 pm. Closed major holidays; also 12/24, 12/31, Sun & Mon. **Reservations:** accepted. **Features:** The menu incorporates many non-dairy vegetarian dishes, such as miso soup, tempura with tofu and stir-fried vegetables, as well as chicken and seafood. Salads contain hydroponically grown, pesticide-free lettuce. The owner/chef has cooked for many famous people, such as Bob Dylan, Kenny G, Busta Rhymes and members of the band Phish. Casual dress. **Parking:** on-site. **Cards:** AX, DS, MC, VI.

BLASDELL —See Buffalo p. 255.

BLOOMFIELD pop. 1,267—See also FINGER LAKES.

——— **WHERE TO DINE** ———

THE ORIGINAL HOLLOWAY HOUSE   **Lunch:** $7-$14   **Dinner:** $15-$25   **Phone:** 585/657-7120
American
Location: Jct SR 332, 8 mi w on US 20 and SR 5; 8 mi w of Canandaigua. 29 State St 14443. **Hours:** Open 5/1-12/10 & 4/1-4/30; 11:30 am-2 & 5-9 pm, Sun 11:30 am-7:30 pm; Sunday brunch. Closed: Mon except Labor Day. **Reservations:** suggested. **Features:** The quaint 1808 country inn is decorated in the Early American style, with lace curtains, wreaths and country accents. Home-style favorites, such as roast turkey dinner with gravy and mashed potatoes, fresh seafood and steak, mingle with fresh house-baked bread and sumptuous desserts. Finger Lakes wines are featured. Casual dress; cocktails. **Parking:** on-site. **Cards:** AX, DS, MC, VI. **Historic**

BOHEMIA pop. 9,871

——— **WHERE TO STAY** ———

LA QUINTA INN & SUITES-ISLIP   *Book great rates at AAA.com*   **Phone:** (631)881-7700
Small-scale Hotel

4/1-4/30	1P: $179-$229	2P: $189-$239	XP: $10	F18
5/1-10/31	1P: $159-$209	2P: $169-$219	XP: $10	F18
11/1-3/31	1P: $149-$209	2P: $159-$219	XP: $10	F18

Location: I-495, exit 57, 5.1 mi se on SR 454, just s on Johnson Ave, then just e. 10 Aero Rd 11716. **Fax:** 631/881-7740. **Facility:** 132 one-bedroom standard units. 4 stories, interior corridors. **Bath:** combo or shower only. **Parking:** on-site. **Amenities:** video games (fee), high-speed Internet, dual phone lines, voice mail, irons, hair dryers. **Leisure Activities:** whirlpool, exercise room. **Guest Services:** valet and coin laundry, area transportation, wireless Internet. **Business Services:** meeting rooms, business center. **Cards:** AX, CB, DC, DS, MC, VI. *(See color ad p 360)*   SOME UNITS

BOLTON LANDING (See map and index starting on p. 330)—See also ADIRONDACK MOUNTAINS.

——— **WHERE TO STAY** ———

BONNIE VIEW RESORT   **Phone:** 518-644-5591   32
Motel

7/21-9/3	1P: $113-$168	2P: $113-$168	XP: $8
6/23-7/20	1P: $91-$135	2P: $91-$135	XP: $8
5/11-6/22 & 9/4-9/17	1P: $65-$84	2P: $65-$84	XP: $3

Location: 1.5 mi s on SR 9N. Located on a lake. 4654 Lake Shore Dr 12814-0330 (PO Box 330). **Facility:** 50 units. 22 one-bedroom standard units, some with efficiencies. 28 cottages ($113-$211). 1 story, exterior corridors. **Bath:** combo or shower only. **Parking:** on-site. **Terms:** open 5/11-9/17, 3-7 night minimum stay - seasonal and/or weekends, 28 day cancellation notice, weekly rates available, package plans. **Pool(s):** heated outdoor. **Leisure Activities:** fishing, tennis court, playground, basketball, horseshoes, shuffleboard. **Fee:** paddleboats, boat dock. **Cards:** DC, DS, MC, VI.

MELODY MANOR RESORT   **Phone:** 518-644-9750   33
Motel

6/22-9/3	1P: $165-$250	2P: $165-$250	XP: $15
5/5-6/21 & 9/4-10/20	1P: $125-$180	2P: $125-$180	XP: $10

Location: 1.8 mi s on SR 9N. Located on a lake. 4610 Lake Shore Dr 12814 (PO Box 366). **Fax:** 518-644-9750. **Facility:** 40 one-bedroom standard units. 2 stories (no elevator), exterior corridors. **Parking:** on-site. **Terms:** open 5/5-10/20, 30 day cancellation notice-fee imposed, weekly rates available, [MAP] meal plan available. **Amenities:** Some: hair dryers. **Dining:** Villa Napoli, see separate listing. **Pool(s):** heated outdoor. **Business Services:** meeting rooms. **Cards:** AX, MC, VI. **Free Special Amenities:** local telephone calls and high-speed Internet.

(See map and index starting on p. 330)

THE SAGAMORE *Book great rates at AAA.com* **Phone:** (518)644-9400 **31**

(AAA) (SAVE) All Year 1P: $155-$465 2P: $155-$466 XP: $25 F6

▽▽▽▽ ▽▽▽▽ **Location:** I-87 N, exit 22, 0.3 mi e. Located on Green Island. 110 Sagamore Rd 12814 (PO Box 450).

Resort **Fax:** 518/743-6036. **Facility:** This sprawling resort sits on a 72-acre private island. It offers traditional decor in its hotel units and Adirondack-style furnishings in the lodges. 30 day cancellation notice 7/1-8/31. 350 units. 176 one-bedroom standard units. 174 one-bedroom suites ($295-$840), some with efficiencies. 2-3 stories, interior/exterior corridors. *Bath:* combo or shower only. **Parking:** on-site. **Terms:** check-in 4 pm, 2 night minimum stay - seasonal and/or weekends, 30 day cancellation notice-fee imposed, [BP] meal plan available, package plans, $9 service charge. **Amenities:** video games (fee), dual phone lines, voice mail, safes, irons, hair dryers. **Dining:** 4 restaurants, 7 am-midnight, cocktails, entertainment. **Pool(s):** heated indoor. **Leisure Activities:** whirlpool, rental boats, fishing, cross country skiing, ice skating, snowshoeing, recreation programs, carriage rides, bicycles, playground, spa, basketball. *Fee:* saunas, steamrooms, sailboats, marina, waterskiing, charter fishing, charter sailboats, parasailing, kayaks, lunch & dinner cruises, golf-18 holes, 6 tennis courts (1 indoor, 5 lighted), racquetball court. **Guest Services:** gift shop, valet laundry, area transportation-within 3 mi, beauty salon, wireless Internet. **Business Services:** conference facilities, business center. **Cards:** AX, CB, DC, DS, MC, VI. *(See color ad p 342)*
Large-scale Hotel

SOME UNITS

[icons] FEE

──────── **WHERE TO DINE** ────────

ALGONQUIN RESTAURANT **Lunch:** $7-$12 **Dinner:** $19-$33 **Phone:** 518/644-9442 **13**

▽▽▽ ◆◆ **Location:** 1 mi s on SR 9N. 4770 Lake Shore Dr 12814. **Hours:** 11:30 am-10 pm. Closed: 11/22, 12/25; also 1/2-1/31 & 3/1-3/31. **Reservations:** suggested, for Topside. **Features:** Overlooking Lake George, the casual restaurant is especially popular in summer, when diners gather in the Topside room and on the patio to enjoy great views and good food. Salmon, veal and steak are among well-prepared choices. Vegetarian selections are also available. Casual dress; cocktails. **Parking:** on-site. **Cards:** AX, DC, DS, MC, VI.
American

CATE'S ITALIAN GARDEN
RESTAURANT AND BAR **Lunch:** $5-$10 **Dinner:** $11-$22 **Phone:** 518/644-2041

(AAA) **Location:** Corner of Congress Point Way; center. 7054 Main St 12814. **Hours:** Open 5/1-2/29 & 4/16-4/30; noon-11 pm. **Reservations:** accepted. **Features:** At the bustling little bistro, mom and dad can opt for a glass of wine and sea bass encrusted with basil pesto and leave the kids to enjoy delicious homemade pizza. Patio seating is an option. Casual dress; cocktails. **Parking:** street. **Cards:** AX, DS, MC, VI.
Italian

VILLA NAPOLI *Menu on AAA.com* **Dinner:** $17-$30 **Phone:** 518/644-9047 **14**

(AAA) **Location:** 1.8 mi s on SR 9N; in Melody Manor Resort. 4610 Lake Shore Dr 12814. **Hours:** Open 5/1-10/31; 8 am-11 & 5-10 pm; weekends only 5/1-6/30 & 9/1-10/31. **Reservations:** suggested. **Features:** A hand-carved marble fireplace, European oil paintings and antique Tiffany lamps grace this charming restaurant on the property of a former estate. Stuffed artichokes, veal shanks and veal parmigiana are examples of delectable entrees perfected by the chef. Dishes made from original recipes and home-grown herbs and vegetables take the food to a different level. Casual dress; cocktails. **Parking:** on-site. **Cards:** AX, MC, VI.
Italian

BOONVILLE pop. 2,138

──────── **WHERE TO STAY** ────────

HEADWATERS MOTOR LODGE **Phone:** 315/942-4493

(AAA) (SAVE) All Year [CP] 1P: $53-$89 2P: $63-$89 XP: $8 F12

▽▽▽ **Location:** Jct SR 12 and 120, 0.7 mi n. 13524 Rt 12 13309 (PO Box 337). **Fax:** 315/942-4626. **Facility:** 37 one-bedroom standard units, some with kitchens. 1-2 stories (no elevator), interior corridors. **Parking:** on-site, winter plug-ins. **Terms:** 2-3 night minimum stay - seasonal and/or weekends, small pets only. **Leisure Activities:** *Fee:* game room. **Cards:** AX, DS, MC, VI. **Free Special Amenities:** continental breakfast and high-speed Internet.
Motel

SOME UNITS

BOWMANSVILLE —*See Buffalo p. 256.*

BRENTWOOD pop. 53,917

──────── **WHERE TO STAY** ────────

WINGATE INN *Book at AAA.com* **Phone:** (631)434-1818

▽◆◆▽ 5/1-9/30 1P: $109-$159 2P: $119-$159

10/1-4/30 1P: $99-$139 2P: $99-$139

Small-scale Hotel **Location:** I-495, exit 52 (Commack Rd) eastbound; exit 53 (Commack Rd) westbound, follow signs to Crooked Hill Rd. 801 Crooked Hill Rd 11717. **Fax:** 631/434-1919. **Facility:** 111 units. 107 one-bedroom standard units, some with whirlpools. 4 one-bedroom suites with whirlpools. 5 stories, interior corridors. *Bath:* combo or shower only. **Parking:** on-site. **Terms:** package plans. **Amenities:** video games (fee), high-speed Internet, dual phone lines, voice mail, safes, irons, hair dryers. **Leisure Activities:** whirlpool, exercise room. **Guest Services:** complimentary evening beverages: Tues, valet and coin laundry, area transportation, wireless Internet. **Business Services:** meeting rooms, business center. **Cards:** AX, CB, DC, DS, JC, MC, VI.

SOME UNITS

BREWERTON pop. 3,453

──── WHERE TO STAY ────

BEL AIR MOTEL

Motel

5/1-10/31 & 4/1-4/30	1P: $66-$71	2P: $73-$76	XP: $5	F18
11/1-3/31	1P: $61-$66	2P: $68-$73	XP: $5	F18

Phone: 315/699-5991

Location: I-81, exit 30, just w on SR 31 to SR 11, then 2.1 mi n. Located in a rural setting. 8961 Rt 11 13029. **Fax:** 315/505-6740. **Facility:** 14 one-bedroom standard units. 1 story, exterior corridors. **Parking:** on-site, winter plug-ins. **Terms:** weekly rates available. **Amenities:** hair dryers. **Cards:** DS, MC, VI.

SOME UNITS

HOLIDAY INN EXPRESS *Book at AAA.com*

Small-scale Hotel

5/12-9/8 [CP]	1P: $109-$119	2P: $109-$119
9/9-4/30 [CP]	1P: $99-$109	2P: $99-$109
5/1-5/11 [CP]	1P: $89-$99	2P: $89-$99

Phone: 315/676-3222

Location: I-81, exit 31 (Bartell Rd), just s to 5552 Bartell Rd 13029 (PO Box 589). **Fax:** 315/676-7497. **Facility:** 64 one-bedroom standard units. 2 stories, interior corridors. **Bath:** combo or shower only. **Parking:** on-site, winter plug-ins. **Terms:** package plans. **Amenities:** irons, hair dryers. **Leisure Activities:** exercise room. **Guest Services:** coin laundry, wireless Internet. **Business Services:** meeting rooms, PC. **Cards:** AX, DC, DS, MC, VI.

SOME UNITS

──── WHERE TO DINE ────

DG'S OF BREWERTON

American

Lunch: $6-$7   **Dinner:** $9-$16   **Phone:** 315/676-4235

Location: I-81, exit 31 (Bartell Rd), just s 0.8 mi s. 9334 Brewerton Rd 13029. **Hours:** 11 am-10 pm, Fri & Sat-11 pm, Sun-8:30 pm; hours vary in winter. Closed: 1/1, 12/25. **Features:** Diners relax in the cozy spot and dig into home-style cooking. Offerings range from Italian favorites and oven-baked pasta to fresh seafood, tempting appetizers and steak, chop and veal creations. Prime rib is served on Saturday and Sunday. Casual dress; cocktails. **Parking:** on-site. **Cards:** AX, DS, MC, VI.

BRIDGEHAMPTON pop. 1,381

──── WHERE TO STAY ────

THE ENCLAVE INN-BRIDGEHAMPTON

Motel

All Year   1P: $89-$399

Phone: 631/537-2900

Location: Just w of town. Located in a quiet area. 2668 Montauk Hwy 11932 (PO Box 623). **Fax:** 631/283-3292. **Facility:** Smoke free premises. 10 one-bedroom standard units. 1 story, exterior corridors. **Bath:** shower only. **Parking:** on-site. **Terms:** 2-4 night minimum stay - seasonal and/or weekends, cancellation fee imposed, weekly rates available, package plans, 5% service charge. **Amenities:** high-speed Internet, irons, hair dryers. **Pool(s):** outdoor. **Leisure Activities:** bocci, horseshoes. **Cards:** AX, DS, MC, VI.
Free Special Amenities: high-speed Internet.

──── WHERE TO DINE ────

BOBBY VAN'S STEAKHOUSE

Steak House

Lunch: $8-$12   **Dinner:** $23-$32   **Phone:** 631/537-0590

Location: Between Church Ln and School St; center. 2393 Montauk Hwy 11932. **Hours:** 11:30 am-4:30 & 5:30-11 pm, Fri & Sat-midnight; hours vary off season. Closed: 11/22, 12/25. **Reservations:** accepted. **Features:** On Main Street, the restaurant is a favorite for steak and seafood preparations, including lobster spring rolls and fresh fish. On a warm day, French doors open to the street to allow for good people-watching. Burgers, sandwiches and salads are typically available for lunch. Dressy casual; cocktails. **Parking:** street. **Cards:** AX, DC, DS, MC, VI.

WORLD PIE

Pizza

Lunch: $10-$16   **Dinner:** $13-$20   **Phone:** 631/537-7999

Location: On SR 27A; center. 2402 Montauk Hwy 11932. **Hours:** 11:30 am-midnight. **Features:** This casual trattoria is known for their thin crust pizza baked in their wood-burning brick oven. There is a long laundry list of toppings to choose from, ranging from your classic pepperoni and cheese to the exotic such as clams, goat cheese, calamari and artichokes. Casual dress; cocktails. **Parking:** street. **Cards:** AX, MC, VI.

BRIGHTON pop. 35,584   (See map and index starting on p. 599)

──── WHERE TO STAY ────

COURTYARD BY MARRIOTT BRIGHTON *Book great rates at AAA.com*

Small-scale Hotel

All Year   1P: $89-$259   2P: $89-$259

Phone: (585)292-1000 [27]

Location: I-390, exit 16B (Henrietta Rd) southbound; exit 16 (Henrietta Rd) northbound, just s, then just w on Crittenden Rd. 33 Corporate Woods 14623. **Fax:** 585/292-0905. **Facility:** Smoke free premises. 149 units. 137 one-bedroom standard units. 12 one-bedroom suites. 3 stories, interior corridors. **Parking:** on-site. **Amenities:** video games (fee), high-speed Internet, dual phone lines, voice mail, irons, hair dryers. **Pool(s):** small heated indoor. **Leisure Activities:** whirlpool, exercise room. **Guest Services:** valet and coin laundry, wireless Internet. **Business Services:** meeting rooms, business center. **Cards:** AX, CB, DC, DS, JC, MC, VI.

SOME UNITS

(See map and index starting on p. 599)

HAMPTON INN-ROCHESTER SOUTH

Book great rates at AAA.com Phone: (585)272-7800 **28**

(AAA) [SAVE]
◊◊◊◊

Small-scale Hotel

| 5/1-10/31 [ECP] | 1P: $105-$179 | XP: $5 | F18 |
| 11/1-4/30 [ECP] | 1P: $85-$169 | XP: $5 | F18 |

Location: I-390, exit 16B (Henrietta Rd) southbound; exit 16 (Henrietta Rd) northbound. 717 E Henrietta Rd 14623. Fax: 585/272-1211. **Facility:** 112 one-bedroom standard units. 5 stories, interior corridors. *Bath:* combo or shower only. **Parking:** on-site. **Terms:** cancellation fee imposed. **Amenities:** video games (fee), voice mail, irons, hair dryers. **Guest Services:** valet laundry, area transportation-local hospital & colleges, wireless Internet. **Business Services:** meeting rooms, PC. **Cards:** AX, CB, DC, DS, MC, VI. **Free Special Amenities:** continental breakfast and local telephone calls.

SOME UNITS

HOLIDAY INN EXPRESS-ROCHESTER/BRIGHTON

Book great rates at AAA.com Phone: (585)784-8400 **26**

(AAA) [SAVE]
◊◊◊◊

Small-scale Hotel

| 5/1-10/27 [ECP] | 1P: $119-$219 | 2P: $119-$219 |
| 10/28-4/30 [ECP] | 1P: $99-$189 | 2P: $99-$189 |

Location: I-590, exit 2, just e on SR 31 (Monroe Ave). 2835 Monroe Ave 14618. Fax: 585/784-8411. **Facility:** 68 units. 62 one-bedroom standard units. 6 one-bedroom suites ($159-$259), some with whirlpools. 2 stories, interior corridors. *Bath:* combo or shower only. **Parking:** on-site. **Amenities:** voice mail, irons, hair dryers. **Leisure Activities:** exercise room. **Guest Services:** valet laundry, wireless Internet. **Business Services:** PC. **Cards:** AX, CB, DC, DS, JC, MC, VI. **Free Special Amenities:** expanded continental breakfast and high-speed Internet.

SOME UNITS

TOWPATH MOTEL

Phone: (585)271-2147 **25**

(AAA) [SAVE]
◊

Motel

| 5/1-10/30 [CP] | 1P: $65-$85 | 2P: $70-$95 | XP: $10 | F15 |
| 10/31-4/30 [CP] | 1P: $45-$65 | 2P: $55-$85 | XP: $5 | F15 |

Location: I-590, exit 2 northbound, just w; exit 2A southbound. 2323 Monroe Ave (US 31) 14618. Fax: 585/271-2147. **Facility:** 20 one-bedroom standard units. 2 stories (no elevator), exterior corridors. *Bath:* combo or shower only. **Parking:** on-site. **Amenities:** irons, hair dryers. **Cards:** AX, CB, DC, DS, JC, MC, VI. **Free Special Amenities:** continental breakfast and high-speed Internet. *(See color ad p 602)*

SOME UNITS

WELLESLEY INN (ROCHESTER/SOUTH)

Book at AAA.com Phone: 585/427-0130 **29**

◊◊

Small-scale Hotel

Property failed to provide current rates

Location: I-390, exit 16 (Henrietta Rd) northbound; exit 16B (Henrietta Rd) southbound, just s. 797 E Henrietta Rd 14623. Fax: 585/427-0903. **Facility:** 96 one-bedroom standard units. 4 stories, interior corridors. *Bath:* combo or shower only. **Parking:** on-site. **Amenities:** video games (fee), voice mail, irons, hair dryers. **Guest Services:** valet laundry, wireless Internet.

SOME UNITS

———— WHERE TO DINE ————

BAZIL

Dinner: $8-$18 Phone: 585/427-7420 **21**

◊◊

Italian

Location: I-390, exit 16B (Henrietta Rd) southbound; exit 16 (Henrietta Rd) northbound. 749 E Henrietta Rd 14623. **Hours:** 5 pm-10 pm, Sat noon-11 pm, Sun noon-9 pm; hours vary in winter. Closed major holidays. **Features:** The huge lunch buffet incorporates traditional pasta dishes, as well as meat, chicken and seafood specialties. Casual dress; cocktails. **Parking:** on-site. **Cards:** AX, DC, DS, MC, VI.

DELMONICO'S ITALIAN STEAKHOUSE

Dinner: $9-$20 Phone: 585/424-4242 **22**

◊◊

Steak & Seafood

Location: I-390, exit 16B southbound; exit 16 northbound. 125 White Spruce Blvd 14623. **Hours:** 4 pm-10:30 pm, Fri-11:30 pm, Sat 2 pm-11:30 pm, Sun noon-10 pm. Closed: 11/22, 12/25. **Reservations:** accepted. **Features:** The 24-ounce Delmonico steak is the namesake of this lively restaurant, which also is known for its great Italian fare. Caricatures line the walls of the casual spot. Casual dress; cocktails. **Parking:** on-site. **Cards:** AX, DS, MC, VI.

DIBELLA'S OLD FASHIONED SUBMARINES

Lunch: $3-$6 Dinner: $3-$6 Phone: 585/256-2060 **16**

◊

American

Location: I-390, exit 16A (SR 15 N), 1 mi to Elmwood Ave, then just s. 1900 S Clinton Ave 14618. **Hours:** 10 am-9 pm. Closed: 11/22, 12/25. **Features:** Great subs start with the freshest rolls baked at their in-house bakery. Add top quality meats, cheeses, condiments and choice of toppings for your customized hot or cold favorite. Don't forget one of Grandma DiBella's old fashioned chocolate chip cookies for dessert. Casual dress. **Parking:** on-site. **Cards:** AX, MC, VI.

(See map and index starting on p. 599)

MARIO'S VIA ABRUZZI

▼▼▼▼

Italian

Dinner: $14-$30   **Phone:** 585-271-1111   ⑰
Location: I-590, exit 2, just w. 2740 Monroe Ave 14618. **Hours:** 5 pm-10 pm, Fri-11 pm, Sat 4 pm-11 pm, Sun 10 am-3 & 4:30-9 pm. Closed major holidays. **Reservations:** suggested. **Features:** A warm welcome and attentive service mark the dining experience at the Italian restaurant. On the menu are pleasing appetizers from antipasto to ravioli, a wide variety of pasta dishes, and house-designed specials including rabbit, seafood, veal shanks and duck. Among delectable desserts are classic cannoli and tiramisu. Dressy casual; cocktails. **Parking:** on-site. **Cards:** AX, DC, DS, MC, VI.

MUNDO GRILL

▼▼▼ ▼▼▼

American

Dinner: $13-$19   **Phone:** 585/442-2840   ⑱
Location: I-590, exit 2, just w. 2833 Monroe Ave 14618. **Hours:** 5 pm-10 pm, Fri & Sat-11 pm. Closed major holidays; also Sun. **Features:** New cuisine offerings reflect the influences of many countries. The casually upscale setting includes a seasonal patio. Casual dress; cocktails. **Parking:** on-site. **Cards:** AX, DS, MC, VI.

PHILLIPS EUROPEAN RESTAURANT   *Menu on AAA.com*

ⒶⒶⒶ

▼▼▼▼

Continental

Lunch: $7-$13
Dinner: $13-$30   **Phone:** 585/272-9910   ⑲
Location: I-390, exit 16B (Henrietta Rd) southbound; exit 16 northbound. 26 Corporate Woods 14623. **Hours:** 11 am-midnight. Closed: 11/22, 12/25; also Sun. **Reservations:** suggested. **Features:** Continental cuisine has been carefully prepared to order for more than 16 years. The on-premises bakery churns out 30 European pastries and desserts daily. Casual dress; cocktails. **Parking:** on-site. **Cards:** AX, CB, DC, DS, MC, VI.

PORTOBELLO

▼▼▼ ▼▼

Nouvelle Italian

Lunch: $8-$13   **Dinner:** $14-$22   **Phone:** 585/427-0110   ⑳
Location: I-390, exit 16B northbound, follow service road to W Henrietta Rd, then just s; exit 16A southbound. 2171 W Henrietta Rd 14623. **Hours:** 11:30 am-2:30 & 4:30-10 pm, Sat from 4:30. Closed major holidays; also Sun. **Reservations:** accepted. **Features:** Known for its Italian wine selection, this friendly neighborhood restaurant features pasta, risotto, grilled fish and sauteed meat dishes. Hot homemade bread is hard to resist. Italian music plays softly in the background as friendly staff mill about serving patrons. Casual dress; cocktails. **Parking:** on-site. **Cards:** AX, CB, DC, DS, MC, VI.

BRISTOL CENTER —See FINGER LAKES.

BROADALBIN pop. 1,411

——— **WHERE TO DINE** ———

RAINDANCER STEAK PARLOUR

▼▼▼ ▼▼

Steak & Seafood

Lunch: $5-$10   **Dinner:** $12-$25   **Phone:** 518/842-2606
Location: I-90, exit 27, 4.5 mi n; jct SR 67, 3.8 mi n. 4582 SR 30 12010. **Hours:** 11:30 am-10 pm, Sun 12:30 pm-8 pm. Closed major holidays. **Reservations:** suggested. **Features:** Prime rib and Alaskan king crab legs are specialties on a menu of mostly steak, seafood and pasta dishes, which are served in generous portions. Fireplaces and antiques decorate the rustic dining room. The casual atmosphere is welcoming to families. Casual dress; cocktails. **Parking:** on-site. **Cards:** AX, DS, MC, VI.

BROCKPORT pop. 8,103

——— **WHERE TO STAY** ———

HOLIDAY INN EXPRESS   *Book at AAA.com*

▼▼▼▼

Small-scale Hotel

All Year   1P: $93-$143   2P: $93-$143   **Phone:** (585)395-1000
XP: $10   F14
Location: Just s of jct SR 31, on SR 195. 4908 Lake Rd S 14420. Fax: 585/395-9492. **Facility:** 41 one-bedroom standard units, some with whirlpools. 2 stories, interior corridors. **Parking:** on-site. **Terms:** pets ($15 fee). **Amenities:** high-speed Internet, voice mail, irons, hair dryers. **Guest Services:** wireless Internet. **Cards:** AX, DC, DS, MC, VI.

SOME UNITS

ⒶⓈⓀ ⓈⒹ 🛒 🍴 🔊M 🎦 💻 / ⊠ 🔋 🖥 /
FEE

——— **WHERE TO DINE** ———

MERCHANT STREET SMOKE HOUSE

▼▼ ▼▼

Barbecue

Lunch: $6-$13   **Dinner:** $9-$21   **Phone:** 585/637-6020
Location: SR 19, just w on Clinton St, just n. 48 Merchant St 14420. **Hours:** 11 am-11 pm, Fri & Sat-midnight. Closed: 12/25. **Features:** Tender ribs, brisket, chicken and pulled pork slow cooked in a smoker keep patrons coming back. Varied sauces complement the deep-smoked flavor. Also on the menu are choices geared toward seafood lovers, including king crab legs, broiled scallops, grilled Cajun shrimp and Friday fish fry. Casual dress; cocktails. **Parking:** on-site. **Cards:** AX, MC, VI.

TWO BROTHERS

▼

American

Lunch: $3-$5   **Dinner:** $6-$9   **Phone:** 585/637-7280
Location: Jct SR 31 and 19. 6305 Spencerport Rd (SR 31) 14220. **Hours:** 6 am-9 pm, Fri-10 pm. Closed: 1/1, 12/25. **Features:** The popular, college-town diner offers some upscale appointments, friendly service and ample portions of comfort food. Casual dress; beer & wine only. **Parking:** on-site. **Cards:** AX, DS, MC, VI.

BRONX —See New York p. 485.

BROOKLYN —See New York p. 485.

Destination Buffalo
pop. 292,648

O ften described as a European-looking city, Buffalo has been sculpted by the hands of architectural greats.

F rom the bucolic city park system designed by Frederick Law Olmsted and the handful of Frank Lloyd Wright masterpieces, to Henry Hobson Richardson's Psychiatric Center and the Louis Sullivan Guaranty Building, Buffalo offers a varied palette of architectural styles.

© Lawrence Worcester
Lonely Planet Images

Shea's Performing Arts Center. This beautifully restored 1926 movie palace, one of only a few theaters with an interior designed by the Tiffany Studios, is central to Buffalo's cultural scene. (See mention page 71)

Buffalo waterfront. For a different perspective, take a harbor cruise with an extended excursion to Lake Erie and beyond. (See listing page 70)

Buffalo Niagara CVB and Angel Art Ltd.

Buffalo Niagara CVB and Angel Art Ltd.

City Hall, Buffalo. The 28th-floor observation deck is a great place to begin a self-guiding sightseeing tour of the city.

Buffalo Niagara CVB and Angel Art Ltd.

A Taste of Buffalo. Wings done Buffalo-style are a hot item on most restaurant menus.

See Vicinity map page 243

P laces included in this AAA Destination City:

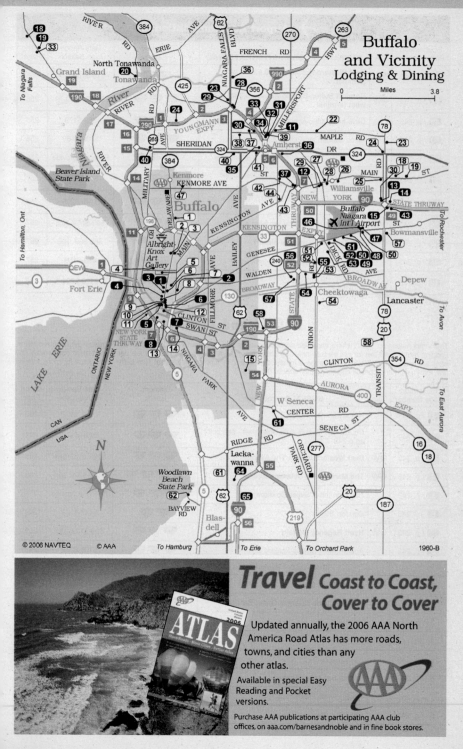

Buffalo and Vicinity
Lodging & Dining

0   Miles   3.8

© 2006 NAVTEQ   © AAA   To Hamburg   To Erie   To Orchard Park   1960-B

✈ Airport Accommodations

Spotter/Map Page Number	OA	**BUFFALO NIAGARA INTERNATIONAL**	Diamond Rating	Rate Range High Season	Listing Page
47 / p. 243	AAA	Best Western-Norstar Inn, 0.4 mi e of terminal	◇◇	$79-$159 SAVE	256
52 / p. 243	AAA	Comfort Suites-Buffalo Airport, 0.7 mi w of west terminal	◇◇◇	$99-$159 SAVE	256
49 / p. 243		Days Inn-Buffalo Airport, just e of terminal	◇◇◇	$69-$179	256
50 / p. 243		Hilton Garden Inn-Buffalo Airport, at airport	◇◇◇	$109-$169	256
48 / p. 243		Holiday Inn-Buffalo Airport, just e of terminal	◇◇◇	Failed to provide	256
51 / p. 243		Holiday Inn Express Hotel & Suites-Buffalo Airport, across from entrance	◇◇◇	$120-$160	257
53 / p. 243		Homewood Suites by Hilton, 0.5 mi w of west terminal	◇◇◇	$149-$209	257
54 / p. 243	AAA	Millennium Hotel, 3 mi sw from entrance	◇◇◇	$99-$159 SAVE	257
55 / p. 243	AAA	Oak Tree Inn, 2 mi w of airport	◇◇	$60-$99 SAVE	257
46 / p. 243		Sleep Inn & Suites, just e of terminal	◇◇	$99-$169	257
12 / p. 243		Hampton Inn at Williamsville, 2.4 mi n of terminal	◇◇◇	$129-$209	263

Buffalo and Vicinity

This index helps you "spot" where approved accommodations and restaurants are located on the corresponding detailed maps. Lodging rate ranges are for comparison only and show the property's high season; rates are per night, unless only weekly (W) rates are available. Restaurant rate range is for dinner, unless only lunch (L) is served. Turn to the listing page for more detailed rate information and consult display ads for special promotions.

Spotter/Map Page Number	OA	**BUFFALO - Lodgings**	Diamond Rating	Rate Range High Season	Listing Page
1 / p. 243		Holiday Inn-Downtown	◇◇◇	$132-$152	250
2 / p. 243		DoubleTree Club Buffalo Downtown - see color ad p 249	◇◇◇	$119-$179	249
3 / p. 243	AAA	Best Western Inn-On The Avenue	◇◇◇	$109-$159 SAVE	248
4 / p. 243	AAA	The Mansion on Delaware Avenue	◇◇◇◇	$169-$325 SAVE	250
5 / p. 243		Hampton Inn & Suites-Downtown	◇◇◇	Failed to provide	249
6 / p. 243		Comfort Suites	◇◇	$119-$169	249
7 / p. 243	AAA	Hyatt Regency Buffalo	◇◇◇	$99-$189 SAVE	250
8 / p. 243		Adam's Mark Buffalo-Niagara Hotel	◇◇◇	$109-$209	248
		BUFFALO - Restaurants			
1 / p. 243		Oliver's Restaurant	◇◇◇	$23-$34	252
2 / p. 243		The Park Lane Tavern & Oyster Bar	◇◇◇	$16-$20	252
3 / p. 243		Hutch's	◇◇◇	$12-$26	251
4 / p. 243		Left Bank	◇◇	$9-$22	251
5 / p. 243		Nektar	◇◇◇	$7-$24	251
6 / p. 243		Anchor Bar & Restaurant	◇◇	$7-$18	251
7 / p. 243		Fiddle Heads Restaurant	◇◇◇	$14-$25	251
8 / p. 243		Chris' NY Sandwich Co	◇	$6-$9(L)	251

Spotter/Map Page Number	OA	BUFFALO - Restaurants (continued)	Diamond Rating	Rate Range High Season	Listing Page
9 / p. 243		Rue Franklin	◆◆◆	$22-$29	252
10 / p. 243		Hemingway's	◆◆	$10-$11	251
11 / p. 243		Papaya Asian Kitchen & Bar	◆◆◆	$10-$26	252
12 / p. 243		E B Green's Steakhouse	◆◆◆	$18-$55	251
13 / p. 243		Pettibone's Grille	◆◆	$6-$22	252
14 / p. 243		Chef's Restaurant	◆◆	$4-$16	251
15 / p. 243		The Blackthorn	◆◆	$11-$16	251
		WILLIAMSVILLE - Lodgings			
11 / p. 243		Residence Inn by Marriott Buffalo/Amherst	◆◆◆	$79-$219	263
12 / p. 243		Hampton Inn at Williamsville	◆◆◆	$129-$209	263
13 / p. 243	◆◆◆	Clarion Hotel-Buffalo Airport - see color ad p 248	◆◆◆	$90-$160 SAVE	262
14 / p. 243		Fairfield Inn-Lancaster	◆◆	$99-$139	262
15 / p. 243		Garden Place Hotel	◆◆◆	$89-$279	262
		WILLIAMSVILLE - Restaurants			
22 / p. 243		Daffodil's	◆◆◆	$17-$28	263
23 / p. 243		Kabab & Curry	◆◆	$9-$18	263
24 / p. 243	◆◆◆	Tandoori's	◆	$8-$30	264
25 / p. 243		Buffalo Brew Pub	◆◆	$6-$16	263
26 / p. 243		Marinaccio's Restaurant	◆◆◆	$16-$40	264
27 / p. 243		Eagle House Restaurant	◆◆	$14-$28	263
28 / p. 243		Creekview Restaurant	◆◆	$8-$22	263
29 / p. 243	◆◆◆	The Original Pancake House	◆◆	$6-$9	264
30 / p. 243		Protocol	◆◆◆	$11-$30	264
		GRAND ISLAND - Lodgings			
18 / p. 243	◆◆◆	Budget Motel	◆	$49-$89 SAVE	259
19 / p. 243		Cinderella Motel	◆	$52-$75	260
20 / p. 243	◆◆◆	Holiday Inn Grand Island Resort	◆◆◆	$129-$189 SAVE	260
		GRAND ISLAND - Restaurant			
33 / p. 243		Jalapeno Loco	◆	$8-$15	260
		TONAWANDA - Lodgings			
23 / p. 243	◆◆◆	Econo Lodge	◆◆	$69-$179 SAVE	262
24 / p. 243		Microtel-Tonawanda	◆◆	$54-$90	262
		AMHERST - Lodgings			
28 / p. 243		Sleep Inn	◆◆	$100-$165	254
29 / p. 243		Holiday Inn Buffalo-Amherst	◆◆◆	$109-$189	253
30 / p. 243		Motel 6 Buffalo-Amherst #1298	◆◆	$49-$65	254
31 / p. 243	◆◆◆	Comfort Inn University	◆◆◆	$99-$139 SAVE	253
32 / p. 243		Hampton Inn-Buffalo/Amherst	◆◆	Failed to provide	253

Spotter/Map Page Number	OA	**AMHERST - Lodgings (continued)**	Diamond Rating	Rate Range High Season	Listing Page
33 / p. 243		Red Roof Inn #7104	▽▽	$63-$104	254
34 / p. 243	⏺	**Buffalo Marriott-Niagara**	▽▽▽	$89-$179 SAVE	253
35 / p. 243		Homewood Suites Buffalo/Amherst	▽▽▽	$149-$199	253
36 / p. 243		Buffalo/Amherst Courtyard by Marriott	▽▽▽	$89-$275	253
37 / p. 243	⏺	**Lord Amherst Hotel**	▽▽	$69-$115 SAVE	254
		AMHERST - Restaurants			
36 / p. 243		The Grapevine	▽▽	$7-$17	254
37 / p. 243		Dakota Grill	▽▽▽	$14-$23	254
38 / p. 243		Scotch 'N Sirloin	▽▽	$16-$31	255
39 / p. 243		Santora's-Phase II	▽	$4-$9	254
40 / p. 243		Taste of India	▽▽	$10-$17	255
41 / p. 243		Duff's Famous Wings	▽	$7-$10	254
42 / p. 243		Siena	▽▽▽	$10-$36	255
43 / p. 243		Sonoma Grille	▽▽▽	$16-$35	255
44 / p. 243		San Marco	▽▽▽	$17-$22	254
		KENMORE - Lodgings			
40 / p. 243		Super 8-Buffalo/Niagara Falls	▽▽	$65-$84	261
		KENMORE - Restaurant			
47 / p. 243		Tsunami	▽▽▽	$15-$29	261
		BOWMANSVILLE - Lodgings			
43 / p. 243		Red Roof Inn-Buffalo Airport #7137	▽▽	Failed to provide	256
		CHEEKTOWAGA - Lodgings			
46 / p. 243		Sleep Inn & Suites	▽▽	$99-$169	257
47 / p. 243	⏺	**Best Western-Norstar Inn**	▽▽	$79-$159 SAVE	256
48 / p. 243		Holiday Inn-Buffalo Airport	▽▽▽	Failed to provide	256
49 / p. 243		Days Inn-Buffalo Airport	▽▽▽	$69-$179	256
50 / p. 243		Hilton Garden Inn-Buffalo Airport	▽▽▽	$109-$169	256
51 / p. 243		Holiday Inn Express Hotel & Suites-Buffalo Airport	▽▽▽	$120-$160	257
52 / p. 243	⏺	**Comfort Suites-Buffalo Airport**	▽▽▽	$99-$159 SAVE	256
53 / p. 243		Homewood Suites by Hilton	▽▽▽	$149-$209	257
54 / p. 243	⏺	**Millennium Hotel -** see color ad p 248	▽▽▽	$99-$159 SAVE	257
55 / p. 243	⏺	**Oak Tree Inn -** see color ad p 250	▽▽	$60-$99 SAVE	257
56 / p. 243		Hampton Inn-Airport/Galleria	▽▽▽	$149-$199	256
57 / p. 243		Residence Inn by Marriott	▽▽▽	$150-$175	257
58 / p. 243		Holiday Inn Express Hotel & Suites	▽▽▽	$120-$170	257
		CHEEKTOWAGA - Restaurants			
50 / p. 243		Olympic Family Restaurant	▽▽	$3-$9	258
51 / p. 243		Danny's	▽▽	$8-$10	258

Spotter/Map Page Number	OA	**CHEEKTOWAGA - Restaurants (continued)**	Diamond Rating	Rate Range High Season	Listing Page
52 / p. 243		Holiday Showcase Restaurant	◈	$6-$11	258
53 / p. 243		Alton's Restaurant	◈	$8-$12	258
54 / p. 243		Adam's Steak and Seafood Restaurant	◈◈	$12-$25	258
		WEST SENECA - Lodgings			
61 / p. 243		Hampton Inn Buffalo-South/I-90	◈◈◈	$79-$189	262
		BLASDELL - Lodgings			
64 / p. 243	AAA	**Econo Lodge South -** see color ad p 250	◈◈	$46-$99 SAVE	255
65 / p. 243	AAA	**Clarion Hotel**	◈◈	$89-$199 SAVE	255
		BLASDELL - Restaurants			
61 / p. 243	AAA	**Ilio DiPaolo's Restaurant**	◈◈	$7-$18	255
62 / p. 243		The Dock at the Bay	◈◈	$10-$25	255
		CLARENCE - Restaurants			
18 / p. 243		Old Red Mill Inn	◈◈	$9-$25	258
19 / p. 243		Hirsch's Restaurant	◈◈	$16-$27	258
		DEPEW - Restaurants			
57 / p. 243	AAA	**Salvatore's Italian Gardens**	◈◈◈	$19-$45	259
58 / p. 243		El-Canelo	◈	$6-$11	259

BUFFALO pop. 292,648   (See map and index starting on p. 243)

——— WHERE TO STAY ———

ADAM'S MARK BUFFALO-NIAGARA HOTEL   *Book great rates at AAA.com*   Phone: (716)845-5100   **8**

| | 5/1-10/31 | 1P: $109-$209 | 2P: $109-$209 | XP: $10 | F17 |
| | 11/1-4/30 | 1P: $109-$179 | 2P: $109-$179 | XP: $10 | F17 |

Large-scale Hotel **Location:** I-190, exit 7, at Church and Lower Terrace sts; downtown. 120 Church St 14202. Fax: 716/845-5377. **Facility:** 486 units. 480 one-bedroom standard units, some with whirlpools. 6 one-bedroom suites. 9 stories, interior corridors. *Bath:* combo or shower only. **Parking:** on-site (fee) and valet. **Terms:** cancellation fee imposed, [AP] meal plan available, package plans. **Amenities:** video games (fee), high-speed Internet, voice mail, irons, hair dryers. **Pool(s):** heated indoor. **Leisure Activities:** sauna. **Guest Services:** gift shop, valet and coin laundry, area transportation, wireless Internet. **Business Services:** conference facilities, business center. **Cards:** AX, CB, DC, DS, JC, MC, VI.

SOME UNITS

(ASK) (SD) ✈ ⏹ 24 🍴 ⓜ ⓖ ⌗ 🅿 ✦ 🎖 💻 / ✕ VCR 🔒 🖨 /
FEE   FEE   FEE

BEST WESTERN INN-ON THE AVENUE   *Book great rates at AAA.com*   Phone: (716)886-8333   **3**

(AAA) (SAVE)   All Year   1P: $109-$149   2P: $119-$159   XP: $7   F16

Small-scale Hotel **Location:** Between Virginia and Allen sts; downtown. 510 Delaware Ave 14202. Fax: 716/884-3070. **Facility:** 61 one-bedroom standard units, some with whirlpools. 5 stories, interior corridors. *Bath:* combo or shower only. **Parking:** on-site. **Terms:** small pets only (in designated units, with prior approval). **Amenities:** irons, hair dryers. **Guest Services:** valet laundry. **Business Services:** meeting rooms. **Cards:** AX, CB, DC, DS, JC, MC, VI. **Free Special Amenities:** expanded continental breakfast and early check-in/late check-out.

SOME UNITS

(SD) 🛏 ⏹ 🍴 ⓖ ✦ 📷 💻 / ✕ VCR 🔒 🖨 /

(See map and index starting on p. 243)

COMFORT SUITES   *Book great rates at AAA.com*   Phone: (716)854-5500   **6**

All Year [ECP]   1P: $119-$159   2P: $129-$169   XP: $10   F18
Location: Between Main and Washington sts, at Chippewa St; downtown. Located in the theater district. 601 Main St
Small-scale Hotel   14203. Fax: 716/854-4836. **Facility:** 146 one-bedroom suites. 7 stories, interior corridors. **Parking:** no self-
parking. **Amenities:** voice mail, irons, hair dryers. **Leisure Activities:** exercise room. **Guest Services:** valet
laundry, area transportation, wireless Internet. **Business Services:** meeting rooms, PC. **Cards:** AX, CB, DC, DS, MC, VI.

SOME UNITS

(ASK) (S₀) (⊞) (¶⊦) (★) (🖥) (🧳) (💻) / (✕) /

DOUBLETREE CLUB BUFFALO DOWNTOWN   *Book great rates at AAA.com*   Phone: (716)845-0112   **2**

All Year   1P: $119-$179   XP: $10   F18
Location: I-90, exit 51W to Buffalo; I-90 W to SR 33 W, exit Locust St to Michigan Ave, 0.4 mi n to High St, then just w.
Small-scale Hotel   125 High St 14203. Fax: 716/845-0125. **Facility:** 100 units. 88 one-bedroom standard units. 12 one-bedroom
suites. 8 stories, interior corridors. *Bath:* combo or shower only. **Parking:** valet. **Terms:** [AP], [BP] & [CP]
meal plans available, package plans. **Amenities:** video library, high-speed Internet, dual phone lines, voice mail, irons, hair
dryers. **Leisure Activities:** exercise room. **Guest Services:** valet and coin laundry, area transportation, wireless Internet.
Business Services: meeting rooms, business center. **Cards:** AX, DC, DS, MC, VI. *(See color ad below)*

SOME UNITS

(ASK) (S₀) (⊞) (¶⊦) (♿) (★) (🖥) (🧳) (💻) / (✕) /
FEE

HAMPTON INN & SUITES-DOWNTOWN   *Book great rates at AAA.com*   Phone: 716/855-2223   **5**

Property failed to provide current rates
Location: At Chippewa St; downtown. 220 Delaware Ave 14202. Fax: 716/856-5221. **Facility:** 137 units. 106 one-
Small-scale Hotel   bedroom standard units, some with whirlpools. 31 one-bedroom suites, some with efficiencies and/or
whirlpools. 6 stories, interior corridors. *Bath:* combo or shower only. **Parking:** on-site. **Amenities:** video
games (fee), high-speed Internet, dual phone lines, voice mail, irons, hair dryers. **Pool(s):** heated indoor. **Leisure
Activities:** whirlpool, exercise room. **Guest Services:** sundries, valet and coin laundry, wireless Internet. **Business Services:**
meeting rooms, business center.

SOME UNITS

(⊞) (¶⊦) (♿M) (★) (📷) (🏊) (★) (💻) / (✕) (🧳) (📻) /

(See map and index starting on p. 243)

HOLIDAY INN-DOWNTOWN   *Book at AAA.com*   Phone: (716)886-2121   **1**
♦♦♦♦♦   5/1-10/31   1P: $132-$152   2P: $132-$152   XP: $10   F19
          11/1-4/30   1P: $123-$132   2P: $123-$132   XP: $10   F19
Small-scale Hotel   **Location:** Between Allen and North sts; downtown. Located in a historic district. 620 Delaware Ave 14202.
Fax: 716/886-7942. **Facility:** 167 one-bedroom standard units. 8 stories, interior corridors. **Parking:** on-site.
Terms: cancellation fee imposed, small pets only ($30 fee, in designated units). **Amenities:** voice mail, irons, hair dryers.
Pool(s): heated outdoor. **Leisure Activities:** lifeguard on duty, exercise room. **Guest Services:** valet and coin laundry, area
transportation, wireless Internet. **Business Services:** meeting rooms, fax. **Cards:** AX, DC, DS, MC, VI.

SOME UNITS
🅷 🐕 🍴 Ⓨ ➹ 🎦 🖥 / ✕ 🛄 🖨 /
FEE   FEE FEE

HYATT REGENCY BUFFALO   *Book great rates at AAA.com*   Phone: (716)856-1234   **7**
(AAA) [SAVE]   All Year   1P: $99-$189   2P: $99-$189   XP: $25   F18
♦♦♦♦♦   **Location:** On Pearl St at W Huron St; downtown. 2 Fountain Plaza 14202. **Fax:** 716/852-6157. **Facility:** 396 units.
384 one-bedroom standard units, some with whirlpools. 12 one-bedroom suites. 16 stories, interior
Large-scale Hotel   corridors. **Bath:** combo or shower only. **Parking:** on-site (fee). **Terms:** cancellation fee imposed.
Amenities: voice mail, irons, hair dryers. *Some:* CD players, high-speed Internet (fee), dual phone lines.
Dining: 2 restaurants, 6:30 am-10 pm, cocktails, also, E B Green's Steakhouse, see separate listing. **Guest**
Services: gift shop, valet laundry. **Business Services:** conference facilities, business center. **Cards:** AX, CB, DC, DS, JC,
MC, VI.

SOME UNITS
🍴 Ⓨ ♿ ➹ 🎦 🖥 / ✕ [VCR] 🛄 🖨 /

THE MANSION ON DELAWARE AVENUE   *Book great rates at AAA.com*   Phone: (716)886-3300   **4**
(AAA) [SAVE]   All Year [ECP]   1P: $169-$325   2P: $169-$325   XP: $20   F16
♦♦♦ ♦♦♦   **Location:** Jct Edward St; downtown. 414 Delaware Ave 14202. **Fax:** 716/883-3923. **Facility:** Meticulous
renovation details combine Old World elegance with contemporary style and modern amenities including
Historic   butler service. Seven rooms with fireplaces. Smoke free premises. 28 units. 25 one-bedroom standard units,
Small-scale Hotel   some with whirlpools. 3 one-bedroom suites ($325) with whirlpools. 4 stories, interior corridors. **Bath:** combo
or shower only. **Parking:** on-site and valet. **Terms:** check-in 4 pm, 2-3 night minimum stay - seasonal
and/or weekends, cancellation fee imposed, [BP] meal plan available, package plans, 2% service charge.
Amenities: DVD players, high-speed Internet, dual phone lines, voice mail, hair dryers. **Leisure Activities:** exercise room. *Fee:*
massage. **Guest Services:** complimentary evening beverages, valet laundry, area transportation-within 3 mi. **Business**
Services: meeting rooms, administrative services, PC. **Cards:** AX, CB, DC, DS, MC, VI. **Free Special Amenities:** expanded
continental breakfast and high-speed Internet.

SOME UNITS
🍴 ♿ ✕ [VCR] 🎦 🖥 / 🛄 /

(See map and index starting on p. 243)

——— **WHERE TO DINE** ———

ANCHOR BAR & RESTAURANT
Lunch: $5-$8   **Dinner:** $7-$18   **Phone:** 716/886-8920   ⑥
Location: Jct Main and North sts; downtown. 1047 Main St 14209. **Hours:** 11 am-11 pm, Fri-1 am, Sat noon-1 am, Sun noon-11 pm. Closed: 11/22, 12/25. **Features:** The self-proclaimed "home of the original buffalo chicken wings," the family-owned restaurant first served buffalo chicken wings in 1964. Open since 1935, this place also prepares salads, subs, hot and cold sandwiches and pasta dishes. Casual dress; cocktails. **Parking:** on-site. **Cards:** AX, DC, DS, MC, VI.
American

THE BLACKTHORN
Lunch: $6-$8   **Dinner:** $11-$16   **Phone:** 716/825-9327   ⑮
Location: I-90, exit 54, 1.5 mi n on SR 16; at Seneca St and Cazenovia. 2134 Seneca St 14210. **Hours:** 11:30 am-10 pm, Fri & Sat-11 pm, Sun noon-10 pm. Closed major holidays. **Features:** Since 1968, the attractive, nicely-decorated restaurant has welcomed the neighborhood crowd to enjoy an extensive array of snacks, sandwiches, soup and entrees. Lunch patrons can sample the buffet. The Friday fish fry and weekend prime rib specials are popular. Casual dress; cocktails. **Parking:** on-site. **Cards:** AX, DS, MC, VI.
Steak & Seafood

CHEF'S RESTAURANT
Lunch: $4-$9   **Dinner:** $4-$16   **Phone:** 716/856-9187   ⑭
Location: Jct Chicago St. 291 Seneca St 14204. **Hours:** 11 am-9 pm. Closed major holidays; also Sun. **Features:** This casual spot has been an understandable choice for traditional fine dining for 75 years. Delicious homemade sauce is the element that keeps western New Yorkers coming back. Casual dress; cocktails. **Parking:** on-site. **Cards:** AX, DS, MC, VI.
Italian

CHRIS' NY SANDWICH CO
Lunch: $6-$9   **Phone:** 716/854-6642   ⑧
Location: Between Tupper and Edward sts. 395 Delaware Ave 14202. **Hours:** 11 am-2:30 pm. Closed major holidays; also Sat & Sun. **Features:** Friendly, laid-back staffers serve generous gourmet sandwiches made from the freshest breads and quality ingredients. The patio opens seasonally. Casual dress. **Parking:** on-site. **Cards:** AX, DS, MC, VI.
American

E B GREEN'S STEAKHOUSE
Dinner: $18-$55   **Phone:** 716/855-4870   ⑫
Location: On Pearl St at W Huron St; downtown; in Hyatt Regency Buffalo. 2 Fountain Plaza 14202. **Hours:** 5 pm-11 pm; call for holiday hours. **Reservations:** suggested. **Features:** Consistency is the key to success at the no-nonsense, high-quality steak house. Among enduring favorites are the 48-ounce porterhouse, 32-ounce prime rib and two- to three-pound lobsters. Enormous portions, including steak fries and baked sweet potatoes, are a challenge for meat-lovers. Dressy casual; cocktails. **Parking:** valet. **Cards:** AX, DC, DS, MC, VI.
Steak & Seafood

FIDDLE HEADS RESTAURANT
Dinner: $14-$25   **Phone:** 716/883-4166   ⑦
Location: Corner of Franklin St. 62 Allen St 14202. **Hours:** 5 pm-10 pm. Closed: 11/22, 12/25; also Sun & Mon. **Reservations:** suggested. **Features:** The tiny restaurant presents an interesting menu of innovative, well-prepared dishes which are served with unusual sides that complement. Two offerings to try are the pizza made from real fiddleheads and the steamed sea bass. Servers are friendly. Casual dress; cocktails. **Parking:** street. **Cards:** AX, DS, MC, VI.
American

HEMINGWAY'S
Lunch: $5-$7   **Dinner:** $10-$11   **Phone:** 716/852-1937   ⑩
Location: In theater district. 492 Pearl St 14202. **Hours:** 11:30 am-11 pm, Fri & Sat-1 am, Sun noon-10 pm. Closed major holidays. **Reservations:** accepted. **Features:** Well-aged brick walls act as a backdrop for stained glass windows, wooden Indians, brass and wood carvings and guns to create an eclectic atmosphere, a favorite spot of the theater-going crowd. The menu dabbles in sandwiches and salads, as well as burgers and full entrees. Chocolate cheesecake is a sinful temptation. Casual dress; cocktails. **Parking:** on-site. **Cards:** AX, DS, MC, VI.
American

HUTCH'S
Dinner: $12-$26   **Phone:** 716/885-0074   ③
Location: 1 blk from Gates Cir. 1375 Delaware Ave 14209. **Hours:** 5 pm-10 pm, Fri & Sat-midnight, Sun 4 pm-9 pm. Closed major holidays. **Reservations:** suggested. **Features:** Patrons can savor prime steak, lamb chops and fresh seafood, such as sesame-crusted tuna. Innovative appetizers include Thai calamari and ceviche. Leopard-skin rugs and a brick-walled bar stand out in the dining room. Dressy casual; cocktails. **Parking:** street. **Cards:** AX, DC, MC, VI.
American

LEFT BANK
Dinner: $9-$22   **Phone:** 716/882-3509   ④
Location: Near Kleinhans Music Hall. 511 Rhode Island St 14213. **Hours:** 5 pm-11 pm, Fri & Sat-midnight, Sun 11 am-2:30 & 4-10 pm. Closed major holidays. **Reservations:** suggested. **Features:** The comfortable, bistro-like restaurant offers many tempting and unusual items, such as its signature eggplant, a large, thick slice of breaded eggplant "steak" sandwiched with ricotta and grilled veggies and topped with fresh mozzarella. Dressy casual; cocktails. **Parking:** street. **Cards:** AX, DS, MC, VI.
American

NEKTAR
Dinner: $7-$24   **Phone:** 716/881-1829   ⑤
Location: Between Bryant St and Hodge. 451 Elmwood Ave 14222. **Hours:** 4:30 pm-11 pm, Sun 11:30 am-10 pm. Closed major holidays. **Reservations:** accepted. The chic martini-bar-style restaurant provides a setting for casually upscale dining. High-quality foods are prepared a la minute and presented with eye appeal. Creative twists to Mediterranean cuisine are the hallmark of chef James Richert, a Culinary Institute of America graduate. Among small plates are octopus with lemon-basil hummus, Cajun grilled shrimp with andouille sausage and corn-breaded banana peppers stuffed with jack and goat cheese. Exotic dessert creations are an event in themselves. Casual dress; cocktails. **Parking:** on-site. **Cards:** AX, MC, VI.
Nouvelle Mediterranean

(See map and index starting on p. 243)

OLIVER'S RESTAURANT
Dinner: $23-$34 Phone: 716/877-9662 ①
Location: SR 384, 0.5 mi n of jct SR 198 at Delaware and Amherst aves; uptown. 2095 Delaware Ave 14216. **Hours:** 5 pm-10 pm, Fri & Sat-midnight, Sun 4:30 pm-9:30 pm. **Closed:** 5/28, 7/4, 9/3. **Reservations:** suggested, weekends. **Features:** Elegant table appointments add to the contemporary sophistication of the informal dining room. International influences punctuate innovative, creatively presented dishes. The food and wine sampler menu, available Tuesday through Friday, is a treat. Dressy casual; cocktails. **Parking:** on-site. **Cards:** AX, MC, VI.

Continental

PAPAYA ASIAN KITCHEN & BAR
Lunch: $7-$11 Dinner: $10-$26 Phone: 716/856-2444 ⑪
Location: At Delaware St; downtown. 118 W Chippewa St 14202. **Hours:** 11 am-11 pm, Thurs & Fri-3 am, Sat 3 pm-3 am, Sun 3 pm-10 pm. **Reservations:** suggested. **Features:** Delicious New Asian cuisine created with imagination gives downtown diners a light, healthy choice. The food is as fresh as the decor and even more pleasing. Pad thai, satay, spring and summer rolls, Thai basil seafood, Singapore duck and other mouthwatering entrees make for a tough decision. Dressy casual; cocktails. **Parking:** on-site (fee) and street. **Cards:** AX, MC, VI.

Asian

THE PARK LANE TAVERN & OYSTER BAR
Lunch: $8-$13 Dinner: $16-$20 Phone: 716/881-2603 ②
Location: Delaware Ave at Gates Cir. 33 Gates Cir 14209. **Hours:** 11:30 am-3 & 5-10 pm, Sat 5-10:30 pm, Sun 10:30 am-2 pm. **Closed:** 12/25; also Mon. **Reservations:** accepted. **Features:** A stylish and upscale aura is provided by the solid background of classic Tudor architecture. Brick, wood, brocades, stained glass, fireplaces and black wrought iron offer timeless style. The menu presents cuisine with a Mediterranean flair, including homemade pasta and other dishes made with fresh ingredients. Desserts are delicious. Casual dress; cocktails. **Parking:** on-site and valet. **Cards:** AX, MC, VI.

American

PETTIBONE'S GRILLE
Lunch: $5-$10 Dinner: $6-$22 Phone: 716/846-2100 ⑬
Location: At Swan and Washington sts; I-190, exit 6, Seneca St ramp to Swan St to Washington St; at Dunn Tire Park. 275 Washington St 14203. **Hours:** 11:30 am-2 pm; dinner during HSBC events. Closed major holidays. **Reservations:** suggested, during games. **Features:** Perched above the baseball park, the casual restaurant lays out a menu of such dishes as steak, chops, seafood and pasta. The grilled portobello sandwich is particularly tasty. Plaques commemorate players being inducted in the local Hall of Fame. Casual dress; cocktails. **Parking:** no self-parking. **Cards:** AX, DS, MC, VI.

American

RUE FRANKLIN
Dinner: $22-$29 Phone: 716/852-4416 ⑨
Location: Just n of Tupper St. 341 Franklin St 14202. **Hours:** 5:30 pm-10 pm. Closed major holidays; also Sun, Mon & 3 weeks in late summer. **Reservations:** suggested. **Features:** Summer dining with a view of the landscaped courtyard or the Provencal-inspired dining room provides an atmosphere of sophisticated grace. The limited, seasonal menu unveils such interesting, contemporary French-inspired cuisine, such as Muscovy duck breast, squab breasts with b'steeya or lamb loin chops with green lentils. Irresistible housemade desserts are served with panache and are as rich as Trump. The espresso is made the old-fashioned way. Dressy casual; cocktails. **Parking:** on-site. **Cards:** AX, DC, DS, MC, VI.

French

The Buffalo Vicinity

AMHERST pop. 116,510 (See map and index starting on p. 243)

—— WHERE TO STAY ——

BUFFALO/AMHERST COURTYARD BY MARRIOTT *Book great rates at AAA.com* **Phone:** (716)626-2300 **36**
All Year 1P: $89-$275 2P: $89-$275
Location: I-290, exit 6, just ne. 4100 Sheridan Dr 14221. Fax: 716/626-2322. **Facility:** Smoke free premises. 108
Small-scale Hotel units. 101 one-bedroom standard units. 7 one-bedroom suites. 4 stories, interior corridors. *Bath:* combo or
shower only. **Parking:** on-site. **Amenities:** video games (fee), high-speed Internet, dual phone lines, voice
mail, irons, hair dryers. **Pool(s):** small heated indoor. **Leisure Activities:** whirlpool, exercise room. **Guest Services:** valet and
coin laundry, wireless Internet. **Business Services:** meeting rooms, PC. **Cards:** AX, CB, DC, DS, JC, MC, VI.

SOME UNITS
(ASK) (S/D) ✈ 🐕 🍽 🏋M 🚫 📶 🏊 ✕ 🐾 🖥 / 🛗 🖼 /

BUFFALO MARRIOTT-NIAGARA *Book great rates at AAA.com* **Phone:** (716)689-6900 **34**
(AAA) (SAVE) All Year 1P: $89-$179 2P: $89-$179
Location: I-290, exit 5B, 0.5 mi n on SR 263 (Millersport Hwy). Located across from the SUNY at Buffalo, North
Campus. 1340 Millersport Hwy 14221. Fax: 716/689-0483. **Facility:** Smoke free premises. 356 units. 350 one-
bedroom standard units. 6 one-bedroom suites ($250). 10 stories, interior corridors. *Bath:* combo or shower
Large-scale Hotel only. **Parking:** on-site, winter plug-ins. **Terms:** pets ($50 fee). **Amenities:** high-speed Internet (fee), voice
mail, honor bars, irons, hair dryers. **Dining:** 6:30 am-10 pm, cocktails. **Pool(s):** heated indoor/outdoor.
Leisure Activities: whirlpool. *Fee:* game room. **Guest Services:** gift shop, valet laundry, area transportation-within 1.5 mi,
wireless Internet. **Business Services:** conference facilities, business center. **Cards:** AX, CB, DC, DS, JC, MC, VI.
Free Special Amenities: newspaper.

SOME UNITS
(S/D) ✈ 🐕 🍽 🍷 🏋M 🚫 📶 🏊 🚐 ✕ 🐾 🖥 / 🛗 /
FEE FEE

COMFORT INN UNIVERSITY *Book great rates at AAA.com* **Phone:** (716)688-0811 **31**
(AAA) (SAVE) 7/1-9/3 1P: $99-$129 2P: $109-$139 XP: $10 F18
5/1-6/30 & 9/4-4/30 1P: $79-$119 2P: $89-$129 XP: $10 F18
Location: I-290, exit 5B, just n on SR 263 (Millersport Hwy), then just w. 1 Flint Rd 14226. Fax: 716/688-2365.
Facility: 102 one-bedroom standard units. 4 stories, interior corridors. **Parking:** on-site. **Terms:** [ECP] meal
Small-scale Hotel plan available, 5% service charge, small pets only ($10 extra charge). **Amenities:** voice mail, irons, hair
dryers. *Some: Fee:* high-speed Internet. **Pool(s):** small heated indoor. **Leisure Activities:** exercise room. **Business**
Guest Services: valet and coin laundry, area transportation-within 5 mi & local business, wireless Internet. **Business**
Services: PC. **Cards:** AX, DC, DS, MC, VI. **Free Special Amenities: expanded continental breakfast and high-speed**
Internet.

SOME UNITS
(S/D) 🐕 🍽 🚐 🐾 🖥 / ✕ 🛗 🖼 /
FEE FEE FEE

HAMPTON INN-BUFFALO/AMHERST *Book great rates at AAA.com* **Phone:** 716/689-4414 **32**
Property failed to provide current rates
Location: I-290, exit 5B, just n on SR 263 (Millersport Hwy). 10 Flint Rd 14226. Fax: 716/689-4382. **Facility:** 196
Small-scale Hotel units. 194 one-bedroom standard units. 2 one-bedroom suites with efficiencies. 4 stories, interior corridors.
Parking: on-site. **Amenities:** voice mail, irons, hair dryers. **Pool(s):** heated indoor. **Leisure**
Activities: whirlpool, exercise room. **Guest Services:** valet laundry, area transportation, wireless Internet. **Business Services:**
meeting rooms.

SOME UNITS
✈ 🍽 🏋M 📶 🚐 🐾 🖥 / ✕ 🛗 🖼 /
FEE

HOLIDAY INN BUFFALO-AMHERST *Book at AAA.com* **Phone:** (716)691-8181 **29**
5/1-10/1 1P: $109-$179 2P: $109-$189 XP: $10 F18
10/2-4/30 1P: $99-$179 2P: $99-$189 XP: $10 F18
Small-scale Hotel **Location:** I-290, exit 3 westbound; exit 3B eastbound, just n on US 62 (Niagara Falls Blvd). 1881 Niagara Falls Blvd
14228. Fax: 716/691-4965. **Facility:** 199 one-bedroom standard units. 2 stories (no elevator), interior
corridors. **Parking:** on-site. **Amenities:** voice mail, irons, hair dryers. **Pool(s):** heated indoor. **Leisure Activities:** whirlpool,
exercise room. **Guest Services:** valet and coin laundry, area transportation, wireless Internet. **Business Services:** conference
facilities. **Cards:** AX, DC, DS, JC, MC, VI.

SOME UNITS
(ASK) (S/D) ✈ 🍽 🍷 🚐 🐾 🖥 / ✕ 🛗 🖼 /
FEE FEE

HOMEWOOD SUITES BUFFALO/AMHERST *Book at AAA.com* **Phone:** (716)833-2277 **35**
All Year [ECP] 1P: $149-$199 F
Location: I-290, exit 5A, just w. 1138 Millersport Hwy 14226. Fax: 716/833-9599. **Facility:** 93 units. 30 one-
bedroom standard units with efficiencies. 63 one-bedroom suites ($149-$199) with efficiencies. 5 stories,
Small-scale Hotel interior corridors. *Bath:* combo or shower only. **Parking:** on-site. **Terms:** package plans, pets ($75 fee).
Amenities: video games (fee), high-speed Internet, dual phone lines, voice mail, irons, hair dryers. *Some:* DVD players (fee).
Pool(s): heated indoor. **Leisure Activities:** whirlpool, exercise room. **Guest Services:** sundries, complimentary evening
beverages: Mon-Thurs, valet and coin laundry, area transportation, wireless Internet. **Business Services:** meeting rooms,
business center. **Cards:** AX, DC, DS, MC, VI.

SOME UNITS
(ASK) (S/D) ✈ 🐕 🏋M 🚐 🐾 🛗 🖼 🖥 / ✕ (VCR) /
FEE FEE

(See map and index starting on p. 243)

LORD AMHERST HOTEL *Book great rates at AAA.com*   Phone: (716)839-2200   37

(AAA) [SAVE]

| | 5/1-9/2 [ECP] | 1P: $69-$99 | 2P: $79-$115 | XP: $10 | F18 |
| | 9/3-4/30 [ECP] | 1P: $59-$89 | 2P: $69-$95 | XP: $10 | F18 |

Motel

Location: I-290, exit 7A, just w on SR 5. 5000 Main St 14226. Fax: 716/839-1538. **Facility:** 95 units. 94 one-bedroom standard units, some with efficiencies. 1 two-bedroom suite with kitchen. 2 stories (no elevator), interior/exterior corridors. **Parking:** on-site. **Terms:** small pets only. **Amenities:** hair dryers. *Some:* CD players. **Pool(s):** heated outdoor. **Leisure Activities:** exercise room. *Fee:* game room. **Guest Services:** valet and coin laundry. **Business Services:** meeting rooms. **Cards:** AX, DC, DS, MC, VI. **Free Special Amenities:** expanded continental breakfast and high-speed Internet.

SOME UNITS
[icons]

MOTEL 6 BUFFALO-AMHERST #1298 *Book at AAA.com*   Phone: 716/834-2231   30

	6/16-8/31	1P: $49-$59	2P: $55-$65	XP: $3	F17
	9/1-10/28	1P: $39-$49	2P: $45-$55	XP: $3	F17
	5/1-6/15 & 10/29-4/30	1P: $37-$47	2P: $43-$53	XP: $3	F17

Motel

Location: I-290, exit 5B, just n to Maple Rd, then 0.7 mi w. 4400 Maple Rd 14226. Fax: 716/834-0872. **Facility:** 93 one-bedroom standard units. 2 stories (no elevator), interior corridors. *Bath:* combo or shower only. **Parking:** on-site. **Cards:** AX, CB, DC, DS, MC, VI.

SOME UNITS
[icons]

RED ROOF INN #7104 *Book at AAA.com*   Phone: (716)689-7474   33

	6/15-9/3	1P: $63-$99	2P: $68-$104	XP: $5	F18
	5/1-6/14	1P: $54-$85	2P: $59-$90	XP: $5	F18
	9/4-11/1	1P: $58-$79	2P: $63-$84	XP: $5	F18
	11/2-4/30	1P: $52-$70	2P: $57-$75	XP: $5	F18

Motel

Location: I-290, exit 5B, just n on SR 263 (Millersport Hwy). Located across from SUNY at Buffalo, North Campus. 42 Flint Rd 14226. Fax: 716/689-2051. **Facility:** 108 one-bedroom standard units. 2 stories (no elevator), exterior corridors. **Parking:** on-site. **Terms:** pets (limit 1). **Amenities:** video games (fee), voice mail. **Guest Services:** wireless Internet. **Cards:** AX, CB, DC, DS, MC, VI.

SOME UNITS
[icons]

SLEEP INN *Book great rates at AAA.com*   Phone: (716)691-6510   28

| | 5/1-9/4 | 1P: $100-$165 | 2P: $100-$165 |
| | 9/5-4/30 | 1P: $85-$165 | 2P: $85-$165 |

Small-scale Hotel

Location: I-290, exit 3, just n on US 62 (Niagara Falls Blvd) to access road. 75 Inn Keepers Ln 14228. Fax: 716/691-3454. **Facility:** 92 one-bedroom standard units. 5 stories, interior corridors. *Bath:* combo or shower only. **Parking:** on-site. **Terms:** 2 night minimum stay - seasonal and/or weekends, cancellation fee imposed, package plans. **Amenities:** video games (fee), high-speed Internet, dual phone lines, voice mail, irons, hair dryers. **Pool(s):** small heated indoor. **Leisure Activities:** whirlpool, exercise room. **Guest Services:** valet laundry, wireless Internet. **Business Services:** PC. **Cards:** AX, DC, DS, MC, VI.

SOME UNITS
[icons]

——— **WHERE TO DINE** ———

DAKOTA GRILL   Dinner: $14-$23   Phone: 716/834-6600   37

American

Location: At Sweethome and Maple rds; in Maple Ridge Plaza. 4224 Maple Rd 14226. **Hours:** 5 pm-10 pm, Fri & Sat-11 pm. Closed major holidays. **Reservations:** suggested. **Features:** The restaurant presents a warm, inviting atmosphere with a touch of Southwest feel and Aboriginal artifacts. The steak is served juicy, hot and sizzling, and the fish and seafood are ocean fresh. Dressy casual; cocktails. **Parking:** on-site. **Cards:** AX, DC, DS, MC, VI.

DUFF'S FAMOUS WINGS   Lunch: $5-$8   Dinner: $7-$10   Phone: 716/834-6234   41

American

Location: Corner of Sheridan Dr and SR 263 (Millersport Hwy). 3651 Sheridan Dr 14226. **Hours:** 11 am-11 pm, Fri & Sat-midnight, Sun noon-10 pm. Closed: Super Bowl Sun. **Features:** An area fixture for more than 50 years, the eatery serves some of the city's best wings. Hot wings come with a warning to "eat at your own risk." Also on the menu are great sandwiches, dinner salads and finger food. Casual dress; beer & wine only. **Parking:** on-site. **Cards:** AX, DS, MC, VI.

THE GRAPEVINE   Lunch: $7-$9   Dinner: $7-$17   Phone: 716/691-7799   36

American

Location: Jct Ellicott Creek Rd. 2545 Niagara Falls Blvd 14228. **Hours:** 11:30 am-10 pm, Fri & Sat-11 pm, Sun 10 am-9 pm; Sunday brunch. Closed: 12/25. **Features:** A larger-than-life fish tank is the central focus of the cozy, comfortable dining space. The friendly, attentive staff serves trendy American favorites. Casual dress; cocktails. **Parking:** on-site. **Cards:** AX, DS, MC, VI.

SAN MARCO   Dinner: $17-$22   Phone: 716/839-5876   44

Northern Italian

Location: I-290, exit 7 (Main St W), 1.2 mi sw. 2082 Kensington Ave 14226. **Hours:** 5:30 pm-10:30 pm. Closed major holidays; also Mon. **Reservations:** suggested. **Features:** Northern Italian cuisine is individually prepared to each guest's palate by the owner/chef. Renown for their wild game creations with venison tenderloin, wild boar, rabbit and quail are a few choices accompanied by creative sauces using porcini mushrooms, truffles, balsamic vinaigrette, red peppercorns and other exotic ingredients. Personal attention by doting professional staff is the norm. Dressy casual; beer & wine only. **Parking:** on-site. **Cards:** AX, MC, VI.

SANTORA'S-PHASE II   Lunch: $4-$9   Dinner: $4-$9   Phone: 716/688-3081   39

Italian

Location: I-290, exit 5B, 0.5 mi n on SR 263 (Millersport Hwy). 1402 Millersport Hwy 14221. **Hours:** 10 am-midnight, Fri & Sat-1 am, Sun 11 am-11 pm. Closed major holidays. **Features:** Prepared as ordered for eat-in or take-out, the restaurant's dishes include traditional and gourmet pizzas, salads, subs, wings, calzones, wraps, burritos, soups and pasta dinners. Casual dress. **Parking:** on-site. **Cards:** AX, MC, VI.

(See map and index starting on p. 243)

SCOTCH 'N SIRLOIN

Steak & Seafood

Dinner: $16-$31   **Phone:** 716/837-4900   (38)
Location: I-290, exit 5B, just n to Maple Rd, then 0.8 mi w. 3999 Maple Rd 14226. **Hours:** 5 pm-10 pm, Fri & Sat-11 pm, Sun 4 pm-9 pm. Closed major holidays. **Reservations:** suggested. **Features:** Welcoming rustic decor, an open-pit fireplace and Coppertop Lounge help set the mood for comfortable, casual dining. Choices from the award-winning wine list complement such specialties as aged USDA steaks and fresh Boston seafood. Casual dress; cocktails. **Parking:** on-site. **Cards:** AX, DS, MC, VI.

SIENA

Italian

Lunch: $8-$13   **Dinner:** $10-$36   **Phone:** 716/839-3108   (42)
Location: I-290, exit 7A, just w on SR 5. 4516 Main St 14226. **Hours:** 11:30 am-3 & 5-10 pm, Fri & Sat-11 pm, Sun 4:30 pm-9 pm. Closed major holidays. **Reservations:** accepted, for lunch. **Features:** Italian fare with a Northern slant is prepared in the trendy bistro-style restaurant. Specialty pizzas cooked in a wood-burning oven are popular, as are grilled dishes, delicious antipasto and daily traditional specials. Dressy casual; cocktails. **Parking:** on-site. **Cards:** AX, MC, VI.

SONOMA GRILLE

Nouvelle California

Lunch: $7-$13   **Dinner:** $16-$35   **Phone:** 716/204-0251   (43)
Location: I-290, exit 7A, just w on SR 5 (Main St). 5010 Main St 14226. **Hours:** 11 am-10 pm, Fri & Sat-11 pm, Sun 4 pm-9 pm. Closed: 12/25. **Reservations:** accepted. **Features:** Fresh decor in relaxing modern tones sets the mood for an enjoyable meal. Menu choices fuse elements of Northern Californian and Mediterranean cuisines. Dressy casual; cocktails. **Parking:** on-site. **Cards:** AX, DS, MC, VI.

TASTE OF INDIA

Indian

Lunch: $5-$8   **Dinner:** $10-$17   **Phone:** 716/837-0460   (40)
Location: In Northtown Plaza. 3093 Sheridan Dr 14226. **Hours:** 11:30 am-2:30 & 4:30-10 pm. **Features:** The simple, casual Indian restaurant prepares traditional cuisine with exotic spices and herbs that satisfy and comfort those who seek something a little unusual. Casual dress; cocktails. **Parking:** on-site. **Cards:** AX, DS, MC, VI.

BLASDELL pop. 2,718 (See map and index starting on p. 243)

——— **WHERE TO STAY** ———

CLARION HOTEL   *Book great rates at AAA.com*

Small-scale Hotel

Phone: (716)648-5700   (65)

7/1-9/10	1P: $89-$199	2P: $89-$199	XP: $10	F17
6/1-6/30	1P: $79-$149	2P: $79-$149	XP: $10	F17
5/1-5/31	1P: $69-$149	2P: $69-$149	XP: $10	F17
9/11-4/30	1P: $69-$139	2P: $69-$139	XP: $10	F17

Location: I-90, exit 56, 0.4 mi e on SR 179, then 0.8 mi s. 3950 McKinley Pkwy 14219. Fax: 716/648-5700. **Facility:** 78 one-bedroom standard units, some with whirlpools. 2 stories (no elevator), interior corridors. **Bath:** combo or shower only. **Parking:** on-site. **Terms:** cancellation fee imposed, package plans, pets ($10 extra charge). **Amenities:** high-speed Internet, voice mail, irons, hair dryers. **Leisure Activities:** exercise room. **Guest Services:** valet and coin laundry. **Business Services:** conference facilities, business center. **Cards:** AX, DC, DS, MC, VI. **Free Special Amenities: continental breakfast and high-speed Internet.**

SOME UNITS

ECONO LODGE SOUTH   *Book great rates at AAA.com*

Motel

Phone: (716)825-7530   (64)

All Year	1P: $46-$99	2P: $46-$99	XP: $7	F18

Location: I-90, exit 56, just e on SR 179. 4344 Milestrip Rd 14219. Fax: 716/825-7530. **Facility:** 85 one-bedroom standard units. 1-2 stories (no elevator), exterior corridors. **Parking:** on-site, winter plug-ins. **Terms:** [CP] meal plan available, package plans, pets ($10 fee, in designated units). **Amenities:** hair dryers. *Some:* irons. **Guest Services:** coin laundry, wireless Internet. **Cards:** AX, CB, DC, DS, JC, MC, VI. **Free Special Amenities: continental breakfast and local telephone calls.** *(See color ad p 250)*

SOME UNITS

——— **WHERE TO DINE** ———

THE DOCK AT THE BAY

American

Lunch: $7-$12   **Dinner:** $10-$25   **Phone:** 716/823-8247   (62)
Location: I-90, exit 56, follow SR 179 W to SR 5 W, then just w. 3800 Hoover Rd 14219. **Hours:** 11:30 am-10 pm, Fri & Sat-11 pm; seasonal hours vary. Closed major holidays. **Reservations:** accepted. **Features:** Overlooking Lake Erie, the waterfront restaurant serves fresh seafood, Certified Angus beef, Australian lobster tails, steaks, prime rib and a huge selection of appetizers. Outside seating is a popular request on warm summer evenings. Casual dress; cocktails. **Parking:** on-site. **Cards:** AX, DC, DS, MC, VI.

ILIO DIPAOLO'S RESTAURANT   *Menu on AAA.com*   **Lunch:** $6-$10 **Dinner:** $7-$18 **Phone:** 716/825-3675   (61)

Italian

Location: I-90, exit 56, on US 62; 0.3 mi n of jct SR 179 and 90. 3785 S Park Ave 14219. **Hours:** 11:30 am-10 pm, Fri-midnight, Sat 2 pm-midnight, Sun 1 pm-10 pm. Closed: 3/23, 11/22, 12/25. **Reservations:** suggested. **Features:** Guests dine among memorabilia honoring the restaurant's founder, a former wrestling champion, and among many other photographs of sports legends. The family eatery is casual. On the impressive menu of amply portioned Italian selections are veal saltimbocca, cannelloni Florentine and other preparations of homemade pasta. Also available are steak, chops and seafood. Casual dress; cocktails. **Parking:** on-site. **Cards:** AX, DC, DS, MC, VI.

BOWMANSVILLE (See map and index starting on p. 243)

──── WHERE TO STAY ────

RED ROOF INN-BUFFALO AIRPORT #7137 *Book at AAA.com* Phone: 716/633-1100 **43**
▼▼▼ ▼
Property failed to provide current rates
Motel **Location:** Just e of SR 78; just n of entrance to I-90 (New York State Thruway), exit 49. 146 Maple Dr 14026. **Fax:** 716/633-2297. **Facility:** 109 one-bedroom standard units. 2 stories (no elevator), exterior corridors. **Parking:** on-site. **Terms:** small pets only. **Amenities:** video games (fee), voice mail. **Guest Services:** wireless Internet.

SOME UNITS

CHEEKTOWAGA pop. 79,988 (See map and index starting on p. 243)

──── WHERE TO STAY ────

BEST WESTERN-NORSTAR INN *Book great rates at AAA.com* Phone: (716)631-8966 **47**

5/1-9/4	1P: $79-$159	2P: $79-$159	XP: $6	F17
9/5-4/30	1P: $69-$149	2P: $69-$149	XP: $6	F17

▼▼ ▼▼
Small-scale Hotel **Location:** Jct SR 78, 1 mi w on SR 33. 4630 Genesee St 14225. **Fax:** 716/631-8977. **Facility:** 77 one-bedroom standard units. 4 stories, interior corridors. *Bath:* combo or shower only. **Parking:** on-site. **Terms:** 7 day cancellation notice-fee imposed, [CP] meal plan available, package plans. **Amenities:** video games (fee), high-speed Internet, irons, hair dryers. **Leisure Activities:** exercise room. **Guest Services:** valet laundry, airport transportation-Buffalo International Airport, area transportation-Amtrak station, wireless Internet. **Business Services:** PC. **Cards:** AX, DC, DS, MC, VI. **Free Special Amenities:** continental breakfast and local telephone calls.

SOME UNITS

COMFORT SUITES-BUFFALO AIRPORT *Book great rates at AAA.com* Phone: (716)633-6000 **52**

5/1-10/31	1P: $99-$149	2P: $109-$159
11/1-4/30	1P: $89-$139	2P: $99-$149

▼▼ ▼▼
Small-scale Hotel **Location:** SR 33, exit Dick Rd, just sw. 901 Dick Rd 14225. **Fax:** 716/633-6858. **Facility:** 100 one-bedroom standard units, some with whirlpools. 2 stories (no elevator), interior corridors. **Parking:** on-site. **Terms:** package plans, small pets only ($10 extra charge). **Amenities:** dual phone lines, voice mail, irons, hair dryers. *Fee:* video games, safes. **Pool(s):** small heated indoor. **Leisure Activities:** whirlpool, exercise room. **Guest Services:** valet and coin laundry, area transportation-within 5 mi, wireless Internet. **Business Services:** meeting rooms, PC. **Cards:** AX, CB, DC, DS, JC, MC, VI. **Free Special Amenities:** expanded continental breakfast and high-speed Internet.

SOME UNITS

FEE

DAYS INN-BUFFALO AIRPORT *Book great rates at AAA.com* Phone: (716)631-0800 **49**
▼▼▼ ▼
All Year [CP] 1P: $69-$169 2P: $79-$179
Small-scale Hotel **Location:** I-90, exit 51, 1.6 mi e on SR 33. 4345 Genesee St 14225. **Fax:** 716/631-7589. **Facility:** 129 one-bedroom standard units. 6 stories, interior corridors. **Parking:** on-site. **Terms:** [BP] meal plan available, package plans. **Amenities:** voice mail, irons, hair dryers. **Pool(s):** small heated indoor. **Leisure Activities:** whirlpool, exercise room. **Guest Services:** valet laundry, area transportation, wireless Internet. **Business Services:** meeting rooms. **Cards:** AX, CB, DC, DS, JC, MC, VI.

SOME UNITS

HAMPTON INN-AIRPORT/GALLERIA *Book great rates at AAA.com* Phone: 716/894-8000 **56**

1/1-4/30	1P: $149-$189	2P: $159-$199
7/1-8/31	1P: $159-$179	2P: $169-$189
5/1-6/30	1P: $139-$169	2P: $149-$179
9/1-12/31	1P: $139-$169	2P: $144-$179

Small-scale Hotel
Location: I-90, exit 52, just w. 1745 Walden Ave 14225. **Fax:** 716/894-3554. **Facility:** 133 one-bedroom standard units, some with whirlpools. 5 stories, interior corridors. *Bath:* combo or shower only. **Parking:** on-site. **Terms:** cancellation fee imposed, [ECP] meal plan available. **Amenities:** video games (fee), voice mail, irons, hair dryers. **Pool(s):** heated indoor. **Leisure Activities:** whirlpool, exercise room. **Guest Services:** valet and coin laundry, area transportation, wireless Internet. **Business Services:** meeting rooms, business center. **Cards:** AX, DC, DS, MC, VI.

SOME UNITS

HILTON GARDEN INN-BUFFALO AIRPORT *Book great rates at AAA.com* Phone: (716)565-0040 **50**
▼▼ ▼▼
All Year 1P: $109-$169 2P: $109-$169 XP: $10 F18
Small-scale Hotel **Location:** I-90, exit 51E (SR 33), 0.5 mi e. Located across from Buffalo Niagara International Airport. 4201 Genesee St 14225. **Fax:** 716/565-0063. **Facility:** 158 units. 157 one-bedroom standard units. 1 one-bedroom suite. 5 stories, interior corridors. *Bath:* combo or shower only. **Parking:** on-site. **Terms:** cancellation fee imposed, [BP] meal plan available, package plans. **Amenities:** video games (fee), high-speed Internet, dual phone lines, voice mail, irons, hair dryers. **Pool(s):** heated indoor. **Leisure Activities:** whirlpool, exercise room. **Business Services:** conference facilities, business center. **Cards:** AX, CB, DC, DS, JC, MC, VI.

SOME UNITS

HOLIDAY INN-BUFFALO AIRPORT *Book at AAA.com* Phone: 716/634-6969 **48**
▼▼▼ ▼
Property failed to provide current rates
Small-scale Hotel **Location:** I-90, exit 51, 1 mi e on SR 33. 4600 Genesee St 14225. **Fax:** 716/634-0920. **Facility:** 207 units. 203 one-bedroom standard units. 4 one-bedroom suites with whirlpools. 2 stories (no elevator), interior corridors. **Parking:** on-site. **Amenities:** voice mail, irons, hair dryers. **Pool(s):** heated outdoor. **Leisure Activities:** whirlpool, exercise room. *Fee:* game room. **Guest Services:** complimentary evening beverages: Tues, valet and coin laundry, area transportation, wireless Internet. **Business Services:** conference facilities, PC.

SOME UNITS

(See map and index starting on p. 243)

HOLIDAY INN EXPRESS HOTEL & SUITES   *Book at AAA.com*   Phone: (716)896-2900   58

▼▼▼▼ All Year   1P: $120-$170   2P: $120-$170   XP: $10   F19
Location: I-190, exit 1, just ne; I-90, exit 53: 601 Dingens St 14206. Fax: 716/896-3765. **Facility:** 117 units. 116
Small-scale Hotel   one-bedroom standard units. 1 one-bedroom suite ($130-$180) with efficiency and whirlpool. 2 stories (no
elevator), interior corridors. *Bath:* combo or shower only. **Parking:** on-site. **Amenities:** dual phone lines,
voice mail, irons, hair dryers. **Pool(s):** heated outdoor. **Leisure Activities:** whirlpool, exercise room. **Guest Services:**
complimentary evening beverages: Tues, valet and coin laundry, area transportation, wireless Internet. **Business Services:**
meeting rooms. **Cards:** AX, CB, DC, DS, JC, MC, VI.

SOME UNITS
(ASK) (S) ✈ 🍽 🍷 ⛹ 🏊 📹 ☕ / ✕ 🔒 🖥 /

HOLIDAY INN EXPRESS HOTEL & SUITES-BUFFALO AIRPORT   *Book at AAA.com*   Phone: (716)631-8700   51

▼▼▼▼ 7/1-8/31 [ECP]   1P: $120-$160   2P: $120-$160   XP: $10   F18
5/1-6/30 & 9/1-4/30 [ECP]   1P: $110-$150   2P: $110-$150   XP: $10   F18
Small-scale Hotel   **Location:** I-90, exit 51 (SR 33), just e. Located adjacent to SR 33) then just s. Located across from Buffalo Niagara
International Airport. 131 Buell Ave 14225. Fax: 716/631-8787. **Facility:** 110 units. 101 one-bedroom standard
units. 9 one-bedroom suites ($120-$190) with whirlpools. 4 stories, interior corridors. *Bath:* combo or shower only. **Parking:** on-
site. **Terms:** pets ($30 fee). **Amenities:** high-speed Internet, dual phone lines, voice mail, irons, hair dryers. **Pool(s):** heated
indoor. **Leisure Activities:** whirlpool, exercise room. *Fee:* game room. **Guest Services:** complimentary evening beverages:
Tues, valet laundry, area transportation, wireless Internet. **Business Services:** meeting rooms. **Cards:** AX, CB, DC, DS, JC,
MC, VI.

SOME UNITS
(ASK) (S) ✈ 🛏 (&M) 🍷 🏊 ✕ 📹 ☕ / ✕ 🔒 🖥 /
FEE

HOMEWOOD SUITES BY HILTON   *Book at AAA.com*   Phone: 716/685-0700   53

▼▼▼▼ All Year   1P: $149   2P: $209
Location: SR 33, exit Dick Rd, 0.3 mi sw. 760 Dick Rd 14225. Fax: 716/685-2034. **Facility:** 77 units. 68 one- and
Small-scale Hotel   9 two-bedroom suites with kitchens, some with whirlpools. 3 stories, interior corridors. *Bath:* combo or
shower only. **Parking:** on-site. **Terms:** cancellation fee imposed, weekly rates available, [ECP] meal plan
available, small pets only ($100 fee). **Amenities:** video games (fee), high-speed Internet, dual phone lines, voice mail, irons,
hair dryers. **Pool(s):** heated indoor. **Leisure Activities:** whirlpool, exercise room. **Guest Services:** sundries, complimentary
evening beverages: Mon-Thurs, valet and coin laundry, area transportation, wireless Internet. **Business Services:** meeting
rooms, business center. **Cards:** AX, DC, DS, MC, VI.

SOME UNITS
✈ 🛏 🍽 🍷 🏊 📹 🔒 🖥 ☕ / ✕ /
FEE

MILLENNIUM HOTEL   *Book great rates at AAA.com*   Phone: (716)681-2400   54

(AAA) (SAVE) All Year   1P: $99-$159   2P: $99-$159   XP: $10   F17
Location: I-90, exit 52, 0.3 mi e. Located adjacent to Walden Galleria Mall. 2040 Walden Ave 14225.
▼▼▼▼ Fax: 716/681-8067. **Facility:** 300 one-bedroom standard units. 2-8 stories, interior/exterior corridors.
Large-scale Hotel   **Parking:** on-site. **Terms:** small pets only ($75 fee, in designated units). **Amenities:** high-speed Internet,
dual phone lines, voice mail, irons, hair dryers. **Dining:** 6:30 am-11 pm, Sun 7 am-10 pm, cocktails.
Pool(s): heated indoor. **Leisure Activities:** saunas, indoor recreation area with sliding roof, exercise room.
Fee: game room. **Guest Services:** valet and coin laundry, area transportation-Depew train station, wireless Internet. **Business
Services:** conference facilities, business center. **Cards:** AX, CB, DC, DS, MC, VI. *(See color ad p 248)*

SOME UNITS
(S) ✈ 🍽 🍷 🏊 ✕ 📹 🖥 ☕ / ✕ 🖥 /
FEE   FEE

OAK TREE INN   *Book great rates at AAA.com*   Phone: (716)681-2600   55

(AAA) (SAVE) All Year   1P: $60-$99
Location: I-90, exit 52, 0.3 mi e on Walden Ave, just n on SR 277 (Union Rd). 3475 Union Rd 14225.
▼▼▼▼ Fax: 716/681-2660. **Facility:** 56 one-bedroom standard units. 3 stories, interior corridors. *Bath:* combo or
shower only. **Parking:** on-site. **Terms:** weekly rates available, pets ($5 extra charge). **Amenities:** irons, hair
Small-scale Hotel   dryers. **Leisure Activities:** whirlpool, exercise room. **Guest Services:** coin laundry, wireless Internet.
Cards: AX, DC, DS, MC, VI. **Free Special Amenities: continental breakfast and local telephone calls.**
(See color ad p 250)

SOME UNITS
(S) 🛏 🍽 (&M) 🍷 🏊 📹 🔒 🖥 / ✕ 🖥 🖥
FEE

RESIDENCE INN BY MARRIOTT   *Book great rates at AAA.com*   Phone: (716)892-5410   57

▼▼▼▼ All Year   1P: $150-$170   2P: $155-$175   XP: $5   F18
Location: I-90, exit 52 westbound, stay to left off exit ramp. Located across from Walden Galleria Mall. 107 Anderson
Small-scale Hotel   Rd 14225. Fax: 716/892-5409. **Facility:** Smoke free premises. 113 units. 49 one-bedroom standard units,
some with efficiencies or kitchens. 45 one- and 19 two-bedroom suites, some with efficiencies or kitchens. 3
stories, interior corridors. *Bath:* combo or shower only. **Parking:** on-site. **Terms:** pets ($75 fee). **Amenities:** video library, high-
speed Internet, dual phone lines, voice mail, irons, hair dryers. *Some:* DVD players (fee). **Pool(s):** small heated indoor. **Leisure
Activities:** whirlpool, exercise room, sports court, basketball. **Guest Services:** complimentary evening beverages: Mon-Thurs,
valet and coin laundry, wireless Internet. **Business Services:** PC. **Cards:** AX, DC, DS, MC, VI.

SOME UNITS
(ASK) (S) 🛏 🍽 (&M) 🍷 🏊 ✕ ✕ 📹 🔒 🖥 🖥 / (VCR) /
FEE   FEE

SLEEP INN & SUITES   *Book great rates at AAA.com*   Phone: (716)626-4000   46

▼▼▼▼ 5/16-9/15   1P: $99-$169   2P: $99-$169   XP: $10   F18
5/1-5/15 & 9/16-4/30   1P: $79-$149   2P: $79-$149   XP: $10   F18
Small-scale Hotel   **Location:** I-90, exit 51, 1.1 mi e on SR 33, then just n. 100 Holtz Rd 14225. Fax: 716/626-3370. **Facility:** 86 one-
bedroom standard units, some with whirlpools. 3 stories, interior corridors. *Bath:* combo or shower only.
Parking: on-site. **Terms:** check-in 3:30 pm. **Amenities:** voice mail, irons, hair dryers. *Some:* high-speed Internet, dual phone
lines. **Leisure Activities:** whirlpool, limited exercise equipment. **Guest Services:** valet and coin laundry, area transportation,
wireless Internet. **Business Services:** meeting rooms, PC. **Cards:** AX, CB, DC, DS, JC, MC, VI.

SOME UNITS
(ASK) (S) ✈ 🍽 (&M) 🍷 📹 🖥 / ✕ 🔒 🖥 /

(See map and index starting on p. 243)

──────── **WHERE TO DINE** ────────

ADAM'S STEAK AND SEAFOOD RESTAURANT **Dinner:** $12-$25 **Phone:** 716/683-3784 54
Steak & Seafood
Location: Just e of jct Union Rd. 204 Como Park Blvd 14227. **Hours:** 3 pm-10 pm, Fri & Sat-11 pm. Closed: 12/25. **Reservations:** accepted. **Features:** Serving delicious steak and seafood since 1959, the restaurant keeps diners coming back because of its friendly service and the quality ingredients in its food. Among specialties are prime rib dinners, steak Lauren, baked salmon Oscar and chicken and rib combinations. Casual dress; cocktails. **Parking:** on-site. **Cards:** AX, DC, MC, VI.

ALTON'S RESTAURANT **Lunch:** $5-$6 **Dinner:** $8-$12 **Phone:** 716/681-7055 53
American
Location: I-90, exit 52, jct Union Rd. 2250 Walden Ave 14225. **Hours:** 24 hours. Closed major holidays; also Sun 11 pm-6 am. **Features:** Since 1982, the restaurant has offered fast, friendly service and breakfast made all day. Greek specialties such as souvlaki and gyros—as well as steaks, seafood, burgers, beef on weck, chicken wings, large salads and hearty sandwiches—are served in generous portions. The dessert selection is varied. Casual dress; beer & wine only. **Parking:** on-site. **Cards:** AX, DS, MC, VI.

DANNY'S **Lunch:** $5-$7 **Dinner:** $8-$10 **Phone:** 716/634-1780 51
American
Location: I-90, exit 52, just w. 3715 Genesee St 14225. **Hours:** 11 am-11 pm, Fri & Sat-midnight, Sun noon-8 pm. Closed: 12/25; also Sun before Memorial Day & Labor Day. **Reservations:** accepted. **Features:** Prompt service and an abundant salad bar with five breads and two homemade soups make the airport-area restaurant a popular choice. Casual dress; cocktails. **Parking:** on-site. **Cards:** AX, DC, MC, VI.

HOLIDAY SHOWCASE RESTAURANT **Lunch:** $4-$8 **Dinner:** $6-$11 **Phone:** 716/684-3382 52
American
Location: I-90, exit 52 westbound, Galleria Dr to Union Rd; exit eastbound, just n. 3765 Union Rd (SR 277) 14225. **Hours:** 7 am-11 pm. Closed: 12/25. **Features:** The classic all-American diner prepares American food. The dining room has an interesting appeal. Casual dress; beer & wine only. **Parking:** on-site. **Cards:** AX, DS, MC, VI.

OLYMPIC FAMILY RESTAURANT **Lunch:** $3-$9 **Dinner:** $3-$9 **Phone:** 716/839-4022 50
Greek
Location: Jct SR 78, 1 mi w on SR 33. 4611 Genesee St 14225. **Hours:** 7 am-midnight. Closed: 12/25. **Features:** Near the airport, the casual restaurant presents a menu of Greek and American fare. The friendly staff serves good food fast. Casual dress; beer & wine only. **Parking:** on-site. **Cards:** AX, DS, MC, VI.

CLARENCE pop. 26,123 (See map and index starting on p. 243)

──────── **WHERE TO STAY** ────────

ASA RANSOM HOUSE **Phone:** (716)759-2315
Historic Country Inn
All Year [BP] **1P:** $89-$145 **2P:** $105-$175 **XP:** $20 F10
Location: Jct SR 78 (Transit Rd), 5.3 mi e on SR 5 (Main St). 10529 Main St 14031. **Fax:** 716/759-2791. **Facility:** Built in 1853, this property maintains its Colonial feel with finely furnished suites, a community library and picturesque gardens with a waterfall. Smoke free premises. 9 units. 7 one-bedroom standard units. 2 one-bedroom suites, some with whirlpools. 2 stories (no elevator), interior corridors. **Parking:** on-site. **Terms:** 7 day cancellation notice, [MAP] meal plan available, package plans, 10% service charge, pets ($50 deposit, in designated units). **Amenities:** irons, hair dryers. Some: CD players. **Dining:** restaurant, see separate listing. **Leisure Activities:** pool privileges, bicycle trails, hiking trails. **Guest Services:** gift shop, wireless Internet. **Business Services:** meeting rooms. **Cards:** DS, MC, VI. **Free Special Amenities:** full breakfast and room upgrade (subject to availability with advance reservations).

SOME UNITS

──────── **WHERE TO DINE** ────────

ASA RANSOM HOUSE DINING ROOM *Menu on AAA.com* **Lunch:** $9-$15 **Dinner:** $12-$34 **Phone:** 716/759-2315
American
Location: Jct SR 78 (Transit Rd), 5.3 mi e on SR 5 (Main St); in Asa Ransom House. 10529 Main St 14031. **Hours:** Open 5/1-1/31 & 2/10-4/30; 4 pm-8 pm, Wed also 11:30 am-2 pm, Fri & Sat 5:30 pm-7:30 pm; limited seating. Closed: 12/25; also Mon. **Reservations:** suggested. **Features:** Intimate dining at the 1853 inn, with seating fireside or on the veranda, pleases all the senses in any season. Chef Robb Perrott prepares country cuisine with a gourmet flair. Seasonal vegetables and fruits lay the basis for inspiring dishes that change seasonally. The devoted local following gives raves to savory dishes such as raspberry mint rack of lamb, corn-crusted catfish or Riesling salmon with asparagus sabayon. The dessert tray can't be missed if only to admire the baker's work of art. Dressy casual; cocktails. **Parking:** on-site. **Cards:** DS, MC, VI. **Country Inn**

HIRSCH'S RESTAURANT **Lunch:** $6-$9 **Dinner:** $16-$27 **Phone:** 716/634-7148 19
American
Location: Jct Transit Rd (SR 78), 0.6 mi e. 8445 Main St 14221. **Hours:** 11 am-10 pm, Sat-11 pm, Sun 3 pm-10 pm. Closed: 12/25. **Reservations:** accepted. **Features:** A local favorite for more than 30 years, the family-owned restaurant is known for its huge baked potatoes, Black Angus beef steaks, generous portions and friendly service. All desserts are made on the premises. Casual dress; cocktails. **Parking:** on-site. **Cards:** AX, DC, DS, MC, VI.

OLD RED MILL INN **Lunch:** $7-$8 **Dinner:** $9-$25 **Phone:** 716/633-7878 18
American
Location: Jct SR 78 (Transit Rd), 0.5 mi e on SR 5 (Main St). 8326 Main St 14221. **Hours:** 11:30 am-3:30 & 4-9 pm, Fri & Sat-10 pm, Sun 10 am-2 & 3-9 pm. Closed: 1/1, 12/25. **Reservations:** suggested. **Features:** Built in 1858, the bright-red grist mill is appointed in a rustic theme with antique farm tools and railroad motifs prevailing. Meat and seafood selections show subtle, International influences. Warm apple pie is just one great choice from an array of fresh desserts. Casual dress; cocktails. **Parking:** on-site. **Cards:** AX, DC, DS, MC, VI.

(See map and index starting on p. 243)

ORAZIO'S RESTAURANT

▼▼▼ ▼▼▼
Italian

Lunch: $6-$8   **Dinner:** $10-$23   **Phone:** 716/759-8888
Location: Jct SR 78 (Transit Rd), 3 mi e on SR 5 (Main St). 9415 Main St 14031. **Hours:** 11 am-11 pm, Sat from 4 pm, Sun noon-9 pm. Closed: 12/25; also Tues. **Reservations:** accepted. **Features:** Italian dishes, such as the award-winning pasta con vodka, and other traditional specialties—including steaks, chops and seafood—make the casual restaurant a popular gathering place for hungry diners. The friendly staff serves generous portions. Casual dress; cocktails. **Parking:** on-site. **Cards:** AX, DS, MC, VI.   ⛄

DEPEW pop. 16,629 (See map and index starting on p. 243)

——— WHERE TO DINE ———

EL-CANELO

▼▼▼
Mexican

Lunch: $4-$6   **Dinner:** $6-$11   **Phone:** 716/897-1195   58
Location: On SR 78 (Transit Rd), just n of French Rd. 6036 Transit Rd 14043. **Hours:** 11 am-10 pm, Fri & Sat-10:30 pm. **Features:** Enjoy authentic Mexican fare served your way, either mild or hot. Generous platters and combination dinners satisfy the hungriest diners. Children's plates are also available. Casual dress; cocktails. **Parking:** on-site. **Cards:** AX, DS, MC, VI.

SALVATORE'S ITALIAN GARDENS   *Menu on AAA.com*   **Dinner:** $19-$45   **Phone:** 716/683-7990   57

ⓐⓐⓐ
▼▼▼ ▼▼▼
American

Location: Jct SR 33, just s on SR 78 (Transit Rd). 6461 Transit Rd 14043. **Hours:** 5 pm-10 pm, Fri & Sat-11 pm, Sun 4 pm-9 pm. Closed major holidays; also 12/24. **Reservations:** suggested. **Features:** Diners can step into another world, where crystal chandeliers, etched glass, classic sculptures, Remington bronzes and marble define elegant, elaborate, Italian-style architecture. The attentive, pampering wait staff serves rack of lamb, Chateaubriand, shrimp scampi, veal steak and prime rib, as well as pasta favorites. This truly is a place for special occasions, where everything is overdone except the food. Dressy casual; cocktails.
Parking: on-site. **Cards:** AX, CB, DS, MC, VI.   ⛄

EAST AURORA pop. 6,673

——— WHERE TO STAY ———

HAMPTON INN EAST AURORA & OAKWOOD EVENT CENTER   *Book great rates at AAA.com*   **Phone:** (716)655-3300

ⓐⓐⓐ ⓢⓐⓥⓔ
▼▼▼ ▼▼▼
Small-scale Hotel

All Year [ECP]	1P: $99-$139	2P: $109-$149	XP: $10 F

Location: Just s of Main St on SR 16. 49 Olean St 14052. **Fax:** 716/655-4740. **Facility:** 80 units. 64 one-bedroom standard units. 16 one-bedroom suites, some with whirlpools. 4 stories, interior corridors. *Bath:* combo or shower only. **Parking:** on-site. **Amenities:** video games (fee), high-speed Internet, dual phone lines, voice mail, irons, hair dryers. **Pool(s):** heated indoor. **Leisure Activities:** whirlpool, exercise room. *Fee:* game room. **Guest Services:** sundries, valet and coin laundry, wireless Internet. **Business Services:** conference facilities, business center. **Cards:** AX, DC, DS, MC, VI. **Free Special Amenities:** full breakfast and local telephone calls.
SOME UNITS

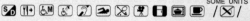

THE ROYCROFT INN   *Book at AAA.com*   **Phone:** 716/652-5552

▼▼▼ ▼▼▼
Historic
Country Inn

Property failed to provide current rates
Location: Off Main St, just s; downtown. Located adjacent to The Roycroft Colony Buildings. 40 S Grove St 14052. **Fax:** 716/655-5345. **Facility:** This 1905 mansion features original and reproduction furniture and fixtures from the arts and crafts movement. Smoke free premises. 29 one-bedroom standard units, some with whirlpools. 2-3 stories (no elevator), interior corridors. *Bath:* combo or shower only. **Parking:** on-site. **Terms:** check-in 4 pm. **Amenities:** voice mail, irons, hair dryers. **Dining:** restaurant, see separate listing. **Guest Services:** valet laundry, wireless Internet. **Business Services:** meeting rooms.
SOME UNITS

🍴 📶 ✕ VCR 🎦 / 🖥 🖨 /

——— WHERE TO DINE ———

OLD ORCHARD INN

▼▼▼ ▼▼
American

Lunch: $8-$14   **Dinner:** $14-$25   **Phone:** 716/652-4664
Location: Jct US 20A, 2.4 mi s on Old SR 16, under SR 400 to Blakeley Rd, then 0.4 mi w, follow signs. 2095 Blakeley Rd 14052. **Hours:** 11:30 am-2:30 & 4-9 pm, Sat-10 pm, Sun noon-8 pm. Closed: 12/25; also Mon. **Reservations:** suggested. **Features:** On manicured grounds overlooking a lake, the restored lodge has a convivial, rustic appeal. Homemade rolls and desserts—particularly the luscious lemon angel—make mouths water. In season, terrace seating is a nice alternative to the dining room. Dressy casual; cocktails. **Parking:** on-site. **Cards:** AX, DS, MC, VI. **Historic**

THE ROYCROFT INN DINING ROOM

▼▼▼ ▼▼▼
American

Lunch: $7-$13   **Dinner:** $12-$32   **Phone:** 716/652-5552
Location: Off Main St, just w; downtown; in The Roycroft Inn. 40 S Grove St 14052. **Hours:** 11:30 am-3 & 5-9 pm, Fri & Sat-10 pm, Sun 4:30 pm-9 pm. **Reservations:** suggested. **Features:** Reflections of the arts and crafts movement—including pictures dating back to the inn's 1900s origin—are evident in the cozy dining room. The restaurant is known for its fresh sunflower seed bread, lamb chops with mustard demi-glace and spectacularly displayed desserts made with the freshest seasonal fruits. Dressy casual; cocktails. **Parking:** on-site. **Cards:** AX, DC, DS, MC, VI. **Historic**
⛄

GRAND ISLAND pop. 18,621 (See map and index starting on p. 243)

——— WHERE TO STAY ———

BUDGET MOTEL   **Phone:** (716)773-3902   18

ⓐⓐⓐ ⓢⓐⓥⓔ
▼▼▼
Motel

5/1-8/31	1P: $49-$55	2P: $59-$89
9/1-12/31	1P: $45-$52	2P: $55-$69
1/1-4/30	1P: $39-$45	2P: $42-$49

Location: I-190, exit 20 northbound, 2 mi se on SR 324; exit 20B southbound, just e on SR 324. 3080 Grand Island Blvd 14072. **Fax:** 716/774-2775. **Facility:** 22 one-bedroom standard units. 2 stories (no elevator), exterior corridors. **Parking:** on-site, winter plug-ins. **Terms:** 3 day cancellation notice. **Cards:** AX, DS, MC, VI.
SOME UNITS

🖥 🖨 / ✕ 🖨 /

(See map and index starting on p. 243)

CINDERELLA MOTEL　　　　　　　　　　　　　　　　　　Phone: (716)773-2872　**19**

▼▼	5/1-10/31	1P: $52-$69	2P: $57-$75
	11/1-4/30	1P: $42-$48	2P: $46-$52

Motel　**Location:** I-190, exit 19 northbound, 1.3 mi w on SR 324; exit 20B southbound, just e on SR 324. 2797 Grand Island Blvd 14072-1210. **Facility:** 16 units. 15 one-bedroom standard units, some with whirlpools. 1 two-bedroom suite with kitchen. 1 story, exterior corridors. **Bath:** combo or shower only. **Parking:** on-site, winter plug-ins. **Terms:** 10 day cancellation notice, weekly rates available, package plans. **Guest Services:** coin laundry. **Cards:** DS, MC, VI.

SOME UNITS
(A$K) (S⊡) (⊞◦) (☎) (⊟) / (✕) (⊡) (⊡) /

HOLIDAY INN GRAND ISLAND RESORT　*Book great rates at AAA.com*　　Phone: (716)773-1111　**20**

(AAA) (SAVE)	6/24-9/6	1P: $129-$189	2P: $129-$189
	5/1-6/23	1P: $99-$159	2P: $99-$159
▼▼▼▼	9/7-10/31	1P: $109-$149	2P: $109-$149
	11/1-4/30	1P: $99-$109	2P: $99-$109

Resort
Large-scale Hotel　**Location:** I-190, exit 19, 4 mi e. 100 Whitehaven Rd 14072. Fax: 716/773-1229. **Facility:** Extensive conference facilities are featured at this activity-oriented, family-friendly riverfront resort. 261 units. 257 one-bedroom standard units. 4 one-bedroom suites ($139-$189) with whirlpools. 4-6 stories, interior corridors. **Bath:** combo or shower only. **Parking:** on-site, winter plug-ins. **Terms:** [AP], [BP] & [CP] meal plans available, package plans, pets ($25 extra charge, in designated units). **Amenities:** dual phone lines, voice mail, irons, hair dryers. **Dining:** 7 am-2 & 6-10 pm; hours vary off season, cocktails. **Pool(s):** heated indoor, heated outdoor, wading, lap. **Leisure Activities:** sauna, whirlpool, boat dock, fishing, Grand Lady boat cruises, 2 tennis courts. *Fee:* golf-18 holes, massage. **Guest Services:** sundries, coin laundry, wireless Internet. **Business Services:** conference facilities. **Cards:** AX, DC, DS, MC, VI. **Free Special Amenities:** newspaper and high-speed Internet.

SOME UNITS
(S⊡) (⊟) (⊞) (Y) (⊡) (⊘) (⊃) (⊞) (✕) (⊡) / (✕) (VCR) (⊟) (⊡) /
　　FEE　　　　　　　　　　　　　　　　　　　　　　　　FEE　FEE　FEE

──────── **WHERE TO DINE** ────────

JALAPENO LOCO　　　**Lunch:** $5-$8　　　**Dinner:** $8-$15　　　Phone: 716/773-8748　**33**

▼▼　**Location:** I-190, exit 19 northbound, 1.3 mi w on SR 324; exit 20B southbound, just e on SR 324. 2800 Grand Island Blvd 14072. **Hours:** 11 am-9:30 pm, Thurs-10 pm, Sat noon-10 pm, Sun noon-8:30 pm. Closed major holidays. **Features:** The jazzy Mexican joint invites guests to unwind in the dining room or grab their food for takeout. The full menu is loaded with favorites prepared from fresh ingredients and served in a jiffy. Casual dress. **Parking:** on-site. **Cards:** AX, DS, MC, VI.

Mexican

HAMBURG pop. 10,116

──────── **WHERE TO STAY** ────────

COMFORT INN & SUITES　*Book great rates at AAA.com*　　　　　Phone: (716)648-2922

(AAA) (SAVE)	5/1-9/8	1P: $89-$179	2P: $89-$179	XP: $10	F
	9/9-11/30	1P: $64-$159	2P: $64-$159	XP: $10	F
▼▼▼	4/1-4/30	1P: $69-$139	2P: $69-$139	XP: $10	F
	12/1-3/31	1P: $59-$129	2P: $59-$129	XP: $10	F

Small-scale Hotel　**Location:** I-90, exit 57, just w. 3615 Commerce Pl 14075. Fax: 716/648-2904. **Facility:** 61 one-bedroom standard units, some with efficiencies (no utensils) and/or whirlpools. 2 stories (no elevator), interior corridors. **Bath:** combo or shower only. **Parking:** on-site. **Terms:** cancellation fee imposed, pets ($10 extra charge). **Amenities:** voice mail, safes (fee), irons, hair dryers. **Pool(s):** heated indoor. **Leisure Activities:** exercise room. **Guest Services:** valet laundry, wireless Internet. **Business Services:** meeting rooms, PC. **Cards:** AX, DC, DS, JC, MC, VI. **Free Special Amenities:** expanded continental breakfast and high-speed Internet.

SOME UNITS
(S⊡) (⊟) (⊧M) (⊡) (⊃) (⊞) (⊡) / (✕) (⊟) (⊡) /
　　FEE

HOLIDAY INN HAMBURG　*Book great rates at AAA.com*　　　　　Phone: (716)649-0500

(AAA) (SAVE)	All Year	1P: $69-$189	2P: $69-$189

▼▼ ▼▼　**Location:** I-90, exit 57, 0.3 mi se on SR 75. 5440 Camp Rd 14075. Fax: 716/648-2278. **Facility:** 130 units. 128 one-bedroom standard units. 2 one-bedroom suites ($79-$199). 2 stories (no elevator), interior corridors. **Bath:** combo or shower only. **Parking:** on-site. **Terms:** check-in 4 pm, package plans, small pets only ($10 extra charge). **Amenities:** voice mail, irons, hair dryers. **Dining:** 6:30 am-2 & 5-9 pm, Sat-10 pm, Sun-2 pm, cocktails. **Pool(s):** heated outdoor. **Leisure Activities:** exercise room. **Guest Services:** valet and coin laundry, wireless Internet. **Business Services:** meeting rooms, PC. **Cards:** AX, DC, DS, MC, VI.

Small-scale Hotel

SOME UNITS
(S⊡) (⊟) (⊞) (Y) (⊡) (⊃) (⊞) (⊡) / (✕) (VCR) (⊟) (⊡) /
　　FEE　　　　　　　　　　　　　　　　　　　　FEE　FEE　FEE

RED ROOF INN #7055　*Book at AAA.com*　　　　　　　　　　Phone: (716)648-7222

▼▼ ▼▼	6/15-9/9	1P: $58-$93	2P: $64-$99	XP: $6	F18
	9/10-10/28	1P: $54-$93	2P: $60-$99	XP: $6	F18
Motel	5/1-6/14	1P: $49-$88	2P: $55-$94	XP: $6	F18
	10/29-4/30	1P: $44-$75	2P: $50-$81	XP: $6	F18

Location: I-90, exit 57, just se on SR 75. 5370 Camp Rd 14075. Fax: 716/648-7324. **Facility:** 108 one-bedroom standard units. 2 stories (no elevator), exterior corridors. **Parking:** on-site. **Terms:** small pets only. **Amenities:** voice mail. **Guest Services:** wireless Internet. **Cards:** AX, CB, DC, DS, MC, VI.

SOME UNITS
(⊟) (⊞◦) (⊘) (⊞) / (✕) (⊟) (⊡) /
　　　　　　　　　　　　FEE

TALLYHO-TEL　　　　　　　　　　　　　　　　　　　Phone: 716/648-2000

(AAA) (SAVE)	All Year	1P: $50-$125	2P: $50-$125	XP: $7　F18

▼▼ ▼▼　**Location:** I-90, exit 57, just nw on SR 75. 5245 Camp Rd 14075. Fax: 716/648-9718. **Facility:** 117 one-bedroom standard units, some with efficiencies. 1 story, exterior corridors. **Parking:** on-site. **Terms:** check-in 4 pm, weekly rates available, pets ($15 fee). **Pool(s):** outdoor. **Guest Services:** coin laundry. **Cards:** AX, DS, MC, VI.

Motel

SOME UNITS
(⊟) (⊃) (⊞) / (✕) (⊟) (⊡) /
　　FEE

——— WHERE TO DINE ———

COYOTE CAFE INC

Mexican

Lunch: $4-$6   Dinner: $8-$15   Phone: 716/649-1837

Location: Center. 36 Main St 14075. **Hours:** 11 am-9 pm, Fri & Sat-10 pm. Closed major holidays; also Sun. **Reservations:** accepted. **Features:** The cozy little Mexican cafe's friendly staff serves traditional favorites. Spicy or not, the varied dishes include something for everyone. Casual dress; cocktails. **Parking:** on-site and street. **Cards:** AX, DC, DS, MC, VI.

DANIEL'S

American

Dinner: $18-$30   Phone: 716/648-6554

Location: On US 62; across from Hamburg Village Plaza. 174 Buffalo St 14075. **Hours:** 5 pm-9 pm, Sat-9:30 pm. Closed major holidays; also Sun & Mon. **Reservations:** suggested. **Features:** Rich sauces and many wines complement lavish dishes of fresh seafood, meat and pasta. The former house is cozy and inviting, with piped-in classical music. The experience is understated, elegant and intimate. Dressy casual; cocktails. **Parking:** on-site. **Cards:** AX, MC, VI.

NEW MANCHURIAN HOUSE

Chinese

Lunch: $4-$9   Dinner: $4-$12   Phone: 716/648-7173

Location: I-90, exit 57, 2 mi s on SR 75; jct US 62. 16 Pierce Ave 14075. **Hours:** 11 am-10 pm, Fri & Sat-11 pm, Sun noon-10 pm. Closed: 11/22. **Reservations:** accepted. **Features:** Extensive selections of freshly-made dishes are made to order for the dining room or to go. The staff is friendly and polite. Casual dress. **Parking:** on-site. **Cards:** AX, DS, MC, VI.

ROMANELLO'S SOUTH

Italian

Dinner: $19-$39   Phone: 716/649-0450

Location: Jct US 20 and 62, 1.7 mi s. 5793 S Park Ave 14075. **Hours:** 4 pm-9 pm, Fri & Sat-10 pm, Sun 3 pm-9 pm. Closed major holidays. **Reservations:** accepted. **Features:** A sophisticated, yet casually friendly, presence is accented by a fireplace set in brick. Bookcases and a variety of plants complete the setting. The competent wait staff serves nicely presented Italian/American cuisine. Dressy casual; cocktails. **Parking:** on-site. **Cards:** AX, DS, MC, VI.

KENMORE pop. 16,426 (See map and index starting on p. 243)

——— WHERE TO STAY ———

SUPER 8-BUFFALO/NIAGARA FALLS   *Book at AAA.com*   Phone: (716)876-4020   **40**

Small-scale Hotel

6/1-9/1 [CP]	1P: $65-$73	2P: $73-$84
9/2-10/31 [CP]	1P: $55-$65	2P: $63-$70
5/1-5/31 [CP]	1P: $52-$57	2P: $60-$67
11/1-4/30 [CP]	1P: $42-$45	2P: $53-$56

Location: I-190, exit 15, 1.5 mi e on SR 324 (Sheridan Dr). 1288 Sheridan Dr 14217. Fax: 716/876-4729. **Facility:** 59 one-bedroom standard units. 2 stories (no elevator), interior corridors. **Parking:** on-site, winter plug-ins. **Amenities:** dual phone lines, voice mail, hair dryers. **Cards:** AX, DS, MC, VI.

SOME UNITS

——— WHERE TO DINE ———

TSUNAMI

Nouvelle Pacific Rim

Dinner: $15-$29   Phone: 716/447-7915   **47**

Location: Just w of Colvin Ave. 1141 Kenmore Ave 14217. **Hours:** 5 pm-10 pm, Fri & Sat-10 pm. Closed: Sun. **Reservations:** suggested. **Features:** Fresh and distinctive seafood, vegetables and meats, such as Kobe beef, are prepared at the culinary oasis for Pacific Rim cuisine. Complex ingredients and imagination come together in artistic presentations with varied colors and textures. The staff is knowledgeable and helpful with all courses. Casual dress; cocktails. **Parking:** on-site. **Cards:** AX, DC, DS, MC, VI.

SPRINGVILLE pop. 4,252

——— WHERE TO STAY ———

MICROTEL INN & SUITES   *Book at AAA.com*   Phone: (716)592-3141

Small-scale Hotel

All Year [CP]   1P: $54-$94   2P: $54-$94   XP: $5   F16

Location: On SR 219 S. Located in the business district. 270 S Cascade Dr 14141. Fax: 716/592-2565. **Facility:** 60 one-bedroom standard units. 2 stories, interior corridors. *Bath:* combo or shower only. **Parking:** on-site. **Terms:** pets ($10 extra charge). **Amenities:** voice mail. *Some:* hair dryers. **Guest Services:** wireless Internet. **Business Services:** meeting rooms. **Cards:** AX, DC, DS, MC, VI.

SOME UNITS

——— WHERE TO DINE ———

APPLE DUMPLIN'

American

Lunch: $4-$6   Dinner: $7-$13   Phone: 716/592-0171

Location: Jct SR 219 and 39, 0.8 mi s on SR 219. 521 S Cascade Dr (SR 219) 14141. **Hours:** 7 am-4 pm, Sun from 8 am. Closed: 1/1, 11/22, 12/25; also Mon. **Reservations:** accepted. **Features:** Cozy cottage decor contributes to the perfect setting for home-style comfort food. Slow-roasted turkey, St. Louis-style ribs, buffalo burgers and an old-fashioned fish fry top the list of popular choices. Breakfast favorites include cinnamon apple and buckwheat pancakes served with maple syrup made at a local farm. Casual dress; beer & wine only. **Parking:** on-site.

TONAWANDA pop. 61,729 (See map and index starting on p. 243)

──────── WHERE TO STAY ────────

ECONO LODGE   *Book great rates at AAA.com*   **Phone:** (716)694-6696   **23**

5/1-9/10	1P: $69-$169	2P: $74-$179	XP: $10
9/11-11/30	1P: $59-$100	2P: $59-$110	XP: $10
3/1-4/30	1P: $55-$89	2P: $55-$89	XP: $10
12/1-2/29	1P: $49-$69	2P: $49-$79	XP: $10

Motel   **Location:** I-290, exit 3 (Niagara Falls Blvd), 0.5 mi n on US 62. 2000 Niagara Falls Blvd 14150. Fax: 716/694-0371. **Facility:** 31 one-bedroom standard units, some with whirlpools. 1 story, exterior corridors. **Parking:** on-site. **Terms:** pets ($10 extra charge). **Amenities:** voice mail, hair dryers. **Cards:** AX, DC, DS, MC, VI.

SOME UNITS

MICROTEL-TONAWANDA   *Book at AAA.com*   **Phone:** (716)693-8100   **24**

6/1-9/4	1P: $54-$90	2P: $54-$90	XP: $5 F16
5/1-5/31	1P: $52-$63	2P: $52-$63	XP: $5 F16
9/5-10/31	1P: $54-$60	2P: $54-$60	XP: $5 F16
11/1-4/30	1P: $46	2P: $46	XP: $5 F16

Small-scale Hotel   **Location:** I-290, exit 1B westbound; exit 1 eastbound, 0.5 mi e on Crestmount Ave, then just n on SR 384 (Delaware St). 1 Hospitality Centre Way 14150. Fax: 716/693-8750. **Facility:** 100 one-bedroom standard units. 2 stories (no elevator), interior corridors. **Parking:** on-site. **Terms:** $1 service charge, pets ($10 fee). **Amenities:** high-speed Internet, safes (fee). **Guest Services:** wireless Internet. **Cards:** AX, DC, DS, MC, VI.

SOME UNITS

WEST SENECA pop. 45,943 (See map and index starting on p. 243)

──────── WHERE TO STAY ────────

HAMPTON INN BUFFALO-SOUTH/I-90   *Book great rates at AAA.com*   **Phone:** (716)824-2030   **61**

All Year [CP]	1P: $79-$179	2P: $89-$189

Location: I-90, exit 55 (Ridge Rd E), just n. 1750 Ridge Rd 14224. Fax: 716/332-1200. **Facility:** 106 units. 101 one-bedroom standard units. 5 one-bedroom suites, some with whirlpools. 5 stories, interior corridors. *Bath:* Small-scale Hotel   combo or shower only. **Parking:** on-site. **Terms:** package plans. **Amenities:** video games (fee), high-speed Internet, dual phone lines, voice mail, irons, hair dryers. **Pool(s):** small heated indoor. **Leisure Activities:** whirlpool, exercise room. **Guest Services:** valet laundry, wireless Internet. **Business Services:** meeting rooms. **Cards:** AX, CB, DC, DS, JC, MC, VI.

SOME UNITS

WILLIAMSVILLE pop. 5,573 (See map and index starting on p. 243)

──────── WHERE TO STAY ────────

CLARION HOTEL-BUFFALO AIRPORT   *Book great rates at AAA.com*   **Phone:** (716)634-7500   **13**

5/1-9/30	1P: $90-$160	2P: $90-$160	XP: $10 F18
10/1-4/30	1P: $80-$110	2P: $80-$110	XP: $10 F18

Location: I-90, exit 49 (SR 78), 0.3 mi n. 6700 Transit Rd 14221. Fax: 716/634-7502. **Facility:** 80 one-bedroom standard units. 2 stories (no elevator), interior corridors. **Parking:** on-site. **Terms:** cancellation fee imposed, Small-scale Hotel   package plans. **Amenities:** high-speed Internet, dual phone lines, voice mail, irons, hair dryers. *Some:* DVD players. **Pool(s):** heated indoor. **Leisure Activities:** whirlpool, exercise room. **Guest Services:** complimentary evening beverages: Mon-Thurs, valet and coin laundry, area transportation-within 5 mi, wireless Internet. **Business Services:** meeting rooms, business center. **Cards:** AX, CB, DC, DS, MC, VI. **Free Special Amenities:** expanded continental breakfast and high-speed Internet. *(See color ad p 248)*

SOME UNITS

FAIRFIELD INN-LANCASTER   **Phone:** (716)626-1500   **14**

5/25-9/1	1P: $99-$139
5/1-5/24 & 9/2-4/30	1P: $79-$119

Small-scale Hotel   **Location:** I-90, exit 49 (SR 78), just e. 52 Freeman Rd 14221. Fax: 716/626-1500. **Facility:** Smoke free premises. 130 one-bedroom standard units. 3 stories, interior/exterior corridors. **Parking:** on-site. **Terms:** cancellation fee imposed. **Amenities:** voice mail, irons, hair dryers. **Pool(s):** heated outdoor. **Guest Services:** valet laundry. **Cards:** AX, CB, DC, DS, JC, MC, VI.

SOME UNITS

GARDEN PLACE HOTEL   *Book at AAA.com*   **Phone:** 716/635-9000   **15**

All Year [ECP]	1P: $89-$279	2P: $89-$279	XP: $20

Location: I-90, exit 49, just e. 6615 Transit Rd 14221. Fax: 716/635-9098. **Facility:** 166 units. 151 one-bedroom Small-scale Hotel   standard units, some with whirlpools. 15 one-bedroom suites with whirlpools. 3 stories, interior corridors. *Bath:* combo or shower only. **Parking:** on-site. **Terms:** package plans. **Amenities:** DVD players, CD players, dual phone lines, voice mail, honor bars, irons, hair dryers. **Dining:** restaurant, see separate listing. **Leisure Activities:** sauna, exercise room. *Fee:* massage. **Guest Services:** valet and coin laundry, area transportation, wireless Internet. **Business Services:** meeting rooms, PC. **Cards:** AX, DC, DS, MC, VI.

SOME UNITS

(See map and index starting on p. 243)

HAMPTON INN AT WILLIAMSVILLE   *Book great rates at AAA.com*   **Phone: (716)632-0900**   🄬

All Year   1P: $129-$209   2P: $139-$209

Small-scale Hotel   **Location:** I-290, exit 7B, 0.7 mi e on SR 5 (Main St). 5455 Main St 14221. Fax: 716/632-1300. **Facility:** 80 units. 76 one-bedroom standard units, some with whirlpools. 4 one-bedroom suites ($189-$209) with whirlpools. 4 stories, interior corridors. *Bath:* combo or shower only. **Parking:** on-site. **Terms:** cancellation fee imposed, package plans. **Amenities:** video games (fee), high-speed Internet, dual phone lines, voice mail, irons, hair dryers. **Pool(s):** heated indoor. **Leisure Activities:** whirlpool, exercise room. **Guest Services:** valet and coin laundry, area transportation, wireless Internet. **Business Services:** meeting rooms, PC. **Cards:** AX, DC, DS, JC, MC, VI.

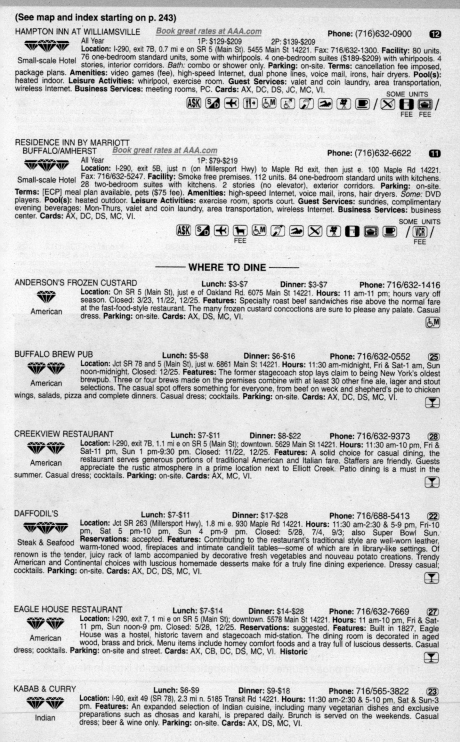

RESIDENCE INN BY MARRIOTT
BUFFALO/AMHERST   *Book great rates at AAA.com*   **Phone: (716)632-6622**   🄫

All Year   1P: $79-$219

Small-scale Hotel   **Location:** I-290, exit 5B, just n (on Millersport Hwy) to Maple Rd exit, then just e. 100 Maple Rd 14221. Fax: 716/632-5247. **Facility:** Smoke free premises. 112 units. 84 one-bedroom standard units with kitchens. 28 two-bedroom suites with kitchens. 2 stories (no elevator), exterior corridors. **Parking:** on-site. **Terms:** [ECP] meal plan available, pets ($75 fee). **Amenities:** high-speed Internet, voice mail, irons, hair dryers. *Some:* DVD players. **Pool(s):** heated outdoor. **Leisure Activities:** exercise room, sports court. **Guest Services:** sundries, complimentary evening beverages: Mon-Thurs, valet and coin laundry, area transportation, wireless Internet. **Business Services:** business center. **Cards:** AX, DC, DS, MC, VI.

—— WHERE TO DINE ——

ANDERSON'S FROZEN CUSTARD   **Lunch:** $3-$7   **Dinner:** $3-$7   **Phone:** 716/632-1416

American   **Location:** On SR 5 (Main St), just e of Oakland Rd. 6075 Main St 14221. **Hours:** 11 am-11 pm; hours vary off season. Closed: 3/23, 11/22, 12/25. **Features:** Specialty roast beef sandwiches rise above the normal fare at the fast-food-style restaurant. The many frozen custard concoctions are sure to please any palate. Casual dress. **Parking:** on-site. **Cards:** AX, DS, MC, VI.

BUFFALO BREW PUB   **Lunch:** $5-$8   **Dinner:** $6-$16   **Phone:** 716/632-0552   🄴

American   **Location:** Jct SR 78 and 5 (Main St), just w. 6861 Main St 14221. **Hours:** 11:30 am-midnight, Fri & Sat-1 am, Sun noon-midnight. Closed: 12/25. **Features:** The former stagecoach stop lays claim to being New York's oldest brewpub. Three or four brews made on the premises combine with at least 30 other fine ale, lager and stout selections. The casual spot offers something for everyone, from beef on weck and shepherd's pie to chicken wings, salads, pizza and complete dinners. Casual dress; cocktails. **Parking:** on-site. **Cards:** AX, DC, DS, MC, VI.

CREEKVIEW RESTAURANT   **Lunch:** $7-$11   **Dinner:** $8-$22   **Phone:** 716/632-9373   🄸

American   **Location:** I-290, exit 7B, 1.1 mi e on SR 5 (Main St); downtown. 5629 Main St 14221. **Hours:** 11:30 am-10 pm, Fri & Sat-11 pm, Sun 1 pm-9:30 pm. Closed: 11/22, 12/25. **Features:** A solid choice for casual dining, the restaurant serves generous portions of traditional American and Italian fare. Staffers are friendly. Guests appreciate the rustic atmosphere in a prime location next to Elliott Creek. Patio dining is a must in the summer. Casual dress; cocktails. **Parking:** on-site. **Cards:** AX, MC, VI.

DAFFODIL'S   **Lunch:** $7-$11   **Dinner:** $17-$28   **Phone:** 716/688-5413   🄢

Steak & Seafood   **Location:** Jct SR 263 (Millersport Hwy), 1.8 mi e. 930 Maple Rd 14221. **Hours:** 11:30 am-2:30 & 5-9 pm, Fri-10 pm, Sat 5 pm-10 pm, Sun 4 pm-9 pm. Closed: 5/28, 7/4, 9/3; also Super Bowl Sun. **Reservations:** accepted. **Features:** Contributing to the restaurant's traditional style are well-worn leather, warm-toned wood, fireplaces and intimate candlelit tables—some of which are in library-like settings. Of renown is the tender, juicy rack of lamb accompanied by decorative fresh vegetables and nouveau potato creations. Trendy American and Continental choices with luscious homemade desserts make for a truly fine dining experience. Dressy casual; cocktails. **Parking:** on-site. **Cards:** AX, DC, DS, MC, VI.

EAGLE HOUSE RESTAURANT   **Lunch:** $7-$14   **Dinner:** $14-$28   **Phone:** 716/632-7669   🄧

American   **Location:** I-290, exit 7, 1 mi e on SR 5 (Main St); downtown. 5578 Main St 14221. **Hours:** 11 am-10 pm, Fri & Sat-11 pm, Sun noon-9 pm. Closed: 5/28, 12/25. **Reservations:** suggested. **Features:** Built in 1827, Eagle House was a hostel, historic tavern and stagecoach mid-station. The dining room is decorated in aged wood, brass and brick. Menu items include homey comfort foods and a tray full of luscious desserts. Casual dress; cocktails. **Parking:** on-site and street. **Cards:** AX, CB, DC, DS, MC, VI. **Historic**

KABAB & CURRY   **Lunch:** $6-$9   **Dinner:** $9-$18   **Phone:** 716/565-3822   🄣

Indian   **Location:** I-90, exit 49 (SR 78), 2.3 mi n. 5185 Transit Rd 14221. **Hours:** 11:30 am-2:30 & 5-10 pm, Sat & Sun-3 pm. **Features:** An expanded selection of Indian cuisine, including many vegetarian dishes and exclusive preparations such as dhosas and karahi, is prepared daily. Brunch is served on the weekends. Casual dress; beer & wine only. **Parking:** on-site. **Cards:** AX, DS, MC, VI.

(See map and index starting on p. 243)

MARINACCIO'S RESTAURANT   Dinner: $16-$40   Phone: 716/633-7755   26
Mediterranean
Location: I-290, exit 7B, 1.1 mi e on SR 5 (Main St). 5877 Main St 14221. **Hours:** 5 pm-close. Closed: 7/4, 12/25; also Sun. **Reservations:** suggested. **Features:** New on the scene to fine dining, the restaurant presents a seasonally changing menu that guarantees fresh preparations. Mediterranean accents punctuate sophisticated dishes. The staff is professional. Dressy casual; cocktails. **Parking:** on-site and valet.
Cards: AX, DS, MC, VI.

THE ORIGINAL PANCAKE HOUSE   Lunch: $8   Dinner: $6-$9   Phone: 716/634-5515   29
American
Location: I-290, exit 7B, 0.8 mi e on SR 5 (Main St). 5479 Main St 14221. **Hours:** 6:45 am-9 pm. Closed: 12/25.
Reservations: accepted, Mon-Fri. **Features:** Originating in 1953, the restaurant has endured due to its use of high-quality ingredients in award-winning recipes. Representative of breakfast fare are classic omelets, wonderful waffles and incredible crepes accompanied by freshly squeezed orange juice. Casual dress.
Parking: on-site. **Cards:** AX, MC, VI.

PROTOCOL   Lunch: $7-$11   Dinner: $11-$30   Phone: 716/632-9556   30
Seafood
Location: I-90, exit 49 (SR 78), 0.5 mi n. 6766 Transit Rd 14221. **Hours:** 11 am-11:30 pm. Closed major holidays; also Sun. **Reservations:** suggested. **Features:** Family-owned since 1972, the restaurant prepares fresh Boston seafood with originality. Sesame-crusted tuna is only one of the most popular dishes. Also tempting are the stuffed filet, baby back ribs, steaks and chicken Protocol. The feel is casual and friendly. Casual dress; cocktails. **Parking:** on-site. **Cards:** AX, MC, VI.

TANDOORI'S   Lunch: $8-$15   Dinner: $8-$30   Phone: 716/632-1112   24
Indian
Location: Jct Sheridan and SR 78. 7740 Transit Rd 14221. **Hours:** 11 am-2:30 & 5-10 pm, Fri & Sat 5 pm-11 pm.
Reservations: suggested, weekends. **Features:** Carefully chosen exotic spices and herbal seasonings are used to create delicious vegetarian and non-vegetarian gourmet dishes. The culinary experience is memorable. Dressy casual; cocktails. **Parking:** on-site. **Cards:** AX, CB, DC, DS, MC, VI.

Naval and Military Park / © Andre Jenny

This ends listings for the Buffalo Vicinity.
The following page resumes the alphabetical listings of cities in New York.

BURNT HILLS

———— WHERE TO DINE ————

CARNEY'S TAVERN

Irish

Lunch: $5-$7   **Dinner:** $13-$18   **Phone:** 518/399-9926

Location: Center. 17 Main St 12019. **Hours:** 11 am-9 pm, Tues-Sat to 10 pm, Sun noon-9 pm. Closed: 3/23, 11/22, 12/25. **Features:** The original tin ceiling and bar back add to the authentic feel of the mid-19th-century Colonial tavern. Traditional Irish pub fare, including the specialty Celtic steak, is at the heart of the menu. Homemade bread pudding is a mouthwatering treat. Casual dress; cocktails. **Parking:** on-site.
Cards: AX, DS, MC, VI.

CALCIUM pop. 3,346

———— WHERE TO STAY ————

MICROTEL INN WATERTOWN   *Book at AAA.com*

Small-scale Hotel

Phone: 315/629-5000

All Year   1P: $58-$64

Location: 4 mi e on SR 342; jct US 11. 8000 Virginia Smith Dr 13616. Fax: 315/629-5393. **Facility:** 100 one-bedroom standard units. 2 stories (no elevator), interior corridors. **Parking:** on-site. **Terms:** pets ($3 extra charge). **Guest Services:** valet laundry, wireless Internet. **Cards:** CB, DC, DS, MC, VI.

SOME UNITS

ASK SD 🐾 🍴 🎥 📶 🗄 / ✕ /
       FEE

CAMILLUS pop. 1,249

———— WHERE TO DINE ————

INN BETWEEN RESTAURANT

American

Dinner: $20-$30   **Phone:** 315/672-3166

Location: 2.3 mi w on SR 5; 10 mi w of Syracuse; 10 mi e of Skaneatles. 2290 W Genesee St 13031. **Hours:** 5 pm-9 pm, Fri & Sat-10 pm, Sun 2 pm-8 pm. Closed: 1/1, 12/24, 12/25; also Mon. **Reservations:** suggested. **Features:** The 19th-century Victorian manor house has a sophisticated feel, with crisp linens and elegant table settings. Beef Wellington and roast duckling are among well-prepared entrees of beef, poultry, veal and seafood. Desserts are delicately presented. Dressy casual; cocktails. **Parking:** on-site. **Cards:** AX, MC, VI.

CANANDAIGUA pop. 11,264—See also FINGER LAKES.

———— WHERE TO STAY ————

1795 ACORN INN
AAA SAVE

Historic Bed
& Breakfast

Phone: (585)229-2834

All Year [BP]   1P: $148-$260   2P: $148-$260   XP: $35

Location: From Canandaigua, SR 420 W, just s on SR 21 (becomes CR 32), 8 mi s on CR 32, then just s. 4508 SR 64 S 14424-9309. **Facility:** A former stagecoach inn dating from 1795, this Finger Lakes B&B is near many wineries and features four-poster beds and rooms with fireplaces. Check-in between 3 pm-5 pm. Smoke free premises. 4 one-bedroom standard units, some with whirlpools. 2 stories (no elevator), interior corridors. **Parking:** on-site. **Terms:** 2 night minimum stay - seasonal and/or weekends, age restrictions may apply, 14 day cancellation notice-fee imposed, package plans. **Amenities:** video library, DVD players, CD players, hair dryers. **Leisure Activities:** whirlpool. **Guest Services:** wireless Internet. **Cards:** AX, DS, MC, VI.
Free Special Amenities: full breakfast and local telephone calls.

✕ VCR ☎

1885 SUTHERLAND HOUSE

Bed & Breakfast

Phone: 585/396-0375

All Year   1P: $105-$195   2P: $105-$195   XP: $25

Location: I-90, exit 44 (Canandaigua/SR 332), s into city, 1.5 mi w on Bristol (SR 21 S). 3179 SR 21 S 14424. Fax: 585/396-9281. **Facility:** Original woodwork adds charm to this 1885 Victorian home. The hilly grounds feature gardens and a 200-year-old copper beech tree. Smoke free premises. 5 one-bedroom standard units, some with whirlpools. 2 stories (no elevator), interior corridors. **Bath:** combo or shower only. **Parking:** on-site. **Terms:** 2 night minimum stay - weekends, age restrictions may apply, 14 day cancellation notice-fee imposed, [BP] meal plan available, package plans, no pets allowed (owner's pet on premises). **Amenities:** video library, CD players, hair dryers. **Guest Services:** wireless Internet. **Cards:** AX, DS, MC, VI.

SOME UNITS

SD ✕ VCR 🐾 / ☎ /

ECONO LODGE CANANDAIGUA   *Book great rates at AAA.com*
AAA SAVE

Small-scale Hotel

Phone: (585)394-9000

5/1-9/30	1P: $79-$122	2P: $84-$127	XP: $10 F18
10/1-4/30	1P: $54-$74	2P: $59-$79	XP: $10 F18

Location: Jct SR 332, 5 and US 20, 0.5 mi e. Located next to Roseland Water Park. 170 Eastern Blvd 14424. Fax: 585/396-2560. **Facility:** 65 one-bedroom standard units. 2 stories (no elevator), interior corridors. **Parking:** on-site. **Terms:** cancellation fee imposed, package plans, pets ($10 fee). **Amenities:** voice mail, irons. *Fee:* video library, safes. *Some:* hair dryers. **Guest Services:** valet and coin laundry, wireless Internet. **Cards:** AX, CB, DC, DS, JC, MC, VI. **Free Special Amenities:** continental breakfast and high-speed Internet.

SOME UNITS

SD 🐾 🍴 🎥 / ✕ VCR 🗄 📶 📺 /
     FEE   FEE FEE FEE

THE INN ON THE LAKE   *Book great rates at AAA.com*
AAA SAVE

Small-scale Hotel

Phone: (585)394-7800

7/1-8/31	1P: $174-$344	2P: $179-$349
5/14-6/30	1P: $134-$344	2P: $139-$349
9/1-10/31	1P: $139-$324	2P: $144-$329
11/1-4/30	1P: $99-$214	2P: $104-$219

Location: I-90, exit 44 (Canandaigua/SR 332), just s across US 20 and SR 5. 770 S Main St 14424. Fax: 585/394-5003. **Facility:** Smoke free premises. 134 units. 88 one-bedroom standard units. 46 one-bedroom suites, some with whirlpools. 2 stories, interior corridors. **Bath:** combo or shower only. **Parking:** on-site. **Terms:** 30 day cancellation notice-fee imposed, [BP] meal plan available, package plans, small pets only ($5 extra charge). **Amenities:** voice mail, safes (fee), irons. *Some:* hair dryers. **Dining:** 6:30 am-10 pm, cocktails. **Pool(s):** heated outdoor, small heated indoor. **Leisure Activities:** whirlpool, boat dock, fishing, patio, exercise room. **Guest Services:** wireless Internet. **Business Services:** conference facilities. **Cards:** AX, DC, DS, MC, VI. **Free Special Amenities:** full breakfast and high-speed Internet.

SOME UNITS

SD 🐾 🍴 🍸 ⛨M ♿ 🎥 🏊 ✕ ✕ 🎥 📺 📺 / 📺 📺 /
   FEE   FEE FEE

MORGAN-SAMUELS INN

Phone: (585)394-9232

AAA [SAVE]

9/15-11/20 [BP]	1P: $149-$235	2P: $159-$295	XP: $50	F
5/25-9/14 [BP]	1P: $139-$199	2P: $139-$285	XP: $50	F
5/1-5/24 [BP]	1P: $89-$129	2P: $139-$255	XP: $50	F
11/21-4/30 [BP]	1P: $89-$129	2P: $139-$225	XP: $50	F

Bed & Breakfast **Location:** I-90, exit 43, 4.1 mi s on SR 21, just e on SR 488 to East Ave/Smith Rd, then 2 mi s. 2920 Smith Rd 14424. **Fax:** 585/394-8044. **Facility:** Mixing modern conveniences with fine antiques, this 1810 mansion sits on a 46-acre estate eminating an aura of Victorian elegance. Smoke free premises. 6 one-bedroom standard units, some with whirlpools. 3 stories (no elevator), interior/exterior corridors. *Bath:* combo or shower only. **Parking:** on-site. **Terms:** 2-3 night minimum stay - seasonal and/or weekends, age restrictions may apply, 14 day cancellation notice-fee imposed, weekly rates available, [MAP] meal plan available, 5% service charge. **Amenities:** video library, hair dryers. **Leisure Activities:** whirlpool, tennis court, bicycles, hiking trails. **Business Services:** fax (fee). **Cards:** AX, MC, VI. **Free Special Amenities: full breakfast and local telephone calls.**

SOME UNITS

🛠️ ⊠ ⊠ ☎ / 🅿 VCR 🔌 /
FEE

RED CARPET INN

Book great rates at AAA.com

Phone: (585)394-4140

AAA [SAVE]

6/1-8/31	1P: $70-$250	XP: $10	F15
5/1-5/31	1P: $60-$150	XP: $10	F15
9/1-11/30	1P: $55-$150	XP: $10	F15
12/1-4/30	1P: $40-$150	XP: $10	F15

Small-scale Hotel Location: 1 mi e of jct SR 332. 4232 Rt 5 & 20 14424. **Fax:** 585/394-5484. **Facility:** 30 units. 26 one-bedroom standard units, some with whirlpools. 4 one-bedroom suites ($90-$250) with efficiencies. 2 stories (no elevator), interior/exterior corridors. **Parking:** on-site. **Terms:** cancellation fee imposed, weekly rates available. **Amenities:** irons, hair dryers. **Business Services:** meeting rooms. **Cards:** AX, DS, MC, VI. **Free Special Amenities: continental breakfast and local telephone calls.**

SOME UNITS

🆘 / ⊠ 🔌 📷 /

SUPER 8

Book at AAA.com

Phone: 585/396-7224

All Year	1P: $60-$110	2P: $60-$110	XP: $10	F17

Location: Jct SR 332, 5 and US 20, 0.5 mi e. 4450 Eastern Blvd 14424. **Fax:** 585/396-7333. **Facility:** 50 one-bedroom standard units, some with whirlpools. 2 stories (no elevator), interior corridors. **Parking:** on-site. **Small-scale Hotel Terms:** cancellation fee imposed, pets ($10 extra charge, with prior approval). **Amenities:** *Some:* irons, hair dryers. **Guest Services:** wireless Internet. **Business Services:** meeting rooms. **Cards:** AX, DC, DS, MC, VI.

SOME UNITS

[ASK] 🆘 🛏️ 📷 / ⊠ 🔌 📷 📷 /
FEE

WHERE TO DINE

AKROPOLIS FAMILY RESTAURANT

Lunch: $4-$7 **Dinner:** $6-$10 **Phone:** 585/394-8721

American

Location: 2.7 mi e on SR 5 and US 20. 4025 Rt 5 & 20 14424. **Hours:** 6 am-9 pm, Thurs to Sat-10 pm. **Closed:** 12/25. **Reservations:** accepted. **Features:** Family-owned since 1985, the family-style restaurant serves up Greek and Italian specialties as well as steaks and seafood. There is also a fabulous famous fish fry on Friday. Casual dress; cocktails. **Parking:** on-site. **Cards:** AX, DS, MC, VI.

CASA DE PASTA

Dinner: $9-$19 **Phone:** 585/394-3710

Italian

Location: Downtown. 125 Bemis St 14424. **Hours:** 5 pm-9 pm, Fri & Sat-10 pm. **Closed:** 11/22, 12/25; also Mon. **Features:** Quality ingredients go into traditional dishes of pasta, seafood, veal and beef. An established local clientele frequents the restaurant—in a mid-19th-century house—for its friendly atmosphere. Soft lighting and background music enhance the ambience. Casual dress; cocktails. **Parking:** on-site. **Cards:** MC, VI.

⊤

KOOZINA'S RESTAURANT

Lunch: $5-$12 **Dinner:** $6-$13 **Phone:** 585/396-0360

Mediterranean

Location: Jct SR 322 and US 20, just e. 699 S Main St 14424. **Hours:** 11 am-10 pm. **Closed:** 11/22, 12/25. **Reservations:** accepted. **Features:** The eclectic bistro prepares Mediterranean cuisine, as well as pizzas made in a wood-fired oven in an open kitchen. Fresh market-priced fish and an impressive choice of pastas also add to the menu. Casual dress; cocktails. **Parking:** on-site. **Cards:** AX, DC, DS, MC, VI.

[M] ⊤

LUMBERYARD GRILLE

Lunch: $6-$11 **Dinner:** $10-$30 **Phone:** 585/393-5550

Nouvelle American

Location: Jct Coy St. 106 Bemis St 14424. **Hours:** 3 pm-10 pm. **Closed:** 12/25; also Mon. **Reservations:** accepted. **Features:** The new restaurant has transformed a historical lumberyard business from remaining structures. Cajun seasonings spice up some of the delicious preparations of steak, chops, seafood, chicken, pasta and vegetarian choices. The rustic decor is pleasant, and servers are friendly and helpful. Casual dress; cocktails. **Parking:** on-site. **Cards:** AX, MC, VI.

⊤

STEAMBOAT LANDING

Lunch: $7-$12 **Dinner:** $10-$26 **Phone:** 585/396-7350

Continental

Location: In resort area. 205 Lakeshore Dr 14424. **Hours:** 11:30 am-4 & 5-9 pm, Fri & Sat-10 pm, Sun 5 pm-9 pm; hours vary in winter. Closed major holidays; also Mon in winter. **Reservations:** accepted. **Features:** Continental cuisine is prepared and presented with flair at the lakefront restaurant. Two-story windows take advantage of the vista at every turn. Warm contemporary accents and such rustic touches as exposed beams lend to the relaxed appeal of the dining room. Casual dress; cocktails. **Parking:** on-site. **Cards:** AX, DS, MC, VI.

⊤

THENDARA INN & RESTAURANT

Dinner: $22-$32 **Phone:** 585/394-4868

American

Location: 4 mi s on SR 364. 4356 E Lake Rd 14424. **Hours:** Open 6/1-10/1; 5 pm-9 pm, Sun 4 pm-8 pm. **Closed:** 9/3, 12/25; also Sun-Thurs in winter. **Reservations:** suggested. **Features:** The handsome lakefront property offers seating in the cozy, old great room and on the enclosed porch, which looks out over the water. Carefully prepared dishes, such as chicken with prosciutto and mozzarella in a phyllo pastry, are nicely presented. Casual dress; cocktails. **Parking:** on-site. **Cards:** AX, DS, MC, VI.

⊤

CANASTOTA pop. 4,425

------- WHERE TO STAY -------

DAYS INN   *Book great rates at AAA.com*   Phone: (315)697-3309
All Year [CP]   1P: $59-$149   2P: $59-$169   XP: $10   F18
Location: I-90, exit 34 on SR 13. Across from the International Boxing Hall of Fame. 377 N Peterboro St 13032.
Small-scale Hotel   Fax: 315/697-5541. **Facility:** 60 one-bedroom standard units. 2 stories (no elevator), interior corridors.
Parking: on-site, winter plug-ins. **Terms:** 7 day cancellation notice, pets ($15 extra charge). **Amenities:** hair
dryers. *Some:* DVD players (fee). **Guest Services:** coin laundry, wireless Internet. **Business Services:** meeting rooms.
Cards: AX, CB, DC, DS, JC, MC, VI.

CANTON pop. 5,882

------- WHERE TO STAY -------

BEST WESTERN UNIVERSITY INN   *Book great rates at AAA.com*   Phone: (315)386-8522
All Year   1P: $109-$169   2P: $119-$169
Location: Jct US 11, 68 and 310, 1 mi e on US 11. 90 E Main St 13617-1452. Fax: 315/386-1025. **Facility:** 99 one-
bedroom standard units. 2-3 stories (no elevator), interior corridors. *Bath:* combo or shower only. **Parking:**
Small-scale Hotel   on-site, winter plug-ins. **Terms:** 7 day cancellation notice, package plans. **Amenities:** voice mail, irons, hair
dryers. **Dining:** 6:30 am-2 & 4:30-9 pm, Sun 7 am-2 pm, cocktails. **Pool(s):** small heated outdoor. **Leisure
Activities:** exercise room. *Fee:* golf-18 holes. **Guest Services:** wireless Internet. **Business Services:**
meeting rooms. **Cards:** AX, CB, DC, DS, MC, VI. **Free Special Amenities: local telephone calls and high-speed Internet.**

CANTON/POTSDAM COMFORT SUITES   *Book great rates at AAA.com*   Phone: (315)386-1161
All Year [ECP]   1P: $99-$229   2P: $99-$229   XP: $12   F18
Location: Jct US 11, 68 and 310, just e. 6000 US 11 13617. Fax: 315/386-2515. **Facility:** 69 one-bedroom
standard units, some with whirlpools. 3 stories, interior corridors. *Bath:* combo or shower only. **Parking:** on-
site, winter plug-ins. **Amenities:** high-speed Internet, irons, hair dryers. **Pool(s):** heated indoor. **Leisure
Small-scale Hotel   **Activities:** sauna, whirlpool, pool table, exercise room. *Fee:* game room. **Guest Services:** sundries, coin
laundry, wireless Internet. **Business Services:** meeting rooms. **Cards:** AX, CB, DC, DS, JC, MC, VI.
Free Special Amenities: expanded continental breakfast and high-speed Internet.

------- WHERE TO DINE -------

PHOEBE'S RESTAURANT   **Dinner:** $7-$19   Phone: 315/386-2128
Location: Jct US 11, 68 and 310, just e. 5994 US 11 13617. **Hours:** 5 pm-9 pm. Closed major holidays.
Reservations: accepted. **Features:** A special twist on American and Italian favorites makes dining at the
American   restaurant special. Cozy decor and a garden room contribute to a pleasant setting for casual fine dining.
Casual dress; cocktails. **Parking:** on-site. **Cards:** AX, MC, VI.

CARLE PLACE pop. 5,247

------- WHERE TO STAY -------

HOLIDAY INN-WESTBURY   *Book at AAA.com*   Phone: (516)997-5000
All Year   1P: $189   2P: $189   XP: $15   F
Location: Meadow Brook Pkwy, exit M1, 0.5 mi e. Located across from a shopping mall. 369 Old Country Rd 11514.
Small-scale Hotel   Fax: 516/997-3623. **Facility:** 152 units. 150 one-bedroom standard units. 2 one-bedroom suites. 3 stories,
interior corridors. *Bath:* combo or shower only. **Parking:** on-site. **Terms:** [AP], [BP] & [ECP] meal plans
available. **Amenities:** video games (fee), dual phone lines, voice mail, irons, hair dryers. **Pool(s):** outdoor. **Leisure
Activities:** exercise room. **Guest Services:** valet and coin laundry, wireless Internet. **Business Services:** meeting rooms,
business center. **Cards:** AX, DC, DS, MC, VI.

------- WHERE TO DINE -------

WEST END CAFE   **Lunch:** $10-$16   **Dinner:** $12-$27   Phone: 516/294-5608
Location: Meadow Brook Pkwy, exit 31, 0.5 mi s; in shopping center. 187 Glen Cove Rd 11514. **Hours:** 11:30 am-
3:30 & 5-10 pm, Fri & Sat-11 pm, Sun 3 pm-9 pm. Closed: 12/25. **Reservations:** suggested. **Features:** A
Nouvelle American   large hand-painted mural, cloth runners draped across the ceiling and fine linens on the tables dramatically
accentuate the welcoming dining room. The best way to sample the exquisite made-from-scratch food is
from the three-course fixed-price menu, typically offered in the twilight hours and an exceptional value. Meals start with bread
and finish with delicious desserts. Diners are made to feel at home with attentive and friendly service and long glass bottles
filled with water. Dressy casual; cocktails. **Parking:** on-site. **Cards:** AX, MC, VI.

CARMEL —See New York p. 498.

CASTILE pop. 1,051

------- WHERE TO DINE -------

GLEN IRIS INN

American

Lunch: $9-$11   **Dinner:** $18-$27   **Phone:** 585/493-2622
Location: 1 mi n off SR 19A and 436; in Letchworth State Park. 7 Letchworth State Park 14427. **Hours:** Open 5/1-10/30 & 3/25-4/30; 8-10:30 am, 11:30-4 & 5-8 pm, Fri & Sat-9 pm. **Reservations:** suggested.
Features: Victorian furnishings decorate the former country estate, near a waterfall. Although the steaks, seafood and chicken are well-prepared and tasty, what guests remember is the berry hill dessert, made tableside. Casual dress; cocktails. **Parking:** on-site. **Cards:** AX, DS, MC, VI.

CASTLETON-ON-HUDSON pop. 1,619

------- WHERE TO STAY -------

COMFORT INN & SUITES-ALBANY/EAST GREENBUSH   *Book great rates at AAA.com*
(AAA) (SAVE)
Small-scale Hotel

Phone: (518)479-3217
All Year	1P: $80-$500	2P: $80-$500	XP: $10 F19

Location: I-90, exit 10 (Schodack-Miller Rd). 99 Miller Rd 12033. **Fax:** 518/479-3167. **Facility:** Smoke free premises. 89 units. 87 one-bedroom standard units. 2 one-bedroom suites ($99-$750) with kitchens. 3 stories, interior corridors. *Bath:* combo or shower only. **Parking:** on-site, winter plug-ins. **Terms:** [ECP] meal plan available. **Amenities:** high-speed Internet, dual phone lines, voice mail, irons, hair dryers. *Some:* DVD players. **Pool(s):** small heated indoor. **Leisure Activities:** whirlpool, exercise room. **Guest Services:** valet laundry, airport transportation (fee)-Albany Airport, area transportation-within 4 mi & local businesses. **Business Services:** conference facilities, PC. **Cards:** AX, CB, DC, DS, JC, MC, VI. **Free Special Amenities: expanded continental breakfast and high-speed Internet.**

SOME UNITS

RODEWAY INN   *Book great rates at AAA.com*
(AAA) (SAVE)
Motel

Phone: (518)477-2606
8/1-10/31	1P: $79-$279	2P: $79-$279	XP: $10 F
5/1-7/31	1P: $74-$279	2P: $74-$279	XP: $10 F
11/1-4/30	1P: $69-$265	2P: $69-$265	XP: $10 F

Location: I-90, exit 11, just nw on US 9 and 20. 1666 Columbia Tpke 12033. **Fax:** 518/479-4660. **Facility:** 22 one-bedroom standard units, some with whirlpools. 1 story, exterior corridors. **Parking:** on-site, winter plug-ins. **Terms:** 2-3 night minimum stay - seasonal, cancellation fee imposed, weekly rates available. **Amenities:** voice mail, hair dryers. **Leisure Activities:** *Fee:* game room. **Cards:** AX, DS, MC, VI. **Free Special Amenities: continental breakfast.**

SOME UNITS

CATSKILL pop. 4,392

------- WHERE TO STAY -------

CARL'S RIP VAN WINKLE MOTOR LODGE
(AAA) (SAVE)
Cabin

Phone: 518/943-3303
5/1-11/15 & 4/15-4/30	1P: $75-$90	2P: $75-$90	XP: $15

Location: I-87 (New York State Thruway), exit 21, 0.3 mi nw. 810 CR 23B 12451. **Fax:** 518/943-2309. **Facility:** 37 units. 14 one-bedroom standard units. 23 cabins. 1 story, exterior corridors. *Bath:* combo or shower only. **Parking:** on-site. **Terms:** open 5/1-11/15 & 4/15-4/30, 7 day cancellation notice, weekly rates available. **Amenities:** *Some:* high-speed Internet (fee). **Pool(s):** outdoor, wading. **Leisure Activities:** fishing, hibachis, hiking trails, playground, shuffleboard. **Business Services:** fax (fee). **Cards:** AX, MC, VI.

SOME UNITS

CATSKILL QUALITY INN & CONFERENCE CENTER   *Book great rates at AAA.com*
(AAA) (SAVE)
Small-scale Hotel

Phone: (518)943-5800
All Year	1P: $59-$269	2P: $59-$269	XP: $10 F17

Location: I-87 (New York State Thruway), exit 21, just w. 704 Rt 23B 12414 (PO Box 5759, ALBANY, 12205). **Fax:** 518/943-7084. **Facility:** 74 one-bedroom standard units, some with kitchens (no utensils) or whirlpools. 2 stories (no elevator), interior/exterior corridors. **Parking:** on-site. **Terms:** 2-3 night minimum stay - weekends, package plans, pets ($20 extra charge, in designated units). **Amenities:** high-speed Internet, irons, hair dryers. *Some:* safes. **Dining:** 6 am-10 & 5-9 pm, cocktails. **Pool(s):** outdoor. **Guest Services:** coin laundry, wireless Internet. **Business Services:** meeting rooms. **Cards:** AX, CB, DC, DS, JC, MC, VI. **Free Special Amenities: full breakfast and high-speed Internet.**

SOME UNITS

RED RANCH MOTEL
(AAA) (SAVE)
Motel

Phone: (518)678-3380
6/8-9/4	1P: $55-$85	2P: $55-$85	XP: $10 F14
9/5-1/2	1P: $48-$85	2P: $48-$85	XP: $10 F14
5/1-6/7 & 4/1-4/30	1P: $48-$65	2P: $48-$65	XP: $10 F14

Location: I-87 (New York State Thruway), exit 20, 9 mi n; exit 21, jct SR 23A, 0.5 mi s. 4555 Rt 32 12414. **Facility:** 39 units. 38 one- and 1 two-bedroom standard units, some with kitchens. 1-2 stories (no elevator), exterior corridors. *Bath:* combo or shower only. **Parking:** on-site, winter plug-ins. **Terms:** open 5/1-1/2 & 4/1-4/30, office hours 9 am-10 pm, 2 night minimum stay - seasonal and/or weekends. **Amenities:** *Some:* hair dryers. **Pool(s):** outdoor. **Leisure Activities:** kiddie pool, playground. *Fee:* game room. **Cards:** AX, CB, DC, DS, MC, VI. **Free Special Amenities: local telephone calls.**

SOME UNITS

------- WHERE TO DINE -------

ANTHONY'S RESTAURANT
American

Dinner: $10-$25   **Phone:** 518/943-3754
Location: I-87 (New York State Thruway), exit 21, just w. 746 Rt 23B 12414. **Hours:** 5 pm-9:30 pm. Closed major holidays; also Mon-Wed. **Features:** The popular, casual restaurant has been family-owned for more than 33 years. The friendly staff serves Italian specialties, seafood, steak and prime rib. Desserts are rich. Casual dress; cocktails. **Parking:** on-site. **Cards:** MC, VI.

LA CONCA D'ORO

Italian

Lunch: $4-$9 **Dinner: $9-$25** **Phone:** 518/943-3549
Location: Center. 440 Main St 12414. **Hours:** 11:30 am-9 pm, Sat 3 pm-10 pm, Sun 2 pm-9 pm, Mon 4 pm-9 pm. Closed: 11/22, 12/25; also Tues. **Reservations:** suggested. **Features:** Representative of tasty choices is the lobster tail Contidinia, which is served with shrimp and clams in a mushroom marinara sauce over fresh linguine. Specials include contemporary American cuisine. Homemade desserts, such as cheesecake, bread pudding, tarts and tiramisu quiet the sweet tooth. Casual dress; cocktails. **Parking:** street. **Cards:** MC, VI.

LOGSIDER CAFE

American

Lunch: $10-$20 **Dinner: $10-$20** **Phone:** 518/943-2581
Location: I-87 (New York State Thruway), exit 21, 0.3 mi w. 800 23B 12451. **Hours:** 7 am-9 pm. **Reservations:** suggested, weekends. **Features:** The 1934 log cabin has an Adirondack atmosphere, with timbers, massive stone fireplaces and varied antique appointments. Well-seasoned dishes include traditional preparations of Angus beef and fresh seafood. The barbecue ribs are outstanding. Casual dress; cocktails. **Parking:** on-site. **Cards:** AX, MC, VI.

CAYUGA HEIGHTS pop. 3,273—See also FINGER LAKES.

——— WHERE TO DINE ———

THE HEIGHTS CAFE & GRILL

American

Lunch: $10-$17 **Dinner: $13-$30** **Phone:** 607/257-4144
Location: SR 13, exit Triphammer Rd, 0.9 mi e to Community Corners Plaza. 903 Hanshaw Rd 14850. **Hours:** 11:30 am-2:30 & 5-9 pm, Fri-10 pm, Sat 5 pm-10 pm. Closed major holidays; also Sun. **Reservations:** suggested. **Features:** An award-winning wine list complements sophisticated cuisine, which is prepared with fresh ingredients and imagination. Much attention is paid to artful plate presentation. Tasteful jazz music plays in the background of the art deco dining room. Dressy casual; cocktails. **Parking:** on-site. **Cards:** AX, DC, DS, MC, VI.

CAZENOVIA pop. 2,614

——— WHERE TO STAY ———

BRAE LOCH INN

Country Inn

Phone: (315)655-3431

5/1-10/31 [CP]	1P: $65-$155	2P: $100-$155	XP: $15	F12
11/1-4/30 [CP]	1P: $65-$155	2P: $85-$140	XP: $15	F12

Location: On US 20. 5 Albany St 13035. Fax: 315/655-4844. **Facility:** Tartan plaids, stained glass and Scottish heirlooms define the Scottish theme of this property which has been family-owned and -operated since 1946. 12 one-bedroom standard units, some with whirlpools. 2 stories (no elevator), interior corridors. **Parking:** on-site. **Terms:** 10 day cancellation notice, package plans. **Amenities:** hair dryers. **Dining:** restaurant, see separate listing. **Leisure Activities:** lake & golf privileges. *Fee:* massage. **Guest Services:** gift shop, wireless Internet. **Business Services:** meeting rooms, PC, fax. **Cards:** AX, DS, MC, VI. **Free Special Amenities: continental breakfast and local telephone calls.**

SOME UNITS

THE BREWSTER INN

Historic Country Inn

Property failed to provide current rates **Phone:** 315/655-9232
Location: On US 20, just w of center. 6 Ledyard Ave 13035 (PO Box 507). Fax: 315/655-2130. **Facility:** Exquisite woodwork distinguishes this 1890 summer home enjoyed by John D. Rockefeller, Sr; it offers unpretentious elegance on scenic Cazenovia Lake. Smoke free premises. 17 one-bedroom standard units, some with whirlpools. 3 stories (no elevator), interior corridors. *Bath:* combo or shower only. **Parking:** on-site. **Amenities:** video library (fee), DVD players, irons, hair dryers. **Dining:** restaurant, see separate listing. **Leisure Activities:** marina, fishing. *Fee:* massage. **Guest Services:** gift shop, wireless Internet. **Business Services:** meeting rooms.

——— WHERE TO DINE ———

BRAE LOCH INN

American

Dinner: $13-$28 **Phone:** 315/655-3431
Location: On US 20; in Brae Loch Inn. 5 Albany St 13035. **Hours:** 5 pm-10 pm, Sun 4 pm-9 pm; hours may vary off season. Closed: 12/24, 12/25. **Reservations:** suggested. **Features:** The prime minister—prime rib served in natural juices with a side of Yorkshire pudding—stands out on a menu of steak, lamb and seafood choices. A Scottish influence shows in the memorabilia and tartan carpets of the warm, intimate dining room. Dressy casual; cocktails. **Parking:** on-site. **Cards:** AX, DS, MC, VI. **Country Inn**

THE BREWSTER INN

Continental

Dinner: $20-$25 **Phone:** 315/655-9232
Location: On US 20, 0.5 mi w of center; in The Brewster Inn. 6 Ledyard Ave 13035. **Hours:** 5 pm-9 pm; Sun also 10:30 am-1:30 pm 4/1-12/31. Closed major holidays. **Reservations:** suggested. **Features:** On Cazenovia Lake, the Victorian mansion exudes an upscale charm. Particularly well-prepared is veal Atlantis, a sauteed cut of veal topped with lobster, served on a bed of wild greens and finished with tarragon beurre blanc sauce. Dessert changes daily. Dressy casual; cocktails. **Parking:** on-site. **Cards:** DC, DS, MC, VI. **Country Inn**

CHAPPAQUA —See New York p. 498.

CHARLOTTEVILLE

——— WHERE TO STAY ———

CHARLOTTE VALLEY INN B & B AND ANTIQUES

Historic Bed & Breakfast

Phone: 607/397-8164

All Year [BP]	1P: $85-$110	2P: $90-$125	XP: $20	D12

Location: SR 23, 5.0 mi n on CR 9/40. 480 County Hwy 40 12197. **Facility:** Handmade quilts cover the four-poster beds at this stagecoach inn overlooking a quiet valley. Smoke free premises. 5 one-bedroom standard units. 2 stories (no elevator), interior corridors. *Bath:* some shared or private, combo or shower only. **Parking:** on-site. **Terms:** 14 day cancellation notice-fee imposed, no pets allowed (owner's pets on premises). **Guest Services:** TV in common area.

CHAZY pop. 4,181

──────── WHERE TO DINE ────────

──────── *The following restaurant has not been evaluated by AAA* ────────
but is listed for your information only.

IRENE'S FINE DINING RESTAURANT **Phone:** 518/846-8804
[fyi] Not evaluated. **Location:** 1305 Fiske Rd 12921. **Features:** Located in a charming bed and breakfast, this cozy dining room is open for both lunch and dinner.

CHEEKTOWAGA —*See Buffalo p. 256.*

CHESTER pop. 3,445

──────── WHERE TO STAY ────────

HOLIDAY INN EXPRESS HOTEL & SUITES *Book great rates at AAA.com* **Phone:** (845)469-3000

5/1-10/31	1P: $129-$250	2P: $129-$250	XP: $15 F16
11/1-4/30	1P: $109-$250	2P: $109-$250	XP: $15 F16

Small-scale Hotel

Location: SR 17, exit 126, just n on SR 94, then just w on SR 17M (Brookside Ave). 2 Bryle Pl 10918. Fax: 845/469-5242. **Facility:** 80 one-bedroom standard units. 3 stories, interior corridors. *Bath:* combo or shower only. **Parking:** on-site. **Terms:** cancellation fee imposed, weekly rates available, [ECP] meal plan available, package plans, pets ($30 fee, in designated units). **Amenities:** video games (fee), high-speed Internet, voice mail, irons, hair dryers. **Pool(s):** heated indoor. **Leisure Activities:** whirlpool, exercise room. **Guest Services:** valet laundry, wireless Internet. **Business Services:** meeting rooms, PC. **Cards:** AX, CB, DC, DS, MC, VI. **Free Special Amenities:** expanded continental breakfast and local telephone calls.

SOME UNITS

CHESTERTOWN pop. 3,614—*See also ADIRONDACK MOUNTAINS.*

──────── WHERE TO STAY ────────

FRIENDS LAKE INN **Phone:** (518)494-4751
All Year [MAP] 2P: $285-$500 XP: $80

Historic Country Inn

Location: I-87, exit 25, 3.5 mi w on SR 8, then 3.2 mi s. Located in a rural area. 963 Friends Lake Rd 12817. Fax: 518/494-4616. **Facility:** This rural inn offers pleasantly-decorated guest rooms, some with fireplaces. The lake is only a short walk away. Smoke free premises. 17 units. 16 one-bedroom standard units, some with whirlpools. 1 one-bedroom suite with whirlpool. 3 stories (no elevator), interior corridors. *Bath:* combo or shower only. **Parking:** on-site. **Terms:** office hours 8 am-11:30 pm, 1-2 night minimum stay - seasonal and/or weekends, 14 day cancellation notice-fee imposed, [BP] meal plan available, package plans. **Amenities:** CD players, voice mail, irons, hair dryers. *Some:* honor bars. **Dining:** restaurant, see separate listing. **Pool(s):** heated outdoor. **Leisure Activities:** sauna, canoeing, paddleboats, kayaks, cross country skiing, hiking trails. *Fee:* cross country equipment & snowshoes. **Guest Services:** TV in common area, complimentary evening beverages: Fri & Sat, wireless Internet. **Cards:** AX, DC, MC, VI. **Free Special Amenities:** early check-in/late check-out and room upgrade (subject to availability with advance reservations).

SOME UNITS

──────── WHERE TO DINE ────────

FRIENDS LAKE INN **Lunch:** $8-$12 **Dinner:** $22-$34 **Phone:** 518/494-4751

Nouvelle American

Location: I-87, exit 25, 3.5 mi w on SR 8, then 3.2 mi s; in Friends Lake Inn. 963 Friends Lake Rd 12817. **Hours:** 8 am-10:30, noon-4 & 5:30-9 pm, Fri-9:30 pm, Sat 8 am-4 & 5:30-9:30 pm, Sun 8 am-4 & 5-9 pm. **Reservations:** suggested. **Features:** The dining room invites relaxed, upscale dining. To pair with gourmet American cuisine, guests can choose any wine from the award-winning, 21,000-bottle collection or let the sommelier do the work. Those who fall in love with a wine will more than likely be able to buy it at the on-site wine shop. Dressy casual; cocktails. **Parking:** on-site. **Cards:** AX, DS, MC, VI.

MAIN STREET ICE CREAM PARLOR **Lunch:** $4-$10 **Dinner:** $10-$15 **Phone:** 518/494-7940

American

Location: Center. 6339 Main St 12817. **Hours:** 10 am-10 pm; to 6 pm, Fri & Sat-9 pm, Sun-4 pm 9/15-6/25. Closed major holidays. **Features:** An air of nostalgia drifts through the 1950s soda fountain, decorated with Coca-Cola antiques and Adirondack memorabilia. The menu focuses on home-style lighter fare: delicious soups, hearty delicatessen sandwiches and ice cream sundaes made the old-fashioned way. Dinner entrees are served on weekends. Casual dress. **Parking:** on-site. **Cards:** DS, MC, VI.

CLARENCE —*See Buffalo p. 258.*

CLARKSON pop. 6,072

──────── WHERE TO DINE ────────

THE APPLE TREE INN **Lunch:** $7-$10 **Dinner:** $12-$23 **Phone:** 585/637-6440

American

Location: Jct SR 19, 2.4 mi e on SR 104 (Ridge Rd). 7407 Ridge Rd W 14420. **Hours:** 11 am-2, Thurs-Sat also 5 pm-8 pm, Sun 11:30 am-2 pm. Closed major holidays; also Mon. **Reservations:** not accepted. **Features:** Upscale country decor provides the backdrop for relaxed dining. Innovative comfort foods served with flair by a friendly wait staff make even lunches memorable. Dressy casual; beer & wine only. **Parking:** on-site. **Cards:** AX, DS, MC, VI.

CLAY pop. 58,805

──────── WHERE TO STAY ────────

FAIRFIELD INN BY MARRIOTT-SYRACUSE   **Phone:** (315)622-2576
All Year   1P: $100-$120   2P: $105-$125   XP: $5   F18
Location: Jct SR 481, exit 12, just w. 3979 SR 31 13041. **Fax:** 315/622-2576. **Facility:** Smoke free premises. 63
Small-scale Hotel   one-bedroom standard units. 3 stories, interior corridors. *Bath:* combo or shower only. **Parking:** on-site.
Terms: pets ($50 fee). **Amenities:** video library (fee), irons, hair dryers. **Pool(s):** small heated indoor.
Leisure Activities: whirlpool. **Guest Services:** valet laundry, wireless Internet. **Business Services:** PC. **Cards:** AX, DC, DS,
MC, VI.

SOME UNITS

(ASK) (S/D) (🛏) (📶) (&M) (🛋) (🏊) (✕) (🎦) (💻) / (🍴) / FEE   FEE

──────── WHERE TO DINE ────────

EUCLID RESTAURANT   *Menu on AAA.com*   **Lunch:** $3-$9   **Dinner:** $6-$24   **Phone:** 315/622-2750
Location: Jct SR 31 and Morgan Rd. 4285 Rt 31 13041. **Hours:** 11 am-10 pm, Fri & Sat-10:30 pm, Sun noon-9
pm. Closed major holidays. **Reservations:** suggested. **Features:** Friendly service is the hallmark at the
busy restaurant. Daily specials focus on delicious comfort food. A $2 children's meal is available. Hearty
American   helpings are served in a casual setting. Casual dress; cocktails. **Parking:** on-site. **Cards:** AX, DC, DS,
MC, VI.

(Y)

CLAYTON pop. 1,821

──────── WHERE TO STAY ────────

FAIR WIND LODGE   **Phone:** 315/686-5251
(AAA) (SAVE)   6/15-9/3   2P: $60-$85   XP: $5   F6
5/1-6/14 & 9/4-10/15   2P: $50-$70   XP: $5   F6
Location: 2.3 mi sw. Located in a quiet area. 38201 NYS Rt 12E 13624. **Fax:** 315/686-3828. **Facility:** 18 units. 9
Motel   one- and 1 two-bedroom standard units. 2 cabins ($70-$85) and 6 cottages ($600-$800). 1 story, exterior
corridors. *Bath:* combo or shower only. **Parking:** on-site. **Terms:** open 5/1-10/15, office hours 8 am-10 pm,
7 day cancellation notice-fee imposed, pets (with prior approval). **Pool(s):** heated outdoor. **Leisure**
Activities: boat dock, fishing, picnic area with grills. **Business Services:** PC. **Cards:** AX, DS, MC, VI.
Free Special Amenities: continental breakfast and high-speed Internet.

SOME UNITS

(🐕) (🏊) (✕) (✕) (🎦) / (🍴) (💻) (💻) /

──────── WHERE TO DINE ────────

HARBOR INN & RESTAURANT   **Lunch:** $4-$8   **Dinner:** $12-$17   **Phone:** 315/686-2293
Location: Center; across from Antique Boat Museum and public docks. 625 Mary St 13624. **Hours:** 6 am-9 pm;
seasonal hours may vary. Closed major holidays. **Reservations:** accepted, for dinner. **Features:** After a
American   tour of the museum, guests can stop at the casual dining spot for a light snack, such as fresh cinnamon
rolls or doughnuts, or heartier fare, including red pepper soup or scallops with French white wine sauce.
Casual dress; beer & wine only. **Parking:** street. **Cards:** AX, DS, MC, VI.

THOUSAND ISLANDS INN   **Lunch:** $4-$9   **Dinner:** $10-$27   **Phone:** 315/686-3030
(AAA)   **Location:** On St. Lawrence River. 335 Riverside Dr 13624. **Hours:** Open 5/16-9/15; 7 am-11:30 & 5-9 pm.
Reservations: suggested. **Features:** This family restaurant delivers such tasty fare as homemade beef
vegetable soup, filet of Lake Ontario walleye and Grenadier Island chicken. Thousand Island salad dressing
American   first was served here. Friendly, prompt servers are adept at follow-up. Casual dress; cocktails. **Parking:** on-
site. **Cards:** CB, DC, DS, MC, VI.

(Y)

CLIFTON PARK pop. 32,995

──────── WHERE TO STAY ────────

COMFORT INN   *Book great rates at AAA.com*   **Phone:** 518/373-0222
(AAA) (SAVE)   7/26-9/5 [CP]   1P: $109-$179   2P: $109-$179   XP: $10   F18
5/1-7/25 & 9/6-4/30 [CP]   1P: $99-$149   2P: $99-$149   XP: $10   F18
Location: I-87, exit 9 northbound; exit 9E southbound. 41 Fire Rd, Old Rt 146 12065. **Fax:** 518/373-0278.
Facility: Smoke free premises. 60 one-bedroom standard units, some with whirlpools. 2 stories (no
Small-scale Hotel   elevator), interior corridors. **Parking:** on-site. **Amenities:** voice mail, irons, hair dryers. **Pool(s):** small
heated outdoor. **Leisure Activities:** exercise room. **Guest Services:** valet laundry, wireless Internet.
Business Services: meeting rooms. **Cards:** AX, DS, MC, VI. **Free Special Amenities:** continental breakfast and high-
speed Internet.

SOME UNITS

(S/D) (🏊) (✕) (🎦) (💻) / (🍴) (💻) /

COMFORT SUITES   *Book great rates at AAA.com*   **Phone:** (518)373-2255
(AAA) (SAVE)   7/26-9/3   1P: $169-$399   2P: $169-$399
9/4-4/30   1P: $109-$299   2P: $109-$299
5/1-7/25   1P: $109-$299   2P: $109-$299
Location: I-87, exit 9 southbound; exit 9E northbound. 7 Northside Dr 12065. **Fax:** 518/373-7888. **Facility:** 75 units.
Small-scale Hotel   72 one-bedroom standard units, some with whirlpools. 3 one-bedroom suites with kitchens, some with
whirlpools. 4 stories, interior corridors. *Bath:* combo or shower only. **Parking:** on-site. **Terms:** 14 day
cancellation notice, [BP] meal plan available. **Amenities:** dual phone lines, voice mail, safes (fee), irons, hair dryers. **Pool(s):**
heated indoor. **Leisure Activities:** exercise room. **Guest Services:** valet and coin laundry, wireless Internet. **Business**
Services: conference facilities. **Cards:** AX, CB, DC, DS, JC, MC, VI.

(S/D) (📶) (&) (🏊) (✕) (🎦) (💻) (💻) (💻)

HAMPTON INN   *Book great rates at AAA.com*   Phone: (518)373-2345

AAA SAVE

7/22-9/2	1P: $199-$249	2P: $199-$269
5/1-7/21	1P: $129-$199	2P: $139-$199
9/3-4/30	1P: $119-$179	2P: $119-$179

Small-scale Hotel **Location:** I-87, exit 9E northbound; exit 9 southbound, just w. 620 Plank Rd 12065. **Fax:** 518/373-0775. **Facility:** 80 one-bedroom standard units. 4 stories, interior corridors. *Bath:* combo or shower only. **Parking:** on-site. **Amenities:** video games (fee), high-speed Internet, dual phone lines, voice mail, irons, hair dryers. **Pool(s):** small heated indoor. **Leisure Activities:** whirlpool, exercise room. **Guest Services:** valet and coin laundry. **Business Services:** meeting rooms, PC. **Cards:** AX, CB, DC, DS, MC, VI. **Free Special Amenities:** expanded continental breakfast and high-speed Internet.

SOME UNITS

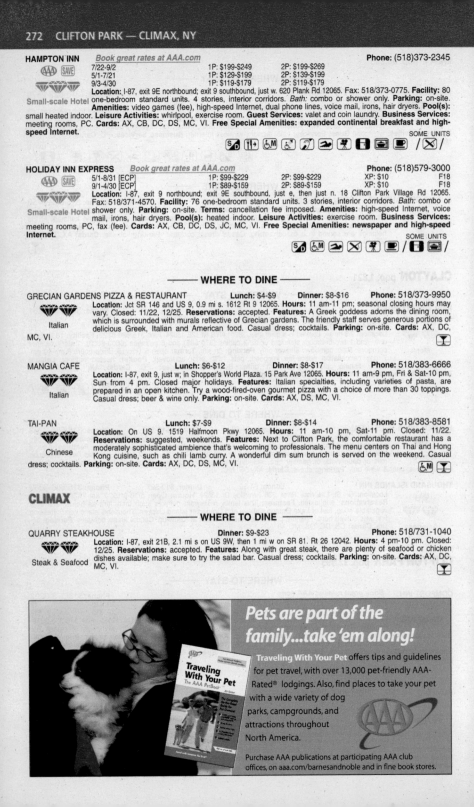

HOLIDAY INN EXPRESS   *Book great rates at AAA.com*   Phone: (518)579-3000

AAA SAVE

5/1-8/31 [ECP]	1P: $99-$229	2P: $99-$229	XP: $10	F18
9/1-4/30 [ECP]	1P: $89-$159	2P: $89-$159	XP: $10	F18

Small-scale Hotel **Location:** I-87, exit 9 northbound; exit 9E southbound, just e, then just n. 18 Clifton Park Village Rd 12065. **Fax:** 518/371-4570. **Facility:** 76 one-bedroom standard units. 3 stories, interior corridors. *Bath:* combo or shower only. **Parking:** on-site. **Terms:** cancellation fee imposed. **Amenities:** high-speed Internet, voice mail, irons, hair dryers. **Pool(s):** heated indoor. **Leisure Activities:** exercise room. **Business Services:** meeting rooms, PC, fax (fee). **Cards:** AX, CB, DC, DS, JC, MC, VI. **Free Special Amenities:** newspaper and high-speed Internet.

SOME UNITS

──────── **WHERE TO DINE** ────────

GRECIAN GARDENS PIZZA & RESTAURANT   **Lunch:** $4-$9   **Dinner:** $8-$16   Phone: 518/373-9950

Italian

Location: Jct SR 146 and US 9, 0.9 mi s. 1612 Rt 9 12065. **Hours:** 11 am-11 pm; seasonal closing hours may vary. **Closed:** 11/22, 12/25. **Reservations:** accepted. **Features:** A Greek goddess adorns the dining room, which is surrounded with murals reflective of Grecian gardens. The friendly staff serves generous portions of delicious Greek, Italian and American food. Casual dress; cocktails. **Parking:** on-site. **Cards:** AX, DC, MC, VI.

MANGIA CAFE   **Lunch:** $6-$12   **Dinner:** $8-$17   Phone: 518/383-6666

Italian

Location: I-87, exit 9, just w; in Shopper's World Plaza. 15 Park Ave 12065. **Hours:** 11 am-9 pm, Fri & Sat-10 pm, Sun from 4 pm. **Closed** major holidays. **Features:** Italian specialties, including varieties of pasta, are prepared in an open kitchen. Try a wood-fired-oven gourmet pizza with a choice of more than 30 toppings. Casual dress; beer & wine only. **Parking:** on-site. **Cards:** AX, DS, MC, VI.

TAI-PAN   **Lunch:** $7-$9   **Dinner:** $8-$14   Phone: 518/383-8581

Chinese

Location: On US 9. 1519 Halfmoon Pkwy 12065. **Hours:** 11 am-10 pm, Sat-11 pm. **Closed:** 11/22. **Reservations:** suggested, weekends. **Features:** Next to Clifton Park, the comfortable restaurant has a moderately sophisticated ambience that's welcoming to professionals. The menu centers on Thai and Hong Kong cuisine, such as chili lamb curry. A wonderful dim sum brunch is served on the weekend. Casual dress; cocktails. **Parking:** on-site. **Cards:** AX, DC, DS, MC, VI.

CLIMAX

──────── **WHERE TO DINE** ────────

QUARRY STEAKHOUSE   **Dinner:** $9-$23   Phone: 518/731-1040

Steak & Seafood

Location: I-87, exit 21B, 2.1 mi s on US 9W, then 1 mi w on SR 81. Rt 26 12042. **Hours:** 4 pm-10 pm. **Closed:** 12/25. **Reservations:** accepted. **Features:** Along with great steak, there are plenty of seafood or chicken dishes available; make sure to try the salad bar. Casual dress; cocktails. **Parking:** on-site. **Cards:** AX, DC, MC, VI.

CLINTON pop. 727

——— WHERE TO STAY ———

AMIDST THE HEDGES
Phone: 315/853-3031
▼▼▼ All Year [BP]   1P: $120-$150   2P: $120-$150   XP: $10   F3
Location: College St, 0.3 mi n on Elm St. Located in a residential area. 180 Sanford Ave 13323. Fax: 315/853-5705.
Bed & Breakfast   **Facility:** The bed and breakfast is in a quiet neighborhood within walking distance of the town center.
Smoke free premises. 5 units. 2 one-bedroom standard units, some with whirlpools. 2 one-bedroom suites.
1 cottage. 2 stories (no elevator), interior corridors. *Bath:* combo or shower only. **Parking:** on-site. **Terms:** check-in 4 pm, 10
day cancellation notice-fee imposed, weekly rates available, package plans, pets (owner's pet on premises). **Amenities:** video
library, hair dryers. *Some:* DVD players, CD players. **Pool(s):** outdoor. **Leisure Activities:** *Fee:* massage. **Business Services:**
PC, fax. **Cards:** AX, MC, VI.

SOME UNITS
🛏 🐾 🔧 ✕ / VCR 🔌 📺 🖥 /
FEE

THE ARTFUL LODGER
Phone: 315/853-3672
▼▼▼ All Year [BP]   1P: $89-$135   2P: $99-$145   XP: $15
Location: Center. Located on the village green. 7 E Park Row 13323. Fax: 315/853-1489. **Facility:** Themed art
Historic Bed   exhibits, which are changed seasonally, enhance this cozy inn. Smoke free premises. 5 one-bedroom
& Breakfast   standard units. 2 stories (no elevator), interior corridors. *Bath:* combo or shower only. **Parking:** on-site.
Terms: check-in 4 pm, 7 day cancellation notice. **Amenities:** hair dryers. **Guest Services:** TV in common
area, gift shop, wireless Internet. **Business Services:** fax. **Cards:** AX, DC, DS, MC, VI.

ASK S🐾 🛎 ✕ 📺

——— WHERE TO DINE ———

O'CONNOR'S ALEXANDER HAMILTON INN
Dinner: $18-$26   **Phone: 315/853-2061**
▼▼▼ **Location:** Center. 21 W Park Row 13323. **Hours:** 5 pm-9 pm, Fri & Sat-10 pm. Closed: 1/1, 12/24, 12/25; also
Sun & Mon. **Reservations:** suggested. **Features:** An elegant fine dining atmosphere and attentive service
Continental   are the hallmarks that distinguish the beautifully restored inn. Dressy casual; cocktails. **Parking:** street.
Cards: AX, DS, MC, VI. **Historic**

📺

COBLESKILL pop. 4,533

——— WHERE TO STAY ———

BEST WESTERN INN OF COBLESKILL   *Book great rates at AAA.com*   **Phone: (518)234-4321**
AAA SAVE   7/1-9/3   1P: $99-$199   2P: $99-$199   XP: $10   F18
▼▼▼   5/1-6/30 & 9/4-4/30   1P: $79-$159   2P: $79-$159   XP: $10   F18
Location: I-88, exit 21 eastbound on SR 7, 0.8 mi e of jct SR 10; exit 22 westbound, 2.9 mi w on SR 27. 121 Burgin Dr
Small-scale Hotel   12043. Fax: 518/234-3869. **Facility:** 76 one-bedroom standard units. 2 stories (no elevator), interior
corridors. **Parking:** on-site, winter plug-ins. **Terms:** package plans, pets ($15 fee). **Amenities:** irons, hair
dryers. **Dining:** 7 am-9 pm; to 10 pm in summer, cocktails. **Pool(s):** heated indoor, wading. **Leisure
Activities:** exercise room. *Fee:* bowling. **Guest Services:** valet laundry, wireless Internet. **Business Services:** meeting rooms.
Cards: AX, CB, DC, DS, JC, MC, VI. **Free Special Amenities: local telephone calls and high-speed Internet.**

SOME UNITS
S🌡 🛏 🍽 📺 🔗 🐾 🎥 🖥 / ✕ 🔌 📺 /
FEE

SUPER 8   *Book at AAA.com*   **Phone: (518)234-4888**
▼▼ ▼▼   5/1-9/3   1P: $99-$125   2P: $99-$125   XP: $10   F17
  9/4-10/28   1P: $79   2P: $79   XP: $10   F17
Small-scale Hotel   10/29-4/30   1P: $69-$75   2P: $69-$75   XP: $10   F17
Location: I-88, exit 22 westbound, 2.4 mi w on SR 7; exit 21 eastbound, 3.1 mi e on SR 7. 955 E Main St 12043.
Fax: 518/234-4888. **Facility:** 50 one-bedroom standard units. 2 stories (no elevator), interior corridors. *Bath:* combo or shower
only. **Parking:** on-site. **Terms:** pets ($10 fee). **Leisure Activities:** *Fee:* game room. **Guest Services:** coin laundry. **Cards:** AX,
DC, DS, MC, VI.

SOME UNITS
ASK S🌡 🛏 🔗M 🔒 🐾 🎥 / ✕ /
FEE

COLONIE pop. 7,916   (See map and index starting on p. 218)

——— WHERE TO STAY ———

ALBANY MARRIOTT   *Book great rates at AAA.com*   **Phone: (518)458-8444**   32
▼▼▼ All Year   1P: $149-$229   2P: $149-$229
Location: I-87, exit 4, 0.3 mi se. 189 Wolf Rd 12205. Fax: 518/482-7809. **Facility:** Smoke free premises. 359
Large-scale Hotel   units. 356 one-bedroom standard units. 3 one-bedroom suites. 8 stories, interior corridors. *Bath:* combo or
shower only. **Parking:** on-site. **Terms:** check-in 4 pm. **Amenities:** video games (fee), high-speed Internet,
voice mail, irons, hair dryers. *Some:* CD players. **Pool(s):** heated outdoor, heated indoor. **Leisure Activities:** sauna, whirlpool,
exercise room. **Guest Services:** gift shop, valet and coin laundry. **Business Services:** conference facilities, business center.
Cards: AX, DC, DS, MC, VI.

SOME UNITS
ASK S🌡 🔌 🍽 📺 🔗M 🔒 🐾 ✕ ✕ 🎥 🖥 / 🔌 /

AMERICA'S BEST VALUE INN   *Book at AAA.com*   **Phone: (518)456-8982**   36
▼▼▼   5/1-9/30   1P: $69-$99   2P: $69-$99   XP: $10   F13
  10/1-4/30   1P: $49-$99   2P: $49-$99   XP: $10   F13
Motel   **Location:** I-87, exit 2 (SR 5), 0.8 mi w. 1600 Central Ave 12205. Fax: 518/456-8743. **Facility:** 56 one-bedroom
standard units. 2 stories (no elevator), exterior corridors. **Parking:** on-site, winter plug-ins. **Terms:** 3 day
cancellation notice, pets ($50 deposit). **Cards:** AX, CB, DC, DS, MC, VI.

SOME UNITS
ASK S🌡 🛏 🛎 🎥 / ✕ /
FEE

(See map and index starting on p. 218)

BEST WESTERN ALBANY AIRPORT INN
Book great rates at AAA.com
Phone: (518)458-1000   30

AAA [SAVE]

5/1-9/30 [ECP]	1P: $99-$159	2P: $99-$159	XP: $10	F13
1/1-4/30 [ECP]	1P: $89-$149	2P: $89-$149	XP: $10	F13
10/1-12/31 [ECP]	1P: $79-$139	2P: $79-$139	XP: $10	F13

Small-scale Hotel
Location: I-87, exit 4, just se to Wolf Rd, then just sw. 200 Wolf Rd 12205. Fax: 518/458-2807. **Facility:** 153 one-bedroom standard units. 2 stories (no elevator), interior corridors. **Parking:** on-site, winter plug-ins. **Terms:** package plans. **Amenities:** voice mail, irons, hair dryers. **Dining:** 4 pm-midnight, cocktails. **Pool(s):** heated indoor. **Guest Services:** valet laundry, area transportation-mall & local restaurants, wireless Internet. **Business Services:** meeting rooms, PC. **Cards:** AX, CB, DC, DS, MC, VI. **Free Special Amenities: early check-in/late check-out and room upgrade (subject to availability with advance reservations).**

SOME UNITS
FEE

COCCA'S INN & SUITES, WOLF RD
Phone: (518)459-2240   38

AAA [SAVE]

6/16-9/6	1P: $89-$149	2P: $99-$149	XP: $5	F16
5/1-6/15	1P: $79-$149	2P: $89-$149	XP: $5	F16
9/7-4/30	1P: $79-$149	2P: $89-$149	XP: $5	F16

Motel
Location: I-87, exit 2E, just e. 2 Wolf Rd 12205. Fax: 518/459-9758. **Facility:** 45 one-bedroom standard units, some with whirlpools. 2 stories (no elevator), interior/exterior corridors. *Bath:* combo or shower only. **Parking:** on-site. **Terms:** package plans, pets (with prior approval). **Amenities:** high-speed Internet, irons. *Some:* DVD players, hair dryers. **Guest Services:** airport transportation-Albany International Airport, wireless Internet. **Business Services:** business center. **Cards:** AX, DS, MC, VI. **Free Special Amenities: continental breakfast and high-speed Internet.** *(See color ad p 223)*

SOME UNITS

COMFORT INN & SUITES
Book great rates at AAA.com
Phone: (518)869-5327   35

AAA [SAVE]

7/21-9/2	1P: $99-$129	2P: $99-$129	XP: $10	F18
9/3-4/30	1P: $79-$129	2P: $89-$129	XP: $10	F18
5/1-7/20	1P: $79-$112	2P: $89-$112	XP: $10	F18

Small-scale Hotel
Location: I-87, exit 2, 0.8 mi w. 1606 Central Ave 12205. Fax: 518/456-8971. **Facility:** 109 units. 108 one-bedroom standard units, some with whirlpools. 1 one-bedroom suite ($109-$250) with whirlpool. 2-3 stories (no elevator), interior/exterior corridors. *Bath:* combo or shower only. **Parking:** on-site. **Terms:** [ECP] meal plan available. **Amenities:** video games (fee), voice mail, irons, hair dryers. *Some:* high-speed Internet, dual phone lines. **Pool(s):** small heated indoor. **Leisure Activities:** whirlpool, exercise room. **Guest Services:** valet and coin laundry. **Business Services:** meeting rooms, business center. **Cards:** AX, CB, DC, DS, JC, MC, VI. **Free Special Amenities: expanded continental breakfast and high-speed Internet.**

SOME UNITS
FEE

COURTYARD BY MARRIOTT
Book great rates at AAA.com
Phone: (518)482-8800   33

All Year	1P: $104-$179	2P: $104-$179

Small-scale Hotel
Location: I-87, exit 4, 0.4 mi se. 168 Wolf Rd 12205. Fax: 518/482-0001. **Facility:** Smoke free premises. 78 one-bedroom standard units. 3 stories, interior corridors. *Bath:* combo or shower only. **Parking:** on-site. **Terms:** [BP] & [CP] meal plans available. **Amenities:** high-speed Internet, dual phone lines, voice mail, irons, hair dryers. **Pool(s):** small heated indoor. **Leisure Activities:** whirlpool, exercise room. **Guest Services:** valet and coin laundry. **Business Services:** meeting rooms. **Cards:** AX, CB, DC, DS, JC, MC, VI.

SOME UNITS

THE DESMOND HOTEL
Book great rates at AAA.com
Phone: (518)869-8100   27

AAA [SAVE]

All Year	1P: $189-$199

Small-scale Hotel
Location: I-87, exit 4, just w. 660 Albany Shaker Rd 12211. Fax: 518/869-7659. **Facility:** 324 units. 306 one-bedroom standard units. 18 one-bedroom suites ($219-$264), some with whirlpools. 3-4 stories, interior corridors. *Bath:* combo or shower only. **Parking:** on-site. **Terms:** check-in 4 pm, package plans. **Amenities:** high-speed Internet, dual phone lines, voice mail, irons, hair dryers. *Some:* safes. **Dining:** 3 restaurants, 6:30 am-midnight, cocktails, also, Scrimshaw, see separate listing. **Pool(s):** 2 heated indoor. **Leisure Activities:** saunas, billiards, exercise room. **Guest Services:** gift shop, valet laundry, airport transportation-Albany International Airport. **Business Services:** conference facilities, business center. **Cards:** AX, DC, DS, MC, VI. **Free Special Amenities: newspaper and high-speed Internet.**

SOME UNITS
FEE

ECONO LODGE
Book great rates at AAA.com
Phone: (518)459-5670   37

AAA [SAVE]

5/1-10/31	1P: $89	2P: $99	XP: $10	F16
11/1-4/30	1P: $69	2P: $79	XP: $10	F16

Motel
Location: I-87, exit 2E, just e, then just n. 44 Wolf Rd 12205. Fax: 518/459-0069. **Facility:** 91 one-bedroom standard units. 2 stories (no elevator), interior corridors. *Bath:* combo or shower only. **Parking:** on-site. **Amenities:** high-speed Internet, voice mail, irons, hair dryers. **Guest Services:** coin laundry. **Business Services:** fax (fee). **Cards:** AX, DC, DS, MC, VI.

SOME UNITS

HAMPTON INN WOLF ROAD
Book great rates at AAA.com
Phone: (518)438-2822   28

AAA [SAVE]

7/15-8/30	1P: $135-$154	2P: $139-$159
5/1-7/14 & 11/2-4/30	1P: $99-$149	2P: $109-$149
8/31-11/1	1P: $109-$139	2P: $109-$139

Small-scale Hotel
Location: I-87, exit 4, just se on Wolf Rd, then just e. 10 Ulenski Dr 12205. Fax: 518/438-2931. **Facility:** 154 one-bedroom standard units. 5 stories, interior corridors. **Parking:** on-site. **Terms:** cancellation fee imposed. **Amenities:** video games (fee), voice mail, irons, hair dryers. **Pool(s):** small outdoor. **Guest Services:** valet and coin laundry, wireless Internet. **Business Services:** meeting rooms. **Cards:** AX, DC, DS, MC, VI. **Free Special Amenities: expanded continental breakfast and newspaper.** *(See color ad p 223)*

SOME UNITS

(See map and index starting on p. 218)

HILTON GARDEN INN-ALBANY AIRPORT · *Book great rates at AAA.com* · **Phone:** (518)464-6666 · **26**

AAA SAVE
WWW

All Year · 1P: $99-$199 · 2P: $99-$199

Location: I-87, exit 4, 1.8 mi nw. Located opposite the terminal. 800 Albany Shaker Rd 12211. Fax: 518/464-9400. **Facility:** 155 one-bedroom standard units. 6 stories, interior corridors. *Bath:* combo or shower only. **Parking:** on-site. **Terms:** check-in 4 pm, package plans. **Amenities:** video games (fee), dual phone lines, voice mail, irons, hair dryers. **Dining:** 6 am-1 & 5-10 pm, Sat & Sun 6:30 am-noon, cocktails. **Pool(s):** small heated indoor. **Leisure Activities:** whirlpool, exercise room. **Guest Services:** sundries, valet and coin laundry, wireless Internet. **Business Services:** meeting rooms, business center. **Cards:** AX, DC, DS, MC, VI. **Free Special Amenities:** newspaper and high-speed Internet.

Small-scale Hotel

SOME UNITS

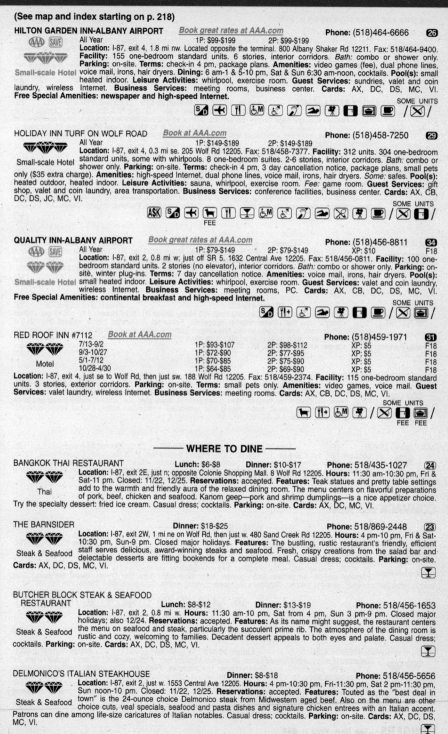

HOLIDAY INN TURF ON WOLF ROAD · *Book at AAA.com* · **Phone:** (518)458-7250 · **29**

WWW

All Year · 1P: $149-$189 · 2P: $149-$189

Location: I-87, exit 4, 0.3 mi se. 205 Wolf Rd 12205. Fax: 518/458-7377. **Facility:** 312 units. 304 one-bedroom standard units, some with whirlpools. 8 one-bedroom suites. 2-6 stories, interior corridors. *Bath:* combo or shower only. **Parking:** on-site. **Terms:** check-in 4 pm, 3 day cancellation notice, package plans, small pets only ($35 extra charge). **Amenities:** high-speed Internet, dual phone lines, voice mail, irons, hair dryers. *Some:* safes. **Pool(s):** heated outdoor, heated indoor. **Leisure Activities:** sauna, whirlpool, exercise room. *Fee:* game room. **Guest Services:** gift shop, valet and coin laundry, area transportation. **Business Services:** conference facilities, business center. **Cards:** AX, CB, DC, DS, JC, MC, VI.

Small-scale Hotel

SOME UNITS

FEE

QUALITY INN-ALBANY AIRPORT · *Book great rates at AAA.com* · **Phone:** (518)456-8811 · **34**

AAA SAVE
WWW

All Year · 1P: $79-$149 · 2P: $79-$149 · XP: $10 · F18

Location: I-87, exit 2, 0.8 mi w; just off SR 5. 1632 Central Ave 12205. Fax: 518/456-0811. **Facility:** 100 one-bedroom standard units. 2 stories (no elevator), interior corridors. *Bath:* combo or shower only. **Parking:** on-site, winter plug-ins. **Terms:** 7 day cancellation notice. **Amenities:** voice mail, irons, hair dryers. **Pool(s):** small heated indoor. **Leisure Activities:** whirlpool, exercise room. **Guest Services:** valet and coin laundry, wireless Internet. **Business Services:** meeting rooms, PC. **Cards:** AX, CB, DC, DS, MC, VI. **Free Special Amenities:** continental breakfast and high-speed Internet.

Small-scale Hotel

SOME UNITS

RED ROOF INN #7112 · *Book at AAA.com* · **Phone:** (518)459-1971 · **31**

WWW

7/13-9/2	1P: $93-$107	2P: $98-$112	XP: $5 · F18
9/3-10/27	1P: $72-$90	2P: $77-$95	XP: $5 · F18
5/1-7/12	1P: $70-$85	2P: $75-$90	XP: $5 · F18
10/28-4/30	1P: $64-$85	2P: $69-$90	XP: $5 · F18

Motel

Location: I-87, exit 4, just se to Wolf Rd, then just sw. 188 Wolf Rd 12205. Fax: 518/459-2374. **Facility:** 115 one-bedroom standard units. 3 stories, exterior corridors. **Parking:** on-site. **Terms:** small pets only. **Amenities:** video games, voice mail. **Guest Services:** valet laundry, wireless Internet. **Business Services:** meeting rooms. **Cards:** AX, CB, DC, DS, MC, VI.

SOME UNITS

FEE FEE

──────── **WHERE TO DINE** ────────

BANGKOK THAI RESTAURANT · **Lunch:** $6-$8 · **Dinner:** $10-$17 · **Phone:** 518/435-1027 · **24**

WWW

Thai

Location: I-87, exit 2E, just n; opposite Colonie Shopping Mall. 8 Wolf Rd 12205. **Hours:** 11:30 am-10:30 pm, Fri & Sat-11 pm. Closed: 11/22, 12/25. **Reservations:** accepted. **Features:** Teak statues and pretty table settings add to the warmth and friendly aura of the relaxed dining room. The menu centers on flavorful preparations of pork, beef, chicken and seafood. Kanom geep—pork and shrimp dumplings—is a nice appetizer choice. Try the specialty dessert: fried ice cream. Casual dress; cocktails. **Parking:** on-site. **Cards:** AX, DC, MC, VI.

THE BARNSIDER · **Dinner:** $18-$25 · **Phone:** 518/869-2448 · **23**

WWW

Steak & Seafood

Location: I-87, exit 2W, 1 mi ne on Wolf Rd, then just w. 480 Sand Creek Rd 12205. **Hours:** 4 pm-10 pm, Fri & Sat-10:30 pm, Sun-9 pm. Closed major holidays. **Features:** The bustling, rustic restaurant's friendly, efficient staff serves delicious, award-winning steaks and seafood. Fresh, crispy creations from the salad bar and delectable desserts are fitting bookends for a complete meal. Casual dress; cocktails. **Parking:** on-site. **Cards:** AX, DC, DS, MC, VI.

BUTCHER BLOCK STEAK & SEAFOOD RESTAURANT · **Lunch:** $8-$12 · **Dinner:** $13-$19 · **Phone:** 518-456-1653 ·

WWW

Steak & Seafood

Location: I-87, exit 2, 0.8 mi w. **Hours:** 11:30 am-10 pm, Sat from 4 pm, Sun 3 pm-9 pm. Closed major holidays; also 12/24. **Reservations:** accepted. **Features:** As its name might suggest, the restaurant centers the menu on seafood and steak, particularly the succulent prime rib. The atmosphere of the dining room is rustic and cozy, welcoming to families. Decadent dessert appeals to both eyes and palate. Casual dress; cocktails. **Parking:** on-site. **Cards:** AX, DC, DS, MC, VI.

DELMONICO'S ITALIAN STEAKHOUSE · **Dinner:** $8-$18 · **Phone:** 518-456-5656 ·

WWW

Steak & Seafood

Location: I-87, exit 2, just w. 1553 Central Ave 12205. **Hours:** 4 pm-10:30 pm, Fri-11:30 pm, Sat 2 pm-11:30 pm, Sun noon-10 pm. Closed: 11/22, 12/25. **Reservations:** accepted. **Features:** Touted as the "best deal in town" is the 24-ounce choice Delmonico steak from Midwestern aged beef. Also on the menu are other choice cuts, veal specials, seafood and pasta dishes and signature chicken entrees with an Italian accent. Patrons can dine among life-size caricatures of Italian notables. Casual dress; cocktails. **Parking:** on-site. **Cards:** AX, DC, DS, MC, VI.

(See map and index starting on p. 218)

GARCIA'S MEXICAN RESTAURANT   Lunch: $5-$9   Dinner: $7-$14   Phone: 518/456-4116   22
Tex-Mex
Location: I-87, exit 2, 1 mi w, then 6 mi w on SR 5. 1614 Central Ave 12205. **Hours:** 11:30 am-10 pm, Fri & Sat-11 pm, Sun noon-9 pm. **Closed:** 11/22, 12/24, 12/25. **Reservations:** suggested, weekends. **Features:** Popular choices on a menu of mostly Tex-Mex fare are ultimate fajitas, Olivia's sampler and quesadillas. The atmosphere is lively and energetic, enhanced by colorful decorations and upbeat music. A varied lunch buffet is laid out on weekdays. Casual dress; cocktails. **Parking:** on-site. **Cards:** AX, CB, DC, DS, MC, VI.

GRANDMA'S COUNTRY RESTAURANT   Lunch: $5-$10   Dinner: $8-$15   Phone: 518/459-4585   26
American
Location: I-87, exit 2, 1 mi e. 1273 Central Ave 12205. **Hours:** 6 am-11:30 pm, Fri & Sat-midnight. **Closed:** 12/24, 12/25. **Features:** Home-style flavors characterize such tried-and-true favorites as turkey soup and meatloaf with mashed potatoes and gravy. The challenge at dessert is to choose from more than 25 varieties of homemade pies, including a delicious lemon meringue. Casual dress; beer & wine only. **Parking:** on-site. **Cards:** AX, CB, DC, DS, MC, VI.

RALPH'S TAVERN   Lunch: $5-$13   Dinner: $5-$13   Phone: 518/489-8290   25
American
Location: I-87, exit 2, 0.6 mi e. 1328 Central Ave 12205. **Hours:** 11 am-midnight, Fri & Sat-2 am, Sun noon-midnight. **Closed:** 4/8, 11/22, 12/25. **Reservations:** accepted, weekdays. **Features:** Guests can come early or wait with other diners hungry for great food at a good price. On the no-frills menu are delicious Italian favorites, finger foods, steaks and prime rib. Casual dress; cocktails. **Parking:** on-site. **Cards:** AX, DC, DS, MC, VI.

REAL SEAFOOD CO   Lunch: $8-$10   Dinner: $14-$28   Phone: 518/458-2068   21
Seafood
Location: I-87, exit 4, 0.3 mi e. 195 Wolf Rd 12205. **Hours:** 11 am-10:30 pm, Fri-11 pm, Sat 3 pm-11 pm, Sun 3 pm-9:30 pm. **Closed:** 11/22, 12/25. **Reservations:** suggested. **Features:** The freshest, best-quality seafood is prepared in abundance. The attentive staff serves palate-tempting creations. Dressy casual; cocktails. **Parking:** on-site. **Cards:** AX, DC, DS, MC, VI.

SCRIMSHAW   Dinner: $18-$30   Phone: 518/869-8100   19
Continental
Location: I-87, exit 4, just w; in The Desmond Hotel. 660 Albany Shaker Rd 12211. **Hours:** 5:30 pm-10 pm. Closed major holidays; also Sun. **Reservations:** suggested. **Features:** A Colonial theme weaves through the upscale dining room, where professionals and couples gather to enjoy a sophisticated atmosphere. Seafood is the specialty, with such well-prepared dishes as citrus-grilled lobster over artichoke hearts. Dressy casual; cocktails. **Parking:** on-site. **Cards:** AX, CB, DC, DS, MC, VI.

SMOKEY BONES BARBECUE & GRILL
RESTAURANT   Lunch: $4-$9   Dinner: $8-$17   Phone: 518/464-9971
Barbecue
Location: I-87, exit 2, 0.5 mi w. 1557 Central Ave 12205. **Hours:** 11 am-10 pm, Fri & Sat-11 pm. **Closed:** 11/22, 12/25. **Features:** Guests can feast on hand-pulled pork, St. Louis-style ribs, smoked turkey breast and other barbecue dishes in a casual, rustic setting that resembles a mountain lodge. Casual dress; cocktails. **Parking:** on-site. **Cards:** AX, DC, DS, MC, VI.

WOLF ROAD DINER   Lunch: $5-$9   Dinner: $8-$11   Phone: 518/459-5214   20
American
Location: I-87, exit 4, just se. 219 Wolf Rd 12205. **Hours:** 6 am-1 am, Fri & Sat-2 am. **Closed:** 11/22, 12/25. **Reservations:** accepted. **Features:** Comfortable diner decor characterizes the eatery, which serves American and Greek comfort food in a flash. Delicious breakfasts and hearty lunches and dinners satisfy a hearty appetite. Casual dress; cocktails. **Parking:** on-site. **Cards:** AX, CB, DC, DS, MC, VI.

COMMACK pop. 36,367

--------- WHERE TO STAY ---------

HAMPTON INN   *Book great rates at AAA.com*   Phone: (631)462-5700
Small-scale Hotel
All Year   1P: $139-$145   2P: $149-$155
Location: I-495, exit 52 eastbound; exit 53 westbound, just n on CR 4. Located in a commercial area. 680 Commack Rd 11725. Fax: 631/462-9735. **Facility:** 143 one-bedroom standard units. 5 stories, interior corridors. **Parking:** on-site. **Amenities:** video games (fee), voice mail, irons, hair dryers. **Guest Services:** valet laundry, area transportation, wireless Internet. **Business Services:** meeting rooms, business center. **Cards:** AX, DS, MC, VI.

SOME UNITS

--------- WHERE TO DINE ---------

CHARLIE BROWN'S STEAKHOUSE   Lunch: $6-$10   Dinner: $12-$21   Phone: 631/462-4206
Steak & Seafood
Location: In King Kullen Shopping Center. 88 Veterans Memorial Hwy 11725. **Hours:** 11:30 am-2:30 & 3-10 pm, Fri & Sat-10:30 pm, Sun-9 pm. **Reservations:** not accepted. **Features:** This budget-friendly steakhouse, famous for its prime rib, offers top quality fare without hurting your pocketbook. The young ones will not be disappointed with the kid's menu, and just might even try something green from the salad bar. Adults will love the quality steaks, chicken and rib dishes. The express lunches are great for those saddled with time constraints. Casual dress; cocktails. **Parking:** on-site. **Cards:** AX, DC, DS, MC, VI.

CONGERS —*See New York p. 498.*

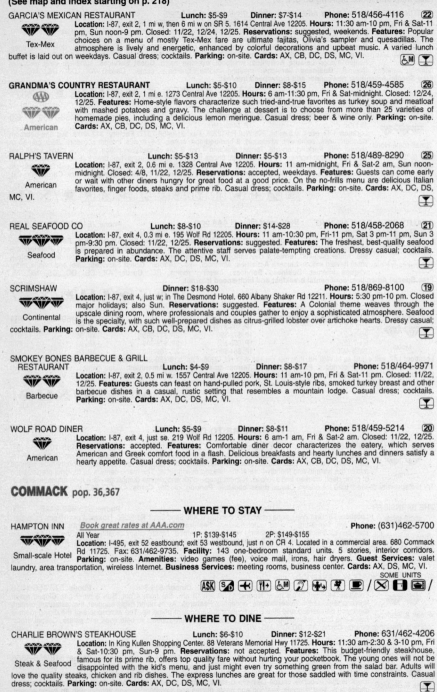

COOPERSTOWN pop. 2,032—See also HARTWICK SEMINARY, INDEX & SPRINGFIELD CENTER.

─────── WHERE TO STAY ───────

BEST WESTERN INN & SUITES AT THE COMMONS   Phone: (607)547-7100
(AAA) (SAVE) 6/2-9/3   1P: $195-$400   2P: $195-$400
          5/1-6/1 & 9/4-4/30   1P: $55-$230   2P: $65-$230
Small-scale Hotel **Location:** On SR 28; center. 50 Commons Dr (Rt 28) 13326. Fax: 607/547-7082. **Facility:** 99 one-bedroom standard units. 2 stories, interior corridors. *Bath:* combo or shower only. **Parking:** on-site, winter plug-ins. *Some:* DVD players. **Pool(s):** small heated indoor. **Leisure Activities:** whirlpool, picnic pavilion with grills, exercise room. *Fee:* game room. **Guest Services:** gift shop, coin laundry, wireless Internet. **Business Services:** meeting rooms. **Cards:** AX, DC, DS, MC, VI. **Free Special Amenities: continental breakfast and high-speed Internet.**
(See color ad below)

SOME UNITS

DIASTOLE BED & BREAKFAST   Phone: (607)547-2665
All Year   1P: $149-$249   2P: $149-$249   XP: $25
Bed & Breakfast **Location:** From Main St, e through town to CR 31, 2.6 mi n, then 0.6 mi ne on Van Yahres Rd (dirt road). 276 Van Yahres Rd 13326. **Facility:** A soothing ambience enhances this secluded country B&B overlooking Lake Otsego; featuring upscale country decor, it has a large deck and a hot tub. Smoke free premises. 4 one-bedroom standard units, some with whirlpools. 2 stories (no elevator), interior corridors. *Bath:* combo or shower only. **Parking:** on-site. **Terms:** 10 day cancellation notice-fee imposed. **Amenities:** video library, DVD players, irons, hair dryers. **Leisure Activities:** whirlpool, hiking trails. **Guest Services:** wireless Internet.

HOLIDAY INN EXPRESS HOTELS & SUITES HARTWICK/COOPERSTOWN

Phone: (607)547-8000

	6/7-9/4 [CP]	1P: $219-$499	2P: $219-$499
AAA SAVE	5/1-6/6 & 9/5-10/31 [CP]	1P: $99-$199	2P: $99-$199
	11/1-4/30 [CP]	1P: $79-$179	2P: $79-$179

Location: On SR 28. 4758 State Hwy 28 13326. Fax: 607/547-2400. **Facility:** Smoke free premises. 74 one-
Small-scale Hotel bedroom standard units. 2-3 stories, interior corridors. *Bath:* combo or shower only. **Parking:** on-site.
Terms: cancellation fee imposed, package plans. **Amenities:** high-speed Internet, voice mail, irons, hair
dryers. *Some:* DVD players, video games, CD players. **Pool(s):** small heated indoor. **Leisure Activities:** whirlpool, exercise
room. **Guest Services:** valet and coin laundry. **Business Services:** meeting rooms, PC. **Cards:** AX, CB, DC, DS, JC, MC, VI.
Free Special Amenities: continental breakfast and high-speed Internet.

SOME UNITS

(&M) (icons) / VCR /

LAKE FRONT MOTEL

Phone: 607/547-9511

	6/1-9/3	1P: $125-$190	2P: $125-$190	XP: $20
(diamonds)	5/1-5/31	1P: $85-$190	2P: $85-$190	XP: $20
Motel	9/4-10/31	1P: $85-$150	2P: $85-$150	XP: $20
	11/1-4/30	1P: $70-$150	2P: $70-$150	XP: $20

Location: Just n of center. 10 Fair St 13326. Fax: 607/547-2792. **Facility:** Smoke free premises. 47 units. 46 one-bedroom standard
units. 1 one-bedroom suite. 1-2 stories (no elevator), exterior corridors. *Bath:* combo or shower only. **Parking:** on-site.
Terms: cancellation fee imposed, package plans. **Amenities:** voice mail. **Dining:** restaurant, see separate listing. **Leisure
Activities:** *Fee:* marina. **Cards:** MC, VI.

(icons)

THE OTESAGA RESORT HOTEL

Phone: (607)547-9931

	5/25-10/7 [MAP]	1P: $343-$523	2P: $405-$585	XP: $130	F6
AAA SAVE	4/18-4/30 [MAP]	1P: $318-$488	2P: $380-$550	XP: $130	F6
(diamonds)	5/1-5/24 & 10/8-11/25 [MAP]	1P: $308-$478	2P: $370-$540	XP: $130	F6

Location: On SR 80 E; center. 60 Lake St 13326 (PO Box 311). Fax: 607/547-9675. **Facility:** Guests will find fine
Historic craftsmanship within and sweeping views of Lake Otsego from the front porch of this restored 1910 hotel.
Large-scale Hotel 135 units. 125 one-bedroom standard units. 10 one-bedroom suites, some with whirlpools. 5 stories, interior
corridors. *Bath:* combo or shower only. **Parking:** on-site and valet. **Terms:** open 5/1-11/25 & 4/18-4/30, 2
night minimum stay - weekends, 14 day cancellation notice-fee imposed, package plans, $15 service charge. **Amenities:** dual
phone lines, voice mail, safes, irons, hair dryers. *Some:* DVD players. **Dining:** 3 restaurants, 7 am-10, noon-2 & 6-9:30 pm,
cocktails. **Pool(s):** heated outdoor. **Leisure Activities:** rental canoes, boat dock, 2 tennis courts, recreation programs, hiking
trails, exercise room. *Fee:* golf-18 holes. **Guest Services:** gift shop, valet laundry. **Business Services:** meeting rooms,
business center. **Cards:** AX, MC, VI. **Free Special Amenities: local telephone calls and high-speed Internet.**

SOME UNITS

(icons) / VCR (icon) /

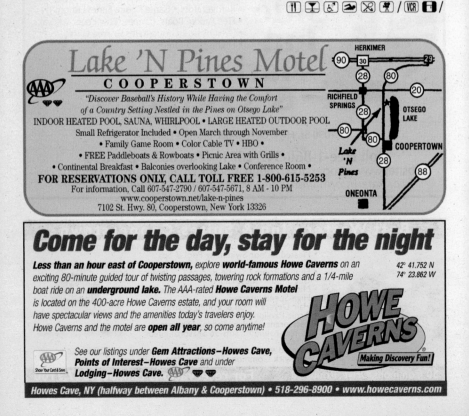

ROSE AND THISTLE B & B

Phone: (607)547-5345

(AAA) [SAVE]	5/1-10/31 [BP]	1P: $125-$175	2P: $125-$175	XP: $25	F7
▼▼▼	11/1-4/30 [BP]	1P: $115-$135	2P: $115-$135	XP: $25	F7

Location: On SR 28, south end of town. 132 Chestnut St 13326. **Fax:** 607/547-5917. **Facility:** Smoke free premises. 4 one-bedroom standard units. 2 stories (no elevator), interior corridors. *Bath:* combo or shower only. **Parking:** on-site. **Terms:** age restrictions may apply, 14 day cancellation notice-fee imposed, package plans, no pets allowed (owner's cat on premises). **Amenities:** video library, hair dryers. **Cards:** AX, DS, MC, VI. **Free Special Amenities:** full breakfast and high-speed Internet.

Bed & Breakfast

SOME UNITS

[X] [☎] / [VCR] /

──────── WHERE TO DINE ────────

THE BLUE MINGO GRILL

| **Lunch:** $4-$11 | **Dinner:** $19-$26 | Phone: 607/547-7496 |

▼▼▼

Location: 2.5 mi n. 6098 Hwy 80 13326. **Hours:** Open 5/15-9/1; 11:30 am-10 pm. **Reservations:** suggested. **Features:** Boaters, sightseers and travelers find the attentive service, delectable entrees and lakefront setting of the marina-centered eatery a delight. Chef Joe Ford chooses fresh seasonal ingredients for his ever-changing menu. Casual dress; cocktails. **Parking:** on-site. **Cards:** MC, VI.

Continental

[K]

THE DOUBLEDAY CAFE

| **Lunch:** $3-$10 | **Dinner:** $6-$20 | Phone: 607/547-5468 |

▼

Location: Center. 93 Main St 13326. **Hours:** 7 am-9 pm, Fri & Sat-10 pm; hours vary. Closed: 11/22, 12/25. **Features:** Wholesome familiar fare—steaks, salads, sandwiches, burgers and daily specials—makes up the restaurant's menu. Savory soups and desserts are particularly noteworthy. Baseball memorabilia decorates the walls of the popular family spot. Casual dress; beer & wine only. **Parking:** street. **Cards:** DS, MC, VI.

American

HOFFMAN LANE BISTRO

| **Dinner:** $12-$19 | Phone: 607/547-7055 |

▼▼▼

Location: Downtown. 2 Hoffman Ln 13326. **Hours:** 5 pm-10 pm. Closed: 3/23, 11/22, 12/25. **Reservations:** suggested. **Features:** Eclectic decor and such menu items as tuna au poivre and pan-seared salmon make the bistro lively in taste and color. Casual dress; cocktails. **Parking:** street. **Cards:** AX, MC, VI.

Continental

[Y]

LAKE FRONT RESTAURANT

| **Lunch:** $7-$13 | **Dinner:** $15-$25 | Phone: 607/547-8188 |

▼▼

Location: Just n of center; in Lake Front Motel. 10 Fair St 13326. **Hours:** Open 5/1-10/31; 7 am-9 pm. **Reservations:** accepted. **Features:** Two blocks from downtown, the lakefront setting includes plenty of windows for viewing, as well as tables on the seasonal patio. Service has a casual, hometown charm. Menu selections are tasty. Casual dress; cocktails. **Parking:** on-site. **Cards:** MC, VI.

American

[Y]

THE PEPPER MILL

| **Dinner:** $9-$19 | Phone: 607/547-8550 |

▼▼

Location: 0.5 mi s. 5418 State Hwy 28 13326. **Hours:** Open 5/1-12/31 & 4/2-4/30; 5 pm-10 pm. Closed: 11/22, 12/24, 12/25. **Reservations:** suggested. **Features:** Baseball Hall of Fame pictures on the wall set the scene for casual dining that is far from ballpark style. Wonderful house sauces flavor preparations of steak and chicken. To top off the meal, enjoy a cup of robust coffee with cinnamon bread pudding. Casual dress; cocktails. **Parking:** on-site. **Cards:** DS, MC, VI.

American

CORFU pop. 795

──────── WHERE TO STAY ────────

DARIEN LAKES ECONO LODGE

Phone: (585)599-4681

▼▼▼	6/15-9/3 [CP]	1P: $79-$139	2P: $79-$139	XP: $5	F18
	5/1-6/14 & 9/4-10/31 [CP]	1P: $50-$90	2P: $50-$90	XP: $5	F18
	11/1-4/30 [CP]	1P: $45-$80	2P: $45-$80	XP: $5	F18

Small-scale Hotel

Location: I-90, exit 48A, just s. 8493 SR 77 14036. **Fax:** 585/599-3040. **Facility:** 73 one-bedroom standard units. 2 stories (no elevator), interior corridors. **Parking:** on-site. **Leisure Activities:** *Fee:* game room. **Guest Services:** coin laundry. **Cards:** AX, DC, DS, MC, VI.

SOME UNITS

[ASK] [S☎] [🛏] [▥+] [✦] / [X] [VCR] [🖥] [📠] /
FEE FEE

CORNING pop. 10,842—*See also FINGER LAKES.*

──────── WHERE TO STAY ────────

COMFORT INN *Book great rates at AAA.com*

Phone: (607)962-1515

▼▼▼	5/1-10/20	1P: $89-$249	2P: $89-$249	XP: $10	F18
	10/21-4/30	1P: $69-$109	2P: $69-$109	XP: $10	F18

Small-scale Hotel

Location: I-86/SR 17, exit 46, just s on SR 414, then 0.5 mi w on SR 415 (Pulteney St). 66 W Pulteney St 14830. **Fax:** 607/962-1899. **Facility:** 62 one-bedroom standard units, some with whirlpools. 2 stories (no elevator), interior corridors. **Parking:** on-site, winter plug-ins. **Terms:** 2 night minimum stay - seasonal, cancellation fee imposed. **Amenities:** video library, DVD players, high-speed Internet, voice mail, irons, hair dryers. **Pool(s):** heated indoor. **Leisure Activities:** exercise room. **Guest Services:** valet laundry, wireless Internet. **Cards:** AX, DC, DS, MC, VI.

SOME UNITS

[ASK] [S☎] [&M] [📶] [➰] [✦] [🖥] / [X] [📠] [🖥] /

CORNING DAYS INN *Book great rates at AAA.com*

Phone: (607)936-9370

▼▼	5/1-10/31 [CP]	1P: $89-$159	2P: $89-$159	XP: $10	F17
	11/1-4/30 [CP]	1P: $79-$149	2P: $79-$149	XP: $10	F17

Small-scale Hotel

Location: Corner of Ferris St and Riverside Dr; just w of Corning Glass Center; center. 23 Riverside Dr 14830. **Fax:** 607/936-0513. **Facility:** 56 one-bedroom standard units, some with efficiencies and/or whirlpools. 3 stories, interior corridors. *Bath:* combo or shower only. **Parking:** on-site. **Amenities:** voice mail, irons, hair dryers. **Dining:** Garcia's Mexican Restaurant, see separate listing. **Pool(s):** heated indoor. **Leisure Activities:** whirlpool. **Guest Services:** valet laundry, wireless Internet. **Cards:** AX, DC, DS, MC, VI.

SOME UNITS

[ASK] [S☎] [▥] [➰] [Y] [&] [➰] [✦+] [✦] [🖥] / [X] [📠] [🖥] /
FEE FEE FEE

FAIRFIELD INN BY MARRIOTT CORNING/RIVERSIDE   *Book great rates at AAA.com*

Phone: 607/937-9600

▼▼▼▼

Property failed to provide current rates

Location: I-86/SR 17, exit 45 eastbound, just n; exit westbound, just e on SR 415 (High St), then just s. 3 S Buffalo St 14830. Fax: 607/937-3155. **Facility:** Smoke free premises. 62 one-bedroom standard units. 3 stories, interior corridors. *Bath:* combo or shower only. **Parking:** on-site. **Amenities:** video games (fee), high-speed Internet, irons, hair dryers. **Pool(s):** small heated indoor. **Leisure Activities:** exercise room. **Guest Services:** valet laundry, wireless Internet.

Small-scale Hotel

SOME UNITS

[🍴↑] [🔲M] [⛬] [🌀] [🏊] [✕] [📷] [💻] / [📠] /

GATE HOUSE MOTEL

Phone: (607)936-4131

AAA [SAVE]	5/1-11/30	1P: $42-$50	2P: $49-$66	XP: $10	F18
	12/1-4/30	1P: $37-$49	2P: $45-$56	XP: $10	F18

▼▼

Motel

Location: I-86/SR 17, exit 47 (SR 352) eastbound, 0.8 mi e; exit 48 (SR 352) westbound, 1.5 mi w. 11409 E LPGA Dr (SR 352) 14830-3663. Fax: 607/936-8730. **Facility:** 20 one-bedroom standard units. 1 story, interior/exterior corridors. *Bath:* combo or shower only. **Parking:** on-site, winter plug-ins. **Terms:** 10 day cancellation notice, [BP] meal plan available. **Guest Services:** coin laundry. **Cards:** AX, MC, VI. **Free Special Amenities:** local telephone calls and preferred room (subject to availability with advance reservations).

SOME UNITS

[S🅳] / [✕] [📠] /

RADISSON HOTEL CORNING   *Book at AAA.com*

Phone: (607)962-5000

	5/1-10/31	1P: $120-$159	2P: $120-$159	XP: $10	F21
	11/1-4/30	1P: $99-$139	2P: $99-$139	XP: $10	F21

▼▼▼▼

Small-scale Hotel   **Location:** On I-86/SR 17; center. 125 Denison Pkwy E 14830-2786. Fax: 607/962-4166. **Facility:** 177 one-bedroom standard units, some with whirlpools. 3 stories, interior corridors. *Bath:* combo or shower only. **Parking:** on-site. **Terms:** cancellation fee imposed, [AP] meal plan available, package plans, small pets only ($35 fee, must be attended). **Amenities:** video games (fee), high-speed Internet, voice mail, irons, hair dryers. *Some:* safes, honor bars. **Pool(s):** heated indoor. **Leisure Activities:** whirlpool, exercise room. **Guest Services:** valet and coin laundry, wireless Internet. **Business Services:** conference facilities, PC. **Cards:** AX, CB, DC, DS, MC, VI.

SOME UNITS

[ASK] [S🅳] [🐾] [🍴↑] [🍸] [🏊] [💻] / [✕] [📠] [🖨] /
FEE

ROSEWOOD INN

Phone: (607)962-3253

	5/1-10/31		2P: $125-$185	XP: $50	
	11/1-4/30		2P: $95-$165	XP: $35	

▼▼▼

Historic Bed & Breakfast   **Location:** Just off SR 352; corner of 1st and Chemung sts. 134 E 1st St 14830. **Facility:** This seven-room, English Tudor-style 1855 mansion features art-glass chandeliers and numerous antiques. Smoke free premises. 7 one-bedroom standard units, some with kitchens. 2 stories (no elevator), interior/exterior corridors. *Bath:* combo or shower only. **Parking:** on-site. **Terms:** age restrictions may apply, 3 day cancellation notice-fee imposed, package plans. **Amenities:** *Some:* hair dryers. **Cards:** AX, CB, DC, DS, MC, VI.

SOME UNITS

[ASK] [🍴↑] [✕] / [🅦] [🌀] [📠] [💻] /

STAYBRIDGE SUITES BY HOLIDAY INN   *Book at AAA.com*

Phone: 607/936-7800

▼▼▼

All Year [ECP]   1P: $150-$185   2P: $150-$185

Small-scale Hotel   **Location:** I-86/SR 17, exit 46, just s. 201 Townley Ave 14830. Fax: 607/936-7900. **Facility:** 115 units. 59 one-bedroom standard units with efficiencies. 38 one- and 18 two-bedroom suites with efficiencies. 3 stories, interior corridors. *Bath:* combo or shower only. **Parking:** on-site. **Terms:** pets ($75 fee). **Amenities:** high-speed Internet, dual phone lines, voice mail, irons, hair dryers. **Pool(s):** heated indoor. **Leisure Activities:** whirlpool, exercise room, sports court. **Guest Services:** sundries, complimentary evening beverages: Tues-Thurs, complimentary and valet laundry, wireless Internet. **Business Services:** meeting rooms, business center. **Cards:** AX, DC, DS, MC, VI.

SOME UNITS

[ASK] [S🅳] [🐾] [🔲M] [⛬] [🌀] [🏊] [✕] [📷] [📠] [🖨] [💻] / [✕] [VCR] /
FEE   FEE

—— WHERE TO DINE ——

CANTINA

◆◆	Lunch: $2-$5	Dinner: $2-$5	Phone: 607/974-8226

Mexican

Location: Downtown; next to Rockwell Museum of Western Art. 111 Cedar St 14830. **Hours:** 11 am-8 pm. Closed major holidays; also Sun. **Features:** At the Rockwell Museum of Art, this colorful eatery prepares traditional made-to-order Mexican choices with fresh, top-quality ingredients. Green Mountain Coffee is brewed freshly all day. Casual dress; beer only. **Parking:** on-site. **Cards:** AX, MC, VI.

GAFFER GRILL AND TAP ROOM

▼▼ ▼▼	Lunch: $6-$9	Dinner: $13-$24	Phone: 607/962-4649

American

Location: Center. 58 W Market St 14830. **Hours:** 11:30 am-3 & 4:30-10:30 pm, Sat from 4:30 pm. Closed major holidays; also Sun. **Reservations:** suggested. **Features:** Contributing to a turn-of-the-20th-century feel are dark woods, brass and glass in the dining and lounge area. Dining experiences here are pleasant thanks to the friendly staff and American fare with some upscale touches. Dressy casual; cocktails. **Parking:** street. **Cards:** AX, DC, DS, MC, VI.

[🍸]

GARCIA'S MEXICAN RESTAURANT

◆▼	Lunch: $3-$8	Dinner: $7-$11	Phone: 607/937-3992

Mexican

Location: Corner of Ferris St and Riverside Dr; just w of Corning Glass Center; center; in Corning Days Inn. 58 Ferris St 14830. **Hours:** 11 am-9 pm, Fri-10 pm, Sat noon-10 pm, Sun noon-9 pm. Closed major holidays. **Reservations:** accepted. **Features:** Patrons can browse the large selection of traditional Mexican dishes in a festive, casual setting. The friendly staff aims to please with fast, courteous service. Casual dress; cocktails. **Parking:** on-site. **Cards:** AX, DS, MC, VI.

[🍸]

LONDON UNDERGROUND CAFE

Lunch: $8-$13   **Dinner:** $13-$30   **Phone:** 607/962-2345

Location: Just n of I-86/SR 17; downtown. 69 E Market St 14830. **Hours:** 11:30 am-9 pm, Fri & Sat-9:30 pm, Sun 11:30 am-7 pm. **Closed:** 11/22, 12/25. **Reservations:** suggested. **Features:** Palate-pleasing flavors are consistent characteristics of the cafe's gourmet Continental cuisine. Favorites include the memorable Wixon's fall flower honey-pecan-crusted rack of lamb and halibut with Finger Lakes wine butter sauce. The casual, three-level dining room is decorated in a British theme. A pianist entertains on Saturday evening. Casual dress; cocktails. **Parking:** street. **Cards:** AX, DS, MC, VI.

Continental

PUDGIE'S PIZZA & SUBS

Lunch: $4-$8   **Dinner:** $4-$8   **Phone:** 607/962-4674

Location: On old SR 17; downtown. 80 Denison E Pkwy 14830. **Hours:** 11 am-10 pm, Thurs-Sat to 11 pm. **Closed:** 3/23, 11/22, 12/25. **Features:** This basic eatery serves up pizza, subs and pasta dishes for hungry diners to eat in or take out. Party packs and delivery are available. Casual dress. **Parking:** on-site. **Cards:** AX, MC, VI.

Pizza

SORGE'S RESTAURANT

Lunch: $4-$6   **Dinner:** $7-$20   **Phone:** 607/937-5422

Location: Historic downtown Gaffer District. 66-68 W Market St 14830. **Hours:** 7 am-10 pm. **Closed:** 3/23, 11/22, 12/25. **Reservations:** suggested. **Features:** Operated by the same family since 1951, the restaurant is a local favorite for steak, seafood and pasta. The downstairs dining room is bright and casual; upstairs, the feeling is more romantic and subdued. The friendly staff provides timely follow-up. Casual dress; cocktails. **Parking:** on-site. **Cards:** AX, DS, MC, VI.

Italian

SPENCER'S RESTAURANT & MERCANTILE

Lunch: $4-$7   **Dinner:** $6-$16   **Phone:** 607/936-9196

Location: SR 352, just n on Conhocton St to Market St Ext, just e. 359 E Market St Ext 14830. **Hours:** 11 am-10 pm. **Closed:** 11/22, 12/25. **Features:** In a semi-commercial neighborhood near downtown, the popular family restaurant delivers a wide array of made-to-order pasta selections, as well as well-prepared steaks, chicken and chops. Patrons can dine next to one of four fireplaces in winter. Prices are moderate, and the food tastes great. Casual dress; cocktails. **Parking:** on-site. **Cards:** AX, DS, MC, VI.

American

THREE BIRDS RESTAURANT

Dinner: $16-$30   **Phone:** 607/936-8862

Location: Center of downtown. 73 E Market St 14830. **Hours:** 5 pm-9 pm, Fri & Sat-10 pm. Closed major holidays; also Sun. **Reservations:** suggested. **Features:** Fresh seasonal ingredients are the basis for progressive American dishes at this cozy, inviting downtown restaurant. Signature items include crispy Chesapeake crab and corn cakes, Three Birds Harbor fish soup, honey-roasted pecan-crusted pork tenderloin and oven-roasted New Zealand rack of lamb. Classic and seasonal martinis are served at the martini bar. Dressy casual; cocktails. **Parking:** street. **Cards:** AX, DS, MC, VI.

Nouvelle American

CORNWALL

------- WHERE TO STAY -------

CROMWELL MANOR INN

Phone: (845)534-7136

All Year [BP]   2P: $165-$370   XP: $35

Location: Jct US 9W and SR 94, 5.5 mi s on US 9W, then 0.5 mi w. 174 Angola Rd 12518. **Facility:** A natural setting overlooking the valley, complemented by spacious, upscale rooms in the main building, makes this brick Colonial mansion stand out. Smoke free premises. 12 one-bedroom standard units, some with whirlpools. 1-2 stories (no elevator), interior/exterior corridors. **Parking:** on-site. **Terms:** 2 night minimum stay - seasonal and/or weekends, age restrictions may apply, 14 day cancellation notice. **Amenities:** CD players, high-speed Internet, hair dryers. **Cards:** AX, MC, VI. **Free Special Amenities:** full breakfast and high-speed Internet.

Bed & Breakfast

CORTLAND pop. 18,740

------- WHERE TO STAY -------

COMFORT INN

Book great rates at AAA.com   **Phone:** (607)753-7721

All Year [ECP]   1P: $79-$199   2P: $79-$199   XP: $12   F18

Location: I-81, exit 11, just e. 2 1/2 Locust Ave 13045. **Fax:** 607/753-7608. **Facility:** 66 one-bedroom standard units, some with whirlpools. 2 stories (no elevator), interior corridors. **Parking:** on-site. **Terms:** small pets only ($10 fee, in smoking units). **Amenities:** irons, hair dryers. **Leisure Activities:** exercise room. **Fee:** game room. **Guest Services:** valet laundry, wireless Internet. **Cards:** AX, CB, DC, DS, JC, MC, VI.

Small-scale Hotel

SOME UNITS

FEE

COUNTRY INN & SUITES

Book at AAA.com   **Phone:** (607)753-8300

1/1-4/30 [ECP]   1P: $110-$215   2P: $110-$215   XP: $10   F18
5/1-12/31 [ECP]   1P: $103-$205   2P: $103-$205   XP: $10   F18

Location: I-81, exit 12, 3 mi s on SR 281 (West Rd). 3707 Rt 281 13045. **Fax:** 607/753-8301. **Facility:** 81 units. 56 one-bedroom standard units, some with whirlpools. 25 one-bedroom suites ($140-$250). 3 stories, interior corridors. **Bath:** combo or shower only. **Parking:** on-site. **Terms:** package plans. **Amenities:** high-speed Internet, voice mail, irons, hair dryers. **Some:** DVD players (fee), dual phone lines. **Pool(s):** small heated indoor. **Leisure Activities:** whirlpool, exercise room. **Guest Services:** valet and coin laundry, wireless Internet. **Business Services:** meeting rooms, business center. **Cards:** AX, DC, DS, MC, VI.

Small-scale Hotel

SOME UNITS

FEE

ECONO LODGE

(AAA) (SAVE)

Motel

Phone: (607)756-2856

All Year   1P: $59-$179   2P: $59-$179   XP: $10   F18
Location: I-81, exit 11, 0.8 mi s on SR 13/41 and US 11. 10 Church St 13045. Fax: 607/758-7555. **Facility:** 42 one-bedroom standard units. 2 stories (no elevator), exterior corridors. **Parking:** on-site. **Terms:** cancellation fee imposed, [CP] meal plan available, package plans, pets ($20 extra charge, in designated units). **Amenities:** high-speed Internet, hair dryers. *Some:* DVD players (fee). **Cards:** AX, DS, MC, VI.
Free Special Amenities: continental breakfast and high-speed Internet.

SOME UNITS

HAMPTON INN

Small-scale Hotel

Phone: (607)662-0007

Book great rates at AAA.com
All Year   1P: $61-$209   2P: $61-$209   Phone: (607)662-0007
Location: I-81, exit 11, just s on SR 13, then just e. 26 River St 13045. Fax: 607/662-0678. **Facility:** 68 one-bedroom standard units, some with whirlpools. 3 stories, interior corridors. **Bath:** combo or shower only. **Parking:** on-site. **Amenities:** video library, DVD players, high-speed Internet, voice mail, irons, hair dryers. **Pool(s):** heated indoor. **Leisure Activities:** exercise room. **Guest Services:** valet and coin laundry. **Business Services:** meeting rooms, PC. **Cards:** AX, DC, DS, MC, VI.

SOME UNITS

HOLIDAY INN CORTLAND   *Book at AAA.com*

Small-scale Hotel

Phone: (607)756-4431

All Year   1P: $69-$189   2P: $69-$189
Location: I-81, exit 11, just s on SR 13. 2 River St 13045. Fax: 607/753-3511. **Facility:** 148 units. 146 one-bedroom standard units. 2 one-bedroom suites, some with whirlpools. 2 stories (no elevator), interior corridors. **Parking:** on-site. **Terms:** cancellation fee imposed, [AP] meal plan available, pets ($25 extra charge). **Amenities:** voice mail, irons, hair dryers. **Pool(s):** small heated indoor. **Leisure Activities:** exercise room. *Fee:* game room. **Guest Services:** valet and coin laundry. **Business Services:** conference facilities. **Cards:** AX, DS, MC, VI.

SOME UNITS

QUALITY INN CORTLAND   *Book great rates at AAA.com*

(AAA) (SAVE)

Small-scale Hotel

Phone: (607)756-5622

All Year [ECP]   1P: $79-$199   2P: $79-$199   XP: $12   F18
Location: I-81, exit 11, just n. 188 Clinton St 13045. Fax: 607/753-6171. **Facility:** 56 one-bedroom standard units. 2 stories (no elevator), interior corridors. **Parking:** on-site. **Terms:** pets ($20 fee). **Amenities:** irons, hair dryers. **Leisure Activities:** limited exercise equipment. **Guest Services:** valet laundry, wireless Internet. **Cards:** AX, CB, DC, DS, JC, MC, VI. **Free Special Amenities: expanded continental breakfast and high-speed Internet.**

SOME UNITS

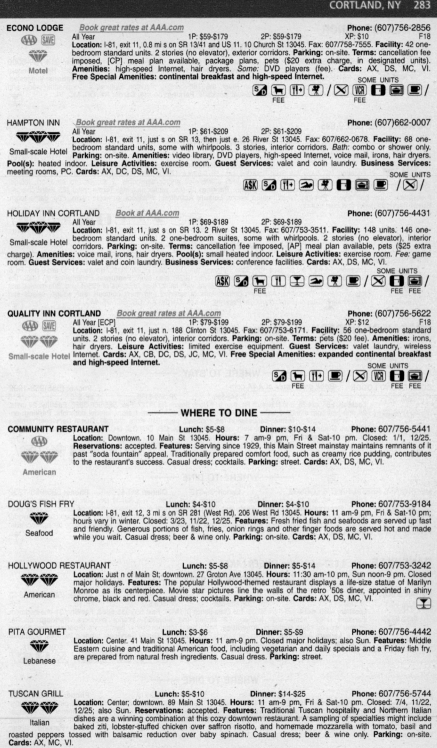

——— **WHERE TO DINE** ———

COMMUNITY RESTAURANT   **Lunch:** $5-$8   **Dinner:** $10-$14   Phone: 607/756-5441

(AAA)

American

Location: Downtown. 10 Main St 13045. **Hours:** 7 am-9 pm, Fri & Sat-10 pm. Closed: 1/1, 12/25. **Reservations:** accepted. **Features:** Serving since 1929, this Main Street mainstay maintains remnants of it past "soda fountain" appeal. Traditionally prepared comfort food, such as creamy rice pudding, contributes to the restaurant's success. Casual dress; cocktails. **Parking:** street. **Cards:** AX, DS, MC, VI.

DOUG'S FISH FRY   **Lunch:** $4-$10   **Dinner:** $4-$10   Phone: 607/753-9184

Seafood

Location: I-81, exit 12, 3 mi s on SR 281 (West Rd). 206 West Rd 13045. **Hours:** 11 am-9 pm, Fri & Sat-10 pm; hours vary in winter. Closed: 3/23, 11/22, 12/25. **Features:** Fresh fried fish and seafoods are served up fast and friendly. Generous portions of fish, fries, onion rings and other finger foods are served hot and made while you wait. Casual dress; beer & wine only. **Parking:** on-site. **Cards:** AX, DS, MC, VI.

HOLLYWOOD RESTAURANT   **Lunch:** $5-$8   **Dinner:** $5-$14   Phone: 607/753-3242

American

Location: Just n of Main St; downtown. 27 Groton Ave 13045. **Hours:** 11:30 am-10 pm, Sun noon-9 pm. Closed major holidays. **Features:** The popular Hollywood-themed restaurant displays a life-size statue of Marilyn Monroe as its centerpiece. Movie star pictures line the walls of the retro '50s diner, appointed in shiny chrome, black and red. Casual dress; cocktails. **Parking:** on-site. **Cards:** AX, DS, MC, VI.

PITA GOURMET   **Lunch:** $3-$6   **Dinner:** $5-$9   Phone: 607/756-4442

Lebanese

Location: Center. 41 Main St 13045. **Hours:** 11 am-9 pm. Closed major holidays; also Sun. **Features:** Middle Eastern cuisine and traditional American food, including vegetarian and daily specials and a Friday fish fry, are prepared from natural fresh ingredients. Casual dress. **Parking:** street.

TUSCAN GRILL   **Lunch:** $5-$10   **Dinner:** $14-$25   Phone: 607/756-5744

Italian

Location: Center; downtown. 89 Main St 13045. **Hours:** 11 am-9 pm, Fri & Sat-10 pm. Closed: 7/4, 11/22, 12/25; also Sun. **Reservations:** accepted. **Features:** Traditional Tuscan hospitality and Northern Italian dishes are a winning combination at this cozy downtown restaurant. A sampling of specialties might include baked ziti, lobster-stuffed chicken over saffron risotto, and homemade mozzarella with tomato, basil and roasted peppers tossed with balsamic reduction over baby spinach. Casual dress; beer & wine only. **Parking:** on-site. **Cards:** AX, MC, VI.

CORTLANDT MANOR

──── WHERE TO DINE ────

MONTEVERDE AT OLDSTONE MANOR **Lunch:** $15-$25 **Dinner:** $24-$36 **Phone:** 914/739-5000
Continental
Location: On US 6 and 202, 2.5 mi se of Bear Mountain Bridge. 28 Bear Mountain Bridge Rd 10567. **Hours:** noon-9 pm, Fri-10 pm, Sat 11:30 am-10 pm, Sun 11:30 am-8 pm. Closed major holidays. **Reservations:** suggested. **Features:** Overlooking the Hudson River, the 18th-century mansion features a Continental menu and formally dressed servers. Dressy casual; cocktails. **Parking:** on-site. **Cards:** AX, DC, MC, VI.

COXSACKIE pop. 2,895

──── WHERE TO STAY ────

BEST WESTERN NEW BALTIMORE INN **Phone:** 518/731-8100
Property failed to provide current rates
Small-scale Hotel
Location: I-87 (New York State Thruway), exit 21B, 0.5 mi s. 12600 Rt 9W 12192. Fax: 518/731-6266. **Facility:** 63 one-bedroom standard units, some with efficiencies and/or whirlpools. 2 stories (no elevator), interior corridors. *Bath:* combo or shower only. **Parking:** on-site, winter plug-ins. **Terms:** pets ($5 extra charge). **Amenities:** irons, hair dryers. **Pool(s):** small heated indoor. **Leisure Activities:** whirlpool, exercise room. *Fee:* game room. **Guest Services:** valet and coin laundry.

SOME UNITS

──── WHERE TO DINE ────

RED'S RESTAURANT *Menu on AAA.com* **Lunch:** $5-$8 **Dinner:** $10-$25 **Phone:** 518/731-8151
American
Location: 1.5 mi s of I-87 (New York State Thruway), exit 21B. 12005 Rt 9W 12192. **Hours:** 11:30 am-9 pm, Fri & Sat-9:30 pm, Sun 10:30 am-8 pm. Closed: 1/1, 12/25; also Mon. **Features:** Established in 1945, the restaurant is decorated in a roadside country style, with knotty pine, pictures of 1950s and '60s movies and lots of plants. Traditional American preparations of seafood and meat combine with soups, salads and sandwiches. Casual dress; cocktails. **Parking:** on-site. **Cards:** AX, CB, DC, DS, MC, VI.

CROTON-ON-HUDSON —*See New York p. 498.*

CUBA pop. 1,633

──── WHERE TO STAY ────

CUBA ECONO LODGE *Book great rates at AAA.com* **Phone:** (585)968-1992
Motel
All Year 1P: $49-$99 2P: $59-$109 XP: $10 F16
Location: I-86, exit 28, n to N Branch Rd, then e. 1 North Branch Rd 14727. Fax: 585/968-3826. **Facility:** 27 units. 26 one-bedroom standard units. 1 one-bedroom suite with kitchen. 1 story, interior corridors. **Parking:** on-site, winter plug-ins. **Terms:** cancellation fee imposed, pets ($10 extra charge). **Guest Services:** wireless Internet. **Business Services:** meeting rooms. **Cards:** AX, CB, DC, DS, MC, VI. **Free Special Amenities:** continental breakfast and high-speed Internet.

SOME UNITS

──── WHERE TO DINE ────

MOONWINKS RESTAURANT & LOUNGE **Lunch:** $5-$12 **Dinner:** $11-$27 **Phone:** 585/968-1232
American
Location: I-86, exit 28, 1 mi n. Rt 305 14727. **Hours:** noon-10 pm, Fri & Sat-11 pm, Sun 11 am-9 pm. Closed: 12/25. **Reservations:** accepted. **Features:** The pleasant, rural atmosphere welcomes diners to relax over entrees of pasta, chicken, veal, pork, seafood and beef. Rack of lamb stands out as a particularly flavorful selection. Wonderful desserts are made on the premises. Servers are attentive. Casual dress; cocktails. **Parking:** on-site. **Cards:** AX, DS, MC, VI.

DANSVILLE pop. 4,832—*See also FINGER LAKES.*

──── WHERE TO STAY ────

LOGAN'S INN **Phone:** (585)335-5840
Small-scale Hotel
All Year 1P: $62-$68 2P: $68-$73 XP: $6 F16
Location: I-390, exit 4, just n on SR 36. 106 Clara Barton St 14437. Fax: 585/335-5863. **Facility:** 31 one-bedroom standard units, some with kitchens. 2 stories (no elevator), interior corridors. **Parking:** on-site. **Terms:** weekly rates available. **Amenities:** high-speed Internet, irons, hair dryers. **Pool(s):** small heated indoor. **Leisure Activities:** saunas, whirlpool. *Fee:* massage. **Guest Services:** tanning facilities. **Business Services:** meeting rooms. **Cards:** AX, DS, MC, VI.

SOME UNITS

──── WHERE TO DINE ────

JACK'S PLACE **Lunch:** $6-$9 **Dinner:** $13-$19 **Phone:** 585/335-3725
American
Cards: MC, VI.
Location: Center. 110-112 Main St 14437. **Hours:** 11:30 am-2 & 5-9 pm, Sat & Mon from 5 pm. Closed major holidays; also Sun. **Reservations:** accepted. **Features:** Established in 1974, the restaurant offers casual dining in a pleasant, subdued atmosphere or on the tavern side. Tasty sauces and accompaniments enhance pasta, seafood, chicken, pork and veal dishes. Casual dress; cocktails. **Parking:** street.

DARIEN CENTER

——— WHERE TO STAY ———

SIX FLAGS HOTEL LODGE ON THE LAKE   **Phone:** 585/599-5500
▼▼▼▼ ▼   Property failed to provide current rates
                Location: I-90, exit 48A, 5 mi s on SR 77. 9993 Allegheny Rd 14040 (PO Box 91). Fax: 585/599-5521.
Small-scale Hotel   **Facility:** Smoke free premises. 162 units. 160 one-bedroom standard units. 2 one-bedroom suites. 3
                stories, interior corridors. *Bath:* combo or shower only. **Parking:** on-site. **Terms:** open 5/5-10/29.
Amenities: hair dryers. **Pool(s):** heated outdoor, wading. **Guest Services:** wireless Internet.

SOME UNITS

——— WHERE TO DINE ———

BEACHY'S PIZZA & WING CAFE   **Lunch:** $3-$5   **Dinner:** $5-$10   **Phone:** 585/547-9339
▼▼   **Location:** Just e of jct SR 77 and US 20 (Broadway). 1415 Broadway 14040. **Hours:** Open 5/1-10/31 & 4/1-4/30;
                11 am-9 pm; hours vary in winter. **Features:** Bright white walls and red-checked tablecloths accent the neat-
American   as-a-pin drive-in. A short drive from Six Flags Darien Lake, this spot is popular for ice cream and fast food,
                such as subs, pizza, burgers and salads. Casual dress. **Parking:** on-site.

DELHI pop. 2,583

——— WHERE TO STAY ———

BUENA VISTA MOTEL   **Phone:** 607/746-2135
(AAA) [SAVE]   All Year   1P: $89-$92   2P: $99-$110   XP: $10   F11
                Location: Jct SR 10, 0.8 mi e. Located next to the Delaware River. 18718 State Hwy 28 13753. Fax: 607/746-6008.
▼▼   **Facility:** Smoke free premises. 33 one-bedroom standard units. 1-2 stories (no elevator), exterior corridors.
Motel   *Bath:* combo or shower only. **Parking:** on-site, winter plug-ins. **Terms:** office hours 7 am-11 pm, pets (dogs
                only, $15 extra charge). **Guest Services:** wireless Internet. **Cards:** AX, DC, DS, MC, VI.

SOME UNITS

FEE   FEE FEE

DEPEW —See Buffalo p. 259.

DE WITT pop. 24,071   (See map and index starting on p. 629)

——— WHERE TO STAY ———

ECONO LODGE   *Book great rates at AAA.com*   **Phone:** (315)446-3300   [47]
(AAA) [SAVE]   5/1-10/31   1P: $70-$130   2P: $75-$140   XP: $10   F18
                11/1-4/30   1P: $64-$140   2P: $70-$140   XP: $10   F18
▼▼▼▼ ▼▼   **Location:** I-481, exit 3, 1.2 mi w on SR 5; I-690, exit 17 S (Bridge St), just e on Erie Blvd (SR 5). Located across from
Motel   Shoppingtown Mall. 3400 Erie Blvd E 13214. Fax: 315/449-3606. **Facility:** 44 one-bedroom standard units,
                some with whirlpools. 1 story, exterior corridors. **Parking:** on-site. **Terms:** [CP] meal plan available, pets
                ($10 extra charge). **Amenities:** irons, hair dryers. **Guest Services:** wireless Internet. **Cards:** AX, CB, DC,
DS, MC, VI. **Free Special Amenities: continental breakfast and high-speed Internet.**

SOME UNITS

FEE

——— WHERE TO DINE ———

DELMONICO'S ITALIAN STEAKHOUSE   **Dinner:** $9-$20   **Phone:** 315/445-1111
▼▼▼▼ ▼▼   **Location:** Just w of jct Thompson Rd and SR 5. 2950 Erie Blvd E 13224. **Hours:** 4 pm-10:30 pm, Fri-11:30 pm, Sat
                2 pm-11:30 pm, Sun noon-10 pm. Closed: 11/22, 12/25. **Reservations:** accepted. **Features:** As the name
Steak & Seafood implies, the restaurant prides itself on its popular 24-ounce Delmonico steak they like to call the "best deal
                in town." Sharing menu space are Italian dishes and meat and seafood choices. The friendly spot invites
dining or just meeting with friends. Casual dress; cocktails. **Parking:** on-site. **Cards:** AX, DS, MC, VI.

SARATOGA STEAKS AND SEAFOOD   **Lunch:** $6-$11   **Dinner:** $15-$30   **Phone:** 315/445-1976   [45]
▼▼▼▼ ▼▼   **Location:** I-481, exit 2 (Jamesville), just n, w on Nottingham Rd to 1st stop sign, then right. 200 Waring Rd 13224.
                Hours: 11:30 am-2 & 5-10 pm, Sun 4 pm-9 pm. Closed: 1/1, 12/25. **Reservations:** accepted. **Features:** Sit
American   by a raised brick fireplace or overlook the golf putting green in a glass-enclosed porch to enjoy this popular
                restaurant. Try the tender scrod with Italian-seasoned breadcrumbs or one of the hand-cut steaks
complemented with a warm loaf of braided egg bread. A doting staff will then serve one of their in-house-made desserts such as
creme brulee or warmed pecan pie. Casual dress; cocktails. **Parking:** on-site. **Cards:** AX, CB, DC, DS, MC, VI.

SCOTCH N' SIRLOIN   **Dinner:** $13-$40   **Phone:** 315/446-1771   [44]
▼▼▼▼ ▼▼   **Location:** 5.5 mi e on SR 5; in Shoppingtown Mall. 3687 Erie Blvd E 13214. **Hours:** 5 pm-10 pm, Fri & Sat-10:30
                pm, Sun 10:30 am-1:30 & 5-9 pm. Closed major holidays; also Sun 7/1-8/31. **Reservations:** suggested.
Steak & Seafood **Features:** Since 1967, this popular eatery has served USDA Choice beef, aged and hand-cut on-premises
                and fresh seafood shipped in daily from Boston. Professional servers will make this a pleasant dining
experience. Casual dress; cocktails. **Parking:** on-site. **Cards:** AX, CB, DC, DS, MC, VI.

TOKYO SEOUL   **Lunch:** $8-$15   **Dinner:** $9-$18   **Phone:** 315/449-2688   [43]
▼▼▼▼ ▼▼   **Location:** I-690 E, exit 17, s on Bridge St, then just e on SR 5. 3180 Erie Blvd E 13210. **Hours:** 11:30 am-10 pm, Fri
                & Sat-11 pm, Sun 2 pm-9 pm. Closed: 11/22. **Reservations:** accepted. **Features:** Classic hibachi, sushi
Japanese   bar and Korean barbecue make for an entertaining and delicious meal. Fresh quality seafood and meat go
                into the pleasant restaurant's food. Servers are friendly. Casual dress; cocktails. **Parking:** on-site.
Cards: AX, DS, MC, VI.

DIAMOND POINT (See map and index starting on p. 330)—*See also ADIRONDACK MOUNTAINS.*

─────── WHERE TO STAY ───────

CAPRI VILLAGE
Phone: 518/668-4829 🔷 41

Motel

	2P:	XP:	
6/29-9/2 Wkly	2P: $768-$1170	XP: $10	F9
6/15-6/28 Dly	2P: $80-$138	XP: $10	F9
5/18-6/14 & 9/3-10/7 Dly	2P: $64-$112	XP: $5	F9

Location: I-87, exit 22, 4.5 mi n on SR 9N. 3926 Lake Shore Dr 12824. Fax: 518/668-4918. **Facility:** 58 units. 20 one- and 38 two-bedroom standard units, some with efficiencies. 1-2 stories (no elevator), interior/exterior corridors. **Parking:** on-site. **Terms:** open 5/18-10/7, 3-4 night minimum stay - seasonal, 56 day cancellation notice-fee imposed, weekly rates available. **Amenities:** voice mail. **Pool(s):** outdoor. **Leisure Activities:** fishing, playground, volleyball, game room. *Fee:* boat dock. **Cards:** DS, MC, VI.

SOME UNITS
🏊 ⊠ 🍴 / ⊠ VCR 📺 🖥 / FEE

CHELKA LODGE
Phone: 518/668-4677 🔷 40

AAA SAVE

Motel

6/22-9/2 [ECP]	1P: $150-$185	2P: $150-$185	XP: $15
5/18-6/21 & 9/3-10/14	1P: $99-$150	2P: $99-$150	XP: $10

Location: I-87, exit 22, 5.8 mi n on SR 9N. 4204 Lake Shore Dr 12824. Fax: 518/668-3496. **Facility:** 25 units. 23 one- and 2 two-bedroom standard units, some with efficiencies or kitchens. 1-2 stories (no elevator), interior/exterior corridors. **Parking:** on-site. **Terms:** open 5/18-10/14, 2-3 night minimum stay - seasonal and/or weekends, 15 day cancellation notice-fee imposed, weekly rates available, no pets allowed (owner's pet on premises). **Amenities:** irons. **Leisure Activities:** canoeing, fishing, kayaks, rowboats, table tennis, badminton, basketball, shuffleboard. *Fee:* boat dock. **Cards:** MC, VI. **Free Special Amenities: expanded continental breakfast and local telephone calls.** *(See color ad p 335)*

SOME UNITS
⊠ ⊠ 🍴 / 📺 🖥 /

DIAMOND COVE COTTAGES
Phone: 518/668-3161 🔷 43

Cottage

5/1-10/1	1P: $95-$165	2P: $95-$165	XP: $20

Location: I-87, exit 22, 3.3 mi n on SR 9N. 3648 Lake Shore Dr 12824 (PO Box 363). Fax: 518/668-3319. **Facility:** 25 units. 6 one-bedroom standard units with efficiencies. 19 cottages ($125-$1915). 1 story, exterior corridors. *Bath:* shower only. **Parking:** on-site. **Terms:** open 5/1-10/1, weekly rates available. **Leisure Activities:** canoeing, playground, basketball, shuffleboard, volleyball. *Fee:* boat dock. **Business Services:** fax (fee).

⊠ ⊠ 🎥 🍴 🖥

GOLDEN SANDS RESORT
Phone: 518/668-2203 🔷 42

Motel

	2P:
7/12-9/3	2P: $125-$175
6/21-7/11	2P: $105-$150
5/15-6/20 & 9/4-9/17	2P: $75-$115

Location: I-87, exit 22, 3.3 mi n on SR 9N. 3654 Lake Shore Dr 12845 (PO Box 11, 12824). **Facility:** 26 units. 18 one- and 8 two-bedroom standard units, some with kitchens. 1-2 stories (no elevator), exterior corridors. *Bath:* shower only. **Parking:** on-site. **Terms:** open 5/15-9/17, 30 day cancellation notice-fee imposed, package plans. **Amenities:** video library (fee), DVD players, CD players. **Pool(s):** small heated outdoor. **Leisure Activities:** fishing, playground, basketball. *Fee:* boat dock. **Cards:** MC, VI.

SOME UNITS
🏊 ⊠ ⊠ VCR 🍴 🖥 / 🖥 /

─────── WHERE TO DINE ───────

MCGOWANS
Lunch: $4-$8 **Dinner:** $9-$10 **Phone: 518/668-4800** 🔲 21

American
DS, MC, VI.

Location: Center. 3712 Lake Shore Dr 12845. **Hours:** 7 am-2 pm; Wed-Sun also 4:30 pm-9 pm 5/1-10/31. Closed: 4/8, 12/25. **Features:** The casual restaurant is a local favorite for generously portioned breakfasts, from simple eggs with toast to the McGowan special breakfast sandwich, as well as hearty brunches and hot and cold lunch sandwiches. Service is quiet and attentive. Casual dress. **Parking:** on-site. **Cards:** AX,

◳

DOVER PLAINS pop. 1,996

─────── WHERE TO DINE ───────

OLD DROVERS INN
Lunch: $12-$33 **Dinner:** $14-$38 **Phone: 845/832-9311**

American

Location: 3 mi s of SR 22 on Old Rt 22 (CR 6); in Old Drovers Inn. 196 E Duncan Hill Rd 12522. **Hours:** 5:30 pm-9 pm, Fri noon-3 & 5:30-10 pm, Sat noon-10 pm, Sun noon-9 pm. Closed: 12/25; also Wed & 3 weeks in Jan. **Reservations:** suggested. **Features:** The tavern-turned-restaurant reflects an 1800s ambience, much as the state's early herd drovers would have experienced. With seasonally created menus, the contemporary cuisine centers on meats, fowl and seafood. Desserts range from decadent cakes and ice cream to the homey sticky toffee pudding. Dressy casual; cocktails. **Parking:** on-site. **Cards:** AX, DC, DS, MC, VI. **Country Inn**

DRYDEN pop. 1,832

─────── **WHERE TO DINE** ───────

A1 PIZZERIA AND FAMILY RESTAURANT **Lunch:** $3-$8 **Dinner:** $7-$25 **Phone:** 607/844-4466
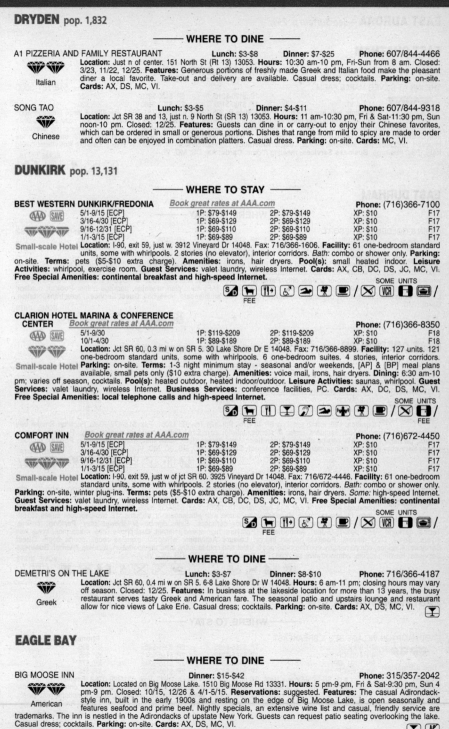
Italian

Location: Just n of center. 151 North St (Rt 13) 13053. **Hours:** 10:30 am-10 pm, Fri-Sun from 8 am. Closed: 3/23, 11/22, 12/25. **Features:** Generous portions of freshly made Greek and Italian food make the pleasant diner a local favorite. Take-out and delivery are available. Casual dress; cocktails. **Parking:** on-site. **Cards:** AX, DS, MC, VI.

SONG TAO **Lunch:** $3-$5 **Dinner:** $4-$11 **Phone:** 607/844-9318

Chinese

Location: Jct SR 38 and 13, just n. 9 North St (SR 13) 13053. **Hours:** 11 am-10:30 pm, Fri & Sat-11:30 pm, Sun noon-10 pm. Closed: 12/25. **Features:** Guests can dine in or carry-out to enjoy their Chinese favorites, which can be ordered in small or generous portions. Dishes that range from mild to spicy are made to order and often can be enjoyed in combination platters. Casual dress. **Parking:** on-site. **Cards:** MC, VI.

DUNKIRK pop. 13,131

─────── **WHERE TO STAY** ───────

BEST WESTERN DUNKIRK/FREDONIA *Book great rates at AAA.com* **Phone:** (716)366-7100

	5/1-9/15 [ECP]	1P: $79-$149	2P: $79-$149	XP: $10	F17
	3/16-4/30 [ECP]	1P: $69-$129	2P: $69-$129	XP: $10	F17
	9/16-12/31 [ECP]	1P: $69-$110	2P: $69-$110	XP: $10	F17
	1/1-3/15 [ECP]	1P: $69-$89	2P: $69-$89	XP: $10	F17

Small-scale Hotel **Location:** I-90, exit 59, just w. 3912 Vineyard Dr 14048. Fax: 716/366-1606. **Facility:** 61 one-bedroom standard units, some with whirlpools. 2 stories (no elevator), interior corridors. *Bath:* combo or shower only. **Parking:** on-site. **Terms:** pets ($5-$10 extra charge). **Amenities:** irons, hair dryers. **Pool(s):** small heated indoor. **Leisure Activities:** whirlpool, exercise room. **Guest Services:** valet laundry, wireless Internet. **Cards:** AX, CB, DC, DS, JC, MC, VI. **Free Special Amenities:** continental breakfast and high-speed Internet.

SOME UNITS

CLARION HOTEL MARINA & CONFERENCE CENTER *Book great rates at AAA.com* **Phone:** (716)366-8350

| | 5/1-9/30 | 1P: $119-$209 | 2P: $119-$209 | XP: $10 | F18 |
| | 10/1-4/30 | 1P: $89-$189 | 2P: $89-$189 | XP: $10 | F18 |

Location: Jct SR 60, 0.3 mi w on SR 5. 30 Lake Shore Dr E 14048. Fax: 716/366-8899. **Facility:** 127 units. 121 one-bedroom standard units, some with whirlpools. 6 one-bedroom suites. 4 stories, interior corridors.
Small-scale Hotel **Parking:** on-site. **Terms:** 1-3 night minimum stay - seasonal and/or weekends, [AP] & [BP] meal plans available, small pets only ($10 extra charge). **Amenities:** voice mail, irons, hair dryers. **Dining:** 6:30 am-10 pm; varies off season, cocktails. **Pool(s):** heated outdoor, heated indoor/outdoor. **Leisure Activities:** saunas, whirlpool. **Guest Services:** valet laundry, wireless Internet. **Business Services:** conference facilities, PC. **Cards:** AX, DC, DS, MC, VI. **Free Special Amenities:** local telephone calls and high-speed Internet.

SOME UNITS

COMFORT INN *Book great rates at AAA.com* **Phone:** (716)672-4450

	5/1-9/15 [ECP]	1P: $79-$149	2P: $79-$149	XP: $10	F17
	3/16-4/30 [ECP]	1P: $69-$129	2P: $69-$129	XP: $10	F17
	9/16-12/31 [ECP]	1P: $69-$110	2P: $69-$110	XP: $10	F17
	1/1-3/15 [ECP]	1P: $69-$89	2P: $69-$89	XP: $10	F17

Small-scale Hotel **Location:** I-90, exit 59, just w of jct SR 60. 3925 Vineyard Dr 14048. Fax: 716/672-4446. **Facility:** 61 one-bedroom standard units, some with whirlpools. 2 stories (no elevator), interior corridors. *Bath:* combo or shower only. **Parking:** on-site, winter plug-ins. **Terms:** pets ($5-$10 extra charge). **Amenities:** irons, hair dryers. *Some:* high-speed Internet. **Guest Services:** valet laundry, wireless Internet. **Cards:** AX, CB, DC, DS, JC, MC, VI. **Free Special Amenities:** continental breakfast and high-speed Internet.

SOME UNITS

─────── **WHERE TO DINE** ───────

DEMETRI'S ON THE LAKE **Lunch:** $3-$7 **Dinner:** $8-$10 **Phone:** 716/366-4187

Greek

Location: Jct SR 60, 0.4 mi w on SR 5. 6-8 Lake Shore Dr W 14048. **Hours:** 6 am-11 pm; closing hours may vary off season. Closed: 12/25. **Features:** In business at the lakeside location for more than 13 years, the busy restaurant serves tasty Greek and American fare. The seasonal patio and upstairs lounge and restaurant allow for nice views of Lake Erie. Casual dress; cocktails. **Parking:** on-site. **Cards:** AX, DS, MC, VI.

EAGLE BAY

─────── **WHERE TO DINE** ───────

BIG MOOSE INN **Dinner:** $15-$42 **Phone:** 315/357-2042

American

Location: Located on Big Moose Lake. 1510 Big Moose Rd 13331. **Hours:** 5 pm-9 pm, Fri & Sat-9:30 pm, Sun 4 pm-9 pm. Closed: 10/15, 12/26 & 4/1-5/15. **Reservations:** suggested. **Features:** The casual Adirondack-style inn, built in the early 1900s and resting on the edge of Big Moose Lake, is open seasonally and features seafood and prime beef. Nightly specials, an extensive wine list and casual, friendly service are trademarks. The inn is nestled in the Adirondacks of upstate New York. Guests can request patio seating overlooking the lake. Casual dress; cocktails. **Parking:** on-site. **Cards:** AX, DS, MC, VI.

EAST AURORA —See Buffalo p. 259.

EAST CHATHAM

———— WHERE TO STAY ————

THE INN AT SILVER MAPLE FARM   Phone: 518/781-3600

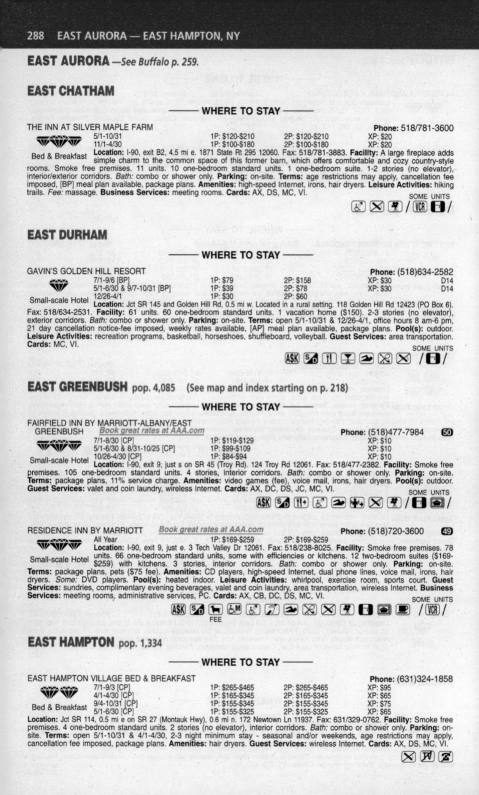

| | 5/1-10/31 | 1P: $120-$210 | 2P: $120-$210 | XP: $20 |
| | 11/1-4/30 | 1P: $100-$180 | 2P: $100-$180 | XP: $20 |

Bed & Breakfast **Location:** I-90, exit B2, 4.5 mi e. 1871 State Rt 295 12060. Fax: 518/781-3883. **Facility:** A large fireplace adds simple charm to the common space of this former barn, which offers comfortable and cozy country-style rooms. Smoke free premises. 11 units. 10 one-bedroom standard units. 1 one-bedroom suite. 1-2 stories (no elevator), interior/exterior corridors. *Bath:* combo or shower only. **Parking:** on-site. **Terms:** age restrictions may apply, cancellation fee imposed, [BP] meal plan available, package plans. **Amenities:** high-speed Internet, irons, hair dryers. **Leisure Activities:** hiking trails. *Fee:* massage. **Business Services:** meeting rooms. **Cards:** AX, DS, MC, VI.

SOME UNITS

EAST DURHAM

———— WHERE TO STAY ————

GAVIN'S GOLDEN HILL RESORT   Phone: (518)634-2582

	7/1-9/6 [BP]	1P: $79	2P: $158	XP: $30	D14
	5/1-6/30 & 9/7-10/31 [BP]	1P: $39	2P: $78	XP: $30	D14
	12/26-4/1	1P: $30	2P: $60	

Small-scale Hotel **Location:** Jct SR 145 and Golden Hill Rd, 0.5 mi w. Located in a rural setting. 118 Golden Hill Rd 12423 (PO Box 6). Fax: 518/634-2531. **Facility:** 61 units. 60 one-bedroom standard units. 1 vacation home ($150). 2-3 stories (no elevator), exterior corridors. *Bath:* combo or shower only. **Parking:** on-site. **Terms:** open 5/1-10/31 & 12/26-4/1, office hours 8 am-6 pm, 21 day cancellation notice-fee imposed, weekly rates available, [AP] meal plan available, package plans. **Pool(s):** outdoor. **Leisure Activities:** recreation programs, basketball, horseshoes, shuffleboard, volleyball. **Guest Services:** area transportation. **Cards:** MC, VI.

SOME UNITS

EAST GREENBUSH pop. 4,085   (See map and index starting on p. 218)

———— WHERE TO STAY ————

FAIRFIELD INN BY MARRIOTT-ALBANY/EAST GREENBUSH   *Book great rates at AAA.com*   Phone: (518)477-7984   50

	7/1-8/30 [CP]	1P: $119-$129		XP: $10
	5/1-6/30 & 8/31-10/25 [CP]	1P: $99-$109		XP: $10
	10/26-4/30 [CP]	1P: $84-$94		XP: $10

Small-scale Hotel **Location:** I-90, exit 9; just s on SR 45 (Troy Rd). 124 Troy Rd 12061. Fax: 518/477-2382. **Facility:** Smoke free premises. 105 one-bedroom standard units. 4 stories, interior corridors. *Bath:* combo or shower only. **Parking:** on-site. **Terms:** package plans, 11% service charge. **Amenities:** video games (fee), voice mail, irons, hair dryers. **Pool(s):** outdoor. **Guest Services:** valet and coin laundry, wireless Internet. **Cards:** AX, DC, DS, JC, MC, VI.

SOME UNITS

RESIDENCE INN BY MARRIOTT   *Book great rates at AAA.com*   Phone: (518)720-3600   49

| | All Year | 1P: $169-$259 | 2P: $169-$259 | |

Small-scale Hotel **Location:** I-90, exit 9, just e. 3 Tech Valley Dr 12061. Fax: 518/238-8025. **Facility:** Smoke free premises. 78 units. 66 one-bedroom standard units, some with efficiencies or kitchens. 12 two-bedroom suites ($169-$259) with kitchens. 3 stories, interior corridors. *Bath:* combo or shower only. **Parking:** on-site. **Terms:** package plans, pets ($75 fee). **Amenities:** CD players, high-speed Internet, dual phone lines, voice mail, irons, hair dryers. *Some:* DVD players. **Pool(s):** heated indoor. **Leisure Activities:** whirlpool, exercise room, sports court. **Guest Services:** sundries, complimentary evening beverages, valet and coin laundry, area transportation, wireless Internet. **Business Services:** meeting rooms, administrative services, PC. **Cards:** AX, CB, DC, DS, MC, VI.

SOME UNITS

FEE

EAST HAMPTON pop. 1,334

———— WHERE TO STAY ————

EAST HAMPTON VILLAGE BED & BREAKFAST   Phone: (631)324-1858

	7/1-9/3 [CP]	1P: $265-$465	2P: $265-$465	XP: $95
	4/1-4/30 [CP]	1P: $165-$345	2P: $165-$345	XP: $65
	9/4-10/31 [CP]	1P: $155-$345	2P: $155-$345	XP: $75
	5/1-6/30 [CP]	1P: $155-$325	2P: $155-$325	XP: $65

Bed & Breakfast **Location:** Jct SR 114, 0.5 mi e on SR 27 (Montauk Hwy), 0.6 mi n. 172 Newtown Ln 11937. Fax: 631/329-0762. **Facility:** Smoke free premises. 4 one-bedroom standard units. 2 stories (no elevator), interior corridors. *Bath:* combo or shower only. **Parking:** on-site. **Terms:** open 5/1-10/31 & 4/1-4/30, 2-3 night minimum stay - seasonal and/or weekends, age restrictions may apply, cancellation fee imposed, package plans. **Amenities:** hair dryers. **Guest Services:** wireless Internet. **Cards:** AX, DS, MC, VI.

The following lodging was either not evaluated or did not meet AAA rating requirements but is listed for your information only.

ACCOMMODATIONS PLUS VACATION HOMES   Phone: 631/324-1858
[fyi]   Not evaluated. **Location:** 172 Newtown Ln 11937. Facilities, services, and decor characterize a mid-range property.

--------- WHERE TO DINE ---------

CITTANUOVA   **Lunch:** $9-$22   **Dinner:** $14-$29   **Phone:** 631/324-6300
▼▼▼▼   **Location:** Just w of SR 27 (Montauk Hwy). 29 Newtown Ln 11937. **Hours:** 11:30 am-10:30 pm, Fri & Sat-11:30
           pm. **Features:** Located in the middle of many upscale boutique shops, this restaurant is a great place to
Italian   people-watch; there are many cafe-style tables available due to the walls that open up on warm days. This
retro-modern, Milan-inspired cafe is styled with chocolate colored banquettes, black and white mosaic tile
artwork and unique De Padova tables and chairs. Prices are on the higher end for smaller sized portions but the taste and
unique dining experience is hard to beat. Dressy casual; cocktails. **Parking:** street. **Cards:** AX, MC, VI.

THE PALM AT THE HUNTTING INN   **Dinner:** $16-$36   **Phone:** 631/324-0411
▼▼▼▼   **Location:** Center; in Huntting Inn. 94 Main St 11937. **Hours:** 5 pm-close, Sat & Sun from noon. Closed: 11/22,
           12/25. **Reservations:** accepted. **Features:** This bustling restaurant is noted for prime, dry-aged steaks and
Steak & Seafood   Nova Scotia lobsters, huge portions are delivered by an attentive staff in an atmosphere that is fun and
lively. At the end of the meal, servers present tempting pastries tableside. Caricature-lined walls lend to the
feeling that patrons are dining in an art gallery. Even if you bring a big appetite you still may leave with a doggy bag. Dressy
casual; cocktails. **Parking:** valet. **Cards:** AX, MC, VI. **Country Inn**   [Y]

EAST MEADOW pop. 37,461

--------- WHERE TO STAY ---------

COLISEUM MOTOR INN   Phone: (516)794-2100
[AAA] [SAVE]   All Year   1P: $95   2P: $110
▼▼   **Location:** Meadowbrook Pkwy, exit M5, 0.3 mi e. Located in a commercial area. 1650 Hempstead Tpke 11554.
Motel   Fax: 516/794-2278. **Facility:** 110 one-bedroom standard units. 2 stories (no elevator), interior/exterior
corridors. *Bath:* combo or shower only. **Parking:** on-site. **Terms:** package plans. **Pool(s):** outdoor.
Business Services: meeting rooms, fax (fee). **Cards:** AX, DC, DS, MC, VI. *(See color ad p 359)*
                                                                           SOME UNITS
                                                        [⊞] [↦] [🏊] [🎦] / [✕] /

--------- WHERE TO DINE ---------

ARTHUR AVE RESTAURANT   **Lunch:** $7-$10   **Dinner:** $7-$16   **Phone:** 516/520-9447
▼▼ ▼▼   **Location:** Meadowbrook Pkwy, exit M5, 1.5 mi e. 2367 Hempstead Tpke 11554. **Hours:** 11:45 am-10 pm, Fri & Sat-
           11 pm, Sun 2 pm-9 pm. Closed: 7/4, 11/22, 12/25. **Reservations:** suggested. **Features:** The restaurant is
Italian   named for the "Little Italy" section of the Bronx, which is depicted by a mural. Relax in the comfortable, laid-
back setting and enjoy home-style Italian fare, including pasta, traditional and gourmet pizza, and even hero
sandwiches. Outdoor patio dining is also available. Casual dress; cocktails. **Parking:** on-site. **Cards:** AX, DC, DS, MC, VI.
                                                                                              [Y]

EAST NORWICH pop. 2,675

--------- WHERE TO STAY ---------

EAST NORWICH INN   *Book great rates at AAA.com*   Phone: (516)922-1500
[AAA] [SAVE]   5/1-10/31   1P: $124   2P: $140   XP: $15   F12
           11/1-4/30   1P: $120   2P: $135   XP: $15   F12
▼▼ ▼▼   **Location:** SR 25A (N Hempstead Tpke), jct SR 106 (Oyster Bay Rd), just nw. Located in a commercial area. 6321
Small-scale Hotel   Northern Blvd 11732. Fax: 516/922-1089. **Facility:** 72 units. 66 one-bedroom standard units, some with
efficiencies. 5 one-bedroom suites ($260). 1 vacation home. 2 stories (no elevator), interior corridors. *Bath:*
combo or shower only. **Parking:** on-site. **Terms:** 4 day cancellation notice. **Amenities:** voice mail, irons,
hair dryers. **Pool(s):** small outdoor. **Leisure Activities:** sauna, exercise room. **Guest Services:** valet laundry, wireless Internet.
Business Services: meeting rooms, business center. **Cards:** AX, CB, DC, DS, JC, MC, VI. **Free Special Amenities:**
expanded continental breakfast and high-speed Internet.
                                                                           SOME UNITS
                                       [S🄳] [⊞] [↦] [🎦] [🛡] [▣] / [✕] [VCR] [▭] /

EAST QUOGUE pop. 4,265

--------- WHERE TO STAY ---------

CAROLE'S BED & BREAKFAST   Phone: (631)653-5152
           5/1-10/1   1P: $125-$185   2P: $125-$185   XP: $40   F10
▼▼ ▼▼   10/2-4/30   1P: $125-$150   2P: $125-$150   XP: $40   F10
Bed & Breakfast   **Location:** Just s of St. Rosalie's Church; center. Located in a residential area. 7 Walnut Ave 11942 (PO Box 1646).
Facility: Smoke free premises. 5 units. 4 one-bedroom standard units. 1 one-bedroom suite. 2 stories (no
elevator), interior corridors. *Bath:* combo or shower only. **Parking:** on-site. **Terms:** 2-3 night minimum stay - seasonal, 7 day
cancellation notice, weekly rates available, [BP] meal plan available. **Pool(s):** small outdoor. **Cards:** MC, VI.
                                                        [A$K] [⊞] [↦] [✕] [🄵]

EAST SYRACUSE pop. 3,178 (See map and index starting on p. 629)—See also SYRACUSE.

——— WHERE TO STAY ———

CANDLEWOOD SUITES SYRACUSE
Book at AAA.com
Phone: (315)432-1684 **38**
All Year 1P: $109-$159
Small-scale Hotel
Location: I-90, exit 35 (Carrier Cir) to SR 298 E to Old Collamer Rd, just n. 6550 Baptist Way 13057. Fax: 315/433-9959. **Facility:** 92 units. 74 one-bedroom standard units with efficiencies. 12 one- and 6 two-bedroom suites ($109-$159) with efficiencies. 3 stories, interior corridors. *Bath:* combo or shower only. **Parking:** on-site, winter plug-ins. **Terms:** office hours 7 am-11 pm, cancellation fee imposed, weekly rates available, package plans, pets ($25 fee). **Amenities:** video library, DVD players, CD players, dual phone lines, voice mail, irons, hair dryers. **Leisure Activities:** exercise room. **Guest Services:** sundries, complimentary and valet laundry, wireless Internet. **Cards:** AX, CB, DC, DS, MC, VI.
SOME UNITS

COMFORT INN-CARRIER CIRCLE
Book great rates at AAA.com
Phone: (315)437-0222 **41**
All Year [ECP] 1P: $59-$134 2P: $59-$134 XP: $10 F
Small-scale Hotel
Location: I-90, exit 35 (Carrier Cir) 6491 Thompson Rd S 13206. Fax: 315/437-4510. **Facility:** 109 units. 108 one-bedroom standard units, some with whirlpools. 1 one-bedroom suite with whirlpool. 4 stories, interior/exterior corridors. **Parking:** on-site. **Terms:** small pets only. **Amenities:** high-speed Internet, irons, hair dryers. **Leisure Activities:** exercise room. **Guest Services:** valet and coin laundry, wireless Internet. **Business Services:** meeting rooms, PC. **Cards:** AX, DS, MC, VI. **Free Special Amenities:** expanded continental breakfast and high-speed Internet.
SOME UNITS

COURTYARD BY MARRIOTT
Book great rates at AAA.com
Phone: (315)432-0300 **35**
All Year 1P: $89-$189 2P: $99-$209
Small-scale Hotel
Location: I-90, exit 35 (Carrier Cir) to SR 298, just e to Old Collamer Rd, then 0.5 mi n. 6415 Yorktown Cir 13057. Fax: 315/432-9950. **Facility:** Smoke free premises. 149 units. 137 one-bedroom standard units. 12 one-bedroom suites ($159-$229). 3 stories, interior corridors. *Bath:* combo or shower only. **Parking:** on-site. **Terms:** package plans. **Amenities:** high-speed Internet, voice mail, irons, hair dryers. **Pool(s):** small heated indoor. **Leisure Activities:** whirlpool, exercise room. **Guest Services:** sundries, valet and coin laundry. **Business Services:** meeting rooms, PC, fax (fee). **Cards:** AX, CB, DC, DS, JC, MC, VI.
SOME UNITS

CRESTHILL SUITES
Book at AAA.com
Phone: (315)432-5595 **37**
5/1-10/31 & 4/1-4/30 1P: $129-$219 2P: $129-$219 XP: $10 F18
11/1-3/31 1P: $119-$199 2P: $119-$199 XP: $10 F18
Small-scale Hotel
Location: I-90, exit 35 (Carrier Cir) to SR 298 E, just s. 6410 New Venture Gear Dr 13057. Fax: 315/432-5686. **Facility:** 86 units. 14 one-bedroom standard units with kitchens. 60 one- and 12 two-bedroom suites with kitchens. 2 stories, interior corridors. *Bath:* combo or shower only. **Parking:** on-site. **Terms:** 7 day cancellation notice, [BP] meal plan available, pets ($50-$150 fee). **Amenities:** high-speed Internet, dual phone lines, voice mail, irons, hair dryers. **Pool(s):** heated outdoor. **Leisure Activities:** exercise room. **Guest Services:** sundries, complimentary evening beverages: Mon-Thurs, complimentary and valet laundry, area transportation. **Business Services:** business center. **Cards:** AX, CB, DC, DS, MC, VI.
SOME UNITS

DOUBLETREE HOTEL SYRACUSE
Phone: (315)432-0200 **40**
All Year 1P: $99-$299 2P: $99-$299
Large-scale Hotel
Location: I-90, exit 35 (Carrier Cir), 0.5 mi e. 6301 Rt 298 13057. Fax: 315/433-1210. **Facility:** 250 units. 248 one-bedroom standard units. 2 one-bedroom suites. 7 stories, interior corridors. *Bath:* combo or shower only. **Parking:** on-site. **Terms:** cancellation fee imposed. **Amenities:** dual phone lines, voice mail, irons, hair dryers. *Fee:* video library, video games. *Some:* CD players. **Dining:** 6:30 am-10 pm, cocktails. **Pool(s):** heated indoor. **Leisure Activities:** sauna, whirlpool, exercise room. **Guest Services:** valet and coin laundry, wireless Internet. **Business Services:** conference facilities, PC. **Cards:** AX, DC, DS, MC, VI.
SOME UNITS
FEE FEE

EMBASSY SUITES HOTEL
Book at AAA.com
Phone: 315/446-3200 **29**
Property failed to provide current rates
Large-scale Hotel
Location: I-90, exit 35 (Carrier Cir) to SR 298 E, just n. 6646 Old Collamer Rd 13057. Fax: 315/437-3302. **Facility:** 215 units. 213 one- and 2 two-bedroom suites. 5 stories, interior corridors. **Parking:** on-site. **Terms:** check-in 4 pm. **Amenities:** video games (fee), dual phone lines, voice mail, irons, hair dryers. **Pool(s):** heated indoor. **Leisure Activities:** sauna, whirlpool, exercise room. *Fee:* massage, game room. **Guest Services:** sundries, complimentary evening beverages, valet and coin laundry, area transportation, wireless Internet. **Business Services:** conference facilities.
SOME UNITS
FEE

EXTENDED STAYAMERICA HOTELS-SYRACUSE-DEWITT
Book at AAA.com
Phone: (315)463-1958 **31**
8/20-9/3 1P: $45-$85 2P: $50-$90 XP: $5 F17
9/4-4/30 1P: $40-$70 2P: $45-$75 XP: $5 F17
5/1-8/19 1P: $40-$65 2P: $45-$65 XP: $5 F17
Small-scale Hotel
Location: I-90, exit 35 (Carrier Cir) to SR 298 E, just n. 6630 Old Collamer Rd 13057. Fax: 315/463-7966. **Facility:** 121 one-bedroom standard units with efficiencies. 3 stories, interior corridors. *Bath:* combo or shower only. **Parking:** on-site. **Terms:** office hours 7 am-11 pm, pets ($25 extra charge). **Amenities:** voice mail, irons. **Guest Services:** coin laundry, wireless Internet. **Cards:** AX, CB, DC, DS, MC, VI.
SOME UNITS
FEE

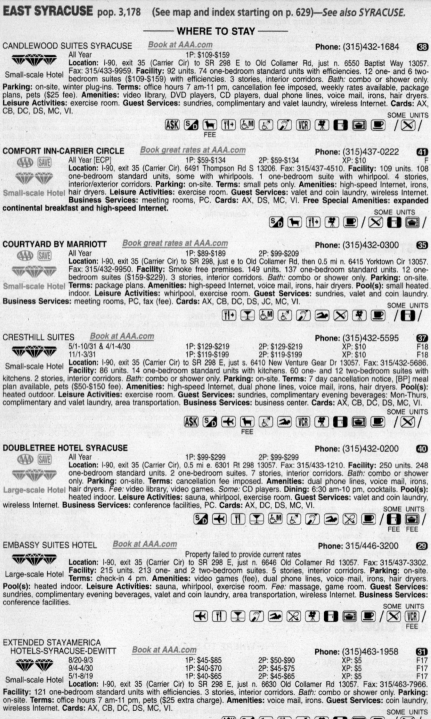

(See map and index starting on p. 629)

FAIRFIELD INN SYRACUSE   *Book great rates at AAA.com*   **Phone:** (315)432-9333   33

5/1-9/30	1P: $89-$139
10/1-11/30 & 3/1-4/30	1P: $79-$109
12/1-2/29	1P: $69-$99

Small-scale Hotel   **Location:** I-90, exit 35 (Carrier Cir) to SR 298 E. 6611 Old Collamer Rd 13057. Fax: 315/432-9197. **Facility:** Smoke free premises. 135 one-bedroom standard units. 3 stories, interior/exterior corridors. **Parking:** on-site. **Amenities:** video games (fee), voice mail, irons, hair dryers. **Pool(s):** outdoor. **Guest Services:** valet laundry, wireless Internet. **Cards:** AX, CB, DC, DS, MC, VI.

SOME UNITS

HAMPTON INN-CARRIER CIRCLE   *Book great rates at AAA.com*   **Phone:** 315/463-6443   36

All Year   1P: $79-$139

Location: I-90, exit 35 (Carrier Cir), just e on SR 298, then just n. 6605 Old Collamer Rd 13057. Fax: 315/432-1080. **Facility:** 115 one-bedroom standard units. 4 stories, interior corridors. *Bath:* combo or shower only. **Parking:** on-site. **Amenities:** video games (fee), dual phone lines, voice mail, irons, hair dryers. **Guest Services:** valet and coin laundry, wireless Internet. **Business Services:** meeting rooms. **Cards:** AX, DC, DS, MC, VI. **Free Special Amenities:** newspaper and high-speed Internet.

Small-scale Hotel

SOME UNITS

FEE

HILTON GARDEN INN-SYRACUSE   *Book great rates at AAA.com*   **Phone:** 315/431-4800   34

All Year   1P: $89-$209

Location: I-90, exit 35 (Carrier Cir) to SR 298 E, 0.7 mi to New Venture Gear Dr, then just e; in Pioneer Business Park. 6004 Fair Lakes Rd 13057. Fax: 315/431-4999. **Facility:** 100 units. 94 one-bedroom standard units, some with whirlpools. 6 one-bedroom suites. 3 stories, interior corridors. *Bath:* combo or shower only. **Parking:** on-site. **Terms:** cancellation fee imposed, [BP] & [CP] meal plans available, package plans. **Amenities:** video games (fee), high-speed Internet, dual phone lines, voice mail, irons, hair dryers. *Some:* DVD players (fee). **Pool(s):** small heated indoor. **Leisure Activities:** whirlpool, exercise room. **Guest Services:** sundries, valet and coin laundry, wireless Internet. **Business Services:** meeting rooms, business center. **Cards:** AX, CB, DC, DS, JC, MC, VI. **Free Special Amenities:** newspaper and high-speed Internet.

Small-scale Hotel

SOME UNITS

FEE

HOLIDAY INN EAST-CARRIER CIRCLE   *Book great rates at AAA.com*   **Phone:** (315)437-2761   39

7/1-10/31	1P: $117-$169
5/1-6/30	1P: $108-$169
1/1-4/30	1P: $99-$108
11/1-12/31	1P: $90-$108

Small-scale Hotel   **Location:** I-90, exit 35 (Carrier Cir) to SR 298 E, just n. 6555 Old Collamer Rd 13057. Fax: 315/463-0028. **Facility:** 201 one-bedroom standard units. 2-3 stories (no elevator), interior/exterior corridors. **Parking:** on-site. **Terms:** package plans, small pets only ($25 fee). **Amenities:** video games (fee), voice mail, irons, hair dryers. **Dining:** 6 am-11 & 5-10 pm, Sat & Sun 7 am-noon & 5-10 pm, cocktails. **Pool(s):** heated indoor. **Leisure Activities:** whirlpool, exercise room. *Fee:* game room. **Guest Services:** valet and coin laundry, wireless Internet. **Business Services:** conference facilities, PC. **Cards:** AX, DC, DS, MC, VI.

SOME UNITS

FEE   FEE FEE

RED ROOF INN #7157   *Book at AAA.com*   **Phone:** (315)437-3309   30

6/10-10/20	1P: $56-$84	2P: $62-$84	XP: $6	F18
5/1-6/9	1P: $49-$70	2P: $55-$70	XP: $6	F18
10/21-4/30	1P: $46-$64	2P: $52-$64	XP: $6	F18

Motel   **Location:** I-90, exit 35 (Carrier Cir), just n. 6614 N Thompson Rd 13206. Fax: 315/437-7865. **Facility:** 114 one-bedroom standard units. 3 stories, exterior corridors. *Bath:* combo or shower only. **Parking:** on-site, winter plug-ins. **Amenities:** video games (fee), voice mail. **Guest Services:** wireless Internet. **Cards:** AX, CB, DC, DS, MC, VI.

SOME UNITS

RESIDENCE INN BY MARRIOTT   *Book great rates at AAA.com*   **Phone:** (315)432-4488   32

All Year   1P: $169-$229   2P: $169-$229

Location: I-90, exit 35 (Carrier Cir) to SR 298, just e to Old Collamer Rd, then 0.5 mi n. 6420 Yorktown Cir 13057. Fax: 315/432-1042. **Facility:** Smoke free premises. 102 units. 78 one-bedroom standard units with kitchens. 24 two-bedroom suites with kitchens. 2 stories (no elevator), exterior corridors. *Bath:* combo or shower only. **Parking:** on-site. **Terms:** cancellation fee imposed, pets ($10 fee). **Amenities:** high-speed Internet, dual phone lines, voice mail, irons, hair dryers. **Pool(s):** small heated outdoor. **Leisure Activities:** whirlpool, exercise room, sports court. **Guest Services:** complimentary evening beverages: Mon-Thurs, valet and coin laundry, wireless Internet. **Business Services:** meeting rooms. **Cards:** AX, CB, DC, DS, JC, MC, VI.

Small-scale Hotel

FEE

——— **WHERE TO DINE** ———

JALAPENO'S   **Lunch:** $6-$8   **Dinner:** $5-$11   **Phone:** 315/431-0322   34

Mexican   **Location:** I-90, exit 35 (Carrier Cir) to SR 298 E, 1.7 mi (becomes Collamer Rd). 6491 Collamer Rd 13057. **Hours:** 11 am-9 pm, Fri-10 pm, Sat 9 am-10 pm. Closed major holidays; also Sun. **Features:** This saucy little joint deserves kudos for its Sonoran-Mexican food. Friendly servers are quick to please in the no-frills atmosphere. Casual dress; beer only. **Parking:** on-site. **Cards:** AX, MC, VI.

(See map and index starting on p. 629)

JOEY'S RESTAURANT   **Lunch:** $7-$10   **Dinner:** $12-$20   **Phone:** 315/432-0315   36

Italian

Location: I-90, exit 35 (Carrier Cir), just n. 6594 Thompson Rd 13206. **Hours:** 11:30 am-11 pm, Sat from 5 pm, Sun 5 pm-10 pm. Closed: 11/22, 12/25; also Super Bowl Sun. **Reservations:** suggested. **Features:** Hearty traditional and regional Italian dishes combined with deft service in a warm, intimate dining room will satisfy the most discriminating diner. An extensive wine list enhances the many choices of creative dishes—from veal and seafood to pasta, chicken and beef. Great entree accompaniments include the spinach bread appetizer, greens and beans soup, Caesar salad made tableside and varied dessert temptations that include tiramisu and white chocolate creme brulee. Dressy casual; cocktails. **Parking:** on-site. **Cards:** AX, DC, DS, MC, VI.

JUSTIN'S GRILL   **Lunch:** $7-$11   **Dinner:** $16-$29   **Phone:** 315/437-1461   35

Steak & Seafood

Location: I-90, exit 35 (Carrier Cir) to SR 298 E, just n. 6400 Yorktown Cir 13057. **Hours:** 11:30 am-2 & 5-9:30 pm, Fri & Sat-10:30 pm. Closed major holidays; also Sun. **Reservations:** suggested. **Features:** In an ocean of hotels, the restaurant builds its menu around USDA Prime meats. The relaxed dining room sustains a stylish, casual elegance. Dressy casual; cocktails. **Parking:** on-site. **Cards:** AX, DC, DS, MC, VI.

————— *The following restaurant has not been evaluated by AAA* —————
but is listed for your information only.

GRIMALDI'S LUNA PARK   **Phone:** 315/432-4614

fyi   Not evaluated. **Location:** I-90, exit 35 (Carrier Cir) to SR 298, just e to Old Collamer Rd, then 0.5 mi n. 6430 Yorktown Cir 13057. **Features:** Casual Italian restaurant.

ELIZABETHTOWN pop. 1,315—*See also ADIRONDACK MOUNTAINS.*

————— **WHERE TO STAY** —————

PARK MOTOR INN   **Phone:** (518)873-2233

AAA SAVE

Motel

All Year   1P: $54-$74   2P: $54-$74   XP: $10
Location: I-87, exit 31, 5 mi w on SR 9N. 7529 Court St 12932 (PO Box 786). **Facility:** 8 one-bedroom standard units. 1 story, exterior corridors. **Parking:** on-site, winter plug-ins. **Terms:** 4 day cancellation notice, weekly rates available. **Cards:** MC, VI.

ELLICOTTVILLE pop. 472

————— **WHERE TO STAY** —————

BLACK DOG LODGE   **Phone:** 716/699-6900

AAA SAVE

Bed & Breakfast

12/27-4/30   2P: $130-$210
5/1-12/26   2P: $90-$150
Location: 5.6 mi n. 7975 Rt 219 14731 (PO Box 1563). Fax: 716/699-8209. **Facility:** Secluded on 66 acres, this country retreat features beautifully appointed rooms with luxury upgrades and decorative touches in a Scottish theme. Smoke free premises. 4 one-bedroom standard units with whirlpools. 2 stories (no elevator), interior corridors. **Parking:** on-site. **Terms:** 2 night minimum stay - seasonal, 14 day cancellation notice-fee imposed, package plans, no pets allowed (owner's dog on premises). **Amenities:** hair dryers. **Leisure Activities:** paddleboats, snowshoes. **Cards:** AX, DS, MC, VI. **Free Special Amenities: full breakfast and preferred room (subject to availability with advance reservations).**

ILEX INN

Bed & Breakfast

Phone: 716/699-2002

12/25-3/12 [BP]   2P: $125-$265
5/1-12/24 & 3/13-4/30 [BP]   2P: $85-$155

Location: Eastern jct US 219 and SR 242, just w; western jct, 0.6 mi e. 6416 E Washington St 14731-0775 (PO Box 775). Fax: 716/699-8790. **Facility:** This country-casual B&B offers luxury guest-room appointments such as bathrobes, French matelasse bedspreads and fine antiques. Smoke free premises. 7 units. 5 one-bedroom standard units. 1 one-bedroom suite. 1 cottage. 1-2 stories (no elevator), interior corridors. *Bath:* combo or shower only. **Parking:** on-site, winter plug-ins. **Terms:** check-in 4 pm, age restrictions may apply, 30 day cancellation notice-fee imposed, package plans. **Amenities:** video library, hair dryers. *Some:* CD players. **Pool(s):** heated outdoor. **Leisure Activities:** whirlpool. **Cards:** AX, DS, MC, VI. **Free Special Amenities:** full breakfast and room upgrade (subject to availability with advance reservations).

THE INN AT HOLIDAY VALLEY RESORT

Resort
Small-scale Hotel

Phone: (716)699-2345

12/25-3/8 [ECP]	1P: $127-$250	2P: $127-$250	XP: $20	F17
10/21-12/24 [ECP]	1P: $96-$160	2P: $96-$160	XP: $20	F17
5/1-10/20 [ECP]	1P: $101-$147	2P: $101-$147	XP: $20	F17
3/9-4/30 [ECP]	1P: $110-$145	2P: $110-$145	XP: $20	F17

Location: Jct US 219 and SR 242, 0.6 mi e. Rt 219 and Holiday Valley Rd 14731 (PO Box 370). Fax: 716/699-5861. **Facility:** The resort features mountain views from many guest rooms and several rooms have patios or balconies. 102 units. 97 one-bedroom standard units, some with whirlpools. 5 one-bedroom suites ($152-$435) with whirlpools. 2 stories (no elevator), interior/exterior corridors. *Bath:* combo or shower only. **Parking:** on-site, winter plug-ins. **Terms:** 2 night minimum stay - seasonal and/or weekends, 14 day cancellation notice-fee imposed, package plans. **Amenities:** voice mail, irons, hair dryers. *Some:* DVD players. **Dining:** 11:30 am-2:30 & 5-9 pm; hours may vary off season, cocktails. **Pool(s):** 2 outdoor, heated indoor/outdoor, wading. **Leisure Activities:** sauna, whirlpool, 53 ski trails & slopes for skiing with 12 lifts, extensive recreational facilities, hiking trails, exercise room. *Fee:* golf-18 holes, downhill & cross country skiing, bicycles, massage. **Guest Services:** coin laundry, wireless Internet. **Business Services:** meeting rooms. **Cards:** AX, CB, DC, DS, MC, VI. **Free Special Amenities:** expanded continental breakfast and newspaper.

THE JEFFERSON INN OF ELLICOTTVILLE

Bed & Breakfast

Phone: (716)699-5869

12/14-3/31 [BP]   2P: $119-$219   XP: $15
5/1-12/13 & 4/1-4/30 [BP]   2P: $95-$159   XP: $15

Location: Western jct US 219 and SR 242, just n; eastern jct US 219 and 242, 0.8 mi w. Located in a quiet area. 3 Jefferson St 14731 (PO Box 1566). Fax: 716/699-5758. **Facility:** Smoke free premises. 7 units. 6 one-bedroom standard units. 1 one-bedroom suite. 1-2 stories (no elevator), interior/exterior corridors. **Parking:** on-site, winter plug-ins. **Terms:** 2 night minimum stay - seasonal and/or weekends, age restrictions may apply, 30 day cancellation notice, package plans. **Amenities:** video library, hair dryers. **Leisure Activities:** whirlpool. **Business Services:** meeting rooms, fax. **Cards:** AX, DS, MC, VI. **Free Special Amenities:** full breakfast and local telephone calls.

SUGAR PINE LODGE

Bed & Breakfast

Phone: 716/699-4855

12/26-3/31 [BP]   1P: $125-$258   2P: $125-$258
5/1-12/25 [BP]   1P: $95-$157   2P: $95-$157

Location: Jct US 219 and SR 242, 0.5 mi s on US 219. 6158 Jefferson St, Rt 219 S 14731. Fax: 716/699-2103. **Facility:** Finely appointed rooms and baths offer style, comfort and modern amenities; the property is traditional with upscale appeal. Smoke free premises. 5 units. 1 one-bedroom standard unit. 4 one-bedroom suites with whirlpools. 2 stories (no elevator), interior/exterior corridors. **Parking:** on-site. **Terms:** open 5/1-3/31, off-site registration, age restrictions may apply, 30 day cancellation notice-fee imposed, package plans, pets (owner's pet on premises, in designated units). **Amenities:** video library, irons, hair dryers. **Pool(s):** small heated outdoor. **Cards:** AX, DC, DS, MC, VI. **Free Special Amenities:** full breakfast and local telephone calls.

WINGATE INN

Book at AAA.com

Small-scale Hotel

Phone: (716)699-6000

All Year   1P: $99-$409   2P: $99-$409

Location: US 219, just s; downtown. 11 Mill St 14731 (PO Box 759). **Facility:** 82 units. 76 one-bedroom standard units, some with whirlpools. 6 one-bedroom suites with whirlpools. 4 stories, interior corridors. *Bath:* combo or shower only. **Parking:** on-site. **Terms:** 10 day cancellation notice, package plans. **Pool(s):** small heated indoor. **Leisure Activities:** whirlpool, exercise room. **Guest Services:** coin laundry, wireless Internet. **Business Services:** meeting rooms, business center. **Cards:** AX, CB, DC, DS, JC, MC, VI.

WHERE TO DINE

THE BARN RESTAURANT

American

Dinner: $10-$25   **Phone:** 716/699-4600

Location: Center. 7 Monroe St 14731. **Hours:** 5 pm-10 pm, Fri & Sat from 4 pm, Sun 3 pm-9 pm. Closed: 11/22, 12/25. **Reservations:** accepted. **Features:** A fireplace accents the relaxed, rustic dining room. The ski-town restaurant's menu covers many popular dishes. The staff is friendly. Casual dress; cocktails. **Parking:** on-site. **Cards:** AX, DS, MC, VI.

DINA'S

American

Lunch: $6-$10   **Dinner:** $13-$25   **Phone:** 716/699-5330

Location: On US 219; center. 15 Washington St 14731. **Hours:** 7 am-10 pm. Closed: 11/22, 12/25. **Features:** In a restored 1840 building, the restaurant has the ambience of a cozy bistro. Stop by for breakfast, lunch or dinner selections, many of which exhibit Italian and Mexican influences. Homemade pastries are among tempting dessert choices. Casual dress; cocktails. **Parking:** on-site. **Cards:** AX, DS, MC, VI.

TIPS UP-CAFE
Italian

Dinner: $8-$22   **Phone:** 716/699-2136
Location: On SR 242; center. 32 Washington St (Rt 242/219) 14731. **Hours:** 4 pm-10 pm, Fri & Sat-11 pm. Closed: 11/22, 12/25; also 3 weeks during Easter. **Features:** Popular with the locals, the often-busy restaurant is in a restored historical building that's loaded with friendly charm. The limited menu of well-prepared dishes features Italian and American offerings. The wait staff provides prompt, pleasant service. Casual dress; cocktails. **Parking:** street. **Cards:** MC, VI.

ELMIRA pop. 30,940

——— WHERE TO STAY ———

COACHMAN MOTOR LODGE
Motel

Phone: 607/733-5526
All Year   1P: $65-$90   2P: $75-$120   XP: $10   F18
Location: SR 17, exit 56 (Church St), 0.5 mi w on SR 352, 0.5 mi s on Madison Ave, then 1.4 mi s. 908 Pennsylvania Ave 14904. Fax: 607/733-0961. **Facility:** 18 one-bedroom suites with efficiencies. 2 stories (no elevator), exterior corridors. **Parking:** on-site, winter plug-ins. **Terms:** weekly rates available, small pets only. **Amenities:** irons. **Guest Services:** coin laundry, wireless Internet. **Cards:** AX, DS, MC, VI. **Free Special Amenities:** local telephone calls and high-speed Internet.

ECONO LODGE *Book great rates at AAA.com*
Small-scale Hotel

Phone: 607/739-2000
Property failed to provide current rates
Location: SR 17, exit 51, just s. Located across from a shopping center and mall. 871 CR 64 14903. Fax: 607/739-3552. **Facility:** 48 one-bedroom standard units, some with whirlpools. 2 stories (no elevator), interior/exterior corridors. **Parking:** on-site. **Amenities:** video library, high-speed Internet, voice mail, irons, hair dryers. **Guest Services:** coin laundry.
SOME UNITS

HOLIDAY INN-ELMIRA RIVERVIEW *Book at AAA.com*
Small-scale Hotel

Phone: (607)734-4211
5/1-10/31   1P: $89-$121   2P: $89-$121
11/1-4/30   1P: $89-$99   2P: $89-$99
Location: SR 17, exit 56 (Water St), 0.5 mi s. 760 E Water St 14901. Fax: 607/734-3549. **Facility:** 149 units. 148 one-bedroom standard units. 1 one-bedroom suite ($139-$225). 2 stories, interior/exterior corridors. **Bath:** combo or shower only. **Parking:** on-site, winter plug-ins. **Terms:** [AP] meal plan available, package plans. **Amenities:** high-speed Internet, voice mail, irons, hair dryers. *Some:* dual phone lines. **Pool(s):** outdoor, heated indoor, wading. **Leisure Activities:** saunas, lifeguard on duty, exercise room. **Guest Services:** valet and coin laundry, wireless Internet. **Business Services:** conference facilities. **Cards:** AX, CB, DC, DS, JC, MC, VI.
SOME UNITS

——— WHERE TO DINE ———

BEIJING GARDEN
Chinese

Lunch: $4-$6   **Dinner:** $7-$14   **Phone:** 607/732-7464
Location: SR 17, exit 56 (Water St), 1 mi w on SR 352 (Church St), s on Main St, then just e. 145 W Gray St 14901. **Hours:** 11:30 am-10 pm, Fri-10:30 pm, Sat noon-10:30 pm, Sun noon-9:30 pm. Closed major holidays. **Reservations:** accepted. **Features:** The friendly staff serves traditional Chinese food prepared with fresh, tender ingredients. Owned by the same family for more than 14 years, the downtown restaurant is next to Clemens Center. Casual dress; cocktails. **Parking:** street. **Cards:** AX, DS, MC, VI.

HILL TOP INN
American

Dinner: $12-$28   **Phone:** 607/732-6728
Location: SR 17, exit 56 (Water St), 0.5 mi to top of hill. 171 Jerusalem Hill Rd 14901. **Hours:** Open 5/1-12/31 & 3/1-4/30; 5 pm-8:30 pm. Closed major holidays; also Sun. **Reservations:** accepted. **Features:** As the name implies, the rustic restaurant is set atop a hill, from which it affords a panoramic view of the Chemung Valley and Elmira. The family-owned spot has been serving diners for more than 70 years. The atmosphere is casual and friendly. The patio opens seasonally. Casual dress; cocktails. **Parking:** on-site. **Cards:** AX, DC, DS, MC, VI.

MORETTI'S RESTAURANT
Italian

Dinner: $8-$32   **Phone:** 607/734-1535
Location: 0.5 mi n, 0.3 mi e on E Washington Ave, then just s. 800 Hatch St 14901. **Hours:** 5 pm-9:30 pm, Fri & Sat-10 pm. Closed major holidays; also Super Bowl Sun. **Reservations:** suggested. **Features:** A regional favorite since 1917, the restaurant delivers many Italian staples, as well as traditional American preparations of veal, steak, chicken and chops. Dining rooms are decorated in a local nostalgic theme. Fish is a popular choice on Friday and Saturday. Casual dress; cocktails. **Parking:** on-site. **Cards:** AX, DS, MC, VI. **Historic**

PIETRO & SON PIZZERIA & RESTAURANT
Italian

Lunch: $4-$8   **Dinner:** $6-$13   **Phone:** 607/733-4400
Location: Corner of Washington Ave and Davis. 400 W Washington Ave 14901. **Hours:** 11 am-10 pm, Sun 3 pm-9 pm. Closed: 3/23, 11/22, 12/25. **Reservations:** accepted. **Features:** Traditional fare makes up the menu at the friendly, family-owned restaurant. Guests can eat in either of two dining rooms or request food for takeout or delivery. The popular, casual spot is near Elmira College. Casual dress; beer & wine only. **Parking:** on-site. **Cards:** AX, DS, MC, VI.

PUDGIE'S PIZZA & SUBS
Pizza

Lunch: $4-$8   **Dinner:** $4-$8   **Phone:** 607/734-3366
Location: SR 17, exit 56 (Church St), 1.1 mi w on SR 352 (Church St), then just n. 526 N Main St 14901. **Hours:** 11 am-10 pm, Thurs-11 pm, Fri & Sat-2 am, Sun noon-10 pm. Closed major holidays. **Features:** Open since 1963, this is the original Pudgie's Pizza, specializing in pizza, cold and hot subs made with house-baked rolls, calzones, Buffalo wings, salads and specials including their party packs. Casual dress. **Parking:** on-site. **Cards:** MC, VI.

ELMIRA HEIGHTS pop. 4,170

———— WHERE TO DINE ————

GARCIA'S MEXICAN RESTAURANT   **Lunch:** $4-$7   **Dinner:** $6-$14   **Phone:** 607/737-7695
Location: SR 17, exit 52 (SR 14 S), 1 mi s. 2446B Corning Rd-Miracle Mile 14903. **Hours:** 11 am-9 pm, Fri & Sat-10 pm. Closed: Sun. **Reservations:** accepted. **Features:** The restaurant offers a large selection of traditional Mexican dishes in a festive, casual setting. Combination plates, vegetarian and American choices are available, and friendly staff aim to please with fast, courteous service. Casual dress; cocktails. **Parking:** on-site. **Cards:** AX, DS, MC, VI.

Mexican

LEGENDS BAR & GRILLE   **Lunch:** $3-$10   **Dinner:** $3-$20   **Phone:** 607/733-0074
Location: Jct 14th St. 229 Oakwood Ave 14903. **Hours:** 11 am-11 pm, Sun noon-10 pm. Closed: 12/25. **Reservations:** accepted. **Features:** Sports memorabilia and decor set the mood in the corner neighborhood bar. Quality ingredients and careful preparation make this a popular place to dine. Early-bird times and the Friday fish fry usher in crowds, so guests should plan ahead. Worth trying is the "legend," a 14-ounce filet mignon. Casual dress; cocktails. **Parking:** street. **Cards:** AX, MC, VI.

American

PIERCE'S 1894 RESTAURANT   *Menu on AAA.com*   **Dinner:** $15-$28   **Phone:** 607/734-2022
Location: 2.5 mi n; jct 14th St and Oakwood Ave; 2.5 mi s of jct SR 14, 17 and 328; just w of SR 14. 228 Oakwood Ave 14903. **Hours:** 5 pm-9 pm. Closed: 12/25; also Sun & Mon. **Reservations:** accepted. **Features:** Gourmet dishes, as well as varied Continental entrees, pepper the innovative menu. Selections in the wine cellar are extensive. Distinctive, well-appointed dining rooms contribute to a sophisticated and relaxing experience. For dessert, the whiskey macaroon torte is delightful. Casual dress; cocktails. **Parking:** on-site. **Cards:** AX, DS, MC, VI.

American

ELMSFORD —See New York p. 499.

ENDICOTT pop. 13,038

———— WHERE TO DINE ————

RUSSELL'S STEAK & SEAFOOD HOUSE   **Dinner:** $7-$25   **Phone:** 607/754-2333
Location: Jct SR 17C (Main St) and 26 N, 1.2 mi w on SR 17C (Main St). 1001 W Main St 13760. **Hours:** 4 pm-9 pm, Fri & Sat-10 pm. Closed: 11/22, 12/24, 12/25; also Mon. **Reservations:** suggested, weekends. **Features:** Diners can treat themselves to tender, juicy steaks that are prepared to order. Seafood lovers won't be disappointed with dishes that bring out robust flavors in shrimp, scallops and lobster. Friendly servers contribute to the pleasant atmosphere. Casual dress; cocktails. **Parking:** on-site. **Cards:** AX, DC, DS, MC, VI.

Steak & Seafood

ENDWELL pop. 11,706

———— WHERE TO DINE ————

TONY'S ITALIAN GRILL   **Lunch:** $4-$6   **Dinner:** $6-$13   **Phone:** 607/785-0127
Location: SR 17 W, exit 69, 2.5 mi w on SR 17C (Main St); SR 17 E, exit 67N, 1.4 mi e. 2315 E Main St 13760. **Hours:** 11 am-10 pm, Fri & Sat-11 pm. Closed: Sun. **Features:** The restaurant offers traditional Italian fare, including pastas and classic dinners and specialties from their hickory wood-fired grill or from the brick oven. Casual dress; cocktails. **Parking:** on-site. **Cards:** AX, DS, MC, VI.

Italian

FAIRPORT pop. 5,740

———— WHERE TO STAY ————

THE LODGE AT WOODCLIFF   *Book at AAA.com*   **Phone: 585/381-4000**
▼▼▼▼▼   All Year   1P: $155-$195   2P: $155-$195   XP: $10   F
Location: I-490, exit 28 eastbound, just s on SR 96; exit 27 westbound, 1.5 mi s on SR 96. 199 Woodcliff Dr 14450 (PO
Large-scale Hotel   Box 22850, ROCHESTER, 14692). Fax: 585/381-2673. **Facility:** 234 units. 227 one-bedroom standard units,
some with whirlpools. 7 one-bedroom suites ($195), some with whirlpools. 6 stories, interior corridors. *Bath:*
combo or shower only. **Parking:** on-site. **Amenities:** voice mail, irons, hair dryers. *Some:* high-speed Internet. **Pool(s):** heated
indoor/outdoor. **Leisure Activities:** saunas, whirlpool, jogging, spa. *Fee:* golf-9 holes. **Guest Services:** gift shop, valet laundry,
area transportation, wireless Internet. **Business Services:** conference facilities, business center. Cards: AX, DS, MC, VI.

SOME UNITS
(A$K) (S/D) [✈] (¶1) (Y) (&M) (&) (∅) (≈) (⊞) (✕) (🎥) (📶) (🖳) / (✕) (VCR) (📷)
FEE

FALCONER pop. 2,540

———— WHERE TO STAY ————

RED ROOF INN JAMESTOWN/FALCONER #7273   *Book at AAA.com*   **Phone: (716)665-3670**
◆◆◆◆   5/1-9/1   1P: $72-$83   2P: $77-$83
9/2-4/30   1P: $53-$68   2P: $59-$74
Small-scale Hotel   **Location:** I-86, exit 13, just w. 1980 E Main St 14733. Fax: 716/664-7651. **Facility:** 80 one-bedroom standard
units. 2 stories (no elevator), interior corridors. *Bath:* combo or shower only. **Parking:** on-site.
Amenities: video games (fee), voice mail. Cards: AX, CB, DC, DS, MC, VI.

SOME UNITS
(🐾) (🎥) / (✕) /

———— WHERE TO DINE ————

HULTMAN'S RESTAURANT & LOUNGE   **Dinner:** $9-$20   **Phone: 716/665-6837**
◆◆◆◆   **Location:** I-86, exit 13, 1 mi w on SR 394. 232 W Main St 14733. **Hours:** 5 pm-9 pm; hours vary off season.
Closed major holidays; also 12/24 & Sun except Mother's Day. **Reservations:** accepted.
American   **Features:** Victorian tables and antiques decorate the casual restaurant, a family favorite for comfortable
dining. A variety of seafood, beef, chicken and pasta preparations lines the menu. Casual dress; cocktails.
Parking: on-site. Cards: AX, DS, MC, VI.

(Y)

FARMINGTON pop. 10,585—*See FINGER LAKES.*

FARMINGVILLE

———— WHERE TO STAY ————

HAMPTON INN BROOKHAVEN   *Book great rates at AAA.com*   **Phone: (631)732-7300**
(AAA) (SAVE)   All Year   1P: $99-$199
Location: I-495, exit 63 (N Ocean Ave), just n. 2000 N Ocean Ave 11738. Fax: 631/732-5522. **Facility:** 161 units.
▼▼▼▼   154 one-bedroom standard units. 7 one-bedroom suites ($279-$329) with whirlpools. 6 stories, interior
corridors. *Bath:* combo or shower only. **Parking:** on-site. **Terms:** [ECP] meal plan available.
Small-scale Hotel   **Amenities:** video games (fee), dual phone lines, voice mail, irons, hair dryers. **Pool(s):** heated indoor.
Leisure Activities: exercise room. **Guest Services:** sundries, valet and coin laundry, airport transportation-
Long Island MacArthur Airport, area transportation-within 5 mi, wireless Internet. **Business Services:** meeting rooms, business
center. Cards: AX, CB, DC, DS, JC, MC, VI. **Free Special Amenities:** full breakfast and high-speed Internet.

SOME UNITS
(S/D) (✈) (&M) (&) (∅) (≈) (🎥) (🖳) (📶) (🖳) / (✕) /

FAYETTEVILLE pop. 4,190   (See map and index starting on p. 629)

———— WHERE TO STAY ————

CRAFTSMAN INN   *Book at AAA.com*   **Phone: 315/637-8000**   (44)
▼▼▼▼   All Year   1P: $95-$165   2P: $95-$165
Location: Across from Fayetteville Towne Center. 7300 E Genesee St (SR 5) 13066. Fax: 315/637-2440.
Small-scale Hotel   **Facility:** Smoke free premises. 90 one-bedroom standard units, some with whirlpools. 2 stories, interior
corridors. *Bath:* combo or shower only. **Parking:** on-site, winter plug-ins. **Terms:** [CP] meal plan available,
pets (in designated units). **Amenities:** voice mail, irons, hair dryers. *Some:* high-speed Internet, dual phone lines.
Dining: restaurant, see separate listing. **Guest Services:** valet laundry, wireless Internet. **Business Services:** meeting rooms,
PC. Cards: AX, CB, DC, DS, MC, VI.

SOME UNITS
(A$K) (🐾) (¶1) (&M) (&) (📶) (✕) (🎥) / (VCR) (🖳) (📶) (🖳) /
FEE

———— WHERE TO DINE ————

ARAD EVANS INN   **Dinner:** $16-$25   **Phone: 315/637-2020**   (40)
▼▼▼   **Location:** 1.5 mi e of SR 481 S; 0.5 mi w of Lower Fayetteville. 7206 Genesee St 13066. **Hours:** 5 pm-10 pm, Fri &
Sat-11 pm. Closed major holidays; also Sun. **Reservations:** suggested. **Features:** Period furniture and
Continental   Oriental rugs decorate the renovated 1840s Federal-style country house. Upscale fusion cuisine blends
French, Italian and nouveau influences. The signature New Zealand rack of lamb is memorable, as are such
showy homemade desserts as the chocolate tower. Dressy casual; cocktails. **Parking:** on-site. Cards: AX, MC, VI. **Historic**

(Y)

(See map and index starting on p. 629)

CRAFTSMAN INN   Lunch: $6-$9   Dinner: $14-$22   Phone: 315/637-9999   (39)
Location: Across from Fayetteville Towne Center; in Craftsman Inn. 7300 E Genesee St (SR 5) 13066. Hours: 11:30 am-2 & 5-10 pm, Sun 5 pm-9 pm. Closed: 7/4, 12/25. Reservations: accepted. Features: Craftsman-style
Nouvelle American oak furnishings enhance the feel of elegance. Menu favorites include rack of lamb, Nantucket chowder, pan-roasted pecan-crusted Atlantic salmon and other fresh seafood. Casual dress; cocktails. Parking: on-site.
Cards: AX, DC, DS, MC, VI.

KYOKO JAPANESE RESTAURANT   Dinner: $8-$22   Phone: 315/637-9000
Location: SR 5, 2.5 mi e of jct SR 481. 111 Brooklea Dr 13066. Hours: 5 pm-9 pm, Fri & Sat-10 pm. Closed
major holidays. Reservations: suggested. Features: Relaxed dining in the intimate feel of a garden tea
Japanese house with pleasantly arrayed Japanese artwork is found at Kyoko. The friendly staff offers a wide variety of
sushi, tempura and teriyaki preparations. Gyoza—steamed and fried meat-filled dumplings—are perfect to
start. Beautifully arrayed sushi, grilled shrimp or chicken stir-fry and all dishes are prepared to order. Each is an art piece
intended to satisfy the eye and palate. Casual dress; beer & wine only. Parking: on-site. Cards: AX, DC, DS, MC, VI.

FILLMORE

———— **WHERE TO STAY** ————

JUST A "PLANE" BED & BREAKFAST   Phone: 585/567-8338
5/1-11/30 & 3/1-4/30   1P: $65   2P: $80   XP: $15   D5
Location: Jct SR 19 and 19A, 1.9 mi n. Located in a rural area next to a grass airstrip. 11152 Rt 19A 14735.
Bed & Breakfast Facility: Smoke free premises. 4 one-bedroom standard units. 3 stories (no elevator), interior corridors.
Bath: combo or shower only. Parking: on-site. Terms: open 5/1-11/30 & 3/1-4/30, check-in 4:30 pm, age
restrictions may apply, cancellation fee imposed. Amenities: hair dryers. Leisure Activities: hiking trails. Guest Services: TV
in common area. Business Services: meeting rooms. Cards: AX, MC, VI.
SOME UNITS

FINDLEY LAKE

———— **WHERE TO STAY** ————

HOLIDAY INN EXPRESS HOTEL & SUITES   *Book great rates at AAA.com*   Phone: (716)769-7900

9/1-4/30 [ECP]	1P: $89-$149	2P: $89-$149	XP: $10	F18
7/1-8/31 [ECP]	1P: $108-$118	2P: $108-$118	XP: $10	F18
5/1-6/30 [ECP]	1P: $89-$118	2P: $89-$118	XP: $10	F18

Location: I-86, exit 4. 3025 Rt 426 14736. Fax: 716/769-7903. Facility: 87 one-bedroom standard units. 3
Small-scale Hotel stories, interior corridors. Bath: combo or shower only. Parking: on-site. Terms: check-in 4 pm.
Amenities: video library, high-speed Internet, dual phone lines, voice mail, irons, hair dryers. Some: DVD
players, video games, CD players. Dining: I-86 Express, see separate listing. Pool(s): heated indoor. Leisure
Activities: exercise room. Guest Services: valet laundry, wireless Internet. Business Services: meeting rooms. Cards: AX,
CB, DC, DS, JC, MC, VI. Free Special Amenities: expanded continental breakfast and high-speed Internet.
SOME UNITS

PEEK'N PEAK RESORT & CONFERENCE CENTER   Phone: (716)355-4141

12/22-4/30	1P: $200-$230	2P: $220-$240	XP: $20	F18
5/26-10/8	1P: $185-$215	2P: $195-$225	XP: $20	F18
10/9-12/21	1P: $135-$165	2P: $135-$165	XP: $20	F18
5/1-5/25	1P: $130-$160	2P: $130-$160	XP: $20	F18

Resort Location: I-86, exit 4, 4 mi s via SR 426, follow signs. 1405 Olde Rd 14736 (1405 Olde Rd, PO Box 360).
Small-scale Hotel Fax: 716/355-4542. Facility: This European-style lodge has Tudor architecture and features some guest
rooms with lofts, fireplaces and balconies. 144 units. 72 one-bedroom standard units. 72 one-bedroom
suites, some with kitchens and/or whirlpools. 2 stories (no elevator), interior/exterior corridors. Bath: combo or shower only.
Parking: on-site. Terms: check-in 5 pm, 2 night minimum stay - weekends, 7 day cancellation notice-fee imposed, package
plans. Amenities: irons, hair dryers. Some: high-speed Internet. Dining: 2 restaurants, 6:30 am-9 pm, Fri & Sat-10 pm, Sun
6:30 am-2 & 5-9 pm, cocktails. Pool(s): heated outdoor, heated indoor. Leisure Activities: sauna, whirlpool, waterslide,
lifeguard on duty, indoor tennis court, winter tubing, child care in winter, bicycles, playground, exercise room, sports court,
basketball, horseshoes, shuffleboard, volleyball. Fee: golf-36 holes, miniature golf, downhill & cross country skiing, game room.
Guest Services: gift shop, coin laundry, wireless Internet. Business Services: conference facilities. Cards: AX, DC, DS,
MC, VI.
SOME UNITS

———— **WHERE TO DINE** ————

I-86 EXPRESS   Lunch: $5-$9   Dinner: $5-$9   Phone: 716/769-7950
Location: I-86, exit 4; next to Holiday Inn Express Hotel & Suites. 3025 Rt 426 14736. Hours: 11 am-10 pm.
American Features: Everything is made fresh on the premises. Among selections are rotisserie chicken and ribs,
tossed salad, potato salad, spaghetti and meatballs, pizza, hot stuffed sandwiches and subs.
Travelers appreciate the easy-off, easy-on interstate access. Casual dress. Parking: on-site. Cards: AX,
DC, DS, MC, VI.

Finger Lakes Area

FINGER LAKES —*See AUBURN, AVON, BATH, BLOOMFIELD, BRISTOL CENTER, CANANDAIGUA, CAYUGA HEIGHTS, CORNING, DANSVILLE, FARMINGTON, GENESEO, GENEVA, GLENORA, GROTON, HAMMONDSPORT, HECTOR, HONEOYE, HORNELL, HORSEHEADS, ITHACA, LANSING, LODI, MANCHESTER, MONTOUR FALLS, NAPLES, NORTH HORNELL, OVID, PAINTED POST, PENN YAN, PINE VALLEY, ROMULUS, SENECA FALLS, SKANEATELES, TRUMANSBURG, VICTOR, WATERLOO, WATKINS GLEN & WEEDSPORT.*

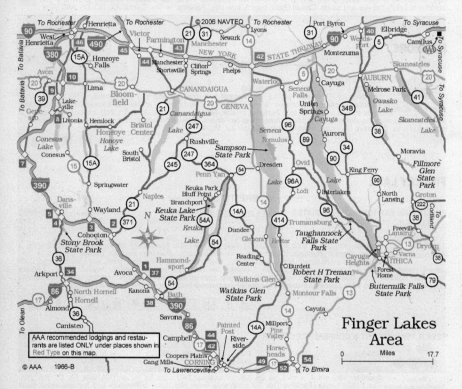

Finger Lakes Area

Traveling is about possibilities...

photo by Theres Angelo

...and when you have more than 9,000 square miles
of lakes, hills, villages and vineyards,
the possibilities are endless in New York's Finger Lakes.

photo by Onondaga County

NEW YORK'S
Finger Lakes

Finger Lakes Tourism Alliance
800-530-7488
www.discoverfingerlakes.com

FISHKILL pop. 1,735

——— WHERE TO STAY ———

COURTYARD BY MARRIOTT *Book great rates at AAA.com*   **Phone:** (845)897-2400
(AAA) [SAVE]
All Year   1P: $119-$289   2P: $119-$289
Location: I-84, exit 13, just n. 17 Westage Dr 12524. Fax: 845/897-2274. **Facility:** Smoke free premises. 152 units. 140 one-bedroom standard units. 12 one-bedroom suites. 4 stories, interior corridors. *Bath:* combo or shower only. **Parking:** on-site, winter plug-ins. **Terms:** cancellation fee imposed, package plans.
Small-scale Hotel **Amenities:** high-speed Internet, voice mail, irons, hair dryers. **Pool(s):** heated indoor. **Leisure Activities:** whirlpool, exercise room. **Guest Services:** sundries, valet and coin laundry. **Business Services:** meeting rooms, business center. **Cards:** AX, CB, DC, DS, JC, MC, VI.
SOME UNITS

EXTENDED STAYAMERICA-FISHKILL-POUGHKEEPSIE *Book at AAA.com*   **Phone:** (845)896-0592
All Year   1P: $104-$124   2P: $109-$129   XP: $17 F17
Location: I-84, exit 13, just n. 55 W Merritt Blvd 12524. Fax: 845/896-0851. **Facility:** 104 one-bedroom standard
Small-scale Hotel units. 3 stories, interior corridors. *Bath:* combo or shower only. **Parking:** on-site. **Terms:** weekly rates available, pets ($25 extra charge). **Amenities:** voice mail, irons, hair dryers. *Some:* DVD players. **Guest Services:** coin laundry, wireless Internet. **Cards:** AX, CB, DC, DS, MC, VI.

HAMPTON INN FISHKILL *Book great rates at AAA.com*   **Phone:** (845)896-4000
(AAA) [SAVE]
10/1-11/10   1P: $129-$169   2P: $129-$169   XP: $10   F17
5/1-9/30   1P: $119-$149   2P: $119-$149   XP: $10   F17
11/11-4/30   1P: $89-$129   2P: $89-$129   XP: $10   F17
Location: I-84, exit 13, just n; behind Holiday Inn. 544 Rt 9 12524. Fax: 845/896-2799. **Facility:** 99 one-bedroom
Small-scale Hotel standard units. 4 stories, interior corridors. *Bath:* combo or shower only. **Parking:** on-site. **Terms:** package plans. **Amenities:** video games (fee), high-speed Internet, voice mail, irons, hair dryers. **Pool(s):** small heated indoor. **Guest Services:** valet laundry. **Cards:** AX, DC, DS, MC, VI. **Free Special Amenities:** expanded continental breakfast and high-speed Internet.
SOME UNITS

HILTON GARDEN INN *Book great rates at AAA.com*   **Phone:** 845/896-7100
All Year   1P: $124-$184   2P: $124-$184   XP: $10   F17
Location: I-84, exit 13, just n, then just w. Located in a commercial area. 25 Westage Dr 12524. Fax: 845/896-7111.
Small-scale Hotel **Facility:** 111 one-bedroom standard units. 4 stories, interior corridors. *Bath:* combo or shower only. **Parking:** on-site. **Terms:** package plans. **Amenities:** high-speed Internet, dual phone lines, voice mail, irons, hair dryers. **Pool(s):** small heated indoor. **Leisure Activities:** whirlpool, exercise room. **Guest Services:** sundries, coin laundry. **Business Services:** meeting rooms, business center. **Cards:** AX, DC, DS, MC, VI.
SOME UNITS

HOMESTEAD STUDIO SUITES HOTEL-FISHKILL-POUGHKEEPSIE *Book at AAA.com*   **Phone:** (845)897-2800
5/1-10/6   1P: $119-$139   2P: $124-$144   XP: $5   F17
10/7-4/30   1P: $109-$129   2P: $114-$134   XP: $5   F17
Location: I-84, exit 13, just n. 25 Merritt Blvd 12524. Fax: 845/897-2616. **Facility:** 106 units. 82 one-bedroom
Small-scale Hotel standard units with efficiencies. 24 one-bedroom suites with efficiencies. 3 stories, interior corridors. *Bath:* combo or shower only. **Parking:** on-site. **Terms:** weekly rates available, pets ($25 extra charge). **Amenities:** dual phone lines, voice mail, irons, hair dryers. *Fee:* video games, high-speed Internet. **Leisure Activities:** limited exercise equipment, sports court. **Guest Services:** sundries, valet and coin laundry. **Cards:** AX, CB, DC, DS, MC, VI.
SOME UNITS

RAMADA FISHKILL POUGHKEEPSIE *Book great rates at AAA.com*   **Phone:** (845)896-4995
(AAA) [SAVE]
All Year [ECP]   1P: $89-$159   2P: $89-$159   XP: $10   F17
Location: I-84, exit 13, just n. 20 Schuyler Blvd 12524. Fax: 845/896-6631. **Facility:** 81 one-bedroom standard units. 4 stories, interior corridors. *Bath:* combo or shower only. **Parking:** on-site. **Terms:** small pets only ($25 extra charge, in 1st floor smoking units, with prior approval). **Amenities:** video games (fee), voice mail,
Small-scale Hotel irons, hair dryers. *Some:* dual phone lines. **Guest Services:** valet and coin laundry, wireless Internet. **Business Services:** meeting rooms, fax (fee). **Cards:** AX, DC, DS, JC, MC, VI. **Free Special Amenities:** expanded continental breakfast and newspaper.
SOME UNITS

RESIDENCE INN BY MARRIOTT *Book great rates at AAA.com*   **Phone:** 845/896-5210
Property failed to provide current rates
Location: I-84, exit 13, just n. 14 Schuyler Blvd 12524. Fax: 845/896-9689. **Facility:** Smoke free premises. 139 units. 105 one- and 34 two-bedroom standard units with kitchens. 2 stories (no elevator), exterior corridors.
Small-scale Hotel *Bath:* combo or shower only. **Parking:** on-site. **Terms:** pets ($75 fee). **Amenities:** video games (fee), dual phone lines, voice mail, irons, hair dryers. **Pool(s):** outdoor. **Leisure Activities:** whirlpool, exercise room, sports court. **Guest Services:** complimentary evening beverages: Mon-Thurs, valet and coin laundry, wireless Internet. **Business Services:** meeting rooms, PC, fax.

SIERRA SUITES POUGHKEEPSIE-FISHKILL *Book at AAA.com* Phone: (845)897-5757
1/1-4/30 [BP] 1P: $159-$189 2P: $159-$189
5/1-12/31 [BP] 1P: $139-$169 2P: $139-$169
Small-scale Hotel **Location:** I-84, exit 13, just n to Merritt Blvd, then left at first light. 100 Westage Business Center Dr 12524. Fax: 845/897-4774. **Facility:** 135 units. 49 one-bedroom standard units. 70 one- and 16 two-bedroom suites with efficiencies. 4 stories, interior corridors. *Bath:* combo or shower only. **Parking:** on-site. **Terms:** pets (with prior approval). **Amenities:** video library, DVD players, high-speed Internet, voice mail, irons, hair dryers. **Pool(s):** outdoor. **Leisure Activities:** exercise room. **Guest Services:** sundries, complimentary evening beverages, valet and coin laundry, wireless Internet. **Business Services:** meeting rooms, business center. **Cards:** AX, CB, DC, DS, JC, MC, VI.

SOME UNITS

(ASK) [icons] / X /

────── WHERE TO DINE ──────

CHARLIE BROWN'S STEAKHOUSE **Lunch:** $7-$10 **Dinner:** $10-$25 Phone: 845/896-2666
Location: In Hudson Valley Towne Center. 18 Westage Dr, Suite 22 12524. **Hours:** 11:30 am-2:30 & 3-10 pm, Fri & Sat-10:30 pm, Sun-9 pm. Closed: 12/25. **Features:** This budget-friendly steakhouse, famous for its prime Steak & Seafood rib, offers top quality fare without hurting your pocketbook. The young ones will not be disappointed with the kid's menu, and just might even try something green from the salad bar. Adults will love the quality steaks, chicken and rib dishes. The express lunches are great for those saddled with time constraints. Casual dress; cocktails. **Parking:** on-site. **Cards:** AX, DS, MC, VI.

[icon]

HUDSON'S RIBS & FISH **Dinner:** $15-$26 Phone: 845/297-5002
Location: I-84, exit 13, 3 mi n. 1099 Rt 9 12524. **Hours:** 5 pm-10 pm, Fri & Sat-11 pm, Sun 2 pm-9 pm. Closed: 1/1, 11/22, 12/25. **Features:** Baby back ribs, prime rib and fresh fish are the focus of the menu. Lacquered tables with maps of New York riverways contribute to the nautical decor. Delicious popovers are served with strawberry honey butter. Service is pleasant and prompt. Casual dress; cocktails. **Parking:** on-site.
Steak & Seafood **Cards:** AX, CB, DC, DS, MC, VI.

[icon]

NORTH STREET GRILL **Lunch:** $6-$10 **Dinner:** $12-$22 Phone: 845/896-1000
Location: I-84, exit 13, 0.9 mi n on US 9, then just w on SR 52. 1111 Main St 12524. **Hours:** 11:30 am-10 pm, Fri & Sat-11 pm, Sun 4 pm-9 pm. Closed major holidays. **Features:** The friendly staff welcomes patrons to the casual atmosphere in the historic building. Locals and families find the variety of Italian-influenced American American dishes to be just right for hearty appetites. The specialty penne Louisiana with shrimp and tasso ham in cream sauce and filet mignon with rosemary sauce are good choices. Finish with rich tiramisu or light zabaglione over fresh fruit. Casual dress; cocktails. **Parking:** on-site. **Cards:** AX, DC, DS, MC, VI.

FLORAL PARK pop. 15,967 (See map and index starting on p. 396)

────── WHERE TO STAY ──────

FLORAL PARK MOTOR LODGE *Book great rates at AAA.com* Phone: (516)775-7777 [9]
All Year 1P: $101-$122 2P: $101-$136
Location: Cross Island Pkwy (Belt Pkwy), exit 27E, 0.8 mi e on SR 25. 30 Jericho Tpke 11001. Fax: 516/775-0451. **Facility:** 107 one-bedroom standard units. 3 stories, interior corridors. *Bath:* combo or shower only. **Parking:** on-site, winter plug-ins. **Terms:** 1-2 night minimum stay. **Amenities:** voice mail, irons, hair dryers. Motel **Guest Services:** valet laundry, wireless Internet. **Business Services:** meeting rooms. **Cards:** AX, DC, DS, MC, VI. **Free Special Amenities:** continental breakfast and high-speed Internet. *(See color ad p 491)*

SOME UNITS

[icons] / X [icon] /

────── WHERE TO DINE ──────

ARTURO'S **Lunch:** $13-$28 **Dinner:** $14-$30 Phone: 516/352-7418 [15]
Location: Belt Pkwy to Cross Island Pkwy, exit 27, 0.3 mi e on SR 25 (Jericho Tpke). **Hours:** noon-3 & 5:30-10 pm, Fri-11 pm, Sat 5 pm-11 pm, Sun 3 pm-9:30 pm. Closed major holidays. **Reservations:** suggested. **Features:** Guests can savor dinner in the "old school" style. Attentive servers in semi-formal attire deliver Northern Italian Northern Italian cuisine, such as osso buco, grilled veal chops, fine risottos, sole in white wine and garlic, and, of course, pasta preparations. A roving guitarist serenades with song of diners' choosing on most nights. A large bowl of fresh fruit comes to the table before the dessert cart rolls through. This place is good for a nice evening out. Casual dress; cocktails; entertainment. **Parking:** valet. **Cards:** AX, DC, DS, MC, VI.

[icon]

POPPY'S PLACE **Lunch:** $7-$14 **Dinner:** $12-$28 Phone: 516/358-2705 [16]
Location: Tulip Ave and Railroad Station, just e. 12 Verbena Ave 11001. **Hours:** 11 am-3 & 5-10 pm, Fri & Sat-11 pm, Sun 4 pm-9 pm. Closed major holidays; also Mon. **Features:** The unpretentious neighborhood restaurant is a local favorite for made-from-scratch American and Italian food. Reasonably priced dishes, Italian such as poached calamari with pasta, are served in generous portions. A few specials are always available. Casual dress; cocktails. **Parking:** street. **Cards:** AX, DC, DS, MC, VI.

[icon]

FORT MONTGOMERY pop. 1,418

────── WHERE TO STAY ──────

HOLIDAY INN EXPRESS HOTEL & SUITES *Book at AAA.com* Phone: 845/446-4277
Property failed to provide current rates
Location: Jct US 6 and SR 9W, 1.5 mi n. 1106 Rt 9W 10922. Fax: 845/446-4288. **Facility:** 86 one-bedroom standard units, some with whirlpools. 3 stories, interior corridors. **Parking:** on-site. **Amenities:** high-speed Small-scale Hotel Internet, dual phone lines, voice mail, irons, hair dryers. **Pool(s):** indoor. **Leisure Activities:** sauna, exercise room. **Fee:** game room. **Guest Services:** coin laundry. **Business Services:** meeting rooms, business center. *(See color ad p 206)*

SOME UNITS

[icons] / X /

FRANKFORT pop. 2,537

──────── WHERE TO DINE ────────

KITLAS RESTAURANT **Lunch:** $6-$8 **Dinner:** $10-$18 **Phone:** 315/732-9616
▼▼ ▼▼ **Location:** SR 5 S, exit Turner Rd, then n. 2242 Broad St 13340. **Hours:** 11:30 am-2 & 4:30-8:30 pm, Sat from 4:30 pm, Mon 11:30 am-2 pm. Closed major holidays; also Sun. **Reservations:** accepted.
American **Features:** Owned by the same family since 1939, the restaurant delivers classic fare, including the slow-roasted pork loin over herbed mashed potatoes and lemon-horseradish-crusted haddock. The atmosphere is casual and comfy, making the place popular with families. Dressy casual; cocktails. **Parking:** on-site. **Cards:** AX, DS, MC, VI.

FREDONIA pop. 10,706

──────── WHERE TO STAY ────────

DAYS INN DUNKIRK-FREDONIA *Book great rates at AAA.com* **Phone:** 716/673-1351

	6/26-9/15	1P: $95-$115	XP: $10	F17
	5/1-6/25 & 9/16-10/31	1P: $75-$95	XP: $10	F17
	11/1-4/30	1P: $75-$85	XP: $10	F17

Location: I-90, exit 59, just s on SR 60. 10455 Bennett Rd 14063. Fax: 716/672-6909. **Facility:** 134 one-bedroom
Small-scale Hotel standard units, some with whirlpools. 2 stories (no elevator), interior corridors. **Parking:** on-site.
Terms: cancellation fee imposed, pets ($10 fee). **Amenities:** high-speed Internet, hair dryers. *Some:* irons.
Dining: 5 pm-10 pm; closed Sun. **Pool(s):** small heated indoor. **Leisure Activities:** whirlpool, grills, picnic tables. **Guest Services:** valet and coin laundry, wireless Internet. **Business Services:** meeting rooms. **Cards:** AX, CB, DC, DS, JC, MC, VI.
Free Special Amenities: continental breakfast and newspaper.

SOME UNITS

THE WHITE INN *Book great rates at AAA.com* **Phone:** (716)672-2103
  All Year [BP] 1P: $89-$199 2P: $89-$199 XP: $15 F12
  Location: I-90, exit 59, 0.5 mi s on SR 60, then 1.3 mi sw on US 20 (Main St); center. 52 E Main St 14063.
Historic Fax: 716/672-2107. **Facility:** Guest rooms appointed with antiques give the inn a pampered atmosphere;
Country Inn accommodations vary from spacious to compact. 23 units. 19 one-bedroom standard units. 4 one-bedroom suites ($109-$199), some with whirlpools. 3 stories, interior corridors. *Bath:* combo or shower only. **Parking:** on-site. **Terms:** [MAP] meal plan available, package plans, pets ($20 fee). **Amenities:** voice mail, irons, hair dryers. **Dining:** restaurant, see separate listing. **Guest Services:** wireless Internet. **Business Services:** meeting rooms. **Cards:** AX, DC, DS, MC, VI. **Free Special Amenities: full breakfast and local telephone calls.**

SOME UNITS

──────── WHERE TO DINE ────────

THE WHITE INN DINING ROOM **Lunch:** $5-$13 **Dinner:** $15-$21 **Phone:** 716/672-2103
▼▼▼▼ **Location:** I-90, exit 59, 0.5 mi s on SR 60, then 1.3 mi sw on US 20 (Main St); center; in The White Inn. 52 E Main St 14063. **Hours:** 7-10 am, 11:30-2 & 5-8:30 pm, Fri & Sat-9 pm, Sun 8-10:30 am, 11:30-2 & 5-8:30 pm.
American **Reservations:** suggested. **Features:** Casual dining with an elegant flair, soft candlelight and attentive service make for a relaxing evening in a finely appointed dining room. The cozy veranda welcomes diners to unwind. Neatly attired servers are prompt and friendly. Semi-formal attire; cocktails. **Parking:** on-site and street. **Cards:** AX, DC, DS, MC, VI. **Historic**

FREEHOLD

──────── WHERE TO DINE ────────

FREEHOLD COUNTRY INN RESTAURANT **Lunch:** $7-$9 **Dinner:** $15-$35 **Phone:** 518/634-2705
▼▼▼ **Location:** Jct SR 32 and CR 67; center. Rt 32 & 67 12431. **Hours:** noon-3 & 4-9 pm, Sun noon-9 pm. Closed: 12/25; also Tues & 1/7-1/21. **Reservations:** suggested, weekends. **Features:** The house dates from the
American late 1700s but has been fully renovated to a fresh and light farmhouse style. Ample-size portions, well-garnished courses and homemade desserts will appeal to many travelers. Casual dress; cocktails. **Parking:** on-site. **Cards:** AX, MC, VI.

FREEPORT pop. 39,900

──────── WHERE TO STAY ────────

FREEPORT MOTOR INN & BOATEL **Phone:** (516)623-9100
  All Year 1P: $95-$105 2P: $105-$120 XP: $7 D16
  Location: 1 mi s from SR 27 (Sunrise Hwy). Located in a residential area adjacent to a marina. 445 S Main St 11520.
Motel Fax: 516/546-5739. **Facility:** 60 one-bedroom standard units, some with whirlpools. 2 stories (no elevator), exterior corridors. *Bath:* combo or shower only. **Parking:** on-site. **Terms:** [CP] meal plan available, package plans. **Amenities:** *Some:* hair dryers. **Leisure Activities:** *Fee:* marina. **Guest Services:** wireless Internet. **Cards:** AX, DC, MC, VI. **Free Special Amenities: continental breakfast and high-speed Internet.**

SOME UNITS

FEE FEE FEE

——— WHERE TO DINE ———

E.B. ELLIOT'S   Lunch: $10-$14   Dinner: $23-$39   Phone: 516/378-8776
▼▼▼ ▼▼▼
Location: SR 27 (Sunrise Hwy), 1.1 mi s on S Ocean Ave, then just e on Front St. 23 Woodcleft Ave 11520.
Regional American   **Hours:** noon-10 pm, Fri & Sat-11 pm. Closed: 11/22, 12/25. **Reservations:** suggested. **Features:** At the
start of Freeport's "Nautical Mile," a road known for quaint shops and restaurants next to a large marina, the
three-story contemporary building devotes its second floor to a large bar and lounge where live music plays
most weekends and its third floor to the main dining room, which affords amazing views of the marina and shops below.
Excellent steaks and local seafood, including lobster and steamer clams with ale bath and drawn butter, are the main draws.
Dressy casual; cocktails. **Parking:** on-site. **Cards:** AX, MC, VI.

FULTON pop. 11,855

——— WHERE TO STAY ———

RIVERSIDE INN   Phone: (315)593-2444
▼▼ ▼▼
                        7/1-10/31   1P: $69-$145   2P: $69-$145
                        5/1-6/30 & 11/1-4/30   1P: $59-$125   2P: $59-$125
Small-scale Hotel   **Location:** On SR 481. 930 S 1st St 13069. Fax: 315/593-1730. **Facility:** 69 one-bedroom standard units. 2
stories (no elevator), interior corridors. **Parking:** on-site, winter plug-ins. **Terms:** [BP] meal plan available,
pets ($100 deposit). **Amenities:** voice mail. *Some:* hair dryers. **Pool(s):** outdoor. **Guest Services:** valet laundry, wireless
Internet. **Business Services:** meeting rooms. **Cards:** AX, DC, DS, MC, VI.

SOME UNITS
(A$K) (S⌀) 🛏 🍽 🍸 🐾 🐕 🖥 / ✕ 💻 /
FEE

GANSEVOORT

——— WHERE TO DINE ———

CHEZ PIERRE RESTAURANT   Dinner: $16-$23   Phone: 518/793-3350
▼▼▼ ▼▼▼
Location: I-87, exit 17S, 3 mi w. 979 Rt 9 12831. **Hours:** 5 pm-10 pm, Sun-9 pm. Closed: 12/24, 12/25; also
French   Mon. **Reservations:** suggested. **Features:** Find the red Eiffel Tower in Wilton and you will also find
provincial French cuisine, carefully prepared by the same family for over 30 years. Polished service will
smooth the way from complimentary pate to crispy salad and on to seafood, veal and beef prepared in
tempting sauces. One attractive dessert is ice cream with candied chestnuts. Casual dress; cocktails. **Parking:** on-site.
Cards: AX, MC, VI.

🍸 ◥

GARDEN CITY pop. 21,672

——— WHERE TO STAY ———

WINGATE INN   *Book at AAA.com*   Phone: 516/705-9000
▼▼▼ ▼▼▼   Property failed to provide current rates
Location: Meadowbrook Pkwy, exit 3, 0.5 mi w. 821 Stewart Ave 11530. Fax: 516/705-9100. **Facility:** 128 units.
Small-scale Hotel   125 one-bedroom standard units. 3 one-bedroom suites. 5 stories, interior corridors. *Bath:* combo or shower
only. **Parking:** on-site. **Terms:** small pets only ($50 fee, $50 deposit). **Amenities:** video games (fee), high-
speed Internet, dual phone lines, voice mail, safes, irons, hair dryers. **Leisure Activities:** whirlpool, exercise room. **Guest
Services:** complimentary evening beverages, valet laundry, wireless Internet. **Business Services:** meeting rooms, business
center.

SOME UNITS
🛏 🍸 ⌂M 🔧 🐕 💻 / ✕ 🖥 📠 /
FEE

——— WHERE TO DINE ———

WALK STREET   Lunch: $10-$13   Dinner: $16-$24   Phone: 516/746-2592
▼▼ ▼▼
Location: Just w of Franklin Ave. 176 Seventh St 11530. **Hours:** noon-3 & 5-10 pm, Fri-11 pm, Sat 5 pm-11 pm,
American   Sun 5 pm-9 pm. Closed: 12/25. **Reservations:** suggested. **Features:** Spacious and comfortable with a
modern decor and an eclectic menu of tempting dishes, the restaurant invites guests to come with friends.
Yellowfin tuna tartare with yuzu-mustard dressing, chilled lobster salad with basil dressing and three-
mushroom risotto with herbs, Parmigiano-Reggiano and truffle oil are a sample of the starters. Marinated hanger steak with old
bay fries and soft shell crab tempura with warm lemon-soy vinaigrette show the range in entrees. Casual dress; cocktails.
Parking: on-site. **Cards:** AX, DS, MC, VI.

⌂M

GARDEN CITY PARK

——— WHERE TO DINE ———

CHARLIE BROWN'S STEAKHOUSE   Lunch: $6-$10   Dinner: $12-$21   Phone: 516/294-7320
▼▼▼ ▼▼▼
Location: On SR 25. 2349 Jericho Tpke 11040. **Hours:** 11:30 am-2:30 & 3-midnight, Sun-11 pm. Closed: 12/25.
Features: This budget-friendly steakhouse, famous for its prime rib, offers top quality fare without hurting
Steak & Seafood   your pocketbook. The young ones will not be disappointed with the kid's menu, and just might even try
something green from the salad bar. Adults will love the quality steaks, chicken and rib dishes. The express
lunches are great for those saddled with time constraints. Casual dress; cocktails. **Parking:** on-site. **Cards:** AX, DS, MC, VI.

🍸

GARDINER pop. 856

———— **WHERE TO STAY** ————

MINNEWASKA LODGE
Phone: (845)255-1110
All Year   1P: $135-$329   2P: $135-$329
▼▼▼▼ **Location:** Jct SR 299 and US 44/SR 55, just e. Located in a rural area. 3116 Rt 44/55 12525. Fax: 845/255-5069.
Small-scale Hotel **Facility:** Smoke free premises. 26 units. 25 one-bedroom standard units. 1 one-bedroom suite ($299-$349).
3 stories (no elevator), interior corridors. **Parking:** on-site. **Terms:** 2 night minimum stay - weekends, 30 day
cancellation notice-fee imposed, 10% service charge, no pets allowed (owner's cat on premises). **Amenities:** DVD players, dual
phone lines, voice mail, irons, hair dryers. **Leisure Activities:** exercise room. **Guest Services:** gift shop, wireless Internet.
Cards: AX, MC, VI.

SOME UNITS
⬚ ⬚ ⬚ ⬚ / ⬚ ⬚ /

GATES pop. 29,275   (See map and index starting on p. 599)

———— **WHERE TO STAY** ————

COMFORT INN CENTRAL   *Book great rates at AAA.com*
Phone: (585)436-4400   ⓴
AAA SAVE All Year   1P: $79-$129   2P: $89-$129   XP: $10   F17
Location: I-390, exit 18B (SR 204), 0.3 mi w; opposite entrance to Greater Rochester International Airport. 395 Buell Rd
▼▼ ▼▼ 14624. Fax: 585/436-6496. **Facility:** 73 one-bedroom standard units. 2 stories (no elevator), interior
corridors. **Parking:** on-site. **Terms:** cancellation fee imposed, package plans, pets ($25 deposit).
Small-scale Hotel **Amenities:** video games, voice mail, irons, hair dryers. **Guest Services:** valet laundry, area transportation-
local businesses, wireless Internet. **Cards:** AX, DS, MC, VI. **Free Special Amenities: continental
breakfast and high-speed Internet.**

SOME UNITS
⬚ ⬚ ⬚ ⬚ ⬚ ⬚ ⬚ / ⬚ ⬚ ⬚ /
FEE

FAIRFIELD INN ROCHESTER AIRPORT   *Book great rates at AAA.com*   **Phone: 585/529-5000**   ㉑
All Year   1P: $134   2P: $134
▼▼▼▼ **Location:** I-390, exit 18B (SR 204). Located at the Greater Rochester International Airport. 1200 Brooks Ave 14624.
Small-scale Hotel Fax: 585/529-5011. **Facility:** Smoke free premises. 62 one-bedroom standard units. 3 stories, interior
corridors. *Bath:* combo or shower only. **Parking:** on-site. **Terms:** [CP] meal plan available. **Amenities:** video
games (fee), high-speed Internet, irons, hair dryers. **Pool(s):** small heated indoor. **Leisure Activities:** exercise room. **Guest
Services:** valet laundry, wireless Internet. **Cards:** AX, DC, DS, MC, VI.

SOME UNITS
⬚ ⬚ ⬚ ⬚ ⬚ ⬚ ⬚ ⬚ ⬚ ⬚ / ⬚ /

HOLIDAY INN-ROCHESTER AIRPORT   *Book great rates at AAA.com*   **Phone: (585)328-6000**   ㉒
All Year   1P: $109-$149   2P: $109-$149
▼▼▼▼ **Location:** I-390, exit 18A (SR 204), just e. 911 Brooks Ave 14624. Fax: 585/328-1012. **Facility:** 279 one-bedroom
standard units, some with whirlpools. 2 stories (no elevator), interior corridors. **Parking:** on-site.
Small-scale Hotel **Terms:** [AP], [BP], [CP], [ECP] & [MAP] meal plans available, small pets only ($50 deposit).
Amenities: high-speed Internet, voice mail, irons, hair dryers. *Some:* dual phone lines. **Pool(s):** heated indoor. **Leisure
Activities:** sauna, whirlpool, exercise room. **Guest Services:** gift shop, valet and coin laundry, area transportation, wireless
Internet. **Business Services:** meeting rooms, business center. **Cards:** AX, CB, DC, DS, JC, MC, VI.

SOME UNITS
⬚ ⬚ ⬚ ⬚ ⬚ ⬚ ⬚ ⬚ ⬚ ⬚ / ⬚ ⬚ /
FEE   FEE

GENESEO pop. 7,579—*See also FINGER LAKES.*

———— **WHERE TO STAY** ————

BIG TREE INN
Phone: 585/243-5220
All Year   1P: $110-$185   2P: $110-$185
▼▼▼▼ **Location:** I-390, exit 8; center. 46 Main St 14454 (PO Box 387). Fax: 585/243-5248. **Facility:** Built in 1833, this
Historic historic property has been totally renovated and now boasts period decor and the ultimate in luxury and
Country Inn modern comforts. Smoke free premises. 8 one-bedroom standard units, some with whirlpools. 3 stories (no
elevator), interior corridors. *Bath:* combo or shower only. **Parking:** on-site. **Terms:** cancellation fee imposed,
package plans. **Amenities:** CD players, high-speed Internet, voice mail, irons, hair dryers. *Some:* DVD players. **Dining:** Big
Tree Inn, see separate listing. **Business Services:** meeting rooms. **Cards:** AX, DC, DS, MC, VI.

⬚ ⬚ ⬚ ⬚ ⬚

QUALITY INN GENESEO   *Book great rates at AAA.com*
Phone: (585)243-0500
5/1-6/30 [CP]   1P: $95-$165   2P: $95-$165   XP: $10   F
▼▼ ▼▼ 7/1-8/31 [CP]   1P: $105-$135   2P: $105-$135   XP: $10   F
9/1-10/31 [CP]   1P: $95-$125   2P: $95-$125   XP: $10   F
Small-scale Hotel 11/1-4/30 [CP]   1P: $95-$115   2P: $95-$115   XP: $10   F
Location: I-390, exit 8, 3.4 mi w on SR 20A. 4242 Lakeville Rd 14454. Fax: 585/243-9007. **Facility:** 76 one-bedroom standard units. 2
stories (no elevator), interior corridors. **Parking:** on-site. **Terms:** cancellation fee imposed, pets ($10 extra charge).
Amenities: voice mail, irons, hair dryers. **Pool(s):** outdoor. **Guest Services:** wireless Internet. **Business Services:** meeting
rooms. **Cards:** AX, DC, DS, MC, VI.

SOME UNITS
⬚ ⬚ ⬚ ⬚ ⬚ ⬚ ⬚ ⬚ / ⬚ /
FEE

———— **WHERE TO DINE** ————

BIG TREE INN
Lunch: $5-$13   **Dinner:** $10-$36   **Phone:** 585/243-5220
▼▼▼▼ **Location:** I-390, exit 8; center; in Big Tree Inn. 46 Main St 14454. **Hours:** 11:30 am-2 & 4-8 pm. Closed: 12/25;
also Sun & Mon. **Reservations:** suggested. **Features:** Guests experience relaxed, elegant dining in the
American beautifully maintained 1833 inn. Seasonal entrees rise above the ordinary, and creative sauces add zest for
ultimate flavor. Prime rib can be savored only on Thursday and Saturday. Casual dress; cocktails. **Parking:**
on-site. **Cards:** AX, DC, DS, MC, VI.

⬚

GENEVA pop. 13,617—*See also FINGER LAKES.*

──── WHERE TO STAY ────

BELHURST

Phone: 315/781-0201

Historic
Country Inn

All Year [CP]   2P: $65-$365

Location: 2 mi s of town. 4069 SR 14 S 14456 (PO Box 609). Fax: 315/781-0201. **Facility:** This lakefront property was built in 1885 and offers spacious, castle-like common areas accented with massive, original, carved woodwork. 34 one-bedroom standard units, some with whirlpools. 3 stories (no elevator), interior corridors. *Bath:* combo or shower only. **Parking:** on-site. **Terms:** 7 day cancellation notice-fee imposed, package plans. **Amenities:** voice mail, irons, hair dryers. *Some:* DVD players, CD players, honor bars. **Leisure Activities:** boat dock, fishing. **Guest Services:** gift shop, wireless Internet. **Business Services:** conference facilities. **Cards:** AX, MC, VI.

SOME UNITS

CLARK'S MOTEL

Motel

Phone: 315/789-0780

5/1-11/30 & 4/1-4/30   1P: $42-$52   2P: $42-$52   XP: $3

Location: Jct US 20/SR 5 and 14A, 2.3 mi w. 824 Canandaigua Rd 14456. **Facility:** 10 one-bedroom standard units. 1 story, exterior corridors. **Parking:** on-site, winter plug-ins. **Terms:** open 5/1-11/30 & 4/1-4/30. **Cards:** MC, VI.

SOME UNITS

FEE

GENEVA-ON-THE-LAKE   *Book great rates at AAA.com*

AAA [SAVE]

Historic
Country Inn

Phone: (315)789-7190

5/24-11/20 [ECP]	1P: $227-$370	2P: $237-$380	XP: $50	F6
5/1-5/23 & 4/1-4/30 [ECP]	1P: $180-$294	2P: $190-$304	XP: $50	F6
11/21-3/31 [ECP]	1P: $132-$218	2P: $142-$228	XP: $50	F6

Location: 1.5 mi s on SR 14. 1001 Lochland Rd 14456. Fax: 315/789-0322. **Facility:** Within the Finger Lakes area, the inn offers manicured lawns, an upscale restaurant and Stickley furniture in the rooms. Smoke free premises. 29 units. 6 one-bedroom standard units with kitchens. 13 one- and 10 two-bedroom suites ($369-$847) with kitchens, some with whirlpools. 3 stories (no elevator), interior corridors. *Bath:* combo or shower only. **Parking:** on-site. **Terms:** 2-3 night minimum stay - seasonal and/or weekends, 14 day cancellation notice-fee imposed, [BP] & [MAP] meal plans available, package plans. **Amenities:** video library, DVD players, CD players, irons, hair dryers. **Dining:** 8 am-10 & 6-9 pm; also noon-2 pm in season, cocktails. **Pool(s):** outdoor. **Leisure Activities:** rental canoes, rental paddleboats, boat dock, fishing, lawn games, bicycles, limited exercise equipment, basketball, horseshoes. *Fee:* sailboats, pontoon boat, massage. **Guest Services:** gift shop, complimentary evening beverages: Fri, valet laundry, wireless Internet. **Business Services:** meeting rooms. **Cards:** AX, DS, MC, VI. **Free Special Amenities: expanded continental breakfast.**

(See color ad p 300)

SOME UNITS

HAMPTON INN GENEVA   *Book great rates at AAA.com*

Small-scale Hotel

Phone: (315)781-2035

All Year [BP]   1P: $104-$182   2P: $114-$192   XP: $10   F18

Location: Jct Exchange St. 43 Lake St 14456. Fax: 315/781-2037. **Facility:** 55 one-bedroom standard units. 3 stories, interior corridors. *Bath:* combo or shower only. **Parking:** on-site. **Terms:** pets ($10 extra charge). **Amenities:** high-speed Internet, voice mail, irons, hair dryers. *Fee:* video library, video games. *Some:* DVD players (fee). **Pool(s):** small heated indoor. **Leisure Activities:** whirlpool, exercise room. **Guest Services:** valet and coin laundry, wireless Internet. **Business Services:** meeting rooms, business center. **Cards:** AX, DC, DS, MC, VI.

SOME UNITS

FEE   FEE

RAMADA INN GENEVA LAKEFRONT   *Book great rates at AAA.com*

AAA [SAVE]

Small-scale Hotel

Phone: 315/789-0400

5/1-11/5	1P: $110-$300	2P: $120-$325	XP: $10	F18
11/6-4/30	1P: $82-$240	2P: $92-$240	XP: $10	F18

Location: I-90, exit 42, 8 mi s on SR 14. 41 Lakefront Dr 14456. Fax: 315/789-4351. **Facility:** 148 one-bedroom standard units, some with whirlpools. 6 stories, interior corridors. *Bath:* combo or shower only. **Parking:** on-site. **Terms:** package plans, pets ($10 extra charge). **Amenities:** voice mail, irons, hair dryers. *Fee:* video games, safes. **Dining:** 6:30 am-3 & 5-10 pm, Fri & Sat 7 am-3 & 5-11 pm, cocktails. **Pool(s):** small heated indoor. **Leisure Activities:** exercise room. **Guest Services:** valet and coin laundry, wireless Internet. **Business Services:** meeting rooms, business center. **Cards:** AX, DC, DS, MC, VI. **Free Special Amenities: newspaper.**

SOME UNITS

FEE   FEE FEE

──── WHERE TO DINE ────

LING LING CHINESE BUFFET

Chinese

DS, MC, VI.

Lunch: $4-$7   **Dinner:** $5-$11   **Phone:** 315/781-0668

Location: 1.5 mi w on SR 20, in Hamilton Square. 481 Hamilton St 14456. **Hours:** 11 am-10:30 pm, Fri & Sat-11:30 pm, Sun 11:30 am-10 pm. Closed: 11/22. **Features:** In a small shopping center, the restaurant sets up a lunch buffet that attracts flocks of hungry diners. Choices include Chinese, Cantonese, Szechuan and Hunan dishes, none of which includes monosodium glutamate. Casual dress. **Parking:** on-site. **Cards:** AX,

NONNA'S TRATTORIA

Italian

Lunch: $5-$9   **Dinner:** $9-$20   **Phone:** 315/789-1638

Location: Just e off Exchange St; center. 1 Railroad Pl 14456. **Hours:** 11:30 am-3:30 & 4:30-9:30 pm, Fri & Sat 4:30 pm-10 pm, Sun 4 pm-9 pm. Closed major holidays; also Tues. **Reservations:** accepted. **Features:** Patrons can nosh on classic fare either inside or on the seasonal patio. The daily lunch buffet is a local favorite, along with Uncle Joe's Pizzeria for eat-in or take-out. Casual dress; cocktails. **Parking:** on-site. **Cards:** AX, DS, MC, VI.

PASTA ONLY'S COBBLESTONE   Lunch: $6-$8   Dinner: $10-$22   Phone: 315/789-8498

Italian

Location: Jct US 20 and SR 5, 1.5 mi w. 3610 PreEmption Rd 14456. **Hours:** 11:30 am-2 & 5-9 pm, Fri & Sat-10 pm. Closed: 1/1, 12/25; also Mon off season. **Reservations:** suggested. **Features:** Although the restored 1825 farmhouse delivers a menu of Italian cuisine, wood-grilled steak, chops and fresh seafood, this place is known for its exquisite dessert. The pastry chef whips up outstanding creations, including the sunken chocolate souffle. Casual dress; cocktails. **Parking:** on-site. **Cards:** AX, DS, MC, VI.

WING TAI ORIENTAL RESTAURANT   Dinner: $6-$9   Phone: 315/789-8892

Chinese

Location: Just off SR 14. 164 Castle St 14456. **Hours:** 5 pm-9:30 pm, Fri & Sat-10 pm, Sun-9 pm. Closed major holidays. **Reservations:** suggested, weekends. **Features:** In business since the late 1970s, the restaurant is decorated in an Oriental style, with Chinese lanterns and painted wallpaper. "Seven stars around the moon"—a seafood, beef and chicken dish for two—is popular, as is the irresistible flaming cherry dessert. Casual dress; beer & wine only. **Parking:** on-site. **Cards:** AX, DC, DS, MC, VI.

GHENT pop. 586

——— WHERE TO DINE ———

RED BARN RESTAURANT   Lunch: $3-$18   Dinner: $8-$26   Phone: 518/828-6677

American

Location: Jct SR 66 and 9H, 2.5 mi n. 47 Old Post Rd/Rt 9H 12075. **Hours:** noon-8 pm, Sat & Sun 7:30 am-9 pm; hours may vary. Closed: 11/22. **Features:** An old-fashioned atmosphere lends to the quaint, homespun charm of the converted barn. Patrons can relax in the smoke-free dining room and enjoy selections including sandwiches and daily specials. When it's time for dessert, opt for the delicious, homemade ice cream. Casual dress. **Parking:** on-site.

GIBBSBORO pop. 2,435

——— WHERE TO DINE ———

THE CHOPHOUSE   Dinner: $24-$39   Phone: 856/566-7300

Steak House

Location: I-295, exit 32, 4 mi e on Haddonfield-Berlin Rd (CR 561). 4 S Lakeview Dr 08026. **Hours:** 5 pm-10 pm, Fri & Sat-11 pm, Sun & Mon-9 pm. Closed major holidays. **Reservations:** suggested, weekends. **Features:** Fine steaks, classic martinis and stellar service are hallmarks of this popular local favorite. The dining room, with its floor-to-ceiling windows, is bright and airy, and wood accents and a hearth makes it warm and cozy. Steaks, though, are the real draw, and they're all that and more. Decadent desserts and traditional steakhouse sides are worth the extra calories. Casual dress; cocktails. **Parking:** on-site. **Cards:** AX, DS, MC, VI.

GLEN COVE pop. 26,622

——— WHERE TO DINE ———

LA PACE   Lunch: $9-$29   Dinner: $20-$42   Phone: 516/671-2970

Northern Italian

Location: Jct Glen Cove Rd, 0.5 mi e. 51 Cedar Swamp Rd 11542. **Hours:** 11:30 am-3 & 5:30-10:30 pm, Fri & Sat 6 pm-11 pm, Sun 4 pm-9 pm. Closed: 3/23, 12/25; also Mon. **Reservations:** suggested. **Features:** A Gold Coast tradition since the late 1970s, the restaurant exudes a sophisticated European ambience that is reflective of an earlier time. The specialty veal chop with wild mushrooms is well-prepared and flavorful. Service is reserved and professional. Semi-formal attire; cocktails. **Parking:** valet and street. **Cards:** AX, DC, MC, VI.

GLENMONT (See map and index starting on p. 218)

——— WHERE TO STAY ———

COMFORT INN   *Book great rates at AAA.com*   Phone: (518)465-8811   [53]

Small-scale Hotel

All Year   1P: $99-$169   2P: $99-$169   XP: $10   F12

Location: I-87, exit 23, 0.5 mi s on US 9W. 37 SR 9W 12077. Fax: 518/465-5732. **Facility:** 100 one-bedroom standard units. 2 stories, interior corridors. *Bath:* combo or shower only. **Parking:** on-site. **Terms:** [CP] meal plan available. **Amenities:** high-speed Internet, voice mail, irons, hair dryers. **Dining:** 4 pm-9:30 pm; closed Sun, cocktails. **Pool(s):** heated indoor. **Leisure Activities:** whirlpool, exercise room, game room. **Guest Services:** coin laundry, wireless Internet. **Business Services:** fax (fee). **Cards:** AX, DC, DS, MC, VI.
Free Special Amenities: continental breakfast and high-speed Internet.

SOME UNITS

GLENORA —See FINGER LAKES.

GLENS FALLS pop. 14,354 (See map and index starting on p. 330)—See also ADIRONDACK MOUNTAINS & SOUTH GLENS FALLS.

——— WHERE TO STAY ———

QUEENSBURY HOTEL   *Book great rates at AAA.com*   Phone: (518)792-1121   [61]

Historic
Small-scale Hotel

All Year   1P: $94-$179   2P: $94-$179

Location: Corner of Maple St; center. 88 Ridge St 12801. Fax: 518/792-9259. **Facility:** Traditional Victorian decor and furnishings enhance this red-brick downtown hotel overlooking a park. 125 units. 114 one-bedroom standard units. 11 one-bedroom suites. 5 stories, interior corridors. *Bath:* combo or shower only. **Parking:** on-site, winter plug-ins. **Terms:** package plans. **Amenities:** high-speed Internet, irons, hair dryers. **Dining:** 6:30-10:30 am, 11:30-2 & 5-9:30 pm. **Pool(s):** heated indoor. **Leisure Activities:** whirlpool, exercise room. *Fee:* massage. **Guest Services:** valet laundry, wireless Internet. **Business Services:** conference facilities, business center. **Cards:** AX, DC, DS, MC, VI. **Free Special Amenities: high-speed Internet.**

SOME UNITS

FEE FEE

——— WHERE TO DINE ———

132 GLEN BISTRO

American

Dinner: $15-$28   **Phone:** 518/743-9138   ④⓪

Location: Center. 132 Glen St 12801. **Hours:** 5:30 pm-9:30 pm. Closed major holidays. **Reservations:** suggested. **Features:** The cozy downtown bistro affords a nice view of the city streets. From season to season, the menu changes to highlight entrees such as blackened catfish, Italian meatloaf and the cowboy cut pork chop. Locally made Davidson Brothers beer is on tap. Casual dress; beer & wine only. **Parking:** street. **Cards:** AX, MC, VI.

DAVIDSON BROTHERS RESTAURANT & BREWERY

American

Lunch: $6-$9   **Dinner:** $11-$20   **Phone:** 518/743-9026   ③⑨

Location: Center. 184 Glen St 12801. **Hours:** 11:30 am-10 pm, Fri-11 pm, Sat noon-11 pm, Sun noon-9 pm. Closed: 4/8, 11/22, 12/25; also Sun 10/1-5/31. **Reservations:** accepted. **Features:** This two-story English brew house offers the typical "pub fare" which is well-complemented by a selection of hand-crafted ales made on the premises. Both levels are decorated using a variety of odd pieces of machinery from the city's industrial past. Upstairs holds a game room and dining outdoors is popular, weather permitting. Casual dress; cocktails. **Parking:** street. **Cards:** AX, MC, VI.

FIDDLEHEADS

Continental

Lunch: $6-$15   **Dinner:** $15-$26   **Phone:** 518/793-5789   ③⑥

Location: I-87, exit 18, follow signs toward hospital 2 mi, just beyond to 2nd traffic light, bear left on SR 9L. 21 Ridge St 12801. **Hours:** 11:30 am-3 & 5-9 pm. Closed: 12/24, 12/25; also Sun & Mon. **Reservations:** suggested. **Features:** A country ambience is pervasive in the charming restaurant. Maryland crab cakes stand out on a menu of beef, lamb, fowl and seafood preparations, all thoughtfully arranged by the owner-chef. In addition to being delicious, desserts have great eye appeal. Casual dress; cocktails. **Parking:** street. **Cards:** DS, MC, VI.

THE GOURMET CAFE

American

Lunch: $6-$10   **Dinner:** $6-$20   **Phone:** 518/761-0864   ③⑦

Location: Center. 185 Glen St (Rt 9) 12801. **Hours:** 11 am-9 pm, Mon & Tues-4 pm. Closed major holidays; also Sun. **Reservations:** accepted. **Features:** The little downtown cafe applies a distinctive twist to some traditional items. The menu changes periodically, so it's a good idea to stop back often to get a sampling of everything. Beer & wine only. **Parking:** street. **Cards:** AX, MC, VI.

SIAM THAI SUSHI

Sushi

Lunch: $5-$8   **Dinner:** $5-$30   **Phone:** 518/792-6111   ③⑧

Location: Center of downtown. 196 Glen St 12801. **Hours:** 11:30 am-3 & 5-10 pm, Fri & Sat-10:30 pm. Closed: 11/22, 12/25. **Reservations:** accepted. **Features:** Traditional Thai dishes, as well as an extensive sushi menu and stir-fry, are available. Casual dress; beer & wine only. **Parking:** street. **Cards:** AX, DS, MC, VI.

GOSHEN pop. 5,676

——— WHERE TO STAY ———

COMFORT INN & SUITES - GOSHEN   *Book great rates at AAA.com*

Large-scale Hotel

Phone: (845)291-1282

All Year   1P: $119-$279   2P: $119-$279   XP: $10   F18

Location: SR 17, exit 124, straight off exit. 20 Hatfield Ln 10924. Fax: 845/291-1283. **Facility:** 95 units. 58 one-bedroom standard units, some with whirlpools. 37 one-bedroom suites ($149-$279), some with whirlpools. 3 stories, interior corridors. *Bath:* combo or shower only. **Parking:** on-site. **Terms:** cancellation fee imposed, package plans. **Amenities:** high-speed Internet, voice mail, irons, hair dryers. **Pool(s):** outdoor. **Leisure Activities:** exercise room. **Guest Services:** valet and coin laundry, wireless Internet. **Business Services:** meeting rooms, business center. **Cards:** AX, CB, DC, DS, MC, VI.

SOME UNITS

GRAND ISLAND —See Buffalo p. 259.

GREAT NECK pop. 9,538

——— WHERE TO STAY ———

THE ANDREW HOTEL   *Book at AAA.com*

Small-scale Hotel

Phone: (516)482-2900

All Year   1P: $279-$299   XP: $25   F12

Location: Jct SR 25A, 0.8 mi n on Middle Neck Rd, just e. Located in a commercial/residential area. 75 N Station Plaza 11021. Fax: 516/482-4643. **Facility:** 62 one-bedroom standard units. 4 stories, interior corridors. **Parking:** valet and street. **Terms:** cancellation fee imposed, [ECP] meal plan available, pets ($150 fee). **Amenities:** video library (fee), DVD players, CD players, high-speed Internet, dual phone lines, voice mail, safes, honor bars, hair dryers. **Guest Services:** valet laundry. **Business Services:** meeting rooms. **Cards:** AX, DC, DS, MC, VI.

SOME UNITS
FEE   FEE

INN AT GREAT NECK   *Book at AAA.com*

Small-scale Hotel

Phone: (516)773-2000

All Year   1P: $219   2P: $269   XP: $20   F16

Location: Jct SR 25A, 0.8 mi n on Middle Neck Rd, just w. Located in a commercial area. 30 Cutter Mill Rd 11021. Fax: 516/773-2020. **Facility:** 85 units. 79 one-bedroom standard units, some with whirlpools. 6 one-bedroom suites ($329-$379). 5 stories, interior corridors. *Bath:* combo or shower only. **Parking:** valet. **Terms:** pets ($50 fee, with prior approval). **Amenities:** video library, DVD players, CD players, high-speed Internet, dual phone lines, voice mail, safes, honor bars, irons, hair dryers. **Leisure Activities:** exercise room. **Guest Services:** valet laundry, wireless Internet. **Business Services:** meeting rooms, business center. **Cards:** AX, CB, DC, DS, JC, MC, VI.

SOME UNITS
FEE   FEE

─────── **WHERE TO DINE** ───────

PETER LUGER   **Lunch:** $9-$25   **Dinner:** $16-$37   **Phone:** 516/487-8800
♦♦♦♦ ♦♦♦♦   **Location:** I-495, exit 33 (Lakeville Rd), 0.8 mi n, then 0.6 mi w. 255 Northern Blvd 11021. **Hours:** 11:45 am-10 pm,
          Fri & Sat-11 pm, Sun from 1 pm. **Reservations:** required. **Features:** Succulent prime porterhouse steaks,
Steak House   which are dry-aged on premise, are this sophisticated restaurant's specialty and they are exceptional. Many
          by-the-glass selections line the excellent wine list. The dining room exudes an elegant, Old World charm.
Casual dress; cocktails. **Parking:** valet and street.

GREECE pop. 14,614   (See map and index starting on p. 599)

─────── **WHERE TO STAY** ───────

COURTYARD BY MARRIOTT-ROCHESTER WEST .   *Book great rates at AAA.com*   **Phone:** (585)621-6050   **14**
♦♦♦ ♦♦♦   1/1-4/30   1P: $109-$169   2P: $109-$169
          5/1-12/31   1P: $104-$159   2P: $104-$159
Small-scale Hotel   **Location:** I-390, exit 24A, just s on SR 104 (Paddy Rd), just s on Hoover Dr, then just w. 400 Paddy Creek Cir 14615.
Fax: 585/621-6115. **Facility:** Smoke free premises. 78 units. 70 one-bedroom standard units. 8 one-
bedroom suites. 3 stories, interior corridors. *Bath:* combo or shower only. **Parking:** on-site. **Amenities:** high-speed Internet,
dual phone lines, voice mail, irons, hair dryers. **Pool(s):** small heated indoor. **Leisure Activities:** whirlpool, exercise room.
Guest Services: valet and coin laundry, area transportation, wireless Internet. **Business Services:** meeting rooms. **Cards:** AX,
CB, DC, DS, JC, MC, VI.

(ASK) (SD) + (♦) (|♦) (♦) (⊘) (♦) (X) (♦) (♦) / (♦) (♦) /   SOME UNITS

EXTENDED STAY AMERICA-ROCHESTER-GREECE   *Book at AAA.com*   **Phone:** (585)663-5558   **9**
♦♦♦ ♦♦♦   5/31-9/8   1P: $60-$85   2P: $65-$90   XP: $5   F17
          9/9-4/30   1P: $60-$80   2P: $65-$85   XP: $5   F17
          5/1-5/30   1P: $55-$80   2P: $60-$85   XP: $5   F17
Small-scale Hotel   **Location:** I-390, exit 24A, just e on SR 104 (Ridge Rd), then just n on Buckman Rd. 600 Center Place Dr 14615.
Fax: 585/663-6750. **Facility:** 125 one-bedroom standard units with efficiencies. 2 stories, interior corridors. *Bath:* combo or
shower only. **Parking:** on-site. **Terms:** pets ($25-$75 fee, in designated units). **Amenities:** voice mail, irons. **Guest Services:**
coin laundry. **Cards:** AX, CB, DC, DS, MC, VI.

(ASK) (SD) (♦) (|♦) (♦M) (♦) (⊘) (♦) (♦) (♦) (♦) / (X) /   SOME UNITS
          FEE

HAMPTON INN-ROCHESTER NORTH   *Book great rates at AAA.com*   **Phone:** (585)663-6070   **10**
♦♦♦ ♦♦♦   All Year [BP]   1P: $119-$149   2P: $125-$155
Small-scale Hotel   **Location:** I-390, exit 24A, just e on SR 104 (Ridge Rd), then just n on Buckman Rd. 500 Center Place Dr 14615.
Fax: 585/663-9158. **Facility:** 118 units. 116 one-bedroom standard units. 2 one-bedroom suites ($149-$169)
with whirlpools. 4 stories, interior corridors. *Bath:* combo or shower only. **Parking:** on-site. **Amenities:** high-
speed Internet, voice mail, irons, hair dryers. **Leisure Activities:** exercise room. **Guest Services:** valet laundry, wireless
Internet. **Business Services:** meeting rooms, PC. **Cards:** AX, DC, DS, MC, VI.

(ASK) (SD) (♦) (|♦) (♦M) (♦) (♦) (♦) / (X) (♦) (♦) /   SOME UNITS
          FEE FEE

HOLIDAY INN EXPRESS ROCHESTER-GREECE   **Phone:** 585/621-2060   **12**
(fyi)   Property failed to provide current rates
          Under major renovation, scheduled to be completed December 2006. Last rated: ♦♦ **Location:** I-390, exit
Small-scale Hotel   24A, just e on SR 104 (Ridge Rd). 1635 W Ridge Rd 14615. **Fax:** 585/621-7102. **Facility:** 97 one-bedroom
          standard units. 4 stories, interior corridors. *Bath:* combo or shower only. **Parking:** on-site. **Amenities:** video
games (fee), voice mail, irons, hair dryers. **Guest Services:** valet laundry.

(|♦) (♦M) (♦) (⊘) (♦♦) (♦) (♦) / (X) (♦) (♦) /   SOME UNITS

MARRIOTT AIRPORT HOTEL   **Phone:** 585/225-6880   **11**
♦♦♦   Property failed to provide current rates
          Location: I-390, exit 24B, just w on SR 104 (Ridge Rd); 3.5 mi n of I-490. 1890 W Ridge Rd 14615.
Small-scale Hotel   **Fax:** 585/225-8188. **Facility:** Smoke free premises. 210 units. 208 one-bedroom standard units. 2 one-
          bedroom suites. 7 stories, interior corridors. **Parking:** on-site. **Amenities:** high-speed Internet, dual phone
lines, voice mail, irons, hair dryers. **Pool(s):** heated indoor. **Leisure Activities:** sauna, whirlpool, exercise room. **Guest
Services:** valet laundry, wireless Internet. **Business Services:** conference facilities, business center.

(+) (|♦) (24♦) (♦) (⊘) (♦) (X) (X) (♦) (♦) / (♦) (♦) /   SOME UNITS

RESIDENCE INN BY MARRIOTT-WEST   *Book great rates at AAA.com*   **Phone:** 585/865-2090   **13**
♦♦♦   Property failed to provide current rates
          Location: I-390, exit 24A, just e on SR 104 (Ridge Rd), just s on Hoover Dr, then just w. 500 Paddy Creek Cir 14615.
Small-scale Hotel   **Fax:** 585/865-2990. **Facility:** Smoke free premises. 90 units. 51 one-bedroom standard units with kitchens.
          26 one- and 13 two-bedroom suites with kitchens. 3 stories, interior corridors. *Bath:* combo or shower only.
Parking: on-site. **Terms:** pets ($75 extra charge). **Amenities:** high-speed Internet, dual phone lines, voice mail, irons, hair
dryers. **Pool(s):** small heated indoor. **Leisure Activities:** whirlpool, exercise room, sports court. **Guest Services:**
complimentary evening beverages: Mon-Thurs, valet and coin laundry, wireless Internet.

(+) (|♦) (♦) (♦) (♦) (X) (X) (♦) (♦) (♦) / (VCR) /   SOME UNITS
          FEE   FEE

——— **WHERE TO DINE** ———

THE LAMPLIGHTER RESTAURANT **Lunch:** $6-$9 **Dinner:** $15-$29 **Phone:** 585/225-2500
▼▼▼▼ **Location:** I-390, exit 24A, just w on SR 104 (Ridge Rd), then 0.5 mi n; in Creekside Plaza. 831 Fetzner Rd 14626.
Hours: 11:30 am-2 & 4:30-10 pm, Mon & Sat from 4:30 pm. Closed major holidays; also Sun except Easter
Italian & Mother's Day. **Reservations:** accepted. **Features:** For 37 years, this restaurant's owner has served locals
and out-of-towners tasty Black Angus beef, fresh seafood and Italian specialties. The house specialty
portofino combines luscious lobster, shrimp, scallops and crab sauteed in a white wine sauce with black olives and artichoke
hearts over a bed of pasta. Friendly, professional servers circulate through the charming restaurant. Casual dress; cocktails.
Parking: on-site. **Cards:** AX, MC, VI.

GREENPORT pop. 4,180

——— **WHERE TO STAY** ———

THE BARTLETT HOUSE INN **Phone:** 631/477-0371
▼▼▼▼ All Year 2P: $175-$250 XP: $50
Location: SR 25 (Front St), just w of town. 503 Front St 11944. Fax: 631/477-3541. **Facility:** This large, cedar-
Bed & Breakfast shingled Victorian home dates from 1908 and features beautifully decorated rooms with International
themes. Smoke free premises. 10 one-bedroom standard units. 3 stories (no elevator), interior corridors.
Bath: combo or shower only. **Parking:** on-site. **Terms:** office hours 9 am-9 pm, age restrictions may apply, 14 day cancellation
notice-fee imposed. **Amenities:** voice mail, hair dryers. *Some:* DVD players, irons. **Guest Services:** wireless Internet.
Business Services: fax (fee). **Cards:** MC, VI.
SOME UNITS
(ASK) (S/D) (✕) (🖥) / (VCR) /

——— *The following lodging was either not evaluated or did not* ———
meet AAA rating requirements but is listed for your information only.

SILVER SANDS MOTEL **Phone:** 631/477-0011
(fyi) Did not meet all AAA rating requirements for locking devices in some guest rooms at time of last
Motel evaluation. **Location:** SR 25, 1 mi w. 1400 Silvermere Rd 11944 (PO Box 285). Facilities, services, and decor
characterize a basic property.

——— **WHERE TO DINE** ———

CLAUDIO'S RESTAURANT **Lunch:** $9-$17 **Dinner:** $19-$39 **Phone:** 631/477-0627
▼▼ ▼▼ **Location:** SR 25 to corner of Main and Front sts SE, just s to harbor. 111 Main St 11944. **Hours:** Open 5/1-11/30 &
4/15-4/30; 11:30 am-10 pm, Fri & Sat-11 pm; seasonal hours vary. Closed: Tues 9/6-5/30.
Steak & Seafood **Reservations:** suggested. **Features:** Overlooking the marina and fishing harbor, the established restaurant
has been operated by generations of the same family since 1870. Traditional preparations of mostly seafood
are wholesome and flavorful. A nautical theme weaves through the dining areas. Casual dress; cocktails. **Parking:** on-site.
Cards: MC, VI. **Historic**

GREENWICH pop. 1,902

——— **WHERE TO STAY** ———

SUNSHINE INN **Phone:** 518/692-2997
▼▼ ▼▼ All Year 1P: $60-$125 2P: $65-$125
Location: 0.5 mi n. Located in a rural area. 2624 SR 40 12834. Fax: 518/692-2601. **Facility:** 10 one-bedroom
Motel standard units, some with efficiencies. 1 story, exterior corridors. *Bath:* combo or shower only. **Parking:** on-
site, winter plug-ins. **Terms:** office hours 9 am-10 pm, 7 day cancellation notice. **Amenities:** voice mail.
Cards: AX, DS, MC, VI.
SOME UNITS
(ASK) (S/D) (🖥) / (✕) (VCR) (▢) (▣) /

GROTON pop. 2,470—See also *FINGER LAKES.*

——— **WHERE TO DINE** ———

BENN CONGER INN **Dinner:** $9-$20 **Phone:** 607/898-5817
▼▼▼▼ **Location:** Just w of SR 38. 206 W Cortland St 13073. **Hours:** 4:30 pm-11 pm. Closed: Mon.
Reservations: suggested. **Features:** The 1919 Southern mansion reflects elegant decor in an otherwise
American casual atmosphere. An immediate favorite is fried ripe olives stuffed with seasoned cream cheese. Other top
comfort foods include chicken and mushroom casserole with puff pastry, coconut shrimp, Mom's meatloaf,
chicken-fried steak and the Friday fish fry. Casual dress; cocktails. **Parking:** on-site. **Cards:** AX, DC, DS, MC, VI. **Historic**

GUILDERLAND pop. 32,688 (See map and index starting on p. 218)

——— **WHERE TO STAY** ———

BEST WESTERN SOVEREIGN HOTEL ALBANY *Book great rates at AAA.com* **Phone:** (518)489-2981 (42)
(AAA) (SAVE) All Year [BP] 1P: $89-$109 2P: $99-$159 XP: $10 F16
Location: I-87/90, exit 24, follow signs to US 20 (Western Ave), then 1 mi e. Located across from the state university.
▼▼ ▼▼ 1228 Western Ave 12203. Fax: 518/489-8967. **Facility:** 192 one-bedroom standard units. 5 stories, interior
Small-scale Hotel corridors. *Bath:* combo or shower only. **Parking:** on-site. **Terms:** cancellation fee imposed, package plans,
small pets only ($10 extra charge). **Amenities:** video games (fee), voice mail, irons, hair dryers.
Dining: 6:30 am-10 pm. **Pool(s):** small heated indoor. **Leisure Activities:** saunas, exercise room. *Fee:*
game room. **Guest Services:** valet laundry, area transportation-bus & train station. **Business Services:** conference facilities,
business center. **Cards:** AX, CB, DC, DS, JC, MC, VI. **Free Special Amenities:** full breakfast and room upgrade (subject to
availability with advance reservations).
SOME UNITS
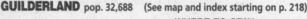
(S/D) (📞) (🛏) (🍴) (Y) (😊) (🏊) (✕) (🖥) (▢) (▣) / (✕) /
FEE

HOLIDAY INN EXPRESS TURF ON WESTERN AVE   *Book at AAA.com*   Phone: (518)438-0001   **41**

7/6-8/31	1P: $129-$199	2P: $129-$199
5/1-7/5	1P: $109-$179	2P: $109-$179
9/1-4/30	1P: $89-$179	2P: $89-$179

Small-scale Hotel   **Location:** I-87/90, exit 24, 0.5 mi e on US 20 (Western Ave). 1442 Western Ave 12203. Fax: 518/438-0690. **Facility:** 121 units. 117 one-bedroom standard units. 4 one-bedroom suites ($139-$209). 4 stories, interior corridors. *Bath:* combo or shower only. **Parking:** on-site. **Terms:** check-in 4 pm, 3 day cancellation notice, [CP] meal plan available. **Amenities:** video games (fee), high-speed Internet, voice mail, safes, irons, hair dryers. **Pool(s):** small heated indoor. **Leisure Activities:** exercise room. **Guest Services:** sundries, valet and coin laundry. **Business Services:** meeting rooms, business center. **Cards:** AX, CB, DC, DS, JC, MC, VI.

SOME UNITS

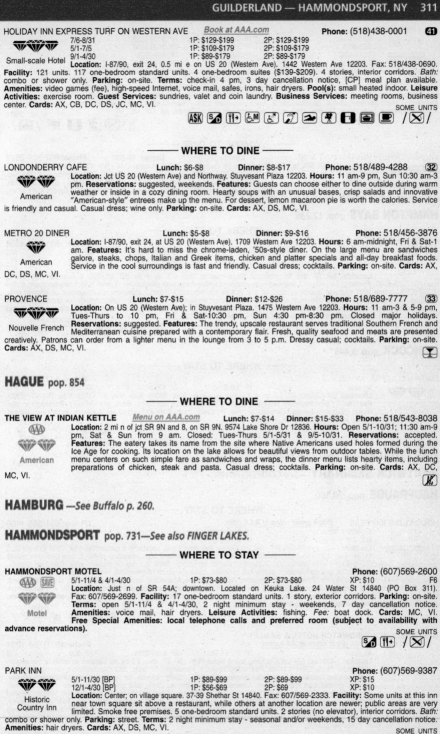

——— WHERE TO DINE ———

LONDONDERRY CAFE   **Lunch:** $6-$8   **Dinner:** $8-$17   Phone: 518/489-4288   **32**

American   **Location:** Jct US 20 (Western Ave) and Northway. Stuyvesant Plaza 12203. **Hours:** 11 am-9 pm, Sun 10:30 am-3 pm. **Reservations:** suggested, weekends. **Features:** Guests can choose either to dine outside during warm weather or inside in a cozy dining room. Hearty soups with an unusual bases, crisp salads and innovative "American-style" entrees make up the menu. For dessert, lemon macaroon pie is worth the calories. Service is friendly and casual. Casual dress; wine only. **Parking:** on-site. **Cards:** AX, DS, MC, VI.

METRO 20 DINER   **Lunch:** $5-$8   **Dinner:** $9-$16   Phone: 518/456-3876

American   **Location:** I-87/90, exit 24, at US 20 (Western Ave). 1709 Western Ave 12203. **Hours:** 6 am-midnight, Fri & Sat-1 am. **Features:** It's hard to miss the chrome-laden, '50s-style diner. On the large menu are sandwiches galore, steaks, chops, Italian and Greek items, chicken and platter specials and all-day breakfast foods. Service in the cool surroundings is fast and friendly. Casual dress; cocktails. **Parking:** on-site. **Cards:** AX, DC, DS, MC, VI.

PROVENCE   **Lunch:** $7-$15   **Dinner:** $12-$26   Phone: 518/689-7777   **33**

Nouvelle French   **Location:** On US 20 (Western Ave); in Stuyvesant Plaza. 1475 Western Ave 12203. **Hours:** 11 am-3 & 5-9 pm, Tues-Thurs to 10 pm, Fri & Sat-10:30 pm, Sun 4:30 pm-8:30 pm. Closed major holidays. **Reservations:** suggested. **Features:** The trendy, upscale restaurant serves traditional Southern French and Mediterranean cuisine prepared with a contemporary flair. Fresh, quality seafood and meats are presented creatively. Patrons can order from a lighter menu in the lounge from 3 to 5 p.m. Dressy casual; cocktails. **Parking:** on-site. **Cards:** AX, DS, MC, VI.

HAGUE pop. 854

——— WHERE TO DINE ———

THE VIEW AT INDIAN KETTLE   *Menu on AAA.com*   **Lunch:** $7-$14   **Dinner:** $15-$33   Phone: 518/543-8038

American   **Location:** 2 mi n of jct SR 9N and 8, on SR 9N. 9574 Lake Shore Dr 12836. **Hours:** Open 5/1-10/31; 11:30 am-9 pm, Sat & Sun from 9 am. Closed: Tues-Thurs 5/1-5/31 & 9/5-10/31. **Reservations:** accepted. **Features:** The eatery takes its name from the site where Native Americans used holes formed during the Ice Age for cooking. Its location on the lake allows for beautiful views from outdoor tables. While the lunch menu centers on such simple fare as sandwiches and wraps, the dinner menu lists hearty items, including preparations of chicken, steak and pasta. Casual dress; cocktails. **Parking:** on-site. **Cards:** AX, DC, MC, VI.

HAMBURG *—See Buffalo p. 260.*

HAMMONDSPORT pop. 731—*See also FINGER LAKES.*

——— WHERE TO STAY ———

HAMMONDSPORT MOTEL   Phone: (607)569-2600

5/1-11/4 & 4/1-4/30	1P: $73-$80	2P: $73-$80	XP: $10 F6

Motel   **Location:** Just n of SR 54A; downtown. Located on Keuka Lake. 24 Water St 14840 (PO Box 311). Fax: 607/569-2699. **Facility:** 17 one-bedroom standard units. 1 story, exterior corridors. **Parking:** on-site. **Terms:** open 5/1-11/4 & 4/1-4/30, 2 night minimum stay - weekends, 7 day cancellation notice. **Amenities:** voice mail, hair dryers. **Leisure Activities:** fishing. *Fee:* boat dock. **Cards:** MC, VI. **Free Special Amenities:** local telephone calls and preferred room (subject to availability with advance reservations).

SOME UNITS

PARK INN   Phone: (607)569-9387

5/1-11/30 [BP]	1P: $89-$99	2P: $89-$99	XP: $15
12/1-4/30 [BP]	1P: $56-$69	2P: $69	XP: $10

Historic Country Inn   **Location:** Center; on village square. 37-39 Shethar St 14840. Fax: 607/569-2333. **Facility:** Some units at this inn near town square sit above a restaurant, while others at another location are newer; public areas are very limited. Smoke free premises. 5 one-bedroom standard units. 2 stories (no elevator), interior corridors. *Bath:* combo or shower only. **Parking:** street. **Terms:** 2 night minimum stay - seasonal and/or weekends, 15 day cancellation notice. **Amenities:** hair dryers. **Cards:** AX, DS, MC, VI.

SOME UNITS

VILLAGE TAVERN INN

Phone: (607)569-2528

8/24-11/14	1P: $109-$289	2P: $109-$289
5/25-8/23	1P: $109-$250	2P: $109-$250
11/15-4/30	1P: $99-$225	2P: $99-$225
5/1-5/24	1P: $89-$200	2P: $89-$200

Historic Country Inn

Location: On SR 54A. Located in the village square. 30 Mechanic St 14840 (PO Box 92). Fax: 607/569-3560. **Facility:** Rooms located over the restaurant at this inn, which lacks public areas, have homelike decor. Smoke free premises. 8 units. 6 one-bedroom standard units, some with efficiencies (no utensils). 1 one- and 1 two-bedroom suites with efficiencies (no utensils). 2 stories (no elevator), interior corridors. **Bath:** combo or shower only. **Parking:** street. **Terms:** off-site registration, 2 night minimum stay - seasonal, 11 day cancellation notice-fee imposed. **Amenities:** irons, hair dryers. **Dining:** restaurant, see separate listing. **Cards:** AX, DS, MC, VI.

SOME UNITS

──────── **WHERE TO DINE** ────────

VILLAGE TAVERN RESTAURANT & INN **Lunch:** $10-$15 **Dinner:** $8-$37 Phone: 607/569-2528

American

Location: On SR 54A; in Village Tavern Inn. 30 Mechanic St 14840. **Hours:** Open 5/1-1/3 & 2/9-4/30; 11:30 am-9 pm; Fri & Sat-10 pm. Closed: 11/22, 12/24, 12/25; also Mon-Wed 11/1-5/1. **Reservations:** suggested. **Features:** An extensive selection of wine and exotic beer matches well with thoughtfully prepared steak, seafood and pasta dishes. Airplane photographs hang on the walls of the comfortable, tavern-style dining room. Casual dress; cocktails. **Parking:** street. **Cards:** AX, DC, MC, VI.

HAMPTON BAYS pop. 12,236

──────── **WHERE TO STAY** ────────

OCEAN VIEW TERRACE MOTEL

Phone: (631)728-4036

7/12-9/12	2P: $150-$325	XP: $30	F12
5/24-7/11	2P: $135-$305	XP: $30	F12
5/1-5/23 & 9/13-4/30	2P: $100-$275	XP: $30	F12

Motel

Location: SR 27, exit 65 (Hampton Bays), just s, then 2.5 mi e on SR 80. 285 E Montauk Hwy 11946. Fax: 631/723-3287. **Facility:** 16 units. 13 one-bedroom standard units, some with efficiencies. 2 one- and 1 two-bedroom suites ($230-$325), some with kitchens and/or whirlpools. 1-2 stories (no elevator), exterior corridors. **Bath:** combo or shower only. **Parking:** on-site. **Terms:** 2 night minimum stay - seasonal and/or weekends, 14 day cancellation notice-fee imposed, weekly rates available, package plans. **Amenities:** voice mail. **Pool(s):** outdoor. **Leisure Activities:** beach access, playground. **Guest Services:** valet laundry. **Business Services:** fax (fee). **Cards:** AX, CB, DC, DS, JC, MC, VI.

SOME UNITS

HANCOCK pop. 3,449

──────── **WHERE TO STAY** ────────

SMITH'S COLONIAL MOTEL

Phone: 607/637-2989

All Year	1P: $65-$130	2P: $75-$130	XP: $10
			F12

Motel

Location: SR 17, exit 87, 2.7 mi s. Located in a quiet area. 23085 State Hwy 97 13783. Fax: 607/637-2989. **Facility:** 17 one-bedroom standard units. 1 story, exterior corridors. **Bath:** shower only. **Parking:** on-site, winter plug-ins. **Terms:** cancellation fee imposed, pets ($10 extra charge). **Leisure Activities:** fishing. **Guest Services:** wireless Internet. **Cards:** AX, DS, MC, VI.

SOME UNITS

FEE

HARTSDALE —See New York p. 499.

HARTWICK SEMINARY —See COOPERSTOWN.

HAUPPAUGE pop. 20,100

──────── **WHERE TO STAY** ────────

HOLIDAY INN EXPRESS *Book great rates at AAA.com*

Phone: 631/348-1400

5/1-9/29 & 3/2-4/30	1P: $149-$199	
9/30-3/1	1P: $119-$189	

Small-scale Hotel

Location: I-495, exit 56 (SR 111), just s to Central Ave, then just w. Located in a commercial area. 2050 Express Dr S 11788. Fax: 631/348-1411. **Facility:** 133 units. 131 one-bedroom standard units. 2 one-bedroom suites ($209-$329) with whirlpools. 7 stories, interior corridors. **Bath:** combo or shower only. **Parking:** on-site. **Terms:** 14 day cancellation notice-fee imposed, package plans. **Amenities:** video games (fee), dual phone lines, voice mail, irons, hair dryers. **Pool(s):** small heated indoor. **Leisure Activities:** sauna, exercise room. **Guest Services:** valet and coin laundry, airport transportation-Long Island MacArthur Airport, area transportation-within 1 mi & train station, wireless Internet. **Business Services:** meeting rooms, business center. **Cards:** AX, DS, MC, VI. **Free Special Amenities:** expanded continental breakfast and high-speed Internet.

SOME UNITS

HYATT REGENCY WINDWATCH HOTEL & HAMLET GOLF CLUB *Book great rates at AAA.com*

Phone: (631)784-1234

All Year	1P: $129-$329	2P: $129-$329	XP: $20
			F18

Large-scale Hotel

Location: I-495, exit 57, just n to Long Island Motor Pkwy (SR 67), then 1.3 mi ne. Located adjacent to golf course. 1717 Motor Pkwy (SR 67) 11788. Fax: 631/232-9853. **Facility:** 360 units. 352 one-bedroom standard units. 8 one-bedroom suites. 10 stories, interior corridors. **Bath:** combo or shower only. **Parking:** on-site. **Terms:** cancellation fee imposed. **Amenities:** video games (fee), dual phone lines, voice mail, irons, hair dryers. **Dining:** 6:30 am-2 & 5-11 pm, Sat & Sun 6:30 am-11 pm, cocktails. **Pool(s):** heated outdoor, heated indoor. **Leisure Activities:** saunas, whirlpool, 2 lighted tennis courts, playground, basketball, volleyball. **Fee:** golf-18 holes, driving range, massage. **Guest Services:** gift shop, valet laundry, airport transportation-Long Island MacArthur Airport, area transportation-train station, wireless Internet. **Business Services:** conference facilities, business center. **Cards:** AX, CB, DC, DS, JC, MC, VI. *(See color ad p 313)*

SOME UNITS

RESIDENCE INN BY MARRIOTT   *Book great rates at AAA.com*   **Phone:** (631)724-4188

(AAA) (SAVE)   All Year   1P: $129-$229   2P: $129-$229

Small-scale Hotel

Location: I-495, exit 57, 1.2 mi nw. 850 Veterans Memorial Hwy 11788. Fax: 631/724-4186. **Facility:** Smoke free premises. 100 units. 44 one-bedroom standard units, some with efficiencies or kitchens. 44 one- and 12 two-bedroom suites, some with efficiencies or kitchens. 3 stories, interior corridors. *Bath:* combo or shower only. **Parking:** on-site. **Terms:** cancellation fee imposed, package plans, pets ($75 fee). **Amenities:** high-speed Internet, voice mail, irons, hair dryers. *Some:* dual phone lines. **Pool(s):** small heated indoor. **Leisure Activities:** whirlpool, barbecue grills, limited exercise equipment. **Guest Services:** complimentary evening beverages: Mon-Thurs, valet and coin laundry, airport transportation-Long Island MacArthur Airport, area transportation-within 5 mi. **Business Services:** meeting rooms, fax (fee). **Cards:** AX, DC, DS, MC, VI. **Free Special Amenities: expanded continental breakfast and newspaper.**

FEE

SHERATON LONG ISLAND HOTEL   *Book great rates at AAA.com*   **Phone:** (631)231-1100

(AAA) (SAVE)   All Year   1P: $109-$229   XP: $25   F18

Large-scale Hotel

Location: I-495, exit 53 (Wicks Rd), just n, then 0.3 mi e. Located in a commercial area. 110 Vanderbilt Motor Pkwy 11788. Fax: 631/231-1143. **Facility:** 209 units. 201 one-bedroom standard units. 8 one-bedroom suites. 6 stories, interior corridors. *Bath:* combo or shower only. **Parking:** on-site. **Terms:** cancellation fee imposed, package plans, 9% service charge, pets (dogs only). **Amenities:** dual phone lines, voice mail, irons, hair dryers. *Fee:* video games, high-speed Internet. **Dining:** 6:30 am-10:30 pm, Sat & Sun from 7 am, cocktails. **Pool(s):** heated indoor. **Leisure Activities:** sauna, whirlpool, steamroom, exercise room. *Fee:* game room. **Guest Services:** valet laundry, airport transportation-Long Island MacArthur Airport, area transportation-within 5 mi. **Business Services:** conference facilities, business center. **Cards:** AX, CB, DC, DS, JC, MC, VI. **Free Special Amenities: newspaper and room upgrade (subject to availability with advance reservations).** *(See color ad below)*   SOME UNITS

FEE

------- **WHERE TO DINE** -------

BERTUCCI'S BRICK OVEN RISTORANTE   **Lunch:** $7-$15   **Dinner:** $10-$15   **Phone:** 631/952-2100
▼▼▼   **Location:** Jct Expressway Dr and Long Island Motor Pkwy, then 0.5 mi w. 358 Vanderbilt Motor Pkwy 11788.
Italian   **Hours:** 11 am-10 pm, Fri & Sat-11 pm. Closed: 11/22, 12/25. **Features:** This popular chain is known for
their signature brick oven cooking which creates the distinctive flavors you'll taste in the fresh roasted
vegetables, the seafood and entree specialties, and of course, the restaurant's top notch pizza. Every dish
is made to order and all breads are made from scratch throughout the day. A sample meal may include pasta with the rich
flavors of fresh garlic, basil and oven roasted tomatoes and for dessert a divine lemon cream dessert with berries. Casual
dress; cocktails. **Parking:** on-site. **Cards:** AX, CB, DC, DS, MC, VI.

KOTOBUKI   **Lunch:** $8-$25   **Dinner:** $15-$25   **Phone:** 631/360-3969
▼▼▼   **Location:** Jct SR 111, just w; in Hauppauge Shopping Center. 377 Nesconset Hwy 11787. **Hours:** noon-2:30 & 5:30-
Japanese   10 pm, Sat 5 pm-10:30 pm, Sun 5 pm-9:30 pm. Closed major holidays; also Mon. **Features:** Drive up to the
unpretentious restaurant, and you'll see "sushi" before you see the name. Among other selections are
regionally-inspired rolls, sashimi, and nigiri, as well as a variety of savory cooked dishes, such as teriyaki,
yakitori and tempura. Casual dress; beer & wine only. **Parking:** on-site. **Cards:** AX, CB, DC, DS, JC, MC, VI.

PACE'S STEAKHOUSE   **Lunch:** $10-$30   **Dinner:** $17-$36   **Phone:** 631/979-7676
▼▼▼   **Location:** On SR 347, just ne of jct SR 454. 325 Nesconset Hwy 11788. **Hours:** noon-11 pm, Fri-midnight, Sat 4
Steak House   pm-midnight, Sun 3 pm-10 pm. Closed: 12/25. **Reservations:** suggested. **Features:** The restaurant is
known for its high-quality steaks, fresh seafood and attentive service. Decorating the formal dining room are
crown-molded ceilings, gilded framed mirrors and antique pictures of New York City. Dressy casual;
cocktails. **Parking:** on-site and valet. **Cards:** AX, CB, DC, DS, MC, VI.   Ⓨ

SEMPRE VIVOLO   **Lunch:** $16-$24   **Dinner:** $24-$30   **Phone:** 631/435-1737
▼▼▼   **Location:** I-495, exit 55, just n. 696 Vanderbilt Motor Pkwy 11788. **Hours:** noon-2:30 & 5-9:30 pm. Closed major
Italian   holidays; also Sun. **Reservations:** suggested. **Features:** A knowledgeable and attentive wait staff serves
diners in the upscale, elegant setting. Sophisticated Italian dishes include delicious roasted salmon and a
pasta dish with pancetta and fresh and sun-dried tomatoes. Roman artwork decorates the dining room.
Dressy casual; cocktails. **Parking:** on-site and valet. **Cards:** AX, DC, DS, MC, VI.   Ⓨ

HAWTHORNE —See New York p. 500.

HECTOR pop. 4,854—See also FINGER LAKES.

------- **WHERE TO DINE** -------

THE BISTRO AT RED NEWT CELLARS   **Lunch:** $7-$10   **Dinner:** $17-$23   **Phone:** 607/546-4100
▼▼▼   **Location:** Off SR 414. 3675 Tichenor Rd 14841. **Hours:** Open 5/31-12/12 & 2/13-4/29; noon-4 & 5-9 pm;
seasonal hours may vary. Closed: Wed 11/1-4/30, Mon & Tues. **Reservations:** suggested. **Features:** The
Regional American   winery-restaurant offers sumptuous and innovative regional cuisine made from ingredients sold by local
producers. Prix fixe, vegan and vegetarian choices also are offered. Casual dress; beer & wine only.
Parking: on-site. **Cards:** AX, MC, VI.

HENRIETTA pop. 39,028   (See map and index starting on p. 599)—See also WEST HENRIETTA.

------- **WHERE TO STAY** -------

BEST WESTERN-ROCHESTER MARKETPLACE INN   *Book great rates at AAA.com*   **Phone:** (585)427-2700   **33**
ⓐⓐ SAVE   All Year   1P: $109-$149   2P: $119-$159   XP: $10   F18
▼▼ ▼   **Location:** I-390, exit 14A southbound; exit 14 northbound, just w on SR 252 (Jefferson Rd). 940 Jefferson Rd 14623.
Small-scale Hotel   Fax: 585/427-8504. **Facility:** 98 one-bedroom standard units, some with whirlpools. 3 stories, interior
corridors. *Bath:* combo or shower only. **Parking:** on-site. **Terms:** 5 day cancellation notice-fee imposed.
Amenities: video library, DVD players, irons, hair dryers. **Leisure Activities:** exercise room. **Guest
Services:** valet and coin laundry, area transportation-local universities & hospitals, wireless Internet.
Business Services: meeting rooms, PC. **Cards:** AX, CB, DC, DS, MC, VI. **Free Special Amenities:** full breakfast and high-
speed Internet.

SOME UNITS
🅂🄳 ➡️ 🍽️ 🄴 🐾 🖥️ 📷 💻 / ✕ /

COMFORT SUITES BY CHOICE HOTELS OF
ROCHESTER   *Book great rates at AAA.com*   **Phone:** (585)334-6620   **38**
▼▼▼   All Year   1P: $130-$150   2P: $135-$155   XP: $5   F18
Small-scale Hotel   **Location:** I-390, exit 13, just e. 2085 Hylan Dr 14623. Fax: 585/334-9649. **Facility:** 66 one-bedroom standard
units. 3 stories, interior corridors. *Bath:* combo or shower only. **Parking:** on-site. **Terms:** pets ($75 fee).
Amenities: irons, hair dryers. **Pool(s):** heated indoor. **Leisure Activities:** whirlpool. **Guest Services:** valet
laundry, wireless Internet. **Cards:** AX, DC, DS, MC, VI.

SOME UNITS
ASK 🅂🄳 🛏️ 🍽️ 🄶🄼 🄴 🌊 🐾 🖥️ 📷 💻 / ✕ /
FEE

COUNTRY INN & SUITES BY CARLSON   *Book great rates at AAA.com*   **Phone:** (585)486-9000   **41**
ⓐⓐ SAVE   5/1-10/31   1P: $189-$210   2P: $189-$239   XP: $10   F16
▼▼▼   11/1-4/30   1P: $179-$219   2P: $179-$229   XP: $10   F16
Small-scale Hotel   **Location:** I-390, exit 12 northbound; exit 12A southbound, 0.5 mi w on SR 253, then just n on SR 15 (Henrietta Rd).
4635 W Henrietta Rd 14467. Fax: 585/486-9010. **Facility:** 77 units. 56 one-bedroom standard units, some with
whirlpools. 21 one-bedroom suites. 2 stories, interior corridors. *Bath:* combo or shower only. **Parking:** on-
site. **Amenities:** video games (fee), high-speed Internet, voice mail, irons, hair dryers. *Some:* dual phone
lines. **Pool(s):** small heated indoor. **Leisure Activities:** whirlpool, exercise room. **Guest Services:** valet and coin laundry,
wireless Internet. **Business Services:** meeting rooms, business center. **Cards:** AX, DC, DS, MC, VI. **Free Special Amenities:**
continental breakfast and high-speed Internet.

SOME UNITS
🅂🄳 🍽️ 🄴 🌊 🐾 💻 / ✕ 🖥️ 📷 /

DOUBLETREE HOTEL ROCHESTER   *Book great rates at AAA.com*   Phone: (585)475-1510   **36**

▼▼▽▼▽▼   All Year   1P: $109-$179   2P: $109-$179
         Location: I-390, exit 14, on SR 252 (Jefferson Rd). 1111 Jefferson Rd 14623. Fax: 585/427-8673. **Facility:** 249
Small-scale Hotel   units. 247 one-bedroom standard units. 2 one-bedroom suites. 6 stories, interior corridors. *Bath:* combo or
shower only. **Parking:** on-site. **Terms:** [AP] & [CP] meal plans available. **Amenities:** high-speed Internet,
voice mail, irons, hair dryers. **Pool(s):** heated indoor. **Leisure Activities:** whirlpool, lifeguard on duty, exercise room. **Guest**
Services: sundries, valet laundry, wireless Internet. **Business Services:** conference facilities, business center. **Cards:** AX, DC,
DS, JC, MC, VI.

SOME UNITS
(ASK) (S▽D) (✈) (†¶) (Y) (&M) (✍) (⌂) (➤) (✕) (✦) (▣) / (✕) (目) /
FEE

EXTENDED
STAYAMERICA-ROCHESTER-HENRIETTA   *Book at AAA.com*   Phone: (585)427-7580   **37**

▼▽▼ ▽▼   5/31-9/8   1P: $55-$90   2P: $60-$95   XP: $5   F17
         9/9-4/30   1P: $55-$80   2P: $60-$85   XP: $5   F17
Small-scale Hotel   5/1-5/30   1P: $50-$80   2P: $55-$85   XP: $5   F17
Location: I-390, exit 14B southbound; exit 14 northbound, just e on SR 252 (Jefferson Rd), then just s. 700 Commons
Way 14623. Fax: 585/427-8849. **Facility:** 127 one-bedroom standard units with efficiencies. 3 stories, interior corridors. *Bath:*
combo or shower only. **Parking:** on-site. **Terms:** office hours 7 am-11 pm. **Amenities:** voice mail, irons. **Guest Services:** coin
laundry. **Cards:** AX, CB, DC, DS, MC, VI.

(ASK) (S▽D) (🛏) (†¶✦) (&M) (✍) (✦) (目) (▣) (🖥)

FAIRFIELD INN BY MARRIOTT-ROCHESTER/SOUTH   *Book great rates at AAA.com*   Phone: (585)334-3350   **40**

▼▼▽▼▽   All Year   1P: $113-$119   2P: $113-$119
         Location: Jct SR 253 and 15 (Henrietta Rd). 4695 W Henrietta Rd 14467. Fax: 585/334-2295. **Facility:** Smoke free
Small-scale Hotel   premises. 62 one-bedroom standard units. 3 stories, interior corridors. *Bath:* combo or shower only.
Parking: on-site. **Terms:** [CP] meal plan available. **Amenities:** high-speed Internet, irons, hair dryers. *Fee:*
video library, video games. **Pool(s):** small heated indoor. **Leisure Activities:** exercise room. **Guest Services:** valet laundry,
wireless Internet. **Cards:** AX, DC, DS, MC, VI.

SOME UNITS
(ASK) (S▽D) (†¶✦) (&M) (✍) (⌂) (➤) (✕) (✦) (▣) / (目) /

HOLIDAY INN HOTEL & SUITES   Phone: 585/475-9190   **35**

(fyi)   Property failed to provide current rates
         Under major renovation, scheduled to be completed January 2007. **Last rated:** ▼▽ ▼▽ **Location:** I-390, exit 14A
Small-scale Hotel   southbound; exit 14 northbound, 0.5 mi w on SR 252 (Jefferson Rd). Located in a light-commercial area. 800 Jefferson
Rd 14623. **Facility:** Smoke free premises. 120 units. 96 one-bedroom standard units. 24 one-bedroom
suites, some with whirlpools. 3 stories, interior corridors. *Bath:* combo or shower only. **Parking:** on-site. **Amenities:** DVD
players, irons, hair dryers. **Pool(s):** heated indoor. **Guest Services:** valet and coin laundry, area transportation, wireless
Internet. **Business Services:** meeting rooms, business center.

SOME UNITS
(✈) (†¶) (Y) (➤) (✕) (✦) (▣) / (目) (🖥) /

HOMEWOOD SUITES BY HILTON-ROCHESTER   *Book at AAA.com*   Phone: (585)334-9150   **39**

▼▼▽▼▽   All Year   1P: $170-$190   2P: $175-$195   XP: $5   F18
         Location: I-390, exit 13, just e. 2095 Hylan Dr 14623. Fax: 585/334-1226. **Facility:** 90 units. 85 one- and 5 two-
Small-scale Hotel   bedroom suites with efficiencies. 3 stories, interior corridors. *Bath:* combo or shower only. **Parking:** on-site.
Terms: pets ($75 fee). **Amenities:** video library (fee), dual phone lines, voice mail, irons, hair dryers. *Some:*
high-speed Internet. **Pool(s):** small heated indoor. **Leisure Activities:** exercise room. **Guest Services:** sundries,
complimentary evening beverages: Mon-Thurs, valet and coin laundry, wireless Internet. **Business Services:** meeting rooms,
business center. **Cards:** AX, DC, DS, MC, VI.

SOME UNITS
(ASK) (S▽D) (🛏) (†¶✦) (&M) (✍) (⌂) (➤) (VCR) (✦) (目) (🖥) (🖥) / (✕) /
FEE

MICROTEL-ROCHESTER   *Book at AAA.com*   Phone: (585)334-3400   **42**

▼▽▼ ▽▼   8/1-10/31   1P: $60-$99   2P: $65-$99   XP: $5   F18
         5/1-7/31   1P: $52-$99   2P: $57-$99   XP: $5   F18
Small-scale Hotel   4/1-4/30   1P: $50-$65   2P: $55-$70   XP: $5   F18
         11/1-3/31   1P: $45-$65   2P: $45-$65   XP: $5   F18
Location: I-390, exit 12 northbound; exit 12A southbound, just w on SR 253. 905 Lehigh Station Rd 14467. Fax: 585/334-5042.
Facility: 98 one-bedroom standard units. 2 stories (no elevator), interior corridors. *Bath:* combo or shower only. **Parking:** on-
site. **Terms:** cancellation fee imposed, [CP] meal plan available, small pets only ($10 fee). **Amenities:** *Fee:* video games, safes.
Cards: AX, DC, DS, MC, VI.

SOME UNITS
(ASK) (S▽D) (🛏) (†¶✦) (✍) (✦) / (✕) (目) (🖥)
FEE

RADISSON ROCHESTER AIRPORT   *Book at AAA.com*   Phone: (585)475-1910   **32**

▼▽▼ ▽▼   5/1-10/31   1P: $119-$159   2P: $119-$159   XP: $10   F18
         11/1-4/30   1P: $109-$149   2P: $109-$149   XP: $10   F18
Small-scale Hotel   **Location:** I-390, exit 14A southbound; exit 14 northbound, 3 mi w on SR 252 (Jefferson Rd). 175 Jefferson Rd 14623.
Fax: 585/475-9633. **Facility:** 171 one-bedroom standard units. 4 stories, interior corridors. *Bath:* combo or
shower only. **Parking:** on-site. **Terms:** 3 day cancellation notice, [AP], [BP] & [CP] meal plans available, pets ($25 extra
charge). **Amenities:** video games (fee), high-speed Internet, voice mail, irons, hair dryers. **Pool(s):** heated indoor. **Leisure**
Activities: exercise room. **Guest Services:** valet laundry, area transportation, wireless Internet. **Business Services:**
conference facilities, business center. **Cards:** AX, CB, DC, DS, JC, MC, VI.

SOME UNITS
(ASK) (S▽D) (✈) (†¶) (Y) (&M) (✍) (⌂) (➤) (✦) (▣) / (✕) (目) /
FEE

RED ROOF INN-HENRIETTA #7042   *Book at AAA.com*   Phone: (585)359-1100   43

5/1-6/16	1P: $54-$83	2P: $59-$88	XP: $5 F18
6/17-10/20	1P: $59-$75	2P: $64-$80	XP: $5 F18
1/1-4/30	1P: $48-$74	2P: $53-$79	XP: $5 F18
10/21-12/31	1P: $48-$65	2P: $53-$70	XP: $5 F18

Motel

Location: I-390, exit 12 northbound; exit 12A southbound, 0.5 mi w on SR 253, then just s on SR 15 (Henrietta Rd). 4820 W Henrietta Rd 14467. Fax: 585/359-1121. **Facility:** 108 one-bedroom standard units. 2 stories (no elevator), exterior corridors. *Bath:* combo or shower only. **Parking:** on-site. **Terms:** small pets only. **Amenities:** video games (fee), voice mail. **Cards:** AX, CB, DC, DS, MC, VI.

SOME UNITS

RESIDENCE INN BY MARRIOTT   *Book great rates at AAA.com*   Phone: 585-272-8850   34

All Year   1P: $159-$289   2P: $169-$299   XP: $10   F

Small-scale Hotel

Location: I-390, exit 14A southbound, 0.5 mi e on SR 252 (Jefferson Rd); exit 14 northbound, just n on SR 15A, then 0.5 mi e on SR 252 (Jefferson Rd). 1300 Jefferson Rd 14623. Fax: 585/272-7822. **Facility:** Smoke free premises. 152 units. 81 one-bedroom standard units with kitchens. 38 one- and 33 two-bedroom suites with kitchens. 2 stories (no elevator), interior/exterior corridors. *Bath:* combo or shower only. **Parking:** on-site. **Terms:** package plans, pets ($75 fee). **Amenities:** video games (fee), high-speed Internet, dual phone lines, voice mail, irons, hair dryers. **Pool(s):** small heated outdoor. **Leisure Activities:** whirlpool, exercise room, sports court. **Guest Services:** complimentary evening beverages: Mon-Thurs, valet and coin laundry. **Business Services:** PC. **Cards:** AX, CB, DC, DS, JC, MC, VI.

FEE

R I T INN & CONFERENCE CENTER   *Book at AAA.com*   Phone: (585)359-1800   44

All Year   1P: $89-$115

Small-scale Hotel

Location: I-390, exit 12 northbound; exit 12A southbound, 0.5 mi w on SR 253, then 0.7 mi s. 5257 W Henrietta Rd 14586 (PO Box 20551, ROCHESTER, 14602). Fax: 585/359-1349. **Facility:** 305 one-bedroom standard units. 5 stories, interior corridors. **Parking:** on-site. **Terms:** cancellation fee imposed, pets ($50 deposit). **Amenities:** dual phone lines, voice mail, irons, hair dryers. *Some:* high-speed Internet. **Pool(s):** heated outdoor, heated indoor. **Leisure Activities:** sauna, whirlpool, exercise room. **Guest Services:** sundries, valet and coin laundry, wireless Internet. **Business Services:** conference facilities, PC. **Cards:** AX, DC, DS, MC, VI.

SOME UNITS

FEE   FEE

——— WHERE TO DINE ———

BILL GRAY'S   Lunch: $3-$9   Dinner: $3-$9   Phone: 585/424-2350   34

American

Location: I-390, exit 14 northbound, just n on SR 15A; exit 14 southbound, just e on SR 252 (Jefferson Rd); exit 14A southbound, just e on SR 252 (Jefferson Rd). 1225 Jefferson Rd 14467. **Hours:** 10:30 am-9 pm, Fri & Sat-10 pm. Closed: 5/28, 11/22, 12/25. **Features:** Since 1938, locals have come to the fast-food alternative for made-to-order burgers, slow-roasted roast beef, salads and fries. Casual dress. **Parking:** on-site. **Cards:** AX, DS, MC, VI.

BUGABOO CREEK STEAK HOUSE   Lunch: $7-$12   Dinner: $9-$23   Phone: 585/292-5800

American

Location: I-390, exit 14A, just w on SR 252 (Jefferson Rd). 935 Jefferson Rd 14623. **Hours:** 11 am-10 pm, Fri & Sat-10:30 pm, Sun noon-9 pm. Closed: 11/22, 12/25. **Reservations:** accepted, weekdays. **Features:** Families will love the friendly service at this mythical Canadian Rockies ski lodge. The north-country decor is brought to life with dancing trees and talking moose heads. Also of note are its featured dry-aged beef specialties, burgers and chicken dishes. Portions are large, particularly of the desserts. While reservations are not taken, call-ahead seating is offered. Casual dress; cocktails. **Parking:** on-site. **Cards:** AX, DC, DS, MC, VI.

DIBELLA'S   Lunch: $4-$6   Dinner: $4-$6   Phone: 585/475-1831   33

American

Location: Jct SR 15 (Henrietta Rd). 420 Jefferson Rd 14623. **Hours:** 10 am-9 pm. Closed: 11/22, 12/25. **Features:** Family owned since 1918, the eatery prepares old-fashioned hot and cold submarine sandwiches with fresh quality meats and breads baked in the in-house bakery. Casual dress. **Parking:** on-site. **Cards:** AX, DS, MC, VI.

THE KING AND I   Lunch: $3-$7   Dinner: $8-$15   Phone: 585/427-8090   31

Thai

Location: I-390, exit 14, just n of Jefferson St. 1455 E Henrietta Rd 14623. **Hours:** 11 am-10 pm, Fri & Sat-11 pm, Sun noon-9:30 pm. Closed: 11/22. **Features:** Award-winning preparations of Thai cuisine, including an extensive selection of vegetarian fare, are made daily. Take-out, catering and banquet services are available. Casual dress; cocktails. **Parking:** on-site. **Cards:** AX, DS, MC, VI.

SHANGHAI RESTAURANT   Lunch: $6-$7   Dinner: $5-$16   Phone: 585/424-4000   30

Asian

Location: Just n of jct SR 252 (Jefferson St). 2920 W Henrietta Rd 14623. **Hours:** 11:30 am-10 pm, Fri & Sat-11 pm. Closed: 11/22. **Features:** Extensive choices include lunch special menus, such as the Thai cuisine luncheon. All the favorites are served a la carte or in combination platters. Casual dress; cocktails. **Parking:** on-site. **Cards:** AX, DS, MC, VI.

TANDOOR OF INDIA   Lunch: $6-$8   Dinner: $10-$15   Phone: 585/427-7080   32

Indian

Location: I-390, exit 14A southbound; exit 14 northbound, 2 mi w on SR 252 (Jefferson Rd); in Jefferson Plaza. 376 Jefferson Rd 14623. **Hours:** 11:30 am-3 & 5-9 pm, Tues-9:30 pm. Closed major holidays; also Mon. **Features:** Exotic dishes in the tradition of Bombay, Manchurian and Southern India are a delicious break from the routine. Sharply dressed staff serve healthful dishes carefully prepared with fresh vegetables, lean meats and aromatic spices. Casual dress; beer & wine only. **Parking:** on-site. **Cards:** AX, DC, DS, MC, VI.

TOKYO JAPANESE RESTAURANT & STEAK HOUSE   **Lunch:** $6-$9   **Dinner:** $12-$20   **Phone:** 585/424-4166   (29)

Japanese

Location: I-390, exit 14 northbound; exit 14A southbound, just w on SR 252 (Jefferson Rd), then just n. 2930 W Henrietta Rd 14623. **Hours:** 11:30 am-10 pm, Fri & Sat-11 pm, Sun 4 pm-10 pm. Closed: 11/22.
Reservations: accepted. **Features:** Family owned since 1988, the restaurant gives patrons a taste of Japan through offerings of sushi, teriyaki, sukiyaki, shabu shabu, bento and dishes entertainingly prepared tableside at hibachi grills. Quality, fresh ingredients are used in every individual preparation. Casual dress; cocktails. **Parking:** on-site. **Cards:** AX, DC, DS, MC, VI.

TULLY'S   **Lunch:** $6-$10   **Dinner:** $6-$10   **Phone:** 585/272-8900

American

Location: I-390, exit 14A southbound, just e on SR 252 (Jefferson Rd); exit 14 northbound, just e on SR 252 (Jefferson Rd). 1225 Jefferson Rd 14623. **Hours:** 11 am-midnight, Fri & Sat-1 am, Sun noon-11 pm. Closed: 11/22, 12/25. **Features:** The sports-themed family restaurant offers plenty of choices for casual dining: chicken fingers, 13 huge burgers, 20 appetizers and mega-salads. More than 80 TVs ensure diners get a view from every table. Casual dress; cocktails. **Parking:** on-site. **Cards:** AX, DS, MC, VI.

HERKIMER pop. 7,498

——— WHERE TO STAY ———

HERKIMER MOTEL   **Phone:** (315)866-0490

Motel

| | All Year | 1P: $64 | 2P: $68-$88 | XP: $7 | F12 |

Location: I-90, exit 30, just n on SR 28. 100 Marginal Rd 13350. Fax: 315/866-0416. **Facility:** 60 units. 56 one-bedroom standard units, some with kitchens. 4 two-bedroom suites ($99-$125) with kitchens. 2 stories (no elevator), interior/exterior corridors. *Bath:* combo or shower only. **Parking:** on-site, winter plug-ins. **Terms:** [ECP] meal plan available, small pets only. **Amenities:** voice mail, hair dryers. *Some:* irons. **Pool(s):** heated outdoor. **Leisure Activities:** exercise room. **Guest Services:** sundries, coin laundry. **Business Services:** fax (fee). **Cards:** AX, DS, MC, VI. **Free Special Amenities:** expanded continental breakfast and local telephone calls.

SOME UNITS

——— WHERE TO DINE ———

CRYSTAL CHANDELIER RESTAURANT   **Dinner:** $10-$15   **Phone:** 315/891-3366

American

Location: Jct SR 28, 29 and 169, 1 mi s. 4579 SR 28 13350. **Hours:** Open 5/1-11/1; 5 pm-9:30 pm, Fri & Sat-10 pm, Sun 1 pm-8 pm. Closed: 1/1, 12/24, 12/25; also Mon-Wed. **Reservations:** accepted. **Features:** Smoked baby back ribs stand out on a menu of well-prepared beef, seafood and poultry selections. Flowers and fine artwork decorate the moderately upscale dining room. The restaurant caters to a diverse clientele, ranging from families to professionals. Casual dress; cocktails. **Parking:** on-site. **Cards:** AX, CB, DC, DS, MC, VI.

WATERFRONT GRILLE   **Lunch:** $7-$10   **Dinner:** $12-$24   **Phone:** 315/717-0700

American

Location: I-90, exit 30, just off SR 5; on the waterfront. 800 Mohawk St 13350. **Hours:** 11:30 am-2:30 & 5-9 pm, Fri-10 pm, Sat 11:30 am-3:30 & 5-10 pm, Sun noon-7 pm. Closed major holidays. **Reservations:** accepted. **Features:** The restaurant is a spot for casual waterfront dining in the "Gems Along the Mohawk" at the marina. Guests can sit on the seasonal patio to sample favorite American and Italian fare. Casual dress; cocktails. **Parking:** on-site. **Cards:** AX, DS, MC, VI.

——— *The following restaurant has not been evaluated by AAA but is listed for your information only.* ———

HEIDELBERG CAFE   **Phone:** 315/866-0999

[fyi]

Not evaluated. **Location:** Jct SR 5, 1.5 mi n. 3056 SR 28 N 13350. **Features:** A casual, friendly open dining room doubles as this bakery's store with tempting baked goods displayed to whet the appetite.

HICKSVILLE pop. 41,260

——— WHERE TO STAY ———

ECONO LODGE   *Book great rates at AAA.com*   **Phone:** (516)433-3900

Small-scale Hotel

| | All Year [CP] | 1P: $89-$139 | 2P: $89-$139 | XP: $10 | F16 |

Location: I-495, exit 41, 1.3 mi s on SR 106, then 1.2 mi w on Old Country Rd. Located in a commercial area. 429 Duffy Ave 11801. Fax: 516/433-3909. **Facility:** 82 one-bedroom standard units. 2 stories (no elevator), interior corridors. *Bath:* combo or shower only. **Parking:** on-site. **Amenities:** voice mail. **Guest Services:** valet laundry, wireless Internet. **Cards:** AX, CB, DC, DS, JC, MC, VI. **Free Special Amenities:** continental breakfast and high-speed Internet.

SOME UNITS

——— WHERE TO DINE ———

LUIGI Q   **Lunch:** $20-$25   **Dinner:** $22-$35   **Phone:** 516/932-7450

Italian

Location: I-495, exit 43, 1 mi n. 400B S Oyster Bay Rd 11801. **Hours:** noon-3 & 5-10 pm, Fri & Sat-11 pm. Closed major holidays; also Sun. **Reservations:** accepted. **Features:** This Mediterranean-styled restaurant is a great place for a business lunch or dinner date. Warm terra cotta walls and white table linens accentuate the room. Italian cuisine is prepared to perfection, from al dente pasta, veal and chicken dishes to homemade desserts. Dressy casual; cocktails. **Parking:** on-site. **Cards:** AX, MC, VI.

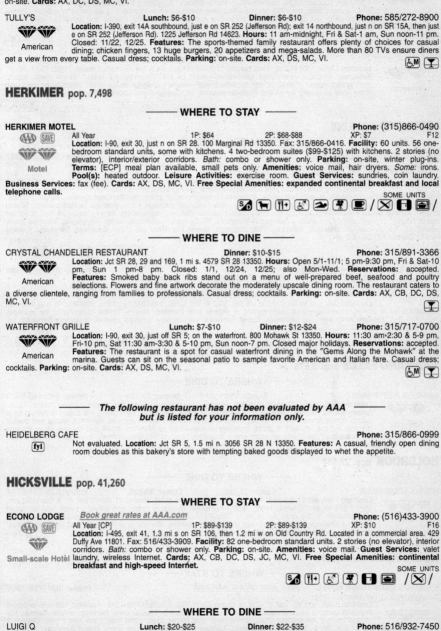

HIGH FALLS pop. 627

——— WHERE TO DINE ———

DEPUY CANAL HOUSE
WWWWW
American
Historic
Dinner: $20-$45
Phone: 845/687-7700
Location: Center. 103 Main St 12440. **Hours:** Open 5/1-1/22 & 2/14-4/30; 5:30 pm-10 pm, Sun 11:30 am-2 & 4:30-9 pm. Closed: 12/25; also Mon-Wed. **Reservations:** suggested. **Features:** Along the historic Delaware and Hudson Canal, the 1797 landmark has been meticulously restored and is appointed in antiques. Whole lobster taken out of the shell and presented encrusted with panko crumbs and steamed claws is one example of the creative, internationally influenced cuisine. Casual dress; cocktails. **Parking:** on-site. **Cards:** AX, MC, VI.

THE EGG'S NEST
WWW WW
American
Lunch: $6-$10
Dinner: $8-$14
Phone: 845/687-7255
Location: Center. 1300 Rt 213 12440. **Hours:** 11:30 am-11 pm, Fri & Sat-midnight. Closed: 11/22, 12/24, 12/25.
Features: Inventive overstuffed sandwiches—such as the "Thanksgiving feast," which stacks turkey, stuffing and melted cheese on egg-battered bread—are as wonderful as the decor, which brims with such funky finds as toaster lamps and three-dimensional art. Casual dress; cocktails. **Parking:** on-site.

HIGHLAND pop. 5,060

——— WHERE TO STAY ———

ROCKING HORSE RANCH RESORT
WWWWW
Resort Ranch
Phone: (845)691-2927
5/25-9/3 [MAP]	1P: $210-$245	2P: $420-$490	XP: $110	D16
5/1-5/24 & 9/4-4/30 [MAP]	1P: $135-$225	2P: $270-$450	XP: $85	D16

Location: Jct US 9W and US 44/SR 55, 4 mi w. Located in a quiet area. 600 Rt 44-55 12528. Fax: 845/691-6434. **Facility:** Extensive recreational facilities are one of the highlights of this family-oriented ranch resort. Smoke free premises. 119 one-bedroom standard units. 2 stories, interior/exterior corridors. **Parking:** on-site, winter plug-ins. **Terms:** check-in 4 pm, 28 day cancellation notice, weekly rates available, package plans. **Pool(s):** heated outdoor, heated indoor, wading. **Leisure Activities:** saunas, whirlpool, waterslide, paddleboats, waterskiing, fishing, miniature golf, 2 lighted tennis courts, downhill skiing, ice skating, recreation programs, hiking trails, horseback riding, playground, exercise room, basketball, horseshoes, shuffleboard, volleyball. *Fee:* massage. **Guest Services:** gift shop. **Business Services:** meeting rooms. **Cards:** AX, DC, DS, MC, VI.

SOME UNITS

SUPER 8 MOTEL *Book at AAA.com*
WW WW
Motel
Phone: (845)691-6888
5/1-10/31	1P: $63-$130	2P: $69-$141	XP: $5	F
11/1-12/31	1P: $56-$85	2P: $70-$135	XP: $5	F
1/1-4/30	1P: $65-$90	2P: $65-$90	XP: $5	F

Location: Just s of jct SR 299 and US 9W. 3423 Rt 9W 12528. Fax: 845/691-6888. **Facility:** 44 one-bedroom standard units. 2 stories, interior corridors. *Bath:* combo or shower only. **Parking:** on-site. **Terms:** cancellation fee imposed, pets ($10 fee). **Leisure Activities:** spa privileges. **Guest Services:** coin laundry, wireless Internet. **Business Services:** fax (fee). **Cards:** AX, CB, DC, DS, JC, MC, VI.

SOME UNITS

HIGHLAND FALLS pop. 3,678

——— WHERE TO DINE ———

SCHADES RESTAURANT
WW WWW
American
Lunch: $5-$9
Dinner: $9-$20
Phone: 845/446-2626
Location: Downtown. 457 Main St 10928. **Hours:** 11 am-9 pm, Fri & Sat-10 pm. Closed: 11/22, 12/25. **Reservations:** required, weekdays. **Features:** Near the West Point front gates, the eatery is perfect for a casual family dinner. On the varied menu are Mexican and Italian entrees, sandwich wraps and basket dinners, but the highlight is pizza. Specialty pizzas—such as Mexican, steak and cheese, Hawaiian and seafood—are popular, as are the "rolled" pizzas, which (more accurately) are stuffed. Casual dress; cocktails. **Parking:** street. **Cards:** DS, MC, VI.

HOLBROOK pop. 27,512

——— WHERE TO DINE ———

MAMMA LOMBARDI'S
WWWWW
Italian
Lunch: $7-$15
Dinner: $9-$26
Phone: 631/737-0774
Location: I-495, exit 61, 0.8 mi s, then just w. 400 Furrows Rd 11741. **Hours:** 11 am-10 pm, Fri & Sat-11:30 pm, Sun 1 pm-10 pm. Closed: 11/22, 12/25. **Features:** Burgundy tones and gilded artwork lend an air of sophistication to the cozy dining room. Bow tie pasta with Gorgonzola sauce is representative of well-prepared offerings, which are served in abundant portions. Service is professional and attentive. Casual dress; cocktails. **Parking:** on-site. **Cards:** AX, DC, DS, MC, VI.

HOLTSVILLE pop. 5,100

——— WHERE TO STAY ———

RADISSON MACARTHUR HOTEL *Book great rates at AAA.com*
AAA SAVE
WWWW
Small-scale Hotel
Phone: (631)758-2900
All Year 1P: $129
Location: I-495, exit 63, just s. 1730 N Ocean Ave 11742. Fax: 631/758-2612. **Facility:** 188 one-bedroom standard units. 3 stories, interior corridors. *Bath:* combo or shower only. **Parking:** on-site. **Terms:** 9% service charge. **Amenities:** video games (fee), dual phone lines, voice mail, irons, hair dryers. **Dining:** 6 am-11 pm, Fri & Sat-midnight, cocktails. **Leisure Activities:** exercise room. **Guest Services:** sundries, valet and coin laundry, airport transportation-MacArthur Airport, area transportation-railroad station, wireless Internet. **Business Services:** meeting rooms. **Cards:** AX, CB, DC, DS, JC, MC, VI. **Free Special Amenities:** newspaper and high-speed Internet.

SOME UNITS

HONEOYE —See also FINGER LAKES.

—————— WHERE TO STAY ——————

GREENWOODS BED & BREAKFAST INN   *Book great rates at AAA.com*   Phone: (585)229-2111

(AAA) (SAVE)   5/1-11/15 & 2/29-4/30 [BP]   1P: $109-$169   2P: $109-$169   XP: $20

▽▽▽▽   **Location:** 2.5 mi e on SR 20A, just n. 8136 Quayle Rd 14471. **Facility:** Quality appointments are the signature of this Adirondack-themed B&B overlooking a scenic valley; three rooms have fireplaces, all have feather beds. Smoke free premises. 5 units. 3 one-bedroom standard units. 2 one-bedroom suites. 2 stories (no

Bed & Breakfast elevator), interior/exterior corridors. **Parking:** on-site. **Terms:** open 5/1-11/15 & 2/29-4/30, 2 night minimum stay - weekends, age restrictions may apply, 14 day cancellation notice-fee imposed, package plans. **Amenities:** video library, CD players, irons, hair dryers. **Leisure Activities:** whirlpool, board games, puzzles, hiking trails. **Guest Services:** wireless Internet. **Business Services:** PC, fax. **Cards:** AX, DS, MC, VI. **Free Special Amenities:** full breakfast and high-speed Internet.

SOME UNITS

[✕$] [✕] [VCR] [☎] / [🖥] /

HORNELL pop. 9,019—See also FINGER LAKES.

—————— WHERE TO STAY ——————

COMFORT INN   *Book great rates at AAA.com*   Phone: (607)324-4300

▽▽▽▽   5/1-11/30 [ECP]   1P: $99-$129   2P: $99-$129   XP: $10   F18
        12/1-4/30 [ECP]   1P: $89-$129   2P: $89-$129   XP: $10   F18

Small-scale Hotel **Location:** Jct US 36 and SR 17, 3 mi s. 1 Canisteo Square 14843. Fax: 607/324-4311. **Facility:** 62 one-bedroom standard units, some with whirlpools. 2 stories (no elevator), interior corridors. **Bath:** combo or shower only. **Parking:** on-site, winter plug-ins. **Amenities:** video library, DVD players, high-speed Internet, voice mail, irons, hair dryers. **Pool(s):** small heated indoor. **Leisure Activities:** exercise room. **Guest Services:** valet and coin laundry, wireless Internet. **Business Services:** meeting rooms. **Cards:** AX, CB, DC, DS, MC, VI.

SOME UNITS

[A$K] [S☐] [¶†] [♿M] [🖥] [🚤] [🛠] [🖥] [🖥] [🖥] / [✕] [VCR] /

HORSEHEADS pop. 6,452—See also FINGER LAKES.

—————— WHERE TO STAY ——————

COUNTRY INN & SUITES BY CARLSON-BIG FLATS   *Book at AAA.com*   Phone: (607)739-9205

▽▽▽▽   All Year   1P: $100-$120   2P: $105-$125   XP: $5   F18

Location: SR 17 (I-86), exit 51A eastbound; exit 51B westbound. 105 E Mall Rd 14845. Fax: 607/739-9205.

Small-scale Hotel **Facility:** 70 units. 50 one-bedroom standard units. 19 one- and 1 two-bedroom suites. 3 stories, interior corridors. **Bath:** combo or shower only. **Parking:** on-site. **Amenities:** voice mail, irons, hair dryers. **Pool(s):** small heated indoor. **Leisure Activities:** whirlpool, exercise room. **Guest Services:** valet and coin laundry, wireless Internet. **Business Services:** meeting rooms. **Cards:** AX, DC, DS, MC, VI.

SOME UNITS

[A$K] [S☐] [¶†] [🖥] [🚤] [🛠] [🖥] / [✕] [🖥] [🖥] /

HILTON GARDEN INN ELMIRA/CORNING   *Book great rates at AAA.com*   Phone: (607)795-1111

▽▽▽▽   All Year   1P: $89-$164   2P: $89-$164   XP: $20   F19

Location: SR 17 (I-86), exit 51A eastbound; exit 51B westbound. Located across from Arnot Mall. 35 Arnot Rd 14845.

Small-scale Hotel Fax: 607/795-4103. **Facility:** 119 units. 116 one-bedroom standard units, some with whirlpools. 3 one-bedroom suites ($109-$350) with whirlpools. 4 stories, interior corridors. **Bath:** combo or shower only. **Parking:** on-site. **Terms:** cancellation fee imposed, [BP] meal plan available, package plans. **Amenities:** video games (fee), high-speed Internet, dual phone lines, voice mail, irons, hair dryers. **Pool(s):** heated indoor. **Leisure Activities:** whirlpool, exercise room. **Guest Services:** sundries, valet and coin laundry, wireless Internet. **Business Services:** meeting rooms, business center. **Cards:** AX, CB, DC, DS, JC, MC, VI. **(See color ad p 300)**

SOME UNITS

[A$K] [S☐] [¶] [Ⓣ] [♿M] [🖥] [🚤] [🛠] [🖥] [🖥] [🖥] / [✕] /

HOLIDAY INN EXPRESS   *Book at AAA.com*   Phone: (607)739-3681

▽▽▽▽   All Year   1P: $99-$125   2P: $99-$125

Location: Jct SR 14, 17 and 328, exit 52 off SR 17. 2666 Corning Rd 14845. Fax: 607/796-6927. **Facility:** 99 one-bedroom standard units. 2 stories, interior corridors. **Bath:** combo or shower only. **Parking:** on-site.

Small-scale Hotel **Terms:** package plans. **Amenities:** Some: dual phone lines. **Pool(s):** outdoor. **Leisure Activities:** exercise room, basketball, volleyball. **Guest Services:** valet and coin laundry, wireless Internet. **Business Services:** conference facilities, PC. **Cards:** AX, DC, DS, MC, VI.

SOME UNITS

[A$K] [S☐] [✈] [♿] [🚤] [✕] [🛠] [🖥] / [✕] [VCR] [🖥] [🖥] /

—————— WHERE TO DINE ——————

PUDGIE'S PIZZA   Lunch: $4-$6   Dinner: $4-$6   Phone: 607/739-8781

▽▽   **Location:** Jct SR 14 and 13; in Hanover Square. 134 W Franklin St 14845. **Hours:** 11 am-10 pm, Fri & Sat-12:30 am, Sun noon-10 pm. Closed: 3/23, 11/22, 12/25. **Features:** For over 25 years, this location has served

Pizza   their pizza, subs and pasta dishes for hungry diners to eat in or take out. Party packs and delivery are available. Casual dress. **Parking:** on-site. **Cards:** DS, MC, VI.

SUGAR & SPICE RESTAURANT   *Menu on AAA.com*   Lunch: $5-$8   Dinner: $5-$9   Phone: 607/739-5303

(AAA)   **Location:** Just n of Hanover Square; center. 300 Watkins Rd 14845. **Hours:** 6 am-3 pm, Fri-7:30 pm, Sat & Sun 7

▽▽   am-1 pm. Closed major holidays. **Reservations:** accepted. **Features:** Daily specials coordinate with fresh seasonal fruits and vegetables in the popular little diner. Old-fashioned comfort food is made on the

American premises. Casual dress. **Parking:** on-site. **Cards:** AX, DS, MC, VI.

HOUGHTON pop. 1,748

──────── WHERE TO STAY ────────

THE INN AT HOUGHTON CREEK   **Phone: 585/567-8400**

All Year   1P: $59-$74   2P: $63-$79   XP: $5   F12

Location: I-86, exit 30, 14 mi n on CR 19; center. Located next to the college. 9722 Genesee St 14744.

Small-scale Hotel   Fax: 585/567-4842. **Facility:** Smoke free premises. 17 one-bedroom standard units. 2 stories (no elevator), interior corridors. *Bath:* combo or shower only. **Parking:** on-site. **Terms:** package plans. **Amenities:** video library (fee), irons, hair dryers. *Some:* DVD players (fee). **Guest Services:** wireless Internet. **Business Services:** PC.
Cards: AX, DS, MC, VI.

SOME UNITS

(A$K) (S℗) (ⓜ) (&) (♥+) (✕) (🏃) (▣) / (VCR)
FEE

HOWES CAVE

──────── WHERE TO STAY ────────

HOWE CAVERNS MOTEL   **Phone: 518/296-8950**

All Year   1P: $45-$170   2P: $45-$170

Location: I-88, exit 22, 1.2 mi e on SR 7, 1.3 mi n on CR 8, then e, follow signs. 255 Discovery Dr 12092.
Fax: 518/296-8958. **Facility:** 21 units. 19 one- and 2 two-bedroom standard units, some with whirlpools. 1 story, exterior corridors. *Bath:* combo or shower only. **Amenities:** hair dryers. **Dining:** 11 am-7 pm; closed 10/12-4/30, cocktails. **Pool(s):** outdoor. **Leisure**
Motel   **Activities:** *Fee:* cavern tours, gemstone mining. **Cards:** AX, DS, MC, VI. **Free Special Amenities:**
continental breakfast and local telephone calls. *(See color ad p 278)*

SOME UNITS

(¶¶) (&) (➔) (▣) / (✕) (🛄) (▦) /

HUNTER pop. 490

──────── WHERE TO STAY ────────

HUNTER INN   **Phone: (518)263-3777**

11/21-3/30 [ECP]   1P: $89-$245   2P: $89-$245   XP: $10   F16
6/29-10/21 [ECP]   1P: $89-$140   2P: $89-$140   XP: $10   F16

Location: Jct SR 296, 1.9 mi e. Located in a commercial area. Rt 23A 12442 (PO Box 355). Fax: 518/263-3981.
Small-scale Hotel   **Facility:** 40 one-bedroom standard units, some with whirlpools. 3 stories (no elevator), interior corridors.
Parking: on-site. **Terms:** open 6/29-10/21 & 11/21-3/30, 2-3 night minimum stay - seasonal and/or weekends, 14 day cancellation notice, package plans, pets ($20 extra charge). **Amenities:** video library, hair dryers. *Some:* DVD players. **Leisure Activities:** whirlpool, exercise room, game room. **Guest Services:** coin laundry. **Cards:** AX, DS, MC, VI.

SOME UNITS

(A$K) (🛏) (Ⓨ) (✕) (🏃) / (✕) (AC) (VCR) (🛄) /
FEE   FEE   FEE

SCRIBNER HOLLOW LODGE   **Phone: (518)263-4211**

All Year [MAP]   1P: $110-$170   2P: $110-$170

Location: 0.5 mi e. Located in a commercial area. Rt 23A 12442 (PO Box 156). Fax: 518/263-5266. **Facility:** 37
Small-scale Hotel   units. 35 one-bedroom standard units, some with whirlpools. 2 one-bedroom suites ($250-$750). 2-3 stories (no elevator), interior corridors. **Parking:** on-site. **Terms:** package plans, 10% service charge.
Amenities: hair dryers. *Some:* DVD players, CD players. **Dining:** The Prospect Restaurant, see separate listing. **Pool(s):** outdoor, small heated indoor. **Leisure Activities:** saunas, whirlpool, tennis court. *Fee:* massage, game room. **Guest Services:** area transportation. **Business Services:** meeting rooms. **Cards:** AX, DC, DS, MC, VI.

SOME UNITS

(A$K) (S℗) (¶¶) (➔) (✕) / (VCR) (🛄) /

──────── WHERE TO DINE ────────

MOUNTAIN BROOK DINING AND SPIRITS   **Dinner:** $12-$29   **Phone:** 518/263-5351

Location: Center. 625 Main St 12442. **Hours:** 5 pm-9 pm, Fri & Sat-10 pm; seasonal hours may vary. Closed major holidays. **Reservations:** suggested, weekends. **Features:** Perched along the creek side at the entrance to the ski area, the casual eatery offers warm ambience, attentive service and a selection of foods
American   made with the freshest ingredients, from delicate seafood to veal, fowl and beef. Casual dress; cocktails.
Parking: street. **Cards:** MC, VI.

THE PROSPECT RESTAURANT   **Dinner:** $18-$27   **Phone:** 518/263-4211

Location: 0.5 mi e; in Scribner Hollow Lodge. Rt 23A 12442. **Hours:** 8 am-10 & 5-10 pm, Fri & Sat-11 pm, Sun 8 am-11 & 5-11 pm. **Reservations:** suggested. **Features:** Wide windows offer views to the ski area from every table. The friendly and competent staff brings pleasant selections from the kitchen, including poultry,
American   fish and beef items. The wine list is extensive. Casual dress; cocktails. **Parking:** on-site. **Cards:** AX, DS,
MC, VI.

(Ⓨ)

HUNTINGTON STATION pop. 29,910

──────── WHERE TO STAY ────────

HUNTINGTON COUNTRY INN   *Book great rates at AAA.com*   **Phone: (631)421-3900**

All Year   1P: $109-$189   2P: $109-$189

Location: Jct SR 110, just w on SR 25 (Jericho Tpke). Located in a commercial area. 270 W Jericho Tpke 11746.
Fax: 631/421-5287. **Facility:** 62 units. 61 one-bedroom standard units with whirlpools. 1 one-bedroom suite ($249-$299) with whirlpool. 2 stories (no elevator), interior/exterior corridors. **Parking:** on-site. **Terms:** [CP]
Motel   meal plan available, package plans. **Amenities:** CD players, voice mail, irons, hair dryers. *Some:* fax.
Pool(s): heated outdoor. **Leisure Activities:** exercise room. **Guest Services:** valet laundry, wireless Internet. **Business Services:** meeting rooms, business center. **Cards:** AX, CB, DC, DS, JC, MC, VI. **Free Special Amenities:** expanded continental breakfast and high-speed Internet.

SOME UNITS

(S℗) (¶+) (➔) (VCR) (🏃) (🛄) (▦) (▣) / (✕) /

WHITMAN MOTOR LODGE

AAA SAVE

Motel

Phone: (631)271-2800

All Year   1P: $90-$110   2P: $90-$110   XP: $25   F12
Location: On SR 25 (Jericho Tpke), 0.6 mi e of SR 110. Located in a commercial area. 295 E Jericho Tpke 11746. Fax: 631/271-2804. **Facility:** 44 units. 36 one-bedroom standard units. 8 one-bedroom suites ($125-$150), some with efficiencies or kitchens. 1-2 stories (no elevator), interior/exterior corridors. *Bath:* combo or shower only. **Parking:** on-site. **Terms:** weekly rates available, small pets only ($20 extra charge, with prior approval). **Guest Services:** wireless Internet. **Cards:** AX, DC, DS, MC, VI. **Free Special Amenities: expanded continental breakfast and high-speed Internet.**

SOME UNITS

🐾 🍴 📷 / ⊠ 🛏 🖥 /
FEE   FEE FEE

───── **WHERE TO DINE** ─────

PANAMA HATTIE'S

American

Lunch: $21   **Dinner:** $26-$37   Phone: 631/351-1727
Location: Jct SR 110, 1.8 mi e of SR 25 (Jericho Tpke). 872 E Jericho Tpke 11746. **Hours:** noon-2 & 5:30-9 pm, Fri & Sat-10 pm, Sun 4:30 pm-8:30 pm. Closed: 12/25. **Reservations:** required. **Features:** Chic restaurant designed with an art deco flair is a wonderful accompaniment to the eclectic cuisine. The restaurant features a prix fixe lunch and weekend dinner menu but offers a la carte dinner selections during the week. The chef's superior skill is readily apparent in each dish, and desserts are not only decadent but artful as well. Dressy casual; cocktails. **Parking:** on-site. **Cards:** AX, DC, DS, MC, VI.

🍸

HYDE PARK pop. 20,851

───── **WHERE TO STAY** ─────

GOLDEN MANOR MOTEL

AAA SAVE

Motel

Phone: 845-229-2157

All Year [CP]   1P: $45-$75   2P: $55-$85   XP: $10   F5
Location: Jct CR 41, 1.5 mi s. Located opposite the Roosevelt Mansion. 4100 Albany Post Rd (US Rt 9) 12538. Fax: 845/229-6127. **Facility:** 38 units. 37 one-bedroom standard units, some with efficiencies. 1 one-bedroom suite with efficiency. 1 story, exterior corridors. **Parking:** on-site, winter plug-ins. **Terms:** office hours 7:30 am-11 pm, weekly rates available. **Pool(s):** outdoor. **Cards:** AX, DC, DS, MC, VI. **Free Special Amenities: continental breakfast and newspaper.**

SOME UNITS

🆘 🏊 / ⊠ 🛏 🖥 /

QUALITY INN-HYDE PARK   *Book great rates at AAA.com*

AAA SAVE

Motel

Phone: (845)229-0088

All Year   1P: $55-$179   2P: $55-$179   XP: $10   F
Location: Jct CR 41, 1.3 mi s. Located in a quiet area. 4142 Albany Post Rd (US Rt 9) 12538. Fax: 845/229-8088. **Facility:** 61 one-bedroom standard units. 2 stories (no elevator), interior corridors. **Parking:** on-site. **Amenities:** irons, hair dryers. **Guest Services:** wireless Internet. **Cards:** AX, CB, DC, DS, JC, MC, VI. **Free Special Amenities: continental breakfast and high-speed Internet.**

SOME UNITS

🆘 🍴 📶 📷 / ⊠ 🛏 🖥 /
FEE FEE

───── **WHERE TO DINE** ─────

AMERICAN BOUNTY

Regional American

Lunch: $12-$18   **Dinner:** $20-$26   Phone: 845/471-6608
Location: 3 mi n of Poughkeepsie on US 9; in The Culinary Institute of America. 1946 Campus Dr 12538-1499. **Hours:** 11:30 am-1 & 6:30-8:30 pm. Closed: Sun, Mon & 3 weeks in July & Dec. **Reservations:** required. **Features:** In Roth Hall, the restaurant prepares diverse cuisine that reflects the country's rich heritage via homegrown ingredients. A few tables face the open kitchen, where tempting desserts come to life. Dressy casual; cocktails. **Parking:** on-site. **Cards:** AX, CB, DC, DS, MC, VI.

🍸

THE APPLE PIE BAKERY CAFE

Deli/Subs
Sandwiches

Lunch: $5-$7   Phone: 845/905-4500
Location: 3 mi n of Poughkeepsie on US 9; in The Culinary Institute of America. 1946 Campus Dr 12538-1499. **Hours:** 8 am-6:30 pm. Closed major holidays; also Sat, Sun & 3 weeks in July & Dec. **Features:** In Roth Hall, the restaurant blends organic and fresh ingredients in offerings of coffee, tea, salad, delicatessen-style sandwiches and baked goods. Casual dress; beer & wine only. **Parking:** on-site. **Cards:** AX, CB, DC, DS, MC, VI.

THE BRASS ANCHOR

Seafood

Lunch: $8-$12   **Dinner:** $17-$28   Phone: 845/452-3232
Location: Jct CR 41, 3.7 mi s on US 9, 0.5 mi sw. 31 River Point Rd 12601. **Hours:** 11:30 am-10 pm. Closed: 12/25. **Reservations:** accepted. **Features:** Green awnings decorate the front of the blue, wood-sided building, while nautical decor brightens the dining room, which overlooks the Hudson River. The menu centers on seafood, with such choices as fried clams and fish and chips. Service is responsive both inside and on the seasonal patio. Casual dress; cocktails. **Parking:** on-site. **Cards:** AX, DC, DS, MC, VI.

🍸

CATERINA DE MEDICI

Regional Italian

Lunch: $9-$19   **Dinner:** $20-$25   Phone: 845/471-6608
Location: 3 mi n of Poughkeepsie on US 9; in The Culinary Institute of America. 1946 Campus Dr 12538-1499. **Hours:** 11:30 am-1 & 6-8 pm. Closed major holidays; also Sat, Sun & 3 weeks in July & Dec. **Reservations:** required. **Features:** In Colavita Center, the restaurant lets patrons escape to the Old World and indulge in rich, hearty Italian flavors. Dressy casual; cocktails. **Parking:** on-site. **Cards:** AX, DC, DS, MC, VI.

**COPPOLA'S ITALIAN AMERICAN
BISTRO** *Menu on AAA.com*   **Lunch:** $6-$14   **Dinner:** $7-$18   **Phone:** 845/229-9113

Italian

Location: Jct CR 41 on US 9, 1 mi s. 4167 Albany Post Rd 12538. **Hours:** 11:30 am-9:30 pm, Fri & Sat-10 pm, Sun 10:30 am-9 pm. Closed: 11/22, 12/25. **Reservations:** suggested, for dinner. **Features:** Traditional preparations of American and Italian foods, including lots of pasta and pizzas, are well-presented and flavorful. The menu also offers a selection of lighter fare. The casual, laid-back atmosphere makes the restaurant a favorite of families. Casual dress; cocktails. **Parking:** on-site. **Cards:** AX, DC, DS, MC, VI.

ESCOFFIER   **Lunch:** $17-$25   **Dinner:** $24-$28   **Phone:** 845/471-6608

French

Location: 3 mi n of Poughkeepsie on US 9; in The Culinary Institute of America. 1946 Campus Dr 12538-1499. **Hours:** 11:30 am-1 & 6:30-8:30 pm. Closed major holidays; also Sun, Mon & 3 weeks in July & Dec. **Reservations:** required. **Features:** In Roth Hall, the restaurant mixes high elegance with traditional Provencal flavors and the upscale tastes of Paris. Dressy casual; cocktails. **Parking:** on-site. **Cards:** AX, CB, DC, DS, MC, VI.

ST. ANDREW'S CAFE   **Lunch:** $14-$20   **Dinner:** $16-$24   **Phone:** 845/471-6608

American

Location: 3 mi n of Poughkeepsie on US 9; in The Culinary Institute of America. 1946 Campus Dr 12538-1499. **Hours:** 11:30 am-1 & 6:30-8:30 pm. Closed major holidays; also Sat, Sun & 3 weeks in July & Dec. **Reservations:** required. **Features:** In the General Foods Nutrition Center, the restaurant hints at an Asian influence in some preparations, which are offered along with wood-fired pizza and other chicken and seafood dishes. Formal service is the norm in what could pass as an exclusive country club dining room. Dressy casual; cocktails. **Parking:** on-site. **Cards:** AX, CB, DC, DS, MC, VI.

INDEX—See COOPERSTOWN.

INLET pop. 406—See also ADIRONDACK MOUNTAINS.

——— WHERE TO STAY ———

MARINA MOTEL   **Phone:** 315/357-3883

Motel

5/1-4/1   1P: $69-$129   2P: $69-$149   XP: $10   F10
Location: Center. Located across from Fourth Lake. 6 S Shore Rd 13360 (PO Box 480). **Fax:** 315/357-2247. **Facility:** 16 one-bedroom standard units. 1 story, exterior corridors. **Parking:** on-site, winter plug-ins. **Terms:** open 5/1-4/1, office hours 9 am-9 pm, 2 night minimum stay - weekends, 14 day cancellation notice-fee imposed, package plans, pets (in designated units). **Leisure Activities:** adjacent to cross country & snowmobile trails, bicycles. **Fee:** game room. **Cards:** MC, VI. **Free Special Amenities:** continental breakfast and local telephone calls.

SOME UNITS

IRONDEQUOIT pop. 52,354 (See map and index starting on p. 599)

——— WHERE TO STAY ———

HOLIDAY INN EXPRESS *Book at AAA.com*   **Phone:** (585)342-0430   **17**

Small-scale Hotel

All Year   1P: $110-$130   2P: $115-$135   XP: $5   F18
Location: SR 104, exit Goodman St, just n. Located adjacent to Irondequoit Mall. 2200 Goodman St N 14609. **Fax:** 585/342-0430. **Facility:** 66 one-bedroom standard units. 3 stories, interior corridors. **Bath:** combo or shower only. **Parking:** on-site. **Terms:** pets ($75 fee). **Amenities:** dual phone lines, voice mail, irons, hair dryers. **Pool(s):** small heated indoor. **Leisure Activities:** whirlpool, exercise room. **Guest Services:** valet laundry, wireless Internet. **Business Services:** business center. **Cards:** AX, DC, DS, MC, VI.

SOME UNITS
FEE

ISLANDIA pop. 3,057

——— WHERE TO STAY ———

HAMPTON INN *Book great rates at AAA.com*   **Phone:** (631)234-0400

Small-scale Hotel

5/1-11/30   1P: $139-$164   2P: $139-$164
12/1-4/30   1P: $119-$149   2P: $119-$149
Location: I-495, exit 57, on south service road. Located in a commercial area. 1600 Veterans Hwy 11749. **Fax:** 631/234-0415. **Facility:** 120 one-bedroom standard units. 4 stories, interior corridors. **Parking:** on-site. **Terms:** package plans. **Amenities:** voice mail, irons, hair dryers. **Leisure Activities:** limited exercise equipment. **Guest Services:** valet laundry, area transportation, wireless Internet. **Business Services:** meeting rooms, business center. **Cards:** AX, DC, DS, MC, VI.

SOME UNITS
FEE FEE

ISLANDIA MARRIOTT LONG ISLAND   **Phone:** (631)232-3000

Large-scale Hotel

All Year   1P: $119-$229   2P: $119-$229
Location: I-495, exit 58, 0.3 mi w on north service road. Located in a commercial area. 3635 Express Dr N 11749. **Fax:** 631/232-3029. **Facility:** Smoke free premises. 278 one-bedroom standard units. 10 stories, interior corridors. **Bath:** combo or shower only. **Parking:** on-site. **Terms:** package plans. **Amenities:** voice mail, irons, hair dryers. **Fee:** video games, high-speed Internet. **Pool(s):** heated indoor. **Leisure Activities:** whirlpool, exercise room. **Guest Services:** gift shop, valet laundry, area transportation. **Business Services:** conference facilities, business center. **Cards:** AX, CB, DC, DS, JC, MC, VI.

SOME UNITS

ISLIP pop. 20,575

✈ Airport Accommodations

Spotter/Map Page Number	OA	LONG ISLAND MACARTHUR AIRPORT	Diamond Rating	Rate Range High Season	Listing Page
N/A		La Quinta Inn & Suites-Islip, 1 mi s of terminal	▽▽▽	$179-$239	237
N/A		Hilton Garden Inn Islip/MacArthur Airport, 2 mi w of terminal	▽▽▽	$139-$279	606

——— WHERE TO DINE ———

TELLERS
▽▽▽
American

Lunch: $14-$42   **Dinner:** $19-$45   **Phone:** 631/277-7070
Location: Jct SR 111, just w on SR 27A (Montauk Hwy). 605 Main St 11751. **Hours:** 11:30 am-3 & 5-10 pm, Fri-11 pm, Sat 5 pm-11 pm, Sun 3 pm-10 pm. Closed: 12/25. **Reservations:** suggested. **Features:** The grand 1927 stone bank has been meticulously transformed into this great American chophouse. On the menu are many well-prepared prime-aged steaks and seafood dishes. The classic yet contemporary space features 30-foot windows, art deco friezes and a clubby bar and cocktail area. The wine cellar housed through the old vault door offers a diverse selection of more than 8,000 bottles. Dressy casual; cocktails. **Parking:** on-site. **Cards:** AX, DC, DS, MC, VI.   ⓨ

ITHACA pop. 29,287—*See also FINGER LAKES.*

——— WHERE TO STAY ———

BEST WESTERN UNIVERSITY INN   *Book great rates at AAA.com*   **Phone:** (607)272-6100
🔺🔺 [SAVE]
▽▽▽
Motel

7/1-8/31	1P: $159-$209	2P: $159-$209	XP: $10
9/1-11/17	1P: $149-$209	2P: $149-$209	XP: $10
5/1-6/30 & 11/18-4/30	1P: $139-$169	2P: $139-$169	XP: $10

Location: From SR 79, 1 mi ne on Pine Tree Rd, just n; in East Hill Plaza. 1020 Ellis Hollow Rd 14850. **Fax:** 607/272-1518. **Facility:** 101 one-bedroom standard units, some with whirlpools. 1 story, interior corridors. **Bath:** combo or shower only. **Parking:** on-site, winter plug-ins. **Terms:** 14 day cancellation notice, small pets only ($10 extra charge). **Amenities:** high-speed Internet, dual phone lines, voice mail, irons, hair dryers. *Some:* DVD players. **Pool(s):** outdoor. **Leisure Activities:** exercise room. **Guest Services:** valet laundry, area transportation-bus station, Cornell & Ithaca Colleges, wireless Internet. **Business Services:** meeting rooms, PC. **Cards:** AX, CB, DC, DS, JC, MC, VI. **Free Special Amenities: expanded continental breakfast and high-speed Internet.**

SOME UNITS
🅢🅓 ✈ 🔌 🍽 ♿ ⊇ 📷 🞵 🖨 🖵 / ✕ ⓋⒸⓇ /
FEE

COMFORT INN   *Book great rates at AAA.com*   **Phone:** (607)272-0100
🔺🔺 [SAVE]
▽▽
Small-scale Hotel

5/1-8/31	1P: $109-$250	2P: $109-$250	XP: $10	F18
9/1-12/31	1P: $99-$169	2P: $99-$169	XP: $10	F18
1/1-4/30	1P: $99-$149	2P: $99-$149	XP: $10	F18

Location: Jct SR 96, 89 and 79, 1.5 mi sw on SR 13. Located in a light-commercial area. 356 Elmira Rd 14850. **Fax:** 607/272-2405. **Facility:** 79 one-bedroom standard units, some with whirlpools. 2 stories (no elevator), interior corridors. **Parking:** on-site, winter plug-ins. **Terms:** cancellation fee imposed, pets ($25 fee). **Amenities:** voice mail, irons, hair dryers. **Leisure Activities:** exercise room. **Guest Services:** valet laundry, wireless Internet. **Cards:** AX, CB, DC, DS, JC, MC, VI. **Free Special Amenities: expanded continental breakfast and high-speed Internet.**

SOME UNITS
🅢🅓 🔌 🍽 ♿M 🞵 🖨 🖵 / ✕ ⓋⒸⓇ 🖵
FEE

ECONOMY INN   *Book at AAA.com*   **Phone:** 607/277-0370
▽
Motel

5/1-11/30	1P: $49-$59	2P: $85-$149	XP: $10	F18
12/1-4/30	1P: $45-$55	2P: $59-$69	XP: $10	F18

Location: 2 mi s on SR 13. 658 Elmira Rd 14850. **Fax:** 607/277-3618. **Facility:** 13 one-bedroom standard units. 1 story, exterior corridors. **Bath:** shower only. **Parking:** on-site. **Terms:** cancellation fee imposed. **Amenities:** high-speed Internet, irons. *Some:* video games, hair dryers. **Cards:** AX, DS, MC, VI.

SOME UNITS
[ASK] 🅢🅓 🖨 / ✕ ⓋⒸⓇ 🖵 /

EMBASSY INN MOTEL   **Phone:** 607/272-3721
▽▽
Motel

All Year	1P: $55-$75	2P: $69-$99	XP: $10	D12

Location: 4 mi e; 2 mi e of Cornell University. Located in a quiet area. 1083 Dryden Rd (Rt 366) 14850. **Fax:** 607/272-3722. **Facility:** Smoke free premises. 25 one-bedroom standard units, some with efficiencies (no utensils). 1-2 stories (no elevator), exterior corridors. **Bath:** combo or shower only. **Parking:** on-site, winter plug-ins. **Terms:** 3 day cancellation notice, package plans. **Amenities:** irons, hair dryers. **Cards:** AX, DS, MC, VI.

SOME UNITS
[ASK] 🅢🅓 ✕ / 🖨 /

HAMPTON INN   *Book great rates at AAA.com*   **Phone:** 607/277-5500
🔺🔺 [SAVE]
▽▽▽
Small-scale Hotel

5/1-10/31 [ECP]	1P: $129-$250	2P: $129-$250	
11/1-4/30 [ECP]	1P: $119-$189	2P: $119-$189	

Location: On SR 13. 337 Elmira Rd 14850. **Fax:** 607/277-5700. **Facility:** 66 one-bedroom standard units, some with whirlpools. 4 stories, interior corridors. **Bath:** combo or shower only. **Parking:** on-site. **Terms:** package plans, small pets only ($100 deposit, in designated units). **Amenities:** video games (fee), high-speed Internet, dual phone lines, voice mail, irons, hair dryers. **Pool(s):** heated indoor. **Leisure Activities:** exercise room. **Guest Services:** valet laundry, wireless Internet. **Business Services:** meeting rooms, PC. **Cards:** AX, DC, DS, MC, VI. **Free Special Amenities: local telephone calls and high-speed Internet.**

SOME UNITS
🅢🅓 🐾 🍽 ♿M ⊘ ⊇ 🞵 🖨 🖵 🖵 / ✕ /
FEE

HILTON GARDEN INN ITHACA   *Book great rates at AAA.com*   Phone: (607)277-8900

▼▼▼▼
Large-scale Hotel

All Year   1P: $129-$399
Location: Jct Tioga St; downtown. 130 E Seneca St 14850. **Fax:** 607/277-8910. **Facility:** Smoke free premises. 104 units. 96 one-bedroom standard units. 8 one-bedroom suites ($179-$450) with whirlpools. 9 stories, interior corridors. *Bath:* combo or shower only. **Parking:** on-site. **Terms:** check-in 4 pm, [BP] meal plan available, package plans. **Amenities:** high-speed Internet, dual phone lines, voice mail, irons, hair dryers. *Fee:* video library, video games. **Pool(s):** small heated indoor. **Leisure Activities:** whirlpool, exercise room. **Guest Services:** sundries, valet and coin laundry, area transportation, wireless Internet. **Business Services:** conference facilities, business center. **Cards:** AX, CB, DC, DS, JC, MC, VI.

SOME UNITS

HOLIDAY INN ITHACA DOWNTOWN   *Book at AAA.com*   Phone: 607/272-1000

▼▼▼▼
Small-scale Hotel

All Year   1P: $152-$171   2P: $152-$171
Location: Just n of SR 96B. 222 S Cayuga St 14850. **Fax:** 607/277-1275. **Facility:** 181 units. 179 one-bedroom standard units. 2 one-bedroom suites with whirlpools. 2-10 stories, interior corridors. *Bath:* combo or shower only. **Parking:** on-site. **Terms:** package plans, 5% service charge, small pets only ($25 fee). **Amenities:** voice mail, irons, hair dryers. **Pool(s):** heated indoor. **Leisure Activities:** exercise room. **Guest Services:** valet and coin laundry, area transportation, wireless Internet. **Business Services:** conference facilities, business center. **Cards:** AX, DS, MC, VI.

SOME UNITS
FEE   FEE FEE

LA TOURELLE RESORT AND SPA   Phone: (607)273-2734

▼▼▼▼
Country Inn

All Year   1P: $125-$375   2P: $125-$375   XP: $10
Location: 2.7 mi s on SR 96B. Located adjacent to Buttermilk Falls State Park entrance. 1150 Danby Rd 14850. **Fax:** 607/273-4821. **Facility:** Set on a 70-acre country estate near Ithaca College and Cornell, the inn offers distinctively furnished rooms and the all-new August Moon Spa. Smoke free premises. 54 units. 53 one-bedroom standard units, some with whirlpools. 1 one-bedroom suite. 1-3 stories, interior corridors. *Bath:* combo or shower only. **Parking:** on-site. **Terms:** 3 day cancellation notice-fee imposed, package plans, pets (in designated units). **Amenities:** video library, DVD players, CD players, high-speed Internet, voice mail, safes, irons, hair dryers. **Dining:** John Thomas Steakhouse, see separate listing. **Leisure Activities:** fishing, 2 lighted tennis courts, bicycles, hiking trails, exercise room, spa. **Guest Services:** valet laundry, wireless Internet. **Business Services:** meeting rooms, PC. **Cards:** AX, DC, MC, VI.

MEADOW COURT INN   Phone: (607)273-3885

ⒶⒶⒶ [SAVE]
▼▼ ▼▼
Motel

All Year   1P: $50-$275   2P: $55-$295   XP: $10   F
Location: 1.5 mi s on SR 13 and 96. Located across from shopping, close to state parks. 529 S Meadow St 14850. **Fax:** 607/277-0758. **Facility:** 75 one-bedroom standard units, some with whirlpools. 2 stories (no elevator), interior/exterior corridors. **Parking:** on-site. **Terms:** cancellation fee imposed, pets ($10 extra charge, in designated units). **Amenities:** voice mail, hair dryers. *Some:* high-speed Internet. **Dining:** 7 am-9 pm, Sat from 5 pm; closed Sun, cocktails. **Guest Services:** wireless Internet. **Business Services:** meeting rooms. **Cards:** AX, DC, DS, MC, VI.

SOME UNITS
FEE   FEE FEE

THE STATLER HOTEL AT CORNELL UNIVERSITY   *Book at AAA.com*   Phone: (607)257-2500

▼▼▼▼
Small-scale Hotel

All Year   1P: $229   2P: $350   XP: $10   F18
Location: On campus of Cornell University. 130 Statler Dr 14853. **Fax:** 607/257-6432. **Facility:** Smoke free premises. 153 units. 138 one-bedroom standard units. 15 one-bedroom suites ($385-$550), some with whirlpools. 9 stories, interior corridors. *Bath:* combo or shower only. **Parking:** on-site. **Terms:** 2-3 night minimum stay - weekends, cancellation fee imposed, 6% service charge. **Amenities:** CD players, high-speed Internet, dual phone lines, voice mail, irons, hair dryers. *Some:* safes. *Fee:* DVD players. **Dining:** Banfi's at The Statler Hotel, see separate listing. **Leisure Activities:** exercise room. **Guest Services:** gift shop, valet laundry, area transportation, wireless Internet. **Business Services:** conference facilities, PC. **Cards:** AX, DC, DS, MC, VI.

SOME UNITS
FEE FEE

SUPER 8 MOTEL   *Book at AAA.com*   Phone: (607)273-8088

▼▼ ▼▼
Small-scale Hotel

All Year   1P: $79-$325   2P: $79-$325   XP: $7   F17
Location: Jct SR 96B and 13, just s. 400 S Meadow St 14850. **Fax:** 607/273-4832. **Facility:** 63 one-bedroom standard units. 2 stories (no elevator), interior corridors. **Parking:** on-site. **Terms:** cancellation fee imposed. **Amenities:** hair dryers. **Leisure Activities:** exercise room. **Guest Services:** wireless Internet. **Business Services:** PC. **Cards:** AX, DC, DS, MC, VI.

SOME UNITS

——— WHERE TO DINE ———

BANFI'S AT THE STATLER HOTEL   Dinner: $17-$30   Phone: 607/254-2565

▼▼▼▼
Italian

Location: On campus of Cornell University; in The Statler Hotel at Cornell University. 130 Statler Dr 14853. **Hours:** 5:30 pm-9 pm, Fri & Sat-9:30 pm. Closed: 11/22; also 12/25-1/1. **Reservations:** suggested. **Features:** First-timers are encouraged to take a "course" at the "institute of fine dining." Wine pairings enhance the delicious cuisine, including nightly specials. The professional and accommodating wait staff assist with every aspect of the dining experience. Dressy casual; cocktails. **Parking:** valet. **Cards:** MC, VI.

BOATYARD GRILL   Lunch: $8-$12   Dinner: $14-$25   Phone: 607/256-2628

▼▼ ▼▼
American

Location: Just off SR 89. 525 Taughannock Blvd 14850. **Hours:** 5 pm-10 pm, Fri & Sat 11:30 am-11 pm, Sun 11:30 am-10 pm. Closed: 1/1, 11/22, 12/25. **Features:** The waterside restaurant affords great views from every seat. This place displays suspended antique wooden boats and canoes along with other nautical decor. The menu centers on fresh seafood and other popular Continental and American fare. Call-ahead seating is accepted. Casual dress; cocktails. **Parking:** on-site. **Cards:** AX, DC, DS, MC, VI.

CHINESE BUFFET RESTAURANT
Lunch: $5-$6 **Dinner:** $8-$9 **Phone:** 607/277-3399

Chinese

Location: On SR 13; in Buttermilk Falls Plaza. 401 Elmira Rd 14850. **Hours:** 11:30 am-9:30 pm, Fri & Sat-10:30 pm. **Closed:** 11/22. **Reservations:** accepted. **Features:** More than 160 items line the buffet, a wise, economical choice for hot and delicious Chinese and American fare. The menu lists items available for carrying out. Casual dress. **Parking:** on-site. **Cards:** AX, DS, MC, VI.

GLENWOOD PINES
Lunch: $3-$16 **Dinner:** $3-$16 **Phone:** 607/273-3709

American

Location: 4 mi n on SR 89. 1213 Taughannock Blvd 14850. **Hours:** 11 am-10 pm. Closed major holidays. **Features:** Perched atop a hillside overlooking Cayuga Lake, the restaurant caters to friends and families. Tasty food is reasonably priced and traditionally prepared with quality ingredients. Casually dressed servers capably handle the generally hopping business. Casual dress; cocktails. **Parking:** on-site. **Cards:** MC, VI.

ITHACA BAKERY
Lunch: $4-$8 **Dinner:** $5-$12 **Phone:** 607/273-7110

American

Location: On SR 13. 400 N Meadow St 14850. **Hours:** 6 am-8 pm, Fri & Sat-9 pm; hours may vary in winter. **Closed:** 1/1, 11/22, 12/25. **Features:** The heart and soul of the operation, the bakery supplies numerous businesses with quality breads and pastries. This is a great place to grab some tasty homemade soup or chili with a fresh delicatessen sandwich and fresh varieties of coffee and tea. Casual dress. **Parking:** on-site. **Cards:** AX, DS, MC, VI.

JOHN THOMAS STEAKHOUSE
Dinner: $15-$40 **Phone:** 607/273-3464

American

Location: 2.7 mi s on SR 96B; in La Tourelle Resort and Spa. 1152 Danby Rd 14850. **Hours:** 5:30 pm-10 pm, Fri & Sat-11 pm. Closed major holidays. **Reservations:** required, college events. **Features:** Prime, dry-aged beef—such as the specialty porterhouse steak for two—and fresh seafood are what the restaurant is all about. The mid-1800s farmhouse has beam ceilings and wide-plank floors. An extensive selection of wines provides a fitting complement. Dressy casual; cocktails. **Parking:** on-site. **Cards:** AX, DS, MC, VI.

LOST DOG CAFE/COFFEEHOUSE
Lunch: $7-$10 **Dinner:** $14-$17 **Phone:** 607/277-9143

International

Location: Center. 106-112 S Cayuga St 14850. **Hours:** 11:30 am-2:30 & 5-10 pm, Sat 11:30 am-10 pm, Sun 11:30 am-9 pm. Closed major holidays; also Mon. **Features:** Eclectic, Bohemian-inspired decor sets a relaxing atmosphere for health-conscious diners. The nouvelle cuisine with an International flair also features many vegetarian dishes, all complemented by fresh specialty brewed coffees, lattes, cappuccinos and herbal teas. Casual dress; beer & wine only. **Parking:** street. **Cards:** AX, DC, DS, MC, VI.

MOOSEWOOD RESTAURANT
Lunch: $7-$8 **Dinner:** $12-$16 **Phone:** 607/273-9610

American

Location: Downtown; in Dewitt Mall (old Ithaca High School). 215 N Cayuga St 14850. **Hours:** 11:30 am-3 & 5:30-8:30 pm, Fri & Sat-9 pm, Sun 5:30 pm-8:30 pm; hours vary in summer. Closed major holidays. **Features:** Celebrating more than 30 years, the restaurant is acclaimed as a driving force in the world of creative vegetarian cooking. Organic ingredients are used whenever possible. The innovative daily changing menu draws on many inspirations, ranging from regional American to ethnic. The atmosphere is casual and relaxed. Casual dress; cocktails. **Parking:** on-site (fee). **Cards:** AX, DS, MC, VI.

OLIVIA
Lunch: $8-$15 **Dinner:** $10-$22 **Phone:** 607/272-1020

American

Location: SR 79, 1 mi ne; next to East Park Plaza. 381 Pine Tree Rd 14850. **Hours:** 11 am-3 & 4-11 pm. **Closed:** 12/25. **Reservations:** accepted. **Features:** The restaurant offers a classical structure and contemporary design with a trendy menu offering top-quality meats and fish as well as gourmet sandwiches and burgers, pleasingly presented with seasonal vegetables and fruits. Dressy casual; cocktails. **Parking:** on-site. **Cards:** AX, DC, DS, MC, VI.

PUDGIE'S PIZZA
Lunch: $3-$5 **Dinner:** $5-$8 **Phone:** 607/272-7600

Italian

Location: Just n off SR 13. 215 Elmira Rd 14867. **Hours:** 11 am-10 pm, Fri & Sat-midnight. **Closed:** 3/23, 11/22, 12/25. **Features:** This basic eatery serves up their pizza, subs and pasta dishes for hungry diners to eat in or take out. Party packs and delivery are available. Casual dress. **Parking:** on-site. **Cards:** MC, VI.

SIMEON'S
Lunch: $7-$10 **Dinner:** $15-$22 **Phone:** 607/272-2212

Continental

Location: Corner of State and Aurora sts; on The Commons. 224 E State St 14850. **Hours:** 11 am-midnight; hours may vary in winter. **Closed:** 3/23, 11/22, 12/25. **Features:** Since 1975, the restaurant has prepared Continental dishes with a Mediterranean flair. The full menu—which includes monstrous healthy salads, jumbo sandwiches, generous and creative pasta dishes, rack of lamb, duck, tuna and some vegetarian fare—is offered all day. Casual dress; cocktails. **Parking:** street. **Cards:** AX, DC, DS, MC, VI.

THAI CUISINE
Dinner: $9-$18 **Phone:** 607/273-2031

Thai

Location: 1.5 mi s on SR 13 and 96. 501 S Meadow St 14850. **Hours:** 5 pm-9:30 pm, Fri-10 pm, Sat 11:30 am-2:30 & 5-10 pm, Sun 11:30 am-2 & 5-9:30 pm. **Closed:** Tues. **Reservations:** suggested. **Features:** Authentic Thai cuisine—including many preparations of beef, chicken, pork and seafood—is made from traditional recipes. Dishes are seasoned to the diner's preference, from mild to piquant to hot. Casual servers exhibit good menu knowledge and are helpful to new guests. Casual dress; beer & wine only. **Parking:** on-site. **Cards:** AX, DS, MC, VI.

VIVA TAQUERIA AND CANTINA
Lunch: $6-$8 **Dinner:** $7-$12 **Phone:** 607/277-1752

Mexican

Location: Corner of State and Aurora sts. 101 N Aurora St 14850. **Hours:** 11 am-10 pm. **Closed:** 1/1, 11/22, 12/25. **Features:** Patrons can nosh on fast, healthy and reasonably priced food in the lively cantina, on the patio or to go. Generous servings go well with Mexican and local beers, premium tequilas and fresh sangria. Casual dress; cocktails. **Parking:** on-site (fee) and street. **Cards:** DS, MC, VI.

JAMESTOWN pop. 31,730

——— WHERE TO STAY ———

BEST WESTERN DOWNTOWN JAMESTOWN   *Book great rates at AAA.com*   Phone: (716)484-8400
(AAA) (SAVE)   All Year [ECP]   1P: $79-$189   2P: $79-$189
▼▼▼   **Location:** I-86, exit 12, 2 mi s on SR 60 (Washington St). 200 W 3rd St 14701. Fax: 716/484-8405. **Facility:** 61 one-bedroom standard units, some with whirlpools. 3 stories, interior corridors. *Bath:* combo or shower only.
Small-scale Hotel   **Parking:** on-site. **Terms:** package plans. **Amenities:** high-speed Internet, voice mail, irons, hair dryers. **Pool(s):** small heated indoor. **Leisure Activities:** exercise room. **Guest Services:** valet laundry, wireless Internet. **Business Services:** meeting rooms, business center. **Cards:** AX, CB, DC, DS, MC, VI.
Free Special Amenities: expanded continental breakfast and high-speed Internet.
SOME UNITS
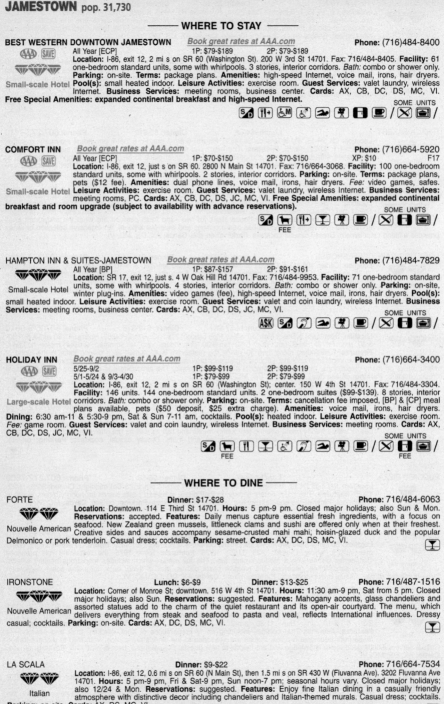

COMFORT INN   *Book great rates at AAA.com*   Phone: (716)664-5920
(AAA) (SAVE)   All Year [ECP]   1P: $70-$150   2P: $70-$150   XP: $10   F17
▼▼▼   **Location:** I-86, exit 12, just s on SR 60. 2800 N Main St 14701. Fax: 716/664-3068. **Facility:** 100 one-bedroom standard units, some with whirlpools. 2 stories, interior corridors. **Parking:** on-site. **Terms:** package plans, pets ($12 fee). **Amenities:** dual phone lines, voice mail, irons, hair dryers. *Fee:* video games, safes.
Small-scale Hotel   **Leisure Activities:** exercise room. **Guest Services:** valet laundry, wireless Internet. **Business Services:** meeting rooms, PC. **Cards:** AX, CB, DC, DS, JC, MC, VI. **Free Special Amenities:** expanded continental breakfast and room upgrade (subject to availability with advance reservations).
SOME UNITS
FEE

HAMPTON INN & SUITES-JAMESTOWN   *Book great rates at AAA.com*   Phone: (716)484-7829
▼▼▼   All Year [BP]   1P: $87-$157   2P: $91-$161
Location: SR 17, exit 12, just s. 4 W Oak Hill Rd 14701. Fax: 716/484-9953. **Facility:** 71 one-bedroom standard units, some with whirlpools. 4 stories, interior corridors. *Bath:* combo or shower only. **Parking:** on-site,
Small-scale Hotel   winter plug-ins. **Amenities:** video games (fee), high-speed Internet, voice mail, irons, hair dryers. **Pool(s):** small heated indoor. **Leisure Activities:** exercise room. **Guest Services:** valet and coin laundry, wireless Internet. **Business Services:** meeting rooms, business center. **Cards:** AX, CB, DC, DS, JC, MC, VI.
SOME UNITS
(ASK)

HOLIDAY INN   *Book great rates at AAA.com*   Phone: (716)664-3400
(AAA) (SAVE)   5/25-9/2   1P: $99-$119   2P: $99-$119
▼▼▼   5/1-5/24 & 9/3-4/30   1P: $79-$99   2P: $79-$99
Location: I-86, exit 12, 2 mi s on SR 60 (Washington St); center. 150 W 4th St 14701. Fax: 716/484-3304.
Facility: 146 units. 144 one-bedroom standard units. 2 one-bedroom suites ($99-$139). 8 stories, interior
Large-scale Hotel   corridors. *Bath:* combo or shower only. **Parking:** on-site. **Terms:** cancellation fee imposed, [BP] & [CP] meal plans available, pets ($50 deposit, $25 extra charge). **Amenities:** voice mail, irons, hair dryers.
Dining: 6:30 am-11 & 5:30-9 pm, Sat & Sun 7-11 am, cocktails. **Pool(s):** heated indoor. **Leisure Activities:** exercise room. *Fee:* game room. **Guest Services:** valet and coin laundry, wireless Internet. **Business Services:** meeting rooms. **Cards:** AX, CB, DC, DS, JC, MC, VI.
SOME UNITS
FEE   FEE

——— WHERE TO DINE ———

FORTE   Dinner: $17-$28   Phone: 716/484-6063
▼▼   **Location:** Downtown. 114 E Third St 14701. **Hours:** 5 pm-9 pm. Closed major holidays; also Sun & Mon. **Reservations:** accepted. **Features:** Daily menus capture essential fresh ingredients, with a focus on
Nouvelle American   seafood. New Zealand green mussels, littleneck clams and sushi are offered only when at their freshest. Creative sides and sauces accompany sesame-crusted mahi mahi; hoisin-glazed duck and the popular
Delmonico or pork tenderloin. Casual dress; cocktails. **Parking:** street. **Cards:** AX, DC, DS, MC, VI.

IRONSTONE   Lunch: $6-$9   Dinner: $13-$25   Phone: 716/487-1516
▼▼▼   **Location:** Corner of Monroe St; downtown. 516 W 4th St 14701. **Hours:** 11:30 am-9 pm, Sat from 5 pm. Closed major holidays; also Sun. **Reservations:** suggested. **Features:** Mahogany accents, glass chandeliers and
Nouvelle American   assorted statues add to the charm of the quiet restaurant and its open-air courtyard. The menu, which delivers everything from steak and seafood to pasta and veal, reflects International influences. Dressy
casual; cocktails. **Parking:** on-site. **Cards:** AX, DC, DS, MC, VI.

LA SCALA   Dinner: $9-$22   Phone: 716/664-7534
▼▼   **Location:** I-86, exit 12, 0.6 mi s on SR 60 (N Main St), then 1.5 mi s on SR 430 W (Fluvanna Ave). 3202 Fluvanna Ave 14701. **Hours:** 5 pm-9 pm, Fri & Sat-9 pm, Sun noon-7 pm; seasonal hours vary. Closed major holidays;
Italian   also 12/24 & Mon. **Reservations:** suggested. **Features:** Enjoy fine Italian dining in a casually friendly atmosphere with distinctive decor including chandeliers and Italian-themed murals. Casual dress; cocktails.
Parking: on-site. **Cards:** AX, DS, MC, VI.

MACDUFF'S
▼▼▼
Continental

Dinner: $18-$28 **Phone: 716/664-9414**
Location: E of SR 60 (Washington St), at 4th St and Pine; downtown. 317 Pine St 14701. **Hours:** 5:30 pm-close. Closed major holidays; also Sun. **Reservations:** suggested. **Features:** The intimate restaurant boasts a sophisticated verbal menu that changes nightly. Personal service and comfortable surroundings add to the dining experience. Offerings include distinctive signature dishes, more than 40 single-malt scotches, a nice wine list and homemade ice cream. Dressy casual; cocktails. **Parking:** on-site and street. **Cards:** AX, MC, VI.

VULLO'S
▼▼ ▼▼
Italian

Dinner: $9-$15 **Phone: 716/487-9568**
Location: I-86, exit 12, 0.5 mi s on SR 60, then 1.4 mi w on SR 430; next to Ellery Park. 2953 Rt 430 14701. **Hours:** 5 pm-9 pm, Fri & Sat-10 pm. Closed major holidays; also Sun. **Reservations:** suggested, weekends. **Features:** Since 1988, the family-friendly restaurant has been pleasing diners with Italian preparations of seafood, chicken and steak, in addition to award-winning veal dishes and in-house-made ravioli. The large portions pair well with impressive and affordable choices from the wine list. Casual dress; cocktails. **Parking:** on-site. **Cards:** AX, DC, DS, MC, VI.

JAMESVILLE

-------- **WHERE TO DINE** --------

GLEN LOCH RESTAURANT *Menu on AAA.com*
ⒶⒶ
▼▼ ▼▼
Continental

Dinner: $14-$29 **Phone: 315/469-6969**
Location: I-481, exit 2, 1.4 mi s. 4626 North St 13078. **Hours:** 5 pm-10 pm, Sun 10 am-9 pm; Sunday brunch. Closed: 12/24, 12/25. **Reservations:** suggested. **Features:** Attractive Scots Highland decor in the old rustic feed mill lends to an enjoyable, relaxed evening. Friendly service and Continental entrees combine pleasantly with the lovely view across the Butternut Creek. Outdoor deck seating can be requested from early June through early September. Dressy casual; cocktails. **Parking:** on-site. **Cards:** AX, DS, MC, VI.
Historic

JEFFERSONVILLE pop. 420

-------- **WHERE TO STAY** --------

THE GRIFFIN HOUSE
▼▼▼▼
Historic Bed
& Breakfast

Phone: 845/482-3371
All Year 1P: $199-$259 2P: $199-$259 XP: $50 D10
Location: Just n; center. 27 Maple Ave 12748. **Facility:** Architecturally pristine features add an ambience of Victorian elegance at this two-acre estate, which claims Franklin Roosevelt as a one-time guest. Smoke free premises. 4 one-bedroom standard units. 2 stories (no elevator), interior corridors. *Bath:* combo or shower only. **Parking:** on-site. **Terms:** 2 night minimum stay - seasonal and/or weekends, age restrictions may apply, 30 day cancellation notice-fee imposed, no pets allowed (owner's pet on premises). **Amenities:** hair dryers. **Guest Services:** wireless Internet. **Business Services:** fax. **Cards:** MC, VI.

JOHNSON CITY pop. 15,535

-------- **WHERE TO STAY** --------

BEST WESTERN OF JOHNSON CITY *Book great rates at AAA.com*
ⒶⒶ SAVE
▼▼ ▼▼
Small-scale Hotel

Phone: (607)729-9194
All Year 1P: $55-$155 2P: $65-$165 XP: $10 F12
Location: SR 17, exit 70N, 0.3 mi n. Located opposite Oakdale Mall. 569 Harry L Dr 13790. Fax: 607/729-3205. **Facility:** 101 one-bedroom standard units. 4 stories, interior corridors. **Parking:** on-site, winter plug-ins. **Terms:** pets ($10 extra charge, in designated units). **Amenities:** high-speed Internet, voice mail, irons, hair dryers. *Some:* DVD players (fee). **Leisure Activities:** pool privileges, pool privileges. **Guest Services:** valet and coin laundry, wireless Internet. **Business Services:** meeting rooms, business center. **Cards:** AX, DC, DS, MC, VI. **Free Special Amenities:** expanded continental breakfast and local telephone calls.

HAMPTON INN BY HILTON *Book great rates at AAA.com*
▼▼▼▼
Small-scale Hotel

Phone: (607)729-9125
All Year 1P: $125-$145 2P: $130-$150 XP: $5 F18
Location: SR 17, exit 70N, just w on Harry L Dr (go through Wegman's lot). 630 Field St 13790. Fax: 607/729-9816. **Facility:** 63 one-bedroom standard units. 3 stories, interior corridors. *Bath:* combo or shower only. **Parking:** on-site. **Amenities:** voice mail, irons, hair dryers. **Pool(s):** small heated indoor. **Leisure Activities:** whirlpool. **Guest Services:** valet laundry, wireless Internet. **Business Services:** PC. **Cards:** AX, DC, DS, MC, VI.

LA QUINTA INN *Book great rates at AAA.com*
▼▼▼▼
Small-scale Hotel

Phone: (607)770-9333
All Year 1P: $65-$199 2P: $65-$199
Location: SR 17, exit 70, 0.3 mi n. Located opposite Oakdale Mall. 581 Harry L Dr 13790. Fax: 607/770-7526. **Facility:** 59 one-bedroom standard units. 4 stories, interior corridors. **Parking:** on-site. **Amenities:** high-speed Internet, voice mail, irons, hair dryers. *Some:* DVD players. **Guest Services:** valet and coin laundry, wireless Internet. **Business Services:** business center. **Cards:** AX, DC, DS, MC, VI. *(See color ad p 360)*

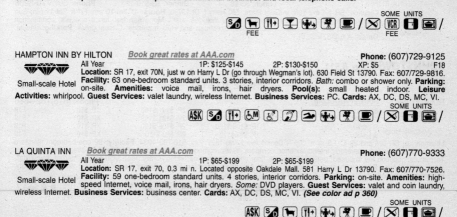

RED ROOF INN-BINGHAMTON #7203   *Book at AAA.com*   Phone: (607)729-8940

6/28-9/7	1P: $57-$91	2P: $67-$96	XP: $5 F18
5/1-6/27	1P: $53-$86	2P: $58-$91	XP: $5 F18
9/8-11/26	1P: $57-$75	2P: $62-$80	XP: $5 F18
11/27-4/30	1P: $50-$72	2P: $55-$77	XP: $5 F18

Motel

Location: SR 17, exit 70, 0.3 mi n, then just n on Reynolds Rd. 590 Fairview St 13790. Fax: 607/729-8949. **Facility:** 107 one-bedroom standard units. 2 stories (no elevator), exterior corridors. *Bath:* combo or shower only. **Parking:** on-site. **Terms:** small pets only. **Amenities:** video games (fee), voice mail. **Guest Services:** valet laundry, wireless Internet. **Cards:** AX, CB, DC, DS, MC, VI.

SOME UNITS

TRADITIONS AT THE GLEN RESORT &
CONFERENCE CENTER   *Book great rates at AAA.com*   Phone: (607)797-2381

All Year [CP]   1P: $119   2P: $119

AAA SAVE

Small-scale Hotel

Location: SR 17, exit 70N, 1.3 mi on Harry L Dr W (becomes Watson Blvd). 4101 Watson Blvd 13790. Fax: 607/584-5386. **Facility:** Smoke free premises. 18 units. 13 one-bedroom standard units, some with whirlpools. 5 one-bedroom suites ($159). 3 stories, interior corridors. **Parking:** on-site. **Terms:** check-in 4 pm. **Amenities:** DVD players, high-speed Internet, voice mail, safes, irons, hair dryers. **Leisure Activities:** hiking trails, exercise room. *Fee:* golf-18 holes. **Guest Services:** valet laundry, wireless Internet. **Business Services:** conference facilities, business center. **Cards:** AX, DS, MC, VI. **Free Special Amenities:** continental breakfast and high-speed Internet.

SOME UNITS

──────── WHERE TO DINE ────────

CACCIATORE'S   **Dinner:** $8-$18   Phone: 607/798-7699

Italian

Location: SR 17, exit 70N, 0.5 mi e. 365 Harry L Dr E 13790. **Hours:** 4 pm-10 pm. Closed major holidays; also Sun. **Features:** The popular restaurant is tucked away in a small shopping center. Established favorites are dished in abundant servings. Casual dress; cocktails. **Parking:** on-site. **Cards:** AX, DS, MC, VI.

CHRISTIE'S GRILL   **Lunch:** $6-$9   **Dinner:** $9-$24   Phone: 607/729-3100

American

Location: SR 17, exit 70N; in Giant Plaza. 560 Harry L Dr 13790. **Hours:** 11 am-10 pm, Fri & Sat-11 pm, Sun-9 pm. Closed: 11/22, 12/25. **Reservations:** accepted. **Features:** The American grill reflects an Italian flair. Certified Angus beef is used in specialties such as steak au poivre or juicy, slow-roasted prime rib. All soup is made in-house and served in bottomless helpings. Among other generous entrees are fresh seafood, pasta favorites, tender chicken and ribs. The family atmosphere is friendly. Casual dress; cocktails. **Parking:** on-site. **Cards:** AX, DC, DS, MC, VI.

DELGADO'S CAFE   **Lunch:** $4-$7   **Dinner:** $7-$12   Phone: 607/798-7306

Mexican

Location: SR 17, exit 71, just w. 119 Harry L Dr 13790. **Hours:** 11:30 am-11 pm, Sat from 4 pm. Closed major holidays; also Sun. **Features:** Popular with the neighborhood crowd, the casual restaurant is a nice place to take the family for good food. Although the menu centers on Mexican fare—burritos, enchiladas, tacos and nachos—guests also find a number of traditional American choices. Casual dress; cocktails. **Parking:** on-site. **Cards:** DC, DS, MC, VI.

GREAT CHINA BUFFET   **Lunch:** $3-$8   **Dinner:** $3-$10   Phone: 607/770-8938

Chinese

Location: SR 17, exit 70N; in Giant Plaza. 560 Harry L Dr 13790. **Hours:** 11 am-10 pm, Fri & Sat-11 pm, Sun noon-10 pm. **Features:** The extensive menu includes sushi, Mongolian bar, lunch specials, combination platters and chef's specials of Cantonese, Szechuan and Hunan cuisine. Casual dress. **Parking:** on-site. **Cards:** AX, DS, MC, VI.

JOHNSTOWN pop. 8,511

──────── WHERE TO STAY ────────

HOLIDAY INN   *Book at AAA.com*   Phone: (518)762-4686

8/1-8/31	1P: $141-$160	2P: $141-$160	XP: $10 F19
7/1-7/31	1P: $131-$150	2P: $131-$150	XP: $10 F19
5/1-6/30	1P: $108-$120	2P: $108-$120	XP: $10 F19
9/1-4/30	1P: $93-$110	2P: $93-$110	XP: $10 F19

Small-scale Hotel

Location: Jct SR 30A and 29 E, 1.3 mi n. 308 N Comrie Ave 12095-1095. Fax: 518/762-4034. **Facility:** 99 one-bedroom standard units. 2-3 stories (no elevator), interior/exterior corridors. *Bath:* combo or shower only. **Parking:** on-site, winter plug-ins. **Terms:** cancellation fee imposed, pets ($10 fee, 1st floor units). **Amenities:** video library (fee), high-speed Internet, voice mail, irons, hair dryers. **Pool(s):** heated outdoor. **Leisure Activities:** exercise room. **Guest Services:** valet and coin laundry. **Business Services:** meeting rooms. **Cards:** AX, CB, DC, DS, JC, MC, VI.

SOME UNITS

SUPER 8 MOTEL   *Book at AAA.com*   Phone: 518/736-1800

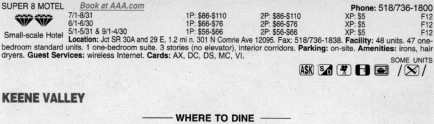

	7/1-8/31	1P: $86-$110	2P: $86-$110	XP: $5	F12
	6/1-6/30	1P: $66-$76	2P: $66-$76	XP: $5	F12
Small-scale Hotel	5/1-5/31 & 9/1-4/30	1P: $56-$66	2P: $56-$66	XP: $5	F12

Location: Jct SR 30A and 29 E, 1.2 mi n. 301 N Comrie Ave 12095. Fax: 518/736-1838. **Facility:** 48 units. 47 one-bedroom standard units. 1 one-bedroom suite. 3 stories (no elevator), interior corridors. **Parking:** on-site. **Amenities:** irons, hair dryers. **Guest Services:** wireless Internet. **Cards:** AX, DC, DS, MC, VI.

SOME UNITS

KEENE VALLEY

———— **WHERE TO DINE** ————

KEENE VALLEY MARKET PLACE   Lunch: $4-$7   Phone: 518/576-9731

American

Location: On SR 73; center. 87 Main St 12943. **Hours:** 11 am-3 pm. Closed: 2/1-3/31 & 1st 3 weeks of Nov. **Features:** Keene Valley Market Place has very limited indoor seating with only a few tables and some self-service aspects. The menu is made up of a few soups, a good variety of creative sandwiches and homemade casseroles. Casual dress; beer & wine only. **Parking:** on-site. **Cards:** MC, VI.

KEESEVILLE pop. 1,850—*See ADIRONDACK MOUNTAINS.*

KENMORE —*See Buffalo p. 261.*

KINGSTON pop. 23,456

———— **WHERE TO STAY** ————

HOLIDAY INN   *Book great rates at AAA.com*   Phone: (845)338-0400

| | 5/1-11/25 | 1P: $139-$189 | 2P: $139-$189 |
| | 11/26-4/30 | 1P: $139-$149 | 2P: $139-$149 |

Location: I-87, exit 19, just e of traffic circle. Located in a quiet area. 503 Washington Ave 12401. Fax: 845/340-1908. **Facility:** 212 one-bedroom standard units. 2 stories (no elevator), interior corridors. *Bath:* combo or shower Small-scale Hotel only. **Parking:** on-site. **Terms:** 2-5 night minimum stay - seasonal and/or weekends, 3 day cancellation notice-fee imposed, [BP] meal plan available, small pets only ($10 extra charge). **Amenities:** voice mail, irons, hair dryers. **Dining:** 6:30 am-2 & 5-10 pm, cocktails. **Pool(s):** heated indoor, wading. **Leisure Activities:** sauna, whirlpool, lifeguard on duty, exercise room. *Fee:* game room. **Guest Services:** coin laundry, wireless Internet. **Business Services:** meeting rooms, business center. **Cards:** AX, CB, DC, DS, JC, MC, VI. **Free Special Amenities: newspaper and high-speed Internet.**

SOME UNITS

FEE   FEE FEE

QUALITY INN AND SUITES   *Book great rates at AAA.com*   Phone: (845)339-3900

| | All Year | 1P: $105-$130 | 2P: $115-$140 | XP: $10 | F18 |

Location: I-87, exit 19, just w. 114 Rt 28 12401. Fax: 845/338-8464. **Facility:** 142 one-bedroom standard units. 2 stories (no elevator), interior corridors. **Parking:** on-site. **Amenities:** voice mail, irons, hair dryers. **Pool(s):** heated indoor. **Guest Services:** coin laundry, wireless Internet. **Business Services:** meeting Small-scale Hotel rooms, fax (fee). **Cards:** AX, CB, DC, DS, MC, VI. **Free Special Amenities: newspaper and high-speed Internet.**

SOME UNITS

———— **WHERE TO DINE** ————

ARMADILLO BAR & GRILL   Lunch: $6-$8   Dinner: $9-$14   Phone: 845/339-1550

Tex-Mex

Location: Just s of Broadway; 1.8 mi e of jct US 587 and SR 28; in Rondout Historic Region. 97 Abeel St 12401. **Hours:** noon-3 & 4:30-10 pm, Fri & Sat noon-3 & 5-11 pm, Sun noon-3 & 4-9 pm; hours may vary in winter. Closed major holidays; also Mon. **Features:** Soft colors decorate the dining room, where a wide array of regulars gather to enjoy Southwestern cuisine, particularly Tex-Mex specialties. Frozen margaritas and Mexican beers complement such selections as shrimp stuffed jalapenos and grilled tuna. Casual dress; cocktails. **Parking:** street. **Cards:** AX, DS, MC, VI.

THE HOFFMAN HOUSE   Lunch: $8-$12   Dinner: $16-$22   Phone: 845/338-2626

American

Location: I-87, exit 19, 0.5 mi e on Washington Ave, left at bus station. 94 N Front St 12401. **Hours:** Open 5/1-2/1 & 3/1-4/29; 11:30 am-9 pm, Fri & Sat-10 pm. Closed major holidays; also Sun. **Reservations:** suggested. **Features:** The late-17th-century, Dutch rubble house exudes historic charm, with three fireplaces and lots of original woodwork. Representative of traditional fare are fish and chips, as well as the Saturday special of prime rib with Yorkshire pudding. Casual dress; cocktails. **Parking:** on-site. **Cards:** AX, CB, DC, DS, MC, VI. **Historic**

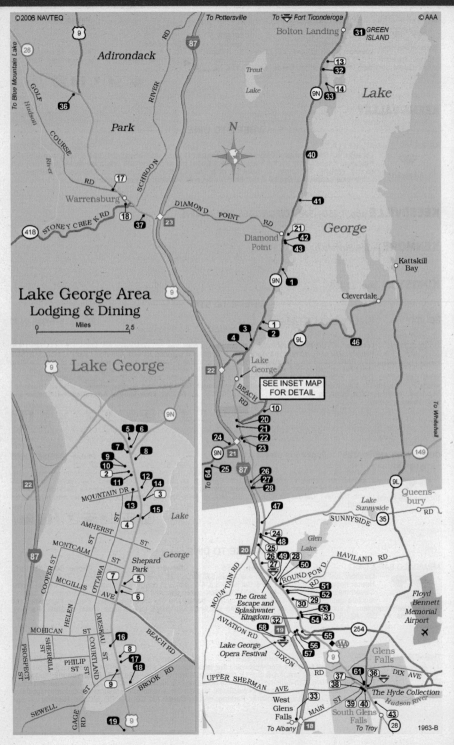

© 2006 NAVTEQ

To Pottersville
To Fort Ticonderoga

© AAA

Bolton Landing

31 GREEN ISLAND

Adirondack

To Blue Mountain Lake

Trout Lake

13
32

9N 33
14

Lake

Hudson River

GOLF COURSE

36

Park

SCHROON

40

41

George

17

Warrensburg

DIAMOND POINT RD

21
42
43

Diamond Point

Kattskill Bay

418 STONEY CREEK RD

18
37

23

9N 1

Cleverdale

Lake George Area
Lodging & Dining

Miles
0   2.5

9

3
4

1
2

9L

46

Lake George

SEE INSET MAP
FOR DETAIL

BEACH RD

To Whitehall

149

Lake George

9

22

9N

10

20
21
22
23

24

To 64
25

9N 21
87

26
27
28

47

9L

Queensbury

Lake Sunnyside

35

SUNNYSIDE RD

5 6

7
9
10
2
11

8

24
48
25
26 49 28
27 50

Glen Lake

HAVILAND RD

Floyd Bennett Memorial Airport

12
14
3
13
15

ROUND POND RD

51
52

MOUNTAIN DR

AMHERST ST

4

Lake George

MONTCALM ST

The Great Escape and Splashwater Kingdom

30 29
53
54 31

MOUNTAIN RD

COOPER ST

MCGILLIS

VANDLOVT

Shepard Park

7
5
6

32
58 19

AVIATION RD

DIXON

55
56
57

254

AAA

Glens Falls

22

87

HELEN ST

DIESSAU ST

MOHICAN ST

16
8
17
18

Lake George Opera Festival

DIX AVE

61 36
37
38

The Hyde Collection

Hudson River

SHERRILL ST

PHILIP ST

COURTLAND ST

BEACH RD

BROOK RD

UPPER SHERMAN AVE

33

MAIN ST

39 40

43

PROSPECT ST

SEWELL

GAGE RD

9

19

9

West Glens Falls

To Albany
18

South Glens Falls

To Troy
28

1963-B

Lake George Area

This index helps you "spot" where approved accommodations and restaurants are located on the corresponding detailed maps. Lodging rate ranges are for comparison only and show the property's high season; rates are per night, unless only weekly (W) rates are available. Restaurant rate range is for dinner, unless only lunch (L) is served. Turn to the listing page for more detailed rate information and consult display ads for special promotions.

Spotter/Map Page Number	OA	LAKE GEORGE - Lodgings	Diamond Rating	Rate Range High Season	Listing Page
1 / p. 330	AAA	Still Bay Resort	◆◆	$150-$205 SAVE	343
2 / p. 330		Green Haven	◆	$59-$109	337
3 / p. 330	AAA	Gentleman Johnny's Inn	◆	$60-$95 SAVE	337
4 / p. 330		Inn on the Hill	◆◆	$100-$115	339
5 / p. 330		Lake Haven Motel - see color ad p 340	◆◆	$89-$129	339
6 / p. 330		Balmoral Motel/Lake George Inn - see color ad p 334	◆◆	$75-$125	334
7 / p. 330	AAA	Econo Lodge Lake George Motel - see color ad p 336	◆◆	$79-$174 SAVE	335
8 / p. 330	AAA	Motel Montreal - see color ad p 340	◆◆	$85-$125 SAVE	341
9 / p. 330		Mohawk Motel & Cottages	◆◆	$89-$179	340
10 / p. 330		Choice Inn & Suites	◆◆	$89-$179	334
11 / p. 330		Heritage of Lake George	◆◆	$75-$185	337
12 / p. 330	AAA	Surfside On The Lake - see color ad p 343	◆◆	$89-$245 SAVE	343
13 / p. 330	AAA	Admiral Motel	◆◆	$110-$125 SAVE	334
14 / p. 330	AAA	The Georgian Resort & Conference Center - see color ad p 338	◆◆◆	$170-$369 SAVE	337
15 / p. 330	AAA	Marine Village Resort	◆◆	$85-$310 SAVE	340
16 / p. 330	AAA	Quality Inn - see color ad p 342	◆◆◆	$79-$199 SAVE	341
17 / p. 330	AAA	Fort William Henry Resort Hotel & Conference Center	◆◆◆	$189-$329 SAVE	336
18 / p. 330	AAA	Howard Johnson Tiki Resort Inn - see color ad p 339	◆◆	$69-$249 SAVE	339
19 / p. 330		Holiday Inn Lake George-Turf	◆◆◆	$209-$299	339
20 / p. 330		Super 8 Lake George Downtown	◆◆	$67-$245	343
21 / p. 330		Hampton Inn & Suites	◆◆◆	$99-$329	337
22 / p. 330	AAA	Best Western of Lake George	◆◆	$149-$189 SAVE	334
23 / p. 330	AAA	Travelodge of Lake George	◆◆	$84-$168 SAVE	344
24 / p. 330		Ramada Lake George	◆◆◆	$69-$139	341
25 / p. 330	AAA	Roaring Brook Ranch & Tennis Resort - see color ad p 342	◆◆	$208-$218 SAVE	343
26 / p. 330	AAA	Colonel Williams Resort & Suites	◆◆	$102-$126 SAVE	335
27 / p. 330	AAA	Tall Pines Motel	◆◆	$115-$130 SAVE	344
28 / p. 330	AAA	Lyn Aire Motel	◆◆	$99-$219 SAVE	340
		LAKE GEORGE - Restaurants			
1 / p. 330		The Inn at Erlowest	◆◆◆◆	$26-$50	344
2 / p. 330	AAA	Mario's Restaurant	◆◆	$9-$22	344
3 / p. 330		The Georgian Dining Room	◆◆	$17-$30	344
4 / p. 330		Taste of Poland	◆◆	$8-$19	345
5 / p. 330		Shoreline Restaurant	◆◆	$11-$33	344
6 / p. 330		SJ Garcia's	◆◆	$6-$20	345

Spotter/Map Page Number	OA	LAKE GEORGE - Restaurants (continued)	Diamond Rating	Rate Range High Season	Listing Page
⑦ / p. 330		Sopranos	◆◆	$6-$18	345
⑧ / p. 330		J T Kelly's	◆◆	$16-$30	344
⑨ / p. 330		Adirondack Pub & Brewery	◆◆	$8-$21	344
⑩ / p. 330	AAA	**East Cove Restaurant**	◆◆	$8-$26	344
		BOLTON LANDING - Lodgings			
㉛ / p. 330	AAA	**The Sagamore -** see color ad p 342	◆◆◆◆	$155-$466 SAVE	238
㉜ / p. 330		Bonnie View Resort	◆	$113-$168	237
㉝ / p. 330	AAA	**Melody Manor Resort**	◆◆◆	$165-$250 SAVE	237
		BOLTON LANDING - Restaurants			
⑬ / p. 330		Algonquin Restaurant	◆◆	$19-$33	238
⑭ / p. 330	AAA	**Villa Napoli**	◆◆◆	$17-$30	238
		WARRENSBURG - Lodgings			
㊱ / p. 330		Alynn's Butterfly Inn Bed & Breakfast	◆◆	$109-$189	645
㊲ / p. 330		Super 8 Warrensburg	◆◆	$125-$155	645
		WARRENSBURG - Restaurants			
⑰ / p. 330		Merrill Magee House	◆◆	$19-$25	645
⑱ / p. 330		Grist Mill on the Schroon	◆◆◆	$15-$24	645
		DIAMOND POINT - Lodgings			
㊵ / p. 330	AAA	**Chelka Lodge -** see color ad p 335	◆◆	$150-$185 SAVE	286
㊶ / p. 330		Capri Village	◆	$80-$138	286
㊷ / p. 330		Golden Sands Resort	◆◆	$125-$175	286
㊸ / p. 330		Diamond Cove Cottages	◆◆	$95-$165	286
		DIAMOND POINT - Restaurant			
㉑ / p. 330		McGowans	◆	$9-$10	286
		QUEENSBURY - Lodgings			
㊻ / p. 330	AAA	**Dunham's Bay Resort**	◆◆	$105-$275 SAVE	594
㊼ / p. 330	AAA	**Mohican Motel -** see color ad p 341	◆◆◆	$105-$145 SAVE	594
㊽ / p. 330		Days Inn of Lake George - see color ad p 336	◆◆	$89-$186	593
㊾ / p. 330		Six Flags Great Escape Lodge & Indoor Water Park	◆◆◆	$219-$529	594
㊿ / p. 330	AAA	**The Wakita Motel**	◆◆	$74-$199 SAVE	595
51 / p. 330		Country Inn & Suites - see color ad p 335	◆◆◆	Failed to provide	593
52 / p. 330	AAA	**Graycourt Motel -** see color ad p 337	◆◆	$85-$120 SAVE	594
53 / p. 330		Budget Inn	◆◆	$98-$125	593
54 / p. 330	AAA	**Sleep Inn & Suites**	◆◆	$84-$199 SAVE	595
55 / p. 330		Alpenhaus Motel	◆	$69-$149	593
56 / p. 330		Quality Inn of Glens Falls	◆◆◆	$69-$149	594
57 / p. 330		Econo Lodge & Suites of Glens Falls/Lake George	◆◆	$49-$139	594
58 / p. 330	AAA	**Ramada Glens Falls**	◆◆	$74-$169 SAVE	594
		QUEENSBURY - Restaurants			
㉔ / p. 330		Log Jam	◆◆	$13-$22	595

Spotter/Map Page Number	OA	QUEENSBURY - Restaurants (continued)	Diamond Rating	Rate Range High Season	Listing Page
25 / p. 330		The Meeting Place	▽▽	$12-$20	595
26 / p. 330		The Montcalm	▽▽	$13-$33	595
27 / p. 330		Olde Post Grille	▽▽	$6-$15	595
28 / p. 330	AAA	Trapper's Adirondack Grille	▽▽▽	$15-$26	596
29 / p. 330		Sutton's Country Cafe	▽▽	$9-$16	596
30 / p. 330		Smokey Bear BBQ & Gril	▽▽	$6-$18	595
31 / p. 330		Gamble's Bakery & Coffee Shop	▽	$3-$8(L)	595
32 / p. 330		Flower Drum Song Restaurant	▽▽	$6-$18	595
33 / p. 330	AAA	Carl R's Cafe	▽▽	$9-$12	595
		GLENS FALLS - Lodgings			
61 / p. 330	AAA	Queensbury Hotel	▽▽▽	$94-$179 SAVE	307
		GLENS FALLS - Restaurants			
36 / p. 330		Fiddleheads	▽▽▽	$15-$26	308
37 / p. 330		The Gourmet Cafe	▽	$6-$20	308
38 / p. 330		Siam Thai Sushi	▽▽	$5-$30	308
39 / p. 330	AAA	Davidson Brothers Restaurant & Brewery	▽▽	$11-$20	308
40 / p. 330		132 Glen Bistro	▽▽	$15-$28	308
		LAKE LUZERNE - Lodgings			
64 / p. 330	AAA	Pine Point Cottages & Motel	▽	$78-$86 SAVE	345
		SOUTH GLENS FALLS - Restaurant			
43 / p. 330		Jake's Round Up	▽▽	$6-$20	625

LAKE GEORGE pop. 985 (See map and index starting on p. 330)—*See also ADIRONDACK MOUNTAINS.*

─── WHERE TO STAY ───

ADMIRAL MOTEL
Phone: 518/668-2097 **13**

AAA SAVE

Motel

7/25-9/3	1P: $110-$125	2P: $110-$125	XP: $10	F12
6/29-7/24	1P: $100-$115	2P: $100-$115	XP: $10	F12
5/14-6/28 & 9/4-10/21	1P: $70-$80	2P: $70-$80	XP: $10	F12

Location: I-87, exit 22, 0.5 mi s on US 9. 401 Canada St 12845. Fax: 518/668-3250. **Facility:** 27 one-bedroom standard units. 2 stories (no elevator), exterior corridors. *Bath:* combo or shower only. **Parking:** on-site. **Terms:** open 5/14-10/21, 10 day cancellation notice-fee imposed. **Pool(s):** heated outdoor. **Cards:** DS, MC, VI. **Free Special Amenities: local telephone calls and room upgrade (subject to availability with advance reservations).**

SOME UNITS

BALMORAL MOTEL/LAKE GEORGE INN
Phone: (518)668-2673 **6**

Motel

7/1-8/31	1P: $75-$109	2P: $85-$125	XP: $10	F16
5/1-6/30	1P: $49-$65	2P: $49-$75	XP: $10	F16
9/1-10/22	1P: $49-$59	2P: $59-$69	XP: $10	F16

Location: I-87, exit 22, 0.3 mi s on US 9. 444 Canada St 12845. Fax: 518/668-9248. **Facility:** 32 units. 29 one- and 2 two-bedroom standard units, some with efficiencies. 1 one-bedroom suite ($83-$195). 2 stories (no elevator), exterior corridors. *Bath:* combo or shower only. **Parking:** on-site. **Terms:** open 5/1-10/22, office hours 8 am-11 pm, 10 day cancellation notice-fee imposed, weekly rates available, pets ($15 extra charge). **Amenities:** hair dryers. **Pool(s):** heated outdoor. **Guest Services:** coin laundry. **Cards:** DS, MC, VI. *(See color ad below)*

SOME UNITS

BEST WESTERN OF LAKE GEORGE
Book great rates at AAA.com
Phone: (518)668-5701 **22**

AAA SAVE

Motel

6/22-9/2	1P: $149-$189	2P: $149-$189	XP: $15	F12
5/1-6/21 & 9/3-10/7	1P: $89-$129	2P: $89-$129	XP: $15	F12
10/8-4/30	1P: $69-$99	2P: $69-$99	XP: $15	F12

Location: I-87, exit 21, just e. Exit 21 off I-87 12845. Fax: 518/668-5701. **Facility:** 87 units. 79 one- and 4 two-bedroom standard units. 3 one- and 1 two-bedroom suites ($139-$459), some with kitchens. 2 stories (no elevator), interior/exterior corridors. **Parking:** on-site, winter plug-ins. **Terms:** 2 night minimum stay - seasonal and/or weekends, 3 day cancellation notice-fee imposed, [CP] meal plan available, package plans. **Amenities:** voice mail, safes, irons, hair dryers. *Some:* high-speed Internet. **Pool(s):** outdoor, small heated indoor, wading. **Leisure Activities:** whirlpool. **Guest Services:** valet laundry. **Cards:** AX, CB, DC, DS, MC, VI. **Free Special Amenities: continental breakfast and high-speed Internet.**

SOME UNITS

CHOICE INN & SUITES
Phone: 518/668-2143 **10**

Motel

6/22-9/3	1P: $89-$149	2P: $119-$179	XP: $10	F18
5/1-6/21 & 9/4-10/9	1P: $59-$89	2P: $69-$129	XP: $10	F18
10/10-4/30	1P: $45-$89	2P: $49-$119	XP: $10	F18

Location: I-87, exit 22, 0.3 mi s on US 9/SR 9N. 435 Canada St 12845. Fax: 518/668-3025. **Facility:** 39 one-bedroom standard units. 2 stories (no elevator), exterior corridors. **Parking:** on-site, winter plug-ins. **Terms:** 2 night minimum stay, 14 day cancellation notice, weekly rates available, 5% service charge. **Amenities:** voice mail. **Pool(s):** heated indoor. **Leisure Activities:** whirlpool, playground, basketball, volleyball. **Business Services:** fax (fee). **Cards:** DS, MC, VI.

SOME UNITS

(See map and index starting on p. 330)

COLONEL WILLIAMS RESORT & SUITES   Phone: (518)668-5727   **26**

(AAA) (SAVE)   6/25-9/1   1P: $102-$126   2P: $102-$126   XP: $10
            6/1-6/24   1P: $78-$92   2P: $78-$92   XP: $10

◆◆◆   **Location:** I-87, exit 21, 1.3 mi s on US 9. 1787 Historic Dr 12845 (PO Box 268). Fax: 518/668-2996.
Motel   **Facility:** Smoke free premises. 45 units. 30 one-bedroom standard units. 9 one- and 6 two-bedroom suites
            ($160-$230). 1 story, interior/exterior corridors. *Bath:* combo or shower only. **Parking:** on-site. **Terms:** open
            6/1-9/1, 2-3 night minimum stay - seasonal and/or weekends, 14 day cancellation notice-fee imposed.
Amenities: voice mail. *Some:* irons. **Pool(s):** heated outdoor, heated indoor, wading. **Leisure Activities:** sauna, whirlpools,
lawn games, barbecue grills, playground, exercise room. *Fee:* game room. **Guest Services:** coin laundry, wireless Internet.
Cards: AX, DS, MC, VI. **Free Special Amenities: local telephone calls and high-speed Internet.**

SOME UNITS

[icons]

COMFORT SUITES   Phone: 518/761-0001

(fyi)   All Year   1P: $120-$200   2P: $120-$200   XP: $10   F18
            Too new to rate, opening scheduled for April 2007. **Location:** I-87 W, exit 20. 1533 SR 9 12845. **Amenities:** 98
Small-scale Hotel   units, restaurant, coffeemakers, microwaves, refrigerators, pool. **Terms:** 10 day cancellation notice.
            Cards: AX, DC, DS, MC, VI.

ECONO LODGE LAKE GEORGE MOTEL   *Book great rates at AAA.com*   Phone: (518)668-2689   **7**

(AAA) (SAVE)   6/15-9/2   1P: $79-$174   2P: $79-$174   XP: $10   F17
            5/1-6/14 & 9/3-10/31   1P: $52-$94   2P: $52-$94   XP: $10   F17

◆◆◆   **Location:** I-87, exit 22, 0.3 mi s on US 9. 439 Canada St 12845. Fax: 518/668-4129. **Facility:** 50 one-bedroom
Motel   standard units, some with whirlpools. 2-3 stories, interior/exterior corridors. *Bath:* combo or shower only.
            Parking: on-site. **Terms:** open 5/1-10/31, 7 day cancellation notice-fee imposed. **Amenities:** hair dryers.
            Pool(s): outdoor, small heated indoor. **Leisure Activities:** whirlpool, pool table. *Fee:* game room. **Guest
Services:** wireless Internet. **Business Services:** meeting rooms. **Cards:** AX, CB, DC, DS, JC, MC, VI.
Free Special Amenities: continental breakfast and high-speed Internet. *(See color ad p 336)*

SOME UNITS

[icons]

(See map and index starting on p. 330)

FORT WILLIAM HENRY RESORT HOTEL & CONFERENCE CENTER *Book great rates at AAA.com*   Phone: (518)668-3081   **17**

6/22-9/2	1P: $189-$329	2P: $189-$329	XP: $15	F12
5/1-6/21 & 9/3-10/7	1P: $129-$249	2P: $129-$249	XP: $15	F12
10/8-4/30	1P: $89-$169	2P: $89-$169	XP: $15	F12

Historic
Large-scale Hotel

Location: I-87, exit 21, 1 mi n on US 9/SR 9N. 48 Canada St 12845. Fax: 518/668-4926. **Facility:** Overlooking Lake George, the property's location affords a quick walk to the beach. 195 units. 98 one-bedroom standard units. 97 one-bedroom suites ($159-$499), some with whirlpools. 2-5 stories, interior/exterior corridors. **Parking:** on-site. **Terms:** 2 night minimum stay - weekends, 3 day cancellation notice-fee imposed, package plans. **Amenities:** video games, high-speed Internet, voice mail, safes, irons, hair dryers. *Some:* dual phone lines. **Dining:** 4 restaurants, 6:30 am-1 am, cocktails. **Pool(s):** outdoor, heated indoor. **Leisure Activities:** sauna, whirlpool, yoga instruction, exercise room, horseshoes, shuffleboard, volleyball. **Guest Services:** gift shop, valet and coin laundry. *Fee:* airport transportation-Albany International Airport, area transportation. **Business Services:** conference facilities, business center. **Cards:** AX, CB, DC, DS, MC, VI. **Free Special Amenities:** local telephone calls and room upgrade (subject to availability with advance reservations).

SOME UNITS

(See map and index starting on p. 330)

GENTLEMAN JOHNNY'S INN

AAA SAVE
Motel

Phone: 518/668-2096 **3**

| | | | F12 |
| 5/1-9/30 | 1P: $60-$95 | 2P: $60-$95 | XP: $10 |

Location: I-87, exit 22, 0.5 mi n on SR 9N. 3057 Lake Shore Dr 12845. **Facility:** 17 units. 14 one- and 3 two-bedroom standard units, some with kitchens. 1 story, exterior corridors. *Bath:* combo or shower only. **Parking:** on-site. **Terms:** open 5/1-9/30, 15 day cancellation notice-fee imposed, package plans. **Pool(s):** outdoor. **Leisure Activities:** grills, picnic tables, table tennis, basketball, horseshoes. **Cards:** MC, VI. **Free Special Amenities: continental breakfast and local telephone calls.**

SOME UNITS

[icons]

THE GEORGIAN RESORT & CONFERENCE CENTER *Book great rates at AAA.com*

AAA SAVE
Small-scale Hotel

Phone: (518)668-5401 **14**

6/15-9/5	1P: $170-$188	2P: $329-$369	XP: $10	F10
5/1-6/14 & 9/6-11/1	1P: $95-$110	2P: $259-$299	XP: $10	F10
11/2-4/30	1P: $85-$110	2P: $239-$279	XP: $10	F10

Location: I-87, exit 22, 0.5 mi s on US 9/SR 9N. 384 Canada St 12845. Fax: 518/668-5870. **Facility:** 163 units. 161 one-bedroom standard units, some with whirlpools. 1 one- and 1 two-bedroom suites ($189-$329) with whirlpools. 1-3 stories (no elevator), exterior corridors. **Parking:** on-site, winter plug-ins. **Terms:** 3 night minimum stay - weekends, 3 day cancellation notice. **Amenities:** voice mail, irons, hair dryers. **Dining:** restaurant, see separate listing, entertainment. **Pool(s):** heated outdoor. **Leisure Activities:** limited beach access. **Guest Services:** valet laundry. **Business Services:** meeting rooms. **Cards:** AX, DC, DS, MC, VI. **Free Special Amenities: high-speed Internet.**
(See color ad p 338)

SOME UNITS

[icons]

GREEN HAVEN

Motel

Phone: 518/668-2489 **2**

11/1-4/30 [CP]		2P: $59-$109	XP: $10	D3
5/1-6/30 & 9/6-10/31 [CP]		2P: $54-$109	XP: $10	D3
7/1-9/5 [CP]		2P: $69-$79	XP: $10	D3

Location: I-87, exit 22, 0.8 mi n on SR 9N. 3136 Lake Shore Dr 12845. Fax: 518/668-2575. **Facility:** 20 units. 8 one-bedroom standard units. 2 two-bedroom suites ($94-$129) with kitchens. 10 cottages ($94-$129). 1-2 stories (no elevator), exterior corridors. *Bath:* combo or shower only. **Parking:** on-site. **Terms:** 10 day cancellation notice, pets ($10 fee, with prior approval). **Pool(s):** outdoor, wading. **Leisure Activities:** whirlpool, playground, horseshoes, shuffleboard, volleyball. *Fee:* game room. **Cards:** AX, DS, MC, VI.

SOME UNITS

[icons] FEE

HAMPTON INN & SUITES *Book great rates at AAA.com*

Small-scale Hotel

Phone: (518)668-4100 **21**

| All Year [BP] | 1P: $99-$329 | 2P: $99-$329 | XP: $10 | F18 |

Location: I-87, exit 21, 0.4 mi n. 2133 SR 9 12845. Fax: 518/668-4104. **Facility:** 93 one-bedroom standard units. 4 stories, interior corridors. *Bath:* combo or shower only. **Parking:** on-site. **Terms:** check-in 4 pm, package plans. **Amenities:** video games, high-speed Internet, voice mail, irons, hair dryers. **Pool(s):** heated outdoor. **Leisure Activities:** whirlpool, snowmobiling, hiking trails, exercise room. **Guest Services:** valet and coin laundry. **Business Services:** PC, fax. **Cards:** AX, CB, DC, DS, JC, MC, VI.

SOME UNITS

[icons]

HERITAGE OF LAKE GEORGE

Motel

Phone: 518/668-3357 **11**

| 6/21-9/3 | 1P: $75-$185 | 2P: $75-$185 | XP: $15 | F16 |
| 5/19-6/20 & 9/4-10/10 | 1P: $70-$145 | 2P: $70-$145 | XP: $15 | F16 |

Location: I-87, exit 22, 0.3 mi s on US 9/SR 9N. 419 Canada St 12845. Fax: 518/668-9784. **Facility:** Designated smoking area. 38 units. 32 one-bedroom standard units. 6 cottages. 1-2 stories (no elevator), exterior corridors. *Bath:* combo or shower only. **Parking:** on-site. **Terms:** open 5/19-10/10, 2-3 night minimum stay - weekends, 14 day cancellation notice-fee imposed, weekly rates available, package plans. **Pool(s):** heated outdoor. **Leisure Activities:** shuffleboard. **Cards:** AX, DS, MC, VI.

[icons]

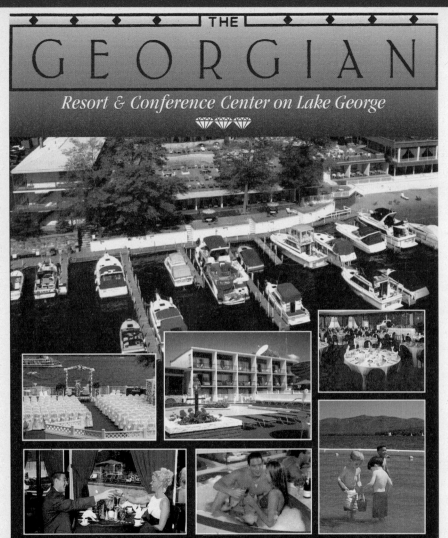

(See map and index starting on p. 330)

HOLIDAY INN LAKE GEORGE-TURF — *Book at AAA.com* — Phone: 518/668-5781 **19**

7/1-8/31	1P: $209-$299	2P: $209-$299
5/1-6/30 & 9/1-10/31	1P: $149-$159	2P: $149-$159
11/1-4/30	1P: $109-$159	2P: $109-$159

Small-scale Hotel **Location:** I-87, exit 21, 0.8 mi n. 2223 Rt 9 (Canada St) 12845 (Rt 9, Box 231). Fax: 518/668-9213. **Facility:** 105 units. 104 one-bedroom standard units, some with efficiencies (no utensils) and/or whirlpools. 1 one-bedroom suite. 2 stories, interior corridors. *Bath:* combo or shower only. **Parking:** on-site, winter plug-ins. **Terms:** 3 day cancellation notice, [BP] meal plan available, package plans. **Amenities:** video games (fee), high-speed Internet, dual phone lines, voice mail, safes, irons, hair dryers. **Pool(s):** heated outdoor, heated indoor, wading. **Leisure Activities:** sauna, whirlpool, playground, exercise room, shuffleboard, game room. **Guest Services:** sundries, valet and coin laundry, wireless Internet. **Business Services:** meeting rooms, business center. **Cards:** AX, DC, DS, MC, VI.

SOME UNITS

🅰🆂🅳 🍴 🍸 🔥 🏊 ✕ 🐾 🔌 📺 💻 / ✕ /

HOWARD JOHNSON TIKI RESORT INN — *Book great rates at AAA.com* — Phone: (518)668-5744 **18** — XP: $15

5/1-10/31 — 1P: $69-$249 — 2P: $69-$249

Location: I-87, exit 21, 0.7 mi n on US 9/SR 9N. 2 Canada St 12845. Fax: 518/668-3544. **Facility:** 110 one-bedroom standard units, some with efficiencies (no utensils). 2 stories (no elevator), interior/exterior corridors. **Parking:** on-site. **Terms:** open 5/1-10/31, 1-4 night minimum stay - seasonal, 30 day cancellation notice-fee imposed. **Amenities:** voice mail, irons, hair dryers. **Dining:** 7 am-noon; dinner theater 5:45 pm-8 pm 7/1-8/31, cocktails. **Pool(s):** outdoor, small heated indoor, wading. **Leisure Activities:** exercise room. **Guest Services:** valet laundry, wireless Internet. **Business Services:** meeting rooms. **Cards:** AX, CB, DC, DS, MC, VI. **Free Special Amenities:** local telephone calls and newspaper. *(See color ad below)*

Small-scale Hotel

SOME UNITS

🍴 🍸 🏊 🐾 🔌 💻 / ✕ /

INN ON THE HILL — Phone: (518)668-2572 **4**

7/27-9/2	1P: $100-$115	2P: $100-$115	XP: $15	F16
6/29-7/26	1P: $80-$90	2P: $80-$90	XP: $15	F16
5/18-6/28 & 9/3-10/28	1P: $60-$70	2P: $60-$70	XP: $15	F16

Motel **Location:** I-87, exit 22, 1 mi n on SR 9N. 3007 Lake Shore Dr 12845. Fax: 518/668-3728. **Facility:** Smoke free premises. 22 units. 20 one- and 2 two-bedroom standard units. 2 stories (no elevator), exterior corridors. **Parking:** on-site. **Terms:** open 5/18-10/28, office hours 8 am-10 pm, 2 night minimum stay - weekends, 7 day cancellation notice. **Amenities:** hair dryers. **Pool(s):** heated outdoor. **Leisure Activities:** volleyball. **Cards:** AX, MC, VI.

🍴 🐾 ✕ 🔌 💻

LAKE HAVEN MOTEL — Phone: 518/668-2260 **5**

7/21-9/4	1P: $89-$129	2P: $89-$129	XP: $10	F15
6/30-7/20	1P: $74-$109	2P: $74-$109	XP: $10	F15
5/11-6/29 & 9/5-11/19	1P: $45-$79	2P: $49-$89	XP: $10	F15

Motel **Location:** I-87, exit 22, 0.4 mi s on US 9. 442 Canada St 12845 (PO Box 581). **Facility:** 31 one-bedroom standard units. 2 stories (no elevator), exterior corridors. *Bath:* combo or shower only. **Parking:** on-site. **Terms:** open 5/11-11/19, 10 day cancellation notice-fee imposed, weekly rates available, package plans, pets ($10 extra charge, with prior approval). **Amenities:** Some: DVD players, irons, hair dryers. **Pool(s):** heated outdoor. **Guest Services:** area transportation. **Cards:** AX, DC, DS, MC, VI. *(See color ad p 340)*

SOME UNITS

🅰🆂🅳 🛏 🍴 🐾 🔌 / ✕ / VCR 🖥 /
FEE

(See map and index starting on p. 330)

LYN AIRE MOTEL

(AAA) SAVE

Motel

Phone: (518)668-4612   **28**

6/16-9/4 [CP]	1P: $99-$159	2P: $119-$219	XP: $10	F12
5/25-6/15 [CP]	1P: $69-$119	2P: $69-$139	XP: $10	F12

Location: I-87, exit 21, 1 mi s. 1872 US 9 12845. **Fax:** 518/668-5804. **Facility:** 36 units. 35 one- and 1 two-bedroom standard units. 2 stories, exterior corridors. **Parking:** on-site. **Terms:** open 5/25-9/4, 3 night minimum stay - weekends, 14 day cancellation notice. **Amenities:** voice mail. Some: hair dryers. **Pool(s):** heated outdoor. **Leisure Activities:** whirlpool, game pavilion, barbecue grills, playground, basketball, volleyball. **Cards:** DS, MC, VI. **Free Special Amenities: continental breakfast and local telephone calls.**

SOME UNITS

MARINE VILLAGE RESORT

(AAA) SAVE

Motel

Phone: 518/668-5478   **15**

5/1-10/31	1P: $85-$310	2P: $85-$310

Location: I-87, exit 22, 0.5 mi s; center; on Lake George. 370 Canada St 12845. **Fax:** 518/668-5546. **Facility:** 100 units. 95 one-bedroom standard units. 5 one-bedroom suites, some with kitchens. 1-2 stories (no elevator), exterior corridors. **Parking:** on-site. **Terms:** open 5/1-10/31, cancellation fee imposed. **Amenities:** voice mail, safes, irons, hair dryers. Some: DVD players. **Dining:** 7 am-noon. **Pool(s):** heated outdoor. **Leisure Activities:** rental paddleboats, fishing, barbecue grills, picnic tables, shuffleboard. Fee: canoes, boat dock, rowboats, kayaks, game room. **Cards:** AX, DS, MC, VI.

SOME UNITS

MOHAWK MOTEL & COTTAGES

Motel

Phone: 518/668-2143   **9**

6/22-9/3	1P: $89-$149	2P: $119-$179	XP: $10	F18
5/1-6/21 & 9/4-10/9	1P: $59-$89	2P: $69-$129	XP: $10	F18
10/10-4/30	1P: $45-$89	2P: $49-$119	XP: $10	F18

Location: I-87, exit 22, 0.3 mi s on US 9/SR 9N. 435 Canada St 12845. **Fax:** 518/668-3025. **Facility:** 23 units. 17 one-bedroom standard units, some with efficiencies and/or whirlpools. 6 cottages ($159-$425). 2 stories (no elevator), exterior corridors. **Parking:** on-site, winter plug-ins. **Terms:** 2 night minimum stay, 14 day cancellation notice, weekly rates available, 5% service charge. **Amenities:** voice mail. **Pool(s):** heated indoor. **Leisure Activities:** whirlpool, playground, basketball, volleyball. **Guest Services:** wireless Internet. **Business Services:** fax (fee). **Cards:** DS, MC, VI.

SOME UNITS

(See map and index starting on p. 330)

MOTEL MONTREAL   Phone: (518)668-5439   **8**

(AAA) (SAVE)

	7/1-9/7	1P: $85-$125	2P: $85-$125	XP: $10	F15
	5/10-6/30	1P: $49-$85	2P: $49-$109	XP: $10	F15
	9/8-10/16	1P: $49-$85	2P: $49-$95	XP: $10	F15

Motel   **Location:** I-87, exit 22, 0.3 mi s on US 9/SR 9N, then just e. 3 Lake Ave 12845. Fax: 518/668-5439. **Facility:** 40 units. 39 one-bedroom standard units. 1 two-bedroom suite ($975-$1450) with kitchen. 1-2 stories, exterior corridors. *Bath:* combo or shower only. **Parking:** on-site. **Terms:** open 5/10-10/16, 7 day cancellation notice-fee imposed. **Amenities:** voice mail. **Pool(s):** heated outdoor. **Leisure Activities:** grills, picnic tables. **Guest Services:** wireless Internet. **Cards:** DS, MC, VI. **Free Special Amenities:** early check-in/late check-out and room upgrade (subject to availability with advance reservations).** (See color ad p 340)*

SOME UNITS

🅢🄳 〽 ➰ / ⊠ 🔌 / FEE

QUALITY INN   *Book great rates at AAA.com*   Phone: (518)668-3525   **16**

(AAA) (SAVE)

| | 5/1-9/8 [ECP] | 1P: $79-$199 | 2P: $79-$199 | XP: $15 | F18 |
| | 9/9-4/30 [ECP] | 1P: $69-$159 | 2P: $69-$159 | XP: $15 | F18 |

Motel   **Location:** I-87, exit 21, 1 mi n on US 9/SR 9N. 57 Canada St 12845. Fax: 518/668-3598. **Facility:** 54 one-bedroom standard units. 2 stories (no elevator), exterior corridors. **Parking:** on-site. **Terms:** check-in 4 pm, 2-3 night minimum stay - seasonal, 5 day cancellation notice-fee imposed. **Amenities:** high-speed Internet, voice mail, safes, irons, hair dryers. **Pool(s):** heated outdoor. **Leisure Activities:** whirlpool, exercise room. *Fee:* game room. **Guest Services:** valet laundry, wireless Internet. **Business Services:** PC. **Cards:** AX, CB, DC, DS, JC, MC, VI. **Free Special Amenities:** expanded continental breakfast and high-speed Internet.** (See color ad p 342)*

SOME UNITS

🅢🄳 ➰ ⊠ 👤 🔌 🔌 🖥 / ⊠ /

RAMADA LAKE GEORGE   *Book at AAA.com*   Phone: (518)668-4141   **24**

🔻🔺🔻🔺   5/1-10/31 [CP]   1P: $69-$139   2P: $69-$139   XP: $10   F15

Small-scale Hotel   **Location:** I-87, exit 21, just e. 2447 SR 9N 12845 (547 Aviation Rd, QUEENSBURY, 12804). Fax: 518/668-2075. **Facility:** 88 one-bedroom standard units, some with whirlpools. 2 stories (no elevator), interior corridors. **Parking:** on-site. **Terms:** open 5/1-10/31, cancellation fee imposed, package plans. **Amenities:** voice mail, irons, hair dryers. **Pool(s):** outdoor. **Business Services:** fax (fee). **Cards:** AX, DC, DS, MC, VI.

SOME UNITS

(ASK) 🅢🄳 ♿M ➰ ⟲ 📹 🔌 🖨 🖥 / ⊠ /

(See map and index starting on p. 330)

ROARING BROOK RANCH & TENNIS RESORT
Phone: (518)668-5767 [25]

6/29-9/2 [MAP]	2P: $208-$218	XP: $52	D8
5/25-6/28 & 9/3-10/7 [MAP]	2P: $168-$178	XP: $52	D8

Resort
Small-scale Hotel
Location: I-87, exit 21, 1 mi s. Rt 9N S 12845 (Lake George 3). Fax: 518/668-4019. **Facility:** This family-oriented resort, a sprawling complex on spacious grounds, is in a mountain setting away from the hubbub of the village. 135 units. 118 one-bedroom standard units. 17 one-bedroom suites ($218-$264). 1-2 stories (no elevator), interior/exterior corridors. **Parking:** on-site. **Terms:** open 5/25-10/7, 10 day cancellation notice, weekly rates available, package plans. **Dining:** 8 am-8 pm, cocktails. **Pool(s):** 2 outdoor, heated indoor. **Leisure Activities:** saunas, 5 tennis courts (2 lighted), pool tables, children's counselor 7/1-8/31, archery, hiking trails, horseback riding, playground, exercise room, basketball, shuffleboard, volleyball. *Fee:* riding instruction, massage, horseshoes, game room. **Guest Services:** gift shop, coin laundry, area transportation-Lake George Bus Station. **Business Services:** conference facilities. **Cards:** AX, MC, VI. *(See color ad p 342)*

SOME UNITS

STILL BAY RESORT
Phone: 518/668-2584 [1]

6/22-9/3	2P: $150-$205	
5/25-6/21 & 9/4-10/7	2P: $90-$125	

Motel
Location: I-87, exit 22, 3 mi n on SR 9N. Located on the lake. 3458 Lake Shore Dr 12845 (PO Box 333, DIAMOND POINT, 12824). Fax: 518/668-3880. **Facility:** 24 units. 18 one- and 4 two-bedroom standard units, some with efficiencies. 1 two-bedroom suite ($950-$1650). 1 cottage ($950-$1650). 2 stories (no elevator), exterior corridors. *Bath:* combo or shower only. **Parking:** on-site. **Terms:** open 5/25-10/7, office hours 9 am-9 pm, 10 day cancellation notice, weekly rates available. **Leisure Activities:** limited beach access, paddleboats, boat dock, fishing, lawn games, grills, picnic tables. **Cards:** MC, VI. **Free Special Amenities:** local telephone calls and high-speed Internet.

SOME UNITS

SUPER 8 LAKE GEORGE DOWNTOWN *Book at AAA.com*
Phone: (518)668-2470 [20]

6/1-9/12	1P: $67-$245	2P: $67-$245	XP: $10	F17
5/1-5/31	1P: $49-$139	2P: $49-$139	XP: $10	F17
9/13-4/30	1P: $49-$129	2P: $49-$129	XP: $10	F17

Motel
Location: I-87, exit 21, 0.4 mi n. 2159 SR 9 (Canada St) 12845 (PO Box 448). Fax: 518/668-5355. **Facility:** 54 one-bedroom standard units, some with efficiencies. 1-2 stories (no elevator), exterior corridors. **Parking:** on-site, winter plug-ins. **Terms:** 3 day cancellation notice-fee imposed, [CP] meal plan available. **Amenities:** voice mail, hair dryers. **Pool(s):** heated outdoor. **Leisure Activities:** playground, basketball. **Guest Services:** wireless Internet. **Cards:** AX, DS, MC, VI.

SOME UNITS

SURFSIDE ON THE LAKE
Phone: 518/668-2442 [12]

7/13-9/2	1P: $89-$245	2P: $89-$245	XP: $10	F12
6/14-7/12	1P: $69-$190	2P: $69-$190	XP: $10	F12
5/1-6/13	1P: $46-$165	2P: $46-$165	XP: $10	F12
9/3-11/4	1P: $46-$155	2P: $46-$155	XP: $10	F12

Small-scale Hotel **Location:** I-87, exit 22, 0.3 mi s on US 9/SR 9N. Located on the lake. 400 Canada St 12845. Fax: 518/668-3202. **Facility:** 144 units. 117 one-bedroom standard units, some with efficiencies. 11 one-bedroom suites ($95-$255) with efficiencies. 16 cabins. 1-2 stories, interior/exterior corridors. *Bath:* combo or shower only. **Parking:** on-site. **Terms:** open 5/1-11/4, 2-3 night minimum stay - weekends, 10 day cancellation notice-fee imposed, package plans. **Amenities:** irons, hair dryers. **Dining:** 7:30-11 am 6/1-9/1; hours may vary. **Pool(s):** heated outdoor. **Leisure Activities:** limited beach access, barbecue grills, playground. *Fee:* paddleboats. **Guest Services:** wireless Internet. **Business Services:** meeting rooms. **Cards:** AX, DS, MC, VI. *(See color ad below)*

SOME UNITS

(See map and index starting on p. 330)

TALL PINES MOTEL　　　　　　　　　　　　　　　　　　**Phone: 518/668-5122** 🔲27

AAA (SAVE)

7/1-8/31	2P: $115-$130	XP: $10
9/1-10/20	2P: $80-$120	XP: $10
5/1-6/30	2P: $75-$105	XP: $10

Motel

Location: I-87, exit 20, 1.5 mi n; exit 21, 2 mi s. 1747 SR 9 12845 (1747 US 9). Fax: 518/668-5128. **Facility:** 26 one-bedroom standard units. 1-2 stories, exterior corridors. **Parking:** on-site. **Terms:** open 5/1-10/20, office hours 8 am-10 pm, 10 day cancellation notice-fee imposed, no pets allowed (owner's pet on premises). **Pool(s):** heated outdoor, wading. **Leisure Activities:** sauna, whirlpools, picnic tables, barbecue grills, playground, basketball. **Cards:** AX, DS, MC, VI. **Free Special Amenities: local telephone calls.**

SOME UNITS

🏊 ⊗ ⊠ 🅱 / 📺 /

TRAVELODGE OF LAKE GEORGE　　*Book great rates at AAA.com*　　**Phone: (518)668-5421** 🔲23

AAA (SAVE)

5/19-10/9　　　　1P: $84-$168　　　　2P: $84-$168　　　　XP: $15　　　　F16

Motel

Location: I-87, exit 21, just s. 2011 SR 9 12845. Fax: 518/668-2696. **Facility:** 100 units. 99 one-bedroom standard units. 1 one-bedroom suite. 2 stories, exterior corridors. *Bath:* combo or shower only. **Parking:** on-site. **Terms:** open 5/19-10/9, cancellation fee imposed, [BP] meal plan available, small pets only ($20 fee, with prior approval). **Amenities:** safes, irons, hair dryers. **Dining:** 6:30-11 am; hours may vary, beer only. **Pool(s):** outdoor. **Leisure Activities:** playground. **Guest Services:** valet laundry. **Cards:** AX, CB, DC, DS, JC, MC, VI. **Free Special Amenities: continental breakfast and high-speed Internet.**

SOME UNITS

🆂 ⓕ 🍴 🏊 🐾 / ⊠ 🅱 📺 📶 /
　　　FEE

WINGATE INN LAKE GEORGE　　　　　　　　　　　　　　**Phone: 518/668-4884**

(fyi)

Under construction, scheduled to open May 2007. **Location:** I-87, exit 21, 0.3 mi n on SR 9N, then just n. 4054 SR 9L 12845 (PO Box 432). **Planned Amenities:** 96 units, coffeemakers, microwaves, refrigerators, pool.

Small-scale Hotel

──────── **WHERE TO DINE** ────────

ADIRONDACK PUB & BREWERY　　**Lunch:** $7-$11　　**Dinner:** $8-$21　　**Phone:** 518/668-0002　🔲9

American

Location: I-87, exit 21, 1 mi n on US 9/SR 9N. 33 Canada St 12845. **Hours:** Open 5/1-10/31; 11:30 am-10 pm. **Reservations:** not accepted. **Features:** Renovated building made to look like an Adirondack lodge. Pub fare and craft-brewed ales on premises. Casual dress; cocktails. **Parking:** on-site. **Cards:** AX, DS, MC, VI.

♿M

EAST COVE RESTAURANT　　　　　　**Dinner:** $8-$26　　　　　**Phone:** 518/668-5265　🔲10

AAA American

Location: 0.8 mi e. 3873 Rt 9L 12845. **Hours:** 5 pm-10 pm, Sun from 11 am. Closed: Mon 4/1-11/1. **Reservations:** suggested. **Features:** Informal dining in a rustic log cabin, East Cove serves a great American fare. One can enjoy early bird specials such as prime rib and then top it off with a great slice of carrot cake. Casual dress; cocktails. **Parking:** on-site. **Cards:** AX, CB, DC, DS, MC, VI.

🍸

THE GEORGIAN DINING ROOM　　**Lunch:** $6-$14　　**Dinner:** $17-$30　　**Phone:** 518/668-5401　🔲3

American

Location: I-87, exit 22, 0.5 mi s on US 9/SR 9N; in The Georgian. 384 Canada St 12845. **Hours:** Open 5/19-10/21; 7:30 am-10 pm; 7:30 am-1 & 5:30-9 pm 5/19-7/1. Closed major holidays. **Reservations:** suggested, in season. **Features:** The attractive dining room, as well as the luncheon patio, overlook Lake George. In addition to tableside-carved Chateaubriand and thick-cut prime rib, the restaurant serves tasty breakfast selections. Entertainers perform on summer nights. Dressy casual; cocktails. **Parking:** on-site. **Cards:** AX, DC, DS, MC, VI.

🍸

THE INN AT ERLOWEST　　　　　　**Dinner:** $26-$50　　　　　**Phone:** 518/668-5928　🔲1

Continental

Location: I-87, exit 22, 0.9 mi n on SR 9N. 3178 Lake Shore Dr 12845. **Hours:** 5:30 pm-8:30 pm. Closed: Mon & Tues. **Reservations:** suggested. **Features:** Overlooking Lake George, this restaurant was once a single-family home. It sits amid trees away from the road noise. The setting is peaceful and the decor beautiful. Dressy casual; cocktails. **Parking:** on-site. **Cards:** AX, DS, MC, VI.

J T KELLY'S　　　　　　　　　　**Dinner:** $16-$30　　　　　　**Phone:** 518/668-3165　🔲8

Steak & Seafood

Location: I-87, exit 21, 1 mi n. 48 Canada St 12845. **Hours:** Open 5/15-10/15; 4 pm-9 pm, Sat-10 pm. Closed: Tues 5/15-6/22. **Reservations:** accepted. **Features:** Serving up steak and seafood, J T Kelly's is a great place to have a meal. Families enjoy this local spot because it is only minutes from downtown Lake George where shopping and fun can be had. Casual dress; cocktails. **Parking:** on-site. **Cards:** AX, CB, DC, DS, MC, VI.

🍸 🚭

MARIO'S RESTAURANT　　　　　　**Dinner:** $9-$22　　　　　　**Phone:** 518/668-2665　🔲2

AAA Italian

Location: I-87, exit 22, 0.3 mi n, then 0.3 mi s on US 9/SR 9N. 429 Canada St 12845. **Hours:** Open 5/1-11/30 & 12/16-4/30; 3:30 pm-11 pm; also 8-11:30 am 7/1-8/31; 4:30 pm-close, Sun 3 pm-close 12/16-4/30. Closed: Tues & Wed 12/16-4/30. **Reservations:** suggested. **Features:** A favorite local restaurant that's been family-operated since 1954, Mario's serves a variety of dishes including steak, chicken and seafood. Hearty portions of pasta, veal and chops can also be found on the menu. Casual dress; cocktails. **Parking:** on-site. **Cards:** AX, CB, DC, DS, MC, VI.

🍸 🚭

SHORELINE RESTAURANT　　　　**Lunch:** $6-$10　　**Dinner:** $11-$33　　**Phone:** 518/668-2875　🔲5

American

Location: At the foot of Kurosaka Ln; center. 4 Kurosaka Ln 12845. **Hours:** Open 5/1-10/31 & 4/20-4/30; 11 am-10 pm, Fri & Sat-11 pm. **Reservations:** accepted. **Features:** Overlooking the lake, the contemporary dining room is handsome and casual, while the seasonal terrace is warm and breezy. Among oven-cooked and grilled entrees are inventive chicken selections. The Sunday breakfast buffet is particularly popular. Casual dress; cocktails. **Parking:** on-site. **Cards:** AX, MC, VI.

🍸 🚭

(See map and index starting on p. 330)

SJ GARCIA'S

Mexican

Lunch: $6-$15   Dinner: $6-$20   Phone: 518/668-5111   ⑥
Location: On US 9; center. 192 Canada St 12845. **Hours:** noon-10 pm. Closed: 11/22, 12/25. **Reservations:** accepted. **Features:** The downtown restaurant maintains a fun, festive atmosphere and offers outdoor seating in the summer. Plenty of combination dishes lead into delicious flan for dessert. Casual dress; cocktails. **Parking:** street. **Cards:** AX, DC, MC, VI.

SOPRANOS

Italian

Lunch: $6-$18   Dinner: $6-$18   Phone: 518/668-4379   ⑦
Location: On US 9/SR 9N; center. 157 Canada St 12845. **Hours:** 11:30 am-11 pm. Closed: 1/1, 11/22, 12/24-12/26. **Features:** There's a "pasta fa u" on the menu at the casual eatery. For those in the mood for something else, the joint also prepares "fuhgeddaboutit" heroes and New York-style pizza, including the "stuffed trunk," "godfather" and "empty suit." Everyone here is treated like a "goomba". Casual dress. **Parking:** street. **Cards:** MC, VI.

TASTE OF POLAND

Polish

Lunch: $8-$19   Dinner: $8-$19   Phone: 518/668-4386   ④
Location: I-87, exit 22, 0.4 mi s on US 9/SR 9N. 375 Canada St 12845. **Hours:** 8 am-10 pm; from 5 pm 11/1-4/30. **Reservations:** accepted. **Features:** With the feel of a cozy cottage, the restaurant presents a large menu of Bavarian-influenced Polish food. Among choices are pierogies, potato pancakes, kielbasa and a variety of soups and salads. A favorite is the "taste of Poland," a sampler of menu selections. Authenticity is seen even in the beverage selections, which include traditional Polish juices. Casual dress; beer & wine only. **Parking:** on-site. **Cards:** AX, DC, DS, MC, VI.

LAKE GROVE pop. 10,250

———— WHERE TO DINE ————

JOHN HARVARD'S BREWHOUSE

American

Lunch: $7-$10   Dinner: $8-$18   Phone: 631/979-2739
Location: On SR 347 (Nesconset Hwy); in parking lot of Smith Haven Mall. 2093 Smith Haven Plaza 11755. **Hours:** 11:30 am-midnight, Fri & Sat-1 am. Closed: 12/25. **Features:** Known for their onsite micro-brewery, diners may enjoy one of the 8 freshly brewed lagers or ales as they view the production of the beer through a glass wall in the dining room. The recipe for the beer is believed to have originated from William Shakespeare and brought to America in 1637 by John Harvard, after whom Harvard University is named. The menu offers chicken sandwiches and burgers as well as some home-style favorites such as grilled meatloaf and chicken pot pie. Casual dress; cocktails. **Parking:** on-site. **Cards:** AX, DC, DS, MC, VI.

LAKE LUZERNE pop. 2,240   (See map and index starting on p. 330)—*See also ADIRONDACK MOUNTAINS.*

———— WHERE TO STAY ————

LAMPLIGHT INN BED & BREAKFAST

Historic Bed
& Breakfast

Phone: (518)696-5294

	2P: $135-$239	XP: $35
7/25-9/2 [BP]		
5/1-7/24 & 9/3-10/31 [BP]	2P: $119-$219	XP: $35
11/1-4/30 [BP]	2P: $110-$199	XP: $35

Location: I-87, exit 21, 10.2 mi s on SR 9N. 231 Lake Ave (PO Box 130, 12846-0130). Fax: 518/696-4914. **Facility:** Themed rooms are featured at this 1890 hilltop home; furnished with antiques, it offers a sunny breakfast room and spacious traditional parlor area. Smoke free premises. 13 units. 6 one-bedroom standard units. 7 one-bedroom suites, some with whirlpools. 1-2 stories (no elevator); interior corridors. *Bath:* combo or shower only. **Parking:** on-site. **Terms:** 2-3 night minimum stay - weekends, age restrictions may apply, 14 day cancellation notice, package plans. **Amenities:** voice mail. *Some:* hair dryers. **Dining:** Sunday brunch 10:30 am-noon 5/15-10/15. **Leisure Activities:** cross country skiing, hiking trails. **Guest Services:** gift shop. **Cards:** AX, MC, VI. **Free Special Amenities:** full breakfast and local telephone calls.

SOME UNITS

LUZERNE COURT

Motel

Phone: 518/696-2734

| 5/15-10/15 | 2P: $75-$180 | XP: $15 | F12 |

Location: I-87, exit 21, 8.7 mi s on SR 9N. 508 Lake Ave 12846. Fax: 518/696-3290. **Facility:** 10 one-bedroom standard units, some with efficiencies. 1 story, exterior corridors. *Bath:* combo or shower only. **Parking:** on-site. **Terms:** open 5/15-10/15, 2-3 night minimum stay - seasonal and/or weekends, 14 day cancellation notice-fee imposed. **Dining:** 7:30-11 am 7/1-9/6. **Pool(s):** outdoor. **Cards:** AX, DS, MC, VI.

SOME UNITS

PINE POINT COTTAGES & MOTEL

Cottage

Phone: (518)696-3015   ⑥④

| 6/16-9/4 | 1P: $78-$86 | 2P: $78-$86 | XP: $5 |
| 5/15-6/15 & 9/5-10/15 | 1P: $71-$78 | 2P: $71-$78 | XP: $5 |

Location: I-87, exit 21, 4.9 mi s on SR 9N. Located in a quiet area. 1369 Lake Ave 12846. Fax: 518/696-3015. **Facility:** 18 units. 10 one-bedroom standard units. 8 cottages ($89-$125). 1 story, exterior corridors. *Bath:* shower only. **Parking:** on-site. **Terms:** open 5/15-10/15, 14 day cancellation notice-fee imposed. **Amenities:** hair dryers. **Leisure Activities:** paddleboats, boat dock, fishing, rowboats, barbecue grills, picnic tables, table tennis, horseshoes, shuffleboard, volleyball. **Cards:** AX, DS, MC, VI.

SOME UNITS

———— WHERE TO DINE ————

PAPA'S ICE CREAM PARLOR RESTAURANT

American

Lunch: $3-$11   Dinner: $3-$11   Phone: 518/696-3667
Location: Center. 29 Main St 12846. **Hours:** Open 5/15-9/4; 8 am-10 pm. **Reservations:** accepted. **Features:** The classic, old-fashioned ice cream parlor sits on the banks of the Hudson River and offers outdoor seating on the deck. On the menu is mostly simple fare, such as sandwiches and salads, as well as a few dinner platters. Don't leave without trying the scrumptious ice cream desserts. Breakfast is served all day, and a barbershop quartet entertains guests on Thursday. Casual dress. **Parking:** on-site and street. **Cards:** MC, VI.

(See map and index starting on p. 330)

THE WATERHOUSE
Lunch: $5-$10   Dinner: $13-$28   Phone: 518/696-3115

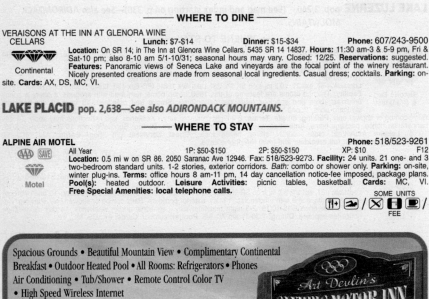

American

Location: On SR 9N; center. 85 Lake Ave 12846. **Hours:** 11:30 am-3:30 & 4-10 pm. **Reservations:** suggested. **Features:** Beyond the characterless walls of the exterior, with its neon Michelob sign, hides a magical little room aglow with the sparkle of lights and the charm of walls filled with antique knickknacks and pictures. The cozy place prepares good food ranging from the simple to the creative. Casual dress; cocktails. **Parking:** on-site. **Cards:** AX, MC, VI.

LAKEMONT

——————— **WHERE TO STAY** ———————

THE INN AT GLENORA WINE CELLARS   Phone: (607)243-9500

7/1-10/31	1P: $159-$299	2P: $159-$299	XP: $20	F12
5/1-6/30	1P: $149-$299	2P: $149-$299	XP: $20	F12
11/1-4/30	1P: $119-$239	2P: $119-$239	XP: $20	F12

Small-scale Hotel **Location:** On SR 14. 5435 Rt 14 14837. Fax: 607/243-9595. **Facility:** Smoke free premises. 30 one-bedroom standard units, some with whirlpools. 1-2 stories, interior corridors. *Bath:* combo or shower only. **Parking:** on-site. **Terms:** cancellation fee imposed. **Amenities:** high-speed Internet, voice mail, irons, hair dryers. *Some:* DVD players. **Dining:** Veraisons at The Inn at Glenora Wine Cellars, see separate listing. **Guest Services:** complimentary evening beverages, wireless Internet. **Business Services:** meeting rooms, PC. **Cards:** AX, DS, MC, VI.

SOUTH GLENORA TREE FARM BED & BREAKFAST   Phone: 607/243-7414

7/1-8/31 [BP]	1P: $119-$135	2P: $119-$135	XP: $40
5/1-6/30 [BP]	1P: $107-$135	2P: $107-$135	XP: $40
9/1-4/30 [BP]	1P: $99-$135	2P: $99-$135	XP: $40

Bed & Breakfast **Location:** SR 14, 1 mi w via S Glenora Rd, follow signs. Located in a quiet area. 546 S Glenora Rd 14837. Fax: 607/243-7414. **Facility:** Originally a barn, this renovated B&B offers country-themed rooms and plenty of acreage in which to explore and bird-watch. Smoke free premises. 5 one-bedroom standard units. 1 story, interior/exterior corridors. *Bath:* combo or shower only. **Parking:** on-site. **Terms:** 14 day cancellation notice-fee imposed. **Amenities:** video library, hair dryers. **Leisure Activities:** fishing, hiking trails. **Business Services:** fax. **Cards:** DS, MC, VI.

SOME UNITS

——————— **WHERE TO DINE** ———————

VERAISONS AT THE INN AT GLENORA WINE
CELLARS   Lunch: $7-$14   Dinner: $15-$34   Phone: 607/243-9500

Continental

Location: On SR 14; in The Inn at Glenora Wine Cellars. 5435 SR 14 14837. **Hours:** 11:30 am-3 & 5-9 pm, Fri & Sat-10 pm; also 8-10 am 5/1-10/31; seasonal hours may vary. Closed: 12/25. **Reservations:** suggested. **Features:** Panoramic views of Seneca Lake and vineyards are the focal point of the winery restaurant. Nicely presented creations are made from seasonal local ingredients. Casual dress; cocktails. **Parking:** on-site. **Cards:** AX, DS, MC, VI.

LAKE PLACID pop. 2,638—See also *ADIRONDACK MOUNTAINS.*

——————— **WHERE TO STAY** ———————

ALPINE AIR MOTEL   Phone: 518/523-9261

All Year	1P: $50-$150	2P: $50-$150	XP: $10	F12

Motel **Location:** 0.5 mi w on SR 86. 2050 Saranac Ave 12946. Fax: 518/523-9273. **Facility:** 24 units. 21 one- and 3 two-bedroom standard units. 1-2 stories, exterior corridors. *Bath:* combo or shower only. **Parking:** on-site, winter plug-ins. **Terms:** office hours 8 am-11 pm, 14 day cancellation notice-fee imposed, package plans. **Pool(s):** heated outdoor. **Leisure Activities:** picnic tables, basketball. **Cards:** MC, VI. **Free Special Amenities:** local telephone calls.

SOME UNITS
FEE

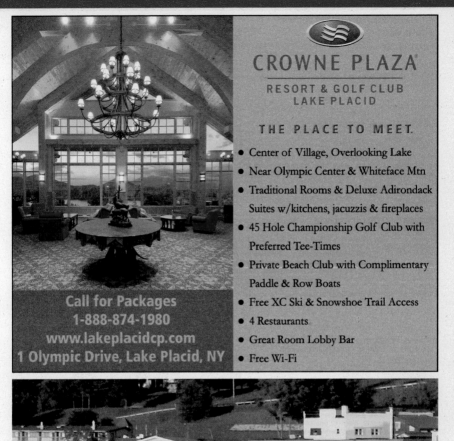

ART DEVLIN'S OLYMPIC MOTOR INN, INC.

Phone: 518/523-3700

(AAA) (SAVE)
Motel

	1P: $74-$168	2P: $74-$168	XP: $10
6/22-9/2			
5/1-6/21 & 9/3-4/30	1P: $64-$168	2P: $64-$168	XP: $10

Location: 0.5 mi e on SR 86. 2764 Main St 12946. Fax: 518/523-3893. **Facility:** 44 one-bedroom standard units. 1-2 stories (no elevator), exterior corridors. **Parking:** on-site. **Terms:** 1-3 night minimum stay - seasonal and/or weekends, 14 day cancellation notice, pets (dogs only). **Amenities:** hair dryers. **Pool(s):** heated outdoor, wading. **Guest Services:** wireless Internet. **Business Services:** meeting rooms. **Cards:** AX, DC, DS, MC, VI. **Free Special Amenities:** local telephone calls and high-speed Internet. *(See color ad p 346)*

SOME UNITS

CARRIAGE HOUSE MOTOR INN

Phone: (518)523-2260

Motel

5/25-10/20 & 12/21-4/30	1P: $70-$200	2P: $80-$200	XP: $10	F18
10/21-12/20	1P: $60-$130	2P: $70-$130	XP: $10	F18
5/1-5/24	1P: $60-$110	2P: $70-$110	XP: $10	F18

Location: 3 mi s on SR 73 from jct SR 86. 5825 Cascade Rd 12946 (PO Box 527). Fax: 518/523-4160. **Facility:** 17 one-bedroom standard units. 1-2 stories (no elevator), interior/exterior corridors. **Parking:** on-site, winter plug-ins. **Terms:** cancellation fee imposed, package plans. **Amenities:** hair dryers. **Pool(s):** outdoor. **Cards:** AX, DC, DS, MC, VI.

SOME UNITS

COMFORT INN ON LAKE PLACID

Book great rates at AAA.com

Phone: (518)523-9555

(AAA) (SAVE)
Small-scale Hotel

| All Year | 1P: $100-$200 | 2P: $100-$200 | XP: $10 | F18 |

Location: 0.5 mi w on SR 86. 2125 Saranac Ave 12946. Fax: 518/523-4765. **Facility:** 92 units. 88 one- and 1 two-bedroom standard units. 3 one-bedroom suites, some with kitchens. 1-2 stories (no elevator), interior/exterior corridors. **Parking:** on-site, winter plug-ins. **Terms:** cancellation fee imposed, [ECP] meal plan available, package plans. **Amenities:** high-speed Internet, voice mail, irons, hair dryers. *Some:* DVD players. **Dining:** 6:15 am-10 pm, cocktails. **Pool(s):** heated indoor. **Leisure Activities:** whirlpool, canoeing, paddleboats, boat dock, fishing, rowboats, 2 tennis courts, cross country skiing, picnic areas with charcoal grills, hiking trails. **Guest Services:** complimentary and valet laundry, wireless Internet. **Business Services:** conference facilities. **Cards:** AX, CB, DC, DS, JC, MC, VI. **Free Special Amenities:** expanded continental breakfast and local telephone calls.

SOME UNITS

CROWNE PLAZA RESORT & GOLF CLUB LAKE PLACID

Book great rates at AAA.com

Phone: (518)523-2556

(AAA) (SAVE)
Small-scale Hotel

6/25-9/2	1P: $139-$299	2P: $139-$299	XP: $10	F19
9/3-3/3	1P: $109-$299	2P: $109-$299	XP: $10	F19
5/1-6/24	1P: $109-$209	2P: $109-$209	XP: $10	F19
3/4-4/30	1P: $99-$199	2P: $99-$199	XP: $10	F19

Location: Downtown. 1 Olympic Dr 12946. Fax: 518/523-9410. **Facility:** 208 units. 193 one-bedroom standard units. 13 one-bedroom suites, some with whirlpools. 2 cottages with whirlpools. 2-4 stories, interior/exterior corridors. **Parking:** on-site, winter plug-ins. **Terms:** check-in 4 pm, 30 day cancellation notice-fee imposed, [BP] meal plan available, package plans, pets ($10 fee). **Amenities:** video games (fee), CD players, voice mail, irons, hair dryers. **Dining:** 4 restaurants, 7 am-10 pm, cocktails, also, Veranda Restaurant, see separate listing. **Pool(s):** heated indoor. **Leisure Activities:** sauna, whirlpool, paddleboats, 7 tennis courts, cross country skiing, hiking trails, exercise room. *Fee:* golf-45 holes. **Guest Services:** valet and coin laundry, wireless Internet. **Business Services:** conference facilities. **Cards:** AX, CB, DC, DS, JC. MC. VI. **Free Special Amenities:** newspaper and high-speed Internet. *(See color ad p 347)*

FEE

ECONO LODGE

Book great rates at AAA.com

Phone: (518)523-2817

(AAA) (SAVE)
Small-scale Hotel

5/25-10/20 & 12/21-4/30	1P: $70-$200	2P: $80-$200	XP: $10	F18
10/21-12/20	1P: $60-$130	2P: $70-$130	XP: $10	F18
5/1-5/24	1P: $60-$110	2P: $70-$110	XP: $10	F18

Location: 3 mi s on SR 73 from jct SR 86. 5828 Cascade Rd 12946 (PO Box 527). Fax: 518/523-4160. **Facility:** 61 one-bedroom standard units. 2 stories (no elevator), interior/exterior corridors. **Parking:** on-site. **Terms:** cancellation fee imposed, package plans. **Amenities:** *Some:* irons, hair dryers. **Pool(s):** heated indoor. **Leisure Activities:** whirlpool. **Guest Services:** coin laundry. **Business Services:** meeting rooms. **Cards:** AX, DC, DS, JC, MC, VI. **Free Special Amenities:** continental breakfast and local telephone calls.

SOME UNITS

FEE

GOLDEN ARROW LAKESIDE RESORT

Phone: (518)523-3353

(AAA) (SAVE)
Small-scale Hotel

| All Year | 1P: $89-$300 | 2P: $89-$300 | XP: $12 |

Location: On SR 86; center. 2559 Main St 12946. Fax: 518/523-8063. **Facility:** Smoke free premises. 152 units. 137 one-bedroom standard units, some with efficiencies and/or whirlpools. 15 one-bedroom suites ($159-$500) with whirlpools, some with efficiencies or kitchens. 2-5 stories, interior corridors. **Parking:** on-site, winter plug-ins. **Terms:** 2-4 night minimum stay - weekends, 30 day cancellation notice, [MAP] meal plan available, package plans, pets ($50 fee, in designated units). **Amenities:** video games, high-speed Internet, voice mail, irons, hair dryers. *Some:* DVD players, safes. **Dining:** 7 am-9:30 pm, cocktails, nightclub. **Pool(s):** heated indoor, wading. **Leisure Activities:** saunas, whirlpool, steamroom, canoeing, paddleboats, boat dock, fishing, kayaks, rowboats, downhill & cross country skiing, snowmobiling, ice skating, pool table, table tennis, playground. *Fee:* racquetball court, massage, game room. **Guest Services:** gift shop, valet and coin laundry, airport transportation-Saranac Lake Airport. **Business Services:** conference facilities. **Cards:** AX, CB, DC, DS, MC, VI. **Free Special Amenities:** local telephone calls and early check-in/late check-out. *(See color ad p 347)*

SOME UNITS

FEE

HILTON LAKE PLACID RESORT   *Book great rates at AAA.com*   **Phone:** (518)523-4411

▼▼◇◇◇

	7/1-8/31	1P: $149-$289	2P: $149-$289	XP: $15	F18
	9/1-4/30	1P: $99-$289	2P: $99-$289	XP: $15	F18
	5/1-6/30	1P: $89-$269	2P: $89-$269	XP: $15	F18

Small-scale Hotel   **Location:** 0.3 mi w on SR 86. 1 Mirror Lake Dr 12946. Fax: 518/523-1120. **Facility:** 178 one-bedroom standard units. 2-5 stories, interior corridors. **Bath:** combo or shower only. **Parking:** on-site, winter plug-ins. **Terms:** check-in 4 pm, 2 night minimum stay - weekends, 7 day cancellation notice-fee imposed, [BP] & [MAP] meal plans available, package plans, pets ($25 deposit). **Amenities:** video games, voice mail, irons, hair dryers. **Dining:** Terrace Room Restaurant, see separate listing. **Pool(s):** 2 heated outdoor, 2 heated indoor. **Leisure Activities:** whirlpools, paddleboats, fishing, exercise room. *Fee:* game room. **Guest Services:** valet laundry, wireless Internet. **Business Services:** conference facilities. **Cards:** AX, CB, DC, DS, JC, MC, VI.

SOME UNITS

🏨 🍽 🍸 🔊ℳ 🛗 📶 🏊 🖅 📷 🖨 / 🖂 🛡 🖵 /
FEE

MAPLE LEAF INN   **Phone:** 518/523-2471

(AAA) [SAVE]
▼▼◇◇
▼▼ ◇

| | All Year | 1P: $70-$350 | 2P: $70-$350 | XP: $25 | F12 |

Motel   **Location:** 0.5 mi w on SR 86. 2234 Saranac Ave 12946. Fax: 518/523-5378. **Facility:** 18 units. 15 one-bedroom standard units, some with efficiencies and/or whirlpools. 3 one-bedroom suites, some with efficiencies and/or whirlpools. 1-2 stories (no elevator), interior/exterior corridors. **Parking:** on-site. **Terms:** 2 night minimum stay - weekends, 14 day cancellation notice-fee imposed, package plans. **Amenities:** irons, hair dryers. **Pool(s):** heated outdoor. **Leisure Activities:** picnic & charcoal grill area. **Cards:** AX, DS, MC, VI.

Free Special Amenities: local telephone calls.

SOME UNITS

🔊🅳 🍽 🏊 🖅 📷 🛡 🖵 / 🖵 /

MIRROR LAKE INN RESORT AND SPA   *Book great rates at AAA.com*   **Phone:** (518)523-2544

(AAA) [SAVE]

	5/1-10/7	1P: $300-$650	2P: $300-$650	XP: $65	D18
	12/22-4/30	1P: $250-$650	2P: $250-$650	XP: $65	D18
	10/8-12/21	1P: $240-$650	2P: $240-$650	XP: $65	D18

▼▼▼◇◇ Small-scale Hotel   **Location:** Just off SR 86, 0.5 mi w. 77 Mirror Lake Dr 12946. Fax: 518/523-2871. **Facility:** Guests can enjoy views of Mirror Lake from the balconies of most guest rooms at this traditional resort. 128 units. 125 one- and 1 two-bedroom standard units, some with whirlpools. 1 two- and 1 three-bedroom suites ($420-$1275), some with efficiencies and/or whirlpools. 2-4 stories, interior/exterior corridors. **Parking:** on-site, winter plug-ins. **Terms:** 14 day cancellation notice, [BP] & [MAP] meal plans available, package plans, $7 service charge. **Amenities:** CD players, voice mail, safes, irons, hair dryers. *Some:* DVD players. **Dining:** 3 restaurants, 7:30 am-10 & 5:30-9 pm, Sat & Sun 7:30 am-11 & 5:30-9 pm, also, The View Restaurant, see separate listing. **Pool(s):** heated outdoor, heated indoor. **Leisure Activities:** sauna, whirlpool, canoeing, paddleboats, boat dock, fishing, rowboats, tennis court, cross country skiing, ice skating, guided snowshoe hikes, hiking trails, spa. **Guest Services:** gift shop. **Business Services:** conference facilities, fax (fee). **Cards:** AX, DC, DS, MC, VI.

SOME UNITS

🍽 🍸 🔊 🏊 🛗 🖅 🖂 🛡 / (VCR) /

MOUNTAIN VIEW INN   **Phone:** 518/523-2439

(AAA) [SAVE]
▼▼◇◇
▼▼ ◇

| | 6/20-10/31 & 12/1-4/1 | | 2P: $125-$155 | XP: $10 | F13 |
| | 5/15-6/19 | | 2P: $105-$125 | XP: $10 | F13 |

Motel   **Location:** On SR 86; center. 2548 Main St 12946. Fax: 518/523-8974. **Facility:** 18 one-bedroom standard units. 2-3 stories (no elevator), interior/exterior corridors. **Parking:** on-site. **Terms:** open 5/15-10/31 & 12/1-4/1, 2-5 night minimum stay - seasonal and/or weekends, 30 day cancellation notice, package plans. **Amenities:** hair dryers. **Leisure Activities:** beach privileges. **Cards:** AX, DC, DS, MC, VI.

Free Special Amenities: local telephone calls and high-speed Internet.

SOME UNITS

🔊🅳 🍽 🖅 🛡 / 🖵 🖵 /

THE NORTHWAY MOTEL   **Phone:** 518/523-3500

(AAA) [SAVE]
▼▼◇◇
▼▼ ◇

| | 6/21-10/31 & 12/15-3/31 | 1P: $85-$125 | 2P: $85-$125 | XP: $10 | F12 |
| | 5/1-6/20 | 1P: $65-$100 | 2P: $65-$100 | XP: $10 | F12 |

Motel   **Location:** On SR 86, 0.5 mi e of jct SR 73. 2795 Wilmington Rd 12946. **Facility:** 11 units. 9 one- and 2 two-bedroom standard units. 1-2 stories, exterior corridors. **Parking:** on-site. **Terms:** open 5/1-10/31 & 12/15-3/31, 2-3 night minimum stay - weekends, 7 day cancellation notice-fee imposed. **Pool(s):** outdoor. **Cards:** AX, DS, MC, VI. **Free Special Amenities:** local telephone calls and preferred room (subject to availability with advance reservations).

SOME UNITS

🏊 🖅 🅺 / 🛡 /
FEE

SWISS ACRES INN

Phone: (518)523-3040

All Year   2P: $58-$148   XP: $10   F12
Location: 1 mi w on SR 86. 1970 Saranac Ave 12946. Fax: 518/523-2196. **Facility:** 44 units. 33 one-bedroom standard units, some with efficiencies. 7 one-bedroom suites ($98-$219), some with efficiencies or kitchens. 4 cabins ($118-$249) with whirlpools. 1-2 stories (no elevator), interior/exterior corridors. *Bath:* combo or shower only. **Parking:** on-site, winter plug-ins. **Terms:** 7 day cancellation notice, [BP] meal plan available, package plans, pets ($15 fee). **Dining:** 7 am-11 pm, cocktails. **Pool(s):** heated outdoor. **Leisure Activities:** sauna, whirlpool, picnic tables, barbecue grill. **Business Services:** meeting rooms. **Cards:** MC, VI. **Free Special Amenities:** full breakfast and newspaper.

Small-scale Hotel

SOME UNITS

TOWN & COUNTRY MOTOR INN   *Book at AAA.com*

Phone: 518/523-9268

5/1-10/15 & 12/21-3/31   1P: $69-$79   2P: $69-$98   XP: $10   F10
10/16-12/20 & 4/1-4/30   1P: $59-$69   2P: $59-$69   XP: $10   F10
Location: 0.5 mi w on SR 86. 2200 Saranac Ave 12946. Fax: 518/523-8058. **Facility:** 24 units. 22 one-bedroom standard units. 1 one-bedroom suite ($150-$180) with kitchen. 1 cottage ($150-$180). 2 stories (no elevator), exterior corridors. **Parking:** on-site. **Terms:** 2-3 night minimum stay - seasonal and/or weekends, 10 day cancellation notice, package plans. **Pool(s):** heated outdoor. **Guest Services:** wireless Internet. **Cards:** MC, VI.

Motel

SOME UNITS

TOWN HOUSE LODGE "BY THE LAKE"

Phone: 518/523-2532

6/22-9/3   2P: $88-$155   XP: $10   F12
9/4-4/30   2P: $68-$155   XP: $10   F12
5/1-6/21   2P: $68-$88   XP: $10   F12
Location: 0.5 mi w on SR 86. 2267 Saranac Ave 12946. **Facility:** 25 units. 23 one-bedroom standard units. 2 two-bedroom suites ($98-$165). 1-2 stories (no elevator), exterior corridors. *Bath:* combo or shower only. **Parking:** on-site, winter plug-ins. **Terms:** 2-5 night minimum stay - seasonal and/or weekends, 15 day cancellation notice-fee imposed. **Amenities:** *Some:* hair dryers. **Pool(s):** heated outdoor, wading. **Leisure Activities:** *Fee:* game room. **Cards:** AX, MC, VI.

Motel

SOME UNITS

THE WHITEFACE LODGE   *Book great rates at AAA.com*

Phone: (518)523-0500

All Year   1P: $295-$1950   XP: $50   F18
Location: 1 mi w on SR 86. 7 Whiteface Inn Ln 12946. Fax: 518/523-0559. **Facility:** Relax in the peaceful setting of an Adirondack lodge with modern comforts, an indoor/outdoor pool and the look of a handmade property. 85 units. 13 one-bedroom standard units. 48 one-, 9 two- and 15 three-bedroom suites. *Bath:* combo or shower only. **Parking:** on-site. **Terms:** check-in 4 pm, 30 day cancellation notice-fee imposed. **Amenities:** video library, DVD players, high-speed Internet, dual phone lines, voice mail, safes, irons, hair dryers. **Pool(s):** heated outdoor, heated indoor. **Leisure Activities:** whirlpools, limited beach access, canoeing, paddleboats, 2 lighted tennis courts, sleigh rides, table tennis, ice skating, hiking trails, jogging, exercise room. *Fee:* downhill skiing, kayaks. **Guest Services:** sundries, complimentary and valet laundry, area transportation-downtown. **Business Services:** meeting rooms, PC. **Cards:** AX, DS, MC, VI. **Free Special Amenities:** local telephone calls and newspaper.

Large-scale Hotel

─────── WHERE TO DINE ───────

THE BOAT HOUSE

Dinner: $8-$20   **Phone:** 518/523-4822
Location: 1.5 mi n of jct SR 86. 89 Mirror Lake Dr 12946. **Hours:** 5 pm-10 pm. **Reservations:** suggested. **Features:** Along with a fine Continental menu, the eatery boasts a warm Adirondack ambience, spectacular views and sunsets and a covered deck extending over Mirror Lake. Selections range from juicy hamburgers and filet mignon to pasta and seafood dishes. For dessert, guests can prepare true Adirondack s'mores over an open flame at the table. Casual dress; cocktails. **Parking:** on-site. **Cards:** AX, DC, DS, MC, VI.

Continental

THE BROWN DOG CAFE & WINE BAR

Lunch: $6-$8   **Dinner:** $7-$32   **Phone:** 518/523-3036
Location: Downtown. 3 Main St 12946. **Hours:** 11 am-10 pm. Closed: 3/23, 11/22, 12/25; also last week of Nov. **Reservations:** accepted. **Features:** Don't let the carry-out aspect of this bistro-type establishment throw you. Fine creative dinners are served in the small restaurant portion at the rear, while traditional delicatessen fare is offered during the day. More than 50 wines are available by the glass. Saturday night wine dinners are popular. Casual dress; cocktails. **Parking:** street. **Cards:** AX, MC, VI.

American

CAFFE RUSTICA

Lunch: $8-$22   **Dinner:** $8-$22   **Phone:** 518/523-7511
Location: 1.1 mi w on SR 86. 1936 Saranac Ave 12946. **Hours:** 11 am-3 & 5-9 pm. Closed: Sun & for lunch Mon. **Features:** Located in a shopping center, this cozy caf?? will win you over. With its open floor plan and open kitchen you'll feel like one of the family. The chef prepares some creative dishes with shrimp, chicken or beef. Enjoy! Dressy casual; beer & wine only. **Parking:** on-site. **Cards:** AX, DS, MC, VI.

American

THE CHARCOAL PIT

Dinner: $11-$33   **Phone:** 518/523-3050
Location: 1 mi w. 100 Saranac Ave 12946. **Hours:** 5 pm-10 pm. Closed: 12/25; also Mon-Thurs 4/1-4/30 & 11/1-11/30. **Reservations:** accepted. **Features:** Located at the edge of picturesque Lake Placid Village, this restaurant has been family-owned and -operated since 1957. The variety of dishes offered assures that any craving will be met. Casual dress; cocktails. **Parking:** on-site. **Cards:** AX, CB, DC, DS, MC, VI.

American

DESPERADOS

Lunch: $6-$10   **Dinner:** $6-$10   **Phone:** 518/523-1507
Location: 0.5 mi w on SR 86. 97 Saranac Ave 12946. **Hours:** 11:30 am-9 pm, Sun-Tues from 4 pm. Closed: 4/8, 11/22, 12/25. **Features:** Hand-made nachos, big fat burritos and hot sauces! Add to this the bright, bold citrus colours of the interior and the rhythmic sounds of salsa and you will no doubt find yourself transported to the fine white sandy beaches and hot tropical sun of Mexico. And, well, if that doesn't do it, try a shot of one of the fifty premium brands of tequila that the owner keeps in stock. Casual dress; cocktails. **Parking:** on-site. **Cards:** MC, VI.

Tex-Mex

THE GREAT ADIRONDACK STEAK & SEAFOOD COMPANY & GREAT ADIRONDACK BREWING CO
Lunch: $5-$15   Dinner: $8-$20   Phone: 518/523-1629

Steak & Seafood

Location: Center. 34 Main St 12946. **Hours:** 11:30 am-9:30 pm; from 8:30 am 5/1-6/14; 8:30 am-10 pm 6/15-9/15 & 12/24-3/1. **Features:** In the heart of the village, the casual restaurant offers a little something for everyone, ranging from flavorful French onion soup to exquisite flatbread. An interesting story is behind the name of every beer made at the on-site microbrewery. Casual dress; cocktails. **Parking:** street. **Cards:** AX, CB, DC, DS, MC, VI.

GRILL 211
Lunch: $8-$15   Dinner: $10-$30   Phone: 518/523-5853

Steak House

Location: Downtown; across from Olympic Center. 211 Main St 12946. **Hours:** 5 pm-11 pm, Sat & Sun noon-4 & 5-11 pm. **Reservations:** accepted. **Features:** The name says it all. The grill gets a workout with steak, which is probably the most popular choice, and how you would like it prepared is up to you. The restaurant has plenty of options, so enjoy. Dressy casual; cocktails. **Parking:** on-site. **Cards:** AX, MC, VI.

LUNA LOCA
Lunch: $7-$20   Dinner: $7-$20   Phone: 518/523-1160

Tex-Mex

Location: 1.1 mi w on SR 86. 211 Saranac Ave 12946. **Hours:** 11:30 am-10 pm. Closed: 11/22, 12/25. **Reservations:** accepted. **Features:** Bring your appetite and you'll enjoy these hearty portions of several classic Mexican favorites as well as some new dishes that are sure to become classics. A happy and helpful staff round out the experience. Casual dress; cocktails. **Parking:** on-site. **Cards:** AX, MC, VI.

MYKONOS
Lunch: $7-$13   Dinner: $9-$20   Phone: 518/523-1164

Greek

Location: 0.5 mi w on SR 86. 38 Saranac Ave 12946. **Hours:** Open 5/1-10/31 & 12/1-3/31; 11:30 am-10 pm. Closed: Mon & Tues 12/1-3/31 & 5/1-5/31. **Reservations:** accepted. **Features:** The menu selections at Mykonos are varied and include not only the standard gyro and souflaki but many wonderful traditional appetizers and soups as well. If you're are not sure what to order, try one of the combination platters for a little sampling of their best Greek specialties. But, do come with your appetite, the servings are hardy. Casual dress; cocktails. **Parking:** on-site. **Cards:** AX, DC, DS, MC, VI.

NICOLA'S ON MAIN
Lunch: $8-$20   Dinner: $8-$32   Phone: 518/523-0198

Mediterranean

Location: Downtown; across from Olympic Center. 211 Main St 12946. **Hours:** 5 pm-11 pm; Sat & Sun from noon. **Reservations:** accepted. **Features:** The specialty here is the wood-fired pizza; with plenty of topping choices, it's very tasty. The menu is rounded out with several Mediterranean dishes. Casual dress; cocktails. **Parking:** on-site. **Cards:** AX, DS, MC, VI.

TERRACE ROOM RESTAURANT
Lunch: $7-$9   Dinner: $14-$32   Phone: 518/523-4411

American

Location: 0.3 mi w on SR 86; in Hilton Lake Placid Resort. 1 Mirror Lake Dr 12946. **Hours:** 7 am-10:30, noon-2 & 5:30-9 pm, Sun 11 am-2 & 5:30-9 pm; Sunday brunch. **Reservations:** suggested, for dinner. **Features:** The Terrace Room offers great American fare with a choice of buffet for breakfast and lunch. Casual dress; cocktails. **Parking:** on-site. **Cards:** AX, DC, DS, MC, VI.

VERANDA RESTAURANT
Dinner: $15-$30   Phone: 518/523-3339

Continental

Location: Downtown; in Crowne Plaza Resort & Golf Club Lake Placid. 1 Olympic Dr 12946. **Hours:** 5:30 pm-9:30 pm. Closed: 11/22, 12/24, 12/25; also Mon. **Reservations:** suggested. **Features:** Intimate dining rooms throughout the attractively restored house boast tasteful decor and afford lovely lake views. The casual fine-dining restaurant offers a nice selection of seafood, meat and fowl, along with a few pasta dishes, all thoughtfully presented. Outdoor terrace seating is a seasonal option. Casual dress; cocktails. **Parking:** on-site. **Cards:** AX, CB, DC, DS, MC, VI. **(See color ad p 347)**

THE VIEW RESTAURANT
Menu on AAA.com   Dinner: $16-$35   Phone: 518/523-2544

Regional American

Location: Just off SR 86, 0.5 mi w; in Mirror Lake Inn Resort and Spa. 77 Mirror Lake Dr 12946. **Hours:** 7:30 am-10 & 5:30-9 pm, Sat & Sun 7:30 am-11 & 5:30-9 pm. **Reservations:** suggested. **Features:** The one of the region's most elegant dining rooms is the place for a cozy tete-a-tete or a leisurely meal in the company of good friends. The cuisine here is creative, and even dishes on the spa menu are sure to please any palate. Casual dress; cocktails. **Parking:** on-site. **Cards:** AX, DC, DS, MC, VI. **Historic**

LANSING pop. 3,417—See also FINGER LAKES.

——— WHERE TO STAY ———

ECONO LODGE
Book great rates at AAA.com   Phone: (607)257-1400

Small-scale Hotel

5/1-8/31 [ECP]	1P: $75-$135	2P: $75-$135	XP: $10	F18
9/1-11/15 [ECP]	1P: $65-$125	2P: $65-$125	XP: $10	F18
11/16-4/30 [ECP]	1P: $55-$115	2P: $55-$115	XP: $10	F18

Location: SR 13, exit Triphammer Rd. Adjoins Cayuga Mall. 2303 N Triphammer Rd 14850. Fax: 607/257-6359. **Facility:** 72 one-bedroom standard units, some with whirlpools. 2 stories (no elevator); interior corridors. **Parking:** on-site, winter plug-ins. **Terms:** pets ($15 extra charge). **Guest Services:** valet laundry, wireless Internet. **Business Services:** meeting rooms, PC. **Cards:** AX, DC, DS, MC, VI.

SOME UNITS

ITHACA COURTYARD BY MARRIOTT
Book great rates at AAA.com   Phone: (607)330-1000

Small-scale Hotel

All Year   1P: $99-$309

Location: Jct SR 13 N and Warren Rd, just w to Brown Rd, just e. Located next to Tompkins County Airport. 29 Thornwood Dr 14850. Fax: 607/330-1500. **Facility:** Smoke free premises. 106 units. 99 one-bedroom standard units. 6 one- and 1 two-bedroom suites. 4 stories, interior corridors. *Bath:* combo or shower only. **Parking:** on-site. **Terms:** [BP] meal plan available. **Amenities:** video games (fee), high-speed Internet, dual phone lines, voice mail, irons, hair dryers. **Pool(s):** heated indoor. **Leisure Activities:** whirlpool, exercise room. **Guest Services:** sundries, valet and coin laundry, area transportation, wireless Internet. **Business Services:** meeting rooms, PC. **Cards:** AX, DC, DS, MC, VI.

SOME UNITS

RAMADA INN EXECUTIVE TRAINING & CONFERENCE CTR

Book great rates at AAA.com

Phone: (607)257-3100

(AAA) (SAVE) | All Year | 1P: $99-$299 | 2P: $99-$299 | XP: $12 | F18

Small-scale Hotel

Location: Jct SR 13 and 34, 3.5 mi n on SR 13, exit Triphammer Rd, just w. 2310 N Triphammer Rd 14850. Fax: 607/257-4425. **Facility:** 121 one-bedroom standard units, some with whirlpools. 2 stories, interior corridors. *Bath:* combo or shower only. **Parking:** on-site, winter plug-ins. **Terms:** [AP] meal plan available, package plans, pets ($25 fee). **Amenities:** voice mail, irons, hair dryers. **Dining:** 6:30 am-2 & 5-10 pm, cocktails. **Pool(s):** outdoor, heated indoor, wading. **Leisure Activities:** sauna, whirlpool, exercise room. **Guest Services:** valet laundry, area transportation-Ithaca and Cornell colleges, wireless Internet. **Business Services:** conference facilities. **Cards:** AX, CB, DC, DS, JC, MC, VI. **Free Special Amenities:** full breakfast and high-speed Internet.

SOME UNITS

ROGUE'S HARBOR INN

Phone: 607/533-3535

Historic Bed & Breakfast

| | 5/1-11/30 & 4/1-4/30 | 1P: $125-$165 | 2P: $125-$165 |
| | 12/1-3/31 | 1P: $100 | 2P: $100 |

Location: Corner of SR 34 and 34B; 6 mi n of Ithaca. 2079 E Shore Dr 14882 (PO Box 97). Fax: 607/533-9494. **Facility:** Some guest rooms at this 1830s B&B feature brass beds. Smoke free premises. 7 one-bedroom standard units. 3 stories (no elevator), interior corridors. *Bath:* some shared or private, combo or shower only. **Parking:** on-site. **Terms:** check-in 4 pm, 14 day cancellation notice, weekly rates available, package plans. **Amenities:** hair dryers. **Dining:** Rogue's Harbor Steak & Ale Inc, see separate listing. **Cards:** AX, MC, VI.

———— WHERE TO DINE ————

THE ANTLERS

Dinner: $10-$20

Phone: 607/273-9725

American

Location: Jct SR 13, just e on SR 366 (Dryden Rd). 1159 Dryden Rd 14850. **Hours:** 5 pm-9:30 pm, Fri & Sat-10 pm. Closed: 12/24, 12/25. **Reservations:** accepted. **Features:** A cozy, pub-like atmosphere makes the restaurant a favorite for casual dining. The covered patio is a fun spot when the weather cooperates. This place is known for its great homemade soups and sandwiches. Casual dress; cocktails. **Parking:** on-site. **Cards:** AX, DS, MC, VI.

CTB APPETIZERS

Lunch: $4-$6

Dinner: $5-$12

Phone: 607/257-2255

American

Location: SR 13, exit Triphammer Rd. Triphammer Marketplace Mall 14850. **Hours:** 7 am-7:30 pm, Sun-5 pm. Closed: 1/1, 11/22, 12/25. **Features:** The cafe is known for its wide selection of coffees, including espresso and cappuccino. Sold by weight, delicatessen sandwiches are made to order in innumerable combinations. Among other offerings are vegetarian items, pasta dishes, smoked fish, inventive appetizers and bread and desserts made in this place's own bakery. Casual dress. **Parking:** on-site. **Cards:** MC, VI.

KYUSHU

Lunch: $5-$9

Dinner: $12-$26

Phone: 607/257-6788

Sushi

Location: SR 13, exit Triphammer Rd, just w. 2300 Triphammer Rd 14850. **Hours:** 11:30 am-3 & 5-10 pm, Fri & Sat-11 pm, Sun noon-10 pm. Closed: 11/22. **Reservations:** accepted. **Features:** Bright, uncomplicated and modern decor provides the background for the hibachi and sushi bar, at which patrons can sample healthy, fresh and delicious seafood prepared by a professionally trained staff. Casual dress. **Parking:** on-site. **Cards:** AX, DS, MC, VI.

ROGUE'S HARBOR STEAK & ALE INC

Dinner: $8-$23

Phone: 607/533-3535

American

Location: Corner of SR 34 and 34B; 6 mi n of Ithaca; in Rogue's Harbor Inn. 2079 E Shore Dr 14882. **Hours:** 4 pm-10 pm, Sun 3 pm-9 pm. Closed: 1/1, 12/25; also 1/1-1/14. **Features:** Antiques, local memorabilia and 13 fireplaces add to the ambience of the 19th-century historic landmark. The menu centers on prime rib, fresh seafood and interesting pasta combinations. Seasonal outdoor seating is a warm-weather option. Casual dress; cocktails. **Parking:** on-site. **Cards:** AX, MC, VI.

LATHAM pop. 10,100 (See map and index starting on p. 218)

———— WHERE TO STAY ————

THE CENTURY HOUSE, A CLARION HOTEL

Book great rates at AAA.com

Phone: (518)785-0931 **11**

(AAA) (SAVE) | 7/24-9/3 [BP] | 1P: $140-$230 | 2P: $140-$230 | XP: $20 | F18
| 5/1-7/23 & 9/4-4/30 [BP] | 1P: $130-$230 | 2P: $130-$230 | XP: $20 | F18

Small-scale Hotel

Location: I-87, exit 7 (SR 7), just e, then 0.5 mi n on US 9 (New Loudon Rd). 997 New Loudon Rd 12110 (PO Box 1100). Fax: 518/785-3274. **Facility:** 68 units. 64 one-bedroom standard units. 2 one- and 2 two-bedroom suites ($160-$230) with kitchens. 2 stories (no elevator), interior corridors. **Parking:** on-site. **Terms:** cancellation fee imposed, pets ($15 extra charge). **Amenities:** dual phone lines, voice mail, irons, hair dryers. **Dining:** Century House, see separate listing. **Pool(s):** small outdoor. **Leisure Activities:** tennis court, nature trail, exercise room. **Guest Services:** sundries, valet laundry, area transportation-Amtrak station, wireless Internet. **Business Services:** conference facilities, PC. **Cards:** AX, CB, DC, DS, MC, VI. **Free Special Amenities:** full breakfast and high-speed Internet.

SOME UNITS

COMFORT INN ALBANY AIRPORT & CONFERENCE CENTER

Book great rates at AAA.com

Phone: (518)783-1900 **15**

(AAA) (SAVE) | 7/24-8/28 | 1P: $109-$149 | 2P: $109-$149 | XP: $10 | F
| 5/1-7/23 | 1P: $99-$129 | 2P: $99-$129 | XP: $10 | F
| 8/29-4/30 | 1P: $89-$129 | 2P: $89-$129 | XP: $10 | F

Small-scale Hotel

Location: I-87, exit 4, 2.2 mi nw on Albany Shaker Rd. 20 Airport Park Blvd 12110. Fax: 518/783-4085. **Facility:** 96 one-bedroom standard units, some with whirlpools. 2 stories (no elevator), interior corridors. **Parking:** on-site. **Terms:** cancellation fee imposed, [ECP] meal plan available, pets ($10 fee). **Amenities:** voice mail, irons, hair dryers. **Leisure Activities:** exercise room. **Guest Services:** valet and coin laundry, wireless Internet. **Business Services:** meeting rooms, PC. **Cards:** AX, DC, DS, MC, VI. **Free Special Amenities:** expanded continental breakfast and high-speed Internet.

SOME UNITS

(See map and index starting on p. 218)

HAMPTON INN-LATHAM *Book great rates at AAA.com* Phone: 518/785-0000 **12**
Property failed to provide current rates
Location: I-87, exit 7 (SR 7), just e, then just n on US 9 (New Loudon Rd). 981 New Loudon Rd 12047.
Small-scale Hotel Fax: 518/785-1285. **Facility:** 126 one-bedroom standard units. 4 stories, interior corridors. **Parking:** on-site.
Amenities: high-speed Internet, voice mail, irons, hair dryers. **Pool(s):** small outdoor. **Leisure**
Activities: exercise room. **Guest Services:** valet laundry. **Business Services:** meeting rooms.

SOME UNITS

HOLIDAY INN EXPRESS-AIRPORT *Book great rates at AAA.com* Phone: 518/783-6161 **14**
7/21-9/5 [ECP] 1P: $130
5/1-7/20 [ECP] 1P: $110
9/6-4/30 [ECP] 1P: $99
Location: I-87, exit 7 (SR 7), just e, then just n on US 9 (New Loudon Rd). 946 New Loudon Rd 12110.
Small-scale Hotel Fax: 518/783-0154. **Facility:** 120 one-bedroom standard units. 2 stories (no elevator), exterior corridors.
Bath: combo or shower only. **Parking:** on-site, winter plug-ins. **Terms:** pets ($20 fee). **Amenities:** dual
phone lines, voice mail, irons, hair dryers. *Some:* high-speed Internet. **Pool(s):** outdoor. **Leisure Activities:** exercise room.
Guest Services: valet and coin laundry, area transportation-train and bus station. **Business Services:** meeting rooms, PC, fax
(fee). **Cards:** AX, DC, DS, MC, VI. **Free Special Amenities: expanded continental breakfast and local telephone calls.**

FEE SOME UNITS FEE

LA QUINTA INN & SUITES - ALBANY AIRPORT *Book great rates at AAA.com* Phone: (518)640-2200 **18**
7/1-10/31 1P: $119-$149 2P: $119-$149
5/1-6/30 1P: $109-$139 2P: $109-$139
3/1-4/30 1P: $109-$119 2P: $109-$119
11/1-2/29 1P: $99-$119 2P: $99-$119
Location: I-87, exit 7, just s on US 9 to Latham Circle, then n on US 9. 833 New Loudon Rd 12110. Fax: 518/640-2215. **Facility:** 78
units. 72 one-bedroom standard units. 6 one-bedroom suites ($139-$199). 3 stories, interior corridors. *Bath:* combo or shower
only. **Parking:** on-site. **Terms:** [ECP] meal plan available, package plans, pets (with prior approval). **Amenities:** voice mail,
irons, hair dryers. **Pool(s):** heated indoor. **Leisure Activities:** whirlpool, limited exercise equipment. **Guest Services:** coin
laundry, area transportation, wireless Internet. **Business Services:** meeting rooms, PC, fax. **Cards:** AX, CB, DC, DS, MC, VI.
(See color ad p 360)

MICROTEL INN, ALBANY AIRPORT *Book great rates at AAA.com* Phone: (518)782-9161 **16**
All Year 1P: $45-$169 2P: $45-$169
Location: I-87, exit 6, just w. 7 Rensselaer Ave 12110. Fax: 518/782-9162. **Facility:** 100 one-bedroom standard
units. 2 stories (no elevator), interior corridors. *Bath:* combo or shower only. **Parking:** on-site. **Terms:** [CP]
meal plan available, package plans, pets ($10 extra charge). **Amenities:** voice mail, safes (fee). **Guest**
Small-scale Hotel **Services:** valet laundry, wireless Internet. **Business Services:** meeting rooms. **Cards:** AX, DC, DS,
MC, VI. **Free Special Amenities: continental breakfast.**

FEE SOME UNITS

QUALITY INN & SUITES *Book great rates at AAA.com* Phone: (518)785-5891 **17**
5/1-9/30 & 4/1-4/30 [CP] 1P: $107-$140 2P: $107-$140
10/1-3/31 [CP] 1P: $99-$130 2P: $99-$130
Location: I-87, exit 6, just w on SR 7. 611 Troy-Schenectady Rd 12110. Fax: 518/785-5805. **Facility:** 132 units.
119 one-bedroom standard units. 6 one-bedroom suites ($125-$145) with whirlpools. 2
Small-scale Hotel stories, interior/exterior corridors. *Bath:* combo or shower only. **Parking:** on-site. **Terms:** package plans,
18% service charge, pets (in designated units). **Amenities:** voice mail, irons, hair dryers. **Pool(s):** outdoor.
Leisure Activities: exercise room. **Guest Services:** valet laundry, area transportation-local businesses, wireless Internet.
Business Services: meeting rooms, business center. **Cards:** AX, CB, DC, DS, JC, MC, VI. **Free Special Amenities:**
expanded continental breakfast and high-speed Internet.

SOME UNITS

RESIDENCE INN BY MARRIOTT ALBANY AIRPORT *Book great rates at AAA.com* Phone: 518/783-0600 **13**
All Year 1P: $149-$269
Location: I-87, exit 6, 2 mi w on SR 7. 1 Residence Inn Dr 12110. Fax: 518/783-0709. **Facility:** Smoke free
premises. 112 units. 68 one-bedroom standard units with kitchens. 44 one-bedroom suites with kitchens. 2
Small-scale Hotel stories (no elevator), exterior corridors. **Parking:** on-site. **Terms:** pets ($75 fee). **Amenities:** high-speed
Internet, voice mail, irons, hair dryers. **Pool(s):** small outdoor. **Leisure Activities:** whirlpool, exercise room, sports court. **Guest**
Services: complimentary evening beverages: Mon-Thurs, valet and coin laundry. **Business Services:** meeting rooms, business
center. **Cards:** AX, CB, DC, DS, JC, MC, VI.

FEE

WINGATE INN *Book at AAA.com* Phone: (518)869-9100 **19**
7/25-8/31 [ECP] 1P: $144-$146 2P: $146-$156 XP: $10 F
5/1-7/24 & 9/1-4/30 [ECP] 1P: $126-$136 2P: $136-$146 XP: $10 F
Location: I-87, exit 4, just w on Albany Shaker Rd. 254 Old Wolf Rd 12110. Fax: 518/869-0114. **Facility:** 107 one-
bedroom standard units. 5 stories, interior corridors. *Bath:* combo or shower only. **Parking:** on-site.
Small-scale Hotel **Amenities:** video games (fee), dual phone lines, voice mail, safes, irons, hair dryers. **Leisure Activities:** sauna, exercise room.
Guest Services: valet laundry, wireless Internet. **Business Services:** meeting rooms, business center. **Cards:** AX, CB, DC,
DS, MC, VI.

SOME UNITS

(See map and index starting on p. 218)

——— WHERE TO DINE ———

CENTURY HOUSE *Menu on AAA.com*   **Lunch:** $7-$13   **Dinner:** $16-$27   **Phone:** 518/785-0834   ⑪
Regional American
Location: I-87, exit 7 (SR 7), just e, then 0.5 mi n on US 9 (New Loudon Rd); in The Century House, a Clarion Hotel. 997 New Loudon Rd 12110. **Hours:** 11 am-3 & 4-9 pm, Fri-10 pm, Sat 4 pm-10 pm, Sun 4 pm-9 pm. Closed: 7/4, 12/25. **Reservations:** suggested. **Features:** The New England Federal-style restaurant is a relaxed spot for fine dining by candlelight. Hunter-style, free-range chicken and Vermont maple-glazed salmon are a couple of tempting choices. The casual tavern is a nice place to unwind and enjoy conversation. Casual dress; cocktails. **Parking:** on-site. **Cards:** AX, DC, DS, MC, VI.

DAKOTA STEAKHOUSE   **Dinner:** $9-$18   **Phone:** 518/786-1234
Steak & Seafood
Location: I-87, exit 6, just e; in Latham Circle Farms. 579 Troy-Schenectady Rd 12110. **Hours:** 4:30 pm-10 pm, Fri-11 pm, Sat 4 pm-11 pm, Sun 1 pm-9 pm. Closed: 11/22, 12/25. **Reservations:** accepted. **Features:** The restaurant presents a warm, inviting atmosphere with a touch of Southwest feel and Aboriginal artifacts. The steak is served juicy, hot and sizzling, and the fish and seafood are ocean fresh. Casual dress; cocktails. **Parking:** on-site. **Cards:** AX, DS, MC, VI.

KIRKER'S STEAK & SEAFOOD   **Lunch:** $6-$10   **Dinner:** $12-$22   **Phone:** 518/785-3653   ⑫
Steak & Seafood
Location: I-87, exit 7 (SR 7), just e, then just n on US 9 (New Loudon Rd). 959 New Loudon Rd 12110. **Hours:** 11:30 am-3 & 4-9:30 pm, Sat from 4 pm, Sun 1 pm-8 pm. Closed: 12/24, 12/25. **Reservations:** accepted. **Features:** Serving delicious steak and seafood and other popular American fare for more than 50 years, the well-established restaurant has a warm, inviting charm with gracious, friendly hospitality. Reduced portions and healthy choices are available. Casual dress; cocktails. **Parking:** on-site. **Cards:** AX, DS, MC, VI.

——— *The following restaurants have not been evaluated by AAA* ———
but are listed for your information only.

MILANO   **Phone:** 518/783-3334
[fyi]   **Not evaluated. Location:** In Newton Plaza. 594 New Loudon Rd, Rt 9 12110. **Features:** The restaurant offers distinctive Northern Italian cuisine such as freshly made pastas, pizzas from the wood-burning oven and exotic appetizers. Main entrees include tender veal, chicken, steak and specially prepared seafoods to please the most discriminating palate.

TOKYO SUSHI   **Phone:** 518/783-7838
[fyi]   **Not evaluated. Location:** 571 Watervliet Shaker Rd 12110. **Features:** This casual Japanese restaurant is open for both lunch and dinner.

LEONARDSVILLE

——— WHERE TO DINE ———

——— *The following restaurant has not been evaluated by AAA* ———
but is listed for your information only.

THE HORNED DORSET INN   **Phone:** 315/855-7898
[fyi]   **Not evaluated. Location:** Jct SR 8 and US 20, 4 mi s; center. Rt 8 13364. **Features:** On a village main street tucked away in the countryside, the hidden restaurant is a bona fide treat. Elaborate wood trim and a heavy stone hearth decorate the upscale dining room. Fish, red meat and fowl are prepared with both care and flair.

LE ROY pop. 4,462

——— WHERE TO STAY ———

EDSON HOUSE BED & BREAKFAST   **Phone:** (585)768-8579
Bed & Breakfast
All Year   1P: $89-$109
Location: I-90, exit 47, just s on SR 19. 7863 Griswold Circle Rd 14482-0296 (PO Box 296). Fax: 585/768-2063. **Facility:** Smoke free premises. 4 one-bedroom standard units. 2 stories (no elevator); interior corridors. **Parking:** on-site. **Terms:** 7 day cancellation notice, [CP] meal plan available. **Amenities:** video library. *Some:* hair dryers. **Cards:** AX, DS, MC, VI.
SOME UNITS

——— WHERE TO DINE ———

D & R DEPOT RESTAURANT *Menu on AAA.com*   **Lunch:** $5-$8   **Dinner:** $8-$17   **Phone:** 585/768-6270
American
Location: Jct SR 5 and 19, just n. 63 Lake St (SR 19) 14482. **Hours:** 7 am-9 pm. Closed: 12/25. **Reservations:** suggested, weekends. **Features:** Near the historic town, the former 1901 train depot offers a heart-smart menu that incorporates such choices as ostrich meat, fresh seafood, prime rib and chicken pot pie. Casual dress; beer & wine only. **Parking:** on-site. **Cards:** AX, DS, MC, VI.

L.B. GRAND STEAK AND SPAGHETTI HOUSE   **Lunch:** $4-$9   **Dinner:** $7-$20   **Phone:** 585/768-6707
Italian
Location: Center. 37-39 Main St 14482. **Hours:** 11 am-9 pm, Fri & Sat-10 pm. Closed major holidays; also Sun. **Reservations:** accepted, Sat-Thurs. **Features:** The downtown local favorite serves fresh Italian fare, seafood and USDA Choice steaks in a friendly, casual atmosphere. Sunday brunch is by reservation only. Casual dress; cocktails. **Parking:** on-site. **Cards:** AX, DS, MC, VI.

PONTILLO'S PIZZA & PASTA   **Lunch:** $5-$7   **Dinner:** $7-$8   **Phone:** 585/768-6660

Italian

Location: Jct SR 19 and 5; downtown. 49 Main St 14482. **Hours:** 11 am-11 pm, Fri & Sat-midnight. Closed: 1/1, 11/22, 12/25. **Features:** The casual eatery lays out a popular lunch buffet and presents a menu of stone-hearth pizza, chicken wings, hot subs and pasta dishes. Casual dress; beer & wine only. **Parking:** on-site. **Cards:** AX, DC, DS, MC, VI.

LEWISTON —See Niagara Falls p. 527.

LIBERTY pop. 3,975

———— WHERE TO STAY ————

DAYS INN   *Book great rates at AAA.com·*   **Phone:** (845)292-7600

5/1-9/2	1P: $88-$135	2P: $93-$135	XP: $10 F12
9/3-4/30	1P: $79-$135	2P: $79-$135	XP: $10 F12

Small-scale Hotel

Location: SR 17, exit 101, 0.5 mi w. 52 Sullivan Ave 12754. Fax: 845/292-3303. **Facility:** 118 one-bedroom standard units. 2-3 stories (no elevator), interior corridors. **Parking:** on-site. **Amenities:** voice mail, irons, hair dryers. **Pool(s):** small outdoor, small indoor. **Leisure Activities:** *Fee:* game room. **Guest Services:** wireless Internet. **Business Services:** meeting rooms. **Cards:** AX, DC, DS, MC, VI. **Free Special Amenities:** continental breakfast and high-speed Internet.

SOME UNITS

———— WHERE TO DINE ————

MANNY'S STEAKHOUSE   **Lunch:** $7-$13   **Dinner:** $12-$29   **Phone:** 845/295-3170

Steak & Seafood

Location: SR 17, exit 100, 0.4 mi e. 79 Sullivan Ave 12754. **Hours:** 11:30 am-9:30 pm, Fri-Sun to 10 pm. Closed: 1/1, 12/25; also Tues. **Reservations:** suggested. **Features:** An upscale, refreshing atmosphere makes the restaurant an ideal place to enjoy steaks, prime rib and fresh seafood. The prime rib sandwich layers tender, juicy, thinly sliced prime rib on a garlic-butter toasted roll au jus. All luscious desserts are made in-house. Casual dress; cocktails. **Parking:** on-site. **Cards:** AX, DS, MC, VI.

PICCOLO PAESE   **Lunch:** $16-$23   **Dinner:** $16-$23   **Phone:** 845/292-7210

Northern Italian

Location: SR 17, exit 100 westbound, just n; exit eastbound, just s. 2071 SR 52 12754. **Hours:** noon-10 pm, Fri-11 pm, Sat 4 pm-11 pm, Sun 4 pm-10 pm. Closed major holidays; also Mon. **Reservations:** suggested. **Features:** The fine-dining establishment specializes in Northern Italian cuisine made from the freshest quality ingredients. Pastas are made on the premises. An extensive wine list and in-house desserts complement a perfect meal. Casual dress; cocktails. **Parking:** on-site. **Cards:** AX, DS, MC, VI.

LITTLE FALLS pop. 5,188

———— WHERE TO STAY ————

BEST WESTERN LITTLE FALLS MOTOR INN   *Book great rates at AAA.com*   **Phone:** (315)823-4954

5/20-9/30	1P: $85-$105	2P: $95-$120	XP: $6 F12
5/1-5/19 & 10/1-4/30	1P: $65-$85	2P: $70-$90	XP: $6 F12

Small-scale Hotel

Location: On SR 5 and 167. 20 Albany St 13365. Fax: 315/823-4507. **Facility:** 56 one-bedroom standard units. 2 stories (no elevator), interior corridors. **Parking:** on-site, winter plug-ins. **Terms:** [AP] & [BP] meal plans available, package plans, pets ($10 deposit). **Amenities:** irons, hair dryers. *Some:* high-speed Internet. **Dining:** 6:30 am-2 & 5-9 pm, Sun 7 am-1 & 5-9 pm, cocktails. **Leisure Activities:** *Fee:* movie theaters. **Guest Services:** valet laundry. **Business Services:** meeting rooms. **Cards:** AX, CB, DC, DS, MC, VI. **Free Special Amenities:** local telephone calls and high-speed Internet.

SOME UNITS
FEE

———— WHERE TO DINE ————

BEARDSLEE CASTLE   **Dinner:** $15-$26   **Phone:** 315/823-3000

American

Location: On SR 5; just w of East Canada Creek. 123 Old State Rd 13365. **Hours:** 5 pm-9 pm, Sun 4 pm-8 pm. Closed: 1/1, 12/25; also Mon-Wed. **Reservations:** suggested. **Features:** Guests can read through the written history of the castle as they enjoy the quaint surroundings. Stone walls and fireplaces enhance the atmosphere of the dining room. The innovative, daily changing menu dabbles in steak, seafood and lamb, just to name a few. Appetizers, such as alligator fritters and grilled buffalo satay, are intriguing. Desserts are all made on the premises and are ample enough to share. Dressy casual; cocktails. **Parking:** on-site. **Cards:** AX, DS, MC, VI.

BELLA VISTA RESTAURANT   **Dinner:** $13-$26   **Phone:** 315/823-2861

Italian

Location: Jct SR 167 and 5, 1.3 mi s. 3622 SR 167 13365. **Hours:** 5 pm-9 pm, Fri & Sat-10 pm. Closed: 1/1, 12/24, 12/25; also Sun-Tues. **Reservations:** required. **Features:** Patrons can sample hearty, tasty food—such as the pleasantly presented chicken Christina, a chicken breast stuffed with crabmeat, spinach and cheese—in the casual, friendly restaurant. Look across the street for beautiful views of Shoemaker Mountain. Casual dress; cocktails. **Parking:** on-site. **Cards:** AX, DS, MC, VI.

CANAL SIDE INN   **Dinner:** $16-$25   **Phone:** 315/823-1170

French

Location: Just s of SR 5, follow SR 167 S. 395 S Ann St 13365. **Hours:** Open 5/1-2/1 & 3/1-4/30; 5 pm-9 pm, Fri & Sat-10 pm. Closed major holidays; also Sun & Mon. **Reservations:** suggested. **Features:** In the historic area near the Erie Canal Project is a French dining experience waiting to delight. Expert service smoothes the way through a pleasing meal of the chef/owner's traditionally prepared cuisine. The house Caesar salad, made tableside, is mouthwatering. Choose from a variety of pates, soup and appetizers. Beef, chicken, seafood and lamb are presented with sauce, garnish and fresh seasonal vegetables. Casual dress; cocktails. **Parking:** on-site. **Cards:** AX, DS, MC, VI. **Historic**

LIVERPOOL pop. 2,505 (See map and index starting on p. 629)

———— WHERE TO STAY ————

BEST WESTERN INN & SUITES *Book great rates at AAA.com*
Phone: (315)701-4400 **18**
All Year 1P: $89-$189 2P: $89-$189 XP: $5 F12
Location: I-90, exit 37 (Electronics Pkwy), just n; I-81, exit 25 (7th North St), 1.3 mi w, just n on Electronics Pkwy, then just w. 136 Transistor Pkwy 13088. Fax: 315/701-2712. **Facility:** 61 one-bedroom standard units, some with whirlpools. 2 stories, interior corridors. *Bath:* combo or shower only. **Parking:** on-site. **Terms:** [CP] meal plan available, small pets only ($20 fee, must remain caged). **Amenities:** voice mail, irons, hair dryers. **Pool(s):** small heated indoor. **Leisure Activities:** whirlpool, exercise room. **Guest Services:** valet and coin laundry, wireless Internet. **Business Services:** meeting rooms. **Cards:** AX, DS, MC, VI. **Free Special Amenities: continental breakfast and high-speed Internet.**
SOME UNITS

CLARION INN *Book great rates at AAA.com*
Phone: (315)451-6000 **21**
All Year 1P: $60-$139 2P: $60-$139 XP: $10 F18
Location: I-81, exit 25 (7th North St), straight off exit. 401 7th North St 13088. Fax: 315/451-0193. **Facility:** 80 one-bedroom standard units. 4 stories, interior corridors. *Bath:* combo or shower only. **Terms:** cancellation fee imposed, package plans. **Amenities:** irons, hair dryers. **Leisure Activities:** exercise room. **Guest Services:** valet laundry, wireless Internet. **Business Services:** business center. **Cards:** AX, CB, DC, DS, MC, VI. **Free Special Amenities: continental breakfast and high-speed Internet.**
SOME UNITS

HAMPTON INN *Book great rates at AAA.com*
Phone: (315)457-9900 **20**
All Year [CP] 1P: $104-$129 2P: $104-$129
Location: I-81, exit 25 (7th North St); I-90, exit 36. 417 7th North St 13088. Fax: 315/457-6600. **Facility:** 105 one-bedroom standard units. 3 stories, interior corridors. *Bath:* combo or shower only. **Parking:** on-site. **Terms:** [ECP] meal plan available. **Amenities:** video games (fee), voice mail, irons, hair dryers. **Leisure Activities:** exercise room. **Guest Services:** valet and coin laundry, wireless Internet. **Business Services:** meeting rooms, PC. **Cards:** AX, CB, DC, DS, JC, MC, VI. **Free Special Amenities: expanded continental breakfast and high-speed Internet.**
SOME UNITS
FEE FEE

HOLIDAY INN SYRACUSE AIRPORT *Book at AAA.com*
Phone: (315)457-1122 **15**
All Year 1P: $99-$229 2P: $99-$229
Location: I-90, exit 37 (Electronics Pkwy); I-81, exit 25 (7th North St), 1.3 mi nw. 441 Electronics Pkwy 13088. Fax: 315/451-1269. **Facility:** 274 units. 272 one-bedroom standard units. 2 two-bedroom suites. 2-8 stories, interior corridors. *Bath:* combo or shower only. **Parking:** on-site. **Terms:** check-in 4 pm, small pets only (in designated units). **Amenities:** video games (fee), voice mail, irons, hair dryers. **Pool(s):** heated indoor. **Leisure Activities:** sauna, whirlpool, exercise room, volleyball. *Fee:* game room. **Guest Services:** valet laundry, wireless Internet. **Business Services:** conference facilities, business center. **Cards:** AX, CB, DC, DS, JC, MC, VI.
SOME UNITS
FEE

HOMEWOOD SUITES *Book at AAA.com*
Phone: (315)451-3800 **17**
All Year 1P: $149-$199 2P: $149-$199 XP: $10
Location: I-81, exit 25 (7th North St), 1 mi w; I-90, exit 36. 275 Elwood Davis Rd 13088. Fax: 315/451-5838. **Facility:** 102 units. 98 one- and 4 two-bedroom suites with efficiencies. 3 stories, interior corridors. *Bath:* combo or shower only. **Parking:** on-site. **Terms:** pets ($100 fee). **Amenities:** video library (fee), DVD players, high-speed Internet, dual phone lines, voice mail, irons, hair dryers. **Pool(s):** outdoor. **Leisure Activities:** exercise room, basketball, game room. **Guest Services:** sundries, complimentary evening beverages: Mon-Thurs, valet and coin laundry. **Business Services:** meeting rooms, business center. **Cards:** AX, CB, DC, DS, JC, MC, VI.
SOME UNITS
FEE

KNIGHTS INN *Book great rates at AAA.com*
Phone: (315)453-6330 **16**
All Year 1P: $49-$189 2P: $49-$199 XP: $8 F12
Location: I-90, exit 37 (Electronics Pkwy), just s; I-81, exit 25 (7th North St), 1.3 mi nw, then just s. 430 Electronics Pkwy 13088. Fax: 315/457-9240. **Facility:** 80 one-bedroom standard units, some with whirlpools. 1 story, exterior corridors. **Parking:** on-site. **Terms:** pets ($12 extra charge). **Amenities:** high-speed Internet, irons, hair dryers. **Guest Services:** coin laundry. **Business Services:** PC. **Cards:** AX, CB, DC, DS, MC, VI. **Free Special Amenities: expanded continental breakfast and high-speed Internet.**
(See color ad p 633)
SOME UNITS
FEE

SUPER 8 MOTEL ROUTE 57 *Book great rates at AAA.com*
Phone: (315)451-8550 **14**
All Year 1P: $69-$119 2P: $69-$119 XP: $5 F12
Location: I-90, exit 38, 1 mi n on CR 57. Located in a quiet area. 7360 Oswego Rd 13090. Fax: 315/451-6205. **Facility:** 43 one-bedroom standard units, some with whirlpools. 2 stories (no elevator), interior corridors. **Parking:** on-site. **Terms:** [CP] meal plan available. **Amenities:** irons, hair dryers. **Guest Services:** wireless Internet. **Cards:** AX, DS, MC, VI. **Free Special Amenities: continental breakfast and high-speed Internet.**
SOME UNITS

(See map and index starting on p. 629)

SUPER 8 MOTEL SYRACUSE/LIVERPOOL   *Book at AAA.com*   **Phone:** (315)451-8888   **19**
All Year   1P: $50-$129   2P: $60-$129
Small-scale Hotel   **Location:** I-81, exit 25 (7th North St), just nw; I-90, exit 36. 421 7th North St 13088. **Fax:** 315/451-0043. **Facility:** 99 one-bedroom standard units. 4 stories, interior corridors. **Parking:** on-site. **Amenities:** *Some:* high-speed Internet. **Guest Services:** valet laundry, wireless Internet. **Cards:** AX, CB, DC, DS, JC, MC, VI.

SOME UNITS

──────── **WHERE TO DINE** ────────

BANGKOK THAI RESTAURANT   **Lunch:** $7-$8   **Dinner:** $12-$14   **Phone:** 315/451-4621
Thai   **Location:** I-90, exit 38, 1.2 mi n on CR 57. 7421 Oswego Rd 13090. **Hours:** 11:30 am-2:30 & 5-9:30 pm. Closed major holidays; also Sun. **Reservations:** accepted. **Features:** The friendly owner Adisak has been pleasing ravenous diners for more than five years. Healthy, original Thai recipes are prepared with the freshest ingredients. Whether mild, medium or spicy, dishes are rich and deep in flavors. Casual dress; beer & wine only. **Parking:** on-site. **Cards:** AX, MC, VI.

HEID'S OF LIVERPOOL   **Lunch:** $2-$7   **Dinner:** $2-$7   **Phone:** 315/451-0786   **29**
American   **Location:** Old Liverpool Rd and Onondaga Pkwy. 305 Oswego St 13088. **Hours:** 9 am-10 pm. Closed major holidays. **Reservations:** not accepted. **Features:** Since 1917, the restaurant has served hungry diners all-American food in a hurry. On the menu are Texas hots, burgers, fries, onion rings, shakes and plenty of other mouthwatering favorites. Outdoor seating is a summer option. Casual dress; beer only. **Parking:** on-site.

ICHIBAN JAPANESE STEAK HOUSE   *Menu on AAA.com*   **Dinner:** $14-$27   **Phone:** 315/457-0000   **31**
Japanese   **Location:** 1 mi nw of SR 370 and Buckley Rd. 302 Old Liverpool Rd 13088-6219. **Hours:** 5 pm-9 pm, Fri & Sat-10 pm, Sun 4 pm-9 pm. Closed major holidays. **Reservations:** suggested. **Features:** Polite service and fresh ingredients are hallmarks of the hibachi-style restaurant. Sushi can be ordered from the sushi bar or off the menu. Meals prepared in front of guests provide for a fun, lively experience. Casual dress; cocktails. **Parking:** on-site. **Cards:** AX, DC, DS, MC, VI.

PIER 57   **Lunch:** $6-$8   **Dinner:** $10-$15   **Phone:** 315/457-8109   **27**
American   **Location:** I-90, exit 38, 1 mi n on CR 57. 7376 Oswego Rd 13090. **Hours:** 11 am-10 pm, Fri & Sat-11 pm, Sun noon-9 pm. Closed: 1/1, 11/22, 12/25. **Reservations:** accepted. **Features:** The busy favorite serves traditional American fare, including many pasta dishes, seafood, steaks and hearty sandwiches. Casual dress; cocktails. **Parking:** on-site. **Cards:** AX, DC, DS, MC, VI.

THE RETREAT   **Lunch:** $5-$7   **Dinner:** $11-$15   **Phone:** 315/457-6358   **28**
American   **Location:** I-90, exit 38, 0.5 mi on CR 57, then just s. 302 Vine St 13088. **Hours:** 11 am-11 pm. Closed: for lunch Thanksgiving & 12/25. **Reservations:** accepted. **Features:** A cozy, pub-like atmosphere invites diners to this eatery, known for their great homemade soups and sandwiches, a favorite for casual dining. A covered patio offers fun dining in season. Casual dress; cocktails. **Parking:** on-site. **Cards:** AX, DC, DS, MC, VI.

SANTANGELO'S RESTAURANT   **Lunch:** $7-$13   **Dinner:** $12-$22   **Phone:** 315/457-4447   **30**
Italian   **Location:** I-90, exit 37 (Electronics Pkwy), just sw, then just se. 673 Old Liverpool Rd 13088. **Hours:** 11:30 am-10 pm, Sun 4 pm-9 pm. Closed major holidays. **Reservations:** accepted. **Features:** Family-secret recipes have helped make the Italian restaurant a success since 1986. Some of the traditional seafood, chop, veal, pork and pasta dishes are prepared with a creative twist. Sam's cake is a perfect meal ending. Casual dress; cocktails. **Parking:** on-site. **Cards:** AX, DS, MC, VI.

TULLY'S   **Lunch:** $5-$10   **Dinner:** $5-$10   **Phone:** 315/451-6766
American   **Location:** I-81, exit 25 (7th North St), straight off exit. 311 7th North St 13088. **Hours:** 11 am-midnight, Sat-1 am, Sun noon-11 pm. Closed: 11/22, 12/25. **Features:** The lively and casual sports bar has wall-to-wall TVs that broadcast all the sports channels. Menu highlights include chicken tenders, huge 10-ounce burgers, hearty homemade soups, super appetizers, colossal salads and pasta entrees. A pool table and video games provide additional entertainment. Casual dress; cocktails. **Parking:** on-site. **Cards:** AX, DS, MC, VI.

LOCKPORT —*See Niagara Falls p. 527.*

LODI pop. 338—*See also FINGER LAKES.*

──────── **WHERE TO DINE** ────────

DANO'S HEURIGER ON SENECA   **Lunch:** $10-$15   **Dinner:** $15-$25   **Phone:** 607/582-7555
Hungarian   **Location:** On SR 414, south of town. 9564 Rt 414 14860. **Hours:** noon-9 pm; seasonal hours vary. Closed: Thurs (Jan-Apr), Mon-Wed (Nov-Apr), Tues (May-Oct). **Reservations:** accepted. **Features:** Derived from the word "heurige," or new wine, Dano's Heuriger sits on Seneca Lake in the heart of wine country. The newer casual spot presents a list of mostly Finger Lakes wines to pair with its preparations of Austrian cuisine. This is a place to unwind, enjoy a meal and take in the spectacular view. Casual dress; beer & wine only. **Parking:** on-site. **Cards:** MC, VI.

THE GINNY LEE CAFE   **Lunch:** $6-$12   **Phone:** 607/582-6574
Regional American   **Location:** On SR 414. 9322 SR 414 14860. **Hours:** Open 5/1-12/1 & 4/1-4/30; 11 am-4 pm. **Reservations:** accepted. **Features:** From gourmet deli-style sandwiches to true Italian-style pizza, the quality of fresh ingredients is evident. Try a complimentary glass of wine from their on-site winery. Casual dress; beer & wine only. **Parking:** on-site. **Cards:** DS, MC, VI.

LONG ISLAND

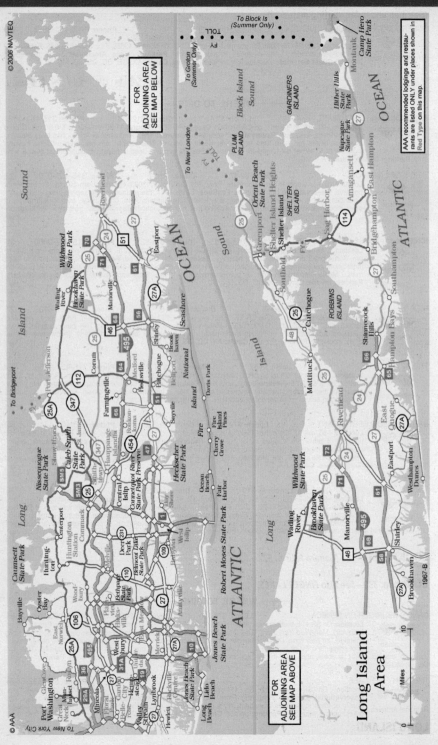

© 2006 NAVTEQ

FOR
ADJOINING AREA
SEE MAP BELOW

To Block Is
(Summer Only)

To Groton
(Summer Only)

To New London

AAA recommended lodgings and restaurants are listed ONLY under places shown in Red Type on this map.

Camp Hero
State Park

Montauk

Hither Hills
State Park

Napeague
State Park

GARDINERS
ISLAND

Block Island
Sound

PLUM
ISLAND

Orient Beach
State Park

Shelter Island Heights

SHELTER
ISLAND

Sag Harbor

Amagansett

East Hampton

Bridgehampton

Southampton

ATLANTIC

OCEAN

Greenport

Southold

Cutchogue

ROBBINS
ISLAND

Shinnecock
Hills

Hampton Bays

Mattituck

Riverhead

East
Quogue

Eastport

Westhampton
Dunes

Long
Island

Sound

Wading
River

Brookhaven
State Park

Wildwood
State Park

Manorville

Shirley

Brookhaven

FOR
ADJOINING AREA
SEE MAP ABOVE

Long Island
Area

0   Miles   10

1967-B

To Bridgeport

© AAA

To New York City

Caumsett
State Park

Bayville

Oyster
Bay

East
Norwich

Woodbury

Port
Washington

Great
Neck

Man-
hasset

Roslyn

Glen Cove

Nissequogue
State Park

Northport

Huntington

Huntington
Station

Commack

Caleb Smith
State Park

St. James

Stony Brook

Port Jefferson

Smithtown

Hauppauge

Islandia

Ronkonkoma

Central
Islip

Connetquot River
State Park Preserve

Heckscher
State Park

Ocean
Beach

Fair
Harbor

Cherry
Grove

Fire Island
Pines

Davis Park

Fire Island
National
Seashore

Bellport

Patchogue

Brookhaven

Shirley

Eastport

Medford

Bayville

Coram

Farmingville

Selden

Holbrook

Ronkonkoma

Wildwood
State Park

Brookhaven
State Park

Wading
River

Manorville

Riverhead

West
Sayville

Bay
Shore

West Islip

Babylon

Amityville

Robert Moses State Park

Jones Beach
State Park

Deer
Park

Melville

Bethpage
State Park

Plain-
view

Hicks-
ville

Bethpage

West
Bury

East Meadow

Levittown

Uniondale

Merrick

Mineola

Floral
Park

Belle-
rose

Garden
City

Rockville
Centre

Lynbrook

Hewlett

Valley
Stream

Long
Beach

Little
Neck

Telmont Lake
State Park

Nissequogue
State Park

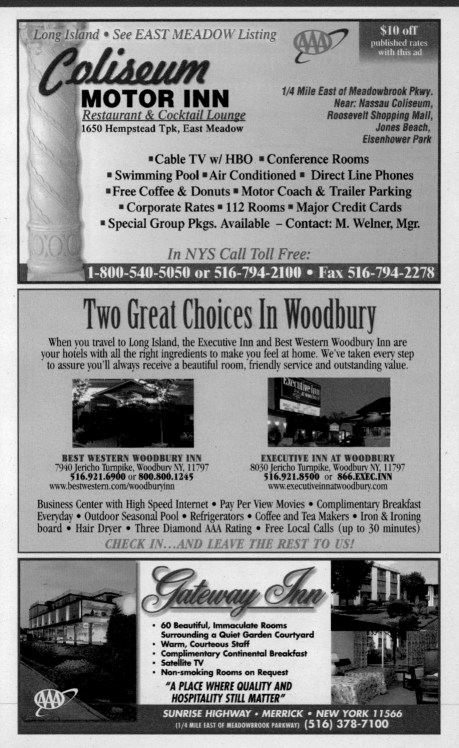

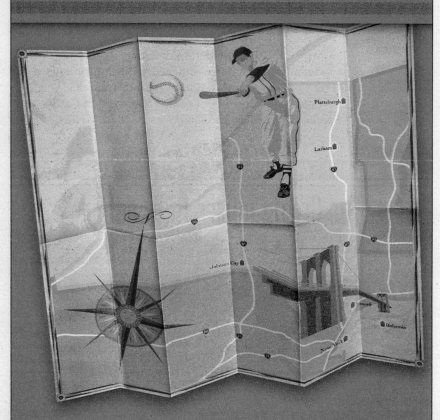

LONG LAKE pop. 852—See also ADIRONDACK MOUNTAINS.

──────── WHERE TO STAY ────────

JOURNEY'S END COTTAGES
Phone: 518/624-5381

(AAA) (SAVE)
▽▽ ▽▽
Cottage

6/25-9/10 Wkly	2P: $800-$1000
9/11-11/15 Wkly	2P: $600-$800
5/1-6/24 Wkly	2P: $500-$700

Location: On SR 30/28 N, 1 mi s. 941 Deerland Rd (Rt 30) 12847 (PO Box 96). **Facility:** 4 cottages ($650-$1000). 1 story, exterior corridors. **Parking:** on-site. **Terms:** open 5/1-11/15, 3-7 night minimum stay - seasonal, 60 day cancellation notice, weekly rates available, pets ($10 fee). **Amenities:** hair dryers. **Leisure Activities:** canoeing, boat dock, fishing, grills, picnic tables. **Cards:** DS, MC, VI. **Free Special Amenities: local telephone calls and high-speed Internet.**

🛒 ⊠ 🎧 (VCR) 🕿 🖥 🖨 🖵
FEE

LONG VIEW LODGE
Phone: (518)624-2862

▽▽ ▽▽
Historic
Country Inn

6/15-10/15	1P: $90-$130	XP: $10
5/1-6/14 & 10/16-4/30	1P: $60-$120	XP: $10

Location: On SR 30/28 N, 2.2 mi s. 681 Deerland Rd 12847. **Fax:** 518/624-2862. **Facility:** There are many antiques located throughout the property and also a great room for functions. The lake is a quick walk down the property. Designated smoking area. 15 units. 9 one- and 4 two-bedroom standard units. 2 cottages. 2 stories (no elevator), interior/exterior corridors. *Bath:* combo or shower only. **Parking:** on-site. **Terms:** check-in 4 pm, 2-4 night minimum stay - seasonal, 7 day cancellation notice-fee imposed, pets (in cottages). **Leisure Activities:** canoeing, boat dock, fishing. **Cards:** DS, MC, VI.

SOME UNITS
🛒 🍴 🛎 ⊠ ⊠ 🎧 / 🖥 🖨 /

SANDY POINT MOTEL
Phone: (518)624-3871

(AAA) (SAVE)
▽▽ ▽▽
Motel

5/1-10/31	1P: $65-$105	2P: $65-$105	XP: $10
			F5

Location: On SR 30/28 N, 1.3 mi s. 865 Deerland Rd (Rt 30) 12847 (PO Box 8). **Fax:** 518/624-3348. **Facility:** 11 one-bedroom standard units, some with efficiencies. 2 stories (no elevator), exterior corridors. **Parking:** on-site. **Terms:** open 5/1-10/31, 10 day cancellation notice-fee imposed. **Leisure Activities:** sauna, rental boats, rental canoes, rental paddleboats, boat dock, fishing. **Guest Services:** wireless Internet. **Cards:** AX, DS, MC, VI. **Free Special Amenities: preferred room (subject to availability with advance reservations) and high-speed Internet.**

SOME UNITS
(S🄳) ⊠ 🎧 🕿 🖵 / ⊠ 🖥 /

──────── WHERE TO DINE ────────

ADIRONDACK BLARNEY STONE, AN IRISH PUB
Lunch: $5-$10   **Dinner:** $8-$22   **Phone:** 518/624-5366

▽▽ ▽▽
Irish

Location: Center. Rt 30 12847. **Hours:** 11:30 am-9 pm, Fri & Sat-10 pm. **Closed:** 11/22, 12/24, 12/25. **Reservations:** suggested, in summer. **Features:** This restaurant has Irish classics like bangers and mashed or fish and chips. The menu also has salads, burgers and sandwiches to round out this Irish-feeling pub. Casual dress; cocktails. **Parking:** on-site. **Cards:** AX, DC, DS, MC, VI.

🛎

LOUDONVILLE pop. 10,900 (See map and index starting on p. 218)

──────── WHERE TO DINE ────────

PEARL OF THE ORIENT
Lunch: $6-$7   **Dinner:** $7-$17   **Phone:** 518/459-0903   (29)

▽▽ ▽▽
Chinese

Location: I-87, exit 4 (Kimberly Square), 1.7 mi e; just w of jct Albany Shaker and Osborn rds. 471 Albany Shaker Rd 12211. **Hours:** 11 am-10 pm, Fri-11 pm, Sat noon-11 pm, Sun noon-10 pm. **Closed:** 7/4, 11/22, 12/25. **Reservations:** accepted. **Features:** The variety of regional Chinese dishes includes Hunan, Szechuan and Cantonese preparations. Luncheon buffets and weekend dinner buffets allow for a sampling of some of each of these styles. Shrimp with black bean sauce and vegetables is a standard dish, and there are a number of chef's specials, including empress duck and chow steak kew. Other seafood, beef and poultry options can be ordered to varying degrees of spiciness. Casual dress; cocktails. **Parking:** on-site. **Cards:** AX, DC, DS, MC, VI.

LOWVILLE pop. 3,476

──────── WHERE TO STAY ────────

RIDGE VIEW MOTOR LODGE
Phone: 315/376-2252

▽▽ ▽▽
Motel

All Year	1P: $59-$89	2P: $69-$99	XP: $10
			F12

Location: 1.5 mi n. Located in a quiet rural area. 7491 SR 12 13367. **Fax:** 315/376-2977. **Facility:** 40 one-bedroom standard units, some with whirlpools. 1 story, interior corridors. **Parking:** on-site, winter plug-ins. **Terms:** 7 day cancellation notice-fee imposed. **Leisure Activities:** playground. *Fee:* game room. **Business Services:** meeting rooms. **Cards:** AX, DS, MC, VI.

SOME UNITS
🎥 / ⊠ (VCR) 🖥 🖨 /
FEE   FEE   FEE

LYNBROOK pop. 19,911

──────── WHERE TO DINE ────────

CHARLIE BROWN'S STEAKHOUSE
Lunch: $6-$10   **Dinner:** $12-$21   **Phone:** 516/256-3273

▽▽ ▽▽
Steak & Seafood

Location: 0.6 mi s of jct Sunrise Hwy (SR 27). 161 Union Ave 11563. **Hours:** 11:30 am-2:30 & 3-10 pm, Fri & Sat-10:30 pm, Sun-9 pm. **Closed:** 12/25. **Features:** This budget-friendly steakhouse, famous for its prime rib, offers top quality fare without hurting your pocketbook. The young ones will not be disappointed with the kid's menu, and young and old, and might even try something green from the salad bar. Adults will love the quality steaks, chicken and rib dishes. The express lunches are great for those saddled with time constraints. Casual dress; cocktails. **Parking:** on-site. **Cards:** AX, DS, MC, VI.

🛎

LYONS FALLS pop. 591

------ **WHERE TO STAY** ------

THE EDGE HOTEL   Phone: 315/348-4211
WWWW   All Year [ECP]   1P: $79-$169   2P: $79-$169
        Location: On SR 12, just n. 3952 SR 12 13368. Fax: 315/348-8111. **Facility:** 65 one-bedroom standard units,
Small-scale Hotel some with whirlpools. 2 stories (no elevator), interior corridors. *Bath:* combo or shower only. **Parking:** on-
        site. **Terms:** cancellation fee imposed, package plans. **Amenities:** high-speed Internet, voice mail, hair
dryers. *Some: Fee:* DVD players. **Cards:** AX, DS, MC, VI.

SOME UNITS

[icons] FEE FEE FEE

MALONE pop. 6,075

------ **WHERE TO STAY** ------

FOUR SEASONS MOTEL   Phone: (518)483-3490
AAA SAVE 5/1-10/20   1P: $55-$79   2P: $65-$89   XP: $5   F12
          10/21-4/30   1P: $50-$59   2P: $55-$79   XP: $5   F12
WWWW   **Location:** 1 mi w on US 11. 206 W Main St 12953. Fax: 518/483-1693. **Facility:** 26 units. 25 one-bedroom
          standard units. 1 one-bedroom suite with kitchen. 1 story, exterior corridors. *Bath:* combo or shower only.
Motel   **Parking:** on-site, winter plug-ins. **Terms:** 3 day cancellation notice, package plans, pets ($5 extra charge).
          Pool(s): outdoor. **Guest Services:** valet laundry, wireless Internet. **Cards:** AX, CB, DC, DS, JC, MC, VI.
Free Special Amenities: high-speed Internet.

SOME UNITS

[icons] FEE

SUNSET INN   Phone: (518)483-3367
AAA SAVE All Year   1P: $40-$80   2P: $50-$80   XP: $5   F12
          Location: 1.5 mi e. 3899 US 11 12953. Fax: 518/481-6172. **Facility:** 27 units. 26 one-bedroom standard units.
WW   1 two-bedroom suite with kitchen. 1 story, exterior corridors. **Parking:** on-site, winter plug-ins.
Motel   **Terms:** weekly rates available, pets (in designated units). **Pool(s):** outdoor. **Cards:** AX, DS, MC, VI.

SOME UNITS

[icons]

SUPER 8 MOTEL AT JONS   *Book great rates at AAA.com*   Phone: 518/483-8123
AAA SAVE All Year   1P: $84-$150   2P: $90-$150   XP: $6   F12
          Location: On SR 30, just s of jct US 11. 42 Finney Blvd 12953. Fax: 518/483-8058. **Facility:** 44 one-bedroom
WW   standard units. 2 stories (no elevator), interior corridors. **Parking:** on-site, winter plug-ins.
          Terms: cancellation fee imposed, [CP] meal plan available, small pets only (in designated units).
Small-scale Hotel **Amenities:** video library (fee). **Guest Services:** valet laundry, wireless Internet. **Cards:** AX, CB, DC, DS,
          MC, VI. **Free Special Amenities: continental breakfast and high-speed Internet.**

SOME UNITS

[icons] FEE

------ **WHERE TO DINE** ------

JONS FAMILY RESTAURANT   **Lunch:** $2-$10   **Dinner:** $2-$10   Phone: 518/483-6230
WW   **Location:** Jct US 11/SR 30/37, just s on SR 30. 44 Finney Blvd 12953. **Hours:** 5:30 am-8 pm, Fri & Sat-8 pm.
          Closed: 11/22, 12/25. **Features:** The menu at Jons is all about traditional comfort food that's both tasty and
American filling. This simple, casual restaurant offers family-style dining with table, booth and counter seating
          available. For dessert, choose from a variety of homemade pies; for breakfast, try a homemade donut.
Casual dress; cocktails. **Parking:** on-site. **Cards:** AX, DS, MC, VI.

VILLA FIORE   **Lunch:** $4-$7   **Dinner:** $7-$16   Phone: 518/481-6557
WW   **Location:** On US 11/SR 30; center. 18 E Main St 12953. **Hours:** 11 am-10 pm, Fri & Sat-11 pm, Sun 4 pm-9 pm.
          Closed: 11/22, 12/25. **Reservations:** accepted. **Features:** The family restaurant serves Italian-American
Italian   cuisine. In addition to traditional pasta dishes, the dinner menu lists prime rib and seafood selections.
          Casual dress; cocktails. **Parking:** on-site. **Cards:** AX, MC, VI.

[icon]

MANCHESTER pop. 1,475—*See FINGER LAKES.*

MARGARETVILLE pop. 643

------ **WHERE TO STAY** ------

MARGARETVILLE MTN INN B&B & VILLAGE SUITES   Phone: 845/586-3933
WWWW   All Year [BP]   1P: $85-$300   2P: $85-$300   XP: $20   F12
          Location: 2 mi n on Walnut St/Margaretville Mountain Rd. 1478 Margaretville Mountain Rd 12455.
Historic Bed Fax: 845/586-1699. **Facility:** This restored Victorian home, which dates from 1886, features wide porches.
& Breakfast Smoke free premises. 8 units. 5 one- and 1 two-bedroom standard units. 2 two-bedroom suites ($140-$300)
          with kitchens. 2 stories (no elevator), interior corridors. *Bath:* combo or shower only. **Parking:** on-site.
Terms: office hours 8 am-10 pm, check-in 4 pm, 10 day cancellation notice-fee imposed, package plans, $5 service charge, no
pets allowed (owner's pet on premises). **Amenities:** video library. **Leisure Activities:** whirlpools. **Guest Services:** TV in
common area. **Cards:** AX, MC, VI.

SOME UNITS

[icons]

MASSAPEQUA PARK pop. 17,499

──────── WHERE TO STAY ────────

BEST WESTERN BAR HARBOUR INN   **Phone:** (516)541-2000

(AAA) (SAVE)
(fyi)

Motel

All Year [CP]   1P: $125-$199   2P: $125-$199   XP: $10   F18
Under major renovation, scheduled to be completed September 2006. **Last rated:** ▼▼ **Location:** SR 27, 2.5 mi e of SR 135. Located in a commercial area. 5080 Sunrise Hwy (SR 27 E) 11762. Fax: 516/541-2004. **Facility:** 72 one-bedroom standard units. 2 stories, interior/exterior corridors. *Bath:* combo or shower only. **Parking:** on-site. **Amenities:** high-speed Internet, irons, hair dryers. **Pool(s):** heated indoor. **Leisure Activities:** exercise room. **Guest Services:** coin laundry. **Business Services:** business center. **Cards:** AX, CB, DC, DS, MC, VI. **Free Special Amenities:** continental breakfast and newspaper.

SOME UNITS

(ᴴ⁺) (ᵈ) (⊸) (⨂) (▭) / (⨉) /

MASSENA pop. 11,209

──────── WHERE TO STAY ────────

ECONO LODGE-MEADOW VIEW MOTEL   *Book great rates at AAA.com*   **Phone:** (315)764-0246

(AAA) (SAVE)
▼▼ ▼▼

Small-scale Hotel

All Year [CP]   1P: $65-$99   2P: $72-$99   XP: $10   F
Location: On SR 37, 2.7 mi sw. 15054 SR 37 13662. Fax: 315/764-9615. **Facility:** 52 one-bedroom standard units. 2 stories (no elevator), interior/exterior corridors. **Parking:** on-site, winter plug-ins. **Terms:** cancellation fee imposed, [BP] meal plan available, package plans, small pets only ($5 fee, in designated units). **Amenities:** voice mail, irons, hair dryers. *Some:* DVD players. **Dining:** 6 am-10:30 & 5-10 pm, Mon from 5 pm; Sun 7 am-2 pm 5/1-10/31, cocktails. **Leisure Activities:** exercise room. **Guest Services:** valet laundry, wireless Internet. **Business Services:** meeting rooms, PC. **Cards:** AX, CB, DC, DS, JC, MC, VI. **Free Special Amenities:** continental breakfast and high-speed Internet.

SOME UNITS

(Sᴰ) (⊸) (†↑†) (⨂) (▤) (▦) (▭) / (⨉) (ᴠᶜᴿ) /
FEE

SUPER 8 MOTEL   *Book great rates at AAA.com*   **Phone:** (315)764-1065

(AAA) (SAVE)
▼▼ ▼▼

Small-scale Hotel

5/1-10/31   1P: $60-$95   2P: $65-$95   XP: $7   F17
11/1-4/30   1P: $60-$70   2P: $65-$75   XP: $7   F17
Location: Jct SR 56, 2 mi e on SR 37. 84 Grove St 13662. Fax: 315/764-9710. **Facility:** 43 one-bedroom standard units. 3 stories (no elevator), interior corridors. **Parking:** on-site, winter plug-ins. **Terms:** [CP] meal plan available. **Amenities:** *Some:* irons, hair dryers. **Guest Services:** wireless Internet. **Business Services:** PC. **Cards:** AX, DC, DS, MC, VI. **Free Special Amenities:** continental breakfast and high-speed Internet.

SOME UNITS

(Sᴰ) (†↑†) (⨂) / (⨉) (▤) (▦) /

MAYVILLE pop. 1,756

──────── WHERE TO DINE ────────

THE WATERMARK RESTAURANT   **Lunch:** $8-$20   **Dinner:** $8-$27   **Phone:** 716/753-2900

▼▼ ▼▼

Seafood

Location: 1.2 mi sw on SR 394. 188 S Erie St 14757. **Hours:** 11:30 am-9 pm. Closed: 11/22, 12/25; also Mon-Wed in winter. **Reservations:** accepted. **Features:** The casual, waterfront restaurant serves grilled steaks and fresh seafood, including crab cakes and other coastal varieties. From the open dining room or one of three summer decks, guests can enjoy sunset views along the shore of Lake Chautauqua. Diners also have access to a private tie-up dock. Casual dress; cocktails. **Parking:** on-site. **Cards:** AX, DS, MC, VI.

(Y)

WEBB'S CAPTAINS TABLE   *Menu on AAA.com*   **Lunch:** $7-$10   **Dinner:** $14-$30   **Phone:** 716/753-3960

(AAA)
▼▼ ▼▼ ▼▼

American

Location: 1.3 mi s on SR 394. 115 W Lake Rd 14757. **Hours:** 11:30 am-11 pm. Closed: 11/22, 12/24, 12/25. **Reservations:** suggested, weekends. **Features:** Many tables in the interestingly decorated dining room overlook Lake Chautauqua. Regional dishes, as well as weekend specials and vegetarian choices, line the menu. Half portions are available. The neatly dressed wait staff provides attentive service. Dressy casual; cocktails. **Parking:** on-site. **Cards:** AX, DS, MC, VI.

(ᴹ) (Y)

MCGRAW pop. 1,000

──────── WHERE TO STAY ────────

CORTLAND DAYS INN   *Book great rates at AAA.com*   **Phone:** 607/753-7594

(AAA) (SAVE)
▼▼ ▼▼

Small-scale Hotel

All Year   1P: $49-$175   2P: $59-$175   XP: $10   F
Location: I-81, exit 10 (McGraw/Cortland), just n. 3775 US Rt 11 13101. Fax: 607/753-6508. **Facility:** 72 one-bedroom standard units, some with whirlpools. 2 stories (no elevator), interior corridors. **Parking:** on-site. **Terms:** weekly rates available, [CP] meal plan available, package plans, small pets only ($10 extra charge). **Amenities:** hair dryers. **Cards:** AX, CB, DC, DS, JC, MC, VI. **Free Special Amenities:** continental breakfast and local telephone calls.

SOME UNITS

FEE

MEDFORD pop. 21,985

——— WHERE TO STAY ———

THE COMFORT INN   *Book great rates at AAA.com*   **Phone:** (631)654-3000

(AAA) (SAVE)	5/1-9/15	1P: $99-$189	2P: $99-$189	XP: $10	F17
▼▼▼ ▼▼▼	9/16-10/31	1P: $89-$189	2P: $89-$189	XP: $10	F17
	11/1-4/30	1P: $79-$189	2P: $79-$189	XP: $10	F17

Location: I-495, exit 64 (SR 112), just s. Located in a commercial area. 2695 Rt 112 11763. Fax: 631/654-1281.
Small-scale Hotel **Facility:** 75 one-bedroom standard units, some with whirlpools. 2 stories (no elevator), interior/exterior corridors. **Parking:** on-site. **Terms:** cancellation fee imposed, [ECP] meal plan available, small pets only ($30 extra charge, in limited units). **Amenities:** video games (fee), dual phone lines, voice mail, irons, hair dryers. **Dining:** cocktails. **Pool(s):** outdoor. **Leisure Activities:** saunas, exercise room. *Fee:* game room. **Guest Services:** valet and coin laundry, wireless Internet. **Business Services:** meeting rooms, fax (fee). **Cards:** AX, CB, DC, DS, JC, MC, VI.
Free Special Amenities: continental breakfast and high-speed Internet.

SOME UNITS

🄂 🛏 🕩 📺 🖥 ➰ ✕ 📷 💻 / ✕ 🔋 📶 /
FEE

MELVILLE pop. 14,533

——— WHERE TO STAY ———

HILTON LONG ISLAND/HUNTINGTON   *Book great rates at AAA.com*   **Phone:** (631)845-1000

▼▼▼	3/1-4/30	1P: $149-$309	2P: $149-$309	XP: $10	F18
	5/1-12/31	1P: $149-$289	2P: $149-$289	XP: $10	F18
	1/1-2/29	1P: $99-$249	2P: $99-$249	XP: $10	F18

Large-scale Hotel **Location:** I-495 (Long Island Expwy), exit 49, 1 mi s on SR 110. Located in a business park. 598 Broad Hollow Rd (SR 110) 11747. Fax: 631/845-1223. **Facility:** 305 units. 296 one-bedroom standard units. 9 one-bedroom suites. 5 stories, interior corridors. *Bath:* combo or shower only. **Parking:** on-site. **Terms:** check-in 4 pm. **Amenities:** dual phone lines, voice mail, irons, hair dryers. *Fee:* video games, high-speed Internet. **Pool(s):** outdoor, heated indoor. **Leisure Activities:** whirlpool, lighted tennis court, exercise room, basketball. *Fee:* massage, game room. **Guest Services:** gift shop, valet and coin laundry, wireless Internet. **Business Services:** conference facilities. **Cards:** AX, CB, DC, DS, JC, MC, VI.

SOME UNITS

(ASK) 🕩 📺 🖥 📠 🌀 ➰ ✕ 📷 💻 / ✕ 🔋 📶 /
FEE FEE

MELVILLE MARRIOTT LONG ISLAND   *Book great rates at AAA.com*   **Phone:** (631)423-1600

▼▼▼	All Year	1P: $139-$269	2P: $139-$269		

Location: I-495 (Long Island Expwy), exit 49S eastbound, just n; exit 49N westbound, off north service road; just w of
Large-scale Hotel SR 110. Located in a business park. 1350 Old Walt Whitman Rd 11747. Fax: 631/423-1790. **Facility:** Smoke free premises. 369 one-bedroom standard units. 4 stories, interior corridors. *Bath:* combo or shower only.
Parking: on-site. **Terms:** check-in 4 pm, cancellation fee imposed, package plans. **Amenities:** voice mail, irons, hair dryers. *Fee:* video games, high-speed Internet. **Pool(s):** heated indoor. **Leisure Activities:** whirlpool, exercise room. **Guest Services:** gift shop, valet laundry, area transportation. **Business Services:** conference facilities, business center. **Cards:** AX, CB, DC, DS, JC, MC, VI.

SOME UNITS

(ASK) 🄂 🕩 📺 🖥 ➰ ✕ 📷 💻 / 🔋 📶 /

——— WHERE TO DINE ———

BERTUCCI'S BRICK OVEN RISTORANTE   **Lunch:** $7-$15   **Dinner:** $10-$15   **Phone:** 631/427-9700

▼▼ **Location:** Northern Pkwy E, exit 40 n, 0.4 mi n. 881 Walt Whitman Rd 11747. **Hours:** 11 am-10 pm, Fri & Sat-11
pm. Closed: 11/22, 12/25. **Features:** This popular chain is known for their signature brick oven cooking
Italian which creates the distinctive flavors you'll taste in the fresh roasted vegetables, the seafood and entree specialties, and of course, the restaurant's top notch pizza. Every dish is made to order and all breads are made from scratch throughout the day. A sample meal may include pasta with the rich flavors of fresh garlic, basil and oven roasted tomatoes and for dessert a divine lemon cream dessert with berries. Casual dress; cocktails. **Parking:** on-site.
Cards: AX, CB, DC, DS, MC, VI.

MERRICK pop. 22,764

―――――― WHERE TO STAY ――――――

GATEWAY INN

AAA **SAVE**

Motel

Phone: 516/378-7100

All Year   1P: $99-$119   2P: $99-$119   XP: $7   F12
Location: Meadowbrook Pkwy, exit M8, 0.3 mi e. Located in a commercial area. 1780 Sunrise Hwy 11566. Fax: 516/378-5745. **Facility:** 60 units. 59 one-bedroom standard units. 1 one-bedroom suite ($149). 2 stories, interior/exterior corridors. *Bath:* combo or shower only. **Parking:** on-site. **Cards:** AX, CB, DC, DS, MC, VI. **Free Special Amenities: continental breakfast and newspaper.** *(See color ad p 359)*

SOME UNITS

FEE

MIDDLETOWN pop. 25,388

―――――― WHERE TO STAY ――――――

COURTYARD BY MARRIOTT   *Book great rates at AAA.com*

Small-scale Hotel

Phone: (845)695-0606

All Year   1P: $144-$184   2P: $144-$184
Location: SR 17, exit 122, just ne. 24 Crystal Run Crossing 10941. Fax: 845/695-0607. **Facility:** Smoke free premises. 134 units. 130 one-bedroom standard units, some with whirlpools. 4 one-bedroom suites. 4 stories, interior corridors. *Bath:* combo or shower only. **Parking:** on-site. **Terms:** package plans. **Amenities:** video games (fee), high-speed Internet, dual phone lines, voice mail, irons, hair dryers. **Pool(s):** small heated indoor. **Leisure Activities:** whirlpool, exercise room. **Guest Services:** sundries, valet and coin laundry, wireless Internet. **Business Services:** meeting rooms, business center. **Cards:** AX, DC, DS, MC, VI.

SOME UNITS

HOLIDAY INN   *Book at AAA.com*

Small-scale Hotel

Phone: 845/343-1474

Property failed to provide current rates
Location: SR 17, exit 122, 0.3 mi ne. 68 Crystal Run Rd 10941. Fax: 845/692-7155. **Facility:** 100 one-bedroom standard units. 2 stories, interior corridors. *Bath:* combo or shower only. **Parking:** on-site, winter plug-ins. **Amenities:** video games (fee), high-speed Internet, dual phone lines, voice mail, safes, irons, hair dryers. **Pool(s):** outdoor, heated indoor. **Leisure Activities:** sauna, exercise room. **Guest Services:** valet and coin laundry. **Business Services:** conference facilities, business center.

SOME UNITS
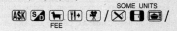

MIDDLETOWN HAMPTON INN   *Book great rates at AAA.com*

Small-scale Hotel

Phone: (845)344-3400

All Year   1P: $119-$159   2P: $129-$169
Location: SR 17, exit 122, just ne. 20 Crystal Run Crossing 10941. Fax: 845/344-3403. **Facility:** 127 units. 119 one-bedroom standard units. 8 one-bedroom suites ($169-$219). 4 stories, interior corridors. *Bath:* combo or shower only. **Parking:** on-site. **Terms:** [ECP] meal plan available. **Amenities:** dual phone lines, voice mail, irons, hair dryers. **Pool(s):** heated outdoor. **Leisure Activities:** exercise room. **Guest Services:** valet and coin laundry, wireless Internet. **Business Services:** meeting rooms, business center. **Cards:** AX, DC, DS, MC, VI.

SOME UNITS
[ASK] images

SUPER 8 MOTEL   *Book at AAA.com*

Small-scale Hotel

Phone: (845)692-5828

All Year   1P: $65-$100   2P: $70-$110   XP: $10   F12
Location: I-84, exit 4, 0.5 mi w on SR 17 to exit 120, then 0.3 mi e. Located next to a shopping mall and near Galleria Mall. 563 Rt 211 E 10940. Fax: 845/692-5828. **Facility:** 82 one-bedroom standard units. 2 stories (no elevator), interior corridors. **Parking:** on-site. **Terms:** cancellation fee imposed, pets ($25 deposit). **Amenities:** voice mail. *Some:* hair dryers. **Guest Services:** coin laundry. **Cards:** AX, DC, DS, MC, VI.

SOME UNITS
[ASK] images
FEE

―――――― WHERE TO DINE ――――――

CHARLIE BROWN'S STEAKHOUSE

Steak & Seafood

Lunch: $6-$10   Dinner: $12-$21   Phone: 845/342-0601

Location: From jct CR 67, just n on CR 108. 505 Schutt Rd Ext 10940. **Hours:** 11:30 am-2:30 & 3-10 pm, Fri & Sat-10:30 pm, Sun-9 pm. Closed: 12/25. **Features:** This budget-friendly steakhouse, famous for its prime rib, offers top quality fare without hurting your pocketbook. The young ones will not be disappointed with the kid's menu, and might even try something green from the salad bar. Adults will love the quality steaks, chicken and rib dishes. The express lunches are great for those saddled with time constraints. Casual dress; cocktails. **Parking:** on-site. **Cards:** AX, DS, MC, VI.

COSIMO'S BRICK OVEN

Italian

Cards: MC, VI.

Lunch: $8-$13   Dinner: $10-$24   Phone: 845/692-3242

Location: SR 17, exit 120 eastbound; exit 121 westbound, 0.6 mi e. 620 Rt 211 E 10940. **Hours:** 11:30 am-10 pm, Fri & Sat-11 pm, Sun noon-10 pm. Closed: 3/23, 11/22, 12/25. **Reservations:** accepted. **Features:** Chandeliers and Italy-themed murals are elements of the distinctive decor in the casually friendly setting. Delicious Italian and American fare is prepared to order. Casual dress; cocktails. **Parking:** on-site.

EL BANDITOS
Mexican
Lunch: $5-$10   **Dinner:** $8-$18   **Phone:** 845/343-2958
Location: SR 17, exit 122, just sw; jct Dunning St. 536 E Main St 10940. **Hours:** 11 am-11 pm. **Features:** Mexican food is served in a cantina-like atmosphere marked by colorful wall murals. A serenader complements the meal and sets the mood. Casual dress; cocktails. **Parking:** on-site. **Cards:** AX, DC, DS, MC, VI.

HANA FUSION DINING & SUSHI
Nouvelle Asian
Lunch: $8-$12   **Dinner:** $12-$25   **Phone:** 845/342-6634
Location: SR 17, exit 120, 1 mi w. 339 Rt 211 E 10940. **Hours:** noon-9:30 pm, Sun 4 pm-9 pm. Closed major holidays. **Reservations:** suggested, weekends. **Features:** A red brick base lines the bottom of the attractive, stone-sided building. Soft Japanese music plays in the background as diners enjoy traditional Japanese and Korean cuisine, including a nice array of sushi. The tatami room is available by reservation. Casual dress; cocktails. **Parking:** on-site. **Cards:** AX, MC, VI.

MILTON pop. 1,251

———— WHERE TO DINE ————

SHIP LANTERN INN   *Menu on AAA.com*
American
Lunch: $8-$20   **Dinner:** $15-$25   **Phone:** 845/795-5400
Location: Jct US 44 and SR 55, 4.3 mi s on US 9W; at Mid-Hudson Bridge. 1725 Rt 9W 12547. **Hours:** noon-2 & 5-9:30 pm, Sat 5 pm-10:30 pm, Sun 1 pm-8 pm. Closed: 12/24, 12/25; also Mon & 1/5-1/20. **Reservations:** suggested. **Features:** Three generations of the Foglia family have hosted guests. Their grandfather was a founding owner of Chef Boyardi, but they style the food served now as "New American." Traditional pasta, such as spaghetti con vongole e cozze with mussels and clams, is served. A new chef, Dana Calabrese, conjures up delectable caramelized salmon or braised spinach or filet of beef tenderloin with piquant salsa verde. The nautical decor, including ship models and lanterns, warms the dining room and cozy bar. Casual dress; cocktails. **Parking:** on-site. **Cards:** AX, DC, DS, MC, VI.

MOHEGAN LAKE

———— WHERE TO DINE ————

CHARLIE BROWN'S STEAKHOUSE
Steak & Seafood
Lunch: $6-$10   **Dinner:** $12-$21   **Phone:** 914/528-0074
Location: On SR 6; in shopping plaza. 1745 E Main St 10547. **Hours:** 11:30 am-2:30 & 3-10:30 pm, Fri & Sat-11 pm, Sun-10 pm. Closed: 12/25. **Features:** This budget-friendly steakhouse, famous for its prime rib, offers top quality fare without hurting your pocketbook. The young ones will not be disappointed with the kid's menu, and just might even try something green from the salad bar. Adults will love the quality steaks, chicken and rib dishes. The express lunches are great for those saddled with time constraints. Casual dress; cocktails. **Parking:** on-site. **Cards:** AX, DS, MC, VI.

MONTAUK pop. 3,851

———— WHERE TO STAY ————

MONTAUK YACHT CLUB RESORT & MARINA   *Book at AAA.com*
Resort
Small-scale Hotel

6/16-9/8	1P: $239-$439	2P: $239-$439	XP: $25 F18
5/1-6/15	1P: $129-$309	2P: $129-$309	XP: $25 F18
3/17-4/30	1P: $119-$309	2P: $119-$309	XP: $25 F18
9/9-11/25	1P: $119-$289	2P: $119-$289	XP: $25 F18

Phone: (631)668-3100

Location: 1 mi e on SR 27, 2 mi n on W Lake Dr (CR 77), then just e. Located on the waterfront. 32 Star Island Rd 11954 (PO Box 5048). Fax: 631/668-6181. **Facility:** Guests may boat to this Star Island resort, where many of the beige-and-white rooms, each with a patio, overlook a marina; villas also are available. Smoke free premises. 107 units. 105 one-bedroom standard units. 2 one-bedroom suites. 2 stories (no elevator), interior corridors. **Parking:** on-site. **Terms:** open 5/1-11/25 & 3/17-4/30, check-in 4 pm, 2 night minimum stay - weekends, 10 day cancellation notice-fee imposed, package plans, $7 service charge. **Amenities:** voice mail, safes, irons, hair dryers. **Pool(s):** outdoor, heated outdoor, small heated indoor. **Leisure Activities:** saunas, putting green, 9 tennis courts (4 lighted), playground, exercise room, volleyball. *Fee:* marina, massage, game room. **Guest Services:** gift shop, coin laundry, area transportation, wireless Internet. **Business Services:** meeting rooms, fax (fee). **Cards:** AX, CB, DC, DS, MC, VI.

———— WHERE TO DINE ————

GOSMAN'S DOCK RESTAURANT
Seafood
Lunch: $14-$25   **Dinner:** $14-$25   **Phone:** 631/668-5330
Location: 1 mi e on SR 27, 2.5 mi n on W Lake Dr (CR 77). 500 W Lake Dr 11954. **Hours:** Open 5/1-10/15 & 4/15-4/30; noon-10 pm. Closed: Tues off season. **Features:** From the flower-filled patio to the open dining dock, the setting here is perfect for a summer meal. The menu offers the sea's bounty—particularly excellent local lobster—and Long Island produce in traditional and modern dishes. Casual dress; cocktails. **Parking:** on-site. **Cards:** AX, MC, VI.

SEA GRILL AT GURNEY'S INN   *Menu on AAA.com*
Italian
Dinner: $18-$35   **Phone:** 631/668-2660
Location: 3 mi w; in Gurney's Inn Resort, Spa & Conference Center. 290 Old Montauk Hwy 11954. **Hours:** 5:30 pm-10 pm. **Reservations:** suggested, in season. **Features:** Mouthwatering aromas hang in the air as the on-site bakery produces tempting fresh bread. Enjoy breathtaking views of the ocean from the modestly decorated dining room. The menu lists Internationally influenced entrees of fresh seafood and prime meat. Dressy casual; cocktails; entertainment. **Parking:** on-site and valet. **Cards:** AX, DC, DS, MC, VI.

MONTICELLO pop. 6,512

——— WHERE TO STAY ———

BEST WESTERN MONTICELLO   *Book great rates at AAA.com*   Phone: (845)796-4000

AAA (SAVE)

7/1-9/2 [CP]	1P: $115-$165	2P: $125-$225	XP: $20	F12
5/1-6/30 & 9/3-12/31 [CP]	1P: $105-$125	2P: $115-$200	XP: $20	F12
1/1-4/30 [CP]	1P: $95-$115	2P: $105-$200	XP: $20	F12

Location: SR 17, exit 104, 0.3 mi s on SR 17B. 16 Raceway Rd 12701. Fax: 845/796-4000. **Facility:** 62 one-

Small-scale Hotel bedroom standard units, some with whirlpools. 2 stories, interior corridors. **Parking:** on-site, winter plug-ins. **Terms:** 2-3 night minimum stay - seasonal and/or weekends, 3 day cancellation notice-fee imposed, package plans. **Amenities:** voice mail, irons, hair dryers. *Some:* high-speed Internet. **Pool(s):** small heated indoor. **Leisure Activities:** sauna, exercise room. *Fee:* game room. **Guest Services:** coin laundry, wireless Internet. **Business Services:** meeting rooms. **Cards:** AX, CB, DC, DS, MC, VI. **Free Special Amenities: continental breakfast and high-speed Internet.**

SOME UNITS

———— WHERE TO DINE ————

HANA RESTAURANT   **Lunch:** $5-$14   **Dinner:** $12-$20   Phone: 845/794-3700

Japanese

Location: SR 17; exit 107, just w. 162 Bridgeville Rd 12701. **Hours:** noon-10 pm, Fri & Sat-10:30 pm, Sun-9:30 pm. Closed: 11/22. **Reservations:** suggested, weekends. **Features:** Deliciously fresh preparations of Japanese and Korean cuisine include sushi, sashimi and tempura. The Asian atmosphere is relaxing. Casual dress; cocktails. **Parking:** on-site. **Cards:** AX, MC, VI.

OLD HOMESTEAD RESTAURANT   **Dinner:** $21-$40   Phone: 845/794-8973

American

Location: SR 17, exit 107, 1 mi se. 472 Bridgeville Rd 12701. **Hours:** Open 5/1-3/31 & 4/16-4/30; 4:30 pm-9:30 pm, Fri-10 pm, Sat-10:30 pm, Sun 4 pm-9 pm. Closed: 11/22, 12/25; also Mon & Tues 10/15-3/14. **Features:** For more than 40 years, delicious American fare has been served in a comfortable, homey and country-like setting. Generously plated food is prepared to the guest's liking. Homemade banana cream pie is to die for. Casual dress; cocktails. **Parking:** on-site. **Cards:** AX, DC, DS, MC, VI.

MONTOUR FALLS pop. 1,797—*See also FINGER LAKES.*

——— WHERE TO STAY ———

RELAX INN   Phone: 607/535-7183

AAA (SAVE)

| 5/1-10/31 [CP] | 1P: $49-$125 | 2P: $59-$135 | XP: $10 | F5 |
| 11/1-4/30 [CP] | 1P: $39-$59 | 2P: $39-$59 | XP: $5 | F5 |

Location: Jct SR 14 and 224. Located in a residential area. 100 Clawson Blvd 14865. Fax: 607/535-6199. **Facility:** 12 one-bedroom standard units. 1 story, exterior corridors. *Bath:* combo or shower only. **Parking:** Motel on-site. **Terms:** 4 day cancellation notice-fee imposed, weekly rates available, pets ($10 extra charge). **Guest Services:** wireless Internet. **Cards:** AX, DS, MC, VI. **Free Special Amenities: continental breakfast and local telephone calls.**

SOME UNITS
FEE

———— WHERE TO DINE ————

CHEF'S DINER   **Lunch:** $4-$7   **Dinner:** $4-$14   Phone: 607/535-9975

American

Location: 1 mi n; 2.4 mi s on SR 14 from Watkins Glen State Park entrance. Rt 14 Montour-Watkins Rd 14865. **Hours:** 6 am-8 pm, Fri & Sat-9 pm. Closed: 12/25. **Features:** An area institution since 1949, the family restaurant delivers a diverse menu of traditional favorites, ranging from salads, sandwiches and quiche to meatloaf and pork chops. Big portions and reasonable prices mean excellent value. Casual dress. **Parking:** on-site.

MOUNT KISCO —*See New York p. 500.*

MOUNT MORRIS pop. 3,266

——— WHERE TO STAY ———

COUNTRY INN AND SUITES   *Book great rates at AAA.com*   Phone: (585)658-4080

AAA (SAVE)

| 5/1-10/31 | 1P: $103-$169 | 2P: $103-$169 | XP: $10 | F18 |
| 11/1-4/30 | 1P: $90-$149 | 2P: $90-$149 | XP: $10 | F18 |

Location: On SR 36; center. Located near entrance to Lechworth St Park & Genesee River. 130 N Main St 14510. Fax: 585/658-4020. **Facility:** 60 units. 43 one-bedroom standard units, some with whirlpools. 17 one-

Small-scale Hotel bedroom suites. 2 stories, interior corridors. *Bath:* combo or shower only. **Parking:** on-site, winter plug-ins. **Terms:** cancellation fee imposed, package plans. **Amenities:** voice mail, irons, hair dryers. *Some:* high-speed Internet. **Pool(s):** small heated indoor. **Leisure Activities:** whirlpool, exercise room. **Guest Services:** coin laundry, wireless Internet. **Business Services:** meeting rooms. **Cards:** AX, DC, DS, MC, VI. **Free Special Amenities: expanded continental breakfast and high-speed Internet.**

SOME UNITS

MOUNT UPTON

———— WHERE TO DINE ————

THE OLD MILL   **Dinner:** $10-$25   Phone: 607/764-8300

American

Location: Jct SR 51, 1.5 mi n. Rt 8 13809. **Hours:** Open 5/1-11/28 & 3/29-4/30; 4:30 pm-9 pm, Sun noon-7:30 pm; hours may vary 11/1-11/28. Closed: 12/25; also Mon. **Reservations:** suggested. **Features:** The converted old mill, featuring tables set with hand-painted china, sits alongside the river and affords beautiful views. Such dishes as the signature chicken Old Mill are well-prepared, tasty and served in ample portions. Homemade desserts are a treat. Casual dress; cocktails. **Parking:** on-site. **Cards:** AX, DS, MC, VI.

NANUET —*See New York p. 500.*

NAPLES pop. 1,072—*See also FINGER LAKES.*

────── **WHERE TO STAY** ──────

BRISTOL HARBOUR RESORT   Phone: (585)396-2200

AAA [SAVE]   5/1-10/31   1P: $179-$219   2P: $179-$219
             11/1-4/30   1P: $129-$159   2P: $129-$159
◇◇◇◇   **Location:** From Canandaigua, 7.7 mi s on SR 21, 0.5 mi e on CR 16, then 1.1 mi s. 5410 Seneca Point Rd 14424.
Resort   Fax: 585/394-9254. **Facility:** In a sophisticated Adirondack style, these roomy lodgings, each with a
Small-scale Hotel   fireplace, offer heated bath floors and balconies overlooking a lake. Smoke free premises. 31 units. 30 one-
             bedroom standard units. 1 one-bedroom suite with whirlpool. 1-3 stories (no elevator), exterior corridors.
Parking: on-site. **Terms:** office hours 7 am-midnight, 7 day cancellation notice-fee imposed, weekly rates
available, [MAP] meal plan available, package plans. **Amenities:** voice mail, irons, hair dryers. *Some:* DVD players.
Dining: Lodge at Bristol Harbour, see separate listing. **Pool(s):** lap. **Leisure Activities:** whirlpool, putting green, 4 tennis
courts, exercise room. *Fee:* golf-18 holes, massage. **Guest Services:** gift shop, wireless Internet. **Business Services:** meeting
rooms, PC. **Cards:** AX, DS, MC, VI.

SOME UNITS

🍽 🏊 ✖ ✉ 🎥 💻 / VCR 🛗 🖭 /

────── **WHERE TO DINE** ──────

LODGE AT BRISTOL HARBOUR   **Lunch:** $7-$11   **Dinner:** $15-$26   **Phone:** 585/396-2200
◇◇◇   **Location:** From Canandaigua, 7.7 mi s on SR 21, 0.5 e on CR 16, then 1.1 mi s; in Bristol Harbour Resort. 5410
American   Seneca Point Rd 14424. **Hours:** 7 am-10 pm, Fri & Sat-11 pm, Sun-9 pm; hours may vary in winter.
             Reservations: accepted. **Features:** Seasonal patio seats afford spectacular views of Canandaigua Lake.
             The golf resort hotel lets guests peruse the trendy menu in a casual, log cabin-like atmosphere. Casual
dress; cocktails. **Parking:** on-site. **Cards:** AX, DS, MC, VI.   [Y]

REDWOOD RESTAURANT   **Lunch:** $4-$8   **Dinner:** $10-$15   **Phone:** 585/374-6360
◇   **Location:** 0.5 mi s on SR 21. 6 Cohocton St 14512. **Hours:** 6 am-8 pm, Fri & Sat-9 pm. Closed: 12/25.
American   **Reservations:** suggested, weekends. **Features:** Many windows let in lots of light at the bright, family-
             oriented restaurant. The menu includes seafood and steak, as well as soup, sandwiches and Italian entrees.
             The Friday fish fry is popular, as are the delicious and tempting homemade desserts. Casual dress;
cocktails. **Parking:** on-site. **Cards:** MC, VI.   [Y]

NEWBURGH pop. 28,259

-------- WHERE TO STAY --------

COMFORT INN NEWBURGH   *Book great rates at AAA.com*   **Phone:** (845)567-0567
WWWW All Year   1P: $99-$129   2P: $99-$129   XP: $8   F18
Location: I-84, exit 6, just w. 5 Lakeside Rd 12550. **Fax:** 845/567-0582. **Facility:** 130 one-bedroom standard
Small-scale Hotel units, some with whirlpools. 3 stories, interior corridors. **Parking:** on-site, winter plug-ins.
Terms: cancellation fee imposed. **Amenities:** irons, hair dryers. **Pool(s):** outdoor. **Leisure**
Activities: exercise room. **Guest Services:** coin laundry, wireless Internet. **Business Services:** meeting rooms, fax (fee).
Cards: AX, DC, DS, MC, VI.
SOME UNITS
(ASK) (S/D) (+) (1l+) (⌐) (⇌) (⚄) (▭) / (☒) (VCR) (⊟) (⊡) /

COURTYARD BY MARRIOTT STEWART/NEWBURGH   *Book great rates at AAA.com*   **Phone:** 845/567-4800
WWWW All Year   1P: $152   2P: $152
Location: I-84, exit 6. Located in Stewart International Airport Industrial Park. 4 Governor Dr 12550.
Small-scale Hotel **Fax:** 845/567-9550. **Facility:** Smoke free premises. 78 units. 70 one-bedroom standard units. 8 one-
bedroom suites. 3 stories, interior corridors. *Bath:* combo or shower only. **Parking:** on-site. **Amenities:** high-
speed Internet, dual phone lines, voice mail, irons, hair dryers. **Pool(s):** small heated indoor. **Leisure Activities:** whirlpool,
exercise room. **Guest Services:** coin laundry. **Business Services:** meeting rooms, fax. **Cards:** AX, DC, DS, MC, VI.
SOME UNITS
(ASK) (S/D) (⚅) (⇌) (☒) (⚄) (▭) / (⊟) (⊡) /

HAMPTON INN-NEWBURGH   *Book great rates at AAA.com*   **Phone:** (845)567-9100
WWWW All Year   1P: $129-$269   2P: $129-$269
Location: I-87, exit 17, w to SR 300 (Union Ave), then just n; I-84, exit 7S. 1292 SR 300 (Union Ave) 12550.
Small-scale Hotel **Fax:** 845/567-6331. **Facility:** 116 one-bedroom standard units. 2 stories, interior corridors. *Bath:* combo or
shower only. **Parking:** on-site. **Terms:** cancellation fee imposed. **Amenities:** video games (fee), high-speed
Internet, voice mail, irons, hair dryers. **Pool(s):** heated indoor. **Leisure Activities:** whirlpool, exercise room. **Guest Services:**
valet laundry. **Business Services:** meeting rooms. **Cards:** AX, CB, DC, DS, MC, VI.
SOME UNITS
(ASK) (S/D) (1l+) (⚅) (⇌) (⚄) (▭) / (☒) (⊟) /
FEE

HILTON GARDEN INN NEWBURGH/STEWART
AIRPORT   **Phone:** 845/567-9500
(fyi)   11/2-4/30   1P: $189-$269   2P: $189-$269
5/1-11/1   1P: $189-$249   2P: $189-$249
Small-scale Hotel Too new to rate. **Location:** I-87, exit 17 to SR 17K W. 15 Crossroads Ct 12550. **Fax:** 845/567-9502.
Amenities: 119 units, microwaves, refrigerators. **Cards:** AX, CB, DC, DS, JC, MC, VI.

HOWARD JOHNSON INN   *Book great rates at AAA.com*   **Phone:** (845)564-4000
(AAA) (SAVE) All Year   1P: $59-$149   2P: $69-$159   XP: $8   F17
WW WW **Location:** I-87, exit 17, just w; I-84, exit 7S westbound to SR 17K W; exit 6 eastbound, 2 mi e. 95 RT 17K 12550.
Fax: 845/564-0620. **Facility:** 74 one-bedroom standard units. 2 stories (no elevator), interior corridors.
Parking: on-site, winter plug-ins. **Terms:** [CP] meal plan available. **Amenities:** video library (fee), voice
Small-scale Hotel mail, irons, hair dryers. **Pool(s):** outdoor, wading. **Leisure Activities:** tennis court. **Guest Services:** coin
laundry, wireless Internet. **Business Services:** meeting rooms, fax. **Cards:** AX, DC, DS, MC, VI.
Free Special Amenities: expanded continental breakfast and high-speed Internet. *(See color ad below)*
SOME UNITS
(S/D) (1l+) (⇌) (⚄) (▭) / (☒) (VCR) (⊟) (⊡) /

RAMADA INN & SUITES   *Book at AAA.com*   **Phone:** 845/564-4500
WWWW   Property failed to provide current rates
Location: I-87, exit 17 via SR 17K W to SR 300 (Union Ave), just n; I-84, exit 7S. 1289 Rt 300 (Union Ave) 12550.
Small-scale Hotel **Fax:** 845/564-4524. **Facility:** 164 units. 124 one-bedroom standard units. 40 one-bedroom suites, some
with whirlpools. 2 stories (no elevator), interior corridors. **Parking:** on-site. **Amenities:** voice mail, irons, hair
dryers. **Pool(s):** outdoor. **Leisure Activities:** limited exercise equipment. **Guest Services:** coin laundry. **Business Services:**
conference facilities.
SOME UNITS
(+) (1l) (Y) (⇌) (⚄) (▭) / (☒) (⊟) /

SUPER 8   *Book at AAA.com*   **Phone:** (845)564-5700

5/1-10/31 & 4/1-4/30	1P: $80-$100	2P: $90-$120	XP: $10	F17
11/1-3/31	1P: $50-$65	2P: $55-$75	XP: $10	F17

Motel   **Location:** I-87, exit 17, just w; I-84, exit 6, 2 mi e. 1287 Rt 300 12550. **Fax:** 845/564-7338. **Facility:** 108 one-bedroom standard units. 2 stories (no elevator), interior corridors. **Parking:** on-site. **Terms:** package plans, pets ($10 fee, in designated units). **Amenities:** hair dryers. **Guest Services:** coin laundry, wireless Internet. **Cards:** AX, DC, DS, MC, VI.

SOME UNITS

---------- **WHERE TO DINE** ----------

ALEXIS DINER RESTAURANT   **Lunch:** $5-$10   **Dinner:** $8-$15   **Phone:** 845/565-1400

American   **Location:** I-84, exit 10. 5023 Rt 9W 12550. **Hours:** 24 hours. Closed: 12/25. **Features:** This spacious diner is a favorite for locals and celebrities alike. A splendid menu selection, ample portions and an on-site fine bakery make this a must-stop. Casual dress; cocktails. **Parking:** on-site. **Cards:** AX, DC, MC, VI.

THE BIG EASY BISTRO   **Lunch:** $5-$15   **Dinner:** $8-$28   **Phone:** 845/565-3939

Cajun   **Location:** Jct US 9, 0.7 mi e on Broadway, just ne on Washington Pl, then just s. 40 Front St 12550. **Hours:** 11:30 am-9 pm, Fri & Sat 6 pm-11 pm, Sun noon-8 pm. Closed: 11/22, 12/25. **Reservations:** accepted. **Features:** On the Hudson River, the bistro has outdoor seats that are great for relaxing and watching the sailboats. Among favorites are crab-stuffed sole and the meat on a stick with horseradish dipping sauce appetizer. Casual dress; cocktails. **Parking:** on-site. **Cards:** AX, DS, MC, VI.

CENA 2000   **Lunch:** $13-$19   **Dinner:** $15-$24   **Phone:** 845/561-7676

Italian   **Location:** Jct US 9, 0.7 mi e on Broadway, just ne on Washington Pl, then just s. 50 Front St 12550. **Hours:** noon-3 & 5-10 pm, Fri & Sat-11 pm. Closed: 11/22, 12/25. **Reservations:** accepted. **Features:** On the trendy waterfront, the eatery serves traditional Tuscan dishes, and daily specials are sure to entice. The patio overlooks the Hudson. Casual dress; cocktails. **Parking:** on-site. **Cards:** AX, MC, VI.

IL CENA'COLO   **Lunch:** $10-$22   **Dinner:** $15-$26   **Phone:** 845/564-4494

Northern Italian   **Location:** Jct SR 300 (Union Ave) and 52, just w on SR 52. 228 S Plank Rd (SR 52) 12550. **Hours:** noon-2:30 & 5-9 pm, Fri & Sat 4 pm-11 pm, Sun 4 pm-9 pm. Closed major holidays; also Tues. **Reservations:** suggested. **Features:** An outstanding example of true Tuscan cuisine is the ravioli, which is stuffed with cheese and spinach, with pureed mushrooms in cream sauce. The wine list concentrates exclusively on Italian selections. Melt-in-your-mouth dessert is homemade. Casual dress; cocktails. **Parking:** on-site. **Cards:** AX, DC, MC, VI.

THE RIVER GRILL   **Lunch:** $7-$25   **Dinner:** $7-$30   **Phone:** 845/561-9444

American   **Location:** Jct US 9, 0.7 mi e on Broadway, just ne on Washington Pl, then just s. 40 Front St 12550. **Hours:** 11:30 am-9:30 pm, Fri & Sat-10:30 pm. **Reservations:** suggested. **Features:** Located on the Hudson River, the restaurant features some classic American dishes with a new twist. Outdoor seating in the summer makes for nice boat watching. Casual dress; cocktails. **Parking:** on-site. **Cards:** AX, DC, DS, MC, VI.

TORCHES ON THE HUDSON   **Lunch:** $8-$14   **Dinner:** $12-$21   **Phone:** 845/568-0100

American   **Location:** Jct US 9, 0.7 mi e on Broadway, just ne on Washington Pl, then just n. 120 Front St 12550. **Hours:** 11:30 am-10 pm, Fri & Sat 11:30-11 pm. Closed: 12/25. **Reservations:** required. **Features:** Guests can come by car or boat—dockage is available—to the fresh and popular riverfront restaurant. Contemporary dishes, such as panko-encrusted crab cakes and oak-fired chicken breast, are complemented by friendly and efficient service. Entertainers perform on weekends. Dressy casual; cocktails; entertainment. **Parking:** on-site. **Cards:** AX, CB, DC, DS, JC, MC, VI.

YOBO ORIENTAL RESTAURANT   **Lunch:** $5-$10   **Dinner:** $10-$23   **Phone:** 845/564-3848

Asian   **Location:** I-87, exit 17 to SR 300 (Union Ave) via SR 17K W, then just n. 1297 SR 300 12550. **Hours:** 11:30 am-10 pm, Fri-11 pm, Sat 12:30 pm-11 pm, Sun 12:30 pm-10 pm. Closed: 11/22. **Reservations:** accepted. **Features:** Despite covering broad territory, the menu does a good job with cuisines of China, Japan, Thailand, Korea and Indonesia. Among selections are sushi, sashimi, tempura, dim sum and Korean bolgogi. The wait staff provides capable, well-executed service. Casual dress; cocktails. **Parking:** on-site. **Cards:** AX, MC, VI.

NEWFANE —*See Niagara Falls p. 528.*

NEW HAMPTON

---------- **WHERE TO STAY** ----------

DAYS INN   *Book great rates at AAA.com*   **Phone:** (845)374-2411

5/1-10/31	1P: $79-$139	2P: $79-$139	XP: $10	F17
11/1-4/30	1P: $74-$139	2P: $74-$139	XP: $10	F17

Motel   **Location:** I-84, exit 3, 0.8 mi e on US 6 and SR 17M. 4939 Rt 17M 10958 (PO Box 279). **Fax:** 845/374-0011. **Facility:** 45 one-bedroom standard units. 1-2 stories (no elevator), interior/exterior corridors. **Bath:** combo or shower only. **Parking:** on-site. **Terms:** pets ($50 deposit, in smoking units). **Amenities:** hair dryers. *Some:* irons. **Pool(s):** outdoor. **Guest Services:** wireless Internet. **Cards:** AX, DC, DS, MC, VI. **Free Special Amenities:** continental breakfast and high-speed Internet.

SOME UNITS

NEW HARTFORD pop. 1,886

———— WHERE TO STAY ————

HOLIDAY INN UTICA *Book at AAA.com* **Phone:** (315)797-2131

7/1-8/31	1P: $139-$209	2P: $149-$219
9/1-10/31	1P: $129-$199	2P: $139-$209
5/1-6/30	1P: $119-$189	2P: $129-$199
11/1-4/30	1P: $109-$179	2P: $119-$189

Small-scale Hotel

Location: I-90 (New York State Thruway), exit 31, 4.5 mi w on SR 5 W and 12 S, exit Burrstone Rd, then 1 mi nw. 1777 Burrstone Rd 13413. Fax: 315/797-5817. **Facility:** 100 units. 96 one-bedroom standard units. 4 one-bedroom suites ($179-$279) with kitchens. 2 stories (no elevator), interior corridors. *Bath:* combo or shower only. **Parking:** on-site, winter plug-ins. **Terms:** cancellation fee imposed, [BP] meal plan available, package plans, small pets only ($25 deposit). **Amenities:** video games (fee), irons, hair dryers. **Pool(s):** outdoor. **Leisure Activities:** whirlpool, exercise room. *Fee:* game room. **Guest Services:** sundries, valet and coin laundry, wireless Internet. **Business Services:** conference facilities. **Cards:** AX, CB, DC, DS, JC, MC, VI.

SOME UNITS

ASK SD 🐾 ❨↑❩ 🍸 🗟M 🐕 📷 🏊 ⊠ 🎥 ▣ / ⊠ 🛢 🖭 /
FEE — FEE FEE

RAMADA *Book at AAA.com* **Phone:** (315)735-3392

	1P	2P	XP
5/1-10/31	1P: $99-$129	2P: $109-$139	XP: $10	F12
11/1-4/30	1P: $89-$109	2P: $99-$129	XP: $10	F12

Small-scale Hotel

Location: SR 8, 12 and 5, exit French Rd, just w, then just n. 141 New Hartford St 13413. Fax: 315/738-7642. **Facility:** 104 units. 102 one-bedroom standard units. 2 one-bedroom suites ($140-$175). 2 stories (no elevator), interior corridors. **Parking:** on-site. **Amenities:** voice mail, irons, hair dryers. **Pool(s):** heated outdoor. **Guest Services:** valet laundry, wireless Internet. **Business Services:** meeting rooms. **Cards:** AX, DC, DS, MC, VI.

SOME UNITS

ASK SD ❨↑❩ 🍸 🏊 ♿ ▣ / ⊠ VCR 🛢 🖭 /
FEE FEE

———— WHERE TO DINE ————

BELLA CUCINA **Dinner:** $10-$23 **Phone:** 315-736-4885

Italian

MC, VI.

Location: Jct SR 5, just n. 4479 Commercial Dr 13413. **Hours:** 4 pm-9:30 pm, Fri & Sat-10:30 pm, Sun 2 pm-8 pm. Closed major holidays; also Mon & Tues. **Reservations:** accepted. **Features:** The Italian garden-like setting allows for pleasant, casual dining. Delicious Italian favorites, including seafood, chicken and veal specialties, are served by a friendly staff. Casual dress; cocktails. **Parking:** on-site. **Cards:** AX, DC, DS,

🍸

CARMELLA'S CAFE **Lunch:** $5-$11 **Dinner:** $6-$14 **Phone:** 315-797-3350

American

Location: 0.5 mi w on SR 5. 8530 Seneca Tpke 13413. **Hours:** 11 am-midnight, Thurs-Sat to 1 am, Sun 9 am-midnight. Closed: 11/22, 12/25. **Reservations:** accepted. **Features:** A festive mood prevails in the energized dining room, which is decorated with eclectic antiques. Chicken riggies, which blends rigatoni noodles, charbroiled chicken, mushrooms, peppers, olives and onions, has long been a favorite dinner selection. Casual dress; cocktails. **Parking:** on-site. **Cards:** AX, CB, DC, DS, MC, VI.

🍸

HOOK, LINE & SINKER PUB **Lunch:** $5-$7 **Dinner:** $11-$16 **Phone:** 315-732-3636

Seafood

Location: SR 12 and 5, 0.8 mi w on SR 5. 8471 Seneca Tpke 13413. **Hours:** 11:30 am-10 pm, Sat from 4 pm, Sun 1 pm-9 pm. Closed: 11/22, 12/25. **Reservations:** accepted. **Features:** Casual dining is the bait for families, groups and those looking for hearty meals and tasty desserts, all served with a smile. Although the fish displayed on the walls might subtly lead you to choose a seafood entree, at least consider the beef, chicken, vegetarian and pasta choices. The grilled portobello sandwich is a delectable, juicy "two-napkin" selection. Choose prime rib in servings from a half-pound up to a full-pound. Crispy salad and tummy-warming soup fill out any meal. Casual dress; cocktails. **Parking:** on-site. **Cards:** AX, CB, DC, DS, MC, VI.

🍸

MICHAEL T'S *Menu on AAA.com* **Dinner:** $7-$17 **Phone:** 315-724-4882

Italian

Location: Jct SR 12 and 5, 1 mi w on SR 5. 8390 Seneca Tpke 13413. **Hours:** 4 pm-9 pm, Fri & Sat-10 pm, Sun 3 pm-9 pm. Closed major holidays. **Reservations:** accepted. **Features:** Representative of regional Italian specialties are "greens," which are not salads but tasty blends of cooked escarole with spicy Italian meats. Haddock delivered fresh daily along with Certified Angus beef make options in the casual atmosphere a delight. Friendly, familiar service place diners at ease to enjoy any number of traditional pasta, seafood, chicken and beef dishes. Casual dress; cocktails. **Parking:** on-site. **Cards:** AX, DS, MC, VI.

🍸

THE PHOENICIAN RESTAURANT **Lunch:** $4-$7 **Dinner:** $7-$16 **Phone:** 315/733-2709

Lebanese

Location: I-90 (New York State Thruway), exit 31, 4.5 mi w on SR 5 W and 12 S, exit Burrstone Rd, then just ne. 623 French Rd 13413. **Hours:** 11 am-10 pm. Closed: 11/22, 12/24, 12/25; also Sun. **Reservations:** accepted. **Features:** The restaurant offers authentic Lebanese fare made with only the freshest ingredients—no canned or preserved foods. Exotic spices bring out the full flavor of meats and fish. Casual dress; beer & wine only. **Parking:** on-site. **Cards:** AX, MC, VI.

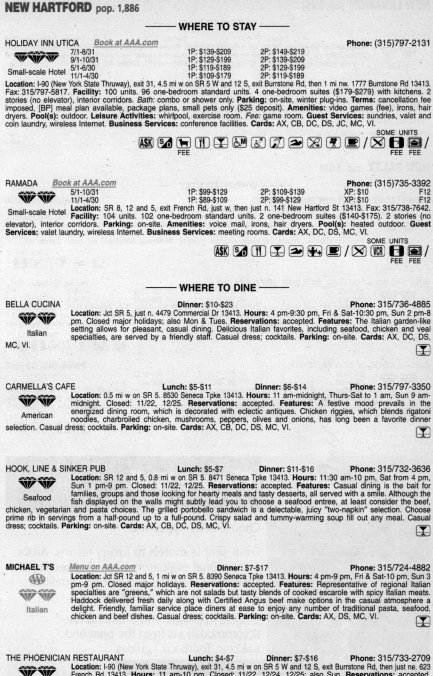

NEW LEBANON pop. 2,454

── WHERE TO DINE ──

FRESCO'S
▼▼ ▼▼
Italian

Lunch: $7-$12   **Dinner:** $7-$12   **Phone:** 518/794-9339
Location: Jct US 20 and SR 22, just n. 569 Rt 20 12125. **Hours:** 11:30 am-10 pm, Fri & Sat-midnight. Closed major holidays. **Features:** Known for its wood-fired pizza, the casual restaurant also serves a good array of popular Italian favorites. Casual dress; cocktails. **Parking:** on-site. **Cards:** AX, DS, MC, VI.

MARIO'S RESTAURANT
▼▼ ▼▼
Northern Italian

Dinner: $14-$22   **Phone:** 518/794-9495
Location: Jct US 20 and SR 22, just n on SR 22. **Hours:** 4 pm-9:30 pm, Fri & Sat-10 pm, Sun-9 pm. Closed: 11/22, 12/25; also Tues. **Reservations:** suggested. **Features:** The restaurant's pleasant wait staff serves a fine selection of traditional and seasonal Northern Italian dishes, including preparations of pasta, veal, seafood and chicken. Enjoy the serene mountain setting and the elegant surroundings. Casual dress; cocktails. **Parking:** on-site. **Cards:** AX, CB, DC, DS, MC, VI.

NEW PALTZ pop. 6,034

── WHERE TO STAY ──

ECONO LODGE
(AAA) (SAVE)
▼▼ ▼▼
Motel

Book great rates at AAA.com   **Phone:** (845)255-6200
All Year [CP]   1P: $55-$125   2P: $65-$135   XP: $6
Location: I-87, exit 18, 0.5 mi e on SR 299. Located in a quiet area. 530 Main St 12561. Fax: 845/255-5841. **Facility:** 34 one-bedroom standard units. 2 stories (no elevator), interior/exterior corridors. *Bath:* combo or shower only. **Parking:** on-site, winter plug-ins. **Terms:** office hours 7:30 am-1 am, cancellation fee imposed. **Pool(s):** outdoor. **Guest Services:** wireless Internet. **Business Services:** fax (fee). **Cards:** AX, DS, MC, VI.

SOME UNITS

RODEWAY INN & SUITES
▼▼ ▼▼
Motel

Book great rates at AAA.com   **Phone:** (845)883-7373
5/1-10/31   1P: $89-$209   2P: $89-$229   XP: $10   F18
11/1-4/30   1P: $69-$189   2P: $69-$189   XP: $10   F18
Location: I-87, exit 18, 0.5 mi e on SR 299. 601 Main St (SR 299) 12561. Fax: 845/883-7383. **Facility:** 39 one-bedroom standard units. 1 story, interior/exterior corridors. **Parking:** on-site, winter plug-ins. **Terms:** 2-3 night minimum stay - seasonal, 3 day cancellation notice-fee imposed, [ECP] meal plan available. **Amenities:** high-speed Internet, irons, hair dryers. **Business Services:** fax. **Cards:** AX, CB, DC, DS, JC, MC, VI.

SOME UNITS

SUPER 8 MOTEL OF NEW PALTZ
▼▼ ▼▼
Motel

    Phone: 845/255-8865
5/1-10/31   1P: $59-$125   2P: $59-$125
11/1-4/30   1P: $63-$85   2P: $63-$85
Location: I-87, exit 18, just w. Located in a quiet area. 7 Terwilliger Ln 12561. Fax: 845/255-1629. **Facility:** 69 one-bedroom standard units, some with whirlpools. 2 stories (no elevator), interior corridors. **Parking:** on-site, winter plug-ins. **Terms:** [CP] meal plan available. **Amenities:** voice mail, hair dryers. **Leisure Activities:** sauna, exercise room. **Guest Services:** coin laundry, wireless Internet. **Cards:** AX, DC, DS, MC, VI.

SOME UNITS

——— **The following lodging was either not evaluated or did not** ———
meet AAA rating requirements but is listed for your information only.

MOHONK MOUNTAIN HOUSE **Phone:** 845/255-1000
(fyi) Not evaluated. **Location:** 1000 Mountain Rest Rd 12561. Facilities, services, and decor characterize a mid-range property.

NEW ROCHELLE —*See New York p. 501.*

NEW WINDSOR pop. 9,077

——— **WHERE TO STAY** ———

DAYS INN NEWBURGH *Book great rates at AAA.com* **Phone:** (845)564-7550

5/1-11/30 [CP]	1P: $85-$125	2P: $85-$125	XP: $6	F13
12/1-4/30 [CP]	1P: $68-$90	2P: $68-$90	XP: $6	F13

(AAA) (SAVE) **Location:** On SR 300, just s, follow signs for Stewart International Airport; I-84, exit 7 southbound; I-87, exit 17 via SR 17K W to SR 300, 1 mi s. 915 Union Ave (SR 300) 12553. **Fax:** 845/564-7560. **Facility:** 97 one-bedroom standard units. 2 stories, interior corridors. **Parking:** on-site, winter plug-ins. **Amenities:** voice mail, hair dryers.
Small-scale Hotel *Some:* irons. **Pool(s):** heated outdoor. **Guest Services:** coin laundry, wireless Internet. **Business Services:** fax (fee). **Cards:** AX, DC, DS, MC, VI. **Free Special Amenities: continental breakfast and newspaper.**

SOME UNITS
[icons] / FEE

WINDSOR MOTEL **Phone:** 845/562-7777

(AAA) (SAVE) All Year 1P: $50-$179 2P: $55-$199
Location: Jct SR 17K and 32, 2.4 mi s. 2976 Rt 9W 12553. **Fax:** 845/562-7889. **Facility:** 30 one-bedroom standard units. 1 story, exterior corridors. *Bath:* combo or shower only. **Parking:** on-site. **Amenities:** *Some:*
Motel high-speed Internet. **Cards:** AX, DS, MC, VI. **Free Special Amenities: expanded continental breakfast and high-speed Internet.**

SOME UNITS
[icons] / FEE

——— **WHERE TO DINE** ———

JOHNNY D'S **Lunch:** $4-$8 **Dinner:** $7-$19 **Phone:** 845/567-1600
Location: I-87, exit 17 via SR 17K, w to SR 300, then 2 mi s. 909 Union Ave (SR 300) 12553. **Hours:** 24 hours.
American **Features:** The charming 1950s-style diner is all chrome and neon, with Coca Cola memorabilia and lots of windows that overlook the lake. The 15-page menu includes a little bit of everything, from eggs to lobster tail. Tempting desserts are made on the premises. Casual dress; cocktails. **Parking:** on-site. **Cards:** AX, DS, MC, VI.
[icon]

SCHLESINGER'S STEAK HOUSE **Lunch:** $7-$23 **Dinner:** $14-$33 **Phone:** 845/561-1762
Location: 2 mi s on SR 300. 475 Temple Hill Rd 12553. **Hours:** 11:30 am-9 pm, Fri-10 pm, Sat 4:30 pm-10 pm, Sun 3 pm-9 pm. Closed major holidays. **Reservations:** accepted. **Features:** Casual dining in the steak
Steak & Seafood house's historic atmosphere makes for a relaxed evening. The house, dating from 1762, has picturesque stone walls and beam ceilings. Steak and ribs are house specialties, as are the Rocky Mountain mashed potatoes. Seafood and pasta choices cater to diverse taste buds. Lighter fare is offered at lunch, along with the steaks. Casual dress; cocktails. **Parking:** on-site. **Cards:** AX, CB, DC, DS, MC, VI.
[icon]

Destination
New York City
pop. 8,008,278

*F*rom pastrami and corned beef
on rye to spicy Indian curry,
the Big Apple dishes up varied
cuisine.

*T*ake a bite out of New York
and visit Little Italy for eggplant
parmigiana, or Chinatown for dim
sum. While in Harlem, stop for some
soul food, or grab a slice of pizza
at one of the city's many pizzerias.
Don't forget about New York's favorite
street fare—jumbo hot dogs, giant
soft pretzels and bags of roasted
chestnuts—all served from pushcarts.

*Ice skating,
Central Park.*
Wollman Rink is
one of two places
in the park where
skaters can glide
across sparkling
ice day or night.
(See mention
page 146)

© NYC & Company

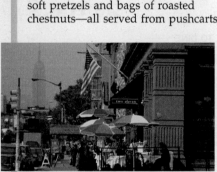

© R. Kord / Robertstock

*Dining,
New York-style.*
There's a place to
suit any pace or
taste—inside and el-
egant, outside and
casual, or curbside
on-the-run.

*P*laces included in this AAA Destination City:

*Chinatown,
Lower Manhattan.*
A riot of color, an
array of aromas and
a cacophony of
sounds await
visitors in this
historic district. (See
listing page 115)

© Gibson Stock Photography

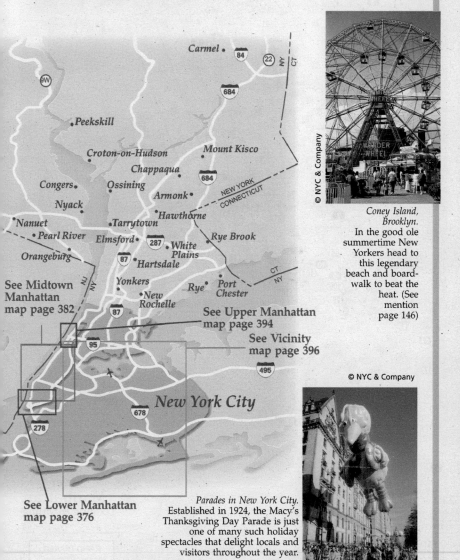

Carmel •
84
22
NY
CT

684

• Peekskill

Croton-on-Hudson
Chappaqua
Congers •
Ossining
Nyack •
Armonk •
NEW YORK
CONNECTICUT

Mount Kisco

684

• Nanuet
• Pearl River
Orangeburg
Elmsford •
287
Yonkers
87
Hartsdale
• New
Rochelle
87

• Hawthorne
• Tarrytown
White
Plains
Rye Brook •
CT
NY
Rye •
Port
Chester

**See Midtown
Manhattan
map page 382**

**See Upper Manhattan
map page 394**

**See Vicinity
map page 396**

95

495

New York City

678

278

**See Lower Manhattan
map page 376**

Coney Island,
Brooklyn.
In the good ole
summertime New
Yorkers head to
this legendary
beach and board-
walk to beat the
heat. (See
mention
page 146)

© NYC & Company

© NYC & Company

Parades in New York City.
Established in 1924, the Macy's
Thanksgiving Day Parade is just
one of many such holiday
spectacles that delight locals and
visitors throughout the year.

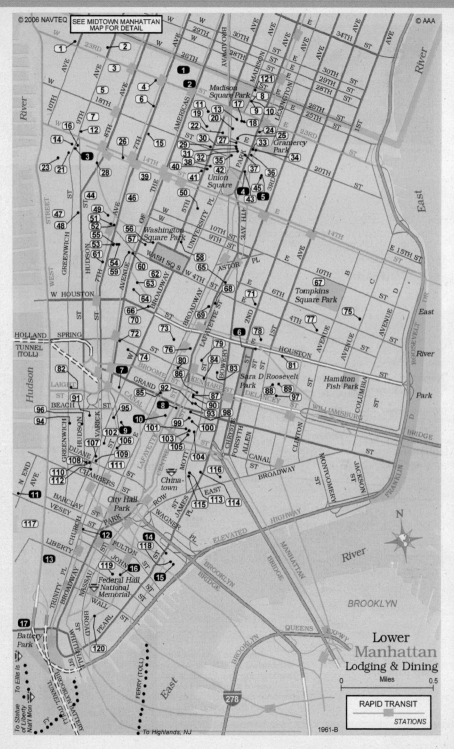

© 2006 NAVTEQ

SEE MIDTOWN MANHATTAN
MAP FOR DETAIL

© AAA

Lower
Manhattan
Lodging & Dining

0   Miles   0.5

RAPID TRANSIT

STATIONS

1961-B

IF YOU HAVEN'T SEEN DOWNTOWN, YOU HAVEN'T SEEN NEW YORK.

It's the birthplace of the nation. It's Wall Street, the South Street Seaport and the Brooklyn Bridge. It's breathtaking views of the harbor and Statue of Liberty. It's narrow winding streets and skyscraper canyons. It's parks, plazas and esplanades. It's museums, concerts and outdoor sculpture. It's diverse shopping, superb dining and world-class hotels. Best of all, it's a short walk from one great attraction to the next.

DOWNTOWN NEW YORK

Downtown
ALLiANCE

visit www.DowntownNY.com

Lower Manhattan New York City

This index helps you "spot" where approved accommodations and restaurants are located on the corresponding detailed maps. Lodging rate ranges are for comparison only and show the property's high season; rates are per night, unless only weekly (W) rates are available. Restaurant rate range is for dinner, unless only lunch (L) is served. Turn to the listing page for more detailed rate information and consult display ads for special promotions.

Spotter/Map Page Number	OA	LOWER MANHATTAN - Lodgings	Diamond Rating	Rate Range High Season	Listing Page
1 / p. 376		Four Points by Sheraton Manhattan Chelsea	◆◆◆	$295-$625	400
2 / p. 376	AAA	Hampton Inn-Manhattan/Chelsea - see color ad p 432	◆◆◆	$199-$460 SAVE	400
3 / p. 376		Hotel Gansevoort	◆◆◆◆	$555	401
4 / p. 376		W New York-Union Square	◆◆◆◆	Failed to provide	403
5 / p. 376		The Inn at Irving Place	◆◆◆	Failed to provide	401
6 / p. 376	AAA	Howard Johnson Express Inn	◆◆	$139-$309 SAVE	401
7 / p. 376		The SoHo Grand Hotel	◆◆◆	$749	402
8 / p. 376	AAA	The Solita SoHo Hotel-Clarion Collection	◆◆	$229-$599 SAVE	402
9 / p. 376		Tribeca Grand Hotel	◆◆◆	Failed to provide	402
10 / p. 376	AAA	Holiday Inn Downtown/Soho - see color ad p 401	◆◆◆	$499-$529 SAVE	400
11 / p. 376		Embassy Suites Hotel New York - see color ad starting on p 436	◆◆◆	$209-$559	400
12 / p. 376	AAA	Millenium Hilton - see color ad starting on p 436	◆◆◆◆	$199-$879 SAVE	401
13 / p. 376		New York Marriott Financial Center	◆◆◆	$249-$529	401
14 / p. 376	AAA	Hampton Inn-Manhattan/Seaport/Financial District - see color ad p 432	◆◆◆	$232-$444 SAVE	400
15 / p. 376	AAA	Best Western Seaport Inn Downtown	◆◆◆	$289-$399 SAVE	400
16 / p. 376		The Wall Street District Hotel	◆◆◆	$349-$579	403
17 / p. 376		The Ritz-Carlton New York, Battery Park	◆◆◆◆◆	$750-$1025	402
		LOWER MANHATTAN - Restaurants			
① / p. 376		The Red Cat	◆◆◆	$20-$25	413
② / p. 376		Grand Sichuan International	◆◆	$6-$20	408
③ / p. 376		Chelsea Bistro & Bar	◆◆◆	$18-$29	406
④ / p. 376	AAA	El Quijote Restaurant	◆◆	$10-$30	407
⑤ / p. 376		O Mai Restaurant	◆◆	$12-$16	411
⑥ / p. 376		Le Zie 2000	◆◆◆	$6-$16	409
⑦ / p. 376		Matsuri	◆◆◆	$15-$26	410
⑧ / p. 376		Tabla	◆◆◆	$64	414
⑨ / p. 376		Bread Bar at Tabla	◆◆	$7-$19	405
⑩ / p. 376		Eleven Madison Park	◆◆◆	$68	407
⑪ / p. 376		Arezzo	◆◆	$18-$39	404
⑫ / p. 376		The Old Homestead	◆◆◆	$25-$45	411
⑬ / p. 376		Bolo	◆◆◆	$22-$32	405
⑭ / p. 376		Spice Market	◆◆◆	$15-$29	413

Spotter/Map Page Number	OA	LOWER MANHATTAN - Restaurants (continued)	Diamond Rating	Rate Range High Season	Listing Page
⑮ / p. 376		Cafeteria	◈◈	$8-$22	405
⑯ / p. 376		Vento Trattoria	◈◈◈	$18-$22	415
⑰ / p. 376		Tamarind	◈◈◈	$11-$32	414
⑱ / p. 376		Beppe	◈◈◈	$17-$35	404
⑲ / p. 376		Periyali	◈◈◈	$18-$29	412
⑳ / p. 376		Mayrose Comfortable Food	◈◈	$7-$15	410
㉑ / p. 376		Pastis	◈◈	$12-$26	412
㉒ / p. 376		Fleur de Sel	◈◈◈	$67-$82	407
㉓ / p. 376		Restaurant Florent	◈◈	$10-$26	413
㉔ / p. 376		Novita	◈◈	$12-$25	411
㉕ / p. 376		Veritas	◈◈◈◈	$76	415
㉖ / p. 376		Crispo	◈◈	$15-$20	407
㉗ / p. 376		Gramercy Tavern	◈◈◈◈	$76-$98	408
㉘ / p. 376		Corner Bistro	◈	$6-$8	406
㉙ / p. 376		City Bakery	◈	$8-$16	406
㉚ / p. 376		Craft	◈◈◈◈	$26-$46	406
㉛ / p. 376		Pipa	◈◈	$10-$25	412
㉜ / p. 376		Craftbar	◈◈◈	$17-$33	406
㉝ / p. 376		L'Express	◈◈	$11-$21	409
㉞ / p. 376		SushiSamba Park	◈◈	$18-$34	414
㉟ / p. 376		Lucy Latin Kitchen	◈◈◈	$20-$32	409
㊱ / p. 376		Angelo & Maxie's	◈◈◈	$12-$25	403
㊲ / p. 376		Old Town Bar & Restaurant	◈◈	$5-$11	411
㊳ / p. 376		Union Square Cafe	◈◈◈	$23-$31	415
㊴ / p. 376		Sumile	◈◈◈◈	$14-$28	414
㊵ / p. 376		Chat 'n Chew	◈◈	$9-$14	406
㊶ / p. 376		Mesa Grill	◈◈◈	$18-$40	410
㊷ / p. 376		Blue Water Grill	◈◈◈	$19-$34	404
㊸ / p. 376		Olives	◈◈◈	$22-$29	411
㊹ / p. 376		The Magnolia Bakery	◈	$2-$7	409
㊺ / p. 376		Casa Mono	◈◈◈	$3-$15	406
㊻ / p. 376		Sapore	◈◈	$15-$30	413
㊼ / p. 376		Wallse Restaurant	◈◈◈	$16-$35	415
㊽ / p. 376	AAA	**Alfama, Fine Portuguese Cuisine**	◈◈◈	$22-$34	403
㊾ / p. 376		Mary's Fish Camp	◈◈	$18-$25	410
㊿ / p. 376		Gotham Bar and Grill	◈◈◈	$28-$44	408

Spotter/Map Page Number	OA	LOWER MANHATTAN - Restaurants (continued)	Diamond Rating	Rate Range High Season	Listing Page
51 / p. 376		Chow Bar	◆◆	$17-$22	406
52 / p. 376		Riviera Cafe & Sports Bar	◆◆	$8-$13	413
53 / p. 376		Sushi Samba 7	◆◆	$9-$39	414
54 / p. 376		Annisa	◆◆◆	$27-$33	404
55 / p. 376		One If By Land, Two If By Sea	◆◆◆◆	$69-$85	411
56 / p. 376		Babbo	◆◆◆	$16-$28	404
57 / p. 376		Blue Hill	◆◆◆	$28-$32	404
58 / p. 376		Otto Enoteca Pizzeria	◆◆◆	$8-$14	411
59 / p. 376		Po	◆◆◆	$13-$24	412
60 / p. 376		Pearl Oyster Bar	◆	$18-$28	412
61 / p. 376		Snack Taverna	◆◆	$12-$19	413
62 / p. 376		Il Mulino	◆◆◆	$50-$75	408
63 / p. 376	ⒶⒶⒶ	**Monte's Restaurant**	◆◆	$9-$25	410
64 / p. 376	ⒶⒶⒶ	**Villa Mosconi Restaurant**	◆◆	$11-$28	415
65 / p. 376		Butter	◆◆◆◆	$17-$34	405
66 / p. 376		Lupa	◆◆◆	$10-$20	409
67 / p. 376		Cafe Pick Me Up	◆	$5-$7	405
68 / p. 376		Five Points	◆◆◆	$15-$25	407
69 / p. 376		BOND ST	◆◆◆◆	$18-$32	405
70 / p. 376		Jean-Claude	◆◆◆	$15-$19	408
71 / p. 376		Sea Thai Restaurant	◆◆	$8-$15	413
72 / p. 376		Aquagrill	◆◆◆◆	$19-$50	404
73 / p. 376		Woo Lae Oak	◆◆	$8-$28	415
74 / p. 376		Country Cafe	◆◆◆	$16-$21	406
75 / p. 376		Bao 111	◆◆◆	$12-$25	404
76 / p. 376		Savoy Restaurant	◆◆	$25-$29	413
77 / p. 376		Mamlouk	◆◆	$30	410
78 / p. 376		Prune	◆◆◆	$19-$30	412
79 / p. 376		Eight Mile Creek	◆◆◆	$15-$30	407
80 / p. 376		Balthazar	◆◆◆	$15-$24	404
81 / p. 376		Katz's Deli	◆	$3-$20	408
82 / p. 376		Dylan Prime	◆◆◆	$19-$62	407
83 / p. 376		Peasant	◆◆◆	$12-$29	412
84 / p. 376		Lombardi's Coal Oven Pizzeria	◆◆	$12-$16	409
85 / p. 376		L'Ecole, the Restaurant of the French Culinary Institute	◆◆◆	$40	409
86 / p. 376		Umberto's Clam House	◆◆◆	$12-$40	414

Spotter/Map Page Number	OA	LOWER MANHATTAN - Restaurants (continued)	Diamond Rating	Rate Range High Season	Listing Page
87 / p. 376	◈◈◈	**Grotta Azzurra**	◈◈◈	$14-$29	408
88 / p. 376		Teany	◈◈	$5-$10	414
89 / p. 376		inoteca	◈◈	$7-$15	408
90 / p. 376		Lunella Ristorante	◈◈◈	$14-$35	409
91 / p. 376		Bubby's Restaurant	◈◈	$10-$23	405
92 / p. 376		Amici II	◈◈◈	$12-$28	403
93 / p. 376		Da Nico Ristorante	◈◈◈	$14-$30	407
94 / p. 376		Tribeca Grill	◈◈◈	$19-$35	414
95 / p. 376		Montrachet	◈◈◈	$24-$32	410
96 / p. 376		Nobu	◈◈◈◈	$12-$25	411
97 / p. 376		Suba	◈◈◈	$24-$28	413
98 / p. 376		Il Palazzo Ristorante Italiano	◈◈◈	$14-$37	408
99 / p. 376		Sal Anthony's S P Q R	◈◈	$20-$30	413
100 / p. 376		Pellegrino's	◈◈◈	$14-$34	412
101 / p. 376		Il Cortile	◈◈◈	$19-$68	408
102 / p. 376		Landmarc	◈◈◈	$15-$30	409
103 / p. 376		Buona Notte Ristorante	◈◈◈	$13-$26	405
104 / p. 376		New Chao Chow Restaurant	◈	$5-$14	410
105 / p. 376		Luna	◈◈	$10-$20	409
106 / p. 376		66	◈◈◈	$19-$29	403
107 / p. 376		The Odeon	◈◈	$19-$28	411
108 / p. 376		Danube	◈◈◈◈	$28-$35	407
109 / p. 376		Takahachi Tribeca	◈◈	$16-$23	414
110 / p. 376		Bouley	◈◈◈◈	$38-$45	405
111 / p. 376		City Hall	◈◈◈◈	$10-$34	406
112 / p. 376		NAM	◈◈	$10-$20	410
113 / p. 376		Peking Duck House	◈◈	$12-$36	412
114 / p. 376		NY Noodle Town	◈◈	$4-$21	411
115 / p. 376		Ping's	◈◈	$20-$40	412
116 / p. 376		Canton	◈◈	$15	405
117 / p. 376		South West NY	◈◈◈	$10-$26	413
118 / p. 376		MarkJoseph Steakhouse	◈◈◈	$28-$51	410
119 / p. 376		Lemongrass Grill	◈◈	$6-$17	409
120 / p. 376		Delmonico's	◈◈◈	$19-$48	407
121 / p. 376		A Voce	◈◈◈	$22-$30	404

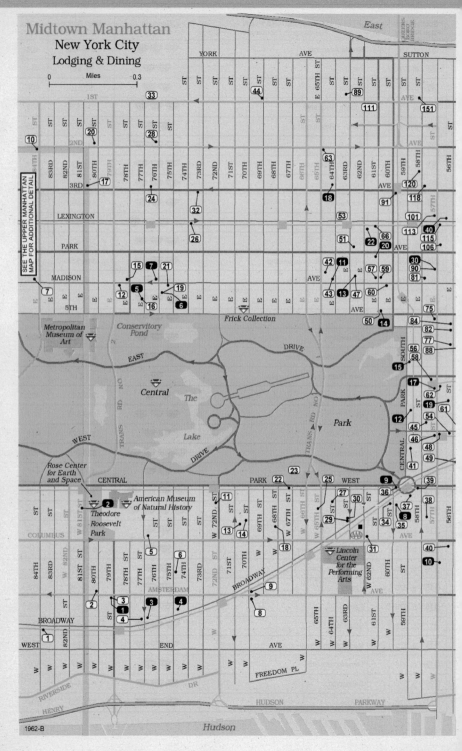

Midtown Manhattan
New York City
Lodging & Dining

Miles
0   0.3

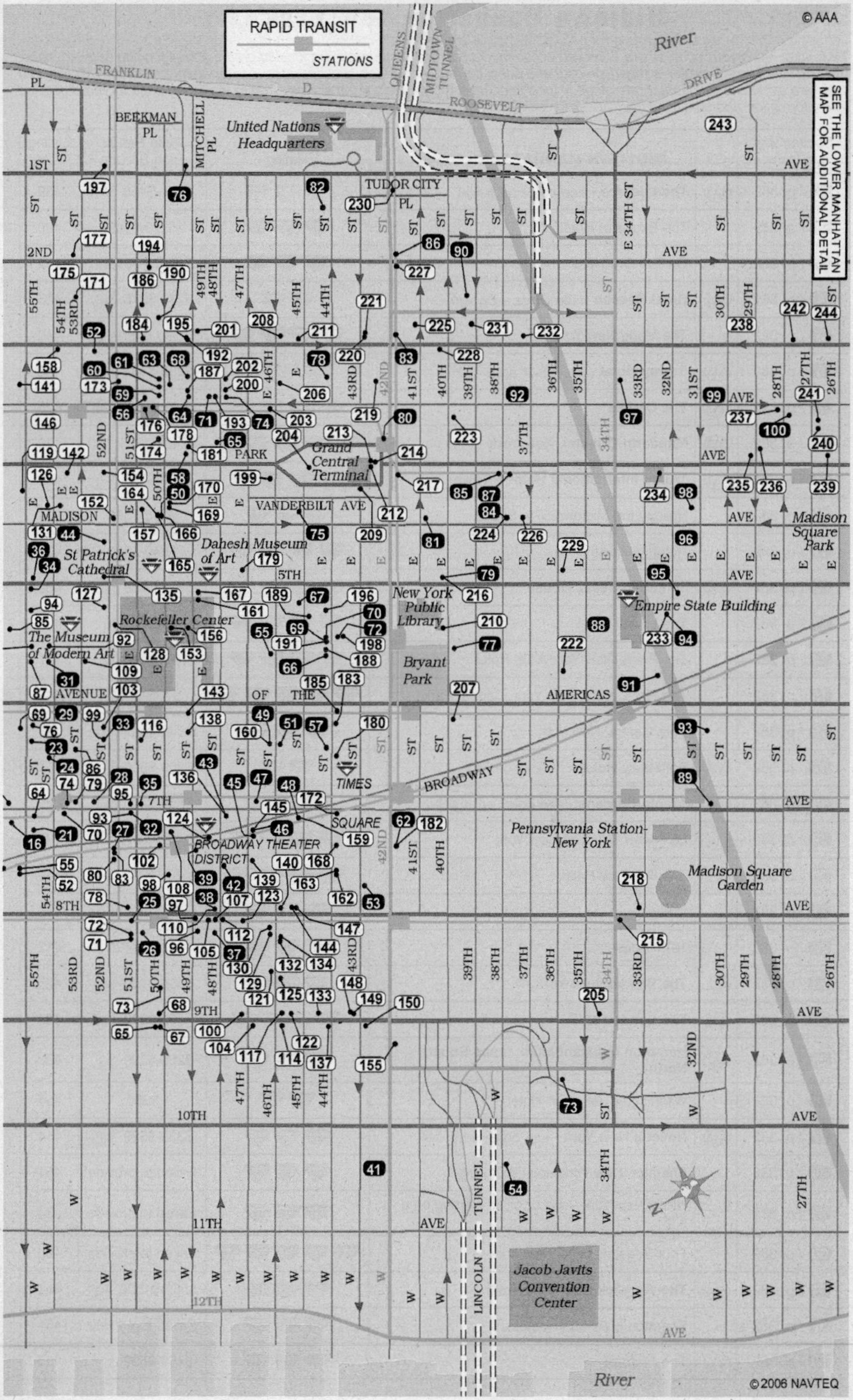

© AAA

RAPID TRANSIT
STATIONS

FRANKLIN

River

QUEENS MIDTOWN TUNNEL

ROOSEVELT

DRIVE

PL

BEEKMAN PL

MITCHELL PL

United Nations Headquarters

SEE THE LOWER MANHATTAN MAP FOR ADDITIONAL DETAIL

1ST ST

2ND ST

TUDOR CITY PL

E 34TH ST

AVE

55TH 54TH 53RD 52ND 51ST 50TH

MADISON

St Patrick's Cathedral

Dahesh Museum of Art

VANDERBILT AVE

5TH

Grand Central Terminal

Rockefeller Center

The Museum of Modern Art

AVENUE

Empire State Building

Madison Square Park

AVE

New York Public Library

Bryant Park

AMERICAS

OF THE

TIMES SQUARE

BROADWAY

Pennsylvania Station-New York

BROADWAY THEATER DISTRICT

Madison Square Garden

AVE

55TH 53RD 52ND 51ST 50TH 49TH 48TH

9TH

47TH 46TH 45TH 44TH

10TH

43RD

39TH 38TH 37TH 36TH 35TH 34TH 33RD

32ND

30TH 29TH 28TH 27TH 26TH

8TH

54TH

7TH

W

11TH

AVE

LINCOLN TUNNEL

34TH

N

Z

W

Jacob Javits Convention Center

W

12TH

W

AVE

River

© 2006 NAVTEQ

Midtown Manhattan New York City

This index helps you "spot" where approved accommodations and restaurants are located on the corresponding detailed maps. Lodging rate ranges are for comparison only and show the property's high season; rates are per night, unless only weekly (W) rates are available. Restaurant rate range is for dinner, unless only lunch (L) is served. Turn to the listing page for more detailed rate information and consult display ads for special promotions.

Spotter/Map Page Number	OA	MIDTOWN MANHATTAN - Lodgings	Diamond Rating	Rate Range High Season	Listing Page
1 / p. 382	AAA	**The Lucerne** - see color ad p 440	◈◈◈	$270-$450 SAVE	439
2 / p. 382		The Excelsior Hotel	◈◈◈	$229-$399	430
3 / p. 382		On The Ave Hotel	◈◈◈	$279-$379	445
4 / p. 382	AAA	**Hotel Beacon** - see color ad p 434	◈◈	$240-$275 SAVE	435
5 / p. 382		The Mark, New York	◈◈◈◈	Failed to provide	440
6 / p. 382	AAA	**Surrey Hotel** - see color ad p 452	◈◈◈	$299-$489 SAVE	453
7 / p. 382	AAA	**The Carlyle**	◈◈◈◈	$540-$1360 SAVE	425
8 / p. 382	AAA	**Mandarin Oriental, New York**	◈◈◈◈◈	$745-$1125 SAVE	440
9 / p. 382	AAA	**Trump International Hotel & Tower**	◈◈◈◈	$750-$795 SAVE	453
10 / p. 382		Holiday Inn Midtown-57th Street	◈◈◈	$335-$395	434
11 / p. 382		Hotel Plaza Athenee	◈◈◈◈	$640-$890	435
12 / p. 382	AAA	**Jumeirah-Essex House**	◈◈◈◈	$329-$869 SAVE	438
13 / p. 382		The Lowell Hotel	◈◈◈◈	$545-$7500	439
14 / p. 382		The Pierre New York-A Taj Hotel	◈◈◈◈	$610-$1400	447
15 / p. 382		The Ritz-Carlton New York, Central Park	◈◈◈◈◈	$795-$1475	449
16 / p. 382		Park Central New York	◈◈◈	Failed to provide	445
17 / p. 382	AAA	**Salisbury Hotel**	◈◈	$309-$339 SAVE	451
18 / p. 382	AAA	**Affinia Gardens** - see color ad p 439	◈◈◈	$259-$449 SAVE	420
19 / p. 382		Le Parker Meridien New York	◈◈◈◈	$860-$1110	438
20 / p. 382		The Regency Hotel	◈◈◈◈	$749-$4500	449
21 / p. 382		Dream	◈◈◈	Failed to provide	430
22 / p. 382		1871 House	◈◈◈	$225-$495	417
23 / p. 382	AAA	**The Blakely New York**	◈◈◈	$350-$450 SAVE	425
24 / p. 382	AAA	**The London NYC**	◈◈◈◈	$499-$999 SAVE	439
25 / p. 382	AAA	**Hampton Inn Manhattan Times Square North**	◈◈◈	$269-$599 SAVE	432
26 / p. 382		Washington Jefferson Hotel	◈◈	$350	454
27 / p. 382	AAA	**Novotel New York** - see color ad p 444	◈◈◈	$339-$529 SAVE	444
28 / p. 382		Sheraton New York Hotel & Towers	◈◈◈	Failed to provide	451
29 / p. 382		Hilton New York - see color ad starting on p 436	◈◈◈	Failed to provide	434
30 / p. 382		Four Seasons Hotel New York	◈◈◈◈◈	Failed to provide	430
31 / p. 382	AAA	**The Warwick New York Hotel**	◈◈◈	$550-$1500 SAVE	454
32 / p. 382		Sheraton Manhattan Hotel	◈◈◈	Failed to provide	451
33 / p. 382	AAA	**The Flatotel**	◈◈◈	$459-$599 SAVE	430

Spotter/Map Page Number	OA	**MIDTOWN MANHATTAN - Lodgings (continued)**	Diamond Rating	Rate Range High Season	Listing Page
34 / p. 382	AAA	The Peninsula New York	◇◇◇◇◇	$675-$895 SAVE	447
35 / p. 382		The Michelangelo	◇◇◇◇	$525-$575	440
36 / p. 382	AAA	The St. Regis Hotel, New York	◇◇◇◇◇	$895-$1095 SAVE	450
37 / p. 382	AAA	Belvedere Hotel - see color ad p 423	◇◇	$299-$599 SAVE	421
38 / p. 382		Hilton Garden Inn Times Square	◇◇◇	$299-$599	434
39 / p. 382		The Time	◇◇◇	$539-$889	453
40 / p. 382		Fitzpatrick Manhattan Hotel	◇◇◇	Failed to provide	430
41 / p. 382	AAA	Travel Inn - see color ad p 452	◇◇	$125-$250 SAVE	453
42 / p. 382	AAA	Best Western President Hotel	◇◇	$149-$549 SAVE	425
43 / p. 382	AAA	Renaissance New York Hotel Times Square - see color ad p 449	◇◇◇◇	$399-$779 SAVE	449
44 / p. 382		Omni Berkshire Place	◇◇◇◇	Failed to provide	445
45 / p. 382		Hotel Edison	◇◇	$190-$215	435
46 / p. 382		W New York Times Square	◇◇◇	Failed to provide	455
47 / p. 382	AAA	DoubleTree Guest Suites Times Square/New York City - see color ad starting on p 436	◇◇◇	$299-$899 SAVE	427
48 / p. 382		New York Marriott Marquis	◇◇◇	Failed to provide	442
49 / p. 382	AAA	The Muse Hotel - see color ad p 419	◇◇◇◇	$329-$999 SAVE	442
50 / p. 382	AAA	The New York Palace	◇◇◇◇	$775-$975 SAVE	444
51 / p. 382	AAA	Comfort Inn Midtown - see color ad p 422	◇	$259-$279 SAVE	427
52 / p. 382		New York Midtown East Courtyard by Marriott	◇◇◇	$329-$639	444
53 / p. 382	AAA	The Westin New York at Times Square	◇◇◇◇	$279-$899 SAVE	454
54 / p. 382	AAA	Best Western Convention Center Hotel - see color ad p 424	◇◇	$179-$334 SAVE	424
55 / p. 382		Super 8 Hotel-Times Square - see color ad p 422	◇◇	$259-$279	451
56 / p. 382		DoubleTree Metropolitan Hotel New York City - see color ad starting on p 436	◇◇◇	$199-$699	427
57 / p. 382	AAA	Millennium Broadway - see color ad p 417	◇◇◇	$599-$2500 SAVE	442
58 / p. 382		The Waldorf=Astoria - see color ad starting on p 436	◇◇◇◇	$499-$939	453
59 / p. 382	AAA	The Benjamin Hotel - see color ad p 420	◇◇◇◇	$239-$669 SAVE	424
60 / p. 382	AAA	The Kimberly A Boutique Hotel	◇◇◇	$315-$1200 SAVE	438
61 / p. 382	AAA	Affinia 50 - see color ad p 439	◇◇◇	$189-$529 SAVE	417
62 / p. 382	AAA	Hilton Times Square - see color ad starting on p 436	◇◇◇	$279-$999 SAVE	434
63 / p. 382		San Carlos Hotel	◇◇◇	Failed to provide	451
64 / p. 382		W New York	◇◇◇	Failed to provide	455
65 / p. 382		InterContinental The Barclay New York	◇◇◇	Failed to provide	435
66 / p. 382	AAA	Algonquin Hotel - see color ad p 423	◇◇◇	$299-$469 SAVE	421
67 / p. 382		Holiday Inn Express Fifth Ave	◇◇	$279-$399	434
68 / p. 382	AAA	Best Western Hospitality House - see color ad p 424 & coupon in Savings Section	◇◇	$189-$599 SAVE	424

Spotter/Map Page Number	OA	MIDTOWN MANHATTAN - Lodgings (continued)	Diamond Rating	Rate Range High Season	Listing Page
69 / p. 382		The Iroquois Hotel	▽▽▽	$499-$750	435
70 / p. 382	AAA	Sofitel New York - see color ad p 452	▽▽▽▽	$399-$809 SAVE	451
71 / p. 382		New York Marriott East Side	▽▽▽	$239-$679	442
72 / p. 382		Royalton	▽▽▽	Failed to provide	450
73 / p. 382	AAA	Comfort Inn Javits Center	▽▽	$189-$399 SAVE	425
74 / p. 382		Radisson Lexington Hotel New York	▽▽▽	$319-$379	447
75 / p. 382	AAA	The Roosevelt Hotel - see color ad p 450	▽▽▽	$209-$509 SAVE	450
76 / p. 382		Beekman Tower Hotel	▽▽▽	$139-$449	421
77 / p. 382	AAA	The Bryant Park Hotel	▽▽▽▽	$445-$800 SAVE	425
78 / p. 382		Fitzpatrick Grand Central Hotel	▽▽▽	$399-$499	430
79 / p. 382		Courtyard by Marriott New York Manhattan/5th Avenue	▽▽▽	Failed to provide	427
80 / p. 382	AAA	Grand Hyatt New York	▽▽▽	$349-$639 SAVE	432
81 / p. 382		Library Hotel	▽▽▽	$385-$565	438
82 / p. 382	AAA	Millennium UN Plaza Hotel New York - see color ad p 417	▽▽▽	$199-$639 SAVE	442
83 / p. 382		The New York Helmsley Hotel	▽▽▽	$289-$429	442
84 / p. 382	AAA	Jolly Hotel Madison Towers	▽▽▽	$320-$604 SAVE	435
85 / p. 382	AAA	70 Park Avenue Hotel - see color ad p 419	▽▽▽	$325-$750 SAVE	417
86 / p. 382		Crowne Plaza at the United Nations	▽▽▽	$159-$799	427
87 / p. 382	AAA	The Kitano New York	▽▽▽▽	$345 SAVE	438
88 / p. 382	AAA	Comfort Inn-Manhattan - see color ad p 427	▽▽	$189-$369 SAVE	425
89 / p. 382	AAA	Affinia Manhattan - see color ad p 439	▽▽▽	$159-$469 SAVE	420
90 / p. 382		Eastgate Tower Hotel	▽▽	Failed to provide	430
91 / p. 382	AAA	Radisson Martinique on Broadway - see color ad p 448	▽▽▽	$429-$734 SAVE	447
92 / p. 382		Shelburne Murray Hill Hotel - see color ad p 439	▽▽▽	$179-$599	451
93 / p. 382	AAA	Hampton Inn-Madison Square Garden Area - see color ad p 432	▽▽▽	$149-$519 SAVE	432
94 / p. 382		La Quinta Inn Manhattan - see color ad p 422, p 360	▽▽▽	$189-$329	438
95 / p. 382		Red Roof Inn Manhattan - see color ad p 422	▽▽	$259-$279	449
96 / p. 382		Vinnci Avalon	▽▽▽	$474-$700	453
97 / p. 382	AAA	Affinia Dumont - see color ad p 439	▽▽▽	$189-$499 SAVE	420
98 / p. 382		Hotel Roger Williams	▽▽▽	$480-$510	435
99 / p. 382		Ramada Eastside - see color ad p 422	▽▽	$249-$269	447
100 / p. 382	AAA	Park South Hotel	▽▽▽	$286-$323 SAVE	447
		MIDTOWN MANHATTAN - Restaurants			
1 / p. 382		Ouest	▽▽▽	$25-$36	473
2 / p. 382		Sarabeth's	▽▽	$14-$25	477
3 / p. 382		Nice Matin	▽▽	$16-$25	472

Spotter/Map Page Number	OA	MIDTOWN MANHATTAN - Restaurants (continued)	Diamond Rating	Rate Range High Season	Listing Page
④ / p. 382		Ruby Foo's Dim Sum & Sushi Palace	◆◆◆	$6-$19	476
⑤ / p. 382		Isabella's	◆◆	$16-$28	467
⑥ / p. 382		Cesca	◆◆◆	$19-$33	461
⑦ / p. 382		Le Pain Quotidien	◆◆	$7-$13	470
⑧ / p. 382		Compass	◆◆◆	$18-$38	463
⑨ / p. 382		Cafe Luxembourg	◆◆◆	$20-$32	460
⑩ / p. 382		Jasmine	◆◆	$8-$22	467
⑪ / p. 382		Dallas BBQ	◆◆	$7-$15	463
⑫ / p. 382		Serafina Fabulous Pizza	◆◆	$10-$26	477
⑬ / p. 382		Pasha Restaurant	◆◆	$15-$24	473
⑭ / p. 382		Metsovo	◆◆	$15-$25	471
⑮ / p. 382		Viand Restaurant-Cafe	◆◆	$10-$25	479
⑯ / p. 382		Mark's	◆◆◆◆	$29-$42	470
⑰ / p. 382		Beyoglu	◆◆	$13-$19	458
⑱ / p. 382		La Boite en Bois	◆◆◆	$18-$27	468
⑲ / p. 382		Cafe Boulud	◆◆◆◆	$26-$50	460
⑳ / p. 382		Pig Heaven	◆◆	$9-$16	474
㉑ / p. 382		3 Guys Restaurant	◆◆	$5-$25	456
㉒ / p. 382		Cafe des Artistes	◆◆◆	$27-$46	460
㉓ / p. 382		Tavern on the Green	◆◆◆	$23-$39	478
㉔ / p. 382		Atlantic Grill	◆◆◆	$20-$32	457
㉕ / p. 382		Shun Lee	◆◆◆	$12-$26	477
㉖ / p. 382		Payard Patisserie & Bistro	◆◆◆	$26-$33	474
㉗ / p. 382		Picholine	◆◆◆◆	$78-$105	474
㉘ / p. 382		Il Monello	◆◆◆	$16-$32	466
㉙ / p. 382		Cafe Fiorello	◆◆	$25-$35	460
㉚ / p. 382		Josephina	◆◆◆	$20-$34	468
㉛ / p. 382		Rosa Mexicano	◆◆◆	$17-$27	476
㉜ / p. 382		Lenox Room	◆◆◆	$19-$32	469
㉝ / p. 382		Canyon Road	◆◆	$14-$24	461
㉞ / p. 382		Gabriel's Bar & Restaurant	◆◆◆	$19-$34	466
㉟ / p. 382	▲▲▲	**Asiate**	◆◆◆◆	$75-$95	457
㊱ / p. 382	▲▲▲	**Jean Georges Restaurant**	◆◆◆◆◆	$95-$125	467
㊲ / p. 382		Bar Masa	◆◆◆	$12-$75	458
㊳ / p. 382		Hudson Cafeteria	◆◆◆	$11-$38	466
㊴ / p. 382		Cafe Gray	◆◆◆◆	$26-$38	460
㊵ / p. 382		Bello Restaurant	◆◆◆	$15-$30	458

Spotter/Map Page Number	OA	MIDTOWN MANHATTAN - Restaurants (continued)	Diamond Rating	Rate Range High Season	Listing Page
(41) / p. 382	AAA	San Domenico	◆◆◆◆	$25-$35	476
(42) / p. 382		Daniel	◆◆◆◆◆	$92-$168	463
(43) / p. 382		Arabelle	◆◆◆◆	$29-$38	457
(44) / p. 382		Cafe Evergreen	◆◆	$7-$16	460
(45) / p. 382		Petrossian	◆◆◆	$29-$37	474
(46) / p. 382		Cafe Europa	◆◆	$7-$13	460
(47) / p. 382		The Post House	◆◆	$22-$50	475
(48) / p. 382		Trattoria Dell'Arte	◆◆	$16-$28	479
(49) / p. 382		Patsy's Italian Restaurant	◆◆◆	$21-$39	474
(50) / p. 382		Cafe Pierre	◆◆◆◆	$18-$36	460
(51) / p. 382		Park Avenue Cafe	◆◆◆	$20-$39	473
(52) / p. 382		Nocello	◆◆◆	$12-$23	472
(53) / p. 382		Jo Jo	◆◆◆◆	$18-$65	468
(54) / p. 382		Redeye Grill	◆◆◆	$12-$35	475
(55) / p. 382		Sugiyama	◆◆◆	$32-$175	478
(56) / p. 382		Mickey Mantle's	◆◆	$9-$30	471
(57) / p. 382		Geisha	◆◆◆	$19-$34	466
(58) / p. 382		Jekyll & Hyde Club	◆◆	$13-$25	467
(59) / p. 382		Aureole	◆◆◆◆◆	$79-$125	457
(60) / p. 382		Fred's at Barney's	◆◆◆	$18-$32	465
(61) / p. 382		Molyvos	◆◆◆	$20-$29	471
(62) / p. 382		Norma's	◆◆◆	$10-$24(L)	472
(63) / p. 382		Asia Grill	◆◆	$7-$20	457
(64) / p. 382		Carnegie Delicatessen & Restaurant	◆	$10-$20	461
(65) / p. 382		Uncle Nick's Greek Cuisine	◆	$10-$25	479
(66) / p. 382		davidburke & donatella	◆◆◆◆	$22-$44	463
(67) / p. 382		Grand Sichuan International Midtown	◆◆	$8-$20	466
(68) / p. 382		Rice 'n' Beans	◆	$14-$23	475
(69) / p. 382		Estiatorio Milos	◆◆◆	$45-$75	465
(70) / p. 382		Stage Deli	◆	$10-$20	478
(71) / p. 382		ViceVersa	◆◆◆	$15-$28	479
(72) / p. 382		Rene Pujol	◆◆◆	$44	475
(73) / p. 382		Costa del Sol Restaurant	◆◆	$13-$36	463
(74) / p. 382		Famous Original Ray's Pizza	◆	$3-$23	465
(75) / p. 382		Brasserie 8 1/2	◆◆◆	$25-$37	459
(76) / p. 382		Osteria del Circo	◆◆◆	$20-$37	473
(77) / p. 382		Bay Leaf Indian Brasserie	◆◆	$20-$35	458

Spotter/Map Page Number	OA	MIDTOWN MANHATTAN - Restaurants (continued)	Diamond Rating	Rate Range High Season	Listing Page
78 / p. 382		Siam Inn	◆◆	$10-$17	477
79 / p. 382		Lindy's	◆◆	$13-$25	470
80 / p. 382		Victor's Cafe 52	◆◆	$10-$32	480
81 / p. 382		Tao	◆◆◆	$16-$28	478
82 / p. 382		Beacon	◆◆◆	$27-$38	458
83 / p. 382		Gallagher's Steak House	◆◆	$19-$40	466
84 / p. 382		Town	◆◆◆	$22-$36	479
85 / p. 382		Zona Rosa	◆◆◆	$18-$27	481
86 / p. 382		Remi	◆◆◆	$18-$38	475
87 / p. 382		LCB Brasserie Rachou	◆◆◆◆	$22-$39	469
88 / p. 382		Cafe Spice	◆◆	$10-$22	461
89 / p. 382		Pongal South Indian Vegetarian Restaurant	◆◆	$8-$15	474
90 / p. 382		Fifty-Seven Restaurant & Bar	◆◆◆◆	$28-$45	465
91 / p. 382		Brasserie 360	◆◆◆	$8-$22	459
92 / p. 382	◭◭◭	**Murals on 54 Restaurant**	◇◇◇	$26-$34	472
93 / p. 382		Russo's Steak & Pasta	◆◆◆	$16-$32	476
94 / p. 382		Michael's Restaurant	◆◆◆	$26-$38	471
95 / p. 382		Le Bernardin	◆◆◆◆	$105	469
96 / p. 382	◭◭◭	**Churrascaria Plataforma**	◇◇	$52	462
97 / p. 382		Ciro	◆◆	$18-$40	462
98 / p. 382		New York Palm-Times Square	◆◆◆	$19-$43	472
99 / p. 382		Moda	◆◆◆	$18-$33	471
100 / p. 382		Amarone Ristorante	◆◆	$11-$27	456
101 / p. 382		Le Cirque	◆◆◆◆	$42-$48	469
102 / p. 382	◭◭◭	**Mars 2112**	◇◇	$13-$26	470
103 / p. 382		Ben Benson's Steak House	◆◆◆	$16-$39	458
104 / p. 382		Hell's Kitchen	◆◆	$15-$25	466
105 / p. 382		Sombrero Mexican Restaurant	◆◆	$17-$19	477
106 / p. 382		BLT Steak	◆◆◆◆	$24-$79	458
107 / p. 382		Social Bar & Grill	◆◆	$8-$11	477
108 / p. 382		Ruby Foo's Dim Sum & Sushi Palace	◆◆◆	$16-$35	476
109 / p. 382		China Grill	◆◆◆	$13-$39	462
110 / p. 382		Pigalle	◆◆	$7-$24	474
111 / p. 382		East River Cafe	◆◆	$12-$20	464
112 / p. 382		Brazil Grill	◆◆	$20-$35	459
113 / p. 382		Le Colonial	◆◆◆	$15-$24	469
114 / p. 382		Zen Palate	◆◆	$13-$19	480

Spotter/Map Page Number	OA	**MIDTOWN MANHATTAN - Restaurants (continued)**	Diamond Rating	Rate Range High Season	Listing Page
(115) / p. 382		Opia	▽▽▽	$6-$16	472
(116) / p. 382	⊕	**Cite**	▽▽▽	$20-$33	462
(117) / p. 382		Cara Mia	▽▽	$9-$26	461
(118) / p. 382		dawat	▽▽▽	$13-$23	463
(119) / p. 382		Aquavit	▽▽▽▽	$80-$105	457
(120) / p. 382		Felidia	▽▽▽	$18-$32	465
(121) / p. 382		Becco	▽▽	$22	458
(122) / p. 382		Yum Yum Bangkok	▽	$7-$15	480
(123) / p. 382		The Delta Grill	▽▽	$10-$22	464
(124) / p. 382		Noche	▽▽▽	$17-$30	472
(125) / p. 382		Bangkok House	▽▽	$8-$17	457
(126) / p. 382		Oceana	▽▽▽▽	$78	472
(127) / p. 382	⊕	**21 Club**	▽▽▽	$30-$45	456
(128) / p. 382		ACQUA PAZZA	▽▽▽	$20-$40	456
(129) / p. 382		Barbetta	▽▽▽	$24-$35	458
(130) / p. 382		La Rivista	▽▽	$19-$33	469
(131) / p. 382		The Steakhouse at Monkey Bar	▽▽▽	$18-$36	478
(132) / p. 382		Joe Allen	▽▽	$14-$27	467
(133) / p. 382		Marseille	▽▽▽	$17-$28	471
(134) / p. 382		Orso	▽▽▽	$18-$28	473
(135) / p. 382		La Grenouille	▽▽▽▽	$90	469
(136) / p. 382	⊕	**Foley's Restaurant & Bar**	▽▽▽	$25-$39	465
(137) / p. 382		L'Allegria Ristorante	▽▽▽	$13-$29	469
(138) / p. 382		Sushiden Sixth Avenue	▽▽▽	$10-$30	478
(139) / p. 382		Raku-It's Japanese!	▽	$12-$125	475
(140) / p. 382		Kyma	▽▽	$16-$23	468
(141) / p. 382		Shun Lee Palace	▽▽▽	$14-$39	477
(142) / p. 382		Lever House Restaurant	▽▽▽▽	$29-$40	470
(143) / p. 382		City Lobster and Crab Company	▽▽▽	$19-$39	463
(144) / p. 382		The Playwright Tavern	▽▽	$14-$25	474
(145) / p. 382		Blue Fin	▽▽▽	$19-$28	459
(146) / p. 382		Korea Palace	▽▽	$15-$40	468
(147) / p. 382		Daniela's Trattoria	▽▽	$9-$18	463
(148) / p. 382		Rachel's American Bistro	▽▽	$8-$22	475
(149) / p. 382		Chimichurri Grill	▽▽▽	$17-$28	462
(150) / p. 382		Esca	▽▽▽	$19-$35	465
(151) / p. 382		March	▽▽▽▽	$55-$95	470

Spotter/Map Page Number	OA	MIDTOWN MANHATTAN - Restaurants (continued)	Diamond Rating	Rate Range High Season	Listing Page
(152) / p. 382		Fresco by Scotto	◈◈◈	$18-$46	465
(153) / p. 382		Rock Center Cafe	◈◈	$20-$39	476
(154) / p. 382		The Four Seasons	◈◈◈◈	$85-$100	465
(155) / p. 382	◬	**Chez Josephine**	◈◈◈◈	$18-$32	461
(156) / p. 382		The Sea Grill	◈◈◈	$28-$45	477
(157) / p. 382		Sushi Ann	◈◈◈	$20	478
(158) / p. 382		Vong Restaurant	◈◈◈	$19-$40	480
(159) / p. 382		The View	◈◈◈	$55	480
(160) / p. 382		District	◈◈◈	$26-$36	464
(161) / p. 382		Morrell Wine Bar & Cafe	◈◈◈	$19-$37	471
(162) / p. 382		John's Pizzeria-Times Square	◈◈	$8-$16	468
(163) / p. 382		Angus McIndoe Restaurant	◈◈	$11-$28	456
(164) / p. 382		Maloney & Porcelli	◈◈	$22-$40	470
(165) / p. 382		Gilt	◈◈◈◈	$55-$105	466
(166) / p. 382		Istana	◈◈◈	$20-$38	467
(167) / p. 382		The Rainbow Grill	◈◈◈	$22-$47	475
(168) / p. 382		Sardi's	◈◈◈	$19-$35	477
(169) / p. 382		Giambelli 50th	◈◈◈	$29-$35	466
(170) / p. 382		Cinquanta Ristorante	◈◈◈	$13-$29	462
(171) / p. 382		Il Nido	◈◈◈	$19-$35	467
(172) / p. 382		Ollie's	◈	$8-$20	472
(173) / p. 382		Restaurant Nippon	◈◈	$22-$45	475
(174) / p. 382		Cafe St. Bart's	◈◈	$17-$32	460
(175) / p. 382	◬	**Jaipur's Indian Cuisine**	◈◈	$11-$27	467
(176) / p. 382	◬	**Mr. K's**	◈◈◈◈	$18-$38	471
(177) / p. 382		La Mangeoire	◈◈	$12-$32	469
(178) / p. 382		Ocean 50	◈◈◈	$25-$50	472
(179) / p. 382		Kuruma Zushi	◈◈◈	$20-$200	468
(180) / p. 382		Virgil's Real Barbecue	◈◈	$7-$24	480
(181) / p. 382		Oscar's American Brasserie	◈◈◈	$15-$27	473
(182) / p. 382		Above	◈◈◈	$10-$28	456
(183) / p. 382	◬	**St. Andrews**	◈◈	$17-$27	476
(184) / p. 382		Ess-a-Bagel	◈	$2-$10	465
(185) / p. 382		SushiZen	◈◈◈	$19-$31	478
(186) / p. 382		Amma	◈◈	$12-$28	456
(187) / p. 382	◬	**San Martin Restaurant**	◈◈	$15-$32	476
(188) / p. 382		db bistro moderne	◈◈◈◈	$27-$38	463

Spotter/Map Page Number	OA	MIDTOWN MANHATTAN - Restaurants (continued)	Diamond Rating	Rate Range High Season	Listing Page
189 / p. 382		Bread and Olive	◆	$5-$10	459
190 / p. 382		DeGrezia	◆◆◆	$25-$50	464
191 / p. 382		Triomphe New York	◆◆◆	$20-$50	479
192 / p. 382		Smith & Wollensky	◆◆◆	$18-$48	477
193 / p. 382		AVRA Estiatorio	◆◆◆	$20-$36	457
194 / p. 382		Zarela	◆◆	$14-$19	480
195 / p. 382		Pampano	◆◆◆	$23-$30	473
196 / p. 382		Jewel of India	◆◆	$10-$26	467
197 / p. 382	▲▲▲	**Le Perigord**	◆◆◆	$62	470
198 / p. 382		44 at Royalton	◆◆◆	$13-$32	456
199 / p. 382		Junior's	◆	$6-$11	468
200 / p. 382		Diwan	◆◆	$13-$26	464
201 / p. 382		Chin Chin	◆◆◆	$15-$22	462
202 / p. 382		Chiam	◆◆◆	$20-$25	462
203 / p. 382		Django	◆◆◆	$19-$28	464
204 / p. 382		Cafe Centro	◆◆◆	$20-$27	460
205 / p. 382		Uncle Jack's Steakhouse	◆◆◆	$40-$60	479
206 / p. 382		Patroon	◆◆◆	$25-$38	474
207 / p. 382		Croton Reservoir Tavern	◆◆◆	$18-$32	463
208 / p. 382		Sparks Steak House	◆◆	$25-$38	477
209 / p. 382		Michael Jordan's The Steakhouse N.Y.C.	◆◆◆	$22-$38	471
210 / p. 382		Bryant Park Grill	◆◆	$19-$35	459
211 / p. 382	▲▲▲	**Riingo** - see color ad p 421	◆◆◆◆	$17-$28	475
212 / p. 382		Charlie Palmer's Metrazur	◆◆◆	$19-$30	461
213 / p. 382		Zocalo Grand Central	◆◆	$10-$20	481
214 / p. 382		Paninoteca Italiana	◆	$4-$9	473
215 / p. 382		Tick Tock Diner	◆	$8-$19	478
216 / p. 382		Salmon River	◆◆◆	$12-$26	476
217 / p. 382		Pershing Square Cafe	◆◆	$18-$35	474
218 / p. 382		Tupelo Grill	◆◆	$15-$30	479
219 / p. 382		The Capital Grille	◆◆◆	$21-$38	461
220 / p. 382		Sushi Yasuda	◆◆◆	$18-$29	478
221 / p. 382	▲▲▲	**Malika**	◆◆	$10-$21	470
222 / p. 382		Keens Steakhouse	◆◆◆	$18-$45	468
223 / p. 382		Domenico	◆◆	$16-$34	464
224 / p. 382	▲▲▲	**Ristorante Cinque Terre**	◆◆◆	$9-$35	476
225 / p. 382		Docks Oyster Bar & Seafood Grill	◆◆	$15-$28	464

Spotter/Map Page Number	OA	MIDTOWN MANHATTAN - Restaurants (continued)	Diamond Rating	Rate Range High Season	Listing Page
226 / p. 382		Asia de Cuba	▽▽▽	$23-$36	457
227 / p. 382		Cibo	▽▽▽	$15-$35	462
228 / p. 382		English is Italian	▽▽▽	$20-$42	464
229 / p. 382		Toledo Restaurant	▽▽▽	$23-$45	479
230 / p. 382		L'Impero	▽▽▽	$15-$29	470
231 / p. 382		Byblos	▽▽	$30-$35	459
232 / p. 382		Josie's	▽▽	$12-$22	468
233 / p. 382		Dae Dong Manhattan	▽▽	$10-$36	463
234 / p. 382		Artisanal	▽▽▽	$17-$25	457
235 / p. 382		Park Bistro	▽▽	$20-$32	473
236 / p. 382		Brasserie Les Halles	▽▽▽	$13-$28	459
237 / p. 382		Chinese Mirch	▽▽	$7-$14	462
238 / p. 382		Vatan	▽▽	$24	479
239 / p. 382		Dos Caminos	▽▽▽	$11-$28	464
240 / p. 382		I Trulli	▽▽▽	$19-$36	467
241 / p. 382		Blue Smoke	▽▽	$9-$24	459
242 / p. 382		L'Annam	▽▽	$7-$14	469
243 / p. 382	AAA	**The Water Club**	▽▽▽	$25-$38	480
244 / p. 382		Anh	▽▽	$7-$17	456

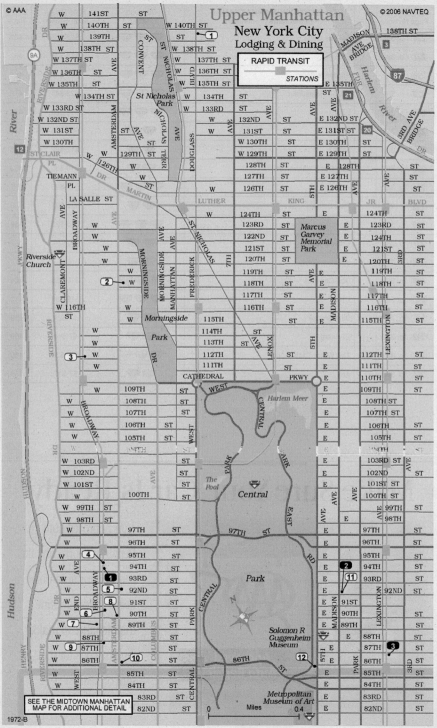

Upper Manhattan New York City

This index helps you "spot" where approved accommodations and restaurants are located on the corresponding detailed maps. Lodging rate ranges are for comparison only and show the property's high season; rates are per night, unless only weekly (W) rates are available. Restaurant rate range is for dinner, unless only lunch (L) is served. Turn to the listing page for more detailed rate information and consult display ads for special promotions.

Spotter/Map Page Number	OA	UPPER MANHATTAN - Lodgings	Diamond Rating	Rate Range High Season	Listing Page
❶ / p. 394	🔺🔺🔺	Hotel Newton - see color ad p 482	◈ ◈	$150-$200 SAVE	482
❷ / p. 394	🔺🔺🔺	Hotel Wales - see color ad p 482	◈ ◈ ◈	$249-$450 SAVE	483
❸ / p. 394		The Franklin Hotel	◈ ◈	Failed to provide	482
		UPPER MANHATTAN - Restaurants			
① / p. 394		Londel's	◈ ◈	$12-$21	483
② / p. 394		Radio Perfecto Restaurant and Bar	◈ ◈	$9-$16	484
③ / p. 394		Tom's Restaurant	◈	$4-$16	484
④ / p. 394		Lemongrass Grill	◈ ◈	$6-$14	483
⑤ / p. 394		Gennaro	◈ ◈	$9-$19	483
⑥ / p. 394		Carmine's-Upper West Side	◈ ◈	$20-$73	483
⑦ / p. 394		Docks Oyster Bar	◈ ◈	$17-$30	483
⑧ / p. 394		Saigon Grill	◈	$8-$14	484
⑨ / p. 394		AIX	◈ ◈ ◈	$26-$39	483
⑩ / p. 394		Barney Greengrass	◈ ◈	$4-$38(L)	483
⑪ / p. 394		Sarabeth's	◈ ◈	$11-$25	484
⑫ / p. 394		Cafe Sabarsky	◈ ◈	$10-$25	483

New York City
And Vicinity
Lodging & Dining

0   Miles   3.1

© AAA   To Staten Island   1964-B ©2006 NAVTEQ

✈ Airport Accommodations

Spotter/Map Page Number	OA	LA GUARDIA	Diamond Rating	Rate Range High Season	Listing Page
14 / p. 396	AAA	Clarion Hotel at La Guardia Airport, opposite airport	◇◇◇	$225-$285 SAVE	489
15 / p. 396		Courtyard by Marriott New York/La Guardia Airport, opposite airport	◇◇◇	$329-$429	490
17 / p. 396	AAA	Crowne Plaza Hotel La Guardia, 0.4 mi from entrance	◇◇◇	$399 SAVE	491
16 / p. 396		New York La Guardia Airport Marriott, opposite terminal	◇◇◇	$199-$369	493
24 / p. 396	AAA	Sheraton La Guardia East Hotel, 3 mi se of terminal	◇◇◇	$199-$429 SAVE	495

✈ Airport Accommodations

Spotter/Map Page Number	OA	JOHN F. KENNEDY INTERNATIONAL	Diamond Rating	Rate Range High Season	Listing Page
44 / p. 396	AAA	Best Western Kennedy Airport, 0.5 mi e of airport	◇◇	$99-$239 SAVE	488
46 / p. 396		Comfort Inn at JFK Airport, 0.5 mi e of terminal	◇◇	Failed to provide	490
40 / p. 396		Courtyard by Marriott JFK Airport, 1 mi n of terminal	◇◇◇	$159-$269	490
45 / p. 396		Days Inn JFK Airport, 0.5 mi e of airport	◇◇	$89-$189	491
39 / p. 396		DoubleTree Hotel JFK Airport, 0.5 mi ne of terminal	◇◇◇	Failed to provide	491
41 / p. 396	AAA	Fairfield Inn New York JFK Airport, 1.5 mi w of entrance	◇◇◇	$139-$179 SAVE	492
42 / p. 396		Holiday Inn Express, 0.5 mi e of terminal	◇◇◇	$99-$299	492
37 / p. 396	AAA	Holiday Inn-JFK Airport, just n of terminal	◇◇◇	$159-$209 SAVE	493
47 / p. 396		Ramada Plaza Hotel at JFK, at entrance to terminal	◇◇	$165-$225	494

New York City and Vicinity

This index helps you "spot" where approved accommodations and restaurants are located on the corresponding detailed maps. Lodging rate ranges are for comparison only and show the property's high season; rates are per night, unless only weekly (W) rates are available. Restaurant rate range is for dinner, unless only lunch (L) is served. Turn to the listing page for more detailed rate information and consult display ads for special promotions.

Spotter/Map Page Number	OA	BROOKLYN - Lodgings	Diamond Rating	Rate Range High Season	Listing Page
1 / p. 396		New York Marriott at the Brooklyn Bridge	◇◇◇	$399-$609	486
2 / p. 396		Howard Johnson-Brooklyn	◇◇	$100-$270	486
3 / p. 396		Bed & Breakfast on the Park	◇◇◇	$155-$300	485
4 / p. 396		Avenue Plaza Hotel	◇◇◇	$129-$449	485
5 / p. 396	AAA	Best Western Gregory Hotel - see color ad p 485	◇◇	$189-$219 SAVE	485
6 / p. 396	AAA	Comfort Inn	◇◇◇	$129-$229 SAVE	486
		BROOKLYN - Restaurants			
① / p. 396		Peter Luger's	◇◇	$35-$70	487
② / p. 396		River Cafe	◇◇◇◇	$85	487
③ / p. 396		Grimaldi's Pizzeria	◇	$12-$18	487
④ / p. 396		Kapadokya	◇◇	$10-$22	487
⑤ / p. 396		Fragole	◇◇	$10-$15	486

Spotter/Map Page Number	OA	BROOKLYN - Restaurants (continued)	Diamond Rating	Rate Range High Season	Listing Page
6 / p. 396	AAA	Aunt Suzie's Restaurant	◆◆	$13-$17	486
7 / p. 396		Amin Indian Restaurant	◆◆	$9-$20	486
8 / p. 396		Blue Ribbon Sushi	◆◆	$12-$27	486
9 / p. 396		Blue Ribbon Brooklyn	◆◆◆	$13-$49	486
10 / p. 396		Bar Minnow	◆◆	$15-$25	486
11 / p. 396		Tommaso's	◆◆	$9-$30	487
12 / p. 396		Ocean View Cafe	◆	$7-$18	487
		FLORAL PARK - Lodgings			
9 / p. 396	AAA	Floral Park Motor Lodge - see color ad p 491	◆◆	$101-$136 SAVE	302
		FLORAL PARK - Restaurants			
15 / p. 396		Arturo's	◆◆◆	$14-$30	302
16 / p. 396		Poppy's Place	◆◆	$12-$28	302
		QUEENS - Lodgings			
12 / p. 396		Extended StayAmerica-Whitestone	◆◆	$139-$164	491
13 / p. 396		Fairfield Inn by Marriot La Guardia Airport	◆◆◆	Failed to provide	492
14 / p. 396	AAA	Clarion Hotel at La Guardia Airport	◆◆◆	$225-$285 SAVE	489
15 / p. 396		Courtyard by Marriott New York/La Guardia Airport	◆◆◆	$329-$429	490
16 / p. 396		New York La Guardia Airport Marriott	◆◆◆	$199-$369	493
17 / p. 396	AAA	Crowne Plaza Hotel La Guardia	◆◆◆	$399 SAVE	491
18 / p. 396	AAA	Super 8 Motel	◆◆	$99-$199 SAVE	495
19 / p. 396		Wingate Inn & Suites La Guardia Airport	◆◆◆	$129-$399	495
20 / p. 396	AAA	Adria Hotel and Conference Center	◆◆	$129-$169 SAVE	488
21 / p. 396	AAA	Ramada Inn Adria	◆◆	$129-$169 SAVE	494
22 / p. 396	AAA	Anchor Inn - see color ad p 488	◆◆	$129-$169 SAVE	488
23 / p. 396	AAA	Comfort Inn La Guardia	◆◆	$109-$299 SAVE	490
24 / p. 396	AAA	Sheraton La Guardia East Hotel - see color ad p 494	◆◆◆	$199-$429 SAVE	495
25 / p. 396	AAA	Best Western Queens Court Hotel	◆◆◆	$219-$349 SAVE	489
26 / p. 396		Ramada Plaza La Guardia	◆◆◆	Failed to provide	494
27 / p. 396	AAA	Comfort Inn Long Island City	◆◆	$139-$189 SAVE	490
28 / p. 396		Best Western Eden Park Hotel	◆◆	Failed to provide	488
29 / p. 396	AAA	Pan American Hotel - see color ad p 493, p 445	◆◆	$109-$229 SAVE	494
30 / p. 396	AAA	Holiday Inn Express	◆◆	$199-$259 SAVE	493
31 / p. 396	AAA	Best Western City View - see color ad p 489	◆◆	$139-$199 SAVE	488
32 / p. 396		Comfort Inn & Suites	◆◆◆	$129-$299	489
33 / p. 396	AAA	Quality Inn Jamaica	◆◆	$95-$105 SAVE	494
34 / p. 396		Econo Lodge	◆	$89-$189	491
35 / p. 396		Howard Johnson Express Inn-JFK Airport	◆◆	$90-$180	493
36 / p. 396		Hampton Inn-JFK Airport	◆◆◆	$159-$289	492
37 / p. 396	AAA	Holiday Inn-JFK Airport	◆◆◆	$159-$209 SAVE	493

Spotter/Map Page Number	OA	QUEENS - Lodgings (continued)	Diamond Rating	Rate Range High Season	Listing Page
38 / p. 396		Crowne Plaza Hotel-JFK Airport	♦♦♦	Failed to provide	491
39 / p. 396		DoubleTree Hotel JFK Airport	♦♦♦	Failed to provide	491
40 / p. 396		Courtyard by Marriott JFK Airport - see color ad p 490	♦♦♦	$159-$269	490
41 / p. 396	AAA	**Fairfield Inn New York JFK Airport**	♦♦♦	$139-$179 [SAVE]	492
42 / p. 396		Holiday Inn Express	♦♦♦	$99-$299	492
43 / p. 396	AAA	**Hilton Garden Inn-Queens/JFK Airport** - see color ad p 492	♦♦♦	$159-$269 [SAVE]	492
44 / p. 396	AAA	**Best Western Kennedy Airport**	♦♦	$99-$239 [SAVE]	488
45 / p. 396		Days Inn JFK Airport	♦♦	$89-$189	491
46 / p. 396		Comfort Inn at JFK Airport	♦♦	Failed to provide	490
47 / p. 396		Ramada Plaza Hotel at JFK	♦♦	$165-$225	494
		QUEENS - Restaurants			
19 / p. 396		Mombar	♦♦	$16-$25	495
20 / p. 396		Uncle Jack's Steakhouse	♦♦♦	$40-$60	496
21 / p. 396		First Edition	♦	$8-$17	495
22 / p. 396	AAA	**Erawan Thai Cuisine**	♦♦	$10-$20	495
23 / p. 396		Lailla Bar & Restaurant	♦♦	$11-$15	495
24 / p. 396		Green Papaya	♦♦	$8-$19	495
25 / p. 396		Mythos	♦♦	$10-$20	496
26 / p. 396		Buddha Bodai Restaurant	♦♦	$6-$15	495
27 / p. 396		Water's Edge	♦♦♦♦	$58-$78	496
28 / p. 396		Ping's	♦♦	$8-$20	496

LOWER MANHATTAN (See map and index starting on p. 376)

———— WHERE TO STAY ————

BEST WESTERN SEAPORT INN DOWNTOWN *Book great rates at AAA.com*   Phone: (212)766-6600   **15**

(AAA) (SAVE)

9/1-12/31	1P: $289-$379	2P: $299-$399	XP: $10 F12
5/1-6/30	1P: $269-$349	2P: $279-$359	XP: $10 F12
7/1-8/31	1P: $259-$349	2P: $269-$359	XP: $10 F12
1/1-4/30	1P: $209-$349	2P: $219-$359	XP: $10 F12

Historic
Small-scale Hotel

Location: North end of South St Seaport. 33 Peck Slip on Front St 10038. Fax: 212/766-6615. **Facility:** This 19th-century guest house features some units with terraces overlooking the seaport. 72 one-bedroom standard units, some with whirlpools. 7 stories, interior corridors. *Bath:* combo or shower only. **Parking:** no self-parking. **Terms:** cancellation fee imposed. **Amenities:** video library, video games (fee), high-speed Internet, dual phone lines, voice mail, safes, irons, hair dryers. **Leisure Activities:** exercise room. **Guest Services:** complimentary evening beverages: Wed, valet laundry. **Business Services:** meeting rooms, PC. **Cards:** AX, DC, DS, MC, VI. **Free Special Amenities:** continental breakfast and high-speed Internet.

SOME UNITS

EMBASSY SUITES HOTEL NEW YORK *Book great rates at AAA.com*   Phone: (212)945-0100   **11**

All Year [AP]	1P: $209-$559	2P: $209-$559	XP: $30 F

Large-scale Hotel

Location: Between Murray and Vesey sts. 102 N End Ave 10282. Fax: 212/945-3012. **Facility:** 463 units. 462 one- and 1 two-bedroom suites. 15 stories, interior corridors. *Bath:* combo or shower only. **Parking:** valet. **Terms:** check-in 4 pm, pets ($75 fee). **Amenities:** dual phone lines, voice mail, safes, honor bars, irons, hair dryers. *Fee:* video games, high-speed Internet. *Some:* CD players, fax. **Guest Services:** gift shop, complimentary evening beverages, valet and coin laundry, wireless Internet. **Business Services:** conference facilities, business center. **Cards:** AX, CB, DC, DS, JC, MC, VI. *(See color ad starting on p 436)*

SOME UNITS

FEE

FOUR POINTS BY SHERATON MANHATTAN
CHELSEA *Book great rates at AAA.com*   Phone: 212/627-1888   **1**

All Year	1P: $295-$625	2P: $295-$625	XP: $20 F17

Small-scale Hotel

Location: Between 6th (Ave of the Americas) and 7th aves. 160 W 25th St 10001. Fax: 212/627-1611. **Facility:** 158 units. 156 one-bedroom standard units. 2 one-bedroom suites. 22 stories, interior corridors. *Bath:* combo or shower only. **Parking:** on-site (fee). **Terms:** cancellation fee imposed, [AP] meal plan available. **Amenities:** high-speed Internet, dual phone lines, voice mail, safes, irons, hair dryers. **Leisure Activities:** exercise room. **Guest Services:** valet laundry. **Business Services:** meeting rooms, PC. **Cards:** AX, DC, DS, MC, VI.

SOME UNITS

HAMPTON INN-MANHATTAN/CHELSEA *Book great rates at AAA.com*   Phone: (212)414-1000   **2**

(AAA) (SAVE)

9/11-12/15	1P: $199-$430	2P: $229-$460	
5/1-6/30	1P: $189-$349	2P: $219-$379	
7/1-9/10 & 12/16-4/30	1P: $179-$329	2P: $209-$359	

Small-scale Hotel

Location: Between 6th (Ave of the Americas) and 7th aves. 108 W 24th St 10011. Fax: 212/647-1511. **Facility:** 144 one-bedroom standard units. 20 stories, interior corridors. *Bath:* combo or shower only. **Parking:** no self-parking. **Terms:** small pets only ($20 fee). **Amenities:** high-speed Internet, dual phone lines, voice mail, irons, hair dryers. *Some:* DVD players, CD players. **Leisure Activities:** Patio, exercise room. **Guest Services:** valet and coin laundry, wireless Internet. **Cards:** AX, CB, DC, DS, JC, MC, VI. **Free Special Amenities:** high-speed Internet. *(See color ad p 432)*

SOME UNITS

FEE

HAMPTON INN-MANHATTAN/SEAPORT/FINANCIAL
DISTRICT *Book great rates at AAA.com*   Phone: (212)571-4400   **14**

(AAA) (SAVE)

8/27-12/31 [BP]	1P: $232-$444	2P: $232-$444	XP: $10 F
3/26-4/30 [BP]	1P: $198-$410	2P: $198-$410	XP: $10 F
5/1-8/26 [BP]	1P: $173-$410	2P: $173-$410	XP: $10 F
1/1-3/25 [BP]	1P: $148-$334	2P: $148-$334	XP: $10 F

Small-scale Hotel

Location: Between deck slip and Dover St. 320 Pearl St 10038. Fax: 212/571-3300. **Facility:** 65 one-bedroom standard units. 9 stories, interior corridors. *Bath:* combo or shower only. **Parking:** no self-parking. **Terms:** cancellation fee imposed, package plans, pets ($20 fee). **Amenities:** high-speed Internet, dual phone lines, voice mail, irons, hair dryers. **Leisure Activities:** limited exercise equipment. **Guest Services:** valet laundry, wireless Internet. **Business Services:** PC. **Cards:** AX, CB, DC, DS, JC, MC, VI. **Free Special Amenities:** high-speed Internet. *(See color ad p 432)*

SOME UNITS

FEE

HOLIDAY INN DOWNTOWN/SOHO *Book great rates at AAA.com*   Phone: (212)966-8898   **10**

(AAA) (SAVE)

9/5-12/31	1P: $499	2P: $529	XP: $20 F12
5/1-6/30	1P: $399	2P: $419	XP: $20 F12
1/1-4/30	1P: $299	2P: $329	XP: $20 F12
7/1-9/4	1P: $299	2P: $319	XP: $20 F12

Small-scale Hotel

Location: In Chinatown; corner of Howard St; just n of Canal St. 138 Lafayette St 10013. Fax: 212/966-3933. **Facility:** 227 one-bedroom standard units. 14 stories, interior corridors. *Bath:* combo or shower only. **Parking:** valet. **Terms:** 3 day cancellation notice-fee imposed. **Amenities:** CD players, high-speed Internet, dual phone lines, voice mail, irons, hair dryers. *Some:* fax. **Guest Services:** valet laundry. **Business Services:** meeting rooms, PC. **Cards:** AX, CB, DC, DS, JC, MC, VI. **Free Special Amenities:** newspaper and high-speed Internet. *(See color ad p 401)*

SOME UNITS

FEE FEE FEE

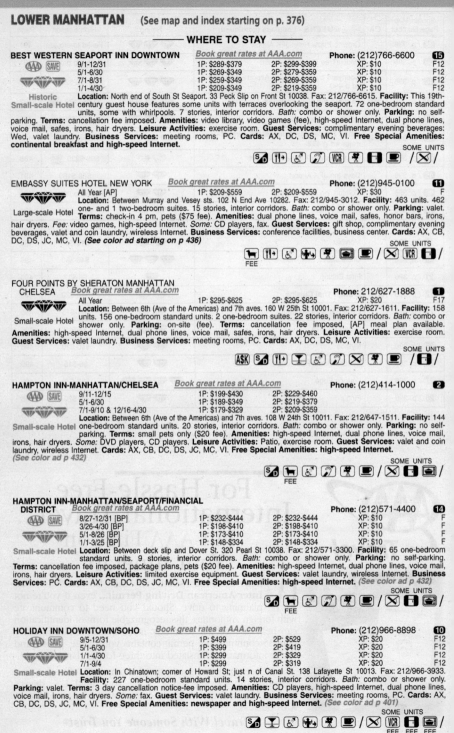

(See map and index starting on p. 376)

HOTEL GANSEVOORT   **Phone: (212)660-6700**   **3**

5/1-6/30	1P: $555	2P: $555 XP: $20 F
9/6-4/30	1P: $505	2P: $505 XP: $20 F
7/1-9/5	1P: $495	2P: $495 XP: $20 F

Small-scale Hotel   **Location:** At 13th St. 18 9th Ave 10014. Fax: 212/255-5858. **Facility:** Luxury is modern and comforts very gracious at this stylish property which glows at night and offers fine service, generous extras and water views. 187 units. 166 one-bedroom standard units. 20 one- and 1 two-bedroom suites, some with whirlpools. 14 stories, interior corridors. *Bath:* combo or shower only. **Parking:** valet. **Terms:** cancellation fee imposed, [AP] & [BP] meal plans available, small pets only ($65 deposit). **Amenities:** video library (fee), video games, CD players, high-speed Internet, dual phone lines, voice mail, safes, honor bars, irons, hair dryers. *Some:* DVD players. **Pool(s):** small heated indoor/outdoor. **Leisure Activities:** exercise room, spa. **Guest Services:** gift shop, valet laundry, wireless Internet. **Business Services:** meeting rooms, business center. **Cards:** AX, DC, DS, MC, VI.

SOME UNITS

HOWARD JOHNSON EXPRESS INN   *Book great rates at AAA.com*   **Phone: 212-358-8844**   **6**

All Year   1P: $139-$299   2P: $139-$309   XP: $10
Location: Jct Forsythe; between 1st and 2nd aves. 135 E Houston St 10002. Fax: 212/473-3500. **Facility:** 45 one-bedroom standard units. 6 stories, interior corridors. **Parking:** no self-parking. **Terms:** cancellation fee imposed. **Amenities:** voice mail, safes, irons, hair dryers. **Guest Services:** valet laundry, wireless Internet.

Small-scale Hotel   **Cards:** AX, CB, DC, DS, JC, MC, VI. **Free Special Amenities: continental breakfast and local telephone calls.**

SOME UNITS

THE INN AT IRVING PLACE   *Book at AAA.com*   **Phone: 212/533-4600**   **5**

Property failed to provide current rates

Historic Bed & Breakfast   **Location:** Between 17th and 18th sts. 56 Irving Pl 10003. Fax: 212/533-4611. **Facility:** 1834 Greek Revival in historic Gramercy Park. Period antiques in guest rooms. Smoke free premises. 12 one-bedroom standard units. 4 stories (no elevator), interior corridors. *Bath:* combo or shower only. **Parking:** on-site (fee) and valet. **Terms:** age restrictions may apply. **Amenities:** video library (fee), CD players, honor bars, irons, hair dryers. **Guest Services:** valet laundry, wireless Internet. **Business Services:** meeting rooms.

MILLENIUM HILTON   *Book great rates at AAA.com*   **Phone: (212)693-2001**   **12**

All Year   1P: $199-$849   2P: $229-$879   XP: $30   F18
Location: Between Dey and Fulton sts. Located next to Ground Zero. 55 Church St 10007. Fax: 212/571-2316. **Facility:** This hotel offers magnificent views of the city, including some river views. 569 units. 472 one-bedroom standard units. 93 one- and 4 two-bedroom suites ($779-$5549). 55 stories, interior corridors. **Parking:** on-site (fee) and valet. **Terms:** 1-5 night minimum stay - seasonal, 3 day cancellation notice-fee imposed, [AP], [BP] & [CP] meal plans available, package plans. **Amenities:** dual phone lines, voice mail, safes, honor bars, irons, hair dryers. *Fee:* video games, high-speed Internet. **Dining:** 6:30 am-10 pm, cocktails. **Pool(s):** heated indoor. **Leisure Activities:** sauna, exercise room. *Fee:* massage. **Guest Services:** gift shop, valet laundry. **Business Services:** meeting rooms, business center. **Cards:** AX, CB, DC, DS, JC, MC, VI. **Free Special Amenities: newspaper and preferred room (subject to availability with advance reservations).** *(See color ad starting on p 436)*

SOME UNITS

NEW YORK MARRIOTT FINANCIAL CENTER   *Book great rates at AAA.com*   **Phone: (212)385-4900**   **13**

9/2-12/15	1P: $249-$529	2P: $249-$529
12/16-4/30	1P: $249-$479	2P: $249-$479
5/1-6/30	1P: $219-$459	2P: $219-$459
7/1-9/1	1P: $209-$369	2P: $209-$369

Large-scale Hotel

Location: Between Albany and Carlyle sts. 85 West St 10006. Fax: 212/227-8136. **Facility:** Smoke free premises. 500 units. 493 one-bedroom standard units. 7 one-bedroom suites ($650-$1250). 38 stories, interior corridors. *Bath:* combo or shower only. **Parking:** valet. **Terms:** check-in 4 pm, cancellation fee imposed, package plans. **Amenities:** dual phone lines, voice mail, safes, honor bars, irons, hair dryers. *Fee:* video games, high-speed Internet. *Some:* fax. **Pool(s):** heated indoor. **Leisure Activities:** saunas. **Guest Services:** gift shop, valet laundry, wireless Internet. **Business Services:** conference facilities, business center. **Cards:** AX, CB, DC, DS, JC, MC, VI.

SOME UNITS

(See map and index starting on p. 376)

THE RITZ-CARLTON NEW YORK, BATTERY PARK   *Book at AAA.com*   **Phone:** (212)344-0800 ⑰

9/5-12/31	1P: $750-$1025	
5/1-7/4	1P: $695-$920	
Small-scale Hotel	1/1-4/30	1P: $650-$850
	7/5-9/4	1P: $600-$800

Location: Jct Battery Park. Located opposite Battery Park. Two West St 10004. Fax: 212/344-3801. **Facility:** This luxury waterfront hotel features telescopes in some rooms and offers sweeping views of the Statue of Liberty and Ellis Island. Smoke free premises. 298 units. 258 one-bedroom standard units. 40 one-bedroom suites ($800-$6000), some with whirlpools. 14 stories, interior corridors. *Bath:* combo or shower only. **Parking:** valet. **Terms:** cancellation fee imposed, small pets only ($125 fee). **Amenities:** CD players, dual phone lines, voice mail, safes, honor bars, irons, hair dryers. *Fee:* video library, video games, high-speed Internet. *Some:* DVD players. **Leisure Activities:** spa. **Guest Services:** gift shop, valet laundry, area transportation. **Business Services:** conference facilities, business center. **Cards:** AX, CB, DC, DS, JC, MC, VI.

SOME UNITS

THE SOHO GRAND HOTEL   *Book at AAA.com*   **Phone:** (212)965-3000 ⑦

9/4-12/31	1P: $749	2P: $749
1/1-4/30	1P: $729	2P: $729
Small-scale Hotel	5/1-6/28	1P: $689	2P: $689
	6/29-9/3	1P: $639	2P: $639

Location: In SoHo; jct Grand St. 310 W Broadway 10013. Fax: 212/965-3200. **Facility:** 363 units. 361 one-bedroom standard units. 2 two-bedroom suites ($5000). 17 stories, interior corridors. *Bath:* combo or shower only. **Parking:** valet. **Terms:** cancellation fee imposed, $4 service charge. **Amenities:** CD players, high-speed Internet (fee), dual phone lines, voice mail, safes, honor bars, hair dryers. *Some:* DVD players, irons. **Leisure Activities:** exercise room. **Guest Services:** valet laundry, beauty salon. **Business Services:** meeting rooms, business center. **Cards:** AX, DC, DS, JC, MC, VI.

SOME UNITS

THE SOLITA SOHO HOTEL-CLARION COLLECTION   *Book great rates at AAA.com*   **Phone:** (212)925-3600 ⑧

9/4-12/31	1P: $229-$599	2P: $229-$599	XP: $10	F12
5/1-6/30	1P: $199-$399	2P: $199-$399	XP: $10	F12
1/1-4/30	1P: $179-$399	2P: $179-$399	XP: $10	F12
7/1-9/3	1P: $189-$349	2P: $189-$349	XP: $10	F12

Small-scale Hotel **Location:** Between Lafayette and Centre sts. 159 Grand St 10013. Fax: 212/925-3385. **Facility:** 42 one-bedroom standard units. 12 stories, interior corridors. **Parking:** no self-parking. **Terms:** cancellation fee imposed. **Amenities:** high-speed Internet, voice mail, safes, irons, hair dryers. **Dining:** 6 pm-2 am. **Cards:** AX, DC, DS, MC, VI. **Free Special Amenities:** local telephone calls and high-speed Internet.

SOME UNITS

TRIBECA GRAND HOTEL   *Book at AAA.com*   **Phone:** 212/519-6600 ⑨

Property failed to provide current rates

Location: At 6th Ave (Ave of the Americas) and White St. 2 Ave of the Americas 10013. Fax: 212/519-6700. **Facility:** 203 units. 189 one-bedroom standard units. 14 one-bedroom suites. 8 stories, interior corridors. *Bath:* combo or shower only. **Parking:** valet. **Amenities:** DVD players, video games (fee), CD players, dual phone lines, voice mail, safes, honor bars, irons, hair dryers. **Leisure Activities:** exercise room. **Guest Services:** valet laundry, wireless Internet. **Business Services:** meeting rooms, business center.

SOME UNITS

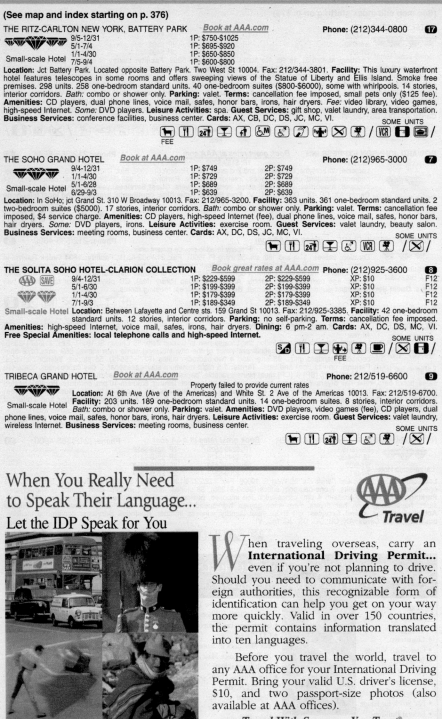

(See map and index starting on p. 376)

THE WALL STREET DISTRICT HOTEL   *Book at AAA.com*   Phone: (212)232-7700   **16**

	9/3-4/30	1P: $349-$579	2P: $349-$579	XP: $30	F
	5/1-6/30	1P: $299-$509	2P: $299-$509	XP: $30	F
	7/1-9/2	1P: $249-$449	2P: $249-$449	XP: $30	F

Large-scale Hotel   **Location:** Corner of Gold and Platt sts. 15 Gold St 10038. Fax: 212/425-0330. **Facility:** 138 units. 137 one-bedroom standard units. 1 one-bedroom suite. 18 stories, interior corridors. *Bath:* combo or shower only. **Parking:** on-site (fee). **Terms:** cancellation fee imposed, small pets only ($25 extra charge). **Amenities:** CD players, dual phone lines, voice mail, safes, honor bars, irons, hair dryers. *Fee:* video games, high-speed Internet. **Leisure Activities:** exercise room. **Guest Services:** valet laundry, personal trainer. **Business Services:** meeting rooms, business center. **Cards:** AX, CB, DC, DS, MC, VI.

SOME UNITS

W NEW YORK-UNION SQUARE   *Book great rates at AAA.com*   Phone: 212/253-9119   **4**

Property failed to provide current rates

Small-scale Hotel   **Location:** At 17th St. 201 Park Ave S 10003. Fax: 212/253-9229. **Facility:** Surfaces reminiscent of mother-of-pearl give the lobby a glittering ambience while guest rooms are handsomely outfitted and luxurious. 270 units. 252 one-bedroom standard units. 18 one-bedroom suites, some with whirlpools. 21 stories, interior corridors. *Bath:* combo or shower only. **Parking:** valet. **Terms:** pets ($100 fee, $25 extra charge). **Amenities:** DVD players, CD players, high-speed Internet (fee), dual phone lines, voice mail, safes, honor bars, irons, hair dryers. **Leisure Activities:** exercise room. *Fee:* massage. **Guest Services:** valet laundry, wireless Internet. **Business Services:** conference facilities, business center.

SOME UNITS

The following lodgings were either not evaluated or did not meet AAA rating requirements but are listed for your information only.

CLARION HOTEL PARK AVENUE   Phone: 212/532-4860

[fyi]   Not evaluated. **Location:** 429 Park Ave S 10016. Facilities, services, and decor characterize a mid-range property.

HOTEL GIRAFFE   Phone: 212/685-7700

[fyi]   Not evaluated. **Location:** At E 26th St. 365 Park Ave S 10016. Facilities, services, and decor characterize a mid-range property.

THE MARITIME HOTEL   Phone: 212/242-4300

[fyi]   Not evaluated. **Location:** Between 8th and 9th aves. 363 W 16th St 10011. Facilities, services, and decor characterize an upscale property.

WHERE TO DINE

---

66   **Dinner:** $19-$29   Phone: 212/925-0202   **106**

Chinese   **Location:** In TriBeCa; between Worth and Leonard sts. 241 Church St 10013. **Hours:** 5:30 pm-11 pm, Thurs-Sat to midnight. **Reservations:** suggested. **Features:** A highly polished and minimally embellished series of rooms includes a large tropical fish tank with a through-kitchen view. It's easy to order a lot from a menu of either small tastes or slightly larger ones. Some of the familiar-sounding dishes are stellar, with rich, clear flavors. Stir-fried shrimp, chive dumplings, beef short ribs and steamed cod with caramelized onion, ginger and scallion look spectacular. Tapioca fruit parfait is texture-filled and fun. Dressy casual; cocktails. **Parking:** street. **Cards:** AX, DC, DS, MC, VI.

ALFAMA, FINE PORTUGUESE CUISINE   **Lunch:** $10-$15   **Dinner:** $22-$34   Phone: 212/645-2500   **48**

Portuguese   **Location:** At Perry St. 551 Hudson St 10014. **Hours:** 6 pm-11 pm, Fri-midnight, Sat noon-3 & 6-midnight, Sun noon-3 & 4:30-11 pm. **Closed:** 5/28, 9/3. **Reservations:** suggested. **Features:** The cozy dining room is pleasant and fresh looking with pressed linen and a charming blue and white Portugese theme. The menu is reflective of the fish and shellfish so abundant in Portugal, but there is also a selection of meats like braised chicken with smoked ham or roasted skewered lamb with garlic. The menu changes but always offers homey hearty dishes though prepared with a somewhat delicate touch. The selection of Portugese wines is considerable. Dressy casual; cocktails. **Parking:** street. **Cards:** AX, DC, DS, MC.

AMICI II   **Lunch:** $10-$20   **Dinner:** $12-$28   Phone: 212/334-3869   **92**

South Italian   **Location:** In Little Italy; between Broome and Grand sts. 165 Mulberry St 10013. **Hours:** 11:30 am-11:30 pm. **Closed:** 12/25. **Reservations:** suggested, weekends. **Features:** Family takes special care at the this restaurant. The setting is friendly, and the menu tempts with such homemade offerings as lobster ravioli. All of the recipes from Amici I, this place's sister restaurant in Naples, Italy, made the trip across the Atlantic Ocean. Casual dress; cocktails. **Parking:** street. **Cards:** MC, VI.

ANGELO & MAXIE'S   **Lunch:** $12-$25   **Dinner:** $12-$25   Phone: 212/220-9200   **36**

Steak House   **Location:** Corner of 19th St. 233 Park Ave 10003. **Hours:** 11:30 am-3 & 5-11 pm, Fri-midnight, Sat 5 pm-midnight, Sun 4 pm-11 pm. **Closed:** 12/25. **Reservations:** suggested. **Features:** This large, contemporary restaurant is quite elegant for a steak house. The high ceilings are filled with decorative lighting and large ornate columns. Indulge in top quality steaks, veal chops and some seafood dishes. Dressy casual; cocktails. **Parking:** street. **Cards:** AX, DC, MC, VI.

(See map and index starting on p. 376)

ANNISA

Asian

Dinner: $27-$33   **Phone:** 212/741-6699   54

Location: In Greenwich Village; w of Washington Square; just s of W 4th St. 13 Barrow St 10014. **Hours:** 5:30 pm-10:30 pm, Sun-9:30 pm. Closed major holidays. **Features:** This is an intimate, upscale, contemporary restaurant located in the heart of Greenwich Village. They have an extensive wine list that celebrates women in the wine industry; almost all wines on their list were made by female vintners and/or made at vineyards with female proprietors. Casual dress; cocktails. **Parking:** street. **Cards:** AX, CB, DC, DS, JC, MC, VI.

AQUAGRILL

French

Lunch: $16-$25   **Dinner:** $19-$50   **Phone:** 212/274-0505   72

Location: In SoHo; between Sullivan St and 6th Ave (Ave of the Americas). 210 Spring St 10012. **Hours:** noon-3 & 6-10:45 pm, Sat & Sun noon-3:45 & 6-10 pm. **Reservations:** accepted. **Features:** This is a must stop for a memorable dining experience supported with exceptional flavors, creativity and high-quality dishes. Gazpacho is incredible, salmon is meticulously poached, and apple-cinnamon tart is imaginative. The menu mostly comprises fresh seafood, all delicious, and some steak and poultry items. Dressy casual; cocktails. **Parking:** street. **Cards:** AX, DC, MC, VI.

AREZZO

Northern Italian

Lunch: $13-$34   **Dinner:** $18-$39   **Phone:** 212/206-0555   11

Location: Between 5th and 6th (Ave of the Americas) aves. 46 W 22nd St 10010. **Hours:** 11:30 am-3 & 5-11 pm, Fri & Sat 5 pm-midnight. Closed major holidays; also Sun. **Reservations:** suggested. **Features:** In the Flatiron district, the cozy, intimate restaurant builds its menu on Tuscan and Northern Italian cuisine. Superb focaccia alla robiola a spinaci is the signature dish. Dressy casual; cocktails. **Parking:** no self-parking. **Cards:** AX, DS, MC, VI.

A VOCE

Italian

Lunch: $21-$30   **Dinner:** $22-$30   **Phone:** 212/545-8555   121

Location: At 26th St, just e of Madison Square Park. 41 Madison Ave 10010. **Hours:** 11:30 am-3 & 5:30-11 pm, Sun-3 pm. Closed major holidays. **Reservations:** suggested. **Features:** Dressy casual; cocktails. **Parking:** street. **Cards:** AX, MC, VI.

BABBO

Italian

Dinner: $16-$28   **Phone:** 212/777-0303   56

Location: Between 6th Ave (Ave of the Americas) and MacDougal St; just w of Washington Square Park. 110 Waverly Pl 10011. **Hours:** 5:30 pm-11:30 pm, Sun 5 pm-11 pm. Closed: 11/22, 12/25. **Reservations:** suggested. **Features:** The hard-to-get Village favorite has received a lot of press for showcasing innovative, new Italian cuisine. Mario Batali uses only fresh global products in designing a most discerning and modern menu. Black tagliatelle with charred corn, rock shrimp and budding chives, along with foie gras ravioli with balsamic vinegar reduction, take the place of traditional fare. The seven-course and pasta-tasting menus are worth their weight in calories. Dressy casual; cocktails. **Parking:** street. **Cards:** AX, DC, MC, VI.

BALTHAZAR

French

Lunch: $11-$23   **Dinner:** $15-$24   **Phone:** 212/965-1414   80

Location: In SoHo; between Broadway and Lafayette St. 80 Spring St 10012. **Hours:** 7:30 am-11:30, noon-5 & 6-midnight, Sat & Sun 10 am-4 & 6-midnight. Closed: 12/25. **Reservations:** required. **Features:** The trendy hot spot is still a favorite hangout in which to see and be seen. Styled as a traditional brasserie, it feels warm and authentic, with large depressed mirrors, decorative microtile floors, a pressed-tin ceiling towering over the cavernous space and delightful art deco touches. Savory, flavorful and textural dishes—such as brandade, steak frites, duck confit, duck shepherd's pie and skate—span the range from traditional to modern and would delight any Frenchman. Casual dress; cocktails. **Parking:** no self-parking. **Cards:** AX, MC, VI.

BAO 111

Vietnamese

Dinner: $12-$25   **Phone:** 212/254-7773   75

Location: Between 7th and 8th aves. 111 Ave C 10009. **Hours:** 6 pm-2 am, Sun-midnight. Closed major holidays. **Reservations:** suggested. **Features:** It's difficult to explain in so short a space the range and depth of flavors on a menu in which each dish sounds like a jewel worth tasting. Aromas from glistening food make the mouth water. Among teasers to the menu are grilled short ribs on lemongrass skewers; crispy frog legs with spicy basil mayonnaise; guava-lacquered quail with anise and lemongrass reduction; ginger-braised chicken; and king prawns simmered in garlic-tofu sauce. The casual space is dimly lit, sleek and seductive. Casual dress; cocktails. **Parking:** no self-parking. **Cards:** MC, VI.

BEPPE

Italian

Lunch: $17-$35   **Dinner:** $17-$35   **Phone:** 212/982-8422   18

Location: Between Broadway and Park Ave S. 45 E 22nd St 10010. **Hours:** noon-2:30 & 5:30-10:30 pm, Fri & Sat-11:30 pm. Closed major holidays; also Sun. **Reservations:** required. **Features:** A pleasant dining room manages to be both modern and provincial with dark woods, beautiful burnt hues, warm brick walls and shelves of grain- and bean-filled mason jars. Utterly charming and comfortable. Fine country cooking from Tuscany means all house-made pastas, sausages and custom farm-grown produce. Simple cooking methods leave nothing to be desired but more, more, more. Dressy casual; cocktails. **Parking:** no self-parking. **Cards:** AX, DC, DS, MC, VI.

BLUE HILL

American

Dinner: $28-$32   **Phone:** 212/539-1776   57

Location: Between Washington Square W and 6th Ave (Ave of the Americas). 75 Washington Pl 10011. **Hours:** 5:30 pm-11 pm, Sun-10 pm. Closed: 12/24. **Reservations:** suggested. **Features:** Located in the lower floor of a brownstone near Washington Square, this sublime casual sophisticate is intimate and warm with the feel of an exclusive hideaway. Service is relaxed, though gracious and highly skilled. Artful presentations are not showy yet beautifully show off the food which is market fresh and prepared with creativity and skill, always highlighting fine flavors united by the chef's studied hands. Dressy casual; cocktails. **Parking:** no self-parking. **Cards:** AX, DC, MC, VI.

BLUE WATER GRILL

Seafood

Lunch: $12-$25   **Dinner:** $19-$34   **Phone:** 212/675-9500   42

Location: At 16th St. 31 Union Square W 10003. **Hours:** 11:30 am-4 & 5-midnight, Fri & Sat-12:30 am, Sun 10:30 am-4 & 5-midnight. Closed: 12/25. **Reservations:** suggested. **Features:** Patrons should phone ahead for reservations when planning to dine at the popular restaurant, a favorite with locals and tourists in the mood for fresh seafood. Many selections, including sushi and shrimp dumplings, are prepared with an Asian flair. The dining room is in a restored bank and has seasonal outdoor patio seating. Casual dress; cocktails. **Parking:** no self-parking. **Cards:** AX, MC, VI.

(See map and index starting on p. 376)

BOLO
Spanish

Lunch: $12-$19   Dinner: $22-$32   Phone: 212/228-2200 (13)
Location: Between Broadway and Park Ave S. 23 E 22nd St 10010. **Hours:** noon-2:30 & 5:30-10 pm, Sat from 5:30 pm. Closed: 1/1, 11/22, 12/25. **Reservations:** suggested. **Features:** Superstar chef Bobby Flay pays homage to the flavors of the Iberian Peninsula. The walls of the casual Flatiron eatery are brilliantly colored and lend a modern, Picasso-like feel to the space. The vibrant, sophisticated food—everything from the delicious Spanish tortilla to octopus with grilled lemons to sea bass with artichokes and black olives—serves as the perfect introduction to nouveau Spanish cuisine prepared with a creative flair. Casual dress; cocktails. **Parking:** street. **Cards:** AX, DC, DS, MC, VI.

BOND ST
Japanese

Dinner: $18-$32   Phone: 212/777-2500 (69)
Location: In Noho; between Broadway and Lafayette sts. 6 Bond St 10012. **Hours:** 6 pm-11:30 pm, Sun & Mon 10:30 pm. Closed: 7/4, 12/24. **Reservations:** required. **Features:** In a non-descript brick townhouse, the restaurant exudes style and sophistication from every corner and every plate. Patrons can experience some of the finest modern Japanese cuisine around, from duck pho to fantastic sushi—both classic and innovative. Dressy casual; cocktails. **Parking:** no self-parking. **Cards:** AX, MC, VI.

BOULEY
French

Lunch: $38-$44   Dinner: $38-$45   Phone: 212/964-2525 (110)
Location: At Duane St. 120 W Broadway 10013. **Hours:** 11:30 am-3 & 5-11:30 pm. **Reservations:** required. **Features:** Two glorious dining rooms—one a rich red, the other a silvery white—are architecturally sophisticated and as romantic as could be, with elaborate flowers, flickering candlelight, the scent of warm apple and bedecked mantels. This also happens to be food nirvana. Dishes are lovely to behold, and preparatory skill is evident from the first glance to the last dab with a pristine linen napkin. A meal here is a dining event for sure. Dressy casual; cocktails. **Parking:** no self-parking. **Cards:** AX, DC, MC, VI.

BREAD BAR AT TABLA
Indian

Lunch: $7-$19   Dinner: $7-$19   Phone: 212/889-0667 (9)
Location: At 25th St. 11 Madison Ave 10010. **Hours:** noon-11 pm, Sun 5:30 pm-10:30 pm. Closed major holidays. **Reservations:** accepted. **Features:** Creative Indian-style tapas plates meant for sharing are tasty choices, and droves of people indulge in the aromatic, sweet, savory and sometimes pungent flavors. Because there is much to sample, it's best to come with friends so there are more mouths, and thus more reason to order additional dishes. Patio seats are popular in warmer months. A frequently changing seasonal menu means return trips are rewarded with new tastes. A prix fixe family-style menu is another option. Casual dress; cocktails. **Parking:** no self-parking. **Cards:** AX, DC, DS, MC, VI.

BUBBY'S RESTAURANT
American

Lunch: $8-$16   Dinner: $10-$23   Phone: 212/219-0666 (91)
Location: In TriBeCa; jct N Moore St. 120 Hudson St 10013. **Hours:** 8 am-close, Sat & Sun from 9 am; Saturday & Sunday brunch. Closed: 11/22, 12/25. **Reservations:** accepted, except for brunch. **Features:** Bubby's is the place in Lower Manhattan for comfort food, such as matzo ball soup, meat loaf, pulled pork barbecue and buttermilk fried chicken. Also always on the menu are several Mexican dishes, such as chicken tacos and spinach quesadillas. Save room for a wedge of pie. Casual dress; cocktails. **Parking:** street. **Cards:** DC, DS, MC, VI.

BUONA NOTTE RISTORANTE
Italian

Lunch: $8-$17   Dinner: $13-$26   Phone: 212-965-1111 (103)
Location: In Little Italy; between Canal and Hester sts. 120 Mulberry St 10013. **Hours:** noon-midnight. Closed: 12/25. **Reservations:** suggested, weekends. **Features:** Cozy and elegant surroundings help guests unwind as they sit down to such specialties as homemade lobster ravioli. Servers are knowledgeable. The outdoor garden area provides seating when the weather is agreeable. Casual dress; cocktails. **Parking:** street. **Cards:** AX, MC, VI.

BUTTER
American

Dinner: $17-$34   Phone: 212/253-2828 (65)
Location: In Noho; between E 4th St and Astor Pl. 415 Lafayette St 10003. **Hours:** 5:30 pm-11:30 pm. Closed major holidays; also Sun. **Reservations:** suggested. **Features:** The eatery offers a memorable dining experience: from fantastic aromas emanating from the kitchen to the smell of rich woods to the distinctive visual appeal of entering a short tunnel resembling the hollowed out interior of a great redwood. A blend of wonderful woods and antique butter dishes creates a wonderful dining experience. Dressy casual; cocktails. **Parking:** street. **Cards:** AX, DC, MC, VI.

CAFE PICK ME UP
Bakery/Desserts

Lunch: $5-$7   Dinner: $5-$7   Phone: 212/673-7231 (67)
Location: Corner of 9th St. 145 Ave A 10009. **Hours:** 7 am-1:30 am. **Features:** Located across from a park in the NYU district, this contemporary, hip coffee shop serves up some excellent specialty coffees, sandwiches and bakery items. Floor-to-ceiling glass doors open to outdoor bistro tables during warmer months. Guests are encouraged to bring their own laptops or use one of the Internet access stations available. Casual dress; beer & wine only. **Parking:** street.

CAFETERIA
American

Lunch: $7-$18   Dinner: $8-$22   Phone: 212-414-1717 (15)
Location: Corner of W 17th St. 119 7th Ave 10011. **Hours:** 24 hours. **Reservations:** accepted. **Features:** Despite the name, the fun restaurant is not a cafeteria. Guests can expect, however, a mixed menu, generous portions and efficient, friendly service. This is a great spot for those interested in all-day breakfast items. Roll-up garage doors create a sidewalk cafe atmosphere in the dining room, while the streetside patio allows for seasonal outdoor meals. Casual dress; cocktails. **Parking:** street. **Cards:** AX, MC, VI.

CANTON
Chinese

Lunch: $15   Dinner: $15   Phone: 212/226-4441 (116)
Location: In Chinatown; between Bowery and Market sts. 45 Division St 10002. **Hours:** Open 5/1-7/5 & 8/16-4/30; noon-10 pm, Fri & Sat-11 pm. Closed: Mon & Tues. **Reservations:** suggested. **Features:** In business for more than 40 years, this place on the outskirts of Chinatown is one of the last stalwartly authentic outposts of Cantonese cuisine. The dishes will be familiar to generations of devotees of fine Chinese cooking. Owner and hostess Eileen Leong assists diners with choices and tells them when they have ordered enough. The shrimp and lobster sauce is a fine choice with a kick of black bean sauce to add flavor. Bring cash, as no cards are accepted. Casual dress; beer & wine only. **Parking:** no self-parking.

(See map and index starting on p. 376)

CASA MONO   **Lunch:** $3-$15   **Dinner:** $3-$15   **Phone:** 212/253-2773   ㊺
▼▼▼▼   **Location:** At 17th St. 52 Irving Pl 10003. **Hours:** noon-midnight. Closed: 7/4. **Reservations:** suggested.
Spanish   **Features:** Spanish tapas delight folks who happen upon this treasure of a place. Plum seating spots are at the bar, which offers elbow room and an up-close view of chefs grilling over the iron plancha, as well as a chance to speak with them. Hearty, rustic food—some of it exotic, such as the cock's comb or lamb's tongue—is richly flavored. Grilled razor clams, soft-shell crab with artichoke aioli, skirt steak with onion marmalada and lamb with fava and mint are great options. Casual dress; beer & wine only. **Parking:** street. **Cards:** AX, MC, VI.   ⅄

CHAT 'N CHEW   **Lunch:** $9-$14   **Dinner:** $9-$14   **Phone:** 212/243-1616   ㊵
▼▼ ▼▼   **Location:** Between 5th Ave and Union Square. 10 E 16th St 10003. **Hours:** 11 am-midnight, Sat 10 am-midnight, Sun 10 am-11 pm. **Features:** Some come for the gooey and oh-so-good macaroni and cheese, and others
American   are devotees of the delectable BLT. Both are worthy of the extra calories, as are the nachos, milk shakes, pork chops and, well, just about anything the kitchen prepares. Home-style cooking and kitschy Americana—the decor that makes this spot so appealing to its loyal clientele—are the order of the day. Casual dress; cocktails. **Parking:** street. **Cards:** AX, DC, MC, VI.

CHELSEA BISTRO & BAR   **Dinner:** $18-$29   **Phone:** 212/727-2026   ③
▼▼▼▼   **Location:** Between 8th and 9th aves. 358 W 23rd St 10011. **Hours:** 5:30 pm-11 pm, Fri & Sat 5 pm-midnight, Sun 5 pm-10:30 pm. Closed: 5/28, 7/4, 9/3. **Reservations:** accepted. **Features:** The classic Parisian bistro focuses on delivering modernized classics, from leg of lamb to the famed goat cheese tart. Warm tones and
French   an inviting brick hearth lend to the cozy atmosphere of the relaxed dining room. The glass-enclosed Garden Terrace Room has a more romantic appeal. The wine book is comprehensive. Dressy casual; cocktails. **Parking:** street. **Cards:** AX, DC, DS, MC, VI.

CHOW BAR   **Dinner:** $17-$22   **Phone:** 212/633-2212   ㉛
▼▼ ◆◆   **Location:** At W 10th St. 230 W 4th St 10014. **Hours:** 5 pm-11 pm, Fri & Sat-midnight, Sun 11:30 am-10 pm. Closed: 9/3, 11/22, 12/25. **Reservations:** suggested. **Features:** In the heart of the West Village, the trendy
Asian   but casual place is nothing exotic, nor is the food, but crowds gather for the good Asian dishes. Among them is Szechuan steak frites with cilantro, shallots, garlic, ginger, soy and chili peppers. These spices tend to be the basis for seasoning throughout the menu, as are white miso dressing and lime, miso and hot oil vinaigrette. Daily special plates and house chows also are savory. Casual dress; cocktails. **Parking:** no self-parking. **Cards:** AX, DS, MC, VI.

CITY BAKERY   **Lunch:** $5-$12   **Dinner:** $8-$16   **Phone:** 212/366-1414   ㉙
▼▼   **Location:** Between 5th and 6th (Ave of the Americas) aves. 3 W 18th St 10011. **Hours:** 7:30 am-7 pm, Sat-6:30 pm, Sun 9 am-6 pm. Closed major holidays. **Reservations:** not accepted. **Features:** Sample New York's
Bakery/Desserts   most creative salad bar with dishes wide-ranging in inspiration, from Asian rice noodle salad to cornmeal crusted catfish. Alternatively, grab a seat at the soda fountain for hot items like mac n' cheese, ice creams or the best hot cocoa with homemade marshmallows. Don't forget to save room for dessert; cookies, cakes, tarts and the famed pretzel croissant are the specialties that originally made this spot a favorite. Casual dress. **Parking:** no self-parking. **Cards:** AX, MC, VI.

CITY HALL   **Lunch:** $10-$34   **Dinner:** $10-$34   **Phone:** 212/227-7777   ⑪⑪
▼▼◆ ▼▼◆   **Location:** Between Church St and W Broadway. 131 Duane St 10013. **Hours:** 7 am-11 & noon-11 pm, Sat from 5:30 pm. Closed: 1/1, 12/25; also Sun. **Reservations:** suggested. **Features:** This spacious brasserie,
American   decorated with black and white photos of old New York, is decidedly American in theme. The d[00c3][00a9]cor is classic country; the food upscale metropolitan that keeps this dining room tops on the list for powerbrokers and politicians. Chef/owner Henry Meer relies on farmers market produce and quality ingredients to craft homespun American favorites, including a knockout brisket and a superlative shellfish pan roast. Casual dress; cocktails. **Parking:** street. **Cards:** AX, DC, DS, MC, VI.   ⅄

CORNER BISTRO   **Lunch:** $6-$8   **Dinner:** $6-$8   **Phone:** 212/242-9502   ㉘
▼▼   **Location:** Corner of Jane St. 331 W 4th St 10014. **Hours:** 11:30 am-3:30 am, Sun from noon. Closed: 11/22, 12/25. **Features:** The crowded tavern is a popular spot with locals and offers a limited menu of belly-busting
American   hamburgers, crispy french fries, chili and monster grilled chicken sandwiches. Casual dress; cocktails. **Parking:** no self-parking.   ⅄

COUNTRY CAFE   **Lunch:** $12-$18   **Dinner:** $16-$21   **Phone:** 212/966-5417   ㊼
▼▼▼   **Location:** In SoHo; between Broome and Spring sts. 69 Thompson St 10012. **Hours:** noon-11 pm, Sat & Sun from 10:30 am. Closed: 7/4. **Reservations:** accepted. **Features:** The family-operated bistro serves fantastic
French   French and Moroccan cuisine in a cozy atmosphere. Flavorful dishes are created using fresh, homemade ingredients. Outdoor dining is an option in warmer months. Casual dress; cocktails. **Parking:** street. **Cards:** MC, VI.

CRAFT   **Dinner:** $26-$46   **Phone:** 212/780-0880   ㉚
▼▼◆ ▼▼◆   **Location:** Between Broadway and Park Ave S. 43 E 19th St 10003. **Hours:** 5:30 pm-10 pm, Fri & Sat 11 pm. Closed major holidays; also 12/24. **Reservations:** required. **Features:** When the restaurant first opened its
American   doors, the concept of crafting a meal around small plates broken down by food type and cooking method was groundbreaking. Everyone was, and still is, gaga over chef Tom Colicchio's expertise in the kitchen and the integrity he brings to the ingredients in his dishes. Everything is farmers-market fresh and smacks of goodness and purity. Not only is the food something to talk about, but the stunning dining room also is a conversation piece in its own right. Dressy casual; cocktails. **Parking:** street. **Cards:** AX, DC, DS, MC, VI.

CRAFTBAR   **Lunch:** $12-$29   **Dinner:** $17-$33   **Phone:** 212/461-4300   ㉜
▼▼▼   **Location:** Between Broadway and Park Ave S. 900 Broadway St 10003. **Hours:** noon-2:30 & 5:30-11 pm, Sun & Mon-10 pm. Closed major holidays. **Reservations:** suggested. **Features:** This contemporary yet
Mediterranean   sophisticated restaurant has some unique features, such as a hidden restroom entry that looks as though it is part of the wall; luckily, attentive servers will always show you the way. The creative menu may include peekey toe crab soup, duck and pecorino-stuffed risotto balls. Dressy casual; cocktails. **Parking:** street. **Cards:** AX, CB, DC, DS, JC, MC, VI.

(See map and index starting on p. 376)

CRISPO

Italian

Dinner: $15-$20   Phone: 212/229-1818   **26**

Location: Between 7th and 8th aves. 240 W 14th St 10011. **Hours:** 5 pm-11:30 pm, Fri & Sat-12:30 am, Sun 4 pm-11:30 pm. **Closed:** 11/22, 12/25. **Reservations:** accepted. **Features:** In a casual setting with exposed brick walls and a sidewalk terrace, the restaurant serves up delicious regional Italian dishes. Start with an assortment of antipasto that ranges from bruschetta to a wide variety of Italian cheeses before moving on to a savory pasta such as spaghetti carbonara. Entrees range from daily seafood specials to veal or osso buco. Casual dress; entertainment. **Parking:** street. **Cards:** AX, MC, VI.

DA NICO RISTORANTE

Italian

Lunch: $7-$12   Dinner: $14-$30   Phone: 212/343-1212   **93**

Location: In Little Italy; between Broome and Grand sts. 164 Mulberry St 10013. **Hours:** noon-midnight. **Closed:** 11/22, 12/25. **Reservations:** suggested, weekends. **Features:** Patrons unwind in a casual, family-friendly setting over plates of Northern and Southern Italian cuisine. Table spacing may be tight in the cozy, romantic setting, but the background music is good. The wait staff is knowledgeable. Casual dress; cocktails. **Parking:** street. **Cards:** AX, CB, DC, DS, JC, MC, VI.

DANUBE

Hungarian

Dinner: $28-$35   Phone: 212/791-3771   **108**

Location: Between Duane and Reade sts. 30 Hudson St 10013. **Hours:** 5:30 pm-11 pm. **Closed:** Sun. **Reservations:** required. **Features:** A hint of Eastern European mystique is evident at this grand and enchanting TriBeCa fantasy. Dangling fringed lanterns softly illuminate the jewel tones, eccentric portraits, mosaic wall murals and accents of gold leaf. The deep banquette seats and throne-like chairs are color-rich, plush and velvety. David Bouley breathes new life into traditional Austro-Hungarian dishes, as the selections are contemporary and beguiling. What began as a whisper is now a steady murmur around town. Dressy casual; cocktails. **Parking:** no self-parking. **Cards:** AX, DC, DS, JC, MC, VI.

DELMONICO'S

American

Lunch: $15-$30   Dinner: $19-$48   Phone: 212/509-1144   **120**

Location: Between William and Stone sts; in financial district. 56 Beaver St 10004. **Hours:** 11:30 am-10 pm, Sat from 5 pm. **Closed:** 11/22, 12/25; also Sun. **Reservations:** suggested. **Features:** Old-fashioned and dignified, the restaurant offers immaculate tables draped in white linen, a varied menu and a professionally attired wait staff. Close to Wall Street, this place enjoys a big following and is great for business entertaining. Casual dress; cocktails. **Parking:** street. **Cards:** AX, CB, DC, DS, JC, MC, VI.

DYLAN PRIME

Steak House

Lunch: $12-$59   Dinner: $19-$62   Phone: 212/334-4783   **82**

Location: Jct Greenwich St. 62 Laight St 10013. **Hours:** noon-2:30 & 5:30-11 pm, Thurs & Fri-midnight, Sat 5:30 pm-midnight, Sun 5:30 pm-10 pm. **Closed:** 3/23, 11/22, 12/25. **Reservations:** suggested. The upscale steak house is noted for creative dishes such as the carpetbagger steak: an 11 oz. filet mignon stuffed with blue point oysters and served with spinach, mashed potatoes, and a sauce of Guinness and brown sugar. The restaurant offers diners a choice of "chapeaux," or crusts baked on their steaks (maytag blue cheese and chive, foie gras butter, mushroom and truffle and other creations). Diners also have the option of various steak sauces, including black truffle beurre blanc and Maker's Mark bourbon sauce. Dressy casual; cocktails. **Parking:** no self-parking. **Cards:** AX, DC, MC, VI.

EIGHT MILE CREEK

Australian

Lunch: $12-$18   Dinner: $15-$30   Phone: 212/431-4635   **79**

Location: In Nolita Little Italy; between Prince and Spring sts. 240 Mulberry St 10012. **Hours:** 5:30 pm-4 am, Sat & Sun from 11 am. **Closed:** 12/25. **Features:** Exotic dishes, an amazing wine list, casually elegant surroundings and a friendly staff await. The restaurant treats patrons to Australian dining. Casual dress; cocktails. **Parking:** street. **Cards:** AX, CB, DC, DS, JC, MC, VI.

ELEVEN MADISON PARK

American

Lunch: $24-$34   Dinner: $68   Phone: 212/889-0905   **10**

Location: At 24th St. 11 Madison Ave 10010. **Hours:** 11:30 am-2 & 5:30-10:30 pm, Fri & Sat-11 pm, Sun-10 pm. **Closed:** 12/24. **Reservations:** suggested. **Features:** Another Danny Meyer restaurant devoted to service but delivering culinary hits using fine ingredients and perfect dish pairings, thus ensuring continued popularity. The dining room itself, a reclaimed grand bank lobby, is something to behold in all its elegance and glory. This place seems to have it all: food, service and decor. Dressy casual; cocktails. **Parking:** no self-parking. **Cards:** AX, DC, DS, MC, VI.

EL QUIJOTE RESTAURANT

AAA

Spanish

Lunch: $7-$12   Dinner: $10-$30   Phone: 212/929-1855   **4**

Location: In Chelsea; between 7th and 8th aves. 226 W 23rd St 10011. **Hours:** noon-midnight, Fri & Sat-1 am. **Reservations:** accepted. **Features:** This place is the city's oldest Spanish restaurant, and little has changed since its inception. Older decor is accentuated with colorful murals and windmills. Lobster is brought in straight from the owner's fishing fleet. Paella and sangria are divine. Casual dress; cocktails. **Parking:** no self-parking. **Cards:** AX, DC, DS, MC, VI.

FIVE POINTS

Nouvelle American

Lunch: $12-$15   Dinner: $15-$25   Phone: 212/253-5700   **68**

Location: Between Bowery and Lafayette sts. 31 Great Jones St 10012. **Hours:** 11:30 am-3 & 6-midnight. **Closed:** 12/25. **Reservations:** suggested. **Features:** Crisp white walls and natural elements, such as a line of small trees and a hollowed tree trunk with water trickling through the middle, make this a tranquil setting. A homemade pickle plate is given along with a choice of breads. Among excellent selections that may appear on the menu are warm gulf shrimp with borlotti beans, seared day-boat scallops with braised leeks and grilled lamb with yellow wax beans. Dressy casual; cocktails. **Parking:** street. **Cards:** AX, DC, MC, VI.

FLEUR DE SEL

French

Lunch: $25-$33   Dinner: $67-$82   Phone: 212/460-9100   **22**

Location: Between 5th Ave and Broadway. 5 E 20th St 10003. **Hours:** noon-2 & 5:30-10:30 pm, Sun-9 pm. **Closed:** 1/1, 12/25. **Reservations:** suggested. **Features:** This gem, with casual refinement, serves French food with flair and civility. Seating is tight, other conversations easy to hear, but no one seems to care as they focus on lovely dishes prepared with skill and wisdom. Crisp baby chicken with chanterelles and a foie gras emulsion, olive-marinated lamb loin with a fennel and rosemary lamb jus, and seared sea scallops with honey sherry wine gastric and sage shine. The chef is not only master in the kitchen but his original art is on display. Dressy casual; cocktails. **Parking:** no self-parking. **Cards:** AX, DC, MC, VI.

(See map and index starting on p. 376)

GOTHAM BAR AND GRILL   Lunch: $16-$23   Dinner: $28-$44   Phone: 212/620-4020   [50]
▼▼▼ ▼▼▼ **Location:** Between 5th Ave and University Pl. 12 E 12th 10003. **Hours:** noon-2:15 & 5:30-10:30 pm, Fri-11:30 pm,
American   Sat 5 pm-11 pm, Sun 5 pm-10:30 pm. Closed: 12/25. **Reservations:** suggested. **Features:** New York
sophisticates have kept this bastion of Gotham chic busy from its opening. The music, black and white art
photos, tall ceilings with enormous fabric hung lights, deep mahogany bar and soft jazz in the background
suit the city just fine. The food, creative and beautiful and decadently good, is the work of a master chef who all who have eaten
here revere. Desserts are no less marvelous. Many say this is among the best. Dressy casual; cocktails. **Parking:** no self-
parking. **Cards:** AX, DC, DS, MC, VI.

GRAMERCY TAVERN   Lunch: $21-$55   Dinner: $76-$98   Phone: 212/477-0777   [27]
▼▼▼ ▼▼▼ **Location:** Between Park Ave S and Broadway. 42 E 20th St 10003. **Hours:** noon-2 & 5:30-10 pm, Fri & Sat noon-
11 pm, Sun 5:30 pm-11 pm. Closed major holidays. **Reservations:** suggested. **Features:** A rustic, yet first-
Continental   class event, patrons of the traditional American tavern never had it so good. The use of the finest
ingredients, linens and tableware, in contrast to wooden floors, copper enhancements, fresh flowers and
trellised vines evoke the atmosphere of old New England with all the best of New World refinement. This NYC institution
bestows true hospitality as an accent to its flawless pioneering approach to food. Semi-formal attire; cocktails. **Parking:** no self-
parking. **Cards:** AX, DC, DS, MC, VI.

GRAND SICHUAN INTERNATIONAL   Lunch: $6-$20   Dinner: $6-$20   Phone: 212/620-5200   [2]
▼▼▼ ▼▼▼ **Location:** At 24th St; downtown. 229 9th Ave 10001. **Hours:** 11:30 am-11 pm. Closed: 11/22. **Features:** While
the usual suspects make their way onto the menu at the local haunt, those with more adventurous palates
Chinese   would be wise to try the doughy and delicious soup dumplings, five-spice beef or any of the dishes under
the "General Mao's Homecoming" heading, especially the beguiling vinegared potatoes, the spicy and sour
sea cucumber, the preserved turnip Szechuan-style and chicken and loofah soup. Those unwilling to try something different
should stick with the out-of-this-world mu shu. Casual dress. **Parking:** street. **Cards:** AX, DC, DS, MC, VI.

GROTTA AZZURRA   *Menu on AAA.com*   Lunch: $8-$25   Dinner: $14-$29   Phone: 212/925-8775   [87]
Ⓐ   **Location:** In Little Italy; between Broome and Grand sts. 177 Mulberry St 10013. **Hours:** noon-3:30 & 5:30-
midnight, Fri & Sat-2 am, Sun 11:30 am-3:30 & 4-10 pm. Closed: 12/25. **Reservations:** suggested,
▼▼▼   weekends. **Features:** A Little Italy staple since 1908, the restaurant presents a diverse menu that pairs with
Italian   its good line list. The building in in the process of being restored, and the decor is beautiful and ornate.
Casual dress; cocktails. **Parking:** street. **Cards:** AX, CB, DC, DS, JC, MC, VI.

IL CORTILE   Lunch: $19-$68   Dinner: $19-$68   Phone: 212/226-6060   [101]
▼▼▼ **Location:** Between Canal and Hester sts. 125 Mulberry St 10013. **Hours:** noon-midnight, Fri & Sat-1 am. Closed:
11/22, 12/24, 12/25. **Reservations:** suggested. **Features:** The restaurant, in the bustling heart of Little Italy,
Italian   has the inviting feel of a terrace garden, with open skylights, natural wood tables and brick walls. Specialties
center on seafood, veal and homemade pasta. Seating is available on the seasonal patio. Casual dress;
cocktails. **Parking:** no self-parking. **Cards:** AX, DC, DS, MC, VI.

IL MULINO   Lunch: $50-$75   Dinner: $50-$75   Phone: 212/673-3783   [62]
▼▼▼ **Location:** In Greenwich Village; between Sullivan and Thompson sts. 86 W 3rd St 10012. **Hours:** Open 5/1-6/30 &
8/1-4/30; noon-2:30 & 5-11 pm, Sat from 5 pm. Closed major holidays; also Sun. **Reservations:** required.
Italian   **Features:** If you hope to dine here, call well in advance. The charming haven is quite small and extremely
popular. The magnificent cuisine is pure Old World Italian—rich, bountiful and among the city's finest. The
specialty rack of lamb is accented by fresh sage. Semi-formal attire; cocktails. **Parking:** no self-parking. **Cards:** AX, DC,
MC, VI.

IL PALAZZO RISTORANTE ITALIANO   Lunch: $10-$20   Dinner: $14-$37   Phone: 212/343-7000   [98]
▼▼▼ **Location:** In Little Italy; between Grand and Hester sts. 151 Mulberry St 10013. **Hours:** 11:30 am-11 pm, Fri & Sat-
midnight. Closed: 12/25. **Reservations:** suggested, weekends. **Features:** Traditional Italian cuisine is
Italian   served in a family-centric atmosphere. Soothing background music, a great wine list and a knowledgeable
staff contribute to a low-stress meal. Old-school sauce recipes are standouts. Casual dress; cocktails.
Parking: street. **Cards:** AX, CB, DC, DS, JC, MC, VI.

INOTECA   Lunch: $7-$15   Dinner: $7-$15   Phone: 212/614-0473   [89]
▼▼ ▼▼ **Location:** Corner of Ludlow St. 98 Rivington St 10002. **Hours:** noon-3 am, Sat & Sun from 10 am. Closed: 11/22,
12/25. **Reservations:** suggested. **Features:** This Tuscan-inspired restaurant encourages guests to share by
Italian   specializing in small plates. Menu items may include antipasto plates filled with cured meats, artesian
cheeses and olives, pasta or jumbo shrimp wrapped in bacon. Casual dress; beer & wine only. **Parking:**
street. **Cards:** AX, MC, VI.

JEAN-CLAUDE   Dinner: $15-$19   Phone: 212/475-9232   [70]
▼▼▼ **Location:** Between Prince and W Houston sts. 137 Sullivan St 10012. **Hours:** 6 pm-11 pm. Closed major holidays.
Reservations: accepted. **Features:** The romantic atmosphere of a French bistro can be experienced at this
French   SoHo neighborhood eatery. The a-la-carte menu items are made to order and include fresh seafood, steak,
lamb and poultry. Remember: no credit cards are accepted. Casual dress; cocktails. **Parking:** no
self-parking.

KATZ'S DELI   Lunch: $3-$20   Dinner: $3-$20   Phone: 212/254-2246   [81]
▼▼▼ **Location:** At Ludlow St; on Lower East Side. 205 E Houston St 10002. **Hours:** 8 am-10 pm, Fri & Sat-3 am, Sun-
11 pm. **Features:** Katz's has been the quintessential New York deli for over 113 years, serving up heaping
Deli/Subs   portions of great kosher food such as steaming pastrami sandwiches, knishes and more. If it looks familiar,
Sandwiches   a scene from "When Harry Met Sally" was filmed here. Casual dress; beer & wine only. **Parking:** street.

(See map and index starting on p. 376)

LANDMARC
American
Lunch: $6-$24   **Dinner:** $15-$30   **Phone:** 212/343-3883   102
Location: Between Leonard and Worth sts. 179 W Broadway 10013. **Hours:** noon-2 am. Closed: 1/1, 11/22, 12/25. **Features:** This modern industrial-like restaurant with exposed brick walls and wood-beam ceiling features an open brick oven and grill where guests can view chefs preparing their meals. Tender steaks with choice of homemade sauce and fresh seafood are always an excellent option. Casual dress; cocktails.
Parking: street. **Cards:** AX, DC, DS, MC, VI.

**L'ECOLE, THE RESTAURANT OF THE FRENCH
    CULINARY INSTITUTE**
Nouvelle French
Lunch: $27   **Dinner:** $40   **Phone:** 212/219-3300   85
Location: In SoHo; at Grand St. 462 Broadway 10013. **Hours:** 12:15 pm-2:30 & 5:30-9:30 pm. Closed major holidays; also Sun. **Reservations:** suggested, for dinner. **Features:** Students of the institute prepare the innovative, daily changing menu, which includes a prix fixe lunch as well as four- and five-course prix fixe menus at dinner. Set in a trendy environment, the restaurant displays an elegant simplicity. Casual dress; cocktails. **Parking:** no self-parking. **Cards:** AX, DC, DS, MC, VI.

LEMONGRASS GRILL
Thai
Lunch: $6-$17   **Dinner:** $6-$17   **Phone:** 212/809-8038   119
Location: Between Maiden Ln and Platt St; 1 blk w of Pearl St. 84 William St 10038. **Hours:** 11:30 am-10:30 pm, Sat & Sun 1 pm-10 pm. Closed major holidays. **Reservations:** not accepted. **Features:** The intimate dining room glows with a green hue and Thai wall medallions. The menu offers a wide range of items from vegetarian dishes to duck, fish, noodle and curry dishes. Casual dress; cocktails. **Parking:** no self-parking.
Cards: AX, DC, MC, VI.

L'EXPRESS
French
Lunch: $9-$13   **Dinner:** $11-$21   **Phone:** 212/254-5858   33
Location: Between 19th and 20th sts. 249 Park Ave S 10003. **Hours:** 24 hours. **Features:** This popular French bistro serves up an excellent brunch menu that is available 24 hours a day. Casual dress; cocktails. **Parking:** street. **Cards:** AX, MC, VI.

LE ZIE 2000
Italian
Lunch: $6-$16   **Dinner:** $6-$16   **Phone:** 212/206-8686   6
Location: Between 20th and 21st sts. 172 7th Ave 10011. **Hours:** noon-11:30 pm. Closed: 7/4, 11/22, 12/25. **Reservations:** accepted. **Features:** The restaurant offers great value, a traditional Venetian menu that changes frequently and a comfortable, trendy environment frequented by locals. Select an appetizer such as baked goat cheese, a salad such as tricolore salad with sauteed shiitake and applewood smoked bacon, or an entree such as the Venetian-style calf's liver sauteed with onions. The dessert sepection includes tiramisu, creme brulee, cheesecake, and profiteroles. An extensive wine list will complement any menu choice. Casual dress; cocktails. **Parking:** street. **Cards:** AX, MC, VI.

LOMBARDI'S COAL OVEN PIZZERIA
Pizza
Lunch: $12-$16   **Dinner:** $12-$16   **Phone:** 212/941-7994   84
Location: Between Mott and Mulberry sts. 32 Spring St 10012. **Hours:** 11:30 am-11 pm, Fri & Sat-midnight, Sun-10 pm. Closed: 11/22, 12/25. **Features:** Since 1905 this restaurant has been serving crisp-crust pizza from their coal oven that has made New York pizzerias famous. The standard favorite has a sweet sauce, basil and fresh mozzarella. A wide variety of toppings are offered; the fresh clam pie and the white pizza are other specialties. They do not accept credit cards. Casual dress; cocktails. **Parking:** street.

LUCY LATIN KITCHEN
Latino
Lunch: $20-$32   **Dinner:** $20-$32   **Phone:** 212/475-5829   35
Location: Between Broadway and Park Ave; just n of Union Square. 35 E 18th St 10003. **Hours:** noon-3 & 5:30-11 pm, Fri noon-3 & 5-midnight, Sat 5 pm-midnight, Sun 5:30 pm-10:30 pm. **Reservations:** accepted. **Features:** The sophisticated Nuevo Latino menu offers delightful tastes such as a wide variety of ceviches and empanadas, pork Cubano and sugarcane roasted duck, best accented by their custom sangrias. Homemade ice creams and sorbet are a sweet ending to the meal. Dressy casual; cocktails. **Parking:** street. **Cards:** AX, DS, MC, VI.

LUNA
Italian
Lunch: $10-$15   **Dinner:** $10-$20   **Phone:** 212/226-8657   105
Location: In Little Italy; between Canal and Walker sts. 112 Mulberry St 10013. **Hours:** noon-11:30 pm, Fri & Sat-midnight. Closed major holidays. **Features:** The Italian eatery, now considered an institution, serves decent pasta, sauces, parmigianas and more. Casual dress; cocktails. **Parking:** street. **Cards:** MC, VI.

LUNELLA RISTORANTE
Italian
Lunch: $11-$18   **Dinner:** $14-$35   **Phone:** 212/966-6639   90
Location: In Little Italy; between Broome and Grand sts. 173 Mulberry St 10013. **Hours:** noon-midnight. Closed: 12/25. **Reservations:** suggested, weekends. **Features:** Good background music enhances the cozy, romantic setting, which is characterized by intimate table spacing and fine artwork. In the heart of Little Italy, the restaurant presents a vast menu of choices, including great breads. Casual dress; cocktails. **Parking:** street. **Cards:** AX, CB, DC, DS, JC, MC, VI.

LUPA
Italian
Lunch: $10-$20   **Dinner:** $10-$20   **Phone:** 212/982-5089   66
Location: In Greenwich Village; between Bleecker and Houston sts. 170 Thompson St 10012. **Hours:** noon-midnight. Closed: 11/22, 12/25. **Reservations:** suggested. **Features:** This casual member of the Batali family serves up a rustic version of Italian countryside cuisine not often found stateside. Start with a sampling from their large antipasto selection which includes house-made salami, cheese, cured seafood and marinated vegetables. Savor these while deciding what to try next. Will it be a pasta such as bucatini or the daily ravioli, or the daily roasted meat special such as duck or Braciola or the grilled whole fish? Casual dress; cocktails. **Parking:** street. **Cards:** AX, MC, VI.

THE MAGNOLIA BAKERY
Bakery/Desserts
Lunch: $2-$7   **Dinner:** $2-$7   **Phone:** 212/462-2572   44
Location: In Greenwich Village; at W 11th St. 401 Bleecker St 10014. **Hours:** 9 am-11:30 pm, Sat 10 am-12:30 am, Sun 10 am-11:30 pm, Mon noon-11:30 pm. Closed major holidays. **Features:** The popular bakery is well-known and often crowded. The signature cupcakes make a wait in line worthwhile. Casual dress. **Parking:** street. **Cards:** AX, DS, MC, VI.

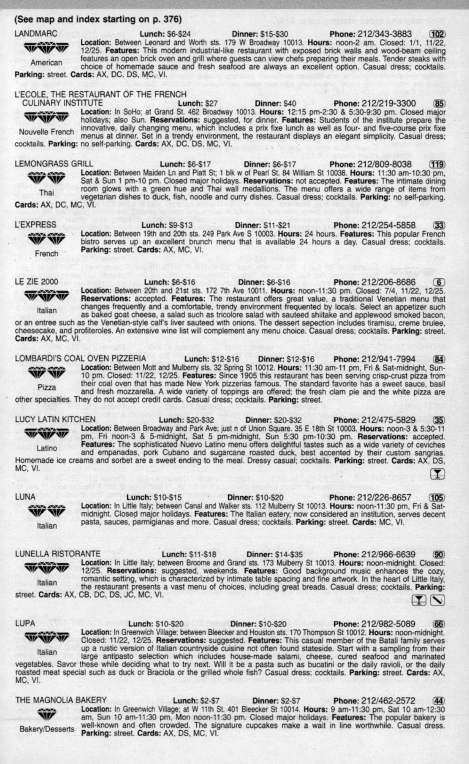

(See map and index starting on p. 376)

MAMLOUK **Dinner:** $30 **Phone:** 212/529-3477 (77)
Middle Eastern
Location: Between Aves A and B. 211 E 4th St 10009. **Hours:** 6 pm-midnight. **Closed:** Mon. **Reservations:** suggested. **Features:** A narrow, little restaurant where diners sit at low tables in short, inlaid chairs and enjoy multi-dish courses of what the chef has prepared. There is no room for disappointment with the fragrantly seasoned, tenderly cooked food that emerges. Salads, dips, breads, olives, meats and braised and stewed vegetables are followed by dessert. For large groups, reserve a couple of couches and ottomans below and follow the meal with the houka whose long pipe can reach easily around the table. Casual dress; cocktails. **Parking:** no self-parking. **Cards:** AX, DC, DS, MC, VI.

MARKJOSEPH STEAKHOUSE **Lunch:** $13-$51 **Dinner:** $28-$51 **Phone:** 212/277-0020 (118)
Steak House
Location: Just n of Peck Slip. 261 Water St 10038. **Hours:** 11:30 am-10 pm, Fri 11:30 am-11 pm, Sat 5 pm-11 pm. Closed major holidays; also Sun. **Reservations:** accepted. **Features:** Tucked off a little cobblestone side street, the traditional steak house serves large, perfectly aged steaks that are cooked to perfection. Guests have their choice of accompanying vegetables. Service is friendly and efficient. Casual dress; cocktails. **Parking:** street. **Cards:** AX, MC, VI.

MARY'S FISH CAMP **Lunch:** $14-$21 **Dinner:** $18-$25 **Phone:** 646/486-2185 (49)
Seafood
Location: Between W 4th and Bleecker sts. 64 Charles St 10014. **Hours:** noon-3 & 6-11 pm. Closed major holidays; also Sun. **Features:** Those who don't arrive early will wait in a line that winds up the block to get into the tiny fish camp. With just a handful of tables and counter seating, the casual restaurant fills up fast. The kitchen is renowned for crafting tempting roadside seafood, including killer lobster rolls, fragrant bouillabaisse and buckets of buttery steamers. Save room for the decadent ice cream sundae topped with peanut brittle. Casual dress; beer & wine only. **Parking:** street. **Cards:** AX, MC, VI.

MATSURI **Dinner:** $15-$26 **Phone:** 212/243-6400 (7)
Japanese
Location: At 9th Ave; in The Maritime Hotel. 369 W 16th St 10011. **Hours:** 6 pm-midnight, Thur-Sat to 1 am. **Reservations:** required. **Features:** Tadashi Ono again is producing food that looks and tastes exquisite, but this time it's traditional Japanese cuisine. Cuts of fish are spectacular, and the displays are exotic, with flying fish wings spread as if in flight and fish arched as if jumping. A walnut staircase leads to a room with a vaulted teak ceiling, rice paper lanterns and Japanese pottery. This place offers what is said to be the city's largest sake selection, with 100 varieties. The wonderful spot is a showcase for fine food. Dressy casual; cocktails. **Parking:** no self-parking. **Cards:** AX, DC, DS, MC, VI.

MAYROSE COMFORTABLE FOOD **Lunch:** $6-$11 **Dinner:** $7-$15 **Phone:** 212/533-3663 (20)
American
Location: At 21st St. 920 Broadway 10010. **Hours:** 7 am-11 pm, Sat from 8:30 am, Sun 8:30 am-4 pm. **Closed:** 7/4, 11/22, 12/25. **Features:** Located on a busy street corner with a bustling atmosphere, the restaurant offers a nice variety of fresh salads, sandwiches, burgers and an all-day breakfast menu. Casual dress; beer & wine only. **Parking:** no self-parking. **Cards:** AX, MC, VI.

MESA GRILL **Lunch:** $10-$18 **Dinner:** $18-$40 **Phone:** 212/807-7400 (41)
Regional American
Location: Between 15th and 16th sts. 102 5th Ave 10011. **Hours:** noon-2:30 & 5:30-10:30 pm, Fri-11 pm, Sat 11:30 am-2:30 & 5-11 pm, Sun 11:30 am-3 & 5:30-10:30 pm. **Closed:** 12/25. **Reservations:** required. **Features:** Among the chef's piquant, Southwest-inspired creations are spice-crusted Angus steak, tuna steak with pineapple/green chile glaze, red chile-rubbed rabbit, ancho-rubbed chicken and yellow corn-crusted chiles rellenos filled with eggplant and goat cheese. Flavors burst from every dish. Weekend brunch is a tasty experience. Dressy casual; cocktails. **Parking:** no self-parking. **Cards:** AX, DC, DS, MC, VI.

MONTE'S RESTAURANT *Menu on AAA.com* **Lunch:** $9-$25 **Dinner:** $9-$25 **Phone:** 212/228-9194 (63)
Italian
Location: In Greenwich Village; between Bleecker and W 3rd sts. 97 MacDougal St 10012. **Hours:** noon-11 pm, Fri & Sat-11:30 pm. **Closed:** 11/22, 12/25. **Reservations:** suggested. **Features:** The charming owner-host delights in welcoming every guest to the family-oriented restaurant in an old New York setting. Representative of home-cooking like Mama made are traditional pasta, veal and seafood dishes. Walls are lined with maps and celebrity pictures. Casual dress; cocktails. **Parking:** street. **Cards:** AX, DC, MC, VI.

MONTRACHET **Lunch:** $16-$21 **Dinner:** $24-$32 **Phone:** 212/219-2777 (95)
French
Location: In TriBeCa; between White and Walker sts. 239 W Broadway 10013. **Hours:** 5:30 pm-10:30 pm, Fri noon-2:15 & 5:30-11 pm, Sat 5:30 pm-11 pm. Closed major holidays; also Sun. **Reservations:** suggested. **Features:** The non-descript entrance, painted red, marks the spot. Settle in at the unpretentious bistro to enjoy modern French cuisine and excellent wines. The dining room is small and intimate, the perfect place to begin a romantic night on the town. The wait staff is focused and professional. Dressy casual; cocktails. **Parking:** no self-parking. **Cards:** AX, DC, MC, VI.

NAM **Lunch:** $10-$20 **Dinner:** $10-$20 **Phone:** 212/267-1777 (112)
Vietnamese
Location: Between Church St and W Broadway. 110 Reade St 10013. **Hours:** noon-2 & 5:30-9:30 pm, Fri-10:30 pm, Sat 5:30 pm-10:30 pm, Sun 5:30 pm-9:30 pm. **Closed:** 1/1, 11/22, 12/25. **Reservations:** accepted. **Features:** Casual and attractive with a serene, grown-up refinement, the restaurant is a great place to come for not-so-typical, but still traditional, Vietnamese cooking. Wok-seared chopped monkfish with herbs, grilled eggplant with ginger and lime sauce and crispy spring rolls are popular starters, while crispy red snapper in chili-lime sauce, caramelized shrimp and pork in light pepper sauce are popular main courses. Respectful servers are pleased to offer menu advice. Casual dress; cocktails. **Parking:** no self-parking. **Cards:** AX, MC, VI.

NEW CHAO CHOW RESTAURANT **Lunch:** $5-$12 **Dinner:** $5-$14 **Phone:** 212/226-2590 (104)
Chinese
Location: In Chinatown; between Canal and Hester sts. 111 Mott St 10013. **Hours:** 8 am-10 pm. **Features:** Many Chinatown shops are near the casual Chinese restaurant, which prepares a diverse selection of dishes in its open-air kitchen. Casual dress. **Parking:** street.

(See map and index starting on p. 376)

NOBU   Lunch: $12-$20   Dinner: $12-$25   Phone: 212/219-0500   96
▼▼▼ ▼▼▼ **Location:** In TriBeCa; at Franklin St. 105 Hudson St 10013. **Hours:** 11:45 am-2:15 & 5:45-10:15 pm, Sat & Sun
            from 5:45 pm. Closed major holidays. **Reservations:** required. **Features:** Continually voted one of New
Japanese   York's best and for good reason. The menu is a melange of flavors and textures, featuring mainly finest
            quality fish and seafood, best experienced "family-style," sharing with the table so as to experience a range
of exquisite dishes with explosive flavors. The server will expertly guide you through the menu and you will find yourself on the
edge of your seat with anticipation. Casual dress; cocktails. **Parking:** no self-parking. **Cards:** AX, DC, DS, MC, VI.

NOVITA   Lunch: $12-$25   Dinner: $12-$25   Phone: 212/677-2222   24
▼▼▼ ▼▼   **Location:** In Gramercy Park; between Park Ave S and Lexington Ave. 102 E 22nd St 10010. **Hours:** noon-3 & 5:30-
            11 pm, Fri & Sat-midnight, Sun 5 pm-10 pm. Closed major holidays. **Reservations:** suggested. **Features:**
Northern Italian Polished wood floors, crisp linen and butter-yellow walls lend a soothing hand to the tailored
            decor. Pappardelle with lamb ragu and porcini mushrooms, pan-roasted sea bass with artichoke fricassee
and roasted breast of duck with Barolo wine sauce are among modern dishes on a menu of Northern Italian fare. Casual dress;
cocktails. **Parking:** no self-parking. **Cards:** AX, DC, MC, VI.

NY NOODLE TOWN   Lunch: $4-$21   Dinner: $4-$21   Phone: 212/349-2690   114
▼▼ ▼▼   **Location:** At Bayard St. 28 1/2 Bowery 10013. **Hours:** 9 am-4 am. **Features:** It doesn't get more rough and
            tumble than this: a gritty restaurant in the heart of Chinatown. Guests can wait for their own table or share a
Chinese   communal one with others who can't wait to get their chopsticks into lushly braised pig or Chinese loofah.
            The usual suspects, along with more intriguing dishes, are served well into the wee hours. The decor is
largely non-existent, save for the few ducks and fowl hanging in the front window. Only cash is accepted, and limited English is
spoken. Casual dress; beer only. **Parking:** street.

THE ODEON   Lunch: $17-$26   Dinner: $19-$28   Phone: 212/233-0507   107
▼▼▼ ▼▼   **Location:** Between Thomas and Duane sts. 145 W Broadway 10013. **Hours:** noon-2 am, Sat from 11 am, Sun
            from 10:30 am. **Reservations:** accepted. **Features:** The TriBeCa legend remains the place to see and be
American   seen. Famous, infamous and regular folk stop in at all hours of the night and day for classic French-
            American bistro fare, including steak au poivre, a perfect omelet and knockout frisee salad with lardons.
Don't miss the mighty fine creme brulee. Casual dress; cocktails. **Parking:** street. **Cards:** AX, CB, DC, DS, JC, MC, VI.

THE OLD HOMESTEAD Lunch: $12-$25   Dinner: $25-$45   Phone: 212/242-9040   12
▼▼▼ ▼▼   **Location:** Between 14th and 15th sts. 56 9th Ave 10011. **Hours:** noon-10:45 pm, Sat 1 pm-11:45 pm, Sun 1 pm-
            9:45 pm. **Reservations:** suggested. **Features:** In the historic Chelsea meat market district, the restaurant
Steak House has specialties that range from succulent prime sirloin steak, filet mignon and prime rib to creamed spinach
            and cottage fries. The restaurant has been operated by the same family since 1954. Casual dress;
cocktails. **Parking:** no self-parking. **Cards:** AX, CB, DC, MC, VI.   ⬙

OLD TOWN BAR & RESTAURANT Lunch: $5-$11   Dinner: $5-$11   Phone: 212/529-6732   37
▼▼▼ ▼▼   **Location:** Between Park Ave and Broadway. 45 E 18th St 10003. **Hours:** 11:30 am-11:30 pm, Sat from noon, Sun
            1 pm-10 pm. Closed major holidays. **Reservations:** not accepted. **Features:** Housed in an 1892 structure,
American   the old, New York establishment still features many of historic architectural elements, including a pressed-tin
            ceiling, magnificent bar and beveled glass mirrors. Expect generous portions of hearty tavern food. Casual
dress; cocktails. **Parking:** street. **Cards:** AX, MC, VI. **Historic**

OLIVES   Lunch: $17-$28   Dinner: $22-$29   Phone: 212/353-8345   43
▼▼▼▼▼▼   **Location:** In Union Square; at 17th St. 201 Park Ave S 10003. **Hours:** 7 am-10:30, noon-2:30 & 6-10:30 pm, Fri-
            11 pm, Sat 10 am-2:30 & 6-11 pm, Sun 10 am-2:30 & 5:30-10 pm. **Reservations:** suggested.
American   **Features:** The mesmerizing space—with loud, rhythmic music, suave warmth, blown-glass-shaded light
            fixtures and energy wafting in from the bar—exudes style. The more important half of the equation is the
superb food. Plate envy could be a problem, but there are flexible tasting menus and knowledgeable servers to assist. The
dishes, which merge time-tested flavor combinations and scrumptious textures, are the brainchild of skilled staffers who must,
themselves, love to eat. Dressy casual; cocktails. **Parking:** no self-parking. **Cards:** AX, MC, VI.   ♿ ⬙

O MAI RESTAURANT   Dinner: $12-$16   Phone: 212/633-0550   5
▼▼▼ ▼▼   **Location:** Between 19th and 20th sts. 158 9th Ave 10011. **Hours:** 5:30 pm-10 pm, Fri & Sat-11 pm. Closed: 1/1,
            11/22, 12/25. **Reservations:** accepted. **Features:** The restaurant is a bit difficult to find and the decor is
Vietnamese sparing, but the food is a definite attraction. Traditional Vietnamese fare is complemented by some Western
            influences. Start with an appetizer of grilled calamari with tamarind vinaigrette or wok-seared monkfish with
peanut, chili and basil. Progress to an entree of crispy red snapper in chili-lime sauce or jumbo shrimp sauteed in curry-coconut
sauce. Although desserts are limited, warm banana bread is a treat. Casual dress; cocktails. **Parking:** no self-parking.
Cards: AX, MC, VI.   ⬙

ONE IF BY LAND, TWO IF BY SEA   Dinner: $69-$85   Phone: 212/228-0822   55
▼▼▼ ▼▼▼ **Location:** Between W 4th St and 7th Ave; just off 7th Ave. 17 Barrow St 10014. **Hours:** 5:30 pm-11:15 pm. Closed:
            5/28, 9/3. **Reservations:** suggested. **Features:** Overlooking a small courtyard garden, the beautifully
American   restored, 18th-century carriage house once owned by Aaron Burr offers candlelight dining in a room filled
            with the sounds of piano music. Beef Wellington and souffles are specialties on a menu of classic and
creative cuisine. Parking across the street. Semi-formal attire; cocktails; entertainment. **Parking:** no self-parking. **Cards:** AX,
DC, DS, MC, VI.   ⬙

OTTO ENOTECA PIZZERIA   Lunch: $8-$14   Dinner: $8-$14   Phone: 212/995-9559   58
▼▼▼ ▼▼   **Location:** At 8th St; entrance on 8th St. 1 5th Ave 10003. **Hours:** 11:30 am-midnight. Closed: 11/22, 12/25.
            Features: The collaboration of four chefs, including Mario Batali and Joseph Bastianich, helped create a
Italian   pizzeria unlike any other. Pizza with cured salt pork—more a flatbread with savory essences unhampered
            by tomato products—and other pies, some more traditional, are loved by many. Among appetizers are
cauliflower with lemon and garlic, eggplant caponata and fried tidbits, such as chickpea fritters and whitebait. The large menu
offers plenty over which to ogle. Casual dress; cocktails. **Parking:** no self-parking. **Cards:** AX, DC, MC, VI.   ♿ ⬙

(See map and index starting on p. 376)

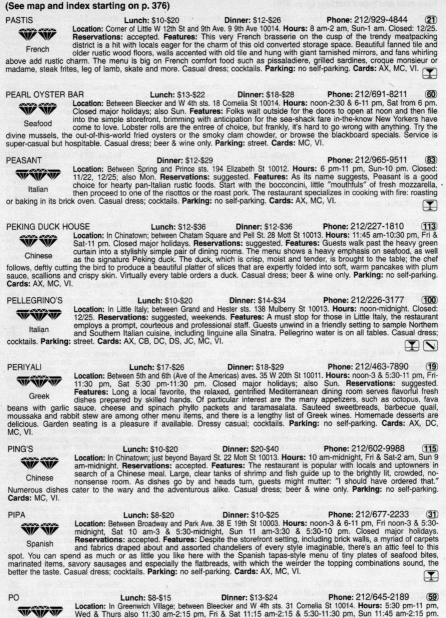

PASTIS

French

Lunch: $10-$20   Dinner: $12-$26   Phone: 212/929-4844   ㉑
Location: Corner of Little W 12th St and 9th Ave. 9 9th Ave 10014. **Hours:** 8 am-2 am, Sun-1 am. **Closed:** 12/25.
Reservations: accepted. **Features:** This very French brasserie on the cusp of the trendy meatpacking district is a hit with locals eager for the charm of this old converted storage space. Beautiful fanned tile and older rustic wood floors, walls accented with old tile and hung with giant tarnished mirrors, and fans whirling above add rustic charm. The menu is big on French comfort food such as pissaladiere, grilled sardines, croque monsieur or madame, steak frites, leg of lamb, skate and more. Casual dress; cocktails. **Parking:** no self-parking. **Cards:** AX, MC, VI.

PEARL OYSTER BAR

Seafood

Lunch: $13-$22   Dinner: $18-$28   Phone: 212/691-8211   ㉖
Location: Between Bleecker and W 4th sts. 18 Cornelia St 10014. **Hours:** noon-2:30 & 6-11 pm, Sat from 6 pm. Closed major holidays; also Sun. **Features:** Folks wait outside for the doors to open at noon and then file into the simple storefront, brimming with anticipation for the sea-shack fare in-the-know New Yorkers have come to love. Lobster rolls are the entree of choice, but frankly, it's hard to go wrong with anything. Try the divine mussels, the out-of-this-world fried oysters or the smoky clam chowder, or browse the blackboard specials. Service is super-casual but hospitable. Casual dress; beer & wine only. **Parking:** street. **Cards:** MC, VI.

PEASANT

Italian

Dinner: $12-$29   Phone: 212/965-9511   ㉝
Location: Between Spring and Prince sts. 194 Elizabeth St 10012. **Hours:** 6 pm-11 pm, Sun-10 pm. **Closed:** 11/22, 12/25; also Mon. **Reservations:** suggested. **Features:** As its name suggests, Peasant is a good choice for hearty pan-Italian rustic foods. Start with the bocconcini, little "mouthfuls" of fresh mozzarella, then proceed to one of the risottos or the roast pork. The restaurant specializes in cooking with fire: roasting or baking in its brick oven. Casual dress; cocktails. **Parking:** no self-parking. **Cards:** AX, MC, VI.

PEKING DUCK HOUSE

Chinese

Lunch: $12-$36   Dinner: $12-$36   Phone: 212/227-1810   ⑪③
Location: In Chinatown; between Chatam Square and Pell St. 28 Mott St 10013. **Hours:** 11:45 am-10:30 pm, Fri & Sat-11 pm. Closed major holidays. **Reservations:** suggested. **Features:** Guests walk past the heavy green curtain into a stylishly simple pair of dining rooms. The menu shows a heavy emphasis on seafood, as well as the signature Peking duck. The duck, which is crisp, moist and tender, is brought to the table; the chef follows, deftly cutting the bird to produce a beautiful platter of slices that are expertly folded into soft, warm pancakes with plum sauce, scallions and crispy skin. Virtually every table orders a duck. Casual dress; beer & wine only. **Parking:** no self-parking. **Cards:** AX, MC, VI.

PELLEGRINO'S

Italian

Lunch: $10-$20   Dinner: $14-$34   Phone: 212/226-3177   ⑩⓪
Location: In Little Italy; between Grand and Hester sts. 138 Mulberry St 10013. **Hours:** noon-midnight. **Closed:** 12/25. **Reservations:** suggested, weekends. **Features:** A must stop for those in Little Italy, the restaurant employs a prompt, courteous and professional staff. Guests unwind in a friendly setting to sample Northern and Southern Italian cuisine, including linguine alla Sinatra. Pellegrino water is on all tables. Casual dress; cocktails. **Parking:** street. **Cards:** AX, CB, DC, DS, JC, MC, VI.

PERIYALI

Greek

Lunch: $17-$26   Dinner: $18-$29   Phone: 212/463-7890   ⑲
Location: Between 5th and 6th (Ave of the Americas) aves. 35 W 20th St 10011. **Hours:** noon-3 & 5:30-11 pm, Fri-11:30 pm, Sat 5:30 pm-11:30 pm. Closed major holidays; also Sun. **Reservations:** suggested. **Features:** Long a local favorite, the relaxed, gentrified Mediterranean dining room serves flavorful fresh dishes prepared by skilled hands. Of particular interest are the many appetizers, such as octopus, fava beans with garlic sauce, cheese and spinach phyllo packets and taramasalata. Sauteed sweetbreads, barbecue quail, moussaka and rabbit stew are among other menu items, and there is a lengthy list of Greek wines. Homemade desserts are delicious. Garden seating is a pleasure if available. Dressy casual; cocktails. **Parking:** no self-parking. **Cards:** AX, DC, MC, VI.

PING'S

Chinese

Lunch: $10-$20   Dinner: $20-$40   Phone: 212/602-9988   ⑪⑤
Location: In Chinatown; just beyond Bayard St. 22 Mott St 10013. **Hours:** 10 am-midnight, Fri & Sat-2 am, Sun 9 am-midnight. **Reservations:** accepted. **Features:** The restaurant is popular with locals and uptowners in search of a Chinese meal. Large, clear tanks of shrimp and fish guide up to the brightly lit, crowded, non-nonsense room. As dishes go by and heads turn, guests might mutter: "I should have ordered that." Numerous dishes cater to the wary and the adventurous alike. Casual dress; beer & wine only. **Parking:** no self-parking. **Cards:** MC, VI.

PIPA

Spanish

Lunch: $8-$20   Dinner: $10-$25   Phone: 212/677-2233   ㉛
Location: Between Broadway and Park Ave. 38 E 19th St 10003. **Hours:** noon-3 & 6-11 pm, Fri noon-3 & 5:30-midnight, Sat 10 am-3 & 5:30-midnight, Sun 11 am-3:30 & 5:30-10 pm. Closed major holidays. **Reservations:** accepted. **Features:** Despite the storefront setting, including brick walls, a myriad of carpets and fabrics draped about and assorted chandeliers of every style imaginable, there's an attic feel to this spot. You can spend as much or as little you like here with the Spanish tapas-style menu of tiny plates of seafood bites, marinated items, savory sausages and especially the flatbreads, with which the weirder the topping combinations sound, the better the taste. Casual dress; cocktails. **Parking:** no self-parking. **Cards:** AX, MC, VI.

PO

Italian

Lunch: $8-$15   Dinner: $13-$24   Phone: 212/645-2189   ㉟
Location: In Greenwich Village; between Bleecker and W 4th sts. 31 Cornelia St 10014. **Hours:** 5:30 pm-11 pm, Wed & Thurs also 11:30 am-2:15pm, Fri & Sat 11:15 am-2:15 & 5:30-11:30 pm, Sun 11:45 am-2:15 pm. Closed major holidays. **Reservations:** suggested. **Features:** This is the tiny spot that first made Mario Batali a star; while he has since moved on, the rustic Italian cuisine lives on. Start with the complimentary white bean bruschetta and then possibly move on to the antipasto bar with a selection of marinated veggies and other treats displayed on the small bar. The menu offers unique pastas, meats and daily seafood specialties. The light-as-a-cloud gnocchi is a special treat. Casual dress; cocktails. **Parking:** street. **Cards:** AX.

PRUNE

American

Lunch: $9-$14   Dinner: $19-$30   Phone: 212/677-6221   ㉘
Location: In Greenwich Village; between 1st and 2nd aves. 54 E 1st St 10003. **Hours:** 11:30 am-3 & 6-11 pm, Sat 6 pm-midnight, Sun 5 pm-10 pm. Closed major holidays. **Reservations:** suggested. **Features:** Chef/Owner Gabrielle Hamilton has become known far and wide for the eclectic fare she turns out from this small spot that still nostalgically sports its turn-of-the-century fixtures. The cuisine is unique but cozy and homey, with such seasonal specialties as marinated fresh anchovies, suckling pig, roasted marrow bones, whole grilled fish and pasta kerchief, and a fun snack menu at the bar. Casual dress; cocktails. **Parking:** street. **Cards:** AX, MC, VI.

(See map and index starting on p. 376)

THE RED CAT | **Dinner:** $20-$25 | **Phone:** 212/242-1122 ①

◆◆◆ American

Location: In Chelsea; between 23rd and 24th sts. 227 10th Ave 10011. **Hours:** 5:30 pm-11 pm, Fri & Sat-midnight, Sun 5 pm-10 pm. Closed: 1/1, 12/26. **Reservations:** accepted. **Features:** The casual decor mixes such as elements as red farmhouse siding with oversized Morrocan lanterns at this upscale but casual bar and restaurant. The cuisine mixes classics with the innovative such as tempura green beans, sugarcane rosted pork tenderloin and lobster pierogies. Dressy casual; cocktails. **Parking:** street. **Cards:** AX, DC, DS, MC, VI.

RESTAURANT FLORENT | **Lunch:** $8-$18 | **Dinner:** $10-$26 | **Phone:** 212/989-5779 ㉓

◆◆ American

Location: Between Greenwich and Washington sts; downtown. 69 Gansevoort St 10014. **Hours:** 24 hours. **Reservations:** accepted. **Features:** Long before Stella McCartney and other fashionistas opened shop in the meatpacking district, Florent was satisfying the after-hours crowd with a perfect hybrid of classic French and hip American fare, including a light and fluffy goat cheese omelet with apples, onions and herbs; Louisiana crab cakes topped with Creole mayonnaise; and of course, the late-night standby: a juicy burger with an enormous mound of fries. Befitting the city that never sleeps, this place stays open into the wee hours. Casual dress; cocktails. **Parking:** street.

RIVIERA CAFE & SPORTS BAR | **Lunch:** $8-$16 | **Dinner:** $8-$13 | **Phone:** 212/929-3250 (52)

◆◆ American

Location: Corner of 7th Ave. 225 W 4th St 10014. **Hours:** noon-1 am, Fri & Sat-2 am. Closed: 12/24, 12/25. **Features:** The cafe is the kind of place where folks gather with old friends and meet new ones. Plenty of televisions broadcast sporting events, providing cheering fodder as guests munch on traditional appetizers and entrees. Cocktails. **Parking:** street. **Cards:** AX, DC, JC, MC, VI.

🍸

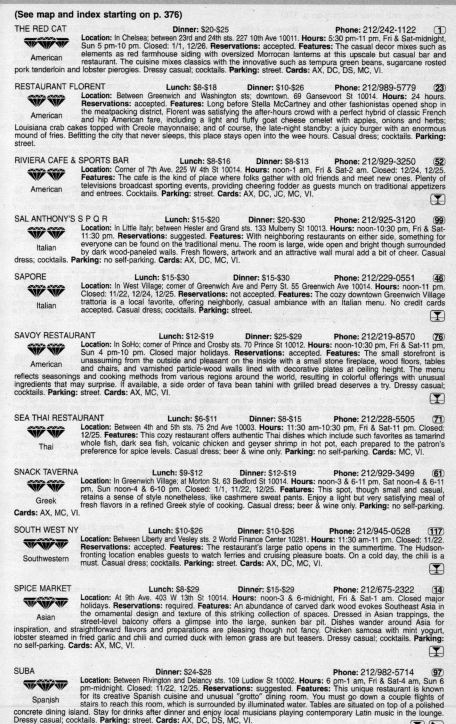

SAL ANTHONY'S S P Q R | **Lunch:** $15-$20 | **Dinner:** $20-$30 | **Phone:** 212/925-3120 (99)

◆◆ Italian

Location: In Little Italy; between Hester and Grand sts. 133 Mulberry St 10013. **Hours:** noon-10:30 pm, Fri & Sat-11:30 pm. **Reservations:** suggested. **Features:** With neighboring restaurants on either side, something for everyone can be found on the traditional menu. The room is large, wide open and bright though surrounded by dark wood-paneled walls. Fresh flowers, artwork and an attractive wall mural add a bit of cheer. Casual dress; cocktails. **Parking:** no self-parking. **Cards:** AX, DC, MC, VI.

SAPORE | **Lunch:** $15-$30 | **Dinner:** $15-$30 | **Phone:** 212/229-0551 ㊻

◆◆ Italian

Location: In West Village; corner of Greenwich Ave and Perry St. 55 Greenwich Ave 10014. **Hours:** noon-11 pm. Closed: 11/22, 12/24, 12/25. **Reservations:** not accepted. **Features:** The cozy downtown Greenwich Village trattoria is a local favorite, offering neighborly, casual ambiance with an Italian menu. No credit cards accepted. Casual dress; cocktails. **Parking:** street.

🍸

SAVOY RESTAURANT | **Lunch:** $12-$19 | **Dinner:** $25-$29 | **Phone:** 212/219-8570 (76)

◆◆ American

Location: In SoHo; corner of Prince and Crosby sts. 70 Prince St 10012. **Hours:** noon-10:30 pm, Fri & Sat-11 pm, Sun 4 pm-10 pm. Closed major holidays. **Reservations:** accepted. **Features:** The small storefront is unassuming from the outside and pleasant on the inside with a small stone fireplace, wood floors, tables and chairs, and varnished particle-wood walls lined with decorative plates at ceiling height. The menu reflects seasonings and cooking methods from various regions around the world, resulting in colorful offerings with unusual ingredients that may surprise. If available, a side order of fava bean tahini with grilled bread deserves a try. Dressy casual; cocktails. **Parking:** street. **Cards:** AX, MC, VI.

🍸

SEA THAI RESTAURANT | **Lunch:** $6-$11 | **Dinner:** $8-$15 | **Phone:** 212/228-5505 (71)

◆◆ Thai

Location: Between 4th and 5th sts. 75 2nd Ave 10003. **Hours:** 11:30 am-10:30 pm, Fri & Sat-11 pm. Closed: 12/25. **Features:** This cozy restaurant offers authentic Thai dishes which include such favorites as tamarind whole fish, dark sea fish, volcanic chicken and geyser shrimp in hot pot, each prepared to the patron's preference for spice levels. Casual dress; beer & wine only. **Parking:** no self-parking. **Cards:** MC, VI.

SNACK TAVERNA | **Lunch:** $9-$12 | **Dinner:** $12-$19 | **Phone:** 212/929-3499 (61)

◆◆ Greek

Location: In Greenwich Village; at Morton St. 63 Bedford St 10014. **Hours:** noon-3 & 6-11 pm, Sat noon-4 & 6-11 pm, Sun noon-4 & 6-10 pm. Closed: 1/1, 11/22, 12/25. **Features:** This spot, though small and casual, retains a sense of style nonetheless, like cashmere sweat pants. Enjoy a light but very satisfying meal of fresh flavors in a refined Greek style of cooking. Casual dress; beer & wine only. **Parking:** no self-parking. **Cards:** AX, MC, VI.

SOUTH WEST NY | **Lunch:** $10-$26 | **Dinner:** $10-$26 | **Phone:** 212/945-0528 (117)

◆◆◆ Southwestern

Location: Between Liberty and Vesley sts. 2 World Finance Center 10281. **Hours:** 11:30 am-11 pm. Closed: 11/22. **Reservations:** accepted. **Features:** The restaurant's large patio opens in the summertime. The Hudson-fronting location enables guests to watch ferries and cruising pleasure boats. On a cold day, the chili is a must. Casual dress; cocktails. **Parking:** street. **Cards:** AX, DC, MC, VI.

🍸

SPICE MARKET | **Lunch:** $8-$29 | **Dinner:** $15-$29 | **Phone:** 212/675-2322 ⑭

◆◆◆ Asian

Location: At 9th Ave. 403 W 13th St 10014. **Hours:** noon-3 & 6-midnight, Fri & Sat-1 am. Closed major holidays. **Reservations:** required. **Features:** An abundance of carved dark wood evokes Southeast Asia in the ornamental design and texture of this striking collection of spaces. Dressed in Asian trappings, the street-level balcony offers a glimpse into the large, sunken bar pit. Dishes wander around Asia for inspiration, and straightforward flavors and preparations are pleasing though not fancy. Chicken samosa with mint yogurt, lobster steamed in fried garlic and chili and curried duck with lemon grass are but teasers. Dressy casual; cocktails. **Parking:** no self-parking. **Cards:** AX, MC, VI.

🍸

SUBA | **Dinner:** $24-$28 | **Phone:** 212/982-5714 (97)

◆◆◆ Spanish

Location: Between Rivington and Delancy sts. 109 Ludlow St 10002. **Hours:** 6 pm-1 am, Fri & Sat-4 am, Sun 6 pm-midnight. Closed: 11/22, 12/25. **Reservations:** suggested. **Features:** This unique restaurant is known for its creative Spanish cuisine and unusual "grotto" dining room. You must go down a couple flights of stairs to reach this room, which is surrounded by illuminated water. Tables are situated on top of a polished concrete dining island. Stay for drinks after dinner and enjoy local musicians playing contemporary Latin music in the lounge. Dressy casual; cocktails. **Parking:** street. **Cards:** AX, DC, DS, MC, VI.

🍸 ⧄

(See map and index starting on p. 376)

SUMILE   Dinner: $14-$28   Phone: 212/989-7699 [39]
Japanese

Location: Between 6th (Ave of the Americas) and 7th aves. 154 W 13th St 10013. **Hours:** 5:30 pm-10:30 pm, Fri & Sat-11 pm, Sun-10 pm. Closed: 11/22, 12/25; also Sun & Mon in summer. **Reservations:** suggested. **Features:** Simple can be a great success if done with poise, elegance and a desire to please. The highly skilled chef prepares dishes with top-quality ingredients. Artful cuisine that draws on Japanese influences uses just the right combinations of spices and herbs. Three tapas-size plates, at $14 each, make a lovely meal. The seductive and clean white space—cozy with cushions and green accents and washed with violet light—is peaceful. Sumile, which means "little violet" in Japanese, is a little jewel. Dressy casual; cocktails. **Parking:** no self-parking. **Cards:** AX, DC, MC, VI.

SUSHI SAMBA 7   Lunch: $6-$20   Dinner: $9-$39   Phone: 212/691-7885 [53]
Sushi

Location: At Barrow St. 87 7th Ave S 10014. **Hours:** noon-1 am, Thurs-Sat to 2 am; Sunday brunch. Closed: 11/22. **Reservations:** accepted. **Features:** Fusion cooking takes a lively twist in the colorful corner restaurant. Interesting high-quality sushi and sashimi choices reflect Latino influences. Late at night, the full menu accompanies lively samba music and dancing. Casual dress; cocktails. **Parking:** on-site. **Cards:** AX, MC, VI.

SUSHISAMBA PARK   Lunch: $12-$30   Dinner: $18-$34   Phone: 212/475-9377 [34]
Japanese

Location: Between 19th and 20th sts. 245 Park Ave S 10003. **Hours:** 11:45 am-1 am, Thurs-Sat to 2 am, Sun 11:30 am-midnight; Sunday brunch. Closed: 11/22, 12/25. **Reservations:** suggested. **Features:** Vibrant colors of mango, red, lime and gold celebrate Brazil's Carnival. Bubble-shaped lights add another jolt of fun. The food is lively, making use of Brazilian, Japanese and Peruvian cuisines in creative fusion, furiously flavorful. The tuna sashimi seviche with orange, ginger, yuzu and white soy, octopus sashimi seviche with sweet sake and mustard, sushi combinations, grilled meats with farofa and chimichurri are examples of cuisines worked together. Cocktails are wild and wonderful. Casual dress; cocktails. **Parking:** no self-parking. **Cards:** AX, MC, VI.

TABLA   Lunch: $19-$24   Dinner: $64   Phone: 212/889-0667 [8]
Indian

Location: At 25th St. 11 Madison Ave 10010. **Hours:** noon-2 & 5:30-10 pm, Sat & Sun 5:30 pm-10:30 pm. Closed major holidays. **Reservations:** suggested. **Features:** A spiral staircase leads from the popular lively scene of the downstairs Bread Bar, which is eye-catching and visually appealing with hints of art deco, to the more subdued and polished scene upstairs. Aromas of spices and herbs virtually waft up from the menu as guests read. Some ingredients are exotic, but the servers can explain. Dishes arrive full of flavor and wonderful texture. The tasting menu is a great way to sample. Dressy casual; cocktails. **Parking:** no self-parking. **Cards:** AX, DC, DS, MC, VI.

TAKAHACHI TRIBECA   Lunch: $5-$15   Dinner: $16-$23   Phone: 212/571-1830 [109]
Sushi

Location: In TriBeCa; between Church St and W Broadway. 145 Duane St 10013. **Hours:** noon-2:30 & 5:30-10:30 pm, Fri-11 pm, Sat 5:30 pm-11 pm, Sun 5:30 pm-10:30 pm. Closed major holidays. **Reservations:** accepted. **Features:** Diners start with one of two miso soups: a mild red or the more potent white. Scads of creative sushi combinations, some taking their name from movies, make it difficult to choose. The Godfather—with fried oysters, cucumber and Gorgonzola—is an offer that can't be refused, as is the case with the Godzilla, with soba noodles, avocado and salmon skin, and the riveting Taxi Driver. Among cooked items are Kyoto-style beef stew and a delightful grilled salmon with green tea salt. Casual dress; beer & wine only. **Parking:** street. **Cards:** AX, DC, DS, MC, VI.

TAMARIND   Lunch: $25   Dinner: $11-$32   Phone: 212/674-7400 [17]
Indian

Location: Between Lexington and Park aves. 41-43 E 22nd St 10010. **Hours:** 11:30 am-3 & 5:30-11:30 pm, Fri & Sat-midnight. **Reservations:** required. **Features:** A very lovely dining room with silk lanterns, gentle lights, soft fabric walls, and a display of old calf bells, sets the mood for the exotic meal. Food is prepared in a exhibition kitchen by masters. Dishes like lotus root dumplings in a spicy sauce, shrimp in aromatic coconut sauce, roasted mint and ginger marinated leg of lamb, and oven roasted cornish game hen are but a few of the anything-but-ordinary selections. Service is gracious and will help with difficult decisions! Dressy casual; cocktails. **Parking:** street. **Cards:** AX, CB, DC, DS, MC, VI.

TEANY   Lunch: $5-$10   Dinner: $5-$10   Phone: 212/475-9190 [88]
Vegetarian

Location: Between Ludlow and Orchard sts. 90 Rivington St 10002. **Hours:** 10 am-10 pm, Fri & Sat-2 am. Closed: 11/22, 12/25; also Mon. **Features:** In the Bargain District on Manhattan's lower east side, the popular meeting spot is aptly named. On the menu is a good selection of sandwiches, soups, great desserts, healthy snacks, teas, coffee and breakfast items. The atmosphere is relaxed, and guests need not be vegetarians to enjoy this place. Streetside seating is a seasonal option. Casual dress; beer & wine only. **Parking:** street.

TRIBECA GRILL   Lunch: $12-$25   Dinner: $19-$35   Phone: 212/941-3900 [94]
American

Location: In TriBeCa; at Franklin St. 375 Greenwich St 10013. **Hours:** 11:30 am-3 & 5:30-11 pm, Fri & Sat-11:30 pm, Sun-10 pm. Closed major holidays; also for lunch Sat. **Reservations:** required. **Features:** Many celebrities enjoy the famous spot, which is owned by Robert DeNiro in partnership with noted restaurateur Drew Nieporent. The unpretentious setting radiates energy, and a down-to-earth mood punctuates the renovated warehouse, which has brick walls hung with original art and high ceilings traversed by large painted pipes. Contemporary cuisine is on the menu. Semi-formal attire; cocktails. **Parking:** no self-parking. **Cards:** AX, DC, DS, MC, VI.

UMBERTO'S CLAM HOUSE Lunch: $12-$40   Dinner: $12-$40   Phone: 212/431-7545 [86]
Italian

Location: In Little Italy; between Broome and Kenmare sts. 178 Mulberry St 10013. **Hours:** 11 am-4 am. **Reservations:** suggested, weekends. **Features:** In the heart of Little Italy, the clam house prepares Italian seafood specialties with homemade red and white clam sauces. This place is a favorite with such celebrities as Robert De Niro, Michael Douglas and Bette Midler. Casual dress; cocktails. **Parking:** street. **Cards:** AX, CB, DC, DS, JC, MC, VI.

(See map and index starting on p. 376)

UNION SQUARE CAFE   **Lunch:** $12-$20   **Dinner:** $23-$31   **Phone:** 212/243-4020   ㊳
▼▼▼▼   **Location:** Between 5th Ave and Union Square W. 21 E 16th St 10003. **Hours:** noon-2:15 & 5:30-10 pm, Fri & Sat-
American   11 pm. Closed major holidays. **Reservations:** suggested. **Features:** Excellent food is served in a casual
atmosphere. Smartly dressed servers describe wonderful dishes, which might include steamed wild salmon,
roasted organic chicken and grilled lamb chops, all with a sampling of seasonal vegetables. Portions are
considered to be large. Dressy casual; cocktails. **Parking:** no self-parking. **Cards:** AX, MC, VI.

VENTO TRATTORIA   **Lunch:** $9-$12   **Dinner:** $18-$22   **Phone:** 212/699-2400   ⑯
▼▼▼▼   **Location:** Corner of 13th St (where Hudson St becomes 9th Ave). 675 Hudson St 10014. **Hours:** noon-10 pm, Tues
& Wed-11 pm, Thurs-midnight, Fri & Sat-1 am, Sun 11:30 am-10 pm; Sunday brunch. Closed: 12/25.
Italian   **Reservations:** suggested. **Features:** In the meatpacking district, the sophisticated yet trendy restaurant
features exposed wood-beam ceilings, brick accent walls and large floor-to-ceiling glass doors that open to
bistro tables outside. Two types of fresh bread are served with a wonderful ricotta cheese spread drenched in olive oil and
ground pepper. Fire-grilled pizza and homemade pasta are always excellent choices. Dressy casual; cocktails. **Parking:** street.
Cards: AX, DC, DS, MC, VI.

VERITAS   **Dinner:** $76   **Phone:** 212/353-3700   ㉕
▼▼▼ ▼▼▼   **Location:** Between Park Ave S and Broadway. 43 E 20th St 10003. **Hours:** 5:30 pm-10:30 pm, Sun 5 pm-10 pm.
Closed major holidays. **Reservations:** required. **Features:** The intimate dining room, modern and hip, with
American   illuminated art glass and original art on red brick walls, soft track lighting and flickering candle light, is
perfect for an unassuming quiet night out with a well-prepared dinner of upscale comfort food, beautifully
presented. For wine lovers, this is Mecca. Dressy casual; cocktails. **Parking:** no self-parking. **Cards:** AX, DC, DS, MC, VI.

VILLA MOSCONI RESTAURANT   **Lunch:** $10-$25   **Dinner:** $11-$28   **Phone:** 212/673-0390   ㊴
AAA   **Location:** In Greenwich Village; between Bleecker and Houston sts. 69 MacDougal St 10012. **Hours:** noon-11 pm.
Closed: 12/25; also Sun. **Reservations:** suggested. **Features:** Special requests are handled expediently at
▼▼ ▼▼   the casual restaurant, which is known for flavorful, traditional preparations of homemade pasta. The down-
to-earth atmosphere is reminiscent of an Old World setting. Servers are prompt and efficient. Casual dress;
South Italian   cocktails. **Parking:** no self-parking. **Cards:** AX, DC, DS, MC, VI.

WALLSE RESTAURANT   **Lunch:** $16-$35   **Dinner:** $16-$35   **Phone:** 212/352-2300   ㊼
▼▼▼   **Location:** Corner of Washington St. 344 W 11th St 10014. **Hours:** 5:30 pm-11:30 pm, Sat & Sun also 11 am-3
pm. **Reservations:** accepted. **Features:** Guests are treated to traditional Austrian dishes and American
Austrian   offerings that are carefully prepared and artfully presented. Servers are professional and friendly. There is a
distinctly neighborhood feel to this restaurant, with an upscale twist. Casual dress; cocktails. **Parking:**
street. **Cards:** AX, MC, VI.

WOO LAE OAK   **Lunch:** $8-$28   **Dinner:** $8-$28   **Phone:** 212/925-8200   ㊷
▼▼▼ ▼   **Location:** Between Prince and Houston sts. 148 Mercer St 10012. **Hours:** noon-10:30 pm, Fri & Sat-11:30 pm.
Reservations: accepted. **Features:** On the basement level, the intimate and warm spot has an open
Korean   kitchen and nurtures a casual, friendly atmosphere. Guests make their own creations from a grill at each
table. Fresh, quality seafood such as cham chi (ahi tuna filet), vegetarian dishes and dak (free-range
chicken) are healthy choices. Casual dress; cocktails. **Parking:** street. **Cards:** AX, DC, MC, VI.

(See map and index starting on p. 376)

──────　*The following restaurants have not been evaluated by AAA*　──────
but are listed for your information only.

2 WEST
Phone: 917/790-2525

[fyi] Not evaluated. **Location:** Jct Battery Pl; in The Ritz-Carlton New York, Battery Park. 2 West St 10004. **Features:** This interesting new gem in the Battery Park area, tucked away just off the lobby of an elegant hotel, offers outstanding quality prime steaks in a sophisticated and modernly appointed space. The cuisine is described as French-American with an emphasis on premium beef and a variety of excellent sauces. The most unique feature of the dining room is the professional chef (called a "saucier") who visits each table with a cart of nine different sauces to accompany the guest's meal.

71 CLINTON FRESH FOOD
Phone: 212/614-6960

[fyi] Not evaluated. **Location:** Between Rivington and Stanton sts. 71 Clinton St 10002. **Features:** Creative dishes that pique interest and taste buds with layered flavors, sometimes sweet and savory together, prepared by a skilled hand. Crowded, close-knit seating but few mind.

BARMARCHE
Phone: 212/219-2399

[fyi] Not evaluated. **Location:** At Elizabeth St. 14 Spring St 10010. **Features:** Ultra-relaxed may describe the attitude of the nifty neighborhood cafe, which serves favorites such as duck confit, croque monsieur, artichoke vinaigrette and steak frites. The charcuterie platter—which displays thinly sliced cured meats, pate, pickles, confit and grilled bread—can make a meal itself.

BOULEY BAKERY
Phone: 212/219-1011

[fyi] Not evaluated. **Location:** At Duane St. 130 W Broadway 10013. **Features:** Chef David Bouley offers patrons a cafe/bakery featuring fresh homemade breads, pastries, soups and sandwiches. Open 7:30 am-7 pm.

CANDELA RESTAURANT
Phone: 212/254-1600

[fyi] Not evaluated. **Location:** Between Park Ave and Irving Pl. 116 E 16th St. **Features:** Open for dinner, the restaurant offers an upscale romantic atmosphere.

CHEZ ES SAADA
Phone: 212/777-5617

[fyi] Not evaluated. **Location:** Between 1st and 2nd aves. 42 E 1st St 10003. **Features:** Moroccan cuisine with a French twist is a good thing at the restaurant, which is hard to find due to lack of signage.

CONES-ICE CREAM ARTISANS
Phone: 212/414-1795

[fyi] Not evaluated. **Location:** Between 7th Ave and Morton St. 272 Bleecker St 10014. **Features:** An Argentinian gelato maker uses his Italian family recipes to deliver 32 flavors of high quality ice cream and sorbet to lines of appreciative folks there to savor unique and pure flavors such as grapefruit, Andian blackberry, ginger, passionfruit, pear, canteloupe hazelnut, dulce de leche and tiramisu. A few new flavors are added each season.

FERRARA PASTICCERIA BAKERY & CAFE
Phone: 212/226-6150

[fyi] Not evaluated. **Location:** In Little Italy; just e of jct Mulberry St. 195 Grand St 10013. **Features:** Since 1892, this cafe has served baked goods and sweet treats.

JOHN'S PIZZERIA
Phone: 212/243-1680

[fyi] Not evaluated. **Location:** Just e of jct 6th Ave (Ave of the Americas). 278 Bleecker St 10014. **Features:** A Greenwich Village institution for 70 years, John's offers coal-fired pizzas and sweet sausage.

KITTICHAI
Phone: 212/219-2000

[fyi] Not evaluated. **Location:** Between Broome and Spring sts. 60 Thompson St 10012. **Features:** Located on the lobby level of the ultra-hip Thompson Hotel, this trendy hot-spot serves up intriguing, deftly prepared Thai cuisine in a Buddhist temple-like setting. The David Rockwell-designed space includes a candle-lit reflecting pool in the middle of the dining room, as well as roomy booths for larger parties. The Bangkok inspired menu includes succulent short ribs in a green curry sauce, and a fiery papaya salad topped with grilled beef.

LIMA'S TASTE
Phone: 212/228-7900

[fyi] Not evaluated. **Location:** Between 1st Ave and Ave A. 432 E 13th St 10009. **Features:** Peruvian cuisine has graduated, and preparations are finely turned out with skill and attention to eye appeal, let alone nose appeal. Fresh citrus flavors buoyed by herbs and spices make easy work of fresh seafood and meats on the tantalizing menu.

L'ORANGE BLEUE
Phone: 212/226-4999

[fyi] Not evaluated. **Location:** At Crosby St. 430 Broome St 10013. **Features:** Exotic good looks and comfortable covered outdoor seating in warmer months are only a small part of the appeal. The inspired Mediterranean/Moroccan/French cuisine is the rest.

NOBU NEXT DOOR
Phone: 212/334-4445

[fyi] Not evaluated. **Location:** In TriBeCa; at Franklin St. 105 Hudson 10013. **Features:** A first-come, first-served solution to the hard-to-get tables at the original Nobu is found at this casual offshoot. Many of the same exciting and innovative dishes are available, along with an extensive raw bar, market and sake bar. Whole fish are cooked to order.

STRIP HOUSE
Phone: 212/328-0000

[fyi] Not evaluated. **Location:** Between 5th Ave and University Pl. 13 E 12th St 10038. **Features:** Upscale steak house.

WD-50
Phone: 212/477-2900

[fyi] Not evaluated. **Location:** Between Rivington and Stanton sts. 50 Clinton St 10002. **Features:** The food prepared by well-known chef Wylie Dufresne is a little quirky, a lot unusual and always very interesting, and the whole town is coming to experience it. Ingredient pairings and preparations are exciting and unexpected.

MIDTOWN MANHATTAN (See map and index starting on p. 382, 393)

──── WHERE TO STAY ────

1871 HOUSE
▼▼◇◇◇▼▼
Bed & Breakfast

Phone: 212/756-8823 [22]
All Year   1P: $225-$495   2P: $225-$495   XP: $50
Location: Between Park and Lexington aves. 130 E 62nd St 10021. Fax: 212/588-0995. **Facility:** The inn features spacious, individually decorated suites, many with fireplaces; morning breakfast baskets are delivered upon request. Smoke free premises. 7 units. 5 one- and 2 two-bedroom standard units, some with kitchens. 6 stories (no elevator), interior corridors. *Bath:* combo or shower only. **Parking:** no self-parking. **Terms:** office hours 9 am-7 pm, check-in 4 pm, 3-4 night minimum stay - seasonal, cancellation fee imposed. **Amenities:** voice mail, irons, hair dryers. **Cards:** AX, DS, MC, VI.

SOME UNITS

70 PARK AVENUE HOTEL   *Book great rates at AAA.com*
[AAA] [SAVE]
▼▼◇◇◇▼▼
Small-scale Hotel

Phone: (212)973-2400 [85]
9/4-4/30   1P: $325-$750   2P: $325-$750   XP: $20   F12
5/1-6/28   1P: $295-$650   2P: $295-$650   XP: $20   F12
6/29-9/3   1P: $249-$625   2P: $249-$625   XP: $20   F12
Location: At 38th St. 70 Park Ave 10016. Fax: 212/973-2401. **Facility:** 205 units. 201 one-bedroom standard units, some with whirlpools. 4 one-bedroom suites with whirlpools. 17 stories, interior corridors. *Bath:* combo or shower only. **Parking:** valet. **Terms:** cancellation fee imposed. **Amenities:** DVD players, video games (fee), CD players, dual phone lines, voice mail, safes, honor bars, irons, hair dryers. **Dining:** 7 am-midnight, cocktails. **Guest Services:** valet laundry, wireless Internet. **Business Services:** meeting rooms, PC. **Cards:** AX, DC, DS, MC, VI.
(See color ad p 419)

SOME UNITS

AFFINIA 50   *Book great rates at AAA.com*
[AAA] [SAVE]
▼▼◇◇◇▼▼
Small-scale Hotel

Phone: (212)751-5710 [61]
All Year   1P: $189-$529   2P: $189-$529   XP: $20   F12
Location: Between 3rd and Lexington aves. 155 E 50th St 10022. Fax: 212/753-1468. **Facility:** 209 units. 151 one-bedroom standard units, some with kitchens. 57 one- and 1 two-bedroom suites with kitchens. 22 stories, interior corridors. **Parking:** valet. **Terms:** package plans. **Amenities:** CD players, dual phone lines, voice mail, safes, irons, hair dryers. *Fee:* video games, high-speed Internet. **Leisure Activities:** exercise room. **Guest Services:** complimentary evening beverages: Mon-Thurs, valet and coin laundry, wireless Internet. **Business Services:** business center. **Cards:** AX, DC, DS, JC, MC, VI. *(See color ad p 439)*

SOME UNITS

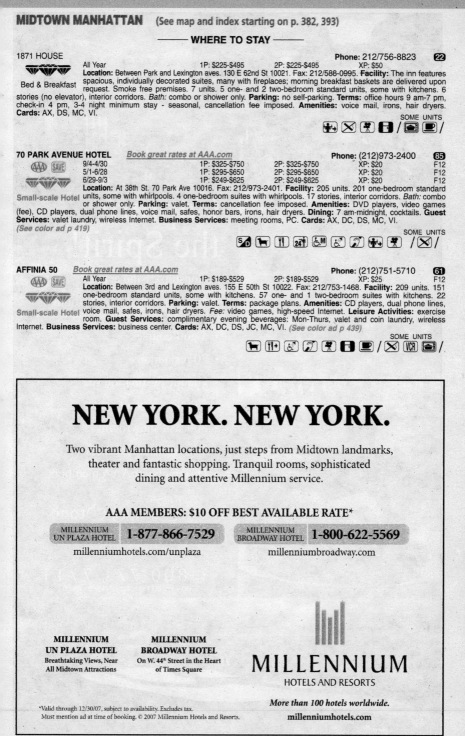

(See map and index starting on p. 382)

AFFINIA DUMONT   *Book great rates at AAA.com*   **Phone:** (212)481-7600   **97**

All Year   1P: $189-$499   2P: $189-$499   XP: $25   F12
Location: Between Lexington and 3rd aves. 150 E 34th St 10016. Fax: 212/889-8856. **Facility:** 241 units. 171 one-bedroom standard units with kitchens. 70 one-bedroom suites with kitchens. 37 stories, interior corridors. *Bath:* combo or shower only. **Parking:** valet. **Terms:** package plans, pets (with prior approval).
Small-scale Hotel **Amenities:** CD players, dual phone lines, voice mail, safes, honor bars, irons, hair dryers. *Fee:* video games, high-speed Internet. *Some:* DVD players, fax. **Dining:** 7 am-11 pm. **Leisure Activities:** exercise room, spa. **Guest Services:** valet and coin laundry. **Business Services:** meeting rooms, PC. **Cards:** AX, DC, DS, JC, MC, VI. *(See color ad p 439)*

SOME UNITS

AFFINIA GARDENS   *Book great rates at AAA.com*   **Phone:** (212)355-1230   **18**

All Year   1P: $259-$449   2P: $259-$449   XP: $25   F12
Location: Between 2nd and 3rd aves. Located in a residential area. 215 E 64th St 10021. Fax: 212/758-7858. **Facility:** 130 units. 81 one-bedroom standard units with kitchens. 46 one- and 2 two-bedroom suites with kitchens. 13 stories, interior corridors. *Bath:* combo or shower only. **Parking:** no self-parking.
Small-scale Hotel **Terms:** package plans. **Amenities:** video games (fee), CD players, dual phone lines, voice mail, safes, irons, hair dryers. *Some:* DVD players (fee). **Leisure Activities:** exercise room. **Guest Services:** valet and coin laundry, wireless Internet. **Business Services:** PC. **Cards:** AX, DC, DS, JC, MC, VI. *(See color ad p 439)*

SOME UNITS

FEE

AFFINIA MANHATTAN   *Book great rates at AAA.com*   **Phone:** (212)563-1800   **89**

All Year   1P: $159-$469   2P: $159-$469   XP: $25   F12
Location: At 31st St. Located opposite Madison Square Garden. 371 7th Ave 10001-3984. Fax: 212/643-8028. **Facility:** 501 units. 329 one-bedroom standard units with efficiencies. 165 one- and 7 two-bedroom suites with kitchens. 28 stories, interior corridors. *Bath:* combo or shower only. **Parking:** valet. **Terms:** package
Large-scale Hotel plans. **Amenities:** dual phone lines, voice mail, safes, irons, hair dryers. *Fee:* video games, high-speed Internet. *Some:* DVD players, CD players. **Dining:** 7 am-11:30 pm, cocktails. **Leisure Activities:** exercise room. **Guest Services:** valet and coin laundry. **Business Services:** conference facilities, business center. **Cards:** AX, DC, DS, JC, MC, VI. *(See color ad p 439)*

SOME UNITS

(See map and index starting on p. 382)

ALGONQUIN HOTEL *Book great rates at AAA.com*   Phone: (212)840-6800 66

	9/6-12/31	1P: $299-$469	2P: $299-$469
	5/1-6/30	1P: $299-$399	2P: $299-$399
	1/1-4/30	1P: $229-$369	2P: $229-$369
	7/1-9/5	1P: $229-$329	2P: $229-$329

Classic
Large-scale Hotel
Location: Between 5th and 6th (Ave of the Americas) aves. 59 W 44th St 10036. Fax: 212/944-1449. **Facility:** History lingers at this classic hotel, where tradition and whimsy combine to create fresh, stylish rooms that are comfortable and elegant. 174 units. 150 one-bedroom standard units. 24 one-bedroom suites. 12 stories, interior corridors. *Bath:* combo or shower only. **Parking:** no self-parking. **Terms:** package plans, pets ($50 fee, owner's pet on premises). **Amenities:** high-speed Internet, dual phone lines, voice mail, safes, irons, hair dryers. *Some:* CD players, honor bars. **Dining:** 3 restaurants, 7 am-10:30 & noon-10:30 pm, Fri & Sat-11:30 pm, cocktails, nightclub, entertainment. **Leisure Activities:** exercise room. **Guest Services:** valet laundry. **Business Services:** meeting rooms, fax (fee). **Cards:** AX, DC, DS, JC, MC, VI. *(See color ad p 423)*

SOME UNITS
(icons) FEE

BEEKMAN TOWER HOTEL *Book at AAA.com*   Phone: (212)355-7300 76

	All Year	1P: $139-$449	2P: $139-$449	XP: $25	F12

Small-scale Hotel
Location: 49th St and 1st Ave. 3 Mitchell Pl 10017. Fax: 212/753-9366. **Facility:** 173 units. 56 one-bedroom standard units with kitchens. 114 one- and 3 two-bedroom suites with kitchens. 25 stories, interior corridors. *Bath:* combo or shower only. **Parking:** valet. **Terms:** package plans. **Amenities:** video games (fee), dual phone lines, voice mail, safes, irons, hair dryers. **Leisure Activities:** saunas, exercise room. **Guest Services:** valet and coin laundry, wireless Internet. **Business Services:** meeting rooms, fax (fee). **Cards:** AX, DC, DS, JC, MC, VI.

SOME UNITS
(icons) FEE

BELVEDERE HOTEL *Book great rates at AAA.com*   Phone: (212)245-7000 37

	9/6-12/31	1P: $299-$599	2P: $299-$599	XP: $15	F12
	5/1-6/30	1P: $299-$499	2P: $299-$499	XP: $15	F12
	1/1-4/30	1P: $229-$499	2P: $229-$499	XP: $15	F12
	7/1-9/5	1P: $229-$399	2P: $229-$329	XP: $15	F12

Large-scale Hotel
Location: Between 8th and 9th aves. 319 W 48th St 10036. Fax: 212/245-4455. **Facility:** 324 units. 323 one-bedroom standard units. 1 one-bedroom suite with whirlpool. 16 stories, interior corridors. *Bath:* combo or shower only. **Parking:** on-site and valet. **Terms:** check-in 4 pm, [AP] & [CP] meal plans available. **Amenities:** video games (fee), dual phone lines, voice mail, safes, irons, hair dryers. *Some:* DVD players, CD players. **Dining:** 2 restaurants, 7-11 am, also, Churrascaria Plataforma, see separate listing. **Leisure Activities:** exercise room. **Guest Services:** gift shop, valet and coin laundry, wireless Internet. **Business Services:** meeting rooms, business center. **Cards:** AX, DC, DS, MC, VI. *(See color ad p 423)*

SOME UNITS
(icons)

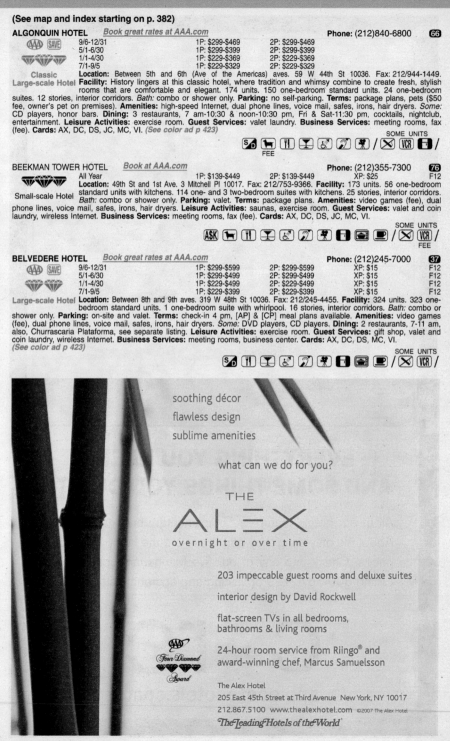

(See map and index starting on p. 382)

THE BENJAMIN HOTEL   *Book great rates at AAA.com*   Phone: (212)715-2500   59
[AAA] [SAVE]   All Year   1P: $239-$669   2P: $239-$669   XP: $25   F12
Location: Between Lexington and 3rd aves. 125 E 50th St 10022. Fax: 212/715-2525. **Facility:** High-tech
amenities meld with art deco-era high style at this 1920s hotel; adorning the exterior are intricate cartouches
and pediments. 209 units. 112 one-bedroom standard units. 96 one- and 1 two-bedroom suites. 26 stories,
Small-scale Hotel   interior corridors. **Parking:** valet. **Terms:** package plans, pets ($500 deposit). **Amenities:** dual phone lines,
voice mail, fax, safes, honor bars, irons, hair dryers. *Fee:* video games, high-speed Internet. *Some:* DVD
players, CD players. **Dining:** 7 am-10, noon-2 & 5-10 pm, Sat 8 am-2 & 5-10 pm, Sun 8 am-2 pm, cocktails, also, Ocean 50,
see separate listing. **Leisure Activities:** steamrooms, exercise room, spa. **Guest Services:** valet laundry. **Business Services:**
meeting rooms, PC (fee). Cards: AX, DC, DS, JC, MC, VI. *(See color ad p 420)*   SOME UNITS

BEST WESTERN CONVENTION CENTER HOTEL   *Book great rates at AAA.com*   Phone: (212)405-1700   54
[AAA] [SAVE]   9/1-12/31   1P: $179-$329   2P: $184-$334   XP: $5   F12
5/1-8/31   1P: $159-$329   2P: $164-$334   XP: $5   F12
1/1-4/30   1P: $159-$289   2P: $164-$294   XP: $5   F12
Location: Between 10th and 11th aves. 522 W 38th St 10018. Fax: 212/947-1545. **Facility:** 83 one-bedroom
Small-scale Hotel   standard units. 11 stories, interior corridors. **Parking:** on-site (fee). **Amenities:** high-speed Internet, voice
mail, safes, irons, hair dryers. **Leisure Activities:** exercise room. **Guest Services:** valet laundry.
Cards: AX, CB, DC, DS, MC, VI. **Free Special Amenities: continental breakfast and local telephone calls.**
(See color ad below)   SOME UNITS

BEST WESTERN HOSPITALITY HOUSE   *Book great rates at AAA.com*   Phone: (212)753-8781   68
[AAA] [SAVE]   All Year [CP]   1P: $189-$599   2P: $189-$599   XP: $20   F13
Location: Between 3rd and Lexington aves. 145 E 49th St 10022. Fax: 212/813-2070. **Facility:** Smoke free
premises. 34 units. 18 one- and 16 two-bedroom suites with kitchens. 10 stories, interior corridors. **Parking:**
no self-parking. **Terms:** cancellation fee imposed. **Amenities:** high-speed Internet, voice mail, safes, irons,
Small-scale Hotel   hair dryers. **Guest Services:** coin laundry. Cards: AX, CB, DC, DS, JC, MC, VI. **Free Special Amenities:
continental breakfast and high-speed Internet.** *(See color ad below & coupon in Savings Section)*

(See map and index starting on p. 382)

BEST WESTERN PRESIDENT HOTEL *Book great rates at AAA.com* Phone: (212)246-8800  42

9/5-12/31	1P: $149-$519	2P: $169-$549	XP: $50 · F10
5/1-9/4	1P: $139-$399	2P: $139-$429	XP: $50 F10
3/7-4/30	1P: $119-$399	2P: $119-$429	XP: $50 F10
1/1-3/6	1P: $109-$349	2P: $135	XP: $50 F10

Small-scale Hotel **Location:** Between Broadway and 8th Ave. 234 W 48th St 10036. Fax: 212/974-3922. **Facility:** 334 units. 309 one-bedroom standard units. 24 one- and 1 two-bedroom suites ($159-$899). 16 stories, interior corridors. *Bath:* combo or shower only. **Parking:** no self-parking. **Terms:** cancellation fee imposed. **Amenities:** dual phone lines, voice mail, irons, hair dryers. **Fee:** video library, safes. *Some:* CD players. **Dining:** 2 restaurants, 7 am-10 pm, cocktails. **Guest Services:** gift shop, valet laundry, wireless Internet. **Cards:** AX, CB, DC, DS, JC, MC, VI. **Free Special Amenities: local telephone calls.**

SOME UNITS

THE BLAKELY NEW YORK *Book great rates at AAA.com* Phone: (212)245-1800 23

1/1-4/30	1P: $350-$450	2P: $350-$450	XP: $20 F16
9/4-12/31	1P: $405	2P: $450	XP: $20 F16
5/1-6/30	1P: $320	2P: $350	XP: $20 F16
7/1-9/3	1P: $315	2P: $335	XP: $20 F16

Small-scale Hotel **Location:** Between 6th (Ave of the Americas) and 7th aves. 136 W 55th St 10019. Fax: 212/582-8332. **Facility:** 118 units. 76 one-bedroom standard units. 42 one-bedroom units, some with whirlpools. 17 stories, interior corridors. *Bath:* combo or shower only. **Parking:** no self-parking. **Terms:** cancellation fee imposed. **Amenities:** DVD players, CD players, dual phone lines, voice mail, safes, honor bars, irons, hair dryers. **Dining:** 6:30 am-2 am. **Leisure Activities:** exercise room. **Guest Services:** valet laundry, wireless Internet. **Business Services:** meeting rooms, PC. **Cards:** AX, CB, DC, DS, MC, VI. **Free Special Amenities: newspaper and high-speed Internet.**

SOME UNITS

THE BRYANT PARK HOTEL *Book great rates at AAA.com* Phone: (212)869-0100 77

5/1-6/24 & 9/5-12/31	1P: $445-$800	2P: $445-$800
6/25-9/4 & 1/1-4/30	1P: $395-$750	2P: $395-$750

Location: Between 5th and 6th (Ave of the Americas) aves. 40 W 40th St 10018. Fax: 212/869-4446. **Facility:** Ultra-fashionable, the hotel bustles with a sleek lounge by day and swanky club in evenings; Small-scale Hotel rooms, slightly spare in design, are not shy on comforts. 128 units. 110 one-bedroom standard units. 18 one-bedroom suites. 21 stories, interior corridors. *Bath:* combo or shower only. **Parking:** valet. **Terms:** cancellation fee imposed, small pets only (with prior approval). **Amenities:** CD players, high-speed Internet (fee), dual phone lines, voice mail, fax, safes, honor bars, hair dryers. *Some:* DVD players. **Dining:** 7 am-11 pm, nightclub. **Leisure Activities:** exercise room. **Fee:** massage. **Guest Services:** valet laundry, beauty salon, wireless Internet. **Business Services:** meeting rooms. **Cards:** AX, DC, JC, MC, VI. **Free Special Amenities: local telephone calls and newspaper.**

SOME UNITS

THE CARLYLE *Book great rates at AAA.com* Phone: (212)744-1600 7

All Year	1P: $540-$1360	2P: $540-$1360

Location: At Madison Ave. 35 E 76th St 10021. Fax: 212/717-4682. **Facility:** Pantries are featured in the suites at this elegant hotel. 179 units. 122 one-bedroom standard units, some with whirlpools. 49 one- and 8 two-bedroom suites, some with efficiencies, kitchens and/or whirlpools. 34 stories, interior corridors. **Parking:** Small-scale Hotel valet. **Terms:** cancellation fee imposed, package plans. **Amenities:** CD players, high-speed Internet (fee), dual phone lines, voice mail, fax, safes, honor bars, hair dryers. *Some:* DVD players. **Dining:** 3 restaurants, 7 am-1 am, cocktails, entertainment. **Leisure Activities:** saunas, steamroom, spa. **Guest Services:** gift shop, valet laundry, personal trainers. **Business Services:** meeting rooms, business center. **Cards:** AX, DC, DS, JC, MC, VI.

SOME UNITS

COMFORT INN JAVITS CENTER *Book great rates at AAA.com* Phone: (212)714-6699 73

5/1-12/31	1P: $189-$389	2P: $199-$399	XP: $10 F12
3/1-4/30	1P: $189-$259	2P: $199-$269	XP: $10 F12
1/1-2/29	1P: $129-$179	2P: $139-$189	XP: $10 F12

Location: Between 9th and 10th aves. 442 W 36th St 10018. Fax: 212/714-6681. **Facility:** 56 one-bedroom Small-scale Hotel standard units. 15 stories, interior corridors. **Parking:** no self-parking. **Terms:** [CP] meal plan available. **Amenities:** high-speed Internet, dual phone lines, voice mail, safes (fee), irons, hair dryers. **Guest Services:** valet laundry. **Business Services:** PC. **Cards:** AX, CB, DC, DS, JC, MC, VI. **Free Special Amenities: continental breakfast and high-speed Internet.**

SOME UNITS

FEE

COMFORT INN-MANHATTAN *Book great rates at AAA.com* Phone: (212)947-0200 88

9/1-12/31	1P: $189-$349	2P: $199-$369	XP: $10 F18
5/1-8/31	1P: $169-$309	2P: $179-$339	XP: $10 F18
2/29-4/30	1P: $149-$249	2P: $159-$269	XP: $10 F18
1/1-2/28	1P: $129-$199	2P: $139-$229	XP: $10 F18

Small-scale Hotel **Location:** Between 5th and 6th (Ave of the Americas) aves; just e of Herald Square. 42 W 35th 10001. Fax: 212/594-0401. **Facility:** 131 one-bedroom standard units. 13 stories, interior corridors. **Parking:** no self-parking. **Amenities:** voice mail, safes (fee), irons, hair dryers. **Dining:** 7 am-11 pm, cocktails. **Guest Services:** valet laundry, wireless Internet. **Cards:** AX, CB, DC, DS, JC, MC, VI. **Free Special Amenities: expanded continental breakfast and high-speed Internet.** *(See color ad p 427)*

SOME UNITS

(See map and index starting on p. 382)

COMFORT INN MIDTOWN   *Book great rates at AAA.com*   Phone: (212)221-2600   🛑 51

11/1-12/31	1P: $259-$269	2P: $269-$279	XP: $12	F13
9/1-10/31	1P: $239-$249	2P: $249-$259	XP: $12	F13
5/1-8/31	1P: $209-$229	2P: $219-$239	XP: $12	F13
1/1-4/30	1P: $129-$139	2P: $139-$149	XP: $12	F13

Small-scale Hotel **Location:** Between 6th (Ave of the Americas) and 7th aves. 129 W 46th St 10036. Fax: 212/764-7481. **Facility:** Smoke free premises. 79 one-bedroom standard units. 9 stories, interior corridors. *Bath:* shower or tub only. **Parking:** no self-parking. **Amenities:** video games, high-speed Internet, voice mail, irons, hair dryers. **Leisure Activities:** limited exercise equipment. **Guest Services:** valet laundry, wireless Internet. **Business Services:** meeting rooms, business center. **Cards:** AX, CB, DC, DS, JC, MC, VI. **Free Special Amenities: continental breakfast and high-speed Internet.** *(See color ad p 422)*

🆂🅳 ✖ 💻

COURTYARD BY MARRIOTT NEW YORK MANHATTAN/5TH AVENUE   *Book great rates at AAA.com*   Phone: 212/447-1500   79

Property failed to provide current rates

Small-scale Hotel **Location:** Between Madison and 5th aves. 3 E 40th St 10016. Fax: 212/213-0972. **Facility:** Smoke free premises. 185 units. 181 one-bedroom standard units. 4 one-bedroom suites. 30 stories, interior corridors. *Bath:* combo or shower only. **Parking:** no self-parking. **Amenities:** high-speed Internet, dual phone lines, voice mail, irons, hair dryers. **Fee:** video games, safes. *Some:* DVD players, CD players. **Dining:** Salmon River, see separate listing. **Leisure Activities:** exercise room. **Guest Services:** valet laundry. **Business Services:** business center.

SOME UNITS
🍴 🔧 🕸 ✖ 📹 💻 / 🛏 /

CROWNE PLAZA AT THE UNITED NATIONS   *Book great rates at AAA.com*   Phone: (212)986-8800   86

All Year	1P: $159-$799	2P: $159-$799	XP: $25 F12

Historic Large-scale Hotel **Location:** Between 1st and 2nd aves. 304 E 42nd St 10017. Fax: 212/986-1758. **Facility:** The hotel offers smaller, though very charming, accommodations, and it has a well-equipped exercise room. 300 units. 286 one-bedroom standard units, some with whirlpools. 14 one-bedroom suites ($249-$999) with whirlpools. 17-20 stories, interior corridors. *Bath:* combo or shower only. **Parking:** valet. **Terms:** 1-4 night minimum stay - seasonal, cancellation fee imposed, [AP] meal plan available, package plans. **Amenities:** CD players, high-speed Internet (fee), dual phone lines, voice mail, safes, honor bars, irons, hair dryers. **Leisure Activities:** saunas, exercise room. **Fee:** massage. **Guest Services:** valet laundry, wireless Internet. **Business Services:** meeting rooms, business center. **Cards:** AX, DC, DS, MC, VI.

SOME UNITS
🔍ASK 🆂🅳 🍴 🔧 🕸 ✖ 📹 💻 / ✖ 📼VCR 🛏 /
FEE

DOUBLETREE GUEST SUITES TIMES SQUARE/NEW YORK CITY   *Book great rates at AAA.com*   Phone: (212)719-1600   🛑 47

9/4-12/31	1P: $299-$899	2P: $299-$899	XP: $20	F17
5/1-9/3	1P: $299-$699	2P: $299-$699	XP: $20	F17
1/1-4/30	1P: $249-$699	2P: $249-$699	XP: $20	F17

Large-scale Hotel **Location:** 47th St and 7th Ave. 1568 Broadway 10036. Fax: 212/921-5212. **Facility:** 460 units. 458 one- and 2 two-bedroom suites. 43 stories, interior corridors. *Bath:* combo or shower only. **Parking:** valet. **Terms:** package plans. **Amenities:** dual phone lines, voice mail, safes, honor bars, irons, hair dryers. **Fee:** video library, video games. *Some:* DVD players (fee). **Dining:** 6:30 am-11 pm, cocktails. **Leisure Activities:** exercise room. **Guest Services:** valet laundry, wireless Internet. **Business Services:** conference facilities, business center. **Cards:** AX, DC, DS, JC, MC, VI. **Free Special Amenities: newspaper.** *(See color ad starting on p 436)*

SOME UNITS
🍴 📺 ♿ 🔧 🕸 ✖ 📹 🛏 🍽 💻 / ✖ 📼VCR 🛏 /
FEE

DOUBLETREE METROPOLITAN HOTEL NEW YORK CITY   *Book great rates at AAA.com*   Phone: (212)752-7000   🛑 56

All Year	1P: $199-$699	2P: $199-$699	XP: $20 F18

Small-scale Hotel **Location:** At E 51st St. 569 Lexington Ave 10022. Fax: 212/758-6311. **Facility:** 755 units. 752 one-bedroom standard units. 3 one-bedroom suites ($499-$1999). 20 stories, interior corridors. *Bath:* combo or shower only. **Parking:** on-site (fee). **Terms:** 10 day cancellation notice-fee imposed, package plans. **Amenities:** high-speed Internet (fee), dual phone lines, voice mail, safes, irons, hair dryers. **Leisure Activities:** exercise room. **Guest Services:** gift shop, valet laundry, barber shop. **Business Services:** conference facilities, business center. **Cards:** AX, CB, DC, DS, JC, MC, VI. *(See color ad starting on p 436)*

SOME UNITS
🍴 📺 ♿ 🔧 🕸 🎬 / ✖ 📼VCR 🛏 /
FEE

SPECIAL SAVINGS
for AAA Members
for performances from May 1, 2007- May 31, 2008

$75* Orch/
Front Mezz
Regularly $110

DISNEP PRESENTS

TARZAN®

BROADWAY'S HIGH-FLYING ADVENTURE
MUSIC AND LYRICS BY PHIL COLLINS

3 EASY WAYS TO ORDER!

1. BOX OFFICE: Show your card and save at the
Richard Rodgers Theatre at B'way & 46th

2. Call: *ticketmaster* at (212) 307-4747 and use code AAA

3. ONLINE: Ticketmaster.com and enter code AAA

*Performance dates, times, prices and cast are subject to change without notice. Not valid with any other offer or previously purchased tickets. ALL SALES FINAL. No exchanges or refunds. Not all seats are discounted. Offer not available 11/16 - 11/24/07, 12/14/07 - 1/5/08, 1/18 - 1/21/08, 2/15 - 2/23/08, 4/1 - 4/30/08. Some additional restrictions and blackout dates may apply. This offer can be revoked at any time without notice. Limit 14 tickets per person per 7-day period. Telephone and internet orders are subject to standard service fees. Offer expires 5/31/08.

TARZAN® owned by Edgar Rice Burroughs, Inc. and used by permission. ©2007 Burroughs and Disney.

(See map and index starting on p. 382)

DREAM   *Book at AAA.com*   **Phone:** 212/247-2000   ㉑

Property failed to provide current rates

Historic Small-scale Hotel
Location: Between Broadway and 7th Ave. 210 W 55th St 10019. Fax: 212/581-2248. **Facility:** Original 1920s relief detailing enhances the hotel's exterior; inside, find post-modern decor, a multi-floor fish tank, a meditation room and a spa. 220 units. 209 one-bedroom standard units, some with whirlpools. 10 one- and 1 two-bedroom suites, some with whirlpools. 14 stories, interior corridors. *Bath:* combo or shower only. **Parking:** valet. **Terms:** pets ($50 extra charge, in designated units, with prior approval). **Amenities:** honor bars. *Some:* DVD players. **Leisure Activities:** exercise room, spa. **Guest Services:** valet laundry. **Business Services:** meeting rooms.

SOME UNITS

EASTGATE TOWER HOTEL   *Book at AAA.com*   **Phone:** 212/687-8000   ㉚

Property failed to provide current rates

Small-scale Hotel
Location: Between 2nd and 3rd aves. 222 E 39th St 10016. Fax: 212/490-2634. **Facility:** 187 units. 133 one-bedroom standard units with kitchens. 36 one- and 18 two-bedroom suites with kitchens. 25 stories, interior corridors. *Bath:* combo or shower only. **Parking:** valet. **Terms:** pets (with prior approval). **Amenities:** video games (fee), dual phone lines, voice mail, irons, hair dryers. *Some:* DVD players (fee), CD players. **Leisure Activities:** exercise room. **Guest Services:** valet and coin laundry, wireless Internet. **Business Services:** meeting rooms, PC.

SOME UNITS

THE EXCELSIOR HOTEL   *Book at AAA.com*   **Phone:** (212)362-9200   ❷

5/1-6/30 & 9/1-12/31	1P: $229-$399	2P: $229-$399	XP: $20 F12
7/1-8/31 & 1/1-4/30	1P: $169-$399	2P: $169-$399	XP: $20 F12

Small-scale Hotel
Location: Between Columbus Ave and Central Park W; on Upper West Side. 45 W 81st St 10024. Fax: 212/580-3972. **Facility:** 199 units. 110 one-bedroom standard units. 89 one-bedroom suites ($279-$599). 16 stories, interior corridors. **Parking:** no self-parking. **Terms:** cancellation fee imposed, [AP] & [CP] meal plans available, package plans. **Amenities:** video games (fee), voice mail, safes, irons, hair dryers. *Some:* dual phone lines. **Leisure Activities:** exercise room. **Guest Services:** gift shop, valet laundry, wireless Internet. **Business Services:** meeting rooms, PC. **Cards:** AX, DC, DS, JC, MC, VI.

SOME UNITS

FITZPATRICK GRAND CENTRAL HOTEL   *Book at AAA.com*   **Phone:** 212/351-6800   ㉘

9/4-12/17	1P: $399-$499
5/1-6/30	1P: $309-$409
12/18-4/30	1P: $229-$329
7/1-9/3	1P: $199-$299

Small-scale Hotel
Location: Between 3rd and Lexington aves. 141 E 44th St 10017. Fax: 212/818-1747. **Facility:** 155 one-bedroom standard units. 9 stories, interior corridors. *Bath:* combo or shower only. **Parking:** valet. **Terms:** cancellation fee imposed, [AP] & [CP] meal plans available, package plans. **Amenities:** video library, video games (fee), dual phone lines, voice mail, safes, irons, hair dryers. *Some:* DVD players, CD players. **Guest Services:** valet laundry, wireless Internet. **Business Services:** meeting rooms. **Cards:** AX, DC, DS, JC, MC, VI.

SOME UNITS

FITZPATRICK MANHATTAN HOTEL   *Book at AAA.com*   **Phone:** 212/355-0100   ㊵

Property failed to provide current rates

Small-scale Hotel
Location: Between 56th and 57th sts. 687 Lexington Ave 10022. Fax: 212/355-1371. **Facility:** 93 units. 40 one-bedroom standard units. 53 one-bedroom suites. 16 stories, interior corridors. *Bath:* combo or shower only. **Parking:** valet. **Amenities:** dual phone lines, voice mail, safes, irons, hair dryers. *Fee:* video games, high-speed Internet. *Some:* DVD players, CD players. **Guest Services:** valet laundry, wireless Internet. **Business Services:** meeting rooms.

SOME UNITS

THE FLATOTEL   *Book great rates at AAA.com*   **Phone:** (212)887-9400   ㉝

9/5-12/16 [CP]	1P: $459-$569	2P: $489-$599
5/1-6/28 [CP]	1P: $339-$469	2P: $369-$489
12/17-4/30 [CP]	1P: $289-$429	2P: $319-$459
6/29-9/4 [CP]	1P: $279-$399	2P: $309-$429

Large-scale Hotel
Location: Between 6th (Ave of the Americas) and 7th ave. 135 W 52nd St 10019. Fax: 212/887-9442. **Facility:** 283 units. 213 one-bedroom standard units, some with efficiencies. 54 one- and 16 two-bedroom suites with kitchens. 46 stories, interior corridors. **Parking:** on-site (fee) and valet. **Terms:** check-in 4 pm, 2-3 night minimum stay - weekends, 3 day cancellation notice, package plans. **Amenities:** CD players, dual phone lines, voice mail, irons, hair dryers. *Some:* safes. *Fee:* DVD players, high-speed Internet. **Dining:** Moda, see separate listing. **Leisure Activities:** exercise room. **Guest Services:** valet laundry. **Business Services:** meeting rooms, business center. **Cards:** AX, DC, DS, JC, MC, VI. **Free Special Amenities:** continental breakfast and high-speed Internet.

SOME UNITS

FOUR SEASONS HOTEL NEW YORK   *Book at AAA.com*   **Phone:** 212/758-5700   ㉚

Property failed to provide current rates

Large-scale Hotel
Location: Between Park and Madison aves. 57 E 57th St 10022. Fax: 212/758-5711. **Facility:** Said to be the tallest hotel in the city, this lavishly-decorated luxury property sets equally lofty standards for service. 368 units. 307 one-bedroom standard units. 61 one-bedroom suites, some with whirlpools. 52 stories, interior corridors. **Parking:** valet. **Terms:** small pets only. **Amenities:** video library, DVD players, CD players, high-speed Internet, dual phone lines, voice mail, fax, safes, honor bars, hair dryers. *Some:* video games. **Dining:** Fifty-Seven Restaurant & Bar, see separate listing. **Leisure Activities:** saunas, whirlpools, steamrooms, spa. **Guest Services:** gift shop, valet laundry, area transportation. **Business Services:** conference facilities, business center.

SOME UNITS

ENTERTAINMENT AT FOXWOODS

THERE'S A LOT MORE TO 🌳 FOXWOODS THAN OUR CASINOS.
RESORT ♦ CASINO
Mashantucket Pequot Tribal Nation

CONVENIENTLY LOCATED OFF I-95 IN THE MYSTIC COUNTRY REGION OF SOUTHEAST CONNECTICUT. CALL 1-800-FOXWOODS OR VISIT FOXWOODS.COM.

(See map and index starting on p. 382)

GRAND HYATT NEW YORK *Book great rates at AAA.com* Phone: (212)883-1234   🟠**80**

9/1-4/30	1P: $349-$639	2P: $349-$639	XP: $25 F18
5/1-6/30	1P: $239-$519	2P: $239-$519	XP: $25 F18
7/1-8/31	1P: $209-$409	2P: $209-$409	XP: $25 F18

Location: Between Lexington and Park aves. Located adjacent to Grand Central Station. 109 E 42nd St 10017.
Large-scale Hotel   **Fax:** 212/697-3772. **Facility:** 1311 units. 1294 one-bedroom standard units. 16 one- and 1 three-bedroom suites, some with whirlpools. 34 stories, interior corridors. *Bath:* combo or shower only. **Parking:** valet. **Terms:** cancellation fee imposed. **Amenities:** CD players, dual phone lines, voice mail, safes, irons, hair dryers. **Dining:** 2 restaurants, 6:30 am-midnight, cocktails. **Leisure Activities:** exercise room. **Guest Services:** gift shop, valet laundry, wireless Internet. **Business Services:** conference facilities, business center. **Cards:** AX, CB, DC, DS, JC, MC, VI.

SOME UNITS

🍽️ 24🛎️ 🍸 ৬M 🐾 📷 📶 / ✕ 📼 🖥️ 🖨️ /
FEE

HAMPTON INN-MADISON SQUARE GARDEN AREA *Book great rates at AAA.com* Phone: (212)947-9700 🟠**93**

9/10-4/30	1P: $149-$499	2P: $169-$519
5/1-9/9	1P: $149-$399	2P: $169-$419

Location: Between 6th (Ave of the Americas) and 7th aves. 116 W 31st St 10001. Fax: 212/947-1800. **Facility:** 136 one-bedroom standard units. Interior corridors. *Bath:* combo or shower only. **Parking:** on-site (fee).
Small-scale Hotel   **Terms:** cancellation fee imposed, small pets only ($20 extra charge, in smoking units). **Amenities:** high-speed Internet, dual phone lines, voice mail, irons, hair dryers. **Leisure Activities:** exercise room. **Guest Services:** valet laundry. **Cards:** AX, CB, DC, DS, JC, MC, VI. **Free Special Amenities:** high-speed Internet.

(See color ad below)

SOME UNITS

$🐕 🛏️ 🍽️➕ 🐾 🖥️ / ✕ 🖥️ 🖨️ /
FEE   FEE FEE

HAMPTON INN MANHATTAN TIMES SQUARE NORTH *Book great rates at AAA.com* Phone: (212)581-4100 🟠**25**

9/4-12/17 [BP]	1P: $269-$599	XP: $30 F16
5/1-6/30 [BP]	1P: $229-$549	XP: $30 F16
12/18-4/30 [BP]	1P: $179-$349	XP: $30 F16
7/1-9/3 [BP]	1P: $189-$339	XP: $30 F16

Large-scale Hotel   **Location:** Between 51st and 52nd sts. 851 8th Ave 10019. Fax: 212/974-7502. **Facility:** 300 one-bedroom standard units. 11 stories, interior corridors. *Bath:* combo or shower only. **Parking:** on-site (fee). **Terms:** cancellation fee imposed. **Amenities:** video games (fee), high-speed Internet, voice mail, safes, irons, hair dryers. **Leisure Activities:** exercise room. **Guest Services:** gift shop, valet laundry, wireless Internet. **Cards:** AX, CB, DC, DS, JC, MC, VI. **Free Special Amenities:** full breakfast and high-speed Internet.

SOME UNITS

🐾 📷 📶 🖥️ / ✕ 🖥️ 🖨️ /

(See map and index starting on p. 382)

HILTON GARDEN INN TIMES SQUARE   *Book great rates at AAA.com*   Phone: (212)581-7000   38

	1P: $299-$599	2P: $299-$599	XP: $20	F18
9/5-12/31				
5/1-6/30	1P: $259-$499	2P: $259-$499	XP: $20	F18
1/1-4/30	1P: $199-$369	2P: $199-$369	XP: $20	F18
7/1-9/4	1P: $209-$349	2P: $209-$349	XP: $20	F18

Small-scale Hotel

Location: At 48th St. 790 Eighth Ave 10019. **Fax:** 212/974-0291. **Facility:** 369 one-bedroom standard units. 15 stories, interior corridors. *Bath:* combo or shower only. **Parking:** no self-parking. **Terms:** 2 night minimum stay - weekends, cancellation fee imposed, [BP] meal plan available, package plans. **Amenities:** video games (fee), high-speed Internet, dual phone lines, voice mail, safes, irons, hair dryers. **Dining:** Pigalle, see separate listing. **Leisure Activities:** exercise room. **Guest Services:** sundries, valet laundry. **Business Services:** business center. **Cards:** AX, DC, DS, JC, MC, VI.

SOME UNITS

HILTON NEW YORK   *Book great rates at AAA.com*   Phone: 212/586-7000   29

Property failed to provide current rates

Large-scale Hotel   **Location:** Between 53rd and 54th sts. 1335 Ave of the Americas 10019-6078. **Fax:** 212/315-1374. **Facility:** 1980 units. 1925 one-bedroom standard units. 40 one-, 12 two- and 3 three-bedroom suites, some with whirlpools. 46 stories, interior corridors. *Bath:* combo or shower only. **Parking:** on-site (fee) and valet. **Terms:** small pets only. **Amenities:** video games (fee), dual phone lines, voice mail, honor bars, irons, hair dryers. *Some:* CD players, safes. *Fee:* DVD players, high-speed Internet. **Leisure Activities:** spa. **Guest Services:** gift shop, valet laundry, wireless Internet. **Business Services:** conference facilities, business center. *(See color ad starting on p 436)*

SOME UNITS
FEE   FEE FEE

HILTON TIMES SQUARE   *Book great rates at AAA.com*   Phone: (212)642-2500   62

| 9/7-4/30 | 1P: $279-$999 | 2P: $279-$999 | XP: $30 | F |
| 5/1-9/6 | 1P: $279-$799 | 2P: $309-$829 | XP: $30 | F |

Location: Between 7th and 8th aves. 234 W 42nd St 10036. **Fax:** 212/840-5516. **Facility:** 444 units. 429 one-bedroom standard units. 14 one- and 1 two-bedroom suites. 44 stories, interior corridors. *Bath:* combo or shower only. **Parking:** valet. **Terms:** cancellation fee imposed, package plans, pets ($250 deposit). *Fee:* video games, high-speed Internet. *Some:* fax. **Dining:** 6:30 am-10 pm, cocktails, also, Above, see separate listing. **Leisure Activities:** exercise room. **Guest Services:** valet laundry. **Business Services:** conference facilities, business center. **Cards:** AX, CB, DC, DS, JC, MC, VI. *(See color ad starting on p 436)*

SOME UNITS
FEE

HOLIDAY INN EXPRESS FIFTH AVE   *Book at AAA.com*   Phone: (212)302-9088   67

9/6-12/31	1P: $279-$399	2P: $279-$399	
1/1-4/30	1P: $209-$309	2P: $209-$309	
5/1-9/5	1P: $199-$299	2P: $199-$299	

Small-scale Hotel   **Location:** At 5th Ave. 15 W 45th St 10036. **Fax:** 212/302-3088. **Facility:** 125 units. 122 one-bedroom standard units. 3 one-bedroom suites. 22 stories. *Bath:* combo or shower only. **Parking:** no self-parking. **Terms:** cancellation fee imposed. **Amenities:** high-speed Internet, dual phone lines, voice mail, irons, hair dryers. *Some:* DVD players. **Guest Services:** valet laundry, wireless Internet. **Business Services:** business center. **Cards:** AX, CB, DC, DS, MC, VI.

SOME UNITS

HOLIDAY INN MIDTOWN-57TH STREET   *Book at AAA.com*   Phone: (212)581-8100   10

9/1-12/31	1P: $335-$395	2P: $335-$395	XP: $20	F18
3/1-4/30	1P: $239-$299	2P: $239-$299	XP: $20	F18
5/1-8/31	1P: $229-$299	2P: $229-$299	XP: $20	F18
1/1-2/29	1P: $209-$259	2P: $209-$259	XP: $20	F18

Large-scale Hotel   **Location:** Between 9th and 10th aves. 440 W 57th St 10019. **Fax:** 212/581-7739. **Facility:** 597 units. 594 one-bedroom standard units. 2 one- and 1 two-bedroom suites. 10-18 stories, interior corridors. **Parking:** on-site (fee) and valet. **Terms:** check-in 4 pm, 2-3 night minimum stay - weekends, cancellation fee imposed. **Amenities:** video games (fee), dual phone lines, voice mail, irons, hair dryers. **Pool(s):** outdoor. **Guest Services:** gift shop, valet laundry, wireless Internet. **Business Services:** conference facilities. **Cards:** AX, CB, DC, JC, MC, VI.

SOME UNITS
FEE FEE

(See map and index starting on p. 382)

HOTEL BEACON
Book great rates at AAA.com

Phone: (212)787-1100 **4**

All Year 1P: $240-$260   2P: $260-$275   XP: $15   F12
Location: At W 75th St. 2130 Broadway 10023. Fax: 212/724-0839. **Facility:** 255 units. 132 one-bedroom standard units with efficiencies. 123 one-bedroom suites ($325-$750), some with kitchens. 25 stories, interior corridors. *Bath:* combo or shower only. **Parking:** no self-parking. **Amenities:** safes, irons, hair dryers. *Some:* DVD players. **Guest Services:** valet and coin laundry, wireless Internet. **Business Services:** meeting rooms, business center. **Cards:** AX, DC, DS, JC, MC, VI. **Free Special Amenities:** newspaper.

Small-scale Hotel
(See color ad p 434)

HOTEL EDISON
Book at AAA.com

Phone: (212)840-5000 **45**

All Year 1P: $190-$215   2P: $200-$215   XP: $20
Location: Between Broadway and 8th Ave. 228 W 47th St 10036. Fax: 212/596-6850. **Facility:** 800 units. 745 one- and 10 two-bedroom standard units. 45 one-bedroom suites ($260-$275). 22 stories, interior corridors. **Parking:** valet. **Amenities:** voice mail. *Some:* irons, hair dryers. **Leisure Activities:** exercise room. **Business Services:** meeting rooms, business center. **Cards:** AX, CB, DC, DS, JC, MC, VI.

Large-scale Hotel

HOTEL PLAZA ATHENEE
Book at AAA.com

Phone: (212)734-9100 **11**

9/4-4/30 1P: $640-$890   2P: $640-$890   XP: $40   F12
5/1-9/3 1P: $590-$825   2P: $590-$825   XP: $40   F12
Location: Between Madison and Park aves. 37 E 64th St 10021. Fax: 212/772-0958. **Facility:** Old World touches add an elegant ambience to this Upper East Side property, which is walking distance from the designer boutiques of Madison Avenue. 149 units. 115 one-bedroom standard units. 34 one-bedroom suites ($1335-$4700). 17 stories, interior corridors. *Bath:* combo or shower only. **Parking:** valet. **Terms:** cancellation fee imposed, package plans, 13% service charge, small pets only. **Amenities:** CD players, high-speed Internet (fee), dual phone lines, voice mail, safes, honor bars, hair dryers. *Some:* DVD players, fax. **Dining:** Arabelle, see separate listing. **Leisure Activities:** exercise room. *Fee:* massage. **Guest Services:** valet laundry. **Business Services:** meeting rooms, business center. **Cards:** AX, CB, DC, DS, JC, MC, VI.

Historic
Small-scale Hotel

HOTEL ROGER WILLIAMS
Book at AAA.com

Phone: (212)448-7000 **98**

9/5-12/31 1P: $480   2P: $510   XP: $20
5/1-6/30 1P: $450   2P: $480   XP: $20
7/1-9/4 1P: $390   2P: $420   XP: $20
Location: Corner of 31st St. 131 Madison Ave 10016. **Facility:** 191 one-bedroom standard units. 16 stories, interior corridors. *Bath:* combo or shower only. **Parking:** valet. **Terms:** open 5/1-12/31, cancellation fee imposed, $10 service charge. **Amenities:** video games (fee), dual phone lines, voice mail, safes, irons, hair dryers. *Some:* DVD players, CD players, high-speed Internet (fee). **Leisure Activities:** exercise room. **Guest Services:** valet laundry, wireless Internet. **Business Services:** meeting rooms, PC. **Cards:** AX, DC, DS, JC, MC, VI.

Small-scale Hotel

INTERCONTINENTAL THE BARCLAY NEW YORK
Book at AAA.com

Phone: 212/755-5900 **65**

Property failed to provide current rates
Location: Between Park and Lexington aves. 111 E 48th St 10017. Fax: 212/644-0079. **Facility:** 686 units. 622 one-bedroom standard units. 62 one- and 2 two-bedroom suites, some with whirlpools. 14 stories, interior corridors. *Bath:* combo or shower only. **Parking:** valet. **Amenities:** high-speed Internet (fee), dual phone lines, voice mail, safes, honor bars, irons, hair dryers. *Some:* DVD players (fee), CD players. **Leisure Activities:** sauna, steamroom, exercise room. *Fee:* massage. **Guest Services:** gift shop, valet laundry. **Business Services:** conference facilities, business center.

Large-scale Hotel

THE IROQUOIS HOTEL
Book at AAA.com

Phone: (212)840-3080 **69**

9/4-12/31 1P: $499-$750   2P: $499-$750
5/1-6/30 1P: $469-$685   2P: $469-$685
1/1-4/30 1P: $459-$685   2P: $459-$685
7/1-9/3 1P: $429-$650   2P: $429-$650
Location: Between 5th and 6th (Ave of the Americas) aves. 49 W 44th St 10036. Fax: 212/398-1754. **Facility:** Intimate and elegant are the best words to describe this historic hotel; guest rooms and bathrooms tend to be small but decor is rich and luxurious. 114 units. 105 one-bedroom standard units. 9 one-bedroom suites ($650-$750) with whirlpools, some with kitchens. 12 stories, interior corridors. *Bath:* combo or shower only. **Parking:** on-site (fee) and valet. **Amenities:** video library, DVD players, video games (fee), CD players, high-speed Internet, dual phone lines, voice mail, safes, honor bars, irons, hair dryers. **Dining:** Triomphe New York, see separate listing. **Leisure Activities:** sauna, exercise room. **Guest Services:** valet laundry, wireless Internet. **Business Services:** PC. **Cards:** AX, CB, DC, DS, MC, VI.

Historic
Small-scale Hotel

JOLLY HOTEL MADISON TOWERS
Book great rates at AAA.com

Phone: (212)802-0600 **84**

9/4-12/31 [ECP] 1P: $320-$604   2P: $320-$604   XP: $55   F12
5/1-6/30 [ECP] 1P: $310-$425   2P: $310-$425   XP: $55   F12
7/1-9/3 & 1/1-4/30 [ECP] 1P: $275-$415   2P: $275-$415   XP: $55   F12
Location: Between Park and Madison aves. 22 E 38th St 10016. Fax: 212/447-0747. **Facility:** 240 units. 233 one-bedroom standard units. 7 one-bedroom suites. 18 stories, interior corridors. *Bath:* combo or shower only. **Parking:** valet. **Terms:** cancellation fee imposed, small pets only. **Amenities:** video games (fee), dual phone lines, voice mail, honor bars, irons, hair dryers. *Some:* high-speed Internet (fee), safes. **Dining:** 2 restaurants, 7 am-10:30 pm, cocktails. **Leisure Activities:** *Fee:* massage. **Guest Services:** valet laundry, wireless Internet. **Business Services:** conference facilities, PC. **Cards:** AX, DC, DS, JC, MC, VI. **Free Special Amenities:** expanded continental breakfast and newspaper.

Large-scale Hotel

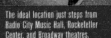

(See map and index starting on p. 382)

JUMEIRAH-ESSEX HOUSE   *Book great rates at AAA.com*   **Phone: (212)247-0300**   ⑫

9/4-12/31	1P: $329-$869	2P: $329-$869	XP: $50	F18
1/1-4/30	1P: $299-$799	2P: $299-$799	XP: $50	F18
5/1-9/3	1P: $259-$629	2P: $259-$629	XP: $50	F18

Location: Between 6th (Ave of the Americas) and 7th aves. 160 Central Park S 10019. Fax: 212/315-1839.
Classic **Facility:** Classic art deco styling and unobstructed views of Central Park are highlights of this luxury hotel.
Large-scale Hotel Smoke free premises. 515 units. 505 one-bedroom standard units. 10 one-bedroom suites ($1000-$5000),
some with whirlpools. 40 stories, interior corridors. *Bath:* combo or shower only. **Parking:** valet.
Terms: cancellation fee imposed, package plans. **Amenities:** dual phone lines, voice mail, safes, honor bars, irons, hair dryers.
Fee: video games, high-speed Internet. **Leisure Activities:** saunas, steamrooms, exercise room, spa. **Guest Services:** gift
shop, valet laundry, personal trainers. **Business Services:** conference facilities, business center. **Cards:** AX, CB, DC, DS, JC,
MC, VI. **Free Special Amenities:** newspaper.

SOME UNITS

THE KIMBERLY A BOUTIQUE HOTEL   *Book great rates at AAA.com*   **Phone: (212)702-1600**   ⑥⓪

All Year	1P: $315-$840	2P: $345-$1200	XP: $30	F17

Location: Between 3rd and Lexington aves. 145 E 50th St 10022. Fax: 212/486-6915. **Facility:** 192 units. 41 one-
bedroom standard units, some with kitchens. 141 one- and 10 two-bedroom suites ($395-$1200), some with
kitchens and/or whirlpools. 31 stories, interior corridors. *Bath:* combo or shower only. **Parking:** valet.
Small-scale Hotel **Terms:** cancellation fee imposed, package plans. **Amenities:** dual phone lines, voice mail, fax, safes, honor
bars, irons, hair dryers. *Fee:* video games, high-speed Internet. *Some:* DVD players, CD players. **Dining:** 2
restaurants, 6:30 am-11 pm, cocktails, nightclub. **Leisure Activities:** *Fee:* massage. **Guest Services:** valet laundry, wireless
Internet. **Business Services:** meeting rooms, business center. **Cards:** AX, CB, DC, DS, JC, MC, VI. **Free Special Amenities:**
newspaper.

SOME UNITS

THE KITANO NEW YORK   *Book great rates at AAA.com*   **Phone: (212)885-7000**   ⑧⑦

5/1-11/22	1P: $345	2P: $345	XP: $25	F12
11/23-4/30	1P: $315	2P: $315	XP: $25	F12

Location: At 38th St. 66 Park Ave 10016. Fax: 212/885-7100. **Facility:** Understatement and elegance come
together in warm woods, gentle lighting and tailored symmetry in this property designed to soothe its guests.
Small-scale Hotel 149 units. 141 one-bedroom standard units. 8 one-bedroom suites. 18 stories, interior corridors. **Parking:**
on-site (fee) and valet. **Terms:** 3 day cancellation notice, in season-fee imposed, [BP] meal plan available.
Amenities: high-speed Internet (fee), dual phone lines, voice mail, safes, honor bars, hair dryers. *Some:* CD players, irons.
Fee: DVD players. **Dining:** 2 restaurants, 7 am-2:30 & 6-10 pm, cocktails. **Guest Services:** gift shop, valet laundry, area
transportation-Wall Street, wireless Internet. **Business Services:** meeting rooms, business center. **Cards:** AX, CB, DC, DS, JC,
MC, VI.

SOME UNITS
FEE   FEE

LA QUINTA INN MANHATTAN   *Book great rates at AAA.com*   **Phone: (212)736-1600**   ⑨④

9/1-12/31	1P: $189-$249	2P: $199-$329	XP: $20	F12
3/1-4/30	1P: $139-$159	2P: $189-$249	XP: $20	F12
5/1-8/31	1P: $129-$159	2P: $199-$239	XP: $20	F12
1/1-2/29	1P: $99-$109	2P: $129-$169	XP: $20	F12

Location: Between 5th Ave and Broadway. 17 W 32nd St 10001. Fax: 212/563-4007. **Facility:** 182 one-bedroom standard units. 12
stories, interior corridors. *Bath:* combo or shower only. **Parking:** valet. **Terms:** 14 day cancellation notice-fee imposed, [ECP]
meal plan available. **Amenities:** video games (fee), high-speed Internet, voice mail, irons, hair dryers. **Leisure
Activities:** limited exercise equipment. **Guest Services:** gift shop, valet laundry, wireless Internet. **Business Services:**
business center. **Cards:** AX, CB, DC, DS, JC, MC, VI. *(See color ad p 422 & p 360)*

SOME UNITS

LE PARKER MERIDIEN NEW YORK   *Book great rates at AAA.com*   **Phone: (212)245-5000**   ⑲

9/4-12/31	1P: $860-$1080	2P: $890-$1110	XP: $30	F12
1/1-4/30	1P: $790-$1010	2P: $820-$1040	XP: $30	F12
5/1-6/30	1P: $760-$980	2P: $790-$1010	XP: $30	F12
7/1-9/3	1P: $660-$880	2P: $690-$910	XP: $30	F12

Location: Between 6th (Ave of the Americas) and 7th aves; vehicle entrance on 56th St. 118 W 57th St 10019. Fax: 212/307-1776.
Facility: Characterized by artful accents in stone, cherry and teak, these sleek-lined accommodations include work spaces and
swiveling entertainment centers. 731 units. 717 one-bedroom standard units. 14 one-bedroom suites ($980-$5000). 42 stories,
interior corridors. *Bath:* combo or shower only. **Parking:** on-site (fee) and valet. **Terms:** cancellation fee imposed, package
plans. **Amenities:** DVD players, CD players, dual phone lines, voice mail, safes, honor bars, irons, hair dryers. *Fee:* video
games, high-speed Internet. **Dining:** Norma's, see separate listing. **Pool(s):** heated indoor. **Leisure Activities:** saunas. *Fee:*
racquetball courts, massage, basketball. **Guest Services:** gift shop, valet laundry. *Fee:* nutritionist, personal trainer. **Business
Services:** meeting rooms, business center. **Cards:** AX, CB, DC, DS, JC, MC, VI.

SOME UNITS

LIBRARY HOTEL   *Book at AAA.com*   **Phone: (212)983-4500**   ⑧①

9/1-12/31 [ECP]	1P: $385-$565	2P: $385-$565	
5/1-6/30 [ECP]	1P: $329-$485	2P: $329-$485	
1/1-4/30 [ECP]	1P: $329-$475	2P: $329-$475	
7/1-8/31 [ECP]	1P: $299-$425	2P: $299-$425	

Location: At 41st St. 299 Madison Ave 10017. Fax: 212/499-9099. **Facility:** 60 one-bedroom standard units. 14 stories, interior
corridors. *Bath:* combo or shower only. **Parking:** no self-parking. **Terms:** cancellation fee imposed, package plans.
Amenities: video library, DVD players, CD players, high-speed Internet, dual phone lines, safes, honor bars, irons, hair dryers.
Leisure Activities: *Fee:* massage. **Guest Services:** valet laundry. **Business Services:** meeting rooms, business center.
Cards: AX, DC, MC, VI.

SOME UNITS

(See map and index starting on p. 382)

THE LONDON NYC   *Book great rates at AAA.com*   **Phone:** (212)307-5000   **24**

12/1-4/30	1P: $499-$999	2P: $499-$999	XP: $34
9/1-11/30	1P: $499-$949	2P: $499-$949	XP: $34
5/1-6/30	1P: $459-$899	2P: $459-$899	XP: $34
7/1-8/31	1P: $359-$799	2P: $359-$799	XP: $34

Large-scale Hotel **Location:** Between 6th (Ave of the Americas) and 7th aves. 151 W 54th St 10019 (475 Seagate Dr, NAPLES, FL, 34103). Fax: 212/765-6530. **Facility:** Seating areas and mirrored French doors add charm to the large guest rooms at this modern hotel, which is decorated in rich fabrics and hardwoods. 507 units. 6 one-bedroom standard units. 460 one- and 41 two-bedroom suites ($499-$6999). 54 stories, interior corridors. *Bath:* combo or shower only. **Parking:** valet. **Terms:** cancellation fee imposed. **Amenities:** video library (fee), dual phone lines, voice mail, safes, honor bars, irons, hair dryers. *Some: Fee:* high-speed Internet. **Dining:** 6:30-11 am, 11:30-2:30 & 5:30-10:30 pm, cocktails. **Leisure Activities:** saunas, exercise room. *Fee:* massage. **Guest Services:** valet laundry, wireless Internet. **Business Services:** meeting rooms, business center. **Cards:** AX, DC, DS, JC, MC, VI. **Free Special Amenities:** newspaper and preferred room (subject to availability with advance reservations).

SOME UNITS
FEE

THE LOWELL HOTEL   *Book at AAA.com*   **Phone:** (212)838-1400   **13**

All Year	1P: $545-$7500	2P: $635-$7500

Historic
Small-scale Hotel **Location:** Between Park and Madison aves. 28 E 63rd St 10021. Fax: 212/319-4230. **Facility:** Luxurious, intimate and service-oriented, this charming European-style hotel offers gracious guest rooms, some with a fireplace. 70 units. 23 one-bedroom standard units. 47 one-bedroom suites with kitchens. 17 stories, interior corridors. **Parking:** valet. **Terms:** cancellation fee imposed, package plans, small pets only. **Amenities:** video library (fee), DVD players, high-speed Internet, dual phone lines, voice mail, safes, honor bars, hair dryers. *Some:* CD players, fax. **Dining:** The Post House, see separate listing. **Leisure Activities:** exercise room. *Fee:* massage. **Guest Services:** valet laundry, wireless Internet. **Business Services:** meeting rooms, business center. **Cards:** AX, CB, DC, DS, JC, MC, VI.

SOME UNITS

THE LUCERNE   *Book great rates at AAA.com*   **Phone:** (212)875-1000   **1**

1/1-4/30	1P: $270-$450	2P: $270-$450	XP: $20 F16
5/1-12/31	1P: $240-$400	2P: $240-$400	XP: $20 F16

Small-scale Hotel **Location:** At Amsterdam and Broadway aves. 201 W 79th St 10024. Fax: 212/362-7251. **Facility:** 185 units. 143 one-bedroom standard units. 42 one-bedroom suites. 13 stories, interior corridors. **Parking:** on-site (fee) and valet. **Terms:** check-in 4 pm, cancellation fee imposed, $4 service charge. **Amenities:** CD players, dual phone lines, voice mail, irons, hair dryers. *Fee:* video games, high-speed Internet. *Some:* safes. **Dining:** 7 am-midnight, Fri & Sat-1 am, cocktails. **Leisure Activities:** exercise room. **Guest Services:** valet laundry, wireless Internet. **Business Services:** meeting rooms, business center. **Cards:** AX, DC, DS, MC, VI. **Free Special Amenities:** newspaper.

(See color ad p 440)

SOME UNITS

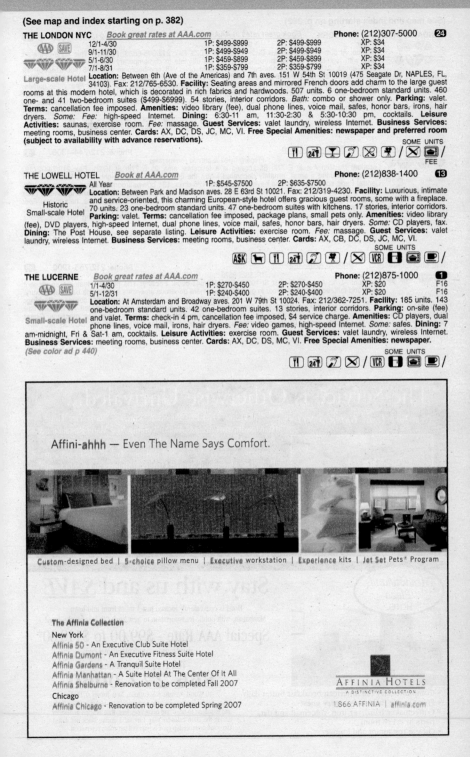

(See map and index starting on p. 382)

MANDARIN ORIENTAL, NEW YORK   *Book great rates at AAA.com*   Phone: 212/805-8800   **8**

All Year   1P: $745-$1125

Location: At 60th St. 80 Columbus Circle at 60th St 10023. Fax: 212/805-8888. **Facility:** This state-of-the-art hotel, with high-tech features throughout, offers the ultimate in contemporary luxury in guest rooms and public areas. 248 units. 202 one-bedroom standard units. 46 one-bedroom suites ($1900-$14000). 19 stories, interior corridors. **Parking:** valet. **Terms:** cancellation fee imposed, package plans. **Amenities:** DVD players, CD players, dual phone lines, voice mail, safes, honor bars, irons, hair dryers. *Fee:* video games, high-speed Internet. **Dining:** Asiate, see separate listing. **Pool(s):** heated indoor. **Leisure Activities:** DVD library, spa. **Guest Services:** gift shop, valet laundry, area transportation-local area. **Business Services:** conference facilities, business center. **Cards:** AX, CB, DC, DS, JC, MC, VI.

Large-scale Hotel

SOME UNITS

THE MARK, NEW YORK   *Book at AAA.com*   Phone: 212/744-4300   **5**

Property failed to provide current rates

Location: Madison Ave at E 77th St. Located in a residential area. 25 E 77th St 10021. Fax: 212/744-2749. **Facility:** Featuring a small, ornately decorated lobby, the hotel is in a quiet neighborhood just steps from Central Park; some guest rooms have kitchenettes. 176 units. 131 one-bedroom standard units, some with efficiencies (no utensils). 45 one-bedroom suites with kitchens (no utensils). 16 stories, interior corridors. **Parking:** on-site (fee) and valet. **Terms:** pets (small dogs only). **Amenities:** dual phone lines, voice mail, safes, honor bars, irons, hair dryers. *Fee:* video games, high-speed Internet. *Some:* CD players. **Dining:** Mark's, see separate listing. **Leisure Activities:** saunas, steamrooms, exercise room. *Fee:* massage. **Guest Services:** valet laundry. **Business Services:** meeting rooms, business center.

Small-scale Hotel

SOME UNITS

THE MICHELANGELO   *Book at AAA.com*   Phone: 212/765-1900   **35**

All Year   1P: $525-$575   2P: $525-$575

Location: At 7th Ave. 152 W 51st St 10019. Fax: 212/541-6604. **Facility:** The property features an elegant lobby and tailored traditional decor in guest rooms, where generous amenities and marble baths add luxury. 178 units. 163 one-bedroom standard units. 15 one-bedroom suites. 5 stories, interior corridors. **Parking:** on-site (fee) and valet. **Terms:** cancellation fee imposed. **Amenities:** CD players, dual phone lines, voice mail, honor bars, hair dryers. *Fee:* video games, high-speed Internet. *Some:* DVD players. **Leisure Activities:** exercise room. *Fee:* massage. **Guest Services:** valet laundry, area transportation. **Business Services:** meeting rooms, PC, fax (fee). **Cards:** AX, DC, DS, MC, VI.

Small-scale Hotel

SOME UNITS

(See map and index starting on p. 382)

MILLENNIUM BROADWAY — *Book great rates at AAA.com* — Phone: (212)768-4400 — **57**

AAA SAVE

9/5-12/31	1P: $599-$2500	2P: $599-$2500
5/1-6/30 & 1/1-4/30	1P: $499-$1900	2P: $499-$1900
7/1-9/4	1P: $399-$1500	2P: $399-$1500

Location: Between 6th (Ave of the Americas) and 7th aves; in Times Square. 145 W 44th St 10036. **Large-scale Hotel** Fax: 212/768-0847. **Facility:** 750 units. 737 one-bedroom standard units. 13 one-bedroom suites ($899-$2500), some with whirlpools. 52 stories, interior corridors. *Bath:* some combo or shower only. **Parking:** on-site (fee) and valet. **Terms:** check-in 4 pm, cancellation fee imposed, [CP] meal plan available, package plans, $2 service charge. **Amenities:** high-speed Internet (fee), dual phone lines, voice mail, safes, honor bars, irons, hair dryers. *Some:* CD players, fax. *Fee:* DVD players. **Dining:** 6:30 am-10:30 pm, cocktails. **Leisure Activities:** exercise room. *Fee:* massage. **Guest Services:** gift shop, valet laundry, wireless Internet. **Business Services:** conference facilities, business center. **Cards:** AX, CB, DC, DS, JC, MC, VI. *(See color ad p 417)*

MILLENNIUM UN PLAZA HOTEL NEW YORK — *Book great rates at AAA.com* — Phone: (212)758-1234 — **82**

AAA SAVE

All Year	1P: $199-$639	2P: $199-$639	XP: $40	F17

Location: Between First and Second aves. Located across from United Nations Headquarters. One UN Plaza, 44th St 10017-3575. Fax: 212/702-5051. **Facility:** 427 units. 383 one-bedroom standard units, some with efficiencies. 34 one- and 10 two-bedroom suites ($369-$5000), some with kitchens. 38-40 stories, interior corridors. **Large-scale Hotel** *Bath:* combo or shower only. **Parking:** on-site (fee) and valet. **Terms:** cancellation fee imposed, [AP], [BP] & [CP] meal plans available. **Amenities:** high-speed Internet (fee), dual phone lines, voice mail, safes, honor bars, irons, hair dryers. *Some:* DVD players, CD players. **Dining:** 6:30 am-2:30 & 6-11 pm, cocktails. **Pool(s):** heated indoor. **Leisure Activities:** saunas. *Fee:* indoor tennis court, massage. **Guest Services:** gift shop, valet laundry, area transportation (fee)-theater. **Business Services:** meeting rooms, business center. **Cards:** AX, MC, VI. *(See color ad p 417)*

THE MUSE HOTEL — *Book great rates at AAA.com* — Phone: (212)485-2400 — **49**

AAA SAVE

9/4-4/30	1P: $329-$999	2P: $329-$999	XP: $20	F12
5/1-6/28	1P: $295-$999	2P: $295-$999	XP: $20	F12
6/29-9/3	1P: $249-$999	2P: $249-$999	XP: $20	F12

Location: Between 6th (Ave of the Americas) and 7th aves. 130 W 46th St 10036. Fax: 212/485-2900. **Facility:** In **Small-scale Hotel** the heart of the theater district, The Muse is a sophisticated and elegant small hotel offering fine service with modern style and personality. 200 one-bedroom standard units. 19 stories, interior corridors. *Bath:* combo or shower only. **Parking:** valet. **Terms:** cancellation fee imposed, [MAP] meal plan available. **Amenities:** CD players, high-speed Internet (fee), dual phone lines, voice mail, safes, honor bars, irons, hair dryers. *Some:* DVD players. **Dining:** District, see separate listing. **Leisure Activities:** exercise room. **Guest Services:** valet laundry. **Business Services:** meeting rooms, administrative services, fax. **Cards:** AX, DC, DS, MC, VI. *(See color ad p 419)*

THE NEW YORK HELMSLEY HOTEL — *Book at AAA.com* — Phone: (212)490-8900 — **83**

5/1-6/30 & 9/4-12/31	1P: $289-$429	2P: $289-$429	XP: $30	F14
1/1-4/30	1P: $209-$369	2P: $209-$369	XP: $30	F14
7/1-9/3	1P: $179-$309	2P: $179-$309	XP: $30	F14

Large-scale Hotel **Location:** Between Second and Third aves. 212 E 42nd St 10017. Fax: 212/986-4792. **Facility:** 779 units. 775 one-bedroom standard units. 3 one- and 1 two-bedroom suites. 41 stories, interior corridors. *Bath:* combo or shower only. **Parking:** valet. **Terms:** check-in 4 pm, [AP], [BP] & [CP] meal plans available, package plans, small pets only. **Amenities:** video games (fee), dual phone lines, voice mail, safes, irons, hair dryers. *Some:* high-speed Internet. **Leisure Activities:** exercise room. **Guest Services:** gift shop, valet laundry. **Business Services:** conference facilities, PC. **Cards:** AX, CB, DC, DS, JC, MC, VI.

NEW YORK MARRIOTT EAST SIDE — *Book great rates at AAA.com* — Phone: 212/755-4000 — **71**

9/4-12/31	1P: $239-$659	2P: $259-$679
1/1-4/30	1P: $199-$599	2P: $219-$619
5/1-6/30	1P: $239-$559	2P: $259-$579
7/1-9/3	1P: $199-$429	2P: $219-$449

Large-scale Hotel **Location:** Between 48th and 49th sts. 525 Lexington Ave 10017. Fax: 212/751-3440. **Facility:** Smoke free premises. 646 units. 629 one-bedroom standard units. 17 one-bedroom suites ($800-$1500), some with whirlpools. 33 stories, interior corridors. *Bath:* some combo or shower only. **Parking:** on-site (fee) and valet. **Terms:** cancellation fee imposed, package plans. **Amenities:** CD players, high-speed Internet (fee), dual phone lines, voice mail, safes, honor bars, irons, hair dryers. **Leisure Activities:** exercise room. **Guest Services:** gift shop, valet laundry. **Business Services:** conference facilities, business center. **Cards:** AX, CB, DC, DS, JC, MC, VI.

NEW YORK MARRIOTT MARQUIS — *Book great rates at AAA.com* — Phone: 212/398-1900 — **48**

Property failed to provide current rates

Location: Between 45th and 46th sts; motor entrance on 46th St. Located in Times Square. 1535 Broadway 10036. **Large-scale Hotel** Fax: 212/704-8930. **Facility:** Smoke free premises. 1944 units. 1893 one-bedroom standard units. 51 one-bedroom suites. 48 stories, interior corridors. *Bath:* combo or shower only. **Parking:** on-site (fee) and valet. **Terms:** small pets only (with prior approval). **Amenities:** dual phone lines, voice mail, safes, irons, hair dryers. *Fee:* video library, video games, high-speed Internet. *Some: Fee:* DVD players. **Dining:** The View, see separate listing. **Guest Services:** gift shop, valet laundry. **Business Services:** conference facilities, business center.

CLEARLY, A SPECTACULAR VIEW OF NEW YORK CITY

The Top of the Rock Observation Deck features crystal clear, completely unobstructed views of New York. High atop 30 Rockefeller Center, the 3-tiered Observation Deck offers an unforgettable experience, with 360-degree views from this historic vantage point, 850 feet in the sky.

Rockefeller Center
50th St. btw. 5th & 6th Aves.

Open daily 8:00 a.m. to midnight

212-698-2000
877-NYC-ROCK (877-692-7625)
www.topoftherocknyc.com

TOP OF THE ROCK
OBSERVATION DECK

(See map and index starting on p. 382)

NEW YORK MIDTOWN EAST COURTYARD BY MARRIOTT *Book great rates at AAA.com*

Phone: (212)644-1300 [52]

▼▼▼

Small-scale Hotel

All Year — 1P: $329-$639

Location: Between 52nd and 53rd sts. 866 3rd Ave 10022. **Fax:** 212/317-7940. **Facility:** Smoke free premises. 307 units. 303 one-bedroom standard units. 4 one-bedroom suites ($299-$699). 31 stories, interior corridors. **Bath:** combo or shower only. **Parking:** valet. **Terms:** package plans. **Amenities:** video games (fee), high-speed Internet, dual phone lines, voice mail, safes, irons, hair dryers. **Leisure Activities:** exercise room. **Guest Services:** valet and coin laundry. **Business Services:** meeting rooms, PC. **Cards:** AX, DC, DS, JC, MC, VI.

SOME UNITS

(ASK) (YI) (⌷) (⌷M) (⌷) (⌷) (✕) (⌷) (⌷) / (⌷) (⌷) /

THE NEW YORK PALACE *Book great rates at AAA.com*

Phone: (212)888-7000 [50]

(AAA) (SAVE)

▼▼▼ ▼▼▼

Historic
Large-scale Hotel

9/4-9/75	1P: $775-$975	2P: $775-$975	XP: $30	F12
5/1-6/24 & 1/1-4/30	1P: $640-$840	2P: $640-$840	XP: $30	F12
6/25-9/3	1P: $570-$770	2P: $570-$770	XP: $30	F12

Location: Between 50th and 51st sts. 455 Madison Ave 10022. **Fax:** 212/303-6000. **Facility:** A grand staircase and marble fireplace accent the Neo-Italian Renaissance lobby at this hotel, which provides polished service and excellent views. 892 units. 838 one-bedroom standard units. 54 one-bedroom suites ($1100-$2600) with kitchens, some with whirlpools. 55 stories, interior corridors. **Bath:** combo or shower only. **Parking:** valet. **Terms:** package plans, small pets only. **Amenities:** dual phone lines, voice mail, fax, safes, honor bars, irons, hair dryers. **Some:** DVD players, video games, CD players. **Dining:** 6:30 am-11 pm, cocktails, also, Istana, see separate listing, entertainment. **Leisure Activities:** steamrooms, spa. **Guest Services:** gift shop, valet laundry, area transportation-Wall Street, wireless Internet. **Business Services:** conference facilities, business center. **Cards:** AX, CB, DC, DS, JC, MC, VI.

SOME UNITS

(⌷) (YI) (24I) (⌷) (⌷M) (⌷) (⌷) (⌷) (⌷) / (✕) (VCR) (⌷) (⌷) (⌷) /

NOVOTEL NEW YORK *Book great rates at AAA.com*

Phone: (212)315-0100 [27]

(AAA) (SAVE)

▼▼▼

Large-scale Hotel

9/6-12/31	1P: $339-$529	2P: $339-$529	XP: $20	F
5/1-6/30	1P: $239-$429	2P: $239-$429	XP: $20	F
7/1-9/5	1P: $219-$409	2P: $219-$409	XP: $20	F
1/1-4/30	1P: $199-$389	2P: $199-$389	XP: $20	F

Location: At Broadway. 226 W 52nd St 10019. **Fax:** 212/765-5365. **Facility:** 480 one-bedroom standard units. 33 stories, interior corridors. **Parking:** no self-parking. **Terms:** cancellation fee imposed. **Amenities:** video games (fee), voice mail, safes, honor bars, irons, hair dryers. **Some:** high-speed Internet, dual phone lines. **Dining:** 6:30 am-11 pm, cocktails. **Leisure Activities:** exercise room. **Guest Services:** gift shop, valet laundry, wireless Internet. **Business Services:** meeting rooms, business center. **Cards:** AX, CB, DC, DS, JC, MC, VI. *(See color ad below)*

SOME UNITS

(S⌷) (⌷) (YI) (⌷) (⌷) (⌷) / (✕) (⌷) /

FEE

(See map and index starting on p. 382)

OMNI BERKSHIRE PLACE *Book at AAA.com* **Phone:** 212/753-5800 **44**

Property failed to provide current rates

Large-scale Hotel

Location: Between Madison and 5th aves. 21 E 52nd St 10022. Fax: 212/754-5020. **Facility:** Setting a tone of elegance at this luxury hotel are sparkling chandeliers, 18th-century-inspired carpets and marble finishes. 396 units. 353 one-bedroom standard units. 43 one-bedroom suites, some with whirlpools. 22 stories, interior corridors. *Bath:* combo or shower only. **Parking:** valet. **Terms:** small pets only ($75 fee). **Amenities:** video games (fee), CD players, dual phone lines, voice mail, safes, honor bars, irons, hair dryers. *Some:* DVD players. **Leisure Activities:** exercise room. *Fee:* massage. **Guest Services:** valet laundry, wireless Internet. **Business Services:** meeting rooms, business center.

SOME UNITS
🛏️ 🍴 🍸 🖥 M 🛋 🐾 📷 / ✕ VCR 🗄 /
FEE

ON THE AVE HOTEL *Book at AAA.com* **Phone:** (212)362-1100 **3**

Small-scale Hotel

	1P:	2P:
9/1-12/31	$279-$379	$279-$379
1/1-4/30	$259-$325	$259-$325
5/1-6/30	$239-$299	$239-$299
7/1-8/31	$225-$259	$225-$259

Location: At 77th St. 2178 Broadway 10024. Fax: 212/787-9521. **Facility:** 266 units. 259 one-bedroom standard units. 7 one-bedroom suites ($525-$995). 16 stories, interior corridors. *Bath:* combo or shower only. **Parking:** no self-parking. **Terms:** pets ($25 extra charge). **Amenities:** CD players, high-speed Internet, dual phone lines, voice mail, irons, hair dryers. *Some:* DVD players. **Guest Services:** valet laundry. **Business Services:** business center. **Cards:** AX, DC, DS, JC, MC, VI.

SOME UNITS
ASK S🅳 🐾 🍴 👥 ✕ 🖥 / VCR 🗄 /
FEE   FEE

PARK CENTRAL NEW YORK *Book at AAA.com* **Phone:** 212/247-8000 **16**

Property failed to provide current rates

Large-scale Hotel

Location: At 56th St. 870 7th Ave 10019. Fax: 212/707-5557. **Facility:** 935 units. 914 one-bedroom standard units. 20 one- and 1 two-bedroom suites. 25 stories, interior corridors. *Bath:* combo or shower only. **Parking:** valet. **Terms:** check-in 4 pm. **Amenities:** video games (fee), dual phone lines, voice mail, safes, irons, hair dryers. **Leisure Activities:** exercise room. **Guest Services:** gift shop, valet laundry, wireless Internet. **Business Services:** conference facilities, business center.

SOME UNITS
🍴 🍸 🖥 M 🛋 🐾 📷 / ✕ VCR 🗄 🖥 /
FEE FEE

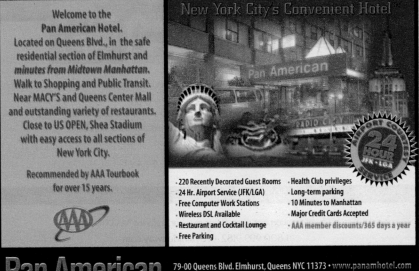

(See map and index starting on p. 382)

PARK SOUTH HOTEL *Book great rates at AAA.com* Phone: (212)448-0888 🔟🔟

(AAA) (SAVE)

9/8-4/30 [CP]	1P: $286-$323	2P: $286-$323	XP: $30	F11
5/1-6/30 [CP]	1P: $281-$318	2P: $281-$318	XP: $30	F11
7/1-9/7 [CP]	1P: $244-$281	2P: $244-$281	XP: $30	F11

Location: Between Park and Lexington aves. 124 E 28th St 10016. Fax: 212/448-0811. **Facility:** 141 one-bedroom standard units. 8 stories, interior corridors. *Bath:* combo or shower only. **Parking:** no self-parking. **Small-scale Hotel** **Terms:** cancellation fee imposed. **Amenities:** video library, DVD players, high-speed Internet, dual phone lines, voice mail, safes, irons, hair dryers. *Some:* CD players, fax. **Dining:** 6 pm-11 pm, cocktails. **Leisure Activities:** limited exercise equipment. **Guest Services:** valet laundry. **Business Services:** meeting rooms, business center. **Cards:** AX, MC, VI.

SOME UNITS

THE PENINSULA NEW YORK *Book great rates at AAA.com* Phone: (212)956-2888 🔢🔢

(AAA) (SAVE)

9/4-12/31	1P: $675-$895	2P: $675-$895	XP: $50	F12
5/1-9/3 & 1/1-4/30	1P: $615-$845	2P: $615-$845	XP: $50	F12

Location: At 55th St. 700 5th Ave 10019. Fax: 212/903-3949. **Facility:** Distinct grandeur and intricate architecture mark this turn-of-the-20th-century beaux arts-style hotel, which offers modern rooms and a **Large-scale Hotel** rooftop health spa. 239 units. 201 one-bedroom standard units. 37 one- and 1 two-bedroom suites ($1250-$17950), some with whirlpools. 23 stories, interior corridors. *Bath:* combo or shower only. **Parking:** valet. **Terms:** cancellation fee imposed, package plans, small pets only. **Amenities:** video library, DVD players, CD players, high-speed Internet, dual phone lines, voice mail, fax, safes, honor bars, hair dryers. *Some:* video games. **Dining:** 6:30-10:30 am, 11:30-2:30 & 5:30-10:30 pm, cocktails. **Pool(s):** heated indoor. **Leisure Activities:** saunas, whirlpool, steamrooms, spa. **Guest Services:** gift shop, valet laundry, area transportation-theater district. **Business Services:** meeting rooms, business center. **Cards:** AX, CB, DC, DS, JC, MC, VI. **Free Special Amenities:** local telephone calls and high-speed Internet.

SOME UNITS

THE PIERRE NEW YORK-A TAJ HOTEL *Book at AAA.com* Phone: (212)838-8000 🔢🔢

5/1-9/3	1P: $610-$1400	2P: $640-$1400	XP: $35
9/4-4/30	1P: $670-$1200	2P: $700-$1200	

Location: At 5th Ave. 2 E 61st St 10021. Fax: 212/940-8109. **Facility:** White-gloved elevator operators add Old **Historic** World charm at this grand 1930s hotel, where high tea is served amid Rococo murals in the rotunda. 200 **Large-scale Hotel** units. 150 one-bedroom standard units. 50 one-bedroom suites ($775-$4000). 42 stories, interior corridors. *Bath:* combo or shower only. **Parking:** valet. **Terms:** cancellation fee imposed, [AP] meal plan available, package plans, small pets only. **Amenities:** dual phone lines, voice mail, safes, honor bars, hair dryers. *Fee:* video library, high-speed Internet. *Some:* DVD players, video games, CD players, fax, irons. **Dining:** Cafe Pierre, see separate listing. **Leisure Activities:** exercise room. *Fee:* massage. **Guest Services:** gift shop, valet laundry, area transportation. **Business Services:** conference facilities, business center. **Cards:** AX, CB, DC, DS, JC, MC, VI.

SOME UNITS

RADISSON LEXINGTON HOTEL NEW YORK *Book at AAA.com* Phone: (212)755-4400 🔢🔢

9/5-12/19	1P: $319-$379	2P: $319-$379	XP: $25	F12
5/1-6/23	1P: $299-$359	2P: $299-$359	XP: $25	F12
12/20-4/30	1P: $239-$299	2P: $239-$299	XP: $25	F12
6/24-9/4	1P: $219-$279	2P: $219-$279	XP: $25	F12

Large-scale Hotel Location: At E 48th St. 511 Lexington Ave 10017. Fax: 212/751-4091. **Facility:** 705 units. 683 one-bedroom standard units. 22 one-bedroom suites ($650-$3500), some with whirlpools. 27 stories, interior corridors. *Bath:* combo or shower only. **Parking:** on-site (fee) and valet. **Terms:** check-in 4 pm, 2-3 night minimum stay - seasonal and/or weekends, cancellation fee imposed. **Amenities:** dual phone lines, voice mail, safes, irons, hair dryers. *Fee:* video games, high-speed Internet. **Leisure Activities:** exercise room. **Guest Services:** valet laundry. **Business Services:** meeting rooms, business center. **Cards:** AX, CB, DC, DS, JC, MC, VI.

SOME UNITS

RADISSON MARTINIQUE ON BROADWAY *Book great rates at AAA.com* Phone: (212)736-3800 🔢🔢

(AAA) (SAVE)

9/1-12/31	1P: $429-$699	2P: $464-$734	XP: $35	F16
5/1-6/30	1P: $279-$429	2P: $314-$465	XP: $35	F16
7/1-8/31 & 1/1-4/30	1P: $239-$339	2P: $274-$374	XP: $35	F16

Location: Corner of Broadway. 49 W 32nd St 10001. Fax: 212/277-2702. **Facility:** 532 units. 522 one-bedroom **Small-scale Hotel** standard units. 10 one-bedroom suites. 19 stories, interior corridors. **Parking:** valet. **Terms:** cancellation fee imposed, [AP] meal plan available, package plans, pets ($100 deposit, $50 extra charge). **Amenities:** dual phone lines, voice mail, honor bars, irons, hair dryers. *Fee:* video library, video games, safes. **Dining:** 3 restaurants, 6:30 am-11 pm, cocktails. **Leisure Activities:** exercise room, spa. **Guest Services:** gift shop, valet laundry, wireless Internet. **Business Services:** meeting rooms, PC. **Cards:** AX, CB, DC, DS, JC, MC, VI. **Free Special Amenities:** newspaper and high-speed Internet. *(See color ad p 448)*

SOME UNITS

FEE

RAMADA EASTSIDE *Book great rates at AAA.com* Phone: (212)545-1800 🔢🔢

11/1-12/31	1P: $249-$259	2P: $259-$269	XP: $12	F13
9/1-10/31	1P: $229-$239	2P: $239-$249	XP: $12	F13
5/1-8/31	1P: $199-$209	2P: $209-$229	XP: $12	F13
1/1-4/30	1P: $119-$129	2P: $129-$139	XP: $12	F13

Small-scale Hotel Location: At 30th St. 161 Lexington Ave 10016. Fax: 212/481-7270. **Facility:** 95 one-bedroom standard units. 12 stories, interior corridors. **Parking:** no self-parking. **Amenities:** video games (fee), voice mail, irons, hair dryers. **Leisure Activities:** limited exercise equipment. **Guest Services:** valet laundry, wireless Internet. **Business Services:** meeting rooms, business center. **Cards:** AX, CB, DC, DS, JC, MC, VI. *(See color ad p 422)*

SOME UNITS

(See map and index starting on p. 382)

RED ROOF INN MANHATTAN   *Book great rates at AAA.com*   Phone: (212)643-7100   **95**

▼▼ ▼▼	11/1-12/31	1P: $259-$269	2P: $269-$279	XP: $12	F13
	9/1-10/31	1P: $239-$249	2P: $249-$259	XP: $12	F13
	5/1-8/31	1P: $209-$219	2P: $219-$239	XP: $12	F13
Small-scale Hotel	1/1-4/30	1P: $129-$139	2P: $139-$149	XP: $12	F13

Location: Between Broadway and 5th Ave. 6 W 32nd St 10001. Fax: 212/643-7101. **Facility:** 171 one-bedroom standard units. 17 stories, interior corridors. **Parking:** no self-parking. **Amenities:** video games (fee), high-speed Internet, voice mail, irons, hair dryers. **Leisure Activities:** exercise room. **Guest Services:** valet laundry, wireless Internet. **Business Services:** meeting rooms. **Cards:** AX, CB, DC, DS, JC, MC, VI. *(See color ad p 422)*

SOME UNITS

ASK 🆂 📺 🎥 💻 / ⊠ 🗄 📷 /

THE REGENCY HOTEL   *Book at AAA.com*   Phone: (212)759-4100   **20**

▼▼▼ ▼▼▼	9/4-12/31	1P: $749-$4500	2P: $749-$4500	XP: $40	F17
	1/1-4/30	1P: $629-$4000	2P: $629-$4000	XP: $40	F17
	5/1-6/28	1P: $619-$4000	2P: $619-$4000	XP: $40	F17
Large-scale Hotel	6/29-9/3	1P: $489-$3500	2P: $489-$3500	XP: $40	F17

Location: At 61st St. 540 Park Ave 10021. Fax: 212/826-5674. **Facility:** Guest rooms at this upscale hotel are done in muted earth tones, wood and granite. 351 units. 265 one-bedroom standard units. 72 one- and 14 two-bedroom suites, some with efficiencies. 21 stories, interior corridors. **Bath:** combo or shower only. **Parking:** valet. **Terms:** cancellation fee imposed. **Amenities:** video library, CD players, dual phone lines, voice mail, safes, honor bars, irons, hair dryers. **Fee:** video games, high-speed Internet. *Some:* DVD players. **Leisure Activities:** sauna. **Guest Services:** gift shop, valet laundry, beauty salon. **Business Services:** conference facilities, business center. **Cards:** AX, DC, DS, JC, MC, VI. Affiliated with Loews Hotels.

SOME UNITS

ASK 🆂 🐾 🍴 24⊤ 📺 ♿ᴹ ♿ 🌀 🐾 VCR 🎥 / ⊠ 🗄 📷 /

RENAISSANCE NEW YORK HOTEL TIMES SQUARE   *Book great rates at AAA.com*   Phone: (212)765-7676   **43**

AAA SAVE	9/2-12/31	1P: $399-$759	2P: $419-$779
	5/1-6/30	1P: $399-$599	2P: $419-$619
▼▼▼ ▼▼▼	7/1-9/1	1P: $399-$559	2P: $419-$579
	1/1-4/30	1P: $379-$579	2P: $359-$499

Large-scale Hotel   **Location:** Broadway and 7th Ave; auto access from 7th Ave, s of W 48th St. 2 Times Square, 7th Ave at W 48th St 10036 (714 7th Ave, NEW YORK). Fax: 212/765-1962. **Facility:** This richly decorated luxury hotel offers large guest rooms and central Times Square location. Smoke free premises. 310 units. 305 one-bedroom standard units. 5 one-bedroom suites. 26 stories, interior corridors. **Parking:** valet. **Terms:** check-in 4 pm, pets ($60 fee). **Amenities:** dual phone lines, voice mail, safes, honor bars, irons, hair dryers. *Fee:* video games, high-speed Internet. *Some:* CD players, fax. **Dining:** Foley's Restaurant & Bar, see separate listing, entertainment. **Leisure Activities:** exercise room. **Guest Services:** valet laundry. **Business Services:** meeting rooms, business center. **Cards:** AX, DC, DS, JC, MC, VI. *(See color ad below)*

🐾 🍴 24⊤ 📺 🌀 ⊠ 🎥 💻
FEE

THE RITZ-CARLTON NEW YORK, CENTRAL PARK   *Book at AAA.com*   Phone: (212)308-9100   **15**

▼▼▼▼ ▼▼▼▼	9/6-12/31	1P: $795-$1475
	5/1-6/30	1P: $745-$1220
	7/1-9/5	1P: $675-$1050
Large-scale Hotel	1/1-4/30	1P: $725-$1025

Location: Between 5th and 6th (Ave of the Americas) aves. 50 Central Park S 10019. Fax: 212/207-8831. **Facility:** This traditionally elegant property offers a plush lounge, quality appointments, a high standard of service and views of Central Park. Smoke free premises. 261 units. 213 one-bedroom standard units. 48 one-bedroom suites ($1195-$15000), some with whirlpools. 22 stories, interior corridors. **Bath:** combo or shower only. **Parking:** valet. **Terms:** cancellation fee imposed, [CP] meal plan available, pets ($125 fee). **Amenities:** video library, DVD players, CD players, high-speed Internet (fee), dual phone lines, voice mail, safes, honor bars, hair dryers. **Leisure Activities:** exercise room, spa. **Fee:** DVD library. **Guest Services:** gift shop, valet laundry, area transportation, wireless Internet. **Business Services:** meeting rooms, business center. **Cards:** AX, CB, DC, DS, JC, MC, VI.

SOME UNITS

🐾 📺 ♿ᴹ ♿ 🌀 ⊠ 🎥 / VCR 🗄 📷 /
FEE

(See map and index starting on p. 382)

THE ROOSEVELT HOTEL *Book great rates at AAA.com* Phone: (212)661-9600 **75**

All Year 1P: $209-$509 2P: $209-$509 XP: $20 F12
Location: Between Madison and Vanderbilt aves. 45 E 45th St 10017. Fax: 212/885-6161. **Facility:** 1015 units.
957 one-bedroom standard units. 55 one-, 2 two- and 1 three-bedroom suites. 19 stories, interior corridors.
Bath: combo or shower only. **Parking:** valet. **Terms:** cancellation fee imposed. **Amenities:** high-speed
Large-scale Hotel Internet (fee), dual phone lines, voice mail, safes, irons, hair dryers. **Dining:** 6:30 am-11 pm, cocktails.
Leisure Activities: exercise room. **Guest Services:** gift shop, valet laundry. **Business Services:**
conference facilities, business center. **Cards:** AX, CB, DC, DS, JC, MC, VI. *(See color ad below)*

SOME UNITS

ROYALTON *Book at AAA.com* Phone: 212/869-4400 **72**

Property failed to provide current rates
Location: Between 5th and 6th (Ave of the Americas) aves. 44 W 44th St 10036. Fax: 212/869-8965. **Facility:** 169
Large-scale Hotel units. 166 one-bedroom standard units. 3 one-bedroom suites. 19 stories, interior
corridors. *Bath:* combo or shower only. **Parking:** valet. **Amenities:** CD players, dual phone lines, voice mail,
safes, honor bars, irons, hair dryers. **Dining:** 44 at Royalton, see separate listing. **Leisure Activities:** exercise room. *Fee:*
massage. **Guest Services:** valet laundry, wireless Internet. **Business Services:** meeting rooms.

SOME UNITS

THE ST. REGIS HOTEL, NEW YORK *Book great rates at AAA.com* Phone: (212)753-4500 **36**

All Year 1P: $895-$1095 XP: $50 F10
Location: Between Madison and 5th aves. 2 E 55th St 10022. Fax: 212/787-3447. **Facility:** A New York landmark
since 1904, the hotel offers personalized butler service and classic Old World decor. 229 units. 164 one-
bedroom standard units. 64 one- and 1 two-bedroom suites, some with whirlpools. 19 stories, interior
Historic corridors. **Parking:** on-site (fee) and valet. **Terms:** cancellation fee imposed, package plans, small pets
Large-scale Hotel only. **Amenities:** DVD players, CD players, dual phone lines, voice mail, fax, safes, honor bars, hair dryers.
Fee: video library, high-speed Internet. *Some:* video games (fee). **Dining:** 7 am-11 pm, cocktails,
entertainment. **Leisure Activities:** steamrooms, exercise room, spa. **Guest Services:** gift shop, valet laundry, personal trainer,
beauty salon. **Business Services:** meeting rooms, business center. **Cards:** AX, CB, DC, DS, JC, MC, VI.

SOME UNITS

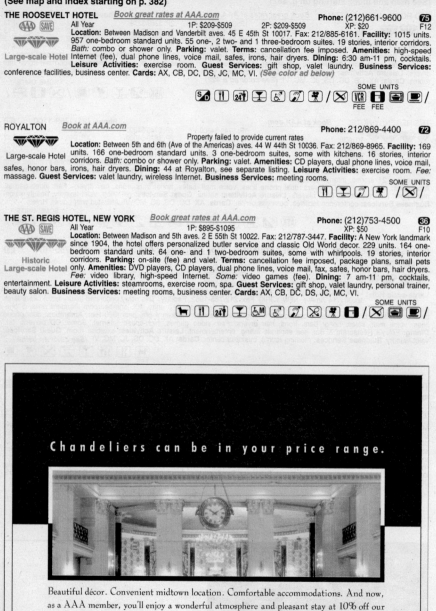

(See map and index starting on p. 382)

SALISBURY HOTEL   *Book great rates at AAA.com*   **Phone:** (212)246-1300   **17**

9/10-4/30	1P: $309-$339	2P: $309-$339	XP: $25	F18
5/1-6/30	1P: $259-$329	2P: $259-$329	XP: $25	F18
7/1-9/9	1P: $225-$279	2P: $225-$279	XP: $25	F18

Location: Between 6th (Ave of the Americas) and 7th aves. 123 W 57th St 10019. Fax: 212/977-7752. **Facility:** 201 units. 120 one-bedroom standard units. 81 one-bedroom suites ($309-$389). 17 stories, interior corridors. *Bath:* combo or shower only. **Parking:** no self-parking. **Terms:** [CP] meal plan available. **Amenities:** voice mail, safes, irons, hair dryers. *Some:* dual phone lines. **Guest Services:** valet laundry, wireless Internet. **Business Services:** meeting rooms, PC. **Cards:** AX, CB, DC, DS, JC, MC, VI. **Free Special Amenities: room upgrade (subject to availability with advance reservations).**

Small-scale Hotel

SAN CARLOS HOTEL   *Book at AAA.com*   **Phone:** 212/755-1800   **63**

Property failed to provide current rates

Location: Between 2nd and 3rd sts. 150 E 50th St 10022. Fax: 212/688-9778. **Facility:** 147 units. 100 one-bedroom standard units. 45 one- and 2 two-bedroom suites. 18 stories, interior corridors. *Bath:* combo or shower only. **Amenities:** video games (fee), CD players, high-speed Internet, dual phone lines, voice mail, safes, honor bars, irons, hair dryers. **Leisure Activities:** exercise room. **Guest Services:** valet laundry. **Business Services:** meeting rooms, business center.

Small-scale Hotel

SHELBURNE MURRAY HILL HOTEL   *Book great rates at AAA.com*   **Phone:** (212)689-5200   **92**

All Year   1P: $179-$599   2P: $179-$599   XP: $25   F12

Location: Between 37th and 38th sts. 303 Lexington Ave 10016. Fax: 212/779-7068. **Facility:** 263 units. 131 one-bedroom standard units, some with efficiencies. 119 one- and 13 two-bedroom suites. 16 stories, interior corridors. *Bath:* combo or shower only. **Parking:** valet. **Terms:** package plans. **Amenities:** dual phone lines, voice mail, safes, irons, hair dryers. **Leisure Activities:** saunas, exercise room. **Guest Services:** valet and coin laundry, wireless Internet. **Business Services:** meeting rooms, fax (fee). **Cards:** AX, DC, DS, JC, MC, VI. *(See color ad p 439)*

Small-scale Hotel

SHERATON MANHATTAN HOTEL   *Book great rates at AAA.com*   **Phone:** 212/581-3300   **32**

Property failed to provide current rates

Location: Between 51st and 52nd sts. 790 7th Ave 10019. Fax: 212/541-9219. **Facility:** 665 units. 657 one-bedroom standard units. 7 one- and 1 two-bedroom suites, some with kitchens and/or whirlpools. 22 stories, interior corridors. *Bath:* combo or shower only. **Parking:** on-site (fee). **Terms:** pets (dogs only). **Amenities:** dual phone lines, voice mail, safes, irons, hair dryers. *Fee:* video games, high-speed Internet. **Dining:** Russo's Steak & Pasta, see separate listing. **Pool(s):** heated indoor. **Leisure Activities:** saunas, exercise room. *Fee:* massage. **Guest Services:** gift shop, valet laundry. **Business Services:** meeting rooms, business center.

Large-scale Hotel

SHERATON NEW YORK HOTEL & TOWERS   *Book great rates at AAA.com*   **Phone:** 212/581-1000   **28**

Property failed to provide current rates

Location: At 52nd St. 811 7th Ave 10019. Fax: 212/262-4410. **Facility:** 1749 units. 1716 one-bedroom standard units. 33 one-bedroom suites, some with whirlpools. 50 stories, interior corridors. *Bath:* combo or shower only. **Parking:** on-site (fee) and valet. **Terms:** pets (dogs only). **Amenities:** dual phone lines, voice mail, safes, irons, hair dryers. *Fee:* video games, high-speed Internet. *Some:* DVD players, CD players. **Leisure Activities:** saunas, steamrooms. *Fee:* massage. **Guest Services:** gift shop, valet laundry. **Business Services:** conference facilities, business center.

Large-scale Hotel

SOFITEL NEW YORK   *Book great rates at AAA.com*   **Phone:** (212)354-8844   **70**

All Year   1P: $399-$809

Location: Between 5th and 6th (Ave of the Americas) aves. 45 W 44th St 10036. Fax: 212/354-2480. **Facility:** The lobby of this property is plush and pleasing while its guest rooms offer a sense of enveloping luxury; the staff is attentive and gracious. 398 units. 346 one-bedroom standard units. 52 one-bedroom suites. 29 stories, interior corridors. *Bath:* combo or shower only. **Parking:** valet. **Amenities:** CD players, high-speed Internet (fee), dual phone lines, voice mail, safes, honor bars, irons, hair dryers. **Dining:** 6 am-midnight, cocktails. **Leisure Activities:** exercise room. *Fee:* massage. **Guest Services:** gift shop, valet laundry, wireless Internet. **Business Services:** conference facilities, business center. **Cards:** AX, CB, DC, DS, JC, MC, VI. **Free Special Amenities: newspaper.** *(See color ad p 452)*

Large-scale Hotel

SUPER 8 HOTEL-TIMES SQUARE   *Book great rates at AAA.com*   **Phone:** (212)719-2300   **55**

11/1-12/31	1P: $259-$269	2P: $269-$279	XP: $12	F13
9/1-10/31	1P: $239-$249	2P: $249-$259	XP: $12	F13
5/1-8/31	1P: $209-$229	2P: $219-$239	XP: $12	F13
1/1-4/30	1P: $129-$139	2P: $139-$149	XP: $12	F13

Location: Between 5th and 6th (Ave of the Americas) aves. 59 W 46th St 10036. Fax: 212/768-3477. **Facility:** 206 units. 196 one- and 10 two-bedroom standard units. 12 stories, interior corridors. *Bath:* combo or shower only. **Parking:** no self-parking. **Amenities:** video games (fee), voice mail, safes, irons, hair dryers. **Leisure Activities:** exercise room. **Guest Services:** valet laundry, wireless Internet. **Business Services:** meeting rooms, business center. **Cards:** AX, CB, DC, DS, JC, MC, VI. *(See color ad p 422)*

Small-scale Hotel

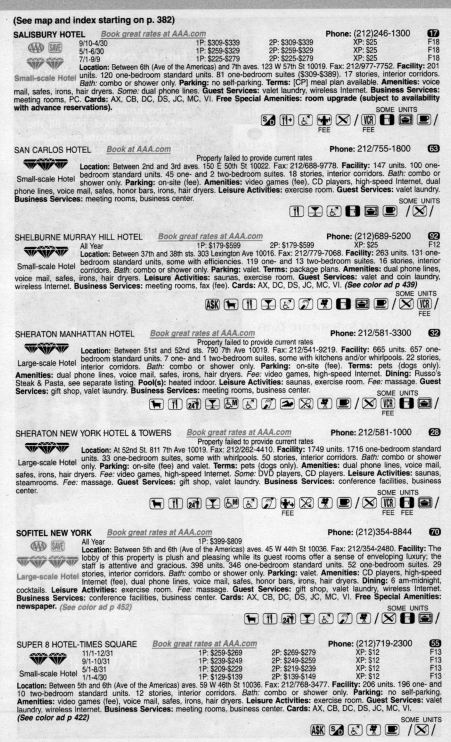

(See map and index starting on p. 382)

SURREY HOTEL — *Book great rates at AAA.com* — Phone: (212)288-3700 — **6**
All Year — 1P: $299-$489 — 2P: $299-$489 — XP: $25 — F12
Location: E 76th St and Madison Ave. 20 E 76th St 10021. Fax: 212/628-1549. **Facility:** 132 units. 37 one-bedroom standard units, some with efficiencies. 90 one- and 5 two-bedroom suites, some with kitchens. 16 stories, interior corridors. *Bath:* combo or shower only. **Parking:** on-site (fee) and valet. **Terms:** package plans. **Amenities:** high-speed Internet (fee), dual phone lines, voice mail, safes, honor bars, irons, hair dryers. *Some:* DVD players, CD players. **Dining:** Cafe Boulud, see separate listing. **Leisure Activities:** exercise room. **Guest Services:** valet and coin laundry. **Business Services:** meeting rooms, PC. **Cards:** AX, DC, DS, JC, MC, VI. *(See color ad p 452)*
SOME UNITS

THE TIME — *Book at AAA.com* — Phone: 212/246-5252 — **39**
9/3-12/31 — 1P: $539-$889 — 2P: $539-$889 — XP: $25 — F12
5/1-6/30 — 1P: $509-$809 — 2P: $509-$809 — XP: $25 — F12
7/1-9/2 & 1/1-4/30 — 1P: $459-$809 — 2P: $459-$809 — XP: $25 — F12
Location: Between 8th Ave and Broadway. 224 W 49th St 10019. Fax: 212/245-2305. **Facility:** 192 units. 163 one-bedroom standard units. 29 one-bedroom suites with whirlpools. 17 stories, interior corridors. *Bath:* combo or shower only. **Parking:** no self-parking. **Terms:** [BP] & [CP] meal plans available. **Amenities:** high-speed Internet (fee), dual phone lines, voice mail, safes, honor bars, irons, hair dryers. *Some:* DVD players, CD players. **Leisure Activities:** *Fee:* massage. **Guest Services:** valet laundry. **Business Services:** meeting rooms. **Cards:** AX, CB, DC, DS, JC, MC, VI.
SOME UNITS
FEE

TRAVEL INN — *Book great rates at AAA.com* — Phone: (212)695-7171 — **41**
All Year — 1P: $125-$250 — 2P: $140-$250 — XP: $15 — F16
Location: Between 10th and 11th aves. 515 W 42nd St 10036. Fax: 212/967-5025. **Facility:** 160 units. 159 one-bedroom standard units. 1 one-bedroom suite. 7 stories, interior/exterior corridors. *Bath:* combo or shower only. **Parking:** on-site. **Terms:** 2 night minimum stay - weekends, cancellation fee imposed. **Amenities:** video games (fee), voice mail, irons, hair dryers. **Dining:** 6 am-8 pm, wine/beer only. **Pool(s):** outdoor. **Leisure Activities:** lifeguard on duty, exercise room. **Guest Services:** gift shop, wireless Internet. **Business Services:** meeting rooms, PC (fee). **Cards:** AX, DC, DS, MC, VI. *(See color ad p 452)*
SOME UNITS

TRUMP INTERNATIONAL HOTEL & TOWER — *Book great rates at AAA.com* — Phone: (212)299-1000 — **9**
1/1-4/30 — 1P: $750-$795 — 2P: $750-$795
9/3-12/31 — 1P: $725-$765 — 2P: $725-$765
5/1-8/31 — 1P: $705-$740 — 2P: $705-$740
Location: Jct Central Park S; at Columbus Circle. 1 Central Park W 10023. Fax: 212/299-1150. **Facility:** Like its namesake, this apartment-type high-rise is upscale all the way, combining white-glove service and decked-out decor. Smoke free premises. 167 units. 36 one-bedroom standard units with efficiencies and whirlpools. 131 one-bedroom suites ($1015-$2400) with whirlpools, some with kitchens. 17 stories, interior corridors. **Parking:** valet. **Terms:** check-in 4 pm, [AP] meal plan available, small pets only ($200 fee). **Amenities:** video library, DVD players, video games (fee), high-speed Internet, dual phone lines, voice mail, fax, safes, honor bars, irons, hair dryers. *Some:* CD players. **Dining:** 6:30 am-10 pm, cocktails, also, Jean Georges Restaurant, see separate listing. **Pool(s):** lap. **Leisure Activities:** saunas, steamrooms, spa. **Guest Services:** valet laundry. **Business Services:** meeting rooms, business center. **Cards:** AX, CB, DC, DS, JC, MC, VI. **Free Special Amenities: newspaper and high-speed Internet.**
SOME UNITS
FEE

VINNCI AVALON — *Book great rates at AAA.com* — Phone: (212)299-7000 — **96**
All Year — 1P: $474-$700 — 2P: $474-$700 — XP: $30 — F12
Location: Between 5th and Madison aves. 16 E 32nd St 10016. Fax: 212/299-7001. **Facility:** 99 units. 20 one-bedroom standard units. 79 one-bedroom suites. 12 stories, interior corridors. *Bath:* combo or shower only. **Parking:** valet. **Terms:** cancellation fee imposed, [BP] meal plan available, package plans. **Amenities:** high-speed Internet, dual phone lines, voice mail, safes, honor bars, irons, hair dryers. *Some:* fax. **Guest Services:** valet laundry. **Business Services:** meeting rooms, PC. **Cards:** AX, DS, MC, VI.
SOME UNITS
FEE

THE WALDORF=ASTORIA — *Book great rates at AAA.com* — Phone: (212)355-3000 — **58**
9/4-12/31 — 1P: $499-$899 — 2P: $539-$939 — XP: $30 — F
5/1-6/27 — 1P: $419-$529 — 2P: $449-$559 — XP: $30 — F
1/1-4/30 — 1P: $299-$529 — 2P: $339-$559 — XP: $30 — F
6/28-9/3 — 1P: $299-$459 — 2P: $339-$489 — XP: $30 — F
Location: Between E 49th and 50th sts. 301 Park Ave 10022. Fax: 212/872-7272. **Facility:** The well-known hotel, which was built in 1931, centers around a grand lobby and offers expectedly elegant accommodations. 1416 units. 1185 one-bedroom standard units. 227 one-, 3 two- and 1 three-bedroom suites, some with efficiencies. 42 stories, interior corridors. *Bath:* combo or shower only. **Parking:** valet. **Terms:** cancellation fee imposed, package plans. **Amenities:** CD players, dual phone lines, voice mail, fax, honor bars, irons, hair dryers. *Fee:* video games, high-speed Internet. *Some:* DVD players (fee), safes. **Dining:** Oscar's American Brasserie, see separate listing. **Leisure Activities:** spa. **Guest Services:** gift shop, valet laundry. **Business Services:** conference facilities, business center. **Cards:** AX, DC, DS, MC, VI. Affiliated with A Hilton Hotel. *(See color ad starting on p 436)*
SOME UNITS
FEE — FEE — FEE

(See map and index starting on p. 382)

THE WARWICK NEW YORK HOTEL   *Book great rates at AAA.com*   Phone: (212)247-2700   [31]

(AAA) (SAVE)	5/1-6/28 & 9/4-12/31	2P: $550-$1500	XP: $30	F12
	6/29-9/3	2P: $425-$1200	XP: $30	F12
▼▼▼▼	1/1-4/30	2P: $425-$1000	XP: $30	F12

Historic
Small-scale Hotel

Location: Corner of 54th St and 6th Ave (Ave of the Americas). 65 W 54th St 10019. Fax: 212/247-2725. **Facility:** Built in 1927 by William Randolph Hearst, the property is close to Rockefeller Center and Central Park; some plush, spacious rooms have terraces. 426 units. 359 one-bedroom standard units. 66 one- and 1 two-bedroom suites, some with whirlpools. 33 stories, interior corridors. *Bath:* combo or shower only. **Parking:** valet. **Terms:** [BP] meal plan available, package plans. **Amenities:** video games (fee), dual phone lines, voice mail, safes, honor bars, irons, hair dryers. *Some:* DVD players, CD players. **Dining:** 2 restaurants, 6:30 am-10:30, noon-3 & 5:30-1 am, Sun 11 am-11 pm, also, Murals on 54 Restaurant, see separate listing. **Leisure Activities:** exercise room. **Guest Services:** valet laundry, wireless Internet. **Business Services:** meeting rooms, business center. **Cards:** AX, CB, DC, DS, JC, MC, VI. **Free Special Amenities:** newspaper and early check-in/late check-out.

SOME UNITS
[icons] FEE

WASHINGTON JEFFERSON HOTEL   *Book at AAA.com*   Phone: (212)246-7550   [26]

▼▼▼▼	9/1-12/31	1P: $350	2P: $350
	5/1-6/30	1P: $250	2P: $250
	7/1-8/31	1P: $240	2P: $240
Small-scale Hotel	1/1-4/30	1P: $225	2P: $225

Location: Between 8th and 9th aves. 318 W 51st St 10019. Fax: 212/246-7622. **Facility:** 135 one-bedroom standard units, some with whirlpools. 6 stories, interior corridors. *Bath:* combo or shower only. **Parking:** valet. **Terms:** 2 night minimum stay - weekends, 7 day cancellation notice-fee imposed. **Amenities:** high-speed Internet, voice mail, safes, irons, hair dryers. *Some:* CD players. **Leisure Activities:** limited exercise equipment. **Guest Services:** valet laundry. **Cards:** AX, DC, DS, MC, VI.

SOME UNITS
[icons]

THE WESTIN NEW YORK AT TIMES SQUARE   *Book great rates at AAA.com*   Phone: (212)201-2700   [53]

(AAA) (SAVE)	9/4-12/31	1P: $279-$899	2P: $279-$899	XP: $30	F
	6/29-6/28	1P: $269-$699	2P: $269-$699	XP: $30	F
▼▼▼ ▼▼▼	1/1-4/30	1P: $249-$699	2P: $249-$699	XP: $30	F
	6/29-9/3	1P: $249-$669	2P: $249-$669	XP: $30	F

Large-scale Hotel **Location:** Corner of 8th Ave. 270 W 43rd St 10036. Fax: 212/201-2701. **Facility:** With a reflective blue-green exterior and modernistic, jewel-toned interior, the property offers accommodations which are stylish and plush. Smoke free premises. 863 units. 857 one-bedroom standard units. 6 one-bedroom suites ($449-$2500). 45 stories, interior corridors. *Bath:* combo or shower only. **Parking:** valet. **Terms:** cancellation fee imposed, [AP], [BP] & [CP] meal plans available, package plans, small pets only. **Amenities:** dual phone lines, voice mail, safes, honor bars, irons, hair dryers. *Fee:* video games, high-speed Internet. *Some:* DVD players, CD players. **Dining:** 6:30 am-11:30 pm, cocktails. **Leisure Activities:** saunas, spa. *Fee:* exercise room. **Guest Services:** gift shop, valet laundry. **Business Services:** conference facilities, business center. **Cards:** AX, CB, DC, DS, JC, MC, VI.

SOME UNITS
[icons]

WINGATE INN MANHATTAN MIDTOWN   Phone: 212/967-7500

[fyi]	9/1-12/31 [ECP]	1P: $299-$569	2P: $299-$569	XP: $20
	5/1-6/30 [ECP]	1P: $269-$429	2P: $269-$429	XP: $20
Small-scale Hotel	1/1-4/30 [ECP]	1P: $219-$429	2P: $219-$429	XP: $20
	7/1-8/31 [ECP]	1P: $209-$429	2P: $209-$429	XP: $20

Too new to rate. **Location:** 235 W 35 St 10001. Fax: 212/967-7599. **Amenities:** 92 units, restaurant, coffeemakers, microwaves, refrigerators. **Terms:** cancellation fee imposed. **Cards:** AX, CB, DC, DS, JC, MC, VI. *(See color ad below)*

(See map and index starting on p. 382)

W NEW YORK   *Book great rates at AAA.com*   **Phone:** 212/755-1200   [64]

Property failed to provide current rates

Location: At 49th St. 541 Lexington Ave 10022. Fax: 212/421-3876. **Facility:** 688 units. 634 one-bedroom

Large-scale Hotel   standard units. 54 one-bedroom suites. 18 stories, interior corridors. *Bath:* combo or shower only. **Parking:** valet. **Terms:** pets ($100 fee, $25 extra charge). **Amenities:** DVD players, CD players, high-speed Internet (fee), dual phone lines, voice mail, safes, honor bars, irons, hair dryers. *Some:* fax. **Leisure Activities:** spa. **Guest Services:** gift shop, valet laundry, wireless Internet. **Business Services:** conference facilities. *Fee:* administrative services, PC.

SOME UNITS

FEE

W NEW YORK TIMES SQUARE   *Book great rates at AAA.com*   **Phone:** 212/930-7400   [46]

Property failed to provide current rates

Location: Corner of 47th St. 1567 Broadway at 47th St 10036. **Facility:** 507 units. 462 one-bedroom standard

Large-scale Hotel   units. 43 one- and 2 two-bedroom suites. 57 stories, interior corridors. *Bath:* combo or shower only. **Parking:** valet. **Terms:** pets ($100 fee, $25 extra charge). **Amenities:** DVD players, CD players, dual phone lines, voice mail, safes, honor bars, irons, hair dryers. *Fee:* video games, high-speed Internet. *Some:* fax. **Leisure Activities:** exercise room, spa. **Guest Services:** gift shop, valet laundry. **Business Services:** conference facilities, business center.

SOME UNITS

FEE   FEE FEE

──────── *The following lodgings were either not evaluated or did not* ────────
meet AAA rating requirements but are listed for your information only.

THE ALEX   **Phone:** 212/867-5100
[fyi]   Not evaluated. **Location:** At 3rd Ave. 205 E 45th St 10017. Facilities, services, and decor characterize an upscale property. *(See color ad p 421)*

AMSTERDAM COURT   **Phone:** 212/459-1000
[fyi]   Not evaluated. **Location:** Between 7th and 8th aves. 226 W 50th St 10019. Facilities, services, and decor characterize a mid-range property.

BENTLEY HOTEL   **Phone:** 212/644-6000
[fyi]   Not evaluated. **Location:** At York Ave. 500 E 62nd St 10021. Facilities, services, and decor characterize a mid-range property.

CASABLANCA HOTEL   **Phone:** 212/869-1212
[fyi]   Not evaluated. **Location:** Between 6th Ave (Ave of the Americas) and Broadway. 147 W 43rd St 10036. Facilities, services, and decor characterize a mid-range property.

COURTYARD BY MARRIOTT/MANHATTAN-TIMES SQUARE SOUTH   **Phone:** 212/391-0088
[fyi]   Not evaluated. **Location:** Between Broadway and 6th Ave (Ave of the Americas). 114 W 40th St 10018. Facilities, services, and decor characterize a mid-range property.

THE GRACIE INN   **Phone:** 212/628-1700
[fyi]   Not evaluated. **Location:** Between York and East End aves. 502 E 81st St 10028. Facilities, services, and decor characterize a mid-range property.

HOTEL 41 AT TIMES SQUARE   **Phone:** 212/703-8600
[fyi]   Not evaluated. **Location:** Between 7th and 8th aves. 206 W 41st St 10036. Facilities, services, and decor characterize a mid-range property.

HOTEL BELLECLAIRE   **Phone:** 212/362-7700
[fyi]   Not evaluated. **Location:** At Broadway. 250 W 77th St 10024. Facilities, services, and decor characterize a basic property.

HOTEL ELYSEE   **Phone:** 212/753-1066
[fyi]   Not evaluated. **Location:** Between Park and Lexington aves. 60 E 54th St 10022. Facilities, services, and decor characterize a mid-range property.

HUDSON HOTEL   **Phone:** 212/554-6000
[fyi]   Not evaluated. **Location:** Between 8th and 9th aves. 356 W 58th St 10019. Facilities, services, and decor characterize an upscale property.

THE MODERNE   **Phone:** 212/397-6767
[fyi]   Not evaluated. **Location:** Between 7th and 8th aves. 243 W 55th St 10019. Facilities, services, and decor characterize a mid-range property.

MORGANS HOTEL   **Phone:** 212/686-0300
[fyi]   Not evaluated. **Location:** Between 37th and 38th sts. 237 Madison Ave 10016. Facilities, services, and decor characterize a mid-range property.

(See map and index starting on p. 382)

W NEW YORK-THE COURT

(fyi) Not evaluated. **Location:** Between Park and Lexington aves. 130 E 39th St 10016. Facilities, services, and decor characterize an upscale property.

Phone: 212/685-1100

W NEW YORK-THE TUSCANY

(fyi) Not evaluated. **Location:** Between Park and Lexington aves. 120 E 39th St 10016. Facilities, services, and decor characterize an upscale property.

Phone: 212/686-1600

──────── **WHERE TO DINE** ────────

3 GUYS RESTAURANT
American
Lunch: $5-$25 **Dinner:** $5-$25 **Phone:** 212/628-8108 (21)
Location: Between 75th and 76th sts. 960 Madison Ave 10021. **Hours:** 6 am-10 pm. Closed: 12/25.
Features: The family-friendly restaurant and coffee shop serves up a wide array of American, Italian and Greek specialties. Casual dress; cocktails. **Parking:** no self-parking. **Cards:** AX, MC, VI.

21 CLUB
American
Lunch: $27-$45 **Dinner:** $30-$45 **Phone:** 212/582-7200 (127)
Location: Between 5th and 6th (Ave of the Americas) aves. 21 W 52nd St 10019. **Hours:** noon-2:30 & 5:30-10 pm, Fri-11 pm, Sat 5:30 pm-11 pm. Closed major holidays; also Sun. **Reservations:** suggested.
Features: Noticeable from the street by miniature statuary and fancy wrought-iron fencing surrounding the entrance, the bastion of old New York is still clubby with dark wood, brass-studded leather banquettes and toys hanging from every corner of the ceiling. Classic "21" dishes have been revived; Senegalese soup, an extraordinary "21" burger and eye-catching game pot pie are among those choices. Although the food isn't fancy, it's top quality and richly satisfying. Service is Old World professional. Semi-formal attire; cocktails. **Parking:** no self-parking. **Cards:** AX, CB, DC, DS, MC, VI.

44 AT ROYALTON
American
Lunch: $13-$26 **Dinner:** $13-$32 **Phone:** 212/944-8844 (198)
Location: Between 5th and 6th (Ave of the Americas) aves; in Royalton Hotel. 44 W 44th St 10036. **Hours:** 7 am-11, noon-3 & 7-10:30 pm, Sat & Sun 8 am-2 & 7-10:30 pm. **Reservations:** suggested. **Features:** An upscale stylish boutique hotel houses this upscale dining room, popular with young professionals. The menu of New American dishes features wild striped bass, crispy roast chicken, seared skate fish, grilled spicy skirt steak, barbecue king salmon, lobster ravioli, seared beef tenderloin, grilled lamb T-bones, grilled tuna and pork chops. Dressy casual; cocktails. **Parking:** on-site (fee). **Cards:** AX, DC, DS, MC, VI.

ABOVE
American
Lunch: $8-$22 **Dinner:** $10-$28 **Phone:** 212/642-2626 (182)
Location: Between 7th and 8th aves; in Hilton Times Square. 234 W 42nd St 10036. **Hours:** 6:30-11 am, 11:30-2 & 5:30-10 pm. **Reservations:** suggested. **Features:** The lounge has become a hot post-theater spot and the view of the lights of theater row below is commanding, but the cuisine is more than an afterthought. The menu focuses on large and small dishes, so sample as you will from appetizers, salads and tasty pastas—some accented by savory veal sausage—served in two sizes; dive into the crunchy breadsticks as you consider your options. Dressy casual; cocktails. **Parking:** on-site (fee) and valet. **Cards:** AX, CB, DC, DS, JC, MC, VI.

ACQUA PAZZA
Italian
Lunch: $17-$26 **Dinner:** $20-$40 **Phone:** 212/582-6900 (128)
Location: Between 5th and 6th (Ave of the Americas) aves. 36 W 52nd St 10019. **Hours:** 11 am-3 & 5:30-10:30 pm, Sat from 5:30 pm. Closed major holidays; also Sun. **Reservations:** suggested. **Features:** Lending to the clean, classic and crisp atmosphere are a brown granite bar and dark wood furniture with light blue walls. Italian dishes center on beef, poultry and game. Formal attire; cocktails. **Parking:** street. **Cards:** AX, DC, DS, MC, VI.

AMARONE RISTORANTE
Italian
Lunch: $11-$27 **Dinner:** $11-$27 **Phone:** 212/245-6060 (100)
Location: Between 47th and 48th sts; in theater district. 686 9th Ave 10036. **Hours:** noon-11 pm, Tues-Sat to midnight. **Reservations:** suggested. **Features:** Popular with the locals, the Italian restaurant serves pasta, chicken and veal dishes, all made from scratch. Guests should make sure to see the wine menu and the restaurant's wine area. The theater is nearby, so pre- and post-show dinners are common here. Casual dress; cocktails. **Parking:** no self-parking. **Cards:** AX, DC, DS, JC, MC, VI.

AMMA
Indian
Lunch: $11-$17 **Dinner:** $12-$28 **Phone:** 212/644-8330 (186)
Location: Between 2nd and 3rd aves. 246 E 51st St 10022. **Hours:** noon-3 & 5-10:15 pm.
Reservations: accepted. **Features:** India isn't likely to immediately come to mind when diners walk into the neat, contemporary dining room, but then the tamarind-yellow walls, persimmon chairs and otherworldly new-age music may make subtle hints at the distinctly ethnic menu to come. Amma, or "mother," serves home-style cooking from the north and south of India. Lamb shank curry or tandoor and moist, fragrant chicken tikka masala are specialties. Casual dress; cocktails. **Parking:** no self-parking. **Cards:** AX, DC, DS, MC, VI.

ANGUS MCINDOE RESTAURANT
American
Lunch: $11-$28 **Dinner:** $11-$28 **Phone:** 212/221-9222 (163)
Location: Between 8th Ave and Broadway; in theater district. 258 W 44th St 10036. **Hours:** noon-12:30 am, Fri & Sat-1 am, Sun-midnight. Closed: 11/22, 12/24, 12/25. **Reservations:** suggested. **Features:** In the heart of the theater district, the busy and casual place is where diners might come across actors from the shows that are playing. Three dining rooms help accommodate the reservations and walk-ins. Casual dress; cocktails. **Parking:** no self-parking. **Cards:** AX, MC, VI.

ANH
Vietnamese
Lunch: $4-$7 **Dinner:** $7-$17 **Phone:** 212/532-2848 (244)
Location: Between 26th and 27th sts. 363 3rd Ave 10016. **Hours:** 11:30 am-11 pm, Fri & Sat-midnight.
Reservations: accepted. **Features:** Anh offers classic Vietnamese fare ranging from pho (oxtail broth with rice, noodles and sliced beef) to tau hu chay (pan-seared tofu skin roll). Desserts have a more Western aspect, ranging from chocolate truffle to lemon raspberry mousse. Casual dress; cocktails. **Parking:** no self-parking. **Cards:** AX, DC, DS, MC, VI.

(See map and index starting on p. 382)

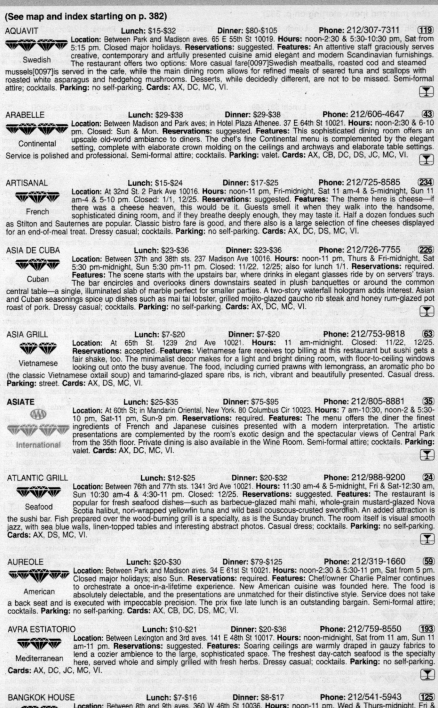

AQUAVIT **Lunch:** $15-$32 **Dinner:** $80-$105 **Phone:** 212/307-7311 `119`
Location: Between Park and Madison aves. 65 E 55th St 10019. **Hours:** noon-2:30 & 5:30-10:30 pm, Sat from
5:15 pm. Closed major holidays. **Reservations:** suggested. **Features:** An attentive staff graciously serves
creative, contemporary and artfully presented cuisine amid elegant and modern Scandinavian furnishings.
Swedish The restaurant offers two options: More casual fare[0097]Swedish meatballs, roasted cod and steamed
mussels[0097]is served in the cafe, while the main dining room allows for refined meals of seared tuna and scallops with
roasted white asparagus and hedgehog mushrooms. Desserts, while decidedly different, are not to be missed. Semi-formal
attire; cocktails. **Parking:** no self-parking. **Cards:** AX, DC, MC, VI.

ARABELLE **Lunch:** $29-$38 **Dinner:** $29-$38 **Phone:** 212/606-4647 `43`
Location: Between Madison and Park aves; in Hotel Plaza Athenee. 37 E 64th St 10021. **Hours:** noon-2:30 & 6-10
pm. Closed: Sun & Mon. **Reservations:** suggested. **Features:** This sophisticated dining room offers an
upscale old-world ambiance to diners. The chef's fine Continental menu is complemented by the elegant
Continental setting, complete with elaborate crown molding on the ceilings and archways and elaborate table settings.
Service is polished and professional. Semi-formal attire; cocktails. **Parking:** valet. **Cards:** AX, CB, DC, DS, JC, MC, VI.

ARTISANAL **Lunch:** $15-$24 **Dinner:** $17-$25 **Phone:** 212/725-8585 `234`
Location: At 32nd St. 2 Park Ave 10016. **Hours:** noon-11 pm, Fri-midnight, Sat 11 am-4 & 5-midnight, Sun 11
am-4 & 5-10 pm. Closed: 1/1, 12/25. **Reservations:** suggested. **Features:** The theme here is cheese—if
there was a cheese heaven, this would be it. Guests smell it when they walk into the handsome,
French sophisticated dining room, and if they breathe deeply enough, they may taste it. Half a dozen fondues such
as Stilton and Sauternes are popular. Classic bistro fare is good, and there also is a large selection of fine cheeses displayed
for an end-of-meal treat. Dressy casual; cocktails. **Parking:** no self-parking. **Cards:** AX, DC, DS, MC, VI.

ASIA DE CUBA **Lunch:** $23-$36 **Dinner:** $23-$36 **Phone:** 212/726-7755 `226`
Location: Between 37th and 38th sts. 237 Madison Ave 10016. **Hours:** noon-11 pm, Thurs & Fri-midnight, Sat
5:30 pm-midnight, Sun 5:30 pm-11 pm. Closed: 11/22, 12/25; also for lunch 1/1. **Reservations:** required.
Cuban **Features:** The scene starts with the upstairs bar, where drinks in elegant glasses ride by on servers' trays.
The bar encircles and overlooks diners downstairs seated in plush banquettes or around the common
central table—a single, illuminated slab of marble perfect for smaller parties. A two-story waterfall hologram adds interest. Asian
and Cuban seasonings spice up dishes such as mai tai lobster, grilled mojito-glazed gaucho rib steak and honey rum-glazed pot
roast of pork. Dressy casual; cocktails. **Parking:** no self-parking. **Cards:** AX, DC, MC, VI.

ASIA GRILL **Lunch:** $7-$20 **Dinner:** $7-$20 **Phone:** 212/753-9818 `63`
Location: At 65th St. 1239 2nd Ave 10021. **Hours:** 11 am-midnight. Closed: 11/22, 12/25.
Reservations: accepted. **Features:** Vietnamese fare receives top billing at this restaurant but sushi gets a
fair shake, too. The minimalist decor makes for a light and bright dining room, with floor-to-ceiling windows
Vietnamese looking out onto the busy avenue. The food, including curried prawns with lemongrass, an aromatic pho bo
(the classic Vietnamese oxtail soup) and tamarind-glazed spare ribs, is rich, vibrant and beautifully presented. Casual dress.
Parking: street. **Cards:** AX, DS, MC, VI.

ASIATE **Lunch:** $25-$35 **Dinner:** $75-$95 **Phone:** 212/805-8881 `35`
Location: At 60th St; in Mandarin Oriental, New York. 80 Columbus Cir 10023. **Hours:** 7 am-10:30, noon-2 & 5:30-
10 pm, Sat-11 pm, Sun-9 pm. **Reservations:** required. **Features:** The menu offers the diner the finest
ingredients of French and Japanese cuisines presented with a modern interpretation. The artistic
presentations are complemented by the room's exotic design and the spectacular views of Central Park
International from the 35th floor. Private dining is also available in the Wine Room. Semi-formal attire; cocktails. **Parking:**
valet. **Cards:** AX, DC, MC, VI.

ATLANTIC GRILL **Lunch:** $12-$25 **Dinner:** $20-$32 **Phone:** 212/988-9200 `24`
Location: Between 76th and 77th sts. 1341 3rd Ave 10021. **Hours:** 11:30 am-4 & 5-midnight, Fri & Sat-12:30 am,
Sun 10:30 am-4 & 4:30-11 pm. Closed: 12/25. **Reservations:** suggested. **Features:** The restaurant is
popular for fresh seafood dishes—such as barbecue-glazed mahi mahi, whole-grain mustard-glazed Nova
Seafood Scotia halibut, nori-wrapped yellowfin tuna and wild basil couscous-crusted swordfish. An added attraction is
the sushi bar. Fish prepared over the wood-burning grill is a specialty, as is the Sunday brunch. The room itself is visual smooth
jazz, with sea blue walls, linen-topped tables and interesting abstract photos. Casual dress; cocktails. **Parking:** no self-parking.
Cards: AX, DS, MC, VI.

AUREOLE **Lunch:** $20-$30 **Dinner:** $79-$125 **Phone:** 212/319-1660 `59`
Location: Between Park and Madison aves. 34 E 61st St 10021. **Hours:** noon-2:30 & 5:30-11 pm, Sat from 5 pm.
Closed major holidays; also Sun. **Reservations:** required. **Features:** Chef/owner Charlie Palmer continues
to orchestrate a once-in-a-lifetime experience. New American cuisine was founded here. The food is
American absolutely delectable, and the presentations are unmatched for their distinctive style. Service does not take
a back seat and is executed with impeccable precision. The prix fixe late lunch is an outstanding bargain. Semi-formal attire;
cocktails. **Parking:** no self-parking. **Cards:** AX, CB, DC, DS, MC, VI.

AVRA ESTIATORIO **Lunch:** $10-$21 **Dinner:** $20-$36 **Phone:** 212/759-8550 `193`
Location: Between Lexington and 3rd aves. 141 E 48th St 10017. **Hours:** noon-midnight, Sat from 11 am, Sun 11
am-11 pm. **Reservations:** suggested. **Features:** Soaring ceilings are warmly draped in gauzy fabrics to
lend a cozier ambience to the large, sophisticated space. The freshest day-catch seafood is the specialty
Mediterranean here, served whole and simply grilled with fresh herbs. Dressy casual; cocktails. **Parking:** no self-parking.
Cards: AX, DC, JC, MC, VI.

BANGKOK HOUSE **Lunch:** $7-$16 **Dinner:** $8-$17 **Phone:** 212/541-5943 `125`
Location: Between 8th and 9th aves. 360 W 46th St 10036. **Hours:** noon-11 pm, Wed & Thurs-midnight, Fri &
Sat-1 am. Closed: 12/25. **Reservations:** accepted. **Features:** A pleasant atmosphere and friendly staff
await patrons. The menu selection is ample and all of the entrees are prepared to order with level of spice
Thai preference in mind. Casual dress; cocktails. **Parking:** no self-parking. **Cards:** AX, DC, DS, MC, VI.

(See map and index starting on p. 382)

BARBETTA   Lunch: $18-$28   Dinner: $24-$35   Phone: 212/246-9171   `129`
▼▼▼▼▼
Location: Between 8th and 9th aves; in theater district; on Restaurant Row. 321 W 46th St 10036. **Hours:** noon-3 &
5-1 am. Closed: Sun. **Reservations:** suggested. **Features:** Opulence abounds in the sophisticated dining
Northern Italian   room, which is appointed with 18th-century antiques. The lovely garden is pleasant. Such preparations as
swordfish over lentils in a balsamic vinaigrette are unequivocally Italian. A prix fixe pre-theater dinner is
featured for $45. The menu includes dishes served since the 1906 opening by the same family still in ownership. Dressy casual;
cocktails. **Parking:** street. **Cards:** AX, DC, DS, MC, VI.   &M Y

BAR MASA   Lunch: $21-$69   Dinner: $12-$75   Phone: 212/823-9800   `37`
▼▼▼
Location: At 59th St; in Time Warner Center. 10 Columbus Circle 10019. **Hours:** 11:30 am-3 & 6-midnight. Closed:
Sun. **Reservations:** not accepted. **Features:** The space is lovely and serene, as one might expect at a
Japanese   more casual yet refined Japanese bar cum cafe. The selection is smaller, but top-quality dishes are simple
yet distinguished. Offerings include sake-steamed clams, sea eel tempura with shiso leaf, such sashimi
salads as salmon with kaiware mustard soy and organic Kobe beef tataki with garlic. Also on the menu are a few rolls, soups
and a platter of sushi canapes. Guests appreciate lighter but no less gratifying meals. Casual dress; cocktails. **Parking:** on-site
(fee) and street. **Cards:** AX, MC, VI.   &M

BAY LEAF INDIAN BRASSERIE   Lunch: $15-$25   Dinner: $20-$35   Phone: 212/957-1818   `77`
▼▼▼
Location: Between 5th and 6th (Ave of the Americas) aves. 49 W 56th St 10019. **Hours:** noon-3 & 5:30-11 pm, Fri
& Sat-11:30 pm. Closed major holidays. **Reservations:** suggested. **Features:** Skilled hands with a light
Northern Indian   touch create dishes from Hydrobad, Kashmir, Bangal, Bombay, Goa and more. Dishes such as grilled jumbo
shrimp marinated in olive oil, garlic and herbs, fish simmered in a sauce of yellow chilis, coconut milk and
spices, and minced lamb with spices rolled onto skewers and broiled in the clay oven hold a certain appeal. The almost
weightless naan, perfectly charred, goes with melt-in-your-mouth chicken saag. Servers are attentive and the host is a pleasure.
Casual dress; cocktails. **Parking:** on-site (fee). **Cards:** AX, JC, MC, VI.   Y

BEACON   Lunch: $18-$34   Dinner: $27-$38   Phone: 212/332-0500   `82`
▼▼▼
Location: Between 5th and 6th (Ave of the Americas) aves. 25 W 56th St 10019. **Hours:** noon-2:30 & 5:30-10 pm,
Fri-10:30 pm, Sat 5 pm-10:30 pm, Sun 4 pm-8 pm; Saturday & Sunday brunch 11:30 am-2:30 pm. Closed
American   major holidays. **Reservations:** required. **Features:** Wielding flame as a tool to enhance the true flavor of
ingredients, the chef uses a wood-burning oven, grill and rotisserie to create impressive dishes that will
satisfy the soul. Try the wood-roasted oysters with shallots, ten-herb rotisserie grilled chicken or any of the fresh-from-the-hearth
meats. A table within the restaurant's pit will afford diners a view of the open kitchen theatrics and the wood-fired ovens, while a
table on the mezzanine level offers a bit more intimacy. Dressy casual; cocktails. **Parking:** street. **Cards:** AX, DC, MC, VI.

BECCO   Lunch: $17   Dinner: $22   Phone: 212/397-7597   `121`
▼▼▼
Location: Between 8th and 9th aves. 355 W 46th St 10036. **Hours:** noon-3 & 4:30-midnight, Sun & Mon noon-10
pm, Tues noon-3 & 5-midnight. Closed: 12/25. **Reservations:** required. **Features:** Symphony de pasta, a
Regional Italian   bottomless dish of three daily pastas, is a signature creation on a menu of farmhouse-style, countrified
Northern Italian cuisine. Osso buco is another. Portions are ample, flavors hearty and fresh, and prices
reasonable. Three dining areas deliver distinct, but altogether pleasant, experiences. The back room is bright with natural light
from the glass pyramid ceiling. This place is a neat find. Casual dress; cocktails. **Parking:** no self-parking. **Cards:** AX, CB, DC,
DS, MC, VI.   &M

BELLO RESTAURANT   Lunch: $15-$30   Dinner: $15-$30   Phone: 212/246-6773   `40`
▼▼▼
Location: At 56th St. 863 9th Ave 10019. **Hours:** 11:30 am-11 pm, Fri-midnight, Sat 3 pm-midnight. Closed:
Sun. **Reservations:** suggested. **Features:** Consistently flavorful food brings locals back again and again for
Northern Italian   fresh marinated anchovies, sauteed portobello mushrooms, stuffed veal chop with cognac sauce and
salmon Dijon. The menu and decor are classic. Italian. Farro and squid ink can't be had here, but
outstanding Alfredo and bolognese help patrons find their bliss. Also on the menu are well-done and delicate interpretations of
Marsalas, piccatas, scampis, scarpiellos and diavolos. Casual dress; cocktails. **Parking:** on-site. **Cards:** AX, DC, DS, MC, VI.   Y

BEN BENSON'S STEAK HOUSE   Lunch: $16-$39   Dinner: $16-$39   Phone: 212/581-8888   `103`
▼▼▼
Location: Between 6th (Ave of the Americas) and 7th aves. 123 W 52nd St 10019. **Hours:** 11:45 am-11 pm, Fri-
midnight, Sat 5 pm-midnight, Sun 5 pm-10 pm. Closed major holidays. **Reservations:** suggested.
Steak & Seafood   **Features:** Great steak plus famous crab cakes, lobster, veal and lamb. Lunch specials daily. Winter and
summer menus. Indoor parking at 31 W 52nd St from 5 pm-midnight. Outdoor cafe, seasonal. Casual dress;
cocktails. **Parking:** no self-parking. **Cards:** AX, DC, DS, JC, MC, VI.   &M Y

BEYOGLU   Lunch: $13-$19   Dinner: $13-$19   Phone: 212/650-0850   `17`
▼▼ ▼▼
Location: At 81st St. 1431 3rd Ave 10028. **Hours:** noon-close. **Reservations:** required. **Features:** The popular
restaurant has a casual, friendly way about it. Neighborhood locals gather in crowds to enjoy the selection
Turkish   of meze—such as hummus, eggplant salad, spicy chopped vegetables, chargrilled octopus or shrimp,
tabbouleh and the like—and grilled meat and fish selections. In warmer months, it's delightful to sit curbside
or just within the wide open doors and watch passersby. Casual dress; cocktails. **Parking:** street. **Cards:** AX, MC, VI.

BLT STEAK   Lunch: $22-$79   Dinner: $24-$79   Phone: 212/752-7470   `106`
▼▼▼ ▼▼▼
Location: Between Park and Lexington aves. 106 E 57th St 10022. **Hours:** 11:45 am-2:30 & 5:30-11 pm, Fri-11:30
pm, Sat 5:30 pm-11:30 pm. Closed: Sun. **Reservations:** suggested. **Features:** A polished steak house like
Steak & Seafood   no other, the restaurant exudes sophistication through its handsome zinc bar, ebony tables and ultrasuede
chairs. An equally distinguished menu lists Angus beef, broiled at 900 degrees and served with a choice of
sauce and steak butter for extra luxury. Fine sauces also accompany seafood. Marvelous potatoes, mushrooms and vegetables
enhance the full meal. The danger is filling up on piping-hot popovers topped with crispy Gruyere cheese before the meal.
Dressy casual; cocktails. **Parking:** no self-parking. **Cards:** AX, DC, DS, MC, VI.   Y

(See map and index starting on p. 382)

BLUE FIN **Lunch:** $12-$23 **Dinner:** $19-$28 **Phone:** 212/918-1400 (145)
⩗⩗⩗⩗⩗ **Location:** Corner of 47th St. 1567 Broadway 10036. **Hours:** 7 am-midnight, Fri & Sat-1 am.
Reservations: suggested. **Features:** The "wow" factor is high at the oh-so-cool eye-pleaser, where fresh
Seafood flavor comes from the kitchen. Predominantly seafood dishes with relatively simple preparations look
beautiful from menu to table, and service leaves a pleasant aftertaste. The sushi bar has a master working
behind. Casual dress; cocktails. **Parking:** no self-parking. **Cards:** AX, DS, MC, VI. ♿Ⓜ Ⓨ

BLUE SMOKE **Lunch:** $9-$24 **Dinner:** $9-$24 **Phone:** 212/447-7733 (241)
⩗⩗⩗⩗ **Location:** Between Lexington and Park aves. 116 E 27th St 10016. **Hours:** 11:30 am-10 pm, Fri-1 am, Sat noon-1
am, Sun noon-10 pm. Closed major holidays. **Reservations:** suggested. **Features:** The famous blend in
Barbecue and dig into reasonably priced ribs, pulled pork and beef brisket that keep lines long at the casual, down-
home eatery. More than just barbecue, the menu lists sides and vegetables, as well as dishes rarely seen
since the '50s: iceberg wedges with green goddess dressing, fry bread with chipotle butter and jalapeno marmalade and
chocolate layer cake and milk. Sticky toffee pudding, banana cream pie or a banana split is a perfect conclusion. Casual dress;
cocktails. **Parking:** no self-parking. **Cards:** AX, DC, DS, MC, VI. Ⓨ

BRASSERIE 8 1/2 **Lunch:** $22-$29 **Dinner:** $25-$37 **Phone:** 212/829-0812 (75)
⩗⩗⩗⩗ **Location:** Between 5th and 6th (Ave of the Americas) aves. 9 W 57th St 10019. **Hours:** 11:30 am-3 & 5:30-10 pm,
Fri & Sat-11 pm, Sun 11 am-3 & 5:30-9 pm; Sunday brunch. Closed: 7/4, 9/3. **Reservations:** suggested.
American **Features:** While the entrance to this upscale restaurant is at street level, diners descend a sweeping semi-
circular staircase into the casually elegant dining room and lounge. The menu reflects French and American
brasserie influences. Lunch and dinner have both prix fixe and a la carte offerings. Dressy casual; cocktails. **Parking:** street.
Cards: AX, CB, DC, DS, MC, VI. Ⓨ

BRASSERIE 360 **Lunch:** $8-$20 **Dinner:** $8-$22 **Phone:** 212/688-8688 (91)
⩗⩗⩗ **Location:** At 3rd Ave. 200 E 60th St 10022. **Hours:** 11 am-11 pm, Fri & Sat-midnight. Closed: 11/22, 12/25.
Reservations: accepted. **Features:** This casual French eatery is the perfect place to regroup and revitalize
American from a harried day of shopping at Bloomingdales, which is just across the street. Healthy salads, a sampling
of pastas and classic brasserie fare, including roasted salmon and a lush tarte tatin, provide all the energy
you'll need for a post-meal shopping spree, perhaps even a jaunt to Bergdof's. Casual dress; cocktails. **Parking:** street.
Cards: AX, DC, DS, MC, VI. Ⓨ

BRASSERIE LES HALLES **Lunch:** $13-$28 **Dinner:** $13-$28 **Phone:** 212/679-4111 (236)
⩗⩗⩗⩗ **Location:** Between 28th and 29th sts. 411 Park Ave S 10016. **Hours:** 8 am-midnight. **Reservations:** accepted.
Features: It's loud, it's crowded, the air is full of energy and this only adds to the experience of this
French brasserie. The dishes are classic hearty French, including top-quality grilled Angus beef ribeyes, the famous
hanger steak with shallot sauce, tartiflette, duck confit, cassoulet, choucroute garni, steak frites, lighter
salads spiked with meat and other classic much-loved classics. Preparations are tasty and not a single, delicious calorie is
spared. Dressy casual; cocktails. **Parking:** no self-parking. **Cards:** AX, DC, DS, MC, VI. ♿Ⓜ

BRAZIL GRILL **Lunch:** $12-$20 **Dinner:** $20-$35 **Phone:** 212/307-9449 (112)
⩗⩗⩗ **Location:** At 48th St. 787 8th Ave 10036. **Hours:** noon-midnight. **Features:** This restaurant features South
American fare and is conveniently located near Times Square and the Theater District. They also offer a
Brazilian very reasonable evening buffet for those wishing to sample a wide variety of selections. Casual dress;
cocktails. **Parking:** street. **Cards:** AX, CB, DC, DS, JC, MC, VI.

BREAD AND OLIVE **Lunch:** $5-$10 **Dinner:** $5-$10 **Phone:** 212/391-7772 (189)
⩗ **Location:** Between 5th and 6th (Ave of the Americas) aves. 24 W 45th St 10036. **Hours:** 11 am-9 pm, Sat 11:30
am-6 pm. Closed major holidays; also Sun. **Features:** The small "quick serve" has attracted much attention
Lebanese in the area by serving some good Middle Eastern eats. Guests can take out grilled kebabs of beef, lamb or
chicken, savory pastries or appetizer salads or carry meals to the tables in the back. Casual dress. **Parking:**
no self-parking. **Cards:** AX, MC, VI. Ⓚ

BRYANT PARK GRILL **Lunch:** $15-$32 **Dinner:** $19-$35 **Phone:** 212/840-6500 (210)
⩗⩗⩗ **Location:** Between 5th and 6th (Ave of the Americas) aves. 25 W 40th St 10018. **Hours:** 11:30 am-3:30 & 5-11 pm;
Saturday & Sunday brunch. **Reservations:** suggested. **Features:** Tempting selections include succulent filet
American mignon, lobster salad and pork tenderloin. The large, glorious building, which overlooks the park for which
the restaurant is named, offers seasonal seating on the patio and rooftop. Casual dress; cocktails. **Parking:**
no self-parking. **Cards:** AX, DC, DS, MC, VI. Ⓨ

BUBBA GUMP SHRIMP COMPANY **Lunch:** $11-$23 **Dinner:** $11-$23 **Phone:** 212/391-7100
⩗⩗⩗ **Location:** Between 43rd and 44th sts; in Times Square. 1501 Broadway 10036. **Hours:** 11 am-midnight, Fri & Sat-1
am. Closed: 11/22, 12/25. **Features:** The menu comprises shrimp, shrimp and more shrimp, as well as
Seafood burgers, ribs and barbecue. The busy atmosphere and outdoor seating are a real treat for the family. Lots of
memorabilia inside appeals to fans of Forrest Gump. Casual dress; cocktails. **Parking:** no self-parking.
Cards: AX, DS, MC, VI. ♿Ⓜ

BYBLOS **Lunch:** $8-$14 **Dinner:** $30-$35 **Phone:** 212/687-0808 (231)
⩗⩗⩗⩗ **Location:** Jct E 39th St and 3rd Ave. 200 E 39th St 10016. **Hours:** 11:30 am-10:30 pm, Fri-1 am, Sat 1 pm-2 am,
Sun 1 pm-10 pm. Closed: 1/1, 11/22, 12/25. **Reservations:** accepted. **Features:** The casual dining spot
Lebanese employs a charming staff and serves authentic Middle Eastern fare. Start with an appetizer assortment to
sample the various tastes, then move on to specialties such as kebabs, lamb and even vegetarian dishes.
Casual dress; cocktails. **Parking:** street. **Cards:** AX, DC, JC, MC, VI. Ⓨ

(See map and index starting on p. 382)

CAFE BOULUD   Lunch: $19-$36   Dinner: $26-$50   Phone: 212/772-2600   (19)
French
Location: E 76th St and Madison Ave; in Surrey Hotel. 20 E 76th St 10021. **Hours:** noon-2:30 & 5:45-11 pm, Sun & Mon from 5:45 pm. Closed major holidays. **Reservations:** suggested. **Features:** A smart sophisticated dining room in subtle hues provides a lovely place for a beautifully prepared meal. The menu features classic French dishes, seasonal market specialties, vegetable garden focused dishes and dishes showcasing exotic world flavors. Dressy casual; cocktails. **Parking:** no self-parking. **Cards:** AX, DC, MC, VI.

CAFE CENTRO   Lunch: $20-$27   Dinner: $20-$27   Phone: 212/818-1222   (204)
French
Location: Between Lexington and Vanderbilt aves. 200 Park Ave on 45th St 10166. **Hours:** 11:30 am-10:30 pm, Sat from 5 pm. Closed major holidays; also Sun. **Reservations:** suggested. **Features:** A massive stone fireplace encloses eight rotisserie spits laden with roasting chicken, rack of lamb, pork and filet mignon. Strong, sleek lines shape the warm, comfortable dining room, trimmed with beautiful wood, heavy moldings and relief-work. Although dishes are French, they reflect Mediterranean influences. Dressy casual; cocktails. **Parking:** no self-parking. **Cards:** AX, DC, DS, MC, VI.

CAFE DES ARTISTES   Lunch: $16-$25   Dinner: $27-$46   Phone: 212/877-3500   (22)
French
Location: Between Columbus Ave and Central Park W. One W 67th St 10023. **Hours:** noon-3 & 5-midnight, Sat from 11 am, Sun 10 am-3 & 5:30-11 pm. Closed: 12/25. **Reservations:** suggested. **Features:** History abounds in the 76-year-old establishment, once a meeting and eating place for artists that lived in apartments above. French food and famous murals of naked nymphs playing in a richly flowered forest remain for the pleasure of a new group of diners, many dressed for the opera or performances at Lincoln Center. Rich flavors punctuate such dishes as steak frites, pan-roasted squab with garlic flan, tea-smoked duck breast, crisp duck confit and Wiener or sturgeon schnitzel. Dressy casual; cocktails. **Parking:** no self-parking. **Cards:** AX, CB, DC, JC, MC, VI.

CAFE EUROPA   Lunch: $7-$13   Dinner: $7-$13   Phone: 212/977-4030   (46)
American
Location: At 7th Ave. 205 W 57th St 10019. **Hours:** 7 am-1 am. **Features:** The unpretentious bakery sticks to a menu of mostly lighter fare, pasta, sandwiches, salad and pizza, as well as exceptional European pastry and dessert. Bright lighting adds to the energetic, upbeat mood of the dining room. Gourmet coffees are a treat. Casual dress; beer & wine only. **Parking:** no self-parking. **Cards:** AX, DC, MC, VI.

CAFE EVERGREEN   Lunch: $6-$8   Dinner: $7-$16   Phone: 212/744-3266   (44)
Chinese
Location: At 69th St. 1288 1st Ave 10021. **Hours:** 11:30 am-10:30 pm. Closed: 11/22. **Features:** This is a comfortable place to take children, and the menu offers something for everyone. Tempting choices include Beijing pork filets, pine-nut crispy sea bass, shredded pork with spicy pickle and the exquisite Grand Marnier prawns. Weekends are busy with patrons vying for seats for an exceptional dim sum offering. Casual dress; cocktails. **Parking:** no self-parking. **Cards:** AX, DC, MC, VI.

CAFE FIORELLO   Lunch: $15-$23   Dinner: $25-$35   Phone: 212/595-5330   (29)
Italian
Location: At 64th St; across from Lincoln Center. 1900 Broadway 10023. **Hours:** 11:30 am-12:30 am, Sat from 10 am, Sun 10 am-11 pm. **Reservations:** suggested. **Features:** Settle into the colorful, festive dining room to enjoy award-winning gourmet pizza, delicacies from the antipasto bar and daily fresh fish selections. The wide sidewalk patio is a delightful spot in good weather. Casual dress; cocktails. **Parking:** street. **Cards:** AX, DC, DS, MC, VI.

CAFE GRAY   Lunch: $26-$32   Dinner: $26-$38   Phone: 212/823-6338   (39)
French
Location: In AOL-Time Warner Building, 3rd floor. 10 Columbus Circle 10019. **Hours:** 11:30 am-2:15 & 5:30-10:30 pm, Wed-Sat to 11 pm, Sun 5 pm-10 pm. Closed: 12/25. **Reservations:** suggested. **Features:** A celebrated chef has put his name on the exceptional cafe. The open kitchen slightly obstructs the impressive views of Central Park and the city. Representative of the incredible food is the chef's signature risotto mushroom fricassee with chicken broth and wild mushrooms, which melts in the mouth. The braised short rib of beef with soft grits and Meaux mustard sauce also is memorable. All dishes are dramatically presented. Dressy casual; cocktails. **Parking:** on-site (fee). **Cards:** AX, DC, DS, MC, VI.

CAFE LUXEMBOURG   Lunch: $12-$30   Dinner: $20-$32   Phone: 212/873-7411   (9)
French
Location: Between Amsterdam and West End aves. 200 W 70th St 10023. **Hours:** 8 am-midnight, Sat & Sun from 9 am. Closed: 11/22, 12/25. **Reservations:** suggested. **Features:** This vibrant art-deco bistro has been a bustling neighborhood favorite for years, due in no small part to the classic French fare served in its bright and casual dining room. The kitchen prepares all the usual suspects, including steak au poivre, roasted chicken and frisee salad with lardons, with great aplomb. When in season, do try the fried baby artichokes served with olive tapenade. Casual dress; cocktails. **Parking:** street. **Cards:** AX, DC, MC, VI.

CAFE PIERRE   Lunch: $18-$36   Dinner: $18-$36   Phone: 212/940-8195   (50)
International
Location: At 5th Ave; in The Pierre New York-A Taj Hotel. 5th Ave at 61st St 10021. **Hours:** 7 am-10:30, noon-2:30 & 6-11 pm. **Reservations:** suggested. **Features:** An old New York style punctuates the richly opulent dining room, in which both creative contemporary and traditional classic entrees are served. Enjoy light lunches and high tea on the trompe l'oeil Queen's Court rotunda. The tasting menu is exquisite. Semi-formal attire; cocktails; entertainment. **Parking:** valet. **Cards:** AX, DC, DS, MC, VI.

CAFE ST. BART'S   Lunch: $17-$32   Dinner: $17-$32   Phone: 212/888-2664   (174)
California
Location: Jct 50th St and Park Ave. 109 E 50th St 10022. **Hours:** 8-11 am, 11:30-3 & 6-10 pm, Sat 11:30 am-4 & 6-10 pm, Sun 11:30 am-4 pm. **Reservations:** suggested. **Features:** The eatery offers stylish American food in a historic setting adjacent to St. Bartholomew's Church. In warm months, eat on the terrace with the background of the church above. The menu is Californian with selections such as grilled baby lamb chops and batter-fried okra with spicy dip. Casual dress; cocktails. **Parking:** street. **Cards:** AX, DC, MC, VI.

(See map and index starting on p. 382)

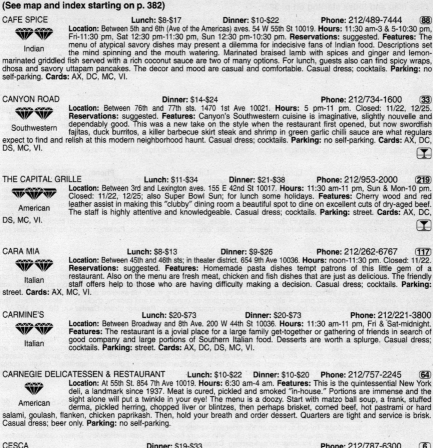

CAFE SPICE　　　　**Lunch:** $8-$17　　　　**Dinner:** $10-$22　　　　**Phone:** 212/489-7444　　(88)
Location: Between 5th and 6th (Ave of the Americas) aves. 54 W 55th St 10019. **Hours:** 11:30 am-3 & 5-10:30 pm,
Indian　Fri-11:30 pm, Sat 12:30 pm-11:30 pm, Sun 12:30 pm-10:30 pm. **Reservations:** suggested. **Features:** The
menu of atypical savory dishes may present a dilemma for indecisive fans of Indian food. Descriptions set
the mind spinning and the mouth watering. Marinated braised lamb with spices and ginger and lemon-
marinated griddled fish served with a rich coconut sauce are two of many options. For lunch, guests also can find spicy wraps,
dhosa and savory uttapam pancakes. The decor and mood are casual and comfortable. Casual dress; cocktails. **Parking:** no
self-parking. **Cards:** AX, DC, MC, VI.

CANYON ROAD　　　　　　　**Dinner:** $14-$24　　　　　　　**Phone:** 212/734-1600　　(33)
Location: Between 76th and 77th sts. 1470 1st Ave 10021. **Hours:** 5 pm-11 pm. Closed: 11/22, 12/25.
Reservations: suggested. **Features:** Canyon's Southwestern cuisine is imaginative, slightly nouvelle and
Southwestern　dependably good. This was a new take on the style when the restaurant first opened, but now swordfish
fajitas, duck burritos, a killer barbecue skirt steak and shrimp in green garlic chilli sauce are what regulars
expect to find and relish at this modern neighborhood haunt. Casual dress; cocktails. **Parking:** no self-parking. **Cards:** AX, DC,
DS, MC, VI.

THE CAPITAL GRILLE　　　**Lunch:** $11-$34　　　　**Dinner:** $21-$38　　　　**Phone:** 212/953-2000　　(219)
Location: Between 3rd and Lexington aves. 155 E 42nd St 10017. **Hours:** 11:30 am-11 pm, Sun & Mon-10 pm.
Closed: 11/22, 12/25; also Super Bowl Sun; for lunch some holidays. **Features:** Cherry wood and red
American　leather assist in making this "clubby" dining room a beautiful spot to dine on excellent cuts of dry-aged beef.
The staff is highly attentive and knowledgeable. Casual dress; cocktails. **Parking:** street. **Cards:** AX, DC,
DS, MC, VI.

CARA MIA　　　　　**Lunch:** $8-$13　　　　**Dinner:** $9-$26　　　　**Phone:** 212/262-6767　　(117)
Location: Between 45th and 46th sts; in theater district. 654 9th Ave 10036. **Hours:** noon-11:30 pm. Closed: 11/22.
Reservations: suggested. **Features:** Homemade pasta dishes tempt patrons of this little gem of a
Italian　restaurant. Also on the menu are fresh meat, chicken and fish dishes that are just as delicious. The friendly
staff offers help to those who are having difficulty making a decision. Casual dress; cocktails. **Parking:**
street. **Cards:** AX, MC, VI.

CARMINE'S　　　　**Lunch:** $20-$73　　　　**Dinner:** $20-$73　　　　**Phone:** 212/221-3800
Location: Between Broadway and 8th Ave. 200 W 44th St 10036. **Hours:** 11:30 am-11 pm, Fri & Sat-midnight.
Features: The restaurant is a jovial place for a large family get-together or gathering of friends in search of
Italian　good company and large portions of Southern Italian food. Desserts are worth a splurge. Casual dress;
cocktails. **Parking:** street. **Cards:** AX, DC, DS, MC, VI.

CARNEGIE DELICATESSEN & RESTAURANT　**Lunch:** $10-$22　**Dinner:** $10-$20　**Phone:** 212/757-2245　(64)
Location: At 55th St. 854 7th Ave 10019. **Hours:** 6:30 am-4 am. **Features:** This is the quintessential New York
deli, a landmark since 1937. Meat is cured, pickled and smoked "in-house." Portions are immense and the
American　sight alone will put a twinkle in your eye! The menu is a doozy. Start with matzo ball soup, a frank, stuffed
derma, pickled herring, chopped liver or blintzes, then perhaps brisket, corned beef, hot pastrami or hard
salami, goulash, flanken, chicken paprikash. Then, hold your breath and order dessert. Quarters are tight and service is brisk.
Casual dress; beer only. **Parking:** no self-parking.

CESCA　　　　　　　**Dinner:** $19-$33　　　　　　　**Phone:** 212/787-6300　　(6)
Location: Between Amsterdam and Columbus aves. 164 W 75th St 10024. **Hours:** 5 pm-11 pm, Fri & Sat-11:30
pm, Sun 5 pm-10 pm. Closed: 12/25. **Reservations:** suggested. **Features:** Be sure to make
Italian　reservations for this popular spot as it is always buzzing with locals in both the lounge and the dining room.
The menu features an upscale mix of "comfort foods" including antipasto selections to start, fresh
homemade pastas and a variety of grilled meats and fishes. The ambience is bustling with tight table spacing and a loud
boisterous feeling. Service is warm and personable. Casual dress; cocktails. **Parking:** no self-parking. **Cards:** AX, DC, MC, VI.

CHARLIE PALMER'S METRAZUR　　**Lunch:** $19-$27　　**Dinner:** $19-$30　　**Phone:** 212/687-4600　　(212)
Location: Grand Central Terminal, East Balcony, Main Concourse. Grand Central Terminal 10017. **Hours:** 11:30 am-3
& 5-10:30 pm, Sat from 5 pm. Closed: Sun. **Reservations:** suggested. **Features:** An innovative menu and a
Continental　fabulous location make this a popular spot for a power lunch or dinner experience. Diners enjoy the creative
menu choice, contemporary decor and the bustling ambiance of the setting. Casual dress; cocktails.
Parking: no self-parking. **Cards:** AX, MC, VI.

CHEVYS FRESH MEX-TIMES SQUARE　　**Lunch:** $10-$18　　**Dinner:** $10-$18　　**Phone:** 212/302-4010
Location: Between 7th and 8th aves. 259 W 42nd St 10036. **Hours:** 11 am-1 am, Fri & Sat-2 am. **Features:** With
a hip Latin/Mexican decor and upscale bar, the cantina nurtures a festive atmosphere. The menu boasts
Mexican　mesquite-grilled chicken, beef, shrimp and vegetable fajitas. Casual dress; cocktails. **Parking:** no self-
parking. **Cards:** AX, DS, MC, VI.

CHEZ JOSEPHINE　　　　　**Dinner:** $18-$32　　　　　**Phone:** 212/594-1925　　(155)
Location: Between 9th and Dyer aves. 414 W 42nd St 10036. **Hours:** 5 pm-1 am, Sun noon-10 pm. Closed major
holidays; also Mon. **Reservations:** suggested. **Features:** Named in honor of Josephine Baker, the cozy
bistro is owned and operated by her adopted son, Jean-Claude. He and his staff have created a wonderfully
romantic dining spot where imaginative dishes are whipped up and served with flair. This is an ideal location
French　for a pre-theater dinner or a night on the town. Dressy casual; cocktails. **Parking:** street. **Cards:** AX,
MC, VI.

(See map and index starting on p. 382)

CHIAM
▼▼▼▼ ▼
Chinese

Lunch: $20-$25 **Dinner:** $20-$25 **Phone:** 212/371-2323 [202]
Location: Between Lexington and 3rd aves. 160 E 48th St 10017. **Hours:** 11:30 am-11 pm, Sat 5 pm-11 pm. Closed: 11/22. **Reservations:** suggested. **Features:** Carefully selected wines complement creative preparations of Cantonese food. Diners face hard choices from a long menu that includes hand-shredded chicken in oyster sauce, filet mignon kew, Grand Marnier prawns, salt and pepper prawns and crispy spicy sea bass. Spa and grill options are also available. The restaurant, which got its name from combining the words "Chinese" and "American," is a favorite for dim sum. Dressy casual; cocktails. **Parking:** no self-parking. **Cards:** AX, DC, DS, MC, VI.

CHIMICHURRI GRILL
▼▼▼▼
Argentine

Lunch: $15-$21 **Dinner:** $17-$28 **Phone:** 212/586-8655 [149]
Location: Between 43rd and 44th sts; in theater district. 606 9th Ave 10036. **Hours:** noon-3 & 5-11:30 pm, Sat & Sun from 4 pm. Closed: 11/22, 12/25. **Reservations:** suggested. **Features:** Named for the addictive Argentinean salsa that accompanies their delicious grilled steaks, this tiny theater district spot has the feel of someone's living room. There are other items on the menu that are also sure to please such as savory empanadas and daily-changing handmade raviolis. Casual dress; cocktails. **Parking:** street. **Cards:** AX, DC, DS, MC, VI.

CHINA GRILL
▼▼▼▼
Asian

Lunch: $13-$39 **Dinner:** $13-$39 **Phone:** 212/333-7788 [109]
Location: Between 5th and 6th (Ave of the Americas) aves. 60 W 53rd St 10019. **Hours:** 11:45 am-5 & 5:30-10:45 pm, Thurs & Fri-midnight, Sat 5:30 pm-midnight, Sun 5:30 pm-10 pm. Closed major holidays. **Reservations:** suggested. **Features:** Reputation has never waned in all the years the renowned businessmen's staple has been open. The space itself is immense and wide. The din may seem like a roar at times, but sleek, shiny black dining rooms draw people to them. The menu holds such promise as lamb spare ribs, spicy beef and scallion dumplings, coriander-dusted shrimp with yuzu glaze, barbecue braised short ribs, miso-glazed black cod and duck two ways. Dishes are sized to share family style with the table. Dressy casual; cocktails. **Parking:** no self-parking. **Cards:** AX, DC, MC, VI.

CHIN CHIN
▼▼▼
Nouvelle Chinese

Lunch: $12-$18 **Dinner:** $15-$22 **Phone:** 212/888-4555 [201]
Location: Between 2nd and 3rd aves. 216 E 49th St 10017. **Hours:** noon-midnight, Sat & Sun from 5 pm. **Reservations:** accepted. **Features:** Chinese food is a treat at the modern, sophisticated restaurant, which presents a menu of traditional and familiar dishes. Assorted dumplings and ribs flow from the kitchen, and many patrons can't resist Grand Marnier prawns. Peking duck, tea-smoked duck with scallion bread and boneless duck l'Orange are most popular, although such standards as orange beef and sesame chicken are also excellent. The $20 four-course lunch is one of the best deals in town. Dressy casual; cocktails. **Parking:** street. **Cards:** AX, CB, DC, MC, VI.

CHINESE MIRCH
▼▼▼ ▼
Chinese

Lunch: $7-$14 **Dinner:** $7-$14 **Phone:** 212/532-3663 [237]
Location: At 28th St. 120 Lexington Ave 10016. **Hours:** noon-3 & 5:30-10:30 pm. Closed: 7/4, 11/22, 12/25. **Features:** The unassuming little place offers efficient service, clean but simple surroundings and an interesting menu. An unusual fusion of Chinese and Indian flavors results in some surprising dishes, including chili chicken, crispy Szechuan lamb, Szechuan prawns and chili-garlic noodles. Chicken lollipops are a spicy, delectable treat, and the crispy okra and fried cauliflower starters are no slouches either. This place is a notable local favorite. Casual dress. **Parking:** no self-parking. **Cards:** AX, DS, MC, VI.

CHURRASCARIA PLATAFORMA
(AAA)
▼▼ ▼
Brazilian

Lunch: $31 **Dinner:** $52 **Phone:** 212/245-0505 [96]
Location: Between 8th and 9th aves; in Belvedere Hotel. 316 W 49th St 10019. **Hours:** noon-midnight. **Reservations:** suggested. **Features:** The lively, festive spot allows for a distinctive Brazilian dining experience. Try not to fill up on the extensive variety of salads and antipasto because the true delights await as servers parade by with sabers filled with savory beef, lamb, pork and poultry. Dressy casual; cocktails; entertainment. **Parking:** no self-parking. **Cards:** AX, DC, DS, MC, VI.

CIBO
▼▼▼▼
Continental

Lunch: $15-$27 **Dinner:** $15-$35 **Phone:** 212/681-1616 [227]
Location: At 41st St. 767 2nd Ave 10017. **Hours:** 11:30 am-3 & 5:30-10 pm, Sat & Sun 11 am-3 & 5-10 pm; Saturday & Sunday brunch. **Reservations:** suggested. **Features:** A romantic aura punctuates the modern and casual dining room, which is accented with floral arrangements and dramatic, freshly cut branches. The seasonal menu centers on Tuscan-American cuisine. Weekend brunches are popular, as are the pastry chef's decadent creations. Dressy casual; cocktails. **Parking:** no self-parking. **Cards:** AX, CB, DC, DS, MC, VI.

CINQUANTA RISTORANTE
▼▼▼▼
Italian

Lunch: $13-$29 **Dinner:** $13-$29 **Phone:** 212/759-5050 [170]
Location: Between Madison and Park aves. 50 E 50th St 10022. **Hours:** noon-11 pm, Sun from 5 pm. Closed: 7/4. **Reservations:** suggested. **Features:** The bright dining room has an art deco feel. Representative of dishes is bass encrusted with shredded potatoes and served in thickened fish broth. Game is available in season. Outfitted in black-and-white attire, the wait staff delivers old-school, professional service. Casual dress; cocktails. **Parking:** street. **Cards:** AX, DC, DS, JC, MC, VI.

CIRO
▼▼ ▼▼
Italian

Lunch: $9-$17 **Dinner:** $18-$40 **Phone:** 212/307-5484 [97]
Location: At 49th St. 813 8th Ave 10019. **Hours:** noon-11 pm, Fri & Sat-midnight, Sun noon-9 pm. Closed: 12/25. **Features:** Located in the heart of the theater district close to Broadway shows and Times Square, the restaurant features many creative selections and homemade pastas. Casual dress; cocktails. **Parking:** street. **Cards:** AX, CB, DC, DS, JC, MC, VI.

CITE
(AAA)
▼▼▼▼
Steak House

Lunch: $20-$33 **Dinner:** $20-$33 **Phone:** 212/956-7100 [116]
Location: Between 6th (Ave of the Americas) and 7th aves. 120 W 51st St 10020. **Hours:** noon-2 & 5-10 pm, Fri-11:30 pm, Sat 5 pm-11:30 pm, Sun 5 pm-10 pm. Closed major holidays. **Reservations:** suggested. **Features:** An upscale steak house with handsome and handsome art deco decor slightly reminiscent of "nouvelle Paris." The popular wine dinners are a bargain. Dressy casual; cocktails. **Parking:** no self-parking. **Cards:** AX, DC, DS, MC, VI.

(See map and index starting on p. 382)

CITY LOBSTER AND CRAB COMPANY   Lunch: $19-$39   Dinner: $19-$39   Phone: 212/354-1717   143
▼▼▼▼   **Location:** Between 6th (Ave of the Americas) and 7th aves. 121 W 49th St 10020. **Hours:** 11:30 am-10 pm, Fri-11 pm, Sat 4:30 pm-11 pm, Sun 10:30 am-10 pm. Closed: 12/25. **Reservations:** suggested. **Features:** Right in the middle of Rockefeller Center and Times Square, this gem of a restaurant is the place to be for diners
Seafood   seeking fresh seafood. Friendly staff members assist guests not only in choosing the best entree but also in picking out the best Broadway show to see. Casual dress; cocktails. **Parking:** no self-parking. **Cards:** AX, DC, DS, JC, MC, VI.

COMPASS   Dinner: $18-$38   Phone: 212/875-8600   8
▼▼▼▼   **Location:** Between Amsterdam and West End aves. 208 W 70th St 10023. **Hours:** 5 pm-11:15 pm, Sun also 11:30 am-2:30 pm; Sunday brunch. **Reservations:** suggested. **Features:** The seats are so comfortable guests
American   could sit all night amid sophisticated, albeit understated, contemporary surroundings. Representative of the offerings are yellowtail snapper tapenade, roast guinea hen with chanterelles, steamed black sea bass and pan-seared hanger steak. Savory dishes reflect a new American flair and creativity. Another selection is the prix fixe meal. Dressy casual; cocktails. **Parking:** street. **Cards:** AX, DS, MC, VI.

COSTA DEL SOL RESTAURANT   Lunch: $8-$29   Dinner: $13-$36   Phone: 212/541-8382   73
▼▼▼   **Location:** Corner of 9th Ave and W 50th St. 369 W 50th St 10019. **Hours:** noon-11 pm, Fri-midnight, Sat 1 pm-midnight, Sun 1 pm-11 pm. **Features:** Authentic Spanish cuisine served in a casual setting. Meals start with
Spanish   traditional appetizers followed by a large menu of paella, mariscada in garlic sauce or green sauce, shrimp Diablo, chicken with almond sauce, chicken and rice, veal with wine sauce, as well as selection of daily specials are among the many choices. Casual dress; cocktails. **Parking:** on-site (fee). **Cards:** AX, CB, DC, DS, JC, MC, VI.

CROTON RESERVOIR TAVERN   Lunch: $13-$27   Dinner: $18-$32   Phone: 212/997-6835   207
▼▼▼   **Location:** Between 6th Ave (Ave of the Americas) and Broadway. 108 W 40th St 10018. **Hours:** 11:30 am-midnight, Thurs & Fri-2 am, Sat 2:30 pm-2 am. Closed: 12/25; also Sun. **Reservations:** accepted. **Features:** Named
American   after the famous 150-million-gallon Croton Reservoir, this delightful upscale tavern offers dining on the main level and additional area in the quieter cellar. Very well prepared pub fare and a more extensive, finer menu are available in the evenings, featuring grilled salmon, Asian pork chops, baby back ribs and yellowfin tuna to name but a few. Casual dress; cocktails. **Parking:** no self-parking. **Cards:** AX, MC, VI.

DAE DONG MANHATTAN   Lunch: $10-$36   Dinner: $10-$36   Phone: 212/967-1900   233
▼▼▼   **Location:** Between 5th Ave and Broadway. 17 W 32nd St 10001. **Hours:** 11 am-midnight. Closed: Sun. **Reservations:** required. **Features:** Named after a famous river in the owner's hometown, this restaurant
Korean   serves authentic Korean dishes and barbecue delights. Be prepared for the tempting selection of appetizers they offer. Casual dress; cocktails. **Parking:** no self-parking. **Cards:** AX, MC, VI.

DALLAS BBQ   Lunch: $5-$10   Dinner: $7-$15   Phone: 212/873-2004   11
▼▼   **Location:** Between Columbus Ave and Central Park W. 27 W 72nd St 10023. **Hours:** noon-midnight, Fri & Sat-1 am. **Features:** Spacious, like Texas, this very popular, upbeat restaurant serves huge portions of everything,
American   including rotisseried chicken, steaks, hickory smoked ribs, burgers and spicy wings. Casual dress; cocktails. **Parking:** no self-parking. **Cards:** AX, DC, MC, VI.

DANIEL   Dinner: $92-$168   Phone: 212/288-0033   42
▼▼▼▼▼   **Location:** Between Park and Madison aves. 60 E 65th St 10021. **Hours:** 5:45 pm-11 pm, Fri & Sat from 5:30 pm. Closed major holidays; also Sun. **Reservations:** required. **Features:** Daniel Boulud masterfully brings the essences of France to the Upper East Side restaurant. Indirect lighting and warm, coppery hues highlight
French   the architectural accents of the turn-of-the-20th-century building. Superb food, wine and service astound even the most refined foodie. Semi-formal attire; cocktails. **Parking:** no self-parking. **Cards:** AX, DC, MC, VI.

DANIELA'S TRATTORIA   Lunch: $9-$18   Dinner: $9-$18   Phone: 212/869-3585   147
▼▼ ▼▼   **Location:** Between 45th and 46th sts. 728 8th Ave 10036. **Hours:** 6 am-midnight. **Reservations:** accepted. **Features:** Located in the theater district, the affordable restaurant serves large portions of freshly prepared
Italian   Italian cuisine. Popular menu items include black pasta made with squid ink, chicken parmigiana and veal florentine. Casual dress; beer & wine only. **Parking:** no self-parking. **Cards:** AX, MC, VI.

DAVIDBURKE & DONATELLA   Lunch: $16-$44   Dinner: $22-$44   Phone: 212/813-2121   66
▼▼▼ ▼▼▼   **Location:** Between Park and Lexington aves. 133 E 61st St 10021. **Hours:** 11:30 am-2:30 & 5-10:30 pm, Fri-11 pm, Sat 5 pm-11 pm, Sun 11 am-2:30 & 4:30-9 pm. Closed: 12/25. **Reservations:** required.
American   **Features:** Stylish, tailored, bold, sophisticated and a little bit swanky describes the dining room and the food, but the dishes go further still with a fun look. But serious is the cooking that brings forth crisp, angry lobster "cocktail," sea scallops Benedict with chorizo oil and lobster foam, gingersnap barbecue squab with foie gras corn torte and specials so notable that the chef hand-writes and signs the menus. A white stretch limousine parked outside is the smoking section. Dressy casual; cocktails. **Parking:** no self-parking. **Cards:** AX, DC, MC, VI.

DAWAT   Lunch: $13-$23   Dinner: $13-$23   Phone: 212/355-7555   118
▼▼▼   **Location:** Between 2nd and 3rd aves. 210 E 58th St 10022. **Hours:** 11:30 am-2:45 & 5:30-10:45 pm, Fri & Sat-11:15 pm, Sun 5 pm-10:30 pm. **Reservations:** suggested. **Features:** Reserved formality is evident in every
Indian   aspect of the restaurant—from its menu of creatively prepared dishes to its servers in crisp uniform. Wonderful ground lamb meatballs are served in a thick puree of onions, tomatoes and chilis. Dressy casual; cocktails. **Parking:** no self-parking. **Cards:** AX, DC, DS, MC, VI.

DB BISTRO MODERNE   Lunch: $27-$38   Dinner: $27-$38   Phone: 212/391-2400   188
▼▼ ▼▼   **Location:** Between 5th and 6th (Ave of the Americas) aves. 55 W 44th St 10036. **Hours:** noon-2:30 & 5-11 pm, Sun 5 pm-10 pm. **Reservations:** suggested. **Features:** Casual yet sleek, with design in mind in every crevice,
French   the dining rooms are handsome and stylish. As for the food, Daniel Boulud may play around but never misses with his dishes. Artful use of the freshest ingredients mean plates go back to the kitchen empty. Dressy casual; cocktails. **Parking:** no self-parking. **Cards:** AX, DC, MC, VI.

(See map and index starting on p. 382)

DEGREZIA   Lunch: $17-$34   Dinner: $25-$50   Phone: 212/750-5353   (190)
Italian
Location: Between 2nd and 3rd aves. 231 E 50th St 10022. **Hours:** noon-3 & 5-10 pm, Sat from 5 pm. Closed: 1/1, 11/22, 12/25; also Sun. **Reservations:** suggested. **Features:** This convenient East Side location serves Italian cuisine featuring veal specialties from Tuscany and other authentic regional Italian dishes, along with a great selection of wines to complement your meal. The dining room is ornate with golden oak wood, etched mirrors, brass fixtures and a comfortable, charming atmosphere. Casual dress; cocktails. **Parking:** street. **Cards:** AX, DC, MC, VI.

THE DELTA GRILL   Lunch: $10-$22   Dinner: $10-$22   Phone: 212/956-0934   (123)
Regional American
Location: At 48th St. 700 9th Ave 10036. **Hours:** noon-midnight, Sat & Sun from 11:30 am. Closed: 12/25. **Features:** Diners here will think they are in a Louisiana roadside restaurant. Large portions of regional favorites such as jambalaya, gumbo and etouffee are on the menu which features Creole and Cajun cuisine as well as barbecue. Casual dress; cocktails. **Parking:** no self-parking. **Cards:** AX, DS, MC, VI.

DISTRICT   Lunch: $24-$32   Dinner: $26-$36   Phone: 212/485-2999   (160)
American
Location: Between 6th (Ave of the Americas) and 7th aves; in The Muse. 130 W 46th St 10036. **Hours:** 6:30 am-10:30, noon-2 & 5-10 pm, Sat 7 am-11 & 5-10 pm, Sun 7 am-11 am. **Reservations:** suggested. **Features:** Richly designed to resemble a theater with the open kitchen being center stage. District, just off Broadway, offers an eclectic menu that ranges from luxury box items, including truffle and foie gras selections to seafood tacos and Tokyo roast. Semi-formal attire; cocktails. **Parking:** valet. **Cards:** AX, CB, DC, DS, JC, MC, VI.

DIWAN   Lunch: $13-$26   Dinner: $13-$26   Phone: 212/593-5425   (200)
Indian
Location: Between Lexington and 3rd aves. 148 E 48th St 10017. **Hours:** 11:30 am-2:30 & 5-10:30 pm, Fri-11 pm, Sat 11:30 am-3 & 5-11 pm, Sun 11:30 am-3 & 5-10:30 pm. **Reservations:** accepted. **Features:** The seasoned chef prepares not only wonderfully cooked, familiar dishes but also more intriguing choices. Stuffed chicken breast with lemon rice and tamarind sauce, basil chicken, tandoori jhinga, tandoori halibut and wild boar chops are a few lively dishes. Starters of Goan shrimp, crab beggar's purses and crisp vegetable fritters are little prizes. Chai- and cardamom-infused pot de creme, richly creamy and smooth, is a refreshing end to the meal. Casual dress; cocktails. **Parking:** no self-parking. **Cards:** AX, DC, MC, VI.

DJANGO   Lunch: $14-$24   Dinner: $19-$28   Phone: 212/871-6600   (203)
French
Location: At 46th St. 480 Lexington Ave 10167. **Hours:** 11:30 am-2 & 5:30-10:30 pm, Sat from 6 pm. Closed major holidays; also Sun. **Reservations:** suggested. **Features:** Spicy, exotic decor evokes the mystery and adventure that come to mind with the word "gypsy," as in famed gypsy jazz musician Django Reinhart. Purple and green jewel tones, gold-stenciled walls, bead curtains, blown-glass chandeliers and leather sofa and armchair seating say anything but brasserie, which this, regardless, is. Tweaking is done to such dishes as mackerel pissaladiere, tuna tartare with yuzu essence, duck confit with Muscat caramel and tagine of beef with lemon grass. Dressy casual; cocktails. **Parking:** no self-parking. **Cards:** AX, DC, MC, VI.

DOCKS OYSTER BAR & SEAFOOD GRILL   Lunch: $15-$28   Dinner: $15-$28   Phone: 212/986-8080   (225)
Seafood
Location: Between 40th and 41st sts. 633 3rd Ave 10017. **Hours:** Open 5/13-4/30; 11:30 am-11 pm, Fri-midnight, Sat 5 pm-midnight, Sun 11:30 am-2:45 & 4-10 pm. Closed: 12/25. **Reservations:** suggested. **Features:** The lively, noisy dining room is not a distraction from the straightforward fresh seafood preparations, which are at the heart of a varied menu that includes some selections of chicken, pasta and steak. The long-running establishment caters to both businessmen and ladies lunching. Generous but not gross portions add to the appeal. The wait staff, in casual dress, delivers knowledgeable service. Casual dress; cocktails. **Parking:** no self-parking. **Cards:** AX, DC, DS, MC, VI.

DOMENICO   Lunch: $16-$34   Dinner: $16-$34   Phone: 212/682-0310   (223)
Italian
Location: Between Park and Lexington aves. 120 E 40th St 10016. **Hours:** noon-9:30 pm, Sat 5 pm-9 pm. Closed: 11/22, 12/24, 12/25; also Sun. **Reservations:** suggested. **Features:** Adjacent to the Bedford Hotel, this old-world Italian restaurant offers a cozy atmosphere with classic Italian specialties in hearty portions. Casual dress; cocktails. **Parking:** street. **Cards:** AX, CB, DS, MC, VI.

DOS CAMINOS   Lunch: $11-$20   Dinner: $11-$28   Phone: 212/294-1000   (239)
Mexican
Location: Between 26th and 27th sts. 373 Park Ave S 10016. **Hours:** 11:30 am-4 & 5-midnight, Fri-12:30 am, Sat 5 pm-12:30 am, Sun 5 pm-11 pm. Closed: 12/25. **Reservations:** suggested. **Features:** A sense of fun and style prevails at the casual space in which patrons enjoy flavorful food. Starters of chipotle meatballs with handmade tortillas, roasted plantain empanadas with chipotle aioli, seviches, tacos with grilled Kobe beef or mahi mahi and slow-roasted pork demonstrate the variety of flavors. Tasty entrees—including chipotle barbecue pork ribs with black bean chorizo chili and cumin-braised cabbage and grilled marinated Angus skirt steak—make a case for multiple meals here. Casual dress; cocktails. **Parking:** no self-parking. **Cards:** AX, DS, MC, VI.

EAST RIVER CAFE   Lunch: $12-$20   Dinner: $12-$20   Phone: 212/980-3144   (111)
Italian
Location: At 61st St. 1111 1st Ave 10021. **Hours:** noon-4 & 5-11 pm. **Reservations:** suggested. **Features:** Lending to the simple decor are small black-and-white photographs, lanterns on the walls and a handsome copper-topped bar. On the menu are such choices as lobster-stuffed pasta with shrimp in fra diavolo sauce, pasta with grilled sausage, broccoli rabe in garlic and oil, monkfish with lemon-thyme-white wine sauce and pasta stuffed with roasted meat and mushrooms in a sauce of shallots, sage, brandy and cream. Creative and well-prepared dishes all are redolent with flavor. Casual dress; cocktails. **Parking:** no self-parking. **Cards:** AX, DC, MC, VI.

ENGLISH IS ITALIAN   Lunch: $14-$34   Dinner: $20-$42   Phone: 212/404-1700   (228)
Italian
Location: At 40th St. 622 3rd Ave 10017. **Hours:** 11:30 am-2 & 5:30-10 pm, Thurs & Fri-11 pm, Sat 5:30 pm-11 pm, Sun 5 pm-10 pm. Closed major holidays. **Reservations:** suggested. **Features:** The handsome, wide-open space—with a striking decor accented in copper, brown and black—offers much visual stimulation both high and low and comfortable seating from which to enjoy the view. Menu options include plates of pasta and risotto; dry-aged steak, which is marinated and grilled over wood embers; and such fish dishes as whole wood-grilled trout and roasted salmon. Dressy casual; cocktails. **Parking:** no self-parking. **Cards:** AX, DC, MC, VI.

(See map and index starting on p. 382)

ESCA
▽▽▽▽
Seafood
Lunch: $16-$28   **Dinner:** $19-$35   **Phone:** 212/564-7272   (150)
Location: 9th Ave; in theater district. 402 W 43rd St 10036. **Hours:** noon-2:30 & 5-11:30 pm, Sun 4:30 pm-10:30 pm, Mon noon-2:30 & 5-10:30 pm. Closed: 11/22, 12/25. **Reservations:** required. **Features:** Celebrity chef Mario Batali and David Pasternack, a James Beard Award winner for '04, interpret the coastal cuisine of Italy, which means all manner of fish and shellfish baked whole, mixed in pasta or served raw, crudo-style, with a little olive oil, spices and maybe some citrus. The not-to-be-missed raw section of the menu will delight those who thought raw fish began and ended with sushi. Casual dress; cocktails. **Parking:** no self-parking. **Cards:** AX, DC, MC, VI. ⵡ

ESS-A-BAGEL
▽
American
Lunch: $2-$10   **Dinner:** $2-$10   **Phone:** 212/980-1010   (184)
Location: Between 50th and 51st sts. 831 3rd Ave 10022. **Hours:** 6 am-9 pm, Sat & Sun 7 am-5 pm. Closed major holidays. **Features:** The unpretentious spot is a favorite for classic New York bagels, which are served with spreads, including vegetarian, tofu and such smoked fish as sturgeon, nova lox, sable, whitefish and baked salmon. Also on the menu are reasonably priced salads, smoked meat and fish platters, pastries and cookies. Casual dress. **Parking:** no self-parking. **Cards:** AX, DC, DS, JC, MC, VI.

ESTIATORIO MILOS
▽▽▽▽
Nouvelle Greek
Lunch: $20-$35   **Dinner:** $45-$75   **Phone:** 212/245-7400   (69)
Location: Between 6th (Ave of the Americas) and 7th aves. 125 W 55th St 10019. **Hours:** noon-2:45 & 5-11:30 pm, Sat from 5 pm, Sun 5 pm-10:45 pm. Closed: 1/1, 11/22, 12/25. **Reservations:** suggested. **Features:** Upscale Greek cuisine is made from choice quality seafood, some exhibited in an agora-like market display. In the open kitchen, chefs show their skill in preparing sushi-quality Mediterranean octopus, varieties of Greek spreads and seafood dishes using the finest olive oils and herbs. Dressy casual; cocktails. **Parking:** street. **Cards:** AX, MC, VI. ⵡ

FAMOUS ORIGINAL RAY'S PIZZA
▽
Pizza
Lunch: $3-$23   **Dinner:** $3-$23   **Phone:** 212/974-9381   (74)
Location: Between W 53rd and W 54th sts. 831 7th Ave 10019. **Hours:** 24 hours. **Features:** Established in 1964, the 24-hour eatery is now considered an institution and a must for pizza lovers. There are several other locations around the city. Casual dress; beer only. **Parking:** street. **Cards:** AX, MC, VI.

FELIDIA
▽▽▽▽
Northern Italian
Lunch: $18-$27   **Dinner:** $18-$32   **Phone:** 212/758-1479   (120)
Location: Between 2nd and 3rd aves. 243 E 58th St 10022. **Hours:** noon-2:30 & 5-11 pm, Sat from 5 pm, Sun 4 pm-10 pm. Closed major holidays. **Reservations:** suggested. **Features:** This place is a breath of fresh air in hectic Manhattan. Saffron-colored walls soothe the soul and prepare guests for satisfying regional dishes delivered with fine attentive service. Pastas are made in-house daily, and many vegetables and herbs are picked from the owner's garden. The extensive wine list represents several regions of Italy. Dressy casual; cocktails. **Parking:** no self-parking. **Cards:** AX, DC, DS, MC, VI.

FIFTY-SEVEN RESTAURANT & BAR
▽▽▽▽ ▽▽▽▽
American
Lunch: $17-$35   **Dinner:** $28-$45   **Phone:** 212/758-5757   (90)
Location: Between Park and Madison aves; in Four Seasons Hotel New York. 57 E 57th St 10022. **Hours:** 6:30 am-3 & 5:30-10 pm; Sunday brunch. **Reservations:** required. **Features:** The warmth and sincerity of the staff overcome the cold nature of the soaring modern marble architecture of the hotel dining room. Ever-changing dishes are of the highest quality and bring out the freshest tastes. Semi-formal attire; cocktails; entertainment. **Parking:** valet. **Cards:** AX, CB, DC, DS, JC, MC, VI. ⵖⵡ

FOLEY'S RESTAURANT & BAR
ⒶⒶⒶ
▽▽▽▽
Seafood
Lunch: $15-$29   **Dinner:** $25-$39   **Phone:** 212/261-5200   (136)
Location: Broadway and 7th Ave; auto access from 7th Ave, s of W 48th St; in Renaissance New York Hotel Times Square. 2 Times Square, 7th Ave at W 48th St 10036. **Hours:** 6:30 am-2:30 & 5-10 pm; Sunday brunch noon-2 pm. Closed major holidays. **Reservations:** suggested. **Features:** Relax and enjoy the feast of lights created by Times Square as you look out from this two-level restaurant. Fin and turf offerings are creatively prepared and served in ample portions. The bread selection is extensive. A pre-theater menu is available. Save plenty of room for one of the decadent desserts. Dressy casual; cocktails. **Parking:** valet. **Cards:** AX, CB, DC, DS, JC, MC, VI. *(See color ad p 449)* ⵖⵡ

THE FOUR SEASONS
▽▽▽▽ ▽▽▽▽
American
Lunch: $30-$40   **Dinner:** $85-$100   **Phone:** 212/754-9494   (154)
Location: Between Park and Lexington aves. 99 E 52nd St 10022. **Hours:** noon-2 & 5-9:30 pm, Sat 5 pm-11 pm. Closed major holidays; also Sun. **Reservations:** required. **Features:** Designed by architects Mies van der Rohe and Philip Johnson, the restaurant has been a notable landmark and modern classic in New York since 1959. It features contemporary cuisine, several dining rooms, an extensive wine cellar and a renowned art collection. Six menus range from the prix fixe bar lunch to the Pool Room's multi-faceted a la carte menu. All feature a good selection of global variety. Semi-formal attire; cocktails. **Parking:** no self-parking. **Cards:** AX, CB, DC, DS, MC, VI. ⵡ

FRED'S AT BARNEY'S
▽▽▽▽
American
Lunch: $18-$32   **Dinner:** $18-$32   **Phone:** 212/833-2200   (60)
Location: Madison Ave at 61st St, 9th floor. 660 Madison Ave 10021. **Hours:** 11:30 am-9 pm, Sat 11 am-8 pm, Sun 11 am-6 pm. Closed: 3/23, 11/22, 12/25. **Reservations:** suggested. **Features:** On the top level of the ultra-chic Barney's Department Store, the pleasant, tucked-away cafe serves more than 50 varieties of International cheeses, as well as fresh bakery items, light lunches and more. Dressy casual; beer & wine only. **Parking:** no self-parking. **Cards:** AX, DC, MC, VI.

FRESCO BY SCOTTO
▽▽▽
Northern Italian
Lunch: $16-$42   **Dinner:** $18-$46   **Phone:** 212/935-3434   (152)
Location: Between Madison and Park aves. 34 E 52nd St 10022. **Hours:** 11:30 am-3 & 5-11 pm, Sat from 5 pm. Closed major holidays; also Sun. **Reservations:** suggested. **Features:** Bright-colored frescoes and mirrors enhance the upbeat and friendly mood of this inviting, comfortable, yet small dining room. Modern Tuscan menu selections featuring homemade pasta and bread are cooked to perfection and served by a most accomplished staff. Dressy casual; cocktails. **Parking:** street. **Cards:** AX, DC, DS, MC, VI. ⵡ

(See map and index starting on p. 382)

GABRIEL'S BAR & RESTAURANT
Lunch: $15-$19   **Dinner:** $19-$34   **Phone:** 212/956-4600   ㉞

American

Location: Between Broadway and Columbus Ave. 11 W 60th St 10023. **Hours:** noon-3 & 5-11 pm, Fri & Sat-midnight. Closed major holidays; also Sun. **Reservations:** suggested. **Features:** A long-time Lincoln Center favorite for music lovers of all ages, the casual spot lets patrons stop in for a quick bite. The kitchen can easily accommodate those with time constraints, but nothing is even remotely akin to fast food here. Dishes, for the most part, exude a Mediterranean accent. Examples include saffron-imbued risottos; salads laced with fennel, orange and olives; and, for the more adventurous, rabbit cacciatore and braised goat with an Andalusian influence. Casual dress; cocktails. **Parking:** street. **Cards:** AX, MC, VI.

GALLAGHER'S STEAK HOUSE
Lunch: $11-$40   **Dinner:** $19-$40   **Phone:** 212/245-5336   ㊋

Steak House

Location: Between Broadway and 8th Ave. 228 W 52nd St 10019. **Hours:** noon-midnight. **Reservations:** suggested. **Features:** A New York landmark since 1927, Gallagher's displays its trademark dry-aged prime beef at the entrance. The years melt away as you enter a large dark-wood-paneled room dominated by photos of famous people and a large old-time bar. The tables are set with red-and-white-checkered cloths and sturdy chairs. Located in the heart of the theater district. Casual dress; cocktails. **Parking:** no self-parking. **Cards:** AX, CB, DC, DS, MC, VI.

🍸

GEISHA
Lunch: $15-$29   **Dinner:** $19-$34   **Phone:** 212/813-1113   ㊹

Japanese

Location: Between Madison and Park aves. 33 E 61st St 10021. **Hours:** noon-3:30 & 5:30-midnight, Fri & Sat 5:30 pm-1 am. Closed major holidays; also Sun. **Features:** The hip, often-crowded eatery's no-reservations policy doesn't deter patrons, but it may annoy. Dishes are beautifully prepared, cooked or not. Simple preparations and seasonings showcase how light broths, sauces, vinaigrettes and seasonings can raise a lovely piece of fish to sublime status. Appetizers, which serve as an opportunity for the chef to wow with delicate yet exciting flavors, must not be neglected. The entree list is short; the fine sushi and roll list is long. Dressy casual; cocktails. **Parking:** no self-parking. **Cards:** AX, DC, JC, MC, VI.

🍸

GIAMBELLI 50TH
Lunch: $27   **Dinner:** $29-$35   **Phone:** 212/688-2760   ⑯⑨

Northern Italian

Location: Between Madison and Park aves. 46 E 50th St 10022. **Hours:** noon-3 & 5-midnight. **Reservations:** accepted. **Features:** An interesting collection of art decorates the moderately upscale restaurant. On the menu is a wide variety of selections, ranging from seafood and pasta to veal and beef. Many wines serve as fitting complements. Servers are knowledgeable. Casual dress; cocktails. **Parking:** no self-parking. **Cards:** AX, CB, DC, DS, JC, MC, VI.

🍸

GILT
Dinner: $55-$105   **Phone:** 212/891-8100   ⑯⑤

Nouvelle American

Location: Between 50th and 51st sts; in The New York Palace. 455 Madison Ave 10022. **Hours:** 5:30 pm-10 pm. Closed: Sun & Mon. **Reservations:** suggested. **Features:** Built in 1882 by railroad magnate Henry Villard, the Villard Mansion at The New York Palace Hotel is now home to this gem of a restaurant tucked inside an opulent box. The place is best summarized in one word: wow. Service is impeccable, the menu is beguiling, and the talent presiding in the kitchen is all about perfection and exceeding expectation. This spot can't be beat for a special occasion or occasional treat. Diners can expect a meal to savor and memories for a lifetime. Semi-formal attire; cocktails. **Parking:** valet. **Cards:** AX, CB, DC, DS, JC, MC, VI.

🍸

GRAND SICHUAN INTERNATIONAL MIDTOWN
Lunch: $8-$20   **Dinner:** $8-$20   **Phone:** 212/582-2288   ㊅⑦

Chinese

Location: Between W 50th and W 51st sts. 745 9th Ave 10019. **Hours:** 11 am-11 pm, Sat & Sun from noon. Closed major holidays. **Features:** Near Times Square but without the heavy foot traffic, the restaurant occupies a prime location. Typical Chinese fare displays an excellent level of preparation. The dishes are very good, and the staff is pleasant. Casual dress; cocktails. **Parking:** street. **Cards:** AX, DS, MC, VI.

HEARTLAND BREWERY AND CHOP HOUSE
Lunch: $6-$17   **Dinner:** $6-$30   **Phone:** 646/366-0235

American

Location: Between 6th (Ave of the Americas) and 7th aves. 127 W 43rd St 10036. **Hours:** 11:30 am-10 pm. Closed: 5/28. **Reservations:** suggested. **Features:** The restaurant's award-winning microbrews pair well with delicious burgers and appetizers. Casual dress; cocktails. **Parking:** street. **Cards:** AX, DC, DS, MC, VI.

🍸

HELL'S KITCHEN
Lunch: $8-$14   **Dinner:** $15-$25   **Phone:** 212/977-1588   ⑩④

Mexican

Location: Between 46th and 47th sts. 679 9th Ave 10036. **Hours:** 11:30 am-3:30 & 5-midnight, Sat from 5 pm, Sun 5 pm-11 pm, Mon & Tues 11:30 am-3:30 & 5-11 pm. Closed: 11/22, 12/25. **Reservations:** accepted. **Features:** This place is not the typical chips-and-salsa Mexican joint. The menu lists creative, artfully presented dishes of which first-timers might never have heard. Flavors pop and please the locals, who enjoy the casual, friendly service and style. Savory choices include chili-rubbed lamb shank and pulled pork posole with a goat cheese, sweet corn flauta. Casual dress; cocktails. **Parking:** street. **Cards:** AX, MC, VI.

HUDSON CAFETERIA
Lunch: $11-$38   **Dinner:** $11-$38   **Phone:** 212/554-6500   ㊳

American

Location: Between 8th and 9th sts. 356 W 58th St 10019. **Hours:** 6:30-11 am, 11:30-4:30 & 5:30-11:30 pm, Thurs & Fri-12:30 am, Sat 6:30 am-3 & 4-12:30 am, Sun 6:30 am-3 & 4-11:30 pm. **Reservations:** suggested. **Features:** The organic-looking space—wide open with a soaring ceiling and brick walls—is dark with richly stained wood and looks a lot like a funky, upscale boarding school dining hall. There are long communal tables with benches, tall kitchen-style cabinets stocked with dry goods and a large, truly open central kitchen with counter seating around much of it. The space is cool, no doubt. The food is homey and good. Casual dress; cocktails. **Parking:** valet. **Cards:** AX, DC, DS, MC, VI.

♿M

IL MONELLO
Lunch: $16-$32   **Dinner:** $16-$32   **Phone:** 212/535-9310   ㉘

Northern Italian

Location: Between 76th and 77th sts. 1460 2nd Ave 10021. **Hours:** noon-3 & 5-11 pm, Fri & Sat-midnight, Sun-10 pm. Closed: 11/22, 12/25. **Reservations:** suggested. **Features:** Elegant table settings and attractive artwork lend to the sophisticated appeal of the comfortably refined dining room. The menu centers on Northern Italian dishes, which are well complemented by an assortment of wines. Desserts are delicious. Dressy casual; cocktails. **Parking:** no self-parking. **Cards:** AX, CB, DC, DS, MC, VI.

(See map and index starting on p. 382)

IL NIDO   Lunch: $18-$27   Dinner: $19-$35   Phone: 212/753-8450   [171]
▼▽▽▼▽   **Location:** Between 2nd and 3rd aves. 251 E 53rd St 10022. **Hours:** noon-3 & 5:30-11 pm. Closed major holidays; also Sun. **Reservations:** suggested. **Features:** An extensive selection of Italian wines complements
Northern Italian   selections of Northern Italian cuisine. Subtle lighting helps to give the quiet, Tuscan-influenced dining room a warm, intimate feel. Among the wonderful desserts are classic tiramisu and zabaglione. Semi-formal attire;
cocktails. **Parking:** no self-parking. **Cards:** AX, CB, DC, MC, VI.

ISABELLA'S   Lunch: $10-$19   Dinner: $16-$28   Phone: 212/724-2100   [5]
▼▽▽ ▼▽▽   **Location:** At 77th St. 359 Columbus Ave 10024. **Hours:** 11:30 am-4 & 5:30-11:30 pm, Fri-midnight, Sat 11 am-4 & 5:30-midnight, Sun 10 am-4:30 & 5-11 pm, Mon 11:30 am-4 & 5:30-11 pm. Closed: 12/25.
Mediterranean   **Reservations:** accepted. **Features:** Value and variety are cornerstones of the big sidewalk cafe, which is always bustling. Herb-crusted salmon, marinated seafood salad, striped bass wrapped in prosciutto and
well-prepared sirloin are among American dishes that exhibit Mediterranean influences. Casual dress; cocktails. **Parking:** no self-parking. **Cards:** AX, DS, MC, VI.

ISTANA   Lunch: $17-$29   Dinner: $20-$38   Phone: 212/303-6032   [166]
▼▽▽▼▽   **Location:** Between 50th and 51st sts; in The New York Palace. 455 Madison Ave 10022. **Hours:** 6:30 am-11, noon-2:30 & 5:30-10:45 pm, Sat & Sun 6:30 am-11:30, noon-2:30 & 5:30-10:45 pm. **Reservations:** suggested.
Continental   **Features:** In the elegant lobby of the hotel, the restaurant offers diners a fine Continental menu and a luxurious yet comfortable setting. During dinner, guests enjoy the pleasant piano music that drifts in from the
lounge. Service is polished and professional. Casual dress; cocktails. **Parking:** on-site (fee). **Cards:** AX, DC, DS, JC, MC, VI.

I TRULLI   Lunch: $18-$28   Dinner: $19-$36   Phone: 212/481-7372   [240]
▼▽▽▼▽   **Location:** Between Park and Lexington aves. 122 E 27th St 10016. **Hours:** noon-3 & 5:30-10 pm, Fri-10:30 pm, Sat 5 pm-10:30 pm, Sun 5 pm-10 pm. Closed: 1/1, 7/4, 12/25. **Reservations:** suggested. **Features:** Distinct
Provincial Italian   Mediterranean style makes for a charming setting for creative and savory dishes, some prepared on the rotisserie or in the wood-burning oven. Warm-weather dining in the walled garden, which has a rush-mat
roof and lovely waterfall, has a hide-away appeal. Dressy casual; cocktails. **Parking:** street. **Cards:** AX, DC, MC, VI.

JAIPUR'S INDIAN CUISINE   Lunch: $11-$27   Dinner: $11-$27   Phone: 212/371-3000   [175]
(AAA)   **Location:** Between 53rd and 54th sts. 1007 2nd Ave 10022. **Hours:** 11:30 am-3 & 5-10:30 pm. **Features:** This cozy storefront serves a very popular Indian buffet lunch, but plan to arrive early; the small dining room gets
▼▽▽ ▼▽▽   crowded in a New York minute. Don't mind the less-than-posh digs: this place is no Taj Mahal, but it does
Indian   serve hearty curries and fragrant, flaky breads fresh from the tandoor. Casual dress; beer & wine only. **Parking:** no self-parking. **Cards:** AX, DS, MC, VI.

JASMINE   Lunch: $8-$22   Dinner: $8-$22   Phone: 212/517-8854   [10]
▼▽▽ ▼▽▽   **Location:** Corner of 84th St and 2nd Ave. 1619 2nd Ave 10021. **Hours:** 11:30 am-10:30 pm, Fri & Sat-11:30 pm, Sun 11 pm-10:30 pm. Closed: 11/2. **Features:** This casual storefront favorite has outdoor street dining in
Thai   warmer weather but is popular all-year-round for the highly flavorful dishes, both traditional and unusual. The lemongrass grilled pork chops are sublime and the ginger chicken and lemongrass shrimp are aromatic
and addictive. But these are just a few of the excellent choices. Casual. Casual dress; cocktails. **Parking:** no self-parking. **Cards:** AX, MC, VI.

JEAN GEORGES RESTAURANT   *Menu on AAA.com* Lunch: $24-$42 Dinner: $95-$125 Phone: 212/299-3900   [36]
(AAA)   **Location:** Jct Central Park S; at Columbus Circle; in Trump International Hotel & Tower. 1 Central Park W 10023. **Hours:** noon-2:30 & 5:30-11 pm, Sat from 5:30 pm. Closed: Sun. **Reservations:** required. **Features:** The
▽▽▽ ▽▽▽   Central Park skyline enhances this serene, center-stage location. Once inside, the elaborate open kitchen
French   fuses the imaginative, art deco elements of the formal dining room with the equally appealing, yet less starched, bistro milieu. Enticing, cultivated aromas feed the frenzy for the sumptuous food, which is always
presented in remarkable Chef Vongererichten's style. Semi-formal attire; cocktails. **Parking:** valet.
Cards: AX, DC, MC, VI.

JEKYLL & HYDE CLUB   Lunch: $13-$25   Dinner: $13-$25   Phone: 212/541-9505   [58]
▼▽▽ ▼▽▽   **Location:** Between 57th and 58th sts. 1409 6th Ave (Ave of the Americas) 10019. **Hours:** 11:30 am-11 pm, Fri-1 am, Sat 11 am-1 am. **Features:** Every inch of this four-story restaurant is designed with a sort of "haunted
American   house" theme. Eyes will follow you from large paintings on the walls, mechanical werewolf heads mounted on walls will come to life and speak to the children, and props of mummies and monsters can be found in
just about every corner. Professional actors entertain the kids making this a not-so-scary experience, and the menu featuring hamburgers, pizzas and pasta dishes will keep everyone in the family happy. Casual dress; cocktails; entertainment. **Parking:** street. **Cards:** AX.

JEWEL OF INDIA   Lunch: $10-$26   Dinner: $10-$26   Phone: 212/869-5544   [196]
▼▽▽▼▽   **Location:** Between 5th and 6th (Ave of the Americas) aves. 15 W 44th St 10036. **Hours:** noon-3 & 5:30-11 pm. **Reservations:** suggested. **Features:** The space is distinctive, with tall ceilings, mirrors and lots of greenery,
Indian   and the food is richly flavored and good. The popular buffet lunch is a bargain. Casual dress; cocktails. **Parking:** no self-parking. **Cards:** AX, DC, DS, MC, VI.

JOE ALLEN   Lunch: $14-$27   Dinner: $14-$27   Phone: 212/581-6464   [132]
▼▽▽ ▼▽▽   **Location:** Between 8th and 9th aves. 326 W 46th St 10036. **Hours:** noon-11:45 pm, Fri-midnight, Sat 11:30 am-midnight, Sun & Wed 11:30 am-11:45 pm. Closed: 11/22, 12/25. **Reservations:** required. **Features:** A
Regional American   theater district classic, the cheerful pub delivers unpretentious, home-style staples, such as meatloaf, liver and roasted chicken. Apple pie is stuffed full of fruit and served warm. Broadway stars are known to gather
here for late night meals. Casual dress; cocktails. **Parking:** no self-parking. **Cards:** MC, VI.

(See map and index starting on p. 382)

JOHN'S PIZZERIA-TIMES SQUARE   **Lunch:** $8-$16   **Dinner:** $8-$16   **Phone:** 212/391-7560   162

American

Location: Between 7th and 8th aves. 260 W 44th St 10036. **Hours:** 11:30 am-11:30 pm. Closed: 3/23, 11/22, 12/25. **Reservations:** not accepted. **Features:** First established in 1929 and now with four New York City locations, this spacious eatery is situated in an historic landmark church. Although famous for thin crust pizza baked in a coal-fired brick oven, the pasta, sandwiches and homemade dessert are worthy of a return visit. Casual dress; cocktails. **Parking:** no self-parking. **Cards:** AX, DS, JC, MC.

JO JO   **Lunch:** $18-$37   **Dinner:** $18-$65   **Phone:** 212/223-5656   53

French

Location: Between Lexington and 3rd aves. 160 E 64th St 10021. **Hours:** noon-2:30 & 5:30-10:30 pm, Fri & Sat-11 pm, Sun-10 pm. **Reservations:** suggested. **Features:** This gem of a brownstone, which has been serving those interested in a superlative food experience for years, has been redone with gracious decor in warm tones. The experience again is both refined and comfortable. Food preparation shows skill, and the changing menu means variety for those returning. Star chef Vongerichten's bistro fare on overdrive itself is the star. Dressy casual; cocktails. **Parking:** no self-parking. **Cards:** AX, DC, DS, JC, MC, VI.

JOSEPHINA   **Lunch:** $12-$18   **Dinner:** $20-$34   **Phone:** 212/799-1000   30

American

Location: Between 63rd and 64th sts. 1900 Broadway 10023. **Hours:** 11:30 am-midnight, Sat from 11 am, Sun 11 am-11 pm. **Features:** Located opposite the New York City Opera, this place is packed the night of performances, so plan ahead. Savor the New American cuisine inside the dining room or watch the crowds from the outdoor cafe. Casual dress; cocktails. **Parking:** no self-parking. **Cards:** AX, MC, VI.

JOSIE'S   **Lunch:** $12-$22   **Dinner:** $12-$22   **Phone:** 212/490-1245   232

Natural/Organic

Location: At E 37th St. 565 3rd Ave 10016. **Hours:** 11:30 am-10:30 pm; hours may vary. **Features:** Health-conscious or not, you'll enjoy the dairy-free organic foods and free-range meats we're all starting to hear more about. Sidewalk and open-air dining are available in season. Casual dress; cocktails. **Parking:** no self-parking. **Cards:** AX, MC, VI.

JUNIOR'S   **Lunch:** $6-$11   **Dinner:** $6-$11   **Phone:** 212/586-4677   199

Deli/Subs
Sandwiches

Location: Between Park and Lexington aves; in Grand Central Terminal. 45 Grand Central Station 10017. **Hours:** 6:30 am-10 pm. **Features:** Since the 1950s, the Brooklyn landmark has been known for its cheesecakes, pastries and delicatessen sandwiches. It now has a location in Midtown within Grand Central Station. Casual dress; beer only. **Parking:** no self-parking. **Cards:** AX, DC, DS, MC, VI.

KEENS STEAKHOUSE   **Lunch:** $8-$37   **Dinner:** $18-$45   **Phone:** 212/947-3636   222

Steak House

Location: Between 5th and 6th (Ave of the Americas) aves. 72 W 36th St 10018. **Hours:** 11:45 am-10:30 pm, Sat from 5 pm, Sun 5 pm-9 pm. Closed: 12/25. **Reservations:** accepted. **Features:** This classic steak house was established in 1885 as a men's pipe-smoking club; the decor features lovely 19th-Century carved oak walls, fine furnishings, pictures and ceilings decorated with thousands of clay pipes. The menu offers a fine selection of choice cuts of beef, some chicken and seafood dishes including live lobster. Casual dress; cocktails. **Parking:** no self-parking. **Cards:** AX, DC, DS, MC, VI.

KOREA PALACE   **Lunch:** $12-$25   **Dinner:** $15-$40   **Phone:** 212/832-2350   146

Korean

Location: Between Park and Lexington aves. 127 E 54th St 10022. **Hours:** 11:30 am-10:30 pm, Sat from 4:30 pm. Closed major holidays; also Sun. **Reservations:** accepted. **Features:** Each table is equipped with a hot plate for popular Korean barbecue. Among many traditional dishes are Korean pancakes, a large selection of hot pot soups and hot-stone-cooked choices. Stewed cod with garlic and soy, the pa jun seafood pancake, barbecue and sushi are favorites. The relaxed dining room is appropriately appointed in ethnic decor. Servers in black and white uniforms are friendly and efficient. Casual dress; cocktails; entertainment. **Parking:** valet and street. **Cards:** AX, DC, JC, MC, VI.

KURUMA ZUSHI   **Lunch:** $20-$200   **Dinner:** $20-$200   **Phone:** 212/317-2802   179

Sushi

Location: Between 5th and Madison aves. 7 E 47th St, 2nd Floor 10017. **Hours:** 11:30 am-2 & 5:30-10 pm. Closed major holidays; also Sun. **Reservations:** suggested. **Features:** No street sign marks this exclusive sushi-only restaurant, located on the second floor of a nondescript building. The understated but bright and spotless dining room is small but there is room at the sushi bar. The menu offers sushi in three different qualities: high, higher and spectacular, as well as special fish flown in from Japan. One orders by quality or price. There is also a menu of various sushi rolls. Service is sweet and demure and ever watchful for the guest's needs. Casual dress; cocktails. **Parking:** no self-parking. **Cards:** AX, JC, MC, VI.

KYMA   **Lunch:** $16-$23   **Dinner:** $16-$23   **Phone:** 212/957-8830   140

Greek

Location: At 8th Ave. 300 W 46th St 10036. **Hours:** 11:45 am-midnight. Closed major holidays. **Reservations:** accepted. **Features:** Typical Greek hot and cold appetizers are perfect for sharing before a meal of moussaka, souvlaki, charcoal-broiled lamb chops or such seafood dishes as jumbo shrimp in a clay pot or grilled or broiled prawns and fish with olive oil and lemon. Lending to the casual dining room's bright feel are large floor-to-ceiling windows and a large, central chandelier. Casual dress; cocktails. **Parking:** no self-parking. **Cards:** AX, MC, VI.

LA BOITE EN BOIS   **Lunch:** $12-$19   **Dinner:** $18-$27   **Phone:** 212/874-2705   18

French

Location: Between Columbus Ave and Central Park W. 75 W 68th St 10023. **Hours:** noon-2:30 & 5:30-10:30 pm, Sun 11:30 am-2:30 & 5-10 pm, Mon 5:30 pm-10 pm. Closed major holidays. **Reservations:** suggested. **Features:** Tucked away down a small flight of stairs into a small, rustic, wood-panelled dining room decorated with touches of brass and other small items is this distinctly provencial French charmer. Small and cozy, local regulars come in pairs or alone with a book and order comfort food such as lentils with sausage and potato, pumpkin soup, duck confit and salmon with honey-mustard glaze and dauphinoise potato. Food is well-prepared and hearty of flavor. Service is casual and there when you need it. Dressy casual; cocktails. **Parking:** no self-parking. **Cards:** AX, MC, VI.

(See map and index starting on p. 382)

LA GRENOUILLE Lunch: $28-$49 Dinner: $90 Phone: 212/752-1495 [135]
French
Location: Between 5th and Madison aves. 3 E 52nd St 10022. **Hours:** Open 5/1-8/31 & 9/8-4/30; noon-3 & 5-10:30 pm, Fri & Sat-11 pm. Closed major holidays; also Sun. **Reservations:** required. **Features:** An abundance of sophistication is apparent in the food, the room and the guests of this long-standing New York favorite. Classic dishes are served by mature and professional staff who will speak French to you, charm you, and most important, help you with the menu, written entirely in French. Enormous and elaborate floral arrangements and brocade walls are reflected in walls of mirror with stunning effect. No need to fly to Paris for a dose of grandeur. Prix fixe menu available lunch and dinner. Semi-formal attire; cocktails. **Parking:** no self-parking. **Cards:** AX, DC, JC, MC, VI.

L'ALLEGRIA RISTORANTE Lunch: $13-$29 Dinner: $13-$29 Phone: 212/265-6777 [137]
Italian
Location: Corner of 44th St. 623 9th Ave 10036. **Hours:** noon-midnight. **Closed:** 12/25. **Reservations:** accepted. **Features:** In the heart of the theater district and catering to late night diners, the restaurant is a pleasant dining room offering a wide variety of delightful Italian dishes, including various pastas, fresh seafood, veal and chicken entrees. Outdoor sidewalk dining is available in season. Casual dress; cocktails. **Parking:** no self-parking. **Cards:** AX, DC, VI.

LA MANGEOIRE Lunch: $12-$32 Dinner: $12-$32 Phone: 212/759-7086 [177]
French
Location: Between 53rd and 54th sts. 1008 2nd Ave 10022. **Hours:** noon-2:30 & 5:30-10:30 pm, Fri-11 pm, Sat 5:30 pm-11 pm, Sun 11:30 am-2:30 & 5:30-10 pm. **Reservations:** suggested. **Features:** Guests step out of New York and into Provence, where bundles of dried herbs and flowers hang from thatched roofs, and hearty cooking with fresh herbs and ingredients makes mealtime special. A charming, rustic appearance prevails inside and out. Fish soup, onion tart, escargot with garlic cream, braised leg of lamb and shepherd's pie all are representative of the dive-right-in menu. The wine list carefully combines French and Californian selections. Dressy casual; cocktails. **Parking:** street. **Cards:** AX, MC, VI.

L'ANNAM Lunch: $5 Dinner: $7-$14 Phone: 212/686-5168 [242]
Vietnamese
Location: Jct E 28th St. 393 3rd Ave 10016. **Hours:** 11:30 am-11:30 pm, Fri & Sat-12:30 am. **Reservations:** accepted. **Features:** The eatery offers a wide variety of Vietnamese dishes including Saigon-style noodle dishes, pho, vegetarian dishes and seafood. Casual dress. **Parking:** no self-parking. **Cards:** AX, MC, VI.

LA RIVISTA Lunch: $12-$20 Dinner: $19-$33 Phone: 212/245-1707 [130]
Italian
Location: Between 8th and 9th aves; in theater district; on restaurant row. 313 W 46th St 10036. **Hours:** noon-midnight. Closed major holidays; also Sun. **Reservations:** suggested. **Features:** A casual, relaxing and romantic dining experience awaits diners. The menu comprises local-favorite Italian dishes. A pianist performs nightly. Casual dress; cocktails. **Parking:** no self-parking. **Cards:** AX, DC, DS, MC, VI. [⅃M]

LCB BRASSERIE RACHOU Lunch: $15-$26 Dinner: $22-$39 Phone: 212/688-6525 [87]
French
Location: Between 5th and 6th (Ave of the Americas) aves. 60 W 55th St 10018. **Hours:** noon-3 & 5-10:30 pm, Fri & Sat-11:30 pm. Closed: Sun in summer. **Reservations:** suggested. **Features:** The incarnation of famed La Cote Basque is a highly polished brasserie that gleams with relaxed elegance. Service remains expert, and the food—purely French and traditional—is excellent. Roast chicken with creamy morel and champagne sauce, roasted honey-glazed duck with cherry Grand Marnier sauce, cassoulet in cooler months, steak frites, seafood platters, choucroute garnie and Dover sole meuniere are just a glimpse of the fine options. Dressy casual; cocktails. **Parking:** no self-parking. **Cards:** AX, DC, DS, MC, VI.

LE BERNARDIN Lunch: $55 Dinner: $105 Phone: 212/489-1515 [95]
Seafood
Location: Between 6th (Ave of the Americas) and 7th aves; in Equitable Building. 155 W 51st St 10019. **Hours:** noon-2:30 & 5:15-10:30 pm, Fri-11 pm, Sat 5:15 pm-11 pm. Closed major holidays; also Sun. **Reservations:** required. **Features:** Simply put, the menu is a who's who of fish. The scope of seafood choices is exciting to any fish lover, especially to those eager to enjoy the fish itself. The varied accompanying flavors creatively and gracefully spotlight the star of the show. The graceful dining room also pays tribute through large still-life paintings of the sea's rich bounty. Many consider this one of New York's premier seafood restaurants. Semi-formal attire; cocktails. **Parking:** no self-parking. **Cards:** AX, DC, DS, MC, VI.

LE CIRQUE Lunch: $34-$48 Dinner: $42-$48 Phone: 212/644-0202 [101]
Nouvelle French
Location: Between Lexington and 3rd aves. 151 E 58th St 10022. **Hours:** 11:45 am-2:30 & 5:30-10:-30 pm, Sat-5:30 pm. Closed major holidays; also Sun. **Reservations:** required. **Features:** In the striking Bloomberg building, the latest incarnation of Sirio Maccioni's homage to all things over-the-top is more subdued than its predecessors. The comfortable room is still the place to see and be seen, and the current menu includes the ultra-refined signature Dover sole and a proper trout amandine. Thrill-seekers might try braised leeks with crispy pig's feet in mustard vinaigrette. For dessert, diners find great comfort in bomboloni: warm brioche filled with lush vanilla cream. Semi-formal attire; cocktails. **Parking:** no self-parking. **Cards:** AX, DC, DS, MC, VI. [Y]

LE COLONIAL Lunch: $15-$24 Dinner: $15-$24 Phone: 212/752-0808 [113]
Vietnamese
Location: Between Lexington and 3rd aves. 149 E 57th St 10022. **Hours:** noon-2:30 & 5:30-11:30 pm, Sat & Sun from 5:30 pm. Closed: 11/22, 12/25. **Reservations:** suggested. **Features:** Twirling fans, tall ferns and an original tin ceiling painted deep, brick red with a black border give the dining room the feel of 1940s Vietnam. The menu centers on excellent Vietnamese cuisine, all priced reasonably. Servers are gentle and efficient. Dressy casual; cocktails. **Parking:** no self-parking. **Cards:** AX, DC, JC, MC, VI. [Y]

LENOX ROOM Lunch: $10-$17 Dinner: $19-$32 Phone: 212/772-0404 [32]
American
Location: Between E 73rd and E 74th sts. 1278 3rd Ave 10021. **Hours:** noon-2:30 & 5:30-10:30 pm, Fri & Sat from 5:30 pm, Sun 11:30 am-2:30 & 5:30-10:30 pm; Sunday brunch. **Reservations:** suggested. **Features:** The restaurant offers creative dishes with an Asian flair; potential delights may include steamed dumplings, sashimi salmon or tuna, grilled strip steak or marinated lamb chops. Diners may sample items from the tapas menu, referred to as the "Tiers of Taste," or a la carte. Outdoor dining in the warmer months resembles an outside cafe. Dressy casual; cocktails. **Parking:** street. **Cards:** AX, CB, DC, DS, MC, VI. [Y]

(See map and index starting on p. 382)

LE PAIN QUOTIDIEN   Lunch: $7-$13   Dinner: $7-$13   Phone: 212/327-4900   ⑦
Location: Between 84th and 85th sts. 1131 Madison Ave 10028. **Hours:** 7:30 am-7 pm. Closed: 12/25.
Features: Fresh from Belgium comes this small chain sandwich and bake shop. Its very casual manner is
typified by a long communal table down the center of one room, though there is individual seating as well.
Belgian   There is no decor to speak of except raw wood floors, unfinished window trim and stripped walls. The
sandwiches and baked goods, especially the breakfast pastries, are quality and typically European in nature, thus there are
usually many full tables. Casual dress. **Parking:** no self-parking. **Cards:** AX, MC, VI.

LE PERIGORD   Lunch: $32   Dinner: $62   Phone: 212/755-6244   ⑲⑦
Location: E of 1st Ave. 405 E 52nd St 10022. **Hours:** noon-3 & 5:30-10:30 pm, Sat from 5:30 pm, Sun 5:30 pm-
9:30 pm. Closed: 1/1, 12/25. **Reservations:** required. **Features:** In a residential area near the United
Nations Building, the long-established restaurant has welcomed guests with grace and dignity. The staid yet
elegant spot employs servers seemingly born ages ago. The broad menu centers on classic dishes, which
French   are nicely complemented by a fine wine list. Semi-formal attire; cocktails. **Parking:** no self-parking.
Cards: AX, DC, DS, MC, VI.

LEVER HOUSE RESTAURANT   Lunch: $19-$34   Dinner: $29-$40   Phone: 212/888-2700   ⑭②
Location: Between 53rd and 54th sts. 390 Park Ave 10022. **Hours:** 11:45 am-2 & 5:30-11 pm, Fri & Sat-11:30
pm, Sun 5 pm-10 pm. **Reservations:** required. **Features:** On the first floor of New York's first glass
American   skyscraper, the restaurant has an edgy, 21st-century design by Marc Newson that ably fits chef Dan
Silverman's grown-up, smartly seasoned food. Wasabi creme fraiche and tobiko enrich his tuna carpaccio;
diver scallops float in an intense celery nage, and the veal chop is impeccable. Dressy casual; cocktails. **Parking:** no self-
parking. **Cards:** AX, MC, VI.

L'IMPERO   Lunch: $13-$27   Dinner: $15-$29   Phone: 212/599-5045   ②③⓪
Location: Between E 41st and E 43rd sts. 45 Tudor City Pl 10017. **Hours:** noon-2:15 & 5:30-10:15 pm, Fri noon-
2:15 & 5-11:15 pm, Sat 5 pm-11:15 pm. Closed major holidays; also Sun. **Reservations:** suggested.
Italian   **Features:** People are talking about this newcomer from star chef Scott Conant. The menu successfully
delivers sophisticated high Italian dishes. Dressy casual; cocktails. **Parking:** street. **Cards:** AX, MC, VI.

LINDY'S   Lunch: $13-$25   Dinner: $13-$25   Phone: 212/767-8343   ⑦⑨
Location: At 53rd St. 825 7th Ave 10019. **Hours:** 7 am-11 pm, Thurs-Sat to 2 am. **Features:** This New York
institution is the place to go when an urge strikes for authentic New York-style cheesecake. Deli sandwiches
American   are the main bill of fare, but there are plenty of hot items as well. This spot is casual and good for a rest
after a day of walking. Breakfast also is served. Casual dress; cocktails. **Parking:** no self-parking.
Cards: AX, DC, DS, MC, VI.

MALIKA   *Menu on AAA.com*   Lunch: $10-$21   Dinner: $10-$21   Phone: 212/681-6775   ②②①
Location: Between 2nd and 3rd aves. 210 E 43rd St 10017. **Hours:** 11:30 am-3 & 5-11 pm. Closed: 12/25.
Reservations: accepted. **Features:** Popular with the lunch crowd for its varied and nicely presented buffet,
the restaurant offers some of the same well-prepared and fragrant items on the dinner menu. Casual decor
Indian   makes this place appropriate for kids. Casual dress; cocktails. **Parking:** on-site (fee). **Cards:** AX, MC, VI.

MALONEY & PORCELLI   Lunch: $19-$30   Dinner: $22-$40   Phone: 212/750-2233   ⑯④
Location: Between Park and Madison aves. 37 E 50th St 10022. **Hours:** 11:45 am-11:30 pm, Sat noon-midnight,
Sun noon-11:30 pm. Closed: 1/1, 12/25. **Reservations:** suggested. **Features:** Excellent quality steaks and
seafood can be savored in an upscale yet masculine-feeling atmosphere. No-nonsense meals are served in
Steak & Seafood   portions best described as hearty, generous and "manly." The professional and attentive staff dotes on and
spoils even the fussiest patrons. Dressy casual; cocktails. **Parking:** street. **Cards:** AX, DC, DS, MC, VI.

MARCH   Dinner: $55-$95   Phone: 212/754-6272   ⑮①
Location: Between 1st Ave and Sutton Pl. 405 E 58th St 10022. **Hours:** 5:30 pm-10:30 pm.
Reservations: required. **Features:** Appointed with elegant, turn-of-the-20th-century decor, this multi-level
townhouse features a Degne chandelier, Chinese needlepoint tapestry and a working fireplace. A myriad of
American   dining rooms provide a romantic intimacy. Alfresco dining is available. The menu accommodates a refined
level of curiosity and appetite featuring distinguished and exquisitely prepared New World selections. An award-winning wine list
complements this warm and comfortable approach to fine dining. Semi-formal attire; cocktails. **Parking:** no self-parking.
Cards: AX, DC, DS, JC, MC, VI.

MARK'S   Lunch: $19-$29   Dinner: $29-$42   Phone: 212/879-1864   ⑯
Location: Madison Ave at E 77th St; in The Mark, New York. 25 E 77th St 10021. **Hours:** 7 am-11, noon-2:30 & 6-
10:30 pm, Sat 7 am-11 & 5:30-midnight, Sun 11:30 am-2:30 & 6-10:30 pm. **Reservations:** suggested.
Continental   **Features:** Roman prints decorate the walls of the plush, terraced dining room. The atmosphere is refined
and comfortable, welcoming diners to unwind. The menu presents traditional choices, with the three-course
prix fixe meals being a particular deal. Dressy casual; cocktails. **Parking:** no self-parking. **Cards:** AX, CB, DC, DS, JC,
MC, VI.

MARS 2112   Lunch: $13-$26   Dinner: $13-$26   Phone: 212/582-2112   ⑩②
Location: Corner of 51st St. 1633 Broadway 10019. **Hours:** 11:30 am-9:30 pm, Sat & Sun from 11 am. Closed:
12/25. **Features:** At this theme park-like restaurant, guests start off their adventure to the "red planet" in a
simulated spaceship ride. Once the ride is over, guests enter into what seems to be a large crater-like room
made to look like Mars. Costumed actors dressed as aliens entertain guests, especially children, at their
American   tables. Cheeseburgers, pasta and buffalo wings can all be found on the menu. Casual dress; cocktails.
Parking: street. **Cards:** AX, DC, MC, VI.

(See map and index starting on p. 382)

MARSEILLE   **Lunch:** $9-$16   **Dinner:** $17-$28   **Phone:** 212/333-2323   133
Location: At 44th St. 630 9th Ave 10036. **Hours:** 11:30 am-3 & 5:15-midnight, Sat from 11 am, Sun 11 am-3 & 5:15-11 pm, Mon 11:30 am-3 & 5:15-11 pm. **Reservations:** suggested. **Features:** Marseille takes the diner
Regional French   to that French city with its 1930s- and 40s-style French Moroccan ambiance. The cuisine reflects the influences of the region and the Mediterranean. The downstairs bar is reminiscent of an old speakeasy and the wine cellar is located in a former bank vault. Open-air dining is available seasonally. Casual dress; cocktails. **Parking:** no self-parking. **Cards:** AX, MC, VI.

METSOVO   **Dinner:** $15-$25   **Phone:** 212/873-2300   14
Location: Between Columbus Ave and Central Park W. 65 W 70th St 10023. **Hours:** 5:30 pm-11 pm, Fri & Sat-midnight. Closed: 1/1, 11/22, 12/25. **Reservations:** accepted. **Features:** The refreshingly different Greek
Greek   option serves hearty home-style dishes of fish and lamb with a nice selection of hot and cold mezze to start; don't look for moussaka here. Brick walls and understated but warm decor softly lit by candlelight present a very comfortable atmosphere which is enhanced by lively music. Platters piled high with powdered and nut-covered cookies are a nice distraction throughout meal. Casual dress; cocktails. **Parking:** no self-parking. **Cards:** AX, DC, MC, VI.

MICHAEL JORDAN'S THE STEAKHOUSE N.Y.C.   **Lunch:** $15-$30   **Dinner:** $22-$38   **Phone:** 212/655-2300   209
Location: Grand Central Terminal, West Balcony. 23 Vanderbilt Ave at Grand Central Ter 10017. **Hours:** 11:30 am-2:30 & 5-11 pm, Sat from 5 pm, Sun 5 pm-10 pm. Closed: 12/25. **Reservations:** suggested. **Features:** On
Steak House   a balcony overlooking the terminal, the view is ever-changing below, there are constellations above and the restaurant is handsome and suave. The rich-looking bar oozes sophistication, offers a warm welcome and is a great meeting place before a dinner of traditional steak house offerings. Choices include glazed Alaskan salmon, steamed Maine lobster, roast chicken and the finest dry-aged steaks with sides of creamed spinach, hash browns, fried onions and macaroni and cheese. Dressy casual; cocktails. **Parking:** no self-parking. **Cards:** AX, DC, DS, MC, VI.

MICHAEL'S RESTAURANT   **Lunch:** $26-$34   **Dinner:** $26-$38   **Phone:** 212/767-0555   94
Location: Between 5th and 6th (Ave of the Americas) aves. 24 W 55th St 10019. **Hours:** 7:30 am-9:30, noon-2:30 & 5-10:30 pm, Sat from 5 pm. Closed major holidays; also Sun. **Reservations:** suggested.
American   **Features:** Diners are frequently surrounded by live famous faces amid walls of original artwork and two life-size ceramic sheep. Well-prepared dishes are light but savory, designed to keep figures svelte and pampered palates satisfied. Large, colorful floral arrangements add even more interest to an already head-turning room. Dressy casual; cocktails. **Parking:** no self-parking. **Cards:** AX, DC, DS, MC, VI.

MICKEY MANTLE'S   **Lunch:** $9-$30   **Dinner:** $9-$30   **Phone:** 212/688-7777   56
Location: Between 5th and 6th (Ave of the Americas) aves. 42 Central Park S 10019. **Hours:** 11:30 am-11 pm, Sat-midnight. **Reservations:** accepted. **Features:** In a terrific location, the popular eatery displays a vast
American   collection of Mickey Mantle memorabilia and serves a wide range of comfort foods. This place is great for families, those looking for a light bite and all sports fans. Casual dress; cocktails. **Parking:** street.
Cards: AX, MC, VI.

MODA   **Lunch:** $13-$33   **Dinner:** $18-$33   **Phone:** 212/887-9880   99
Location: Between 6th (Ave of the Americas) and 7th aves; in The Flatotel. 135 W 52nd St 10019. **Hours:** 7 am-2:30 & 5:30-11 pm, Sat & Sun 7 am-11:30 & 5:30-11 pm. **Reservations:** required. **Features:** Mediterranean and
Continental   Italian bents are evident in creative and substantial dishes, such as roast rack and slow-cooked leg of lamb with white beans and escarole; sauteed skate with fava, artichoke and corn shoots; and grilled pheasant with sage and soft polenta. The food is warm and satisfying, while the room, mainly concrete with candles hung on walls, is a cool space. Dressy casual; cocktails. **Parking:** no self-parking. **Cards:** AX, MC, VI.

MOLYVOS   **Lunch:** $18-$28   **Dinner:** $20-$29   **Phone:** 212/582-7500   61
Location: Between 55th and 56th sts. 871 7th Ave 10019. **Hours:** noon-3 & 5:30-11:30 pm, Fri-midnight, Sat noon-3 & 5-midnight, Sun noon-11 pm. Closed: 12/25. **Reservations:** suggested. **Features:** Inspired from
Greek   the memories of their Mediterranean island, the Livanos family has created Molyvos as a celebration of its cuisine. Start with a meze assortment of small dishes such as tangy cheese in phyllo, tiny lamb meatballs, or various dips with triangles of pita bread. Then on to delicious Greek dishes such as lamb stewed in a clay pot or grilled whole fish. Dressy casual; cocktails. **Parking:** street. **Cards:** AX, DC, DS, MC, VI.

MORRELL WINE BAR & CAFE   **Lunch:** $10-$19   **Dinner:** $19-$37   **Phone:** 212/262-7700   161
Location: Between 5th and 6th (Ave of the Americas) aves. One Rockefeller Plaza, 14 W 49th St 10020. **Hours:** 11:30 am-11 pm; Sunday brunch. Closed: 11/22, 12/25. **Reservations:** suggested. **Features:** A
American   busy place to be any hour of the day, the restaurant is known for its selection of wines from all over the world. The selection of tasty entrees is varied. Because the restaurant is in the Rockefeller Center area, happy hour is busy. The staff makes guests feel welcomed and special. Casual dress; cocktails. **Parking:** no self-parking.
Cards: AX, MC, VI.

MR. K'S   **Lunch:** $18-$33   **Dinner:** $18-$38   **Phone:** 212/583-1668   176
Location: At 51st St. 570 Lexington Ave 10022. **Hours:** 11:30 am-11 pm, Sat & Sun from noon. **Reservations:** suggested. **Features:** This is not your typical Chinese restaurant. Located in one of the city's
Chinese   historic landmarks, the magnificent art deco design is in keeping with the old GE Building tradition. Design features include high ceilings, quality woodwork, plush fabrics and etched glass. Table tops are adorned with the finest place settings accented by a circle of light from below. The food and service are of equal elegance and combine for a unique dining experience. Dressy casual; cocktails. **Parking:** no self-parking.
Cards: AX, DC, DS, JC, MC, VI.

(See map and index starting on p. 382)

MURALS ON 54 RESTAURANT

International

Lunch: $15-$19   **Dinner:** $26-$34   **Phone:** 212/314-7700   92

Location: Corner of 54th St and 6th Ave (Ave of the Americas); in The Warwick New York Hotel. 63 W 54th St 10019. **Hours:** 6:30 am-11 & noon-2:30 pm, Tues-Fri also 5 pm-11 pm, Sat 6:30 am-12:30 & 5-11 pm, Sun 6:30 am-12:30 pm. **Reservations:** suggested. **Features:** Historic restored murals—which depict the queen offering Sir Walter Raleigh a charter to seek new lands and then him being knighted upon return—are the clear focal point of the room, which is modern and stylish, with tailored lines and fabrics. The bistro-style fare of classic favorites that incorporate French, Spanish and Mediterranean flavors is sophisticated yet unfussy. Dressy casual; cocktails. **Parking:** no self-parking. **Cards:** AX, DC, DS, MC, VI.

NEW YORK PALM-TIMES SQUARE

Steak House

Lunch: $17-$43   **Dinner:** $19-$43   **Phone:** 212/333-7256   98

Location: Between Broadway and 8th Ave. 250 W 50th St 10019. **Hours:** 11:45 am-11:30 pm, Sat from 5 pm, Sun 5 pm-10 pm. Closed major holidays. **Reservations:** suggested. **Features:** Huge portions of wholesome dishes, such as Italian beef and seafood favorites, are a staple here. Caricatures of the famous and not-so-famous hang throughout the dining room. Casual dress; cocktails. **Parking:** street. **Cards:** AX, DC, DS, MC, VI.

NICE MATIN

French

Lunch: $10-$20   **Dinner:** $16-$25   **Phone:** 212/873-6423   3

Location: Between Amsterdam Ave and Broadway. 201 W 79th St 10024. **Hours:** 7 am-midnight. **Reservations:** suggested. **Features:** The casual bistro quickly became a neighborhood favorite not only for its cheerful decor but also for its comforting food. Choices include salad nicoise, stuffed baby artichokes, pissaladiere, roast chicken with oyster mushrooms and buttered leeks, roast codfish with ratatouille and anchoiade and daube of beef short ribs with celery root puree and chickpea fries. Of course, there's much more, including rosemary-rubbed grilled leg of lamb with rosemary aioli and the five-napkin burger. Casual dress; cocktails. **Parking:** no self-parking. **Cards:** AX, DC, MC, VI.

NOCELLO

Northern Italian

Lunch: $10-$16   **Dinner:** $12-$23   **Phone:** 212/713-0224   52

Location: Between Broadway and 8th Ave. 257 W 55th St 10019. **Hours:** noon-3 & 5-10 pm, Sat & Sun from 4 pm. Closed: 12/25. **Reservations:** suggested. **Features:** A favorite of the locals, the restaurant has slightly tight table spacing, but the creative homemade Italian entrees make up for it. Large portions make up each course. Casual dress; wine only. **Parking:** no self-parking. **Cards:** AX, DS, MC, VI.

NOCHE

Latino

Lunch: $10-$20   **Dinner:** $17-$30   **Phone:** 212/541-7070   124

Location: Between 48th and 49th sts. 1604 Broadway 10019. **Hours:** 5 pm-10:30 pm. Closed: 1/1, 12/25; also Sun. **Reservations:** suggested. **Features:** The downstairs bar is loud and energetic with crowds having a collective party, but the multi-story dining rooms, each with its own bar tucked into a nook or alcove, are quieter. The menu lists food from not just one Latin nation but favorites from many. Flavor is in the air, the music and the food. Casual dress; cocktails. **Parking:** no self-parking. **Cards:** AX, DC, DS, MC, VI.

NORMA'S

American

Lunch: $10-$24   **Phone:** 212/708-7460   62

Location: Between 6th (Ave of the Americas) and 7th aves; vehicle entrance on 56th St; in Le Parker Meridien New York. 118 W 57th St 10019-3318. **Hours:** 6:30 am-3 pm, Sat & Sun from 7 am. **Features:** Norma's is arguably one of the most stylish spots in the city for breakfast and lunch and the only one that can boast a $1,000 omelet. (Don't worry, the rest of the selections are absolutely affordable). Menu selections are clever, oversize, creative and delectable. The contemporary yet casual atmosphere features European and South American accents and treatments. Casual dress. **Parking:** on-site (fee) and valet. **Cards:** AX, CB, DC, DS, JC, MC, VI.

OCEAN 50

Seafood

Lunch: $20-$32   **Dinner:** $25-$50   **Phone:** 212/715-2700   178

Location: Between 3rd and Lexington aves; in The Benjamin Hotel. 565 Lexington Ave 10022. **Hours:** 7 am-10:30, noon-2:30 & 5-10 pm, Sat 8 am-2 & 5-10 pm, Sun 8 am-2 pm. Closed: 11/22, 12/24, 12/25; also Mon. **Reservations:** suggested. **Features:** With a stylish yet easygoing atmosphere, the restaurant specializes in fresh seafood along with traditional meat and poultry dishes. Casual dress; cocktails. **Parking:** street. **Cards:** AX, DC, DS, MC, VI.

OCEANA

Seafood

Lunch: $48   **Dinner:** $78   **Phone:** 212/759-5941   126

Location: Between Madison and Park aves. 55 E 54th St 10022. **Hours:** noon-2:30 & 5:30-10:30 pm, Sat from 5 pm. Closed major holidays; also Sun. **Reservations:** suggested. **Features:** The dining room presents what looks like a ship-side view of lush cliffs, seaside villages and other ships from windows within a stately ocean vessel's dining room through murals and clever streamlined architectural detail. The entirely seafood menu is enticing and exhibits outstanding visual and vibrant flavor combinations. The staff is welcoming and gracious. Semiformal attire; cocktails. **Parking:** no self-parking. **Cards:** AX, DC, DS, JC, MC, VI.

OLLIE'S

Chinese

Lunch: $8-$20   **Dinner:** $8-$20   **Phone:** 212/921-5988   172

Location: Between 7th and 8th aves. 200B W 44th St 10036. **Hours:** 11:30 am-midnight, Fri & Sat-1 am, Sun-11:30 pm. **Reservations:** required. **Features:** Known for dumplings, barbecue and a good variety of Cantonese wonton and Mandarin noodle soups, the casual and usually bustling Times Square restaurant is a favorite for traditional food. No-nonsense servers are efficient. Casual dress; cocktails. **Parking:** no self-parking. **Cards:** AX, MC, VI.

OPIA

International

Lunch: $6-$16   **Dinner:** $6-$16   **Phone:** 212/688-3939   115

Location: Jct Lexington Ave and 57th St. 130 E 57th St 10022. **Hours:** 11 am-midnight. Closed: 11/22, 12/24, 12/25. **Reservations:** suggested. **Features:** This beautifully designed second floor restaurant features arched windows, high ceilings and low couches: a casual but elegant atmosphere. A separate area called the Corner Lounge has red walls and low lighting; very intimate and romantic. A few appetizer selections are mini-crab cakes, green papaya salad and white soy cream; entrees include striped bass with baby vegetables and port wine glaze. Dessert selections include creme brulee and peach tatin with raspberry sorbet. Dressy casual; cocktails. **Parking:** street. **Cards:** AX, DC, MC, VI.

(See map and index starting on p. 382)

ORSO Lunch: $18-$28 Dinner: $18-$28 Phone: 212/489-7212 (134)
Location: Between 8th and 9th aves; on restaurant row. 322 W 46th St 10036. Hours: noon-11:45 pm, Wed & Sat from 11:30 am; closing hours may vary Sun & Mon. Closed: 11/22, 12/25. Reservations: suggested.
Italian Features: Guests must look hard for the sign to this quaint Mediterranean hideaway, where well-prepared food is flavorful and fresh and complemented by a carefully selected Italian wine list. Dishes look colorful and appetizing and make good use of fresh herbs. Dressy casual; cocktails. Parking: no self-parking. Cards: MC, VI.

OSCAR'S AMERICAN BRASSERIE Lunch: $14-$21 Dinner: $15-$27 Phone: 212/872-4913 (181)
Location: Between E 49th and 50th sts; in The Waldorf=Astoria. 301 Park Ave 10022. Hours: 6:30 am-10 pm. Reservations: suggested, jacket required. Features: Named in honor of The Waldorf=Astoria's longtime
American maitre d', Oscar Tchirky, this lively and informal brasserie does him proud. The cuisine features interesting twists of classic American dishes. Sunday brunch a la carte is offered, as well as a daily lunch buffet. The varied menu features daily specials and specialties like veal Oscar, fresh grouper, fettucini, Reuben sandwich, turkey club, Cobb salad and a prime beef burger. Casual dress; cocktails. Parking: valet. Cards: AX, CB, DC, DS, JC, MC, VI.

OSTERIA DEL CIRCO Lunch: $20-$36 Dinner: $20-$37 Phone: 212/265-3636 (76)
Location: Between 6th (Ave of the Americas) and 7th aves. 120 W 55th St 10019. Hours: 11:30 am-2:30 & 5:30-11:30 pm, Sat from 5:30 pm, Sun 5 pm-10:30 pm, Mon 11:30 am-2:30 & 5:30-10:30 pm. Closed major
Italian holidays; also 12/24. Reservations: suggested. Features: There is much to look at around the whimsically dressed-up space: an illuminated full moon, bronze circus figures standing or hanging around and colorful flags and fabrics draped about. Hearty, savory dishes are prepared with skill and flourish. After starting with pizza or antipasti, diners might try seafood cannelloni with roasted lobster sauce; pappardelle with red mullet, caper and tomato ragu; glazed lamb chops with honey lavender; or perhaps brick-pressed chicken with cipollini. Dressy casual; cocktails. Parking: no self-parking. Cards: AX, DC, MC, VI.

OUEST Dinner: $25-$36 Phone: 212/580-8700 (1)
Location: Between 83rd and 84th sts. 2315 Broadway 10024. Hours: 5 pm-11 pm, Fri & Sat-midnight, Sun 11 am-2 & 5-10 pm. Closed: 7/4, 12/25. Reservations: suggested. Features: The popular eatery offers guests
American a delightful new twist on American cooking. The dining room offers a handsome atmoshere which nicely captures a refined, casual New York feel. Dressy casual; cocktails. Parking: no self-parking. Cards: AX,
DC, MC, VI.

PAMPANO Lunch: $19-$24 Dinner: $23-$30 Phone: 212/751-4545 (195)
Location: Between 2nd and 3rd aves. 209 E 49th St 10017. Hours: 11:30 am-2:30 & 5-10 pm, Thurs & Fri-10:30 pm, Sat 5 pm-10:30 pm, Sun 5 pm-9:30 pm. Closed major holidays. Reservations: suggested.
Mexican Features: The first-floor bar leaves the second floor free to be a tropical retreat, all white with whirring fans high overhead. There is a sense of cool refinement inside and a bit of fun on the outdoor dining terrace, with greenery aplenty and a large fish sculpture perfect for the seafood theme. Seviches and lobster tacos are good for starters, then creatively prepared seafood can be enjoyed with sweet and savory seasonings and spices. Other offerings include specialty tequilas, mezcal and margaritas. Dressy casual; cocktails. Parking: street. Cards: AX, MC, VI.

PANINOTECA ITALIANA Lunch: $4-$9 Dinner: $4-$9 Phone: 212/490-8531 (214)
Location: In Grand Central Terminal, dining concourse, lower level. 18 Grand Central Terminal 10017. Hours: 9 am-9 pm, Sun 11 am-6 pm. Features: This quick-serve outlet has a convenient location inside the terminal with
Deli/Subs seating in the food court area. Casual dress. Parking: street. Cards: AX, DC, MC, VI.
Sandwiches

PARK AVENUE CAFE Lunch: $16-$28 Dinner: $20-$39 Phone: 212/644-1900 (51)
Location: At Park Ave. 100 E 63rd St 10021. Hours: 11:30 am-3 & 5:30-10 pm, Fri & Sat 5:30 pm-11 pm, Sun 11 am-3 & 5:30-10 pm. Closed: 1/1, 12/25. Reservations: suggested. Features: Charm and sophistication
American with a touch of whimsy and the food is excellent. Ingenuity and consistency are the hallmarks of the changing nightly menu which focuses on contemporary cuisine with wide appeal. Bread basket is full of suprises. Side dishes are happy extras. Desserts are both fun and fabulous. Flights of wine are a good option with dinner. Dressy casual; cocktails. Parking: no self-parking. Cards: AX, DC, DS, JC, MC, VI.

PARK BISTRO Lunch: $17-$32 Dinner: $20-$32 Phone: 212/689-1360 (235)
Location: Between 28th and 29th sts. 414 Park Ave S 10016. Hours: noon-3 & 5-11 pm, Sat & Sun from 5 pm. Reservations: suggested. Features: Wonderful food fits the description of bistro cooking: bold, colorful,
French flavorful and hearty. Meaty hangar steak is topped with seasoned cream sauce, and chicken fricassee is in a rich demi-glace spiked with rosemary, black olives and sun-dried tomatoes. Excellent desserts are prepared on site. The small space gets crowded at night and can be a bit loud, but that's part of the charm. Casual dress; cocktails. Parking: street. Cards: AX, MC, VI.

PASHA RESTAURANT Dinner: $15-$24 Phone: 212/579-8751 (13)
Location: Between Columbus Ave and Central Park W. 70 W 71st St 10023. Hours: 5 pm-11 pm, Fri & Sat-11:30 pm, Sun 4 pm-10:30 pm. Closed: 7/4, 11/22, 12/25. Reservations: suggested. Features: Locals are loyal to
Turkish this jewel-red Turkish delight, where fragrant and flavorful dishes are prepared by a chef who knows flavor. The selection of appetizers shouldn't be bypassed, notably manti, a tender steamed dumpling filled with ground lamb and fresh mint drizzled with a light garlic-yogurt sauce. Lamb dishes, especially those with eggplant in the mix, are a standout. A prix fixe menu and outdoor sidewalk seating are available. Casual dress; cocktails. Parking: no self-parking. Cards: AX, MC, VI.

(See map and index starting on p. 382)

PATROON   Lunch: $21-$30   Dinner: $25-$38   Phone: 212/883-7373   206
▼▼▼▼   **Location:** Between Lexington and 3rd aves. 160 E 46th St 10017. **Hours:** noon-2:30 & 5:30-11 pm. Closed major
American   holidays. **Reservations:** suggested. **Features:** Patroon strikes a pose between an art deco steak house and a photo gallery showcasing striking stills in black and white. The menu is mostly American with a touch of a French accent; grilled seafood and a dramatic lobster presentation also make their case; sides such as porcini mashed or garlic roasted potatoes are extra and sized to split so plan accordingly. Dressy casual; cocktails. **Parking:** no self-parking. **Cards:** AX, DS, MC, VI.

PATSY'S ITALIAN RESTAURANT   Lunch: $18-$35   Dinner: $21-$39   Phone: 212/247-3491   49
▼▼▼▼   **Location:** Between Broadway and 8th Ave. 236 W 56th St 10019. **Hours:** noon-9:30 pm, Fri & Sat-10:30 pm.
South Italian   Closed major holidays. **Reservations:** suggested. **Features:** Open since 1944 and having catered to celebrities like Frank Sinatra, Madonna, David Letterman, George Clooney, and Oprah Winfrey, Patsy's offers traditional Neopolitan-style dishes as well as signature dishes such as calamari stuffed with seafood with garlic sauce, spicy lobster fra diavolo and stuffed veal chop Marsala in a cozy and inviting atmosphere with soft lighting and comfortable booths. Pre-theater menu. Parking at Central Park Systems, 235 W 56th. Dressy casual; cocktails. **Parking:** no self-parking. **Cards:** AX, CB, DC, DS, MC, VI.

PAYARD PATISSERIE & BISTRO   Lunch: $13-$29   Dinner: $26-$33   Phone: 212/717-5252   26
▼▼▼▼   **Location:** Between 73rd and 74th sts. 1032 Lexington Ave 10021. **Hours:** noon-3 & 5:45-10:30 pm, Fri & Sat-11
French   pm; pastry 7 am-11 pm. Closed major holidays; also Sun. **Reservations:** required. **Features:** Visually impressive with soft lights, tall ceilings, playful wall moldings and a loft dining room, this place exudes style. Bright cases are filled with the gleaming pastries, individual gateaux and tarts, chocolates and confectionaries that have made this place a staple for exquisite desserts. Dinner is popular with the locals, with satisfying changing specials seasoned and sauced by expert hands. Morning pastry and afternoon tea are other fine pleasures. Dressy casual; cocktails. **Parking:** no self-parking. **Cards:** AX, DC, MC, VI.

PERSHING SQUARE CAFE   Lunch: $15-$28   Dinner: $18-$35   Phone: 212/286-9600   217
▼▼▼   **Location:** At Park Ave. 90 E 42nd St 10017. **Hours:** 7-10:30 am, 11:30-3 & 5:30-10:30 pm, Sat & Sun 8-11 am,
American   11:30-3 & 5:30-10:30 pm. Closed: 5/28, 9/3, 12/25. **Reservations:** suggested. **Features:** Across the street from Grand Central, the lively joint is energized by the sounds of jazz playing and the din of the happy crowd. The handsome room features shaded lanterns that cast light over dark-wood tables flanked by brass-studded red-leather chairs. Sophisticated comfort food is tasty and hearty, with a measure of refinement. Fried oysters with sesame aioli are popular to start. Good choices include beef short ribs and chicken pot pie topped with a golden puff pastry dome. Casual dress; cocktails. **Parking:** no self-parking. **Cards:** AX, DC, DS, MC, VI.

PETROSSIAN   Lunch: $29-$37   Dinner: $29-$37   Phone: 212/245-2214   45
▼▼▼   **Location:** At 7th Ave. 182 W 58th St 10019. **Hours:** 11:30 am-3 & 5:30-11 pm, Sun-10 pm. Closed: 5/28, 7/4.
Continental   **Reservations:** suggested. **Features:** The restaurant's elegant, streamlined, art deco style—which employs marble floors, rose-tinted mirrors, etched glass, rows of shimmering champagne glasses behind the bar and sleek, bronze sculptures—says chic. Caviar, smoked salmon and foie gras are specialties at this New York institution. Semi-formal attire; cocktails. **Parking:** no self-parking. **Cards:** AX, CB, DC, JC, MC, VI.

PICHOLINE   Lunch: $35   Dinner: $78-$105   Phone: 212/724-8585   27
▼▼▼▼   **Location:** Between Broadway and Central Park W. 35 W 64th St 10023. **Hours:** 5 pm-11 pm, Thurs & Fri-11:45
French   pm, Sat 11:45 am-2 & 5-11:45 pm, Sun 5 pm-9 pm. Closed: 12/25; also Sun in summer. **Reservations:** suggested. **Features:** Noted as one of the city's best for good reason. The room is lovely with large, gilded oil paintings, plush seating and elaborately set tables with Italian linen and flowers. There is a menu to match. Layers of flavor that tickle the fancy of any true food lover can be found throughout the menu, unusual ingredients peppered here and there among traditional dishes expertly prepared with such happy results. Service is gracious and refined. Don't pass up the cheese tray, one of the best in town. Semi-formal attire; cocktails. **Parking:** no self-parking. **Cards:** AX, DC, MC, VI.

PIGALLE   Lunch: $7-$20   Dinner: $7-$24   Phone: 212/489-2233   110
▼▼▼   **Location:** At 48th St; in Hilton Garden Inn Times Square. 790 Eighth Ave 10019. **Hours:** 6:30 am-midnight.
Regional French   **Reservations:** accepted, suggested for dinner Fri & Sat. **Features:** The flavor of Paris is on this restaurant's menu, which features the cuisine of the Alsace region of France. Breakfast, lunch and dinner are served at this 1950s-style brasserie. The lively atmosphere and bustling staff make it a pleasant experience for everyone from theatergoers to families. Casual dress; cocktails. **Parking:** no self-parking. **Cards:** AX, DS, MC, VI.

PIG HEAVEN   Lunch: $8-$9   Dinner: $9-$16   Phone: 212/744-4333   20
▼▼▼   **Location:** Between 80th and 81st sts. 1540 2nd Ave 10028. **Hours:** 11:30 am-11:15 pm, Fri & Sat-12:15 am.
Chinese   **Reservations:** suggested. **Features:** Open for more than 20 years, the restaurant continues to offer a wide range of barbecue and pork specialties that draw on Cantonese and Szechuan influences. Also on the menu are lobster with ginger and scallions, whole sea bass with hot bean sauce, crispy prawns with walnuts and the more traditional dishes known to most fans of Chinese-American food. Warmer months allow for charming streetside seating under a canopy. Casual dress; cocktails. **Parking:** no self-parking. **Cards:** AX, DS, MC, VI.

THE PLAYWRIGHT TAVERN   Lunch: $10-$14   Dinner: $14-$25   Phone: 212/354-8404   144
▼▼▼   **Location:** Between 45th and 46th sts. 732 8th Ave 10036. **Hours:** 11 am-4 am. Closed: 12/25. **Features:** This
American   busy brewery features 20 different bottled beers as well as another 20 on tap. The atmosphere is lively and bustling with a friendly staff to keep your brew flowing. Casual dress; cocktails. **Parking:** street. **Cards:** AX, CB, DC, DS, JC, MC, VI.

PONGAL SOUTH INDIAN VEGETARIAN RESTAURANT   Lunch: $5-$12   Dinner: $8-$15   Phone: 212/355-4600   89
▼▼▼   **Location:** Corner of 63rd St. 1154 1st Ave 10021. **Hours:** noon-3 & 5-10:30 pm, Sat & Sun noon-10:30 pm.
Indian   Closed: 12/25. **Reservations:** accepted. **Features:** The small restaurant serves a good selection of vegetarian, (Kosher) Indian dishes which are prepared to order; a limited wine list is also offered. Casual dress; cocktails. **Parking:** no self-parking. **Cards:** AX, MC, VI.

(See map and index starting on p. 382)

THE POST HOUSE **Lunch:** $16-$40 **Dinner:** $22-$50 **Phone:** 212/935-2888 (47)
▼▼▼▼ **Location:** Between Park and Madison aves; in The Lowell Hotel. 28 E 63rd St 10021. **Hours:** noon-11 pm, Sat &
Sun from 5:30 pm. Closed major holidays. **Reservations:** suggested. **Features:** In the bustling, vibrant
Steak & Seafood atmosphere, guests can enjoy a relaxed meal of steak and seafood with a choice of fresh vegetables.
Accompany the entree with a selection from the award-winning wine list and a temptation from the dessert
menu—banana cream pie perhaps. Dressy casual; cocktails. **Parking:** on-site. **Cards:** AX, CB, DC, DS, JC, MC, VI.

RACHEL'S AMERICAN BISTRO **Lunch:** $8-$14 **Dinner:** $8-$22 **Phone:** 212/957-9050 (148)
▼▼ ▼▼ **Location:** Between 43rd and 44th sts. 608 9th Ave 10036. **Hours:** noon-11:30 pm; hours may vary. Closed: 3/23,
12/25. **Reservations:** accepted. **Features:** The eatery has the cozy feel of a neighborhood restaurant yet
American with a quiet, romantic atmosphere. The extensive menu offers New American cuisine with its International
influences. Patio dining is available seasonally. Casual dress; cocktails. **Parking:** no self-parking.
Cards: AX, MC, VI.

THE RAINBOW GRILL **Dinner:** $22-$47 **Phone:** 212/632-5100 (167)
▼▼▼▼ **Location:** 65th floor of Rockefeller Center. 30 Rockefeller Plaza, 65th Floor 10112. **Hours:** 5 pm-11:30 pm.
Reservations: suggested. **Features:** Initially conceived as supper club for the elite and influential of New
Italian York, this restaurant made its debut in 1934. Since then it has become known all over the world for its
breathtaking panoramic views and glamorous dreamlike atmosphere. Romance is alive with fine dining and
formal service. Semi-formal attire; cocktails. **Parking:** on-site (fee). **Cards:** AX, MC, VI.

RAKU-IT'S JAPANESE! **Lunch:** $9-$35 **Dinner:** $12-$125 **Phone:** 212/719-9055 (139)
▼▼ **Location:** Between Broadway and 8th Ave. 252 W 47th St 10036. **Hours:** noon-2:30 & 5-10:45 pm, Sat from 5
pm, Mon & Tues noon-2:30 & 5-10 pm. Closed major holidays; also Sun & President's Day.
Japanese **Reservations:** suggested. **Features:** Specializing in traditional dishes, the cozy little place is tucked away
as a quiet respite from the busy city bustle. "Crazy" rolls and chef's sushi specials made from fresh seafood
are offered daily. Casual dress; beer & wine only. **Parking:** on-site (fee) and street. **Cards:** AX, DC, DS, MC, VI. ☖

REDEYE GRILL **Lunch:** $12-$35 **Dinner:** $12-$35 **Phone:** 212/541-9000 (54)
▼▼▼ **Location:** At 56th St. 890 7th Ave 10019. **Hours:** 11:30 am-11:30 pm, Thurs-Sat to 12:30 am, Sun 11 am-11
pm. **Reservations:** suggested. **Features:** Perhaps only Grand Central Station is busier than the Redeye.
American Directly across from Carnegie Hall, this cavernous spot is a favorite among musicians, patrons of the arts,
and practically everyone else in midtown. Famous for its raw bar and diverse menu that includes everything
from sushi and sandwiches to dancing (yes, dancing) shrimp and prime aged steaks, the Redeye is the ultimate crowd pleaser.
Don't miss the clay-baked sea bass with tomato and capers, it's wonderfully satisfying. Casual dress; cocktails; entertainment.
Parking: street. **Cards:** AX, DC, MC, VI. ☖

REMI **Lunch:** $17-$34 **Dinner:** $18-$38 **Phone:** 212/581-4242 (86)
▼▼▼▼ **Location:** Between 6th (Ave of the Americas) and 7th aves. 145 W 53rd St 10019. **Hours:** noon-11 pm, Sat from 5
pm, Sun 5 pm-10 pm. **Reservations:** suggested. **Features:** Convenient to the theater district, this Italian
Italian eatery offers a contemporary-sleek appeal accented with wood floors, lengthy banquettes and modern
lighting. Casual dress; cocktails. **Parking:** on-site (fee). **Cards:** AX, DC, DS, MC, VI.

RENE PUJOL **Lunch:** $24 **Dinner:** $44 **Phone:** 212/246-3023 (72)
▼▼▼ **Location:** Between 8th and 9th aves. 321 W 51st St 10019. **Hours:** noon-2:30 & 5-10:30 pm, Fri & Sat-11:30 pm,
Sun noon-2:30 & 4:30-7 pm. Closed major holidays; also Mon. **Reservations:** accepted.
Provincial French **Features:** Contemporary presentations of classic French food are the hallmark of the cozy theater district
restaurant. The brick fireplace lends to a comfortable and relaxing atmosphere in which diners enjoy the
finest quality seafood, which is expertly prepared but simply presented. Dressy casual; cocktails. **Parking:** street.
Cards: MC, VI.

RESTAURANT NIPPON **Lunch:** $12-$28 **Dinner:** $22-$45 **Phone:** 212/758-0226 (173)
▼▼ **Location:** Between 3rd and Lexington aves. 155 E 52nd St 10022. **Hours:** noon-2:30 & 5:30-10 pm, Fri-10:30 pm,
Sat 5:30 pm-10:30 pm. Closed: Sun. **Reservations:** suggested. **Features:** The dining room is relaxed and
Japanese tranquil with a few private rooms and tables separated by screens. There is a large menu of homemade
soba noodle dishes, which are among fine traditional dishes served beside familiar standbys. The dessert
menu includes a wonderful choice of yokan, red bean cake. Service is attentive. Dressy casual; cocktails. **Parking:** no self-
parking. **Cards:** AX, DC, JC, MC, VI.

RICE 'N' BEANS **Lunch:** $8-$9 **Dinner:** $14-$23 **Phone:** 212/265-4444 (68)
▼▼ **Location:** Between 50th and 51st sts. 744 9th Ave 10019. **Hours:** noon-11 pm. Closed: 1/1, 11/22, 12/25.
Reservations: accepted. **Features:** The 9th Avenue location means that most people who wander into the
Brazilian seven-table storefront have prior knowledge about the savory offerings of sauced, stewed, grilled, roasted
and sauteed chicken, seafood and meat dishes, which are served with yellow rice and black beans. Home-
style food is simple but flavorful and hearty. The decor could not be more casual. Casual dress; beer & wine only. **Parking:**
street. **Cards:** AX, DS, MC, VI.

RIINGO **Lunch:** $11-$22 **Dinner:** $17-$28 **Phone:** 212/867-4200 (211)
ⒶⒶⒶ **Location:** Between 2nd and 3rd aves. 205 E 45th St 10017. **Hours:** 7 am-11, noon-2:30 & 5:30-10 pm, Thurs &
Fri-midnight, Sat 7 am-3 & 5:30-midnight, Sun 11:30 am-3 & 5:30-10:30 pm. **Reservations:** suggested.
▼▼▼▼ **Features:** Although the look is casual, there are marks of finery, including ebony wood trim, bamboo floors,
red plaster walls and a marble staircase to an intimate dining area. Downstairs dining, hardly larger, makes
American diners feel privileged. Gloriously prepared food arrives looking lovely. Braised pork belly with honey-glazed
garlic, grilled rib eye with onion chutney and seared char with herb-coconut milk only sound simple. Finely
prepared sushi, side dishes and desserts complete a distinguished meal. Dressy casual; cocktails. **Parking:** no self-parking.
Cards: AX, DC, DS, MC, VI. *(See color ad p 421)* ☖

(See map and index starting on p. 382)

RISTORANTE CINQUE TERRE   Lunch: $8-$13   Dinner: $9-$35   Phone: 212/867-2260   [224]
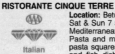
Italian
Location: Between Park and Madison aves. 22 E 38th St 10016. **Hours:** 7 am-10:30, noon-2:30 & 5-10:30 pm, Sat & Sun 7 am-10:30 & 5-10:30 pm. **Reservations:** suggested. **Features:** The decor is simple and faintly Mediterranean, while service is relaxed but efficient. Pleasing dishes are freshly made and nicely flavored. Pasta and meat dishes include fresh tagliolini with sea urchin and gray mullet bottarga and homemade pasta squares sauteed in butter and sage with wild boar ragu perfumed in truffle oil. Richly flavored meat and fish dishes reflect a distinctly authentic soul. Dressy casual; cocktails. **Parking:** valet and street.
Cards: AX, DC, DS, MC, VI.

ROCK CENTER CAFE   Lunch: $17-$35   Dinner: $20-$39   Phone: 212/332-7620   [153]
American
Location: Between 5th and 6th (Ave of the Americas) aves; at Rockefeller Center Skating Rink, concourse level. 20 W 50th St 10020. **Hours:** 7:30-10:30 am, 11:30-3 & 5-10 pm, Sat 11 am-3 & 4-10 pm, Sun 10 am-3 & 4-10 pm. **Reservations:** suggested. **Features:** A bright, simply done dining room of beige looks directly at the Rockefeller Center Fountain year-round and the skating rink in winter. A collection of original Andy Warhol lithographs hang above the bar, adding vibrant color. The menu consists of pasta dishes, cioppino, veal chops, roast chicken, fish and steak. A more modest and limited menu is presented at lunch. Casual dress; cocktails. **Parking:** no self-parking.
Cards: AX, CB, DC, DS, JC, MC, VI.

ROSA MEXICANO   Lunch: $10-$18   Dinner: $17-$27   Phone: 212/977-7700   [31]
Mexican
Location: At 62nd St. 61 Columbus Ave 10023. **Hours:** noon-3 & 5-11:30 pm, Sun & Mon-10:30 pm; Saturday & Sunday brunch 11:30 am-2:30 pm. **Closed:** 11/22. **Reservations:** suggested. **Features:** The space is wide open and handsome with sophisticated, comfortable decor and a water wall falling over high diving figures. Meals usually start with the renowned guacamole, prepared tableside from fresh avacados, onion and cilantro. The menu, rich with unusual flavor pairings which please, isn't typical, but refined with dishes like spicy mahi mahi seviche, wild mushroom tamale with an intense mole or tender aromatic lamb shank braised in banana and avacado leaves. Dressy casual; cocktails. **Parking:** no self-parking. **Cards:** AX, DC, DS, MC, VI.

RUBY FOO'S DIM SUM & SUSHI PALACE   Lunch: $16-$35   Dinner: $16-$35   Phone: 212/489-5600   [108]
Asian
Location: In Time Square; at 49th St and Broadway. 1626 Broadway 10019. **Hours:** 11:30 am-11:30 pm, Fri & Sat-12:30 am. **Closed:** 11/22, 12/25. **Reservations:** suggested. **Features:** Whether it's dim sum, sushi or full meals, this restaurant will please your palate. The Pan-Asian cuisine reflects influences from Japan, China, Thailand and Korea, as well as other Asian countries. The stylish dining room with Asian accents creates a comfortable dining atmosphere for any occasion. Dressy casual; cocktails. **Parking:** no self-parking. **Cards:** AX, CB, DC, DS, MC, VI.

RUBY FOO'S DIM SUM & SUSHI PALACE   Lunch: $6-$19   Dinner: $6-$19   Phone: 212/724-6700   [4]
Asian
Location: At 77th St and Broadway. 2182 Broadway 10024. **Hours:** 11:30 am-11 pm, Wed & Thurs-11:30 pm, Fri & Sat-12:30 am. **Closed:** 12/25. **Reservations:** suggested. **Features:** Whether it's dim sum, sushi or full meals, the food will please the palate. Pan-Asian cuisine reflects influences from Japan, China, Thailand and Korea, as well as other Asian countries. The stylish dining room with Asian accents creates a comfortable atmosphere for any occasion. Dressy casual; cocktails. **Parking:** no self-parking. **Cards:** AX, CB, DC, DS, MC, VI.

RUSSO'S STEAK & PASTA   Lunch: $13-$25   Dinner: $16-$32   Phone: 212/621-8537   [93]
American
Location: Between 51st and 52nd sts; in Sheraton Manhattan Hotel. 790 7th Ave 10019. **Hours:** 6:30 am-10:30 & noon-10:30 pm, Sat & Sun 6:30 am-noon & 4-10:30 pm. **Reservations:** accepted. **Features:** The nice spot is convenient to Time Square. Preparations are tasty, and the staff is cordial. Casual dress; cocktails. **Parking:** street. **Cards:** AX, MC, VI.

ST. ANDREWS   Lunch: $12-$18   Dinner: $17-$27   Phone: 212/840-8413   [183]
Scottish
Location: Between Broadway and 6th Ave (Ave of the Americas). 120 W 44th St 10036. **Hours:** 11:30 am-2 am, Sun noon-midnight. **Closed:** 11/22, 12/25. **Reservations:** suggested. **Features:** In the middle of the theater district, the busy brewpub is the place to be seen. The menu lists plenty from which to choose, and everything is tasty. Homemade cavatelli with grilled chicken is a favorite. It's worth saving room for one of the desserts, which are made on the premises. The beer list is extensive. Casual dress; cocktails. **Parking:** no self-parking. **Cards:** AX, MC, VI.

SALMON RIVER   Lunch: $12-$26   Dinner: $12-$26   Phone: 212/481-7887   [216]
Seafood
Location: Between Madison and 5th aves; in Courtyard by Marriott New York Manhattan/5th Avenue. 3 E 40th St 10016. **Hours:** 7 am-10 & noon-9:30 pm, Sat & Sun 7:30 am-10:30 & noon-9:30 pm. **Closed:** 11/22, 12/24, 12/25. **Reservations:** suggested. **Features:** This contemporary restaurant is a great place for seafood lovers. Dressy casual; cocktails. **Parking:** street. **Cards:** AX, DC, DS, MC, VI.

SAN DOMENICO NY   Lunch: $30   Dinner: $25-$35   Phone: 212/265-5959   [41]
Italian
Location: W 59th St; between Broadway and 7th Ave. 240 Central Park S 10019. **Hours:** noon-2:30 & 5:30-11 pm, Sat 5 pm-11:30 pm, Sun 11:30 am-3 & 5-10 pm; hours vary off season. **Closed:** 12/25. **Reservations:** suggested. **Features:** A seasonal art collection enhances the sophisticated, contemporary dining room. The building was designed by Italian architects and constructed of Italian materials. Risotto parmigiano with beef glaze is an outstanding choice, and the soft, egg-yolk-filled ravioli in truffle butter is a popular signature dish. Service is relaxed though professional. Semi-formal attire; cocktails. **Parking:** no self-parking. **Cards:** AX, CB, DC, MC, VI.

SAN MARTIN RESTAURANT   *Menu on AAA.com*   Lunch: $11-$16   Dinner: $15-$32   Phone: 212/832-0888   [187]
Italian
Location: Between Lexington and 3rd aves. 143 E 49th St 10017. **Hours:** noon-midnight. **Reservations:** accepted. **Features:** Patrons visit the pleasant Italian stop for a traditional meal without any pomp or circumstance. Specialty dishes please regular guests who come for penne pasta with porcini mushrooms, sun-dried tomatoes, green peas in cream sauce, rosemary-scented baby lamb chops or porcini mushroom ravioli with Gorgonzola walnut sauce. The mood is all-around casual and friendly. Casual dress; cocktails. **Parking:** street. **Cards:** AX, CB, DC, DS, MC, VI.

(See map and index starting on p. 382)

SARABETH'S   Lunch: $8-$12   Dinner: $14-$25   Phone: 212/496-6280   ②

American

Location: Between 80th and 81st sts. 423 Amsterdam Ave 10024. **Hours:** 8 am-10:30 pm, Sat 8 am-4 & 5:30-11 pm, Sun 8 am-4 & 5:30-9:30 pm. Closed: 12/25. **Reservations:** accepted, for dinner. **Features:** Menu offerings include Goldi lox, which blends smoked salmon and cream cheese; pumpkin waffles; and Popeye eggs, which are served on homemade English muffins. The home-like atmosphere is reminiscent of a country inn. Baked goods are delicious. Casual dress; cocktails. **Parking:** no self-parking. **Cards:** AX, DC, MC, VI.

SARDI'S   Lunch: $17-$30   Dinner: $19-$35   Phone: 212/221-8440   ⟨168⟩

Continental

Location: Between Broadway and 8th Ave. 234 W 44th St 10036. **Hours:** 11:30 am-3 & 3:30-11:30 pm, Fri & Sat-midnight, Sun noon-3 & 3:30-8 pm. Closed: Mon. **Reservations:** suggested. **Features:** A New York institution, located deep in the theater district, is known for the signed caricatures of famous faces which fill the walls. Professional waiters wait in bright red jackets and black tie to tend to you. Come ready for a dose of nostalgia. It's administered as soon as you walk into the dining room. Cannelloni au gratin, shrimp Sardi and crab cakes are old time favorites. Prix fixe pre-theater dinner available. Casual dress; cocktails. **Parking:** street. **Cards:** AX, DC, DS, MC, VI. **Classic**

THE SEA GRILL   Lunch: $28-$45   Dinner: $28-$45   Phone: 212/332-7610   ⟨156⟩

Seafood

Location: Between 5th & 6th aves; At Rockefeller Center Skating Rink, concourse level. 19 W 49th St 10020. **Hours:** 11:30 am-2:15 & 5-9:45 pm, Sat from 5 pm. Closed: 5/28, 7/4, 9/3; also Sun. **Reservations:** suggested. **Features:** A quick elevator ride brings guests down level with the Rockefeller Center Fountain and skating rink to a lovely dining room of beige and sea blue hues. There is a din of the crowd enjoying fresh seafood, ordered by the piece for create-your-own platters or raw in ceviche, carpaccio or tartare dishes. Appetizers are enlivened with herbs, light vinaigrettes or sauces, and entrees of fresh fish are prepared as diners like. Also offered are pre-designed entrees. Dressy casual; cocktails. **Parking:** no self-parking. **Cards:** AX, CB, DC, DS, MC, VI.

SERAFINA FABULOUS PIZZA   Lunch: $6-$12   Dinner: $10-$26   Phone: 212/734-2676   ⟨12⟩

Italian

Location: Between E 78th and E 79th sts. 1022 Madison Ave 10021. **Hours:** 11:30 am-midnight. **Features:** This busy outlet offers both original and creative Northern Italian fare. The crowd is always a diverse one and the windows are opened in good weather with patio dining also available. Casual dress; cocktails. **Parking:** street. **Cards:** AX, DC, DS, JC, MC, VI.

SHUN LEE   Lunch: $10-$24   Dinner: $12-$26   Phone: 212/595-8895   ⟨25⟩

Chinese

Location: Between Columbus Ave and Central Park W. 43 W 65th St 10023. **Hours:** noon-midnight, Sun-10:30 pm. Closed: 11/22. **Reservations:** suggested. **Features:** Across the street from Lincoln Center, the often-packed restaurant is a neighborhood favorite for pre-theater, ballet or opera dinners. The sleek, black dining room, with red-eyed dragons snaking around the perimeter, is abuzz from the crowd, and some seats are tight. However, traditional preparations of Hunan and Szechuan cuisine are the true draw here. There is also a cafe-like dining room, which is chic, trendy and fun with wild animal lights dangling overhead. Dressy casual; cocktails. **Parking:** no self-parking. **Cards:** AX, DC, DS, MC, VI.

SHUN LEE PALACE   Lunch: $12-$24   Dinner: $14-$39   Phone: 212/371-8844   ⟨141⟩

Chinese

Location: Between Lexington and 3rd aves. 155 E 55th St 10022. **Hours:** noon-11:30 pm, Sun-11 pm. Closed: 11/22. **Reservations:** suggested. **Features:** A gentle ambience—enhanced by subtle lighting, silk lanterns and frosted-glass art—settles over the elegant rooms. The menu of gourmet Szechuan and Cantonese selections lists such excellent, not-to-be-missed selections as sliced duck with fresh ginger, heavenly sea bass and sole with crisp bones. Semi-formal attire; cocktails. **Parking:** no self-parking. **Cards:** AX, DC, MC, VI.

SIAM INN   Lunch: $8-$12   Dinner: $10-$17   Phone: 212/757-4006   ⟨78⟩

Ethnic

Location: Between W 51st and W 52nd sts. 854 8th Ave 10019. **Hours:** 11:45 am-11 pm, Sat noon-11:30 pm, Sun noon-11 pm. Closed major holidays. **Reservations:** suggested. **Features:** Familiar curried, grilled meat, sauteed and noodle dishes are well-prepared and flavorful, taking advantage of the herbs and spices that make the flavors bright and fresh. Presentations are decorative with a delicate touch. Soft and inviting decor, with a rose on each table, is a cut above though still casual. Casual dress; cocktails. **Parking:** no self-parking. **Cards:** AX, CB, DC, MC, VI.

SMITH & WOLLENSKY   Lunch: $15-$42   Dinner: $18-$48   Phone: 212/753-1530   ⟨192⟩

Steak House

Location: At 49th St. 797 3rd Ave 10022. **Hours:** 11:45 am-midnight. Closed: 11/22, 12/25. **Reservations:** required. **Features:** Patrons savor the flavors of New Orleans at the elegant, well-known steakhouse. A tempting menu awaits, as does the clublike atmosphere, which incorporates rich, dark woods and soft lighting. Service is professional and capable. Casual dress; cocktails. **Parking:** street. **Cards:** AX, DC, DS, MC, VI.

SOCIAL BAR & GRILL   Lunch: $8-$11   Dinner: $8-$11   Phone: 212/459-0643   ⟨107⟩

American

Location: Between W 48th and W 49th sts. 795 8th Ave 10019. **Hours:** 11:30 am-4 am, Sun from noon. Closed: 12/25. **Features:** This popular Hells Kitchen bar and grill has three floors of dining plus a large rooftop patio where smoking is permitted. On the menu you will find everything from burgers and sandwiches to chicken, steaks and seafood. Casual dress; cocktails. **Parking:** no self-parking. **Cards:** AX, DC, DS, MC, VI.

SOMBRERO MEXICAN RESTAURANT   Lunch: $13-$18   Dinner: $17-$19   Phone: 212/586-4853   ⟨105⟩

Mexican

Location: Corner of 8th Ave. 303 W 48th St 10036. **Hours:** noon-midnight. **Features:** This cozy restaurant is located on a side street just off 8th Avenue with patio dining available in good weather. They offer daily specials and reasonable prices with friendly service. Casual dress; cocktails. **Parking:** street. **Cards:** AX, DC, DS, MC, VI.

SPARKS STEAK HOUSE   Lunch: $25-$38   Dinner: $25-$38   Phone: 212/687-4855   ⟨208⟩

Steak & Seafood

Location: Between 2nd and 3rd aves. 210 E 46th St 10017. **Hours:** noon-close, Sat from 5 pm. Closed major holidays; also Sun. **Reservations:** suggested. **Features:** The pedestrian New York legend serves ample portions in a boisterous atmosphere. Be prepared to wait even with reservations. Dressy casual; cocktails. **Parking:** no self-parking. **Cards:** AX, CB, DC, DS, MC, VI.

(See map and index starting on p. 382)

STAGE DELI

Lunch: $10-$20   **Dinner:** $10-$20   **Phone:** 212/245-7850   70

Deli/Subs
Sandwiches

Location: At 52nd St. 834 7th Ave 10019. **Hours:** 6 am-2 am. **Reservations:** not accepted. **Features:** Diners are sure to leave very full and very satisfied at this eatery, known for huge portions of fine deli fare and for their slogan, "If you come for lunch, don't make dinner plans." Sandwiches, desserts and meals are sized for sharing and are deliciously decadent. For a real eating challenge, check out the triple decker sandwiches, each named after the celebrities who created them. The cheesecake is not to be missed.
Casual dress; cocktails. **Parking:** no self-parking. **Cards:** AX, MC, VI.

THE STEAKHOUSE AT MONKEY BAR

Lunch: $18-$32   **Dinner:** $18-$36   **Phone:** 212/838-2600   131

American

Location: Between Madison and Park aves. 60 E 54th St 10022. **Hours:** 11:30 am-2:30 & 5:30-11 pm, Sat from 5:30 pm, Mon 11:30 am-2:30 & 5:30-10 pm. Closed: 12/25. **Reservations:** suggested. **Features:** Black-and-white photographs of yesteryear's stars and rich velvet fabrics evoke '40s Hollywood glamour. Adding whimsy are a monkey mural and monkey figures that hang from chandeliers and hide among the railings, ready to swing into the jungle leaf pattern of plush banquettes. The bar has served the signature penny martini and banana highball since 1936. Well-prepared food deserves no less a mention and has kept this place in peanuts. Live piano music is performed weekdays and jazz on weekends. Dressy casual; cocktails; entertainment. **Parking:** no self-parking. **Cards:** AX, DC, DS, MC, VI.

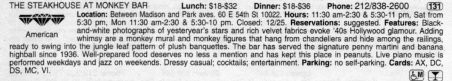

SUGIYAMA

Dinner: $32-$175   **Phone:** 212/956-0670   55

Japanese

Location: Between Broadway and 8th Ave. 251 W 55th St 10019. **Hours:** 5:30 pm-11:45 pm. Closed major holidays; also Sun & Mon. **Reservations:** suggested. **Features:** Not the place for the faint of heart, the restaurant welcomes food-lovers for kaiseki meals, in which the chef prepares a multi-course offering of exotic dishes that are lovely to look at. The food—elegant and amazing in range—may include tiny, translucent baby eels or a small fried crab to be eaten whole. The point of all 8, 10 or 12 courses is to be highly aware of the beauty and flavor of the food. Here, it is easy. Casual dress; beer & wine only. **Parking:** street. **Cards:** AX, DC, MC, VI.

SUSHI ANN

Lunch: $20   **Dinner:** $20   **Phone:** 212/755-1780   157

Japanese

Location: Between Madison and Park aves. 38 E 51st St 10022. **Hours:** noon-2:45 & 6-10 pm, Sat from 6 pm. Closed major holidays; also Sun. **Reservations:** suggested. **Features:** A good selection of authentic and attractively prepared sushi is served at this conveniently located restaurant. The service overall is pleasant and efficient. Casual dress; beer & wine only. **Parking:** street. **Cards:** AX, DC, MC, VI.

SUSHIDEN SIXTH AVENUE

Lunch: $8-$24   **Dinner:** $10-$30   **Phone:** 212/398-2800   138

Japanese

Location: Between 6th (Ave of the Americas) and 7th aves. 123 W 49th St 10020-1101. **Hours:** 11:45 am-2:30 & 5-10 pm, Sat-9 pm. Closed major holidays; also Sun. **Reservations:** accepted. **Features:** Watch the chefs create works of art with sushi at this contemporary upscale restaurant. The menu provides them with plenty of room to work with its extensive offerings of sushi and other Japanese favorites. Casual dress; cocktails.
Parking: no self-parking. **Cards:** AX, DC, MC, VI.

SUSHI YASUDA

Lunch: $18-$29   **Dinner:** $18-$29   **Phone:** 212/972-1001   220

Japanese

Location: Between 2nd and 3rd aves. 204 E 43rd St 10017. **Hours:** noon-2:15 & 6-10:15 pm, Sat from 6 pm. Closed major holidays; also Sun. **Reservations:** suggested. **Features:** Typically handsome and simple decor makes use of the large space, and beautifully grained blond wood is everywhere the eye looks. The fine sushi restaurant serves quality fresh fish, which is well cut and tender. Some fish on the list of available options are unusual. Only one hot dish of grilled sea bass or salmon shares menu space with the sushi, sashimi and rolls. Flexible combination platters give diners variety. Dressy casual; cocktails. **Parking:** no self-parking. **Cards:** AX, DC, MC, VI.

SUSHIZEN

Lunch: $19-$24   **Dinner:** $19-$31   **Phone:** 212/302-0707   185

Japanese

Location: Between Broadway and 6th Ave (Ave of the Americas). 108 W 44th St 10036. **Hours:** noon-2:45 & 5:30-10 pm, Sat from 5 pm. Closed major holidays; also Sun. **Reservations:** suggested. **Features:** A relaxed and well-heeled clientele squeeze into the cozy and serene, if loud, dining room to spoil themselves with the freshest fish, beautifully presented on lacquer trays and attractive pottery dishes. Choose your own meal or leave it to the chef's wise discretion. Dressy casual; cocktails. **Parking:** no self-parking. **Cards:** AX, MC, VI.

TAO

Lunch: $16-$28   **Dinner:** $16-$28   **Phone:** 212/888-2288   81

Asian

Location: Between Madison and Park aves. 42 E 58th St 10022. **Hours:** 11:30 am-midnight, Wed-Fri to 1 am, Sat 5 pm-1 am, Sun 5 pm-midnight. Closed: 11/22, 12/25. **Reservations:** suggested. **Features:** Massive carved doors lead into a dark, candlelit sanctuary resembling a temple in a lost city deep in the jungle. Towering brick walls with inset statuary, huge lanterns, banners and a giant Buddha sitting before a fish pond are good conversation starters. The large menu provides an exercise in self-control. Squab lettuce wraps, dragon-tail spare ribs, miso-glazed sea bass, Mongolian filet mignon and Hong Kong XO shrimp are samples. Prix fixe lunch available. Dressy casual; cocktails. **Parking:** no self-parking. **Cards:** AX, DC, MC, VI.

TAVERN ON THE GREEN

Lunch: $20-$29   **Dinner:** $23-$39   **Phone:** 212/873-3200   23

American

Location: In Central Park. Central Park at W 67th St 10023. **Hours:** 11:30 am-3 & 5-11 pm, Fri-11:30 pm, Sat 10 am-3:15 & 5-11 pm, Sun 10 am-3:15 & 5-10 pm. **Reservations:** suggested. **Features:** One of New York's most enchanting dining rooms has visual delights around every corner. Inside and out, flowers are draped, walls are mural-covered, and all is dripping with lights and lanterns, creating a festival for the eyes. Dishes suit just about every taste, but whatever guests order is beside the point. Casual dress; cocktails; entertainment. **Parking:** valet. **Cards:** AX, CB, DC, DS, MC, VI.

TICK TOCK DINER

Lunch: $8-$19   **Dinner:** $8-$19   **Phone:** 212/268-8444   215

American

Location: At 34th St. 481 8th Ave 10001. **Hours:** 24 hours. **Features:** This corner restaurant offers the comfort foods one would expect from a diner, as well as specials like their choice, thick New York sirloin steak with potatoes and steamed vegetables. Casual dress; beer & wine only. **Parking:** no self-parking. **Cards:** DC, MC, VI.

(See map and index starting on p. 382)

TOLEDO RESTAURANT   Lunch: $23-$45   Dinner: $23-$45   Phone: 212/696-5036   (229)
▼▼▼▼
Spanish
Location: Between 5th and Madison aves. 6 E 36th St 10016. **Hours:** noon-10:30 pm. Closed major holidays; also Sun. **Reservations:** accepted. **Features:** Gracious, attentive service is as pleasant as the handsome room, which displays distinguished still-life paintings softly lit by sconces and a skylight. The menu lists seafood and meats, served with colorful herbs, garlicky sauces and yellow rice. Pitchers of fruit-filled sangria look irresistible. Dishes are brought to the table and served in the traditional style, and then the dessert cart comes by for the finale. Semi-formal attire; cocktails. **Parking:** street. **Cards:** AX, CB, DC, DS, MC, VI.   ⵆ

TOWN   Lunch: $21-$30   Dinner: $22-$36   Phone: 212/582-4445   (84)
▼▼▼▼
American
Location: Between 5th and 6th (Ave of the Americas) aves.; in The Chambers Hotel. 15 W 56th St 10019. **Hours:** 7 am-10:30, noon-2:30 & 5:30-11 pm, Sat from 5:30 pm; Sunday brunch. Closed: 1/1. **Reservations:** suggested. **Features:** The contemporary dining room is a looker, with soft, neutral colors, fine fabric, wood-veneer walls and a glass waterfall. Skillfully conceived and carried out, dishes are modern themselves and devilishly good. The upstairs bar overlooks the dining room and has a small but intriguing menu of its own. Prix fixe menu is available for lunch and dinner. Dressy casual; cocktails. **Parking:** no self-parking. **Cards:** AX, MC, VI.   ⵆⵆ

TRATTORIA DELL'ARTE   Lunch: $16-$28   Dinner: $16-$28   Phone: 212/245-9800   (48)
▼▼ ▼▼
Northern Italian
Location: Between 56th and 57th sts. 900 7th Ave 10019. **Hours:** 11:45 am-11:30 pm, Sun 11 am-10:30 pm. **Reservations:** suggested. **Features:** Convenient to Carnegie Hall, the whimsical, artsy restaurant bustles with energy. The extensive vegetable and seafood antipasto bar is a great place to start, but from there the decisions get harder. From great thin-crust lobster pizzas to savory pasta dishes, nothing disappoints. In fine weather, many diners prefer to take a seat on the sidewalk patio. Dressy casual; cocktails. **Parking:** no self-parking. **Cards:** AX, DC, DS, MC, VI.   ⵆ

TRIOMPHE NEW YORK   Lunch: $10-$26   Dinner: $20-$50   Phone: 212/453-4233   (191)
▼▼▼▼
French
Location: Between 5th and 6th (Ave of the Americas) aves.; in The Iroquois Hotel. 49 W 44th St 10036. **Hours:** 7-10:30 am, 11:45-2:30 & 5:45-11 pm, Sat 7 am-11:30 & 5:45-11 pm, Sun 7-11:30 am. Closed: 11/22, 12/24, 12/25. **Reservations:** suggested. **Features:** The elegant, cozy little restaurant offers French-American cuisine with an International flair. Enjoy refined food with well-balanced flavors and the attentive service. Dressy casual; cocktails. **Parking:** street. **Cards:** AX, DC, DS, MC, VI.   ⵆ

TUPELO GRILL   Lunch: $13-$27   Dinner: $15-$30   Phone: 212/760-2700   (218)
▼▼ ▼▼
American
Location: Between 7th and 8th aves. 1 Penn Plaza 10019. **Hours:** 11:30 am-4 & 5-10 pm. Closed major holidays; also Sat & Sun. **Reservations:** suggested. **Features:** Located directly across the street from Madison Square Garden, the eatery is a great place for business or after-event lunch or dining. Casual dress; cocktails. **Parking:** street. **Cards:** AX, DC, DS, MC, VI.   ⵆ

UNCLE JACK'S STEAKHOUSE   Lunch: $15-$30   Dinner: $40-$60   Phone: 212/244-0005   (205)
▼▼▼▼
Steak & Seafood
Location: At 34th St. 440 9th Ave 10001. **Hours:** 11:30 am-11 pm, Thurs & Fri-midnight, Sat 4 pm-midnight, Sun 3 pm-11 pm. Closed major holidays. **Reservations:** suggested. **Features:** Casual dress; cocktails. **Parking:** street. **Cards:** AX, MC, VI.

UNCLE NICK'S GREEK CUISINE   Lunch: $8-$10   Dinner: $10-$25   Phone: 212/245-7992   (65)
▼▼
Greek
Location: Between 50th and 51st sts. 747 9th Ave 10019. **Hours:** noon-11 pm, Fri & Sat-11:30 pm. Closed: 1/1, 3/23, 12/25. **Reservations:** accepted. **Features:** Quick, no-nonsense Greek cuisine—such as spanakopita, moussaka, kebabs, gyros and monumental salads meant for sharing—is served by a casual clan of staff members. This is a great place to bring children. The tapas dinner menu at the sister restaurant next door is an option, but appetizer variety is plentiful here, too. Casual dress; cocktails. **Parking:** no self-parking. **Cards:** AX, DC, DS, MC, VI.

VATAN   Dinner: $24   Phone: 212/689-5666   (238)
▼▼ ▼▼
Indian
Location: Between 28th and 29th sts. 409 3rd Ave 10016. **Hours:** 5:30 pm-11:30 pm. Closed: Mon. **Reservations:** required. **Features:** There are few like this restaurant in New York. Diners get the sense of being seated in a rural, idyllic Indian village with a leafy tree, village well, thatched-roof huts, fancy doorways and colorful mural scenes. The menu exists only to show what will be served in various courses, but the quantity and level of spice are up to the guest. Aromatic vegetarian dishes, some wonderfully distinctive, provide a brief education in pleasant taste. Casual dress; beer & wine only. **Parking:** on-site. **Cards:** AX, MC, VI.   ⵆ

VIAND RESTAURANT-CAFE   Lunch: $8-$20   Dinner: $10-$25   Phone: 212/249-8250   (15)
▼▼ ▼▼
American
Location: Corner of 78th St. 1011 Madison Ave 10021. **Hours:** 6 am-10 pm. **Features:** The cozy diner and coffee shop is famous for its hot roast turkey carved to order; giant chef salads, deli-style sandwiches and Greek specialties are also offered. Casual dress. **Parking:** no self-parking. **Cards:** AX, MC, VI.

VICEVERSA   Lunch: $13-$20   Dinner: $15-$28   Phone: 212/399-9291   (71)
▼▼▼▼
Italian
Location: Between 8th and 9th aves. 325 W 51st St 10019. **Hours:** noon-2:30 & 5-11 pm, Sat from 5 pm. Closed major holidays; also Sun. **Reservations:** required. **Features:** Located on a charming residential street, this restaurant features contemporary Italian cuisine. The attractive dining room has a clean look and is decorated in neutral tones. Dressy casual; cocktails. **Parking:** no self-parking. **Cards:** AX, DC, MC, VI.

(See map and index starting on p. 382)

VICTOR'S CAFE 52 Lunch: $8-$19   Dinner: $10-$32   Phone: 212/586-7714 (80)
Cuban

Location: Between Broadway and 8th Ave. 236 W 52nd St 10019. **Hours:** noon-11 pm, Wed & Thur-11:30 pm, Fri & Sat noon-midnight. **Reservations:** suggested. **Features:** Wildly colorful wall murals lend energy, boldness and a touch of ethnicity to the upbeat dining room and colorful atrium area. There is no doubt about these Cuban digs when the food arrives—it looks and tastes good. Buttery-soft caramelized plantains, grilled skirt steak with tangy, garlicky chimichurri sauce and, of course, fragrant black beans with fluffy white rice make a lovely meal. Pictures of famous folks who have dined here are on display. Casual dress; cocktails. **Parking:** no self-parking. **Cards:** AX, CB, DC, MC, VI.

THE VIEW   Dinner: $55   Phone: 212/398-1900 (159)
American

Location: Between 45th and 46th sts; motor entrance on 46th St; in New York Marriott Marquis. 1535 Broadway 10036. **Hours:** 5:30 pm-10 pm, Fri & Sat 5 pm-11:30 pm, Sun 10:30 am-2 & 5:30-10 pm. **Reservations:** suggested. **Features:** The city's only revolving rooftop restaurant, The View gets its name for obvious reasons. Chilean sea bass and seared veal chop are among appetizing dishes on a menu of creative fare. In addition to being tasty, desserts are showy and fun. Two prix fixe menus available. Dressy casual; cocktails; entertainment. **Parking:** on-site. **Cards:** AX, CB, DC, DS, JC, MC, VI.

VIRGIL'S REAL BARBECUE Lunch: $7-$24   Dinner: $7-$24   Phone: 212/921-9494 (180)
Barbecue

Location: Between Broadway and 6th Ave (Ave of the Americas). 152 W 44th St 10036. **Hours:** 11:30 am-midnight, Sun & Mon-11 pm. Closed: 12/25. **Reservations:** accepted. **Features:** It's a good thing there are lots of tables because crowds flock here for smoky, meaty, succulent, finger-licking, gooey barbecue ribs, brisket, shrimp and pulled pork, which are served in generous portions with mustard slaw and other sides. Free tea refills might make guests forget they're in New York City. There are no napkins, but towels—clean and dry before the meal and hot and damp after—are plentiful. Service is brisk and friendly. Casual dress; cocktails. **Parking:** no self-parking. **Cards:** AX, DC, DS, MC, VI.

VONG RESTAURANT Lunch: $19-$40   Dinner: $19-$40   Phone: 212/486-9592 (158)
Thai

Location: Between 2nd and 3rd aves. 200 E 54th St 10022. **Hours:** noon-2:30 & 5:30-10:30 pm, Fri-11 pm, Sat 5 pm-11 pm, Sun 5:30 pm-10 pm. Closed major holidays. **Reservations:** suggested. **Features:** Tiki lights at the entrance welcome guests to a memorable room with fabric-covered walls, a shimmering gold-leaf ceiling, softly whirring fans and nooks nestled in the shadows. An elaborate display of spices hints at the flavor of the food. French accents infuse dishes, including the delicious lobster, with Thai herbs. Foremost, however, is the black plate special: a sampling of five appetizers. The prix fixe lunch is a bargain. Dressy casual; cocktails. **Parking:** on-site and street. **Cards:** AX, CB, DC, DS, JC, MC, VI.

THE WATER CLUB Lunch: $15-$24   Dinner: $25-$38   Phone: 212/683-3333 (243)
(AAA)

American

Location: On east end of 23rd St to FDR Dr, then n. 500 E 30th St 10016. **Hours:** noon-3 & 5:30-10 pm, Fri & Sat noon-3 & 5:45-11 pm, Sun 11 am-3 & 5:30-10 pm; Sunday brunch. **Reservations:** suggested. **Features:** A fresh-looking, nautical-themed dining room with a casually sophisticated air and river views makes this a lovely place to enjoy a seafood meal. Preparations are not complex or cutting-edge creative, but fresh seafood is well-seasoned and sauced and served with tasty side dishes. Prix fixe lunch and dinner are an excellent value. Dressy casual; cocktails; entertainment. **Parking:** on-site and valet. **Cards:** AX, DC, DS, JC, MC.

WU LIANG YE   Lunch: $7-$19   Dinner: $11-$19   Phone: 212/398-2308
Regional Chinese

Location: Between 5th and 6th (Ave of the Americas) aves. 36 W 48th St 10036. **Hours:** 11:30 am-9:30 pm, Fri & Sat-10 pm. Closed: 11/22. **Reservations:** accepted. **Features:** The dining room has the feel of a 19th century upscale eatery with the high ceilings and architectural details. The staff provides attentive service and authentic Chinese cuisine. Casual dress; cocktails. **Parking:** no self-parking. **Cards:** AX, MC, VI.

YUM YUM BANGKOK Lunch: $7-$10   Dinner: $7-$15   Phone: 212/262-7244 (122)
Thai

Location: Between 45th and 46th sts. 650 9th Ave 10036. **Hours:** noon-midnight. **Features:** If you're in the neighborhood and need a quick and savory meal, this most casual store front has a good selection of traditional noodles and currys. The mix and match menu allows diners to select from a list of sauces and a list of meats to create their own dish. Casual dress. **Parking:** no self-parking. **Cards:** AX, DC, MC, VI.

ZARELA   Lunch: $10-$15   Dinner: $14-$19   Phone: 212/644-6740 (194)
Mexican

Location: Between 50th and 51st sts. 953 2nd Ave 10022. **Hours:** noon-3 & 5-11 pm, Fri-11:30 pm, Sat 5 pm-11:30 pm, Sun 5 pm-10 pm. Closed major holidays. **Reservations:** suggested. **Features:** Guests who step inside the lively restaurant might feel as though they're inside a pinata. Wild colors and "stuff" are everywhere, live Mexican music is played on the steps for lack of space anywhere else, and the bar is hopping. Creative, well-prepared choices include duck in "tablecloth stainer" sauce, red snapper hash and a killer hanger steak fajita. Black beans with rice and plantains are great side dishes. Traditional Mexican dishes also are listed. Casual dress; cocktails. **Parking:** no self-parking. **Cards:** AX, DC, MC, VI.

ZEN PALATE   Lunch: $7-$10   Dinner: $13-$19   Phone: 212/582-1669 (114)
Vegetarian

Location: At 46th St, southwest corner. 663 9th Ave 10036. **Hours:** 11:30 am-10:45 pm, Sun-10:30 pm. Closed: 7/4, 11/22. **Reservations:** suggested, pre-theater. **Features:** The restaurant affords diners a moment of calm in the midst of the Midtown rush. Warm sconce lighting and skylights are among features of the soothing decor. Dishes creatively blend Asian and Western influences. The Key lime pie is satisfying. BYOB. Dressy casual. **Parking:** no self-parking. **Cards:** AX, DC, MC, VI.

(See map and index starting on p. 382)

ZOCALO GRAND CENTRAL   Lunch: $10-$20   Dinner: $10-$20   Phone: 212/687-5666   (213)
▼▼ ▼▼ **Location:** Between Vanderbilt and Lexington aves. 119 E 42nd St (Grand Central Terminal) 10017. **Hours:** 11:30 am-
9:30 pm, Sat & Mon-9 pm, Sun-7 pm. Closed: 11/22, 12/25. **Reservations:** not accepted. **Features:** In the
Mexican   dining concourse of Grand Central, the open-air restaurant is a step or two up from typical fast-food
Mexican. Among pleasingly embellished dishes is spiced fried calamari with chipotle mayonnaise. Casual
dress; cocktails. **Parking:** no self-parking. **Cards:** AX, DC, DS, MC, VI.

ZONA ROSA   Lunch: $9-$20   Dinner: $18-$27   Phone: 212/247-2800   (85)
▼▼▼ ▼ **Location:** Between 5th and 6th (Ave of the Americas) aves. 40 W 56th St 10019. **Hours:** 11:30 am-3 & 5-10:30 pm,
Sat 5 pm-11 pm. Closed: Sun. **Reservations:** suggested. **Features:** The spare bronze and orange dining
Mexican   room, reminiscent of the Mexican desert, exemplifies the stark beauty of nature. The food, much like the
surroundings, is understated and elegant. Lush guacamole with tomatillo salsa makes for an apt start, as
does one of the many margarita offerings. The short rib tacos will have you wanting more, and the roast pork with mole is
positively dazzling. Tequila aficionados will love the selections; tasting flights are a great way to sample Mexico's finest. Casual
dress; cocktails. **Parking:** street. **Cards:** AX, DC, DS, MC, VI.

──────── *The following restaurants have not been evaluated by AAA* ────────
but are listed for your information only.

DIGBY'S   Phone: 212/977-7272
[fyi]   Not evaluated. **Location:** Between 5th and 6th (Ave of the Americas) aves. 666 5th Ave 10103. **Features:** For a
quick and healthy on-the-go lunch, folks can stop in and choose from pre-made items in the cases. Those
with a few more minutes to spare might wait at the custom sandwich bar, choose from the daily soups and pizzas or get a bowl
of lettuce and have the staff toss a custom-built salad chosen from a menu of ingredients.

DYLAN'S CANDY BAR   Phone: 646/735-0078
[fyi]   Not evaluated. **Location:** At 60th St. 1011 3rd Ave 10021. **Features:** So full of color and overwhelmingly full of
fun, the delight might make you gasp. This is a candy shop of major proportions and seriously sunny
disposition.

GRAY'S PAPAYA   Phone: 212/799-0243
[fyi]   Not evaluated. **Location:** Jct 72nd St. 2090 Broadway 10023. **Features:** The corner counter offers grilled hot
dogs and fresh tropical juice.

GRAY'S PAPAYA   Phone: 212/260-3532
[fyi]   Not evaluated. **Location:** Jct 8th St. 402 Ave of the Americas 10011. **Features:** The corner counter offers grilled
hot dogs and fresh tropical juice.

JOHN'S PIZZERIA EAST   Phone: 212/935-2895
[fyi]   Not evaluated. **Location:** Between 1st and York aves. 408 E 64th St 10021. **Features:** First established in 1929
and now with four New York City locations. Famous for their thin crust pizza.

LILI'S NOODLE SHOP & GRILL   Phone: 212/639-1313
[fyi]   Not evaluated. **Location:** Between 84th and 85th sts. 1500 3rd Ave 10028. **Features:** The bright, casual place is
characterized by bi-level seating amid stylish digs. Guests stop in for better-than-average Chinese favorites
from the enormous menu, as well as steamed and braised fish, Mandarin noodle soups and Cantonese wonton soups, roasted
meat and sizzling platters.

MANHATTAN BRICK OVEN & GRILL   Phone: 212/639-9696
[fyi]   Not evaluated. **Location:** Between 67th and 68th sts. 1159 3rd Ave 10021. **Features:** Noted for their pizzas, this
quick self-serve restaurant also offers a number of Italian dishes and sandwiches. If you order one of the
delicious freshly extracted pure juice drinks, be sure it's a medium or large or you'll be disappointed.

MESKEREM ETHIOPIAN RESTAURANT   Phone: 212/664-0520
[fyi]   Not evaluated. **Location:** Between 9th and 10th aves. 468 W 47th St 10036. **Features:** Open for lunch and
dinner, the restaurant provides an authentic Ethopian dining experience.

OYSTER BAR   Phone: 212/490-6650
[fyi]   Not evaluated. **Location:** Grand Central Station, lower level. 42nd St 10017. **Features:** The extensive seafood
menu includes more than 50 kinds of fresh fish.

PASTICCIO   Phone: 212/679-2551
[fyi]   Not evaluated. **Location:** At 31st St. 447 3rd Ave 10016. **Features:** This Murray Hill restaurant has been
serving Italian dishes to guests in a comfortable setting since 1980.

PER SE   Phone: 212/823-9335
[fyi]   Not evaluated. **Location:** In AOL-Time Warner Building, 4th floor. 10 Columbus Cir 10019. **Features:** This
contemporary Thomas Keller restaurant offers elegance, sophistication and an innovative menu.

V STEAKHOUSE   Phone: 212/823-9500
[fyi]   Not evaluated. **Location:** In AOL-Time Warner Building, 4th floor. 10 Columbus Circle 10019. **Features:** Jean
Georges Vongerichten offers patrons a new twist in steak houses with this stylish upscale restaurant.

UPPER MANHATTAN   (See map and index starting on p. 394)

─── WHERE TO STAY ───

THE FRANKLIN HOTEL   *Book at AAA.com*   **Phone:** 212/369-1000   **3**

▼▼ ▼▼   Property failed to provide current rates

Location: Between 3rd and Lexington aves. 164 E 87th St 10128. **Fax:** 212/369-8000. **Facility:** 49 one-bedroom
Small-scale Hotel   standard units. 9 stories, interior corridors. **Parking:** no self-parking. **Amenities:** video library, CD players,
high-speed Internet, dual phone lines, voice mail, safes, honor bars, hair dryers. *Some:* irons. **Guest**
Services: complimentary evening beverages: Mon-Fri, valet laundry. **Business Services:** PC.

SOME UNITS

🛎️ 📶 ✖️ 🐾 / 🖥️ /
FEE

HOTEL NEWTON   *Book great rates at AAA.com*   **Phone:** (212)678-6500   **1**

🆎 [SAVE]   9/1-12/17   1P: $150-$200   2P: $150-$200   XP: $25   F17
▼▼ ▼▼   5/1-8/31 & 12/18-4/30   1P: $125-$160   2P: $125-$160   XP: $25   F17

Small-scale Hotel   **Location:** Between 94th and 95th sts. 2528 Broadway 10025. **Fax:** 212/678-6758. **Facility:** 110 units. 90 one-
bedroom standard units. 20 one-bedroom suites. 9 stories, interior corridors. *Bath:* some shared or private,
combo or shower only. **Parking:** no self-parking. **Amenities:** voice mail, irons, hair dryers. **Guest Services:**
wireless Internet. **Business Services:** PC. **Cards:** AX, DC, DS, MC, VI. **Free Special Amenities:** room
upgrade and preferred room (each subject to availability with advance reservations). *(See color ad below)*

SOME UNITS

🛎️ ♿ 📶 ✖️ / 🖥️ 🍽️ 💻 /

(See map and index starting on p. 394)

HOTEL WALES

Book great rates at AAA.com

Historic
Small-scale Hotel

Phone: (212)876-6000 **2**
All Year   1P: $249-$450   2P: $249-$450   XP: $20   F16
Location: Between 92nd and 93rd sts E. 1295 Madison Ave 10128. Fax: 212/860-7000. **Facility:** This historic hotel retains its charm with carved wood trim, renovated baths in pre-War style, and a parlor featuring a harpist in the afternoon. 87 units. 44 one-bedroom standard units, some with efficiencies. 42 one- and 1 two-bedroom suites. 10 stories, interior corridors. **Bath:** combo or shower only. **Parking:** valet. **Terms:** small pets only ($75 deposit). **Amenities:** video library, CD players, dual phone lines, voice mail, safes, hair dryers. *Some:* irons. **Dining:** 8 am-10:30 pm, cocktails. **Leisure Activities:** rooftop terrace. *Fee:* massage. **Guest Services:** valet laundry, wireless Internet. **Business Services:** meeting rooms, business center. **Cards:** AX, CB, DC, DS, JC, MC, VI. **Free Special Amenities: continental breakfast and newspaper.** *(See color ad p 482)*

SOME UNITS

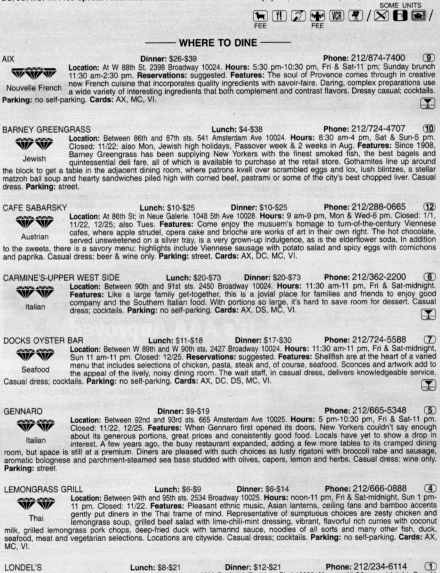

------- WHERE TO DINE -------

AIX

Nouvelle French

Dinner: $26-$39   **Phone: 212/874-7400** **9**
Location: At W 88th St. 2398 Broadway 10024. **Hours:** 5:30 pm-10:30 pm, Fri & Sat-11 pm; Sunday brunch 11:30 am-2:30 pm. **Reservations:** suggested. **Features:** The soul of Provence comes through in creative new French cuisine that incorporates quality ingredients with savoir-faire. Daring, complex preparations use a wide variety of interesting ingredients that both complement and contrast flavors. Dressy casual; cocktails. **Parking:** no self-parking. **Cards:** AX, MC, VI.

BARNEY GREENGRASS

Jewish

Lunch: $4-$38   **Phone: 212/724-4707** **10**
Location: Between 86th and 87th sts. 541 Amsterdam Ave 10024. **Hours:** 8:30 am-4 pm, Sat & Sun-5 pm. **Closed:** 11/22; also Mon, Jewish high holidays, Passover week & 2 weeks in Aug. **Features:** Since 1908, Barney Greengrass has been supplying New Yorkers with the finest smoked fish, the best bagels and quintessential deli fare, all of which is available to purchase at the retail store. Gothamites line up around the block to get a table in the adjacent dining room, where patrons kvell over scrambled eggs and lox, lush blintzes, a stellar matzoh ball soup and hearty sandwiches piled high with corned beef, pastrami or some of the city's best chopped liver. Casual dress. **Parking:** street.

CAFE SABARSKY

Austrian

Lunch: $10-$25   **Dinner: $10-$25**   **Phone: 212/288-0665** **12**
Location: At 86th St; in Neue Galerie. 1048 5th Ave 10028. **Hours:** 9 am-9 pm, Mon & Wed-6 pm. **Closed:** 1/1, 11/22, 12/25; also Tues. **Features:** Come enjoy the musuem's homage to turn-of-the-century Viennese cafes, where apple strudel, opera cake and brioche are works of art in their own right. The hot chocolate, served unsweetened on a silver tray, is a very grown-up indulgence, as is the elderflower soda. In addition to the sweets, there is a savory menu; highlights include Viennese sausage with potato salad and spicy eggs with cornichons and paprika. Casual dress; beer & wine only. **Parking:** street. **Cards:** AX, DC, MC, VI.

CARMINE'S-UPPER WEST SIDE

Italian

Lunch: $20-$73   **Dinner: $20-$73**   **Phone: 212/362-2200** **6**
Location: Between 90th and 91st sts. 2450 Broadway 10024. **Hours:** 11:30 am-11 pm, Fri & Sat-midnight. **Features:** Like a large family get-together, this is a jovial place for families and friends to enjoy good company and the Southern Italian food. With portions so large, it's hard to save room for dessert. Casual dress; cocktails. **Parking:** no self-parking. **Cards:** AX, DS, MC, VI.

DOCKS OYSTER BAR

Seafood

Lunch: $11-$18   **Dinner: $17-$30**   **Phone: 212/724-5588** **7**
Location: Between W 89th and W 90th sts. 2427 Broadway 10024. **Hours:** 11:30 am-11 pm, Fri & Sat-midnight, Sun 11 am-11 pm. **Closed:** 12/25. **Reservations:** suggested. **Features:** Shellfish are at the heart of a varied menu that includes selections of chicken, pasta, steak and, of course, seafood. Sconces and artwork add to the appeal of the lively, noisy dining room. The wait staff, in casual dress, delivers knowledgeable service. Casual dress; cocktails. **Parking:** no self-parking. **Cards:** AX, DC, DS, MC, VI.

GENNARO

Italian

Dinner: $9-$19   **Phone: 212/665-5348** **5**
Location: Between 92nd and 93rd sts. 665 Amsterdam Ave 10025. **Hours:** 5 pm-10:30 pm, Fri & Sat-11 pm. **Closed:** 11/22, 12/25. **Features:** When Gennaro first opened its doors, New Yorkers couldn't say enough about its generous portions, great prices and consistently good food. Locals have yet to show a drop in interest. A few years ago, the busy restaurant expanded, adding a few more tables to its cramped dining room, but space is still at a premium. Diners are pleased with such choices as lusty rigatoni with broccoli rabe and sausage, aromatic bolognese and parchment-steamed sea bass studded with olives, capers, lemon and herbs. Casual dress; wine only. **Parking:** street.

LEMONGRASS GRILL

Thai

Lunch: $6-$9   **Dinner: $6-$14**   **Phone: 212/666-0888** **4**
Location: Between 94th and 95th sts. 2534 Broadway 10025. **Hours:** noon-11 pm, Fri & Sat-midnight, Sun 1 pm-11 pm. **Closed:** 11/22. **Features:** Pleasant ethnic music, Asian lanterns, ceiling fans and bamboo accents gently put diners in the Thai frame of mind. Representative of sumptuous choices are zesty chicken and lemongrass soup, grilled beef salad with lime-chili-mint dressing, vibrant, flavorful rich curries with coconut milk, grilled lemongrass pork chops, deep-fried duck with tamarind sauce, noodles of all sorts and many other fish, duck, seafood, meat and vegetarian selections. Locations are citywide. Casual dress; cocktails. **Parking:** no self-parking. **Cards:** AX, MC, VI.

LONDEL'S

Soul Food

Lunch: $8-$21   **Dinner: $12-$21**   **Phone: 212/234-6114** **1**
Location: Between 139th and 140th sts. 2620 Frederick Douglass Blvd 10030. **Hours:** 11:30 am-midnight, Sun 11 am-5 pm; Sunday brunch. Closed major holidays; also Mon. **Reservations:** required. **Features:** Located on the threshold of Striver's Row, a historical section of Harlem, this restaurant offers friendly service and delicious Southern comfort food made from scratch, such as honey-barbequed ribs, blackened catfish, chicken and waffles and collard greens. Save room for the sweet potato pie. Casual dress; cocktails. **Parking:** street. **Cards:** AX, DC, DS, MC, VI.

(See map and index starting on p. 394)

RADIO PERFECTO RESTAURANT AND BAR   **Lunch:** $8-$13   **Dinner:** $9-$16   **Phone:** 212/932-0707   ②

Location: Between W 118th and W 119th sts. 1187 Amsterdam Ave 10027. **Hours:** 11:30 am-4:30 & 5-midnight. Closed: 12/25. **Features:** Guests enjoy a casual atmosphere and friendly servers who know how to get the
American   job done. The popular patio opens seasonally. Inside, a collection of old radios sits high on a shelf, and chickens can be seen slowly turning on a rotisserie. This restaurant may be busy at peak times. Casual dress; cocktails. **Parking:** street. **Cards:** AX, MC, VI.   Y

SAIGON GRILL   **Lunch:** $5-$8   **Dinner:** $8-$14   **Phone:** 212/875-9072   ⑧
Location: Corner of 90th St. 620 Amsterdam Ave 10024. **Hours:** 11 am-midnight. Closed: 11/22. **Features:** A formidable menu offers unusual and familiar dishes, each replete with vibrant flavor and colors. Fragrant
Vietnamese   seasonings perfume the air, and you'll find your head turning as dishes go by. Red curries, spicy soup and seafood dishes are excellent, and the grilled pork chop marinated in lemongrass is a must. Casual dress; cocktails. **Parking:** no self-parking. **Cards:** AX, DC, DS, MC, VI.

SARABETH'S   **Lunch:** $10-$17   **Dinner:** $11-$25   **Phone:** 212/410-7335   ⑪
Location: At E 92nd St; on Upper East Side. 1295 Madison Ave 10128. **Hours:** 8 am-10:30 pm, Sun-9:30 pm. Closed: 12/25. **Reservations:** accepted. **Features:** Crowded with "ladies who lunch" and their well-heeled
American   offspring, Sarabeth's became famous first for her sweet preserves, and now also for creative egg and brunch dishes, homemade granola, and gourmet sandwich and salad plates. As always, save room for desserts: rich ice creams, sumptuous cakes, scones and, of course, cookies and milk. Casual dress; cocktails. **Parking:** no self-parking. **Cards:** AX, DC, MC, VI.

TOM'S RESTAURANT   **Lunch:** $4-$16   **Dinner:** $4-$16   **Phone:** 212/864-6137   ③
Location: Jct 112th St. 2880 Broadway 10025. **Hours:** 6 am-1:30 am, Fri-Sun 24 hours. Closed: 12/25. **Reservations:** not accepted. **Features:** This inexpensive coffee shop has been made famous by the
American   television series Seinfield. They are also known for their delicious burgers and fries. Casual dress. **Parking:** no self-parking.

YORK GRILL   **Dinner:** $25-$40   **Phone:** 212/772-0261
Location: Between 88th and 89th aves. 1690 York Ave 10128. **Hours:** 4 pm-10:30 pm, Fri & Sat-11:30 pm, Sunday 11:30 am-3 & 4-10:30 pm; Sunday brunch. Closed: 1/1, 12/25. **Reservations:** suggested.
American   **Features:** A neighborhood go-to spot for a nice yet casual evening out for a good meal. Decor is vibrant with yellows and blues and a wall-sized mural of a crowd having fun. Food is creative American with flavorful seasonings and sauces. A very comfortable bar area is also a local draw. Dressy casual; cocktails. **Parking:** street. **Cards:** AX, CB, DC, MC, VI.   Y

BRONX pop. 1,332,650

──── WHERE TO STAY ────

HOWARD JOHNSON YANKEE STADIUM   *Book great rates at AAA.com*   **Phone:** 718/293-1100

(AAA) (SAVE)

▼▼▼ ▼▼

Motel

12/1-1/9 [CP]	1P: $159-$189	2P: $159-$189	XP: $25 F3
11/1-11/30 & 1/10-4/30 [CP]	1P: $129-$139	2P: $129-$139	XP: $25 F3
5/1-10/31 [CP]	1P: $119-$139	2P: $119-$139	XP: $25 F3

Location: I-87 N, exit 5, service road to Sedgwick Ave. 1300 Sedgwick Ave 10452. Fax: 718/293-0044. **Facility:** 45 one-bedroom standard units. 2 stories, interior corridors. **Parking:** on-site. **Terms:** cancellation fee imposed. **Amenities:** voice mail, hair dryers. **Cards:** AX, DS, MC, VI. **Free Special Amenities: continental breakfast and high-speed Internet.**

SOME UNITS

🎦 🖥 / 🖂 /

──── WHERE TO DINE ────

AL BUSTAN   **Lunch:** $20-$28   **Dinner:** $20-$28   **Phone:** 212/759-8439

▼▼▼▼ ▼▼▼▼

Lebanese

Location: Between 50th and 51st sts. 827 3rd Ave 10022. **Hours:** noon-3 & 5:30-10 pm. **Reservations:** suggested. **Features:** Well-known for Lebanese cuisine with a flair, the restaurant presents a long list of hot and cold appetizers that could be a great meal. However, diners would miss such entrees as marinated lamb medallions, grilled quail, steamed fish and the specialty spiced lamb tartare. The tranquil dining room is mirrored and best described as neutral. Dressy casual; cocktails. **Parking:** no self-parking. **Cards:** AX, CB, DC, DS, JC, MC, VI.

BROOKLYN pop. 2,465,326   (See map and index starting on p. 396)

──── WHERE TO STAY ────

AVENUE PLAZA HOTEL   **Phone:** (718)552-3200   **4**

▼▼▼▼ ▼▼

Small-scale Hotel

All Year [BP]   1P: $129-$449   2P: $159-$449   XP: $20   F5

Location: Belt Pkwy W, exit 7N to Ocean Pkwy, 3.4 mi n to 18th Ave, 0.4 mi w to 47th, then 0.7 mi n. 4624 13th Ave 11219. Fax: 718/552-3201. **Facility:** Smoke free premises. 52 units. 51 one-bedroom standard units. 1 one-bedroom suite with whirlpool. 8 stories, interior corridors. *Bath:* combo or shower only. **Parking:** on-site (fee). **Amenities:** dual phone lines, voice mail, safes, hair dryers. **Guest Services:** valet laundry, wireless Internet. **Business Services:** meeting rooms, fax (fee). **Cards:** AX, DC, DS, MC, VI.

🅂🄳 🍴 ♿ 🖂 🖥 💻

BED & BREAKFAST ON THE PARK   **Phone:** 718/499-6115   **3**

▼▼▼ ▼▼

Historic Bed & Breakfast

All Year   1P: $155-$300   2P: $155-$300   XP: $25   F12

Location: Between 6th and 7th sts. Located opposite Prospect Park. 113 Prospect Park W 11215. Fax: 718/499-1385. **Facility:** This opulent Victorian brownstone features stained-glass windows and abundant artwork. Smoke free premises. 7 units. 6 one- and 1 two-bedroom standard units. 4 stories (no elevator), interior corridors. *Bath:* combo or shower only. **Parking:** street. **Terms:** 2-3 night minimum stay, 10 day cancellation notice, 10% service charge, no pets allowed (owner's dog on premises). **Amenities:** voice mail, hair dryers. *Some:* DVD players. **Cards:** AX, MC, VI.

SOME UNITS

(ASK) 🖂 🎦 / (VCR) 💻 /

BEST WESTERN GREGORY HOTEL   *Book great rates at AAA.com*   **Phone:** (718)238-3737   **5**

(AAA) (SAVE)

▼▼▼ ▼▼

Small-scale Hotel

5/1-10/31	1P: $189-$219	2P: $189-$219	XP: $10 F18
11/1-12/31	1P: $179-$209	2P: $179-$209	XP: $10 F18
1/1-4/30	1P: $169-$199	2P: $169-$199	XP: $10 F18

Location: I-278 (Brooklyn-Queens Expwy), exit 86th St southbound; exit 92nd St northbound, w to 4th Ave, then 0.4 mi n; between 83rd and 84th sts. Located in a commercial area. 8315 4th Ave 11209. Fax: 718/680-0827. **Facility:** 70 units. 64 one-bedroom standard units. 6 one-bedroom suites, some with whirlpools. 4 stories, interior corridors. *Bath:* combo or shower only. **Parking:** on-site (fee) and valet. **Terms:** cancellation fee imposed. **Amenities:** video games (fee), high-speed Internet, dual phone lines, voice mail, safes, irons, hair dryers. **Guest Services:** valet laundry, wireless Internet. **Business Services:** meeting rooms, PC. **Cards:** AX, CB, DC, DS, JC, MC, VI. *(See color ad below)*

SOME UNITS

🅂🄳 🍸 ♿ 🐾 🛗 🎦 💻 / 🖂 🖥 🖼 /
FEE

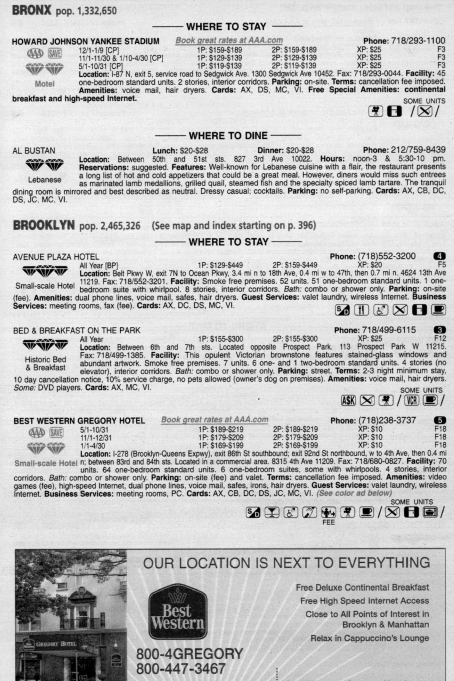

(See map and index starting on p. 396)

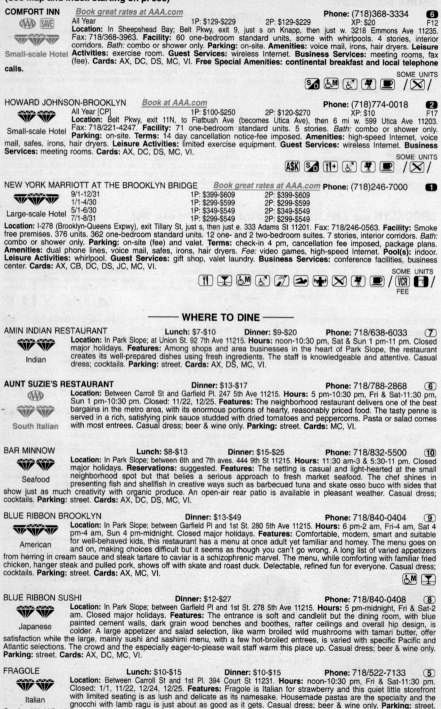

COMFORT INN   *Book great rates at AAA.com*   Phone: (718)368-3334   **6**
AAA SAVE   All Year   1P: $129-$229   2P: $129-$229   XP: $20   F12
Location: In Sheepshead Bay; Belt Pkwy, exit 9, just s on Knapp, then just w. 3218 Emmons Ave 11235.
Fax: 718/368-3963. **Facility:** 60 one-bedroom standard units, some with whirlpools. 4 stories, interior
corridors. *Bath:* combo or shower only. **Parking:** on-site. **Amenities:** voice mail, irons, hair dryers. **Leisure**
Small-scale Hotel   **Activities:** exercise room. **Guest Services:** wireless Internet. **Business Services:** meeting rooms, fax
(fee). **Cards:** AX, DC, DS, MC, VI. **Free Special Amenities: continental breakfast and local telephone**
calls.

SOME UNITS

HOWARD JOHNSON-BROOKLYN   *Book at AAA.com*   Phone: (718)774-0018   **2**
All Year [CP]   1P: $100-$250   2P: $120-$270   XP: $10   F17
Location: Belt Pkwy, exit 11N, to Flatbush Ave (becomes Utica Ave), then 6 mi w. 599 Utica Ave 11203.
Small-scale Hotel   Fax: 718/221-4247. **Facility:** 71 one-bedroom standard units. 5 stories. *Bath:* combo or shower only.
Parking: on-site. **Terms:** 14 day cancellation notice-fee imposed. **Amenities:** high-speed Internet, voice
mail, safes, irons, hair dryers. **Leisure Activities:** limited exercise equipment. **Guest Services:** wireless Internet. **Business
Services:** meeting rooms. **Cards:** AX, DC, DS, MC, VI.

SOME UNITS

NEW YORK MARRIOTT AT THE BROOKLYN BRIDGE   *Book great rates at AAA.com*   Phone: (718)246-7000   **1**
9/1-12/31   1P: $399-$609   2P: $399-$609
1/1-4/30   1P: $299-$599   2P: $299-$599
Large-scale Hotel   5/1-6/30   1P: $349-$549   2P: $349-$549
7/1-8/31   1P: $299-$549   2P: $299-$549
Location: I-278 (Brooklyn-Queens Expwy), exit Tillary St, just s, then just e. 333 Adams St 11201. Fax: 718/246-0563. **Facility:** Smoke
free premises. 376 units. 362 one-bedroom standard units. 12 one- and 2 two-bedroom suites. 7 stories, interior corridors. *Bath:*
combo or shower only. **Parking:** on-site (fee) and valet. **Terms:** check-in 4 pm, cancellation fee imposed, package plans.
Amenities: dual phone lines, voice mail, safes, irons, hair dryers. *Fee:* video games, high-speed Internet. **Pool(s):** indoor.
Leisure Activities: whirlpool. **Guest Services:** gift shop, valet laundry. **Business Services:** conference facilities, business
center. **Cards:** AX, CB, DC, DS, JC, MC, VI.

SOME UNITS

/ VCR / FEE

─────── **WHERE TO DINE** ───────

AMIN INDIAN RESTAURANT   **Lunch:** $7-$10   **Dinner:** $9-$20   Phone: 718/638-6033   **7**
Location: In Park Slope; at Union St. 92 7th Ave 11215. **Hours:** noon-10:30 pm, Sat & Sun 1 pm-11 pm. Closed
major holidays. **Features:** Among shops and area businesses in the heart of Park Slope, the restaurant
creates its well-prepared dishes using fresh ingredients. The staff is knowledgeable and attentive. Casual
Indian   dress; cocktails. **Parking:** street. **Cards:** AX, DS, MC, VI.

AUNT SUZIE'S RESTAURANT   **Dinner:** $13-$17   Phone: 718/788-2868   **6**
AAA   **Location:** Between Carroll St and Garfield Pl. 247 5th Ave 11215. **Hours:** 5 pm-10:30 pm, Fri & Sat-11:30 pm,
Sun 1 pm-10:30 pm. Closed: 11/22, 12/25. **Features:** The neighborhood restaurant delivers one of the best
bargains in the metro area, with its enormous portions of hearty, reasonably priced food. The tasty penne is
served in a rich, satisfying pink sauce studded with dried tomatoes and peppercorns. Pasta or salad comes
South Italian   with most entrees. Casual dress; beer & wine only. **Parking:** street. **Cards:** MC, VI.

BAR MINNOW   **Lunch:** $8-$13   **Dinner:** $15-$25   Phone: 718/832-5500   **10**
Location: In Park Slope; between 6th and 7th aves. 444 9th St 11215. **Hours:** 11:30 am-3 & 5:30-11 pm. Closed
major holidays. **Reservations:** suggested. **Features:** The setting is casual and light-hearted at the small
Seafood   neighborhood spot but that belies a serious approach to fresh market seafood. The chef shines in
presenting fish and shellfish in creative ways such as barbecued tuna and skate osso buco with sides that
show just as much creativity with organic produce. An open-air rear patio is available in pleasant weather. Casual dress;
cocktails. **Parking:** street. **Cards:** AX, DC, DS, MC, VI.

BLUE RIBBON BROOKLYN   **Dinner:** $13-$49   Phone: 718/840-0404   **9**
Location: In Park Slope; between Garfield Pl and 1st St. 280 5th Ave 11215. **Hours:** 6 pm-2 am, Fri-4 am, Sat 4
pm-4 am, Sun 4 pm-midnight. Closed major holidays. **Features:** Comfortable, modern, smart and suitable
American   for well-behaved kids, this restaurant has a menu at once adult yet familiar and homey. The menu goes on
and on, making choices difficult but it seems as though you can't go wrong. A long list of varied appetizers
from herring in cream sauce and steak tartare to caviar is a schizophrenic marvel. The menu, while comforting with familiar fried
chicken, hanger steak and pulled pork, shows off with skate and roast duck. Delectable, refined fun for everyone. Casual dress;
cocktails. **Parking:** street. **Cards:** AX, MC, VI.

BLUE RIBBON SUSHI   **Dinner:** $12-$27   Phone: 718/840-0408   **8**
Location: In Park Slope; between Garfield Pl and 1st St. 278 5th Ave 11215. **Hours:** 5 pm-midnight, Fri & Sat-2
am. Closed major holidays. **Features:** The entrance is soft and candlelit but the dining room, with blue
Japanese   painted cement walls, dark grain wood benches and boothes, rafter ceilings and overall hip design, is
colder. A large appetizer and salad selection, like warm broiled wild mushrooms with tamari butter, offer
satisfaction while the large, mainly sushi and sashimi menu, with a few hot-broiled entrees, is varied with specific Pacific and
Atlantic selections. The crowd and the especially eager-to-please wait staff warm this place up. Casual dress; beer & wine only.
Parking: street. **Cards:** AX, DC, MC, VI.

FRAGOLE   **Lunch:** $10-$15   **Dinner:** $10-$15   Phone: 718/522-7133   **5**
Location: Between Carroll St and 1st Pl. 394 Court St 11231. **Hours:** noon-10:30 pm, Fri & Sat-11:30 pm.
Closed: 1/1, 11/22, 12/24, 12/25. **Features:** Fragole is Italian for strawberry and this quiet little storefront
Italian   with limited seating is as lush and delicate as its namesake. Housemade pastas are the specialty and the
gnocchi with lamb ragu is just about as good as it gets. Casual dress; beer & wine only. **Parking:** street.
Cards: AX, MC, VI.

(See map and index starting on p. 396)

GRIMALDI'S PIZZERIA Lunch: $12-$18 Dinner: $12-$18 Phone: 718/858-4300 ③
◆
American
Location: Between Water and Front sts; adjacent to base of Brooklyn Bridge. 19 Old Fulton St 11201. **Hours:** 11:30 am-11 pm, Fri-midnight, Sat noon-midnight, Sun noon-11 pm. Closed: 3/23, 11/22, 12/25. **Features:** Although the lively, tightly packed restaurant serves calzones, antipasto and pasta, it is known for great brick-oven pizzas. There are no salads, and only one starter is served. The dessert menu tempts with such selections as cannoli, spumoni, tortoni and tartufo. Casual dress; beer & wine only. **Parking:** no self-parking.

KAPADOKYA Lunch: $8-$13 Dinner: $10-$22 Phone: 718/875-2211 ④
◆◆
Turkish
Location: Between Clinton and Henry sts. 142 Montague St 11201. **Hours:** 11:30 am-11:30 pm, Fri & Sat-midnight, Sun-10:30 pm. Closed: 12/24, 12/25. **Reservations:** accepted. **Features:** With Turkish beats emanating from the sound system, exotic light fixtures gleaming overhead and the sultry belly dancer working the room, you might just think you're in Istanbul, but the street below is undoubtedly downtown Brooklyn. Turkish specialties such as kebab, eggplant and stuffed grape leaves will not disappoint, nor will the aforementioned dancers. They keep patrons tapping their feet and swaying to the beat long into the night. Casual dress; cocktails. **Parking:** street. **Cards:** AX, DC, MC, VI.

OCEAN VIEW CAFE Lunch: $5-$18 Dinner: $7-$18 Phone: 718/332-1900 ⑫
◆
Russian
Location: Corner of Brighton 3rd St and Brighton Beach Ave. 290 Brighton Beach Ave 11235. **Hours:** 10 am-10 pm, Sat-11:30 pm. Closed: Yom Kippur. **Reservations:** accepted. **Features:** The small storefront is casual and frequently busy, serving Russian dishes to locals who come for richly flavored Ukrainian borscht with garlic popovers, herring with potato, stuffed cabbage, beef stew, a variety of blintzes and truly terrific potato vareniki with onion. Casual dress; cocktails. **Parking:** no self-parking. **Cards:** AX, DS, MC, VI.

PETER LUGER'S Lunch: $35-$70 Dinner: $35-$70 Phone: 718/387-7400 ①
◆◆
Steak House
Location: From Manhattan, outside lane of Williamsburg Bridge, 1st exit, then sharp right. 178 Broadway 11211. **Hours:** 11:45 am-9:45 pm, Fri & Sat-10:45 pm, Sun & major holidays 12:45 pm-9:45 pm. **Reservations:** suggested. **Features:** A star-studded dining room filled with business professionals hungry for dry-aged prime porterhouse steaks attests to the reputation for excellence that has been the restaurant's hallmark for decades. A tomato and onion salad and side dishes of creamed spinach and potatoes are most typically ordered. The rustic, old dining rooms—with bulky wood tables, plank wood floors, pressed-tin ceilings and little else to distract from dinner—are classic Brooklyn, classic Peter Luger's. Casual dress; cocktails. **Parking:** on-site. Ⓨ

RIVER CAFE Lunch: $18-$30 Dinner: $85 Phone: 718/522-5200 ②
◆◆
American
Location: At base of Brooklyn Bridge. 1 Water St 11201. **Hours:** noon-3 & 5:30-11 pm, Sun 11:30 am-3 & 6-11 pm. **Reservations:** required, for dinner. **Features:** A cobblestone drive leads to a wall festooned with flowers in warmer months and to the fragrant garden entrance of the floating restaurant. Walk over an enclosed gangplank to a lovely flower-filled dining room with a spectacular Manhattan view. A glance at the menu reveals such seafood choices as clams, oyster stew, tuna carpaccio, lump crab cakes and other excellent preparations. Semi-formal attire; cocktails. **Parking:** valet. **Cards:** AX, DC, DS, JC, MC, VI. Ⓨ

TOMMASO'S Lunch: $9-$15 Dinner: $9-$30 Phone: 718/236-9883 ⑪
◆◆
Italian
Location: Belt Pkwy, exit 4 (Bay 8th St), 0.6 mi ne. 1464 86th St 11228. **Hours:** noon-close. Closed: 12/25. **Reservations:** accepted. **Features:** A relaxed and mildly sophisticated mood pervades the friendly neighborhood restaurant. The menu lists traditional pasta, chicken and fish dishes, as well as well-prepared quail, veal and lamb. An assortment of cold antipasto is displayed to awaken the appetite. Casual dress; cocktails; entertainment. **Parking:** valet and street. **Cards:** AX, CB, DC, DS, MC, VI.

The following restaurants have not been evaluated by AAA but are listed for your information only.

AL DI LA Phone: 718/783-4565
[fyi]
Not evaluated. **Location:** In Park Slope; at Carroll St. 248 5th Ave 11215. **Features:** In a neighborhood experiencing a restaurant rebirth, the small jewel is popular for reliably excellent food. Dishes are fresh, and flavors distinctly scrumptious. The daily changing menu keeps patrons returning.

TOTONNO'S Phone: 718/372-8606
[fyi]
Not evaluated. **Location:** Between 15th and 16th sts; 2 blks s of Coney Island Park. 1524 Neptune Ave 11224. **Features:** This very basic restaurant is famous for its thin crust pizza which is made with tomatoes imported from Italy, handmade mozzarella cheese and dough that is made daily on premises.

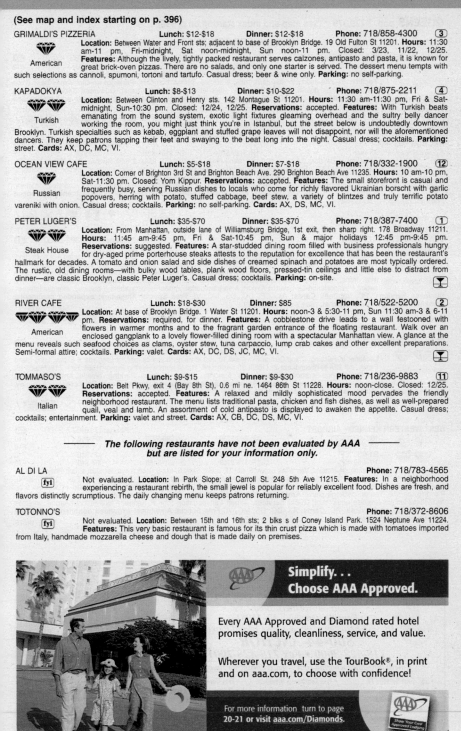

QUEENS pop. 2,229,379 (See map and index starting on p. 396)

------ WHERE TO STAY ------

ADRIA HOTEL AND CONFERENCE CENTER

AAA SAVE

Phone: (718)631-5900 ⑳

Small-scale Hotel

All Year   1P: $129-$159   2P: $139-$169   XP: $10   F12
Location: In Bayside; Cross Island Pkwy, exit 31W (SR 25A). 220-33 Northern Blvd 11361. Fax: 718/279-9080. **Facility:** 57 one-bedroom standard units. 4 stories, interior corridors. **Parking:** on-site. **Amenities:** voice mail, irons, hair dryers. **Guest Services:** valet laundry, wireless Internet. **Business Services:** meeting rooms. **Cards:** AX, CB, DC, DS, JC, MC, VI. **Free Special Amenities:** newspaper and high-speed Internet.

SOME UNITS
🛗 📶 ⊶ 🐾 🔒 🖥 / ✕ 🖨 /

ANCHOR INN

AAA SAVE

Phone: (718)428-8000 ㉒

Small-scale Hotel

All Year   1P: $129-$164   2P: $134-$169   XP: $12   F17
Location: In Bayside; 0.8 mi w of Cross Island Pkwy, exit 31W (SR 25A). 215-34 Northern Blvd (SR 25A) 11361. Fax: 718/428-7001. **Facility:** 66 one-bedroom standard units, some with kitchens and/or whirlpools. 2 stories, interior corridors. **Parking:** on-site. **Amenities:** dual phone lines, voice mail, safes, irons, hair dryers. **Leisure Activities:** limited exercise equipment. **Guest Services:** valet laundry, wireless Internet. **Cards:** AX, CB, DC, DS, MC, VI. **Free Special Amenities:** continental breakfast and high-speed Internet. *(See color ad below)*

SOME UNITS
🆂🅳 🛗 🐾 🔒 🖥 / ✕ 🖨 /

BEST WESTERN CITY VIEW

AAA SAVE

Phone: (718)392-8400 ㉛

Small-scale Hotel

All Year   1P: $139-$159   2P: $159-$199   XP: $12   F
Location: In Long Island City; Long Island Expwy, exit Greenpoint Ave westbound, just s; exit Borden Ave eastbound. 33-17 Greenpoint Ave 11101. Fax: 718/392-2110. **Facility:** 71 one-bedroom standard units, some with whirlpools. 5 stories, interior corridors. **Parking:** on-site. **Amenities:** video library (fee), DVD players, voice mail, irons, hair dryers. **Leisure Activities:** limited exercise equipment. **Guest Services:** valet laundry, airport transportation-La Guardia Airport, area transportation-nearby restaurants & subway, wireless Internet. **Business Services:** PC, fax (fee). **Cards:** AX, CB, DC, DS, MC, VI. **Free Special Amenities:** expanded continental breakfast and high-speed Internet. *(See color ad p 489)*

SOME UNITS
🆂🅳 ✈ 📶 🐾 🖥 / ✕ 🔒 🖨 /

BEST WESTERN EDEN PARK HOTEL

Phone: 718/699-4500 ㉘

Property failed to provide current rates

Small-scale Hotel

Location: In Flushing; Grand Central Pkwy, exit 10, just w via north service road for Long Island Expwy; Long Island Expwy, exit 22A eastbound; exit 21 (108th St) westbound. 113-10 Horace Harding Expwy 11368. Fax: 718/760-3916. **Facility:** 74 one-bedroom standard units. 5 stories, interior corridors. **Parking:** on-site. **Amenities:** voice mail, irons, hair dryers. *Some:* DVD players. **Leisure Activities:** limited exercise equipment. **Guest Services:** valet laundry, area transportation. **Business Services:** meeting rooms, fax (fee).

SOME UNITS
✈ 🍴 🍽 VCR 🐾 🖥 / ✕ 🔒 🖨 /

BEST WESTERN KENNEDY AIRPORT

AAA SAVE

Phone: (718)977-2100 ㊹

Small-scale Hotel

10/1-12/31 [CP]   1P: $99-$239   2P: $99-$239   XP: $10   F10
7/1-9/30 [CP]   1P: $109-$229   2P: $109-$229   XP: $10   F10
5/1-6/30 [CP]   1P: $99-$199   2P: $99-$199   XP: $10   F10
1/1-4/30 [CP]   1P: $79-$159   2P: $79-$159   XP: $10   F10
Location: In Jamaica; Van Wyck Expwy S, exit 1E to Belt Pkwy E, exit S Conduit Ave, then just e; Belt Pkwy E, exit 20; Belt Pkwy W, exit 21A, s at 150th Ln, then e on S Conduit Ave. 144-25 153rd Ln 11434. Fax: 718/977-2200. **Bath:** combo or shower only. **Facility:** 88 one-bedroom standard units, some with whirlpools. 4 stories, interior corridors. **Parking:** on-site. **Terms:** package plans. **Amenities:** high-speed Internet, voice mail, safes (fee), irons, hair dryers. **Leisure Activities:** limited exercise equipment. **Guest Services:** airport transportation-John F. Kennedy International Airport, wireless Internet. **Business Services:** PC. **Cards:** AX, DC, DS, MC, VI. **Free Special Amenities:** expanded continental breakfast and high-speed Internet.

SOME UNITS
🆂🅳 ✈ 🐾 🖥 / ✕ /

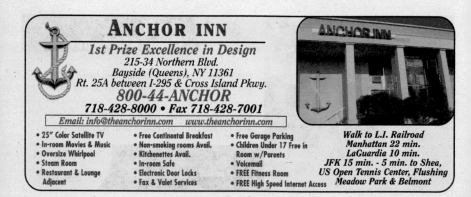

(See map and index starting on p. 396)

BEST WESTERN QUEENS COURT HOTEL　　　　　　　　　　　　Phone: (718)888-1900　㉕

8/26-9/9 [CP]	1P: $219-$329	2P: $239-$349	XP: $20	F12
9/10-4/30 [CP]	1P: $179-$219	2P: $189-$229	XP: $10	F12
5/1-8/25 [CP]	1P: $169-$209	2P: $179-$219	XP: $10	F12

Location: In Flushing; Grand Central Pkwy to Northern Blvd, 1 mi e to Main St, 0.3 mi s to 39th Ave, then just w. 133-51 Small-scale Hotel 39th Ave 11354. Fax: 718/888-1141. **Facility:** 59 one-bedroom standard units, some with whirlpools. 8 stories, interior corridors. *Bath:* combo or shower only. **Parking:** no self-parking. **Terms:** cancellation fee imposed. **Amenities:** voice mail, irons, hair dryers. **Dining:** 5 pm-11 pm, cocktails. **Leisure Activities:** exercise room. **Business Services:** meeting rooms. **Cards:** AX, DS, MC, VI. **Free Special Amenities:** high-speed Internet.

SOME UNITS

CLARION HOTEL AT LA GUARDIA AIRPORT　　　　　　　　　　Phone: (718)335-1200　⓮

9/12-12/31	1P: $225-$285	2P: $225-$285	XP: $10	F12
5/1-9/11 & 1/1-4/30	1P: $225-$265	2P: $225-$265	XP: $10	F12

Location: In East Elmhurst; Grand Central Pkwy, exit 6 (94th St). 9400 Ditmars Blvd 11369. Fax: 718/458-1239. **Facility:** 169 units. 159 one-bedroom standard units. 10 one-bedroom suites, some with whirlpools. 3 Small-scale Hotel stories, interior corridors. *Bath:* combo or shower only. **Parking:** on-site (fee). **Terms:** cancellation fee imposed, weekly rates available. **Amenities:** voice mail, irons, hair dryers. **Dining:** 5 pm-11 pm. **Leisure Activities:** exercise room. **Guest Services:** valet laundry, airport transportation-La Guardia Airport, wireless Internet. **Business Services:** meeting rooms, business center. **Cards:** AX, CB, DC, DS, JC, MC, VI. **Free Special Amenities:** expanded continental breakfast and room upgrade (subject to availability with advance reservations).

SOME UNITS

FEE　FEE

COMFORT INN & SUITES　　　　　　　　　　　　　　　　　　Phone: (718)457-5555　㉜

7/1-9/30	1P: $129-$299	2P: $129-$299	XP: $10	F18
5/1-6/30 & 10/1-12/31	1P: $109-$229	2P: $109-$229	XP: $10	F18
1/1-4/30	1P: $109-$209	2P: $109-$209	XP: $10	F18

Small-scale Hotel **Location:** In Maspeth; I-495 (Long Island Expwy), exit 18, just n. 6030 Maurice Ave 11378. Fax: 718/457-1111. **Facility:** 76 one-bedroom standard units, some with whirlpools. 4 stories, interior corridors. *Bath:* combo or shower only. **Parking:** on-site. **Terms:** cancellation fee imposed, [CP] meal plan available. **Amenities:** high-speed Internet, voice mail, irons, hair dryers. **Leisure Activities:** limited exercise equipment. **Business Services:** PC. **Cards:** AX, CB, DC, DS, JC, MC, VI.

SOME UNITS

(See map and index starting on p. 396)

COMFORT INN AT JFK AIRPORT
Phone: 718/977-0001 **46**

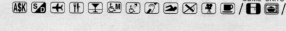

Small-scale Hotel

Property failed to provide current rates

Location: In Jamaica; Van Wyck Expwy S to exit 1E to Belt Pkwy E, exit S Conduit Ave, then just e; Belt Pkwy E, exit 20; Belt Pkwy W, exit 21A, left at 150th St, then left on S Conduit Ave. 144-36 153rd Ln 11434. Fax: 718/977-9166. **Facility:** 59 one-bedroom standard units. 4 stories, interior corridors. *Bath:* combo or shower only. **Parking:** on-site. **Amenities:** high-speed Internet, voice mail, safes (fee), irons, hair dryers. **Business Services:** PC, fax.

SOME UNITS

COMFORT INN LA GUARDIA
Phone: 718/939-5000 **23**

All Year 1P: $109-$299 2P: $109-$299 XP: $10 F18

Small-scale Hotel

Location: In Flushing; from Northern Blvd, just s on Main St, just w. 133-43 37th Ave 11354. Fax: 718/939-4000. **Facility:** 50 one-bedroom standard units. 7 stories, interior corridors. *Bath:* combo or shower only. **Parking:** street. **Amenities:** high-speed Internet, dual phone lines, voice mail, safes (fee), irons, hair dryers. **Cards:** AX, DS, MC, VI. **Free Special Amenities: continental breakfast and high-speed Internet.**

SOME UNITS

COMFORT INN LONG ISLAND CITY
Phone: (718)303-3700 **27**

9/1-4/30	1P: $139-$169	2P: $149-$189	XP: $25 F10
7/1-8/31	1P: $129-$159	2P: $139-$169	XP: $25 F10
5/1-6/30	1P: $119-$149	2P: $129-$159	XP: $25 F10

Small-scale Hotel

Location: In Long Island City; between 24th and 27th sts. 42-24 Crescent St 11101. Fax: 718/303-3800. **Facility:** 80 one-bedroom standard units, some with whirlpools. 8 stories, interior corridors. *Bath:* combo or shower only. **Parking:** no self-parking. **Terms:** cancellation fee imposed. **Amenities:** voice mail, safes, irons, hair dryers. **Leisure Activities:** limited exercise equipment. **Guest Services:** valet laundry, airport transportation (fee)–John F. Kennedy International & La Guardia airports, wireless Internet. **Business Services:** meeting rooms, PC. **Cards:** AX, CB, DC, DS, JC, MC, VI. **Free Special Amenities: expanded continental breakfast and local telephone calls.**

SOME UNITS

FEE

COURTYARD BY MARRIOTT JFK AIRPORT
Phone: (718)848-2121 **40**

All Year 1P: $159-$269

Small-scale Hotel

Location: In Jamaica; Van Wyck Expwy S, exit 2 (Rockaway Blvd), just e, then just w. 145-11 N Conduit Ave 11436. Fax: 718/848-0888. **Facility:** Smoke free premises. 166 units. 164 one-bedroom standard units. 2 one-bedroom suites ($299-$399). 14 stories, interior corridors. *Bath:* combo or shower only. **Parking:** on-site (fee) and valet. **Terms:** [BP] meal plan available, package plans. **Amenities:** video games (fee), high-speed Internet, dual phone lines, voice mail, irons, hair dryers. **Leisure Activities:** exercise room. **Guest Services:** sundries, valet and coin laundry, wireless Internet. **Business Services:** meeting rooms, PC. **Cards:** AX, DC, DS, MC, VI. *(See color ad below)*

SOME UNITS

COURTYARD BY MARRIOTT NEW YORK/LA GUARDIA AIRPORT
Phone: (718)446-4800 **15**

8/26-12/31	1P: $329-$399	2P: $349-$429
5/1-8/25	1P: $309-$359	2P: $329-$379
1/1-4/30	1P: $279-$339	2P: $299-$359

Large-scale Hotel

Location: In East Elmhurst; Grand Central Pkwy, exit 6 (94th St) eastbound; exit 7 westbound, 0.5 mi s on 94th St to 23rd Ave, then just w to 90th St. 90-10 Grand Central Pkwy 11369. Fax: 718/446-5733. **Facility:** Smoke free premises. 288 units. 283 one-bedroom standard units. 5 one-bedroom suites ($399-$599). 1-6 stories, interior corridors. *Bath:* combo or shower only. **Parking:** on-site (fee). **Terms:** cancellation fee imposed, [AP], [BP] & [CP] meal plans available, package plans. **Amenities:** high-speed Internet, voice mail, irons, hair dryers. **Pool(s):** outdoor. **Leisure Activities:** whirlpool, exercise room. **Guest Services:** gift shop, valet and coin laundry. **Business Services:** meeting rooms, business center. **Cards:** AX, CB, DC, DS, JC, MC, VI.

SOME UNITS

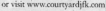

(See map and index starting on p. 396)

CROWNE PLAZA HOTEL-JFK AIRPORT — **Phone:** 718/489-1000 — **38**

Property failed to provide current rates

Small-scale Hotel

Location: In Jamaica; Belt Pkwy E to Farmer's Blvd exit, just n to N Conduit Ave, then just w to Baisley Blvd; Van Wyck Expwy S, exit 2 (Rockaway Blvd), e to Baisley Blvd. 151-20 Baisley Blvd 11434. Fax: 718/276-8212. **Facility:** 182 units. 169 one-bedroom standard units. 13 one-bedroom suites, some with whirlpools. 5 stories, interior corridors. *Bath:* combo or shower only. **Parking:** on-site (fee) and valet. **Amenities:** video games (fee), dual phone lines, voice mail, irons, hair dryers. *Some:* CD players. **Leisure Activities:** exercise room. **Guest Services:** gift shop, valet laundry. **Business Services:** conference facilities, PC.

SOME UNITS

CROWNE PLAZA HOTEL LA GUARDIA — **Phone:** (718)457-6300 — **17**

Large-scale Hotel

8/26-9/30	1P: $399
5/1-7/31 & 10/1-4/30	1P: $339
8/1-8/25	1P: $279

Location: In East Elmhurst; Grand Central Pkwy, exit 7 eastbound to 94th St, 0.5 mi e; exit 6 (94th St) westbound, 0.5 mi e. 104-04 Ditmars Blvd 11369. Fax: 718/899-9768. **Facility:** 358 units. 342 one-bedroom standard units. 16 one-bedroom suites ($399), some with whirlpools. 7 stories, interior corridors. *Bath:* some combo or shower only. **Parking:** on-site (fee). **Terms:** [AP], [BP], [CP] & [ECP] meal plans available, package plans. **Amenities:** video games (fee), CD players, dual phone lines, voice mail, irons, hair dryers. **Dining:** 6 am-11 pm, cocktails, entertainment. **Pool(s):** heated indoor. **Leisure Activities:** sauna, whirlpool, exercise room. **Guest Services:** gift shop, valet and coin laundry, airport transportation-La Guardia Airport, wireless Internet. **Business Services:** conference facilities, business center. **Cards:** AX, CB, DC, DS, JC, MC, VI. **Free Special Amenities:** newspaper and high-speed Internet.

SOME UNITS

DAYS INN JFK AIRPORT — **Phone:** (718)527-9025 — **45**

Small-scale Hotel

All Year	1P: $89-$189	2P: $89-$189	XP: $10 — F12

Location: In Jamaica; Van Wyck Expwy S, exit 1E to Belt Pkwy E, exit S Conduit Ave, then just e; Belt Pkwy E, exit 20; Belt Pkwy W, exit 21A (Rockaway Blvd), s at 150th Ln, then e on S Conduit Ave. 144-26 153rd Ct 11434. Fax: 718/527-9026. **Facility:** 75 one-bedroom standard units, some with whirlpools. 4 stories, interior corridors. **Parking:** on-site. **Amenities:** high-speed Internet, dual phone lines, voice mail, safes (fee), irons, hair dryers. **Cards:** AX, CB, DC, DS, JC, MC, VI.

SOME UNITS
FEE

DOUBLETREE HOTEL JFK AIRPORT — **Phone:** 718/322-2300 — **39**

Property failed to provide current rates

Large-scale Hotel

Location: In Jamaica; Van Wyck Expwy, exit 2 (Rockaway Blvd), just e to 140th St, then s. 135-30 140th St 11436. Fax: 718/322-6894. **Facility:** 386 one-bedroom standard units. 12 stories, interior corridors. *Bath:* combo or shower only. **Parking:** on-site. **Amenities:** video games (fee), high-speed Internet, dual phone lines, voice mail, irons, hair dryers. **Leisure Activities:** exercise room. **Guest Services:** gift shop, valet laundry. **Business Services:** conference facilities, business center.

SOME UNITS

ECONO LODGE — **Phone:** (718)843-4300 — **34**

Motel

All Year	1P: $89-$189	2P: $89-$189	XP: $10 — F

Location: In Ozone Park; Van Wyck Expwy, exit 2 (Rockaway Blvd), 1 mi w to 114th St. 113-18 Rockaway Blvd 11420. Fax: 718/843-0161. **Facility:** 38 one-bedroom standard units, some with whirlpools. 2 stories (no elevator), interior/exterior corridors. *Bath:* combo or shower only. **Parking:** on-site. **Terms:** [CP] meal plan available. **Business Services:** fax. **Cards:** AX, DS, MC, VI.

SOME UNITS

EXTENDED STAYAMERICA-WHITESTONE — **Phone:** (718)357-3661 — **12**

Small-scale Hotel

All Year	1P: $139-$159	2P: $144-$164	XP: $5 — F17

Location: In Flushing; I-678, exit 15, just w; in Whitestone. 18-30 Whitestone Expwy 11357. Fax: 718/357-3644. **Facility:** 117 one-bedroom standard units with efficiencies. 4 stories, interior corridors. *Bath:* combo or shower only. **Parking:** on-site. **Terms:** office hours 7 am-11 pm, cancellation fee imposed, weekly rates available, pets ($25-$75 fee). **Amenities:** dual phone lines, voice mail, irons, hair dryers. **Guest Services:** coin laundry, wireless Internet. **Cards:** AX, CB, DC, DS, MC, VI.

SOME UNITS
FEE

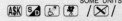

(See map and index starting on p. 396)

FAIRFIELD INN BY MARRIOT LA GUARDIA AIRPORT
Phone: 718/888-9979

Property failed to provide current rates

Location: In Flushing; Whitestone Expwy, exit 14, just s on Linden Pl, just w on 28th Ave, then just s. 28-66 College Park Blvd 11354. Fax: 718/888-9913. **Facility:** Smoke free premises. 84 one-bedroom standard units. 4 stories, interior corridors. *Bath:* combo or shower only. **Parking:** on-site. **Amenities:** video games (fee), high-speed Internet, voice mail, irons, hair dryers. **Leisure Activities:** exercise room. **Guest Services:** valet laundry. **Business Services:** meeting rooms, PC.

Small-scale Hotel

SOME UNITS

FAIRFIELD INN NEW YORK JFK AIRPORT
Phone: (718)977-3300

| All Year [ECP] | 1P: $139-$179 | 2P: $139-$179 | XP: $10 |

F16

Location: In Jamaica; Belt Pkwy E, exit 20, 1 mi e to 156th St; Belt Pkwy W, exit 21B (Rockaway Blvd), left at 1st light, then just s. 156-08 Rockaway Blvd 11434. Fax: 718/977-3301. **Facility:** Smoke free premises. 110 one-bedroom standard units. 5 stories, interior corridors. *Bath:* combo or shower only. **Parking:** on-site. **Terms:** cancellation fee imposed, [AP], [BP] & [MAP] meal plans available. **Dining:** 5 pm-11 pm, cocktails. **Leisure Activities:** exercise room. **Guest Services:** valet laundry, airport transportation-John F. Kennedy International Airport. **Business Services:** meeting rooms, business center. **Cards:** AX, DC, DS, MC, VI. **Free Special Amenities:** expanded continental breakfast and local telephone calls.

Small-scale Hotel

SOME UNITS

HAMPTON INN-JFK AIRPORT
Phone: (718)322-7500

| 5/1-12/23 & 3/1-4/30 [ECP] | 1P: $159-$289 |
| 12/24-2/29 [ECP] | 1P: $159-$249 |

36

Location: In Jamaica; Belt Pkwy W, exit 21A (Rockaway Blvd) to N Conduit Ave; Belt Pkwy E, exit 20 to 150th St, cross over Belt Pkwy, then just w. 144-10 135th Ave 11436. Fax: 718/322-7933. **Facility:** 216 one-bedroom standard units. 13 stories, interior corridors. *Bath:* combo or shower only. **Parking:** on-site. **Terms:** package plans. **Amenities:** video games (fee), dual phone lines, voice mail, irons, hair dryers. **Pool(s):** heated indoor. **Leisure Activities:** exercise room. **Guest Services:** valet laundry. **Business Services:** meeting rooms. **Cards:** AX, CB, DC, DS, JC, MC, VI.

Small-scale Hotel

SOME UNITS
FEE

HILTON GARDEN INN-QUEENS/JFK AIRPORT
Phone: (718)322-4448

| All Year | 1P: $159-$259 | 2P: $169-$269 | XP: $10 |

43
F18

Location: In Jamaica; between S Conduit and 149th aves off Nassau Expwy. 148-18 134th St 11430. Fax: 718/322-3338. **Facility:** 188 one-bedroom standard units. 6 stories, interior corridors. *Bath:* some combo or shower only. **Parking:** on-site. **Terms:** [BP] meal plan available, package plans. **Amenities:** video games (fee), high-speed Internet, dual phone lines, voice mail, irons, hair dryers. **Dining:** 6 am-1 & 5-11 pm, cocktails. **Pool(s):** small heated indoor. **Leisure Activities:** exercise room. **Guest Services:** sundries, valet and coin laundry, airport transportation-John F. Kennedy International Airport. **Business Services:** meeting rooms, business center. **Cards:** AX, CB, DC, DS, JC, MC, VI. **Free Special Amenities:** local telephone calls and high-speed Internet. *(See color ad below)*

Small-scale Hotel

SOME UNITS

HOLIDAY INN EXPRESS
Phone: (718)977-3100

| All Year | 1P: $99-$299 | 2P: $99-$299 | XP: $10 |

42
F18

Location: In Jamaica; Van Wyck Expwy S, exit 1E to Belt Pkwy E, exit S Conduit Ave, then just e; Belt Pkwy E, exit 20; Belt Pkwy W, exit 21A (Rockaway Blvd), s at 150th Ln, then e. 153-70 S Conduit Ave 11434. Fax: 718/977-6100. **Facility:** 129 one-bedroom standard units. 5 stories, interior corridors. *Bath:* combo or shower only. **Parking:** on-site. **Terms:** cancellation fee imposed, [ECP] meal plan available. **Amenities:** high-speed Internet, dual phone lines, voice mail, safes, irons, hair dryers. **Leisure Activities:** exercise room. **Guest Services:** valet laundry. **Business Services:** business center. **Cards:** AX, CB, DC, DS, MC, VI.

Small-scale Hotel

SOME UNITS
FEE

(See map and index starting on p. 396)

HOLIDAY INN EXPRESS *Book great rates at AAA.com* Phone: 718/706-6700 30

AAA SAVE

5/1-11/15	2P: $199-$259	XP: $15	F12
11/16-12/31	2P: $159-$189	XP: $15	F12
1/1-4/30	2P: $129-$169	XP: $15	F12

Small-scale Hotel **Location:** In Long Island City; I-278, exit I-495 (Midtown tunnel) westbound, exit 15 (Van Dam St), just n to Hunters Point Blvd, w on Greenpoint Ave, then n at 39th St; I-278 westbound, exit 35 (Greenpoint Ave), n on Greenpoint Ave, then e on 39th St. 3805 Hunters Point Ave 11101. Fax: 718/784-8532. **Facility:** 79 one-bedroom standard units. 3 stories, interior corridors. *Bath:* combo or shower only. **Parking:** on-site. **Terms:** cancellation fee imposed. **Amenities:** dual phone lines, voice mail, irons, hair dryers. **Guest Services:** valet laundry, wireless Internet. **Cards:** AX, DC, DS, MC, VI.

SOME UNITS

HOLIDAY INN-JFK AIRPORT Phone: (718)659-0200 37

AAA SAVE

All Year	1P: $159-$209	2P: $159-$209	

Large-scale Hotel **Location:** In Jamaica; Van Wyck Expwy, exit 2 (Rockaway Blvd), just e to 143rd St, then just s. 144-02 135th Ave 11436. Fax: 718/322-2533. **Facility:** 360 units. 349 one-bedroom standard units. 11 one-bedroom suites ($250-$289). 12 stories, interior corridors. **Parking:** on-site. **Terms:** package plans, $4 service charge. **Amenities:** video games (fee), high-speed Internet, dual phone lines, voice mail, irons, hair dryers. **Dining:** 2 restaurants, 6 am-1 am, cocktails. **Pool(s):** heated indoor. **Leisure Activities:** sauna, whirlpool, exercise room. **Guest Services:** gift shop, valet and coin laundry, airport transportation-John F. Kennedy International Airport. **Business Services:** conference facilities, business center. **Cards:** AX, CB, DC, DS, JC, MC, VI. **Free Special Amenities:** newspaper.

SOME UNITS

FEE

HOWARD JOHNSON EXPRESS INN-JFK AIRPORT Phone: (718)723-6700 35

All Year	1P: $90-$180	2P: $90-$180	XP: $10	F18

Small-scale Hotel **Location:** In Jamaica; Belt Pkwy, exit 20, 0.4 mi e on service road, then just n; Van Wyck Expwy, s to exit 2 (Rockaway Blvd) service road, then just n. 153-95 Rockaway Blvd 11434. Fax: 718/527-6300. **Facility:** 72 one-bedroom standard units, some with whirlpools. 3 stories, interior corridors. *Bath:* combo or shower only. **Parking:** on-site. **Terms:** [ECP] meal plan available, $4 service charge. **Amenities:** dual phone lines, voice mail, safes (fee), irons, hair dryers. **Cards:** AX, CB, DC, DS, JC, MC, VI.

SOME UNITS

HOWARD JOHNSON INN Phone: 718/264-6600

fyi

Property failed to provide current rates
Too new to rate, opening scheduled for December 2006. **Location:** In Jamaica; Cross Island Pkwy to Jamaica Small-scale Hotel Ave exit; in Queens Village. 220-16 Jamaica Ave 11428. Fax: 718/454-6255. **Amenities:** 53 units.

NEW YORK LA GUARDIA AIRPORT MARRIOTT Phone: (718)565-8900 16

8/26-12/31	1P: $199-$369
5/1-8/25	1P: $179-$339
1/1-4/30	1P: $189-$329

Large-scale Hotel **Location:** In East Elmhurst; Grand Central Pkwy, exit 6 (94th St), 0.3 mi e. 102-05 Ditmars Blvd 11369. Fax: 718/898-4955. **Facility:** Smoke free premises. 438 units. 435 one-bedroom standard units. 3 one-bedroom suites. 9 stories, interior corridors. *Bath:* combo or shower only. **Parking:** on-site (fee). **Terms:** check-in 4 pm. **Amenities:** dual phone lines, voice mail, irons, hair dryers. *Fee:* video games, high-speed Internet. **Pool(s):** heated indoor. **Leisure Activities:** saunas, whirlpool, exercise room. **Guest Services:** gift shop, valet laundry. **Business Services:** conference facilities, business center. **Cards:** AX, CB, DC, DS, MC, VI.

SOME UNITS

FEE

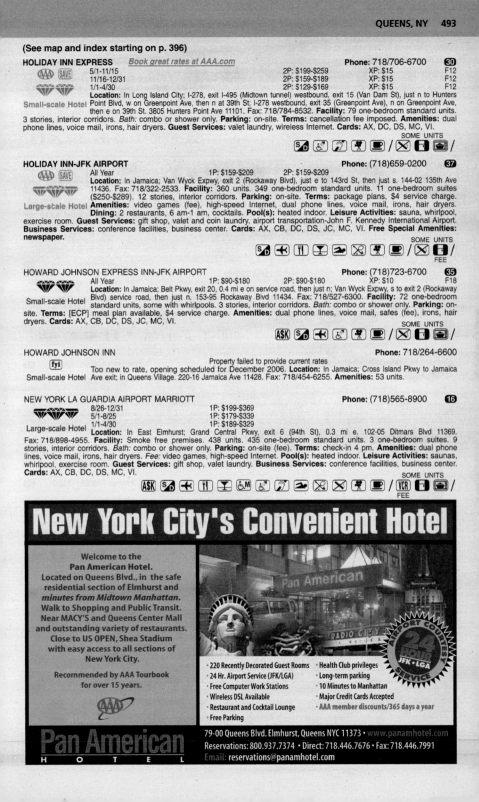

(See map and index starting on p. 396)

PAN AMERICAN HOTEL

Phone: (718)446-7676 **29**

AAA SAVE

All Year   1P: $109-$229   2P: $109-$229   XP: $10   F12
Location: In Elmhurst; I-278, exit 39B, 1 mi e. 79-00 Queens Blvd 11373. Fax: 718/446-7991. **Facility:** 216 one-bedroom standard units. 7 stories, interior corridors. *Bath:* combo or shower only. **Parking:** on-site.
Small-scale Hotel
Terms: cancellation fee imposed. **Amenities:** voice mail, hair dryers. **Dining:** 7 am-midnight, Fri & Sat-4 am, cocktails. **Guest Services:** valet laundry, airport transportation-John F. Kennedy International & La Guardia airports, wireless Internet. **Business Services:** meeting rooms, PC. **Cards:** AX, CB, DC, DS, MC, VI. **Free Special Amenities: newspaper and early check-in/late check-out.** *(See color ad p 493 & p 445)*

SOME UNITS

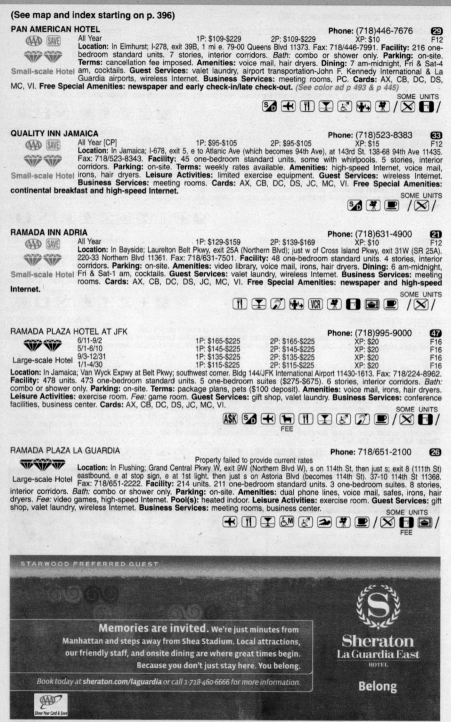

QUALITY INN JAMAICA

Phone: (718)523-8383 **33**

AAA SAVE

All Year [CP]   1P: $95-$105   2P: $95-$105   XP: $15   F12
Location: In Jamaica; I-678, exit 5, e to Atlanic Ave (which becomes 94th Ave), at 143rd St. 138-68 94th Ave 11435.
Fax: 718/523-8343. **Facility:** 45 one-bedroom standard units, some with whirlpools. 5 stories, interior corridors. **Parking:** on-site. **Terms:** weekly rates available. **Amenities:** high-speed Internet, voice mail,
Small-scale Hotel
irons, hair dryers. **Leisure Activities:** limited exercise equipment. **Guest Services:** wireless Internet. **Business Services:** meeting rooms. **Cards:** AX, CB, DC, DS, JC, MC, VI. **Free Special Amenities: continental breakfast and high-speed Internet.**

SOME UNITS

RAMADA INN ADRIA

Phone: (718)631-4900 **21**

AAA SAVE

All Year   1P: $129-$159   2P: $139-$169   XP: $10   F12
Location: In Bayside; Laurelton Belt Pkwy, exit 25A (Northern Blvd); just w of Cross Island Pkwy, exit 31W (SR 25A). 220-33 Northern Blvd 11361. Fax: 718/631-7501. **Facility:** 48 one-bedroom standard units. 4 stories, interior corridors. **Parking:** on-site. **Amenities:** video library, voice mail, irons, hair dryers. **Dining:** 6 am-midnight,
Small-scale Hotel
Fri & Sat-1 am, cocktails. **Guest Services:** valet laundry, wireless Internet. **Business Services:** meeting rooms. **Cards:** AX, CB, DC, DS, JC, MC, VI. **Free Special Amenities: newspaper and high-speed Internet.**

SOME UNITS

RAMADA PLAZA HOTEL AT JFK

Phone: (718)995-9000 **47**

6/11-9/2	1P: $165-$225	2P: $165-$225	XP: $20 F16
5/1-6/10	1P: $145-$225	2P: $145-$225	XP: $20 F16
9/3-12/31	1P: $135-$225	2P: $135-$225	XP: $20 F16
1/1-4/30	1P: $115-$225	2P: $115-$225	XP: $20 F16

Large-scale Hotel

Location: In Jamaica; Van Wyck Expwy at Belt Pkwy; southwest corner. Bldg 144/JFK International Airport 11430-1613. Fax: 718/224-8962. **Facility:** 478 units. 473 one-bedroom standard units. 5 one-bedroom suites ($275-$675). 6 stories, interior corridors. *Bath:* combo or shower only. **Parking:** on-site. **Terms:** package plans, pets ($100 deposit). **Amenities:** voice mail, irons, hair dryers. **Leisure Activities:** exercise room. *Fee:* game room. **Guest Services:** gift shop, valet laundry. **Business Services:** conference facilities, business center. **Cards:** AX, CB, DC, DS, JC, MC, VI.

SOME UNITS

RAMADA PLAZA LA GUARDIA

Phone: 718/651-2100 **26**

Property failed to provide current rates

Large-scale Hotel

Location: In Flushing; Grand Central Pkwy W, exit 9W (Northern Blvd W), s on 114th St, then just s; exit 8 (111th St) eastbound, e at stop sign, e at 1st light, then just s on Astoria Blvd (becomes 114th St). 37-10 114th St 11368. Fax: 718/651-2222. **Facility:** 214 units. 211 one-bedroom standard units. 3 one-bedroom suites. 8 stories, interior corridors. *Bath:* combo or shower only. **Parking:** on-site. **Amenities:** dual phone lines, voice mail, safes, irons, hair dryers. *Fee:* video games, high-speed Internet. **Pool(s):** heated indoor. **Leisure Activities:** exercise room. **Guest Services:** gift shop, valet laundry, wireless Internet. **Business Services:** meeting rooms, business center.

SOME UNITS

(See map and index starting on p. 396)

SHERATON LA GUARDIA EAST HOTEL
Phone: (718)460-6666 24

AAA SAVE

9/10-4/30	1P: $199-$429	2P: $199-$429
5/1-8/24	1P: $189-$429	2P: $189-$429

Location: In Flushing; Grand Central Pkwy to Northern Blvd, 1 mi e to Main St, 0.3 mi s to 39th Ave, then just w. 135-20 39th Ave 11354. **Fax:** 718/445-2655. **Facility:** 173 units. 165 one-bedroom standard units. 8 one-bedroom Large-scale Hotel suites, some with whirlpools. 16 stories, interior corridors. **Bath:** combo or shower only. **Parking:** valet. **Terms:** open 5/1-8/24 & 9/10-4/30, small pets only. **Amenities:** dual phone lines, voice mail, irons, hair dryers. *Some:* DVD players, CD players. **Dining:** 6 am-11 pm, cocktails. **Leisure Activities:** exercise room. **Guest Services:** gift shop, valet laundry, airport transportation-La Guardia Airport, wireless Internet. **Business Services:** conference facilities, business center. **Cards:** AX, DC, DS, VI. *(See color ad p 494)*

SOME UNITS

SUPER 8 MOTEL
Phone: (718)932-2100 18

AAA SAVE

All Year	1P: $99-$199	2P: $99-$199	XP: $15 F12

Location: In Astoria; Grand Central Pkwy, exit 3 (Hoyt Ave), 0.7 mi s on 31st, then 0.5 mi w on Broadway. 31-62 14th St 11106. **Fax:** 718/932-0954. **Facility:** 29 units. 23 one- and 6 two-bedroom standard units, some with efficiencies (no utensils). 2 stories (no elevator), interior corridors. **Bath:** combo or shower only. **Parking:** on-site. **Terms:** [CP] meal plan available. **Amenities:** *Some:* hair dryers. **Guest Services:** wireless Internet. Small-scale Hotel **Cards:** AX, DC, DS, MC, VI. **Free Special Amenities: continental breakfast and local telephone calls.**

SOME UNITS

WINGATE INN & SUITES LA GUARDIA AIRPORT
Phone: (718)445-3300 19

All Year [BP]	1P: $129-$399	2P: $129-$399	XP: $15 F18

Location: In Flushing; I-678 (Van Wick Expwy), exit 14, 0.5 mi s on Linden Pl, then just w. 137-07 Northern Blvd 11354. Small-scale Hotel **Fax:** 718/445-3382. **Facility:** 81 one-bedroom standard units. 8 stories, interior corridors. *Bath:* combo or shower only. **Parking:** no self-parking. **Terms:** cancellation fee imposed, $4 service charge. **Amenities:** video games (fee), high-speed Internet, dual phone lines, voice mail, safes, irons, hair dryers. *Some:* DVD players (fee). **Leisure Activities:** whirlpool, exercise room. **Guest Services:** valet laundry, wireless Internet. **Business Services:** meeting rooms, business center. **Cards:** AX, CB, DC, DS, JC, MC, VI.

SOME UNITS

FEE

——— WHERE TO DINE ———

BUDDHA BODAI RESTAURANT
Lunch: $4-$15 **Dinner:** $6-$15 **Phone:** 718/939-1188 26

Chinese

Location: In Flushing; between Cherry and Blossom aves. 42-96 Main St 11355. **Hours:** 11 am-11 pm, Sat & Sun from 10:30 am. Closed major holidays. **Features:** Strictly vegetarian and kosher food makes up the menu at the Asian restaurant. First-timers shouldn't be deterred by the casual decor and exterior, as the dishes are tasty and well prepared. Casual dress. **Parking:** on-site. **Cards:** MC, VI.

ERAWAN THAI CUISINE
Menu on AAA.com **Lunch:** $7-$12 **Dinner:** $10-$20 **Phone:** 718/428-2112 22

AAA

Thai

Location: In Bayside; between 42nd and 43rd aves. 42-31 Bell Blvd 11361. **Hours:** noon-10:30 pm, Fri & Sat-11:30 pm, Sun 3 pm-10 pm. **Reservations:** accepted. **Features:** Patrons settle into a cool, soothing space with understated Thai accents to enjoy fragrant, well-prepared curries, chicken or seafood with rich sauces and steamed or fried fish with ginger and soy or pungent chili sauce. Also on the menu are noodles and savory specials, including chicken with peanut sauce and watercress and marinated broiled steak with Thai chili dip. Bananas in warm coconut milk is a hard-to-find treat for dessert. Casual dress; cocktails. **Parking:** street. **Cards:** AX, DS, MC, VI.

FIRST EDITION
Lunch: $4-$17 **Dinner:** $8-$17 **Phone:** 718/428-8522 21

American

Location: In Bayside; between 41st and 42nd aves. 4108 Bell Blvd 11361. **Hours:** noon-midnight, Fri & Sat-2 am. Closed: 11/22, 12/25. **Reservations:** accepted. **Features:** This pub has a separate dining room on the second floor, away from the bustle of the bar but fully equipped with TVs. Typical burgers, create your own pizzas and pastas, as well as wraps and a few more complex dinner specials, are served up in most casual fashion. Casual dress; cocktails. **Parking:** street. **Cards:** DC, MC, VI.

GREEN PAPAYA
Lunch: $5-$18 **Dinner:** $8-$19 **Phone:** 718/353-1888 24

Thai

Location: In Flushing; Grand Central Pkwy to Northern Blvd E, 1 mi e to Main St, 0.3 mi s to 39th Ave, then just n. 38-12 Prince St 11354. **Hours:** 11 am-11 pm. Closed: Lunar New Year. **Features:** Authentic Thai cuisine—including the restaurant's namesake, a crunchy and refreshing green papaya salad—doesn't get much better than this. Those unfamiliar to Thai fare will, no doubt, be grateful for the photo album, which depicts each dish offered on the menu, including spicy squid with tamarind, curried blue crab with glass noodles and beef satay. Service is pleasant and accommodating. Casual dress. **Parking:** street.

LAILLA BAR & RESTAURANT
Lunch: $4-$6 **Dinner:** $11-$15 **Phone:** 718/225-2904 23

Turkish

Location: In Bayside; between 42nd and 43rd aves. 4224 Bell Blvd 11361. **Hours:** 11:30 am-10:30 pm, Fri-midnight, Sat & Sun noon-midnight. **Reservations:** accepted. **Features:** This casual Turkish restaurant offers patrons a delicious and delightful meal with attentive and friendly service. Casual dress; cocktails. **Parking:** street. **Cards:** AX, CB, DC, DS, MC, VI.

MOMBAR
Dinner: $16-$25 **Phone:** 718/726-2356 19

Arabic

Location: In Astoria; between 25th and 28th aves. 25-22 Steinway St 11103. **Hours:** 5 pm-11 pm. Closed: 1/1, 11/22, 12/25; also Mon. **Reservations:** accepted. **Features:** Don't look for a sign out front; instead look for the Egyptian eye. Marble-tile floors, a mosaic-tiled ceiling, walls and tables and funky eclectic decor are the hobby of the chef whose first love is the savory food he creates. Lamb and beef sausage with chickpeas and tomato, herb- and rice-stuffed chicken, Egyptian molasses-glazed duck and braised lamb tajine are herbed and spiced. If the choice is too daunting, opt for the tasting menu, which offers a sampling of a good bit of the menu. Casual dress. **Parking:** street.

(See map and index starting on p. 396)

MYTHOS   Lunch: $6-$12   Dinner: $10-$20   Phone: 718/357-6596   (25)

Greek

Location: In Flushing; on SR 25A/Northern Blvd, just w of Cross Island Expwy. 196-29 Northern Blvd 11358. **Hours:** 11 am-11 pm. Closed major holidays. **Reservations:** accepted. **Features:** Enjoy regional Greek cuisine from Cephalunia Island, including a good selection of fish and meat dishes, which are prepared daily. Many interesting, authentic appetizers and salads, as well as traditional Greek dessert such as yummy baklava, grace the menu. The staff is gracious. Casual dress; beer & wine only. **Parking:** street. **Cards:** MC, VI.

PING'S   Lunch: $5-$6   Dinner: $8-$20   Phone: 718/396-1238   (28)

Chinese

Location: In Elmhurst; I-278, exit 36, 1.1 mi e. 83-02 Queens Blvd (SR 25) 11373. **Hours:** 8 am-2 am. **Reservations:** accepted. **Features:** Known and revered for fresh dishes, the restaurant is a bright spot on Queens Boulevard. Lending to the decor are sparkling fish tanks and walls with colorful Chinese accents. The enormous menu spans a great variety, from dungeon crab, conch and cuttlefish dishes to minced squab, clams with black bean sauce, string beans with beef or minced pork and the most familiar standbys. Dim sum is offered every day. Casual dress; beer & wine only. **Parking:** on-site. **Cards:** MC, VI.

UNCLE JACK'S STEAKHOUSE   Lunch: $10-$50   Dinner: $40-$60   Phone: 718/229-1100   (20)

Steak House

Location: In Bayside; 1 mi w of Cross Island Pkwy, exit 31W (SR 25A/Northern Blvd), then 0.5 mi n. 39-40 Bell Blvd 11361. **Hours:** noon-11 pm, Thurs & Fri-midnight, Sat 4 pm-midnight, Sun 3 pm-10 pm. Closed: 7/4, 11/22, 12/25. **Reservations:** suggested. **Features:** A steakhouse with style, the restaurant has atmosphere galore. Instead of bright overhead lights, guests find sawdust on the floor, exposed brick walls, velour curtains and many candles that set the room aglow. Those who don't notice the decor can't help but take notice of the fine, dry-aged steaks and cordial, attentive service. A formidable wine list and martini menu complement the fine steakhouse fare. Dressy casual; cocktails. **Parking:** street. **Cards:** AX, MC, VI.

WATER'S EDGE   Lunch: $29   Dinner: $58-$78   Phone: 718/482-0033   (27)

American

Location: In Long Island City; from Manhattan, 59th St Queensborough Bridge upper level to 21st St exit, left to 44th Dr, 2nd light, then right to river. 44th Dr at the East River 11101. **Hours:** noon-3 & 6-11 pm, Sat 6 pm-11:30 pm. Closed: Sun. **Reservations:** suggested. **Features:** At Water's Edge, the view of Manhattan rivals most others. An extensive selection of wine complements the well-prepared and artfully-presented dishes. Showcase desserts are displayed on a cart to temp those with a sweet tooth. A free water taxi leaves from the 34th Street marina from 6 pm. Seasonal outdoor seating on the deck is pleasant. Dressy casual; cocktails; entertainment. **Parking:** valet. **Cards:** AX, DC, DS, MC, VI.

The following restaurant has not been evaluated by AAA but is listed for your information only.

NO 1 PEOPLE'S & PEOPLE   Phone: 718/460-8686

(fyi)   Not evaluated. **Location:** In Flushing. 38-06 Prince St 11354. **Features:** The name may seem confusing, but the eatery is popular among locals. Exotic dishes—including fish head casserole, salt and pepper frog and duck tongue with basil—may cause a little hesitation, but diners looking for the real McCoy will accomplish their objective here. Also sharing space on the huge menu are such recognizable choices as Mongolian beef with scallion sauce, orange chicken and shrimp with lobster sauce.

STATEN ISLAND pop. 443,728

WHERE TO STAY

HILTON GARDEN INN STATEN ISLAND
Phone: 718/477-2400

(AAA) (SAVE)

All Year   1P: $159-$299   2P: $159-$299   XP: $10   F18

Small-scale Hotel

Location: I-278, exit 6 (South Ave) westbound, just s; exit 5 eastbound to SR 440 S, exit South Ave, just s to South Ave, 1 mi n to Lois Ln, then just w. 1100 South Ave 10314. Fax: 718/477-5620. **Facility:** 148 units. 136 one-bedroom standard units. 12 one-bedroom suites with whirlpools. 6 stories, interior corridors. *Bath:* combo or shower only. **Parking:** on-site. **Terms:** cancellation fee imposed, small pets only ($35 extra charge). **Amenities:** video games (fee), high-speed Internet, dual phone lines, voice mail, irons, hair dryers. **Dining:** 6:30 am-10:30, noon-3:30 & 5-10 pm, Sat & Sun 7 am-11, noon-3 & 5-10 pm; Sunday brunch, cocktails. **Pool(s):** heated indoor. **Leisure Activities:** whirlpool, hiking trails, exercise room, spa. **Guest Services:** sundries, valet and coin laundry, airport transportation-Newark Liberty International Airport, area transportation-Staten Island Ferry. **Business Services:** conference facilities, business center. **Cards:** AX, DS, MC, VI. **Free Special Amenities:** newspaper and high-speed Internet.

SOME UNITS

FEE   FEE

THE STATEN ISLAND HOTEL
Phone: (718)698-5000

(AAA) (SAVE)

All Year   1P: $159-$179   2P: $159-$179

Large-scale Hotel

Location: I-278, exit Richmond Ave, 0.5 mi se. 1415 Richmond Ave 10314. Fax: 718/354-7071. **Facility:** 187 units. 186 one-bedroom standard units. 1 one-bedroom suite ($575). 10 stories, interior corridors. *Bath:* combo or shower only. **Parking:** on-site. **Terms:** package plans, small pets only. **Amenities:** video games (fee), dual phone lines, voice mail, safes, irons, hair dryers. **Dining:** 6:30 am-10 pm, cocktails. **Leisure Activities:** exercise room. **Guest Services:** valet and coin laundry. **Business Services:** meeting rooms. **Cards:** AX, DC, MC, VI. **Free Special Amenities:** local telephone calls and early check-in/late check-out.

SOME UNITS

FEE

WHERE TO DINE

CHARLIE BROWN'S STEAKHOUSE
Lunch: $6-$10   **Dinner:** $12-$21   **Phone:** 718/983-6846

Steak & Seafood

Location: Just w of jct Southern Ave. 1001 Goethals Rd N 10303. **Hours:** 11:30 am-2:30 & 3-10 pm, Fri & Sat-10:30 pm, Sun-9 pm. Closed: 12/25. **Features:** This budget-friendly steakhouse, famous for its prime rib, offers top quality fare without hurting your pocketbook. The young ones will not be disappointed with the kid's menu, and just might even try something green from the salad bar. Adults will love the quality steaks, chicken and rib dishes. The express lunches are great for those saddled with time constraints. Casual dress; cocktails. **Parking:** on-site. **Cards:** AX, DS, MC, VI.

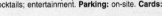

THE HISTORIC OLD BERMUDA INN
Dinner: $30   **Phone:** 718/948-7600

Italian

Location: SR 440, exit 4, just sw. 2512 Arthur Kill Rd 10309. **Reservations:** suggested, weekends. **Features:** The 1830s mansion, restored to resemble a Henry VIII pub, has a cozy, intimate ambience. Eggplant Napoleon and chicken chasseur stand out on a menu of well-prepared choices. Bananas Hamilton, served on a bed of creme anglaise, is exquisite. Casual dress; cocktails; entertainment. **Parking:** on-site. **Cards:** AX, MC, VI.

The New York City Vicinity

ARMONK pop. 3,461

——— WHERE TO STAY ———

WELLESLEY INN · *Book at AAA.com*   **Phone:** 914/273-9090
▼▼▼▼   Property failed to provide current rates
                    Location: I-684, exit 3S northbound; exit 3 southbound, 0.3 mi s on SR 22 to Business Park Dr. 94 Business Park Dr
Small-scale Hotel   10504. Fax: 914/273-4105. **Facility:** 140 one-bedroom standard units. 2 stories (no elevator), interior
                    corridors. *Bath:* combo or shower only. **Parking:** on-site. **Terms:** small pets only ($10 extra charge).
Amenities: voice mail, irons, hair dryers. *Some:* video games (fee). **Pool(s):** outdoor. **Leisure Activities:** exercise room,
volleyball. **Guest Services:** valet and coin laundry, area transportation, wireless Internet. **Business Services:** conference
facilities. *(See color ad p 360)*

SOME UNITS

FEE

CARMEL pop. 5,560

——— WHERE TO DINE ———

CUTILLO'S RESTAURANT   *Menu on AAA.com*   **Lunch:** $7-$12   **Dinner:** $13-$33   **Phone:** 845/225-8903
AAA   **Location:** I-84, exit 17, 1 mi se on SR 52, then just nw. 1196 Farmers Mill Rd 10512. **Hours:** noon-10 pm, Fri & Sat-
▼▼▼   11 pm. Closed: 11/22, 12/25. **Reservations:** suggested. **Features:** The Cutillo family home of stucco and
                    stone is set back among tall trees on a hill and is decorated with many family furnishings and pictures. You
Italian   may sit on the enclosed porch, in the sitting room, the living room or den. On the menu are many dishes
                    named after family members, such as clams Camille, chicken Lucille, shrimp Patricia and cavatelli
MC, VI.   Pasquale. Homemade cheesecake is decadent. Dressy casual; cocktails. **Parking:** on-site. **Cards:** DS,

CHAPPAQUA pop. 9,468

——— WHERE TO DINE ———

CRABTREE'S KITTLE HOUSE   **Lunch:** $11-$19   **Dinner:** $19-$39   **Phone:** 914/666-8044
▼▼▼▼   **Location:** Saw Mill Pkwy, exit 33, 0.9 mi se on Readers Digest and Roaring Brook rds, then 0.5 mi n on CR 117. 11
            Kittle Rd 10514. **Hours:** noon-2:30 & 5:30-9:30 pm, Fri-10:30 pm, Sat 5:30 pm-10:30 pm, Sun noon-2:30 & 3-
American   9 pm. Closed: 12/25. **Reservations:** suggested. **Features:** An award-winning list of wines complements
            such colorfully prepared choices as seafood stew and free-range chicken with couscous, vegetables and
rice vermici. A woodsy setting and large, white pillars distinguish the stately, Colonial-style building. Semi-formal attire; cocktails.
Parking: on-site. **Cards:** AX, CB, DC, DS, MC, VI.

CONGERS pop. 8,303

——— WHERE TO DINE ———

RESTAURANT X   **Lunch:** $10-$15   **Dinner:** $21-$32   **Phone:** 845/268-6555
▼▼▼   **Location:** Jct US 9W, 1 mi s; I-87/287, exit 12, 4 mi n. 117 N SR 303 10920. **Hours:** noon-2:30 & 5:30-10 pm, Fri-
            10:30 pm, Sat 5 pm-11 pm, Sun noon-2:30 & 5-8 pm; Sunday brunch. Closed: 12/25; also Mon.
American   **Reservations:** suggested. **Features:** Upscale country charm envelops the restaurant, which offers serene
            views of a country landscape. Grilled squab and crispy salmon roll tempura stand out on a menu of
contemporary American cuisine. For dessert, savor warm coconut cake or rum raisin ice cream. Dressy casual; cocktails.
Parking: on-site and valet. **Cards:** AX, MC, VI.

ROMOLO'S   **Lunch:** $11-$14   **Dinner:** $12-$26   **Phone:** 845/268-3770
▼▼▼   **Location:** I-87/287, exit 12, 3 mi n. 77 Rt 303 10920. **Hours:** 11:30 am-2:30 & 5-9:30 pm, Fri-10:30 pm, Sat 5
            pm-10:30 pm, Sun 3 pm-8:30 pm. Closed major holidays; also Mon. **Reservations:** suggested.
Italian   **Features:** Excellently seasoned dishes include ravioli stuffed with goat cheese and grilled chicken salad
            with endive and arugula leaves. Photographs of celebrities line the entry area. Polished servers exhibit solid
menu knowledge and timely follow-up. Casual dress; cocktails. **Parking:** on-site. **Cards:** AX, CB, DC, DS, MC, VI.

CROTON-ON-HUDSON pop. 7,606

——— WHERE TO STAY ———

ALEXANDER HAMILTON HOUSE   **Phone:** (914)271-6737
▼▼▼▼   5/1-12/31 [BP]   1P: $110-$125   2P: $125-$350   XP: $25   D15
            1/1-4/30 [BP]   1P: $110-$125   2P: $125-$250   XP: $25   D15
Historic Bed   **Location:** US 9, exit SR 129, e to light, n on Riverside, e on Grand, then n on Hamilton. 49 Van Wyck St 10520.
& Breakfast   Fax: 914/271-3927. **Facility:** Victorian hats and shadowboxes accent the eclectic decor at this quiet inn
            offering fireplaces, a gazebo, a fish pond and homemade cookies. Designated smoking area. 8 one-
bedroom standard units, some with whirlpools. 3 stories (no elevator), interior corridors. *Bath:* combo or shower only. **Parking:**
on-site. **Terms:** office hours 7 am-7 pm, 7 day cancellation notice-fee imposed, weekly rates available, 10% service charge.
Amenities: high-speed Internet, safes, hair dryers. *Some:* DVD players, CD players, irons. **Pool(s):** outdoor. **Leisure
Activities:** *Fee:* massage. **Guest Services:** gift shop. **Business Services:** meeting rooms. **Cards:** AX, CB, DC, DS, JC,
MC, VI.

SOME UNITS
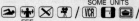
FEE

ELMSFORD pop. 4,676

―――――― WHERE TO STAY ――――――

**EXTENDED STAYAMERICA-WHITE
PLAINS-ELMSFORD** *Book at AAA.com*   **Phone:** (914)347-8073
▼▼ ▼▼ All Year   1P: $139-$159   2P: $144-$164   XP: $5   F17
Location: I-87, exit 8, just w. 118 Tarrytown Rd 10523. Fax: 914/347-8059. **Facility:** 136 one-bedroom standard
Small-scale Hotel units with efficiencies. 7 stories, interior corridors. *Bath:* combo or shower only. **Parking:** on-site.
Terms: office hours 7 am-11 pm, weekly rates available, pets ($75 fee, with prior approval).
Amenities: high-speed Internet, dual phone lines, voice mail, irons, hair dryers. **Leisure Activities:** limited exercise equipment.
Guest Services: coin laundry, wireless Internet. **Cards:** AX, CB, DC, DS, MC, VI.
SOME UNITS

[ASK] [S🄳] [⅃M] [✆] [⟳] [⌖] [🖥] [🖵] [💻] / [✕] /
FEE

HAMPTON INN WHITE PLAINS/TARRYTOWN *Book great rates at AAA.com*   **Phone:** (914)592-5680
[AAA] [SAVE] All Year   1P: $209   2P: $209
▼▼ ▼▼ **Location:** I-287, exit 1; I-87, exit 8, just w. 200 Tarrytown Rd 10523. Fax: 914/592-6727. **Facility:** 156 one-
bedroom standard units. 7 stories, interior corridors. *Bath:* combo or shower only. **Parking:** on-site.
Small-scale Hotel **Terms:** [CP] meal plan available, package plans, small pets only ($25 fee, with prior approval).
Amenities: video games (fee), voice mail, irons, hair dryers. **Pool(s):** outdoor. **Leisure Activities:** exercise
room. **Guest Services:** valet and coin laundry, wireless Internet. **Business Services:** meeting rooms,
business center. **Cards:** AX, DC, DS, MC, VI. **Free Special Amenities:** expanded continental breakfast and high-speed
Internet.
SOME UNITS

[S🄳] [⅃M] [✆] [⟳] [≋] [📷] [💻] / [✕] [🖥] [🖵] /
FEE   FEE FEE

―――――― WHERE TO DINE ――――――

ICHI RIKI RESTAURANT   **Lunch:** $12-$28   **Dinner:** $14-$26   **Phone:** 914/592-2220
▼▼ ▼▼ **Location:** Jct SR 119 (Main St/Tarrytown-White Plains Rd) and 9A, just e on SR 119 (Main St/Tarrytown-White Plains
Rd); downtown. 1 E Main St 10523. **Hours:** 11:45 am-2:30 & 5:30-10 pm, Fri-11 pm, Sat noon-2:30 & 5-11 pm,
Japanese   Sun 5 pm-9:30 pm. Closed major holidays; also Mon. **Reservations:** suggested. **Features:** Japanese music
and art, tatami rooms and servers in kimonos lend to the authentic feel of the comfortable restaurant. The
menu lists varied sushi and sashimi, as well as seasoned preparations of seafood, beef, pork and chicken. Casual dress;
cocktails. **Parking:** on-site. **Cards:** AX, CB, DC, MC, VI.

HARTSDALE pop. 9,830

―――――― WHERE TO DINE ――――――

CAFE MEZE   **Dinner:** $18-$28   **Phone:** 914/428-2400
▼▼ ▼▼ **Location:** Jct Hartsdale and Central Park aves, just n. 20 N Central Park Ave 10530. **Hours:** 5:30 pm-9 pm, Fri &
Sat-10:30 pm. Closed: 7/4, 12/25. **Reservations:** suggested, weekends. **Features:** Varnished wood panel
Mediterranean   walls below numerous Mediterranean pictures and glasses shimmering against votives creates a warm
intimate room in which to enjoy upscale comfort food, full flavored and hearty. The menu changes
seasonally but you can count on creative dishes, a few of which are bound to intrigue you. Casual dress; cocktails. **Parking:** on-
site. **Cards:** AX, DC, DS, MC, VI.
[🍸]

HAWTHORNE pop. 5,083

——— WHERE TO STAY ———

COMFORT INN & SUITES   *Book great rates at AAA.com*   Phone: (914)592-8600

(AAA) (SAVE)   All Year   1P: $160-$250   2P: $160-$250   XP: $10   F16
▼▼▼   **Location:** Saw Mill River Pkwy, exit 25 northbound; exit 23 (Eastview) southbound, 1 mi e on Old Saw Mill River Rd, then 1 mi n on SR 9A. 20 Saw Mill River Rd 10532. Fax: 914/592-7457. **Facility:** 86 units. 72 one-bedroom standard units, some with whirlpools. 12 one- and 2 two-bedroom suites with efficiencies (no utensils). 3 stories, interior corridors. *Bath:* combo or shower only. **Parking:** on-site. **Terms:** check-in 3:30 pm, [ECP]
Small-scale Hotel   meal plan available, package plans. **Amenities:** video games (fee), high-speed Internet, dual phone lines, voice mail, safes, irons, hair dryers. **Pool(s):** heated indoor. **Leisure Activities:** sauna, sun deck, exercise room. **Guest Services:** valet and coin laundry. **Business Services:** meeting rooms, business center. **Cards:** AX, CB, DC, DS, MC, VI.
Free Special Amenities: expanded continental breakfast and high-speed Internet.   SOME UNITS

[S][D] [†¶] [🛏] [🌊] [✕] [🎥] [🎞] [🛗] [📺] [🖥] / [✕] /

MOUNT KISCO pop. 9,983

——— WHERE TO STAY ———

HOLIDAY INN   *Book at AAA.com*   Phone: (914)241-2600
▼▼▼   All Year   1P: $130-$250   2P: $130-$250
Location: Saw Mill River Pkwy, exit 37, just e. 1 Holiday Inn Dr 10549. Fax: 914/241-4742. **Facility:** 122 one-
Small-scale Hotel   bedroom standard units, some with whirlpools. 2 stories (no elevator), interior corridors. *Bath:* combo or shower only. **Parking:** on-site. **Terms:** cancellation fee imposed, package plans, pets ($10 extra charge).
Amenities: high-speed Internet, dual phone lines, voice mail, irons, hair dryers. *Fee:* video library, video games. **Pool(s):** heated outdoor. **Leisure Activities:** exercise room. **Guest Services:** valet and coin laundry, wireless Internet. **Business Services:** conference facilities, business center. **Cards:** AX, CB, DC, DS, JC, MC, VI.
                    SOME UNITS

[ASK] [🛏] [†¶] [🍽] [⌖] [🎥] [🌊] [🎞] [🖥] / [✕] /
FEE   FEE

——— WHERE TO DINE ———

TUSCAN OVEN   **Lunch:** $10-$19   **Dinner:** $16-$29   Phone: 914/666-7711
▼▼▼   **Location:** Saw Mill River Pkwy, exit 38 northound, just e on Green Ln, then 0.4 mi s; exit 39 southbound, just ne on Haines Rd, then 1.5 mi s. 360 N Bedford Rd 10549. **Hours:** noon-10 pm, Fri & Sat-11 pm. Closed: 11/22, 12/25.
Italian   **Features:** Large portions of fresh poultry, steak and pasta are served at the Tuscany-inspired eatery. The wine list is extensive. Dressy casual; cocktails. **Parking:** on-site. **Cards:** AX, MC, VI.
[♿M]

NANUET pop. 16,707

——— WHERE TO STAY ———

CANDLEWOOD SUITES   *Book at AAA.com*   Property failed to provide current rates   Phone: 845/371-4445
▼▼▼   **Location:** I-287/87 (New York State Thruway), exit 14 (SR 59 W) to New Clarkstown Rd. 20 Overlook Blvd 10954.
Small-scale Hotel   Fax: 845/371-4446. **Facility:** 124 units. 100 one-bedroom standard units with efficiencies. 24 one-bedroom suites with efficiencies. 3 stories, interior corridors. *Bath:* combo or shower only. **Parking:** on-site.
Terms: pets ($75-$150 fee). **Amenities:** video library, DVD players, CD players, high-speed Internet, dual phone lines, voice mail, irons, hair dryers. **Leisure Activities:** exercise room. **Guest Services:** sundries, complimentary and valet laundry, wireless Internet.
                    SOME UNITS

[🛏] [†¶] [⌖] [VCR] [🎞] [🛗] [🖥] [📺] / [✕] /
FEE

COMFORT INN & SUITES   *Book great rates at AAA.com*   Phone: (845)623-6000
(AAA) (SAVE)   All Year   1P: $99-$260   2P: $99-$260   XP: $10   F
▼▼▼   **Location:** Palisades Pkwy, exit 8W, jct SR 59/304, then just e. 425 E Rt 59 10954. Fax: 845/623-9338. **Facility:** 156 units. 150 one-bedroom standard units, some with efficiencies and/or whirlpools. 6 one-bedroom suites ($150-$260) with efficiencies and whirlpools. 4 stories, interior corridors. *Bath:* some combo or shower only.
Small-scale Hotel   **Parking:** on-site. **Terms:** [ECP] meal plan available. **Amenities:** video games (fee), high-speed Internet, voice mail, irons, hair dryers. **Dining:** 5 pm-10 pm; closed Sun, cocktails. **Pool(s):** small heated indoor.
Leisure Activities: whirlpool, exercise room. **Guest Services:** valet and coin laundry, area transportation-businesses. **Business Services:** meeting rooms, business center. **Cards:** AX, CB, DC, DS, MC, VI. **Free Special Amenities: expanded continental breakfast and high-speed Internet.**
                    SOME UNITS

[S][D] [†¶] [🍽] [⌖] [🌊] [🎞] [🖥] / [✕] [🛗] [📺] /

DAYS INN NANUET   *Book great rates at AAA.com*   Phone: (845)623-4567
(AAA) (SAVE)   All Year [ECP]   1P: $79-$109   2P: $79-$109   XP: $10   F
▼▼▼   **Location:** I-287/87 (New York State Thruway), exit 14 (SR 59) northbound, just e; exit southbound, just w. 367 W Rt 59 10954. Fax: 845/623-0190. **Facility:** 70 one-bedroom standard units, some with whirlpools. 2 stories (no elevator), interior/exterior corridors. **Parking:** on-site. **Terms:** pets ($8 extra charge). **Amenities:** safes,
Small-scale Hotel   irons, hair dryers. *Some:* DVD players. **Pool(s):** heated outdoor. **Guest Services:** valet and coin laundry.
Business Services: business center. **Cards:** AX, CB, DC, DS, JC, MC, VI. **Free Special Amenities: continental breakfast and high-speed Internet.**
                    SOME UNITS

[S][D] [🛏] [†¶] [🌊] [🍴] [🎞] [🛗] [🖥] [📺] / [✕] [VCR]
FEE

HILTON GARDEN INN *Book great rates at AAA.com*   Phone: (845)623-0600
▼▼▼▼ All Year   1P: $109-$204   2P: $109-$204   XP: $10   F18
Location: I-287/87 (New York State Thruway), exit 14 (SR 59), just se, then U-turn. 270 Rt 59 W 10954.
Small-scale Hotel   Fax: 845/623-6500. **Facility:** 88 units. 80 one-bedroom standard units. 8 one-bedroom suites ($129-$259), some with whirlpools. 5 stories, interior corridors. *Bath:* combo or shower only. **Parking:** on-site. **Terms:** 7 day cancellation notice-fee imposed, [AP] meal plan available, package plans. **Amenities:** video games (fee), high-speed Internet, dual phone lines, voice mail, irons, hair dryers. **Pool(s):** heated indoor. **Leisure Activities:** whirlpool, exercise room. **Guest Services:** sundries, valet and coin laundry, wireless Internet. **Business Services:** meeting rooms, business center. **Cards:** AX, DC, DS, MC, VI.

SOME UNITS
(ASK) (S✆) (TÍ) (ĞM) (🖥) (🅿) (⇆) (🎦) (🖪) (🖵) (📼) / (✕) /

──────── **WHERE TO DINE** ────────

NANUET DINER   **Lunch:** $3-$12   **Dinner:** $10-$19   Phone: 845/623-2200
▼▼▼   **Location:** On SR 59; across from Nanuet Mall; in Rockland Plaza. 120 W Rt 59 10954. **Hours:** 24 hours.
American   **Features:** Guests can choose from a huge selection of Greek, Mexican and American fare in the retro '50s-style diner, which is accented with glass blocks, chrome and neon. The selection of mouthwatering pastries and desserts is impressive. Casual dress; cocktails. **Parking:** on-site. **Cards:** AX, DC, DS, MC, VI.

NEW ROCHELLE pop. 72,182

──────── **WHERE TO STAY** ────────

RADISSON HOTEL   *Book great rates at AAA.com*   Phone: (914)576-3700
(AAA) (SAVE)   5/1-12/15   1P: $157-$202   2P: $157-$202   XP: $10   F17
    3/15-4/30   1P: $152-$197   2P: $152-$197   XP: $10   F17
▼▼▼▼   12/16-3/14   1P: $148-$193   2P: $149-$193   XP: $10   F17
Location: I-95, exit 16, via Cedar St. 1 Radisson Plaza 10801. Fax: 914/576-5864. **Facility:** 130 units. 127 one-bedroom standard units. 3 one-bedroom suites. 10 stories, interior corridors. **Parking:** on-site. **Terms:** 10 day cancellation notice-fee imposed. **Amenities:** voice mail, irons, hair dryers. *Fee:* video games, high-speed Internet. **Dining:** 6:30 am-10 pm, cocktails. **Pool(s):** outdoor. **Leisure Activities:** exercise room. **Guest Services:** valet laundry. **Business Services:** meeting rooms. **Cards:** AX, CB, DC, DS, JC, MC, VI. **Free Special Amenities:** newspaper and early check-in/late check-out. *(See color ad below)*

SOME UNITS
(S✆) (TÍ) (⊥) (🅿) (⇆) (🖪) (🖵) / (✕) (VCR) (📼) /

NYACK pop. 6,737

──────── **WHERE TO STAY** ────────

BEST WESTERN NYACK ON HUDSON   *Book great rates at AAA.com*   Phone: (845)358-8100
(AAA) (SAVE)   5/1-11/26   1P: $109-$119   2P: $109-$119   XP: $5   F18
    11/27-4/30   1P: $99-$109   2P: $99-$109   XP: $5   F18
▼▼ ▼▼   **Location:** I-87 (New York State Thruway), exit 11, just e. Located near Palisades Center Mall and IMAX theater. 26 Rt 59 10960. Fax: 845/358-3644. **Facility:** 80 one-bedroom standard units. 2 stories (no elevator), exterior corridors. **Parking:** on-site, winter plug-ins. **Amenities:** dual phone lines, voice mail, irons, hair dryers.
Motel   **Dining:** 6 am-1 am, wine/beer only. **Guest Services:** wireless Internet. **Business Services:** meeting rooms. **Cards:** AX, CB, DC, DS, MC, VI. **Free Special Amenities:** continental breakfast and high-speed Internet.

SOME UNITS
(S✆) (TÍ) (🏊) (🎦) (🖪) (🖵) (📼) / (✕) /

SUPER 8 MOTEL   *Book great rates at AAA.com*   Phone: 845/353-3880
(AAA) (SAVE)   All Year   1P: $69-$159   2P: $69-$169   XP: $10   F17
Location: I-87 (New York State Thruway), exit 11 eastbound, just e; westbound, 0.5 mi w. 47 Rt 59 W 10960.
Fax: 845/353-0271. **Facility:** 43 one-bedroom standard units. 2 stories (no elevator), interior corridors.
Parking: on-site. **Terms:** [CP] meal plan available. **Amenities:** irons, hair dryers. **Guest Services:** wireless
Small-scale Hotel   Internet. **Cards:** AX, CB, DC, DS, JC, MC, VI. **Free Special Amenities:** expanded continental breakfast and high-speed Internet.

SOME UNITS
(S✆) (T🛏) (🅿) (🎦) / (✕) (🖪) /

——— WHERE TO DINE ———

THE HUDSON HOUSE OF NYACK   **Lunch:** $7-$12   **Dinner:** $18-$26   **Phone:** 845/353-1355
▽▽▽▽   **Location:** Jct Franklin and Main sts, just e; downtown. 134 Main St 10960. **Hours:** 11:30 am-3 & 5:30-10 pm, Fri &
Nouvelle American   Sat-11 pm, Sun 11:30 am-3 & 4:30-9:30 pm. Closed: 11/22, 12/25; also Mon. **Reservations:** suggested.
Features: The restaurant delivers complex cuisine, such as blackened catfish over artichoke hearts,
radicchio, Belgian endive, mesclun, red potatoes and orange slices. The restored storefront building exudes
a quaint, comfortable charm. Homemade desserts are a must. Casual dress; cocktails. **Parking:** street. **Cards:** AX, MC, VI.

⚋

LANTERNA TUSCAN BISTRO   **Lunch:** $8-$15   **Dinner:** $12-$25   **Phone:** 845/353-8361
🅰🅰🅰   **Location:** Downtown. 3 S Broadway 10960. **Hours:** 11:30 am-3:30 & 4:30-10 pm, Fri & Sat-11 pm. Closed: 1/1,
▽▽▽▽   11/22, 12/25. **Reservations:** required. **Features:** This upscale, lively bistro-style restaurant offers authentic
Northern Italian   Tuscan-style cuisine. Careful preparation of the best quality ingredients are served by friendly, efficient staff.
Casual dress; cocktails. **Parking:** street. **Cards:** AX, DC, DS, MC, VI.

ORANGEBURG pop. 3,388

——— WHERE TO STAY ———

ORANGEBURG HOLIDAY INN & REGISTRY HOTEL   *Book at AAA.com*   **Phone:** (845)359-7000
▽▽▽▽   All Year   1P: $109-$159   2P: $109-$159
Location: I-87/287, exit 12, 4 mi s on SR 303; 1 mi n of Palisades Interstate Pkwy, exit 5 northbound; 1 mi e of exit 6.
Small-scale Hotel   329 Rt 303 10962. Fax: 845/359-7196. **Facility:** 168 one-bedroom standard units, some with whirlpools. 3
stories, interior corridors. *Bath:* combo or shower only. **Parking:** on-site. **Amenities:** video games (fee),
voice mail, irons, hair dryers. *Some:* dual phone lines. **Pool(s):** outdoor. **Leisure Activities:** exercise room. **Guest Services:**
valet laundry, area transportation. **Business Services:** meeting rooms. **Cards:** AX, CB, DC, DS, JC, MC, VI.

SOME UNITS
(ASK) 🅂🄳 🐾 🍴 📺 ⊘ ⧖ 📷 📠 / ⊠ 🔌 /
FEE

OSSINING pop. 24,010

——— WHERE TO DINE ———

BRASSERIE SWISS   **Lunch:** $8-$16   **Dinner:** $17-$28   **Phone:** 914/941-0319
▽▽ ▽▽   **Location:** SR 133; between US 9 and SR 9A. 118 Croton Ave 10562. **Hours:** noon-2:30 & 5-9:30 pm, Fri & Sat
Swiss   5:30 pm-10:30 pm, Sun 4 pm-9 pm. Closed: Mon. **Features:** Continental Swiss cuisine, featuring appetizers
such as pate and a variety of schnitzel entrees and gracious service are to be enjoyed at Brasserie Swiss.
Dressy casual; cocktails. **Parking:** on-site. **Cards:** AX, CB, DC, DS, MC, VI.

⚋

GUIDA'S   **Lunch:** $10-$15   **Dinner:** $16-$24   **Phone:** 914/941-2662
▽▽▽   **Location:** Corner of US 9 and Main St; downtown. 199 Main St 10562. **Hours:** 11:30 am-10 pm, Fri & Sat-11 pm,
Italian   Sun 12:30 pm-10 pm. Closed: 11/22, 12/25. **Reservations:** suggested. **Features:** Soft sconce lighting on
yellow walls hung with ornately framed mirrors and upscale table settings enhance the sophisticated appeal
of the restaurant. The menu is traditional and brings in a loyal local crowd. Homemade pastas, veal, filet
mignon, chicken and fish are done many ways, and if you don't see it, ask. Casual dress; cocktails. **Parking:** street. **Cards:** AX,
MC, VI.

PEARL RIVER pop. 15,553

——— WHERE TO STAY ———

HILTON PEARL RIVER   *Book great rates at AAA.com*   **Phone:** 845/735-9000
▽▽▽   All Year   1P: $119-$256   2P: $119-$259   XP: $20   F18
Location: Palisades Interstate Pkwy, exit 6, 2.5 mi w on CR 20 (Veterans Memorial Dr). 500 Veterans Memorial Dr
Small-scale Hotel   10965. Fax: 845/735-9005. **Facility:** 150 one-bedroom standard units. 5 stories, interior corridors. **Parking:**
on-site. **Terms:** package plans. **Amenities:** video games (fee), dual phone lines, voice mail, irons, hair
dryers. **Pool(s):** heated indoor. **Leisure Activities:** saunas, whirlpool, exercise room. *Fee:* massage. **Guest Services:** valet
and coin laundry, area transportation, wireless Internet. **Business Services:** conference facilities, business center. **Cards:** AX,
CB, DC, DS, JC, MC, VI.

SOME UNITS
(ASK) 🍴 📺 🅼 ⊘ 🔁 ⊠ 🎣 📠 / ⊠ 🔌 /

PORT CHESTER pop. 27,867

——— WHERE TO DINE ———

THE WILLETT HOUSE   **Lunch:** $11-$30   **Dinner:** $28-$48   **Phone:** 914/939-7500
▽▽ ▽▽   **Location:** Corner of Willett and Abendroth aves. 20 Willett Ave 10573. **Hours:** 11:45 am-10 pm, Sat noon-10:30
Steak & Seafood   pm, Sun 4 pm-9 pm. **Reservations:** suggested. **Features:** The large and attractive red-brick restaurant
welcomes families to enjoy well-prepared selections of prime steak, plus lobster and grilled seafood. Lighter
lunch fare includes such tasty sandwiches as the BLT, which comes with homemade potato chips. Casual
dress; cocktails. **Parking:** on-site. **Cards:** AX, DC, DS, MC, VI.

⚋

RYE pop. 14,955

———— WHERE TO STAY ————

COURTYARD BY MARRIOTT *Book great rates at AAA.com* Phone: (914)921-1110
(AAA) (SAVE) All Year 1P: $149-$299 2P: $159-$309 XP: $10 F
Location: I-95 (New England Thruway), exit 22 northbound, 0.3 mi n; exit 21 southbound, just s; I-287 (Cross Westchester Exwy), exit 11 eastbound, 0.4 mi s on US 1, 0.4 mi e on Peck Ave, then just n. 631 Midland Ave 10580. Fax: 914/921-2446. **Facility:** Smoke free premises. 145 units. 133 one-bedroom standard units. 12 one-
Small-scale Hotel bedroom suites ($189-$339). 4 stories, interior corridors. *Bath:* combo or shower only. **Parking:** on-site. **Terms:** package plans. **Amenities:** video library (fee), high-speed Internet, dual phone lines, voice mail, irons, hair dryers. **Dining:** 6:30-10 am, Sat & Sun 7 am-noon, wine/beer only. **Pool(s):** heated indoor. **Leisure Activities:** whirlpool, sun deck, exercise room. **Guest Services:** sundries, valet and coin laundry. **Business Services:** meeting rooms, business center. **Cards:** AX, CB, DC, DS, JC, MC, VI.
SOME UNITS

———— WHERE TO DINE ————

CAFE LIVORNO **Lunch:** $10-$15 **Dinner:** $17-$33 Phone: 914/967-1909
Location: Jct US 1, 0.3 mi n; downtown. 92 Purchase St 10580. **Hours:** 11:30 am-2:30 & 5:30-10 pm, Sat 5:30
Northern Italian pm-10:30 pm. Closed major holidays; also Sun. **Reservations:** suggested. **Features:** The established bistro serves authentic food in a cozy atmosphere perfect for an intimate dinner. Casual dress; cocktails. **Parking:** street. **Cards:** AX, DC, MC, VI.

LA PANETIERE **Lunch:** $11-$14 **Dinner:** $48-$62 Phone: 914/967-8140
Location: I-95 (New England Thruway), exit 19, 0.8 mi e on Playland Pkwy, then 0.5 mi s. 530 Milton Rd 10580.
French **Hours:** noon-2:30 & 6-9:30 pm, Sat from 6 pm, Sun noon-2:30 & 5-8:30 pm. Closed: 1/1; also for lunch Mon & Sat. **Reservations:** suggested. **Features:** This lovely dining room is replete with provincial charm from the stenciled stucco walls, imported fabrics, beamed ceilings, to the delightful dishes and the chicken/rooster salt and pepper shakers. Cheerful flower bouquets on each table further brighten the intimate room. Delicate portions of fine, traditionally prepared dishes attract locals again and again. Gracious service is de rigueur. Semi-formal attire; cocktails. **Parking:** on-site and valet. **Cards:** AX, CB, DC, DS, MC, VI.

RYE BROOK pop. 8,602

———— WHERE TO STAY ————

DORAL ARROWWOOD RESORT & GOLF CLUB *Book at AAA.com* Phone: 914/939-5500
Property failed to provide current rates
Resort **Location:** Hutchinson River Pkwy, exit 28, 1 mi nw on Lincoln Ave, then 0.7 mi n. 975 Anderson Hill Rd 10573.
Large-scale Hotel Fax: 914/323-5500. **Facility:** Featuring complete conference facilities, this resort on 114 rolling acres also offers extensive recreational facilities. 374 units. 372 one-bedroom standard units. 2 one-bedroom suites. 5 stories, interior corridors. *Bath:* combo or shower only. **Parking:** on-site and valet. **Amenities:** high-speed Internet, dual phone lines, voice mail, safes, irons, hair dryers. *Fee:* video library, video games. *Some:* CD players. **Pool(s):** heated indoor/outdoor. **Leisure Activities:** saunas, whirlpool, steamrooms, racquetball courts, exercise instruction, basketball, volleyball. *Fee:* golf-9 holes, 2 indoor tennis courts, game room. **Guest Services:** gift shop, complimentary and valet laundry, wireless Internet. **Business Services:** conference facilities, business center.
SOME UNITS
FEE

HILTON RYE TOWN *Book great rates at AAA.com* Phone: (914)939-6300
(AAA) (SAVE) All Year 1P: $129-$369 2P: $129-$369 XP: $20 F18
Location: I-287 (Cross Westchester Expwy), exit 10 eastbound, 0.6 mi ne on SR 120A; exit westbound, 0.3 mi n on Webb Ave, then 0.4 mi ne on SR 120A. 699 Westchester Ave 10573. Fax: 914/939-5328. **Facility:** 437 units. 426 one-bedroom standard units. 5 one- and 6 two-bedroom suites. 4 stories, interior corridors. *Bath:* combo or Large-scale Hotel shower only. **Parking:** on-site and valet. **Terms:** cancellation fee imposed, small pets only ($50 fee). **Amenities:** dual phone lines, voice mail, honor bars, irons, hair dryers. *Fee:* video games, high-speed Internet. **Dining:** 2 restaurants, 6:30 am-11 pm, cocktails. **Pool(s):** outdoor, heated indoor. **Leisure Activities:** saunas, whirlpool, exercise room, basketball, shuffleboard. *Fee:* 3 lighted indoor tennis courts. **Guest Services:** gift shop, valet laundry. **Business Services:** conference facilities, business center. **Cards:** AX, CB, DC, DS, MC, VI.
SOME UNITS
FEE

SPRING VALLEY pop. 25,464

———— WHERE TO STAY ————

FAIRFIELD INN BY MARRIOTT-SPRING VALLEY *Book great rates at AAA.com* Phone: 845/426-2000
All Year 1P: $99-$149 2P: $99-$149
Location: I-87/287, exit 14 (SR 59 W) to New Clarkstown Rd, just e. 100 Spring Valley Marketplace 10977.
Small-scale Hotel Fax: 845/426-2008. **Facility:** Smoke free premises. 105 one-bedroom standard units. 4 stories, interior corridors. *Bath:* combo or shower only. **Parking:** on-site. **Amenities:** video games (fee), voice mail, irons, hair dryers. **Pool(s):** outdoor. **Leisure Activities:** exercise room. **Guest Services:** valet and coin laundry, wireless Internet. **Business Services:** PC. **Cards:** AX, CB, DC, DS, JC, MC, VI.
SOME UNITS

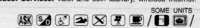

SUFFERN pop. 11,006

———— WHERE TO STAY ————

HOLIDAY INN-SUFFERN   *Book great rates at AAA.com*   Phone: (845)357-4800

(AAA) (SAVE)   All Year [CP]   1P: $109-$129   2P: $109-$129

▼▼▼▼▼   **Location:** I-87 (New York State Thruway), exit 14B, just n. 3 Executive Blvd 10901. Fax: 845/918-1475. **Facility:** 243 units. 238 one-bedroom standard units. 5 one-bedroom suites with whirlpools. 3 stories, interior corridors. *Bath:* combo or shower only. **Parking:** on-site. **Terms:** check-in 4 pm, cancellation fee

Small-scale Hotel   imposed, [BP] meal plan available, pets ($50 fee). **Amenities:** video games (fee), dual phone lines, voice mail, irons, hair dryers. **Dining:** 6:30 am-10:30 & 5-10 pm, Fri & Sat-11 pm, cocktails. **Pool(s):** heated indoor. **Leisure Activities:** sauna, whirlpool, exercise room. *Fee:* game room. **Guest Services:** valet and coin laundry, area transportation-within 5 mi, wireless Internet. **Business Services:** conference facilities, business center. **Cards:** AX, DC, DS, MC, VI. **Free Special Amenities: newspaper and room upgrade (subject to availability with advance reservations).**

SOME UNITS

FEE

———— WHERE TO DINE ————

MARCELLO'S OF SUFFERN   **Lunch:** $13-$18   **Dinner:** $17-$29   Phone: 845/357-9108

(AAA)   **Location:** Between Orange and Chestnut aves; center. 21 Lafayette Ave 10901. **Hours:** noon-2:30 & 5-9:30 pm, Fri & Sat-10 pm, Sun 3 pm-8:30 pm. Closed major holidays. **Reservations:** suggested. **Features:** The chef-

▼▼▼▼▼   owned ristorante uses quality, hand-selected ingredients in traditional Italian dishes such as tangy eggplant

Italian   caponata, rack of lamb, grilled ostrich with spicy Mediterranean salsa and salmon with mustard and mushroom sauce. Pastas are handmade, as are the scrumptious desserts. A professionally trained staff

MC, VI.   accommodates every whim. Dressy casual; cocktails. **Parking:** valet and street. **Cards:** AX, DC, DS,

⟨Y⟩

ORIENTAL GARDEN   **Lunch:** $6-$8   **Dinner:** $8-$14   Phone: 845/368-0011

▼▼▼▼   **Location:** Between Orange and Chestnut aves; center. 25 Lafayette Ave (Rt 59) 10901. **Hours:** 11:30 am-10 pm, Fri-11 pm, Sat noon-11 pm, Sun 2 pm-10 pm. Closed: 11/22. **Reservations:** accepted. **Features:** Simple to

Chinese   look at and unassuming from the outside, the restaurant treats locals to well-prepared dishes, including such standouts as lace shrimp and lobster lover. Ribs and Peking duck are some of the best around.

Service is extra-friendly. Casual dress; cocktails. **Parking:** street. **Cards:** AX, DS, MC, VI.

TARRYTOWN pop. 11,090

———— WHERE TO STAY ————

CASTLE ON THE HUDSON   *Book great rates at AAA.com*   Phone: (914)631-1980

(AAA) (SAVE)   All Year   1P: $320-$625   2P: $320-$625   XP: $50   F16

▼▼▼▼▼   **Location:** I-287 (Cross Westchester Expwy), exit 1, 0.3 mi w on SR 119, then 0.6 mi n; opposite entrance to Hackley School. 400 Benedict Ave 10591. Fax: 914/631-4612. **Facility:** Views of the river and, on clear days, the

Historic   Manhattan skyline, are a feature of this luxurious Gothic-style stone castle set on lush grounds. Smoke free

Country Inn   premises. 31 units. 26 one-bedroom suites ($645-$820). 3-4 stories, interior corridors. **Parking:** valet. **Terms:** check-in 4 pm, 7 day cancellation notice-fee imposed, package plans. **Amenities:** video library, DVD players, video games (fee), CD players, high-speed Internet, dual phone lines, voice mail, safes, honor bars, irons, hair dryers. **Dining:** Equus, see separate listing. **Pool(s):** heated outdoor. **Leisure Activities:** whirlpool, tennis court, giant outdoor chess board, bocci, hiking trails, jogging, exercise room. *Fee:* bicycles, massage. **Guest Services:** valet laundry, wireless Internet. **Business Services:** meeting rooms, business center. **Cards:** AX, CB, DC, DS, MC, VI.

⟨11⟩ ⟨&M⟩ ⟨⊘⟩ ⟨⊅⟩ ⟨⊠⟩ ⟨⊠⟩ ⟨VCR⟩ ⟨❀⟩

COURTYARD BY MARRIOTT   *Book great rates at AAA.com*   Phone: 914/631-1122

Property failed to provide current rates

▼▼▼▼   **Location:** I-287 (Cross Westchester Expwy), exit 1, 1 mi w on SR 119. 475 White Plains Rd 10591.

Small-scale Hotel   Fax: 914/631-1357. **Facility:** Smoke free premises. 139 units. 120 one-bedroom standard units. 19 one-bedroom suites. 3 stories, interior corridors. *Bath:* combo or shower only. **Parking:** on-site. **Amenities:** high-speed Internet, dual phone lines, voice mail, irons, hair dryers. **Pool(s):** heated indoor. **Leisure Activities:** whirlpool, exercise room. **Guest Services:** sundries, valet laundry. **Business Services:** meeting rooms, business center.

SOME UNITS

VCR   FEE

DOUBLETREE TARRYTOWN   Phone: 914/631-5700

Property failed to provide current rates

⟨fyi⟩   Under major renovation, scheduled to be completed January 2007. **Last rated:** ▼▼▼ **Location:** I-87 (New

Large-scale Hotel   York State Thruway), exit 9, just s on US 9. 455 S Broadway 10591. Fax: 914/631-0075. **Facility:** 246 units. 242 one-bedroom standard units. 4 one-bedroom suites. 2 stories, interior corridors. **Parking:** on-site. **Amenities:** dual phone lines, voice mail, irons, hair dryers. *Fee:* video games, high-speed Internet. **Pool(s):** heated outdoor, heated indoor, wading. **Leisure Activities:** saunas, whirlpool, 2 lighted tennis courts, jogging, playground, exercise room, basketball. **Guest Services:** valet laundry. **Business Services:** conference facilities, business center.

SOME UNITS

⟨11⟩ ⟨Y⟩ ⟨⊘⟩ ⟨⊅⟩ ⟨⊠⟩ ⟨❀⟩ ⟨▣⟩ ⟨⊠⟩ ⟨❚⟩
FEE

SPRINGHILL SUITES BY MARRIOTT
TARRYTOWN/GREENBURGH   *Book great rates at AAA.com*   Phone: 914/366-4600

Property failed to provide current rates

▼▼▼▼   **Location:** I-287 (Cross Westchester Expwy), exit 1, just w; I-87 (New York State Thruway), exit 9, just n on US 9, then e

Small-scale Hotel   on SR 119. 480 White Plains Rd 10591. Fax: 914/366-4601. **Facility:** Smoke free premises. 145 one-bedroom standard units. 6 stories, interior corridors. *Bath:* combo or shower only. **Parking:** on-site. **Amenities:** voice mail, irons, hair dryers. **Pool(s):** small heated indoor. **Leisure Activities:** whirlpool, exercise room. **Guest Services:** sundries, valet and coin laundry, wireless Internet. **Business Services:** meeting rooms, business center.

TARRYTOWN HOUSE ESTATE & CONFERENCE CENTER
Book great rates at AAA.com
Phone: (914)591-8200

AAA SAVE
All Year [AP]   1P: $119-$359   2P: $119-$359   XP: $25   F5

Large-scale Hotel
Location: I-87 (New York State Thruway), exit 9, 0.9 mi s on US 9, then just e: I-287 (Cross Westchester Expwy), exit 1, 1.7 mi w on SR 119, 1.1 mi s on US 9, then just e. 49 E Sunnyside Ln 10591. Fax: 914/591-3131. **Facility:** Smoke free premises. 212 units. 206 one-bedroom standard units. 6 one-bedroom suites ($250-$750). 5 stories, interior corridors. *Bath:* combo or shower only. **Parking:** on-site. **Terms:** check-in 4 pm, package plans. **Amenities:** video games (fee), CD players, high-speed Internet, dual phone lines, voice mail, safes, irons, hair dryers. **Dining:** 7 am-10, noon-2 & 6-9 pm, cocktails. **Pool(s):** outdoor, heated indoor. **Leisure Activities:** sauna, whirlpool, 2 tennis courts, racquetball court, 1 lane bowling alley, billiards, bocci, spa, basketball, horseshoes, shuffleboard, volleyball. **Guest Services:** sundries, valet laundry, wireless Internet. **Business Services:** conference facilities, business center. **Cards:** AX, CB, DC, DS, JC, MC, VI. **Free Special Amenities:** full breakfast and newspaper.

SOME UNITS

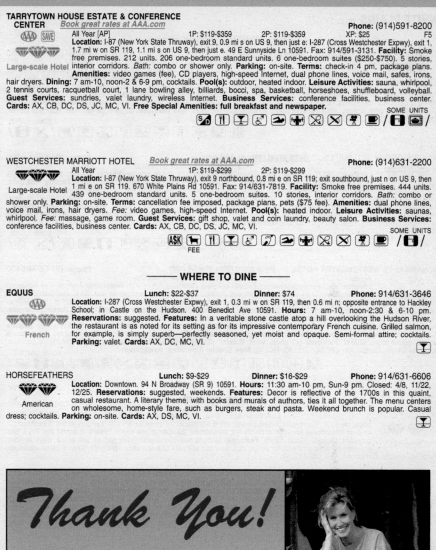

WESTCHESTER MARRIOTT HOTEL
Book great rates at AAA.com
Phone: (914)631-2200

All Year   1P: $119-$299   2P: $119-$299

Large-scale Hotel
Location: I-87 (New York State Thruway), exit 9 northbound, 0.8 mi e on SR 119; exit southbound, just n on US 9, then 1 mi e on SR 119. 670 White Plains Rd 10591. Fax: 914/631-7819. **Facility:** Smoke free premises. 444 units. 439 one-bedroom standard units. 5 one-bedroom suites. 10 stories, interior corridors. *Bath:* combo or shower only. **Parking:** on-site. **Terms:** cancellation fee imposed, package plans, pets ($75 fee). **Amenities:** dual phone lines, voice mail, irons, hair dryers. *Fee:* video games, high-speed Internet. **Pool(s):** heated indoor. **Leisure Activities:** saunas, whirlpool. *Fee:* massage, game room. **Guest Services:** gift shop, valet and coin laundry, beauty salon. **Business Services:** conference facilities, business center. **Cards:** AX, CB, DC, DS, JC, MC, VI.

SOME UNITS

ASK FEE

—— WHERE TO DINE ——

EQUUS
Lunch: $22-$37   Dinner: $74   Phone: 914/631-3646

AAA
French
Location: I-287 (Cross Westchester Expwy), exit 1, 0.3 mi w on SR 119, then 0.6 mi n; opposite entrance to Hackley School; in Castle on the Hudson. 400 Benedict Ave 10591. **Hours:** 7 am-10, noon-2:30 & 6-10 pm. **Reservations:** suggested. **Features:** In a veritable stone castle atop a hill overlooking the Hudson River, the restaurant is as noted for its setting as for its impressive contemporary French cuisine. Grilled salmon, for example, is simply superb—perfectly seasoned, yet moist and opaque. Semi-formal attire; cocktails. **Parking:** valet. **Cards:** AX, DC, MC, VI.

HORSEFEATHERS
Lunch: $9-$29   Dinner: $16-$29   Phone: 914/631-6606

American
Location: Downtown. 94 N Broadway (SR 9) 10591. **Hours:** 11:30 am-10 pm, Sun-9 pm. Closed: 4/8, 11/22, 12/25. **Reservations:** suggested, weekends. **Features:** Decor is reflective of the 1700s in this quaint, casual restaurant. A literary theme, with books and murals of authors, ties it all together. The menu centers on wholesome, home-style fare, such as burgers, steak and pasta. Weekend brunch is popular. Casual dress; cocktails. **Parking:** on-site. **Cards:** AX, DS, MC, VI.

WHITE PLAINS pop. 53,077

------ **WHERE TO STAY** ------

CROWNE PLAZA WHITE PLAINS *Book at AAA.com* **Phone:** (914)682-0050
▼▼▼▼ All Year 1P: $139-$289 2P: $139-$289 XP: $20 F12
Location: I-287 (Cross Westchester Expwy), exit 8 westbound; exit 8W eastbound, just e on Bloomingdale Rd, then just
Large-scale Hotel s on Maple Ave. Located next to a mall. 66 Hale Ave 10601. Fax: 914/682-0405. **Facility:** 401 units. 393 one-
bedroom standard units. 8 one-bedroom suites. 14 stories, interior corridors. *Bath:* combo or shower only.
Parking: on-site and valet. **Terms:** [AP], [BP] & [CP] meal plans available. **Amenities:** video games (fee), CD players, dual
phone lines, voice mail, safes, honor bars, irons, hair dryers. **Leisure Activities:** whirlpool, exercise room. **Guest Services:** gift
shop, valet and coin laundry, area transportation, wireless Internet. **Business Services:** conference facilities, business center.
Cards: AX, CB, DC, DS, JC, MC, VI. SOME UNITS

(ASK) (S/D) (✈) (†|) (Y) (✦M) (✦) (⊘) (✦) (▤) / (✕) (🔒) /
FEE

HYATT SUMMERFIELD SUITES *Book great rates at AAA.com* **Phone:** (914)251-9700
▼▼▼ All Year [CP] 1P: $139-$539 2P: $139-$539 XP: $10 F17
Location: I-287 (Cross Westchester Expwy), exit 9A eastbound, 0.6 mi e on Westchester Ave, then 0.3 mi n; exit 9N-S
Small-scale Hotel westbound, 0.9 mi w on Westchester Ave. 101 Corporate Park Dr 10604. Fax: 914/251-1699. **Facility:** 159 units.
104 one- and 55 two-bedroom suites, some with efficiencies or kitchens. 4 stories, interior corridors. *Bath:*
combo or shower only. **Parking:** on-site. **Terms:** check-in 4 pm, cancellation fee imposed, pets ($50-$250 fee).
Amenities: DVD players, dual phone lines, voice mail, irons, hair dryers. *Fee:* video library, high-speed Internet. **Pool(s):**
heated outdoor. **Leisure Activities:** whirlpool, exercise room, sports court. **Guest Services:** sundries, complimentary evening
beverages: Mon-Thurs, valet and coin laundry. **Business Services:** meeting rooms, business center. **Cards:** AX, CB, DC, DS,
JC, MC, VI. SOME UNITS

(ASK) (🐾) (✦) (⊘) (✦) (✕) (✦) (🔒) (▤) (▤) / (✕) (VCR) /
FEE

RENAISSANCE WESTCHESTER HOTEL *Book great rates at AAA.com* **Phone:** (914)694-5400
(AAA) (SAVE) All Year 1P: $149-$299 2P: $149-$299
Location: I-287 (Cross Westchester Expwy), exit 9N-S eastbound, 0.5 mi e on Westchester Ave, just n on Kenilworth
▼▼▼ Rd, then 0.7 mi w on Westchester Ave; exit westbound, 0.8 mi w on Westchester Ave. 80 W Red Oak Ln 10604.
Fax: 914/694-5616. **Facility:** Smoke free premises. 347 units. 341 one-bedroom standard units. 6 one-
Large-scale Hotel bedroom suites. 6 stories, interior corridors. *Bath:* combo or shower only. **Parking:** on-site.
Terms: cancellation fee imposed. **Amenities:** dual phone lines, voice mail, honor bars, irons, hair dryers.
Fee: video games, high-speed Internet. *Some:* CD players. **Dining:** 6:30 am-10 pm, cocktails. **Pool(s):** heated indoor. **Leisure
Activities:** saunas, whirlpool, bocci, nature trail, exercise room, basketball, horseshoes, volleyball. *Fee:* 2 lighted indoor tennis
courts, game room. **Guest Services:** gift shop, valet laundry, wireless Internet. **Business Services:** conference facilities,
business center. **Cards:** AX, CB, DC, DS, JC, MC, VI. **Free Special Amenities:** newspaper. SOME UNITS

(S/D) (✈) (†|) (24†) (Y) (✦M) (✦) (⊘) (✦) (✕) (✕) (✦) (▤) / (VCR) (🔒) (▤) /
FEE FEE

------ **WHERE TO DINE** ------

CITY LIMITS DINER **Lunch:** $7-$18 **Dinner:** $12-$27 **Phone:** 914/686-9000
▼▼▼ **Location:** I-287 (Cross Westchester Expwy), exit 5 eastbound, 0.4 mi se via SR 100, then just w; exit 8 westbound, 1
mi w on Westchester Ave, 1 mi w on SR 119, then just sw. 200 Central Ave 10606. **Hours:** 8 am-11 pm, Fri & Sat-
American midnight. **Closed:** 11/22, 12/25. **Features:** Multiple televisions and video games are a few ways to keep
entertained while you wait for wings, ribs, seafood specials or a specialty sandwich. Casual dress; cocktails.
Parking: on-site. **Cards:** AX, DC, DS, MC, VI.

P.F. CHANG'S CHINA BISTRO **Lunch:** $6-$14 **Dinner:** $8-$18 **Phone:** 914/997-6100
▼▼▼ **Location:** I-287 (Cross Westchester Expwy), exit 8 westbound, 0.7 mi e; exit 8W eastbound, just n; in Westchester Mall.
125 Westchester Ave 10601. **Hours:** 11 am-11 pm, Fri & Sat-midnight. **Closed:** 12/24, 12/25.
Regional Chinese **Reservations:** suggested. **Features:** Trendy, upscale decor provides a pleasant backdrop for New Age
Chinese dining. Appetizers, soups and salads are a meal by themselves. Vegetarian plates and sides,
noodles, meins, chicken and meat dishes are created from exotic, fresh ingredients. Casual dress; cocktails. **Parking:** on-site
(fee). **Cards:** AX, DC, DS, MC, VI. (✦M)

SPORTS PAGE PUB **Lunch:** $5-$14 **Dinner:** $5-$14 **Phone:** 914/437-8721
▼ **Location:** Jct Hutchison River Pkwy, just n. 200 Hamilton Ave 10601. **Hours:** 11:30 am-11 pm, Sat from noon, Sun
noon-10 pm; from 5 pm weekends in summer. **Closed:** 3/23, 12/25. **Reservations:** accepted.
American **Features:** This place is jock nirvana—if it has to do with sports, you'll find it here. Not only can diners enjoy
a menu that includes Southwestern, Tex-Mex, barbecue, steak and pasta choices, but they also can play all
kinds of games and watch events on 50 TVs. Casual dress; cocktails. **Parking:** on-site. **Cards:** AX, DC, MC, VI. (Y)

YONKERS pop. 196,086

------ **WHERE TO STAY** ------

RAMADA *Book great rates at AAA.com* **Phone:** (914)476-3800
(AAA) (SAVE) All Year 1P: $134-$149 2P: $134-$149
Location: I-87, exit 6, just w. 125 Tuckahoe Rd 10710. Fax: 914/423-3555. **Facility:** 103 one-bedroom standard
▼▼▼ units. 3 stories, interior/exterior corridors. *Bath:* combo or shower only. **Parking:** on-site. **Terms:** package
plans. **Amenities:** video games (fee), voice mail, irons, hair dryers. **Dining:** 6 am-10 pm, Fri & Sat-11 pm,
Small-scale Hotel cocktails. **Pool(s):** outdoor. **Leisure Activities:** exercise room. **Guest Services:** valet laundry, wireless
Internet. **Business Services:** meeting rooms, fax (fee). **Cards:** AX, CB, DC, DS, JC, MC, VI.
Free Special Amenities: newspaper and high-speed Internet. SOME UNITS

(S/D) (†|) (Y) (✦) (✦) (✦) (▤) / (✕) (🔒) (▤) /
FEE

ROYAL REGENCY HOTEL & BANQUET FACILITY   *Book great rates at AAA.com*   **Phone:** (914)476-6200

AAA SAVE   All Year [ECP]   1P: $112-$122   2P: $124-$134   XP: $10   F12
♥♥ ♥♥♥   **Location:** I-87, exit 6, just w. 165 Tuckahoe Rd 10710. **Fax:** 914/375-7017. **Facility:** 91 units. 90 one-bedroom
          standard units, some with whirlpools. 1 one-bedroom suite ($250-$500) with whirlpool. 3 stories,
          interior/exterior corridors. *Bath:* combo or shower only. **Parking:** on-site. **Terms:** 18% service charge.
Small-scale Hotel **Amenities:** voice mail, irons, hair dryers. **Dining:** 4 pm-11 pm; closed Sun, cocktails. **Leisure
          Activities:** exercise room. **Guest Services:** valet laundry, wireless Internet. **Business Services:**
conference facilities. **Cards:** AX, DS, MC, VI. **Free Special Amenities: continental breakfast and newspaper.**

SOME UNITS

[icons] / FEE FEE

──────── **WHERE TO DINE** ────────

CHARLIE BROWN'S STEAKHOUSE   **Lunch:** $6-$10   **Dinner:** $12-$21   **Phone:** 914/779-7227
♥♥ ♥♥   **Location:** On SR 100. 1820 Central Park Ave 10710. **Hours:** 11:30 am-2:30 & 3-10 pm, Fri & Sat-10:30 pm,
          Sun-9 pm. Closed: 12/25. **Features:** This budget-friendly steakhouse, famous for its prime rib, offers top
Steak & Seafood quality fare without hurting your pocketbook. The young ones will not be disappointed with the kid's menu,
          and just might even try something green from the salad bar. Adults will love the quality steaks, chicken and
rib dishes. The express lunches are great for those saddled with time constraints. Casual dress; cocktails. **Parking:** on-site.
Cards: AX, DS, MC, VI.   [icon]

HUNAN VILLAGE   **Lunch:** $9-$23   **Dinner:** $9-$23   **Phone:** 914/779-2272
♥♥ ♥♥   **Location:** I-87, exit 6E southbound; exit 6 northbound, 1.5 mi e on Tuckahoe Rd, then just n. 1828 Central Park Ave
          (SR 100) 10710. **Hours:** noon-10:30 pm, Sun from 1 pm. Closed: 11/22. **Reservations:** suggested,
Chinese   weekends. **Features:** The established local favorite delivers a broad range of cuisines: Hunan, Cantonese,
          Hong Kong, Mandarin and Szechuan. An emphasis is placed on fresh produce and seafood. Attentive
servers and a soothing atmosphere make your experience a memorable one. Casual dress; cocktails. **Parking:** on-site.
Cards: AX, DC, MC, VI.   [icon]

Central Park, Midtown Manhattan / © age fotostock / SuperStock

This ends listings for the New York City Vicinity.
The following page resumes the alphabetical listings of cities in New York.

Destination Niagara Falls
pop. 55,593

Welcome to Niagara Falls, where the mesmerizing cataracts will capture your heart forever. The Honeymoon Capital attracts some 50,000 newlyweds yearly.

There are more ways than one to view the plunging water. Take an evening stroll along the river, when the spectacle of colored lights offers an enchanting experience. Capture the aura of the rolling water with a romantic picnic overlooking the marvelous falls. Or treat yourself to a guided tour.

© Andre Jenny

A spectacular view. See the American and Canadian falls from vantage points within Niagara Falls State Park. (See listing page 164)

Buffalo Niagara CVB and Seneca Niagara Casino

Seneca Niagara Casino, Niagara Falls. Downtown's Las Vegas-style casino offers a glitzy diversion from the natural spectacle just minutes away. (See listing page 165)

Niagara Falls

See Vicinity map page 509

See Vicinity map page 511

Youngstown

Lewiston

Newfane

Lockport
Sanborn

Niagara Falls

Wheatfield

CANADA
USA

QEW
405
20
ON
NY
190
QEW
104
290

© Gibson Stock Photography

Old Fort Niagara, Youngstown. The occupants of this fort, which was built by the French in 1679 and later taken by British troops, controlled access to the Great Lakes region. (See listing page 168)

Places included in this AAA Destination City:

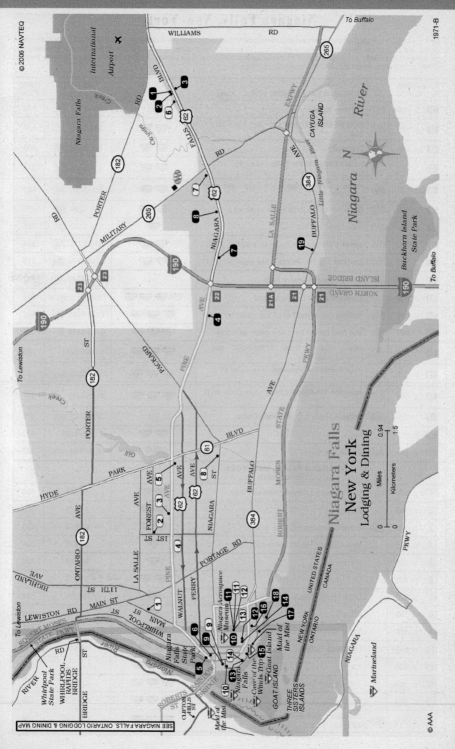

Niagara Falls, New York

This index helps you "spot" where approved accommodations and restaurants are located on the corresponding detailed maps. Lodging rate ranges are for comparison only and show the property's high season; rates are per night, unless only weekly (W) rates are available. Restaurant rate range is for dinner, unless only lunch (L) is served. Turn to the listing page for more detailed rate information and consult display ads for special promotions.

Spotter/Map Page Number	OA	NIAGARA FALLS, NEW YORK - Lodgings	Diamond Rating	Rate Range High Season	Listing Page
1 / p. 509	AAA	Bel Aire Motel	◆	$58-$128 SAVE	516
2 / p. 509	AAA	Best Western Summit Inn - see color ad p 516	◆◆	$99-$159 SAVE	516
3 / p. 509	AAA	Travelodge	◆◆	$69-$150 SAVE	525
4 / p. 509	AAA	Econo Lodge at the Falls - see color ad p 519	◆◆	$55-$229 SAVE	518
5 / p. 509	AAA	Howard Johnson Inn at the Falls - see color ad p 523	◆◆	$85-$255 SAVE	522
6 / p. 509	AAA	Days Inn at the Falls - see color ad p 517	◆◆	$99-$299 SAVE	518
7 / p. 509	AAA	Swiss Cottage Inn	◆	$32-$189 SAVE	525
8 / p. 509	AAA	Super 8 Motel - see color ad p 524	◆◆	$70-$275 SAVE	524
9 / p. 509	AAA	Comfort Inn The Pointe - see color ad p 517	◆◆	$119-$179 SAVE	516
10 / p. 509	AAA	Crowne Plaza-Niagara Falls	fyi	$169-$249 SAVE	517
11 / p. 509		Seneca Niagara Casino & Hotel	◆◆◆◆	Failed to provide	524
12 / p. 509	AAA	Holiday Inn at the Falls - see color ad p 522	◆◆◆	$129-$229 SAVE	522
13 / p. 509	AAA	The Red Coach Inn - see color ad p 524	◆◆◆	$139-$179 SAVE	524
14 / p. 509		Quality Hotel and Suites "At the Falls" - see color ad p 523	◆◆◆	$99-$299	523
15 / p. 509	AAA	Four Points by Sheraton - see color ad p 520	◆◆◆	$85-$225 SAVE	520
16 / p. 509	AAA	Hampton Inn-Niagara Falls - see color ad p 521	◆◆◆	$129-$299 SAVE	521
17 / p. 509	AAA	Fallside Hotel & Conference Center	fyi	$59-$229 SAVE	519
18 / p. 509		Holley Rankine House	◆◆	$65-$125	522
19 / p. 509	AAA	Inn on the River	◆◆	$89-$199 SAVE	522
		NIAGARA FALLS, NEW YORK - Restaurants			
① / p. 509	AAA	Chu's Dining Lounge-Chinese Food	◆◆	$6-$11	525
② / p. 509		Fortuna's	◆◆	$7-$19	525
③ / p. 509	AAA	Como Restaurant & Deli	◆◆	$7-$18	525
④ / p. 509		Pete's Market House Restaurant	◆	$4-$18	526
⑤ / p. 509		Michael's	◆	$8-$10	526
⑥ / p. 509		La Bruschetta	◆◆	$8-$19	525
⑦ / p. 509		Mom's Family Restaurant	◆	$6-$9	526
⑧ / p. 509		Koban's	◆	$8-$12	525
⑨ / p. 509		Top of the Falls Restaurant	◆◆	$18-$30	526
⑩ / p. 509		Hard Rock Cafe	◆◆	$8-$18	525
⑪ / p. 509		Koi	◆◆◆	$12-$25	525
⑫ / p. 509		The Western Door	◆◆◆	$28-$45	526
⑬ / p. 509		La Cascata	◆◆◆	$16-$29	525
⑭ / p. 509	AAA	The Red Coach Inn Restaurant - see color ad p 524	◆◆◆	$10-$25	526

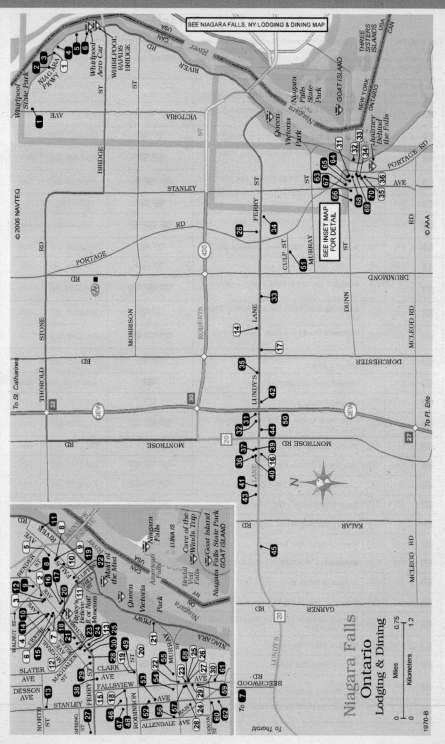

SEE NIAGARA FALLS, NY LODGING & DINING MAP

Niagara Falls
Ontario
Lodging & Dining

Niagara Falls, Ontario

This index helps you "spot" where approved accommodations and restaurants are located on the corresponding detailed maps. Lodging rate ranges are for comparison only and show the property's high season; rates are per night, unless only weekly (W) rates are available. Restaurant rate range is for dinner, unless only lunch (L) is served. Turn to the listing page for more detailed rate information and consult display ads for special promotions.

Spotter/Map Page Number	OA	NIAGARA FALLS, ONTARIO - Lodgings	Diamond Rating	Rate Range High Season	Listing Page
1 / p. 511	CAA	**Great Wolf Lodge Indoor Waterpark Resort** - see color ad p 547	◇◇◇	$359-$599 SAVE	546
2 / p. 511	CAA	**Water's Edge Inn** - see color ad p 529	◇◇	$79-$500 SAVE	567
3 / p. 511	CAA	**Days Inn North of the Falls** - see color ad p 533	◇◇	$98-$228 SAVE	541
4 / p. 511	CAA	**Best Western Fireside Hotel** - see color ad p 533	◇◇◇	$99-$249 SAVE	535
5 / p. 511		Crystal Inn	◇◇	$79-$149	539
6 / p. 511		Hampton Inn North of the Falls - see color ad p 548	◇◇◇	$99-$249	548
7 / p. 511	CAA	**Americas Best Value Inn - Gardens Inn**	◇◇	$69-$129 SAVE	530
8 / p. 511	CAA	**Skyline Inn** - see color ad p 563	◇◇	$99-$369 SAVE	562
9 / p. 511	CAA	**Hampton Inn at the Falls** - see color ad p 546	◇◇◇	$169-$429 SAVE	548
10 / p. 511	CAA	**Americas Best Value Inn and Suites-Chalet Inn**	◇◇	$89-$229 SAVE	530
11 / p. 511	CAA	**Michael's Inn-By the Falls** - see color ad p 553	◇◇◇	$88-$288 SAVE	553
12 / p. 511	CAA	**Days Inn Clifton Hill Casino** - see color ad starting on p 542	◇◇	$49-$429 SAVE	540
13 / p. 511		Camelot Inn - see color ad p 534	◇	Failed to provide	535
14 / p. 511	CAA	**Niagara Family Inn**	◇	$55-$115 SAVE	554
15 / p. 511	CAA	**Days Inn & Suites by the Falls** - see color ad p 540	◇◇◇	$89-$299 SAVE	540
16 / p. 511	CAA	**Thriftlodge Clifton Hill**	◇	$99-$299 SAVE	564
17 / p. 511	CAA	**Travelodge Clifton Hill** - see color ad p 566	◇◇	$99-$349 SAVE	565
18 / p. 511	CAA	**Comfort Inn Clifton Hill** - see color ad p 537	◇◇	$99-$279 SAVE	536
19 / p. 511	CAA	**Brock Plaza Hotel** - see color ad p 534	◇◇◇	$149-$799 SAVE	535
20 / p. 511	CAA	**Quality Inn Clifton Hill** - see color ad p 537	◇◇	$89-$269 SAVE	554
21 / p. 511	CAA	**Imperial Hotel and Suites**	◇◇◇	$69-$359 SAVE	551
22 / p. 511	CAA	**Sheraton on the Falls** - see color ad p 562	◇◇◇◇	$169-$999 SAVE	562
23 / p. 511	CAA	**A Victoria Motor Inn**	◇	$75-$199 SAVE	530
24 / p. 511	CAA	**Days Inn Near the Falls** - see color ad p 544	◇◇	$70-$299 SAVE	540
25 / p. 511	CAA	**Howard Johnson Hotel by the Falls** - see color ad p 551	◇◇	$99-$329 SAVE	549
26 / p. 511	CAA	**Niagara Falls Plaza Hotel**	◇◇	$119-$249 SAVE	553
27 / p. 511		Kings Inn near the Falls	◇◇	$79-$199	551
28 / p. 511		Lodge Near the Falls (Now Known As Country Hearth Inn & Suites) - see color ad p 552	◇◇	$89-$399	552
29 / p. 511	CAA	**Travelodge Hotel by the Falls** - see color ad p 565	◇◇◇	$89-$309 SAVE	565

Spotter/Map Page Number	OA	NIAGARA FALLS, ONTARIO - Lodgings (continued)	Diamond Rating	Rate Range High Season	Listing Page
30 / p. 511	AAA	Courtyard by Marriott Niagara Falls - see color ad p 539	◈◈◈	$99-$399 [SAVE]	536
31 / p. 511	AAA	Ramada All Suites Hotel and Conference Center	◈◈◈	$79-$259 [SAVE]	556
32 / p. 511	AAA	Ramada Coral Hotel - see color ad p 556	◈◈	$69-$169 [SAVE]	556
33 / p. 511	AAA	Best Western Cairn Croft Hotel - see color ad p 532	◈◈◈	$99-$199 [SAVE]	530
34 / p. 511	AAA	Super 8 Hotel	◈◈◈	$59-$299 [SAVE]	563
35 / p. 511	AAA	Knights Inn	◈◈	$79-$249 [SAVE]	551
36 / p. 511	AAA	Travelodge Bonaventure - see color ad p 564	◈◈◈	$89-$209 [SAVE]	564
37 / p. 511	AAA	Flamingo Thriftlodge - see color ad p 546	◈◈	$79-$189 [SAVE]	545
38 / p. 511	AAA	Cadillac Motel	◈	$50-$150 [SAVE]	535
39 / p. 511		Rodeway Inn & Suites	◈◈	$69-$129	560
40 / p. 511	AAA	Advantage Inn	◈	$48-$118 [SAVE]	529
41 / p. 511	AAA	Villager Lodge	◈◈	$69-$199 [SAVE]	567
42 / p. 511	AAA	Days Inn-Lundy's Lane - see color ad starting on p 542	◈◈	$45-$299 [SAVE]	540
43 / p. 511	AAA	Howard Johnson Express Inn	◈◈	$65-$200 [SAVE]	549
44 / p. 511		Comfort Inn Lundy's Lane	◈◈	$89-$199	536
45 / p. 511	AAA	Americana Conference Resort and Spa - see color ad p 531	◈◈◈	$139-$299 [SAVE]	530
46 / p. 511		Econo Lodge near the Falls	◈◈	$55-$120	541
47 / p. 511	AAA	Clarion President Hotel & Suites by the Falls - see color ad p 535	◈◈◈	$99-$299 [SAVE]	536
48 / p. 511	AAA	DoubleTree Resort Lodge & Spa Fallsview - see color ad p 541	◈◈◈◈	$99-$299 [SAVE]	541
49 / p. 511		Old Stone Inn - see color ad starting on p 170	◈◈	$80-$369	554
50 / p. 511	AAA	Peninsula Inn & Resort	◈◈◈	$89-$189 [SAVE]	554
51 / p. 511		Victorian Charm Bed and Breakfast	◈◈	Failed to provide	567
52 / p. 511	AAA	Fallsview Inn - see color ad p 545, starting on p 170	◈◈◈	$49-$199 [SAVE]	545
53 / p. 511	AAA	Stanley Motor Inn - see color ad starting on p 170	◈◈	$60-$140 [SAVE]	562
54 / p. 511	AAA	Best Western Fallsview - see color ad p 534, starting on p 170	◈◈	$119-$299 [SAVE]	530
55 / p. 511	AAA	Holiday Inn by the Falls - see color ad p 550, p 569, starting on p 170	◈◈◈	$99-$275 [SAVE]	549
56 / p. 511	AAA	Knights Inn-By the Falls - see color ad starting on p 170	◈◈	$79-$249 [SAVE]	552
57 / p. 511	AAA	Hilton Niagara Falls Fallsview - see color ad p 549, starting on p 170	◈◈◈	$149-$499 [SAVE]	548
58 / p. 511	AAA	Fallsview Casino Resort	◈◈◈◈	$279-$449 [SAVE]	545
59 / p. 511	AAA	Renaissance Fallsview Hotel - see color ad p 558, starting on p 170	◈◈◈	$149-$499 [SAVE]	557
60 / p. 511		The President Motor Inn - see color ad p 0, starting on p 170	◈	Failed to provide	554

Spotter/Map Page Number	OA	NIAGARA FALLS, ONTARIO - Lodgings (continued)	Diamond Rating	Rate Range High Season	Listing Page
61 / p. 511	ⒶⒶ	The Oakes Hotel Overlooking the Falls - see color ad starting on p 542, starting on p 170	◈◈◈	$49-$729 SAVE	554
62 / p. 511		Days Inn Fallsview Casino - see color ad p 555, starting on p 170	◈◈	$45-$299	540
63 / p. 511	ⒶⒶ	Comfort Inn Fallsview - see color ad p 538, starting on p 170	◈◈	$79-$329 SAVE	536
64 / p. 511	ⒶⒶ	Embassy Suites Niagara Falls Fallsview - see color ad p 539, starting on p 170	◈◈◈◈	$235-$925 SAVE	541
65 / p. 511	ⒶⒶ	Radisson Hotel & Suites Fallsview - see color ad p 556, starting on p 170	◈◈◈	$117-$170 SAVE	555
66 / p. 511	ⒶⒶ	Ritz Inn Niagara - see color ad p 559	◈	$69-$119 SAVE	559
67 / p. 511	ⒶⒶ	Rodeway Inn Fallsview - see color ad p 560, starting on p 170	◈◈◈	$89-$259 SAVE	560
68 / p. 511		Ramada Plaza Hotel Fallsview - see color ad starting on p 170, p 557	◈◈◈	$99-$329	557
69 / p. 511	ⒶⒶ	Marriott Niagara Falls Fallsview Hotel and Spa - see color ad p 539, starting on p 170, inside front cover	◈◈◈◈	$189-$599 SAVE	552
70 / p. 511	ⒶⒶ	Sheraton Fallsview Hotel & Conference Centre - see color ad p 561, starting on p 170 & coupon in Savings Section	◈◈◈◈	$149-$399 SAVE	560
		NIAGARA FALLS, ONTARIO - Restaurants			
1 / p. 511		Frontier Grill House	◈◈	$25-$50	570
2 / p. 511	ⒶⒶ	Monticello Grille House & Wine Bar - see color ad p 571	◈◈	$15-$35	571
3 / p. 511		Remington's of Montana Steak and Seafood - see color ad starting on p 542	◈◈◈	$15-$44	572
4 / p. 511	ⒶⒶ	Big Anthony's Big Eatery and Pub	◈◈	$9-$26	568
5 / p. 511		The Rainbow Fallsview Dining Room	◈◈◈	$25-$50	572
6 / p. 511	ⒶⒶ	The Beef Baron	◈◈	$11-$35	568
7 / p. 511	ⒶⒶ	Mama Mia's	◈◈	$7-$22	570
8 / p. 511		Lucky's Steakhouse	◈◈◈	$15-$35	570
9 / p. 511		Market Buffet	◈◈	$17	570
10 / p. 511		The Secret Garden	◈◈	$10-$30	572
11 / p. 511		Penthouse Restaurant	◈◈◈	$25-$40	571
12 / p. 511		Casa d'Oro Dining Lounge	◈◈◈	$17-$60	569
13 / p. 511	ⒶⒶ	The Keg Steakhouse and Bar	◈◈	$20-$55	570
14 / p. 511		China Buffet	◈◈	$9-$10	569
15 / p. 511	ⒶⒶ	Capri Restaurant	◈◈◈	$15-$40	569
16 / p. 511	ⒶⒶ	Mick and Angelo's Eatery and Bar	◈◈	$10-$29	571
17 / p. 511	ⒶⒶ	Carpaccio Restaurant and Wine Bar	◈◈◈	$9-$35	569
18 / p. 511		Buchanans Chophouse - see color ad p 541	◈◈◈	$19-$34	568
19 / p. 511		The Millery Dining Room	◈◈◈	$21-$58	571
20 / p. 511	ⒶⒶ	The Skylon Tower Dining Rooms - see color ad p 177	◈◈◈	$42-$70	572
21 / p. 511	ⒶⒶ	Edgewaters Tap & Grill	◈◈	$16-$24	569

Spotter/Map Page Number	OA	NIAGARA FALLS, ONTARIO - Restaurants (continued)	Diamond Rating	Rate Range High Season	Listing Page
㉒ / p. 511		Wolfgang Puck Grand Cafe	◈◈◈	$14-$38	573
㉓ / p. 511	ⒶⒶ	**Asian Pearl**	◈◈◈	$13-$28	568
㉔ / p. 511		The Watermark - see color ad p 549	◈◈◈	$25-$65	573
㉕ / p. 511		17 Noir	◈◈◈◈	$20-$50	568
㉖ / p. 511		Pazzo Matto	◈◈	$12-$35	571
㉗ / p. 511		The Famous Coffee Shop	◈◈	$10-$32	569
㉘ / p. 511		Happy Wanderer	◈◈	$10-$40	570
㉙ / p. 511		Canyon Creek Chop House	◈◈	$18-$37	568
㉚ / p. 511	ⒶⒶ	**Rooftop Fallsview Grille**	◈◈◈	$25-$35	572
㉛ / p. 511	ⒶⒶ	**The Keg Steakhouse and Bar**	◈◈	$18-$28	570
㉜ / p. 511	ⒶⒶ	**Table Rock Restaurant**	◈◈	$30-$35	572
㉝ / p. 511		The Pinnacle Restaurant-Atop the Konica Minolta Tower	◈◈◈	$18-$50	572
㉞ / p. 511	ⒶⒶ	**Terrapin Grille**	◈◈◈	$34-$69	572
㉟ / p. 511	ⒶⒶ	**A Cut Above Steakhouse**	◈◈◈	$19-$55	568
㊱ / p. 511		La Piazza Bistro & Cafe	◈◈	$8-$18	570

NIAGARA FALLS　(See map and index starting on p. 509)

Accommodations for the Canadian side are listed under Niagara Falls, Ontario.

───── **WHERE TO STAY** ─────

BEL AIRE MOTEL
Phone: 716/297-2250 　❶

AAA [SAVE]

6/19-9/6	1P: $58-$118	2P: $62-$128	XP: $8
5/1-6/18	1P: $38-$120	2P: $44-$120	XP: $5
9/7-10/13	1P: $38-$80	2P: $44-$80	XP: $6
10/14-4/30	1P: $36-$60	2P: $36-$70	XP: $5

Motel　**Location:** I-190, exit 22, 2 mi e. 9470 Niagara Falls Blvd 14304. Fax: 716/297-8712. **Facility:** 22 units. 19 one-bedroom standard units. 3 one-bedroom suites. 1 story, exterior corridors. *Bath:* combo or shower only. **Parking:** on-site. **Terms:** 3 day cancellation notice-fee imposed, weekly rates available. **Pool(s):** outdoor. **Cards:** AX, MC, VI. **Free Special Amenities: local telephone calls and preferred room (subject to availability with advance reservations).**

SOME UNITS

BEST WESTERN SUMMIT INN　*Book great rates at AAA.com*
Phone: (716)297-5050 　❷

AAA [SAVE]

5/1-9/9	1P: $99-$159	2P: $99-$159	XP: $10　F17
9/10-4/30	1P: $59-$139	2P: $59-$139	XP: $10　F17

Small-scale Hotel　**Location:** I-190, exit 22, 2.1 mi e on US 62 S. 9500 Niagara Falls Blvd 14304. Fax: 716/297-0802. **Facility:** Smoke free premises. 88 one-bedroom standard units, some with whirlpools. 2 stories (no elevator), interior corridors. **Parking:** on-site. **Terms:** [ECP] meal plan available, small pets only ($8 extra charge, in designated units, with prior approval). **Amenities:** video library (fee), voice mail, irons, hair dryers. **Pool(s):** heated indoor. **Leisure Activities:** sauna. **Guest Services:** coin laundry, wireless Internet. **Business Services:** meeting rooms, PC. **Cards:** AX, DC, DS, MC, VI. **Free Special Amenities: continental breakfast and room upgrade (subject to availability with advance reservations).** *(See color ad below)*

SOME UNITS

COMFORT INN THE POINTE　*Book great rates at AAA.com*
Phone: (716)284-6835 　❾

AAA [SAVE]

6/15-9/2	1P: $119-$169	2P: $129-$179	XP: $10　F18
5/1-6/14	1P: $69-$159	2P: $79-$169	XP: $10　F18
10/21-4/30	1P: $59-$139	2P: $69-$149	XP: $10　F18
9/3-10/20	1P: $79-$122	2P: $89-$132	XP: $10　F18

Small-scale Hotel　**Location:** I-190, exit 21 (Robert Moses Pkwy), follow Robert Moses Pkwy to New York State Park/American Falls entrance, exit Falls Parking/Goat Island, stay left to stop sign, just n. At the State Reservation Park entrance. 1 Prospect Pointe 14303. Fax: 716/284-5177. **Facility:** 118 units. 117 one-bedroom standard units, some with whirlpools. 1 one-bedroom suite ($129-$450) with whirlpool. 6 stories, interior corridors. **Parking:** on-site. **Terms:** [ECP] meal plan available, package plans. **Amenities:** video games (fee), voice mail, irons, hair dryers. *Some:* dual phone lines. **Dining:** 11 am-11 pm; hours vary off season, cocktails. **Leisure Activities:** exercise room. **Guest Services:** gift shop, valet laundry, wireless Internet. **Business Services:** meeting rooms. **Cards:** AX, CB, DC, DS, JC, MC, VI. **Free Special Amenities: expanded continental breakfast and high-speed Internet.** *(See color ad p 517)*

SOME UNITS

(See map and index starting on p. 509)

CROWNE PLAZA-NIAGARA FALLS

Phone: (716)285-3361 🔟

	6/29-9/2	1P: $169-$249	2P: $169-$249	XP: $10	F17
AAA SAVE	5/1-6/28 & 9/3-11/3	1P: $119-$189	2P: $119-$189	XP: $10	F17
fyi	11/4-4/30	1P: $109-$169	2P: $109-$169	XP: $10	F17

Small-scale Hotel Under major renovation, scheduled to be completed October 2006. Last rated: ⩌⩌⩌ Location: I-190, exit 21 (Robert Moses Pkwy), exit City Traffic, just w on Rainbow Blvd, then just n. Located across from the Seneca Niagara Casino. 300 Third St 14303. Fax: 716/285-3900. **Facility:** 392 units. 364 one-bedroom standard units. 28 one-bedroom suites. 6 stories, interior corridors. *Bath:* combo or shower only. **Parking:** on-site. **Terms:** check-in 4 pm, [BP] meal plan available, package plans. **Amenities:** dual phone lines, voice mail, irons, hair dryers. **Dining:** 6 am-2 & 5-10 pm, cocktails. **Pool(s):** heated indoor. **Leisure Activities:** sauna, whirlpool, exercise room. *Fee:* game room. **Guest Services:** gift shop, valet and coin laundry. **Business Services:** conference facilities. **Cards:** AX, CB, DC, DS, JC, MC, VI. **Free Special Amenities:** newspaper and high-speed Internet.

SOME UNITS

(See map and index starting on p. 509)

DAYS INN AT THE FALLS   *Book great rates at AAA.com*   Phone: (716)284-8801   **6**

AAA SAVE   6/23-9/3   1P: $99-$299   2P: $99-$299   XP: $10   F
WWWW   9/4-10/31   1P: $69-$189   2P: $69-$189   XP: $10   F
               5/1-6/22 & 11/1-4/30   1P: $59-$159   2P: $59-$159   XP: $10   F
Small-scale Hotel   **Location:** I-190, exit 21 (Robert Moses Pkwy) to City Traffic exit, just w on Rainbow Blvd, just n on 3rd St, then just w. Facing the entrance to Rainbow Bridge. 443 Main St 14301. Fax: 716/284-8633. **Facility:** 168 one-bedroom standard units, some with whirlpools. 9 stories, interior corridors. **Parking:** on-site. **Terms:** package plans. **Amenities:** video games (fee), hair dryers. *Some:* irons. **Dining:** 24 hours, cocktails. **Pool(s):** heated indoor. **Leisure Activities:** sauna, limited exercise equipment. **Guest Services:** valet and coin laundry, wireless Internet. **Business Services:** meeting rooms. **Cards:** AX, CB, DC, DS, JC, MC, VI. *(See color ad p 517)*

SOME UNITS
(S/D) (TI) (Y) (swim) (work) / (X) /

DAYS INN-NIAGARA FALLS/BUFFALO   *Book great rates at AAA.com*   Phone: (716)743-9224

AAA SAVE   5/25-9/3   1P: $79-$249   2P: $89-$269   XP: $10   F12
WWWW   5/1-5/24 & 9/4-4/30   1P: $59-$99   2P: $69-$109   XP: $10   F12
Motel   **Location:** I-190, exit 22, 5.5 mi s on US 62; I-290, exit 3, 7.5 mi n on US 62. 2821 Niagara Falls Blvd 14304. Fax: 716/695-6161. **Facility:** 54 one-bedroom standard units, some with efficiencies and/or whirlpools. 2 stories (no elevator), interior/exterior corridors. *Bath:* combo or shower only. **Parking:** on-site. **Terms:** cancellation fee imposed, weekly rates available, [CP] meal plan available, package plans. **Amenities:** high-speed Internet, voice mail, hair dryers. **Pool(s):** outdoor. **Guest Services:** coin laundry, wireless Internet. **Business Services:** PC. **Cards:** DS, MC, VI. **Free Special Amenities: continental breakfast and high-speed Internet.**
(See color ad below)

SOME UNITS
(S/D) (&) (swim) (work) / (X) (VCR) (|) (=) /
FEE   FEE

ECONO LODGE AT THE FALLS   *Book great rates at AAA.com*   Phone: (716)283-1100   **4**

AAA SAVE   7/1-8/31   1P: $55-$229   2P: $55-$229   XP: $5   F16
WWWW   5/1-6/30   1P: $44-$199   2P: $44-$199   XP: $5   F16
Motel   9/1-4/30   1P: $44-$100   2P: $44-$100   XP: $5   F16
               Location: I-190, exit 22, 0.3 mi n on US 62. 5919 Niagara Falls Blvd 14304. Fax: 716/283-2150. **Facility:** 70 one-bedroom standard units, some with whirlpools. 2 stories (no elevator), exterior corridors. **Parking:** on-site. **Terms:** package plans. **Amenities:** voice mail, irons, hair dryers. **Pool(s):** heated outdoor. **Leisure Activities:** playground. *Fee:* game room. **Guest Services:** coin laundry, wireless Internet. **Cards:** AX, DS, MC, VI. **Free Special Amenities: continental breakfast and high-speed Internet.** *(See color ad p 519)*

SOME UNITS
(S/D) (TI+) (swim) (work) / (X) (|) (=) (work) /
FEE   FEE

(See map and index starting on p. 509)

FALLSIDE HOTEL & CONFERENCE CENTER   **Phone:** (716)285-2541 ⑰

AAA SAVE   All Year   1P: $59-$229   2P: $59-$229   XP: $10   F17

fyi   Under major renovation, scheduled to be completed April 2007. **Location:** I-190, exit 21 (Robert Moses Pkwy),
exit City Traffic, just n. 401 Buffalo Ave 14303. **Fax:** 716/285-6108. **Facility:** 197 one-bedroom standard units. 2-
Small-scale Hotel 4 stories, interior corridors. **Parking:** on-site. **Terms:** cancellation fee imposed, package plans, pets ($10
extra charge). **Dining:** cocktails. **Pool(s):** outdoor. **Leisure Activities:** *Fee:* game room. **Guest Services:**
gift shop. **Business Services:** conference facilities. **Cards:** AX, CB, DC, DS, JC, MC, VI. *(See color ad p 533)*

SOME UNITS

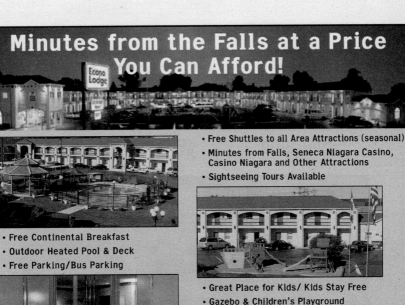

Minutes from the Falls at a Price You Can Afford!

- **Free Continental Breakfast**
- **Outdoor Heated Pool & Deck**
- **Free Parking/Bus Parking**

- Free Shuttles to all Area Attractions (seasonal)
- Minutes from Falls, Seneca Niagara Casino, Casino Niagara and Other Attractions
- Sightseeing Tours Available

- **Great Place for Kids/ Kids Stay Free**
- **Gazebo & Children's Playground**
- **Game Room (free tokens for kids)**
- **Extended Cable & HBO**
- **Guest Laundry**

- **Newly Built**
- **In-room Jacuzzi Suites**

5919 Niagara Falls Blvd.,
Niagara Falls, NY 14304
Phone: 716.283.1100 • Fax: 716.283.2150

800.273.5257
www.econolodgeatthefalls.com

We'll see you there.

© 2006 Choice Hotels International, Inc.

Econo Lodge
BY CHOICE HOTELS

(See map and index starting on p. 509)

FOUR POINTS BY SHERATON   *Book great rates at AAA.com*   Phone: (716)285-2521   **15**

AAA SAVE   7/1-9/4   1P: $85-$225   2P: $85-$225
            11/2-4/30   1P: $55-$225   2P: $55-$225
▽▽▽▽   5/1-6/30 & 9/5-11/1   1P: $65-$175   2P: $65-$175

Location: I-190, exit 21 (Robert Moses Pkwy), eastbound use City Traffic exit, just w on Rainbow Blvd. At the Goat
Large-scale Hotel Island entrance at the Falls. 114 Buffalo Ave 14303. Fax: 716/285-0963. **Facility:** 189 units. 183 one-bedroom
standard units. 6 one-bedroom suites with efficiencies, some with whirlpools. 7 stories, interior corridors.
Bath: combo or shower only. **Parking:** on-site. **Terms:** package plans. **Amenities:** dual phone lines, voice mail, irons, hair
dryers. **Dining:** 6:30 am-11 pm; hours vary off season, cocktails. **Pool(s):** heated indoor. **Leisure Activities:** sauna, whirlpool,
exercise room. *Fee:* game room. **Guest Services:** valet and coin laundry, wireless Internet. **Business Services:** meeting
rooms, PC. **Cards:** AX, DC, DS, MC, VI. *(See color ad below)*

SOME UNITS

[icons] / FEE FEE

(See map and index starting on p. 509)

HAMPTON INN-NIAGARA FALLS   *Book great rates at AAA.com*   **Phone:** (716)285-6666   🔟

(AAA) (SAVE)
▼▼▼▼

6/29-8/31 [ECP]	1P: $129-$289	2P: $139-$299
11/1-4/30 [ECP]	1P: $64-$269	2P: $74-$279
9/1-10/31 [ECP]	1P: $99-$259	2P: $109-$269
5/1-6/28 [ECP]	1P: $94-$239	2P: $109-$249

Small-scale Hotel **Location:** I-190, exit 21 (Robert Moses Pkwy), eastbound use City Traffic exit, just w. 501 Rainbow Blvd 14303. Fax: 716/285-1423. **Facility:** 99 one-bedroom standard units, some with whirlpools. 5 stories, interior corridors. *Bath:* combo or shower only. **Parking:** on-site. **Terms:** check-in 4 pm, package plans. **Amenities:** video games (fee), high-speed Internet, voice mail, safes, irons, hair dryers. **Pool(s):** small heated indoor. **Leisure Activities:** whirlpool, exercise room. **Guest Services:** valet and coin laundry, wireless Internet. **Business Services:** meeting rooms, PC. **Cards:** AX, CB, DC, DS, MC, VI. **Free Special Amenities:** expanded continental breakfast and high-speed Internet. *(See color ad below)*

SOME UNITS

(S🅳) (📶) (🛗) (♿) (➰) (🎦) (💻) / (✉) (🔋) (🖨) /

(See map and index starting on p. 509)

HOLIDAY INN AT THE FALLS *Book great rates at AAA.com* Phone: 716/282-2211 **12**

AAA SAVE

	6/22-9/4	1P: $129-$229	2P: $129-$229	XP: $10	F18
	5/1-6/21	1P: $79-$229	2P: $79-$229	XP: $10	F18
	9/5-4/30	1P: $69-$199	2P: $69-$199	XP: $10	F18

Small-scale Hotel **Location:** I-190, exit 21 (Robert Moses Pkwy) to City Traffic exit, just w on Rainbow Blvd, then just n. Located across from the Seneca Niagara Casino. 231 Third St 14303. **Fax:** 716/282-2748. **Facility:** 161 one-bedroom standard units, some with whirlpools. 8 stories, interior corridors. **Parking:** on-site. **Terms:** package plans. **Amenities:** video games (fee), voice mail, irons, hair dryers. **Dining:** 24 hours, cocktails. **Pool(s):** heated indoor. **Leisure Activities:** sauna, whirlpool, playground, exercise room. *Fee:* game room. **Guest Services:** valet and coin laundry, wireless Internet. **Business Services:** meeting rooms. **Cards:** AX, CB, DC, DS, JC, MC, VI. *(See color ad below)*

SOME UNITS

⬛ 🅢🅓 🍽 🍸 🏋 🐕 🏊 ⊠ 🎥 💻 /⊠ 🛗 /

HOLLEY RANKINE HOUSE Phone: (716)285-4790 **18**

| | All Year [BP] | 1P: $65 | 2P: $125 |

Historic Bed & Breakfast **Location:** I-190, exit 21 (Robert Moses Pkwy), just w on Buffalo Ave, then just s. Located in a residential area. 525 Riverside Dr 14303. **Facility:** The family-owned, 1855 stone house's original woodwork is in pristine condition; stay next to the Niagara River rapids and walk to the falls. Smoke free premises. 5 one-bedroom standard units. 2 stories (no elevator), interior corridors. **Bath:** some shared or private, combo or shower only. **Parking:** on-site. **Terms:** age restrictions may apply, 10 day cancellation notice. **Amenities:** hair dryers.

SOME UNITS

ASK ⊠ CTV 🔌 /🐾 🐾 /

HOWARD JOHNSON INN AT THE FALLS *Book great rates at AAA.com* Phone: (716)285-5261 **5**

AAA SAVE

	6/19-9/5	1P: $85-$255	2P: $85-$255	XP: $10	F
	11/1-4/30	1P: $49-$145	2P: $49-$145	XP: $10	F
	9/6-10/31	1P: $75-$135	2P: $75-$135	XP: $10	F
	5/1-6/18	1P: $65-$129	2P: $65-$129	XP: $10	F

Small-scale Hotel **Location:** I-190, exit 21 (Robert Moses Pkwy), exit City Traffic, just n to Rainbow Blvd, just w. Located adjacent to Rainbow Bridge. 454 Main St 14301. **Fax:** 716/285-8536. **Facility:** 80 one-bedroom standard units, some with whirlpools. 5 stories, interior corridors. **Parking:** on-site. **Terms:** check-in 4 pm, cancellation fee imposed, [ECP] meal plan available, package plans, small pets only ($10 extra charge). **Amenities:** irons, hair dryers. **Pool(s):** heated indoor. **Leisure Activities:** sauna. *Fee:* game room. **Guest Services:** coin laundry. **Cards:** AX, CB, DC, DS, JC, MC, VI. **Free Special Amenities:** expanded continental breakfast and high-speed Internet. *(See color ad p 523)*

SOME UNITS

🅢🅓 🐎 🍽 🏋 🏊 🎥 💻 /⊠ 🛗 🖥 /
FEE   FEE FEE

INN ON THE RIVER *Book great rates at AAA.com* Phone: (716)283-7612 **19**

AAA SAVE

| | All Year | 1P: $89-$199 | 2P: $89-$199 | XP: $10 | F17 |

Small-scale Hotel **Location:** I-190, exit 21 (Robert Moses Pkwy), just e. Located in a quiet area. 7001 Buffalo Ave 14304. **Fax:** 716/283-7613. **Facility:** 148 one-bedroom standard units. 8 stories, interior corridors. **Parking:** on-site. **Terms:** cancellation fee imposed, package plans, pets ($15 fee). **Amenities:** irons, hair dryers. **Dining:** 7 am-2 & 5-9 pm, Fri & Sat-10 pm. **Pool(s):** heated outdoor. **Leisure Activities:** sauna. **Guest Services:** coin laundry. **Business Services:** meeting rooms, PC (fee). **Cards:** AX, CB, DC, DS, JC, MC, VI. *(See color ad p. 533)*

SOME UNITS

🅢🅓 🐾 🏊 🎥 💻 /⊠ 🛗 🖥 /
FEE

(See map and index starting on p. 509)

MOTEL 6 NIAGARA FALLS   **Phone:** 905/356-2000
fyi   Under construction, scheduled to open May 2007. **Location:** Hwy 420, exit Stanley Ave. 5700 Stanley Ave L2G
Motel   3X5. **Planned Amenities:** pets, microwaves, refrigerators, pool.

QUALITY HOTEL AND SUITES "AT THE FALLS"   *Book great rates at AAA.com*   **Phone:** (716)282-1212   **14**

6/18-9/30	1P: $99-$299	2P: $99-$299	XP: $20	F18
5/1-6/17 & 10/1-11/11	1P: $79-$299	2P: $79-$299	XP: $10	F18
11/12-4/30	1P: $59-$199	2P: $59-$199	XP: $10	F18

Small-scale Hotel   **Location:** I-190, exit 21 (Robert Moses Pkwy), eastbound use City Traffic exit, just w; downtown. Adjoins Family Fun Center. 240 Rainbow Blvd 14303. **Fax:** 716/282-0051. **Facility:** 211 units. 197 one-bedroom standard units. 14 one-bedroom suites ($139-$309), some with whirlpools. 4 stories, interior corridors. **Parking:** on-site. **Terms:** [BP] meal plan available, package plans, pets ($20 extra charge). **Amenities:** *Some:* voice mail, irons, hair dryers. **Pool(s):** small heated indoor. **Leisure Activities:** *Fee:* game room. **Guest Services:** gift shop, valet and coin laundry, wireless Internet. **Business Services:** meeting rooms. **Cards:** AX, CB, DC, DS, MC, VI. *(See color ad below)*

SOME UNITS

(ASK) 🛏 🍴 🍸 📶 ➘ 🐾 /✕ 🚫 📺 (VCR) 🌀 📱 📠 💻 /
FEE   FEE

(See map and index starting on p. 509)

THE RED COACH INN

Phone: (716)282-1459   **13**

AAA SAVE

Historic
Country Inn

	7/1-9/3 [ECP]	1P: $139-$179	2P: $139-$179	XP: $20
	5/1-6/30 & 9/4-10/31 [ECP]	1P: $109-$139	2P: $109-$139	XP: $20
	11/1-4/30 [ECP]	1P: $89-$129	2P: $89-$129	XP: $20

Location: I-190, exit 21 (Robert Moses Pkwy) to City Traffic exit, 0.5 mi w. Located next to the Niagara River and state park entrance. 2 Buffalo Ave 14303. Fax: 716/304-1786. **Facility:** Steps away from the Niagara River, attractions and a casino, the Tudor-style inn has been accommodating travelers in luxury since 1923. Smoke free premises. 19 units. 4 one-bedroom standard units with whirlpools. 8 one- and 7 two-bedroom suites ($129-$339) with whirlpools, some with kitchens. 3 stories (no elevator), interior/exterior corridors. **Parking:** on-site. **Terms:** 14 day cancellation notice-fee imposed, package plans, 5% service charge. **Amenities:** CD players, voice mail, irons, hair dryers. **Dining:** restaurant, see separate listing. **Guest Services:** valet laundry, wireless Internet. **Business Services:** meeting rooms. **Cards:** DS, MC, VI. **Free Special Amenities: local telephone calls and high-speed Internet.**
(See color ad below)

SOME UNITS

⑤ 🍽 ✕ 📷 🛢 🖥 💻 / VCR /

SENECA NIAGARA CASINO & HOTEL

Phone: 716/299-1100   **11**

Large-scale Hotel

Property failed to provide current rates

Location: I-190, exit 21 (Robert Moses Pkwy), to City Traffic exit, just n to hotel entrance. 310 4th St 14303. Fax: 716/501-2977. **Facility:** The stately glass high-rise with a waterfall theme towers above the city, providing some great views of the rapids; find luxury and modern amenities. 604 units. 572 one-bedroom standard units, some with whirlpools. 31 one- and 1 two-bedroom suites with whirlpools. 26 stories, interior corridors. *Bath:* combo or shower only. **Parking:** on-site and valet. **Terms:** check-in 4 pm. **Amenities:** CD players, high-speed Internet, dual phone lines, voice mail, safes, irons, hair dryers. *Some:* DVD players. **Dining:** Koi, La Cascata, The Western Door, see separate listings. **Pool(s):** heated outdoor. **Leisure Activities:** saunas, whirlpools, steamrooms, exercise room, spa. **Guest Services:** gift shop, valet laundry, wireless Internet. **Business Services:** conference facilities, business center.

SOME UNITS

🍽 24🕐 🍷 🖥 🌊 ✕ 📷 💻 / ✕ 🛢 /
FEE

SUPER 8 MOTEL

Book great rates at AAA.com

Phone: (716)283-3151   **8**

AAA SAVE

Small-scale Hotel

| | All Year [BP] | 1P: $70-$275 | 2P: $70-$275 | XP: $10 | F12 |

Location: I-190, exit 22, 0.6 mi e. 7680 Niagara Falls Blvd 14304. Fax: 716/215-0296. **Facility:** 73 one-bedroom standard units, some with whirlpools. 2 stories (no elevator), interior corridors. *Bath:* combo or shower only. **Parking:** on-site. **Terms:** cancellation fee imposed, 12% service charge. **Amenities:** high-speed Internet, voice mail, hair dryers. **Pool(s):** heated outdoor. **Guest Services:** area transportation-Seneca Niagara Casino, wireless Internet. **Cards:** AX, DC, DS, MC, VI. **Free Special Amenities: continental breakfast and local telephone calls.** *(See color ad below)*

SOME UNITS

⑤ 🍽 🖥 🌊 ⛲ 📷 🛢 / ✕ 🖥 /
FEE   FEE

(See map and index starting on p. 509)

SWISS COTTAGE INN

AAA [SAVE]

Motel

Phone: (716)283-8142 **7**

All Year [CP]   1P: $32-$99   2P: $42-$189   XP: $10   F12
Location: I-190, exit 22, 0.5 mi e. 6831 Niagara Falls Blvd 14304. Fax: 716/283-2420. **Facility:** 31 one-bedroom standard units. 1 story, exterior corridors. **Bath:** combo or shower only. **Parking:** on-site. **Terms:** weekly rates available, package plans, pets ($10 extra charge). **Pool(s):** heated outdoor. **Cards:** DS, MC, VI.
Free Special Amenities: continental breakfast and high-speed Internet.

SOME UNITS

TRAVELODGE

AAA [SAVE]

Motel

Book great rates at AAA.com

Phone: (716)297-2660 **3**

5/1-8/31	1P: $69-$150	2P: $69-$150	XP: $10	F10
9/1-12/31 & 4/1-4/30	1P: $49-$79	2P: $49-$79	XP: $10	F10
1/1-3/31	1P: $49-$59	2P: $49-$59	XP: $10	F10

Location: I-190, exit 22, 1.8 mi e. 9401 Niagara Falls Blvd 14304. Fax: 716/297-7675. **Facility:** 45 one-bedroom standard units, some with whirlpools. 1 story, exterior corridors. **Parking:** on-site. **Terms:** 1-2 night minimum stay - weekends, weekly rates available, [CP] meal plan available, package plans, small pets only ($10 fee).
Amenities: voice mail. **Pool(s):** outdoor. **Guest Services:** wireless Internet. **Cards:** AX, DS, MC, VI. **Free Special Amenities: continental breakfast and high-speed Internet.**

SOME UNITS

──────── **WHERE TO DINE** ────────

CHU'S DINING LOUNGE-CHINESE FOOD

AAA

Chinese

Lunch: $6-$11   Dinner: $6-$11   Phone: 716/285-7278 **1**
Location: Jct US 62A and SR 104, 0.4 mi ne. 1019 Main St 14301. **Hours:** 11 am-11 pm. Closed: 12/25.
Features: Abundant servings of familiar Chinese choices are prepared individually and served piping hot. Only the freshest and best ingredients are used to produce the most flavorful offerings. Friendly, fast service is the norm in the family-owned and -operated restaurant. Casual dress; cocktails. **Parking:** street. **Cards:** AX, DS, MC, VI.

COMO RESTAURANT & DELI

AAA

Italian

Lunch: $4-$8   Dinner: $7-$18   Phone: 716/285-9341 **3**
Location: Jct SR 104, 1 mi s of US 62A. 2220 Pine Ave 14301. **Hours:** 11:30 am-10 pm, Fri & Sat-11 pm; hours may vary in winter. Closed: 5/28, 7/4, 12/25. **Reservations:** suggested. **Features:** Family-owned since 1927, the restaurant consistently delivers tasty homemade pasta and traditional American dishes. Generous portions and reasonable prices make this a good choice for the value-conscious diner. Casual dress; cocktails. **Parking:** on-site. **Cards:** AX, DS, MC, VI.

FORTUNA'S

Italian

Lunch: $5-$8   Dinner: $7-$19   Phone: 716/282-2252 **2**
Location: Jct 19th St and Forest. 827 19th St 14301. **Hours:** 4 pm-9:30 pm, Fri 11:30 am-10 pm, Sat 4 pm-10:30 pm, Sun noon-8:30 pm. Closed: 7/4, 11/22, 12/24, 12/25; also Mon & Tues. **Reservations:** accepted. **Features:** Classic Italian fare made from the freshest ingredients available and served by the friendly staff in a casual, subdued setting distinguish this restaurant. Longtime favorites include handmade gnocchi and ravioli made from secret family recipes. Casual dress; cocktails. **Parking:** on-site. **Cards:** AX, DS, MC, VI.

HARD ROCK CAFE

American

Lunch: $6-$13   Dinner: $8-$18   Phone: 716/282-0007 **10**
Location: I-190, exit 21 (Robert Moses Pkwy); next to American Falls. 333 Prospect St 14303. **Hours:** 11 am-midnight, Fri & Sat-1 am; closing hours vary off season. Closed: 12/25. **Features:** Rock 'n' roll memorabilia decorates the walls of the popular theme restaurant. Live music on the weekends contributes to the bustling atmosphere. On the menu is a wide variety of American cuisine—from burgers and sandwiches to seafood, steaks and pasta. Casual dress; cocktails. **Parking:** street. **Cards:** AX, DS, MC, VI.

KOBAN'S

American

Dinner: $8-$12   Phone: 716/282-5151 **8**
Location: 2 mi e from center. 3045 Niagara St 14301. **Hours:** 5 pm-10 pm, Sun 4 pm-9 pm. Closed major holidays; also Mon & Tues. **Features:** Specialties at the tavern restaurant include steak, prime rib, seafood and great French onion soup. Casual dress; cocktails. **Parking:** on-site.

KOI

Pacific Rim

Dinner: $12-$25   Phone: 716/299-1100 **11**
Location: In the Seneca Niagara Casino. 310 4th St 14303. **Hours:** 5 pm-10:30 pm. Closed: Mon & Tues. **Reservations:** suggested. **Features:** An explosion of flavors awaits at this Pan-Asian restaurant, where the timeless tradition of quality food and preparation meets modern-day creativity. Flashy decor surrounds patrons as they feast on classics such as pad thai, sushi, sashimi, Vietnamese vegetables rolls and others too numerous to mention. Casual dress; cocktails. **Parking:** on-site. **Cards:** AX, MC, VI.

LA BRUSCHETTA

Italian

Dinner: $8-$19   Phone: 716/297-6222 **6**
Location: I-190, exit 22, 1.8 mi e. 9400 Niagara Falls Blvd 14304. **Hours:** 4 pm-10 pm. Closed major holidays; also Mon. **Reservations:** accepted. **Features:** The chef rules in a dining room decorated with wall art, curios and wallpaper theme of a full-figured chef. Italian specialties come from authentic recipes and are served by a friendly staff. Casual dress; cocktails. **Parking:** on-site. **Cards:** DS, MC, VI.

LA CASCATA

Italian

Dinner: $16-$29   Phone: 716/299-1100 **13**
Location: In the Seneca Niagara Casino. 310 4th St 14303. **Hours:** 5 pm-10:30 pm. Closed: Wed & Thurs. **Reservations:** suggested. **Features:** La Cascata means "the waterfall," and that's what subtly surrounds patrons in the stylish, artsy and upscale dining room. Top-quality ingredients, including daily made pastas and fresh seafood flown in daily, factor into delicious signature dishes such as ravioli di argosta (lobster meat served open-faced and topped with vodka-aurora sauce) and scallops with basil risotto and yellow pepper sauce. Doting, professional staff contribute to a memorable dining experience. Casual dress; cocktails. **Parking:** valet. **Cards:** AX, MC, VI.

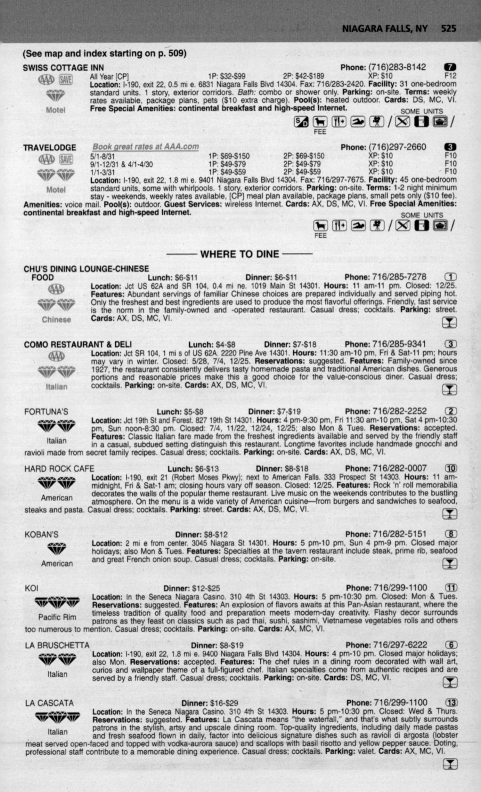

(See map and index starting on p. 509)

MICHAEL'S   Lunch: $6-$8   Dinner: $8-$10   Phone: 716/282-4043   ⑤

Italian

Location: Downtown. 3011 Pine Ave 14301. **Hours:** 11 am-11 pm, Fri & Sat-midnight. Closed: 3/23, 11/22, 12/25. **Features:** The small diner offers generous portions of Italian and American comfort foods at reasonable prices. Servers are friendly and efficient. Casual dress; beer & wine only. **Parking:** on-site. **Cards:** MC, VI.

MOM'S FAMILY RESTAURANT   Lunch: $4-$6   Dinner: $6-$9   Phone: 716/297-6031   ⑦

American

Location: I-190, exit 22, 1.1 mi e on US 62, then just n on Military Rd; in Mil-Pine Plaza. 8420 Niagara Falls Blvd 14304. **Hours:** 5 am-9 pm, Sun 6 am-1:30 pm. Closed: 11/22, 12/25. **Features:** Established in 1954, the family-owned restaurant employs a staff that knows its way around the kitchen. Hungry diners receive the comfort food they crave. Servers are friendly and fast. Credit cards are not accepted. Casual dress; beer & wine only. **Parking:** on-site.

PETE'S MARKET HOUSE RESTAURANT   Lunch: $3-$6   Dinner: $4-$18   Phone: 716/282-7225   ④

Traditional Steak & Seafood

Location: Jct SR 104, 0.8 mi s of US 62A. 1701 Pine Ave 14301. **Hours:** 11:15 am-2:15 & 4-9 pm, Fri 11:15 am-10:30 pm, Sat 11:15 am-11 pm, Sun 1 pm-10 pm. Closed: 5/28, 12/25. **Features:** The casual, popular dining spot occupies an 1800s-style building with original tin-type ceilings. The menu centers on all-American favorites, such as thick sandwiches, homemade soups, juicy steaks, prime rib and lobster. Expect a friendly, hometown atmosphere and service to match. Casual dress; cocktails. **Parking:** on-site. ⓨ

THE RED COACH INN RESTAURANT   *Menu on AAA.com*   Lunch: $7-$12
     Dinner: $10-$25   Phone: 716/282-1459   ⑭

American

Location: I-190, exit 21 (Robert Moses Pkwy) to City Traffic exit, 0.5 mi w; in The Red Coach Inn. 2 Buffalo Ave 14303. **Hours:** 11:30 am-10 pm, Fri & Sat-11 pm, Sun noon-10 pm; 11:30 am-2:30 & 5-9 pm, Fri & Sat 11:30 am-10 pm, Sun noon-9 pm 11/1-4/30. Closed: 12/25. **Reservations:** suggested. **Features:** The Tudor-style, tavern-like dining room has an Old World feel. Selections on the varied menu display creative preparation and nice presentation. The house specialty is succulent prime rib. Servers exhibit good menu knowledge and timely follow-up. Casual dress; cocktails. **Parking:** on-site. **Cards:** AX, DS, MC, VI. *(See color ad p 524)* ⓨ

SUZANNE'S FINE DINING   Dinner: $12-$29   Phone: 716/694-6562

American

Location: I-190, exit 22, 5.5 mi s on US 62; I-290, exit 3, 7.6 mi n on US 62. 2843 Niagara Falls Blvd 14304. **Hours:** 3 pm-9 pm. Closed major holidays; also Sun & Mon. **Reservations:** accepted. **Features:** Soothing, soft tones set the mood for relaxed dining. A sophisticated flair punctuates such delectable menu offerings as chicken Oscar, pork tenderloin and steak Bradley, each embraced by rich sauces and fresh ingredients. It's worth leaving room for one of the homemade desserts. Fine wine offerings, espresso and cappuccino complete a fine-dining experience. Casual dress; cocktails. **Parking:** on-site. **Cards:** AX, DS, MC, VI. ⓨ

TOP OF THE FALLS RESTAURANT   Lunch: $8-$15   Dinner: $18-$30   Phone: 716/278-0340   ⑨

American

Location: On Goat Island; at Terrapin Point. Goat Island-American Falls Park 14302. **Hours:** Open 5/27-9/24; 11 am-9 pm, Fri & Sat-10 pm. **Reservations:** accepted. **Features:** The upscale dining room affords excellent views of Horseshoe Falls from every table. Trendy menu offerings include sandwiches, wraps and seafood and chicken creations similar to those found in finer restaurants. Casual dress; cocktails. **Parking:** on-site (fee). **Cards:** AX, DS, MC, VI. ⓨ

THE WESTERN DOOR   Dinner: $28-$45   Phone: 716/278-3211   ⑫

Steak & Seafood

Location: In Seneca Niagara Casino. 310 4th St 14303. **Hours:** 5 pm-10:30 pm. Closed: Mon. **Reservations:** suggested. **Features:** Servings and taste as big as the West mark this ultra-modern, upscale restaurant. The highest quality meats and seafood flown in daily from Boston are key to the most tender, freshest courses possible. Maryland crab cakes, smoked salmon, hickory-smoked baby back ribs braised with Kentucky bourbon, Alaskan king crab and Australian lobster tail make up the backbone of the solidly popular menu. The professional, knowledgeable staff is friendly and helpful with selections. Casual dress; cocktails. **Parking:** no self-parking. **Cards:** AX, MC, VI.

The Niagara Falls Vicinity

LEWISTON pop. 2,781

——— WHERE TO STAY ———

PORTAGE HOUSE MOTEL   Phone: 716/754-8295

| | | 1P: $59-$75 | 2P: $67-$75 | XP: $7 | F15 |
| | | 1P: $43-$47 | 2P: $50-$54 | XP: $7 | F15 |

5/1-10/31
11/1-4/30

Motel

Location: 0.3 mi w of jct SR 18F and Robert Moses Pkwy; opposite entrance to Artpark. 280 Portage Rd 14092. **Fax:** 716/754-1613. **Facility:** 21 one-bedroom standard units. 2 stories (no elevator), interior/exterior corridors. **Parking:** on-site. **Terms:** 5 day cancellation notice-fee imposed. **Guest Services:** wireless Internet. **Cards:** AX, DS, MC, VI.

SOME UNITS

——— WHERE TO DINE ———

APPLE GRANNY   **Lunch:** $4-$7   **Dinner:** $7-$15   Phone: 716/754-2028

American

Location: Robert Moses Pkwy, exit SR 18F, 1 mi n on SR 104 (Center St). 433 Center St 14092. **Hours:** 11 am-10 pm, Fri & Sat-11 pm. Closed: 3/23, 11/22, 12/25; also Mon. **Reservations:** accepted. **Features:** Rustic decor sets a tone for relaxing in the casual dining room, where patrons sit down to ample portions of American favorites, including super-size salads, extra-large burgers and preparations of seafood, pasta and chicken. A snack menu is presented late at night. Casual dress; cocktails. **Parking:** street. **Cards:** AX, DC, DS, MC, VI.

CLARKSON HOUSE   **Lunch:** $6-$10   **Dinner:** $12-$30   Phone: 716/754-4544

American

Location: 0.4 mi w on SR 104 from jct Robert Moses Pkwy. 810 Center St 14092. **Hours:** 5 pm-9 pm, Fri & Sat-10:30 pm, Sun 4 pm-9 pm. Closed: 1/1, 12/25. **Reservations:** suggested, weekends. **Features:** Since the 1940s, the restaurant has listed steak, live lobster and baked Alaska on its traditional menu. Over the years, such dishes as swordfish with lime salsa, thickly cut lamb chops and cherries jubilee have become exciting additions. Casual dress; cocktails. **Parking:** on-site. **Cards:** AX, DS, MC, VI. **Historic**

LOCKPORT pop. 22,279

——— WHERE TO STAY ———

COMFORT INN   *Book great rates at AAA.com*   Phone: (716)434-4411

		1P: $79-$119	2P: $79-$119	XP: $10	F18
		1P: $69-$99	2P: $69-$99	XP: $10	F18
		1P: $59-$99	2P: $59-$99	XP: $10	F18

5/1-9/9
9/10-10/31 & 3/1-4/30
11/1-2/29

Small-scale Hotel

Location: 1 mi s on SR 78. 551 S Transit Rd 14094. **Fax:** 716/434-9649. **Facility:** 50 one-bedroom standard units, some with whirlpools. 2 stories (no elevator), interior corridors. **Parking:** on-site. **Terms:** [CP] meal plan available, pets ($10 extra charge). **Amenities:** voice mail, irons, hair dryers. **Leisure Activities:** exercise room. **Guest Services:** valet laundry, wireless Internet. **Business Services:** PC. **Cards:** AX, DC, DS, MC, VI.

SOME UNITS
FEE   FEE

HOLIDAY INN LOCKPORT   *Book great rates at AAA.com*   Phone: (716)434-6151

| | | 1P: $90-$150 | | XP: $10 | F18 |
| | | 1P: $70-$110 | | XP: $10 | F18 |

5/1-10/31
11/1-4/30

Small-scale Hotel

Location: 1 mi s on SR 78. 515 S Transit Rd 14094. **Fax:** 716/434-5117. **Facility:** 95 one-bedroom standard units, some with whirlpools. 2 stories, interior corridors. **Bath:** combo or shower only. **Parking:** on-site. **Terms:** pets ($10 extra charge). **Amenities:** high-speed Internet, voice mail, irons, hair dryers. **Pool(s):** heated indoor. **Leisure Activities:** exercise room. **Guest Services:** coin laundry, wireless Internet. **Business Services:** conference facilities, business center. **Cards:** AX, CB, DC, DS, JC, MC, VI. *(See color ad p 521)*

SOME UNITS
FEE

———— WHERE TO DINE ————

FIELDSTONE COUNTRY INN RESTAURANT   Lunch: $5-$7   Dinner: $8-$17   Phone: 716/625-6193

American

Location: 1.5 mi s on SR 78. 5986 S Transit Rd 14094. **Hours:** 11 am-9 pm, Fri & Sat-10 pm, Sun-8 pm. Closed: 12/24, 12/25. **Features:** Recognized by its rounded fieldstone exterior, the casual restaurant is popular for the salad bar, fast service and good, cooked-to-order food. The baby back ribs specialty is tender, smoky and delicious. Casual dress; cocktails. **Parking:** on-site. **Cards:** AX, DC, DS, MC, VI.

GARLOCK'S   Dinner: $11-$30   Phone: 716/433-5595

Steak & Seafood

Location: Jct SR 78 and 31; on Erie Canal. 35 S Transit Rd 14094. **Hours:** 4:30 pm-11:30 pm, Sat-midnight, Sun 3:30 pm-10 pm. Closed: 11/22, 12/25. **Features:** Serving delicious steaks, lamb chops, prime rib, lobster, seafood and more for more than 55 years, the cozy spot has a rustic feel. Friendly hometown service can be expected. Casual dress; cocktails. **Parking:** on-site. **Cards:** AX, DS, MC, VI.

VILLAGE EATERY ITALIAN BISTRO   Lunch: $5-$10   Dinner: $8-$15   Phone: 716/433-0688

Italian

Location: 0.8 mi s of jct SR 31. 429 Davison Rd 14094. **Hours:** 11 am-10 pm, Sun 4 pm-10 pm. Closed major holidays. **Features:** The contemporary, casual dining and upscale bistro bar offered at Village Eatery spotlight abundant, delicious traditional Italian dishes of pasta, steak, veal and chicken, as well as gourmet pizzas. Casual dress; cocktails. **Parking:** on-site. **Cards:** AX, DS, MC, VI.

NEWFANE pop. 3,129

———— WHERE TO STAY ————

LAKE ONTARIO MOTEL   Phone: 716/778-5004

	5/1-11/1	1P: $45-$55	2P: $57-$75	XP: $7	F12
	4/18-4/30	1P: $43-$65	2P: $55-$75	XP: $7	F12

Motel

Location: 2.5 mi n of jct SR 104 on SR 78. 3330 Lockport-Olcott Rd 14108. **Facility:** 11 one-bedroom standard units. 2 stories (no elevator), interior corridors. *Bath:* shower only. **Parking:** on-site. **Terms:** open 5/1-11/1 & 4/18-4/30, pets ($5 fee). **Cards:** AX, DS, MC, VI.

SOME UNITS

(ASK) (SD) (🛏) (🛎) / (✕) (🔒) (🖥) /
FEE

———— WHERE TO DINE ————

GORDIE HARPER'S BAZAAR   Lunch: $4-$8   Dinner: $6-$15   Phone: 716/778-8048

American

Location: 2.5 mi n of jct SR 104 on SR 78. 3333 Lockport-Olcott Rd 14108. **Hours:** 8 am-8 pm, Fri & Sat-9 pm. Closed: 11/22, 12/25. **Features:** Although the experience at the casual roadside bazaar of arts and crafts is unusual, the comfort food tastes great and is served in ample portions. Bakery items are made on the premises. Casual dress; cocktails. **Parking:** on-site. **Cards:** AX, DS, MC, VI.

SANBORN

———— WHERE TO DINE ————

THE NEW SCHIMSCHACK'S RESTAURANT   Dinner: $12-$45   Phone: 716/731-4111

American

Location: 1.3 mi n of jct SR 425 and 31, 2.3 mi w. 2943 Upper Mountain Rd 14132. **Hours:** 4 pm-9 pm, Sat-10 pm, Sun noon-8 pm. Closed: 12/24, 12/25; also Mon 11/1-6/1. **Reservations:** suggested. **Features:** Charbroiled baby back ribs stand out on a menu of traditional favorites. The three-tiered dining room, which affords lovely panoramic views of the vineyards, exudes an informal, romantic ambience. Tempting dessert is prepared on the premises. Marilyn Monroe and Joe DiMaggio dined here during the filming of "Niagara". Casual dress; cocktails. **Parking:** on-site. **Cards:** AX, DC, DS, MC, VI.

WHEATFIELD pop. 14,086

———— WHERE TO DINE ————

OLYMPIA RESTAURANT   Lunch: $6-$8   Dinner: $8-$13   Phone: 716/694-6969

American

Location: Just e of Nash Rd. 3312 Niagara Falls Blvd 14108. **Hours:** 7 am-9 pm. Closed major holidays. **Features:** Attractive new decor follows a Mediterranean theme at this handsome diner, where tender and tangy Greek classics are served in huge portions. Also on the menu are some Italian dishes and traditional American comfort food. Casual dress; cocktails. **Parking:** on-site. **Cards:** MC, VI.

YOUNGSTOWN pop. 1,957

———— WHERE TO STAY ————

CAMEO INN BED & BREAKFAST   Phone: (716)745-3034

	All Year [BP]	1P: $80-$140	2P: $90-$145	XP: $20

Bed & Breakfast

Location: I-190, exit 25B, 0.5 mi e on SR 104, then 4.5 mi n on SR 18F. 3881 Lower River Rd 14174. Fax: 716/745-7455. **Facility:** Smoke free premises. 4 one-bedroom standard units. 2 stories (no elevator), interior corridors. *Bath:* some shared or private. **Parking:** on-site. **Terms:** 2 night minimum stay - seasonal and/or weekends, age restrictions may apply, 14 day cancellation notice-fee imposed, package plans. **Leisure Activities:** bicycles, hiking trails. **Business Services:** meeting rooms. **Cards:** DS, MC, VI.

SOME UNITS

Nearby Ontario

NIAGARA FALLS   (See map and index starting on p. 511)

——— WHERE TO STAY ———

ADVANTAGE INN   *Book great rates at AAA.com*   **Phone:** 905-374-4442   ⓵

CAA SAVE	6/26-9/6	1P: $48-$98	2P: $58-$118	XP: $10 F
	5/1-6/25	1P: $48-$78	2P: $48-$98	XP: $10 F
Motel	9/7-4/30	1P: $42-$58	2P: $48-$78	XP: $10 F

Location: QEW, exit Hwy 20, 2.9 mi (4.6 km) w. 7797 Lundy's Ln L2H 1H3. Fax: 905/357-1854. **Facility:** 35 one-bedroom standard units, some with efficiencies, kitchens and/or whirlpools. 1-2 stories (no elevator), exterior corridors. *Bath:* combo or shower only. **Parking:** on-site, winter plug-ins. **Terms:** 3 day cancellation notice, package plans. **Pool(s):** heated outdoor. **Leisure Activities:** barbecue, playground. **Guest Services:** area transportation (fee)-falls & casino. **Cards:** AX, DC, DS, MC, VI. **Free Special Amenities:** local telephone calls and newspaper.

SOME UNITS

(See map and index starting on p. 511)

AMERICANA CONFERENCE RESORT AND SPA

Phone: (905)356-8444   **45**

(CAA) (SAVE)

	6/22-9/3	1P: $139-$299	2P: $139-$299	XP: $20	F16
	9/4-4/30	1P: $99-$269	2P: $99-$269	XP: $20	F16
	5/1-6/21	1P: $89-$199	2P: $89-$199	XP: $20	F16

Location: QEW, exit Hwy 20, 3.4 mi (5.5 km) w. 8444 Lundy's Ln L2H 1H4. Fax: 905/356-8576. **Facility:** Smoke **Large-scale Hotel** free premises. 204 units. 184 one- and 4 two-bedroom standard units, some with whirlpools. 14 one- and 2 two-bedroom suites ($139-$399), some with whirlpools. 2-3 stories, interior corridors. **Parking:** on-site. **Terms:** check-in 4 pm, cancellation fee imposed, package plans, 3% service charge. **Amenities:** voice mail, hair dryers. **Dining:** 7 am-11 pm, Fri & Sat-midnight, cocktails, entertainment. **Pool(s):** wading. **Leisure Activities:** sauna, whirlpool, steamrooms, waterslide, aqua play structure, indoor water park, wave pool, playground, exercise room, spa, basketball, shuffleboard, volleyball. *Fee:* game room. **Guest Services:** gift shop, valet and coin laundry, area transportation (fee)-casino & falls. **Business Services:** conference facilities, business center. **Cards:** AX, DC, DS, MC, VI. **Free Special Amenities:** newspaper and room upgrade (subject to availability with advance reservations). *(See color ad p 531)*

AMERICAS BEST VALUE INN AND SUITES-CHALET
INN   *Book great rates at AAA.com*

Phone: (905)374-1921   **10**

(CAA) (SAVE)

	5/1-9/6 [CP]	1P: $89-$149	2P: $99-$229	XP: $15	F12
	9/7-9/30 [CP]	1P: $59-$109	2P: $89-$149	XP: $15	F12
	10/1-4/30 [CP]	1P: $59-$109	2P: $69-$129	XP: $15	F12

Small-scale Hotel **Location:** N on Clifton Hill, just e; 0.3 mi (0.6 km) from the falls. 5577 Ellen Ave L2G 3P5. Fax: 905/374-1868. **Facility:** 73 units. 66 one- and 7 two-bedroom standard units, some with whirlpools. 3-5 stories, interior/exterior corridors. **Parking:** on-site. **Terms:** office hours 7 am-2 am, 3 day cancellation notice-fee imposed, package plans. **Pool(s):** heated outdoor, heated indoor. **Cards:** AX, CB, DC, DS, JC, MC, VI.

SOME UNITS

AMERICAS BEST VALUE INN - GARDENS INN   *Book great rates at AAA.com*

Phone: (905)227-0891   **7**

	6/29-9/4	1P: $69-$119	2P: $79-$129	XP: $10	F12
	5/1-6/28	1P: $59-$89	2P: $69-$99	XP: $10	F12
	9/5-4/30	1P: $45-$79	2P: $55-$89	XP: $7	F12

Motel **Location:** 5.8 mi (9.2 km) w on Hwy 20. 13055 Lundys Ln L2E 6S4. Fax: 905/227-3720. **Facility:** 28 one-bedroom standard units, some with whirlpools. 1 story, exterior corridors. **Parking:** on-site. **Terms:** 3 day cancellation notice-fee imposed, package plans. **Amenities:** high-speed Internet. **Pool(s):** heated outdoor. **Leisure Activities:** playground. **Cards:** AX, DC, DS, MC, VI. **Free Special Amenities:** local telephone calls and high-speed Internet.

SOME UNITS

A VICTORIA MOTOR INN

Phone: (905)374-6522   **23**

(CAA) (SAVE)

	7/1-9/2	1P: $75-$129	2P: $99-$199	XP: $15	F16
	9/3-4/30	1P: $59-$99	2P: $79-$129	XP: $15	F16
	5/1-6/30	1P: $59-$79	2P: $79-$99	XP: $15	F16

Motel **Location:** From Clifton Hill, just w. Located in a commercial area. 5869 Victoria Ave L2G 3L6. Fax: 905/374-3038. **Facility:** 33 one-bedroom standard units, some with whirlpools. 3 stories (no elevator), exterior corridors. **Parking:** on-site (fee). **Terms:** 3 day cancellation notice-fee imposed, 3% service charge. **Dining:** 2 noon. **Pool(s):** heated outdoor. **Cards:** AX, DS, MC, VI. **Free Special Amenities:** early check-in/late check-out and room upgrade (subject to availability with advance reservations).

SOME UNITS

BEST WESTERN CAIRN CROFT HOTEL   *Book great rates at AAA.com*

Phone: (905)356-1161   **33**

(CAA) (SAVE)

	6/22-9/2	1P: $99-$199		XP: $10	F16
	9/3-10/27	1P: $79-$169		XP: $10	F16
	10/28-4/30	1P: $59-$139		XP: $10	F16
	5/1-6/21	1P: $59-$129		XP: $10	F16

Small-scale Hotel **Location:** 1.5 mi (2.4 km) w on Hwy 20. 6400 Lundy's Ln L2G 1T6. Fax: 905/356-8664. **Facility:** 165 one-bedroom standard units, some with whirlpools. 2-5 stories, interior/exterior corridors. **Parking:** on-site, winter plug-ins. **Terms:** 2 night minimum stay - weekends, package plans, 3% service charge. **Amenities:** video games (fee), irons, hair dryers. *Some:* high-speed Internet. **Dining:** 7 am-2 & 5-10 pm; to 9 pm weekdays off season, cocktails. **Pool(s):** heated indoor. **Leisure Activities:** whirlpools, indoor children's play area. *Fee:* game room. **Guest Services:** valet laundry, area transportation (fee)-casino & falls. **Business Services:** meeting rooms, PC (fee). **Cards:** AX, DC, DS, MC, VI. **Free Special Amenities:** local telephone calls and high-speed Internet. *(See color ad p 532)*

SOME UNITS

FEE   FEE

BEST WESTERN FALLSVIEW   *Book great rates at AAA.com*

Phone: (905)356-0551   **54**

(CAA) (SAVE)

	6/29-9/2	1P: $119-$299	2P: $119-$299	XP: $10	F12
	5/1-6/28 & 9/3-10/7	1P: $99-$299	2P: $99-$299	XP: $10	F12
	10/8-4/30	1P: $79-$199	2P: $79-$199	XP: $10	F12

Small-scale Hotel **Location:** Jct Niagara River Pkwy, just n on Murray St. 6289 Fallsview Blvd L2G 3V7. Fax: 905/356-7773. **Facility:** Smoke free premises. 243 one-bedroom standard units, some with whirlpools. 4-6 stories, interior/exterior corridors. *Bath:* combo or shower only. **Parking:** on-site (fee). **Terms:** check-in 4 pm, 3 day cancellation notice-fee imposed, [BP] meal plan available, package plans, 3% service charge, small pets only ($10 extra charge). **Amenities:** video games (fee), voice mail, irons, hair dryers. *Some:* high-speed Internet. **Dining:** 7 am-11 & 5-10 pm, Sat & Sun 8 am-9 pm, cocktails. **Pool(s):** outdoor, heated indoor. **Leisure Activities:** whirlpools. **Guest Services:** gift shop. **Cards:** AX, CB, DC, DS, JC, MC, VI. **Free Special Amenities:** local telephone calls and high-speed Internet. *(See color ad p 534 & starting on p 170)*

FEE

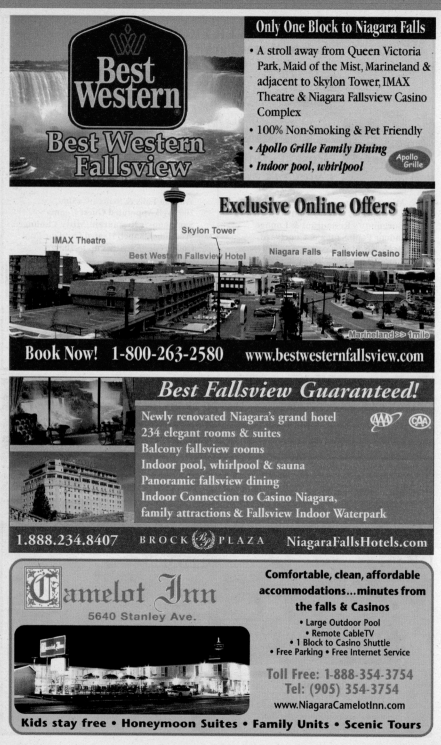

(See map and index starting on p. 511)

BEST WESTERN FIRESIDE HOTEL   *Book great rates at AAA.com*   Phone: (905)374-2027   **④**

6/16-9/4	1P: $99-$249	2P: $99-$249	XP: $10	F16
5/1-6/15 & 9/5-4/30	1P: $69-$199	2P: $69-$199	XP: $10	F16

Location: 1.9 mi (3 km) n of Rainbow Bridge. 4067 River Rd L2E 3E5. Fax: 905/374-7746. **Facility:** 96 one-bedroom standard units, some with whirlpools. 4 stories, interior corridors. **Parking:** on-site. **Small-scale Hotel Terms:** package plans. **Amenities:** high-speed Internet, irons, hair dryers. **Dining:** 7 am-noon. **Pool(s):** heated indoor. **Leisure Activities:** sauna, whirlpool, exercise room. **Guest Services:** area transportation-casino & falls. **Cards:** AX, DC, DS, MC, VI. **Free Special Amenities:** local telephone calls. *(See color ad p 533)*

SOME UNITS

BROCK PLAZA HOTEL   *Book great rates at AAA.com*   Phone: (905)374-4444   **⑲**

6/1-10/31	1P: $149-$799	2P: $149-$799	XP: $20	F18
11/1-4/30	1P: $99-$799	2P: $99-$799	XP: $20	F18
5/1-5/31	1P: $129-$699	2P: $129-$699	XP: $20	F18

Location: Entrance to Rainbow Bridge on Hwy 20; just n of the falls. Located next to a casino. 5685 Falls Ave L2E 6W7. Fax: 905/371-8349. **Facility:** This grand hotel, built in 1929, offers many rooms overlooking the falls; accommodations are cozy and well-appointed with modern amenities. 234 units. 221 one- and 6 two-bedroom standard units, some with whirlpools. 5 one- and 2 two-bedroom suites. 12 stories, interior corridors. *Bath:* combo or shower only. **Parking:** on-site (fee). **Terms:** cancellation fee imposed, package plans, 3% service charge. **Amenities:** video games (fee), voice mail, irons, hair dryers. **Dining:** The Rainbow Fallsview Dining Room, see separate listing. **Pool(s):** heated indoor. *Fee:* waterslide, waterpark & wave pool, exercise room. **Guest Services:** gift shop, valet laundry. **Business Services:** conference facilities. **Cards:** AX, CB, DC, DS, JC, MC, VI. **Free Special Amenities:** high-speed Internet. *(See color ad p 534)*

SOME UNITS

FEE

CADILLAC MOTEL   Phone: (905)356-0830   **㊳**

6/25-9/2	1P: $50-$120	2P: $60-$150	XP: $10	F12
9/3-10/31 & 4/1-4/30	1P: $40-$80	2P: $60-$150	XP: $10	F12
5/1-6/24	1P: $40-$80	2P: $50-$100	XP: $10	F12

Location: On Hwy 20, 0.3 mi (0.6 km) from the falls. Located in a commercial area. 5342 Ferry St L2G 1R7. Fax: 905/356-5624. **Facility:** 23 one-bedroom standard units. 1 story, exterior corridors. **Parking:** on-site. **Terms:** open 5/1-10/31 & 4/1-4/30, cancellation fee imposed, package plans. **Cards:** AX, DS, MC, VI. **Free Special Amenities:** high-speed Internet.

SOME UNITS

CAMELOT INN   Phone: 905/354-3754   **⑬**

Property failed to provide current rates

Location: Just n of Hwy 20; just s of Hwy 420. 5640 Stanley Ave L2G 3X5. Fax: 905/354-6683. **Facility:** 53 one-bedroom standard units, some with whirlpools. 2 stories (no elevator), exterior corridors. **Parking:** on-site. **Terms:** office hours 8 am-2 am, pets ($10 fee). **Amenities:** high-speed Internet. *Some:* hair dryers. **Pool(s):** outdoor. **Business Services:** PC. *(See color ad p 534)*

SOME UNITS

FEE

(See map and index starting on p. 511)

CLARION PRESIDENT HOTEL & SUITES BY THE FALLS   *Book great rates at AAA.com*   **Phone:** (905)374-4142   [47]

5/1-9/30	1P: $99-$199	2P: $99-$299	XP: $10 F18
10/1-4/30	1P: $69-$199	2P: $99-$299	XP: $10 F18

Location: 0.8 mi (1.2 km) w on Hwy 20, then s. 6045 Stanley Ave L2G 3Y3. **Fax:** 905/358-3430. **Facility:** 192 one-bedroom standard units, some with whirlpools. 8 stories, interior corridors. **Parking:** on-site (fee). **Terms:** cancellation fee imposed, [BP] & [MAP] meal plans available, package plans. **Amenities:** video games (fee), voice mail, irons, hair dryers. *Some:* high-speed Internet, dual phone lines. **Dining:** 6:30 am-11 & 5:30-9 pm, cocktails. **Pool(s):** heated indoor. **Leisure Activities:** limited exercise equipment. **Guest Services:** valet laundry. **Business Services:** meeting rooms. **Cards:** AX, CB, DC, DS, MC, VI. **Free Special Amenities:** newspaper and high-speed Internet. *(See color ad p 535)*

SOME UNITS

COMFORT INN CLIFTON HILL   *Book great rates at AAA.com*   **Phone:** (905)358-3293   [18]

7/1-9/2 [ECP]	1P: $99-$279	2P: $99-$279	XP: $10 F18
9/3-12/31 [ECP]	1P: $69-$279	2P: $69-$279	XP: $10 F18
5/1-6/30 [ECP]	1P: $69-$239	2P: $69-$239	XP: $10 F18
1/1-4/30 [ECP]	1P: $59-$189	2P: $59-$189	XP: $10 F18

Location: Jct Victoria Ave and Clifton Hill, just s. 4960 Clifton Hill L2E 6S8 (PO Box 60, NIAGARA FALLS, ON). **Fax:** 905/358-3818. **Facility:** 185 units. 173 one- and 12 two-bedroom standard units, some with whirlpools. 3 stories (no elevator), interior corridors. **Parking:** on-site. **Terms:** package plans. **Amenities:** irons, hair dryers. **Dining:** 11 am-2 am, cocktails, also, Kelsey's, see separate listing. *Some:* heated indoor. **Leisure Activities:** whirlpool. *Fee:* miniature golf. **Business Services:** PC. **Cards:** AX, CB, DC, DS, JC, MC, VI. **Free Special Amenities:** expanded continental breakfast and local telephone calls. *(See color ad p 537)*

SOME UNITS

COMFORT INN FALLSVIEW   *Book great rates at AAA.com*   **Phone:** (905)358-9353   [63]

6/22-9/20	1P: $79-$329	2P: $79-$329	XP: $10
9/21-10/31	1P: $69-$299	2P: $69-$299	XP: $10
5/1-6/21	1P: $59-$249	2P: $59-$249	XP: $10
11/1-4/30	1P: $49-$189	2P: $49-$189	XP: $10

Location: Opposite the new Fallsview Casino. 6645 Fallsview Blvd L2G 3W6. **Fax:** 905/356-7298. **Facility:** 107 units. 105 one-bedroom standard units, some with whirlpools. 2 two-bedroom suites ($139-$429). 2-8 stories, interior corridors. **Parking:** on-site (fee). **Terms:** 4 day cancellation notice-fee imposed, [AP] & [CP] meal plans available, package plans. **Amenities:** high-speed Internet, voice mail, irons, hair dryers. **Dining:** 9:30 am-2 am; to 10:30 pm 4/15-3/15, cocktails. **Pool(s):** heated outdoor, heated indoor. **Leisure Activities:** whirlpools. **Guest Services:** wireless Internet. **Business Services:** meeting rooms. **Cards:** AX, CB, DC, DS, MC, VI. *(See color ad p 538 & starting on p 170)*

SOME UNITS

COMFORT INN LUNDY'S LANE   **Phone:** (905)354-1849   [44]

6/29-9/4 [CP]	1P: $89-$199	2P: $89-$199	XP: $10 F18
9/5-4/30 [CP]	1P: $69-$199	2P: $69-$199	XP: $10 F18
5/1-6/28 [CP]	1P: $69-$179	2P: $69-$179	XP: $10 F18

Location: QEW, exit Hwy 20; 3.1 mi (5 km) from downtown. 7514 Lundy's Ln L2H 1G8. **Fax:** 905/354-6619. **Facility:** 148 one-bedroom standard units. 2-5 stories, interior/exterior corridors. **Parking:** on-site, winter plug-ins. **Terms:** package plans. **Amenities:** video games (fee), voice mail, hair dryers. *Some:* high-speed Internet. **Pool(s):** heated indoor. **Leisure Activities:** whirlpool, exercise room. **Business Services:** meeting rooms, PC (fee). **Cards:** AX, DC, DS, MC, VI.

SOME UNITS

COURTYARD BY MARRIOTT NIAGARA FALLS   *Book great rates at AAA.com*   **Phone:** (905)358-3083   [30]

6/16-9/2	1P: $99-$399	2P: $99-$399	XP: $10
5/1-6/15 & 9/3-4/30	1P: $79-$299	2P: $79-$299	XP: $10

Location: Jct Ferry St. 5950 Victoria Ave L2G 3L7. **Fax:** 905/358-8720. **Facility:** Smoke free premises. 258 one-bedroom standard units, some with whirlpools. 10 stories, interior corridors. *Bath:* combo or shower only. **Parking:** on-site (fee). **Terms:** 3 day cancellation notice-fee imposed, [BP] meal plan available, package plans. **Amenities:** dual phone lines, voice mail, safes, honor bars, irons, hair dryers. *Fee:* video games, high-speed Internet. **Dining:** The Keg Steakhouse and Bar, see separate listing. **Pool(s):** outdoor, heated indoor. **Leisure Activities:** sauna, whirlpool, sun deck, exercise room. *Fee:* game room. **Guest Services:** gift shop, valet and coin laundry, area transportation (fee)-casino, wireless Internet. **Business Services:** meeting rooms, PC (fee). **Cards:** AX, CB, DC, DS, JC, MC, VI. *(See color ad inside front cover & p 539)*

SOME UNITS

(See map and index starting on p. 511)

CRYSTAL INN

				Phone: (905)354-0460	**5**
	6/26-9/6	1P: $79-$149	2P: $79-$149	XP: $10	D12
	5/1-6/25 & 9/7-10/31	1P: $49-$89	2P: $59-$109	XP: $10	D12
Motel	11/1-4/30	1P: $49-$89	2P: $49-$109	XP: $10	D12

Location: 1.8 mi (2.8 km) n of falls on Niagara River Pkwy. 4267 River Rd L2E 3E7. Fax: 905/374-4972.
Facility: 38 one-bedroom standard units, some with whirlpools. 2 stories (no elevator), exterior corridors.
Parking: on-site. **Terms:** cancellation fee imposed, [CP] meal plan available. **Pool(s):** heated outdoor. **Cards:** AX, DS, MC, VI.

SOME UNITS

ASK SD TI↑ ≈ CTV ⚒ 🅱 / ⊠ /

(See map and index starting on p. 511)

DAYS INN & SUITES BY THE FALLS   *Book great rates at AAA.com*   Phone: (905)357-2550   **15**

CAA SAVE

6/23-9/5 [CP]	1P: $89-$299	2P: $89-$299	XP: $10 F16
5/1-6/22 & 9/6-4/30 [CP]	1P: $59-$199	2P: $59-$199	XP: $10 F16

Location: Jct Ellen Ave. 5068 Centre St L2G 3N9. Fax: 905/357-7771. **Facility:** 152 units. 142 one-bedroom standard units, some with whirlpools. 10 one-bedroom suites ($89-$429). 3-6 stories, interior corridors. Small-scale Hotel *Bath:* combo or shower only. **Parking:** on-site. **Terms:** package plans. **Amenities:** high-speed Internet, voice mail, irons, hair dryers. **Pool(s):** heated indoor. **Leisure Activities:** whirlpool, exercise room. **Guest Services:** coin laundry. **Business Services:** meeting rooms. **Cards:** AX, DS, MC, VI. **Free Special Amenities: continental breakfast and high-speed Internet.** *(See color ad below)*

SOME UNITS

DAYS INN CLIFTON HILL CASINO   *Book great rates at AAA.com*   Phone: (905)356-2461   **12**

CAA SAVE

11/1-12/31	1P: $49-$429	2P: $49-$429	XP: $10 F5
5/1-9/6	1P: $49-$399	2P: $49-$399	XP: $10 F5
9/7-10/31 & 1/1-4/30	1P: $49-$299	2P: $49-$299	XP: $10 F5

Location: Just e on Hwy 20. 5657 Victoria Ave L2G 3L5. Fax: 905/356-2467. **Facility:** 138 units. 136 one- and 2 Small-scale Hotel two-bedroom standard units, some with whirlpools. 2-7 stories, interior/exterior corridors. **Parking:** on-site (fee). **Terms:** cancellation fee imposed, package plans. **Amenities:** high-speed Internet, hair dryers. *Some:* voice mail, irons. **Dining:** 2 restaurants, 7 am-midnight; to 10 pm off season, also, Remington's of Montana Steak and Seafood, see separate listing. **Pool(s):** heated indoor. **Leisure Activities:** sauna, whirlpool, game room. **Guest Services:** area transportation-casino. **Business Services:** PC (fee). **Cards:** AX, CB, DC, DS, JC, MC, VI. **Free Special Amenities: high-speed Internet.** *(See color ad starting on p 542)*

SOME UNITS

DAYS INN-LUNDY'S LANE   *Book great rates at AAA.com*   Phone: (905)358-3621   **42**

CAA SAVE

11/1-12/31	1P: $45-$299	2P: $45-$299	
5/1-9/5	1P: $45-$289	2P: $45-$289	
9/6-10/31	1P: $45-$199	2P: $45-$199	
1/1-4/30	1P: $45-$189	2P: $45-$189	

Location: QEW, exit Hwy 20, 2.4 mi (3.8 km) w. 7280 Lundy's Ln L2G 1W2. Fax: 905/356-7693. **Facility:** 136 one-bedroom standard units, some with whirlpools. 2-5 stories, interior/exterior corridors. **Parking:** on-site (fee). **Terms:** cancellation fee imposed, [MAP] meal plan available, package plans. **Amenities:** hair dryers. **Dining:** 24 hours. **Pool(s):** heated indoor. **Leisure Activities:** sauna, whirlpool, playground. *Fee:* miniature golf. **Guest Services:** area transportation-casino. **Business Services:** PC (fee). **Cards:** AX, CB, DC, DS, JC, MC, VI. *(See color ad starting on p 542)*

SOME UNITS

DAYS INN FALLSVIEW CASINO   Phone: (905)356-2461   **62**

11/1-12/31	1P: $45-$299	2P: $45-$299	XP: $10 F16
5/1-9/5	1P: $45-$289	2P: $45-$289	XP: $10 F16
9/6-10/31	1P: $45-$199	2P: $45-$199	XP: $10 F16
1/1-4/30	1P: $45-$189	2P: $45-$189	XP: $10 F16

Small-scale Hotel

Location: Corner of Dixon Ave; 2 blks from Konica Minolta Tower. 6519 Stanley Ave L2G 7L2. Fax: 905/356-3651. **Facility:** 95 one-bedroom standard units, some with whirlpools. 3 stories (no elevator), interior corridors. **Parking:** on-site. **Terms:** cancellation fee imposed, package plans, 3% service charge. **Amenities:** hair dryers. **Pool(s):** heated outdoor. **Business Services:** fax (fee). **Cards:** AX, CB, DC, DS, JC, MC, VI. *(See color ad p 555 & starting on p 170)*

SOME UNITS

DAYS INN NEAR THE FALLS   *Book great rates at AAA.com*   Phone: (905)374-3333   **24**

CAA SAVE

5/1-9/30	1P: $70-$299	2P: $70-$299	XP: $20 F12
10/1-4/30	1P: $60-$280	2P: $60-$280	XP: $20 F12

Location: On Hwy 20, 0.4 mi (0.6 km) from the falls. 5943 Victoria Ave L2G 3L8. Fax: 905/374-0669. **Facility:** 117 one-bedroom standard units, some with whirlpools. 7 stories, interior corridors. **Parking:** on-site (fee). Small-scale Hotel **Terms:** cancellation fee imposed. **Amenities:** hair dryers. *Some:* irons. **Pool(s):** heated indoor. **Leisure Activities:** sauna, whirlpool. *Fee:* pool table. **Guest Services:** gift shop. **Business Services:** PC (fee). **Cards:** AX, DS, MC, VI. *(See color ad p 544)*

SOME UNITS

(See map and index starting on p. 511)

DAYS INN NORTH OF THE FALLS *Book great rates at AAA.com* **Phone:** (905)356-6666 **3**

(AAA) (SAVE)	6/16-9/4	1P: $98-$228	2P: $98-$228	XP: $10	F16
	5/1-6/15	1P: $58-$168	2P: $58-$168	XP: $10	F16
▼▼▼	9/5-4/30	1P: $48-$168	2P: $48-$168	XP: $10	F16

Location: 1.9 mi (3 km) n of Rainbow Bridge. 4029 River Rd L2E 3E5. Fax: 905/356-1800. **Facility:** 94 one-
Small-scale Hotel bedroom standard units, some with whirlpools. 4 stories (no elevator), interior/exterior corridors. **Parking:**
on-site. **Terms:** package plans. **Amenities:** high-speed Internet, voice mail, hair dryers. *Some:* irons.
Dining: noon-10 pm; from 5 pm 10/15-5/14, cocktails. **Pool(s):** heated indoor. **Leisure Activities:** sauna, whirlpool. **Guest
Services:** area transportation-casino & falls. **Cards:** AX, DC, DS, MC, VI. *(See color ad p 533)*

SOME UNITS

DOUBLETREE RESORT LODGE & SPA FALLSVIEW *Book great rates at AAA.com* **Phone:** (905)358-3817 **48**

(AAA) (SAVE)	5/1-10/20	1P: $99-$299	2P: $99-$299	XP: $10	F18
▼▼▼ ▼▼▼	10/21-4/30	1P: $89-$169	2P: $89-$169	XP: $10	F18

Location: Just w via Murray St, then n; adjacent to Skylon Tower. 6039 Fallsview Blvd L2G 3V6. Fax: 905/353-4114.
Large-scale Hotel **Facility:** 224 units. 192 one-bedroom standard units, some with whirlpools. 32 one-bedroom suites ($129-
$359). 18 stories, interior corridors. **Parking:** on-site (fee). **Terms:** [BP] meal plan available, package plans.
Amenities: video games (fee), high-speed Internet, dual phone lines, voice mail, irons, hair dryers.
Dining: Buchanans Chophouse, see separate listing. **Pool(s):** 2 heated indoor. **Leisure Activities:** sauna, whirlpool, hot tub,
exercise room, spa. **Fee:** game room. **Guest Services:** gift shop, valet and coin laundry. **Business Services:** conference
facilities, business center. **Cards:** AX, CB, DC, DS, JC, MC, VI. **Free Special Amenities:** newspaper and high-speed
Internet. *(See color ad below)*

SOME UNITS

ECONO LODGE NEAR THE FALLS *Book great rates at AAA.com* **Phone:** (905)358-6243 **46**

▼▼▼	6/16-9/3	1P: $55-$120	2P: $55-$120	XP: $10	F
	5/1-6/15 & 9/4-4/30	1P: $45-$90	2P: $45-$90	XP: $10	F

Motel **Location:** 0.8 mi (1.3 km) w on Hwy 20, just s. 6000 Stanley Ave L2G 3Y1. Fax: 905/358-1864. **Facility:** 80 one-
bedroom standard units, some with whirlpools. 2 stories (no elevator), interior/exterior corridors. **Parking:**
on-site. **Terms:** small pets only ($10 extra charge, limit 1). **Pool(s):** outdoor. **Business Services:** fax (fee). **Cards:** AX, CB, DC,
DS, MC, VI.

SOME UNITS
FEE

EMBASSY SUITES NIAGARA FALLS FALLSVIEW *Book great rates at AAA.com* **Phone:** (905)356-3600 **64**

(AAA) (SAVE)	7/1-8/31	1P: $235-$925	2P: $235-$925	XP: $25	F17
▼▼▼ ▼▼▼	5/1-6/30 & 9/1-4/30	1P: $135-$825	2P: $135-$825	XP: $25	F17

Location: Adjacent to Konica Minolta Tower. 6700 Fallsview Blvd L2G 3W6. Fax: 905/356-0472. **Facility:** This large
Large-scale Hotel hotel, always bustling, features spacious, well-appointed suites and a central location close to the casino
and area attractions. 512 one-bedroom suites, some with whirlpools. 42 stories, interior corridors. **Terms:** 3
day cancellation notice-fee imposed. **Amenities:** dual phone lines, voice mail, safes, honor bars, irons, hair
dryers. **Fee:** video games, high-speed Internet. *Some:* DVD players (fee). **Dining:** 2 restaurants, 6 am-1 am, also, The Keg
Steakhouse and Bar, see separate listing. **Pool(s):** heated indoor. **Leisure Activities:** whirlpools, sun deck, exercise room,
game room. **Guest Services:** gift shop, complimentary evening beverages, valet and coin laundry, area transportation (fee)-
casino. **Business Services:** meeting rooms, business center. **Cards:** AX, DC, DS, JC, MC, VI.
(See color ad p 539 & starting on p 170)

SOME UNITS
FEE

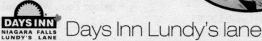

Located in the heart of many Attractions, Restaurants, & the Falls!

Ten Minute Walk to
Casino Niagara &
Fallsview Casino

GREAT LOCATION!

10% Discount for AAA/CAA Members off Published Rates

DAYS INN
NEAR THE FALLS

DIRECT TO HOTEL
1-800-461-9944

5943 Victoria Avenue
Niagara Falls, Ontario • Canada L2G 3L8
Tel. 905-374-3333 • Fax.905-374-0669

⌖120 Attractive Rooms
⌖Heart-Shaped Jacuzzi Rooms ⌖Satellite TV
⌖Indoor Pool, Whirlpool & Sauna
⌖Family Affordable Rates
⌖Kids Stay Free

www.daysinn-nearthefalls.com

(See map and index starting on p. 511)

FALLSVIEW CASINO RESORT

			Phone: 905/358-3255	58
7/1-8/31	1P: $279-$449	2P: $279-$449	XP: $50	F12
5/1-6/30 & 9/1-10/31	1P: $239-$419	2P: $239-$419	XP: $50	F12
11/1-4/30	1P: $209-$419	2P: $209-$419	XP: $50	F12

Large-scale Hotel

Location: Jct Murray St. 6380 Fallsview Blvd L2G 7X5. Fax: 905/371-7950. **Facility:** This hotel features a large casino, a shopping gallery and an entertainment forum in addition to its elegantly appointed guest rooms. 374 units. 365 one-bedroom standard units, some with whirlpools. 9 one-bedroom suites ($339-$2020) with whirlpools. 35 stories, interior corridors. *Bath:* combo or shower only. **Terms:** 3 day cancellation notice-fee imposed, small pets only ($50 extra charge). **Amenities:** high-speed Internet, dual phone lines, voice mail, safes, irons, hair dryers. **Dining:** 8 restaurants, 24 hours, also, 17 Noir, The Famous Coffee Shop, see separate listings, entertainment. **Pool(s):** heated indoor. **Leisure Activities:** saunas, whirlpools, exercise room, spa. *Fee:* steamrooms. **Guest Services:** gift shop, valet laundry. **Business Services:** conference facilities, business center. **Cards:** AX, DS, MC, VI.

SOME UNITS

(icons) FEE

FALLSVIEW INN

			Phone: (905)374-4244	52
All Year	1P: $49-$199	2P: $49-$199		F16

Small-scale Hotel

Location: 0.8 mi (1.2 km) w on Hwy 20, just s. 6170 Stanley Ave L2G 3Y4. Fax: 905/374-6142. **Facility:** 65 one-bedroom standard units, some with whirlpools. 5 stories, interior corridors. **Parking:** on-site. **Terms:** package plans. **Amenities:** irons, hair dryers. **Dining:** 8 am-11 & 5-9 pm, cocktails. **Pool(s):** heated indoor. **Leisure Activities:** sauna, whirlpool, exercise room. **Cards:** AX, DS, MC, VI.
(See color ad below & starting on p 170)

SOME UNITS

(icons) FEE

FLAMINGO THRIFTLODGE   *Book great rates at AAA.com*

			Phone: (905)356-4646	37
6/29-8/25	1P: $79-$169	2P: $79-$189	XP: $10	F
5/1-6/28 & 8/26-10/6	1P: $59-$129	2P: $59-$129	XP: $10	F
10/7-4/30	1P: $49-$99	2P: $59-$99	XP: $10	F

Motel

Location: QEW, exit Hwy 20, 2.1 mi (3.4 km) w. 7701 Lundy's Ln L2H 1H3. Fax: 905/356-9373. **Facility:** 92 one-bedroom standard units, some with whirlpools. 2 stories (no elevator), exterior corridors. **Parking:** on-site, winter plug-ins. **Terms:** package plans, small pets only ($10 extra charge). **Amenities:** high-speed Internet (fee), voice mail. **Pool(s):** heated outdoor. **Leisure Activities:** playground, limited exercise equipment. **Guest Services:** area transportation (fee)-falls & casino. **Business Services:** PC (fee). **Cards:** AX, CB, DC, DS, MC, VI. **Free Special Amenities:** local telephone calls and newspaper. *(See color ad p 546)*

SOME UNITS

(icons) FEE   FEE FEE

(See map and index starting on p. 511)

GREAT WOLF LODGE INDOOR WATERPARK RESORT

Phone: (905)354-4888

7/1-8/31	1P: $359-$599	2P: $359-$599	XP: $20
5/1-6/30	1P: $299-$599	2P: $299-$599	XP: $20
9/1-4/30	1P: $199-$559	2P: $199-$559	XP: $20

Resort
Large-scale Hotel

Location: Jct Niagara Pkwy. 3950 Victoria Ave L2E 7M8. Fax: 905/354-5588. **Facility:** Catering to the family market, this busy resort is very activity-oriented: find a water park, log cabin theme and spacious rooms, some with bunk beds. Smoke free premises. 406 units. 344 one- and 32 two-bedroom standard units, some with whirlpools. 30 one-bedroom suites. 4 stories, interior corridors. *Bath:* combo or shower only. **Parking:** on-site. **Terms:** check-in 4 pm, 3 day cancellation notice-fee imposed, package plans. **Amenities:** video games (fee), high-speed Internet, voice mail, safes, irons, hair dryers. **Dining:** 5 restaurants, 7 am-midnight. **Pool(s):** heated outdoor, 7 heated indoor, wading. **Leisure Activities:** whirlpools, waterslide, wave pool, lazy river water ride, playground, exercise room, spa, basketball, volleyball, game room. **Fee:** miniature golf. **Guest Services:** gift shop, valet and coin laundry, area transportation (fee)-local attractions & falls. **Business Services:** meeting rooms. **Cards:** AX, DC, DS, MC, VI. *(See color ad p 547)*

(See map and index starting on p. 511)

HAMPTON INN AT THE FALLS *Book great rates at AAA.com* Phone: (905)357-1626 **9**

6/1-10/31 [ECP]	1P: $169-$429	2P: $169-$429	XP: $20	F18
5/1-5/31 [ECP]	1P: $129-$389	2P: $129-$389	XP: $20	F18
11/1-4/30 [ECP]	1P: $89-$299	2P: $89-$299	XP: $20	F18

Small-scale Hotel **Location:** At top of Clifton Hill; ne of the falls. 5591 Victoria Ave L2G 3L4. Fax: 905/357-5869. **Facility:** 127 units. 105 one- and 22 two-bedroom standard units, some with whirlpools. 6 stories, interior corridors. **Parking:** on-site. **Terms:** cancellation fee imposed, package plans, 3% service charge. **Amenities:** video games (fee), high-speed Internet, voice mail, irons. *Some:* hair dryers. **Pool(s):** heated indoor. **Leisure Activities:** sauna, whirlpool. **Guest Services:** gift shop, valet laundry. **Business Services:** meeting rooms. **Cards:** AX, DC, DS, MC, VI. **Free Special Amenities: full breakfast.** *(See color ad p 546)*

SOME UNITS

HAMPTON INN NORTH OF THE FALLS *Book great rates at AAA.com* Phone: 905/358-5555 **6**

5/19-9/3	1P: $99-$249	2P: $99-$249	XP: $10	F16
9/4-4/30	1P: $59-$199	2P: $59-$199	XP: $10	F16

Small-scale Hotel **Location:** 1.8 mi (2.8 km) n of the falls. 4357 River Rd L2E 3E8. Fax: 905/358-0140. **Facility:** 105 one-bedroom standard units, some with whirlpools. 5 stories, interior corridors. **Parking:** on-site. **Terms:** 3 day cancellation notice-fee imposed, package plans. **Amenities:** high-speed Internet, voice mail, irons, hair dryers. **Pool(s):** heated indoor. **Leisure Activities:** sauna, whirlpool. **Guest Services:** area transportation. **Cards:** AX, DC, DS, MC, VI. *(See color ad below)*

SOME UNITS

HILTON NIAGARA FALLS FALLSVIEW *Book great rates at AAA.com* Phone: (905)354-7887 **57**

6/15-9/3	1P: $149-$499	2P: $149-$499	XP: $25	F12
5/1-6/14 & 9/4-4/30	1P: $99-$349	2P: $99-$349	XP: $25	F12

Large-scale Hotel **Facility:** Good views of the falls are offered from many of the hotel's rooms as well as from its rooftop restaurant; a waterslide is featured. 516 one-bedroom standard units, some with whirlpools. 34 stories, interior corridors. **Parking:** on-site (fee) and valet. **Terms:** check-in 4 pm, [AP] & [BP] meal plans available, package plans. **Amenities:** dual phone lines, voice mail, irons, hair dryers. *Fee:* video games, high-speed Internet. *Some:* safes. **Dining:** 7 am-10:30 pm, cocktails, also, The Watermark, see separate listing. **Pool(s):** heated indoor. **Leisure Activities:** sauna, whirlpool, steamroom, waterslide, exercise room. **Guest Services:** gift shop, valet laundry, area transportation-casino. **Business Services:** meeting rooms, business center. **Cards:** AX, DC, DS, MC, VI. **Free Special Amenities: newspaper and preferred room (subject to availability with advance reservations).** *(See color ad p 549 & starting on p 170)*

Location: Hwy 20, just s; across from Niagara Fallsview Casino. 6361 Fallsview Blvd L2G 3V9. Fax: 905/357-9300.

SOME UNITS

(See map and index starting on p. 511)

HOLIDAY INN BY THE FALLS

Book great rates at AAA.com   Phone: (905)356-1333   **55**

6/15-9/2	1P: $99-$275	2P: $99-$275	XP: $10	F19
5/1-6/14	1P: $75-$235	2P: $75-$235	XP: $10	F19
9/3-10/8	1P: $99-$225	2P: $99-$225	XP: $10	F19
10/9-4/30	1P: $79-$195	2P: $79-$195	XP: $10	F19

Small-scale Hotel **Location:** Just w of the falls; directly across from casino. Located adjacent to Skylon Tower. 5339 Murray St L2G 2J3. Fax: 905/356-7128. **Facility:** 122 one-bedroom standard units, some with whirlpools. 6 stories, interior corridors. **Parking:** on-site. **Terms:** cancellation fee imposed, package plans. **Amenities:** video games (fee), high-speed Internet, dual phone lines, voice mail, irons, hair dryers. **Dining:** 3 restaurants, 8 am-10 pm; 7 am-11 pm 6/14-10/15, cocktails, also, Wolfgang Puck Grand Cafe, see separate listing. **Pool(s):** heated outdoor, heated indoor. **Leisure Activities:** sauna, whirlpool. **Guest Services:** gift shop. **Cards:** AX, CB, DC, DS, MC, VI. **Free Special Amenities:** newspaper and high-speed Internet. *(See color ad p 550, p 569 & starting on p 170)*

SOME UNITS

HOWARD JOHNSON EXPRESS INN

Phone: (905)358-9777   **43**

6/29-9/2	1P: $65-$200	2P: $65-$200	XP: $10	F16
5/1-6/28 & 9/3-4/30	1P: $45-$150	2P: $45-$150	XP: $10	F16

Location: QEW, exit Hwy 20, 3.1 mi (5 km) w. 8100 Lundy's Ln L2H 1H1. Fax: 905/358-0575. **Facility:** 84 one-bedroom standard units, some with whirlpools. 2 stories (no elevator), exterior corridors. **Parking:** on-site, winter plug-ins. **Terms:** [CP] meal plan available, package plans. **Amenities:** voice mail, irons, hair dryers. **Motel** **Pool(s):** heated outdoor. **Guest Services:** area transportation (fee)-casino. **Cards:** AX, DC, DS, MC, VI. **Free Special Amenities:** continental breakfast and high-speed Internet.

SOME UNITS

FEE

HOWARD JOHNSON HOTEL BY THE FALLS

Book great rates at AAA.com   Phone: (905)357-4040   **25**

6/28-10/15	1P: $99-$329	2P: $99-$329	XP: $10	F16
10/16-12/31	1P: $79-$299	2P: $79-$299	XP: $10	F16
5/1-6/27	1P: $89-$259	2P: $89-$259	XP: $10	F16
1/1-4/30	1P: $69-$229	2P: $69-$229	XP: $10	F16

Small-scale Hotel **Location:** On Hwy 20; 0.4 mi (0.6 km) from the falls. 5905 Victoria Ave L2G 3L8. Fax: 905/357-6202. **Facility:** 199 units. 186 one- and 13 two-bedroom standard units, some with whirlpools. 7 stories, interior corridors. **Parking:** on-site (fee). **Terms:** check-in 4 pm, cancellation fee imposed, package plans. **Amenities:** video games (fee), voice mail, safes, irons, hair dryers. *Some:* high-speed Internet. **Dining:** 24 hours. **Pool(s):** heated indoor/outdoor. **Leisure Activities:** sauna, whirlpool. *Fee:* game room. **Guest Services:** valet and coin laundry, area transportation (fee)-casino. **Business Services:** meeting rooms, PC (fee). **Cards:** AX, DC, DS, JC, MC, VI. **Free Special Amenities:** local telephone calls and high-speed Internet. *(See color ad p 551)*

SOME UNITS

FEE   FEE

(See map and index starting on p. 511)

IMPERIAL HOTEL AND SUITES

Phone: (905)356-2648   **21**

(CAA) (SAVE)

5/1-9/30	1P: $69-$359	2P: $69-$359	XP: $10	F12
10/1-4/30	1P: $49-$259	2P: $49-$259	XP: $10	F12

Location: Hwy 20, 0.3 mi (0.5 km) from the falls. 5851 Victoria Ave L2G 3L6. Fax: 905/356-4068. **Facility:** 104 one-bedroom standard units, some with whirlpools. 10 stories, interior corridors. **Parking:** on-site (fee).

Small-scale Hotel **Terms:** check-in 4 pm, [AP], [BP] & [CP] meal plans available, package plans. **Amenities:** voice mail, safes (fee), hair dryers. *Some:* irons. **Dining:** 7 am-11 pm, cocktails. **Pool(s):** heated indoor. **Leisure Activities:** whirlpool, exercise room. *Fee:* game room. **Guest Services:** gift shop, coin laundry. **Business Services:** *Fee:* PC, fax. **Cards:** AX, CB, DC, DS, JC, MC, VI. **Free Special Amenities:** local telephone calls.

SOME UNITS

(icons)

KINGS INN NEAR THE FALLS   *Book at AAA.com*

Phone: (905)356-1233   **27**

6/17-9/2	1P: $79-$199	2P: $79-$199	XP: $15	F12
9/3-9/30	1P: $49-$199	2P: $49-$199	XP: $10	F12
5/1-6/16	1P: $49-$149	2P: $49-$149	XP: $10	F12
10/1-4/30	1P: $44-$89	2P: $44-$89	XP: $10	F12

Motel

Location: On Hwy 20, 0.6 mi (1 km) from the falls. Located in a commercial area. 5525 Ferry St L2G 1S3. Fax: 905/374-6412. **Facility:** 44 one-bedroom standard units, some with whirlpools. 3 stories (no elevator), exterior corridors. **Parking:** on-site. **Terms:** office hours 8 am-2 am, 3 day cancellation notice-fee imposed, package plans. **Pool(s):** heated outdoor. **Leisure Activities:** *Fee:* game room. **Cards:** AX, CB, DC, DS, JC, MC, VI.

SOME UNITS

(icons)

KNIGHTS INN   *Book great rates at AAA.com*

Phone: (905)354-6939   **35**

(CAA) (SAVE)

6/27-9/6	1P: $79-$249	2P: $79-$249	XP: $10	F16
5/1-6/26	1P: $55-$199	2P: $55-$199	XP: $10	F16
9/7-4/30	1P: $49-$199	2P: $49-$199	XP: $10	F16

Motel

Location: 2.1 mi (3.4 km) w on Hwy 20. Located in a commercial area. 7034 Lundy's Ln L2G 1V9. Fax: 905/354-3699. **Facility:** 64 one-bedroom standard units. 2 stories (no elevator), exterior corridors. **Parking:** on-site. **Amenities:** high-speed Internet. **Pool(s):** heated outdoor. **Guest Services:** area transportation (fee)-casino & falls. **Business Services:** PC, fax (fee). **Cards:** AX, DC, DS, MC, VI. **Free Special Amenities:** local telephone calls.

SOME UNITS

(icons)   FEE   FEE

(See map and index starting on p. 511)

KNIGHTS INN-BY THE FALLS   *Book great rates at AAA.com*   Phone: (905)358-8132   **56**

CAA SAVE

	6/27-9/3	1P: $79-$249	2P: $79-$249	XP: $5	F16
	5/1-6/26	1P: $59-$199	2P: $59-$199	XP: $5	F16
	9/4-4/30	1P: $54-$189	2P: $54-$189	XP: $5	F16

Motel

Location: Jct Murray St. 6276 Main St L2G 6A4. Fax: 905/358-2777. **Facility:** 47 one-bedroom standard units, some with efficiencies and/or whirlpools. 1-2 stories (no elevator), exterior corridors. *Bath:* combo or shower only. **Parking:** on-site. **Terms:** package plans. **Pool(s):** heated outdoor, wading. **Leisure Activities:** whirlpool. **Cards:** AX, DC, DS, MC, VI. **Free Special Amenities:** local telephone calls and newspaper.
(See color ad starting on p 170)

SOME UNITS

⑤Ⓓ 🍴 🏊 🎥 / ✕ ▤ 🖥 /
                              FEE FEE

LODGE NEAR THE FALLS (NOW KNOWN AS COUNTRY HEARTH INN & SUITES)   Phone: (905)374-7771   **28**

	6/16-8/31	1P: $89-$399	2P: $89-$399
	5/1-6/15	1P: $59-$269	2P: $59-$269
	9/1-12/31	1P: $79-$249	2P: $79-$249
	1/1-4/30	1P: $59-$229	2P: $59-$229

Small-scale Hotel

Location: Jct Victoria Ave. 5234 Ferry St L2G 1R5. Fax: 905/374-1996. **Facility:** 86 one-bedroom standard units, some with whirlpools. 2-4 stories, interior/exterior corridors. *Bath:* combo or shower only. **Parking:** on-site (fee). **Terms:** [BP] meal plan available, package plans, 3% service charge. **Amenities:** hair dryers. **Pool(s):** heated indoor. **Leisure Activities:** sauna, whirlpool. **Cards:** AX, DC, MC, VI. *(See color ad below)*

SOME UNITS

ⒶⓈⓀ ⑤Ⓓ 🍴 🏊 🎥 🖥 / ✕

MARRIOTT NIAGARA FALLS FALLSVIEW HOTEL AND SPA   *Book great rates at AAA.com*   Phone: (905)357-7300   **69**

CAA SAVE

	6/16-9/3	1P: $189-$599	2P: $189-$599	XP: $10	F12
	9/4-10/12	1P: $159-$599	2P: $159-$599	XP: $10	F12
	5/1-6/15	1P: $149-$599	2P: $149-$599	XP: $10	F12
	10/13-4/30	1P: $119-$599	2P: $119-$599	XP: $10	F12

Large-scale Hotel **Location:** Next to Konica Minolta Tower. 6740 Fallsview Blvd L2G 3W6. Fax: 905/357-0490. **Facility:** On a hilltop, the hotel offers good views of the falls from many of its guest rooms and common areas. Smoke free premises. 432 units. 342 one-bedroom standard units, some with whirlpools. 90 one-bedroom suites, some with whirlpools. 23 stories, interior corridors. **Parking:** on-site (fee) and valet. **Terms:** 3 day cancellation notice-fee imposed, [BP] & [CP] meal plans available, package plans. **Amenities:** dual phone lines, voice mail, safes, honor bars, irons, hair dryers. *Fee:* video games, high-speed Internet. *Some:* CD players. **Dining:** Terrapin Grille, see separate listing. **Pool(s):** heated indoor. **Leisure Activities:** saunas, whirlpools, steamrooms, exercise room, spa. *Fee:* game room. **Guest Services:** gift shop, valet laundry, area transportation (fee)-casino. **Business Services:** meeting rooms, business center. **Cards:** AX, DC, DS, JC, MC, VI.
(See color ad p 539, starting on p 170 & inside front cover)

⑤Ⓓ 🍴 🍸 🗂M 🍴 🏊 🚫 ✕ 🎥 🖥

(See map and index starting on p. 511)

MICHAEL'S INN-BY THE FALLS

(CAA) (SAVE)

♦♦♦ ♦♦♦ ♦♦♦

Book great rates at AAA.com

6/8-9/15	1P: $88-$288	2P: $88-$288	XP: $5
5/1-6/7 & 9/16-11/3	1P: $58-$178	2P: $58-$178	XP: $5
11/4-4/30	1P: $48-$158	2P: $48-$158	XP: $5

Phone: (905)354-2727   **11**

F12
F12
F12

Location: Just n of Rainbow Bridge and QEW. 5599 River Rd L2E 3H3. Fax: 905/374-7706. **Facility:** 129 units. **Small-scale Hotel** 128 one- and 1 two-bedroom standard units, some with whirlpools. 4 stories, interior corridors. **Parking:** on-site. **Terms:** package plans. **Amenities:** voice mail, irons, hair dryers. *Fee:* video games, high-speed Internet. **Dining:** 7 am-11 pm; 8 am-9 pm 11/1-4/30, cocktails. **Pool(s):** heated indoor, wading. **Leisure Activities:** sauna, whirlpool, sun deck, exercise room. *Fee:* game room. **Guest Services:** sundries, valet laundry. **Business Services:** meeting rooms, business center. **Cards:** AX, CB, DC, JC, MC, VI. **Free Special Amenities: continental breakfast and local telephone calls.** *(See color ad below)*

SOME UNITS

NIAGARA FALLS MOTOR LODGE

♦♦♦ ♦♦♦

Motel

Property failed to provide current rates

Phone: 905/295-3569

Location: 1.3 mi (2 km) s of Horseshoe Falls on Niagara River Pkwy to Portage Rd S; 0.7 mi (1.2 km) s of Marineland. Located in a residential area. 7950 Portage Rd S L2G 5Y8. Fax: 905/295-0022. **Facility:** 21 units. 20 one-bedroom standard units. 1 three-bedroom suite with kitchen. 2 stories (no elevator), exterior corridors. **Parking:** on-site. **Terms:** office hours 7 am-11 pm. **Amenities:** high-speed Internet. **Pool(s):** heated outdoor. **Guest Services:** area transportation (fee). **Business Services:** fax (fee).

SOME UNITS

NIAGARA FALLS PLAZA HOTEL

(CAA) (SAVE)

♦♦♦ ♦♦♦

6/16-8/31	2P: $119-$249	XP: $15
5/1-6/15 & 9/1-10/31	2P: $75-$129	XP: $10
11/1-4/30	2P: $70-$119	XP: $10

Phone: 905/353-1010   **26**

F16
F16
F16

Location: Jct Main and Ferry sts, just s. 5807 Ferry St L2G 1S8. Fax: 905/358-7131. **Facility:** 145 one-bedroom **Large-scale Hotel** standard units, some with whirlpools. 2-11 stories, interior corridors. *Bath:* combo or shower only. **Parking:** on-site. **Terms:** [BP] meal plan available, small pets only (in designated units). **Amenities:** hair dryers. *Some:* high-speed Internet. **Pool(s):** heated outdoor, heated indoor. **Leisure Activities:** whirlpool. **Business Services:** meeting rooms, PC (fee). **Cards:** AX, MC, VI. **Free Special Amenities: local telephone calls and newspaper.**

SOME UNITS

(See map and index starting on p. 511)

NIAGARA FAMILY INN
Phone: 905/354-9844   **14**

CAA SAVE	6/29-9/3	1P: $55-$105	2P: $69-$115	XP: $10	F12
	9/4-4/30	1P: $49-$95	2P: $59-$105	XP: $10	F12
	5/1-6/28	1P: $49-$89	2P: $59-$105	XP: $10	F12

Motel   **Location:** Jct Clifton Hill, just e. 5612 Ellen Ave L2G 7V5. Fax: 905/354-6691. **Facility:** 36 one-bedroom standard units. 2 stories (no elevator), interior/exterior corridors. *Bath:* combo or shower only. **Parking:** on-site. **Terms:** 5 day cancellation notice-fee imposed, package plans. **Dining:** 3 pm-11 pm, cocktails. **Pool(s):** heated outdoor. **Business Services:** meeting rooms. **Cards:** AX, DS, MC, VI. **Free Special Amenities:** early check-in/late check-out and preferred room (subject to availability with advance reservations).

SOME UNITS

NIAGARA PARKWAY COURT MOTEL
Phone: (905)295-3331

CAA SAVE	7/1-9/30	1P: $69-$119	2P: $89-$149	XP: $10	F13
	5/1-6/30	1P: $59-$99	2P: $69-$119	XP: $10	F13
	10/1-1/1	1P: $59-$69	2P: $69-$79	XP: $10	F13
	1/2-4/30	1P: $39-$49	2P: $49-$729	XP: $10	F13

Motel   **Location:** 1.6 mi (2.5 km) s of the falls. Located in a quiet area. 3708 Main St (Niagara River Pkwy S) L2G 6B1. Fax: 905/295-2739. **Facility:** 19 one-bedroom standard units, some with efficiencies and/or whirlpools. 3 stories (no elevator), exterior corridors. **Parking:** on-site. **Terms:** cancellation fee imposed, [CP] meal plan available, package plans, small pets only ($10 extra charge, in designated units). **Cards:** AX, DS, JC, MC, VI. **Free Special Amenities:** local telephone calls and early check-in/late check-out.

SOME UNITS
FEE

THE OAKES HOTEL OVERLOOKING THE FALLS
Book great rates at AAA.com   Phone: (905)356-4514   **61**

CAA SAVE	All Year	1P: $49-$699	2P: $49-$729	XP: $10 F18

Location: By Konica Minolta Tower; adjacent to casino. 6546 Fallsview Blvd L2G 3W2. Fax: 905/356-3651. **Facility:** 239 one-bedroom standard units, some with whirlpools. 2-21 stories, interior/exterior corridors. **Parking:** on-site (fee). **Terms:** cancellation fee imposed, 3% service charge. **Amenities:** voice mail, irons, Large-scale Hotel hair dryers. *Some:* high-speed Internet (fee), dual phone lines. **Dining:** 7 am-midnight, cocktails. **Pool(s):** heated indoor. **Leisure Activities:** sauna, whirlpool, exercise room. **Guest Services:** gift shop, valet laundry, area transportation (fee)-casino. **Business Services:** meeting rooms. *Fee:* PC, fax. **Cards:** AX, DC, DS, JC, MC, VI. *(See color ad starting on p 542 & starting on p 170)*

SOME UNITS

OLD STONE INN
Book at AAA.com   Phone: (905)357-1234   **49**

	10/16-4/30	1P: $80-$369	2P: $80-$369	XP: $15	F12
	6/1-10/15	1P: $129-$299	2P: $129-$299	XP: $15	F12
	5/1-5/31	1P: $95-$249	2P: $95-$249	XP: $15	F12

Small-scale Hotel   **Location:** Just w via Murray St, just n on Buchanan Ave. Located adjacent to Skylon Tower. 5425 Robinson St L2G 7L6. Fax: 905/357-9299. **Facility:** 112 units. 110 one-bedroom standard units, some with whirlpools. 2 one-bedroom suites ($189-$399) with whirlpools. 3 stories, interior/exterior corridors. **Parking:** on-site, winter plug-ins. **Terms:** check-in 4 pm, cancellation fee imposed, package plans. **Amenities:** video games, high-speed Internet, voice mail, hair dryers. *Some:* irons. **Dining:** The Millery Dining Room, see separate listing. **Pool(s):** heated outdoor, heated indoor. **Leisure Activities:** whirlpool. **Guest Services:** valet laundry. **Business Services:** meeting rooms. **Cards:** AX, CB, DC, DS, JC, MC, VI. *(See color ad starting on p 170)*

SOME UNITS

PENINSULA INN & RESORT
Phone: (905)354-8812   **50**

CAA SAVE	6/29-9/4	1P: $89-$189	2P: $89-$189	XP: $10 F12
	5/1-6/28 & 9/5-4/30	1P: $69-$189	2P: $69-$189	XP: $10 F12

Location: QEW, exit McLeod Rd, just w. Located in a quiet area. 7373 Niagara Square Dr L2E 6S5. Fax: 905/354-7174. **Facility:** 95 units. 93 one-bedroom standard units, some with whirlpools. 2 one-Small-scale Hotel bedroom suites. 5 stories, interior corridors. **Parking:** on-site. **Terms:** cancellation fee imposed, package plans, small pets only ($10 fee, with prior approval). **Amenities:** dual phone lines, voice mail, irons, hair dryers. **Dining:** 7:30-11 am; also 5:30 pm-9:30 pm 6/1-9/30, cocktails. **Pool(s):** heated indoor. **Leisure Activities:** sauna, whirlpool, exercise room, spa. *Fee:* game room. **Guest Services:** gift shop, valet laundry, area transportation (fee)-casino & falls. **Business Services:** meeting rooms, PC (fee). **Cards:** AX, MC, VI. **Free Special Amenities:** local telephone calls and early check-in/late check-out.

SOME UNITS
FEE   FEE

THE PRESIDENT MOTOR INN
Phone: 905/358-7272   **60**

Property failed to provide current rates

Motel   **Location:** Corner of Stanley and Dixon aves; just w of Konica Minolta Tower. 6503 Stanley Ave L2G 7L2. Fax: 905/356-0392. **Facility:** 42 one-bedroom standard units. 2 stories (no elevator), exterior corridors. **Parking:** on-site. **Terms:** open 5/1-10/15, office hours 8 am-11 pm. **Pool(s):** outdoor. *(See color ad starting on p 170)*

SOME UNITS

QUALITY INN CLIFTON HILL
Book great rates at AAA.com   Phone: (905)358-3601   **20**

CAA SAVE	7/1-9/2	1P: $89-$269	2P: $89-$269	XP: $10	F18
	9/3-12/31	1P: $59-$269	2P: $59-$269	XP: $10	F18
	5/1-6/30	1P: $59-$229	2P: $59-$229	XP: $10	F18
	1/1-4/30	1P: $49-$179	2P: $49-$179	XP: $10	F18

Small-scale Hotel   **Location:** Jct Victoria Ave and Clifton Hill, just s. 4946 Clifton Hill L2E 6S8 (PO Box 60, NIAGARA FALLS, ON). Fax: 905/358-3818. **Facility:** 251 units. 243 one- and 8 two-bedroom standard units, some with whirlpools. 2-3 stories (no elevator), interior/exterior corridors. **Parking:** on-site. **Terms:** package plans. **Pool(s):** heated outdoor, heated indoor, wading. **Leisure Activities:** whirlpool, playground. **Cards:** AX, CB, DC, DS, JC, MC, VI. **Free Special Amenities:** local telephone calls and newspaper. *(See color ad p 537)*

SOME UNITS

(See map and index starting on p. 511)

RADISSON HOTEL & SUITES FALLSVIEW   *Book great rates at AAA.com*   Phone: 905/356-1944   65

(CAA) (SAVE)	6/30-8/16	1P: $117-$170	2P: $117-$170	XP: $10	F12
	8/17-4/30	1P: $80-$170	2P: $80-$170	XP: $10	F12
◊◊◊◊	5/18-6/29	1P: $107-$161	2P: $107-$161	XP: $10	F12
	5/1-5/17	1P: $81-$135	2P: $81-$135	XP: $10	F12

Large-scale Hotel **Location:** Corner of Stanley Ave and Dunn St. Located across from Konica Minolta Tower. 6733 Fallsview Blvd L2G 3W7. Fax: 905/374-2555. **Facility:** 232 units. 218 one-bedroom standard units, some with whirlpools. 14 one-bedroom suites with whirlpools. 16 stories, interior corridors. **Parking:** on-site (fee) and valet. **Terms:** check-in 4 pm, cancellation fee imposed, package plans, 3% service charge. **Amenities:** dual phone lines, voice mail, irons, hair dryers. *Fee:* video games, high-speed Internet. *Some:* safes. **Dining:** 7 am-midnight, also, Outback Steakhouse, see separate listing. *Some:* safes. **Pool(s):** heated indoor. **Leisure Activities:** exercise room. *Fee:* massage. **Guest Services:** gift shop, valet laundry. **Business Services:** meeting rooms, business center. **Cards:** AX, CB, DC, DS, JC, MC, VI. *(See color ad p 556 & starting on p 170)*

SOME UNITS

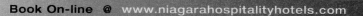

(See map and index starting on p. 511)

RAMADA ALL SUITES HOTEL AND CONFERENCE
CENTER *Book great rates at AAA.com*   **Phone:** (905)356-6119   [31]

(CAA) (SAVE)   9/6-4/30   1P: $79-$259   2P: $79-$259   XP: $10   F
            5/1-9/5   1P: $99-$249   2P: $99-$249   XP: $10   F
▼▼▼▼▼   **Location:** QEW, exit Hwy 20 W; from downtown, 2.5 mi (4 km) w. 7389 Lundy's Ln L2H 2W9. Fax: 905/357-7630.
            Facility: 73 units. 4 one-bedroom standard units with whirlpools. 69 one-bedroom suites, some with
Small-scale Hotel whirlpools. 6 stories, interior corridors. **Parking:** on-site, winter plug-ins. **Terms:** cancellation fee imposed,
            [AP], [BP] & [CP] meal plans available, package plans. **Amenities:** video games (fee), high-speed Internet,
voice mail, irons, hair dryers. **Dining:** 7 am-9 pm, cocktails. **Pool(s):** heated indoor. **Leisure Activities:** whirlpool, steamroom,
exercise room. **Guest Services:** valet laundry, area transportation (fee)-attractions & casino. **Business Services:** conference
facilities, business center. **Cards:** AX, DS, MC, VI.
                                                                                          SOME UNITS
                          [S🄳] [🍴] [🍷] [🛬] [✕] [🐾] [🔒] [📷] [📺] /[✕]/

RAMADA CORAL HOTEL   *Book great rates at AAA.com*   **Phone:** (905)356-6116   [32]

(CAA) (SAVE)   5/1-9/4   1P: $69-$169   2P: $69-$169   XP: $10   F16
            9/5-4/30   1P: $59-$159   2P: $59-$159   XP: $10   F16
▼▼▼ ▼▼▼   **Location:** QEW, exit Hwy 20 W; from downtown, 2.5 mi (4 km) w. 7429 Lundy Ln L2H 1G9. Fax: 905/356-7121.
            Facility: 129 one-bedroom standard units, some with whirlpools. 4 stories, interior corridors. **Parking:** on-
Small-scale Hotel site, winter plug-ins. **Terms:** cancellation fee imposed, package plans, 3% service charge. **Amenities:** video
games (fee), high-speed Internet, voice mail, irons, hair dryers. **Dining:** 11 am-11 pm; from 4 pm 11/1-6/1,
cocktails. **Pool(s):** heated outdoor, heated indoor. **Leisure Activities:** sauna, whirlpool, indoor children's play park. *Fee:* game
room. **Guest Services:** gift shop, valet laundry, area transportation (fee)-attractions & casino. **Business Services:** meeting
rooms. **Cards:** AX, DC, MC, VI. **Free Special Amenities:** high-speed Internet. *(See color ad below)*
                                                                                          SOME UNITS
                          [S🄳] [🍴] [🍷] [🛬] [🌊] [✕] [🐾] [📺] /[✕]/

(See map and index starting on p. 511)

RAMADA PLAZA HOTEL FALLSVIEW   *Book great rates at AAA.com*   Phone: 905/356-1501   **68**

9/5-12/31	1P: $99-$329	2P: $99-$329
7/1-9/4	1P: $139-$279	2P: $139-$279
5/1-6/30	1P: $109-$189	2P: $109-$189
1/1-4/30	1P: $79-$159	2P: $79-$159

Large-scale Hotel

Location: In Konica Minolta Tower. 6732 Fallsview Blvd L2G 3W6. Fax: 905/356-8245. **Facility:** 42 one-bedroom standard units, some with whirlpools. 30 stories, interior corridors. *Bath:* combo or shower only. **Parking:** on-site (fee) and valet. **Terms:** check-in 4 pm, age restrictions may apply, cancellation fee imposed, package plans. **Amenities:** voice mail, safes, irons, hair dryers. **Dining:** The Pinnacle Restaurant-Atop the Konica Minolta Tower, see separate listing. **Guest Services:** gift shop, valet laundry. **Cards:** AX, DC, DS, MC, VI. *(See color ad starting on p 170 & below)*

SOME UNITS

(A$K) (S/D) (TI) (O) (O) (O) / (X) /

RENAISSANCE FALLSVIEW HOTEL   *Book great rates at AAA.com*   Phone: (905)357-5200   **59**

(CAA) (SAVE)	7/1-8/31	1P: $149-$499	2P: $149-$499	XP: $10 F18
	9/1-10/31	1P: $99-$499	2P: $99-$499	XP: $10 F18
	5/1-6/30 & 11/1-4/30	1P: $99-$299	2P: $99-$299	XP: $10 F18

Large-scale Hotel

Location: Corner of Fallsview Blvd and Dixon Ave; across from Niagara Fallsview Casino. 6455 Fallsview Blvd L2G 3V9. Fax: 905/357-3422. **Facility:** This centrally located hotel with distinctive contemporary decor throughout guest rooms and public areas is convenient to the area's attractions. Smoke free premises. 262 one-bedroom standard units, some with whirlpools. 18 stories, interior corridors. **Parking:** on-site (fee) and valet. **Terms:** check-in 4 pm, 3 day cancellation notice-fee imposed, package plans, 3% service charge. **Amenities:** video games (fee), dual phone lines, voice mail, irons, hair dryers. **Dining:** 6 am-11 pm, also, Rooftop Fallsview Grille, see separate listing. **Pool(s):** heated indoor. **Leisure Activities:** saunas, whirlpool. *Fee:* racquetball court, squash court. **Guest Services:** gift shop, valet laundry, wireless Internet. **Business Services:** conference facilities, business center. **Cards:** AX, CB, DC, DS, JC, MC, VI. **Free Special Amenities:** newspaper and high-speed Internet. *(See color ad p 558 & starting on p 170)*

SOME UNITS

(S/D) (TI) (Y) (&M) (O) (O) (X) (X) (O) / (O) /

FEE

(See map and index starting on p. 511)

RITZ INN NIAGARA   *Book great rates at AAA.com*   Phone: (905)356-4490   66

CAA SAVE	7/1-9/9	1P: $69-$119	2P: $69-$119	XP: $10	D12
	5/1-6/30	1P: $59-$99	2P: $59-$99	XP: $10	D12
◇	9/10-1/2	1P: $55-$89	2P: $59-$99	XP: $10	D12
Motel	1/3-4/30	1P: $49-$79	2P: $59-$89	XP: $10	D12

Location: Just w of Konica Minolta Tower; 3 blks from casino. Located in a residential area. 5630 Dunn St L2G 2N7. Fax: 905/374-8401. **Facility:** 29 one-bedroom standard units, some with efficiencies and/or whirlpools. 2 stories (no elevator), exterior corridors. **Parking:** on-site. **Terms:** 3 day cancellation notice-fee imposed, package plans, 4% service charge. **Amenities:** high-speed Internet. **Pool(s):** heated outdoor. **Guest Services:** coin laundry. **Business Services:** PC (fee). **Cards:** AX, DC, MC, VI. **Free Special Amenities:** local telephone calls and early check-in/late check-out. *(See color ad below)*

SOME UNITS
S/D 🚭 / ✕ 🔒 🖨 /

(See map and index starting on p. 511)

RODEWAY INN & SUITES   Phone: (905)358-9833   **39**

6/16-8/31	1P: $69-$129	2P: $69-$129	XP: $5 F16
9/1-10/31	1P: $59-$109	2P: $59-$109	XP: $5 F16
Small-scale Hotel 5/1-6/15 & 11/1-4/30	1P: $59-$99	2P: $59-$99	XP: $5 F16

Location: QEW, exit Hwy 20, 2.5 mi (4 km) w. 7720 Lundy's Ln L2H 1H1. Fax: 905/358-3090. **Facility:** 95 one-bedroom standard units, some with whirlpools. 2-3 stories, interior/exterior corridors. **Parking:** on-site. **Terms:** [CP] meal plan available. **Pool(s):** outdoor, heated indoor. **Leisure Activities:** whirlpool. **Business Services:** PC. **Cards:** AX, CB, DC, DS, JC, MC, VI.

SOME UNITS

(ASK) (SD) (†↑→) (⇆) (▣) / (✕) (▤) (▦) / FEE

RODEWAY INN FALLSVIEW   *Book great rates at AAA.com*   Phone: (905)354-2322   **67**

6/29-9/2	1P: $89-$259	2P: $89-$259	XP: $10 F17
5/1-6/28 & 9/3-4/30	1P: $59-$179	2P: $59-$179	XP: $10 F17

Location: Jct Dunn St. 6663 Stanley Ave L2G 3Y9. Fax: 905/354-4955. **Facility:** 61 one-bedroom standard units, some with whirlpools. 2-3 stories (no elevator), interior/exterior corridors. **Parking:** on-site. **Terms:** cancellation fee imposed, package plans. **Amenities:** voice mail, irons, hair dryers. **Dining:** 2 restaurants, 7 am-midnight, cocktails. **Pool(s):** heated outdoor. **Leisure Activities:** playground. **Guest Services:** gift shop. **Business Services:** meeting rooms, PC (fee). **Cards:** AX, DC, DS, MC, VI. **Free Special Amenities:** local telephone calls and newspaper. *(See color ad below & starting on p 170)*

SOME UNITS

(SD) (†↑) (⇆) (✸) (▣) / (✕) (▦) / FEE

**SHERATON FALLSVIEW HOTEL & CONFERENCE
CENTRE**   *Book great rates at AAA.com*   Phone: (905)374-1077   **70**

5/1-9/30	1P: $149-$399	2P: $149-$399	XP: $20 F18
4/1-4/30	1P: $129-$399	2P: $129-$399	XP: $20 F18
10/1-12/31	1P: $99-$299	2P: $99-$299	XP: $20 F18
1/1-3/31	1P: $89-$299	2P: $89-$299	XP: $20 F18

Location: Near Konica Minolta Tower. 6755 Fallsview Blvd L2G 3W7. Fax: 905/374-6224. **Facility:** Guest rooms in this high-rise have modern, well-appointed decor; many offer very good views of the falls. 402 units. 376 one- and 8 two-bedroom standard units, some with whirlpools. 18 one-bedroom suites ($199-$699) with whirlpools. 32 stories, interior corridors. **Parking:** on-site (fee). **Terms:** 2 night minimum stay - seasonal and/or weekends, cancellation fee imposed, [BP] meal plan available, package plans, pets (small dogs only, $25 fee, with prior approval). **Amenities:** dual phone lines, voice mail, irons, hair dryers. **Fee:** video games, high-speed Internet. *Some:* safes. **Dining:** 7 am-1 am, also, A Cut Above Steakhouse, La Piazza Bistro & Cafe, see separate listings. **Pool(s):** heated indoor. **Leisure Activities:** sauna, whirlpool, exercise room. **Guest Services:** gift shop, valet laundry. **Business Services:** conference facilities, business center. **Cards:** AX, CB, DC, DS, JC, MC, VI. *(See color ad p 561, starting on p 170 & coupon in Savings Section)*

SOME UNITS

(SD) (🛏) (†↑) (Ⳟ) (⌂M) (⇆) (✕) (✸) (▣) / (✕) (VCR) (▦) (▤) / FEE

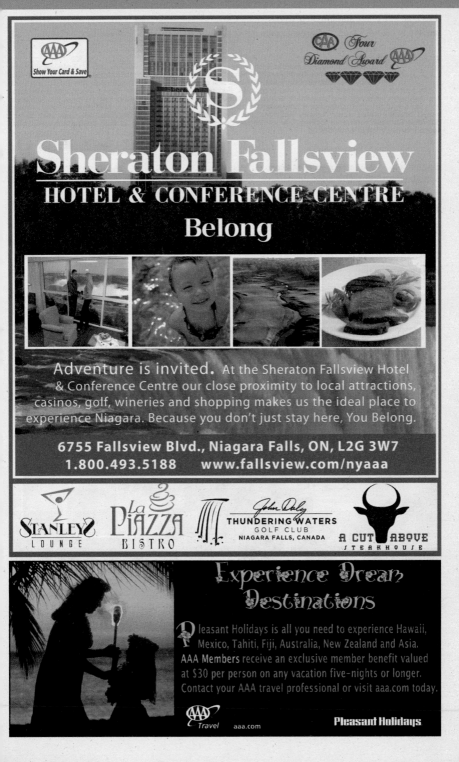

(See map and index starting on p. 511)

SHERATON ON THE FALLS *Book great rates at AAA.com*   Phone: (905)374-4445   [22]

ⓒⒶ SAVE	6/1-10/15	1P: $169-$999	2P: $169-$999	XP: $20	F18
	5/1-5/31	1P: $129-$999	2P: $129-$999	XP: $20	F18
▽▽▽▽▽	10/16-4/30	1P: $99-$999	2P: $99-$999	XP: $20	F18

Large-scale Hotel **Location:** Entrance to Rainbow Bridge on Hwy 20. 5875 Falls Ave L2E 6W7. Fax: 905/371-8349. **Facility:** This large hotel offers a hard-to-beat location; adjacent to a casino and directly across the street from the falls. Many units offer stunning views. 670 units. 659 one-bedroom standard units, some with whirlpools. 11 one-bedroom suites with whirlpools. 24 stories, interior corridors. **Parking:** on-site (fee) and valet. **Terms:** cancellation fee imposed, package plans, small pets only. **Amenities:** dual phone lines, voice mail, irons, hair dryers. **Fee:** video games, high-speed Internet. *Some:* CD players. **Dining:** 6 am-midnight, cocktails, also, Penthouse Restaurant, see separate listing. **Pool(s):** heated outdoor, heated indoor. **Leisure Activities:** spa. **Fee:** exercise room. **Guest Services:** gift shop, valet laundry. **Business Services:** conference facilities, business center. **Cards:** AX, CB, DC, DS, MC, VI. **Free Special Amenities: high-speed Internet.** *(See color ad below)*

SOME UNITS
FEE

SKYLINE INN *Book great rates at AAA.com*   Phone: (905)374-4444   [8]

ⓒⒶ SAVE	6/1-10/31	1P: $99-$369	2P: $99-$369	XP: $20	F18
	5/1-5/31	1P: $79-$329	2P: $79-$329	XP: $20	F18
▽▽▽	11/1-4/30	1P: $59-$299	2P: $59-$299	XP: $20	F18

Small-scale Hotel **Location:** At end of Rainbow Bridge. 4800 Bender Hill L2E 6W7. Fax: 905/371-8349. **Facility:** 206 one-bedroom standard units. 3 stories, interior corridors. **Parking:** on-site (fee). **Terms:** cancellation fee imposed, package plans, 3% service charge. **Amenities:** video games (fee), voice mail, hair dryers. **Dining:** 7 am-midnight; to 9 pm 12/1-3/31. **Leisure Activities:** shared recreational facilities. **Fee:** waterpark, game room. **Guest Services:** gift shop, valet laundry. **Business Services:** fax (fee). **Cards:** AX, CB, DC, DS, JC, MC, VI. *(See color ad p 563)*

SOME UNITS

STANLEY MOTOR INN   Phone: (905)358-9238   [53]

ⓒⒶ SAVE	6/25-9/25	1P: $60-$120	2P: $80-$140	XP: $10	F12
	5/1-6/24 & 9/26-4/30	1P: $50-$60	2P: $60-$70	XP: $10	F12
▽▽▽					

Motel **Location:** 2 blks from the falls; w of Skylon Tower. 6220 Stanley Ave L2G 3Y4. Fax: 905/358-2840. **Facility:** 49 one-bedroom standard units, some with whirlpools. 2 stories (no elevator), interior/exterior corridors. *Bath:* combo or shower only. **Parking:** on-site. **Terms:** office hours 7 am-midnight, pets ($10 extra charge). **Pool(s):** outdoor. **Guest Services:** coin laundry. **Cards:** AX, DC, DS, MC, VI. **Free Special Amenities: local telephone calls and preferred room (subject to availability with advance reservations).** *(See color ad starting on p 170)*

SOME UNITS
FEE   FEE

(See map and index starting on p. 511)

SUPER 8 HOTEL

CAA SAVE

Small-scale Hotel

Phone: (905)356-0052   **34**

All Year   1P: $59-$299   2P: $59-$299   XP: $5   F17
Location: On Hwy 20, 0.9 mi (1.5 km) from the falls. 5706 Ferry St L2G 1S7. Fax: 905/356-7760. **Facility:** 190 units. 181 one-bedroom standard units, some with whirlpools. 9 one-bedroom suites ($99-$499). 7 stories, interior corridors. **Parking:** on-site, winter plug-ins. **Terms:** package plans. **Amenities:** video games (fee), high-speed Internet, voice mail, irons, hair dryers. **Dining:** 6 am-3 pm, cocktails. **Pool(s):** heated outdoor, heated indoor. **Leisure Activities:** sauna, whirlpool, limited exercise equipment. *Fee:* game room. **Guest Services:** gift shop, coin laundry, area transportation (fee)-casino. **Business Services:** meeting rooms, PC (fee). **Cards:** AX, CB, DC, DS, MC, VI. **Free Special Amenities:** local telephone calls and high-speed Internet.

SOME UNITS
FEE

(See map and index starting on p. 511)

SURFSIDE INN   *Book great rates at AAA.com*

(CAA) (SAVE)

◈◈ ◈◈

Motel

5/1-9/30	1P: $99-$129	2P: $99-$129	**Phone:** (905)295-4354
10/1-4/30	1P: $69-$79	2P: $69-$79	XP: $15 D
			XP: $15 D

Location: 2.2 mi (3.5 km) s of Horseshoe Falls on Niagara River Pkwy. Located in a quiet area. 3665 Macklem St L2G 6C8. Fax: 905/295-4374. **Facility:** 31 one-bedroom standard units, some with efficiencies and/or whirlpools. 1 story, exterior corridors. **Parking:** on-site. **Terms:** office hours 7 am-11 pm, cancellation fee imposed. **Amenities:** hair dryers. **Pool(s):** heated outdoor. **Leisure Activities:** barbecue. **Cards:** AX, DS, MC, VI.

SOME UNITS

⧉ 📶 🏊 🎦 🛢 🖥 / ✕ 🖼 /

THRIFTLODGE CLIFTON HILL   *Book great rates at AAA.com*

(CAA) (SAVE)

◈◈◈

◈

Motel

6/1-10/31	1P: $99-$299	2P: $99-$299	**Phone:** (905)357-4330 🔟
11/1-4/30	1P: $49-$299	2P: $49-$299	XP: $10 F18
5/1-5/31	1P: $79-$279	2P: $79-$279	XP: $10 F18
			XP: $10 F18

Location: Just s on jct Victoria Ave. 4945 Clifton Hill L2G 3N5. Fax: 905/357-2223. **Facility:** 38 one-bedroom standard units. 2 stories (no elevator), exterior corridors. **Parking:** on-site. **Terms:** cancellation fee imposed, package plans. **Amenities:** high-speed Internet. **Leisure Activities:** pool privileges. **Guest Services:** coin laundry. **Cards:** AX, MC, VI. **Free Special Amenities:** local telephone calls and newspaper.

SOME UNITS

⧉ 🐾 📶 🖥 / ✕ 🛢 /

TRAVELODGE BONAVENTURE   *Book great rates at AAA.com*

(CAA) (SAVE)

◈◈◈

Small-scale Hotel

6/29-8/25	1P: $89-$209	2P: $89-$209	**Phone:** (905)374-7171 🔟
5/1-6/28 & 8/26-10/6	1P: $69-$159	2P: $69-$159	XP: $10 F17
10/7-4/30	1P: $59-$129	2P: $59-$129	XP: $10 F17
			XP: $10 F17

Location: QEW, exit Hwy 20, 2.8 mi (4.5 km) w. 7737 Lundy Ln L2H 1H3. Fax: 905/374-1151. **Facility:** 118 one-bedroom standard units, some with whirlpools. 3 stories, interior/exterior corridors. **Parking:** on-site, winter plug-ins. **Terms:** package plans. **Amenities:** video games, voice mail, hair dryers. **Dining:** 7:30-11:30 am; closed weekdays off season. **Pool(s):** heated outdoor, heated indoor. **Leisure Activities:** sauna, whirlpool. **Guest Services:** area transportation (fee)-casino & falls. **Business Services:** meeting rooms. **Cards:** AX, DC, DS, MC, VI. **Free Special Amenities:** local telephone calls and high-speed Internet. *(See color ad below)*

SOME UNITS

⧉ 🍴 🏊 🎦 🖥 / ✕ 📼 🛢 /
FEE

(See map and index starting on p. 511)

TRAVELODGE CLIFTON HILL   *Book great rates at AAA.com*   Phone: (905)357-4330   **17**
CAA SAVE   6/1-10/31 [CP]   1P: $99-$349   2P: $99-$349   XP: $10   F18
              5/1-5/31 [CP]   1P: $79-$329   2P: $79-$329   XP: $10   F18
              11/1-4/30 [CP]   1P: $69-$299   2P: $69-$299   XP: $10   F18
Location: Just s of jct Victoria Ave. 4943 Clifton Hill L2G 3N5. Fax: 905/357-2223. **Facility:** 68 units. 67 one- and
Small-scale Hotel 1 two-bedroom standard units, some with kitchens and/or whirlpools. 2 stories (no elevator),
interior/exterior corridors. **Parking:** on-site. **Terms:** cancellation fee imposed, package plans.
Amenities: high-speed Internet, voice mail, irons, hair dryers. **Dining:** 11 am-1 am, cocktails. **Pool(s):** heated outdoor.
Business Services: PC. **Cards:** AX, MC, VI. **Free Special Amenities:** continental breakfast and local telephone calls.
(See color ad p 566)

SOME UNITS

TRAVELODGE HOTEL BY THE FALLS   *Book great rates at AAA.com*   Phone: (905)356-2842   **29**
CAA SAVE   6/15-9/2   1P: $89-$309   2P: $89-$309   XP: $25   F16
              9/3-10/13   1P: $69-$289   2P: $69-$289   XP: $25   F16
              5/1-6/14   1P: $69-$249   2P: $69-$249   XP: $25   F16
              10/14-4/30   1P: $59-$249   2P: $59-$249   XP: $25   F16
Small-scale Hotel **Location:** On Hwy 20, 0.4 mi (0.7 km) from the falls. 5257 Ferry St L2G 1R6. Fax: 905/356-6629. **Facility:** 120
one-bedroom standard units, some with whirlpools. 11 stories, interior corridors. **Parking:** on-site.
Terms: [BP] meal plan available, package plans. **Amenities:** irons, hair dryers. *Fee:* video games, high-speed Internet.
Dining: 7 am-8 pm. **Pool(s):** heated indoor, wading. **Leisure Activities:** sauna, whirlpool, sun deck. **Guest Services:** gift shop.
Business Services: meeting rooms, PC (fee). **Cards:** AX, DS, MC, VI. **Free Special Amenities:** local telephone calls and
early check-in/late check-out. *(See color ad below)*

SOME UNITS

(See map and index starting on p. 511)

VICTORIAN CHARM BED AND BREAKFAST   Phone: 905/357-4221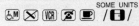

Property failed to provide current rates

Bed & Breakfast

wireless Internet.

Location: Between Main and Drummond sts. 6028 Culp St L2G 2B7. Fax: 905/228-1070. **Facility:** Smoke free premises. 4 one-bedroom standard units, some with whirlpools. 2 stories (no elevator), interior corridors. **Parking:** on-site. **Terms:** office hours 7 am-11 pm. **Amenities:** video library, hair dryers. **Guest Services:**

SOME UNITS

VILLAGER LODGE   Phone: (905)354-3162

6/23-9/4	1P: $69-$199	2P: $69-$199	XP: $10	F12
5/1-6/22	1P: $49-$169	2P: $49-$169	XP: $5	F12
9/5-4/30	1P: $39-$169	2P: $39-$169	XP: $5	F12

Motel

Location: QEW, exit Hwy 20, 3.1 mi (5 km) w. 8054 Lundy's Ln L2H 1H1. Fax: 905/354-8422. **Facility:** 32 one-bedroom standard units, some with efficiencies and/or whirlpools. 2 stories (no elevator), exterior corridors. **Parking:** on-site, winter plug-ins. **Terms:** weekly rates available. **Amenities:** high-speed Internet, voice mail. **Pool(s):** heated outdoor. **Leisure Activities:** barbecue grills, playground. **Guest Services:** area transportation (fee)-casino & falls. **Cards:** AX, DC, DS, MC, VI. **Free Special Amenities: local telephone calls and high-speed Internet.**

SOME UNITS

WATER'S EDGE INN   Phone: 905/356-0131   **2**

7/1-9/30	1P: $79-$500	2P: $79-$500	XP: $10	F14
5/1-6/30	1P: $59-$300	2P: $59-$300	XP: $10	F14
10/1-12/31	1P: $49-$300	2P: $49-$300	XP: $10	F14
1/1-4/30	1P: $49-$199	2P: $49-$199	XP: $10	F14

Motel

Location: 1.9 mi (3 km) n of Rainbow Bridge. 4009 River Rd L2E 3E5. Fax: 905/356-3306. **Facility:** 66 one-bedroom standard units, some with whirlpools. 2 stories (no elevator), exterior corridors. **Parking:** on-site. **Terms:** package plans. **Amenities:** video library (fee), hair dryers. **Dining:** 7:30 am-midnight 6/1-10/31; hours may vary off season. **Pool(s):** outdoor. **Cards:** AX, DC, DS, MC, VI. **Free Special Amenities: local telephone calls and preferred room (subject to availability with advance reservations).** (See color ad p 529)

SOME UNITS

FEE

(See map and index starting on p. 511)

——————— *The following lodging was either not evaluated or did not* ———————
meet AAA rating requirements but is listed for your information only.

A-1 MOTEL   Phone: 905/354-6038
[fyi]   Not evaluated. **Location:** QEW, exit Hwy 20, 2.8 mi (4.5 km) w. 7895 Lundy's Ln L2H 1H3. Facilities, services, and
               decor characterize a mid-range property.

——————— **WHERE TO DINE** ———————

17 NOIR   **Dinner: $20-$50**   Phone: 905/374-6928   25
▼▼▼ ▼▼▼   **Location:** Jct Murray St; in Fallsview Casino Resort. 6380 Fallsview Blvd L2G 7X5. **Hours:** 5 pm-11 pm.
               Reservations: suggested. **Features:** This dining room features an upscale contemporary decor that is sure
Continental   to please, in addition to a fine regional and Continental menu. The chef uses fresh seasonal ingredients in
               the traditional yet innovative menu and can be viewed creating each course in the open-concept kitchen.
Large panoramic windows offer a great view, as does the seasonal outdoor patio. Dressy casual; cocktails. **Parking:** on-site
(fee). **Cards:** AX, DC, DS, MC, VI.   🍸 🔧

A CUT ABOVE STEAKHOUSE   **Lunch: $8-$18**   **Dinner: $19-$55**   Phone: 905/374-1077   35
(CAA)   **Location:** Near Konica Minolta Tower; in Sheraton Fallsview Hotel & Conference Centre. 6755 Fallsview Blvd L2G 3W7.
               Hours: 7 am-10 pm. **Reservations:** suggested. **Features:** Diners are awed by the spectacular views
▼▼▼ ▼▼▼   overlooking the falls and upper river—that and the wonderful selection of salad, appetizer, entree and
Steak House   dessert on the daily buffet. A full a la carte menu is also offered with creative International items. Casual
               dress; cocktails. **Parking:** on-site. **Cards:** AX, DC, DS, JC, MC, VI. *(See color ad p. 561)*
                                                                                                            🍸

ASIAN PEARL   **Lunch: $13-$28**   **Dinner: $13-$28**   Phone: 905/371-0088   23
(CAA)   **Location:** At the Fallsview Casino Resort. 6380 Fallsview Blvd, Unit R-3 L2G 7X5. **Hours:** 11 am-midnight.
               Reservations: suggested. **Features:** A large, airy dining room and a convenient location at the Fallsview
▼▼▼ ▼▼▼   Casino complex make this a popular choice for visitors in the area. The menu features a wide choice of
Chinese   freshly prepared Chinese fare, including many full-course meal selections. The atmosphere is upscale and
               sophisticated. Casual dress; cocktails. **Parking:** on-site (fee). **Cards:** AX, MC, VI.

THE BEEF BARON   **Dinner: $11-$35**   Phone: 905/356-6110   6
(CAA)   **Location:** At top of Clifton Hill. 5019 Centre St L2G 3N5. **Hours:** 4 pm-11 pm, Sat & Sun from 3 pm; to 9 pm, Sat
               & Sun 3 pm-10 pm in winter. Closed: 12/24, 12/25. **Reservations:** suggested, in season.
▼▼▼   **Features:** Hungry? Really hungry? Order Baron's 26 oz. porterhouse. Prime rib and seafood are two more
Steak House   house favourites. Three dining rooms, trimmed in cherry wood, brass and Italian prints, mix well in the
               bustling summer atmosphere and quieter ambience of winter. Casual dress; cocktails. **Parking:** on-site
               (fee). **Cards:** AX, CB, DC, DS, JC, MC, VI.

BETTY'S RESTAURANT   **Lunch: $5-$10**   **Dinner: $9-$15**   Phone: 905/295-4436
▼▼▼   **Location:** Niagara River Pkwy S to Main St, just w; in Chippawa District. 8921 Sodom Rd L2E 6S6. **Hours:** 8 am-9
               pm. Closed: 12/25, 12/26. **Features:** Betty's pleasantly appointed, spacious dining room highlights the
Seafood   good-value home cooking served here. Seafood and fish are what they do best, but many other tasty dishes
               are offered. The fish and chips keeps regular patrons coming back for more. Casual dress; cocktails.
Parking: on-site. **Cards:** AX, MC, VI.

BIG ANTHONY'S BIG EATERY AND
PUB   *Menu on AAA.com*   **Dinner: $9-$26**   Phone: 905/354-9844   4
(CAA)   **Location:** Jct Clifton Hill, at the Niagara Family Inn. 5677 Victoria Ave L2E 3L5. **Hours:** 3 pm-11 pm. Closed: 12/24-
               12/26. **Features:** In a central location in the middle of the tourist zone, the restaurant is a popular choice for
▼▼ ▼▼   its relaxed setting and hearty portions of home-style fare. On the menu are traditional favorites of prime rib,
               ribs, steak and burgers, all served in large portions. A patio area provides more summer seating. Wrestling
American   photographs and memorabilia decorate the dining room of the family-owned-and-operated spot, which is
               known for offering warm and personable service. Casual dress; cocktails. **Parking:** street. **Cards:** AX, DS,
MC, VI.

B JAYS FAMILY RESTAURANT   **Lunch: $6-$11**   **Dinner: $7-$20**   Phone: 905/295-3476
▼▼ ▼▼   **Location:** Jct Main St. 8221 Cummington Sq L2G 6W1. **Hours:** 8 am-8 pm. Closed: 1/1, 12/25, 12/26.
               Features: This casual diner is a favourite with locals in the area in search of a hearty, wholesome meal. It is
Canadian   family oriented and has been in the neighbourhood for years. The eatery is known for its tasty steak
               sandwich and a good mix of Canadian, International and Greek fare. In the summer months, a nice little
outdoor patio is also available. Casual dress; cocktails. **Parking:** on-site. **Cards:** AX, MC, VI.

BUCHANANS CHOPHOUSE   **Lunch: $12-$14**   **Dinner: $19-$34**   Phone: 905/353-4111   18
▼▼ ▼▼   **Location:** Just w via Murray St, then n; adjacent to Skylon Tower; in DoubleTree Resort Lodge & Spa Fallsview. 6039
               Fallsview Blvd L2G 3V6. **Hours:** 7 am-9:30 pm. **Features:** On the second level of the hotel, the dining room
Continental   features a fine menu selection in a warm and cozy setting. Diners enjoy traditional favorites, such as fresh
               salads, homemade soups or baked brie to start, followed by a nice selection of grilled beef, chicken,
seafood or pasta offerings. The service is warm and personable. Casual dress; cocktails. **Parking:** on-site. **Cards:** AX, DC, DS,
JC, MC, VI. *(See color ad p 541)*
                                                                                                            🍸

CANYON CREEK CHOP HOUSE   **Lunch: $12-$26**   **Dinner: $18-$37**   Phone: 905/354-0030   29
▼▼ ▼▼   **Location:** At the Fallsview Casino Resort. 6380 Fallsview Blvd L2G 7Y6. **Hours:** noon-midnight, Thurs-Sat noon-2
               am. **Reservations:** suggested. **Features:** This popular restaurant serves a fine selection of freshly grilled
Steak House   steaks and chops in hearty portions. Diners also enjoy the fabulous location at the Fallsview Casino Resort
               complex and the many tables that afford views of Niagara Falls. Casual dress; cocktails. **Parking:** on-site
(fee). **Cards:** AX, MC, VI.   🍸

(See map and index starting on p. 511)

CAPRI RESTAURANT Lunch: $9-$14 Dinner: $15-$40 Phone: 905/354-7519 ⑮
Italian
Location: Hwy 20, 0.6 mi (1 km) from the falls. 5438 Ferry St L2G 1S1. Hours: 11 am-11 pm, Sat & Sun from 4 pm. Closed: 12/24-12/26; also Sun 1/1-3/31. Reservations: accepted. Features: The dining room offers an elegant, yet relaxed atmosphere for special occasion or family dining. The menu emphasizes Southern Italian cuisine and features a wide selection of homemade pasta as well as a full array of steak, seafood and poultry selections. Casual dress; cocktails. Parking: on-site. Cards: AX, CB, DC, JC, MC, VI.

CARPACCIO RESTAURANT AND WINE BAR Lunch: $7-$15 Dinner: $9-$35 Phone: 905/371-2063 ⑰
Mediterranean
Location: Jct Dorchester Rd. 6840 Lundy's Ln L2G 1V6. Hours: 11:30 am-11 pm, Sat & Sun from 4 pm. Closed: 12/24, 12/25. Reservations: suggested. Features: In the busy Lundy's Lane area, the popular eatery is a local favorite. Diners can enjoy patio seating in season or dine in the large, contemporary dining room. The chef prepares a fine mix of Mediterranean and Italian fare, which pairs with choices from the exceptional wine list. Offerings include gourmet pizzas, fresh pasta dishes, outstanding rack of lamb and preparations of veal, chicken and beef. Fresh, tasty desserts are well worth the calories. Casual dress; cocktails. Parking: on-site. Cards: AX, DC, MC, VI.

CASA D'ORO DINING LOUNGE Lunch: $10-$15 Dinner: $17-$60 Phone: 905/356-5646 ⑫
Italian
Location: Just e of jct Ferry St; jct w of Clifton Hill. 5875 Victoria Ave L2G 3L6. Hours: 11:30 am-10:30 pm, Sat 4 pm-11 pm. Closed: 12/25, 12/26. Reservations: suggested. Features: The restaurant, a popular choice with locals and tourists alike, offers a unique ambience created by elaborate wall murals of Italian and European themes as well as the pleasant outdoor patio area in season. The menu highlights include all the traditional favourites for that special occasion dining including shrimp cocktail, French onion soup, prime rib, steak, lobster and, of course, the excellent selection of fine Italian fare and pastas. Dressy casual; cocktails. Parking: street. Cards: AX, DS, MC, VI.

CHINA BUFFET Lunch: $7-$8 Dinner: $9-$10 Phone: 905/357-6688 ⑭
Chinese
Location: Between Drummond and Dorchester rds. 6661 Lundy's Ln L4G 1V4. Hours: 11:30 am-10 pm. Closed: 12/25. Features: Diners appreciate the casual atmosphere and the flavorful Chinese food lining the buffet's salad, soup and hot bars. Spring rolls are tasty, as are the ice creams and pastries. A full take-out menu also is available. Casual dress; cocktails. Parking: on-site. Cards: MC, VI.

EDGEWATERS TAP & GRILL *Menu on AAA.com* Lunch: $8-$16 Dinner: $16-$24 Phone: 905/356-2217 ㉑
Continental
Location: In Queen Victoria Park; on scenic route. 6345 Niagara River Pkwy L2E 6T2. Hours: Open 5/1-10/15; 11:30 am-10 pm; to 9 pm 5/1-6/18 & 9/5-10/15. Features: What better way to enjoy a breathtaking view of the falls than from an open air balcony while dining on an array of items, including some Canadian fare, prepared with fresh ingredients. A year-round cafeteria with more formal dining in season. Casual dress; cocktails. Parking: street. Cards: AX, MC, VI.

THE FAMOUS COFFEE SHOP Lunch: $10-$32 Dinner: $10-$32 Phone: 905/354-7775 ㉗
American
Location: Jct Murray St; in Fallsview Casino Resort. 6380 Fallsview Blvd L2G 7X5. Hours: 24 hours. Features: This modern diner serves up its menu 24 hours a day which is popular with the casino patrons. Its location at the casino complex makes the all-day breakfast a big hit. The menu also features hearty burgers and deli sandwiches as well as healthy soups, salads and even steak and prime rib specials. Diners can enjoy a quick bite with counter service or booth and table dining. Desserts are decadent and portions are generous. Casual dress; cocktails. Parking: on-site (fee). Cards: AX, MC, VI.

(See map and index starting on p. 511)

FINE KETTLE 'O' FISH　　**Lunch:** $6-$9　　　　**Dinner:** $8-$30　　　　**Phone:** 905/357-3474
　　　　　　　　　　Location: Jct Huggins; in far back section of strip mall. 3641 Portage Rd L2J 2K8. **Hours:** 11 am-10 pm. Closed:
Seafood　　　　3/24, 12/25, 12/26. **Features:** The casual, nautical setting at this popular eatery is enhanced by cozy
　　　　　　　　　　corners and fish aquariums throughout. Good menu selections offer a wide range of fresh seafood—from
on-site. **Cards:** AX, MC, VI.　fish and chips to lobster—as well as steak, chicken and stir-fry options. Casual dress; cocktails. **Parking:**

FRONTIER GRILL HOUSE　　**Lunch:** $6-$11　　　**Dinner:** $25-$50　　　**Phone:** 905/356-8812　　①
　　　　　　　　　　Location: 1.9 mi (3 km) n of Rainbow Bridge at the Days Inn North of the Falls. 4029 River Rd L2E 3E5.
American　　　　**Hours:** noon-10 pm 5/15-10/14; 5 pm-10 pm 10/15-5/14. Closed: 12/25. **Features:** On River Road, this
　　　　　　　　　　restaurant is a nice retreat from the bustling feel of the tourist center. The attractive dining room features
　　　　　　　　　　brick and stone accents and a lodge-like atmosphere. Diners enjoy a fine selection of grilled steaks, prime
rib and the popular barbecue ribs basted in a tangy sauce. Decadent desserts are dished in hearty portions. Casual dress;
cocktails. **Parking:** on-site. **Cards:** AX, MC, VI.

HAPPY WANDERER　　　**Lunch:** $5-$12　　　**Dinner:** $10-$40　　　**Phone:** 905/354-9825　　㉘
　　　　　　　　　　Location: Near Konica Minolta Tower. 6405 Stanley Ave L2G 3Y6. **Hours:** 10 am-10 pm. Closed: 12/24.
　　　　　　　　　　Reservations: accepted. **Features:** If you're looking for a fun, casual restaurant with a European
German　　　　atmosphere, this place is for you. Come hungry as you will be served heaping portions of homemade
　　　　　　　　　　German cuisine. Choose from traditional favourites such as bratwurst, schnitzel, smoked pork or rolled beef
rolls with homemade dumplings. The atmosphere is set by servers in traditional costumes and distinctive Bavarian decor.
Saving room for dessert will be a challenge, but well worth it. Casual dress; cocktails. **Parking:** on-site. **Cards:** AX, MC, VI.

THE KEG STEAKHOUSE AND BAR　　**Lunch:** $10-$18　　**Dinner:** $18-$28　　**Phone:** 905/374-5170　　㉛
　　　　　　　　　　Location: Adjacent to Konica Minolta Tower; in Embassy Suites Niagara Falls Fallsview. 6700 Fallsview Blvd L2G 3W6.
　　　　　　　　　　Hours: noon-close. **Reservations:** accepted. **Features:** Known for its mesquite-grilled steaks and fun, laid-
　　　　　　　　　　back atmosphere, the steak house is a longtime favourite with the local crowd. In addition to great beef, the
　　　　　　　　　　traditional menu lists seafood, grilled chicken, hickory ribs and pasta dishes. Casual dress; cocktails.
Steak House　　　**Parking:** on-site. **Cards:** AX, DC, DS, MC, VI. *(See color ad inside front cover)*

THE KEG STEAKHOUSE AND BAR　　**Lunch:** $10-$20　　**Dinner:** $20-$55　　**Phone:** 905/353-4022　　⑬
　　　　　　　　　　Location: Jct Ferry St; in Courtyard by Marriott Niagara Falls. 5950 Victoria Ave L2G 3L7. **Hours:** 11 am-11 pm, Fri
　　　　　　　　　　& Sat-1 am. **Features:** Known for its mesquite-grilled steaks and fun, laid-back atmosphere, the steak
　　　　　　　　　　house is a longtime favourite with the local crowd. In addition to great beef, the traditional menu lists
　　　　　　　　　　seafood, grilled chicken, hickory ribs and pasta dishes. Casual dress; cocktails. **Parking:** on-site.
Steak House　　　**Cards:** AX, MC, VI.

KELSEY'S　　　　　　**Lunch:** $6-$20　　　**Dinner:** $6-$20　　　　**Phone:** 905/353-0051
　　　　　　　　　　Location: Jct Victoria Ave and Clifton Hill, just s; in Comfort Inn Clifton Hill. 4960 Clifton Hill L2G 3N4. **Hours:** 11 am-
　　　　　　　　　　midnight, Fri & Sat-1:30 am. Closed: 12/25. **Features:** A fun, relaxed atmosphere and tasty menu of casual
Canadian　　　　fare make the restaurant a popular favorite with locals. Diners might start a meal with some tempting
　　　　　　　　　　appetizers, such as wings, loaded potato skins or nachos, and follow them with an old-time favorite, such as
a burger, wrap, pizza or pasta dish. For a heartier meal, it's hard to beat pork back ribs or a steak. The diverse menu has broad
appeal. Casual dress; cocktails. **Parking:** on-site. **Cards:** AX, DC, MC, VI.

LA PIAZZA BISTRO & CAFE　　**Lunch:** $8-$18　　　**Dinner:** $8-$18　　　**Phone:** 905/374-1077　　㊱
　　　　　　　　　　Location: Near Konica Minolta Tower; in Sheraton Fallsview Hotel & Conference Centre. 6755 Fallsview Blvd L2G 3W7.
　　　　　　　　　　Hours: 7 am-10 pm; Fri from 3 pm, Sun 7 am-noon 10/1-4/30. Closed: Mon-Thurs 10/1-4/30.
Italian　　　　　**Features:** This family-oriented eatery offers a nice choice of casual fare and Italian cuisine. Burgers, finger
　　　　　　　　　　foods and sandwiches are featured as well as made-to-order pizza and hearty portions of homemade pasta.
It's a relaxing setting with a comfortable, no-frills ambience. Casual dress; cocktails. **Parking:** on-site. **Cards:** AX, DC, DS,
MC, VI. *(See color ad p. 561)*

LEGENDS ON THE NIAGARA　*Menu on AAA.com*　**Lunch:** $7-$13　　**Dinner:** $9-$23　　**Phone:** 905/295-2241
　　　　　　　　　　Location: 3.1 mi (5 km) s of the falls. 9233 Niagara River Pkwy L2E 6T2. **Hours:** Open 5/1-10/31 & 4/1-4/30; 6
　　　　　　　　　　am-7 pm; to 10 pm 6/15-9/15. **Reservations:** accepted. **Features:** Diners enjoy a wonderful view of the golf
　　　　　　　　　　course through the large panoramic windows or from the large patio. Casual fare—along the lines of wings,
American　　　　burgers and sandwiches—is available for breakfast, lunch and lighter meals, while larger entrees are served
after 4 pm. Casual dress; cocktails. **Parking:** on-site. **Cards:** AX, DC, JC, MC, VI.

LUCKY'S STEAKHOUSE　　**Lunch:** $15-$35　　　**Dinner:** $15-$35　　　**Phone:** 905/374-6928　　⑧
　　　　　　　　　　Location: At Casino Niagara. 5705 Falls Ave L2E 6W7. **Hours:** noon-11 pm. **Reservations:** suggested.
　　　　　　　　　　Features: Inside Casino Niagara, this upbeat restaurant provides casino patrons a pleasant break from their
Steak House　　　gaming activities. The menu compiles many grilled items, including huge steaks and chops as well as
　　　　　　　　　　burgers and sandwich options. Patrons enjoy the extensive wine selection and the club-style decor. Casual
dress; cocktails. **Parking:** on-site (fee). **Cards:** AX, DS, MC, VI.

MAMA MIA'S　　*Menu on AAA.com*　　**Lunch:** $5-$9　　**Dinner:** $7-$22　　　**Phone:** 905/354-7471　　⑦
　　　　　　　　　　Location: At top of Clifton Hill. 5719 Victoria Ave L2G 3L5. **Hours:** 11:30 am-11 pm; seasonal hours vary. Closed:
　　　　　　　　　　12/23-12/25. **Features:** What would an Italian eatery be without a good menu selection of lasagna,
　　　　　　　　　　manicotti and cannelloni? You'll never find out because Mama Mia's serves all these house specialties and
Italian　　　　　more in this quaint dining room. Steak and seafood also make an appearance. Casual dress; cocktails.
　　　　　　　　　　Parking: street. **Cards:** AX, DC, DS, JC, MC, VI.

MARKET BUFFET　　　**Lunch:** $12　　　　**Dinner:** $17　　　　**Phone:** 905/374-6928　　⑨
　　　　　　　　　　Location: At Casino Niagara. 5705 Falls Ave L2E 6W7. **Hours:** 8 am-11 pm. **Features:** An outstanding selection
　　　　　　　　　　of hot and cold items awaits diners at this buffet restaurant in Casino Niagara. Among the extensive choices
　　　　　　　　　　are several roasted meats, pasta dishes, Chinese fare, pizza, salads, several soups and a huge dessert
American　　　　table with fresh pastries, puddings and cakes. Only adults are permitted. Casual dress; cocktails. **Parking:**
on-site (fee). **Cards:** AX, DS, MC, VI.

(See map and index starting on p. 511)

MICK AND ANGELO'S EATERY AND
BAR   Lunch: $10-$16   Dinner: $10-$29   Phone: 905/357-6543   ⑯

Location: QEW, exit Lundy's Ln; corner of Lundy's Ln and Montrose Rd. 7600 Lundy's Ln L2H 1H1. **Hours:** 11 am-midnight. Closed: 12/25. **Reservations:** accepted. **Features:** A diverse crowd patronizes this popular eatery and bar where an extensive menu, large portions and reasonable prices prevail. The specialty white pizza (sans tomato sauce) consists of oil, garlic and three cheeses. Entertainment is offered in season. Casual

Italian   dress; cocktails. **Parking:** on-site. **Cards:** AX, MC, VI.

THE MILLERY DINING ROOM   Lunch: $10-$18   Dinner: $21-$58   Phone: 905/357-1234   ⑲

Location: Just w via Murray St, just n on Buchanan Ave; in Old Stone Inn. 5425 Robinson St L2G 7L6. **Hours:** 7 am-2:30 & 4:30-10 pm. Closed: for dinner 12/24. **Reservations:** suggested. **Features:** Located in a wonderfully converted flour mill, the Millery Dining Room provides upscale dining in an elegant country setting. The

Continental   dining room features high-beam cathedral ceilings and accent stone walls from the original structure of the early 1900s. The innovative menu features fine Continental cuisine with an emphasis on creativity in presentation and freshness of ingredients. It is the perfect choice for special occasion or business dining. Casual dress; cocktails. **Parking:** on-site. **Cards:** AX, DC, DS, JC, MC, VI.

MONTANA'S COOKHOUSE   Lunch: $6-$24   Dinner: $6-$24   Phone: 905/356-7427

Location: Jct Centre St and Victoria Ave. 5759 Victoria Ave L2G 3L6. **Hours:** 11 am-11:30 pm, Fri & Sat-1 am. Closed: 1/1, 12/25. **Features:** Pine boards, exposed beams, a fireplace and Western gear displayed about

Canadian   the dining room give the feeling of a back-country setting. The menu lists hearty portions of comfort fare, such as Yankee pot roast. While the focus is on steaks, ribs and chicken, some seafood entrees also are among offerings. Service is efficient and friendly. Casual dress; cocktails. **Parking:** on-site. **Cards:** AX, CB, MC, VI.

MONTICELLO GRILLE HOUSE & WINE
BAR   *Menu on AAA.com*   Lunch: $9-$35   Dinner: $15-$35   Phone: 905/357-4888   ②

Location: Just e of jct Clifton Hill and Victoria Ave. 5645 Victoria Ave L2G 3L5. **Hours:** noon-10:30 pm. Closed: 12/24, 12/25. **Reservations:** accepted. **Features:** The brick and wood-beamed steak and seafood restaurant gives a nod to New Orleans with such menu items as spicy gumbo. Also offered are more traditional items. The wine list is extensive, and food portions are large. Specialty desserts such as bread

American   pudding add to the theme. Casual dress; cocktails. **Parking:** on-site. **Cards:** AX, CB, DC, JC, MC, VI. *(See color ad below)*

OUTBACK STEAKHOUSE   Dinner: $12-$25   Phone: 905/357-6284

Location: Corner of Stanley Ave and Dunn St; in Radisson Hotel & Suites Fallsview. 6733 Fallsview Blvd L2G 3W7. **Hours:** 4 pm-10 pm, Fri & Sat-11 pm. Closed: 12/25. **Features:** This Aussie themed eatery offers a very

Steak House   laid-back casual and bustling atmosphere. Hearty portions of freshly grilled and barbecued foods include shrimp, steaks, chicken, ribs, burgers and fajitas. Ever popular is the Blooming Onion appetizer with its tasty dipping sauce. Casual dress; cocktails. **Parking:** on-site. **Cards:** AX, DC, DS, JC, MC, VI. *(See color ad p 556)*

PAZZO MATTO   Lunch: $9-$15   Dinner: $12-$35   Phone: 905/358-2672   ㉖

Location: Jct Murray St; in lower level of Fallsview Casino Complex; at food court. 6380 Fallsview Ave L2G 7Y6. **Hours:** noon-11 pm. **Features:** The casual restaurant presents a menu of fresh pasta, veal, chicken and

Italian   beef dishes prepared with rich sauces. Hearty portions of food and good desserts are served in the bustling atmosphere of the food court itself or in the main dining room, which is colorfully decorated with a bright wall mural. Casual dress; cocktails. **Parking:** on-site (fee). **Cards:** AX, CB, DC, DS, JC, MC, VI.

PENTHOUSE RESTAURANT   Lunch: $10-$20   Dinner: $25-$40   Phone: 905/374-4445   ⑪

Location: Entrance to Rainbow Bridge on Hwy 20; in Sheraton on the Falls. 5875 Falls Ave L2E 6W7. **Hours:** 7-11 am, 11:30-2 & 5-9:30 pm. **Reservations:** suggested. **Features:** There's always something to tempt all

American   tastes on the all-you-can-eat breakfast, lunch and dinner buffet. Besides a spectacular view of the falls, the Penthouse offers daily entertainment in season; weekends off season. An a la carte menu is also available. Casual dress; cocktails. **Parking:** on-site (fee). **Cards:** AX, CB, DC, DS, JC, MC, VI.

(See map and index starting on p. 511)

THE PINNACLE RESTAURANT-ATOP THE KONICA MINOLTA TOWER   **Lunch:** $8-$20   **Dinner:** $18-$50   **Phone:** 905/356-1501   (33)

Continental
Location: In Konica Minolta Tower, in Ramada Plaza Hotel Fallsview. 6732 Fallsview Blvd L2G 3W6. **Hours:** 11:30 am-9 pm; hours may vary in season. **Reservations:** suggested. **Features:** Diners can enjoy a bird's-eye view of the falls from atop the tower while relaxing in an upscale, yet relaxed, atmosphere. The menu lists traditional fare served in ample portions and with attractive plate presentations. Full a la carte and prix fixe specials are served. Dressy casual; cocktails. **Parking:** valet. **Cards:** AX, DC, DS, MC, VI.

QUEENSTON HEIGHTS RESTAURANT   *Menu on AAA.com*   **Lunch:** $14-$18 **Dinner:** $21-$30 **Phone:** 905/262-4274

Continental
Location: 6.5 mi (10.4 km) n of Rainbow Bridge, on scenic route. 14184 Niagara River Pkwy L2E 6T2. **Hours:** Open 5/1-12/31 & 4/1-4/30; noon-3 & 5-9 pm; from 11:30 am, Sat-9:30 pm 7/1-8/31. Closed: 12/25, 12/26; also for dinner Sun-Fri 11/1-12/31. **Reservations:** suggested. **Features:** Enjoy a panoramic view of the lower Niagara River and surrounding fruit lands from your table, while scanning a varied menu of such specialties as Atlantic salmon, Angus prime rib and seasonal fruit dessert. Patio lounge dining is offered in season. Casual dress; cocktails. **Parking:** on-site. **Cards:** AX, CB, DC, DS, MC, VI.

THE RAINBOW FALLSVIEW DINING ROOM   **Lunch:** $8-$18   **Dinner:** $25-$50   **Phone:** 905/374-4444   (5)

American
Location: Entrance to Rainbow Bridge on Hwy 20, just n of the falls; in Brock Plaza Hotel. 5685 Falls Ave L2E 6W7. **Hours:** 7-10 am, 11-2 & 5-10 pm. **Reservations:** suggested. **Features:** Creative food presentation and good menu variety are hallmarks at the casually elegant restaurant. Poultry, beef, seafood, fresh vegetables and decadent desserts keep excellent company in the upscale dining room, which affords a fine view of the falls. Casual dress; cocktails. **Parking:** on-site (fee). **Cards:** AX, CB, DC, DS, JC, MC, VI.

REMINGTON'S OF MONTANA STEAK AND SEAFOOD   **Dinner:** $15-$44   **Phone:** 905/356-4410   (3)

Steak & Seafood
Location: Just e on Hwy 20; in Days Inn Clifton Hill Casino. 5657 Victoria Ave L2G 3L5. **Hours:** 4 pm-10:30 pm, Sat-11:30 pm. **Reservations:** suggested. **Features:** A longtime favourite in the busy tourist area, the restaurant presents diners a traditional steak and seafood menu that is sure to please. Starters include French onion soup, shrimp cocktail and Caesar salad, followed by hearty portions of prime rib, steak or surf and turf offerings. Pasta, chicken and ribs also make menu appearances. Service is polished and professional, and the atmosphere is upscale yet comfortable. Dressy casual; cocktails. **Parking:** on-site. **Cards:** AX, CB, DC, DS, JC, MC, VI.
(See color ad starting on p 542)

ROOFTOP FALLSVIEW GRILLE   **Dinner:** $25-$35   **Phone:** 905/357-5200   (30)

Continental
Location: Corner of Fallsview Blvd and Dixon Ave; across from Niagara Fallsview Casino; in Renaissance Fallsview Hotel. 6455 Fallsview Blvd L2G 3V9. **Hours:** 5 pm-10 pm; to 11 pm 5/1-10/31. **Reservations:** suggested. **Features:** Diners here enjoy a fine menu of traditional Continental fare with a Niagara touch, including a wine list featuring selections from the local wineries. Staff members offer warm, personable service to ensure a memorable dining experience. Views of Niagara Falls add to the atmosphere and are particularly enjoyed during the nightly illumination schedule. A perfect choice for a fine meal, personable service and a relaxed setting away from the hustle and bustle of the main tourist area. Dressy casual; cocktails. **Parking:** on-site. **Cards:** AX, DC, DS, JC, MC, VI.

THE SECRET GARDEN   **Lunch:** $10-$22   **Dinner:** $10-$30   **Phone:** 905/358-4588   (10)

American
Location: Directly across from Casino Niagara. 5827 River Rd L2G 3K9. **Hours:** Open 5/1-12/31 & 3/1-4/30; 7:30 am-10 pm; hours may vary off season. Closed: 12/25. **Features:** Families delight in discovering this well-kept secret, a casual spot adjacent to a lovely garden and directly across from the falls. Diners can request to sit in the comfortable indoor dining room or on the seasonal patio. The menu features a good mix of casual fare and is a favorite for breakfast. Lunch and dinner features include hearty burgers, fish and chips, entree salads and steaks. Exotic cocktails are perfect after a hot day touring the local attractions. Casual dress; cocktails. **Parking:** street. **Cards:** AX, DC, DS, JC, MC, VI.

THE SKYLON TOWER DINING ROOMS   **Lunch:** $27-$37   **Dinner:** $42-$70   **Phone:** 905/356-2651   (20)

American
Location: In Skylon Tower. 5200 Robinson St L2G 2A3. **Hours:** 11:30 am-2:30 & 4:30-9 pm. **Reservations:** suggested. **Features:** Affording spectacular, panoramic views of Niagara Falls from its large windows, the revolving restaurant features a traditional menu of Continental fare. The cost to ascend the tower is $2, and diners are welcomed to visit the viewing area after dinner to capture some great photographs. More casual buffet dining is available at the Summit, one floor up. Casual dress; cocktails. **Parking:** on-site (fee). **Cards:** AX, DC, DS, JC, MC, VI. *(See color ad p 177)*

SWISS CHALET   **Lunch:** $7-$20   **Dinner:** $7-$20   **Phone:** 905/356-1028

American
Location: Jct Carlton Ave. 6666 Lundy's Ln L2G 1V5. **Hours:** 11 am-10 pm, Fri & Sat-11 pm. Closed: 12/25. **Features:** The popular restaurant is known for its rotisserie chicken and ribs and the tangy Chalet sauce that gives food its special zip. Diners munch on a half or quarter chicken with sides such as steamed vegetables, fries, baked potatoes and salads. Lunch guests often go for the great soup and sandwich combination. Take-out and delivery service are popular options. Casual dress; cocktails. **Parking:** on-site. **Cards:** AX, MC, VI.

TABLE ROCK RESTAURANT   *Menu on AAA.com*   **Lunch:** $10-$15 **Dinner:** $30-$35 **Phone:** 905/354-3631   (32)

Continental
Location: At Horseshoe Falls. 6650 Niagara Pkwy L2E 6T2. **Hours:** 11:30 am-9 pm; Sat & Sun also 9-11 am 7/1-8/31; hours may vary off season. Closed: 12/25. **Reservations:** accepted. **Features:** It's difficult to take your eyes off the outstanding view of the falls and the upper rapids long enough to make a choice from the menu featuring traditional fare and some Canadian dishes. Attentive and friendly service is the norm. Casual dress; cocktails. **Parking:** street. **Cards:** AX, DC, MC, VI.

TERRAPIN GRILLE   **Lunch:** $14-$45   **Dinner:** $34-$69   **Phone:** 905/357-7300   (34)

Continental
Location: Next to Konica Minolta Tower; in Marriott Niagara Falls Fallsview and Spa. 6740 Fallsview Blvd L2G 3W6. **Hours:** 6 am-11 pm. **Reservations:** suggested. **Features:** The Terrapin Grille features a good selection of fine Continental cuisine. The dining room is dimly lit at dinner, providing a romantic atmosphere with a stunning backdrop of Niagara Falls seen through its panoramic windows. It is spectacular during the lighting up of the falls each evening. Staff members have good menu knowledge and provide professional, attentive service. Casual dress; cocktails. **Parking:** on-site. **Cards:** AX, CB, DC, DS, MC, VI. *(See color ad inside front cover)*

(See map and index starting on p. 511)

THE WATERMARK   Lunch: $10-$25   Dinner: $25-$65   Phone: 905/354-7887 ㉔

Continental

Location: Hwy 20, just s; across from Niagara Fallsview Casino; in Hilton Niagara Falls Fallsview. 6361 Fallsview Blvd L2G 3V9. **Hours:** 7 am-10:30 pm. **Reservations:** required, for dinner. **Features:** The contemporary dining room carries out a distinct water theme, thanks in part to its rooftop location. Large windows offer spectacular, panoramic views of the falls. The menu features a nice mix of traditional Continental fare prepared with market-fresh vegetables. At lunch, lighter options include burgers, sandwiches and pasta. Dressy casual; cocktails. **Parking:** on-site (fee) and valet. **Cards:** AX, CB, DC, DS, JC, MC, VI. *(See color ad p 549)*

WHIRLPOOL RESTAURANT   Lunch: $7-$13   Dinner: $11-$25   Phone: 905/356-7221

American

Location: 5.3 km n of Rainbow Bridge, on scenic route; in Public Whirlpool Golf Complex. 3351 Niagara River Pkwy L2E 6T2. **Hours:** Open 5/1-11/1 & 4/1-4/30; 11 am-9 pm. **Reservations:** accepted. **Features:** Canadian dishes, snacks and daily seasonal featured fare are served in this casual, golf-course-view restaurant across from a whirlpool gorge. Try the very good chicken teriyaki atop angel hair pasta and an eye-appealing fruit plate for dessert. Casual dress; cocktails. **Parking:** on-site. **Cards:** AX, MC, VI.

WOLFGANG PUCK GRAND CAFE   Lunch: $12-$30   Dinner: $14-$38   Phone: 905/354-5000 ㉒

Continental

Location: Just w of the falls; directly across from casino; in Holiday Inn by the Falls. 6300 Fallsview Blvd, Unit A L2G 2J3. **Hours:** 11:30 am-10:30 pm, Fri & Sat-11 pm. **Reservations:** suggested. **Features:** A great location across from the casino and a people-watching outdoor patio in season attract lots of diners to this upbeat cafe. The contemporary setting is the perfect complement to the innovative menu that is characteristic of Wolfgang Puck. Expect the unexpected in taste sensations and get ready to be wowed by some great food combinations. Meat, seafood, poultry, even burgers and pasta are created with flair. Casual dress; cocktails. **Parking:** on-site (fee). **Cards:** AX, DC, MC, VI. *(See color ad p 550)*

Maid of the Mist / © Look GMBH / eStock Photo

This ends listings for the Niagara Falls Vicinity.
The following page resumes the alphabetical listings of cities in New York.

NORTH CREEK —*See also ADIRONDACK MOUNTAINS.*

─────── **WHERE TO STAY** ───────

COPPERFIELD INN

AAA SAVE

▼▼▼ ▼▼▼

Country Inn

Phone: (518)251-2500

12/9-4/30 [BP]	1P: $235-$285	2P: $235-$285	XP: $25	F12
6/30-9/3 [BP]	1P: $225-$275	2P: $225-$275	XP: $25	F12
9/4-10/21 [BP]	1P: $180-$230	2P: $180-$230	XP: $25	F12
5/1-6/29 [BP]	1P: $145-$195	2P: $145-$195	XP: $25	F12

Location: Just e of SR 28; center. 307 Main St 12853 (PO Box 28). Fax: 518/251-4143. **Facility:** Traditionally furnished rooms are offered at this contemporary country inn convenient to dining and shopping. 31 units. 29 one-bedroom standard units, some with whirlpools. 2 one-bedroom suites ($170-$395) with whirlpools. 2 stories, interior corridors. **Parking:** on-site. **Terms:** open 5/1-10/21 & 12/9-4/30, 14 day cancellation notice-fee imposed, [MAP] meal plan available, package plans. **Amenities:** DVD players, video games (fee), voice mail, safes, honor bars, irons, hair dryers. *Some:* CD players, fax. **Dining:** Gardens, Trappers Tavern, see separate listings. **Pool(s):** heated outdoor. **Leisure Activities:** saunas, whirlpool, lighted tennis court, exercise room. *Fee:* massage. **Guest Services:** gift shop, valet laundry, area transportation-ski area, beauty salon, tanning facilities. **Business Services:** meeting rooms, fax (fee). **Cards:** AX, CB, DS, MC, VI. **Free Special Amenities:** full breakfast and newspaper.

GOOSE POND INN

▼▼▼

Historic Bed & Breakfast

Phone: (518)251-3434

All Year	1P: $65-$115	2P: $95-$160	XP: $20

Location: SR 28, 1 mi e, 0.9 mi n. 196 Main St 12853 (PO Box 273). Fax: 518/251-3434. **Facility:** Antiques and individually decorated rooms distinguish this residential-area inn dating from 1894; rooms vary in size. Designated smoking area. 4 one-bedroom standard units. 2 stories (no elevator), interior corridors. **Bath:** combo or shower only. **Parking:** on-site. **Terms:** 2 night minimum stay - seasonal and/or weekends, age restrictions may apply, 14 day cancellation notice-fee imposed, package plans, no pets allowed (owner's pets on premises). **Amenities:** hair dryers. **Guest Services:** area transportation.

─────── **WHERE TO DINE** ───────

GARDENS

▼▼▼

American

DC, DS, MC, VI. **Country Inn**

Dinner: $17-$33

Phone: 518/251-2500

Location: Just e of SR 28; center; in Copperfield Inn. 307 Main St 12853. **Hours:** Open 5/1-10/22 & 12/1-4/30; 7 am-11 & 5:30-10 pm. **Reservations:** accepted. **Features:** In the heart of the Adirondack Mountains one can still enjoy fine dining in an elegant atmosphere at Gardens. Serving gourmet dishes of chicken, lamb, steak and pasta, this restaurant will delight all. Dressy casual; cocktails. **Parking:** on-site and street. **Cards:** AX,

TRAPPERS TAVERN

▼▼ ▼▼

American

Lunch: $3-$16   **Dinner:** $3-$16   **Phone:** 518/251-2500

Location: Just e of SR 28; center; in Copperfield Inn. 307 Main St 12853. **Hours:** Open 5/1-10/31 & 12/16-4/30; noon-midnight. **Reservations:** not accepted. **Features:** The restaurant offers hearty selections, live entertainment on the weekends and a great place to watch a game. Casual dress; cocktails; entertainment. **Parking:** on-site and street. **Cards:** AX, DC, DS, MC, VI.

ECONO LODGE

AAA SAVE

▼▼ ◆

Motel

DS, JC, MC, VI.

Book great rates at AAA.com

Phone: (607)324-0800

All Year	1P: $55-$60	2P: $60-$65	XP: $5	F18

Location: Jct I-86 and SR 36, exit 34, just s to SR 21, just e to Seneca Rd, then just s. 7462 Seneca Rd 14843. Fax: 607/324-0905. **Facility:** 67 one-bedroom standard units. 1-2 stories (no elevator), interior/exterior corridors. **Parking:** on-site. **Terms:** [CP] meal plan available, pets ($7 extra charge). **Amenities:** *Some:* hair dryers. **Dining:** 11 am-3 & 5-9 pm, Sun 9 am-3 pm; closed Mon, cocktails. **Guest Services:** airport transportation-Hornell Airport, wireless Internet. **Business Services:** meeting rooms. **Cards:** AX, CB, DC, **Free Special Amenities:** continental breakfast and high-speed Internet.

SOME UNITS

NORTH SYRACUSE pop. 6,862   (See map and index starting on p. 629)—*See also SYRACUSE.*

─────── **WHERE TO STAY** ───────

BEST WESTERN SYRACUSE AIRPORT INN

AAA SAVE

▼▼▼

Small-scale Hotel

Book great rates at AAA.com   **Phone: (315)455-7362**   **7**

All Year	1P: $77-$118	2P: $82-$148

Location: I-81, exit 27 (Hancock Airport). Hancock Airport 13212. Fax: 315/455-6840. **Facility:** Smoke free premises. 95 units. 91 one-bedroom standard units. 4 one-bedroom suites ($108-$148). 2 stories (no elevator), interior corridors. **Bath:** combo or shower only. **Parking:** on-site. **Terms:** 7 day cancellation notice. **Amenities:** irons, hair dryers. *Some:* high-speed Internet. **Dining:** 7 am-10 & 5-10 pm, cocktails. **Pool(s):** outdoor. **Guest Services:** valet laundry, airport transportation-Syracuse Hancock International Airport. **Business Services:** meeting rooms. **Cards:** AX, CB, DC, DS, JC, MC, VI. **Free Special Amenities:** local telephone calls and newspaper.

SOME UNITS

BUDGET INN

AAA SAVE

▼

Motel

Phone: (315)458-3510

5/1-10/31	1P: $48-$115	2P: $48-$115	XP: $6	F16
11/1-4/30	1P: $48-$100	2P: $48-$100	XP: $6	F16

Location: I-481, exit 10, just n. 901 S Bay Rd 13039. Fax: 315/452-9488. **Facility:** 36 units. 35 one-bedroom standard units, some with efficiencies (no utensils) and/or whirlpools. 1 cottage ($150-$285) with whirlpool. 2 stories (no elevator), exterior corridors. **Parking:** on-site, winter plug-ins. **Terms:** pets ($10 extra charge, in designated units). **Amenities:** hair dryers. **Leisure Activities:** playground. **Cards:** DS, MC, VI. **Free Special Amenities:** early check-in/late check-out and high-speed Internet.

SOME UNITS

(See map and index starting on p. 629)

CANDLEWOOD SUITES SYRACUSE AIRPORT *Book at AAA.com* Phone: (315)454-8999 **8**
1/1-4/30 1P: $109-$159 2P: $119-$169 XP: $10 F18
5/1-12/31 1P: $99-$149 2P: $109-$159 XP: $10 F18
Small-scale Hotel **Location:** I-90, exit 36; I-81, exit 26 (Mattydale Rd), follow South Bay Rd signs, just n. 5414 South Bay Rd 13212. Fax: 315/455-1173. **Facility:** 124 units. 100 one-bedroom standard units with efficiencies. 24 one-bedroom suites ($149-$199) with efficiencies. 4 stories, interior corridors. *Bath:* combo or shower only. **Parking:** on-site. **Terms:** package plans, pets ($75 deposit, in designated units). **Amenities:** video library, DVD players, CD players, high-speed Internet, dual phone lines, voice mail, irons, hair dryers. **Leisure Activities:** exercise room. **Guest Services:** sundries, complimentary and valet laundry, area transportation. **Business Services:** meeting rooms, PC. **Cards:** AX, DC, DS, MC, VI.

SOME UNITS

COMFORT INN & SUITES/SYRACUSE AIRPORT *Book great rates at AAA.com* Phone: (315)457-4000 **9**
All Year 1P: $79-$169 2P: $79-$169 XP: $10 F18
Location: I-81, exit 25 (7th North St), 0.8 mi w; I-90, exit 36. 6701 Buckley Rd 13212. Fax: 315/453-7877. **Facility:** 216 units. 186 one-bedroom standard units. 30 one-bedroom suites ($119-$199). 2 stories (no elevator), interior corridors. **Parking:** on-site. **Terms:** small pets only. **Amenities:** video library (fee). *Some:* video games (fee), voice mail, irons, hair dryers. **Pool(s):** heated indoor. **Leisure Activities:** sauna, whirlpool, exercise room. **Guest Services:** valet and coin laundry, wireless Internet. **Business Services:** conference facilities, business center. **Cards:** AX, DS, MC, VI. **Free Special Amenities:** full breakfast and high-speed Internet. *(See color ad p 633)*

SOME UNITS

QUALITY INN NORTH *Book great rates at AAA.com* Phone: 315/451-1212 **10**
All Year 1P: $62-$109 2P: $72-$119 XP: $10 F18
Location: I-81, exit 25 (7th North St), 0.3 mi w, then just n. 1308 Buckley Rd 13212. Fax: 315/453-8050. **Facility:** 142 units. 141 one-bedroom standard units. 1 one-bedroom suite with whirlpool. 3 stories, interior/exterior corridors. **Parking:** on-site. **Terms:** 7 day cancellation notice, pets ($10 deposit). **Amenities:** voice mail, irons, hair dryers. *Some:* CD players. **Dining:** 4 pm-10 pm, cocktails. **Pool(s):** outdoor, wading. **Leisure Activities:** limited exercise equipment. **Guest Services:** valet and coin laundry, airport transportation-Syracuse Hancock International Airport, area transportation-train & bus station, wireless Internet. **Business Services:** meeting rooms. **Cards:** AX, DC, DS, MC, VI. **Free Special Amenities:** continental breakfast and local telephone calls. *(See color ad p 633)*

SOME UNITS

RAMADA INN *Book at AAA.com* Phone: (315)457-8670 **11**
All Year [BP] 1P: $79-$199 2P: $79-$199 XP: $10 F18
Small-scale Hotel **Location:** I-81, exit 25 (7th North St), just nw; I-90, exit 36. 1305 Buckley Rd 13212. Fax: 315/457-8633. **Facility:** 150 units. 149 one-bedroom standard units. 1 one-bedroom suite with whirlpool. 2 stories (no elevator), interior corridors. *Bath:* combo or shower only. **Parking:** on-site, winter plug-ins. **Terms:** package plans. **Amenities:** voice mail, irons, hair dryers. *Some:* high-speed Internet, dual phone lines, safes. **Pool(s):** heated outdoor. **Leisure Activities:** exercise room. **Guest Services:** valet laundry. **Business Services:** conference facilities, PC. **Cards:** AX, CB, DC, DS, MC, VI.

SOME UNITS

(See map and index starting on p. 629)

─────── **WHERE TO DINE** ───────

BORIO'S RESTAURANT   **Lunch:** $6-$10   **Dinner:** $11-$23   **Phone:** 315/699-2249
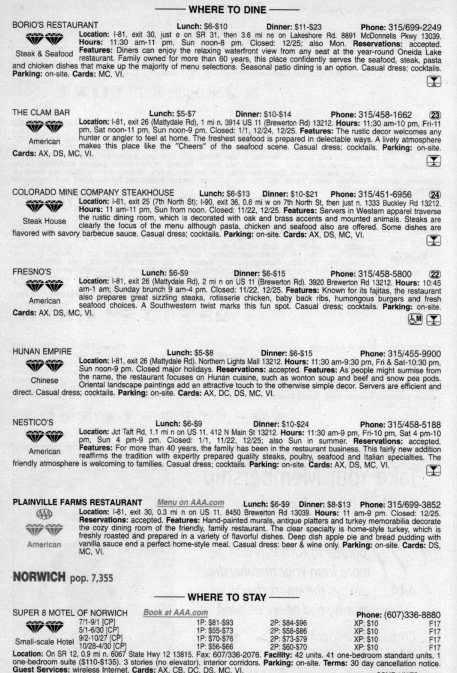
Location: I-81, exit 30, just e on SR 31, then 3.6 mi ne on Lakeshore Rd. 8891 McDonnells Pkwy 13039. **Hours:** 11:30 am-11 pm, Sun noon-8 pm. Closed: 12/25; also Mon. **Reservations:** accepted.
Steak & Seafood **Features:** Diners can enjoy the relaxing waterfront view from any seat at the year-round Oneida Lake restaurant. Family owned for more than 60 years, this place confidently serves the seafood, steak, pasta and chicken dishes that make up the majority of menu selections. Seasonal patio dining is an option. Casual dress; cocktails. **Parking:** on-site. **Cards:** MC, VI.

THE CLAM BAR   **Lunch:** $5-$7   **Dinner:** $10-$14   **Phone:** 315/458-1662   ㉓
Location: I-81, exit 26 (Mattydale Rd), 1 mi n. 3914 US 11 (Brewerton Rd) 13212. **Hours:** 11:30 am-10 pm, Fri-11 pm, Sat noon-11 pm, Sun noon-9 pm. Closed: 1/1, 12/24, 12/25. **Features:** The rustic decor welcomes any
American hunter or angler to feel at home. The freshest seafood is prepared in delectable ways. A lively atmosphere makes this place like the "Cheers" of the seafood scene. Casual dress; cocktails. **Parking:** on-site.
Cards: AX, DS, MC, VI.

COLORADO MINE COMPANY STEAKHOUSE   **Lunch:** $6-$13   **Dinner:** $10-$21   **Phone:** 315/451-6956   ㉔
Location: I-81, exit 25 (7th North St); I-90, exit 36, 0.6 mi w on 7th North St, then just n. 1333 Buckley Rd 13212. **Hours:** 11 am-11 pm, Sun from noon. Closed: 11/22, 12/25. **Features:** Servers in Western apparel traverse
Steak House the rustic dining room, which is decorated with oak and brass accents and mounted animals. Steaks are clearly the focus of the menu although pasta, chicken and seafood also are offered. Some dishes are flavored with savory barbecue sauce. Casual dress; cocktails. **Parking:** on-site. **Cards:** AX, DS, MC, VI.

FRESNO'S   **Lunch:** $6-$9   **Dinner:** $6-$15   **Phone:** 315/458-5800   ㉒
Location: I-81, exit 26 (Mattydale Rd), 2 mi n on US 11 (Brewerton Rd). 3920 Brewerton Rd 13212. **Hours:** 10:45 am-1 am; Sunday brunch 9 am-4 pm. Closed: 11/22, 12/25. **Features:** Known for its fajitas, the restaurant
American also prepares great sizzling steaks, rotisserie chicken, baby back ribs, humongous burgers and fresh seafood choices. A Southwestern twist marks this fun spot. Casual dress; cocktails. **Parking:** on-site.
Cards: AX, DS, MC, VI.

HUNAN EMPIRE   **Lunch:** $5-$8   **Dinner:** $6-$15   **Phone:** 315/455-9900
Location: I-81, exit 26 (Mattydale Rd). Northern Lights Mall 13212. **Hours:** 11:30 am-9:30 pm, Fri & Sat-10 pm, Sun noon-9 pm. Closed major holidays. **Reservations:** accepted. **Features:** As people might surmise from
Chinese the name, the restaurant focuses on Hunan cuisine, such as wonton soup and beef and snow pea pods. Oriental landscape paintings add an attractive touch to the otherwise simple decor. Servers are efficient and direct. Casual dress; cocktails. **Parking:** on-site. **Cards:** AX, DC, DS, MC, VI.

NESTICO'S   **Lunch:** $6-$9   **Dinner:** $10-$24   **Phone:** 315/458-5188
Location: Jct Taft Rd, 1.1 mi n on US 11. 412 N Main St 13212. **Hours:** 11:30 am-9 pm, Fri-10 pm, Sat 4 pm-10 pm, Sun 4 pm-9 pm. Closed: 1/1, 11/22, 12/25; also Sun in summer. **Reservations:** accepted.
American **Features:** For more than 40 years, the family has been in the restaurant business. This fairly new addition reaffirms the tradition with expertly prepared quality steaks, poultry, seafood and Italian specialties. The friendly atmosphere is welcoming to families. Casual dress; cocktails. **Parking:** on-site. **Cards:** AX, DS, MC, VI.

PLAINVILLE FARMS RESTAURANT   *Menu on AAA.com*   **Lunch:** $6-$9   **Dinner:** $8-$13   **Phone:** 315/699-3852
Location: I-81, exit 30, 0.3 mi n on US 11. 8450 Brewerton Rd 13039. **Hours:** 11 am-9 pm. Closed: 12/25. **Reservations:** accepted. **Features:** Hand-painted murals, antique platters and turkey memorabilia decorate
American the cozy dining room of the friendly, family restaurant. The clear specialty is home-style turkey, which is freshly roasted and prepared in a variety of flavorful dishes. Deep dish apple pie and bread pudding with vanilla sauce end a perfect home-style meal. Casual dress; beer & wine only. **Parking:** on-site. **Cards:** DS, MC, VI.

NORWICH pop. 7,355

─────── **WHERE TO STAY** ───────

SUPER 8 MOTEL OF NORWICH   *Book at AAA.com*   **Phone:** (607)336-8880

7/1-9/1 [CP]	1P: $81-$93	2P: $84-$96	XP: $10	F17
5/1-6/30 [CP]	1P: $55-$73	2P: $58-$86	XP: $10	F17
9/2-10/27 [CP]	1P: $70-$76	2P: $73-$79	XP: $10	F17
10/28-4/30 [CP]	1P: $56-$66	2P: $60-$70	XP: $10	F17

Small-scale Hotel
Location: On SR 12, 0.9 mi n. 6067 State Hwy 12 13815. **Fax:** 607/336-2076. **Facility:** 42 units. 41 one-bedroom standard units. 1 one-bedroom suite ($110-$135). 3 stories (no elevator), interior corridors. **Parking:** on-site. **Terms:** 30 day cancellation notice. **Guest Services:** wireless Internet. **Cards:** AX, CB, DC, DS, MC, VI.

SOME UNITS
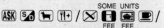

NYACK —See New York p. 501.

OGDENSBURG pop. 12,364

———— WHERE TO STAY ————

QUALITY INN GRAN-VIEW   *Book great rates at AAA.com*   **Phone:** (315)393-4550

7/1-8/31	1P: $104-$128	2P: $117-$159	XP: $10	F18
5/1-6/30	1P: $92-$121	2P: $104-$144	XP: $10	F18
9/1-10/31	1P: $92-$120	2P: $104-$144	XP: $10	F18
11/1-4/30	1P: $82-$99	2P: $91-$110	XP: $10	F18

Motel   **Location:** On SR 37, 3 mi sw. 6765 State Hwy 37 13669. **Fax:** 315/393-3520. **Facility:** 47 units. 44 one-bedroom standard units, some with whirlpools. 2 two-bedroom suites ($95-$165). 1 cottage ($127-$215). 1-2 stories (no elevator), interior/exterior corridors. **Parking:** on-site, winter plug-ins. **Terms:** [ECP] meal plan available, package plans, pets ($10 extra charge, in designated units). **Amenities:** high-speed Internet, voice mail, irons, hair dryers. *Some:* dual phone lines. **Dining:** Gran-View, see separate listing. **Pool(s):** outdoor. **Leisure Activities:** boat dock, fishing, lawn games, exercise room, shuffleboard, volleyball. **Guest Services:** coin laundry, wireless Internet. **Business Services:** meeting rooms. **Cards:** AX, DC, DS, MC, VI. **Free Special Amenities:** expanded continental breakfast and high-speed Internet.

SOME UNITS

THE STONEFENCE RESORT & MOTEL   *Book great rates at AAA.com*   **Phone:** (315)393-1545

5/1-10/31	1P: $69-$179	2P: $75-$179	XP: $10	F
11/1-4/30	1P: $65-$159	2P: $69-$159	XP: $10	F

Motel   **Location:** Jct SR 68, 0.5 mi w. 7191 SR 37 13669. **Fax:** 315/393-1749. **Facility:** 51 units. 45 one-bedroom standard units, some with whirlpools. 6 one-bedroom suites with kitchens. 1-2 stories (no elevator), interior/exterior corridors. **Bath:** combo or shower only. **Parking:** on-site, winter plug-ins. **Terms:** small pets only ($22.50 fee, in designated units). **Amenities:** *Some:* voice mail, irons, hair dryers. **Dining:** Stonefence Dining Room, see separate listing. **Pool(s):** heated outdoor. **Leisure Activities:** paddleboats, marina, fishing, putting green, tennis court, playground, basketball, horseshoes, shuffleboard, volleyball. **Guest Services:** coin laundry, wireless Internet. **Business Services:** meeting rooms. **Cards:** AX, CB, DC, DS, JC, MC, VI. **Free Special Amenities:** full breakfast and high-speed Internet.

SOME UNITS

———— WHERE TO DINE ————

GRAN-VIEW   **Lunch:** $5-$12   **Dinner:** $8-$19   **Phone:** 315/393-4550

Continental   **Location:** On SR 37, 3 mi sw; in Quality Inn Gran-View. 6765 State Hwy 37 13669. **Hours:** 6 am-10 pm, Sun 8 am-9 pm; Fri & Sat 6 am-11 pm in summer. **Closed:** 9/3, 11/22, 12/24. **Reservations:** accepted. **Features:** Overlooking the St. Lawrence River, the restaurant affords stunning views of the Canadian sunset. Italian influences touch selections of Continental cuisine, such as chicken cordon bleu in burgundy currant sauce. The chocolate cheesecake is decadent. Casual dress; cocktails. **Parking:** on-site. **Cards:** AX, CB, DC, DS, JC, MC, VI.

STONEFENCE DINING ROOM   **Lunch:** $4-$10   **Dinner:** $8-$17   **Phone:** 315/393-1545

American   **Location:** Jct SR 68, 0.5 mi w; in The Stonefence Resort & Motel. 7191 State Hwy 37 13669. **Hours:** 7 am-2:30 & 4:30-9 pm. **Closed:** in winter. **Reservations:** accepted. **Features:** The inviting, seasonal patio—as well as both levels of the dining room—overlooks beautifully landscaped grounds and the waterway. London broil is representative of traditionally prepared menu selections. Service is attentive throughout the meal. Casual dress. **Parking:** on-site. **Cards:** AX, DC, DS, MC, VI.

OLD FORGE —See also ADIRONDACK MOUNTAINS.

———— WHERE TO STAY ————

19TH GREEN MOTEL   **Phone:** 315/369-3575

6/26-10/15		2P: $65-$125	XP: $5	F
12/25-4/30		2P: $55-$125	XP: $10	F
5/1-6/25		2P: $50-$75	XP: $5	F
10/16-12/24		2P: $45-$75	XP: $5	F

Motel   **Location:** 0.3 mi s. 2761 SR 28 13420 (PO Box 37). **Fax:** 315/369-4437. **Facility:** 13 one-bedroom standard units. 1 story, exterior corridors. **Bath:** combo or shower only. **Parking:** on-site, winter plug-ins. **Terms:** 14 day cancellation notice-fee imposed. **Amenities:** hair dryers. **Pool(s):** heated outdoor. **Leisure Activities:** cross country skiing, snowmobiling, bicycles, hiking trails. **Guest Services:** wireless Internet. **Cards:** AX, DS, MC, VI. **Free Special Amenities:** local telephone calls and high-speed Internet.

BEST WESTERN SUNSET INN   *Book great rates at AAA.com*   **Phone:** (315)369-6836

6/19-10/18	1P: $89-$209	2P: $89-$209	XP: $10	F13
10/19-4/30	1P: $69-$209	2P: $69-$209	XP: $10	F13
5/1-6/18	1P: $89-$149	2P: $89-$149	XP: $10	F13

Motel   **Location:** 0.3 mi s. 2752 SR 28 13420 (PO Box 261). **Fax:** 315/369-2607. **Facility:** 52 one-bedroom standard units, some with whirlpools. 1-2 stories (no elevator), interior/exterior corridors. **Parking:** on-site, winter plug-ins. **Terms:** 7 day cancellation notice, pets (dogs only, in smoking units). **Amenities:** high-speed Internet, irons, hair dryers. **Pool(s):** heated indoor. **Leisure Activities:** sauna, whirlpool, tennis court. **Guest Services:** coin laundry. **Cards:** AX, DC, DS, MC, VI.

SOME UNITS

BLUE SPRUCE MOTEL

Phone: 315/369-3817

7/1-11/30	2P: $75-$130	XP: $10	F11
12/1-4/1	2P: $55-$125	XP: $10	F11
5/1-6/30	2P: $50-$90	XP: $10	F11

Motel

Location: Just s of town center. 2898 SR 28 13420 (PO Box 604). **Facility:** 13 one-bedroom standard units. 1 story, exterior corridors. **Parking:** on-site, winter plug-ins. **Terms:** open 5/1-4/1, 2 night minimum stay - weekends, 7 day cancellation notice-fee imposed, weekly rates available. **Pool(s):** heated outdoor. **Guest Services:** wireless Internet. **Cards:** AX, DS, MC, VI.

COUNTRY CLUB MOTEL

Phone: 315/369-6340

All Year	1P: $60-$125	2P: $60-$125	XP: $10	F11

Motel

Location: 0.3 mi s. 2747 SR 28 13420 (PO Box 419). Fax: 315/369-2011. **Facility:** 27 one-bedroom standard units. 1 story, exterior corridors. **Parking:** on-site. **Terms:** 2 night minimum stay - seasonal and/or weekends, 14 day cancellation notice. **Pool(s):** heated outdoor. **Cards:** AX, DS, MC, VI.

SOME UNITS

WATER'S EDGE INN & CONFERENCE CENTER

Phone: 315/369-2484

Property failed to provide current rates

Small-scale Hotel

Location: On SR 28; center. Located opposite the Enchanted Forest. 3188 SR 28 13420 (PO Box 181). Fax: 315/369-6782. **Facility:** 75 units. 58 one-bedroom standard units. 17 one-bedroom suites. 2-3 stories (no elevator), interior corridors. **Bath:** combo or shower only. **Parking:** on-site. **Terms:** office hours 8 am-11 pm. **Amenities:** irons, hair dryers. **Pool(s):** heated indoor. **Leisure Activities:** sauna, boat dock, fishing. **Business Services:** meeting rooms.

SOME UNITS

--------- **WHERE TO DINE** ---------

THE OLD MILL RESTAURANT

American

Dinner: $15-$34

Phone: 315/369-3662

Location: 0.3 mi sw. 2888 SR 28 13420. **Hours:** Open 5/10-11/1 & 12/26-3/15; 4:30 pm-9:30 pm, Fri & Sat-10 pm, Sun 4 pm-9 pm; hours may vary in winter. Closed: 3/23, 11/22, 12/25. **Features:** Resembling a rustic, Adirondack log cabin, the dining room is a casual spot for cozy family dining. Patrons can expect large portions of everything from salad to steak. The restaurant often is packed, and it's not unusual to have to wait during peak times. Casual dress; cocktails. **Parking:** on-site. **Cards:** MC, VI.

OLEAN pop. 15,347

--------- **WHERE TO STAY** ---------

HAMPTON INN

Small-scale Hotel

Book great rates at AAA.com

All Year   1P: $65-$209

Phone: (716)375-1000

Location: I-86, exit 26, at SR 16 (Union St). 101 Main St 14760. Fax: 716/375-1279. **Facility:** 76 one-bedroom standard units, some with whirlpools. 3 stories, interior corridors. **Bath:** combo or shower only. **Parking:** on-site. **Amenities:** video library, DVD players, dual phone lines, voice mail, irons, hair dryers. **Pool(s):** small heated indoor. **Leisure Activities:** exercise room. **Guest Services:** valet and coin laundry, wireless Internet. **Business Services:** meeting rooms, PC. **Cards:** AX, DC, DS, MC, VI.

SOME UNITS

OLD LIBRARY INN BED & BREAKFAST

Phone: (716)373-9804

All Year	1P: $85-$135	XP: $10	F5

Historic Bed & Breakfast

Location: I-86, exit 26, 1.4 mi s on SR 16 (Union St); just s of jct SR 417; downtown. 120 S Union St 14760. Fax: 716/373-2462. **Facility:** Hand-carved oak woodwork distinguishes this restored 1895 Victorian home; furnishings include numerous antiques. Smoke free premises. 9 units. 8 one-bedroom standard units. 1 one-bedroom suite. 2 stories (no elevator), interior/exterior corridors. **Bath:** combo or shower only. **Parking:** on-site. **Terms:** office hours 7 am-4 pm, off-site registration, cancellation fee imposed, package plans. **Dining:** restaurant, see separate listing. **Guest Services:** valet laundry, wireless Internet. **Business Services:** meeting rooms. **Cards:** AX, DC, DS, MC, VI.

SOME UNITS

FEE

--------- **WHERE TO DINE** ---------

ANGEE'S

Italian

Lunch: $5-$8   **Dinner:** $9-$16

Phone: 716/373-7070

Location: Center. 475 N Union St 14760. **Hours:** 11 am-10 pm, Fri & Sat-11 pm. Closed major holidays; also Sun. **Reservations:** accepted. **Features:** The restaurant is a top choice of locals for its ever-changing menu of Italian dishes. Fast, friendly service is the norm in the relaxing atmosphere. Casual dress; cocktails. **Parking:** street. **Cards:** AX, DS, MC, VI.

BEEF N' BARREL RESTAURANT

American

Lunch: $5-$8   **Dinner:** $8-$17

Phone: 716/372-2985

Location: Jct SR 16 (Union St) and 417; downtown. 146 N Union St 14760. **Hours:** 11 am-10 pm. Closed major holidays; also Sun. **Features:** The restaurant is popular and with good reason. Selections of USDA Choice beef, especially hand-carved roast beef, are succulent and well-prepared. All dressings—as well as such aromatic baked goods as bread, rolls, pastries, cakes and the like—are made on the premises. Casual dress; cocktails. **Parking:** on-site. **Cards:** AX, DC, DS, MC, VI.

CENTURY MANOR GRILLE HOUSE Dinner: $13-$24 Phone: 716/372-1864
▼▼ ▼▼▼ **Location:** I-86, exit 26, just s of jct SR 16 (Union St) and 417. 401 E State St 14760. **Hours:** 4:30 pm-10:30 pm, Sun-9:30 pm. **Closed:** 12/25. **Reservations:** suggested. **Features:** The fine dining establishment nurtures a relaxed atmosphere. On the menu are Certified Angus beef, seafood, meat and pasta dishes, some prepared on the open pit grill. Mix-and-match items help diners who can't decide among the delicious entrees. Formal attire; cocktails. **Parking:** on-site. **Cards:** AX, DS, MC, VI.

Steak & Seafood

OLD LIBRARY RESTAURANT Lunch: $7-$11 Dinner: $11-$38 Phone: 716/372-2226
◬◬◬ **Location:** I-86, exit 26, 1.4 mi s on SR 16 (Union St); just s of jct SR 417; downtown; in Old Library Inn Bed & Breakfast. 116 S Union St 14760. **Hours:** 11 am-10 pm, Sun-9 pm; Sunday brunch. **Closed:** 5/28, 9/3, 12/25.
▼▼▼▼▼ **Reservations:** accepted. **Features:** The renovated 1909 library serves as a finely appointed yet casually relaxed setting in which to enjoy such creatively prepared dishes as pasta Louis, antelope and steak.
American Chicken, veal and seafood entrees also share menu space. Patrons can choose an appropriate wine from the impressive selection carefully stored in the on-premises cellar. Servers show good menu knowledge.
Casual dress; cocktails. **Parking:** on-site. **Cards:** AX, DC, DS, MC, VI. **Historic**

ONEIDA pop. 10,987

———— **WHERE TO STAY** ————

ONEIDA COMMUNITY MANSION HOUSE Phone: 315/363-0745
▼▼▼▼▼ All Year [BP] 1P: $100-$150 2P: $100-$150
Location: I-90, exit 33, 4 mi s on SR 365 to SR 5, 1.9 mi e to Sherrill Rd, then 1 mi s. 170 Kenwood Ave 13421.
Historic Fax: 315/361-4580. **Facility:** A historically significant mansion, the property offers communal dining and
Small-scale Hotel comfortable, spacious accommodations with a homey style. 8 one-bedroom standard units. 1 story, interior corridors. **Parking:** on-site. **Terms:** package plans. **Amenities:** voice mail, honor bars, irons, hair dryers.
Leisure Activities: Fee: golf-18 holes. **Business Services:** meeting rooms. **Cards:** AX, DS, MC, VI.

SOME UNITS

SUPER 8 MOTEL-ONEIDA *Book at AAA.com* Phone: (315)363-5168
▼▼▼▼ ▼▼▼ 5/1-8/31 1P: $58-$82 2P: $58-$82 XP: $5 F16
5/1-4/30 1P: $99-$199 2P: $99-$199 XP: $5 F16
Small-scale Hotel **Location:** I-90, exit 33, 4 mi s on SR 365 to SR 5, then 0.5 mi w. 215 Genesee St 13421. Fax: 315/363-4628.
Facility: 40 units. 39 one-bedroom standard units. 1 one-bedroom suite. 2 stories (no elevator), interior corridors. **Parking:** on-site. **Terms:** [CP] meal plan available, package plans. **Amenities:** irons, hair dryers. **Guest Services:** wireless Internet. **Business Services:** PC. **Cards:** AX, CB, DC, DS, JC, MC, VI.

SOME UNITS

ONEONTA pop. 13,292

———— **WHERE TO STAY** ————

CLARION HOTEL *Book great rates at AAA.com* Phone: (607)432-7500
▼▼▼▼ ▼▼▼ 6/15-9/3 1P: $179-$299 2P: $179-$299 XP: $12 F18
5/1-6/14 & 9/4-4/30 1P: $99-$199 2P: $99-$199 XP: $12 F18
Small-scale Hotel **Location:** I-88, exit 15 (SR 23 and 28) to Main St, just w, then just s on S Main St; downtown. 55 Market St 13820.
Fax: 607/433-2202. **Facility:** 78 one-bedroom standard units, some with whirlpools. 5 stories, interior corridors. Bath: combo or shower only. **Parking:** on-site. **Terms:** 2-7 night minimum stay - seasonal and/or weekends, 7 day cancellation notice, [AP] meal plan available, package plans, $2 service charge. **Amenities:** dual phone lines, voice mail, irons, hair dryers. **Pool(s):** small heated indoor. **Leisure Activities:** sauna, whirlpool, exercise room. **Business Services:** valet and coin laundry, wireless Internet. **Business Services:** meeting rooms, business center. **Cards:** AX, CB, DC, DS, JC, MC, VI.

SOME UNITS

HAMPTON INN ONEONTA *Book great rates at AAA.com* Phone: 607/433-9000
▼▼▼ ▼▼▼ ▼▼▼ 6/15-9/7 1P: $169-$229 2P: $169-$229
5/1-6/14 1P: $169-$189 2P: $169-$189
Small-scale Hotel 9/8-11/1 1P: $139-$169 2P: $139-$169
11/2-4/30 1P: $99-$129 2P: $99-$129
Location: I-88, exit 13, just n on SR 205, 0.9 mi e on River Street Service Rd. 225 River St 13820. Fax: 607/433-9001. **Facility:** 71 one-bedroom standard units, some with whirlpools. 4 stories, interior corridors. Bath: combo or shower only. **Parking:** on-site. **Terms:** cancellation fee imposed, weekly rates available, package plans. **Amenities:** high-speed Internet, voice mail, irons, hair dryers. **Pool(s):** small heated indoor. **Leisure Activities:** whirlpool, exercise room. **Guest Services:** valet and coin laundry. **Business Services:** meeting rooms, PC. **Cards:** AX, DC, DS, JC, MC, VI.

SOME UNITS
FEE FEE

HOLIDAY INN ONEONTA/COOPERSTOWN AREA *Book great rates at AAA.com* Phone: (607)433-2250
◬◬◬ SAVE 7/1-9/2 1P: $129-$209 2P: $209 XP: $10 F18
5/1-6/30 & 9/3-4/30 1P: $79-$159 2P: $79-$159 XP: $10 F18
▼▼▼▼▼ **Location:** I-88, exit 15 (SR 23 and 28), 1.5 mi e. 5206 State Hwy 23 13820-0634 (PO Box 634). Fax: 607/432-7028.
Small-scale Hotel **Facility:** 120 one-bedroom standard units, some with whirlpools. 2 stories (no elevator), interior corridors.
Bath: combo or shower only. **Parking:** on-site. **Terms:** small pets only ($10 fee, in designated units).
Amenities: voice mail, irons, hair dryers. **Dining:** 6:30 am-10 & 5-10 pm; hours may vary in winter, cocktails. **Pool(s):** outdoor, wading. **Leisure Activities:** soccer field, grill, playground, exercise room, basketball, shuffleboard, volleyball. Fee: game room. **Guest Services:** valet and coin laundry, wireless Internet. **Business Services:** conference facilities, PC. **Cards:** AX, CB, DC, DS, JC, MC, VI. **Free Special Amenities:** newspaper and high-speed Internet.

SOME UNITS
FEE

KOUNTRY LIVING-THE SISTERS B & B   Phone: 607/432-0186

▽▽▽ ▽▽▽   All Year   1P: $110   2P: $125

Historic Bed   **Location:** I-88, exit 14 (SR 23 and 28) eastbound, just s; exit 15 (SR 23 and 28) westbound, 1 mi s. 576 SR 28 13820.
& Breakfast   **Facility:** Casual decor and handcrafted accents bring a country ambience to this near-town B&B. 4 one-bedroom standard units. 2 stories (no elevator), interior corridors. *Bath:* shared. **Parking:** on-site.
                Terms: age restrictions may apply, 30 day cancellation notice-fee imposed.

SOME UNITS

⊠ / ☎ /

RAINBOW INN ONEONTA/COOPERSTOWN AREA   Phone: (607)432-1280

AAA SAVE   5/1-9/1   1P: $119-$189   2P: $129-$200   XP: $10   F18
            9/2-4/30   1P: $79-$158   2P: $89-$178   XP: $10   F18
▽▽▽ ▽▽▽   **Location:** I-88, exit 16 (Emmons/Davenport), 0.3 mi e. 5690 SR 7 13820. Fax: 607/433-2972. **Facility:** 28 one-bedroom standard units, some with whirlpools. 1 story, interior/exterior corridors. **Parking:** on-site, winter
Motel   plug-ins. **Terms:** 30 day cancellation notice-fee imposed. **Amenities:** voice mail. *Some:* DVD players, hair dryers. **Pool(s):** heated outdoor. **Guest Services:** coin laundry. **Cards:** AX, DS, MC, VI.
Free Special Amenities: continental breakfast.

SOME UNITS

S⊘ 🍴 🏊 / ⊠ VCR 🔌 🖥 /

SUPER 8 MOTEL   *Book at AAA.com*   Phone: (607)432-9505

▽▽▽ ▽▽▽   6/19-9/5   1P: $111-$150   2P: $111-$150   XP: $8   F17
            9/6-12/31   1P: $90-$120   2P: $90-$120   XP: $8   F17
Small-scale Hotel 5/1-6/18   1P: $75-$105   2P: $75-$105   XP: $8   F17
            1/1-4/30   1P: $68-$95   2P: $68-$95   XP: $8   F17
Location: I-88, exit 15 (SR 23 and 28), 0.3 mi e. 4973 SR 23 13820. Fax: 607/432-9505. **Facility:** 60 one-bedroom standard units. 2 stories (no elevator), interior corridors. **Parking:** on-site, winter plug-ins. **Amenities:** video library (fee), hair dryers. **Guest Services:** coin laundry, wireless Internet. **Cards:** AX, DC, DS, MC, VI.

SOME UNITS

ASK S⊘ 🐾 🍴 ⚙M / ⊠ VCR 🔌 🖥 /
                                              FEE   FEE FEE

———— The following lodging was either not evaluated or did not ————
meet AAA rating requirements but is listed for your information only.

CHRISTOPHER'S LODGE   Phone: 607/432-2444

fyi   Not evaluated. **Location:** I-88, exit 14 (SR 23 and 28) eastbound, just e; exit 15 (SR 23 and 28) westbound, just w. Rt 28 Southside 13820 (4158 Hwy 28). Facilities, services, and decor characterize a mid-range property.

———— **WHERE TO DINE** ————

AUTUMN CAFE   **Lunch:** $7-$9   **Dinner:** $10-$18   Phone: 607/432-6845

▽▽▽ ▽▽▽   **Location:** Center. 244 Main St 13820. **Hours:** 11 am-9 pm; Sunday brunch 10:30 am-2:30 pm. Closed major
American   holidays; also Mon. **Features:** Since 1980, the cafe has featured daily-changing specials in addition to its tasty sandwiches, omelets, seafood, poultry, Mexican and vegetarian entrees. Most soups, breads and desserts are made on the premises. Patio seating, entertainment and an ever-changing artwork display make this a favorite gathering place. Casual dress; beer & wine only. **Parking:** street. **Cards:** AX, MC, VI.

🍸

BROOKS HOUSE OF BAR-B-Q   **Lunch:** $4-$8   **Dinner:** $6-$14   Phone: 607/432-1782

AAA   **Location:** I-88, exit 16 (Emmons/Davenport), 0.3 mi w, then 2 mi e. 5560 State Hwy 7 13820. **Hours:** 11 am-9 pm;
▽▽▽   Tues, Wed & Sun to 8:30 pm in winter. Closed: 1/1, 11/22, 12/24, 12/25; also 12/31, Tues after Labor Day &
American   Mon except Memorial Day & Labor Day. **Features:** Delicious chicken, ribs, pork, beef and seafood are prepared over a charcoal pit barbecue. The family-oriented restaurant is large and open, while the summer picnic areas encourage guests to kick back and enjoy time among friends. Servers are pleasant. Casual dress. **Parking:** on-site. **Cards:** AX, DS, MC, VI.

CHINA 19 RESTAURANT   **Lunch:** $5-$7   **Dinner:** $6-$10   Phone: 607/433-8888

▽▽▽   **Location:** Center. 156 Main St 13820. **Hours:** 11 am-10 pm, Fri & Sat-11 pm, Sun noon-10 pm. Closed: 7/4,
Chinese   11/22, 12/25. **Reservations:** accepted. **Features:** The restaurant invites patrons to dine in or take out freshly prepared Chinese and Japanese cuisine. The dining room is comfortable. Casual dress. **Parking:** street. **Cards:** AX, DS, MC, VI.

CHRISTOPHER'S RESTAURANT   **Lunch:** $7-$9   **Dinner:** $7-$20   Phone: 607/432-2444

▽▽▽ ▽▽▽   **Location:** I-88, exit 14 (SR 23 and 28) eastbound, just e; exit 15 (SR 23 and 28) westbound, just w. Rt 28 Southside
American   13820. **Hours:** 11 am-9 pm, Fri & Sat-10 pm. **Reservations:** accepted. **Features:** Dine in an Adirondack-like log cabin with genuine rustic decor. Choose one of their steak, pasta, chicken or seafood entrees with salad bar included. Early bird and children's menu items are offered. Casual dress; cocktails. **Parking:** on-site.
Cards: AX, MC, VI.

🍸

CORFU DINER   **Lunch:** $3-$9   **Dinner:** $9-$13   Phone: 607/643-0232

▽▽▽   **Location:** Center. 139 Main St 13820. **Hours:** 7 am-9 pm, Fri & Sat-10 pm. Closed: 12/25.
International **Reservations:** accepted, Fri & Sat. **Features:** The corner diner is alive and well. Delicious, freshly prepared dishes are served from breakfast to dinner. Italian and Thai choices are offered along with the Mediterranean and American. Also available is a long list of hot and cold sandwiches. Casual dress.
Parking: on-site. **Cards:** AX, DS, MC, VI.

FARMHOUSE   **Dinner:** $11-$29   Phone: 607/432-7374

▽▽▽ ▽▽▽   **Location:** I-88, exit 16 (Emmons/Davenport), just n. SR 7 13820. **Hours:** 3 pm-9 pm, Fri & Sat-9:30 pm, Sun
American   noon-9 pm. Closed: 12/25. **Reservations:** accepted. **Features:** Traditional steaks, chops, seafood, chicken and vegetarian choices are the fare in the century-old farmhouse. Guests can enjoy fireside dining under a plethora of stained-glass lamps, under a billowy ceiling in the blue room or on a covered patio in the company of hanging geraniums. The abundant salad bar features peel-and-eat shrimp, soups, salads, homemade breads and pasta. Casual dress; cocktails. **Parking:** on-site. **Cards:** AX, MC, VI. **Historic**

IANNELLI'S RISTORANTE Lunch: $5-$10 Dinner: $11-$21 Phone: 607/433-5230

Regional Italian

Location: SR 7 and 23, 0.4 mi w of jct Main St. 99 Chestnut St 13820. **Hours:** 11:30 am-10 pm, Sun 1 pm-9 pm. Closed major holidays. **Reservations:** suggested. **Features:** The popular restaurant deserves its popularity for distinctive cuisine. Ample, reasonably priced meals are prepared in the nouveau style—affording diners a refreshing change from typical Italian fare. Tiramisu and cheesecake are good dessert choices. Casual dress; cocktails. **Parking:** on-site. **Cards:** AX, DS, MC, VI.

JOE RUFFINO'S PIZZERIA & RESTAURANT Lunch: $2-$9 Dinner: $4-$9 Phone: 607/432-7400

Italian

beer & wine only.

Location: I-88, exit 14 (SR 23 and 28), just n; downtown. 224 Main St 13820. **Hours:** 11 am-10 pm. Closed major holidays; also Sun. **Features:** Since 1972, the Ruffino family has served great prepared-to-order Italian food. Among offerings are weekly specials, pasta dinners, cold and hot submarine sandwiches and salads, as well as pizza and wings. The pizzeria offers free delivery in the city limits from 5 pm-close. Casual dress; **Parking:** street.

NEPTUNE DINER Lunch: $5-$7 Dinner: $9-$18 Phone: 607/432-8820

American

Location: I-88, exit 15 (SR 23 and 28), 0.5 mi e. 5001 SR 23 13820. **Hours:** 24 hours. **Reservations:** accepted. **Features:** Diners can enjoy their favorite American, Greek and Italian comfort foods in this throwback to a '50s diner. Contributing to the decor are a jukebox, neon signs, chrome accents and unusual tropical fish tanks flanking the spare dining room. Casual dress; cocktails. **Parking:** on-site. **Cards:** AX, MC, VI.

SABATINI'S LITTLE ITALY Lunch: $7-$8 Dinner: $11-$18 Phone: 607/432-3000

Italian

brick-oven pizza.

Location: I-88, exit 15 (SR 23 and 28), just s, then just w. Rt 23 Southside 13820. **Hours:** 11:30 am-9 pm, Fri-10 pm, Sat 4 pm-10 pm, Sun 1 pm-9 pm. Closed: 12/25. **Reservations:** accepted. **Features:** The charming dining room is set up to remind diners of Old Italy. Wrought-iron lamps and a suspended ceiling add to the look. The menu centers on large portions of pasta, veal, beef, chicken and seafood, as well as flavorful Casual dress; cocktails. **Parking:** on-site. **Cards:** AX, MC, VI.

STELLA LUNA RISTORANTE Dinner: $10-$30 Phone: 607/433-7646

Italian

MC, VI.

Location: Downtown. 58-60 Market St 13820. **Hours:** 5 pm-9:30 pm, Fri & Sat-10:30 pm; hours may vary off season. Closed: 11/22, 12/25; also Sun. **Reservations:** required, weekends. **Features:** The renovated 1892 train station has been transformed with soft tones into an outdoor courtyard, cantina-type atmosphere. The "sky" room is divine. Among examples of traditional fare are Chilean sea bass, veal chops, homemade ravioli and preparations of Certified Angus beef. Desserts are made on the premises, and wine can be selected from a temperature-controlled room. Casual dress; cocktails. **Parking:** on-site. **Cards:** AX, DS,

ORANGEBURG —See New York p. 502.

ORIENT pop. 709

——— WHERE TO DINE ———

ORIENT BY THE SEA RESTAURANT & MARINA Lunch: $7-$14 Dinner: $14-$28 Phone: 631/323-2424

American

Location: Just w of Long Island Ferry terminal. Main Rd 11957. **Hours:** Open 5/1-10/31; 11:30 am-10 pm; hours vary off season. **Reservations:** accepted. **Features:** In close proximity to the ferry terminal, the restaurant specializes in creative American cuisine, particularly local seafood, steaks and chicken. The decor is a little on the plain side, but the views of Gardiner's Bay and the marina are first rate. Casual dress; cocktails. **Parking:** on-site. **Cards:** MC, VI.

OSSINING —See New York p. 502.

OSWEGO pop. 17,954

——— WHERE TO STAY ———

BEST WESTERN CAPTAIN'S QUARTERS *Book great rates at AAA.com* Phone: (315)342-4040

Small-scale Hotel

All Year [ECP]	1P: $104-$119	2P: $116-$131	XP: $12	F18

Location: Just n on SR 481. 26 E 1st St 13126. Fax: 315/342-5454. **Facility:** 93 units. 90 one-bedroom standard units. 3 one-bedroom suites ($120-$204). 4 stories, interior corridors. **Bath:** combo or shower only. **Parking:** on-site. **Terms:** cancellation fee imposed. **Amenities:** video games (fee), high-speed Internet, voice mail, honor bars, irons, hair dryers. **Pool(s):** heated indoor, lap. **Leisure Activities:** sauna, whirlpool, steamroom. **Guest Services:** valet laundry, wireless Internet. **Business Services:** meeting rooms. **Cards:** AX, CB, DC, DS, MC, VI.

SOME UNITS

ECONO LODGE INN & SUITES *Book great rates at AAA.com* Phone: (315)343-1600

Small-scale Hotel

MC, VI.

5/1-10/29 [CP]	1P: $78-$215	2P: $88-$225	XP: $10	F16
10/30-4/30 [CP]	1P: $68-$137	2P: $80-$149	XP: $10	F16

Location: Just n on SR 481. 70 E 1st St 13126. Fax: 315/343-1222. **Facility:** 93 units. 81 one-bedroom standard units. 12 one-bedroom suites, some with kitchens. 5 stories, interior corridors. **Bath:** combo or shower only. **Parking:** on-site, winter plug-ins. **Amenities:** high-speed Internet, voice mail, irons, hair dryers. **Some:** DVD players. **Guest Services:** valet laundry, wireless Internet. **Business Services:** meeting rooms. **Cards:** AX, CB, DC, DS, JC,

SOME UNITS

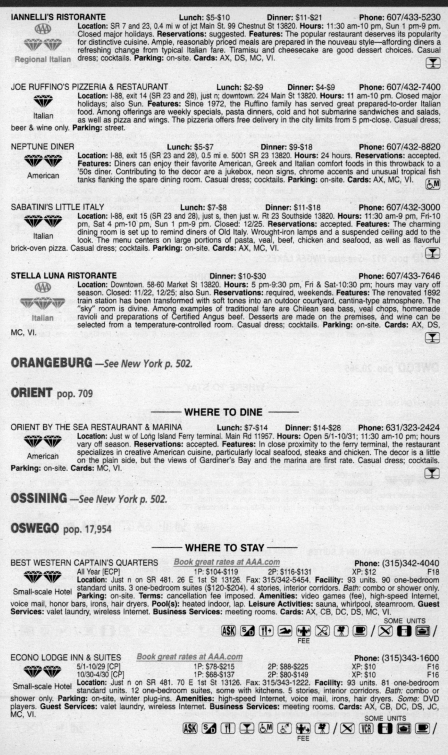

OSWEGO INN LTD

Phone: 315/342-6200

Small-scale Hotel
DS, MC, VI.

All Year 1P: $55-$150 2P: $55-$150 XP: $10 F12
Location: Jct 10th St and SR 104; center. 180 E 10th St 13126. Fax: 315/343-6234. **Facility:** Smoke free premises. 13 one-bedroom standard units. 2 stories (no elevator), interior corridors. **Parking:** on-site. **Terms:** 3 day cancellation notice-fee imposed, weekly rates available, [CP] meal plan available. **Cards:** AX,

---

——— WHERE TO DINE ———

CANALE'S RISTORANTE

Italian

Lunch: $6-$8 Dinner: $8-$20 Phone: 315/343-3540
Location: Jct Utica and Herrick sts; jct SR 481, 0.8 mi w. 156 W Utica St 13126. **Hours:** 11:30 am-10 pm, Fri & Sat-11 pm; open at 4:30 pm in summer. Closed major holidays; also for lunch Sat & Sun in summer. **Reservations:** suggested. **Features:** Vintage artwork, overhead lighting and lots of windows add to the casual warmth of the informal dining room. Diners enjoy good-size portions of steak, veal, pizza, sandwiches and seafood. Servers in attractive uniforms are pleasant and prompt. Casual dress; cocktails. **Parking:** on-site. **Cards:** AX, DC, DS, MC, VI.

COLEMAN'S

Irish

Lunch: $6-$8 Dinner: $8-$18 Phone: 315/343-1433
Location: Bayfront at Seneca and 1st sts W; center. W Seneca St 13126. **Hours:** 11:30 am-10 pm, Fri & Sat-11 pm, Sun noon-9 pm. Closed: 11/22, 12/25. **Reservations:** accepted. **Features:** Overlooking the harbor and Lake Ontario, the cozy pub presents a menu of traditional Irish fare and American favorites. Casual dress; cocktails. **Parking:** on-site. **Cards:** AX, DS, MC, VI.

OVID pop. 612—See also FINGER LAKES.

——— WHERE TO DINE ———

SHELDRAKE POINT VINEYARD & CAFE

Regional American

Lunch: $4-$8 Dinner: $18-$22 Phone: 607/532-9401
Location: Off SR 89, follow signs. 7448 CR 153 14521. **Hours:** Open 5/1-10/31 & 2/1-4/30; 11 am-3 & 6-9:30 pm; seasonal hours vary. Closed: 1/1, 11/22, 12/25. **Reservations:** suggested, for dinner. **Features:** This lakeside cafe offers casual fine dining at their vineyard tasting room. Wine-inspired cuisine can also be enjoyed in their courtyard or on the deck. Casual dress; beer & wine only. **Parking:** on-site. **Cards:** DS, MC, VI.

OWEGO pop. 20,365

——— WHERE TO STAY ———

HAMPTON INN OWEGO

[fyi]

Phone: 607/687-4600

Small-scale Hotel

1/1-4/30 1P: $119-$169 2P: $129-$169
5/1-10/30 1P: $119-$159 2P: $129-$159
10/31-12/31 1P: $119-$149 2P: $129-$149
Too new to rate, opening scheduled for December 2006. **Location:** SR 17, exit 65. 1030 SR 17C 13827. **Amenities:** 66 units, coffeemakers, pool. **Cards:** AX, DC, DS, MC, VI.

HOLIDAY INN EXPRESS *Book at AAA.com*

Phone: (607)687-9000

Small-scale Hotel

All Year [CP] 1P: $90-$100 XP: $15 F18
Location: SR 17, exit 65, at foot of ramp. 20 Hickories Park Rd 13827. Fax: 607/687-3034. **Facility:** 74 one-bedroom standard units, some with efficiencies. 2 stories, interior corridors. **Parking:** on-site. **Terms:** check-in 4 pm. **Amenities:** dual phone lines, voice mail, irons, hair dryers. **Leisure Activities:** fishing. **Guest Services:** valet and coin laundry, wireless Internet. **Business Services:** PC. **Cards:** AX, CB, DC, DS, JC, MC, VI.

SOME UNITS

OWEGO TREADWAY INN & SUITES *Book great rates at AAA.com*

Phone: (607)687-4500

Small-scale Hotel

All Year 2P: $90-$100 XP: $15 F18
Location: SR 17, exit 65. 1100 SR 17C 13827. Fax: 607/687-2456. **Facility:** 92 units. 88 one-bedroom standard units, some with whirlpools. 4 one-bedroom suites with efficiencies. 2 stories, interior corridors. **Bath:** combo or shower only. **Parking:** on-site. **Terms:** check-in 4 pm, [AP] meal plan available. **Amenities:** irons, hair dryers. *Some:* safes. **Dining:** 6:30 am-2 & 5-9:30 pm, Sat-10 pm, Sun 7 am-2 & 5-9 pm, cocktails. **Pool(s):** small heated indoor. **Leisure Activities:** fishing, exercise room. **Guest Services:** valet laundry, wireless Internet. **Business Services:** conference facilities, PC. **Cards:** AX, CB, DC, DS, MC, VI. **Free Special Amenities:** local telephone calls and high-speed Internet.

SOME UNITS

SUNRISE MOTEL

Motel

Phone: (607)687-5667

5/1-11/30 1P: $51-$55 2P: $55-$65 XP: $10 F10
12/1-4/30 1P: $46-$55 2P: $50-$65 XP: $10 F10
Location: SR 17, exit 64 (SR 96 N) across river w to SR 17C, 2 mi w. 3778 Waverly Rd 13827. Fax: 607/687-5666. **Facility:** 20 one-bedroom standard units. 1 story, exterior corridors. **Bath:** combo or shower only. **Parking:** on-site; winter plug-ins. **Terms:** office hours 7 am-11 am, cancellation fee imposed, package plans, pets (small dogs only, $5 extra charge, in designated units). **Cards:** AX, DC, DS, MC, VI. **Free Special Amenities:** continental breakfast and high-speed Internet.

SOME UNITS

——— WHERE TO DINE ———

THE JAIL HOUSE RESTAURANT   **Lunch:** $7-$16   **Dinner:** $8-$25   **Phone:** 607/687-9811
ᗐᗐᗐ ᗐᗐᗐ   **Location:** SR 17, exit 64; jct SR 17C and 96; downtown. 176 Main St 13827. **Hours:** 11 am-9 pm, Fri & Sat-10 pm.
American   Closed: 1/1, 11/22, 12/25; also Sun. **Reservations:** accepted. **Features:** The Jail House locks down
barbecue flavor with its smoky ribs, chicken and pork, which can be enjoyed with great-tasting fixings such
as sweet potato fries, tangy coleslaw and desserts made on the premises. New on the scene is the
Saturday steak and crabmeat Napoleon. Live music pumps up the weekend atmosphere. Casual dress; cocktails. **Parking:**
street. **Cards:** AX, DS, MC, VI.

PAINTED POST pop. 1,842—See also FINGER LAKES.

——— WHERE TO STAY ———

BEST WESTERN LODGE ON THE GREEN   *Book great rates at AAA.com*   **Phone:** (607)962-2456

ᗐᗐᗐ SAVE

5/1-10/31 [CP]	1P: $85-$200	2P: $85-$200	XP: $8 F17
11/1-4/30 [CP]	1P: $50-$90	2P: $50-$90	XP: $8 F17

ᗐᗐ ᗐᗐ

Motel   **Location:** SR 17, exit 44, just s on US 15 to SR 417 and Gang Mills exit, then just n. 3171 Canada Rd 14870.
Fax: 607/962-1769. **Facility:** 135 one-bedroom standard units. 1-2 stories (no elevator), exterior corridors.
Parking: on-site, winter plug-ins. **Terms:** check-in 4 pm, pets (in designated units). **Amenities:** voice mail,
irons, hair dryers. *Some:* high-speed Internet. **Pool(s):** heated outdoor. **Guest Services:** valet and coin
laundry. **Business Services:** meeting rooms. **Cards:** AX, CB, DC, DS, JC, MC, VI. **Free Special Amenities: continental
breakfast and local telephone calls.**

SOME UNITS

ECONO LODGE   *Book great rates at AAA.com*   **Phone:** (607)962-4444

ᗐᗐ ᗐᗐ

5/1-10/20	1P: $69-$129	2P: $69-$129	XP: $10 F18
10/21-4/30	1P: $79-$109	2P: $79-$109	XP: $10 F18

Small-scale Hotel   **Location:** Jct US 15 and SR 17, exit 44, s to Gang Mills exit. 200 Robert Dann Dr 14870. Fax: 607/937-5397.
Facility: 61 one-bedroom standard units, some with whirlpools. 2 stories (no elevator), interior corridors.
Parking: on-site. **Terms:** pets ($10 fee). **Amenities:** video library, voice mail, irons, hair dryers. *Some:* high-speed Internet.
Guest Services: wireless Internet. **Business Services:** PC. **Cards:** AX, DC, DS, MC, VI.

SOME UNITS

ERWIN MOTEL   **Phone:** 607/962-7411

ᗐᗐᗐ SAVE

5/1-10/20 [CP]	1P: $39-$64	2P: $44-$79	XP: $10 F16
10/21-11/30 [CP]	1P: $39-$54	2P: $44-$69	XP: $10 F16
12/1-4/30	1P: $29-$44	2P: $42-$54	XP: $7 F16

ᗐ

Motel   **Location:** US 15, exit Erwin Addison, 0.5 mi e. 806 Addison Rd 14870. Fax: 607/962-6373. **Facility:** 25 one-
bedroom standard units, some with efficiencies. 1 story, exterior corridors. *Bath:* combo or shower only.
Parking: on-site. **Terms:** 4 day cancellation notice, pets ($5 fee, in designated units). **Pool(s):** heated
outdoor. **Leisure Activities:** barbecue grill, picnic table. **Guest Services:** coin laundry. **Cards:** AX, DS, MC, VI.
Free Special Amenities: continental breakfast and high-speed Internet.

SOME UNITS

HAMPTON INN   *Book great rates at AAA.com*   **Phone:** (607)936-3344

ᗐᗐᗐᗐ

5/1-10/31 [ECP]	1P: $99-$249	2P: $99-$249
11/1-4/30 [ECP]	1P: $89-$149	2P: $89-$149

Small-scale Hotel   **Location:** I-86, exit 43, just w. 9775 Victory Hwy 14870. Fax: 607/936-3393. **Facility:** 67 one-bedroom standard
units, some with whirlpools. 3 stories, interior corridors. *Bath:* combo or shower only. **Parking:** on-site,
winter plug-ins. **Terms:** 1-3 night minimum stay - seasonal, [CP] meal plan available. **Amenities:** video library, DVD players,
high-speed Internet, voice mail, irons, hair dryers. **Pool(s):** small heated indoor. **Leisure Activities:** exercise room. **Guest
Services:** valet laundry, wireless Internet. **Business Services:** meeting rooms. **Cards:** AX, CB, DC, DS, MC, VI.

SOME UNITS

HOLIDAY INN   *Book great rates at AAA.com*   **Phone:** (607)962-5021

ᗐᗐᗐ SAVE

7/2-8/30	1P: $89-$179	2P: $89-$179
8/31-10/28	1P: $89-$129	2P: $89-$129
5/1-7/1 & 10/29-4/30	1P: $85-$109	2P: $85-$109

ᗐᗐᗐ ᗐᗐᗐ

Small-scale Hotel   **Location:** Jct US 15 and SR 17, exit 44, s to Gang Mills exit, then s. Located in a light-commercial area. 304 S
Hamilton 14870. Fax: 607/937-4080. **Facility:** 105 one-bedroom standard units. 2 stories, interior corridors.
Bath: combo or shower only. **Parking:** on-site. **Terms:** [BP] meal plan available, package plans.
Amenities: video games (fee), high-speed Internet, voice mail, irons, hair dryers. **Dining:** 6:30 am-11 & 5-9 pm, Sat & Sun from
7 am, cocktails. **Pool(s):** heated outdoor, wading. **Leisure Activities:** exercise room. **Guest Services:** valet and coin laundry,
wireless Internet. **Business Services:** conference facilities, PC. **Cards:** AX, CB, DC, DS, JC, MC, VI. **Free Special Amenities:
newspaper and high-speed Internet.**

SOME UNITS

SUPER 8 MOTEL   **Phone:** (607)937-5383

ᗐᗐᗐ ᗐᗐᗐ

6/1-9/30 [CP]	1P: $60-$135	2P: $65-$135	XP: $5 F12
5/1-5/31 [CP]	1P: $55-$60	2P: $60-$65	XP: $5 F12
1/1-4/30 [CP]	1P: $50-$55	2P: $55-$60	XP: $5 F12
10/1-12/31 [CP]	1P: $46-$50	2P: $50-$55	XP: $5 F12

Small-scale Hotel

Location: Jct US 15 and SR 17, exit 44, s to Gang Mills exit. 255 S Hamilton St 14870. Fax: 607/962-7115. **Facility:** 61 one-bedroom
standard units. 2 stories (no elevator), interior corridors. *Bath:* combo or shower only. **Parking:** on-site, winter plug-ins.
Terms: 30 day cancellation notice, small pets only. **Amenities:** hair dryers. **Cards:** AX, DC, DS, MC, VI.

SOME UNITS

——— WHERE TO DINE ———

CURLEY'S CHICKEN HOUSE
American
Parking: on-site.

Lunch: $5-$6   **Dinner:** $8-$10   **Phone:** 607/937-3010
Location: I-86/SR 17, exit 45 eastbound, just w on SR 415 N (High St); exit 45 westbound, just e on SR 415 N (High St). 414 E High St 14870. **Hours:** 11 am-9 pm, Sun from 8 am. **Closed:** 11/22, 12/25. **Features:** Using the same recipes for 50 years, Curly turns out reliably tender and tasty chicken. This place also is known for its Texas hots and meat sauce recipe, cabbage salad and fresh hot dinners with choice of sides. Casual dress.
Cards: AX, DS, MC, VI.

JELLY BEANS
American
Parking: on-site.

Lunch: $5-$7   **Dinner:** $8-$10   **Phone:** 607/936-2290
Location: Jct US 15 and SR 17, exit 44, s to Gang Mills exit, then just s. 319 S Hamilton St 14870. **Hours:** 6 am-9 pm, Fri & Sat-10 pm. **Closed:** 12/25. **Features:** Bright primary colors surround patrons of the casual restaurant. Generous portions of breakfast, lunch and dinner are served all day. Complimentary Jelly Belly jelly beans accompany every bill and can be purchased separately. Casual dress; beer & wine only.
Cards: AX, DS, MC, VI.

PIERI'S CENTRAL RESTAURANT
American

Lunch: $4-$6   **Dinner:** $5-$25   **Phone:** 607/962-6917
Location: Center; in Village Square. 104 Village Square 14870. **Hours:** 6 am-8:30 pm, Sat from 7 am. Closed major holidays; also Sun. **Features:** From hearty soups, burgers and sandwiches to steaks and lobster tail, the busy restaurant has it all. Lots of popular appetizers and Italian fare, as well as children's items, are offered all day. Casual dress; cocktails. **Parking:** on-site. **Cards:** AX, DS, MC, VI.

PALMYRA pop. 3,490

——— WHERE TO STAY ———

PALMYRA INN
(AAA) (SAVE)
Small-scale Hotel

Phone: (315)597-8888

6/1-10/31	1P: $104-$229	2P: $104-$229
5/1-5/31	1P: $84-$199	2P: $84-$199
11/1-4/30	1P: $74-$159	2P: $74-$159

Location: I-90, exit 43, 4.7 mi n on SR 21. 955 Canandaigua Rd 14522. Fax: 315/597-8889. **Facility:** Smoke free premises. 60 units. 56 one-bedroom standard units, some with efficiencies and/or whirlpools. 4 two-bedroom suites with efficiencies. 2 stories, interior corridors. *Bath:* combo or shower only. **Parking:** on-site. **Terms:** cancellation fee imposed, weekly rates available, [CP] meal plan available. **Amenities:** DVD players, high-speed Internet, voice mail, irons. **Leisure Activities:** whirlpool, exercise room. **Guest Services:** sundries, coin laundry, area transportation-local attractions, wireless Internet. **Business Services:** meeting rooms, PC. **Cards:** AX, DC, DS, MC, VI. **Free Special Amenities:** continental breakfast and high-speed Internet.

PARKSVILLE

——— WHERE TO DINE ———

WEST 17 DINER
American

Lunch: $4-$7   **Dinner:** $4-$13   **Phone:** 845/295-9094
Location: On SR 17, exit 98 westbound side; eastbound U-turn available. 6986 SR 17 12768. **Hours:** 6 am-11 pm. **Reservations:** accepted. **Features:** Friendly staffers serve American comfort food, such as steaks, chicken and seafood, some Greek specialties and all-day breakfast items in the retro '50s-era diner. Casual dress. **Parking:** on-site. **Cards:** AX, DS, MC, VI.

PEARL RIVER —See New York p. 502.

PENFIELD pop. 34,645

——— WHERE TO STAY ———

COURTYARD BY MARRIOTT   *Book great rates at AAA.com*
Small-scale Hotel

Phone: (585)385-1000

1/1-4/30	1P: $169-$179	2P: $169-$179
5/1-12/31	1P: $159-$169	2P: $159-$169

Location: I-490, exit 23 (SR 441 E), 1.7 mi to Washington St exit, then just s to Linden Park. Located in a quiet area. 1000 Linden Park 14625. Fax: 585/385-1005. **Facility:** Smoke free premises. 95 one-bedroom standard units, some with whirlpools. 5 stories, interior corridors. *Bath:* combo or shower only. **Parking:** on-site. **Terms:** cancellation fee imposed, [BP] meal plan available. **Amenities:** high-speed Internet, dual phone lines, voice mail, irons, hair dryers. **Pool(s):** lap. **Leisure Activities:** whirlpool, exercise room. **Guest Services:** valet and coin laundry, wireless Internet. **Business Services:** meeting rooms. **Cards:** AX, DC, DS, MC, VI.

SOME UNITS

PENN YAN pop. 5,219—See also FINGER LAKES.

——— WHERE TO STAY ———

BEST WESTERN VINEYARD INN & SUITES   *Book great rates at AAA.com*
Small-scale Hotel

Phone: (315)536-8473

6/1-10/31	1P: $140-$190	2P: $140-$190	XP: $5 F17
11/1-4/30	1P: $109-$170	2P: $109-$170	XP: $5 F17
5/1-5/31	1P: $110-$140	2P: $110-$140	XP: $5 F17

Location: I-90, exit 43, SR 14 S to SR 54 N; corner of SR 54 and 14A. 142 Lake St 14527. Fax: 315/536-8794. **Facility:** Smoke free premises. 43 one-bedroom standard units, some with whirlpools. 3 stories, interior corridors. **Parking:** on-site. **Terms:** 2 night minimum stay - seasonal and/or weekends, cancellation fee imposed, [CP] meal plan available, package plans, pets ($10 extra charge, in designated units). **Amenities:** high-speed Internet, voice mail, irons, hair dryers. **Pool(s):** small heated indoor. **Leisure Activities:** whirlpool, exercise room. **Guest Services:** wireless Internet. **Cards:** AX, CB, DC, DS, MC, VI.

PERU pop. 1,514

———— WHERE TO DINE ————

CRICKET'S CASUAL FOOD & SPIRITS   **Lunch:** $5-$9   **Dinner:** $6-$24   **Phone:** 518/643-2433

(AAA)
▼▼▼ ▼▼▼

American

Location: I-87, exit 35, just w. Bear Swamp Rd (SR 442) 12972. **Hours:** 11:30 am-10 pm, Sun from 9 am. Closed: 7/4, 9/3, 12/25; also Mon 9/5-5/31. **Reservations:** accepted. **Features:** Pleasant family restaurant open for lunch and dinner. Casual dress; cocktails. **Parking:** on-site. **Cards:** AX, DS, MC, VI.

PINE VALLEY —See also FINGER LAKES.

———— WHERE TO STAY ————

BEST WESTERN MARSHALL MANOR   *Book great rates at AAA.com*   **Phone:** (607)739-3891

(AAA) (SAVE)
▼▼▼ ◆◆

Motel

6/23-10/22	1P: $82-$102	2P: $92-$107	XP: $5	F17
5/1-6/22	1P: $72-$89	2P: $79-$98	XP: $5	F17
10/23-11/26	1P: $62-$74	2P: $69-$80	XP: $5	F17
11/27-4/30	1P: $56-$65	2P: $65-$75	XP: $5	F17

Location: SR 17, exit 52, 5 mi n on SR 14. Located in a quiet area. 3527 Watkins Rd 14845. Fax: 607/739-3892. **Facility:** 40 one-bedroom standard units. 1 story, exterior corridors. **Parking:** on-site. **Terms:** 7 day cancellation notice, pets ($4 extra charge, in designated units). **Amenities:** voice mail, irons, hair dryers. *Some:* high-speed Internet. **Pool(s):** heated outdoor. **Guest Services:** coin laundry. **Cards:** AX, CB, DC, DS, MC, VI.

SOME UNITS

PITTSFORD pop. 27,212   (See map and index starting on p. 599)

———— WHERE TO STAY ————

BROOKWOOD INN ROCHESTER/PITTSFORD   *Book great rates at AAA.com*   **Phone:** (585)248-9000

(AAA) (SAVE)
▼▼▼ ◆◆◆

Small-scale Hotel

All Year   1P: $169-$199

Location: I-490, exit 27 (Bushnell's Basin/SR 96), just n. 800 Pittsford-Victor Rd 14534. Fax: 585/248-8569. **Facility:** 108 one-bedroom standard units, some with whirlpools. 5 stories, interior corridors. **Parking:** on-site. **Amenities:** dual phone lines, voice mail, irons, hair dryers. *Fee:* video games, safes. **Dining:** 6:30-10:30 am, 11:30-2 & 5-10 pm, Sat & Sun 8 am-10:30 & 5-10 pm, cocktails. **Pool(s):** heated indoor. **Leisure Activities:** sauna, whirlpool, exercise room. *Fee:* bicycles. **Guest Services:** valet laundry, wireless Internet. **Business Services:** meeting rooms, business center. **Cards:** AX, CB, DC, DS, MC, VI. **Free Special Amenities:** newspaper and high-speed Internet.

SOME UNITS

THE DEL MONTE LODGE A RENAISSANCE HOTEL AND SPA   *Book great rates at AAA.com*   **Phone:** (585)381-9900

▼▼▼ ◆◆◆

Large-scale Hotel

All Year   1P: $199-$219

Location: Just s on SR 96; center. Located next to Erie Canal path. 41 N Main St 14534. Fax: 585/381-9825. **Facility:** Smoke free premises. 99 units. 97 one-bedroom standard units. 2 one-bedroom suites ($350-$625), some with whirlpools. 3 stories, interior corridors. *Bath:* combo or shower only. **Parking:** on-site. **Terms:** package plans. **Amenities:** video games (fee), high-speed Internet, dual phone lines, voice mail, safes, honor bars, irons, hair dryers. **Dining:** The Erie Grill, see separate listing. **Pool(s):** heated indoor. **Leisure Activities:** whirlpool, exercise room, spa. **Guest Services:** valet laundry, area transportation, beauty salon, wireless Internet. **Business Services:** conference facilities, PC. **Cards:** AX, CB, DC, DS, JC, MC, VI.

SOME UNITS

———— WHERE TO DINE ————

CRYSTAL BARN   **Lunch:** $4-$16   **Dinner:** $14-$35   **Phone:** 585/381-4844   [26]

▼▼▼ ▼▼▼

Continental

Location: Jct Jefferson Rd; in Barn Bazaar. 2851 Clover St 14534. **Hours:** 11:30 am-2 & 5-9 pm, Sat from 5 pm, Sun from 4 pm. Closed major holidays. **Reservations:** suggested. **Features:** In an 1860 barn, the landmark restaurant invites fine American and Continental dining in a setting of Victorian appointments and crystal chandeliers. A skilled staff pampers guests as they savor such International lunch dishes as spanakopita, chicken Mediterranean and seafood di Napoli. Early diners can sample smaller portions of such choices as tournedos Sante Fe, beef or sole Wellington, rack of lamb and prime rib. Dressy casual; cocktails. **Parking:** on-site. **Cards:** AX, DC, DS, MC, VI.

THE ERIE GRILL   **Lunch:** $8-$16   **Dinner:** $25-$35   **Phone:** 585/381-9900

▼▼▼ ▼▼▼

Continental

Location: Just s on SR 96; center; in The Del Monte Lodge A Renaissance Hotel and Spa. 41 N Main St 14534. **Hours:** 6:30 am-2:30 & 5:30-10 pm, Fri & Sat-11 pm. **Reservations:** suggested. **Features:** Enjoy fine dining in a friendly casual atmosphere at this progressive American-style restaurant. Specialty ingredients prepared with finesse complement all courses with intense flavor. Dressy casual; cocktails. **Parking:** on-site. **Cards:** AX, CB, DC, DS, JC, MC, VI.

HAWTHORNE'S RESTAURANT   **Lunch:** $7-$13   **Dinner:** $10-$25   **Phone:** 585/385-4959   [25]

▼▼▼

Steak & Seafood

Location: On SR 96, 2 mi e from center. 3500 East Ave 14534. **Hours:** 11 am-10 pm. Closed major holidays. **Reservations:** suggested. **Features:** The country setting makes a visit to the restaurant worth the drive. Guests unwind in the short but sweet patio dining area to peruse a menu of delicious American fare prepared with a Continental flair. Offerings range from crab cakes with Dijon sauce and cucumber salad to chicken liberty and tender Norwegian salmon. Save room for one of the sinful desserts. Casual dress; cocktails. **Parking:** on-site. **Cards:** AX, MC, VI.

(See map and index starting on p. 599)

RICHARDSON'S CANAL HOUSE
Lunch: $8-$12   **Dinner:** $18-$28   **Phone:** 585/248-5000

American

Location: I-490, exit 27 (Bushnell's Basin/SR 96), just n. 1474 Marsh Rd 14534. **Hours:** 11:30 am-2 & 5-10 pm, Sat & Mon from 5 pm. Closed: 12/25; also 1/1 & Sun in winter. **Reservations:** suggested. **Features:** Sophisticated furnishings decorate the refurbished 1818 Erie Canal tavern, a favorite romantic spot for couples. Freshly-prepared American country and French regional cuisine is complex and flavorful. The focus is on fresh seafood and tantalizing preparations of meats, such as rack of lamb, roasted duck or osso buco. Dressy casual; cocktails. **Parking:** on-site. **Cards:** AX, DS, MC, VI. **Historic**

PLAINVIEW pop. 25,637

——— **WHERE TO STAY** ———

FOUR POINTS BY SHERATON-PLAINVIEW LONG ISLAND   *Book great rates at AAA.com*   **Phone:** 516/694-6500

Property failed to provide current rates

Small-scale Hotel

Location: I-495, exit 48. Located in a commercial area. 333 S Service Rd 11803. Fax: 516/694-4718. **Facility:** 103 units. 97 one-bedroom standard units, some with whirlpools. 6 one-bedroom suites with whirlpools. 2-3 stories, interior corridors. *Bath:* combo or shower only. **Parking:** on-site. **Terms:** pets (small dogs only, $25 extra charge). **Amenities:** video games (fee), high-speed Internet, voice mail, safes, irons, hair dryers. **Pool(s):** heated outdoor. **Leisure Activities:** exercise room. **Guest Services:** sundries, valet laundry, wireless Internet. **Business Services:** meeting rooms, business center.

SOME UNITS

FEE

HOLIDAY INN   *Book at AAA.com*   **Phone:** (516)349-7400

All Year   1P: $129-$199   2P: $129-$269

Small-scale Hotel

Location: I-495, exit 46, just n; Northern State Pkwy, exit 38, just s. Located in a commercial area. 215 Sunnyside Blvd 11803. Fax: 516/349-7491. **Facility:** 125 one-bedroom standard units, some with whirlpools. 2 stories, interior corridors. *Bath:* combo or shower only. **Parking:** on-site. **Terms:** [AP] meal plan available, package plans. **Amenities:** dual phone lines, voice mail, irons, hair dryers. **Pool(s):** small outdoor. **Leisure Activities:** exercise room. *Fee:* game room. **Guest Services:** valet and coin laundry, wireless Internet. **Business Services:** meeting rooms, business center. **Cards:** AX, CB, DC, DS, JC, MC, VI.

SOME UNITS

HOMEWOOD SUITES LONG ISLAND MELVILLE   *Book great rates at AAA.com*   **Phone:** (516)293-4663

All Year   1P: $229-$359   2P: $229-$359   XP: $10   F18

Small-scale Hotel

Location: I-495, exit 48, just s. 1585 Round Swamp Rd 11803. Fax: 516/293-2800. **Facility:** 147 units. 69 one-bedroom standard units with efficiencies. 56 one- and 22 two-bedroom suites with efficiencies. 4 stories, interior corridors. *Bath:* combo or shower only. **Parking:** on-site. **Terms:** [BP] meal plan available, pets ($75 fee). **Amenities:** video games (fee), CD players, high-speed Internet, dual phone lines, voice mail, irons, hair dryers. *Some:* safes. **Pool(s):** heated indoor. **Leisure Activities:** whirlpool, exercise room, sports court, basketball. **Guest Services:** sundries, complimentary evening beverages: Mon-Thurs, valet and coin laundry, area transportation, wireless Internet. **Business Services:** meeting rooms, business center. **Cards:** AX, CB, DC, DS, MC, VI. *(See color ad p 364)*

SOME UNITS

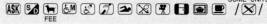

FEE

RESIDENCE INN BY MARRIOTT   *Book great rates at AAA.com*   **Phone:** 516/433-6200

Property failed to provide current rates

Small-scale Hotel

Location: I-495, exit 44, 1.6 mi s on SR 135, exit 10, then just e on Old Country Rd. Located opposite North Shore University Hospital. 9 Gerhard Rd 11803. Fax: 516/433-2569. **Facility:** Smoke free premises. 170 units. 112 one-bedroom standard units with efficiencies. 48 one- and 10 two-bedroom suites with kitchens, some with whirlpools. 2-3 stories, interior corridors. *Bath:* combo or shower only. **Parking:** on-site. **Terms:** check-in 4 pm, pets ($75 fee). **Amenities:** high-speed Internet, dual phone lines, voice mail, irons, hair dryers. **Pool(s):** outdoor, lap. **Leisure Activities:** saunas, whirlpool, putting green, recreation programs, exercise room, basketball. *Fee:* massage, game room. **Guest Services:** sundries, complimentary evening beverages: Mon-Thurs, valet and coin laundry, wireless Internet. **Business Services:** meeting rooms, business center.

FEE

PLATTSBURGH pop. 18,816

——— **WHERE TO STAY** ———

AMERICAS BEST VALUE INN   *Book great rates at AAA.com*   **Phone:** (518)563-0222

All Year [CP]   1P: $49-$129   2P: $49-$129   XP: $10   F14

Motel

Location: I-87, exit 37, just w. 19 Booth Dr 12901. Fax: 518/563-5807. **Facility:** 102 units. 101 one- and 1 two-bedroom standard units, some with kitchens and/or whirlpools. 2 stories (no elevator), exterior corridors. **Parking:** on-site, winter plug-ins. **Terms:** package plans, $2 service charge. **Amenities:** voice mail, irons, hair dryers. *Some:* high-speed Internet. **Pool(s):** outdoor. **Guest Services:** coin laundry, wireless Internet. **Cards:** AX, CB, DC, DS, MC, VI. **Free Special Amenities: continental breakfast and high-speed Internet.**

SOME UNITS

BEST WESTERN THE INN AT SMITHFIELD   *Book great rates at AAA.com*   Phone: (518)561-7750

AAA [SAVE]

6/23-10/21	1P: $89-$179	2P: $89-$179	XP: $5	F18
5/1-6/22	1P: $79-$159	2P: $79-$159	XP: $5	F18
1/1-4/30	1P: $69-$159	2P: $69-$159	XP: $5	F18
10/22-12/31	1P: $69-$149	2P: $69-$149	XP: $5	F18

Small-scale Hotel **Location:** I-87, exit 37, just w. 446 Rt 3 12901. **Fax:** 518/561-9431. **Facility:** 122 units. 116 one-bedroom standard units. 6 one-bedroom suites ($89-$199), some with whirlpools. 2 stories (no elevator), interior corridors. **Parking:** on-site, winter plug-ins. **Terms:** pets ($10 fee). **Amenities:** high-speed Internet, dual phone lines, voice mail, irons, hair dryers. **Dining:** 2 restaurants, 11:30 am-11 pm, Fri & Sat-midnight, Sun-10 pm, cocktails. **Pool(s):** heated indoor. **Leisure Activities:** playground, exercise room. *Fee:* game room. **Guest Services:** valet and coin laundry. **Business Services:** meeting rooms, PC. **Cards:** AX, DC, DS, MC, VI. **Free Special Amenities: expanded continental breakfast and high-speed Internet.**

SOME UNITS

COMFORT INN   *Book great rates at AAA.com*   Phone: (518)562-2730

All Year   1P: $60-$199   2P: $70-$199   XP: $10   F

Small-scale Hotel **Location:** I-87, exit 37, 0.5 mi e. 411 Rt 3 12901. **Fax:** 518/563-1562. **Facility:** 112 units. 85 one-bedroom standard units, some with whirlpools. 27 one-bedroom suites, some with efficiencies (no utensils) and/or whirlpools. 2 stories, interior corridors. **Parking:** on-site, winter plug-ins. **Terms:** package plans. **Amenities:** high-speed Internet, voice mail, irons, hair dryers. **Pool(s):** heated indoor. **Leisure Activities:** sauna, whirlpool, steamroom, waterslide, racquetball courts, playground. *Fee:* miniature golf, game room. **Guest Services:** valet and coin laundry, tanning facilities. **Business Services:** meeting rooms, business center. **Cards:** AX, CB, DC, DS, JC, MC, VI.

SOME UNITS

DAYS INN & SUITES   *Book great rates at AAA.com*   Phone: (518)561-0403

6/23-10/19	1P: $63-$99	2P: $63-$99	XP: $5	F18
5/1-6/22 & 10/20-4/30	1P: $53-$99	2P: $53-$99	XP: $5	F18

Small-scale Hotel **Location:** I-87, exit 37, just w. 8 Everleth Dr 12901. **Fax:** 518/561-4192. **Facility:** 106 units. 100 one-bedroom standard units, some with efficiencies (no utensils). 6 one-bedroom suites ($120-$198) with whirlpools. 3 stories, interior corridors. **Parking:** on-site, winter plug-ins. **Terms:** [CP] meal plan available, package plans. **Amenities:** video games (fee), high-speed Internet, dual phone lines, hair dryers. *Some:* irons. **Pool(s):** outdoor, heated indoor. **Leisure Activities:** whirlpool, exercise room. **Guest Services:** valet and coin laundry, wireless Internet. **Business Services:** meeting rooms, PC. **Cards:** AX, CB, DC, DS, MC, VI.

SOME UNITS

HOLIDAY INN   *Book at AAA.com*   Phone: 518/561-5000

5/1-10/31	1P: $80-$170	2P: $80-$170	XP: $10	F12
11/1-4/30	1P: $76-$150	2P: $76-$150	XP: $10	F12

Small-scale Hotel **Location:** I-87, exit 37, 0.5 mi e. 412 Rt 3 12901. **Fax:** 518/562-2974. **Facility:** 102 one-bedroom standard units. 4 stories, interior corridors. *Bath:* combo or shower only. **Parking:** on-site, winter plug-ins. **Terms:** cancellation fee imposed, [BP] meal plan available, package plans. **Amenities:** video games (fee), high-speed Internet, dual phone lines, voice mail, irons, hair dryers. **Pool(s):** heated indoor, wading. **Leisure Activities:** exercise room. *Fee:* game room. **Guest Services:** valet and coin laundry. **Business Services:** meeting rooms. **Cards:** AX, DC, DS, MC, VI.

SOME UNITS

LA QUINTA   *Book at AAA.com*   Phone: (518)562-4000

7/1-10/31	1P: $84-$139	2P: $89-$144	XP: $5	F18
11/1-4/30	1P: $79-$129	2P: $84-$134	XP: $5	F18
5/1-6/30	1P: $72-$119	2P: $77-$124	XP: $5	F18

Small-scale Hotel   **Location:** I-87, exit 37, just w. 16 Plaza Blvd 12901-6439. Fax: 518/561-3234. **Facility:** 103 units. 100 one-bedroom standard units, some with kitchens. 3 one-bedroom suites. 4 stories, interior corridors. *Bath:* combo or shower only. **Parking:** on-site, winter plug-ins. **Amenities:** video games (fee), voice mail, irons, hair dryers. **Pool(s):** heated indoor. **Leisure Activities:** whirlpool. **Guest Services:** coin laundry, wireless Internet. **Cards:** AX, CB, DC, DS, MC, VI. *(See color ad p 360)*

SOME UNITS

FEE   FEE

MICROTEL INN AND SUITES   *Book great rates at AAA.com*   Phone: (518)324-3800

6/1-10/31	1P: $69-$134	2P: $69-$134	XP: $5	F16
11/1-4/30	1P: $59-$124	2P: $59-$124	XP: $5	F16
5/1-5/31	1P: $54-$119	2P: $54-$119	XP: $5	F16

Small-scale Hotel   **Location:** I-87, exit 37, just w. 554 SR 3 12901. Fax: 518/324-3810. **Facility:** 58 one-bedroom standard units, some with whirlpools. 3 stories, interior corridors. *Bath:* combo or shower only. **Parking:** on-site, winter plug-ins. **Terms:** pets ($10 fee). **Amenities:** high-speed Internet, voice mail, hair dryers. **Guest Services:** coin laundry, wireless Internet. **Business Services:** PC, fax (fee). **Cards:** AX, DC, DS, MC, VI. **Free Special Amenities: continental breakfast and high-speed Internet.**

SOME UNITS

FEE

POINT AU ROCHE LODGE AND BED & BREAKFAST   Phone: 518-563-8714
Property failed to provide current rates

Location: I-87, exit 40, 0.5 mi e on SR 456, 0.4 mi s on US 9, then 2.2 mi e. Located next to Point Au Roche State Park. 463 Point Au Roche Rd 12901. Fax: 518/563-8202. **Facility:** This B&B offers attractive, individually themed guest rooms. Smoke free premises. 8 one-bedroom standard units, some with whirlpools. 2 stories (no elevator), interior corridors. *Bath:* combo or shower only. **Parking:** on-site. **Amenities:** *Some:* hair dryers.

Bed & Breakfast

SOME UNITS

SUPER 8 MOTEL   *Book at AAA.com*   Phone: (518)562-8888

7/1-8/31 [CP]	1P: $69-$79	2P: $78-$89	XP: $10	F16
9/1-10/31 [CP]	1P: $63-$73	2P: $73-$85	XP: $10	F16
5/1-6/30 [CP]	1P: $50-$60	2P: $58-$70	XP: $10	F16
11/1-4/30 [CP]	1P: $49-$59	2P: $53-$69	XP: $10	F16

Motel   **Location:** I-87, exit 39, just e. then just n. 7129 Rt 9 N 12901. Fax: 518/562-8896. **Facility:** 61 one-bedroom standard units, some with efficiencies (no utensils). 2 stories (no elevator), interior corridors. **Parking:** on-site. **Terms:** pets ($10 fee, in designated units). **Amenities:** high-speed Internet, hair dryers. **Pool(s):** heated indoor. **Guest Services:** coin laundry. **Business Services:** meeting rooms, fax (fee). **Cards:** AX, DC, DS, MC, VI.

SOME UNITS

FEE

———— WHERE TO DINE ————

ANTHONY'S RESTAURANT & BISTRO   *Menu on AAA.com*   Lunch: $6-$13   Dinner: $16-$26   Phone: 518/561-6420

Location: I-87, exit 37, just w. 538 Rt 3 12901. **Hours:** 11:30 am-2:30 & 5-9 pm, Fri-10 pm, Sat 5 pm-10 pm, Sun 5 pm-9 pm. Closed major holidays. **Reservations:** suggested. **Features:** Dinner in the cozy and creatively remodeled 150-year-old farmhouse may be mustard and herb-crusted salmon, duckling with figs and pears or a choice of steak broiled to your order. Appetizer, soup and salad blend Continental and American cuisine styles. Imaginatively presented desserts such as cheesecake souffle or Belgium chocolate torte are sure to please. Live entertainment in lounge and bistro menu. Dressy casual; cocktails. **Parking:** on-site. **Cards:** AX, CB, DC, DS, MC, VI.

Continental

BUTCHER BLOCK STEAK & SEAFOOD   Lunch: $6-$8   Dinner: $11-$20   Phone: 518/563-0920

Location: I-87, exit 37. 15 Booth Dr 12901. **Hours:** 11:30 am-3 & 4:30-9:30 pm, Fri & Sat-10 pm. Closed: 11/22, 12/25. **Reservations:** accepted. **Features:** As its name might suggest, the restaurant centers the menu on seafood and steak, particularly succulent prime rib. The atmosphere of the dining room is rustic and cozy, and welcoming to families. Decadent desserts appeal to both eyes and palate. Casual dress; cocktails. **Parking:** on-site. **Cards:** AX, DC, DS, MC, VI.

Steak & Seafood

DANA'S RUSTY ANCHOR   Lunch: $6-$12   Dinner: $13-$30   Phone: 518/563-6000

Location: 5.5 mi s of jct SR 3 and US 9. 4016 Rt 9 S 12901. **Hours:** Open 5/15-12/31; 5 pm-close. Closed: 12/25; also Mon. **Reservations:** suggested. **Features:** This restaurant is located on a bay and offers nice views of the water and the boats as they come and go. Casual dress; cocktails. **Parking:** on-site. **Cards:** AX, DS, MC, VI.

Steak & Seafood

DOMENIC'S RESTAURANT & LOUNGE Lunch: $7-$19 Dinner: $9-$25 Phone: 518/563-6980
AAA
▼▼▼
Italian
Location: I-87, exit 39, 0.5 mi s. 7081 Rt 9N 12901. **Hours:** 11 am-10 pm, Sun-9 pm. Closed: 11/22, 12/25. **Reservations:** suggested. **Features:** Bold shades of red, white and green in the dining room give the place a festive atmosphere. Homemade Italian-American fare centers heavily on "surf and turf." Spumoni and tiramisu satisfy a sweet tooth. Casual dress; cocktails. **Parking:** on-site. **Cards:** AX, CB, DC, DS, MC, VI.

IRISES CAFE AND WINE BAR *Menu on AAA.com* Lunch: $5-$12 Dinner: $10-$20 Phone: 518/566-7000
AAA
▼▼▼
American
Location: Corner of Court St; downtown. 20-22 City Hall Pl 12901. **Hours:** 11:30 am-2:30 & 4:30-9:30 pm, Fri & Sat-10 pm. Closed: 5/28, 9/3, 12/25; also Sun. **Reservations:** suggested. **Features:** Perhaps the trendiest city eatery, the cafe is a good place for those who want a little something out of the ordinary. The menu is eclectic, with pronounced Mediterranean and Asian influences. A wonderful variety of by-the-glass wines can be had along with a good selection of microbrewed beers. Casual dress; cocktails; entertainment. **Parking:** street. **Cards:** AX, DC, DS, MC, VI.

MANGIA Lunch: $6-$17 Dinner: $7-$17 Phone: 518/562-5555
▼▼▼
Italian
Location: I-87, exit 37, 0.5 mi e. 418 SR 3 12901. **Hours:** 11:30 am-9 pm, Fri-10 pm, Sat noon-10 pm, Sun noon-9 pm. **Reservations:** accepted. **Features:** The wood-fired pizza is why people come to this restaurant. Delicious appetizers and desserts are a nice way to round out a meal. Casual dress; cocktails. **Parking:** on-site. **Cards:** AX, DS, MC, VI.

PORT CHESTER —*See New York p. 502.*

PORT JEFFERSON pop. 7,837

——— WHERE TO DINE ———

25 EAST AMERICAN BISTRO Lunch: $12-$20 Dinner: $18-$37 Phone: 631/928-5200
▼▼▼
American
Location: Center; adjacent to ferry dock; in Danford's Inn Marina and Conference Center. 25 E Broadway 11777. **Hours:** 7 am-10:30 & 11:30-9 pm, Sat 8 am-10:30 & 11:30-10 pm, Sun 11:30 am-3 pm. **Reservations:** suggested. **Features:** Overlooking the marina and ferry terminal, the restaurant is decorated with lots of ship memorabilia and nautical accents. Seafood is clearly the focus, with such choices as clams and broiled fish. The casual dining dock has a relaxed, comfortable feel. Dressy casual; cocktails. **Parking:** on-site. **Cards:** AX, DC, DS, MC, VI. **Country Inn**

PORT JERVIS pop. 8,860

——— WHERE TO STAY ———

COMFORT INN *Book great rates at AAA.com* Phone: (845)856-6611
AAA [SAVE]
▼▼▼
Small-scale Hotel

	1P: $89-$149	2P: $89-$149	XP: $10	F18
5/1-10/1				
10/2-4/30	1P: $69-$99	2P: $69-$99	XP: $10	F18

Location: I-84, exit 1, just se. 2247 Greenville Tpke 12771. Fax: 845/856-5299. **Facility:** 103 one-bedroom standard units. 2 stories (no elevator), interior corridors. **Parking:** on-site. **Terms:** cancellation fee imposed, [CP] meal plan available, package plans, pets ($20 fee). **Amenities:** voice mail, safes (fee), irons, hair dryers. **Pool(s):** outdoor. **Leisure Activities:** video games. **Guest Services:** coin laundry, wireless Internet. **Business Services:** meeting rooms, PC. **Cards:** AX, CB, DC, DS, JC, MC, VI. *(See color ad below)*

SOME UNITS

FEE

PORTVILLE pop. 1,024

------ **WHERE TO DINE** ------

SPRAGUE'S MAPLE FARMS PANCAKE HOUSE &
RESTAURANT   **Lunch:** $5-$8   **Dinner:** $8-$16   **Phone:** 716/933-6637

American

Location: I-86, exit 28, 15 mi s; 1 mi n of town. 1048 Rt 305 14770. **Hours:** 8 am-8 pm, Fri & Sat-9 pm. Closed: 12/25. **Features:** The country restaurant's signature recipes are created from maple syrup harvested on the working maple farm. Breakfast is served all day, and a taste of the 100 percent pure maple syrup can be sampled on fluffy pancakes served with double-smoked bacon, country ham or its own recipe of maple sausage patties. Premium, free-range roast turkey comes from its own farm. The Friday night buttermilk-battered fish fry is a local favorite. Casual dress; cocktails. **Parking:** on-site. **Cards:** DS, MC, VI.

POTSDAM pop. 9,425

------ **WHERE TO STAY** ------

THE CLARKSON INN   **Phone:** 315/265-3050
All Year   1P: $109-$199   2P: $119-$199   XP: $20   D10

Small-scale Hotel

Location: Jct US 11 and SR 56; center. 1 Main St 13676. Fax: 315/265-5848. **Facility:** Smoke free premises. 40 one-bedroom standard units. 2 stories (no elevator), interior corridors. **Parking:** on-site, winter plug-ins. **Terms:** 30 day cancellation notice-fee imposed. **Amenities:** voice mail, irons, hair dryers. **Guest Services:** valet laundry, wireless Internet. **Business Services:** meeting rooms, business center. **Cards:** AX, MC, VI.

SOME UNITS

THE SMALLING MOTEL SOUTH   **Phone:** 315/265-0709
All Year   1P: $54   2P: $69   XP: $5   F5

Motel

Location: On US 11, 1.6 mi s. 7518 State Hwy 11 13676. Fax: 315/265-0709. **Facility:** 16 one-bedroom standard units. 1 story, exterior corridors. **Parking:** on-site, winter plug-ins. **Amenities:** hair dryers. **Cards:** AX, DS, MC, VI.

SOME UNITS

------ **WHERE TO DINE** ------

CACTUS GRILL AND CANTINA   **Dinner:** $5-$12   **Phone:** 315/265-0240

Mexican

Location: Center. 11 Raymond St 13676. **Hours:** 5 pm-9 pm, Fri & Sat-10 pm. Closed: 1/1, 11/22, 12/25. **Reservations:** accepted. **Features:** Freshly made Mexican favorites are plated in abundant servings. Festive, sunny decor brightens the boisterous, cantina-like dining room and lounge. The staff is friendly and casual. Casual dress; cocktails. **Parking:** street. **Cards:** AX, MC, VI.

THE LOBSTER HOUSE   **Lunch:** $5-$8   **Dinner:** $11-$20   **Phone:** 315/353-2366

Seafood

Location: 3 mi n on SR 56. 95 S Main St 13668. **Hours:** 11 am-9:30 pm, Fri & Sat-10 pm. Closed: 11/22, 12/25. **Reservations:** suggested, weekends. **Features:** Locally famous for fresh seafoods, delicious pasta creations and abundant combination platters. Baby back ribs and prime rib are also favorites served by friendly wait staff. Casual dress; cocktails. **Parking:** on-site. **Cards:** AX, CB, DS, MC, VI.

MAMA LUCIA   **Dinner:** $8-$14   **Phone:** 315/265-0475

Italian

MC, VI.

Location: Center. 1 Constitution Ave 13676. **Hours:** 5 pm-9 pm, Fri & Sat-10 pm. Closed: 1/1, 11/22, 12/25. **Reservations:** suggested. **Features:** Family-style Italian cuisine is served in this renovated train station. Bright, fresh decor is fun and trendy. Wood-oven pizzas and traditional pastas choices are plated in ample portions and served pass-the-dish, family style. Casual dress; cocktails. **Parking:** on-site. **Cards:** AX,

MAXFIELDS   **Lunch:** $6-$9   **Dinner:** $12-$20   **Phone:** 315/265-3796

American

Location: Center. 5-7 Market St 13676. **Hours:** 11:30 am-2:30 & 5-9 pm, Fri & Sat-9:30 pm. Closed: 1/1, 11/22, 12/25; also Sun. **Reservations:** accepted. **Features:** Patio diners at the historic brick building can watch the Raquette River lull by while dining on fresh, quality Continental cuisine. Servers are pleasant and helpful. Casual dress; cocktails. **Parking:** street. **Cards:** AX, MC, VI.

POUGHKEEPSIE pop. 29,871—See also RED OAKS MILL.

------ **WHERE TO STAY** ------

BEST WESTERN INN & CONFERENCE CENTER   **Phone:** (845)462-4600
All Year   1P: $90-$150   2P: $90-$150   XP: $10   F17

Small-scale Hotel

Location: I-84, exit 13N, 4.7 mi s of Mid Hudson Bridge. 2170 South Rd (Rt 9) 12601. Fax: 845/462-3228. **Facility:** 153 one-bedroom standard units, some with whirlpools. 3 stories (no elevator), interior corridors. **Parking:** on-site. **Terms:** weekly rates available, [MAP] meal plan available, package plans, pets ($50 deposit). **Amenities:** high-speed Internet, voice mail, irons, hair dryers. **Dining:** 6:30 am-10 & 5-10 pm, Sat 8 am-11 & 5-10 pm, Sun 8 am-noon & 5-10 pm, cocktails. **Pool(s):** outdoor. **Guest Services:** valet and coin laundry, wireless Internet. **Business Services:** conference facilities. **Cards:** AX, CB, DC, DS, MC, VI. **Free Special Amenities:** local telephone calls and high-speed Internet. *(See color ad p 591 & coupon in Savings Section)*

SOME UNITS

FEE   FEE   FEE

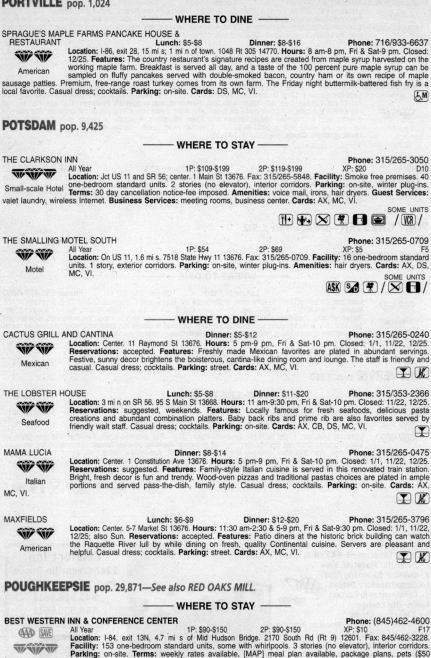

COURTYARD BY MARRIOTT   *Book great rates at AAA.com*
Property failed to provide current rates
Phone: 845/485-6336
Small-scale Hotel
Location: 1.6 mi s of Mid-Hudson Bridge. 2641 South Rd 12601. Fax: 845/485-6514. **Facility:** Smoke free premises. 149 units. 137 one-bedroom standard units. 12 one-bedroom suites. 2 stories, interior corridors. **Bath:** combo or shower only. **Parking:** on-site. **Amenities:** high-speed Internet, voice mail, irons, hair dryers. *Some:* DVD players. **Pool(s):** heated indoor. **Leisure Activities:** whirlpool, exercise room. **Guest Services:** sundries, valet and coin laundry. **Business Services:** meeting rooms, PC, fax (fee).

SOME UNITS

DAYS INN   *Book great rates at AAA.com*
Phone: (845)454-1010
Motel
| | All Year | 1P: $55-$225 | 2P: $55-$225 | XP: $10 | F18 |

Location: 2 mi e of Mid-Hudson Bridge on US 44 and SR 55. Located in a commercial/residental area. 536 Haight Ave 12603. Fax: 845/454-0127. **Facility:** 66 one-bedroom standard units. 1-2 stories (no elevator), interior/exterior corridors. *Bath:* combo or shower only. **Parking:** on-site, winter plug-ins. **Amenities:** voice mail, irons, hair dryers. **Pool(s):** heated indoor. **Leisure Activities:** exercise room. **Guest Services:** wireless Internet. **Business Services:** business center. **Cards:** AX, CB, DC, DS, JC, MC, VI.
Free Special Amenities: expanded continental breakfast and high-speed Internet.

SOME UNITS

ECONO LODGE   *Book great rates at AAA.com*
Phone: (845)452-6600
| | 5/1-10/15 [CP] | 1P: $85-$135 | 2P: $85-$135 | XP: $10 | D15 |
| | 10/16-4/30 [CP] | 1P: $70-$110 | 2P: $70-$110 | XP: $10 | D15 |

Small-scale Hotel
Location: I-84, exit 13N, 1.6 mi s of Mid-Hudson Bridge. 2625 US 9 12601. Fax: 845/454-2210. **Facility:** 112 one-bedroom standard units, some with efficiencies (no utensils). 2 stories (no elevator), exterior corridors. **Parking:** on-site. **Terms:** package plans, pets ($100 deposit). **Amenities:** *Some:* high-speed Internet. **Business Services:** meeting rooms, fax (fee). **Cards:** AX, DC, DS, MC, VI.

SOME UNITS

FEE

HOLIDAY INN EXPRESS   *Book at AAA.com*
Phone: 845/473-1151
Property failed to provide current rates
Small-scale Hotel
Location: 1.5 mi s of Mid-Hudson Bridge. Located in a quiet area. 2750 South Rd (US Rt 9) 12601. Fax: 845/485-8127. **Facility:** 121 units. 119 one-bedroom standard units. 2 one-bedroom suites with whirlpools. 4 stories, interior corridors. *Bath:* combo or shower only. **Parking:** on-site, winter plug-ins. **Amenities:** video games (fee), voice mail, irons, hair dryers. **Pool(s):** outdoor. **Leisure Activities:** exercise room. **Guest Services:** complimentary laundry, wireless Internet. **Business Services:** meeting rooms, fax.

SOME UNITS

POUGHKEEPSIE GRAND HOTEL AND CONFERENCE CENTER   *Book great rates at AAA.com*
Phone: (845)485-5300
| | All Year [BP] | 1P: $129-$189 | 2P: $129-$189 | XP: $10 | F12 |

Small-scale Hotel
Location: Jct US 44 and SR 55 E, just n on Market St; downtown. 40 Civic Center Plaza 12601. Fax: 845/485-4720. **Facility:** 200 units. 198 one-bedroom standard units, some with whirlpools. 2 two-bedroom suites ($250-$350) with whirlpools. 10 stories, interior corridors. *Bath:* combo or shower only. **Parking:** on-site. **Terms:** check-in 4 pm. **Amenities:** video games (fee), high-speed Internet, dual phone lines, voice mail, irons, hair dryers. *Some:* safes. **Dining:** 6:30 am-10:30 pm, cocktails. **Leisure Activities:** *Fee:* massage. **Guest Services:** gift shop, valet and coin laundry, airport transportation-Dutchess County Airport, area transportation-within city limits. **Business Services:** conference facilities, business center. **Cards:** AX, CB, DC, DS, MC, VI.

SOME UNITS

FEE

——— WHERE TO DINE ———

CAPPUCINO BY COPPOLA'S

AAA

Italian

Lunch: $5-$12   Dinner: $7-$18   Phone: 845/462-4545

Location: Jct US 44 and SR 55, 3.7 mi s. 2373 South Rd (US 9) 12601. **Hours:** 11:30 am-10 pm, Fri-11 pm, Sat 10 am-11 pm, Sun 10 am-9 pm. Closed: 11/22, 12/25. **Reservations:** suggested. **Features:** In operation since the late 1960s, the casual restaurant is a favorite for home-style, bistro fare. Six small dining rooms offer warmth and cozy comfort. The extensive menu includes several lighter items. Sunday brunch draws a hungry crowd. Casual dress; cocktails. **Parking:** on-site. **Cards:** AX, DC, DS, MC, VI.

COSIMOS TRATTORIA & BAR

Italian

Lunch: $6-$15   Dinner: $8-$24   Phone: 845/485-7172

Location: 0.6 mi n of Mid-Hudson Bridge. 120 Delafield St 12601. **Hours:** 11:30 am-10 pm, Fri & Sat-11 pm, Sun noon-10 pm. Closed: 3/23, 12/25. **Reservations:** accepted. **Features:** An extensive wine list and several martini choices alone are worth stopping at the trattoria, but the brick-oven pizzas and beautiful atmosphere keep patrons coming back. Casual dress; cocktails. **Parking:** on-site. **Cards:** AX, CB, DC, DS, MC, VI.

COYOTE GRILL

Southwestern

Lunch: $6-$15   Dinner: $6-$29   Phone: 845/471-0600

Location: 1.9 mi s of Mid-Hudson Bridge. 2629 South Rd 12601. **Hours:** 11 am-2 am. Closed: 11/22, 12/25. **Reservations:** accepted. **Features:** The atmosphere is all about having fun. On the menu are traditional American dishes, as well as some Cajun and Southwest favorites. Jambalaya is a must. Casual dress; cocktails. **Parking:** on-site. **Cards:** AX, DC, DS, MC, VI.

CREW

American

Lunch: $7-$16   Dinner: $8-$25   Phone: 845/462-5900

Location: 2.5 mi s of Mid-Hudson Bridge. 2290 South Rd 12601. **Hours:** 11 am-10 pm, Sun-9 pm. Closed: 7/4, 11/22, 12/25. **Reservations:** accepted. **Features:** A trendy scene at night, the restaurant plies guests with a large selection of mixed drinks and traditional American dishes prepared with flair. Casual dress; cocktails. **Parking:** on-site. **Cards:** AX, DC, DS, MC, VI.

THE HAYMAKER

American

Lunch: $8-$16   Dinner: $14-$22   Phone: 845/486-9454

Location: Jct US 9, 44 and SR 55, 4.5 mi e on US 44; in Arlington Plaza. 718 Dutchess Tpke 12603. **Hours:** 11 am-2:30 & 5-9 pm, Fri & Sat-10 pm, Sun 5 pm-9 pm. Closed major holidays. **Reservations:** suggested. **Features:** The intimate restaurant has a bright, modern look. On the menu is a diverse selection of contemporary American dishes that fuse Southwestern and Asian influences. Portobello fries and grilled flat-iron steak are popular. Casual dress; cocktails. **Parking:** on-site. **Cards:** AX, DC, DS, MC, VI.

O'SHO JAPANESE STEAKHOUSE

AAA

Japanese

Lunch: $7-$16   Dinner: $14-$35   Phone: 845/297-0540

Location: Jct US 44 and SR 55, 5.8 mi s; across from Poughkeepsie Galleria Mall. 1998 South Rd (US 9) 12601. **Hours:** 11:30 am-2:30 & 5-10 pm, Sat & Sun from 3:30 pm. Closed: 11/22. **Reservations:** accepted. **Features:** From grill table to yakitori to sushi, the food is fresh and delightful to the taste buds. The country inn exterior changes to Japanese tea house upon entry. The staff is pleasant. Casual dress; cocktails. **Parking:** on-site. **Cards:** AX, DC, DS, MC, VI.

PULASKI pop. 2,398

——— WHERE TO STAY ———

RED CARPET INN & SCOTTISH INNS & SUITES   Phone: (315)298-4717

AAA SAVE

Motel

9/1-10/31 [CP]	1P: $89-$109	2P: $119-$139	XP: $5	F12
5/1-8/31 [CP]	1P: $69-$89	2P: $79-$99	XP: $5	F12
11/1-4/30 [CP]	1P: $64-$84	2P: $74-$94	XP: $5	F12

Location: I-81, exit 36, just e. 3723 SR 13 13142 (309 W Seneca St, OSWEGO, 13126). Fax: 315/298-6645. **Facility:** 50 units. 49 one-bedroom standard units. 1 one-bedroom suite ($125-$150) with kitchen. 1 story, interior/exterior corridors. *Bath:* combo or shower only. **Parking:** on-site. **Terms:** pets ($20 deposit). **Dining:** 11 am-9 pm, Fri & Sat-10 pm, Sun 8 am-9 pm. **Pool(s):** outdoor. **Guest Services:** coin laundry. **Business Services:** meeting rooms. **Cards:** AX, DC, DS, MC, VI. **Free Special Amenities:** continental breakfast and newspaper.

SOME UNITS

SUPER 8 MOTEL   *Book at AAA.com*   Phone: (315)298-4888

Small-scale Hotel

5/1-9/14	1P: $68-$174	2P: $74-$180	XP: $6	F12
9/28-10/23	1P: $103-$150	2P: $109-$150	XP: $6	F12
9/15-9/27	1P: $95-$150	2P: $101-$150	XP: $6	F12
10/24-4/30	1P: $62-$150	2P: $68-$150	XP: $6	F12

Location: I-81, exit 36, just w. 3800 SR 13 13142 (PO Box 532). Fax: 315/298-3293. **Facility:** 40 units. 39 one-bedroom standard units. 1 one-bedroom suite ($90-$300) with efficiency (no utensils). 2 stories (no elevator), interior corridors. **Parking:** on-site, winter plug-ins. **Terms:** [CP] meal plan available. **Amenities:** safes (fee), hair dryers. **Guest Services:** Wireless. **Business Services:** PC. **Cards:** AX, DS, MC, VI.

SOME UNITS

——— WHERE TO DINE ———

C & M DINER

American

Lunch: $3-$6   Dinner: $5-$10   Phone: 315/298-5443

Location: I-81, exit 36, just e. 3739 Rome Rd 13142. **Hours:** 5 am-9 pm. Closed: 12/25. **Features:** The easily accessible old-fashioned diner is great for a delicious, quick bite. Daily homemade specials and traditional American fare make up the offerings. Casual dress. **Parking:** on-site. **Cards:** DS, MC, VI.

QUEENS —See New York p. 488.

QUEENSBURY pop. 25,441 (See map and index starting on p. 330)—*See also ADIRONDACK MOUNTAINS.*

——— WHERE TO STAY ———

ALPENHAUS MOTEL
Phone: (518)792-6941 **55**

5/1-9/30	1P: $69-$129	2P: $69-$149	XP: $10	F
10/1-11/30	1P: $59-$99	2P: $59-$109	XP: $10	F
Motel 12/1-4/30	1P: $49-$89	2P: $49-$99	XP: $10	F

Location: I-87, exit 19, 0.4 mi e, then just n. 851 US 9 12804. Fax: 518/792-0168. **Facility:** 15 one-bedroom standard units. 1 story, exterior corridors. *Bath:* combo or shower only. **Parking:** on-site. **Terms:** weekly rates available. **Business Services:** fax (fee). **Cards:** AX, CB, DC, DS, JC, MC, VI.

SOME UNITS
ASK SD ⊤⊹ ✦ ◻ / ✕ ⊟ ▣ /

BUDGET INN
Phone: 518/792-9576 **53**

6/28-9/6	1P: $98-$125	2P: $98-$125	XP: $15
5/1-6/27	1P: $59-$125	2P: $59-$125	XP: $15
9/7-10/31	1P: $59-$99	2P: $59-$99	XP: $15
Motel 11/1-4/30	1P: $49-$59	2P: $49-$59	XP: $15

Location: I-87, exit 19, 0.8 mi ne. 932 US 9 (Lake George Rd) 12804. Fax: 518/792-8072. **Facility:** 20 one-bedroom standard units. 1 story, exterior corridors. *Bath:* combo or shower only. **Parking:** on-site. **Terms:** 7 day cancellation notice-fee imposed. **Pool(s):** heated outdoor. **Leisure Activities:** playground. **Business Services:** fax. **Cards:** AX, CB, DC, DS, JC, MC, VI.

ASK SD ⊤⊹ ⇌ ✕ ⊟ ◻

COUNTRY INN & SUITES   *Book great rates at AAA.com*
Phone: 518/745-0180 **51**

Property failed to provide current rates

Small-scale Hotel   **Location:** I-87, exit 19, 1.9 mi ne. 1130 US 9 12804. Fax: 518/745-0180. **Facility:** 85 units. 64 one-bedroom standard units. 21 one-bedroom suites. 3 stories, interior corridors. *Bath:* combo or shower only. **Parking:** on-site, winter plug-ins. **Amenities:** high-speed Internet, irons, hair dryers. **Pool(s):** heated outdoor, heated indoor. **Leisure Activities:** whirlpool, playground, exercise room, game room. **Guest Services:** valet and coin laundry. **Business Services:** fax. *(See color ad p 335)*

SOME UNITS
⊤⊹ ⛼M ⓔ 🦶 ⇌ ✕ ◻ / ✕ ⊟ ▣ /

DAYS INN OF LAKE GEORGE   *Book great rates at AAA.com*
Phone: (518)793-3196 **48**

6/22-9/2	1P: $89-$186	2P: $89-$186	XP: $10 F17
5/1-6/21 & 9/3-4/30	1P: $79-$136	2P: $79-$136	XP: $10 F17

Small-scale Hotel   **Location:** I-87, exit 20, just n. Located in a commercial area. 1454 SR 9 12845. Fax: 518/793-6028. **Facility:** 104 units. 101 one- and 3 two-bedroom standard units. 2 stories (no elevator), interior/exterior corridors. **Parking:** on-site. **Terms:** 2 night minimum stay - seasonal and/or weekends, 14 day cancellation notice-fee imposed. **Amenities:** hair dryers. **Dining:** The Meeting Place, see separate listing. **Pool(s):** heated indoor. **Leisure Activities:** whirlpool. **Guest Services:** valet laundry, wireless Internet. **Business Services:** meeting rooms, fax (fee). **Cards:** AX, DC, DS, MC, VI. *(See color ad p 336)*

SOME UNITS
ASK SD ⊤⊹ 🦶 ⇌ ✦ ⊟ / ✕ /

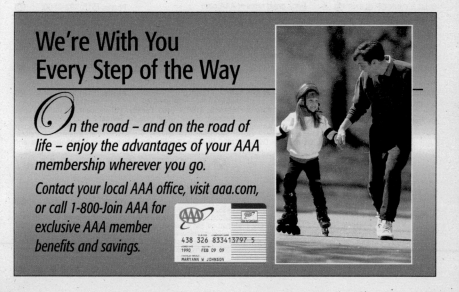

(See map and index starting on p. 330)

DUNHAM'S BAY RESORT
Phone: 518/656-9242   **46**

(AAA) (SAVE)
▼▼▼

Motel

5/1-9/2	1P: $105-$275	2P: $105-$275	XP: $15
9/3-4/30	1P: $60-$220	2P: $60-$220	XP: $15

Location: I-87, exit 21 to US 9N, 5 mi ne. 2999 SR 9L 12845. Fax: 518/656-9250. **Facility:** 50 units. 38 one- and 2 two-bedroom standard units. 2 one- and 8 two-bedroom suites with kitchens. 1-3 stories (no elevator); exterior corridors. **Parking:** on-site. **Terms:** 2-7 night minimum stay - seasonal and/or weekends, 30 day cancellation notice, in season-fee imposed. **Amenities:** voice mail, hair dryers. **Dining:** 7 am-11 & 5-9 pm, cocktails. **Pool(s):** heated indoor, wading. **Leisure Activities:** whirlpool, tennis court, barbecue grills, lawn games, picnic tables, table tennis, hiking trails, jogging, playground, basketball, shuffleboard. *Fee:* game room. **Business Services:** meeting rooms, fax (fee). **Cards:** AX, MC, VI. **Free Special Amenities:** high-speed Internet.

SOME UNITS

ECONO LODGE & SUITES OF GLENS FALLS/LAKE GEORGE
Book great rates at AAA.com
Phone: (518)793-3700   **57**

▼▼▼▼

Motel

5/1-9/30 [CP]	1P: $49-$139	2P: $49-$139	XP: $10	F15
10/1-4/30 [CP]	1P: $49-$79	2P: $49-$79	XP: $5	F15

Location: I-87, exit 19, just e. 543 Aviation Rd 12804. Fax: 518/793-3004. **Facility:** 48 units. 44 one-bedroom standard units. 4 two-bedroom suites ($99-$199) with efficiencies. 2 stories (no elevator). **Parking:** on-site. **Terms:** cancellation fee imposed, package plans. **Amenities:** voice mail, irons, hair dryers. **Cards:** AX, DC, DS, MC, VI.

SOME UNITS

GRAYCOURT MOTEL
Phone: 518/792-0223   **52**

(AAA) (SAVE)
▼▼▼

Motel

6/24-9/3	1P: $85-$95	2P: $110-$120	XP: $5
5/25-6/23 & 9/4-9/25	1P: $75-$90	2P: $75-$90	XP: $5

Location: I-87, exit 19, 1.3 mi ne. 1082 US 9 12804. Fax: 518/792-2003. **Facility:** 25 units. 20 one-bedroom standard units. 5 cottages ($75-$150). 1 story, exterior corridors. *Bath:* combo or shower only. **Parking:** on-site. **Pool(s):** open 5/25-9/25, 2 night minimum stay - in cottages, cancellation fee imposed. **Pool(s):** heated outdoor. **Leisure Activities:** picnic area with barbecue grill, playground. **Business Services:** fax. **Cards:** AX, DS, MC, VI. **Free Special Amenities:** local telephone calls and room upgrade (subject to availability with advance reservations).** *(See color ad p 337)*

SOME UNITS

MOHICAN MOTEL
Phone: (518)792-0474   **47**

(AAA) (SAVE)
▼▼▼▼

Motel

6/22-9/3	1P: $105-$145	2P: $105-$145	XP: $15	F
5/26-6/21	1P: $68-$105	2P: $68-$105	XP: $15	F
5/1-5/25 & 9/4-4/30	1P: $58-$88	2P: $58-$88	XP: $15	F

Location: I-87, exit 20, 0.5 mi n. 1545 US 9 12845. Fax: 518/761-4089. **Facility:** 44 units. 14 one- and 22 two-bedroom standard units, some with efficiencies, kitchens and/or whirlpools. 8 two-bedroom suites ($98-$245) with whirlpools. 1-2 stories (no elevator), exterior corridors. **Parking:** on-site. **Terms:** 21 day cancellation notice-fee imposed. **Amenities:** voice mail. *Some:* hair dryers. **Pool(s):** outdoor, heated indoor, wading. **Leisure Activities:** sauna, whirlpools, playground, sports court. *Fee:* game room. **Guest Services:** coin laundry. **Business Services:** PC, fax. **Cards:** AX, MC, VI. **Free Special Amenities:** preferred room (subject to availability with advance reservations) and high-speed Internet. *(See color ad p 341)*

SOME UNITS

QUALITY INN OF GLENS FALLS
Book great rates at AAA.com
Phone: (518)793-3800   **56**

▼▼▼

Small-scale Hotel

5/1-9/30 [CP]	1P: $69-$149	2P: $69-$149	XP: $10	F15
10/1-4/30 [CP]	1P: $69-$99	2P: $69-$99	XP: $10	F15

Location: I-87, exit 19, just e. 547 Aviation Rd 12804. Fax: 518/793-7800. **Facility:** 38 one-bedroom standard units, some with whirlpools. 2 stories (no elevator), interior corridors. **Parking:** on-site, winter plug-ins. **Terms:** cancellation fee imposed, package plans. **Amenities:** high-speed Internet, voice mail, irons, hair dryers. **Pool(s):** small heated indoor. **Business Services:** fax (fee). **Cards:** AX, DC, DS, MC, VI.

SOME UNITS

RAMADA GLENS FALLS
Book great rates at AAA.com
Phone: (518)793-7701   **58**

(AAA) (SAVE)
▼▼▼

Small-scale Hotel

All Year	1P: $74-$169	2P: $74-$169	XP: $10	F17

Location: I-87, exit 19, just w. 1 Abby Ln 12804. Fax: 518/792-5463. **Facility:** 110 one-bedroom standard units. 2 stories (no elevator), interior corridors. **Parking:** on-site, winter plug-ins. **Terms:** 2-4 night minimum stay - seasonal and/or weekends. **Amenities:** voice mail, irons, hair dryers. **Dining:** 6:30 am-1 & 5-10 pm, cocktails. **Pool(s):** heated indoor. **Guest Services:** valet laundry, wireless Internet. **Business Services:** meeting rooms. **Cards:** AX, DC, DS, MC, VI. **Free Special Amenities:** local telephone calls and newspaper.

SOME UNITS

FEE

SIX FLAGS GREAT ESCAPE LODGE & INDOOR WATER PARK
Phone: (518)824-6000   **49**

▼▼▼

Large-scale Hotel

1/1-4/30	1P: $219-$529	2P: $219-$529	XP: $30
5/1-12/31	1P: $209-$509	2P: $209-$509	XP: $30

Location: I-87, exit 20 northbound, just s; southbound, just e then just s. 89 Six Flags Dr 12804. Fax: 518/824-6006. **Facility:** 200 units. 180 one- and 20 two-bedroom standard units. 4 stories, interior corridors. *Bath:* combo or shower only. **Parking:** on-site. **Terms:** check-in 4 pm, 3 day cancellation notice, [BP] & [MAP] meal plans available, package plans. **Amenities:** video games, dual phone lines, voice mail, safes, irons, hair dryers. **Leisure Activities:** recreation programs, exercise room, spa, game room. **Guest Services:** sundries, valet and coin laundry, wireless Internet. **Business Services:** meeting rooms, fax. **Cards:** AX, DS, MC, VI.

(See map and index starting on p. 330)

SLEEP INN & SUITES   *Book great rates at AAA.com*   Phone: (518)955-3000   54

AAA (SAVE)   All Year [ECP]   1P: $84-$199   2P: $84-$199   XP: $5   F16

WWW WWW   **Location:** I-87, exit 19, 0.3 mi e on Aviation Rd, then 0.5 mi n. 906 Lake George Rd (US 9) 12804. **Fax:** 518/955-3008. **Facility:** 78 one-bedroom standard units, some with whirlpools. 3 stories, interior corridors. *Bath:* combo or shower only. **Parking:** on-site. **Amenities:** high-speed Internet, voice mail, irons,

Small-scale Hotel   hair dryers. **Pool(s):** heated indoor. **Leisure Activities:** exercise room. **Guest Services:** coin laundry. **Business Services:** meeting rooms. **Cards:** AX, CB, DC, DS, JC, MC, VI. **Free Special Amenities:** expanded continental breakfast and high-speed Internet.

SOME UNITS

THE WAKITA MOTEL   Phone: (518)792-0326   50

AAA (SAVE)   5/25-9/4   1P: $74-$199   2P: $74-$199   XP: $5   F16

WWW WWW   **Location:** I-87, exit 19, 1.9 mi ne. 1130 US 9 12804. **Facility:** 12 one-bedroom standard units. 1 story, exterior corridors. **Parking:** on-site. **Terms:** open 5/25-9/4, 2 night minimum stay - weekends,

Motel   7 day cancellation notice-fee imposed. **Pool(s):** heated outdoor. **Leisure Activities:** volleyball. **Business Services:** fax. **Cards:** AX, DS, MC, VI. **Free Special Amenities:** local telephone calls and early check-in/late check-out.

——— WHERE TO DINE ———

CARL R'S CAFE   Lunch: $5-$10   Dinner: $9-$12   Phone: 518/793-7676   33

AAA   **Location:** I-87, exit 18. 124 Corinth Rd 12804. **Hours:** 7 am-11 pm; to 9 pm, Wed & Thurs-10 pm, Fri & Sat-11

WWW WWW   pm 10/2-5/31; hours may vary. **Closed:** 11/22, 12/25. **Reservations:** accepted. **Features:** Sombreros are not needed to enjoy the Mexican/American flavors at Carl R's. A bustling, casual atmosphere and oversize

American   portions are served everyday from 7 am to late. Complimentary chips and salsa to start and then move on to dishes such as chicken fajitas with your choice of toppings, buffalo burgers or steak. Close with a selection of dessert from fried ice cream to apple bread pudding. Casual dress; cocktails. **Parking:** on-site. **Cards:** AX, CB, DC, DS, MC, VI.

FLOWER DRUM SONG RESTAURANT   Lunch: $5-$8   Dinner: $6-$18   Phone: 518/798-0455   32

WWW WWW   **Location:** I-87, exit 19, 0.3 mi e on US 9, then 0.5 mi n. 909 US 9 12804. **Hours:** 11 am-10 pm, Fri & Sat-10:30 pm, Sun noon-9:30 pm. **Closed:** 11/22, 12/25. **Reservations:** accepted. **Features:** Encounter the Orient

Asian   with the variety of Asian cuisines offered here—traditional Chinese, Szechuan and a few Thai and Japanese dishes. The friendly and relaxed service in the pleasant tea house surroundings will delight you. Casual dress; cocktails. **Parking:** on-site. **Cards:** AX, DC, DS, MC, VI.

GAMBLE'S BAKERY & COFFEE SHOP   Lunch: $3-$8   Phone: 518/793-5384   31

WWW   **Location:** I-87, exit 19, 0.3 mi e, then 0.6 mi n. 920 Rt 9 12804. **Hours:** 7 am-3 pm, Sun-2 pm. **Closed:** 1/1, 11/22, 12/25. **Features:** Great spot for breakfast, limited seating. Soup and sandwiches also available for lunch.

American   Casual dress. **Parking:** on-site.

LOG JAM   Lunch: $6-$10   Dinner: $13-$22   Phone: 518/798-1155   24

WWW WWW   **Location:** Jct US 9 and SR 149. 1484 US 9 12804. **Hours:** 11:30 am-2:30 & 5-9 pm, Fri & Sat-9:30 pm, Sun 11:30 am-2:30 & 4:30-9 pm. **Closed:** 11/22, 12/25. **Reservations:** suggested. **Features:** This restaurant is

American   located in the midst of many popular shopping outlets. Wood floors and beamed ceilings lend to the feeling that you're dining in a rustic, Adirondack log cabin. Memorabilia of the logging industry is spread throughout the dining room. Portions are hearty and the service friendly. Casual dress; cocktails. **Parking:** on-site. **Cards:** AX, CB, DC, DS, MC, VI.

THE MEETING PLACE   Lunch: $4-$7   Dinner: $12-$20   Phone: 518/792-9565   25

WWW WWW   **Location:** I-87, exit 20, just n; in Days Inn of Lake George. 1454 US 9 12845. **Hours:** 7 am-9 pm. **Closed:** 11/22, 12/25. **Reservations:** accepted. **Features:** Pizza from a wood-fired brick oven and well-prepared specials

American   are favorites at the casual, cafe-style restaurant. A glassed atrium on each side of the dining room lends warmth. Homemade dessert and gourmet coffee are fitting toppers to any meal. Casual dress; cocktails. **Parking:** on-site. **Cards:** AX, DC, DS, MC, VI.

THE MONTCALM   Lunch: $6-$9   Dinner: $13-$33   Phone: 518/793-6601   26

WWW WWW   **Location:** I-87, exit 20, just n. 1415 US 9 12845. **Hours:** 11:45 am-2:30 & 5-9 pm, Fri & Sat-9:30 pm. **Features:** Diners can sit beside the roaring fire in this spot that's styled after a log home. Steak and

American   seafood specialties, such as the flavorful lobster bisque and New England shore dinner, are delicious. Casual dress; cocktails. **Parking:** on-site. **Cards:** AX, MC, VI.

OLDE POST GRILLE   Lunch: $6-$15   Dinner: $6-$15   Phone: 518/743-9622   27

WWW WWW   **Location:** I-87, exit 20 northbound, just s; exit southbound, just e, then just s. 1300 Rt 9 12845. **Hours:** 11:30 am-10 pm. **Closed:** 4/8, 11/22, 12/25. **Reservations:** suggested, weekends. **Features:** A great place to relax with

American   friends and watch a sporting event of your liking; outdoor seating in the summer months make for a good time. Casual dress; cocktails. **Parking:** on-site. **Cards:** AX, DS, MC, VI.

SMOKEY BEAR BBQ & GRIL   Dinner: $6-$18   Phone: 518/761-7101   30

WWW WWW   **Location:** I-87, exit 19, 1.3 mi n. 1036 Rt 9 12804. **Hours:** Open 5/1-12/31 & 3/1-4/30; 3 pm-10 pm. **Features:** Steamers, hand-battered seafood and slow-cooked barbecue baby back ribs are just some of the

Barbecue   house specialties. Patrons should find room for one of the many delicious flavors of homemade ice cream. Deck seating is a plus. Casual dress; cocktails. **Parking:** on-site. **Cards:** AX, DC, DS, MC, VI.

(See map and index starting on p. 330)

SUTTON'S COUNTRY CAFE | **Lunch:** $4-$8 | **Dinner:** $9-$16 | **Phone:** 518/798-1188 | 29

▼▼ ▼▼ **Location:** I-87, exit 19, 1.3 mi ne. 1066 Rt 9 (Lake George Rd) 12804. **Hours:** 7:30 am-3 pm, Fri also 5 pm-8:30 pm. Closed major holidays. **Features:** Knickknacks and dishes line the shelves around the cozy dining room, which has the aura of a friendly country cafe. The menu revolves around home-style dishes, such as chicken pot pie and pot roast. Particularly tempting are the fresh bread and pies. Casual dress; cocktails.
American
Parking: on-site. **Cards:** AX, DC, DS, MC, VI.

TRAPPER'S ADIRONDACK GRILLE | *Menu on AAA.com* **Lunch:** $6-$13 **Dinner:** $15-$26 **Phone:** 518/824-6000 | 28

ⒶⒶⒶ **Location:** I-87, exit 21, 0.4 mi s. 89 Six Flags Dr 12845. **Hours:** 7 am-3 & 4-9 pm, Fri & Sat-10 pm. **Reservations:** suggested. **Features:** You'll enjoy casual dining in a charming rustic atmosphere, complete
▼▼▼▼ with a cozy fireplace for winter evenings. The eatery also boasts a popular salad bar. Casual dress;
American cocktails. **Parking:** on-site. **Cards:** AX, DC, DS, MC, VI.

RANDOLPH pop. 1,316

——— WHERE TO DINE ———

OREGANO'S FAMILY RESTAURANT | **Lunch:** $4-$7 | **Dinner:** $7-$10 | **Phone:** 716/358-4429

▼▼▼ **Location:** Center. 143 Main St 14772. **Hours:** 7 am-2 pm, Tues & Wed-8 pm, Thurs-9 pm. Closed major holidays; also Sun. **Features:** The small downtown eatery prepares delicious comfort food with guests'
American dietary needs in mind. Offerings include many breakfast dishes, early-bird specials, wings, pasta, sandwiches, burgers, meatloaf, pot roast, scallops, broiled fish and an all-you-can-eat pizza and salad buffet
on Tuesday and Wednesday. Desserts made on the premises are worth a sweet bite. Casual dress. **Parking:** street.
Cards: MC, VI.

R & M RESTAURANT | **Lunch:** $5-$6 | **Dinner:** $7-$10 | **Phone:** 716/358-5141

▼▼▼ **Location:** I-86, exit 16, just n. 265 Main St 14772. **Hours:** 6 am-9 pm, Fri & Sat-10 pm; to 8 pm in winter.
Closed: 1/1, 3/23, 12/25. **Features:** Comfort food is no exaggeration at the neat-as-a-pin diner. Easy-on,
American easy-off access makes this place a convenient spot for a satisfying meal. Casual dress. **Parking:** on-site.
Cards: DS, MC, VI.

RAY BROOK

——— WHERE TO DINE ———

TAIL O' THE PUP | **Lunch:** $5-$15 | **Dinner:** $10-$30 | **Phone:** 518/891-0777

▼▼▼ **Location:** Center. SR 86 12977. **Hours:** Open 5/1-10/31; 11 am-10 pm. **Reservations:** accepted.
Features: Locals and visitors alike flock here to savor the famous smokehouse-barbecued chicken and ribs.
Barbecue It's a "roll up your sleeves and dig in" type of place. Casual dress; cocktails; entertainment. **Parking:** on-site
and street. **Cards:** MC, VI.

RED CREEK pop. 521

——— WHERE TO DINE ———

THE COTTAGE INN | **Lunch:** $3-$8 | **Dinner:** $10-$18 | **Phone:** 315/754-8969

▼▼▼ ▼▼ **Location:** Jct SR 370 and Ridge Rd. 13662 Rt 370 13143. **Hours:** 11 am-2 & 5-9 pm. Closed: 1/1, 11/22, 12/25;
also Sun, Mon & 2 weeks at Easter. **Reservations:** accepted. **Features:** The friendly crossroads restaurant
American offers seating in either the cottage-style room or cozy bar. Examples of fresh homemade-style cooking
include prime rib, steaks, Italian favorites, veal, seafood and at least 10 preparations of chicken. Generous
portions are well priced. Casual dress; cocktails. **Parking:** on-site. **Cards:** MC, VI.

RED HOOK pop. 1,805

——— WHERE TO DINE ———

CAPPUCINO BY COPPOLA'S | **Lunch:** $6-$14 | **Dinner:** $7-$18 | **Phone:** 845/876-1331

ⒶⒶⒶ **Location:** Jct SR 199, 3.4 mi n. 4604 Rt 9G 12571. **Hours:** 11:30 am-9:30 pm, Fri & Sat-10 pm, Sun 10:30 am-9
pm. Closed: 11/22, 12/25. **Reservations:** accepted. **Features:** Offering a wide variety of classic Italian
▼▼ ▼▼ dishes as well as pizza, this roadside eatery is popular with locals and the college crowd. Casual dress;
Italian cocktails. **Parking:** on-site. **Cards:** AX, CB, DC, DS, JC, MC, VI.

RED OAKS MILL pop. 4,930—*See also POUGHKEEPSIE.*

——— WHERE TO STAY ———

INN AT THE FALLS | *Book great rates at AAA.com* | | **Phone:** (845)462-5770

ⒶⒶⒶ SAVE All Year [ECP] | 1P: $149-$239 | 2P: $149-$239
▼▼▼▼ **Location:** Jct SR 376 and CR 113, just se. 50 Red Oaks Mill Rd (CR 44) 12603. Fax: 845/462-5943. **Facility:** 36
units. 22 one-bedroom standard units. 14 one-bedroom suites with whirlpools. 2 stories, interior corridors.
Small-scale Hotel **Parking:** on-site. **Terms:** 3 day cancellation notice-fee imposed, package plans. **Amenities:** DVD players,
voice mail, safes, irons, hair dryers. *Some:* CD players. **Leisure Activities:** whirlpool, fishing, exercise
room. **Guest Services:** complimentary evening beverages, wireless Internet. **Business Services:** meeting
rooms, business center. **Cards:** AX, CB, DC, DS, JC, MC, VI. **Free Special Amenities:** expanded continental breakfast and
local telephone calls.

SOME UNITS

RENSSELAER pop. 7,761   (See map and index starting on p. 218)

──── **WHERE TO STAY** ────

ECONO LODGE   *Book great rates at AAA.com*   Phone: (518)472-1360   **45**
(AAA) (SAVE)   All Year   1P: $59-$129   2P: $69-$139   XP: $10   F12
▼▼▼▼   **Location:** I-787, exit 3, 1.5 mi on US 9 S and 20 E; I-90, exit 9, 2 mi on US 4 S, then 2.5 mi n on US 9 N and 20 W. 110
Motel   Columbia Tpke 12144. Fax: 518/427-2924. **Facility:** 55 one-bedroom standard units, some with whirlpools. 1-
2 stories (no elevator), interior/exterior corridors. *Bath:* combo or shower only. **Parking:** on-site, winter plug-
ins. **Terms:** 2 night minimum stay - seasonal, [CP] meal plan available. **Amenities:** high-speed Internet,
voice mail, irons, hair dryers. **Pool(s):** outdoor. **Guest Services:** coin laundry. **Cards:** AX, DC, DS, MC, VI.
Free Special Amenities: continental breakfast and high-speed Internet.
SOME UNITS

RHINEBECK pop. 3,077

──── **WHERE TO STAY** ────

BEEKMAN ARMS & DELAMATER INN AND
CONFERENCE CENTER   Phone: 845/876-7077
▼▼▼   All Year   1P: $110-$300   2P: $110-$300   XP: $15   D
Historic   **Location:** Jct US 9 and SR 308; center of village. 6387 Mill St (Rt 9) 12572. Fax: 845/876-7077. **Facility:** The
Country Inn property's well-furnished accommodations, some with fireplaces, occupy a main inn as well as several guest
houses. 73 units. 65 one-bedroom standard units. 8 one-bedroom suites. 1-3 stories (no elevator),
interior/exterior corridors. *Bath:* combo or shower only. **Parking:** on-site. **Terms:** 2 night minimum stay -
weekends, 14 day cancellation notice-fee imposed, pets (in designated units). **Amenities:** voice mail, hair dryers. *Some:* CD
players, irons. **Dining:** The Traphagen Restaurant, see separate listing. **Business Services:** meeting rooms. **Cards:** AX, DS,
MC, VI.
SOME UNITS
FEE

──── **WHERE TO DINE** ────

TERRAPIN   Lunch: $6-$13   Dinner: $16-$26   Phone: 845/876-3330
▼▼▼   **Location:** Jct Montgomery and Livingston sts. 6426 Montgomery St 12572. **Hours:** noon-5 & 5:30-10 pm, Fri &
American   Sat-11 pm. Closed: 11/22, 12/25. **Reservations:** suggested. **Features:** After a drive in the countryside,
settle in to choose from 100-plus wines and a wide range of food offerings prepared by Chef Kroner. Dishes
distinctively blend classical French with Southwestern, Italian and Asian influences. Casual dress; cocktails.
Parking: on-site. **Cards:** AX, DS, MC, VI.

THE TRAPHAGEN RESTAURANT   Lunch: $8-$14   Dinner: $19-$36   Phone: 845/876-1766
▼▼▼   **Location:** Jct US 9 and SR 308; in Beekman Arms & Delamater Inn and Conference Center. 6387 Mill St 12572.
Hours: 11:30 am-3 & 5:30-9 pm, Fri & Sat-10 pm, Sun 10:30 am-2 & 4-8:30 pm. **Reservations:** suggested,
Regional American weekends. **Features:** A wide selection of seafood, duck, pork and chicken is offered, and the Traphagen
filet is popular. The 1766 inn has the feel of a cozy tavern, with Colonial furnishings and a charming pewter
Historic   room. The creative menu changes seasonally. Casual dress; cocktails. **Parking:** on-site. **Cards:** AX, CB, DC, DS, MC, VI.

RICHFIELD SPRINGS pop. 1,255

──── **WHERE TO STAY** ────

FOUNTAIN VIEW MOTEL   Phone: 315/858-1360
(AAA) (SAVE)   6/15-9/2   1P: $72-$95   2P: $72-$95   XP: $6
▼▼▼   9/3-11/12   1P: $49-$72   2P: $49-$72   XP: $6
5/1-6/14 & 4/1-4/30 1P: $49-$59   2P: $49-$59   XP: $6
Motel   **Location:** 1 mi e. 3607 US 20 13439. **Facility:** Smoke free premises. 16 one-bedroom standard units. 1 story,
exterior corridors. **Parking:** on-site. **Terms:** open 5/1-11/12 & 4/1-4/30, office hours 7 am-10:30 pm, 3 day
cancellation notice-fee imposed. **Amenities:** DVD players. **Cards:** DS, MC, VI. **Free Special Amenities:**
local telephone calls. *(See color ad p 279)*

STONY BROOK MOTEL   Phone: (315)858-9929
(AAA) (SAVE)   6/15-9/2   1P: $90-$95   2P: $90-$95   XP: $5   F5
▼▼▼   5/1-6/14 & 9/3-4/30   1P: $50-$65   2P: $50-$65   XP: $5   F5
Motel   **Location:** 0.5 mi e. 232 Main St (Rt 20) 13439 (PO Box 1849). Fax: 607/547-5671. **Facility:** 7 one-bedroom
standard units. 1 story, exterior corridors. *Bath:* shower only. **Parking:** on-site, winter plug-ins. **Terms:** office
hours 9 am-9 pm, 5 day cancellation notice. **Leisure Activities:** pool privileges. **Cards:** AX, DS, MC, VI.
Free Special Amenities: local telephone calls and room upgrade (subject to availability with advance
reservations).

VILLAGE MOTEL   Phone: 315/858-1540
(AAA) (SAVE)   6/16-9/5   1P: $90-$95   2P: $100-$110   XP: $6   D18
▼▼   5/1-6/15 & 9/6-4/30   1P: $55-$65   2P: $65-$75   XP: $6   D18
Motel   **Location:** Center. 168 Main St (Rt 20) 13439 (PO Box 766). **Facility:** 11 one-bedroom standard units. 1 story,
exterior corridors. **Terms:** office hours 8 am-11 pm, 2 night minimum stay -
weekends, 7 day cancellation notice-fee imposed. **Cards:** AX, DC, DS, MC, VI. **Free Special Amenities:**
local telephone calls and newspaper.
SOME UNITS

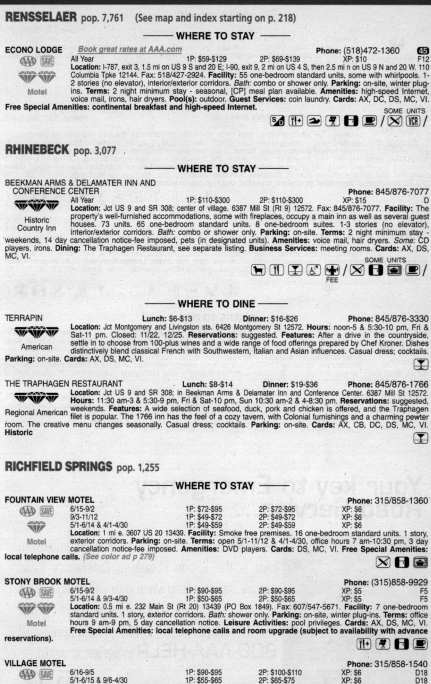

──────── WHERE TO DINE ────────

TALLY-HO RESTAURANT   **Lunch:** $5-$7   **Dinner:** $7-$11   **Phone:** 315/858-0180

American
Location: On US 20; center. 156 Main St 13439. **Hours:** 5 am-7:30 pm, Fri-8:30 pm, Sat-8 pm, Sun-3 pm; hours vary in winter. Closed: 1/1, 12/25. **Features:** The casual eatery makes delicious hot and cold sandwiches to order. All-American favorites, along with daily specials, make up the menu. Casual dress. **Parking:** on-site. **Cards:** DS, MC, VI.

RIVERHEAD pop. 10,513

──────── WHERE TO STAY ────────

BEST WESTERN EAST END   *Book great rates at AAA.com*   **Phone:** (631)369-2200
AAA SAVE   All Year [CP]   1P: $169-$300
Small-scale Hotel   **Location:** I-495, exit 72 (SR 25 E). 1830 SR 25 11901. Fax: 631/369-1202. **Facility:** 100 units. 99 one-bedroom standard units. 1 one-bedroom suite ($300) with whirlpool. 2 stories, interior corridors. *Bath:* combo or shower only. **Parking:** on-site. **Terms:** 3 day cancellation notice-fee imposed, package plans, small pets only ($50 fee). **Amenities:** video games (fee), voice mail, irons, hair dryers. **Dining:** 6:30 am-10 & noon-10 pm, Fri & Sat-11 pm, cocktails. **Pool(s):** heated outdoor. **Leisure Activities:** exercise room. **Guest Services:** valet laundry, wireless Internet. **Business Services:** meeting rooms, business center. **Cards:** AX, CB, DC, DS, MC, VI. **Free Special Amenities: continental breakfast and high-speed Internet.**

SOME UNITS
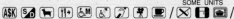
FEE   FEE   FEE

HOLIDAY INN EXPRESS EAST END   *Book at AAA.com*   **Phone:** (631)548-1000
All Year   1P: $179-$399   2P: $179-$399   XP: $10   F18
Small-scale Hotel   **Location:** I-495, exit 73, 0.5 mi e. 1707 Old Country Rd (SR 58) 11901. Fax: 631/548-1010. **Facility:** 89 one-bedroom standard units, some with whirlpools. 4 stories, interior corridors. *Bath:* combo or shower only. **Parking:** on-site. **Terms:** 5 day cancellation notice, [CP] meal plan available, pets (dogs only, $50 fee). **Amenities:** video games (fee), high-speed Internet, voice mail, irons, hair dryers. **Leisure Activities:** exercise room. **Guest Services:** valet laundry, wireless Internet. **Business Services:** meeting rooms, business center. **Cards:** AX, CB, DC, DS, JC, MC, VI.

SOME UNITS

FEE

──────── WHERE TO DINE ────────

THE LOBSTER ROLL/NORTHSIDE   **Lunch:** $7-$20   **Dinner:** $7-$20   **Phone:** 631/369-3039
Seafood
Location: Jct SR 25, 2 mi e on SR 25, 2.2 mi n on Edwards Ave, then 2.6 mi e; at Baitin Hollow Commons Retail complex. 3225 Sound Ave 11901. **Hours:** 11:30 am-8:30 pm, Fri & Sat-9 pm. Closed major holidays; also Tues. **Reservations:** not accepted. **Features:** This is the "country cousin" of the famed Hamptons eatery affectionately known as LUNCH. In a restored country farmhouse, this place serves excellent seafood dishes, great steak, burgers and chicken. Guests also can look forward to deck seating and weekend music in season. Casual dress; cocktails. **Parking:** on-site. **Cards:** AX, MC, VI.

STAR CONFECTIONERY   **Lunch:** $5-$10   **Phone:** 631/727-9873
American
Location: Jct Roanoke Ave. 4 E Main St 11901. **Hours:** 7:30 am-3 pm, Sun-11 pm. Closed major holidays. **Features:** The original pressed-tin ceiling, wooden booths and soda counter with stools create a unique atmosphere of a bygone era. Diners can enjoy a hearty breakfast from the open grill or simply indulge in a sundae topped the way they like it. Casual dress. **Parking:** street.

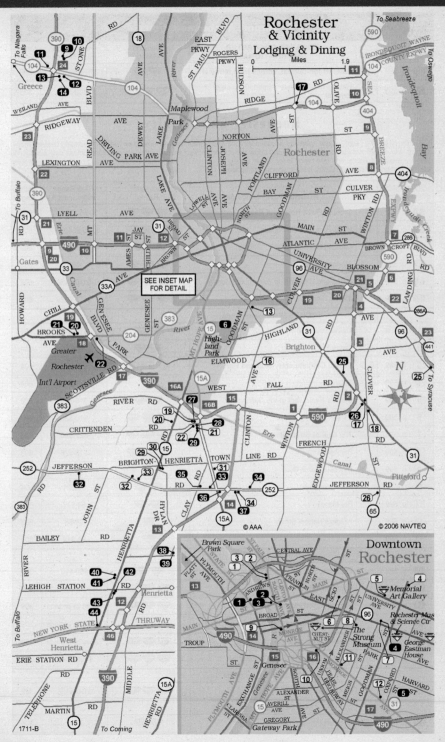

Rochester & Vicinity
Lodging & Dining

✈ Airport Accommodations

Spotter/Map Page Number	OA	GREATER ROCHESTER INTERNATIONAL	Diamond Rating	Rate Range High Season	Listing Page
20 / p. 599	AAA	Comfort Inn Central, across from terminal	◈◈	$79-$129 SAVE	305
22 / p. 599		Holiday Inn-Rochester Airport, 0.3 mi e of terminal	◈◈◈	$109-$149	305

Rochester and Vicinity

This index helps you "spot" where approved accommodations and restaurants are located on the corresponding detailed maps. Lodging rate ranges are for comparison only and show the property's high season; rates are per night, unless only weekly (W) rates are available. Restaurant rate range is for dinner, unless only lunch (L) is served. Turn to the listing page for more detailed rate information and consult display ads for special promotions.

Spotter/Map Page Number	OA	ROCHESTER - Lodgings	Diamond Rating	Rate Range High Season	Listing Page
1 / p. 599	AAA	**Crowne Plaza Hotel and Resort Rochester**	◈◈◈	$99-$169 SAVE	602
2 / p. 599	AAA	**Hyatt Regency Rochester**	◈◈◈	$105-$249 SAVE	602
3 / p. 599		Clarion Riverside Hotel	◈◈	$99-$169	602
4 / p. 599		Strathallan Hotel	◈◈◈	$80	603
5 / p. 599		A Bed and Breakfast at Dartmouth House	◈◈◈	$110-$150	602
6 / p. 599		428 Mt. Vernon	◈◈◈	$110-$125	602
		ROCHESTER - Restaurants			
1 / p. 599		Triphammer Grill	◈◈	$17-$27	604
2 / p. 599		Tapas 177	◈◈	$9-$24	604
3 / p. 599	AAA	**Sienna Contemporary Grill and Bar**	◈◈◈	$16-$34	604
4 / p. 599		Salena's	◈	$9-$16	604
5 / p. 599		Cutler's Restaurant at the Gallery	◈◈	$16-$25	603
6 / p. 599		2 Vine	◈◈◈	$10-$30	603
7 / p. 599	AAA	**The Grill at Strathallan**	◈◈◈	$22-$30	603
8 / p. 599		Bamba Bistro	◈◈◈	$15-$26	603
9 / p. 599		Dinosaur Bar-B-Que	◈	$12-$20	603
10 / p. 599		The Olive Tree	◈◈	$9-$21	604
11 / p. 599		Raj Mahal	◈◈	$9-$17	604
12 / p. 599		Alladin's Natural Eatery	◈	$4-$8	603
13 / p. 599		India House Restaurant	◈	$8-$16	604
		GREECE - Lodgings			
9 / p. 599		Extended Stay America-Rochester-Greece	◈◈	$60-$90	309
10 / p. 599		Hampton Inn-Rochester North	◈◈◈	$119-$155	309
11 / p. 599		Marriott Airport Hotel	◈◈◈	Failed to provide	309
12 / p. 599		Holiday Inn Express Rochester-Greece	fyi	Failed to provide	309
13 / p. 599		Residence Inn by Marriott-West	◈◈◈	Failed to provide	309
14 / p. 599		Courtyard by Marriott-Rochester West	◈◈◈	$109-$169	309
		IRONDEQUOIT - Lodgings			
17 / p. 599		Holiday Inn Express	◈◈◈	$110-$135	322
		GATES - Lodgings			
20 / p. 599	AAA	**Comfort Inn Central**	◈◈	$79-$129 SAVE	305

Spotter/Map Page Number	OA	GATES - Lodgings (continued)	Diamond Rating	Rate Range High Season	Listing Page
21 / p. 599		Fairfield Inn Rochester Airport	◆◆◆	$134	305
22 / p. 599		Holiday Inn-Rochester Airport	◆◆◆	$109-$149	305
		BRIGHTON - Lodgings			
25 / p. 599	AAA	**Towpath Motel - see color ad p 602**	◆	$65-$95 [SAVE]	240
26 / p. 599	AAA	**Holiday Inn Express-Rochester/Brighton**	◆◆◆	$119-$219 [SAVE]	240
27 / p. 599		Courtyard by Marriott Brighton	◆◆◆	$89-$259	239
28 / p. 599	AAA	**Hampton Inn-Rochester South**	◆◆◆	$105-$179 [SAVE]	240
29 / p. 599		Wellesley Inn (Rochester/South)	◆◆	Failed to provide	240
		BRIGHTON - Restaurants			
16 / p. 599		DiBella's Old Fashioned Submarines	◆	$3-$6	240
17 / p. 599		Mario's Via Abruzzi	◆◆◆	$14-$30	241
18 / p. 599		Mundo Grill	◆◆	$13-$19	241
19 / p. 599	AAA	**Phillips European Restaurant**	◆◆◆	$13-$30	241
20 / p. 599		Portobello	◆◆	$14-$22	241
21 / p. 599		Bazil	◆◆	$8-$18	240
22 / p. 599		Delmonico's Italian Steakhouse	◆◆	$9-$20	240
		HENRIETTA - Lodgings			
32 / p. 599		Radisson Rochester Airport	◆◆◆	$119-$159	315
33 / p. 599	AAA	**Best Western-Rochester Marketplace Inn**	◆◆	$109-$159 [SAVE]	314
34 / p. 599		Residence Inn by Marriott	◆◆◆	$159-$299	316
35 / p. 599		Holiday Inn Hotel & Suites	[fyi]	Failed to provide	315
36 / p. 599		DoubleTree Hotel Rochester	◆◆◆	$109-$179	315
37 / p. 599		Extended StayAmerica-Rochester-Henrietta	◆◆	$55-$95	315
38 / p. 599		Comfort Suites by Choice Hotels of Rochester	◆◆◆	$130-$155	314
39 / p. 599		Homewood Suites by Hilton-Rochester	◆◆◆	$170-$195	315
40 / p. 599		Fairfield Inn by Marriott-Rochester/South	◆◆◆	$113-$119	315
41 / p. 599	AAA	**Country Inn & Suites By Carlson**	◆◆◆	$189-$239 [SAVE]	314
42 / p. 599		Microtel-Rochester	◆◆	$60-$99	315
43 / p. 599		Red Roof Inn-Henrietta #7042	◆◆	$54-$88	316
44 / p. 599		R I T Inn & Conference Center	◆◆◆	$89-$115	316
		HENRIETTA - Restaurants			
29 / p. 599		Tokyo Japanese Restaurant & Steak House	◆◆	$12-$20	317
30 / p. 599		Shanghai Restaurant	◆	$5-$16	316
31 / p. 599		The King and I	◆	$8-$15	316
32 / p. 599	AAA	**Tandoor of India**	◆◆	$10-$15	316
33 / p. 599		DiBella's	◆	$4-$6	316
34 / p. 599		Bill Gray's	◆	$3-$9	316
		PITTSFORD - Restaurants			
25 / p. 599		Hawthorne's Restaurant	◆◆◆	$10-$25	585
26 / p. 599		Crystal Barn	◆◆◆	$14-$35	585

ROCHESTER pop. 219,773 (See map and index starting on p. 599)

——— WHERE TO STAY ———

428 MT. VERNON
Phone: (585)271-0792 **6**
▼▼▼ All Year 1P: $110 2P: $125 XP: $15

Historic Bed & Breakfast
Location: I-490, exit 15 eastbound, 1 mi s on South Ave, just e on Rockingham, then just s on Doctor's Rd; exit 17 westbound, 0.6 mi s on Goodman St, 0.3 mi w on Rockingham, then just s on Mt. Vernon Ave to Doctor's Rd. Located next to University Rochester Medical and Highland Park. 428 Mt. Vernon Ave 14620. Fax: 585/271-0946. **Facility:** On two wooded acres next to a large park, this 1917 home has attractive, individually decorated rooms. Smoke free premises. 7 one-bedroom standard units. 3 stories, interior corridors. *Bath:* combo or shower only. **Parking:** on-site. **Terms:** age restrictions may apply, 5 day cancellation notice, weekly rates available. **Amenities:** hair dryers. **Guest Services:** wireless Internet. **Cards:** AX, DC, MC, VI.

(X)

A BED AND BREAKFAST AT DARTMOUTH HOUSE
Phone: (585)271-7872 **5**
▼▼▼ 5/1-12/28 & 4/1-4/30 [BP] 1P: $110-$135 2P: $125-$150 XP: $25

Historic Bed & Breakfast
Location: I-490, exit 18, just w on SR 31 W, then just n. 215 Dartmouth St 14607. Fax: 585/271-7872. **Facility:** The five-course, gourmet, candlelight breakfast is a highlight at this 1905 English Tudor home, part of a Victorian neighborhood near several museums. Smoke free premises. 4 units. 3 one- and 1 two-bedroom standard units. 3 stories (no elevator), interior corridors. *Bath:* combo or shower only. **Parking:** on-site. **Terms:** open 5/1-12/28 & 4/1-4/30, age restrictions may apply. **Amenities:** video library, irons, hair dryers. *Some:* DVD players, CD players. **Guest Services:** wireless Internet. **Business Services:** PC, fax. **Cards:** AX, DS, MC, VI.

(X) (VCR)

CLARION RIVERSIDE HOTEL *Book great rates at AAA.com*
Phone: (585)546-6400 **3**
▼▼ 5/1-10/15 1P: $99-$169 2P: $99-$169 XP: $10 F18
10/16-4/30 1P: $99-$149 2P: $99-$149 XP: $10 F18

Large-scale Hotel
Location: Downtown. Located opposite the convention center. 120 E Main St 14604. Fax: 585/546-1341. **Facility:** 466 units. 458 one-bedroom standard units. 8 one-bedroom suites. 15 stories, interior corridors. *Bath:* combo or shower only. **Parking:** on-site (fee). **Terms:** package plans, pets ($50 deposit). **Amenities:** dual phone lines, voice mail, safes (fee), irons, hair dryers. **Pool(s):** heated outdoor. **Leisure Activities:** sauna, exercise room, spa. **Guest Services:** gift shop, valet and coin laundry, area transportation, wireless Internet. **Business Services:** conference facilities, business center. **Cards:** AX, CB, DC, DS, JC, MC, VI.

SOME UNITS
(ASK) (S/D) (✈) FEE (🍴) (Y) (M) (•) (🖉) (≈) (X) (🐾) (🖥) / (X) (🔒) (🖨) /

CROWNE PLAZA HOTEL AND RESORT
ROCHESTER *Book great rates at AAA.com*
Phone: (585)546-3450 **1**
(AAA) (SAVE) All Year 1P: $109-$169 2P: $99-$159 XP: $10 F
▼▼▼

Large-scale Hotel
Location: Jct Main St; downtown. 70 State St 14614. Fax: 585/546-8712. **Facility:** 362 units. 354 one-bedroom standard units. 6 one- and 2 two-bedroom suites ($149-$209). 7 stories, interior corridors. **Parking:** on-site (fee). **Terms:** cancellation fee imposed, package plans. **Amenities:** video games (fee), CD players, voice mail, irons, hair dryers. *Some:* dual phone lines. **Dining:** 6 am-2 & 4-11 pm, cocktails. **Pool(s):** heated outdoor. **Leisure Activities:** sauna, exercise room. **Guest Services:** valet laundry, area transportation-train & bus stations, wireless Internet. **Business Services:** conference facilities, business center. **Cards:** AX, CB, DC, DS, JC, MC, VI.

SOME UNITS
(S/D) (✈) (🍴) (24) (Y) (🖉) (≈) (🐾) (🖥) / (X) (🔒) (🖨) /

HYATT REGENCY ROCHESTER *Book great rates at AAA.com*
Phone: (585)546-1234 **2**
(AAA) (SAVE) All Year 1P: $105-$249 2P: $105-$249 XP: $25 F18
▼▼▼

Large-scale Hotel
Location: Jct South Ave; downtown. Located next to the convention center connected by skywalk. 125 E Main St 14604. Fax: 585/546-6777. **Facility:** 336 units. 318 one-bedroom standard units. 18 one-bedroom suites. 25 stories, interior corridors. *Bath:* combo or shower only. **Parking:** on-site (fee). **Terms:** cancellation fee imposed. **Amenities:** voice mail, irons, hair dryers. *Some:* DVD players (fee). **Dining:** 6:30 am-2 & 5-10 pm, cocktails. **Pool(s):** heated indoor. **Leisure Activities:** whirlpool, accessible pool lift, exercise room. **Guest Services:** gift shop, valet laundry, area transportation-bus & train station, wireless Internet. **Business Services:** conference facilities, business center. **Cards:** AX, CB, DC, DS, JC, MC, VI.

SOME UNITS
(✈) (🍴) (Y) (M) (•) (🖉) (≈) (X) (🐾) (🖥) / (X) (VCR) (🔒) / FEE

(See map and index starting on p. 599)

STRATHALLAN HOTEL *Book at AAA.com* Phone: (585)461-5010 4
WWWW All Year 1P: $80 2P: $80 XP: $33
Location: I-490, exit 17, 0.8 mi n on Goodman St, then just w. 550 East Ave 14607. Fax: 585/461-3387.
Small-scale Hotel **Facility:** 156 units. 80 one-bedroom standard units. 73 one- and 3 two-bedroom suites ($189-$209), some with efficiencies. 9 stories, interior corridors. **Terms:** cancellation fee imposed, weekly rates available, package plans, small pets only ($75 fee). **Amenities:** high-speed Internet, dual phone lines, voice mail, irons, hair dryers. *Fee:* video games, safes. **Dining:** The Grill at Strathallan, see separate listing. **Leisure Activities:** sauna, exercise room. **Guest Services:** valet and coin laundry, area transportation, wireless Internet. **Business Services:** conference facilities, business center. **Cards:** AX, DS, MC, VI.

SOME UNITS
(ASK) (S/D) (✈) (🛁) (🍽) (Y) (🏃) (🔒) (🖥) (🖨) / (⊠) /
FEE

─────── **WHERE TO DINE** ───────

2 VINE **Lunch:** $8-$16 **Dinner:** $10-$30 Phone: 585-454-6020 6
WWW **Location:** Just e of East Ave; downtown. 24 Winthrop St 14607. **Hours:** 11:30 am-11 pm, Fri-midnight, Sat 5 pm-midnight. Closed major holidays. **Reservations:** suggested. **Features:** Local farm-fresh fruits and vegetables, organic when possible, add flavor to contemporary and innovative cuisine prepared with a French French flair and Italian accents. Seafood is delivered daily from Boston, and only quality meats, such as Certified Angus, are considered. The menu changes seasonally to reflect market availability. Dressy casual; cocktails. **Parking:** on-site. **Cards:** AX, MC, VI.
(♿M) (Y)

ALLADIN'S NATURAL EATERY **Lunch:** $4-$8 **Dinner:** $4-$8 Phone: 585-442-5000 12
W **Location:** Between Oxford and Goodman St; on SR 31. 646 Monroe Ave 14607. **Hours:** 11 am-10 pm, Fri & Sat-11 pm, Sun noon-10 pm; hours vary in winter. Closed: 11/22, 12/25. **Features:** Generous servings of fresh, Greek healthy Greek/Mediterranean meals from an extensive list of choices are tempting and delicious. Casual dress; beer & wine only. **Parking:** on-site. **Cards:** AX, DS, MC, VI.

BAMBA BISTRO **Lunch:** $6-$15 **Dinner:** $15-$26 Phone: 585-244-8680 8
WWW **Location:** Just n of Park Ave; downtown. 282 Alexander St 14607. **Hours:** 11:30 am-2 & 5-10 pm, Fri & Sat 5 pm-11 pm. Closed major holidays; also Sun. **Reservations:** suggested. **Features:** A romantic atmosphere Continental characterized by warm tones and distinctive architecture surrounds guests as they enjoy French-inspired Mediterranean cuisine. A favorite is crab Louis salad, which is fresh and nicely presented. Two daily tasting menus provide a sampling of the chef's expertise. Dressy casual; cocktails. **Cards:** AX, DC, DS, MC, VI.
(Y)

CUTLER'S RESTAURANT AT THE GALLERY **Lunch:** $8-$11 **Dinner:** $16-$25 Phone: 585-473-6380 5
WW **Location:** I-490, exit University Ave/Main St, 1.8 mi ne; in Memorial Art Gallery. 500 University Ave 14607. **Hours:** 11:30 am-2 pm, Thurs-Sat also 5 pm-8 pm. Closed: Mon & for dinner 7/1-8/31. American **Reservations:** suggested. **Features:** The two-tiered restaurant offers a creative menu of popular American entrees served in an elegant atmosphere amid lovely artwork. Casual dress; cocktails. **Parking:** on-site.
Cards: AX, DC, MC, VI.

DINOSAUR BAR-B-QUE **Lunch:** $12-$15 **Dinner:** $12-$20 Phone: 585-325-7090 9
W **Location:** Corner of South Ave. 99 Court St 14604. **Hours:** 11 am-midnight, Fri & Sat-1 am, Sun noon-10 pm. Closed major holidays. **Features:** Prize-winning pit barbecue ribs and chicken come with all the fixings. Live American blues adds to the ambience most every night. This place is next to the Genesee River. Casual dress; cocktails. **Parking:** on-site (fee) and street. **Cards:** AX, DC, DS, MC, VI.
(Y)

THE GRILL AT STRATHALLAN **Lunch:** $8-$13 **Dinner:** $22-$30 Phone: 585-454-1880 7
(AAA) **Location:** I-490, exit 17, 0.8 mi n on Goodman St, then just w; in Strathallan Hotel. 550 East Ave 14607. **Hours:** 6:30-10:30 am, 11:30-2 & 5-9:30 pm, Fri & Sat-10 pm, Sun-9 pm. **Reservations:** suggested. **Features:** Chef WWWW Ethan Drake's dishes delight both the eye and palate. Appetizers appear as art forms, and entrees include Nouvelle such delectable preparations as mustard-crusted salmon, filets of venison and giant scallops wrapped in American leeks. Visually stimulating preparations of steak, scallops, chicken and veal incorporate the highest quality ingredients. Uncomplicated elegance marks a setting characterized by brick walls, high ceilings and Italian oil paintings. Cross-training of the staff in all areas is obvious. Dressy casual; cocktails. **Parking:** on-site and valet. **Cards:** AX, CB, DC, DS, MC, VI.
(Y)

(See map and index starting on p. 599)

INDIA HOUSE RESTAURANT   **Lunch:** $8-$9   **Dinner:** $8-$16   **Phone:** 585/461-0880   ⑬
Indian
Location: I-490, exit 17, sw to Clinton Ave, then just s. 998 S Clinton Ave 14620. **Hours:** 11:30 am-2:30 & 5-9:30 pm, Fri & Sat-10 pm. Closed: 7/4, 11/22, 12/25. **Reservations:** suggested. **Features:** Piquant flavors, pungent aromas and distinctive spices combine in delicious dishes, such as aloo samosa and curried lamb. Tapestries, paintings and carvings are examples of Indian art in the large but intimate dining room. Servers are attentive. Casual dress; cocktails. **Parking:** on-site. **Cards:** AX, DC, DS, MC, VI.

THE OLIVE TREE   **Lunch:** $8-$11   **Dinner:** $9-$21   **Phone:** 585/454-3510   ⑩
Greek
Location: Downtown. 165 Monroe Ave 14607. **Hours:** 11:30 am-2 & 5-9 pm. Closed major holidays; also Sun. **Reservations:** suggested. **Features:** Many light, healthy examples of "nouvelle Greek" cuisine are prepared with the freshest local and imported produce and seafood. Choice Greek wines complement classic yet innovative courses. Patio dining is a seasonal option. Casual dress; cocktails. **Parking:** on-site. **Cards:** AX, DS, MC, VI.

RAJ MAHAL   **Lunch:** $8   **Dinner:** $9-$17   **Phone:** 585/546-2315   ⑪
Indian
Location: I-490, exit 18, 0.5 mi e. 324 Monroe Ave 14607. **Hours:** 11:30 am-2:30 & 5-10 pm. Closed major holidays. **Reservations:** suggested, weekends. **Features:** Patrons can feel like an Indian raja as they dine on well-seasoned curry, brightly colored chicken tandoori, beef samosa, lamb or one of a large selection of vegetarian dishes. Homemade ice cream in such flavors as mango and pistachio is delicious. Relaxed service and a warm, casual atmosphere make for a pleasant meal. A lunch buffet is set up seven days a week. Casual dress; cocktails. **Parking:** on-site. **Cards:** AX, DC, DS, MC, VI.

SALENA'S   **Lunch:** $7-$8   **Dinner:** $9-$16   **Phone:** 585/256-5980   ④
Mexican
Location: Just n of University Ave; in Village Gate Square. 274 N Goodman St 14607. **Hours:** 11:30 am-9 pm, Fri & Sat-10 pm. Closed major holidays; also Sun & Mon. **Reservations:** accepted. **Features:** Lots of herbs and spices accent traditional preparations of Mexican food. The friendly staff serves ample portions. Casual dress; cocktails. **Parking:** on-site. **Cards:** AX, DS, MC, VI.

SIENNA CONTEMPORARY GRILL AND BAR   **Dinner:** $16-$34   **Phone:** 585/546-4070   ③
Continental
Location: Corner of St. Paul St and South Ave. 151 St. Paul St 14604. **Hours:** 5 pm-10 pm, Fri & Sat-11 pm. Closed major holidays; also Sun. **Reservations:** suggested. **Features:** Near downtown businesses and hotels, the metropolitan-style restaurant serves contemporary, trendy dishes, as well as established favorites. Good choices include seared foie gras, perfectly prepared steaks and an impressive selection of fresh seafood. The professional staff spoils patrons. Dressy casual; cocktails. **Parking:** on-site. **Cards:** AX, DC, DS, MC, VI.

TAPAS 177   **Dinner:** $9-$24   **Phone:** 585/262-2090   ②
Mediterranean
Location: Off Inner Loop of I-490, exit 13; downtown. 177 St. Paul St 14604. **Hours:** 5 pm-12:30 am. Closed: 1/1, 11/22, 12/25; also Sun. **Reservations:** accepted. **Features:** The funky little basement bistro features subdued candlelit brick and dark wood walls for intimate table dining. Diverse fusion-style tapas and entrees touch on nearly every ethnic background. Monthly wine tastings are worth a special visit. Casual dress; cocktails. **Parking:** on-site (fee) and valet. **Cards:** AX, DC, DS, MC, VI.

TRIPHAMMER GRILL   **Lunch:** $8-$13   **Dinner:** $17-$27   **Phone:** 585/262-2700   ①
Nouvelle American
Location: Downtown; in Center Brown's Race Historic District. 60 Brown's Race 14614. **Hours:** 11:30 am-2:30 & 5-9:30 pm, Fri-10:30 pm, Sat 5 pm-10:30 pm. Closed major holidays; also Sun & Mon. **Reservations:** suggested. **Features:** Built as a forge in 1816, the Triphammer Building has been home to its namesake restaurant since 1993. Fresh quality ingredients are the hallmark of all courses served in the bistro-like atmosphere. Patio seating is available in season. Dressy casual; cocktails. **Parking:** on-site (fee). **Cards:** AX, DC, DS, MC, VI.

ROCK HILL pop. 1,056

——— WHERE TO STAY ———

THE LODGE AT ROCK HILL   *Book great rates at AAA.com*   **Phone:** (845)796-3100
Small-scale Hotel
	1P: $149-$239
6/29-9/3 [CP]	
5/1-6/28 & 9/4-4/30 [CP]	1P: $99-$189

Location: SR 17, exit 109, just e. 283 Rock Hill Dr 12775 (PO Box 858). Fax: 845/796-3130. **Facility:** 73 one-bedroom standard units, some with whirlpools. 1-2 stories (no elevator), interior corridors. *Bath:* combo or shower only. **Parking:** on-site. **Terms:** 2 night minimum stay - seasonal and/or weekends, cancellation fee imposed, pets ($25 fee). **Amenities:** dual phone lines, voice mail, irons, hair dryers. *Some:* CD players. **Pool(s):** heated indoor. **Leisure Activities:** steamroom, pool table, table tennis. *Fee:* game room. **Guest Services:** wireless Internet. **Business Services:** conference facilities, business center. **Cards:** AX, DC, DS, MC, VI. **Free Special Amenities:** continental breakfast and high-speed Internet.

SOME UNITS

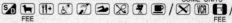

FEE   FEE

——— WHERE TO DINE ———

ROCK HILL COUNTRY GRILL   **Lunch:** $5-$8   **Dinner:** $14-$20   **Phone:** 845/794-5376
American
Location: SR 17, exit 110, just s and e. 227 Lake Marie Louise Rd 12775. **Hours:** 11:30 am-9 pm, Fri & Sat-10 pm. Closed: 1/1, 11/22, 12/25; also Mon & Tues. **Reservations:** accepted. **Features:** Guests can unwind in the casual lounge or in the rustic, fireside setting to savor the highly recommended hickory-smoked barbecue ribs, chicken and brisket. Pasta, chicken and seafood dishes are also intelligent choices. The soup and salad bar is set up all day. Casual dress; cocktails. **Parking:** on-site. **Cards:** AX, DC, DS, MC, VI.

ROCKVILLE CENTRE pop. 24,568

———— WHERE TO STAY ————

BEST WESTERN MILL RIVER MANOR   *Book great rates at AAA.com*   Phone: (516)678-1300
AAA SAVE   All Year   1P: $109-$159
Small-scale Hotel   **Location:** On SR 27; between N Village and N Centre aves. Located adjacent to a train station. 173 Sunrise Hwy 11570. Fax: 516/678-5657. **Facility:** 100 one-bedroom standard units. 5 stories, exterior corridors. *Bath:* combo or shower only. **Parking:** on-site. **Terms:** pets ($15 extra charge). **Amenities:** video games (fee), dual phone lines, voice mail, irons, hair dryers. **Dining:** 7 am-2 & 5-10 pm, cocktails. **Pool(s):** outdoor. **Leisure Activities:** limited exercise equipment. **Guest Services:** valet and coin laundry, wireless Internet. **Business Services:** conference facilities, business center. **Cards:** AX, CB, DC, DS, JC, MC, VI. **Free Special Amenities: continental breakfast and high-speed Internet.**

SOME UNITS

THE DIPLOMAT MOTOR INN   *Book great rates at AAA.com*   Phone: (516)678-1100
AAA SAVE   All Year [ECP]   1P: $94-$199   2P: $94-$199   XP: $5   F12
Small-scale Hotel   **Location:** On SR 27; between Long Beach Rd and Northern State and Meadowbrook pkwys. 1000 Sunrise Hwy 11570. Fax: 516/536-0897. **Facility:** 99 one-bedroom standard units. 2 stories (no elevator), interior/exterior corridors. *Bath:* combo or shower only. **Parking:** on-site. **Amenities:** *Some:* irons, hair dryers. **Pool(s):** outdoor. **Guest Services:** coin laundry, wireless Internet. **Cards:** AX, CB, DC, DS, JC, MC, VI. **Free Special Amenities: expanded continental breakfast and high-speed Internet.**

SOME UNITS

HAMPTON INN & SUITES   *Book great rates at AAA.com*   Phone: (516)599-1700
AAA SAVE   All Year   1P: $169-$269   2P: $169-$269
Small-scale Hotel   **Location:** Jct Merrick Rd and SR 27. Located near railroad station. 125 Merrick Rd 11570. Fax: 516/599-5700. **Facility:** 83 one-bedroom standard units. 4 stories, interior corridors. *Bath:* combo or shower only. **Parking:** on-site. **Amenities:** video games (fee), high-speed Internet, dual phone lines, voice mail, irons, hair dryers. **Leisure Activities:** exercise room. **Guest Services:** sundries, valet laundry, wireless Internet. **Business Services:** meeting rooms, business center. **Cards:** AX, DC, DS, MC, VI. **Free Special Amenities: expanded continental breakfast and local telephone calls.**

SOME UNITS

———— WHERE TO DINE ————

TAIKO   **Lunch:** $8-$15   **Dinner:** $11-$20   **Phone:** 516/678-6149
Japanese   **Location:** Just s of jct Sunrise Hwy. 15 S Village Ave 11570. **Hours:** noon-2:30 & 5:30-10:30 pm, Fri-11 pm, Sat 5:30 pm-11 pm. **Features:** Rice paper screens and tatami tables decorate the simple dining room. Sushi and sashimi choices are excellent, and more timid palates will find plenty of cooked choices, such as teriyaki, tempura and noodle dishes. Ice cream flavors are exquisite. Casual dress; cocktails. **Parking:** street. **Cards:** AX, MC, VI.

ROME pop. 34,950

———— WHERE TO STAY ————

ECONO LODGE   *Book great rates at AAA.com*   Phone: (315)337-9400
Motel   5/1-8/31   1P: $75-$90   2P: $85-$110   XP: $10   F16
9/1-4/30   1P: $65-$80   2P: $70-$90   XP: $10   F16
Location: Just s of jct SR 26 and 46. 145 E Whitesboro St 13440. Fax: 315/337-8660. **Facility:** 57 one-bedroom standard units. 2 stories (no elevator), exterior corridors. **Parking:** on-site, winter plug-ins. **Terms:** [CP] meal plan available, pets ($25 fee). **Amenities:** *Some:* irons, hair dryers. **Guest Services:** wireless Internet. **Business Services:** fax. **Cards:** AX, DC, DS, MC, VI.

SOME UNITS

GREEN LANTERN MOTOR COURT   1P: $50-$60   2P: $65-$75   Phone: (315)336-5200
Motel   All Year   XP: $10
Location: Jct SR 46, 2.9 mi n on SR 26 (Turin Rd). 8189 Turin Rd 13440. Fax: 315/336-5203. **Facility:** Smoke free premises. 11 one-bedroom standard units. 1 story, exterior corridors. *Bath:* combo or shower only. **Parking:** on-site, winter plug-ins. **Terms:** 3 day cancellation notice. **Amenities:** hair dryers. **Cards:** AX, DS, MC, VI.

SOME UNITS

INN AT THE BEECHES   *Book great rates at AAA.com*   Phone: (315)336-1776
AAA SAVE   All Year   1P: $73-$98   2P: $79-$118   XP: $10   F16
Motel   **Location:** Jct SR 46, 2 mi n on SR 26 (Turin Rd). 7900 Turin Rd 13440. Fax: 315/339-2636. **Facility:** 73 units. 72 one-bedroom standard units. 1 one-bedroom suite ($195-$275) with whirlpool. 1 story, exterior corridors. *Bath:* combo or shower only. **Parking:** on-site. **Terms:** weekly rates available, [BP] meal plan available, small pets only ($10 extra charge). **Amenities:** high-speed Internet, irons, hair dryers. **Dining:** 6 am-10 & 11:30-10 pm, Sat 8 am-noon, Sun 8 am-2 pm; closed Mon, cocktails. **Pool(s):** outdoor. **Guest Services:** valet laundry. **Business Services:** conference facilities. **Cards:** AX, DC, DS, MC, VI. **Free Special Amenities: newspaper and early check-in/late check-out.**

SOME UNITS

QUALITY INN OF ROME *Book great rates at AAA.com* Phone: (315)336-4300

AAA SAVE

| | 5/1-9/30 | 1P: $60-$139 | 2P: $73-$159 | XP: $10 | F17 |
| | 10/1-4/30 | 1P: $60-$99 | 2P: $73-$109 | XP: $10 | F17 |

Small-scale Hotel

Location: On SR 49; downtown. 200 S James St 13440. Fax: 315/336-4492. **Facility:** 104 one-bedroom standard units. 2 stories (no elevator), interior/exterior corridors. **Parking:** on-site. **Terms:** cancellation fee imposed, pets ($25 extra charge). **Amenities:** high-speed Internet, irons, hair dryers. **Dining:** 24 hours. **Pool(s):** outdoor. **Leisure Activities:** limited exercise equipment. **Guest Services:** coin laundry. **Business Services:** meeting rooms, PC. **Cards:** AX, DC, DS, MC, VI.

SOME UNITS

─── WHERE TO DINE ───

SAVOY RESTAURANT **Lunch:** $4-$7 **Dinner:** $12-$28 Phone: 315/339-3166

AAA

Italian

Location: Jct SR 26 (Turin Rd) and 46, just s. 255 E Dominick St 13440. **Hours:** 11:30 am-10 pm, Fri-11 pm, Sat 5 pm-11 pm, Sun 4 pm-9 pm. **Closed:** 11/22, 12/25. **Reservations:** suggested. **Features:** In operation since 1908, the family restaurant has a warm, casual atmosphere. El cicco—a seasoned steak with wine, garlic and spices—is particularly flavorful on a menu of mostly Italian choices. Some American specialties also are offered. Casual dress; cocktails. **Parking:** on-site. **Cards:** AX, CB, DC, DS, MC, VI.

ROMULUS pop. 2,036—*See also FINGER LAKES.*

─── WHERE TO DINE ───

KNAPP WINERY & RESTAURANT **Lunch:** $8-$9 **Dinner:** $18-$27 Phone: 607/869-9271

Continental

Location: Off SR 414, just e on CR 128 (Ernsberger Rd). 2770 CR 128 14541. **Hours:** Open 5/1-11/27 & 4/1-4/30; 11 am-4 pm, Fri-Sun also 5 pm-8 pm; weekends only 11/1-11/27; hours may vary. **Closed:** 11/22. **Reservations:** accepted. **Features:** Patrons can dine indoors or on the lovely patio, surrounded by the vineyards and sounds of nature. Fresh local fruits and vegetables complement fresh seafood, chicken and pasta dishes for a memorable lunch. Choose a locally produced wine to enhance the occasion. Casual dress; beer & wine only. **Parking:** on-site. **Cards:** AX, MC, VI.

RONKONKOMA pop. 20,029

─── WHERE TO STAY ───

COURTYARD BY MARRIOTT LONG ISLAND MACARTHUR AIRPORT *Book great rates at AAA.com* Phone: (631)612-5000

| | All Year | 1P: $107-$143 | 2P: $107-$143 | XP: $15 | F |

Small-scale Hotel

Location: I-495, exit 60 (Express Dr S), 0.5 mi e. Located in a commercial area. 5000 Express Dr S 11779. Fax: 631/612-5008. **Facility:** Smoke free premises. 154 units. 142 one-bedroom standard units, some with whirlpools. 12 one-bedroom suites with whirlpools. 7 stories, interior corridors. *Bath:* combo or shower only. **Parking:** on-site. **Amenities:** high-speed Internet, dual phone lines, voice mail, irons, hair dryers. **Pool(s):** small heated indoor. **Leisure Activities:** whirlpool, exercise room. **Guest Services:** valet and coin laundry, area transportation, wireless Internet. **Business Services:** meeting rooms, business center. **Cards:** AX, DC, DS, JC, MC, VI.

ECONO LODGE LONG ISLAND ISLIP MACARTHUR AIRPORT *Book great rates at AAA.com* Phone: (631)588-6800

AAA SAVE

| | All Year [CP] | 1P: $88-$129 | 2P: $92-$169 | XP: $10 | F18 |

Motel

Location: I-495, exit 57, 3 mi se. Located in a commercial area. 3055 Veterans Memorial Hwy (SR 454) 11779. Fax: 631/588-6815. **Facility:** 59 one-bedroom standard units. 1-2 stories (no elevator), interior/exterior corridors. *Bath:* combo or shower only. **Parking:** on-site. **Amenities:** hair dryers. **Guest Services:** wireless Internet. **Business Services:** fax (fee). **Cards:** AX, CB, DC, DS, JC, MC, VI. **Free Special Amenities:** continental breakfast and high-speed Internet.

SOME UNITS

HILTON GARDEN INN ISLIP/MACARTHUR AIRPORT *Book great rates at AAA.com* Phone: (631)738-7800

| | 5/1-10/31 | 1P: $139-$269 | 2P: $149-$279 | XP: $10 | F18 |
| | 11/1-4/30 | 1P: $119-$229 | 2P: $119-$229 | XP: $10 | F18 |

Small-scale Hotel

Location: I-495, exit 57, 3.7 mi se on SR 454. Located in a commercial area. 3485 Veterans Memorial Hwy 11779. Fax: 631/738-7801. **Facility:** 164 units. 162 one-bedroom standard units. 2 one-bedroom suites. 4 stories, interior corridors. *Bath:* combo or shower only. **Parking:** on-site. **Terms:** [BP] meal plan available, package plans. **Amenities:** video games (fee), voice mail, irons, hair dryers. *Some:* DVD players. **Pool(s):** heated indoor. **Leisure Activities:** whirlpool, exercise room. **Guest Services:** sundries, valet and coin laundry, area transportation, wireless Internet. **Business Services:** meeting rooms, business center. **Cards:** AX, DC, DS, MC, VI.

SOME UNITS

HOLIDAY INN *Book at AAA.com* Phone: (631)585-9500

| | All Year | 1P: $129-$169 | | | |

Small-scale Hotel

Location: I-495, exit 57, 4.5 mi se, follow signs to Long Island MacArthur Airport. Located in a commercial area. 3845 Veterans Memorial Hwy 11779. Fax: 631/585-9550. **Facility:** 289 one-bedroom standard units, some with whirlpools. 2 stories, interior corridors. *Bath:* combo or shower only. **Parking:** on-site. **Amenities:** video games (fee), voice mail, honor bars, irons, hair dryers. **Pool(s):** outdoor. **Leisure Activities:** exercise room. **Guest Services:** gift shop, valet and coin laundry, area transportation, wireless Internet. **Business Services:** conference facilities, business center. **Cards:** AX, DC, DS, MC, VI.

SOME UNITS

ROSCOE pop. 597

―――― **WHERE TO STAY** ――――

ROSCOE MOTEL   Phone: 607/498-5220

AAA SAVE — All Year   1P: $55   2P: $70   XP: $10   F5

◈◈◈ — **Location:** SR 17, exit 94, 0.5 mi n on SR 206, then just w. Located in a quiet area. 2054 Old Rt 17 12776 (PO Box
Motel — 609). Fax: 607/498-4643. **Facility:** 18 units. 16 one-bedroom standard units. 2 cabins. 1 story, exterior
corridors. *Bath:* combo or shower only. **Parking:** on-site. **Terms:** 7 day cancellation notice-fee imposed,
small pets only ($10 extra charge). **Amenities:** *Some:* irons, hair dryers. **Leisure Activities:** fishing,
barbecue grills. **Cards:** AX, DS, MC, VI.

SOME UNITS

🖼️📹 / 🗄️ 🛏️ 📺 📼 /
FEE

―――― **WHERE TO DINE** ――――

RAIMONDO'S RESTAURANT & PIZZERIA   **Lunch:** $5-$8   **Dinner:** $11-$25   Phone: 607/498-4702

◈◈ ◈◈ — **Location:** SR 17, exit 94; corner of SR 206 and Main St; downtown. 2 Stewart Ave 12776. **Hours:** 11 am-11 pm; to
Italian — 10 pm in winter. Closed: 3/23, 11/22, 12/25. **Reservations:** accepted. **Features:** Family-owned for 22 years,
the popular restaurant offers carefully prepared Northern Italian dishes that are promptly served. Casual
dress; cocktails. **Parking:** on-site. **Cards:** AX, DS, MC, VI.

🍸

ROSCOE DINER   **Lunch:** $4-$9   **Dinner:** $8-$25   Phone: 607/498-4405

◈◈ — **Location:** SR 17, exit 94, just se. 1908 Old Rt 17 12776. **Hours:** 6 am-midnight. Closed: 12/25.
American — **Features:** Decorated with chrome and teal accents, the casual, '50s-style diner seats up to 300 guests in its
three dining rooms. The on-premises bakery offers a showy display of its creations. American and Greek
MC, VI. — favorites are dished in generous portions. Casual dress; cocktails. **Parking:** on-site. **Cards:** AX, DS,

ROSLYN pop. 2,750

―――― **WHERE TO DINE** ――――

BRYANT & COOPER STEAKHOUSE   **Lunch:** $10-$38   **Dinner:** $19-$42   Phone: 516/627-7270

◈◈◈ — **Location:** I-495, exit 36 (Searingtown), n to Northern Blvd (SR 25A), 0.3 mi e, then just n. 2 Middle Neck Rd 11576.
Steak House — **Hours:** noon-11 pm, Sat 5 pm-midnight, Sun 3 pm-10 pm. Closed: 12/25. **Reservations:** suggested.
Features: Hardwood floors, earth tones and paneling add to the rich, club-like ambience of the upscale
dining room. A comprehensive selection of wines complements preparations of prime rib, chicken, seafood
and rib eye steak. Servers are knowledgeable. Dressy casual; cocktails. **Parking:** valet. **Cards:** AX, DC, MC, VI.

🍸

ROTTERDAM pop. 20,536

―――― **WHERE TO STAY** ――――

MALLOZZI'S BELVEDERE HOTEL   Phone: (518)630-4020

AAA SAVE — 6/4-9/9   1P: $150-$180   2P: $150-$180   XP: $10   F12
5/1-6/3 & 9/10-12/31   1P: $140-$160   2P: $140-$160   XP: $10   F12
◈◈◈ — 1/1-4/30   1P: $125-$145   2P: $125-$145   XP: $10   F12
Small-scale Hotel — **Location:** I-890, exit 9 (Curry Rd), 1.8 mi w; I-90, exit 25. 1926 Curry Rd 12303. Fax: 518/630-4055. **Facility:** 31
units. 29 one-bedroom standard units. 2 one-bedroom suites with whirlpools. 2 stories, interior corridors.
Parking: on-site. **Terms:** cancellation fee imposed. **Amenities:** video library (fee), high-speed Internet, dual
phone lines, voice mail, safes, irons, hair dryers. **Dining:** Mallozzi's Restaurant, see separate listing. **Guest Services:** valet
laundry. **Cards:** AX, DS, MC, VI. **Free Special Amenities: expanded continental breakfast and local telephone calls.**

SOME UNITS

S🄳 🍽️ 🅿️ 📶 VCR 📹 📺 / ✕ 🛏️ /
FEE

QUALITY INN   *Book great rates at AAA.com*   Phone: (518)355-1111

AAA SAVE — 7/1-8/31   1P: $90-$120   2P: $90-$120   XP: $10   F18
5/1-6/30   1P: $80-$110   2P: $80-$110   XP: $10   F18
◈◈◈ — 9/1-4/30   1P: $70-$90   2P: $70-$90   XP: $10   F18
Small-scale Hotel — **Location:** I-890, exit 9 (Curry Rd); jct SR 7 and 146, 0.5 mi ne. 2788 Hamburg St 12303. Fax: 518/356-3817.
Facility: 50 one-bedroom standard units, some with whirlpools. 2 stories (no elevator), interior corridors.
Parking: on-site. **Amenities:** high-speed Internet, voice mail, irons, hair dryers. **Dining:** 11:30 am-3 & 5-10
pm, Fri & Sat-11 pm, cocktails. **Pool(s):** heated indoor. **Business Services:** conference facilities. **Cards:** AX, DC, DS, MC, VI.
Free Special Amenities: continental breakfast and high-speed Internet.

SOME UNITS

🍽️ 🍸 🌊 📹 📺 / ✕ 🛏️ /

SUPER 8 SCHENECTADY   *Book at AAA.com*   Phone: (518)355-2190

◈◈◈ — 5/1-9/4   1P: $85-$99   2P: $85-$99   XP: $10   F17
9/5-4/30   1P: $65-$85   2P: $65-$85   XP: $10   F17
Small-scale Hotel — **Location:** I-890, exit 9 (Curry Rd), 0.4 mi w; I-90, exit 25. 3083 Carman Rd 12303. Fax: 518/355-3843. **Facility:** 99
one-bedroom standard units. 2 stories (no elevator), interior corridors. **Parking:** on-site. **Terms:** pets ($10
extra charge). **Cards:** AX, CB, DC, DS, JC, MC, VI.

SOME UNITS

ASK S🄳 🐾 🍽️ 📹 / ✕ /
FEE

ROUND LAKE pop. 604

------ WHERE TO STAY ------

FAIRFIELD INN & SUITES BY MARRIOTT
Phone: (518)899-6900

▼▼▼
7/25-9/3 — 1P: $239-$339 — 2P: $239-$339
5/1-7/24 — 1P: $119-$179 — 2P: $119-$179
Small-scale Hotel
9/4-11/15 — 1P: $109-$169 — 2P: $109-$169
11/16-4/30 — 1P: $89-$129 — 2P: $89-$129

Location: I-87, exit 12, just e. 101 Saratoga Village Blvd 12020. **Fax:** 518/899-6969. **Facility:** Smoke free premises. 114 units. 111 one-bedroom standard units. 3 one-bedroom suites. 4 stories, interior corridors. *Bath:* combo or shower only. **Parking:** on-site. **Terms:** cancellation fee imposed, [CP] meal plan available, small pets only ($75 fee). **Amenities:** high-speed Internet, voice mail, safes, irons, hair dryers. *Some:* DVD players. **Pool(s):** small heated indoor. **Leisure Activities:** whirlpool, exercise room. **Guest Services:** valet and coin laundry. **Business Services:** business center. **Cards:** AX, DC, DS, MC, VI.

SOME UNITS

A$K S/D 🐾 🍴 &M 🐦 ✖ 📷 🎥 🛢 💻 / VCR 🖥 /
FEE

------ WHERE TO DINE ------

CHEZ SOPHIE BISTRO
Dinner: $26-$38 — Phone: 518/583-3538

▼▼▼
French
Location: I-87, exit 13, just s. 2853 SR 9 12020. **Hours:** 5:30 pm-close; from 5 pm in summer. Closed major holidays; also Sun, Mon in winter. **Reservations:** suggested. **Features:** Fine dining is the mode in the restored 1952 Fodero diner or in either of two elegant dining rooms. With a choice of more than 3,000 French wines from the cellar, diners are sure to find a delicious match for such entrees as Canadian Moulard duck breast with apricot and green peppercorn sauce and marinated quail with truffle butter sauce. Local purveyors provide top-quality organic produce and free-range meats. Professional, courteous staff members can assist with selections. Casual dress; cocktails. **Parking:** on-site. **Cards:** AX, CB, DC, MC, VI.

LAKE RIDGE
Lunch: $5-$8 — Dinner: $13-$18 — Phone: 518/899-6000

🅰🅰🅰
▼▼▼
American
Location: I-87, exit 11, just e on Round Lake Rd. 35 Burlington Ave 12151. **Hours:** 11:30 am-2:30 & 4:30-8:45 pm, Sun 3 pm-8 pm. Closed: 11/22, 12/25; also Mon. **Reservations:** suggested. **Features:** The intimate restaurant offers fine dining in an unpretentious atmosphere either fireside or on the patio. Top-quality ingredients are incorporated into such dishes as the popular crab cakes with garlic citrus aioli and veal Jacqueline with shallots, shiitake mushrooms and king crab meat in garlic-sherry cream sauce. The friendly staff is helpful in recommending good wines to accompany all choices. Desserts made in-house are a perfect end to the feast. Casual dress; cocktails. **Parking:** on-site. **Cards:** AX, MC, VI.

THE RIPE TOMATO-AN AMERICAN GRILL
Lunch: $4-$7 — Dinner: $12-$17 — Phone: 518/581-1530

▼▼ ▼▼
American
Location: I-87, exit 13, 1.9 mi s. 2721 Rt 9 12020. **Hours:** 11:30 am-10 pm, Fri & Sat-11 pm. Closed: 12/25. **Reservations:** suggested. **Features:** From 10 pasta dishes to Yankee pot roast, house ribs and spicy wings, the restaurant's presentations are unbeatable. Eclectic art adorns the walls, and memorable food choices crowd the menu. Chef Tom Clark dishes up ample portions of well-prepared, "all-American" food culled from the backgrounds of those who settled this country. The bustling, friendly atmosphere appeals to families and is great for celebrations. Decadent, homemade desserts cater to the sweet tooth. Casual dress; cocktails. **Parking:** on-site. **Cards:** AX, DC, MC, VI.

🍸

RYE — *See New York p. 503.*

RYE BROOK — *See New York p. 503.*

SACKETS HARBOR pop. 1,386

------ WHERE TO STAY ------

ONTARIO PLACE HOTEL
Phone: (315)646-8000

▼▼
All Year — 1P: $84-$150 — 2P: $84-$150 — XP: $10 — F16
Small-scale Hotel
Location: Center. 103 General Smith Dr 13685 (PO Box 540). **Fax:** 315/646-2506. **Facility:** 38 units. 37 one-bedroom standard units, some with whirlpools. 1 two-bedroom suite ($350-$390) with kitchen and whirlpool. 2-3 stories (no elevator), interior corridors. *Bath:* combo or shower only. **Parking:** on-site. **Terms:** pets ($10 fee, in designated units). **Amenities:** hair dryers. *Some:* DVD players (fee). **Guest Services:** gift shop, wireless Internet. **Business Services:** meeting rooms. **Cards:** AX, DC, MC, VI.

SOME UNITS

🍴 ✖ 🛢 🖥 / VCR 💻 /
FEE — FEE

------ WHERE TO DINE ------

SACKETS HARBOR BREWING CO
Lunch: $8-$10 — Dinner: $15-$25 — Phone: 315/646-2739

▼▼ ▼▼
American
Location: Center. 212 W Main St 13685. **Hours:** call for hours. Closed major holidays. **Reservations:** suggested. **Features:** In a former train station, the waterfront brewpub offers seating in the bi-level dining room and on the patio. The eclectic menu puts a new spin on old favorite dishes, such as chicken pasta pilaf. Custom-prepared microbrewed beers are a nice touch. Casual dress; cocktails. **Parking:** on-site. **Cards:** AX, DS, MC, VI.

🍸

SAG HARBOR pop. 2,313

——— WHERE TO DINE ———

B SMITH'S
Seafood
American cuisine,
Lunch: $13-$18   **Dinner:** $13-$35   **Phone:** 631/725-5858
Location: At end of Bay St, just s of bridge to North Haven. Long Wharf Promenade 11963. **Hours:** Open 5/14-10/31; noon-4 & 6-10 pm; Fri & Sat-11 pm in season. Closed major holidays; also Mon-Fri 5/14-5/28. **Reservations:** suggested. **Features:** Relax in the brightly lit dining room and enjoy views of yachts and boats sailing into and out of the harbor. Mediterranean and Southern influences infuse preparations of new American cuisine, such as caramelized diver scallops over orrechiette pasta. Casual dress; cocktails. **Parking:** street.
Cards: AX, DC, DS, MC, VI.

JLX BISTRO
French
Lunch: $12-$18   **Dinner:** $17-$27   **Phone:** 631/725-9100
Location: Jct SR 114, just se on CR 79. 16 Main St 11963. **Hours:** 11 am-midnight. Closed major holidays. **Reservations:** not accepted. **Features:** Two distinctive elephant sculptures guard the entrance from the outdoor patio. The 1920s bistro feel includes tropical elements, such as rattan chairs, dark wood flooring and potted palms. The diverse menu may feature chicken paillard, pan-roasted Atlantic salmon, New York strip steak and some Asia-inspired dishes. This place became known for its executive chef, Keith Greene, who was head chef on the reality TV show "Devil's Kitchen.". Dressy casual; cocktails. **Parking:** street. **Cards:** AX, MC, VI.

SEN
Sushi
Dinner: $14-$18   **Phone:** 631/725-1774
Location: Just w of SR 114 from south side of bridge; center. 23 Main St 11963. **Hours:** 5:30 pm-11 pm, Fri & Sat-midnight; seasonal hours may vary. Closed: 11/22, 12/25; also Tues. **Features:** Expect ultra-modern, sparse decor and a bustling atmosphere at the highly popular spot. The menu delivers sushi, a wide assortment of traditional and unusual rolls, fun appetizers, noodle soup and steamed fish. Saki varieties are extensive. Casual dress; cocktails. **Parking:** street. **Cards:** AX, MC, VI.

ST. JAMES pop. 13,268

——— WHERE TO DINE ———

MIRABELLE
French
Lunch: $14-$23   **Dinner:** $25-$39   **Phone:** 631/584-5999
Location: 1.6 mi from jct SR 25. 404 N Country Rd (SR 25A) 11780. **Hours:** noon-2 & 6-10 pm, Sat from 5:30 pm, Sun from 5 pm. Closed: 1/1, 11/22, 12/25; also Mon. **Reservations:** suggested. **Features:** In a small house in a small town, the trendy dining room has bright yellow walls, low ceilings and a large painting that is reprinted on the menu cover. Foie gras mousse roulade and eggplant-goat cheese terrine are representative appetizers. Casual dress; cocktails. **Parking:** on-site. **Cards:** AX, DC, DS, MC, VI.

ST. JOHNSVILLE pop. 1,685

——— WHERE TO STAY ———

INN BY THE MILL
Historic Bed
& Breakfast
All Year   1P: $130-$195   2P: $130-$195   XP: $50
Location: 1 mi w on SR 5, 0.5 mi n. 1679 Mill Rd 13452. **Facility:** An 1835 gristmill featuring a self-service soda fountain shares these grounds with a cascading creek, a waterfall, and a cottage with an outdoor spa. Smoke free premises. 5 units. 3 one-bedroom standard units. 1 one-bedroom suite ($175-$375). 1 cottage ($250-$375). 2 stories (no elevator), interior corridors. *Bath:* combo or shower only. **Parking:** on-site.
Terms: 2 night minimum stay - weekends, age restrictions may apply, 14 day cancellation notice-fee imposed. **Amenities:** video library, hair dryers. *Some:* CD players, irons. **Leisure Activities:** whirlpool, game room. **Guest Services:** gift shop, area transportation. **Cards:** AX, MC, VI.

SOME UNITS

SALAMANCA pop. 6,097

——— WHERE TO STAY ———

HOLIDAY INN EXPRESS HOTEL & SUITES   *Book at AAA.com*   **Phone:** (716)945-7600
Small-scale Hotel
12/15-4/14	1P: $139-$179	2P: $139-$179	XP: $10	F18
4/15-4/30	1P: $129-$169	2P: $129-$169	XP: $10	F18
5/1-12/14	1P: $119-$159	2P: $119-$159	XP: $10	F18

Location: I-86, exit 20, just n. 779 Broad St 14779. Fax: 716/945-7200. **Facility:** 68 units. 66 one-bedroom standard units, some with whirlpools. 2 one-bedroom suites ($139-$189) with efficiencies. 2 stories, interior corridors. *Bath:* combo or shower only. **Parking:** on-site. **Terms:** small pets only ($25 fee, $50 deposit). **Amenities:** dual phone lines, voice mail, irons, hair dryers. **Pool(s):** heated indoor. **Leisure Activities:** whirlpool, exercise room. **Guest Services:** sundries, valet and coin laundry, wireless Internet. **Business Services:** meeting rooms, business center. **Cards:** AX, DC, DS, MC, VI.

SOME UNITS
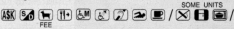

——— WHERE TO DINE ———

RED GARTER RESTAURANT
American
Dinner: $10-$16   **Phone:** 716-945-2503
Location: I-86, exit 21, just w; on top of mountain. 380 Parkway Dr 14779. **Hours:** 4 pm-10:15 pm, Sat 11 am-11 pm, Sun 11 am-8 pm. **Reservations:** accepted. **Features:** On Round Top Mountain and just two miles from Seneca-Allegany Casino, the casual restaurant affords a spectacular view of the valley and mountains below. There is plenty of seasonal patio area seating, as well as a cozy stone fireplace inside for chillier days. Barbecue pork ribs, chicken wings, old-fashioned homemade onion rings and comfort foods such as pot roast and meatloaf are popular. Casual dress; cocktails. **Parking:** on-site. **Cards:** DS, MC, VI.

SANBORN —*See Niagara Falls p. 528.*

SARANAC LAKE pop. 5,041—*See also ADIRONDACK MOUNTAINS.*

———— WHERE TO STAY ————

ADIRONDACK MOTEL
Phone: 518/891-2116

(AAA) (SAVE) ▼ Motel

All Year   1P: $65-$180   2P: $65-$180   XP: $10   F16
Location: 0.7 mi e on SR 86. 248 Lake Flower Ave 12983. Fax: 518/891-0380. **Facility:** 13 units. 11 one-bedroom standard units, some with efficiencies. 2 one-bedroom suites with kitchens. 1-2 stories, exterior corridors. *Bath:* combo or shower only. **Parking:** on-site, winter plug-ins. **Terms:** cancellation fee imposed, package plans, pets (dogs only, $10 extra charge). **Leisure Activities:** canoeing, paddleboats, boat dock, fishing, kayak, rowboat, gazebo, **Guest Services:** wireless Internet. **Cards:** AX, DS, MC, VI.
Free Special Amenities: continental breakfast and high-speed Internet.

SOME UNITS
[icons] FEE

BEST WESTERN MOUNTAIN LAKE INN
Book great rates at AAA.com
Phone: (518)891-1970

(AAA) (SAVE) ▼▼▼ Small-scale Hotel

6/22-10/7   1P: $99-$195   2P: $99-$195   XP: $5   F17
12/21-4/30   1P: $85-$150   2P: $85-$150   XP: $5   F17
5/1-6/21   1P: $76-$110   2P: $76-$110   XP: $5   F17
10/8-12/20   1P: $80-$100   2P: $80-$100   XP: $5   F17
Location: 0.8 mi e on SR 86. 487 Lake Flower Ave 12983. Fax: 518/891-6195. **Facility:** 69 one-bedroom standard units. 2 stories (no elevator), interior corridors. **Parking:** on-site, winter plug-ins. **Terms:** [BP] meal plan available, package plans, pets ($20 extra charge, in ground floor smoking units). **Amenities:** irons, hair dryers. **Dining:** 6 am-2 pm, cocktails. **Pool(s):** heated indoor. **Leisure Activities:** sun deck. **Guest Services:** coin laundry, wireless Internet. **Business Services:** meeting rooms. **Cards:** AX, CB, DC, DS, MC, VI. **Free Special Amenities: local telephone calls and high-speed Internet.** *(See color ad below)*

SOME UNITS
[icons] FEE

THE HOTEL SARANAC OF PAUL SMITH'S COLLEGE
Book great rates at AAA.com
Phone: (518)891-2200

(AAA) (SAVE) ◆ Historic Small-scale Hotel

6/15-10/13   1P: $90-$150   2P: $90-$150   XP: $10   F18
5/1-6/14 & 10/14-4/30   1P: $70-$150   2P: $70-$150   XP: $10   F18
Location: Center. 100 Main St 12983. Fax: 518/891-5664. **Facility:** This restored 1927 hotel is a training facility for hotel-management students. 88 one-bedroom standard units, some with whirlpools. 6 stories, interior corridors. **Parking:** on-site. **Terms:** 2-3 night minimum stay - seasonal and/or weekends, 3 day cancellation notice-fee imposed, [AP], [BP] & [MAP] meal plans available, package plans, pets ($15 extra charge, in designated units). **Amenities:** video library, voice mail, irons, hair dryers. **Dining:** A.P. Smith Restaurant, see separate listing. **Guest Services:** gift shop, valet laundry. **Business Services:** meeting rooms. **Cards:** AX, CB, DC, DS, MC, VI. **Free Special Amenities: local telephone calls and high-speed Internet.**

SOME UNITS
[icons] FEE

LAKE FLOWER INN
Phone: 518/891-2310

◆ Motel

Property failed to provide current rates
Location: 0.6 mi e on SR 86. 234 Lake Flower Ave 12983. Fax: 518/891-0399. **Facility:** 14 one-bedroom standard units. 1 story, exterior corridors. *Bath:* combo or shower only. **Parking:** on-site, winter plug-ins. **Terms:** pets (dogs only, with prior approval). **Pool(s):** outdoor. **Leisure Activities:** canoeing, boat dock, fishing.

SOME UNITS
[icons]

LAKE SIDE MOTEL
Phone: 518/891-4333

▼ Motel

All Year   1P: $59-$109   2P: $69-$119   XP: $10   F12
Location: 0.6 mi e on SR 86. 256 Lake Flower Ave 12983. Fax: 518/891-0577. **Facility:** 22 one-bedroom standard units, some with efficiencies. 1 story, exterior corridors. *Bath:* combo or shower only. **Parking:** on-site. **Terms:** 7 day cancellation notice-fee imposed, weekly rates available, pets ($10 deposit, with prior approval). **Amenities:** *Some:* irons. **Pool(s):** outdoor. **Leisure Activities:** canoeing, paddleboats, boat dock, fishing. **Cards:** DS, MC, VI.

SOME UNITS
[icons] FEE

SARA-PLACID MOTOR INN

Phone: (518)891-2729

◇◇◇ [SAVE]
▽▽▽ ▽▽▽
Motel

All Year   1P: $58-$150   2P: $58-$150   XP: $10
Location: 0.8 mi e on SR 86. 445 Lake Flower Ave 12983. Fax: 518/891-5624. **Facility:** 19 units. 13 one- and 3 two-bedroom standard units, some with efficiencies and/or whirlpools. 3 cottages ($150-$395). 1-2 stories, exterior corridors. **Parking:** on-site, winter plug-ins. **Terms:** 3 day cancellation notice-fee imposed, weekly rates available, package plans. **Amenities:** voice mail, irons, hair dryers. *Some:* DVD players. **Leisure Activities:** paddleboats, fishing, ice skating. *Fee:* boats, kayak. **Guest Services:** valet laundry. **Cards:** AX, DC, DS, MC, VI. **Free Special Amenities:** local telephone calls and early check-in/late check-out.

SOME UNITS

[S⃞D] [🍴] [⊗] [✕] [⌖] [🔲] [🖨] [💻] / [VCR] /

The following lodging was either not evaluated or did not meet AAA rating requirements but is listed for your information only.

THE POINT

Phone: 518/891-5674

[fyi]

Not evaluated. **Location:** SR 3. HCR 1, Box 65 12983. Facilities, services, and decor characterize an upscale property.

WHERE TO DINE

A.P. SMITH RESTAURANT   *Menu on AAA.com*   **Lunch:** $6-$15   **Dinner:** $12-$22   **Phone:** 518/891-2200

◇◇◇
▽▽▽ ▽▽▽
American

Location: Center; in The Hotel Saranac at Paul Smith's College. 100 Main St 12983. **Hours:** 7 am-11 & 11:30-9 pm. **Reservations:** accepted. **Features:** A.P. Smith's offers a good spot for a leisurely afternoon lunch in the company of friends. The dining room is pleasant and the atmosphere casually busy. Light fare is offered at lunch with a more elaborate menu in the evenings. Service is afforded by students in training. Overall, decent food at reasonable prices. Casual dress; cocktails. **Parking:** on-site. **Cards:** AX, CB, DC, DS, MC, VI.

[Y]

CASA DEL SOL

Dinner: $4-$13

Phone: 518/891-0977

▽▽▽
Mexican

Location: 0.8 mi e on SR 86. 154 Lake Flower Ave 12983. **Hours:** 4:30 pm-10 pm. Closed: 11/22, 12/24, 12/25; also Easter week. **Features:** Located between Saranac Lake and Lake Placid, this restaurant serves up some genuine Mexican fare. With six choices of sauces on the table from which to choose, every taste is met from mild to fire-breathing hot. Casual dress; cocktails. **Parking:** on-site.

[Y] [K]

SARATOGA SPRINGS pop. 26,186

WHERE TO STAY

ADELPHI HOTEL

Phone: 518/587-4688

▽▽▽▽▽
Historic
Small-scale Hotel

7/25-9/3 [CP]   1P: $210-$490   2P: $210-$490
5/15-7/24 [CP]   1P: $125-$290   2P: $125-$290
9/4-10/15 [CP]   1P: $125-$245   2P: $125-$245
Location: Between Division and Washington sts; center. 365 Broadway 12866. Fax: 518/587-0851. **Facility:** Period pieces furnish the individually decorated rooms at this 1877 Victorian inn. Smoke free premises. 39 units. 31 one- and 8 two-bedroom standard units. 4 stories, interior corridors. **Bath:** combo or shower only. **Parking:** street. **Terms:** 5/15-10/15, check-in 4 pm, 2-3 night minimum stay - weekends, 14 day cancellation notice. **Amenities:** safes, hair dryers. **Pool(s):** small heated outdoor. **Business Services:** meeting rooms. **Cards:** MC, VI.

[🍴] [Y] [⊿] [⊗]

BEST WESTERN PARK INN   *Book great rates at AAA.com*   **Phone: (518)584-2350**

◇◇◇ [SAVE]
▽▽▽▽▽
Small-scale Hotel

7/25-9/3   1P: $179-$289   2P: $179-$289   XP: $10   F17
5/1-7/24   1P: $139-$189   2P: $139-$189   XP: $10   F17
9/4-12/31   1P: $89-$189   2P: $89-$189   XP: $10   F17
1/1-4/30   1P: $99-$149   2P: $99-$149   XP: $10   F17
Location: I-87, exit 13N, 1.1 mi n on US 9. 3291 S Broadway 12866. Fax: 518/584-2480. **Facility:** 63 one-bedroom standard units. 2 stories, interior corridors. **Bath:** combo or shower only. **Parking:** on-site, winter plug-ins. **Terms:** 7 day cancellation notice, [CP] & [ECP] meal plans available, package plans, pets ($15 fee). **Amenities:** high-speed Internet, voice mail, irons, hair dryers. **Leisure Activities:** hiking trails, exercise room, game room. **Guest Services:** valet and coin laundry, wireless Internet. **Business Services:** meeting rooms. **Cards:** AX, DC, DS, MC, VI. **Free Special Amenities:** expanded continental breakfast and high-speed Internet.

SOME UNITS

[S⃞D] [🛏] [🖼] [⊗] [⌖] [🔲] [🖨] [💻] / [✕] /
FEE

CARRIAGE HOUSE INN

Phone: 518/584-4220

◇◇◇ [SAVE]
▽▽▽▽▽
Small-scale Hotel

7/25-9/3   2P: $229-$269
5/1-7/24 & 9/4-10/31   2P: $109-$149
11/1-4/30   2P: $99-$129
Location: I-87, exit 13, 3.7 mi n on US 9. 198 Broadway 12866. Fax: 518/584-3620. **Facility:** 14 units. 12 one-bedroom standard units, some with efficiencies. 2 one-bedroom suites ($189-$399) with efficiencies and whirlpools. 2 stories (no elevator), interior/exterior corridors. **Parking:** on-site. **Terms:** 30 day cancellation notice, seasonal. **Amenities:** voice mail, irons, hair dryers. **Guest Services:** valet laundry, wireless Internet. **Cards:** AX, DS, MC, VI. **Free Special Amenities:** local telephone calls and high-speed Internet.

SOME UNITS

[⊗] [🔲] [🖨] [💻] / [VCR] /

COURTYARD BY MARRIOTT SARATOGA SPRINGS *Book great rates at AAA.com* Phone: 518/226-0538

AAA SAVE

WWWW

7/25-9/2	1P: $369-$1049	2P: $369-$1049	
5/1-7/24	1P: $159-$374	2P: $159-$374	
9/3-12/31	1P: $149-$364	2P: $149-$364	
1/1-4/30	1P: $129-$294	2P: $129-$294	

Small-scale Hotel **Location:** I-87, exit 15, 1.5 mi on US 9/SR 50, just e, then just n. 11 Excelsior Ave 12866. Fax: 518/226-0542. **Facility:** Smoke free premises. 146 units. 137 one-bedroom standard units. 6 one- and 3 two-bedroom suites ($294-$1049), some with whirlpools. 7 stories, interior corridors. *Bath:* combo or shower only. **Parking:** on-site. **Terms:** 14 day cancellation notice-fee imposed, [BP] meal plan available, package plans. **Amenities:** video games (fee), high-speed Internet, dual phone lines, voice mail, safes, irons, hair dryers. **Pool(s):** small heated indoor. **Leisure Activities:** whirlpool, exercise room. **Guest Services:** valet and coin laundry, area transportation-race track & downtown, wireless Internet. **Business Services:** conference facilities, business center. **Cards:** AX, DC, DS, MC, VI. **Free Special Amenities:** local telephone calls and high-speed Internet.

SOME UNITS

🅂🄳 🛈 📶 🖑 🛏 ⊗ 🎥 📺 / 🛗 📧 /

FOX N' HOUND B & B Phone: (518)584-5959

WWW

7/25-11/14	1P: $295-$400	2P: $295-$400	
5/1-7/24	1P: $165-$245	2P: $165-$245	
11/15-4/30	1P: $150-$220	2P: $150-$245	

Bed & Breakfast **Location:** On SR 29, 1.1 mi w. 142 Lake Ave (SR 29) 12866. **Facility:** This fully restored Victorian inn has a wonderful front porch, a secluded pool and individually decorated rooms. Smoke free premises. 5 one-bedroom standard units, some with whirlpools. 2 stories (no elevator), interior corridors. *Bath:* combo or shower only. **Parking:** on-site. **Terms:** 2-3 night minimum stay - seasonal and/or weekends, age restrictions may apply, 14 day cancellation notice-fee imposed, package plans. **Amenities:** video library, irons, hair dryers. **Pool(s):** outdoor. **Cards:** MC, VI.

SOME UNITS

🛆 ⊗ / VCR /

HILTON GARDEN INN-SARATOGA SPRINGS *Book great rates at AAA.com* Phone: 518/587-1500

WWW

Property failed to provide current rates

Small-scale Hotel **Location:** I-87, exit 13, 3.4 mi n on US 9. 125 S Broadway 12866. Fax: 518/587-7800. **Facility:** 112 one-bedroom standard units. 4 stories, interior corridors. *Bath:* combo or shower only. **Parking:** on-site. **Amenities:** video games (fee), high-speed Internet, dual phone lines, voice mail, safes, irons, hair dryers. **Pool(s):** heated indoor. **Leisure Activities:** whirlpool, exercise room. **Guest Services:** sundries, valet and coin laundry. **Business Services:** meeting rooms, business center.

SOME UNITS

🛈 📶 🄼 🖑 🛆 🎥 🛏 📧 📺 / ⊗ /

HOLIDAY INN *Book great rates at AAA.com* Phone: (518)584-4550

AAA SAVE

WWWW

7/25-9/3	1P: $199-$319	2P: $199-$319	XP: $10	F19
5/1-7/24 & 9/4-11/15	1P: $119-$169	2P: $119-$169	XP: $10	F19
11/16-4/30	1P: $89-$129	2P: $89-$129	XP: $10	F19

Small-scale Hotel **Location:** On US 9, jct SR 50. 232 Broadway 12866. Fax: 518/584-4417. **Facility:** 168 units. 162 one-bedroom standard units. 6 one-bedroom suites with whirlpools. 4 stories, interior corridors. **Parking:** on-site, winter plug-ins. **Terms:** 1-2 night minimum stay - seasonal and/or weekends, [AP] meal plan available, package plans. **Amenities:** high-speed Internet, voice mail, irons, hair dryers. *Some:* dual phone lines, safes. **Dining:** 6:30 am-10 pm, cocktails. **Pool(s):** heated outdoor, heated indoor. **Leisure Activities:** exercise room. **Guest Services:** valet and coin laundry. **Business Services:** conference facilities. **Cards:** AX, DC, DS, MC, VI.

SOME UNITS

🅂🄳 🐾 🛈 📶 🍸 🎛 🛆 🎥 📺 / ⊗ VCR 🛏 📧 /

LONGFELLOWS HOTEL RESTAURANT & CONFERENCE CENTER *Book at AAA.com* Phone: (518)587-0108

WWW

7/25-9/3 [CP]	1P: $305-$495	2P: $305-$495	XP: $10	F18
5/1-7/24 & 9/4-10/28 [CP]	1P: $125-$495	2P: $125-$495	XP: $10	F18
10/29-4/30 [CP]	1P: $105-$495	2P: $105-$495	XP: $10	F18

Country Inn **Location:** I-87, exit 14, 1.4 mi s on SR 9P. 500 Union Ave 12866. Fax: 518/587-6649. **Facility:** Once part of a 1,000-acre dairy farm, this converted barn is now home to modern, stylish guest rooms and charming public areas. Designated smoking area. 50 units. 45 one-bedroom standard units, some with whirlpools. 4 one- and 2 two-bedroom suites ($225-$495) with whirlpools. 3 stories, interior corridors. **Parking:** on-site. **Terms:** 2 night minimum stay - seasonal, 14 day cancellation notice, package plans, $2 service charge. **Amenities:** high-speed Internet, voice mail, irons, hair dryers. **Dining:** restaurant, see separate listing. **Leisure Activities:** exercise room. **Guest Services:** valet laundry. **Business Services:** meeting rooms. **Cards:** AX, DC, DS, MC, VI.

SOME UNITS

ASK 🅂🄳 🍽 ⊗ 🎥 📺 / VCR 🛏 📧 /

RESIDENCE INN BY MARRIOTT-SARATOGA SPRINGS   *Book great rates at AAA.com*

Phone: 518/584-9600

▼▼▼▼

	7/25-9/2 [BP]	1P: $299-$399	2P: $299-$399
	9/3-10/28 [BP]	1P: $169-$219	2P: $169-$219
Large-scale Hotel	5/1-7/24 [BP]	1P: $169-$209	2P: $169-$209
	10/29-4/30 [BP]	1P: $139-$149	2P: $139-$149

Location: I-87, exit 15, just n, just s, then just e. 295 Excelsior Ave 12866. Fax: 518/584-9692. **Facility:** Smoke free premises. 100 units. 42 one-bedroom standard units with kitchens. 58 one-bedroom suites, some with kitchens and/or whirlpools. 4 stories, interior corridors. *Bath:* combo or shower only. **Parking:** on-site. **Terms:** 2-3 night minimum stay - seasonal and/or weekends, package plans, pets ($75 fee). **Amenities:** video games (fee), CD players, high-speed Internet, irons, hair dryers. *Some:* DVD players. **Pool(s):** heated indoor. **Leisure Activities:** whirlpool, exercise room, sports court. **Guest Services:** sundries, complimentary evening beverages, coin laundry, wireless Internet. **Business Services:** meeting rooms, business center. **Cards:** AX, DC, DS, JC, MC, VI.

(ASK) (S🄳) 🐾 (&M) 🖥 🐦 🖾 ⊠ 🎥 🖥 ⊟ ▣ SOME UNITS / (VCR) /
FEE

ROOSEVELT INN & SUITES

Phone: 518/584-0980

▼▼▼

Location: I-87, exit 13N, just n. S Broadway (Box 177, South Broadway). Fax: 518/584-0980. **Facility:** 50 units. 31 one-bedroom standard units. 19 one-bedroom suites ($150-$450), some with whirlpools. 2 stories, interior/exterior corridors. **Parking:** on-site. **Amenities:** video library, CD players, high-speed Internet, voice mail, irons, hair dryers. *Some:* DVD players, safes. **Pool(s):** heated outdoor, heated indoor. **Leisure Activities:** saunas, whirlpool, 2 tennis courts, exercise room. *Fee:* massage. **Guest Services:** sundries, area transportation (fee). **Business Services:** meeting rooms, fax (fee). **Cards:** AX, DS, MC, VI.

All Year   1P: $109-$450   2P: $109-$450   XP: $50   F11

✚ 🍴 (&M) 🏊 🖾 (VCR) 🎥 🖥 / ⊠ 🖥 ▣ / SOME UNITS
FEE

SARATOGA ARMS   *Book at AAA.com*

Phone: (518)584-1775

▼▼▼

| | 7/25-9/3 [BP] | 1P: $315-$595 | 2P: $315-$595 |
| Small-scale Hotel | 5/1-7/24 & 9/4-4/30 [BP] | 1P: $175-$375 | 2P: $175-$375 |

Location: Center. 497 Broadway 12866. Fax: 518/581-4064. **Facility:** 31 units. 29 one-bedroom standard units, some with whirlpools. 2 one-bedroom suites. 4 stories, interior corridors. *Bath:* combo or shower only. **Parking:** on-site. **Terms:** check-in 4 pm, age restrictions may apply, 14 day cancellation notice. **Amenities:** voice mail, safes, irons, hair dryers. *Some:* DVD players. **Leisure Activities:** exercise room. *Fee:* massage. **Guest Services:** sundries, valet laundry, area transportation, wireless Internet. **Business Services:** meeting rooms, PC, fax. **Cards:** AX, DC, DS, MC, VI.

🍴✚ ⊠ 🎥 / ⊟ / SOME UNITS

SARATOGA BED & BREAKFAST

Phone: 518/584-0920

▼▼▼

All Year   1P: $109-$249   2P: $109-$249

Location: 2.3 m w on SR 9N. 434 Church St 12866. Fax: 518/584-7177. **Facility:** This rambling, wood-frame farmhouse, which dates from 1860, offers guest rooms furnished with antiques and quilts; some rooms have a fireplace. Smoke free premises. 5 one-bedroom standard units. 2 stories (no elevator), interior corridors. *Bath:* combo or shower only. **Parking:** on-site. **Terms:** check-in 4 pm, 2-3 night minimum stay, 14 day cancellation notice-fee imposed. **Amenities:** voice mail, irons, hair dryers. **Cards:** AX, MC, VI.

Historic Bed & Breakfast

(ASK) (S🄳) ⊠ 🖥

SARATOGA DOWNTOWNER MOTEL

Phone: (518)584-6160

(AAA) (SAVE)
▼▼ ▼▼
Motel

	7/25-9/2	1P: $199-$229	2P: $199-$229	XP: $15	F
	5/1-7/24 & 9/3-10/27	1P: $105-$115	2P: $105-$115	XP: $10	F
	10/28-4/30	1P: $89-$99	2P: $89-$99	XP: $10	F

Location: On US 9; corner of Division St. 413 Broadway 12866. Fax: 518/584-2907. **Facility:** 42 one-bedroom standard units. 2 stories (no elevator), interior/exterior corridors. **Parking:** on-site. **Terms:** [CP] meal plan available. **Pool(s):** heated indoor. **Cards:** AX, DS, MC, VI. **Free Special Amenities:** continental breakfast and local telephone calls.

(S🄳) 🍴✚ 🐦 / ⊠ 🖥 / SOME UNITS

THE SARATOGA HOTEL & CONFERENCE CENTER *Book great rates at AAA.com*   **Phone:** (518)584-4000

7/26-9/5	1P: $299-$599	2P: $299-$599	XP: $15	F16
12/17-4/30	1P: $159-$279	2P: $159-$279		
5/1-7/25	1P: $139-$239	2P: $139-$239	XP: $15	F16
9/6-12/16	1P: $139-$239	2P: $139-$239		

Small-scale Hotel **Location:** I-87, exit 15, on SR 50. 534 Broadway 12866 (475 Seagate Dr, NAPLES, FL, 34101). Fax: 518/584-7430. **Facility:** 242 one-bedroom standard units. 5 stories, interior corridors. *Bath:* combo or shower only. **Parking:** on-site. **Terms:** 14 day cancellation notice, seasonal-fee imposed, small pets only ($100 deposit). **Amenities:** video games (fee), dual phone lines, voice mail, irons, hair dryers. **Dining:** 7 am-10 pm, cocktails. **Pool(s):** small heated indoor. **Leisure Activities:** exercise room. **Guest Services:** valet laundry, wireless Internet. **Business Services:** conference facilities, business center. **Cards:** AX, DC, DS, JC, MC, VI. **Free Special Amenities:** newspaper and preferred room (subject to availability with advance reservations).

SOME UNITS

SARATOGA MOTEL   **Phone:** 518/584-0920

Motel   All Year   1P: $79-$199   2P: $79-$199   XP: $25   F10
Location: On SR 9N, 2.3 mi w of jct US 9/SR 50. Located in a rural area. 440 Church St 12866. Fax: 518/584-7177. **Facility:** 9 one-bedroom standard units, some with efficiencies. 1 story, exterior corridors. *Bath:* combo or shower only. **Parking:** on-site. **Terms:** check-in 4 pm, 2-3 night minimum stay - seasonal, 14 day cancellation notice-fee imposed, small pets only. **Amenities:** voice mail. **Cards:** AX, MC, VI.

SOME UNITS

SPRINGS MOTEL   **Phone:** 518/584-6336

7/25-9/3	1P: $190	2P: $190	XP: $10	F18
5/1-7/24 & 9/4-10/31	1P: $85	2P: $95	XP: $10	F18
11/1-4/30	1P: $70	2P: $80	XP: $10	F18

Motel **Location:** I-87, exit 13, 3.6 mi n on US 9. 189 Broadway 12866. Fax: 518/587-8164. **Facility:** 28 one-bedroom standard units. 2 stories (no elevator), exterior corridors. **Parking:** on-site, winter plug-ins. **Terms:** 20 day cancellation notice. **Amenities:** irons, hair dryers. **Pool(s):** outdoor. **Guest Services:** wireless Internet. **Cards:** AX, CB, DC, DS, MC, VI. **Free Special Amenities:** local telephone calls and high-speed Internet.

TURF AND SPA MOTEL   **Phone:** 518/584-2550

7/25-9/2	1P: $160-$180	2P: $160-$180	XP: $10	F18
5/1-7/24, 9/3-10/27 & 4/1-4/30	1P: $50-$85	2P: $55-$85	XP: $5	F18

Motel **Location:** I-87, exit 13, 3.4 mi n on US 9. 176 Broadway 12866. Fax: 518/587-8162. **Facility:** 43 one-bedroom standard units. 2 stories (no elevator), exterior corridors. **Parking:** on-site. **Terms:** open 5/1-10/27 & 4/1-4/30, 14 day cancellation notice. **Amenities:** voice mail. **Pool(s):** heated outdoor. **Leisure Activities:** 2 mineral water whirlpools, barbecue & picnic area. **Cards:** AX, CB, DC, DS, MC, VI. **Free Special Amenities: continental breakfast and local telephone calls.** *(See color ad p 613)*

UNION GABLES BED & BREAKFAST   **Phone:** (518)584-1558

7/25-9/5 [CP]	1P: $375-$410	2P: $375-$410	XP: $25	F10
5/1-7/24 [CP]	1P: $195-$230	2P: $195-$230	XP: $25	F10
9/6-11/1 [CP]	1P: $160-$205	2P: $160-$205	XP: $25	F10
11/2-4/30 [CP]	1P: $140-$180	2P: $140-$180	XP: $25	F10

Historic Bed & Breakfast **Location:** I-87, exit 14, 1.5 mi w. 55 Union Ave 12866. Fax: 518/583-0649. **Facility:** This B&B, built in 1901, has been restored and offers well-decorated guest rooms. Designated smoking area. 10 units. 9 one- and 1 two-bedroom standard units. 3 stories (no elevator), interior corridors. *Bath:* combo or shower only. **Parking:** on-site. **Terms:** 2 night minimum stay, 30 day cancellation notice-fee imposed, package plans, pets ($25 fee). **Amenities:** irons, hair dryers. **Business Services:** PC. **Cards:** AX, MC, VI. **Free Special Amenities: continental breakfast and preferred room (subject to availability with advance reservations).**

SOME UNITS

THE WESTCHESTER HOUSE BED & BREAKFAST   **Phone:** (518)587-7613

7/25-9/3	1P: $265-$450	2P: $265-$450	
5/1-7/24, 9/4-12/31 & 2/1-4/30	1P: $125-$245	2P: $125-$245	

Historic Bed & Breakfast **Location:** I-87, exit 13, 3.5 mi n on US 9, then 0.3 mi e. 102 Lincoln Ave 12866 (PO Box 944). Fax: 518/583-9562. **Facility:** This Queen Anne-style inn, built in 1885, is characterized by an Old World ambience yet offers up-to-date amenities. Smoke free premises. 7 one-bedroom standard units. 2 stories (no elevator), interior corridors. *Bath:* combo or shower only. **Parking:** on-site. **Terms:** open 5/1-12/31 & 2/1-4/30, check-in 4 pm, age restrictions may apply, 14 day cancellation notice, [ECP] meal plan available, package plans. **Amenities:** CD players, voice mail. **Guest Services:** wireless Internet. **Cards:** AX, CB, DC, DS, MC, VI.

--- **WHERE TO DINE** ---

43 PHILA BISTRO   **Dinner:** $20-$30   **Phone:** 518/584-2720

American **Location:** Between Caroline and Spring sts; center. 43 Phila St 12866. **Hours:** 5 pm-10 pm. Closed: 5/28, 12/25. **Reservations:** suggested. **Features:** The gaiety of the city's summer life is reflected in the animated conversations that take place around tables at the upscale bistro. Expect creative cuisine, capable service and an excellent wine list. Dressy casual; cocktails. **Parking:** street. **Cards:** AX, DC, DS, MC, VI.

BAILEY'S CAFE   **Lunch:** $6-$12   **Dinner:** $6-$12   **Phone:** 518/583-6060

American **Location:** Between Putnam and Henry sts; downtown. 37 Phila St 12866. **Hours:** 11 am-11 pm. Closed: 11/22, 12/25. **Features:** Wraps and grilled paninis are just a couple of the gourmet sandwiches available. For dessert, you can roast s'mores right at your table. Casual dress; cocktails. **Parking:** street. **Cards:** AX, DC, MC, VI.

BEVERLY'S
American

Lunch: $4-$9   **Phone:** 518/583-2755
Location: Between Caroline and Spring sts. 47 Phila St 12866. **Hours:** 8 am-3 pm. Closed: 12/25. **Reservations:** not accepted. **Features:** The restaurant serves breakfast and light lunches and also will pack picnics for patrons who want them. Casual dress. **Parking:** on-site and street. **Cards:** AX, CB, DC, DS, MC, VI.

THE BREAD BASKET
Bakery/Desserts

Lunch: $3-$6   **Phone:** 518/587-4233
Location: Between Henry St and Circular Dr; center. 65 Spring St 12866. **Hours:** 6 am-6 pm, Sat & Sun-4 pm. Closed: 3/23, 11/22, 12/25; also Mon. **Features:** This small bakery offers a variety of soups and desserts. Limited indoor seating is available. Casual dress. **Parking:** on-site.

BRINDISI'S
Italian

Dinner: $15-$35   **Phone:** 518/587-6262
Location: Center. 390 Broadway 12866. **Hours:** 4 pm-10 pm, Sun noon-9 pm. **Reservations:** accepted. **Features:** Lunch, dinner and late-night dancing are what to expect. Innovative cuisine blends Italian and Continental flavors. Dressy casual; cocktails. **Parking:** street. **Cards:** AX, CB, DC, DS, MC, VI.

CHIANTI IL RISTORANTE
Northern Italian

Dinner: $12-$29   **Phone:** 518/580-0025
Location: 0.5 mi n on US 9. 208 S Broadway 12866. **Hours:** 5 pm-10 pm. Closed major holidays; also Super Bowl Sun. **Reservations:** not accepted. **Features:** A warm and intimate ambience accompanied by attentive and accomplished service set the scene for the simply wonderful food at Chianti's. Salads have unique accompaniments such as roasted eggplant. A great seafood choice is angel hair pasta with shrimp in a lobster, cream and grappa sauce. The classic tiramisu almost floats off the plate, even with a cup of robust espresso. Dressy casual; cocktails. **Parking:** on-site. **Cards:** AX, MC, VI.

CIRCUS CAFE
American

Lunch: $6-$16   **Dinner:** $6-$19   **Phone:** 518/583-1106
Location: Center. 392 Broadway 12866. **Hours:** 11:30 am-10 pm, Fri & Sat-11 pm. Closed: 11/22, 12/25. **Reservations:** accepted. **Features:** You don't have to go far to see the circus. With the long flowing velvet ropes and murals of the circus from the old days, you get the feeling you're under the big top. Great burgers and delicious pasta dishes make it a fun atmosphere. Casual dress; cocktails. **Parking:** street. **Cards:** AX, DC, DS, MC, VI.

DOC'S STEAKHOUSE
Steak & Seafood

Dinner: $16-$31   **Phone:** 518/581-7011
Location: Between Phila and Carolina sts; downtown. 63 Putnam St 12866. **Hours:** 5 pm-10 pm, Fri & Sat-11 pm. Closed: 11/22, 12/25. **Reservations:** suggested. **Features:** Located on a side street, the restaurant features an outdoor deck that is nice and relaxing. There is plenty of steak as well as a nice selection of seafood available. Dressy casual; cocktails. **Parking:** on-site. **Cards:** AX, DS, MC, VI.

FORNO TOSCANO BISTRO
Italian

Lunch: $7-$12   **Dinner:** $7-$27   **Phone:** 518/581-2401
Location: I-87, exit 15, on SR 50; downtown. 541 Broadway 12866. **Hours:** 11:30 am-11 pm. Closed: 11/22; also Sun. **Features:** This trendy yet casual setting offers patrons a variety of creative, fresh Tuscan style Italian dishes. Fresh ingredients are combined to include both traditional dishes and those with more complexity and creativity. Definitely save room for dessert and try their tiramisu or a cannoli. Casual dress; cocktails. **Parking:** on-site. **Cards:** AX, MC, VI.

FOUR SEASONS NATURAL FOODS STORE & CAFE
Vegetarian

Lunch: $5-$15   **Dinner:** $5-$15   **Phone:** 518/584-4670
Location: Corner of Putnam St; center. 33 Phila St 12866. **Hours:** 11:30 am-8 pm. Closed major holidays. **Reservations:** not accepted. **Features:** The city's only vegetarian restaurant also boasts a well-stocked natural foods/products store. Choices at the self-serve cafe are limited and the food is basic and functional. Among offerings are a salad bar, soups and several choices of hot meals. Try one of the many delicious made-to-order shakes and smoothies. Casual dress. **Parking:** street. **Cards:** AX, CB, DC, DS, MC, VI.

HATTIE'S
Southern

Dinner: $13-$18   **Phone:** 518/584-4790
Location: Between Caroline and Spring sts; center. 45 Phila St 12866. **Hours:** 5 pm-10 pm. Closed major holidays; also Mon & Tues 9/1-7/15. **Reservations:** accepted, except 9/1-6/30. **Features:** The restaurant is a part of city history, and the newest owners have done a remarkable job keeping its past alive in the countless photographs and reviews that adorn the walls and, more importantly, in faithful re-creations of some of Hattie's original recipes. Representative of fine down-home cooking are such dishes as Hattie's southern-fried chicken and Creole jambalaya. Chef Alexander also prepares more creative takes on Southern cuisine. Casual dress; cocktails. **Parking:** street. **Cards:** AX, DC, DS, MC, VI.

HIBACHI RESTAURANT
Japanese

Lunch: $8-$10   **Dinner:** $14-$20   **Phone:** 518/580-9343
Location: I-87, exit 13, 1.8 mi n on US 9. 3310 S Broadway 12866. **Hours:** 11:30 am-10 pm, Fri & Sat-11 pm. **Reservations:** accepted. **Features:** Sushi, steak table fare, tempura and teriyaki—all can be found at the Hibachi Restaurant. The charm of a warm, Japanese-style tea house welcomes you to a relaxed and casual lunch or dinner. You will enjoy smooth service with touches of the Orient. A separate sushi menu is offered, as well as a special machine to warm your saki to the correct temperature and dishes prepared to order. A house dessert combines east and west in the fried hibachi split—fried banana and ice cream. Casual dress; beer & wine only. **Parking:** on-site. **Cards:** AX, DS, MC, VI.

LILLIAN'S
American

Lunch: $7-$10   **Dinner:** $15-$20   **Phone:** 518/587-7766
Location: Center. 408 Broadway 12866. **Hours:** 11:30 am-10 pm, Fri & Sat-11 pm, Sun noon-9 pm; to 11 pm 6/1-9/30. **Reservations:** accepted. **Features:** Located on the main street, this restaurant, named after actress Lillian Russell, is appointed in turn-of-the-20th-century decor with Tiffany-style lamps, stained glass and Victorian accents. Prime rib and grilled salmon stand out on a menu of steak and seafood selections. Seasonal outdoor dining is available, weather permitting. Casual dress; cocktails. **Parking:** street. **Cards:** AX, CB, DC, MC, VI.

LONGFELLOWS RESTAURANT   **Dinner:** $15-$30   **Phone:** 518/587-0108

Continental

Location: I-87, exit 14, 1.4 mi s on SR 9P; in Longfellows Inn and Restaurant. 500 Union Ave 12866. **Hours:** 5 pm-10 pm, Fri & Sat-11 pm, Sun 4 pm-9 pm. **Closed:** 5/28, 12/24, 12/25. **Reservations:** suggested. **Features:** The warmth of an old inn combines with attentive service to make any evening memorable. Thick, creamy lobster bisque and Southwestern chicken strudel are two of several tempting appetizers. Entrees range from Kentucky bourbon-glazed salmon to slow-roasted prime rib. Pasta and vegetarian dishes have rich sauces and are served in ample portions. Dressy casual; cocktails. **Parking:** on-site. **Cards:** AX, CB, DC, DS, MC, VI.

O'CALLAGHANS FINE FOOD & SPIRIT   **Lunch:** $6-$18   **Dinner:** $6-$23   **Phone:** 518/450-0205

American

Location: Between Broadway and Putnam St. 14 Phila St 12866. **Hours:** 11:30 am-9 pm. **Closed:** 12/25. **Reservations:** accepted. **Features:** Plenty of spirits on tap and in the bottle make the decision of what to order a difficult one, but with a brewery in house, the homegrown is an easy choice. Wraps, burgers and sandwiches are available for lunch, with more traditional meals for dinner. Casual dress; cocktails. **Parking:** street. **Cards:** AX, DS, MC, VI.

THE OLDE BRYAN INN   **Lunch:** $7-$10   **Dinner:** $11-$20   **Phone:** 518/587-2990

American

Location: I-87, exit 15, 1.5 mi s on SR 50. 123 Maple Ave 12866. **Hours:** 11 am-10 pm, Fri & Sat-11 pm. **Closed:** 5/28, 11/22, 12/25; also for dinner 12/24. **Features:** Originally established as an inn in 1773, the Victorian restaurant is quaintly decorated with red-globe lamps and wood accents. Menu selections are tried and true—prime rib, old-fashioned turkey dinner, homemade apple crisp and chocolate chip pie. Casual dress; cocktails. **Parking:** on-site. **Cards:** AX, DC, DS, MC, VI. **Historic**

PANZA'S RESTAURANT   **Dinner:** $15-$25   **Phone:** 518/584-6882

Continental

Location: On SR 9P; south end of Saratoga Lake. 510 Rt 9P 12866. **Hours:** 5 pm-10 pm, Fri & Sat-11 pm; hours vary off season. **Closed:** 12/24, 12/25; also Mon & Tues. **Features:** Family-owned since 1938, the restaurant is decorated in the art deco style, with purple linens and striking artwork. Chicken Tuscany and shrimp Sorrentino, which blends shrimp, eggplant, mozzarella cheese and butter, are outstanding choices. Casual dress; cocktails. **Parking:** on-site. **Cards:** AX, CB, DS, MC, VI.

RAVENOUS   *Menu on AAA.com*   **Lunch:** $7-$9   **Dinner:** $7-$9   **Phone:** 518/581-0560

Continental

Location: Between Spring and Caroline sts; center. 21 Phila St 12866. **Hours:** 11:30 am-8 pm, Fri & Sat-9 pm; Sunday brunch 10 am-3 pm. **Closed:** Mon & 12/25-1/2. **Features:** The small, funky, contemporary-style cafe has the feel of a local hang-out and offers a nice alternative to a heavy lunch or dinner. Savory lunch and dinner crepes are served with organic lettuces, and lip-smacking, mouthwatering dessert crepes are made with nothing but the freshest, finest ingredients. Guests often are tempted by the pommes frites, Belgian-style fries, as well as by the delicious iced Moroccan mint tea. Casual dress; beer & wine only. **Parking:** street. **Cards:** MC, VI.

SARGO'S AT SARATOGA NATIONAL GOLF CLUB   *Menu on AAA.com*   **Lunch:** $6-$9   **Dinner:** $22-$48   **Phone:** 518/583-4653

American

Location: I-87, exit 14, 1 mi w on SR 9P. 458 Union Ave 12866. **Hours:** 11:30 am-4 & 5-9 pm, Fri & Sat-10 pm, Sun 10 am-7 pm. **Closed:** 12/23-12/25. **Reservations:** suggested. **Features:** The restaurant boasts a very tempting Continental menu and an excellent wine list to go with it. The menu features such favorites as wood-grilled wild king salmon, seared Maine hand-dived scallops, and veal and lobster Lorenzo. With its high ceilings and great lighting, the dining room offers scenic views of the golf course, but if you prefer, you can sit in the lounge for a more casual atmosphere. Dressy casual; cocktails. **Parking:** on-site. **Cards:** AX, DC, DS, MC, VI.

SPRING WATER INN   **Dinner:** $18-$26   **Phone:** 518/584-6440

American

Location: I-87, exit 14, 1.5 mi w; corner of Union Ave and Nelson. 139 Union Ave 12866. **Hours:** 5:30 pm-9:30 pm. **Closed:** 1/1, 11/22, 12/25; also Tues. **Reservations:** suggested. **Features:** For Saratoga racing season dining or anytime of year, the ambience of a private library and relaxed, friendly service at Spring Water Inn is sure to please. The variety of appetizers ranges from pate to crab cakes. Steak is a specialty, but dishes such as veal with shrimp are tempting choices. The house dessert is a "not to be missed" frozen chocolate mousse with chunks of white chocolate and nuts. Valet parking is available 8/1-8/31. Casual dress; cocktails. **Parking:** on-site. **Cards:** AX, DC, MC, VI. **Historic**

THE STADIUM CAFE   **Lunch:** $5-$15   **Dinner:** $5-$15   **Phone:** 518/226-4437

American

Location: Center. 389 Broadway 12866. **Hours:** 11:30 am-11 pm, Fri & Sat-midnight. **Closed:** 3/23, 11/22, 12/25. **Features:** If you have to watch a baseball or football game, this is the place to watch it. There are so many televisions around the restaurant that any seat is a good seat. A list of appetizers will keep you busy and make it hard to choose one of the many sandwiches, wraps or burgers they offer. Outdoor dining in the summer offers views of Broadway. Casual dress; cocktails. **Parking:** street. **Cards:** AX, DS, MC, VI.

SUSHI THAI GARDEN   **Lunch:** $6-$12   **Dinner:** $8-$20   **Phone:** 518/580-0900

Asian

Location: Between Spring and Caroline sts; center. 44-46 Phila St 12866. **Hours:** 11:30 am-3 & 5-10 pm, Fri & Sat-10:30 pm. **Closed:** 11/22, 12/25. **Reservations:** accepted. **Features:** The restaurant offers diners a choice between the milder cuisine of Japan and the spicier foods of Thailand. Opt for teriyaki or tempura, or spice it up with a curry dish. Sushi is another good bet. Casual dress; beer & wine only. **Parking:** street. **Cards:** AX, DS, MC, VI.

TIZNOW   **Dinner:** $14-$36   **Phone:** 518/226-0655

Continental

Location: Between Lake and Caroline sts; downtown. 84 Henry St 12866. **Hours:** 5:30 pm-11 pm, Fri & Sat-midnight. **Closed:** 11/22, 12/25. **Reservations:** suggested. **Features:** Located on a side street, this restaurant has several choices of fresh cuts of meat and fish. The open atmosphere of the restaurant will make everybody fast friends. The walls open up in the summer for almost-outside dining. Dressy casual; cocktails. **Parking:** street. **Cards:** AX, MC, VI.

WEATHERVANE SEAFOOD RESTAURANT | Lunch: $4-$10 | Dinner: $4-$18 | Phone: 518/584-8157

▼▼ ▼▼
Seafood
MC, VI.

Location: I-87, exit 13, 2.5 mi n, then 1.5 mi s on US 9. 3368 S Broadway 12866. **Hours:** 11 am-9:30 pm; to 9 pm in winter. **Closed:** 11/22, 12/24, 12/25. **Features:** The popular, family-oriented restaurant presents a large menu with lobster, fried clams and crisp Cape Cod apple-cranberry cobbler. Flavorful dishes are served in large portions. A fish market is on the premises. Casual dress; cocktails. **Parking:** on-site. **Cards:** AX, DS,

---

WHEATFIELDS | Lunch: $7-$8 | Dinner: $8-$19 | Phone: 518/587-0534

ⒶⒶⒶ
▼▼▼▼
Italian

Location: Center. 440 Broadway 12866. **Hours:** noon-10 pm; hours may vary off season. **Closed:** 11/22, 12/25. **Features:** This moderately upscale restaurant delivers an excellent variety of homemade pasta dishes, as well as preparations of fresh veal and seafood. The inviting dining room, with candlelit tables, is a nice contrast to the more casual patio overlooking the main street. Casual dress; cocktails. **Parking:** street. **Cards:** AX, DS, MC, VI.

THE WINE BAR | Dinner: $18-$30 | Phone: 518/584-8777

▼▼▼▼
California
Cards: AX, DC, DS, MC, VI.

Location: On US 9; center. 417 Broadway 12866. **Hours:** 4 pm-10 pm, Sun-9 pm. **Closed:** 12/25; also Sun 6/1-8/31. **Reservations:** suggested. **Features:** The environment is perfect for sharing a casual evening with friends. Among offerings are lighter fare, including a selection of gourmet cheeses, a full bar with an extensive by-the-glass list, a cigar lounge and an outdoor patio. Dressy casual; cocktails. **Parking:** street.

——— *The following restaurant has not been evaluated by AAA* ———
but is listed for your information only.

ONE CAROLINE STREET BISTRO | Phone: 518/587-2026

[fyi]

Not evaluated. Location: 1 Caroline St 12866. **Features:** The intimate, little bistro offers a lively International menu and nightly live jazz. The premises are entirely smoke-free.

SAUGERTIES pop. 4,955

——— **WHERE TO STAY** ———

COMFORT INN | *Book great rates at AAA.com* | | | Phone: (845)246-1565

ⒶⒶⒶ SAVE
▼▼▼▼
Small-scale Hotel

All Year	1P: $89-$159	2P: $89-$159	XP: $10	F18

Location: I-87, exit 20, just n. Located in a quiet area. 2790 SR 32 12477. **Fax:** 845/246-1631. **Facility:** 65 one-bedroom standard units, some with efficiencies and/or whirlpools. 2 stories (no elevator), interior corridors. **Parking:** on-site. **Terms:** [CP] meal plan available, pets ($25 fee). **Amenities:** high-speed Internet, irons, hair dryers. **Leisure Activities:** exercise room. **Guest Services:** wireless Internet. **Business Services:** meeting rooms. **Cards:** AX, DC, DS, MC, VI. **Free Special Amenities: expanded continental breakfast and high-speed Internet.**

SOME UNITS

HOWARD JOHNSON INN | *Book great rates at AAA.com* | | Phone: (845)246-9511

ⒶⒶⒶ SAVE
▼▼ ▼▼
Small-scale Hotel

5/1-9/5 & 12/1-2/29	1P: $115-$125	2P: $115-$125
9/6-11/30	1P: $89-$99	2P: $89-$99
3/1-4/30	1P: $79-$89	2P: $79-$89

Location: I-90, exit 20, just n. 2764 Rt 32 12477. **Fax:** 845/246-1753. **Facility:** 84 one-bedroom standard units, some with whirlpools. 2 stories, interior corridors. **Parking:** on-site, winter plug-ins. **Terms:** 3 day cancellation notice. **Amenities:** voice mail, irons, hair dryers. *Some:* DVD players. **Pool(s):** heated indoor. **Leisure Activities:** sauna. **Guest Services:** coin laundry, wireless Internet. **Business Services:** meeting rooms, fax. **Cards:** AX, DS, MC, VI. **Free Special Amenities: local telephone calls and high-speed Internet.**

SOME UNITS

——— **WHERE TO DINE** ———

CAFE TAMAYO | Dinner: $14-$22 | Phone: 845/246-9371

▼▼▼▼
Regional American
dress; cocktails. **Parking:** on-site. **Cards:** DS, MC, VI. **Historic**

Location: On SR 32 and US 9W s; center. 89 Partition St 12477. **Hours:** 5 pm-9 pm, Fri & Sat-10 pm. **Closed:** 1/1, 7/4, 12/25; also Mon & Tues. **Reservations:** suggested. **Features:** The attractively restored 1864 building has an original walnut bar, belt-driven paddle fans and plaster on canvas ceilings. Representative of complex preparations is the confit of duck, which is served with wild rice and red onion marmalade. Casual

EMILIANI RISTORANTE | Dinner: $14-$20 | Phone: 845/246-6169

▼▼▼▼
Italian

Location: I-87, exit 20, 0.7 mi s on SR 32. 147-149 Ulster Ave 12477. **Hours:** 4:30 pm-10 pm, Sun 3 pm-9 pm. **Closed:** 11/22, 12/25; also Wed. **Reservations:** suggested, weekends. **Features:** Stenciled and decorated by the owner, the cozy restaurant has a quaint, homey atmosphere. The menu is undeniably sophisticated, with thoughtful preparations of chicken, veal, steak, seafood and pasta. The breads and desserts will make your mouth water. Casual dress; cocktails. **Parking:** on-site. **Cards:** AX, DS, MC, VI.

NEW WORLD HOME COOKING CO. | Lunch: $7-$16 | Dinner: $8-$23 | Phone: 845/246-0900

▼▼▼▼
American

Location: I-87, exit 20, just w to SR 32, just n to CR 212, then 4.5 mi w. 1411 Rt 212 12477. **Hours:** 5 pm-10 pm, Fri-Mon also noon-3 pm. **Closed:** 12/25. **Reservations:** suggested. **Features:** Between Woodstock and Saugerties, the country eatery is bright with artful decorations and palate-pleasing dishes. Chef-owner Ric Orlando's creative menu combines flavors and styles from around the world. Locally produced foods factor heavily in dishes. Casual dress; cocktails. **Parking:** on-site. **Cards:** AX, CB, DC, DS, JC, MC, VI.

SCHENECTADY pop. 61,821

―――― WHERE TO STAY ――――

DAYS INN *Book great rates at AAA.com* **Phone:** (518)370-3297
▼▼ ▼▼ All Year 1P: $69-$99 2P: $69-$99 XP: $5 D16
Small-scale Hotel **Location:** Jct State St (SR 5) and Nott Terrace, 2 bks e; downtown. 167 Nott Terrace 12308. Fax: 518/370-5948. **Facility:** 68 one-bedroom standard units, some with whirlpools. 3 stories, interior corridors. **Parking:** on-site, winter plug-ins. **Terms:** 14 day cancellation notice, [CP] & [ECP] meal plans available, package plans, small pets only ($10 extra charge, in designated units). **Amenities:** high-speed Internet, safes, hair dryers. *Some:* irons. **Guest Services:** valet and coin laundry. **Cards:** AX, CB, DC, DS, MC, VI.

SOME UNITS
(ASK) (S/D) 🐾 (†¶†) 🌀 🐟 / ⊠ 🛢 🖥 🖵 /
FEE

HAMPTON INN DOWNTOWN SCHENECTADY **Phone:** 518/377-4500
(fyi) Property failed to provide current rates
Too new to rate, opening scheduled for December 2006. **Location:** I-890, exit 25, follow 1-90 W to exit 5
Small-scale Hotel (Broadway), continue to State St, then just right. 450 State St 12305. **Amenities:** 93 units, coffeemakers, pool.

HOLIDAY INN-DOWNTOWN SCHENECTADY *Book at AAA.com* **Phone:** (518)393-4141
▼▼▼ All Year 1P: $104-$169 2P: $104-$169 XP: $10 F18
Small-scale Hotel **Facility:** 183 one-bedroom standard units. 4 stories, interior corridors. **Parking:** on-site. **Terms:** [BP], [CP] & [ECP] meal plans available, package plans. **Amenities:** video games (fee), voice mail, irons, hair dryers. **Pool(s):** heated indoor. **Leisure Activities:** whirlpool, putting green, exercise room. *Fee:* game room. **Guest Services:** valet and coin laundry, area transportation, wireless Internet. **Business Services:** conference facilities. **Cards:** AX, CB, DC, DS, JC, MC, VI.

SOME UNITS
(ASK) (S/D) 🕀 (†¶†) 🍽 ⚓ ⊠ 🎥 🖥 / ⊠ 🛢 /
FEE

THE PARKER INN *Book great rates at AAA.com* **Phone:** (518)688-1001
(AAA) (SAVE) All Year 1P: $155-$175 2P: $155-$175 XP: $20 F12
▼▼▼ **Location:** Center. Located next to the Proctor Theater. 434 State St 12305. Fax: 518/688-1002. **Facility:** Smoke free premises. 23 units. 22 one-bedroom standard units. 1 one-bedroom suite ($175-$325). 8 stories, interior corridors. *Bath:* combo or shower only. **Parking:** on-site. **Terms:** cancellation fee imposed, package Small-scale Hotel plans. **Amenities:** high-speed Internet, dual phone lines, voice mail, irons, hair dryers. **Guest Services:** valet laundry, wireless Internet. **Business Services:** meeting rooms, business center. **Cards:** AX, CB, DS, MC, VI. **Free Special Amenities:** continental breakfast and high-speed Internet.

SOME UNITS
(S/D) (†¶†) 🍽 ⊠ 🎥 🖥 / 🛢 /

―――― WHERE TO DINE ――――

FIVE GUYS BURGERS & FRIES **Lunch:** $3-$6 **Dinner:** $3-$6 **Phone:** 518/346-5728
▼ **Location:** On SR 146; in Mohawk Commons Shopping Mall. 418-A Balltown Rd 12304. **Hours:** 11 am-10 pm. **Features:** This is the place if you're in the mood for a good burger. Hand-formed burgers are cooked to American order with a wide selection of toppings to choose from. The fries are cooked in peanut oil; order regular or cajun style. Credit cards are not accepted, however there is an ATM on site. Casual dress. **Parking:** on-site. **Cards:** AX, DS, MC, VI.

PARISI'S **Dinner:** $14-$33 **Phone:** 518/374-0100
▼▼ ▼▼ **Location:** Jct Union and Liberty St. 11 N Broadway 12305. **Hours:** 4 pm-9 pm, Fri & Sat-10 pm. Closed major holidays; also Sun & Mon. **Reservations:** suggested. **Features:** Known locally for its cut-to-order steaks, Steak & Seafood the restaurant also makes comparably delicious pasta and seafood dishes. An impressive list of mouthwatering appetizers and specialty salads makes decisions difficult. Dining rooms have an exotic look. Casual dress; cocktails. **Parking:** on-site. **Cards:** AX, CB, DC, DS, MC, VI.
🍽

SCHOHARIE pop. 1,030

―――― WHERE TO STAY ――――

HOLIDAY INN EXPRESS HOTEL & SUITES
SCHOHARIE *Book at AAA.com* **Phone:** 518/295-6088
▼▼▼▼ 7/1-9/30 1P: $129-$169 2P: $129-$169 XP: $10 F
10/1-4/30 1P: $99-$139 2P: $99-$139 XP: $10 F
6/1-6/30 1P: $98-$139 2P: $98-$139 XP: $10 F
Small-scale Hotel 5/1-5/31 1P: $89-$129 2P: $89-$129 XP: $10 F
Location: I-88, exit 23, just s to Park Pl, then just s. 160 Holiday Way 12157. Fax: 518/295-6099. **Facility:** 56 one-bedroom standard units, some with whirlpools. 3 stories, interior corridors. *Bath:* combo or shower only. **Parking:** on-site. **Terms:** package plans, pets ($17 fee). **Amenities:** dual phone lines, voice mail, irons, hair dryers. **Leisure Activities:** exercise room. *Fee:* game room. **Guest Services:** sundries, valet and coin laundry, wireless Internet. **Business Services:** conference facilities. **Cards:** AX, CB, DC, DS, JC, MC, VI.

SOME UNITS
(ASK) (S/D) 🐾 (&) 🌀 🎥 🖥 / ⊠ 🛢 🖥 /
FEE

―――― WHERE TO DINE ――――

GEORGE MANN'S TORY TAVERN **Dinner:** $30-$35 **Phone:** 518/295-7128
(AAA) **Location:** I-88, exit 23, 2.2 mi s on SR 30, then just e on SR 443. 104 Vrooman Cross Rd 12157. **Hours:** Open 5/1-1/1 & 2/2-4/30; 5 pm-9 pm, Sun 1 pm-7 pm. Closed: Mon & Tues. **Reservations:** suggested. ▼▼▼ **Features:** Colonial furnishings decorate the restored 1700s tavern. The daily-changing menu might include such dishes as veal-mushroom pate, rabbit-white bean soup and flavorful veal gruyere with fresh, al dente American vegetables. Desserts are almost irresistible. Casual dress; cocktails. **Parking:** on-site. **Cards:** AX, MC, VI. **Historic**

THE PARROTT HOUSE   **Lunch:** $4-$8   **Dinner:** $9-$16   **Phone:** 518/295-7111

American

Location: On SR 30; downtown. 294 Main St 12157. **Hours:** 10:30 am-9 pm, Sat from noon. Closed: Sun. **Reservations:** suggested, weekends. **Features:** There are no talking birds or pirates here, just ample servings of good food in a casual family atmosphere. The 1870s tavern specializes in seafood, steak and game. Great soups and hearty sandwiches fill the lunch bill as well. The restaurant is adjacent to other historic buildings in town. Casual dress; cocktails. **Parking:** on-site. **Cards:** AX, DC, DS, MC, VI. **Historic**

SCHROON LAKE —See also ADIRONDACK MOUNTAINS.

——— WHERE TO STAY ———

BLUE RIDGE MOTEL   **Phone:** (518)532-7521

Motel

5/18-9/4 [ECP]   1P: $78-$88   2P: $88-$98   XP: $10   F18

Location: I-87, exit 28, 4 mi n. 2455 US Rt 9 12870. **Facility:** 17 one-bedroom standard units. 1 story, interior/exterior corridors. **Bath:** combo or shower only. **Terms:** open 5/18-9/4, 2 night minimum stay - weekends, 14 day cancellation notice-fee imposed, pets ($5 fee). **Pool(s):** heated outdoor. **Leisure Activities:** recreation programs, barbecue grills, picnic tables, playground. **Business Services:** fax. **Cards:** AX, MC, VI. **Free Special Amenities:** expanded continental breakfast and high-speed Internet.

SOME UNITS

——— WHERE TO DINE ———

DRAKE'S RESTAURANT   **Lunch:** $4-$7   **Dinner:** $8-$18   **Phone:** 518/532-9040

American

Location: I-87, exit 28, 1 mi s; in Drakes Motel. US 9 12870. **Hours:** Open 5/23-10/12; 4:30 pm-9 pm, Sun from 8:30 am. **Reservations:** suggested, for dinner. **Features:** In a seasonal resort town, the cheerful restaurant is appointed with nautical decor. Reasonably priced selections of standard American favorites make this place popular with families. Service is friendly. Casual dress; cocktails. **Parking:** on-site. **Cards:** AX, DS, MC, VI.

SCHUYLERVILLE pop. 1,197

——— WHERE TO STAY ———

BURGOYNE MOTOR INN   **Phone:** 518/695-3282

Motel

Property failed to provide current rates

Location: US 4 and SR 32, just n of jct SR 29. 220 Broad St 12871. **Fax:** 518/695-3328. **Facility:** 14 one-bedroom standard units. 1 story, interior/exterior corridors. **Parking:** on-site. **Terms:** small pets only (with prior approval). **Amenities:** voice mail. **Guest Services:** area transportation. **Business Services:** fax (fee).

SOME UNITS

SCOTIA pop. 7,957

——— WHERE TO DINE ———

GLEN SANDERS MANSION   **Lunch:** $7-$14   **Dinner:** $17-$34   **Phone:** 518/374-7262

Continental

Location: I-890, exit 4C, 1 mi w; SR 5, just 1 Glen Ave 12302. **Hours:** 11:30 am-2 & 5-10 pm, Sat from 5 pm, Sun 10:30 am-1:30 & 4-9 pm. Closed major holidays. **Reservations:** suggested. **Features:** Built in the late 1600s, the elegantly renovated mansion houses a restaurant where accomplished and deft servers bring guests delightful meals. The setting is fitting for sweet corn and crab cake, salmon, roasted sea bass, maple-marinated sirloin, chocolate gooey cake and fine liquors. The new outdoor covered patio opens seasonally. Dressy casual; cocktails. **Parking:** on-site. **Cards:** AX, CB, DC, DS, MC, VI. **Historic**

SEA BREEZE

——— WHERE TO DINE ———

SHAMROCK JACK'S   **Lunch:** $5-$11   **Dinner:** $9-$36   **Phone:** 585/323-9310

Steak & Seafood

Location: Center; next to Sea Breeze Amusement Park. 4554 Culver Rd 14622. **Hours:** 11:30 am-2:30 & 5-9 pm, Fri & Sat-10 pm. Closed: 7/4, 12/25. **Reservations:** accepted. **Features:** The Irish-themed restaurant offers seating in the upbeat pub or in the more quiet dining space, which is appointed in warm, inviting decor. Diners can ponder a generous choice of fresh seafood, pasta, Choice Angus steak and other traditional American favorite dishes. Service is friendly. Casual dress; cocktails. **Parking:** on-site. **Cards:** AX, DS, MC, VI.

SENECA FALLS pop. 6,861—See also FINGER LAKES.

——— WHERE TO STAY ———

BARRISTER'S BED & BREAKFAST   **Phone:** 315/568-0145

Bed & Breakfast

All Year [BP]   1P: $99-$165   2P: $110-$165   XP: $25   F5

Location: I-90 (New York State Thruway), exit 41, 4 mi s on SR 414, then 2 mi e on SR 5 and US 20 (Cayuga St). 56 Cayuga St 13148. **Facility:** 1888 Colonial revival with carved fireplaces and stained glass windows; within walking distance to museums, canal and shops. Smoke free premises. 5 units. 4 one-bedroom standard units, some with whirlpools. 1 one-bedroom suite ($155). 2 stories (no elevator), interior corridors. **Bath:** combo or shower only. **Parking:** on-site. **Terms:** check-in 4 pm, 2 night minimum stay - weekends, 7 day cancellation notice. **Amenities:** Some: CD players. **Cards:** AX, DS, MC, VI.

SOME UNITS

——— WHERE TO DINE ———

HENRY B'S

▼▽▲▽▼

Italian

Dinner: $12-$30

Phone: 315/568-1600

Location: Center. 84 Fall St 13148. **Hours:** 5 pm-9 pm, Fri & Sat-10 pm. Closed: 11/22, 12/24, 12/25; also Sun, Mon & Fri after Thanksgiving. **Reservations:** suggested. **Features:** Authentic Italian cuisine is carefully prepared from quality ingredients and proudly presented by friendly, professional staff who can assist you in your selection. The shared dining concept offers generous portions for two or more in an intimate, upscale but unpretentious atmosphere. Casual dress; cocktails. **Parking:** street. **Cards:** AX, DC, DS, MC, VI.

SHELTER ISLAND HEIGHTS pop. 981

——— WHERE TO STAY ———

DERING HARBOR INN

▼▽ ▼▽

Small-scale Hotel

Phone: 631/749-0900

6/16-9/3	1P: $285-$320	2P: $420-$460	XP: $25	F12
5/18-6/15 & 9/4-10/21	1P: $175-$265	2P: $325-$405	XP: $25	F12

Location: North ferry, 0.5 mi s on SR 114; jct SR 114 and Winthrop Rd, just e. Located on the waterfront. 13 Winthrop Rd 11965 (PO Box 3028). Fax: 631/749-2045. **Facility:** 21 units. 4 one-bedroom standard units. 14 one- and 3 two-bedroom suites ($225-$320) with kitchens. 2 stories (no elevator), exterior corridors. **Parking:** on-site. **Terms:** open 5/18-10/21, 2 night minimum stay, 14 day cancellation notice-fee imposed, weekly rates available, package plans. **Amenities:** voice mail, hair dryers. *Some:* DVD players. **Pool(s):** outdoor. **Leisure Activities:** fishing, 2 tennis courts, basketball, volleyball. *Fee:* boat dock. **Guest Services:** valet and coin laundry, wireless Internet. **Business Services:** meeting rooms, PC. **Cards:** AX, DS, MC, VI.

SOME UNITS

SHERRILL pop. 3,147

——— WHERE TO DINE ———

COLOSSEO ITALIAN & AMERICAN RESTAURANT

▼▽▲▽▼

Italian

Lunch: $3-$5   **Dinner: $6-$12**   **Phone: 315/363-9076**

Location: On SR 5. SR 5 13461. **Hours:** 11 am-10 pm, Fri & Sat-11 pm. Closed major holidays. **Reservations:** suggested. **Features:** A casual ease is evident in the relaxed dining room of this family-oriented restaurant. Traditional entrees are split among American and Italian selections. Manicotti is particularly tasty, as is the scrumptious blueberry pie, served a la mode. Casual dress; cocktails. **Parking:** on-site. **Cards:** AX, DC, DS, MC, VI.

ROSS'S GINGERBREAD HOUSE FAMILY RESTAURANT

▼▽▲▽▼

American

Lunch: $4-$7   **Dinner: $7-$14**   **Phone: 315/363-6644**

Location: On SR 5, just e of Main St. Rt 5 & Betsinger Rd 13461. **Hours:** 11 am-9 pm, Fri & Sat-9:30 pm; Sun noon-6 pm in winter. Closed: 1/1, 11/22, 12/25; also Mon. **Reservations:** accepted. **Features:** Country crafts and Victorian appointments decorate the inviting dining room. Chicken in lemon butter and haddock with white wine sauce are tasty choices, as are the splendid homemade desserts. Casual dress; cocktails. **Parking:** on-site. **Cards:** AX, DC, DS, MC, VI.

SKANEATELES pop. 2,616—See also FINGER LAKES.

——— WHERE TO STAY ———

ARBOR HOUSE INN

▼▽▲▽▼

Bed & Breakfast

Phone: 315/685-8966

5/1-11/1	1P: $150-$250	2P: $150-$250
11/2-4/30	1P: $105-$147	2P: $105-$147

Location: Center of downtown. Located in the historic district. 41 Fennell St 13152. Fax: 315/685-7841. **Facility:** Find gracious luxury at this 1855 inn, with a sun porch, pillow-top beds, antiques and Oriental rugs; some rooms include a Jacuzzi and fireplace. Smoke free premises. 11 units. 10 one-bedroom standard units, some with whirlpools. 1 one-bedroom suite with kitchen and whirlpool. 2 stories (no elevator), interior corridors. *Bath:* combo or shower only. **Parking:** on-site. **Terms:** 2 night minimum stay - seasonal and/or weekends, age restrictions may apply, 10 day cancellation notice. **Amenities:** irons, hair dryers. *Some:* high-speed Internet. **Guest Services:** wireless Internet. **Cards:** AX, DS, MC, VI.

SOME UNITS

BOUTIQUE HOTEL OF SKANEATELES

AAA SAVE

▼▽▲▽▼

Small-scale Hotel

Phone: (315)685-2333

7/1-9/5	1P: $150-$195	2P: $150-$195	XP: $15
5/1-6/30 & 9/6-4/30	1P: $125-$150	2P: $125-$150	XP: $15

Location: Off Jordon St; center. 12 Fennell St 13152 (PO Box 912). Fax: 315/685-7223. **Facility:** Smoke free premises. 5 one-bedroom standard units, some with whirlpools. 2 stories (no elevator), interior corridors. *Bath:* combo or shower only. **Parking:** on-site. **Terms:** 2 night minimum stay - seasonal and/or weekends, cancellation fee imposed. **Amenities:** irons, hair dryers. **Guest Services:** complimentary and valet laundry, wireless Internet. **Cards:** AX, DS, MC, VI. **Free Special Amenities:** continental breakfast and high-speed Internet.

SOME UNITS

FINGER LAKES LODGING

AAA SAVE

▼▽▲▽▼

Motel

Phone: (315)217-4111

5/1-10/31	1P: $120-$265	2P: $120-$265	XP: $10	F13
11/1-4/30	1P: $85-$189	2P: $85-$189	XP: $10	F13

Location: On US 20, just w. 834 W Genesee St 13152. Fax: 315/217-0069. **Facility:** Smoke free premises. 12 units. 10 one-bedroom standard units. 2 one-bedroom suites, some with efficiencies. 1-2 stories (no elevator), interior/exterior corridors. *Bath:* combo or shower only. **Parking:** on-site. **Terms:** off-site registration, check-in 4 pm, 7 day cancellation notice-fee imposed, package plans. **Amenities:** DVD players, CD players, high-speed Internet, dual phone lines, voice mail, irons, hair dryers. **Leisure Activities:** exercise facilities privileges. **Guest Services:** wireless Internet. **Cards:** AX, DC, MC, VI. **Free Special Amenities:** high-speed Internet.

SOME UNITS

HOBBIT HOLLOW FARM BED AND BREAKFAST
Phone: 315/685-2791

▼▼◇◇▼   5/1-12/31 [BP]   1P: $120-$270   2P: $120-$270   XP: $50
        1/1-12/31 [BP]   1P: $100-$250   2P: $100-$250   XP: $30

Historic Bed   **Location:** 1.7 mi s on SR 41A from US 20. Located in a quiet rural area. 3061 W Lake Rd 13152. Fax: 315/685-3426.
& Breakfast   **Facility:** A lake and 460 acres of rolling hills provide a scenic backdrop to this finely furnished B&B; an
adjacent barn houses horses. Smoke free premises. 5 one-bedroom standard units, some with whirlpools. 2
stories (no elevator), interior corridors. *Bath:* combo or shower only. **Parking:** on-site. **Terms:** age restrictions may apply, 10 day
cancellation notice, package plans. **Amenities:** hair dryers. **Leisure Activities:** cross country skiing, hiking trails. **Guest
Services:** complimentary evening beverages, wireless Internet. **Business Services:** fax. **Cards:** AX, MC, VI.

HUMMINGBIRD'S HOME BED & BREAKFAST
Phone: (315)685-5075

▼▼◇◇▼   All Year   1P: $99-$180   2P: $99-$180   XP: $30   D12

Bed & Breakfast   **Location:** 1.5 mi w on US 20. 4273 W Genesee St 13152. **Facility:** Cozy, inviting rooms with hospitality to match
make it easy to relax in this restored 1803 farmhouse; full gourmet breakfast served. 4 one-bedroom
standard units. 2 stories (no elevator), interior corridors. *Bath:* combo or shower only. **Parking:** on-site.
Terms: 14 day cancellation notice-fee imposed, package plans. **Amenities:** irons, hair dryers. **Guest Services:** wireless
Internet. **Cards:** MC, VI.

MIRBEAU INN & SPA   *Book great rates at AAA.com*
Phone: (315)685-5006

(AAA) [SAVE]   5/1-10/31   1P: $185-$520   2P: $185-$520   XP: $25   F13
              11/1-4/30   1P: $160-$360   2P: $160-$360   XP: $25   F13

▼▼◇◇▼   **Location:** On US 20, just w of downtown. 851 W Genesee St 13152. Fax: 315/217-0069. **Facility:** A sublimely
Small-scale Hotel   relaxing atmosphere brings to mind the works of Monet at this inn whose offerings range from spa
treatments to picturesque gardens. Smoke free premises. 34 units. 32 one-bedroom standard units. 2 three-
bedroom suites. 2 stories, interior/exterior corridors. **Parking:** on-site. **Terms:** check-in 4 pm, 7 day
cancellation notice-fee imposed, package plans. **Amenities:** video library, DVD players, CD players, high-speed Internet, dual
phone lines, voice mail, honor bars, irons, hair dryers. **Dining:** Giverny, see separate listing. **Leisure Activities:** saunas,
whirlpool, steamrooms, spa. **Guest Services:** gift shop, valet laundry. **Business Services:** meeting rooms, PC. **Cards:** AX, DC,
MC, VI. **Free Special Amenities: newspaper and high-speed Internet.**

PACKWOOD HOUSE
Phone: 315/217-8100

▼▼◇◇▼   5/1-12/31 [CP]   1P: $150-$230   2P: $150-$230   XP: $25   F
        1/1-4/30 [CP]   1P: $125-$190   2P: $125-$190   XP: $25   F

Small-scale Hotel   **Location:** On US 20; center. Located across from Skaneateles Lake. 14 W Genesee St 13152. Fax: 315/685-8983. **Facility:** Smoke free premises. 19 one-bedroom standard units. 3 stories, interior corridors. **Parking:** on-
site. **Terms:** off-site registration, 10 day cancellation notice, package plans. **Amenities:** CD players, high-speed Internet, voice
mail, irons, hair dryers. **Guest Services:** valet laundry. **Cards:** AX, MC, VI.

SHERWOOD INN
Phone: 315/685-3405

▼▼◇◇▼   5/1-12/31 [BP]   1P: $130-$225   2P: $130-$225   XP: $25   F
        1/1-4/30 [BP]   1P: $120-$200   2P: $120-$200   XP: $25   F

Historic   **Location:** On US 20; center. 26 W Genesee St 13152 (PO Box 529). Fax: 315/685-8983. **Facility:** Recently
Country Inn   renovated, this 1807 landmark hotel offers luxury accommodations across from Skaneateles Lake; a fine
dining room and tavern are on site. Smoke free premises. 24 units. 17 one-bedroom standard units, some
with whirlpools. 7 one-bedroom suites with whirlpools. 3 stories (no elevator), interior corridors. *Bath:* combo or shower only.
Parking: on-site. **Terms:** 10 day cancellation notice, package plans. **Amenities:** hair dryers. *Some:* DVD players.
Dining: restaurant, see separate listing. **Guest Services:** gift shop, valet laundry, wireless Internet. **Business Services:**
meeting rooms. **Cards:** AX, DS, MC, VI.

SOME UNITS

SKANEATELES SUITES
Phone: (315)685-7568

(AAA) [SAVE]   7/1-9/5   1P: $150-$195   2P: $150-$195   XP: $15
              5/1-6/30 & 9/6-4/30   1P: $125-$150   2P: $125-$150   XP: $15

▼▼◇◇▼   **Location:** On US 20, 2 mi w. 4114 W Genesee St 13152 (PO Box 912). Fax: 315/685-7223. **Facility:** Smoke free
Motel   premises. 15 units. 14 one-bedroom standard units, some with kitchens and/or whirlpools. 1 three-bedroom
suite with kitchen. 2 stories (no elevator), exterior corridors. **Parking:** on-site. **Terms:** 2 night minimum stay
- seasonal and/or weekends, cancellation fee imposed, pets ($35 fee). **Amenities:** CD players, irons, hair
dryers. **Leisure Activities:** gas grill, hiking trails. **Guest Services:** valet laundry, wireless Internet. **Cards:** AX, DS, MC, VI.
Free Special Amenities: continental breakfast and high-speed Internet.

FEE

VILLAGE INN OF SKANEATELES
Phone: 315/685-3405

▼▼◇◇▼   All Year   1P: $99-$195   2P: $99-$195

Bed & Breakfast   **Location:** Just n on Fennel St; center. 25 Jordan St 13152. Fax: 315/685-8983. **Facility:** A European-style hotel
decorated in Stickley and Audi, this historic district property offers luxury and privacy in a picturesque Finger
Lakes town. Smoke free premises. 4 one-bedroom standard units. 3 stories (no elevator), interior corridors.
Parking: on-site. **Terms:** off-site registration, 10 day cancellation notice, [BP] meal plan available. **Amenities:** CD players, high-
speed Internet, irons, hair dryers. **Guest Services:** valet laundry. **Cards:** AX, DS, MC, VI.

--- **WHERE TO DINE** ---

BLUEWATER GRILL
Lunch: $5-$9   **Dinner:** $10-$19   **Phone:** 315/685-6600

▼▼▼   **Location:** Center. 11 W Genesee St 13152. **Hours:** 8 am-10 pm; seasonal hours vary. Closed: 1/1, 11/22,
American   12/25. **Reservations:** suggested. **Features:** Sitting on a fishing pier is never as much fun as it is at this
casual grill next to the pier on Lake Skaneateles. Guests can dine outside in fine weather or inside at the
bustling eatery. Baked fresh scrod is a favorite, and Maryland crab cakes and grilled-to-order filet mignon
are also tempting. Bumbleberry pie is a good "catch" for dessert. Casual dress; cocktails. **Parking:** street. **Cards:** AX, DC, DS,
MC, VI.

DOUG'S FISH FRY

Seafood

Lunch: $5-$7 **Dinner:** $7-$15 **Phone:** 315/685-3288
Location: Center. 8 Jordan St 13152. **Hours:** Open 5/1-12/31 & 1/15-4/30; 11 am-10 pm; to 8 pm 9/3-5/26. Closed: 3/23, 11/22, 12/25. **Features:** People flock to the hole-in-the-wall restaurant for a good reason—the food is great. Fried just right, the fish fry is lightly browned, with the fish turning out light and flaky. Crispy, golden fries and tangy slaw are delicious accompaniments. Casual dress; beer & wine only. **Parking:** on-site. **Cards:** MC, VI.

GIVERNY

Continental

Lunch: $15-$30 **Dinner:** $50-$60 **Phone:** 315/685-5006
Location: On US 20, just w of downtown; in Mirbeau Inn & Spa. 851 W Genesee St 13152. **Hours:** 7:30-10:30 am, 11:30-2:30 & 6-9:30 pm. **Reservations:** suggested. **Features:** The ever-changing tasting menu reflects the chef's impressionistic approach. Dishes center on the best of seasonal harvests, often with local selections, when available. Choices are distinctive, stimulating and irresistible. Dressy casual; cocktails. **Parking:** on-site. **Cards:** AX, DC, MC, VI.

KABUKI

Asian

Dinner: $10-$17 **Phone:** 315/685-7234
Location: Center. 12 W Genesee St 13152. **Hours:** 5 pm-9 pm, Fri & Sat-10 pm. Closed: 1/1, 11/22, 12/25. **Reservations:** suggested. **Features:** The eclectic sushi bar sustains a cheery, bistro-style atmosphere in which to enjoy Asian-themed foods made from the freshest ingredients. Casual dress; beer & wine only. **Parking:** street. **Cards:** AX, DS, MC, VI.

THE KREBS

American

Dinner: $10-$47 **Phone:** 315/685-5714
Location: On US 20. 53 W Genesee St 13152. **Hours:** Open 5/1-10/31; 6 pm-9 pm, Fri & Sat-10 pm, Sun 10:30 am-2 & 4-9 pm. Closed: 9/3. **Reservations:** suggested. **Features:** The long-established restaurant delivers a seven-course prix fixe meal that includes country-style entrees of lobster Newburg, prime rib and fried chicken. Early American decor pulls together the dining room in a tidy, cohesive theme. Service is prompt. Dressy casual; cocktails. **Parking:** on-site. **Cards:** AX, CB, DC, DS, MC, VI. **Country Inn**

MANDANA INN

Seafood

Menu on AAA.com **Dinner:** $15-$29 **Phone:** 315/685-7798
Location: 6 mi s on SR 41A. 1937 W Lake Rd 13152. **Hours:** Open 5/1-1/1 & 4/2-4/30; 5 pm-10 pm, Sun 4 pm-9 pm. Closed: 12/24, 12/25; also Mon & Tues 4/2-5/31 & 9/3-10/31 & Mon-Wed 11/1-1/1. **Reservations:** suggested. **Features:** Near Skaneateles Lake, the former stagecoach tavern is decorated with antique grandfather clocks and local artwork. The menu centers on well-prepared entrees of flavorful seafood and steak. The homemade dessert here has been popular for many years. Casual dress; cocktails. **Parking:** street. **Cards:** AX, DC, DS, MC, VI.

ROSALIE'S CUCINA

Italian

Dinner: $20-$35 **Phone:** 315/685-2200
Location: 0.6 mi w. 841 W Genesee St 13152. **Hours:** 5 pm-9 pm, Fri & Sat-10 pm, Sun 4 pm-8 pm. Closed major holidays; also Super Bowl Sun. **Reservations:** suggested. **Features:** Scampi Rosalie—a delicious choice with shrimp, garlic butter, angel hair pasta, artichokes and oven-cured tomatoes—is just one of the creative dishes on the tempting menu. Tuscan furnishings and warm, wood ceilings decorate the dining room. Lucious, generous desserts are made fresh on premises. Dressy casual; cocktails. **Parking:** on-site. **Cards:** AX, MC, VI.

SHERWOOD INN DINING ROOM

American

Lunch: $8-$15 **Dinner:** $12-$28 **Phone:** 315/685-3405
Location: On US 20; center; in Sherwood Inn. 26 W Genesee St 13152. **Hours:** 11:30 am-4 & 5-9 pm, Fri & Sat-10 pm, Sun 4-9 pm; winter hours may vary. Closed: 12/25; also for dinner 12/24, Mon-Wed 1/1-4/30. **Reservations:** suggested. **Features:** Enjoy views of the lake from some seats in the comfortably upscale dining room at this 1807 Inn. Freshness and flavor of seasonal regional ingredients are the foundation for creative American cuisine. Add high quality seafoods and meats such as baked scrod Christopher, herb roasted half chicken, house steaks or hazelnut crusted salmon. Tavern dining is more casual. Casual dress; cocktails. **Parking:** on-site. **Cards:** AX, DS, MC, VI. **Country Inn**

SLINGERLANDS

--------- WHERE TO DINE ---------

MANGIA

Italian

Lunch: $9-$19 **Dinner:** $9-$19 **Phone:** 518/439-5555
Location: I-90, exit 4; center. 1562 New Scotland Rd 12159. **Hours:** 11 am-9 pm, Fri-10 pm, Sat noon-10 pm, Sun noon-9 pm. **Reservations:** accepted. **Features:** The wood-fired pizza is why people come to this restaurant. Delicious appetizers and desserts are a nice way to round out a meal. Casual dress; cocktails. **Parking:** on-site. **Cards:** AX, DS, MC, VI.

SMITHTOWN pop. 26,901

--------- WHERE TO STAY ---------

ECONO LODGE SMITHTOWN

Motel

Book great rates at AAA.com **Phone:** (631)724-9000

All Year [CP]	1P: $90-$149	2P: $92-$169	XP: $8		F18

Location: On SR 347 (Nesconset Hwy/Smithtown Bypass), 2.3 mi e of SR 111. Located in a commercial area. 755 Smithtown Bypass 11787. Fax: 631/724-9017. **Facility:** 39 one-bedroom standard units. 1-2 stories, exterior corridors. **Parking:** on-site. **Amenities:** hair dryers. **Guest Services:** wireless Internet. **Cards:** AX, CB, DC, DS, JC, MC, VI. **Free Special Amenities:** continental breakfast and high-speed Internet.

SOME UNITS

─── WHERE TO DINE ───

CASA RUSTICA
▼▼▼
Northern Italian

Lunch: $15-$24 **Dinner:** $18-$32 **Phone:** 631/265-9265
Location: Jct SR 111/25A/25, 0.7 mi w. 175 W Main St 11787. **Hours:** noon-3 & 5-10 pm, Fri-11 pm, Sat 5 pm-11 pm, Sun 2 pm-9 pm. Closed major holidays. **Reservations:** suggested, for dinner. **Features:** Representative of mouthwatering fare are two specialties: vitello Casa Rustica, which is a breaded rack of veal covered with mozzarella in herb and garlic sauce, and pesce in crosta di sale, a flavorful preparation of the fresh catch of the day. Dressy casual; cocktails. **Parking:** on-site. **Cards:** AX, DC, DS, MC, VI.

H2O SEAFOOD GRILL
▼▼▼
Seafood

Dinner: $17-$48 **Phone:** 631/361-6464
Location: Jct SR 111/25A/25, 0.8 mi w. 215 W Main St 11787. **Hours:** 5 pm-10 pm, Fri & Sat-11 pm, Sun 2 pm-9 pm. Closed: 11/22, 12/25. **Reservations:** suggested. **Features:** The stylish hot spot features fresh tastes from the ocean. Guests should come hungry and order often because the portions allow for the sampling of multiple courses, including artfully presented desserts. Dressy casual; cocktails. **Parking:** on-site. **Cards:** AX, CB, DC, DS, MC, VI.

THE SMITHTOWN HOUSE
▼▼
Continental

Lunch: $12-$17 **Dinner:** $19-$34 **Phone:** 631/979-9113
Location: On SR 25, just w of jct SR 111. 65 E Main St 11787. **Hours:** noon-3 & 5-10 pm, Fri-11 pm, Sat 5 pm-11 pm, Sun 3 pm-9 pm. Closed: Mon. **Reservations:** suggested. **Features:** A romantic atmosphere derives from candlelit tables, fresh flowers and warmly colored walls. Menu specialties include such Continental and traditional German dishes as sauerbraten with potato dumplings and red cabbage, shepherd's pie and lobster ravioli with sun-dried tomatoes and lobster cream sauce. Dressy casual; cocktails. **Parking:** on-site. **Cards:** AX, DS, MC, VI.

SOLVAY pop. 6,845 (See map and index starting on p. 629)

─── WHERE TO STAY ───

BEST WESTERN FAIRGROUNDS
AAA SAVE
▼▼▼
Small-scale Hotel

Book great rates at AAA.com

5/1-10/31	1P: $109	2P: $109	XP: $10	F12
11/1-4/30	1P: $95	2P: $95	XP: $10	F12

Phone: (315)484-0044 **26**

Location: I-690, exit 7, just w. 670 State Fair Blvd 13209. Fax: 315/484-0045. **Facility:** 47 one-bedroom standard units, some with whirlpools. 2 stories, interior corridors. *Bath:* combo or shower only. **Parking:** on-site. **Terms:** 7 day cancellation notice-fee imposed, [ECP] meal plan available, $3 service charge. **Amenities:** high-speed Internet, voice mail, irons, hair dryers. **Dining:** 11 am-2 & 4-10 pm, cocktails. **Leisure Activities:** exercise room. *Fee:* game room. **Guest Services:** valet laundry. **Cards:** AX, DC, DS, MC, VI. **Free Special Amenities:** expanded continental breakfast and high-speed Internet.

SOME UNITS

HOLIDAY INN/FARRELL ROAD
▼▼▼
Small-scale Hotel

Book at AAA.com

	1P:	2P:
7/16-9/5	1P: $119-$139	2P: $119-$139
5/1-7/15	1P: $109-$129	2P: $109-$129
9/6-4/30	1P: $99-$129	2P: $99-$129

Phone: (315)457-8700 **24**

Location: I-690, exit 4 (John Glenn Blvd). 100 Farrell Rd 13209. Fax: 315/457-2379. **Facility:** 150 units. 149 one-bedroom standard units, some with whirlpools. 1 one-bedroom suite. 2 stories (no elevator), interior corridors. *Bath:* combo or shower only. **Parking:** on-site. **Terms:** cancellation fee imposed, pets ($25 fee). **Amenities:** voice mail, irons, hair dryers. *Fee:* video library, video games. **Pool(s):** outdoor. **Leisure Activities:** exercise room. **Guest Services:** valet and coin laundry, wireless Internet. **Business Services:** meeting rooms, PC. **Cards:** AX, CB, DC, DS, JC, MC, VI.

SOME UNITS

WINGATE INN
AAA SAVE
▼▼▼
Small-scale Hotel

5/1-11/30	1P: $109-$159	2P: $109-$159	XP: $10	F17
12/1-4/30	1P: $99-$139	2P: $99-$139	XP: $10	F17

Phone: (315)701-5000 **25**

Location: I-690, exit 5 eastbound, just n on State Fair Blvd; westbound, just s on State Fair Blvd,1 mi w on Walters Rd, then just n. 6947 Winchell Rd 13209. Fax: 315/701-5001. **Facility:** Smoke free premises. 87 one-bedroom standard units, some with whirlpools. 4 stories, interior corridors. *Bath:* combo or shower only. **Parking:** on-site. **Terms:** package plans. **Amenities:** video games (fee), dual phone lines, voice mail, safes, irons, hair dryers. **Pool(s):** small heated indoor. **Leisure Activities:** whirlpool, exercise room. **Guest Services:** valet and coin laundry, wireless Internet. **Business Services:** meeting rooms, business center. **Cards:** AX, CB, DC, DS, MC, VI. **Free Special Amenities:** room upgrade and preferred room (each subject to availability with advance reservations).

SOUTHAMPTON pop. 3,965

─── WHERE TO STAY ───

SOUTHAMPTON INN
AAA SAVE
▼▼▼
Small-scale Hotel

Book great rates at AAA.com

6/1-8/31	1P: $199-$489	2P: $199-$489	XP: $39	F
9/1-12/31	1P: $119-$429	2P: $119-$429	XP: $39	F
5/1-5/31	1P: $199-$299	2P: $199-$299	XP: $39	F
1/1-4/30	1P: $119-$169	2P: $119-$169	XP: $39	F

Phone: (631)283-6500

Location: 0.3 mi n from corner of Main St and Jobs Ln. 91 Hill St 11968. Fax: 631/283-6559. **Facility:** 90 units. 89 one-bedroom standard units. 1 one-bedroom suite ($289-$999). 2 stories (no elevator), exterior corridors. *Bath:* combo or shower only. **Parking:** on-site. **Terms:** check-in 4 pm, 2-3 night minimum stay - seasonal and/or weekends, 30 day cancellation notice-fee imposed, weekly rates available, package plans, small pets only ($39 extra charge). **Amenities:** video games (fee), voice mail, hair dryers. *Some:* CD players. **Dining:** 7:30-11:30 am; closed 10/1-4/30. **Pool(s):** heated outdoor. **Leisure Activities:** tennis court, limited exercise equipment. *Fee:* game room. **Guest Services:** valet laundry, area transportation-beach, train & bus stations, wireless Internet. **Business Services:** meeting rooms, PC, fax (fee). **Cards:** AX, CB, DC, DS, JC, MC, VI.

SOME UNITS

—— WHERE TO DINE ——

BARRISTER'S
Lunch: $10-$13   Dinner: $19-$26   Phone: 631/283-6206
Location: Center. 36 Main St 11968. **Hours:** 11:30 am-5 & 5:30-10:30 pm, Fri & Sat-11 pm, Sun 11:30 am-10 pm. **Closed:** 11/22, 12/25. **Features:** The casual tavern is a favorite haunt in which neighbors dine and chat over simply prepared, flavorful dishes. Penne pasta, peppercorn-rubbed tuna steak and grilled pork loin medallions are representative of menu fare. The covered terrace is relaxing. Casual dress; cocktails. **Parking:** on-site. **Cards:** AX, DC, DS, MC, VI.

American

DRIVERS SEAT RESTAURANT
Lunch: $8-$16   Dinner: $14-$25   Phone: 631/283-6606
Location: Center. 62 Jobs Ln 11968. **Hours:** 11:30 am-10 pm. **Closed:** 11/22, 12/25. **Features:** Known for steak and seafood specials, the casual family restaurant serves traditional American fare with a twist. An inviting patio—dotted with nicely spaced tables covered by umbrellas—sits out back. Service is basic, prompt and friendly. Casual dress; cocktails. **Parking:** on-site. **Cards:** AX, DS, MC, VI.

American

THE GOLDEN PEAR CAFE
Lunch: $7-$12   Dinner: $7-$12   Phone: 631/283-8900
Location: 0.9 mi se of jct SR 27, on CR 38. 99 Main St 11968. **Hours:** 7 am-5:30 pm; hours vary in season. **Closed:** 11/22, 12/25. **Features:** The gourmet cafe is amid many small boutiques on popular Main Street. Guests can sip a cup of house-brand coffee with breakfast or a freshly prepared sandwich or salad for lunch. Cafe-style tables allow for watching busy shoppers. Casual dress. **Parking:** street. **Cards:** AX, MC, VI.

American

LORI RESTAURANT & WINE BAR
Lunch: $15-$28   Dinner: $22-$36.   Phone: 631/283-7575
Location: Jct SR 27, 0.9 mi se on CR 38. 75 Main St 11968. **Hours:** 11 am-3 & 5-10 pm, Fri & Sat-11 pm, Sun-9 pm. **Closed:** 1/1, 11/22, 12/25. **Reservations:** suggested. **Features:** Among many small shops, this contemporary restaurant is nicely decorated with many colorful paintings and unusual lighting fixtures. Prime steaks and seafood ground the menu. In the center of the room is a large bar, which serves as a great spot for a before- or after-dinner cocktail. Dressy casual; cocktails. **Parking:** street. **Cards:** AX, MC, VI.

Nouvelle American

MADAME TONG'S AT JL BEACH CLUB
Dinner: $11-$27   Phone: 631/204-0300
Location: From SR 27, 0.4 mi n; across from railroad station. 256 Elm St 11968. **Hours:** 5:30 pm-midnight; hours vary off season. **Reservations:** suggested. **Features:** This contemporary Asia-inspired restaurant features deep-red walls, golden dragon statues, colorful paper umbrellas hung from ceilings and artwork. French doors in the back open to a large yard with a covered flagstone patio area, outdoor tiki-like sushi bar, fire pit and bar area with plasma HDTV. This place doubles as a dance club on certain nights. Guests can finish a meal of pork and vegetable dumplings, spicy chicken or steak with delicious molten lava cake served with green tea ice cream. Dressy casual; cocktails. **Parking:** street. **Cards:** AX, MC, VI.

Asian

THE PLAZA CAFE
Dinner: $26-$38   Phone: 631/283-9323
Location: 0.3 mi n from corner of Main St and Jobs Ln; downtown. 61 Hill St 11968. **Hours:** 5:30 pm-11 pm. **Closed:** 11/22, 12/25. **Reservations:** suggested, in season. **Features:** Some say this airy East End cottage is a hidden treasure. Yellow textured walls, an iron chandelier, flowers and fireplace make for subdued sophisticated dining. Seafood is the chef's star with choices of brightly flavored and seasoned fish and shellfish. Steamed mussels with lemongrass curry broth anyone? Plaza's generous and soul-satisfying shepherd's pie is the signature dish, filled with chunks of lobster, shrimp, shiitakes and topped with light, chive-flecked potatoes. Dressy casual; cocktails. **Parking:** on-site. **Cards:** AX, DC, MC, VI.

Seafood

RED/BAR BRASSERIE
Dinner: $22-$32   Phone: 631/283-0704
Location: Jct SR 27, 0.8 mi se on CR 38, then 0.4 mi ne. 210 Hampton Rd 11968. **Hours:** 6 pm-10 pm, Thurs-Sat to 11 pm. **Closed:** 11/22, 12/25; also Mon & Tues. **Reservations:** suggested. **Features:** Guests may feel as though they have entered an Old Southern home. White-paned windows, potted palm plants and lit candles on tables and walls contribute to the romantic atmosphere. Angel hair pasta with fresh lump crabmeat in butter-cream sauce is an example of the many excellent selections. Dressy casual; cocktails. **Parking:** on-site. **Cards:** AX, MC, VI.

Nouvelle American

SOUTHAMPTON PUBLICK HOUSE
Lunch: $10-$18   Dinner: $12-$20   Phone: 631/283-2800
Location: Just e; corner of N Sea Rd. 40 Bowden Sq 11968. **Hours:** 11:30 am-4 & 5-10 pm, Fri & Sat-11 pm, Sun noon-3 & 4-9 pm; Sunday brunch. **Closed:** 12/25. **Reservations:** accepted. **Features:** Homemade, award-winning lagers and ales are always on tap to accompany traditional pub favorites. Casual dress; cocktails. **Parking:** on-site. **Cards:** AX, CB, DC, MC, VI.

American

TUSCAN HOUSE
Lunch: $14-$16   Dinner: $24-$36   Phone: 631/287-8703
Location: 0.4 mi s of CR 38. 10 Windmill Ln 11968. **Hours:** 11:30 am-10 pm, Fri & Sat-11 pm, Sun 3 pm-10 pm; hours vary off season. **Closed:** 11/22, 12/25; also 1/1-1/14. **Reservations:** required. **Features:** The contemporary yet traditional restaurant features high ceilings with crown moldings and large windows overlooking the quaint shopping section of town. Pasta, steaks and seafood are all creatively prepared. The pasta with hot and sweet sausage and broccoli rabbe in an oil and garlic sauce is just one of the great menu choices. Dressy casual; cocktails. **Parking:** street. **Cards:** AX, MC, VI.

Northern Italian

SOUTH GLENS FALLS pop. 3,368   (See map and index starting on p. 330)—*See also GLENS FALLS.*

─── WHERE TO STAY ───

LANDMARK MOTOR INN   Phone: 518/793-3441

Motel

7/23-9/2	1P: $135	2P: $135	XP: $10	F18
5/1-7/22	1P: $65	2P: $70-$75	XP: $5	F18
9/3-10/7	1P: $60	2P: $65-$68	XP: $5	F18
10/8-4/30	1P: $55	2P: $59-$64	XP: $5	F18

Location: I-87, exit 17, 1 mi n. US 9 12803 (PO Box 376, GLENS FALLS, 12801). Fax: 518/761-6909. **Facility:** 74 one-bedroom standard units. 1 story, exterior corridors. **Parking:** on-site, winter plug-ins. **Terms:** cancellation fee imposed. **Amenities:** high-speed Internet, hair dryers. **Pool(s):** outdoor, heated indoor. **Leisure Activities:** whirlpool, putting green, playground, exercise room. **Guest Services:** wireless Internet. **Business Services:** meeting rooms, PC, fax. **Cards:** AX, CB, DC, DS, JC, MC, VI. **Free Special Amenities: preferred room (subject to availability with advance reservations) and high-speed Internet.** *(See color ad p 612)*

SOME UNITS

─── WHERE TO DINE ───

JAKE'S ROUND UP   **Lunch:** $5-$15   **Dinner:** $6-$20   **Phone:** 518/761-0015   **(43)**

Tex-Mex

Location: Center. 23 Main St 12803. **Hours:** 11:30 am-9 pm, Fri & Sat-10 pm. Closed: 11/22, 12/25. **Features:** The eclectic decor will have you looking around the entire restaurant. The menu boasts Tex-Mex favorites, as well as a nice burger selection. Casual dress; cocktails. **Parking:** on-site. **Cards:** AX, MC, VI.

LUISA'S ITALIAN BISTRO   **Dinner:** $9-$19   **Phone:** 518/745-5055

Italian

Location: I-87, exit 17N, 1.5 mi n. 1451 Saratoga Rd 12803. **Hours:** 4:30 pm-9 pm, Fri & Sat-10 pm. **Reservations:** accepted. **Features:** Excellent selections of veal, chicken and beef make the meals they come with delicious. Original artwork from the owner adorns the walls. Dressy casual; cocktails. **Parking:** on-site. **Cards:** AX, DC, MC, VI.

SOUTH KORTRIGHT

─── WHERE TO DINE ───

THE HIDDEN INN   **Dinner:** $10-$20   **Phone:** 607/538-9259

American

DS, MC, VI. **Historic**

Location: CR 18, just s of SR 10, follow signs. Main St 13842. **Hours:** 5 pm-9 pm, Sun noon-7 pm. Closed: 12/25; also Mon. **Reservations:** suggested, weekends. **Features:** The restored 1890s Colonial home is decorated in a French country motif, with chandeliers and tableside lighting. Menu offerings include favorite preparations of lamb, veal, duck, beef and seafood. Casual dress; cocktails. **Parking:** on-site. **Cards:** AX,

SPECULATOR pop. 348—*See ADIRONDACK MOUNTAINS.*

SPENCERTOWN

─── WHERE TO STAY ───

SPENCERTOWN COUNTRY HOUSE-A BED & BREAKFAST   Phone: (518)392-5292

Historic Bed & Breakfast

5/1-10/31	1P: $85-$250	2P: $100-$250	XP: $25
11/1-4/30	1P: $85-$185	2P: $100-$185	XP: $25

Location: Jct Taconic State Pkwy, 0.4 mi e on SR 203, 0.9 mi n. 1909 CR 9 12165 (PO Box 279). Fax: 518/392-7453. **Facility:** A brook crosses the grounds of this Federalist-style 1803 mansion in the Berkshires; it also offers a carriage house converted into meeting space. Smoke free premises. 10 one-bedroom standard units. 2 stories (no elevator), interior/exterior corridors. *Bath:* combo or shower only. **Parking:** on-site. **Terms:** 2-3 night minimum stay - seasonal and/or weekends, age restrictions may apply, 14 day cancellation notice-fee imposed. **Amenities:** video library, voice mail. **Business Services:** meeting rooms. **Cards:** AX, DS, MC, VI.

SOME UNITS

SPRINGFIELD CENTER —*See also COOPERSTOWN.*

─── WHERE TO STAY ───

BAYSIDE INN & MARINA   Phone: 607/547-2371

Motel

6/14-9/3	1P: $149-$189	2P: $149-$189	XP: $10
5/25-6/13 & 9/4-10/8	1P: $69-$99	2P: $69-$99	XP: $10

Location: 3 mi s. 7090 State Hwy 80 13468. Fax: 607/547-5856. **Facility:** 29 one-bedroom standard units. 1-2 stories (no elevator), interior/exterior corridors. **Parking:** on-site. **Terms:** open 5/25-10/8, 3 day cancellation notice-fee imposed, weekly rates available. **Amenities:** voice mail, irons, hair dryers. **Leisure Activities:** canoeing, paddleboats, fishing, children's swimming area, kayaks, rowboats, picnic tables, barbecue, gazebos, playground, exercise room. **Fee:** marina, game room. **Guest Services:** wireless Internet. **Cards:** DS, MC, VI. **Free Special Amenities: early check-in/late check-out and high-speed Internet.** *(See color ad p 277)*

SOME UNITS

COOPERSTOWN LAKE 'N PINES MOTEL

AAA SAVE | **Phone:** (607)547-2790

	6/15-9/2 [ECP]	1P: $135-$140	2P: $155-$165	XP: $10	F5
	9/3-11/25 & 3/19-4/30 [ECP]	1P: $55-$75	2P: $65-$85	XP: $10	F5
	5/1-6/14 [ECP]	1P: $55-$65	2P: $65-$85	XP: $10	F5

Motel **Location:** Jct US 20, 3 mi s. 7102 State Hwy 80 13326. Fax: 607/547-5671. **Facility:** 35 one-bedroom standard units. 1 story, exterior corridors. **Parking:** on-site. **Terms:** open 5/1-11/25 & 3/19-4/30, 5 day cancellation notice. **Amenities:** hair dryers. **Pool(s):** heated outdoor, heated indoor. **Leisure Activities:** sauna, whirlpool, paddleboats, boat dock, fishing, rowboats, picnic area with grills. *Fee:* game room. **Cards:** AX, DS, MC, VI. **Free Special Amenities: expanded continental breakfast and local telephone calls.** *(See color ad p 278)*

SOME UNITS

COOPERSTOWN'S HICKORY GROVE MOTOR INN *Book great rates at AAA.com*

AAA SAVE | **Phone:** (607)547-9874

| | 6/15-9/2 | 1P: $120-$140 | 2P: $120-$140 | XP: $5 | F5 |
| | 5/1-6/14 & 9/3-11/11 | 1P: $55-$85 | 2P: $55-$85 | XP: $5 | F5 |

Motel **Location:** Jct US 20, 4.7 mi sw. 6854 State Hwy 80 13326. Fax: 607/547-8567. **Facility:** 12 one-bedroom standard units. 1 story, exterior corridors. *Bath:* shower only. **Parking:** on-site. **Terms:** open 5/1-11/11, 5 day cancellation notice. **Amenities:** hair dryers. *Some:* DVD players. **Leisure Activities:** paddleboats, fishing, small stone beach area. **Guest Services:** wireless Internet. **Cards:** AX, DS, MC, VI. **Free Special Amenities: local telephone calls and high-speed Internet.**

SOME UNITS

LAKE VIEW MOTEL & MARINA *Book great rates at AAA.com*

AAA SAVE | **Phone:** 607/547-9740

| | 6/8-9/3 | 1P: $172-$222 |
| | 5/1-6/7 & 9/4-10/31 | 1P: $81-$144 |

Motel **Location:** Jct US 20, 4 mi s. 6805 State Hwy 80 13326. Fax: 607/547-5080. **Facility:** 35 units. 27 one-bedroom standard units. 3 one-bedroom suites, some with kitchens. 5 cottages. 1-2 stories, exterior corridors. *Bath:* combo or shower only. **Parking:** on-site. **Terms:** open 5/1-10/31, 2-3 night minimum stay - seasonal and/or weekends, 7 day cancellation notice-fee imposed. **Amenities:** video library (fee), CD players, hair dryers. **Leisure Activities:** paddleboats, fishing, horseshoes. *Fee:* boat dock. **Cards:** AX, DS, MC, VI. **Free Special Amenities: high-speed Internet.** *(See color ad p 279)*

SOME UNITS

SPRING VALLEY —*See New York p. 503.*

SPRINGVILLE —*See Buffalo p. 261.*

STAATSBURG pop. 911

——— **WHERE TO DINE** ———

PORTOFINO RISTORANTE

AAA | **Dinner:** $12-$20 | **Phone:** 845/889-4711

Italian **Location:** Center. 57 Old Post Rd 12580. **Hours:** 4 pm-9 pm, Fri & Sat-10 pm. Closed: 11/22, 12/25; also Mon & 1/1-1/20. **Features:** Regional Italian dishes mingle with daily-changing specials that show piquant influences from the Pacific Rim. Art deco prints decorate the walls of the dining room; soft music, ranging from jazz to easy listening pop, plays in the background. Casual dress; cocktails. **Parking:** on-site. **Cards:** AX, DC, DS, MC, VI.

STAFFORD pop. 2,409

——— **WHERE TO DINE** ———

RED OSIER LANDMARK RESTAURANT

| **Dinner:** $10-$30 | **Phone:** 585/343-6972

Steak & Seafood **Location:** On SR 5, 1 mi e of jct SR 237; between I-90 exit 47 and 48. 6492 Main Rd 14143. **Hours:** 4 pm-close, Sun from 1 pm. Closed: 11/22, 12/24, 12/25; also Mon. **Reservations:** accepted. **Features:** Casual country dining offers 'early bird' and famous specials, as well as their signature prime rib and lobster tail dinner value. Generous portions of aged Angus New York strip steaks and filet mignon are available, or create your own seafood combos with lobster, scallops or Alaskan king crab. Dressy casual; cocktails. **Parking:** on-site. **Cards:** AX, DS, MC, VI.

STATEN ISLAND —*See New York p. 497.*

STEPHENTOWN pop. 2,873

——— **WHERE TO STAY** ———

THE MILL HOUSE INN

| All Year | 1P: $125-$135 | 2P: $125-$135 | **Phone:** 518/733-5606

Bed & Breakfast **Location:** Jct SR 22, 1.1 mi e. 86 Rt 43 12168 (PO Box 477). Fax: 518/733-6025. **Facility:** Smoke free premises. 12 units. 7 one-bedroom standard units. 5 one-bedroom suites ($135-$175). 2 stories (no elevator), interior/exterior corridors. *Bath:* combo or shower only. **Parking:** on-site. **Terms:** office hours 8 am-11 pm, 14 day cancellation notice, pets (dogs only, in designated units, with prior approval). **Amenities:** video library, hair dryers. **Pool(s):** small outdoor. **Cards:** AX, CB, DC, DS, JC, MC, VI.

SOME UNITS

STONY BROOK pop. 13,727

———— WHERE TO STAY ————

HOLIDAY INN EXPRESS STONY BROOK   *Book at AAA.com*   **Phone:** (631)471-8000

▼▼▲▲▼   All Year   1P: $139-$309

Small-scale Hotel   **Location:** I-495, exit 62, 8 mi n on Nicolls Rd (CR 97), then 0.6 mi e on SR 347. Located in a commercial area. 3131 Nesconset Hwy 11720. Fax: 631/471-8623. **Facility:** 143 units. 136 one-bedroom standard units, some with whirlpools. 7 one-bedroom suites, some with whirlpools. 6 stories, interior corridors. **Parking:** on-site. **Terms:** cancellation fee imposed, [BP] meal plan available, package plans. **Amenities:** video games (fee), voice mail, irons, hair dryers. **Pool(s):** heated indoor. **Leisure Activities:** putting green, playground, exercise room, horseshoes. **Guest Services:** sundries, valet laundry, wireless Internet. **Business Services:** meeting rooms, business center. **Cards:** AX, DS, MC, VI.

SOME UNITS

(ASK) (SD) (M) (⊘) (≋) (✗) (🐾) (🛏) (🖼) (💻) /(✗)/

THREE VILLAGE INN   **Phone:** 631-751-0555

(AAA) (SAVE)   All Year   1P: $129-$189   2P: $149-$250   XP: $20   F

▼▼▲▲▼   **Location:** Jct SR 25A and Main St, just n. Located opposite the village green. 150 Main St 11790. Fax: 631/751-0593.

Historic   **Facility:** Built as an inn in 1751, this hotel offers a main building and small cottages, all in Colonial style
Country Inn   inside and out. Smoke free premises. 26 one-bedroom standard units. 2 stories (no elevator), interior/exterior corridors. *Bath:* combo or shower only. **Parking:** on-site. **Terms:** package plans. **Amenities:** voice mail, irons, hair dryers. *Some:* high-speed Internet. **Dining:** restaurant, see separate listing. **Guest Services:** wireless Internet. **Business Services:** meeting rooms, business center. **Cards:** AX, DS, MC, VI. **Free Special Amenities:** full breakfast and early check-in/late check-out.

(🍽) (🍸) (✗)

———— WHERE TO DINE ————

THREE VILLAGE INN   **Lunch:** $11-$23   **Dinner:** $17-$37   **Phone:** 631-751-0555

▼▼▲▲▼   **Location:** Jct SR 25A and Main St, just n; in Three Village Inn. 150 Main St 11790. **Hours:** 7 am-10, noon-4 & 5-9 pm, Fri & Sat 8 am-10 pm, Sun 8 am-10, noon-3 & 4-9 pm. Closed: 12/25. **Reservations:** suggested.

Regional American   **Features:** A Colonial theme weaves through the converted 1751 homestead. Enjoy panoramic views of the village and harbor from the charming dining rooms. Yankee pot roast, roast duckling and seafood pie are examples of traditional New England dishes. Dressy casual; cocktails. **Parking:** on-site. **Cards:** AX, DS, MC, VI. **Country Inn**

(🍸)

STORMVILLE

———— WHERE TO DINE ————

FIRE ON THE MOUNTAIN RESTAURANT   **Dinner:** $55   **Phone:** 845/878-6595

▼▼▲▲▼   **Location:** I-84, exit 17, 2.5 mi w. 3760 SR 52 12582. **Hours:** 6 pm-9 pm, Sat seatings 5:30 pm & 9 pm, Sun 11:30 am-2:30 pm. Closed: 12/24, 12/25; also Mon. **Reservations:** required. **Features:** You would take a

Continental   drive up the Taconic Parkway, into the Hudson Valley area, to dine at Harralds. The chef's exceptional six-course meal, complemented by a comprehensive wine list, is an experience in European Continental cuisine. The service is attentive, yet unobtrusive with Old World elegance. Dressy casual; cocktails. **Parking:** on-site. **Cards:** MC, VI.

(🍸)

SUFFERN —*See New York p. 504.*

SYLVAN BEACH pop. 1,071

———— WHERE TO STAY ————

CINDERELLA'S SUITES   **Phone:** 315-762-4280

▼▼▲   5/25-9/4   1P: $79-$179   2P: $79-$179
           9/5-10/31   1P: $69-$129   2P: $69-$129
Motel   5/1-5/24   1P: $59-$129   2P: $59-$129
           11/1-4/30   1P: $59-$119   2P: $59-$119

Location: On SR 13; center. 1208 N Main St 13157. Fax: 315/762-5675. **Facility:** Smoke free premises. 9 one-bedroom standard units, some with whirlpools. 1 story, exterior corridors. *Bath:* combo or shower only. **Parking:** on-site. **Terms:** office hours 8 am-10 pm, 16 day cancellation notice, weekly rates available, package plans, pets ($50 deposit). **Amenities:** irons, hair dryers. **Dining:** Cinderella's Cafe, see separate listing. **Leisure Activities:** playground. **Guest Services:** coin laundry. **Cards:** AX, DC, DS, MC, VI.

(ASK) (SD) (🐾) (🍽) (✗) (🛏) (🖼) (💻)

FEE

———— WHERE TO DINE ————

CANAL VIEW CAFE   **Lunch:** $4-$8   **Dinner:** $7-$14   **Phone:** 315-762-5623

▼▼▲   **Location:** On north side of Erie Canal; w of SR 13 S. 9 Canal St 13157. **Hours:** Open 5/1-11/20 & 3/8-4/30; 11:30 am-9 pm, Fri & Sat-10 pm; to 8 pm, Fri & Sat-9 pm off season. Closed: Tues 3/20-5/29 & Mon-Wed 9/7-11/20.

American   **Features:** Overlooking Oneida Lake and Erie Canal, the casual restaurant has a fresh nautical theme. Patrons can enjoy a meal in the bright dining room or on the deck. Menu favorites include seafood, pasta and steaks. A children's menu is available. Casual dress; beer & wine only. **Parking:** on-site. **Cards:** AX, DS, MC, VI.

(🍸)

CAPTAIN JOHN'S PRIME RIB-PASTA & SEAFOOD HOUSE   *Menu on AAA.com*

Dinner: $9-$24   **Phone:** 315/762-9949

Steak & Seafood

Location: Center. SR 13, 1424 Main St 13157. **Hours:** Open 5/1-10/31 & 2/14-4/30; 4 pm-10 pm, Sat from 3 pm, Sun from 1 pm. Closed: Tues & Wed off season. **Reservations:** accepted. **Features:** Among specialties are two-pound prime rib cuts, two-pound crab legs, one-pound lobster tails. Angus steaks, along with Italian favorites. Nautical appointments set a seafaring tone in the casual dining room. Scrumptious desserts, such as hot apple dumpling served with ice cream, are homemade. Casual dress; cocktails. **Parking:** on-site. **Cards:** AX, CB, DC, DS, MC, VI.

CINDERELLA'S CAFE

Lunch: $5-$8   **Dinner:** $8-$16   **Phone:** 315/762-4280

American

Location: On SR 13; center; in Cinderella's Suites. 1208 Main St 13157. **Hours:** Open 5/1-11/30 & 1/15-4/30; 8 am-9 pm; to 10 pm 6/1-8/31. Closed: 11/22. **Reservations:** accepted. **Features:** Pictures of Cinderella decorate the walls of the whimsical family cafe. Breakfast is served until 2 pm. Menu choices range from charbroiled steaks to grilled lemon-pepper haddock. On Saturday, guests can sample all-you-can-eat crab legs with free shrimp cocktail. For dessert, enjoy a piece of freshly baked pie or choose from an array of more than 40 flavors of ice cream and yogurt. Casual dress; beer & wine only. **Parking:** on-site. **Cards:** AX, DC, DS, MC, VI.

EDDIE'S RESTAURANT

Lunch: $5-$9   **Dinner:** $8-$15   **Phone:** 315/762-5430

American

Location: Center. 901 Main St 13157. **Hours:** Open 5/1-10/30 & 3/15-4/30; 11 am-11 pm; seasonal hours vary. **Features:** Operated by the Stewarts since 1934, the family-oriented restaurant is a local favorite for seafood, steaks and pasta. Homemade fruit and "mile-high" cream pies are specialties. Surrounded by windows, the bright, friendly dining room is decorated with works by local artists. Servers are pleasant and attentive. Casual dress. **Parking:** on-site. **Cards:** MC, VI.

YESTERDAY'S ROYAL-ABBY'S RESTAURANT

Lunch: $6-$8   **Dinner:** $8-$15   **Phone:** 315/762-4677

American

Location: On the canal; next to amusement park. 13 Canal St 13157. **Hours:** Open 5/1-9/30 & 4/14-4/30; 11:30 am-10 pm. Closed: Mon-Wed 9/8-9/30. **Features:** Portions are generous at the old-fashioned family restaurant, which has some old-time memorabilia and a tin-type ceiling. The menu centers on familiar preparations of fish, beef, chicken and pasta. Children of all ages enjoy the ice cream bar and in-house desserts. Casual dress; cocktails. **Parking:** on-site. **Cards:** AX, DC, DS, MC, VI.

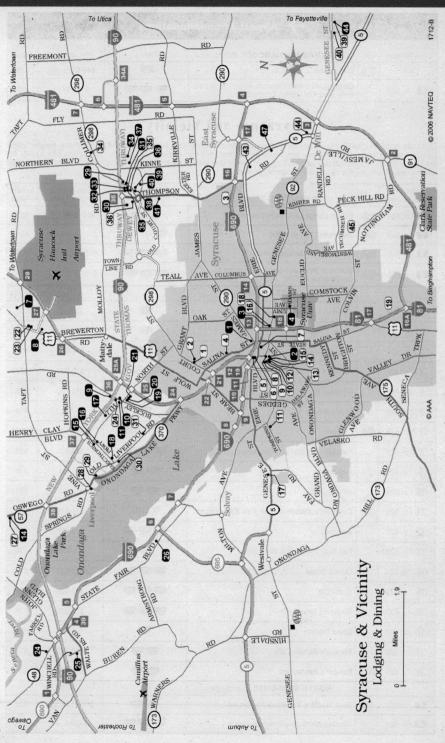

Syracuse & Vicinity
Lodging & Dining

© 2006 NAVTEQ

© AAA

✈ Airport Accommodations

Spotter/Map Page Number	OA	SYRACUSE HANCOCK INT'L	Diamond Rating	Rate Range High Season	Listing Page
N/A	⦿	Budget Inn, 2.8 mi n of terminal	◈	$48-$115 SAVE	574
🔢8 / p. 629		Candlewood Suites Syracuse Airport, at airport entry road, Col. Eileen Collins Blvd	◈◈◈	$109-$169	575

Syracuse and Vicinity

This index helps you "spot" where approved accommodations and restaurants are located on the corresponding detailed maps. Lodging rate ranges are for comparison only and show the property's high season; rates are per night, unless only weekly (W) rates are available. Restaurant rate range is for dinner, unless only lunch (L) is served. Turn to the listing page for more detailed rate information and consult display ads for special promotions.

Spotter/Map Page Number	OA	SYRACUSE - Lodgings	Diamond Rating	Rate Range High Season	Listing Page
❶ / p. 629	⦿	Econo Lodge University/Downtown	◈◈	$49-$299 SAVE	633
❷ / p. 629	⦿	Jefferson Clinton Hotel	◈◈◈	$129-$499 SAVE	634
❸ / p. 629	⦿	Renaissance Syracuse Hotel	◈◈◈	$152-$339 SAVE	634
❹ / p. 629	⦿	Sheraton Syracuse University Hotel & Conference Center	◈◈◈	$129-$409 SAVE	634
		SYRACUSE - Restaurants			
① / p. 629		Juanita's Mexican Kitchen	◈	$5-$12	635
② / p. 629		Weber's Restaurant	◈	$7-$16	636
③ / p. 629		Casa Di Copani	◈◈	$10-$21	634
④ / p. 629		Antonio's Restaurant	◈◈	$15-$30	634
⑤ / p. 629		Dinosaur Bar-B-Que	◈	$10-$25	635
⑥ / p. 629		Mimi's Bakery & Cafe	◈	$2-$7(L)	635
⑦ / p. 629	⦿	L'Adour	◈◈◈	$19-$30	635
⑧ / p. 629		Pascale Wine Bar and Restaurant	◈◈◈	$14-$24	635
⑨ / p. 629		Pastabilities	◈◈	$8-$24	636
⑩ / p. 629		Kitty Hoynes	◈◈	$8-$19	635
⑪ / p. 629	⦿	Coleman's Authentic Irish Pub & Restaurant	◈◈	$11-$18	635
⑫ / p. 629		Ambrosia	◈◈◈	$16-$30	634
⑬ / p. 629		The Blue Tusk Pub & Wine Bar	◈	$7-$12	634
⑭ / p. 629		Lemon Grass	◈◈◈	$14-$20	635
⑮ / p. 629		Bistro 238	◈◈◈	$12-$20	634
⑯ / p. 629		Redfield's Restaurant	◈◈◈	$15-$28	636
⑰ / p. 629		China Pavilion	◈	$6-$13	635
⑱ / p. 629		Phoebe's Garden Cafe	◈◈	$13-$22	636
⑲ / p. 629	⦿	Danzer's Restaurant	◈◈	$10-$14	635
		NORTH SYRACUSE - Lodgings			
🔢7 / p. 629	⦿	Best Western Syracuse Airport Inn	◈◈	$77-$148 SAVE	574
🔢8 / p. 629		Candlewood Suites Syracuse Airport	◈◈◈	$109-$169	575

Spotter/Map Page Number	OA	NORTH SYRACUSE - Lodgings (continued)	Diamond Rating	Rate Range High Season	Listing Page
9 / p. 629	AAA	**Comfort Inn & Suites/Syracuse Airport** - see color ad p 633	▽▽▽	$79-$169 SAVE	575
10 / p. 629	AAA	**Quality Inn North** - see color ad p 633	▽▽	$62-$119 SAVE	575
11 / p. 629		Ramada Inn	▽▽▽	$79-$199	575
		NORTH SYRACUSE - Restaurants			
22 / p. 629		Fresno's	▽▽	$6-$15	576
23 / p. 629		The Clam Bar	▽▽	$10-$14	576
24 / p. 629		Colorado Mine Company Steakhouse	▽▽	$10-$21	576
		LIVERPOOL - Lodgings			
14 / p. 629	AAA	**Super 8 Motel Route 57**	▽▽	$69-$119 SAVE	356
15 / p. 629		Holiday Inn Syracuse Airport	▽▽▽	$99-$229	356
16 / p. 629	AAA	**Knights Inn** - see color ad p 633	▽▽	$49-$199 SAVE	356
17 / p. 629		Homewood Suites	▽▽▽	$149-$199	356
18 / p. 629	AAA	**Best Western Inn & Suites**	▽▽▽	$89-$189 SAVE	356
19 / p. 629		Super 8 Motel Syracuse/Liverpool	▽▽	$50-$129	357
20 / p. 629	AAA	**Hampton Inn**	▽▽▽	$104-$129 SAVE	356
21 / p. 629	AAA	**Clarion Inn**	▽▽▽	$60-$139 SAVE	356
		LIVERPOOL - Restaurants			
27 / p. 629		Pier 57	▽▽	$10-$15	357
28 / p. 629		The Retreat	▽▽	$11-$15	357
29 / p. 629		Heid's of Liverpool	▽	$2-$7	357
30 / p. 629		Santangelo's Restaurant	▽▽	$12-$22	357
31 / p. 629	AAA	**Ichiban Japanese Steak House**	▽▽	$14-$27	357
		SOLVAY - Lodgings			
24 / p. 629		Holiday Inn/Farrell Road	▽▽	$119-$139	623
25 / p. 629	AAA	**Wingate Inn**	▽▽▽	$109-$159 SAVE	623
26 / p. 629	AAA	**Best Western Fairgrounds**	▽▽▽	$109 SAVE	623
		EAST SYRACUSE - Lodgings			
29 / p. 629		Embassy Suites Hotel	▽▽▽	Failed to provide	290
30 / p. 629		Red Roof Inn #7157	▽▽	$56-$84	291
31 / p. 629		Extended StayAmerica Hotels-Syracuse-Dewitt	▽▽	$45-$90	290
32 / p. 629		Residence Inn by Marriott	▽▽▽	$169-$229	291
33 / p. 629		Fairfield Inn Syracuse	▽▽	$89-$139	291
34 / p. 629	AAA	**Hilton Garden Inn-Syracuse**	▽▽▽	$89-$209 SAVE	291
35 / p. 629	AAA	**Courtyard by Marriott**	▽▽▽	$89-$209 SAVE	290
36 / p. 629	AAA	**Hampton Inn-Carrier Circle**	▽▽▽	$79-$139 SAVE	291
37 / p. 629		CrestHill Suites	▽▽▽	$129-$219	290
38 / p. 629		Candlewood Suites Syracuse	▽▽▽	$109-$159	290
39 / p. 629	AAA	**Holiday Inn East-Carrier Circle**	▽▽▽	$117-$169 SAVE	291

Spotter/Map Page Number	OA	EAST SYRACUSE - Lodgings (continued)	Diamond Rating	Rate Range High Season	Listing Page
40 / p. 629	AAA	Doubletree Hotel Syracuse	◇◇◇	$99-$299 SAVE	290
41 / p. 629	AAA	Comfort Inn-Carrier Circle	◇◇	$59-$134 SAVE	290
		EAST SYRACUSE - Restaurants			
34 / p. 629		Jalapeno's	◇	$5-$11	291
35 / p. 629		Justin's Grill	◇◇◇	$16-$29	292
36 / p. 629		Joey's Restaurant	◇◇◇	$12-$20	292
		FAYETTEVILLE - Lodgings			
44 / p. 629		Craftsman Inn	◇◇◇	$95-$165	296
		FAYETTEVILLE - Restaurants			
39 / p. 629		Craftsman Inn	◇◇◇	$14-$22	297
40 / p. 629		Arad Evans Inn	◇◇◇	$16-$25	296
		DE WITT - Lodgings			
47 / p. 629	AAA	Econo Lodge	◇◇	$70-$140 SAVE	285
		DE WITT - Restaurants			
43 / p. 629		Tokyo Seoul	◇◇	$9-$18	285
44 / p. 629		Scotch N' Sirloin	◇◇	$13-$40	285
45 / p. 629		Saratoga Steaks and Seafood	◇◇	$15-$30	285

SYRACUSE pop. 147,306 (See map and index starting on p. 629)—See also EAST SYRACUSE & NORTH SYRACUSE.

──── WHERE TO STAY ────

ECONO LODGE UNIVERSITY/DOWNTOWN
Book great rates at AAA.com
Phone: (315)425-0015
(AAA) (SAVE)
All Year   1P: $49-$299   2P: $49-$299   XP: $10   F17
♦♦♦
Motel
Location: Downtown. 454 James St 13203. Fax: 315/474-7009. **Facility:** 49 one-bedroom standard units. 3 stories, exterior corridors. *Bath:* combo or shower only. **Parking:** on-site. **Amenities:** high-speed Internet, safes, hair dryers. *Some:* DVD players (fee). **Guest Services:** area transportation-bus & train station, local hospitals. **Business Services:** PC. **Cards:** AX, DC, DS, MC, VI. **Free Special Amenities:** expanded continental breakfast and high-speed Internet.

SOME UNITS

(See map and index starting on p. 629)

JEFFERSON CLINTON HOTEL   *Book great rates at AAA.com*   Phone: (315)425-0500   **2**

(AAA) (SAVE)   All Year [BP]   1P: $129-$499   2P: $129-$499   XP: $10   F18

Location: Jct Jefferson St; downtown. 416 S Clinton St 13202. Fax: 315/472-4976. **Facility:** Smoke free premises. 68 units. 28 one-bedroom standard units, some with efficiencies. 40 one-bedroom suites with efficiencies, some with whirlpools. 11 stories, interior corridors. *Bath:* combo or shower only. **Parking:** on-

Small-scale Hotel   site. **Terms:** check-in 5 pm, cancellation fee imposed, package plans. **Amenities:** video library, DVD players, CD players, high-speed Internet, dual phone lines, voice mail, irons, hair dryers. **Leisure Activities:** exercise room. **Guest Services:** complimentary evening beverages: Tues, valet and coin laundry, wireless Internet. **Business Services:** meeting rooms. **Cards:** AX, CB, DC, DS, MC, VI. **Free Special Amenities: full breakfast and high-speed Internet.**

SOME UNITS

RENAISSANCE SYRACUSE HOTEL   *Book great rates at AAA.com*   Phone: 315/479-7000   **3**

(AAA) (SAVE)   8/2-11/27   1P: $152-$329   2P: $162-$339   XP: $10   F

5/1-8/1 & 11/28-4/30   1P: $145-$329   2P: $155-$339   XP: $10   F

Location: Jct Almond St; downtown. 701 E Genesee St 13210. Fax: 315/472-2700. **Facility:** 279 units. 276 one-bedroom standard units. 2 one- and 1 two-bedroom suites. 20 stories, interior corridors. *Bath:* shower only.

Large-scale Hotel   **Parking:** on-site. **Terms:** pets (small dogs only, $50 extra charge, in designated units). **Amenities:** high-speed Internet, dual phone lines, voice mail, safes, irons, hair dryers. **Dining:** Redfield's Restaurant, see separate listing. **Leisure Activities:** exercise room. *Fee:* massage. **Guest Services:** valet laundry, area transportation-local businesses within 5 mi, wireless Internet. **Business Services:** conference facilities, business center. **Cards:** AX, CB, DC, DS, JC, MC, VI.

SOME UNITS

FEE   FEE   FEE

SHERATON SYRACUSE UNIVERSITY HOTEL &

CONFERENCE CENTER   *Book great rates at AAA.com*   Phone: (315)475-3000   **4**

(AAA) (SAVE)   All Year   1P: $129-$409   2P: $129-$409   XP: $10   F12

Location: I-81, exit 18. Located at Syracuse University. 801 University Ave 13210. Fax: 315/475-2266. **Facility:** 236 units. 235 one-bedroom standard units. 1 one-bedroom suite with whirlpool. 9 stories, interior corridors.

Large-scale Hotel   *Bath:* combo or shower only. **Parking:** on-site (fee). **Terms:** cancellation fee imposed, pets (dogs only, in designated units). **Amenities:** high-speed Internet, dual phone lines, voice mail, irons, hair dryers. *Some:* fax, safes. **Dining:** 6:30 am-3 & 5-10 pm, cocktails. **Pool(s):** heated indoor. **Leisure Activities:** sauna, whirlpool, exercise room. **Guest Services:** gift shop, valet and coin laundry, airport transportation-Syracuse Hancock International Airport, wireless Internet. **Business Services:** conference facilities, business center. **Cards:** AX, CB, DC, DS, MC, VI. **Free Special Amenities: newspaper and high-speed Internet.**

SOME UNITS

FEE

WHERE TO DINE

AMBROSIA   **Lunch:** $6-$10   **Dinner:** $16-$30   Phone: 315/426-8800   **12**

Location: Jct S Franklin and Walton sts; in Armory Square. 201 Walton St 13202. **Hours:** 11:30 am-3 & 5-10 pm, Fri & Sat-10:30 pm, Sun 11 am-3 & 4-9 pm; Sunday brunch. Closed major holidays. **Reservations:** accepted. **Features:** Asian cuisine reflecting contemporary, Continental accents make the busy corner restaurant a hit with sushi and sashimi fans. Distinctively creative dishes incorporate exotic

Nouvelle Asian   ingredients for delight and mystery. The happy hour focuses on the great martini selection. Dressy casual; cocktails. **Parking:** street. **Cards:** AX, DC, DS, MC, VI.

ANTONIO'S RESTAURANT   **Lunch:** $7-$13   **Dinner:** $15-$30   Phone: 315/425-1946   **4**

Location: Jct E Division and N Salina sts. 700 N Salina St 13208. **Hours:** noon-2 & 5:30-10 pm, Sat from 5:30 pm. Closed major holidays; also Sun, except Mother's Day. **Reservations:** accepted. **Features:** This restaurant is a locally popular spot to enjoy traditional Italian dishes. The portions are large, the service is

Italian   friendly and the atmosphere is comfortable. Casual dress; cocktails. **Parking:** on-site. **Cards:** AX, MC, VI.

BISTRO 238   **Dinner:** $12-$20   Phone: 315/475-9463   **15**

Location: Center; across from Armory Square. 238 W Jefferson St 13202. **Hours:** 5 pm-9:30 pm, Fri & Sat-11 pm. Closed: 1/1, 11/22, 12/25; also Sun. **Reservations:** suggested. **Features:** The bistro is accommodating in its diverse menu selections. The warm and intimate atmosphere perfectly sets off the Continental choices.

Continental   The menu is changed seasonally to incorporate fresh ingredients. Desserts are fabulous. Casual dress; cocktails. **Parking:** street. **Cards:** AX, DC, DS, MC, VI.

THE BLUE TUSK PUB & WINE BAR   **Lunch:** $5-$8   **Dinner:** $7-$12   Phone: 315/472-1934   **13**

Location: Center; in Armory Square. 165 Walton St 13202. **Hours:** 11 am-11 pm. Closed major holidays; also Sun. **Features:** Among eclectic choices at the casual pub and wine bar are fine gourmet sandwiches, quesadillas, cheese and bread boards, quality salads, international specialty beers and an extensive list of

American   fine wines. Service is friendly. Casual dress; cocktails. **Parking:** on-site (fee) and street. **Cards:** AX, DS, MC, VI.

CASA DI COPANI   **Lunch:** $6-$9   **Dinner:** $10-$21   Phone: 315/463-1031   **3**

Location: Just w of Thompson Rd. 3414 Burnet Ave 13206. **Hours:** 11:30 am-10 pm, Fri & Sat-11 pm, Sun 2 pm-9 pm. Closed: 11/22, 12/25. **Reservations:** accepted. **Features:** Traditional and distinctive Italian dishes top the menu, which also lists prime steaks and delectable veal recipes that have won awards. The mood is

Italian   friendly in the cozy, relaxed dining room. Casual dress; cocktails. **Parking:** on-site. **Cards:** AX, DS, MC, VI.

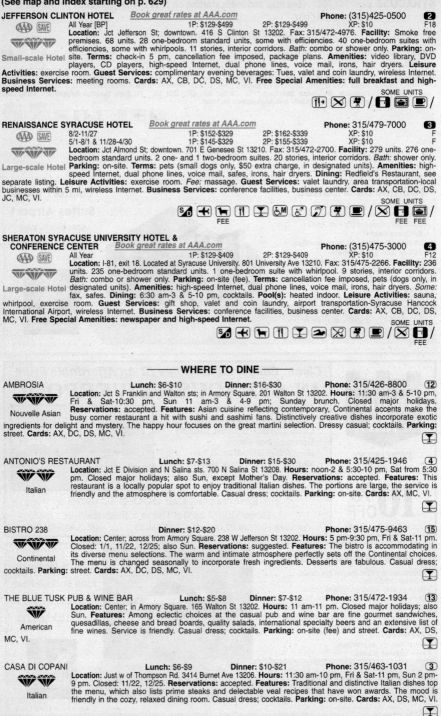

(See map and index starting on p. 629)

CHINA PAVILION   Lunch: $5-$8   Dinner: $6-$13   Phone: 315/488-2828   ⑰
▼▼▼
Asian   **Location:** I-81, exit I-690 W to exit 10 (Geddes St), then s, then w; in Westvale Plaza. 2318 W Genesee St 13219. **Hours:** 11:30 am-9 pm, Fri & Sat-10 pm. Closed major holidays. **Features:** Among cuisines sampled on the extensive menu are Hunan, Cantonese, Peking and Szechuan. Tangerine beef and the treasure-of-the-sea casserole are particularly flavorful. A luncheon buffet is served daily, and dim sum lunch is a Sunday tradition. Casual dress; beer & wine only. **Parking:** on-site. **Cards:** AX, DS, MC, VI.

COLEMAN'S AUTHENTIC IRISH PUB &
RESTAURANT   Lunch: $5-$9   Dinner: $11-$18   Phone: 315/476-1933   ⑪
▲▲▲
▼▼ ▼▼ ▼▼   **Location:** On Tipperary Hill. 100 S Lowell Ave 13204. **Hours:** 11:30 am-10 pm, Fri & Sat-11 pm, Sun noon-9 pm.
Irish   Closed: 11/22, 12/25. **Reservations:** suggested. **Features:** Adding to the cozy, traditional Irish pub decor is a special leprechaun's door. Celtic and regional Irish dishes are served in a bustling atmosphere. Locals often order daily "pub pie" specials, and "green" beer in March makes for a lucky year. Casual dress; cocktails. **Parking:** on-site. **Cards:** AX, DC, DS, MC, VI.   ⵂ

DANZER'S RESTAURANT   Lunch: $3-$7   Dinner: $10-$14   Phone: 315/422-0089   ⑲
▲▲▲
▼▼▼ ▼▼   **Location:** I-81, exit 17, 0.7 mi s on E Brighton Ave, then just e. 153 Ainsley Dr 13210. **Hours:** 11 am-11 pm, Fri &
German   Sat-midnight, Sun noon-11 pm. Closed: 1/1, 11/22, 12/25. **Reservations:** accepted. **Features:** German and American specialties, ranging from steak and seafood to bratwurst and Wiener schnitzel, make up the family-oriented restaurant's menu. In business since 1946, this place resembles a Bavarian chalet. Service is casual but capable. Casual dress; cocktails. **Parking:** on-site. **Cards:** AX, DS, MC, VI.   ⵂ

DINOSAUR BAR-B-QUE   Lunch: $7-$15   Dinner: $10-$25   Phone: 315/476-4937   ⑤
▼▼▼
American   **Location:** Jct Franklin St; downtown. 246 W Willow St 13202. **Hours:** 11 am-midnight, Fri & Sat-1 am, Sun 2 pm-9 pm. Closed major holidays. **Features:** The restaurant is just what you expect: great tasting pork, beef and chicken barbecue, all smokey and delicious. Featuring rough and rustic decor with music and blues offered six nights a week. Casual dress; cocktails. **Parking:** street. **Cards:** AX, DC, DS, MC, VI.   ⵂ

JUANITA'S MEXICAN KITCHEN   Lunch: $5-$10   Dinner: $5-$12   Phone: 315/478-2185   ①
▼▼
Mexican   **Location:** Jct Spring St. 600 Court St 13208. **Hours:** 11:30 am-1:45 & 5-9 pm, Thurs-Sat to 9:30 pm. Closed major holidays; also Sun. **Features:** Modest, casual dining is the mode in the award-winning Mexican/Southwestern restaurant. Traditional dishes are made promptly from fresh ingredients. Casual dress; cocktails. **Parking:** on-site. **Cards:** DS, MC, VI.

KITTY HOYNES   Lunch: $5-$9   Dinner: $8-$19   Phone: 315/424-1974   ⑩
▼▼ ▼▼
Irish   **Location:** Jct Franklin St; downtown. 301 W Fayette St 13202. **Hours:** 11 am-10 pm, Fri & Sat-11 pm. Closed major holidays; also Sun. **Reservations:** accepted. **Features:** Guests can enjoy the ambience of an Irish country cottage while dining on generous portions of creatively prepared food. Warm hospitality envelops the pub, which incorporates authentic Irish artifacts, a mahogany bar, stained glass and gilded mirrors into its decor. Live Irish/Celtic music lends to the atmosphere. Casual dress; cocktails. **Parking:** street. **Cards:** AX, DC, DS, MC, VI.   ⵂ

L'ADOUR   Lunch: $8-$12   Dinner: $19-$30   Phone: 315/475-7653   ⑦
▲▲▲
▼▼▼ ▼▼   **Location:** Jct Washington St; downtown. 110 Montgomery St 13202. **Hours:** 8 am-2 & 5-9 pm, Fri-10 pm, Sat 8
French   am-10 pm, Sun 8 am-2 & 5-8 pm. Closed major holidays. **Reservations:** suggested. **Features:** Classic French cuisine is created from fresh, quality ingredients and presented in artistic harmony for an impressive, tantalizing experience. An extensive French wine list complements the a la carte choices offered in the bistro or the prix fixe menus presented in the formal upstairs restaurant. Dressy casual; cocktails. **Parking:** on-site (fee) and street. **Cards:** AX, DC, DS, MC, VI.   ⵂ⮾ ⵂ

LEMON GRASS   Lunch: $6-$8   Dinner: $14-$20   Phone: 315/475-1111   ⑭
▼▼▼ ▼▼▼
Thai   **Location:** Center; across from Armory Square. 238 W Jefferson St 13202. **Hours:** 11:30 am-2:30 & 5-9:30 pm, Fri & Sat-11 pm, Sun 4:30 pm-9:30 pm. Closed: 1/1, 11/22, 12/25. **Reservations:** suggested. **Features:** Adventuresome diners are treated to a casual atmosphere, intriguing foods with unusual flavor combinations and an extensive wine list. Modern decor, traditional and innovative Thai cuisine choices and Pook Chutinthramond's fabulous dessert all combine to bring guests the quintessential dining event, be it for lunch or dinner. Casual dress; cocktails. **Parking:** street. **Cards:** AX, DC, DS, MC, VI.

MIMI'S BAKERY & CAFE   Lunch: $2-$7   Phone: 315/422-6630   ⑥
▼▼
American   **Location:** I-81, exit Adam St to State northbound, just w on Erie Blvd; exit West and Franklin sts southbound, follow to downtown; across from Clinton Exchange. 260 W Genesee St 13202. **Hours:** 6:30 am-4 pm, Sat 6 am-2 pm. Closed major holidays; also Sun. **Features:** Baked goods are outstanding at the cozy cafe, a favorite for light delicatessen fare. Sandwiches, soups, salads and daily specials have brought this place its devoted clientele. Sidewalk seating lets diners engage in people-watching. Casual dress. **Parking:** on-site. **Cards:** AX, MC, VI.

PASCALE WINE BAR AND RESTAURANT   Dinner: $14-$24   Phone: 315/471-3040   ⑧
▼▼▼ ▼▼▼
American   **Location:** Corner of Clinton and W Fayette sts; downtown. 204 W Fayette St 13202. **Hours:** 5:30 pm-9 pm, Fri & Sat-10:30 pm, Sun 5 pm-8 pm. Closed major holidays. **Reservations:** suggested. **Features:** An extensive wine list complements with rare vintages complements such savory choices as duck breast, venison and king salmon. Stucco walls with original artwork, an open kitchen and marble finishes lend to the contemporary atmosphere. Dressy casual; cocktails. **Parking:** on-site (fee) and valet. **Cards:** AX, DC, MC, VI.   ⵂ

(See map and index starting on p. 629)

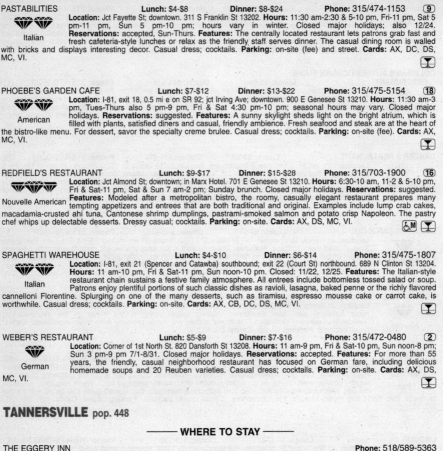

PASTABILITIES   **Lunch:** $4-$8   **Dinner:** $8-$24   **Phone:** 315/474-1153   ⑨
Italian   **Location:** Jct Fayette St; downtown. 311 S Franklin St 13202. **Hours:** 11:30 am-2:30 & 5-10 pm, Fri-11 pm, Sat 5 pm-11 pm, Sun 5 pm-10 pm; hours vary in winter. Closed major holidays; also 12/24. **Reservations:** accepted, Sun-Thurs. **Features:** The centrally located restaurant lets patrons grab fast and fresh cafeteria-style lunches or relax as the friendly staff serves dinner. The casual dining room is walled with bricks and displays interesting decor. Casual dress; cocktails. **Parking:** on-site (fee) and street. **Cards:** AX, DC, DS, MC, VI.

PHOEBE'S GARDEN CAFE   **Lunch:** $7-$12   **Dinner:** $13-$22   **Phone:** 315/475-5154   ⑱
American   **Location:** I-81, exit 18, 0.5 mi e on SR 92; jct Irving Ave; downtown. 900 E Genesee St 13210. **Hours:** 11:30 am-3 pm, Tues-Thurs also 5 pm-9 pm, Fri & Sat 4:30 pm-11 pm; seasonal hours may vary. Closed major holidays. **Reservations:** suggested. **Features:** A sunny skylight sheds light on the bright atrium, which is filled with plants, satisfied diners and casual, friendly ambience. Fresh seafood and steak are at the heart of the bistro-like menu. For dessert, savor the specialty creme brulee. Casual dress; cocktails. **Parking:** on-site (fee). **Cards:** AX, MC, VI.

REDFIELD'S RESTAURANT   **Lunch:** $9-$17   **Dinner:** $15-$28   **Phone:** 315/703-1900   ⑯
Nouvelle American   **Location:** Jct Almond St; downtown; in Marx Hotel. 701 E Genesee St 13210. **Hours:** 6:30-10 am, 11-2 & 5-10 pm, Fri & Sat-11 pm, Sat & Sun 7 am-2 pm; Sunday brunch. Closed major holidays. **Reservations:** suggested. **Features:** Modeled after a metropolitan bistro, the roomy, casually elegant restaurant prepares many tempting appetizers and entrees that are both traditional and original. Examples include lump crab cakes, macadamia-crusted ahi tuna, Cantonese shrimp dumplings, pastrami-smoked salmon and potato crisp Napoleon. The pastry chef whips up delectable desserts. Dressy casual; cocktails. **Parking:** on-site. **Cards:** AX, DS, MC, VI.

SPAGHETTI WAREHOUSE   **Lunch:** $4-$10   **Dinner:** $6-$14   **Phone:** 315/475-1807
Italian   **Location:** I-81, exit 21 (Spencer and Catawba) southbound; exit 22 (Court St) northbound. 689 N Clinton St 13204. **Hours:** 11 am-10 pm, Fri & Sat-11 pm, Sun noon-10 pm. Closed: 11/22, 12/25. **Features:** The Italian-style restaurant chain sustains a festive family atmosphere. All entrees include bottomless tossed salad or soup. Patrons enjoy plentiful portions of such classic dishes as ravioli, lasagna, baked penne or the richly flavored cannelloni Florentine. Splurging on one of the many desserts, such as tiramisu, espresso mousse cake or carrot cake, is worthwhile. Casual dress; cocktails. **Parking:** on-site. **Cards:** AX, CB, DC, DS, MC, VI.

WEBER'S RESTAURANT   **Lunch:** $5-$9   **Dinner:** $7-$16   **Phone:** 315/472-0480   ②
German   **Location:** Corner of 1st North St. 820 Dansforth St 13208. **Hours:** 11 am-9 pm, Fri & Sat-10 pm, Sun noon-8 pm; Sun 3 pm-9 pm 7/1-8/31. Closed major holidays. **Reservations:** accepted. **Features:** For more than 55 years, the friendly, casual neighborhood restaurant has focused on German fare, including delicious homemade soups and 20 Reuben varieties. Casual dress; cocktails. **Parking:** on-site. **Cards:** AX, DS, MC, VI.

TANNERSVILLE pop. 448

―――――― **WHERE TO STAY** ――――――

THE EGGERY INN   **Phone:** 518/589-5363
Bed & Breakfast   Property failed to provide current rates
Location: Jct SR 23A and CR 16, 1.1 mi s. Located in a rural area. 288 Platte Clove Rd (CR 16) 12485. **Fax:** 518/589-5774. **Facility:** Smoke free premises. 15 one-bedroom standard units. 3 stories (no elevator), interior corridors. *Bath:* combo or shower only. **Parking:** on-site. **Amenities:** voice mail, hair dryers.

―――――― **WHERE TO DINE** ――――――

LAST CHANCE ANTIQUES & CHEESE CAFE   **Lunch:** $6-$11   **Dinner:** $8-$16   **Phone:** 518/589-6424
American   **Location:** Center. 602 Main St 12485. **Hours:** 11 am-9 pm; Fri & Sat-9:30 pm 6/16-9/14 & 12/13-3/31. Closed: Mon-Thurs 4/1-6/15 & 9/15-12/12. **Features:** The eclectic eatery has it all—great food, more than 300 beers and 50 cheese selections. The upbeat dining room is hung with old brass instruments. Porch-sidewalk seating is available. Casual dress; cocktails. **Parking:** street. **Cards:** AX, DS, MC, VI.

TARRYTOWN —See New York p. 504.

THENDARA

―――――― **WHERE TO DINE** ――――――

VAN AUKEN'S INNE   **Lunch:** $5-$9   **Dinner:** $10-$18   **Phone:** 315/369-3033
American   **Location:** Just behind Thendara Train Station on SR 28. 108 Forge St 13472. **Hours:** noon-9 pm, Fri & Sat-10 pm. Closed: 11/22, 12/25. **Reservations:** suggested. **Features:** The tastefully restored, turn-of-the-20th-century inn has hardwood floors, decorative wood moldings, pressed-tin ceilings and an understated decor. Popular American fare and Italian specialties topped off with decadent desserts make for a pleasant dining experience. Casual dress; cocktails. **Parking:** on-site. **Cards:** AX, DS, MC, VI.

TICONDEROGA pop. 5,167—*See also ADIRONDACK MOUNTAINS.*

——— WHERE TO STAY ———

CIRCLE COURT MOTEL
Phone: (518)585-7660

AAA SAVE

Motel

	5/25-10/28	1P: $69-$79	2P: $76-$84	XP: $8	F12
	5/1-5/24	1P: $62-$68	2P: $68-$74	XP: $8	F12
	10/29-4/30	1P: $55-$61	2P: $60-$66	XP: $8	F12

Location: SR 9N; at Liberty Monument traffic circle. 6 Montcalm St 12883. Fax: 518/585-3560. **Facility:** 14 one-bedroom standard units. 1-2 stories (no elevator), exterior corridors. *Bath:* combo or shower only. **Parking:** on-site, winter plug-ins. **Cards:** AX, MC, VI. **Free Special Amenities: local telephone calls and high-speed Internet.**

SOME UNITS

STONE HOUSE MOTEL & MOTOR LODGE
Phone: 518/585-7394

AAA SAVE

Motel

| | 5/1-10/31 | 1P: $55-$105 | 2P: $55-$105 |
| | 11/1-4/30 | 1P: $45-$65 | 2P: $45-$65 |

Location: SR 9N, just s of Liberty Monument traffic circle. 9 Montcalm St 12883. Fax: 518/585-7394. **Facility:** 23 units. 20 one- and 3 two-bedroom standard units, some with kitchens. 1-2 stories, interior/exterior corridors. *Bath:* combo or shower only. **Parking:** on-site. **Terms:** 3 day cancellation notice, weekly rates available, package plans. **Amenities:** *Some:* DVD players. **Pool(s):** heated outdoor. **Leisure Activities:** gas & charcoal grills, picnic area, gazebo. **Guest Services:** coin laundry, area transportation-Amtrak Station, wireless Internet. **Business Services:** fax (fee). **Cards:** AX, DC, DS, MC, VI. **Free Special Amenities: local telephone calls and high-speed Internet.**

SOME UNITS

TONAWANDA —*See Buffalo p. 262.*

TROY pop. 49,170 (See map and index starting on p. 218)

——— WHERE TO STAY ———

BEST WESTERN-RENSSELAER INN   *Book great rates at AAA.com*
Phone: (518)274-3210   **23**

AAA SAVE

Small-scale Hotel

| | All Year [BP] | 1P: $84-$89 | 2P: $89-$99 | XP: $5 | F16 |

Location: I-787, exit 9, 0.5 mi e, exit downtown, then 0.5 mi s. 1800 6th Ave 12180. Fax: 518/274-3294. **Facility:** 153 units. 152 one-bedroom standard units. 1 one-bedroom suite. 4 stories, interior corridors. **Parking:** on-site. **Terms:** cancellation fee imposed. **Amenities:** high-speed Internet, irons, hair dryers. **Dining:** 6 am-9:30 & 5-9 pm, Sat & Sun 7 am-11 & 5-9 pm, cocktails. **Pool(s):** outdoor. **Leisure Activities:** exercise room. *Fee:* game room. **Guest Services:** coin laundry, area transportation-train & bus station. **Business Services:** conference facilities. **Cards:** AX, CB, DC, DS, JC, MC, VI. **Free Special Amenities: full breakfast and high-speed Internet.**

SOME UNITS
FEE

FRANKLIN SQUARE INN & SUITES
Phone: (518)274-8800   **22**

AAA SAVE

Small-scale Hotel

| | All Year | 1P: $106-$189 | 2P: $106-$189 | XP: $10 | F18 |

Location: I-787, exit 8, just e on 23rd to Federal, just e to 4th St, then just s; downtown. One 4th St 12180. Fax: 518/274-0427. **Facility:** 62 one-bedroom standard units, some with whirlpools. 3 stories, interior corridors. *Bath:* combo or shower only. **Parking:** on-site. **Terms:** [ECP] meal plan available. **Amenities:** voice mail, irons, hair dryers. *Some:* dual phone lines. **Guest Services:** coin laundry, wireless Internet. **Business Services:** meeting rooms. **Cards:** AX, CB, DC, DS, JC, MC, VI. **Free Special Amenities: expanded continental breakfast and newspaper.**

SOME UNITS
FEE

——— WHERE TO DINE ———

DAISY BAKERS
Lunch: $8-$12   **Dinner:** $15-$35   Phone: 518/266-9200   **16**

American

Location: Downtown. 33 2nd St 12180. **Hours:** 11:30 am-3 & 5-9 pm, Fri & Sat 5 pm-10 pm. Closed major holidays; also Sun. **Reservations:** suggested. **Features:** In an 1892 brownstone, the restaurant—with its heavy, dark oaks and stained and leaded glass—provides a historic setting for pleasant dining. Local purveyors provide the fresh ingredients necessary for tasty dishes. Casual dress; cocktails. **Parking:** street. **Cards:** AX, DS, MC, VI.

HOLMES & WATSON LTD
Lunch: $5-$8   **Dinner:** $11-$15   Phone: 518/273-8526   **15**

American

Location: Downtown. 450 Broadway 12180. **Hours:** 11 am-10 pm, Fri & Sat-11 pm. Closed major holidays; also Sun. **Reservations:** accepted. **Features:** The historic pub atmosphere is themed around Sherlock Holmes. Widely varied menu items are named after book characters or places. Patrons can choose from 70 malt scotches and a world tour beer list with more than 200 selections. Casual style and service surrounded by period decor makes for an interesting meal. Casual dress; cocktails. **Parking:** street. **Cards:** AX, DC, DS, MC, VI. **Historic**

TRUMANSBURG pop. 1,581—*See also FINGER LAKES.*

─────── WHERE TO STAY ───────

TAUGHANNOCK FARMS INN [ECP]   Phone: 607/387-7711

Historic
Country Inn

5/25-9/3 [ECP]	2P: $105-$440	XP: $25	F
9/4-1/1 & 4/1-4/30 [ECP]	2P: $85-$400	XP: $25	F
5/1-5/24 [ECP]	2P: $85-$395	XP: $25	F

Location: From Ithaca, 10 mi n on SR 89. Located next to a state park. 2030 Gorge Rd 14886. Fax: 607/387-7721. **Facility:** The inn offers accommodations in an 1873 Victorian mansion overlooking Cayuga Lake. Smoke free premises. 21 one-bedroom standard units. 2 stories (no elevator), interior/exterior corridors. *Bath:* combo or shower only. **Parking:** on-site. **Terms:** open 5/1-1/1 & 4/1-4/30, cancellation fee imposed. **Amenities:** CD players, voice mail, hair dryers. *Some:* DVD players. **Dining:** restaurant, see separate listing. **Cards:** AX, DS, MC, VI.

SOME UNITS

─────── WHERE TO DINE ───────

TAUGHANNOCK FARMS INN   **Dinner: $24-$38**   Phone: 607/387-7711

Regional American

Location: From Ithaca, 10 mi n on SR 89; in Taughannock Farms Inn. 2030 Gorge Rd 14886. **Hours:** Open 5/1-12/31 & 4/1-4/30; 5 pm-9 pm, Sun 3 pm-8 pm; hours vary in winter. **Reservations:** suggested. **Features:** Overlooking Cayuga Lake, the 1873 Victorian estate is loaded with quaint charm. In addition to such flavorful entrees as prime rib, roast duck, fresh fish and roast turkey, the restaurant serves an excellent chilled strawberry soup. Dinner is prix fixe. Dinner served on New Years Eve. Dressy casual; cocktails. **Parking:** on-site. **Cards:** AX, DS, MC, VI. **Historic**

TULLY pop. 924

─────── WHERE TO STAY ───────

BEST WESTERN TULLY INN   *Book great rates at AAA.com*   Phone: (315)696-6061

Small-scale Hotel

All Year [ECP]	1P: $89-$209	2P: $89-$209	XP: $5	F12

Location: I-81, exit 14, just e. 5779 Rt 80 13159 (PO Box 156). Fax: 315/696-6406. **Facility:** Smoke free premises. 44 one-bedroom standard units, some with whirlpools. 2 stories (no elevator), interior corridors. **Parking:** on-site. **Amenities:** high-speed Internet, voice mail, irons, hair dryers. **Guest Services:** valet laundry. **Cards:** AX, CB, DC, DS, JC, MC, VI. **Free Special Amenities: expanded continental breakfast and high-speed Internet.**

TUPPER LAKE pop. 3,935—*See also ADIRONDACK MOUNTAINS.*

─────── WHERE TO STAY ───────

RED TOP INN   Phone: (518)359-9209

Motel

All Year	1P: $50-$70	2P: $55-$85	XP: $5	F15

Location: 3 mi s. 1562 SR 30 12986. **Facility:** 20 units. 12 one-bedroom standard units. 4 two-bedroom suites ($75-$95) with efficiencies. 4 cabins ($50-$55). 2 stories (no elevator), interior/exterior corridors. *Bath:* combo or shower only. **Parking:** on-site, winter plug-ins. **Terms:** 2 night minimum stay - seasonal and/or weekends, 3 day cancellation notice, weekly rates available, pets (in cabins). **Leisure Activities:** boat dock, fishing. **Cards:** AX, CB, DC, DS, JC, MC, VI. **Free Special Amenities: local telephone calls and newspaper.**

SOME UNITS

SHAHEEN'S MOTEL   Phone: 518-359-3384

Motel

6/15-10/9	1P: $62-$85	2P: $70-$89	XP: $6	F5
12/19-4/30	1P: $58-$78	2P: $65-$87	XP: $6	F5
5/1-6/14 & 10/10-12/18	1P: $58-$74	2P: $64-$75	XP: $6	F5

Location: 0.8 mi e on SR 3/30. 314 Park St 12986. Fax: 518/359-3384. **Facility:** 31 one-bedroom standard units. 2 stories (no elevator), exterior corridors. *Bath:* combo or shower only. **Parking:** on-site, winter plug-ins. **Terms:** 2 night minimum stay - seasonal and/or weekends, 3 day cancellation notice-fee imposed, [CP] meal plan available. **Amenities:** irons, hair dryers. **Pool(s):** outdoor. **Leisure Activities:** picnic area, playground. *Fee:* miniature golf. **Cards:** AX, DS, MC, VI. **Free Special Amenities: continental breakfast and high-speed Internet.**

SOME UNITS

TUPPER LAKE MOTEL   Phone: (518)359-3381

Motel

All Year [CP]	1P: $50-$75	2P: $55-$85	XP: $6	F3

Location: 0.5 mi e on SR 3/30. 255 Park St 12986. Fax: 518/359-8549. **Facility:** 18 one-bedroom standard units. 1 story, exterior corridors. *Bath:* shower only. **Parking:** on-site, winter plug-ins. **Terms:** 2 night minimum stay - weekends, 3 day cancellation notice, package plans. **Pool(s):** outdoor. **Leisure Activities:** picnic table. **Cards:** AX, DS, MC, VI. **Free Special Amenities: continental breakfast and local telephone calls.**

SOME UNITS

─────── WHERE TO DINE ───────

─────── *The following restaurant has not been evaluated by AAA* ───────
but is listed for your information only.

THE WAWBEEK RESTAURANT   Phone: 518/359-2656

[fyi] Not evaluated. **Location:** 553 Panther Mountain Rd (SR 30) 12986. **Features:** Guests can let their eyes bathe in the beauty that surrounds the sprawling, 40-acre resort in the heart of the Adirondacks. The setting is the driving force behind the inspired menu. Reservations are required.

Pick a destination.
Any destination.

Wherever you're headed, there's always
a Choice hotel that fits your travel plans
and budget. And, as a AAA/CAA member,
you'll save at over 4,000 Choice hotels
across the U.S. Plus, it's easy to earn
nights or flights with our reward
programs.* Just contact your local
AAA/CAA office, call 800.228.1222 or
visit choicehotels.com to book.

choicehotels.com
800.228.1222

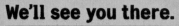

We'll see you there.
CHOICE HOTELS INTERNATIONAL®

We'll see you there.
CHOICE HOTELS INTERNATIONAL®

RODEWAY INN®
Econo Lodge®
MainStay Suites™
CAMBRIA SUITES®
Clarion®
SLEEP INN®
Quality®
Comfort SUITES®
Comfort INN®

Visit your local AAA/CAA office or call **800.228.1222** to book your next stay.

UNIONDALE pop. 23,011

------ **WHERE TO STAY** ------

LONG ISLAND MARRIOTT HOTEL & CONFERENCE
CENTER   *Book great rates at AAA.com*   **Phone:** (516)794-3800
▼▼▼▼   All Year   1P: $169-$299
       Location: Meadowbrook Pkwy, exit M4 (follow signs to coliseum), exit Hempstead Tpke W; in financial district. Located
Large-scale Hotel next to Nassau Coliseum. 101 James Doolittle Blvd 11553. Fax: 516/794-5936. **Facility:** Smoke free premises.
618 units. 610 one-bedroom standard units. 8 one-bedroom suites. 11 stories, interior corridors. **Parking:**
on-site and valet. **Terms:** check-in 4 pm. **Amenities:** high-speed Internet (fee), dual phone lines, voice mail, irons, hair dryers.
Some: CD players. **Pool(s):** heated indoor. **Leisure Activities:** saunas, whirlpool, racquetball courts. *Fee:* massage. **Guest**
Services: gift shop, valet and coin laundry, beauty salon. **Business Services:** conference facilities, business center.
Cards: AX, CB, DC, DS, MC, VI.

SOME UNITS
(ASK) (S/D) ⊟ (Ψ) (Y) (🦢) (✦) (⊠) (⊠) (🎬) (▭) / (VCR) (⊟) (▦) /
FEE

UTICA pop. 60,651

------ **WHERE TO STAY** ------

BEST WESTERN GATEWAY ADIRONDACK INN	*Book great rates at AAA.com*		**Phone:** (315)732-4121	
▼▼▼	7/1-8/31	1P: $99-$169	2P: $109-$169	XP: $10	F18
	9/1-10/31	1P: $89-$129	2P: $99-$139	XP: $10	F18
	5/1-6/30	1P: $79-$129	2P: $89-$139	XP: $10	F18
Small-scale Hotel	11/1-4/30	1P: $69-$99	2P: $79-$109	XP: $10	F18

Location: I-90 (New York State Thruway), exit 31, 0.5 mi s. 175 N Genesee St 13502. Fax: 315/797-8265. **Facility:** 89 units. 88 one-
bedroom standard units. 1 one-bedroom suite ($129-$275) with efficiency. 1-2 stories (no elevator), interior corridors. **Parking:**
on-site, winter plug-ins. **Terms:** pets ($10 fee). **Amenities:** irons, hair dryers. **Leisure Activities:** limited exercise equipment.
Fee: game room. **Guest Services:** sundries, valet and coin laundry. **Business Services:** meeting rooms, PC. **Cards:** AX, CB,
DC, DS, JC, MC, VI. *(See color ad below)*

SOME UNITS
(ASK) (S/D) (🐑) (Ψ🔥) (🚭) (▭) / (⊠) (⊟) (▦) /
FEE

COUNTRY MOTEL			**Phone:** 315/732-4628	
(AAA) (SAVE)	5/1-10/31	1P: $40-$78	2P: $55-$78	XP: $10	F16
▼▼▼	11/1-4/30	1P: $36-$55	2P: $46-$68	XP: $10	F16
Motel				

Location: I-90 (New York State Thruway), exit 31, 2 mi e on SR 5. 1477 Herkimer Rd 13502. Fax: 315/733-8801.
Facility: 25 one-bedroom standard units. 1 story, exterior corridors. *Bath:* combo or shower only. **Parking:**
on-site, winter plug-ins. **Cards:** AX, DS, MC, VI. **Free Special Amenities:** room upgrade and preferred
room (each subject to availability with advance reservations).

SOME UNITS
(▭) / (⊠) (⊟) /

HOTEL UTICA	*Book at AAA.com*		**Phone:** (315)724-7829	
▼▼▼	5/1-10/31 [CP]	1P: $99-$139	2P: $99-$139	XP: $15
	11/1-4/30 [CP]	1P: $89-$129	2P: $89-$129	XP: $15

Location: I-90 (New York State Thruway), exit 31, 1.1 mi s on Genesee St. 102 Lafayette St 13502.
Historic   Fax: 315/733-7621. **Facility:** The 1912 landmark hotel has been meticulously restored to turn-of-the-20th-
Large-scale Hotel century sophisticated elegance. Upscale appointments, modern amenities. 111 units. 97 one-bedroom
standard units. 14 one-bedroom suites ($139-$199), some with whirlpools. 9 stories, interior corridors. *Bath:* combo or shower
only. **Parking:** on-site. **Terms:** check-in 4 pm, cancellation fee imposed. **Amenities:** video games (fee), dual phone lines, voice
mail, irons, hair dryers. **Guest Services:** valet laundry. **Business Services:** conference facilities. **Cards:** AX, DC, DS, MC, VI.

SOME UNITS
(ASK) (S/D) (Ψ) (Y) (&) (🚭) (✦) (🎬) (▭) / (⊠) (VCR) (⊟) /

RADISSON HOTEL-UTICA CENTRE   *Book great rates at AAA.com*   Phone: (315)797-8010

AAA SAVE   All Year   1P: $129-$199   2P: $129-$199   XP: $10   F17

◇◇◇   **Location:** Downtown. 200 Genesee St 13502. Fax: 315/797-1490. **Facility:** 162 one-bedroom standard units. 6 stories, interior corridors. **Parking:** on-site (fee). **Amenities:** video games, high-speed Internet, dual phone lines, voice mail, irons, hair dryers. **Dining:** 6:30 am-10 pm, cocktails. **Pool(s):** heated indoor. **Leisure**

Large-scale Hotel   **Activities:** sauna, whirlpool, exercise room. *Fee:* game room. **Guest Services:** valet and coin laundry, wireless Internet. **Business Services:** conference facilities, business center. **Cards:** AX, CB, DC, DS, JC, MC, VI. **Free Special Amenities: newspaper and high-speed Internet.** *(See color ad below)*

SOME UNITS

🅂 🐾 🎤 🍽 🍸 🏊 ⊗ 🏃 💻 / ⊗ 📼 📠 📧 /
FEE   FEE

RED ROOF INN #7180   *Book at AAA.com*   Phone: (315)724-7128

◇◇◇   6/15-10/27   1P: $76-$99   2P: $82-$105   XP: $6   F18
        5/1-6/14   1P: $63-$73   2P: $69-$89   XP: $6   F18

Motel   10/28-4/30   1P: $54-$73   2P: $60-$79   XP: $6   F18

Location: I-90 (New York State Thruway), exit 31. 20 Weaver St 13502. Fax: 315/724-7158. **Facility:** 112 one-bedroom standard units. 2 stories (no elevator), exterior corridors. **Parking:** on-site. **Terms:** small pets only. **Amenities:** video games, voice mail. **Cards:** AX, CB, DC, DS, MC, VI.

SOME UNITS

🐾 🎤 / ⊗ 📠 📧 /
FEE FEE

ROSEMONT INN BED & BREAKFAST   *Book great rates at AAA.com*   Phone: 315/790-9315

AAA SAVE   5/1-10/31 [BP]   1P: $109-$159   2P: $119-$169   XP: $20
◇◇◇   11/1-4/30 [BP]   1P: $89-$135   2P: $99-$145   XP: $20

Location: I-90 (New York State Thruway), exit 31, 2.5 mi s. 1423 Genesee St 13501. Fax: 315/292-6852. **Facility:** Claw-foot tubs and quality antique period furnishings distinguish this 1860 Italianate-style Victorian

Historic Bed   B&B. Smoke free premises. 7 one-bedroom standard units. 2 stories (no elevator), interior corridors.

& Breakfast   **Parking:** on-site. **Terms:** 2 night minimum stay - seasonal and/or weekends, age restrictions may apply, 7 day cancellation notice-fee imposed. **Amenities:** CD players, hair dryers. **Guest Services:** TV in common area, wireless Internet. **Cards:** AX, DS, MC, VI. **Free Special Amenities: full breakfast and high-speed Internet.**

🅂 ⊗ 📺 📧

SCOTTISH INNS   *Book great rates at AAA.com*   Phone: (315)735-6698

AAA SAVE   6/16-10/27 [CP]   1P: $45-$65   2P: $50-$95   XP: $5   D10
◇   5/1-6/15 [CP]   1P: $40-$49   2P: $50-$60   XP: $5   D10

Motel   10/28-4/30 [CP]   1P: $30-$50   2P: $40-$60   XP: $5   D10

Location: I-90 (New York State Thruway), exit 31, just s. 238 N Genesee St 13502. **Facility:** 20 one-bedroom standard units. 2 stories (no elevator), interior corridors. **Parking:** on-site. **Terms:** 3 day cancellation notice-fee imposed, weekly rates available, package plans, pets (no cats). **Cards:** AX, DC, DS, MC, VI.

Free Special Amenities: local telephone calls and early check-in/late check-out.

SOME UNITS

🅂 🐾 🎤 / ⊗ 📧 /

Easy, hassle-free vehicle battery testing or replacement

A battery jump gets you on your way fast ... but then what? Another breakdown? A trip to the garage for a new battery? AAA Battery Service provides members on-the-scene battery testing and replacement at competitive prices.

Call **800-AAA-HELP** to find out how it works!*

This service is not available in all areas. Contact your AAA representative for details.

Emergency Services

———— **WHERE TO DINE** ————

BABE'S MACARONI GRILL & BAR   **Lunch:** $5-$10   **Dinner:** $6-$18   **Phone:** 315/735-0777
American
Location: I-90 (New York State Thruway), exit 31, 0.8 mi s. 80 N Genesee St 13501. **Hours:** 11 am-midnight, Thurs-Sat to 1 am. Closed: 11/22, 12/25. **Reservations:** accepted. **Features:** The atmosphere is often boisterous at the bustling restaurant, which is decorated with a wide array of memorabilia and movie posters. The broad menu includes chicken, beef and fish dishes, as well as Mexican fare. Service is casual and friendly. Casual dress; cocktails. **Parking:** on-site. **Cards:** AX, CB, DC, DS, MC, VI.

BEI JING HOUSE   **Lunch:** $4-$5   **Dinner:** $4-$10   **Phone:** 315/797-3388
Chinese
Location: 0.5 mi s; center. 1506 Genesee St 13502. **Hours:** 11 am-11 pm, Fri & Sat-midnight, Sun noon-10 pm. Closed: 11/22. **Features:** Menu favorites are cooked in an open kitchen while patrons wait or order take-out. This place is just a short hop from central downtown. Casual dress. **Parking:** on-site. **Cards:** MC, VI.

DELMONICO'S ITALIAN STEAKHOUSE   **Dinner:** $9-$20   **Phone:** 315/732-2300
Italian
Location: I-90 (New York State Thruway), exit 31, 0.6 mi s. 147 N Genesee St 13502. **Hours:** 4 pm-10:30 pm, Fri-11:30 pm, Sat 2 pm-11:30 pm, Sun noon-10 pm. Closed: 11/22, 12/25. **Reservations:** accepted. **Features:** Guests can "dine with the stars" in a room surrounded by caricatures of famous people. The traditional restaurant has a casually upscale feel. The real crowd-pleaser is the 24-ounce Delmonico steak meal. Casual dress; cocktails. **Parking:** on-site. **Cards:** AX, DC, DS, MC, VI.

DOMINIQUE'S CHESTERFIELD RESTAURANT   **Lunch:** $7-$10   **Dinner:** $11-$19   **Phone:** 315/732-9356
Italian
Location: At Niagara St. 1713 Bleecker St 13501. **Hours:** 11:30 am-10 pm. Closed: 12/25. **Reservations:** accepted. **Features:** Since 1988, the family-owned restaurant has been known for its traditional homemade pasta and desserts made on site. Dishes compile fresh, high-quality vegetables, seafood, Certified Angus steak and dry-aged filet mignon. Daily early-bird specials and the fish fry are worth checking out. Casual dress; cocktails. **Parking:** on-site. **Cards:** AX, MC, VI.

THORNBERRY'S RESTAURANT   **Dinner:** $9-$20   **Phone:** 315/735-1409
American
Location: I-90 (New York State Thruway), exit 31, 1.5 mi s to Hopper St, just e, then just s. 1011 King St 13501. **Hours:** 11:30 am-2 & 4:30-9 pm, Fri & Sat-10 pm. Closed: 1/1, 12/25; also Sun. **Reservations:** suggested, weekends. **Features:** Eating downtown won't be ordinary in the bustling restaurant. Relaxed service and ample portions are most satisfying. Original artwork graces the walls and a warm fire brightens any winter day. Hearty soup, salad and dinner specials such as curry chicken with rice or beef and seafood await hungry diners. The worth-waiting-for Thornberry pie is big enough to share. Casual dress; cocktails. **Parking:** on-site. **Cards:** AX, DC, DS, MC, VI.

VALATIE pop. 1,712

———— **WHERE TO STAY** ————

BLUE SPRUCE INN & SUITES   **Phone:** 518/758-9711
Motel

5/1-10/31	1P: $70-$95	2P: $85-$100	XP: $5	D14
11/1-4/30	1P: $65-$95	2P: $80-$90	XP: $5	D14

Location: I-90 (New York State Thruway), exit 12, 4 mi s on US 9 via New York State Thruway Extension, exit B1. 3093 Rt 9 12184. Fax: 518/758-1638. **Facility:** 28 units. 24 one-bedroom standard units. 4 one-bedroom suites ($105-$145) with kitchens. 2 stories (no elevator), exterior corridors. *Bath:* combo or shower only. **Parking:** on-site. **Terms:** 7 day cancellation notice, weekly rates available, package plans. **Amenities:** irons, hair dryers. **Dining:** 7:30-10 am; closed 12/1-4/30. **Pool(s):** outdoor, wading. **Guest Services:** coin laundry. **Business Services:** fax. **Cards:** AX, DC, DS, MC, VI. **Free Special Amenities:** local telephone calls and early check-in/late check-out. *(See color ad p 222)*

VERNON pop. 1,155

———— **WHERE TO DINE** ————

MASON JAR RESTAURANT   **Lunch:** $4-$6   **Dinner:** $8-$12   **Phone:** 315/829-9999
American
Location: Jct SR 31 and 5, 0.3 mi e. SR 5 13476. **Hours:** 8 am-8 pm. Closed: 12/25. **Features:** The restaurant is known for tasty, no-nonsense, home-style cooking. Among favorites are barbecue ribs, roast pork, prime rib and chicken and seafood dishes. The in-house bakery tempts with selections including doughnuts, cakes, pies and other desserts. Casual dress. **Parking:** on-site. **Cards:** AX, MC, VI.

TOWN & COUNTRY RESTAURANT   **Lunch:** $3-$8   **Dinner:** $10-$25   **Phone:** 315/829-2450
American
Location: SR 5, 0.3 mi w of jct SR 31. 5366 E Seneca St 13476. **Hours:** noon-8 pm, Fri-10 pm, Sat 7:30 am-10 pm, Sun 8 am-8 pm. Closed: 1/1, 7/4, 12/25; also Mon & Tues. **Reservations:** accepted. **Features:** Hearty portions and friendly, casual service are hallmarks of the central New York eatery, just a short drive from Turning Stone Casino. The "country-home" atmosphere is welcoming to families, and selections range from soup and sandwiches to pork steak with dressing, gravy and all the "fixins". Casual dress; cocktails. **Parking:** on-site. **Cards:** AX, DS, MC, VI.

VERNON'S APPLE BETTY DINER   **Lunch:** $5-$7   **Dinner:** $9-$14   **Phone:** 315/829-4875
American
Location: Jct SR 31, 0.3 mi e. 5350 SR 5 (Seneca St) 13476. **Hours:** 6 am-8:30 pm, Mon & Tues-2 pm, Sun 7 am-8:30 pm; to 2 pm, Fri & Sat-8:30 pm in winter. Closed major holidays. **Features:** The nifty little diner serves locals and hungry travelers tasty comfort food, such as homemade soups, hot and cold sandwiches and freshly baked desserts. Many breakfast choices are served from 7-11:30 am. Casual dress. **Parking:** on-site.

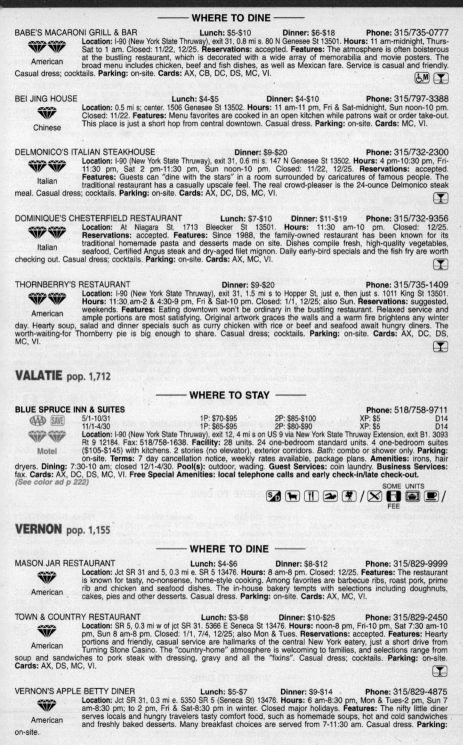

VERONA pop. 6,425

——— WHERE TO STAY ———

THE CASINO HOTEL AT TURNING STONE RESORT

Phone: (315)361-7711

(AAA) (SAVE)

7/1-10/31	1P: $155-$205	2P: $155-$205	XP: $10	F18
5/1-6/30 & 4/1-4/30	1P: $139-$195	2P: $139-$195	XP: $10	F18
11/1-3/31	1P: $119-$165	2P: $119-$165	XP: $10	F18

▽▽▽▽ ▽▽▽▽
Location: I-90 (New York State Thruway), exit 33, just w, follow signs. 5218 Patrick Rd 13478 (PO Box 126).
Large-scale Hotel **Fax:** 315/361-7665. **Facility:** 269 units. 254 one-bedroom standard units, some with whirlpools. 15 one-bedroom suites ($149-$495) with whirlpools. 3 stories, interior corridors. *Bath:* combo or shower only.
Parking: on-site. **Terms:** package plans. **Amenities:** video games (fee), high-speed Internet, voice mail, irons, hair dryers.
Dining: 9 restaurants, 24 hours, nightclub, name entertainment. **Pool(s):** heated indoor. **Leisure Activities:** saunas, whirlpools, steamrooms, driving range. *Fee:* golf-81 holes, massage. **Guest Services:** gift shop, valet laundry, area transportation-RV parks & golf courses, beauty salon, tanning facilities. **Business Services:** conference facilities, business center. **Cards:** AX, DC, DS, MC, VI. *(See color ad p 418)*

SOME UNITS

Sb 🍴 24 &M 🛋 🗐 🏊 🛠 ✗ 🎿 🖳 /✗ 🔋 /

LODGE AT TURNING STONE

Phone: (315)361-7711

(AAA) (SAVE)

All Year	1P: $199-$3000	2P: $199-$3000	XP: $10	F16

▽▽▽▽ ▽▽▽▽
Location: I-90 (New York State Thruway), exit 33, just w, follow signs. 5218 Patrick Rd 13478. **Fax:** 315/361-7637.
Facility: Away from the bustle of the casino, the lodge offers quiet areas for guests to catch up on a good
book or enjoy tranquil views of surrounding trees. 94 units. 93 one- and 1 three-bedroom suites ($375-
Large-scale Hotel $3000), some with whirlpools. 4 stories, interior corridors. **Parking:** on-site. **Terms:** package plans.
Amenities: CD players, high-speed Internet, dual phone lines, voice mail, safes, irons, hair dryers. *Some:*
DVD players. **Dining:** 24 hours. **Leisure Activities:** *Fee:* golf-72 holes, driving range, massage. **Guest Services:** gift shop,
complimentary evening beverages, valet laundry, area transportation. **Business Services:** meeting rooms, fax. **Cards:** AX, DC,
DS, MC, VI. *(See color ad p 418)*

SOME UNITS

Sb 🍴 &M 🎿 🔋 🖳 /✗ VCR 📷 /

THE TOWER HOTEL AT TURNING STONE RESORT

Phone: (315)361-7711

(AAA) (SAVE)

7/1-10/31	1P: $155-$215	2P: $155-$215	XP: $10	F18
4/1-4/30	1P: $139-$205	2P: $139-$205	XP: $10	F18
5/1-6/30	1P: $139-$195	2P: $139-$195	XP: $10	F18
11/1-3/31	1P: $119-$175	2P: $119-$175	XP: $10	F18

▽▽▽▽ ▽▽▽▽
Small-scale Hotel **Location:** I-90 (New York State Thruway), exit 33, just w, follow signs. 5218 Patrick Rd 13478. **Fax:** 315/361-7665.
Facility: Newly constructed rooms offer guests plenty of space to stretch out, and large windows make it
easy to see for miles on a clear day. 287 units. 266 one-bedroom standard units. 20 one- and 1 two-bedroom suites ($189-
$1500), some with whirlpools. 21 stories, interior corridors. *Bath:* combo or shower only. **Parking:** on-site. **Terms:** package
plans. **Amenities:** video games (fee), high-speed Internet, dual phone lines, voice mail, safes, irons, hair dryers. *Some:* CD
players, honor bars. **Dining:** 9 restaurants, 24 hours, nightclub, name entertainment. **Pool(s):** heated indoor. **Leisure
Activities:** saunas, whirlpool, steamrooms, fitness trail, spa. *Fee:* golf-81 holes. **Guest Services:** gift shop, valet laundry, area
transportation, beauty salon, tanning facilities. **Business Services:** conference facilities, business center. **Cards:** AX, DC, DS,
MC, VI. *(See color ad p 418)*

SOME UNITS

Sb 🍴 24 &M 🛋 🗐 🏊 🛠 ✗ 🎿 🖳 /✗ 🔋 /

——— *The following lodging was either not evaluated or did not* ———
meet AAA rating requirements but is listed for your information only.

INN AT TURNING STONE

Phone: 315/363-0096

(fyi)   Not evaluated. **Location:** I-90, exit 33, 0.9 mi e on E365, at jct SR 31. 5558 W Main St 13478. Facilities, services, and
decor characterize a basic property. *(See color ad p 418)*

——— WHERE TO DINE ———

RODIZIO - CHURRASCARIA AT TURNING STONE

Lunch: $10-$20   **Dinner:** $10-$45   **Phone:** 315/361-7711

(AAA)   **Location:** I-90, exit 33, just w follow signs. 5218 Patrick Rd 13478. **Hours:** 11:30 am-2:30 & 5-10 pm, Fri & Sat-11
pm. **Reservations:** suggested. **Features:** With a gourmet salad bar available and the Gouchos serving you
▽▽▽▽   any one of the ten roasted meats tableside you will not go away hungry. Casual dress. **Parking:** on-site and
Brazilian   valet. **Cards:** AX, DC, DS, MC, VI.

&M 🍸

WILDFLOWERS AT TURNING STONE RESORT

Lunch: $16-$26   **Dinner:** $20-$55   **Phone:** 315/361-8620

(AAA)   **Location:** I-90, exit 33, just w, follow signs. 5218 Patrick Rd 13478. **Hours:** 6 am-2 & 5-10 pm, Fri & Sat-11 pm.
Reservations: suggested. **Features:** The quiet and intimate restaurant presents a menu of traditional
▽▽▽▽   Continental cuisine, including some menu items that are prepared tableside. Also offered are some heart-
Continental   healthy choices. Dressy casual. **Parking:** on-site. **Cards:** AX, DS, MC, VI.

&M

VERONA BEACH

——— WHERE TO DINE ———

SPAGHETTI FACTORY

Lunch: $4-$7   **Dinner:** $9-$16   **Phone:** 315/762-9948

▽▽▽ ▽▽   **Location:** Center. 6800 SR 13 13162. **Hours:** Open 5/1-11/6 & 3/23-4/30; 11:30 am-10 pm; Sun noon-9 pm
5/31-9/7. **Reservations:** accepted. **Features:** Family-owned since 1978, the Italian-American restaurant
Italian   prepares made-to-order meals in generous portions. Freshly baked desserts will delight. Skylights and vines
hanging from beams give the dining room the atmosphere of a vineyard. Neatly uniformed servers are
pleasant. Casual dress; cocktails. **Parking:** on-site. **Cards:** AX, DS, MC, VI.

VESTAL pop. 26,535

———— WHERE TO STAY ————

BINGHAMTON COURTYARD BY MARRIOTT *Book great rates at AAA.com* **Phone:** (607)644-1000
▼▽▲▽▼ 1/1-4/30 1P: $119-$169 2P: $119-$169
5/1-12/31 1P: $109-$159 2P: $109-$159
Small-scale Hotel **Location:** SR 17, exit 67 eastbound, just s on SR 26, then 3.3 mi e on SR 434; exit 70 westbound, 2 mi s on SR 201, then just w on SR 434. 3801 Vestal Pkwy E 13850. Fax: 607/644-1022. **Facility:** Smoke free premises. 78 units. 70 one-bedroom standard units. 8 one-bedroom suites. 3 stories, interior corridors. *Bath:* combo or shower only. **Parking:** on-site. **Terms:** [BP] meal plan available. **Amenities:** video games (fee), high-speed Internet, dual phone lines, voice mail, irons, hair dryers. *Some:* DVD players. **Pool(s):** small heated indoor. **Leisure Activities:** whirlpool, exercise room. **Guest Services:** valet and coin laundry, wireless Internet. **Business Services:** meeting rooms, PC. **Cards:** AX, DC, DS, JC, MC, VI.

SOME UNITS
(A$K) (S⚡) (❞⬆) (⬇) (🅿) (⟰) (✕) (📷) (🖥) / (VCR) (🔒) (🍽) /

HAMPTON INN & SUITES *Book great rates at AAA.com* **Phone:** (607)797-5000
▼▽▲▽▼ All Year 1P: $129-$159 2P: $139-$169 XP: $10 F18
Small-scale Hotel **Location:** SR 17, exit 67 eastbound, just s on SR 26, then 3.3 mi e on SR 434; exit 70 westbound, 2 mi s on SR 201, then just w on SR 434. 3708 Vestal Pkwy E 13850. Fax: 607/797-5610. **Facility:** 79 units. 39 one-bedroom standard units. 40 one-bedroom suites with kitchens. 3 stories, interior corridors. *Bath:* combo or shower only. **Parking:** on-site. **Terms:** [BP] meal plan available. **Amenities:** video games (fee), dual phone lines, voice mail, irons, hair dryers. **Pool(s):** small heated indoor. **Leisure Activities:** exercise room. **Guest Services:** sundries, valet and coin laundry, wireless Internet. **Business Services:** meeting rooms. **Cards:** AX, DC, DS, MC, VI.

SOME UNITS
(A$K) (S⚡) (🔨) (❞⬆) (🅿) (⟰) (📷) (🖥) / (✕) (🔒) (🍽) /

HOLIDAY INN AT THE UNIVERSITY *Book at AAA.com* **Phone:** 607/729-6371
▼▽◆▽▼ Property failed to provide current rates
Small-scale Hotel **Location:** SR 17, exit 70, 2.5 mi s on US 201 to SR 434 W, then right on Bunn Hill Rd. 4105 Vestal Pkwy E 13850. Fax: 607/729-6407. **Facility:** 141 units. 139 one-bedroom standard units. 2 one-bedroom suites, some with whirlpools. 2 stories (no elevator), interior corridors. **Parking:** on-site. **Terms:** check-in 4 pm, pets ($25 fee). **Amenities:** video games (fee), high-speed Internet, dual phone lines, voice mail, irons, hair dryers. **Pool(s):** outdoor. **Leisure Activities:** exercise room. **Guest Services:** valet and coin laundry, wireless Internet. **Business Services:** meeting rooms, PC.

SOME UNITS
(🐕) (❞) (⬇) (⅏M) (⟰) (📷) (🖥) / (✕) (🔒) (🍽)
FEE FEE FEE

HOWARD JOHNSON EXPRESS INN (BINGHAMTON UNIVERSITY) *Book at AAA.com* **Phone:** (607)729-6181
▼▽▲▽▼ All Year 1P: $69-$99 2P: $79-$119 XP: $10 F16
Motel **Location:** SR 17, exit 70 westbound, 1 mi s on SR 201 S, then 0.5 mi w on SR 434; exit 67 eastbound, just s on SR 26, then 2.5 mi e on SR 434. Located in a light-commercial area. 3603 Vestal Pkwy E 13850. Fax: 607/797-0309. **Facility:** 58 one-bedroom standard units, some with whirlpools. 1-2 stories (no elevator), interior corridors. **Parking:** on-site. **Terms:** weekly rates available, [CP] meal plan available, package plans. **Amenities:** video library (fee), voice mail, irons, hair dryers. **Pool(s):** outdoor. **Guest Services:** wireless Internet. **Business Services:** meeting rooms. **Cards:** AX, CB, DC, DS, MC, VI.

SOME UNITS
(A$K) (S⚡) (❞⬆) (⟰) (♨) (📷) (🖥) / (✕) (VCR) (🔒) (🍽) /
FEE FEE FEE FEE

———— WHERE TO DINE ————

KAMPAI **Dinner:** $12-$28 **Phone:** 607/798-7521
▼▽▲▽▼ **Location:** SR 17, exit 70, 2.5 mi s on SR 201 to SR 434, 2.5 mi w, then just n. 108 Jensen Rd 13850. **Hours:** 4:30 pm-9:30 pm, Sun 3:30 pm-8:30 pm. Closed major holidays. **Reservations:** suggested. **Features:** A respected area fixture since 1975, the Japanese restaurant offers three dining choices: sushi, hibachi and traditional. Casual dress; cocktails. **Parking:** on-site. **Cards:** AX, DC, MC, VI.
Japanese (🍸)

PLANTATION HOUSE **Dinner:** $18-$22 **Phone:** 607/786-9878
▼▽▲▽▼ **Location:** SR 17, exit 67, just s on SR 26, just w on SR 434, then just n. 2 Pumphouse Rd 13850. **Hours:** 4:30 pm-9:30 pm, Fri & Sat-10:30 pm. Closed: 12/25; also Sun. **Reservations:** suggested. **Features:** In an elegantly restored 1840s inn, the setting welcomes a casual experience. Specialties incorporate Cajun flavorings and garlicky accents. Choices include preparations of prime rib, steak, chops, seafood, pasta, chicken, veal and duck. Private parties can be accommodated. Casual dress; cocktails. **Parking:** on-site. **Cards:** AX, MC, VI.
Steak & Seafood (⅏M) (🍸)

P.S. RESTAURANT **Dinner:** $12-$24 **Phone:** 607/770-0056
▼▽▲▽▼ **Location:** SR 17, exit 70, 2.5 mi s on SR 201 to SR 434, then 3.6 mi w; in Giant Shopping Center. 100 Rano Blvd 13850. **Hours:** 5 pm-9 pm, Fri & Sat-9:30 pm. Closed: 1/1, 11/22, 12/24, 12/25; also Sun & Mon. **Reservations:** suggested. **Features:** The versatile chef/owner of this unassuming but cozy restaurant creates innovative, fusion-style cuisine. Classic French and Thai/Asian influences dominate on a menu that includes filet mignon, poached salmon and vegetarian fare. Diners are encouraged to ask the professional, knowledgeable staff for help with choosing a selection from the award-winning wine list. Casual dress; cocktails. **Parking:** on-site. **Cards:** AX, DC, DS, MC, VI.
Continental (🍸)

TEXAS ROADHOUSE **Lunch:** $6-$8 **Dinner:** $8-$17 **Phone:** 607/729-8200
▼▽▼ **Location:** SR 17, exit 70, 2.5 mi s on US 201 to SR 434, just e, U-turn, then just w. 4399 Vestal Pkwy 13850. **Hours:** 4 pm-10 pm, Fri-11 pm, Sat noon-11 pm, Sun noon-10 pm. Closed: 12/25. **Features:** Buckets of peanuts entice patrons at each table of the popular casual steakhouse, which is known for its fall-off-the bone ribs and hearty steaks. Made-from-scratch yeast rolls are served with cinnamon honey butter at every table. Also featured on the menu are salads, chicken, seafood, and grilled pork chops. Casual dress; cocktails. **Parking:** on-site.
Barbecue (🍸)
Cards: AX, DS, MC, VI.

VICTOR pop. 2,433—See also FINGER LAKES.

——— WHERE TO STAY ———

BUDGET INN
(AAA) (SAVE)
▽▽▽
Motel

Phone: (585)924-5020

All Year — 1P: $43-$59 — 2P: $54-$89 — XP: $8 — F8
Location: I-90, exit 44, 1 mi s on SR 332, then just e. 6001 Rt 96 14425. Fax: 585/924-5020. **Facility:** 20 one-bedroom standard units. 1 story, exterior corridors. **Parking:** on-site. **Terms:** 3 day cancellation notice, small pets only ($5 extra charge). **Amenities:** hair dryers. **Cards:** AX, DS, MC, VI. **Free Special Amenities:** local telephone calls and early check-in/late check-out.

SOME UNITS
[icons]

HAMPTON INN AND SUITES-ROCHESTER/VICTOR *Book great rates at AAA.com* — Phone: (585)924-4400
(AAA) (SAVE)
▽▽▽▽
Small-scale Hotel

All Year — 1P: $139-$179
Location: I-90 (New York State Thruway), exit 45, just n. 7637 SR 96 14564. Fax: 585/924-4478. **Facility:** 123 units. 68 one-bedroom standard units. 55 one-bedroom suites with efficiencies, some with whirlpools. 3 stories, interior corridors. **Bath:** combo or shower only. **Parking:** on-site. **Amenities:** dual phone lines, voice mail, irons, hair dryers. **Pool(s):** small heated indoor. **Leisure Activities:** whirlpool, exercise room. **Guest Services:** valet and coin laundry, area transportation-local businesses. **Business Services:** meeting rooms, fax (fee). **Cards:** AX, CB, DC, DS, MC, VI. **Free Special Amenities:** expanded continental breakfast and high-speed Internet.

SOME UNITS
[icons]

MICROTEL INN VICTOR *Book at AAA.com* — Phone: 585/924-9240
▽▽▽
Small-scale Hotel

Property failed to provide current rates
Location: I-90 (New York State Thruway), exit 45, just s off SR 96. 7498 Main St Fischer 14564. Fax: 585/924-9241. **Facility:** 99 one-bedroom standard units. 2 stories (no elevator), interior corridors. **Bath:** combo or shower only. **Parking:** on-site. **Amenities:** voice mail. **Fee:** video games, safes. **Guest Services:** wireless Internet.

SOME UNITS
[icons]

ROYAL INN *Book great rates at AAA.com* — Phone: (585)924-2121
(AAA) (SAVE)
▽▽▽
Motel

5/1-9/30 — 1P: $49-$79 — 2P: $69-$99 — XP: $5 — F12
10/1-4/30 — 1P: $49-$59 — 2P: $59-$79 — XP: $5 — F12
Location: I-90 (New York State Thruway), exit 45; I-490 (SR 96) exit 29, 0.8 mi s. 7463 SR 96 14564. Fax: 585/924-0468. **Facility:** 30 one-bedroom standard units. 1 story, exterior corridors. **Parking:** on-site. **Terms:** pets ($5 extra charge). **Amenities:** *Some:* DVD players. **Cards:** AX, DC, DS, MC, VI. **Free Special Amenities:** preferred room (subject to availability with advance reservations).

SOME UNITS
[icons]

——— WHERE TO DINE ———

BIAGGI'S RISTORANTE ITALIANO — Lunch: $9-$11 — Dinner: $12-$20 — Phone: 585/223-2290
▽▽▽
Italian
Location: On SR 96; in Eastview Mall. 818 Eastview Mall 14564. **Hours:** 11 am-10 pm, Fri & Sat-11 pm, Sun-9 pm. Closed: 11/22, 12/25. **Reservations:** accepted. **Features:** Cool, upscale decor surrounds diners who savor freshly prepared creations. Delicious combinations of quality, unusual ingredients make for an adventurous dining experience. Casual dress; cocktails. **Parking:** on-site. **Cards:** AX, DS, MC, VI.
[icon]

COLE & PARKS — Lunch: $4-$8 — Dinner: $4-$8 — Phone: 585/924-8710
▽▽
Coffee/Espresso
Location: I-90 (New York State Thruway), exit 45, 0.5 mi s on SR 96, then just e. 607 Rowley Rd 14564. **Hours:** 6:30 am-8 pm, Fri-9 pm, Sat 7 am-9 pm, Sun 7 am-7 pm. Closed: 3/23, 12/25. **Features:** Quality select-roasted coffee beans are the base of the upscale bakery cafe's philosophy. The comfy decor includes a fireplace and plasma TVs. Gourmet confections are a treat. Casual dress. **Parking:** on-site. **Cards:** AX, DS, MC, VI.

INDIA HOUSE — Lunch: $6-$11 — Dinner: $9-$21 — Phone: 585/742-2030
▽▽▽
Indian

MC, VI.
Location: I-90 (New York State Thruway), exit 45, 0.5 mi s. 7343 Rt 96 14564. **Hours:** 11:30 am-2:30 & 5-9:30 pm, Fri & Sat-10 pm. Closed: 7/4, 11/22, 12/25. **Reservations:** accepted. **Features:** A feast for the senses begins with the freshest, quality ingredients, herbs and spices. In addition to vegetarian choices, the menu lists tandoori lamb, chicken, beef and seafood. Casual dress; cocktails. **Parking:** on-site. **Cards:** AX, DS,
[icon]

P.F. CHANG'S CHINA BISTRO — Lunch: $6-$11 — Dinner: $7-$18 — Phone: 585/223-2410
▽▽▽
Chinese

cocktails. **Parking:** on-site. **Cards:** AX, DC, DS, MC, VI.
Location: On SR 96; at Eastview Mall. 820 Eastview Mall 14564. **Hours:** 11 am-10 pm, Fri & Sat-11 pm. Closed: 11/22, 12/25. **Reservations:** accepted. **Features:** Trendy, upscale decor provides a pleasant backdrop for New Age Chinese dining. Appetizers, soups and salads are a meal by themselves. Vegetarian plates and sides, noodles, meins, chicken and meat dishes are created from exotic, fresh ingredients. Casual dress;
[icon]

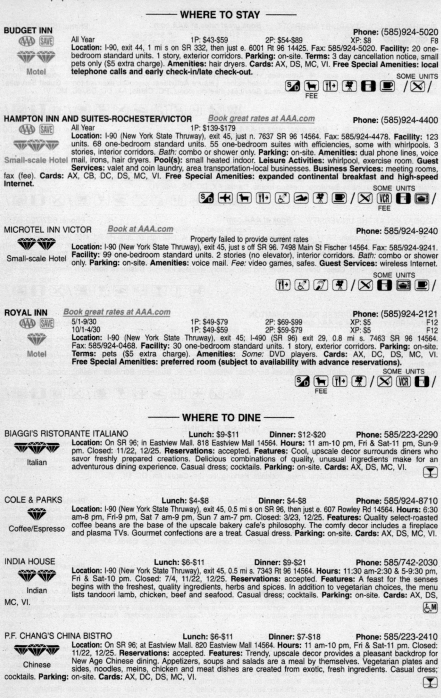

WADING RIVER pop. 6,668

──────── **WHERE TO STAY** ────────

THE INN AND SPA AT EAST WIND   *Book great rates at AAA.com*   Phone: (631)929-3500

(AAA) (SAVE)

5/1-10/31	1P: $199-$299	2P: $199-$299	XP: $15
4/1-4/30	1P: $149-$229	2P: $149-$229	XP: $15
11/1-12/31	1P: $139-$229	2P: $139-$229	XP: $15
1/1-3/31	1P: $139-$199	2P: $139-$199	XP: $15

Small-scale Hotel **Location:** Jct CR 46, 3 mi e on SR 25A. 5720 Rt 25A 11792. Fax: 631/929-4975. **Facility:** Smoke free premises. 50 units. 44 one-bedroom standard units, some with whirlpools. 6 one-bedroom suites ($299-$599). 2 stories, interior corridors. *Bath:* combo or shower only. **Parking:** on-site. **Terms:** check-in 4 pm, 31 day cancellation notice-fee imposed, package plans. **Amenities:** CD players, high-speed Internet, dual phone lines, voice mail, safes, irons, hair dryers. *Some Fee:* DVD players. **Dining:** 7 am-9 pm, Fri & Sat-10 pm, cocktails. **Pool(s):** heated outdoor. **Leisure Activities:** exercise room, spa. **Guest Services:** gift shop, valet laundry, wireless Internet. **Business Services:** conference facilities, fax (fee). **Cards:** AX, CB, DC, JC, MC, VI. **Free Special Amenities:** newspaper and high-speed Internet.

SOME UNITS

[icons] / [VCR] [icon] [icon] /
FEE FEE FEE

WAPPINGERS FALLS pop. 4,929

──────── **WHERE TO DINE** ────────

AROMA OSTERIA   **Lunch:** $9-$13   **Dinner:** $14-$23   Phone: 845/298-6790

Italian

Location: Jct US 9 and CR 28, just se off US 9. 114 Old Post Rd 12590. **Hours:** 11:30 am-2:30 & 5-10 pm, Fri & Sat-11 pm, Sun 4 pm-9 pm. **Closed:** 1/1, 11/22, 12/25; also Mon. **Reservations:** required. **Features:** Patrons might be reminded of an Italian hilltop villa at this restaurant in the heart of the Hudson Valley. This place is nestled away from the hustle of the area's commercial strip. Casual dress; cocktails. **Parking:** on-site. **Cards:** AX, CB, DC, DS, MC, VI.

[icon]

WARRENSBURG pop. 3,208   (See map and index starting on p. 330)—*See also ADIRONDACK MOUNTAINS.*

──────── **WHERE TO STAY** ────────

ALYNN'S BUTTERFLY INN BED & BREAKFAST   Phone: 518/623-9390   **36**

5/1-10/20	1P: $109-$179	2P: $119-$189
10/21-4/30	1P: $85-$145	2P: $95-$155

Bed & Breakfast **Location:** I-87, exit 23, 3.3 mi n on US 9, then just w. Located in a quiet rural area. 69 Rt 28 12885. Fax: 518/623-9396. **Facility:** Smoke free premises. 5 one-bedroom standard units, some with whirlpools. 2 stories (no elevator), interior corridors. *Bath:* combo or shower only. **Parking:** on-site. **Terms:** 2 night minimum stay - seasonal, 14 day cancellation notice-fee imposed, package plans, no pets allowed (owner's pets on premises). **Amenities:** irons, hair dryers. **Leisure Activities:** cross country skiing, hiking trails. **Guest Services:** wireless Internet. **Cards:** MC, VI.

SOME UNITS

[icons] / [W] /

SUPER 8 WARRENSBURG   *Book at AAA.com*   Phone: (518)623-2811   **37**

7/2-9/1 [CP]	1P: $125-$150	2P: $130-$155	XP: $10	F17
9/2-10/2 [CP]	1P: $80-$140	2P: $85-$145	XP: $10	F17
5/1-7/1 [CP]	1P: $75-$140	2P: $80-$145	XP: $10	F17
10/3-4/30 [CP]	1P: $80-$100	2P: $85-$105	XP: $10	F17

Motel

Location: I-87, exit 23, just w. 3619 SR 9 12845. Fax: 518/623-2811. **Facility:** 32 one-bedroom standard units. 2 stories (no elevator), interior corridors. **Parking:** on-site, winter plug-ins. **Terms:** weekly rates available, pets ($10 extra charge, in smoking units). **Cards:** AX, DC, DS, MC, VI.

SOME UNITS

(ASK) [icons] / [icon] /
FEE

──────── **WHERE TO DINE** ────────

GRIST MILL ON THE SCHROON   **Dinner:** $15-$24   Phone: 518/623-8005   **18**

American

Location: I-87, exit 23, 0.9 mi n on US 9; jct CR 418, 0.5 mi w along river. 100 River St 12885. **Hours:** Open 5/1-10/31; 5 pm-9 pm. **Closed:** Mon-Wed 5/1-7/3 & 9/2-10/31. **Reservations:** suggested. **Features:** Whether watching the Schroon River in springtime flood or lazy summer flow, you'll find a delightful vista from your table. Attentive and expert servers bring creations such as orange- and basil-marinated chicken, pan-seared prawns and scallops and pepper-crusted venison. Don't hesitate to blow your diet on a dessert of chocolate mousse with phyllo pastry surrounded with bananas Foster. Casual dress; cocktails. **Parking:** on-site. **Cards:** AX, MC, VI.

[icon]

MERRILL MAGEE HOUSE   **Dinner:** $19-$25   Phone: 518/623-2449   **17**

Continental

Location: Center; opposite bandstand. 3 Hudson St 12885. **Hours:** 5 pm-9 pm, Fri & Sat-10 pm; to 8 pm in winter. **Closed:** 12/24 & Sun. **Reservations:** suggested. **Features:** On the grounds of a historic country inn, the restaurant sustains a romantic and modestly elegant atmosphere, thanks to soft background music and attractive table settings. The menu choices and presentation should please big-city diners. Dressy casual; cocktails. **Parking:** on-site. **Cards:** AX, CB, DC, DS, MC, VI. **Country Inn**

[icon]

WARWICK pop. 6,412

------ WHERE TO DINE ------

CHATEAU HATHORN
▼▼▼▼
Continental
Country Inn

Dinner: $20-$30

Phone: 845/986-6099

Location: Jct SR 17A, 0.6 mi sw on SR 94. 33 Hathorn Rd 10990. **Hours:** 5 pm-9 pm, Sun 3 pm-8 pm. Closed: 12/24, 12/25; also Mon & Tues. **Reservations:** suggested. **Features:** On a small hill surrounded by impressive landscaping and stone walls, the Tudor-style mansion with field stone and red brick face is charming. Vaulted beam ceilings, large arched windows and an ornately carved fireplace are a few of the architectural details. A superior list of wines stored in the cellar complements seafood, chicken and steak dishes. A few German dishes spot the menu, and an exotic dish or two may surprise. Dressy casual; cocktails. **Parking:** on-site. **Cards:** AX, MC, VI.

Ⓨ

WATERLOO pop. 5,111—See also FINGER LAKES.

------ WHERE TO STAY ------

HOLIDAY INN WATERLOO-SENECA FALLS   *Book great rates at AAA.com*   **Phone:** 315/539-5011

Ⓐ SAVE
▼▼▼▼
Small-scale Hotel

7/1-9/2	1P: $99-$179	2P: $179	XP: $10	F18
9/3-4/30	1P: $79-$159	2P: $79-$159	XP: $10	F18
5/1-6/30	1P: $79-$159	2P: $79-$159	XP: $10	F18

Location: I-90 (New York State Thruway), exit 41, 4 mi s; just n of jct SR 414/5 and US 20. 2468 SR 414 13165 (PO Box 149). **Fax:** 315/539-8355. **Facility:** 148 units. 144 one-bedroom standard units. 4 one-bedroom suites with whirlpools. 2 stories (no elevator), interior corridors. **Parking:** on-site. **Terms:** package plans. **Amenities:** high-speed Internet, voice mail, irons, hair dryers. *Some:* DVD players. **Dining:** Our Heritage Cafe, see separate listing. **Pool(s):** heated outdoor. **Leisure Activities:** sauna, whirlpool, lighted tennis court, exercise room, basketball. **Guest Services:** valet and coin laundry, wireless Internet. **Business Services:** conference facilities, PC. **Cards:** AX, CB, DC, DS, JC, MC, VI. **Free Special Amenities:** newspaper and high-speed Internet.

SOME UNITS
🐾 🍴 ⓨ ⤢ ✕ 🎥 ▣ / ✕ VCR 🅗 🖼 /
FEE FEE

MICROTEL INN & SUITES   *Book great rates at AAA.com*   **Phone:** (315)539-8438

Ⓐ SAVE
▼▼▼
Small-scale Hotel

All Year	1P: $46-$94	2P: $46-$94	XP: $10	D16

Location: I-90 (New York State Thruway), exit 41, 4 mi s on SR 414, then just e. 1966 Rt 5 & 20 13148 (PO Box 807, SENECA FALLS). **Fax:** 315/539-4780. **Facility:** 69 one-bedroom standard units. 2 stories, interior corridors. *Bath:* combo or shower only. **Parking:** on-site, winter plug-ins. **Terms:** cancellation fee imposed, pets ($15 extra charge). **Amenities:** video games (fee), irons, hair dryers. **Leisure Activities:** exercise room. **Guest Services:** wireless Internet. **Business Services:** meeting rooms, business center. **Cards:** AX, DC, DS, MC, VI. **Free Special Amenities:** continental breakfast and high-speed Internet.

SOME UNITS
🐾 🍴 ⓜ ♿ 🎥 / ✕ 🅗 🖼 ▣ /
FEE

------ WHERE TO DINE ------

ABIGAIL'S
▼▼
American

Lunch: $5-$9   **Dinner:** $8-$23   **Phone:** 315/539-9300

Location: I-90 (New York State Thruway), exit 41, 4 mi s on SR 414, then just e. 1978 Rt 5 & 20 13165. **Hours:** 11 am-2 & 5-9 pm, Fri & Sat-10 pm, Sun 1 pm-9 pm. Closed major holidays; also 12/24. **Reservations:** suggested, weekends. **Features:** Friendly staff members at the popular, all-American-style restaurant serve homemade comfort food. The weekday lunch buffet is a draw. Casual dress; cocktails. **Parking:** on-site. **Cards:** AX, CB, DC, DS, MC, VI.

Ⓨ

OUR HERITAGE CAFE
Ⓐ
▼▼▼
American

Menu on AAA.com   **Lunch:** $6-$8   **Dinner:** $9-$18   **Phone:** 315/539-6268

Location: I-90 (New York State Thruway), exit 41, 4 mi s; just n of jct SR 414/5 and US 20; in Holiday Inn Waterloo-Seneca Falls. 2468 SR 414 13165. **Hours:** 6:30 am-2 & 5-10 pm, Sun 6:30 am-10 pm. **Reservations:** accepted. **Features:** The restaurant was conceived with a tribute to local history in mind. Genuine artifacts, historical pictures and local facts, trivia and history make this more than a great place to eat. Family favorites are served in ample portions. The salad buffet is plentiful. Casual dress; cocktails. **Parking:** on-site. **Cards:** AX, CB, DC, DS, MC, VI.

ⓜ Ⓨ

WATERTOWN pop. 26,705

------ WHERE TO STAY ------

BEST WESTERN CARRIAGE HOUSE INN &
CONFERENCE CENTER   *Book great rates at AAA.com*   **Phone:** (315)782-8000

Ⓐ SAVE
▼▼▼
Small-scale Hotel

All Year [CP]	1P: $60-$200	2P: $70-$210	XP: $10	F12

Location: Center. 300 Washington St 13601. **Fax:** 315/786-2097. **Facility:** 160 units. 150 one-bedroom standard units. 10 one-bedroom suites ($130-$210), some with whirlpools. 4 stories, interior corridors. **Parking:** on-site. **Terms:** [BP] meal plan available, package plans, pets ($15 fee, in designated units). **Amenities:** irons, hair dryers. **Dining:** 2 restaurants, 6:30 am-2 & 5-9 pm, Fri & Sat-10 pm, Sun-2 pm, cocktails. **Pool(s):** heated indoor. **Leisure Activities:** saunas, exercise room. **Guest Services:** valet laundry, wireless Internet. **Business Services:** conference facilities. **Cards:** AX, DC, DS, MC, VI. **Free Special Amenities:** continental breakfast and local telephone calls.

SOME UNITS
Ⓢⓓ 🐾 🍴 ⓨ ⤢ 🎥 🅗 🖼 ▣ / ✕ VCR /
FEE

DAVIDSON'S MOTEL

Phone: 315/782-3861

AAA SAVE

Motel

4/1-4/30	1P: $70-$75	2P: $75-$80	XP: $5	F5
5/1-12/31	1P: $65-$75	2P: $70-$80	XP: $5	F5
1/1-3/31	1P: $50-$55	2P: $55-$60	XP: $5	F5

Location: From Town Square, 3.5 mi e. 26177 NYS Rt 3 13601. **Fax:** 315/786-0599. **Facility:** 20 one-bedroom standard units, some with kitchens. 1 story, exterior corridors. *Bath:* combo or shower only. **Parking:** on-site. **Terms:** office hours 8:30 am-11 pm, pets ($25 fee). **Amenities:** voice mail. **Pool(s):** small outdoor. **Leisure Activities:** barbecue pit, grills, picnic tables, hiking trails. **Cards:** MC, VI. **Free Special Amenities: continental breakfast and early check-in/late check-out.**

SOME UNITS

🖥️ 📠 ⊘ 🛡️ 🖼️ / ⊠ /
FEE

DAYS INN   *Book great rates at AAA.com*

Phone: (315)782-2700

Small-scale Hotel

7/5-10/10	1P: $89-$95	2P: $94-$100
5/1-7/4 & 10/11-4/30	1P: $75-$81	2P: $80-$86

Location: I-81, exit 45, 0.5 mi e. 110 Commerce Park Dr 13601. **Fax:** 315/782-7691. **Facility:** 135 units. 115 one-bedroom standard units. 20 one-bedroom suites ($90-$109). 6 stories, interior corridors. **Parking:** on-site. **Amenities:** hair dryers. *Some:* irons. **Pool(s):** small heated indoor. **Leisure Activities:** exercise room. *Fee:* game room. **Guest Services:** valet laundry, area transportation, wireless Internet. **Business Services:** meeting rooms, PC. **Cards:** AX, DC, DS, MC, VI.

SOME UNITS

ASK SD ✈ 🍴 24🕐 ▽ 📠 ⊘ 🖥️ / ⊠ 🛡️ 🖼️ /

RAMADA   *Book great rates at AAA.com*

Phone: (315)788-0700

AAA SAVE

Small-scale Hotel

5/1-10/31	1P: $89	2P: $94	XP: $5	F
11/1-4/30	1P: $79	2P: $84	XP: $5	F

Location: I-81, exit 45, just w. Located across from Salmon River Shopping Mall. 6300 Arsenal St 13601. **Fax:** 315/785-9875. **Facility:** 145 one-bedroom standard units. 4 stories, interior corridors. **Parking:** on-site. **Terms:** [CP] meal plan available, package plans, pets ($200 deposit). **Amenities:** voice mail, irons, hair dryers. **Dining:** 6:30 am-10 pm, Sun 8 am-noon, cocktails. **Pool(s):** outdoor. **Leisure Activities:** limited exercise equipment. *Fee:* game room. **Guest Services:** valet laundry, wireless Internet. **Business Services:** conference facilities. **Cards:** AX, DC, DS, MC, VI. **Free Special Amenities: newspaper and high-speed Internet.**

SOME UNITS

SD 🍴 🍴 ▽ 📠 ⊘ 🖥️ / ⊠ 🛡️ 🖼️ /
FEE

REDWOOD MOTOR LODGE

Phone: 315/788-2850

Motel

All Year	1P: $43-$65	2P: $43-$65	XP: $3	F12

Location: I-81, exit 45, 4 mi se on SR 3 E/12 S; jct SR 126, 0.3 mi on SR 12. 24098 Gifford Street Rd 13601. **Facility:** 27 units. 26 one-bedroom standard units. 1 two-bedroom suite ($65). 1-2 stories (no elevator), exterior corridors. *Bath:* combo or shower only. **Parking:** on-site, winter plug-ins. **Terms:** office hours 7 am-11 pm. **Pool(s):** outdoor. **Cards:** AX, MC, VI.

SOME UNITS

ASK 📠 / ⊠ 📱 /

──────── WHERE TO DINE ────────

BENNY'S STEAK HOUSE

Lunch: $5-$10   **Dinner:** $10-$30   **Phone:** 315/788-4110

American

Location: I-81, exit 45, 0.6 mi e. 1050 Arsenal St 13601. **Hours:** 11 am-11 pm. Closed: 11/22. **Reservations:** accepted. **Features:** An established favorite among locals, the casual restaurant is convenient to many lodgings. The menu lists appetizers, pizza, homemade Italian dishes, steaks and seafood. Delivery is available. Casual dress; cocktails. **Parking:** on-site. **Cards:** AX, MC, VI.

🍸

CAVALLARIO'S CUCINA

Lunch: $7-$10   **Dinner:** $12-$20   **Phone:** 315/788-9744

Italian

Location: Jct Prospect St; downtown. 133 N Massey St 13601. **Hours:** 11 am-9 pm, Fri & Sat-9:30 pm. Closed major holidays; also Sun. **Reservations:** accepted. **Features:** Friendly and family-oriented, the new restaurant features gourmet pizza and pasta. Crispy fresh salads, chargrilled Angus beef burgers, stuffed delicatessen sandwiches and such classic dinners as chicken Marsala and veal parmigiana are complemented by Italian wines. Guests can finish off the meal with a rich, homemade dessert. Casual dress; cocktails. **Parking:** on-site. **Cards:** AX, MC, VI.

🚹M

WATKINS GLEN pop. 2,149—See also FINGER LAKES.

————— WHERE TO STAY —————

ANCHOR INN AND MARINA
Phone: (607)535-4159

AAA SAVE
Motel

5/25-9/9 [CP]	1P: $69-$159	2P: $79-$159	XP: $10	F5
9/10-11/21 [CP]	1P: $69-$159	2P: $69-$159	XP: $10	F5
5/1-5/24 [CP]	1P: $59-$99	2P: $69-$99	XP: $10	F5

Location: Just n on SR 14, 0.8 mi n. Located lakeside. 3425 Salt Point Rd 14891. Fax: 607/535-4159. **Facility:** Smoke free premises. 11 one-bedroom standard units. 1 story, exterior corridors. *Bath:* combo or shower only. **Parking:** on-site. **Terms:** open 5/1-11/21, 10 day cancellation notice-fee imposed, weekly rates available, pets ($25 deposit). **Amenities:** voice mail, hair dryers. **Leisure Activities:** rental boats, rental paddleboats, fishing. *Fee:* boat dock, charter fishing, personal watercraft, pontoon boat. **Cards:** AX, DS, MC, VI. **Free Special Amenities:** early check-in/late check-out and high-speed Internet.

SOME UNITS
FEE / FEE FEE

BUDGET INN
Book great rates at AAA.com
Phone: (607)535-4800

AAA SAVE
Motel

5/1-10/31	1P: $69-$135	2P: $99-$145	XP: $10	F12
11/1-4/30	1P: $45	2P: $75	XP: $10	F12

Location: On SR 14. 435 S Franklin St 14891. Fax: 607/535-4800. **Facility:** 21 one-bedroom standard units. 1 story, exterior corridors. *Bath:* combo or shower only. **Parking:** on-site. **Terms:** 10 day cancellation notice-fee imposed, [CP] meal plan available. **Amenities:** high-speed Internet. *Some:* hair dryers. **Cards:** AX, DS, MC, VI.

SOME UNITS
/

CHIEFTAIN MOTEL
Phone: (607)535-4759

AAA SAVE
Motel

5/25-9/9 [CP]	1P: $69-$159	2P: $79-$159	XP: $10	F5
9/10-11/21 [CP]	1P: $69-$159	2P: $69-$159	XP: $10	F5
5/1-5/24 [CP]	1P: $59-$99	2P: $69-$99	XP: $10	F5

Location: Jct SR 14A; 3 mi n of town. 3815 SR 14 14891. Fax: 607/535-6091. **Facility:** 14 units. 12 one- and 2 two-bedroom standard units, some with efficiencies. 1 story, exterior corridors. *Bath:* combo or shower only. **Parking:** on-site. **Terms:** open 5/1-11/21, 10 day cancellation notice-fee imposed, weekly rates available, small pets only ($25 deposit). **Amenities:** voice mail, hair dryers. **Pool(s):** small outdoor. **Cards:** AX, DS, MC, VI. **Free Special Amenities:** continental breakfast and early check-in/late check-out.

SOME UNITS
FEE / FEE FEE FEE /

————— WHERE TO DINE —————

HOUSE OF HONG
Chinese
| Lunch: $5-$11 | Dinner: $5-$11 | Phone: 607/535-7024 |

Location: Corner of 4th St; center. 400 N Franklin St 14891. **Hours:** 11 am-10 pm, Fri & Sat-11 pm, Sun noon-10 pm; winter hours vary. Closed: 11/22, 12/25; also Mon in winter. **Features:** The little corner restaurant is big on taste and choices. Staffers at the friendly, family-owned spot serve all guests' needs. Casual dress; beer & wine only. **Parking:** on-site. **Cards:** AX, DS, MC, VI.

JERLANDO'S RISTORANTE
Italian
| Lunch: $5-$8 | Dinner: $6-$15 | Phone: 607/535-4254 |

Location: Center. 400 N Franklin St 14891. **Hours:** 11 am-10 pm; to 9 pm in winter. Closed: 2 weeks for New Year's & Mon in winter. **Features:** Families gather at the casual restaurant for Italian fare, as well as seafood, steak and veal choices. Pizza, burgers, submarine sandwiches and chicken wings can be carried out. Casual dress; beer & wine only. **Parking:** on-site. **Cards:** AX, DS, MC, VI.

SAVARD'S FAMILY RESTAURANT
American
| Lunch: $4-$7 | Dinner: $7-$15 | Phone: 607/535-4538 |

Location: Center. 601 N Franklin St 14891. **Hours:** 6 am-3 pm, Wed-Sun to 8 pm. Closed: 1/1, 11/22, 12/24, 12/25. **Features:** Comfort food is prepared the old-fashioned way. The popular downtown location serves homemade soups, hot and cold sandwiches, fish fry and daily specials. Casual dress; beer & wine only. **Parking:** on-site. **Cards:** AX, DS, MC, VI.

SENECA HARBOR STATION
American
| Lunch: $7-$10 | Dinner: $9-$30 | Phone: 607/535-6101 |

Location: SR 14; lakefront. 3 N Franklin St 14891. **Hours:** Open 5/1-11/30 & 4/1-4/30; 11:30 am-3:30 & 4:30-9 pm, Fri & Sat-10 pm. Closed: 11/22. **Features:** Guests can dine in casual style in a restored 1876 train station on the Seneca lakefront at the end of the Seneca Lake Wine Trail. The covered patio and raised dining room provide an advantageous view of the lake. Seafood pasta, Bubba Gump shrimp gumbo, crostini fresca and New England clam chowder top the list of popular dishes, which match well with choices from the good wine list, including some made locally. Casual dress; cocktails. **Parking:** on-site. **Cards:** AX, DS, MC, VI.

SENECA LODGE
American
| | Dinner: $11-$23 | Phone: 607/535-2014 |

Location: Just s on SR 329 W; at Watkins Glen State Park, south entrance. Walnut Rd 14891. **Hours:** Open 5/1-10/31; 8 am-11 & 5-9 pm. **Features:** Family operated since 1948, the rustic log cabin-style restaurant offers casual dining with such diverse choices as the most popular slow-baked, cut-to-order prime rib. Also served are generous portions of seafood, chicken, veal, chops, steaks, ribs, pasta, vegetarian dishes and sauteed specialties. The fresh salad bar rounds out a good meal. Casual dress; cocktails. **Parking:** on-site. **Cards:** AX, DC, DS, MC, VI.

WILDFLOWER CAFE
American
| Lunch: $5-$9 | Dinner: $13-$21 | Phone: 607/535-9797 |

Location: SR 14; downtown. 301 N Franklin St 14891. **Hours:** 11:30 am-10 pm, Fri & Sat-11 pm; hours vary off season. Closed major holidays. **Reservations:** accepted. **Features:** Representative of casual New American cuisine are trendy sandwiches, gourmet pizza, steaks, ribs, crispy duck breast and unusual pasta dishes. All are made with only the freshest seasonal ingredients. Homemade breads and desserts, such as the forbidden chocolate trinity and lemon cheesecake with blackberry sauce and homemade ice cream, are a must. Casual dress; cocktails. **Parking:** street. **Cards:** AX, MC, VI.

WEBSTER pop. 5,216

──────── WHERE TO STAY ────────

FAIRFIELD INN BY MARRIOTT ROCHESTER
EAST/WEBSTER   *Book great rates at AAA.com*   **Phone:** (585)671-1500
▼▼▼▼   All Year   1P: $129-$134
Location: I-590, exit 10B (SR 104 E), exit Hard Rd, just s. Located adjacent to a shopping center. 915 Hard Rd 14580.
Small-scale Hotel   Fax: 585/671-1610. **Facility:** Smoke free premises. 63 one-bedroom standard units. 3 stories, interior
corridors. *Bath:* combo or shower only. **Parking:** on-site. **Terms:** cancellation fee imposed, [ECP] meal plan
available. **Amenities:** video games (fee), high-speed Internet, dual phone lines, irons, hair dryers. **Pool(s):** small heated indoor.
Leisure Activities: whirlpool. **Guest Services:** valet laundry, wireless Internet. **Cards:** AX, CB, DC, DS, JC, MC, VI.

SOME UNITS

(ASK) (S/D) (📶) (&M) (🛋) (📷) (🍽) (🛗) (🖻) (📺) (📠) / (🖨) /
FEE

WEBSTER SUPER 8 MOTEL   *Book at AAA.com*   **Phone:** (585)671-6990
▼▼▼ ▼▼▼   5/1-8/31 [CP]   1P: $75-$93   2P: $80-$97   XP: $10   F18
         9/1-10/31 [CP]   1P: $67-$77   2P: $72-$82   XP: $10   F18
Small-scale Hotel   4/1-4/30 [CP]   1P: $60   2P: $65   XP: $10   F18
         11/1-3/31 [CP]   1P: $55   2P: $60   XP: $10   F18
Location: I-590, exit 8, 3.9 mi e on SR 404. 2450 Empire Blvd 14580. Fax: 585/671-7494. **Facility:** 42 one-bedroom standard units,
some with whirlpools. 2 stories (no elevator), interior corridors. **Parking:** on-site. **Terms:** cancellation fee imposed. **Guest
Services:** valet laundry. **Cards:** AX, DC, DS, MC, VI.

SOME UNITS

(ASK) (S/D) (📷) / (X) /

WEEDSPORT pop. 2,017—*See also FINGER LAKES.*

──────── WHERE TO STAY ────────

BEST WESTERN WEEDSPORT INN   *Book great rates at AAA.com*   **Phone:** (315)834-6623
(AAA) (SAVE)   7/1-8/31   1P: $69-$160   2P: $79-$180   XP: $10   F12
         5/1-6/30   1P: $59-$150   2P: $69-$180   XP: $10   F12
▼▼▼ ▼▼▼   9/1-10/31   1P: $54-$150   2P: $59-$160   XP: $10   F12
         11/1-4/30   1P: $54-$99   2P: $59-$110   XP: $10   F12
Motel   **Location:** I-90 (New York State Thruway), exit 40, just s to jct SR 34 and 31, then 0.3 mi w on SR 31. 2709 Erie Dr
13166. Fax: 315/834-6626. **Facility:** 34 one-bedroom standard units. 1 story, exterior corridors. **Parking:** on-
site. **Terms:** cancellation fee imposed, [CP] meal plan available, package plans. **Amenities:** irons, hair dryers. *Some:* high-
speed Internet. **Pool(s):** outdoor. **Guest Services:** wireless Internet. **Cards:** AX, DC, DS, MC, VI. **Free Special Amenities:**
continental breakfast and high-speed Internet.

SOME UNITS

(S/D) (📶) (🛋) (📷) (🛗) (🖻) (📺) / (X) /

DAYS INN-WEEDSPORT   *Book great rates at AAA.com*   **Phone:** 315/834-6198
(AAA) (SAVE)   All Year   1P: $69-$150   2P: $79-$160   XP: $10   D16
▼▼▼ ▼▼▼   **Location:** I-90 (New York State Thruway), exit 40, just s at SR 31 and 34. 9050 SR 34 13166. Fax: 315/834-9849.
Facility: 40 one-bedroom standard units, some with whirlpools. 2 stories (no elevator), exterior corridors.
Motel   *Bath:* combo or shower only. **Parking:** on-site. **Terms:** cancellation fee imposed, [CP] meal plan available.
Amenities: irons, hair dryers. **Guest Services:** wireless Internet. **Cards:** AX, DC, DS, MC, VI.
Free Special Amenities: continental breakfast and high-speed Internet.

SOME UNITS

(S/D) (📶) (🛋) (📷) (🛗) (🖻) (📺) / (X) /

──────── WHERE TO DINE ────────

ARNOLD'S FAMILY RESTAURANT   **Lunch:** $4-$8   **Dinner:** $7-$9   **Phone:** 315/834-6251
▼▼   **Location:** I-90 (New York State Thruway), exit 40, just s to jct SR 34 and 31, then 0.5 mi w on SR 31. 2667 Erie Dr
13166. **Hours:** 9 am-8 pm, Fri & Sat from 8 am, Sun 8 am-1 pm. Closed: 12/25. **Features:** The popular
American   family restaurant is known for friendly, hometown service and a menu of comfort food. Casual dress.
Parking: on-site. **Cards:** AX, DS, MC, VI.

OLD ERIE RESTAURANT   **Lunch:** $4-$8   **Dinner:** $10-$17   **Phone:** 315/834-6641
▼▼▼   **Location:** I-90 (New York State Thruway), exit 40, just s to jct SR 34 and 31, then 0.5 mi s on SR 34. 8924 N Seneca St
13166. **Hours:** 11 am-9 pm, Fri-10 pm, Sat 4 pm-10 pm, Sun 1 pm-9 pm. Closed: 11/22, 12/25.
American   **Reservations:** accepted. **Features:** Culinary Institute of America graduates David and Eileen Gibson refine
their art with such delicious dishes as chicken scampi with lemon-pepper linguine, drunken pork chops,
Wiener schnitzel and St. Louis-style ribs. Eileen makes all the luscious desserts. Guests can expect relaxed dining with a
seasoned, friendly staff. Casual dress; cocktails. **Parking:** on-site. **Cards:** AX, MC, VI.

WELLSVILLE pop. 5,171

──────── WHERE TO STAY ────────

LONG VUE INN & SUITES   *Book great rates at AAA.com*   **Phone:** (585)593-2450
(AAA) (SAVE)   All Year   1P: $49-$64   2P: $54-$64
▼▼   **Location:** Jct SR 19, 3 mi w. 5081 Rt 417 W 14895 (PO Box 463). Fax: 585/593-2450. **Facility:** 19 units. 18 one-
bedroom standard units. 1 one-bedroom suite ($69-$98). 1 story, exterior corridors. *Bath:* combo or shower
Motel   only. **Parking:** on-site, winter plug-ins. **Terms:** cancellation fee imposed, [CP] meal plan available, small
pets only (in designated units). **Amenities:** video library, irons. *Some:* hair dryers. **Guest Services:** valet
laundry. **Cards:** AX, DS, MC, VI. **Free Special Amenities: continental breakfast and room upgrade**
(subject to availability with advance reservations).

SOME UNITS

(S/D) (🐾) (VCR) (🖻) (🖻) (📺) / (X) /

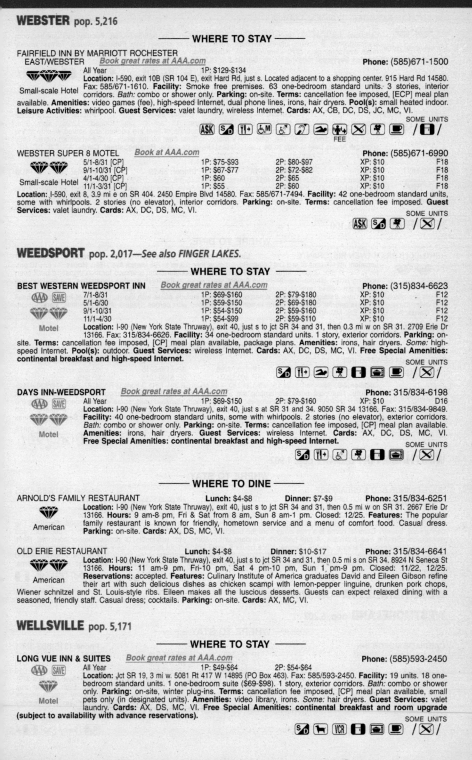

MICROTEL INN & SUITES · *Book at AAA.com*
▽▽ ▽▽
Small-scale Hotel
wireless Internet.
All Year | 1P: $54-$104 | 2P: $54-$104 | XP: $5 | F16
Phone: (585)593-3449
Location: Just n off SR 19 and 417. 30 W Dyke St 14895. **Fax:** 585/593-4288. **Facility:** 60 one-bedroom standard units. 2 stories, interior corridors. *Bath:* combo or shower only. **Parking:** on-site. **Terms:** weekly rates available, pets ($10 extra charge). **Amenities:** voice mail. *Some:* hair dryers. **Guest Services:** **Business Services:** meeting rooms. **Cards:** AX, DC, DS, MC, VI.

SOME UNITS

(ASK) (S✦) 🐾 (𝙔𝙄→) (⅃M) 🎛️ 🎥 / ⊠ 🖥️ 🖨️ 🖵 /
FEE

------ **WHERE TO DINE** ------

THE BEEF HAUS
▽▽ ▽▽
American
MC, VI.
Lunch: $5-$10 | **Dinner:** $8-$18 | **Phone:** 585/593-6222
Location: Center. 176 N Main St 14895. **Hours:** 11 am-10 pm. Closed: 12/25; also Sun. **Reservations:** accepted. **Features:** More than 500 pounds of beef are cooked and served weekly at the busy, popular dining spot. The restaurant's motto is "best beef on the block, and a whole lot more." Only supreme Angus beef is said to be used. Casual dress; cocktails. **Parking:** street. **Cards:** AX, CB, DC, DS,

TEXAS HOT
▽
American
Lunch: $2-$4 | **Dinner:** $5-$9 | **Phone:** 585/593-1400
Location: Center. 132 N Main St 14895. **Hours:** 6 am-11:45 pm. Closed: 3/23, 11/22, 12/25. **Features:** Family-owned since 1921, the busy downtown restaurant serves American fare, good and fast all day. Try the famous Texas hot, with sauce made from a family recipe. Casual dress; beer only. **Parking:** street.

WESTBURY pop. 13,100

------ **WHERE TO DINE** ------

BERTUCCI'S BRICK OVEN RISTORANTE
▽▽ ▽▽
Italian
Lunch: $7-$15 | **Dinner:** $10-$15 | **Phone:** 516/683-8800
Location: Jct Arlington St and Old County Rd. 0.8 mi w, then 0.3 mi s. 795 Merrick Ave 11590. **Hours:** 11 am-10 pm, Fri & Sat-11 pm. Closed: 11/22, 12/25. **Features:** This popular chain is known for their signature brick oven cooking which creates the distinctive flavors you'll taste in the fresh roasted vegetables, the seafood and entree specialties, and of course, the restaurant's top notch pizza. Every dish is made to order and all breads are made from scratch throughout the day. A sample meal may include pasta with the rich flavors of fresh garlic, basil and oven roasted tomatoes and for dessert a divine lemon cream dessert with berries. Casual dress; cocktails. **Parking:** on-site. **Cards:** AX, CB, DC, DS, MC, VI.

WESTFIELD pop. 3,481

------ **WHERE TO STAY** ------

THE WILLIAM SEWARD INN
▽▽▽▽
Historic
Country Inn
elevator), interior corridors.
Phone: 716/326-4151
6/16-9/10 [BP] | 1P: $100-$205 | 2P: $110-$215 | XP: $15
5/1-6/15 & 9/11-4/30 [BP] | 1P: $90-$205 | 2P: $100-$215 | XP: $15
Location: I-90 (New York State Thruway), exit 60, 4 mi se on SR 394. 6645 S Portage Rd 14787. **Fax:** 716/326-4163. **Facility:** High-post beds are among the antiques furnishing individually appointed guest rooms at this historic mansion. Smoke free premises. 12 one-bedroom standard units, some with whirlpools. 2 stories (no elevator), interior corridors. *Bath:* combo or shower only. **Parking:** on-site. **Terms:** 2 night minimum stay - weekends, age restrictions may apply, 7 day cancellation notice. **Amenities:** hair dryers. *Some:* high-speed Internet. **Guest Services:** wireless Internet. **Business Services:** meeting rooms. **Cards:** AX, DS, MC, VI.

SOME UNITS

(𝙔𝙄) ⊠ 🎥 ☎ / 𝖶 /

WESTHAMPTON BEACH pop. 1,902

------ **WHERE TO STAY** ------

SOUTH WINDS BED & BREAKFAST
▽▽ ▽▽
Bed & Breakfast
Phone: (631)288-5505
5/16-10/1 [BP] | 1P: $230-$255 | 2P: $230-$255 | XP: $60
5/1-5/15 & 10/2-11/30 [BP] | 1P: $185-$205 | 2P: $185-$205 | XP: $60
12/1-4/30 [BP] | 1P: $160-$205 | 2P: $160-$205 | XP: $60
Location: Just s of jct CR 31 and Mill Rd; downtown. 91 Potunk Ln 11978. **Fax:** 631/288-5506. **Facility:** The century-old, country Colonial home is a mile away from the beach and within walking distance to many charming boutiques and restaurants. Smoke free premises. 4 one-bedroom standard units, some with whirlpools. 3 stories, interior corridors. *Bath:* combo or shower only. **Parking:** on-site. **Terms:** office hours 8 am-9 pm, 2 night minimum stay - seasonal and/or weekends, age restrictions may apply, cancellation fee imposed, 2% service charge. **Amenities:** video library, hair dryers. **Pool(s):** heated outdoor. **Leisure Activities:** beach access. **Guest Services:** wireless Internet. **Business Services:** meeting rooms. **Cards:** AX, MC, VI.

(ASK) (S✦) (𝙔𝙄→) 🍽️ ⊠ (VCR) ☎ 🖥️

WEST HENRIETTA —See HENRIETTA.

WESTMORELAND pop. 6,207

------ **WHERE TO STAY** ------

CARRIAGE MOTOR INN
(AAA) (SAVE)
▽▽▽▽
Motel
Phone: (315)853-3561
5/1-8/31 | 1P: $45-$55 | 2P: $55-$70 | XP: $7 | D10
9/1-10/31 | 1P: $45-$50 | 2P: $50-$60 | XP: $7 | D10
11/1-4/30 | 1P: $35-$45 | 2P: $45-$55 | XP: $7 | D10
Location: I-90 (New York State Thruway), exit 32, just n. Located in a rural area. 5370 SR 233 13490 (PO Box 379). **Fax:** 315/853-3563. **Facility:** 24 one-bedroom standard units. 1 story, exterior corridors. *Bath:* shower only. **Parking:** on-site, winter plug-ins. **Terms:** 5 day cancellation notice-fee imposed, weekly rates available, [CP] meal plan available, package plans, small pets only ($20 deposit, $5 extra charge). **Guest Services:** coin laundry. **Cards:** AX, CB, DC, DS, MC, VI. **Free Special Amenities:** continental breakfast and local telephone calls.

SOME UNITS

(S✦) 🐾 / ⊠ 🖥️ /
FEE

WEST POINT pop. 7,138

—— WHERE TO STAY ——

THE THAYER HOTEL   *Book great rates at AAA.com*
(AAA) (SAVE)
~~~~~~~~
Historic
Small-scale Hotel

5/1-11/17	1P: $225-$335	Phone: (845)446-4731
11/18-4/30	1P: $179-$269	XP: $10 F12
		XP: $10 F12

Location: Jct US 6 and SR 9W, 2.8 mi n on SR 9W, 1.9 mi n on SR 218 to West Point's South Gate. 674 Thayer Rd 10996. Fax: 845/446-0338. **Facility:** This 1926 hotel has been renovated to preserve its stunning Gothic-style architecture; many rooms offer spectacular views of the Hudson River. 151 units. 149 one-bedroom standard units. 2 one-bedroom suites ($245-$750). 5 stories, interior corridors. **Parking:** on-site. **Terms:** [BP] meal plan available, package plans. **Amenities:** dual phone lines, voice mail, irons, hair dryers. *Fee:* video library, video games. **Dining:** 7-10:30 am, 11:30-2:30 & 5:30-9:30 pm, Sun 10:30 am-2 & 5:30-9:30 pm; Sunday brunch, cocktails. **Leisure Activities:** exercise room. *Fee:* massage. **Guest Services:** valet laundry, beauty salon, wireless Internet. **Business Services:** conference facilities. **Cards:** AX, DC, DS, MC, VI. **Free Special Amenities: full breakfast and local telephone calls.**

SOME UNITS

[icons]

WEST SENECA —*See Buffalo p. 262.*

WHEATFIELD —*See Niagara Falls p. 528.*

WHITE PLAINS —*See New York p. 506.*

WHITNEY POINT pop. 965

—— WHERE TO DINE ——

AIELLO'S RESTAURANT/PIZZERIA   *Menu on AAA.com*   **Lunch:** $4-$8   **Dinner:** $7-$19   **Phone:** 607/692-4114
(AAA)
~~~~~~~~
American

Location: I-81, exit 8; corner of US 11 and Main St. 2677 Main St 13862. **Hours:** 11 am-10 pm, Fri & Sat-10:30 pm. Closed: 3/23, 11/22, 12/25. **Reservations:** required. **Features:** Popular since 1982, the family restaurant features a large selection of fresh seafood, tender veal, prime rib, homemade pasta and sauces. The newly renovated dining room allows for more intimate dining. Casual dress; cocktails. **Parking:** on-site. **Cards:** AX, DS, MC, VI.

WILLIAMSVILLE —*See Buffalo p. 262.*

WILLISTON PARK pop. 7,261

—— WHERE TO DINE ——

RIVERBAY SEAFOOD BAR & GRILL   **Lunch:** $10-$20   **Dinner:** $16-$28   **Phone:** 516/742-9191
~~~~~~~~
Seafood

Location: I-495, exit 37; Northern State Pkwy, exit 28, 1.5 mi s. 700 Willis Ave 11596. **Hours:** noon-10 pm, Fri-11 pm, Sat 5 pm-11 pm, Sun 11:30 am-9:30 pm. Closed: 11/22, 12/25. **Features:** Rich, mahogany beams, antique light fixtures and beveled glass add to the comfortable charm of the relaxed dining room. Many varieties of oysters are among well-prepared selections of fresh seafood, nicely complemented by a lengthy wine list. Casual dress; cocktails. **Parking:** on-site. **Cards:** AX, DC, MC, VI.

[icon]

WILMINGTON pop. 1,131—See also ADIRONDACK MOUNTAINS.

———— **WHERE TO STAY** ————

GRAND VIEW MOTEL
Phone: (518)946-2209

(AAA) [SAVE]

12/26-3/24	1P: $69-$99	2P: $69-$99
5/22-10/9	1P: $59-$99	2P: $59-$99

Motel

Location: On SR 86, 1 mi e. 5941 NYS Rt 86 12997. **Facility:** 16 one-bedroom standard units. 1 story, exterior corridors. *Bath:* shower only. **Parking:** on-site, winter plug-ins. **Terms:** open 5/22-10/9 & 12/26-3/24, package plans, small pets only (with prior approval). **Pool(s):** heated outdoor. **Leisure Activities:** badminton, playground, basketball, horseshoes. **Cards:** MC, VI. **Free Special Amenities: local telephone calls and preferred room (subject to availability with advance reservations).**

SOME UNITS

GREEN MOUNTAIN LODGE
Phone: 518/946-8232

Property failed to provide current rates

Motel

Location: Jct SR 86 and Whiteface Mt Hwy (SR 431). 5675 SR 86 12997. Fax: 518/946-7808. **Facility:** 24 one-bedroom standard units. 2 stories (no elevator), exterior corridors. **Parking:** on-site, winter plug-ins. **Terms:** pets ($10 fee). **Leisure Activities:** playground, horseshoes, game room. **Business Services:** fax.

SOME UNITS

FEE

HUNGRY TROUT RESORT
Phone: 518/946-2217

(AAA) [SAVE]

5/10-10/28	1P: $79-$169	2P: $79-$169
12/26-3/23	1P: $69-$169	2P: $69-$169

Motel

Location: On SR 86, 2 mi w. 5239 Rt 86 12997. Fax: 518/946-7418. **Facility:** 20 units. 18 one- and 2 two-bedroom standard units, some with efficiencies. 1 story, exterior corridors. **Parking:** on-site, winter plug-ins. **Terms:** open 5/10-10/28 & 12/26-3/23, 14 day cancellation notice-fee imposed, [MAP] meal plan available, package plans, pets (dogs only, $5 extra charge). **Dining:** 2 restaurants, 5 pm-10 pm, cocktails, also, The Hungry Trout Restaurant, R. F. McDougall's, see separate listings. **Pool(s):** outdoor, wading. **Leisure Activities:** fishing, guide services for fishing & bird hunting, cross country skiing, hiking trails, playground. **Cards:** AX, DS, MC, VI. **Free Special Amenities: local telephone calls and early check-in/late check-out.**

SOME UNITS

FEE

LEDGE ROCK AT WHITEFACE MOUNTAIN
Book great rates at AAA.com
Phone: (518)946-2379

(AAA) [SAVE]

5/1-10/16	1P: $79-$149	2P: $79-$149
10/17-4/30	1P: $79-$139	2P: $79-$139

Motel

Location: On SR 86, 3 mi w. 5078 NYS Rt 86 12997. Fax: 518/946-7594. **Facility:** 19 units. 16 one-bedroom standard units. 3 two-bedroom suites, some with kitchens. 2 stories (no elevator), exterior corridors. **Parking:** on-site, winter plug-ins. **Terms:** 2 night minimum stay - weekends, 10 day cancellation notice-fee imposed, package plans, pets ($25 fee). **Amenities:** video library, irons, hair dryers. **Pool(s):** outdoor, wading. **Leisure Activities:** paddleboats, cross country skiing, ice skating, tobogganing, ski waxing room, pool table, hiking trails. **Guest Services:** wireless Internet. **Business Services:** meeting rooms. **Cards:** AX, DS, MC, VI. **Free Special Amenities: local telephone calls and high-speed Internet.**

FEE

MOUNTAIN BROOK LODGE
Phone: 518/946-2262

Property failed to provide current rates

Motel

Location: Center. 5712 Rt 86 12997 (PO Box 445). Fax: 518/946-7536. **Facility:** Designated smoking area. 12 one-bedroom standard units. 1 story, exterior corridors. *Bath:* combo or shower only. **Parking:** on-site. **Terms:** pets ($25 fee, in designated units, with prior approval). **Pool(s):** outdoor. **Guest Services:** gift shop.

SOME UNITS

FEE

NORTH POLE INN
Phone: 518/946-7733

(AAA) [SAVE]

All Year	1P: $59-$139	2P: $59-$139	XP: $7 F15

Motel

Location: On SR 86, just w of jct CR 431. 5636 NYS Rt 86 12997 (PO Box 68). Fax: 518/946-7705. **Facility:** 24 units. 19 one-bedroom standard units, some with efficiencies. 1 one-bedroom suite ($99-$149) with efficiency. 1 vacation home ($250-$350) and 3 cottages ($99-$139). 1 story, exterior corridors. *Bath:* combo or shower only. **Parking:** on-site, winter plug-ins. **Terms:** 7 day cancellation notice-fee imposed, package plans, pets ($10 extra charge, with prior approval). **Amenities:** high-speed Internet (fee). **Pool(s):** heated outdoor, wading. **Leisure Activities:** fishing, shared recreational facilities with adjacent campground, bicycles, hiking trails, playground, basketball, horseshoes, volleyball. *Fee:* miniature golf, game room. **Guest Services:** coin laundry. **Business Services:** meeting rooms. **Cards:** DS, MC, VI. **Free Special Amenities: local telephone calls and early check-in/late check-out.**

SOME UNITS

FEE   FEE

WILLKOMMEN HOF BED & BREAKFAST
Phone: (518)946-7669

All Year [BP]	1P: $60-$149	2P: $70-$149	XP: $20 D12

Bed & Breakfast

Location: On SR 86, 1.5 mi of jct CR 431. 5367 Rt 86 12997 (PO Box 240). Fax: 518/946-7626. **Facility:** 6 one-bedroom standard units, some with whirlpools. 2 stories (no elevator), interior corridors. *Bath:* some shared or private, combo or shower only. **Parking:** on-site. **Terms:** 2 night minimum stay - weekends, 21 day cancellation notice-fee imposed, weekly rates available, package plans, pets ($10 fee). **Amenities:** *Some:* hair dryers. **Leisure Activities:** sauna, whirlpool, fishing. **Business Services:** PC. **Cards:** MC, VI.

SOME UNITS

FEE

——— **WHERE TO DINE** ———

THE HUNGRY TROUT RESTAURANT   **Dinner:** $20-$32   **Phone:** 518/946-2217

▼▼▼   **Location:** On SR 86, 2 mi w; in Hungry Trout Resort. Rt 86 12997. **Hours:** 5 pm-10 pm. **Closed:** 3/18-5/8 & 11/1-
12/26. **Reservations:** suggested. **Features:** The setting will enchant you and the atmosphere charm you.
Steak & Seafood   The Hungry Trout offers casual dining with stunning views of the mountains which frame it. Trout, prepared
as simply or as elaborately as you like, is the house specialty. Also on the menu are steak, seafood and
chicken. Reservations are a must for the popular window seats. Casual dress; cocktails. **Parking:** on-site. **Cards:** AX, DS,
MC, VI.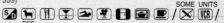

R. F. MCDOUGALL'S   **Dinner:** $8-$15   **Phone:** 518/946-2217

▼▼ ▼▼   **Location:** On SR 86, 2 mi w; in Hungry Trout Resort. 5239 NYS Rt 86 12997. **Hours:** 5 pm-10 pm. **Closed:** 3/23,
11/22, 12/24, 12/25; also 3/18-5/8 & 11/1-12/26. **Reservations:** accepted. **Features:** The old-fashioned
American   neighborhood pub serves fish and chips, steak sandwiches and hamburgers. Bottled and draft beers on tap
are available. Casual dress; cocktails. **Parking:** on-site. **Cards:** AX, DS, MC, VI.

WILTON pop. 12,511

——— **WHERE TO STAY** ———

THE BIRCHES MOTEL   **Phone:** (518)584-1484

▼▼   7/21-9/10   1P: $149-$250   2P: $149-$250   XP: $30
7/1-7/20   1P: $75-$150   2P: $75-$150   XP: $20
Motel   5/1-6/30 & 9/11-4/30   1P: $65-$150   2P: $65-$150   XP: $20
Location: I-87, exit 15, 0.9 mi w, then 2.2 mi n on US 9. 660 Saratoga Rd 12831. **Fax:** 518/584-2178. **Facility:** 11
one-bedroom standard units. 1 story, exterior corridors. *Bath:* combo or shower only. **Parking:** on-site. **Terms:** cancellation fee
imposed, package plans. **Guest Services:** wireless Internet. **Business Services:** fax. **Cards:** MC, VI.

SOME UNITS

WINDHAM pop. 359

——— **WHERE TO STAY** ———

ALBERGO ALLEGRIA HISTORIC BED &
BREAKFAST   **Phone:** (518)734-5560

▲▲▲ [SAVE]   All Year [BP]   1P: $83-$189   2P: $83-$189   XP: $25   D12
Location: SR 23, just s. 43 SR 296 12496 (PO Box 267). **Fax:** 518/734-5570. **Facility:** Near the ski slopes, this
▼▼▼▼   B&B offers individually decorated guest rooms and friendly and accommodating service. Smoke free
Bed & Breakfast   premises. 21 one-bedroom standard units, some with whirlpools. 1-2 stories (no elevator), interior/exterior
corridors. **Parking:** on-site, winter plug-ins. **Terms:** 14 day cancellation notice-fee imposed, package plans.
Amenities: video library, DVD players, dual phone lines, voice mail, hair dryers. *Some:* CD players, irons.
Leisure Activities: rental bicycles, shuffleboard. **Guest Services:** gift shop. **Business Services:** fax (fee). **Cards:** MC, VI.
Free Special Amenities: full breakfast and local telephone calls.

SOME UNITS

——— **WHERE TO DINE** ———

FALVEY'S ON THE MOUNTAIN   **Dinner:** $12-$22   **Phone:** 518/622-8744

▲▲▲   **Location:** On SR 23. SR 23 12405. **Hours:** 4 pm-10 pm, Fri & Sat-11 pm. **Closed:** 12/25.
Reservations: accepted. **Features:** This restaurant features true all-American fare, including a salad bar
and homemade desserts, in a secluded mountaintop location overlooking a valley. Casual dress; cocktails.
Parking: on-site. **Cards:** AX, DS, MC, VI.
Steak & Seafood

WOODBURY pop. 9,010

——— **WHERE TO STAY** ———

BEST WESTERN WOODBURY INN   *Book great rates at AAA.com*   **Phone:** (516)921-6900

▲▲▲ [SAVE]   10/1-11/30   1P: $139-$169   2P: $139-$169
5/1-8/31   1P: $129-$169   2P: $129-$169
▼▼▼▼   9/1-9/30   1P: $119-$149   2P: $119-$149
Motel   12/1-4/30   1P: $109-$129   2P: $109-$129
Location: Jct SR 25 and 135, 0.9 mi e. Located in a commercial area. 7940 Jericho Tpke (SR 25) 11797.
Fax: 516/921-6908. **Facility:** 98 one-bedroom standard units, some with efficiencies. 2-3 stories,
interior/exterior corridors. *Bath:* combo or shower only. **Parking:** on-site. **Terms:** cancellation fee imposed, [CP] meal plan
available, package plans, 12% service charge, small pets only ($50 fee). **Amenities:** video games (fee), high-speed Internet,
voice mail, irons, hair dryers. *Some:* CD players. **Dining:** 11 am-11 pm, Sat 5 pm-midnight, Sun 5 pm-10 pm, cocktails. **Pool(s):**
outdoor. **Leisure Activities:** exercise room. **Guest Services:** valet laundry, wireless Internet. **Business Services:** meeting
rooms, business center. **Cards:** AX, CB, DC, DS, MC, VI. **Free Special Amenities: newspaper and room upgrade (subject
to availability with advance reservations).** *(See color ad p 359)*

SOME UNITS

EXECUTIVE INN AT WOODBURY   *Book great rates at AAA.com*   Phone: (516)921-8500

All Year   1P: $115-$149
Location: Jct SR 25 and 135, 1 mi e. Located in a commercial area. 8030 Jericho Tpke (SR 25) 11797.
Fax: 516/921-1057. **Facility:** 108 one-bedroom standard units. 1-2 stories (no elevator), exterior corridors.
Bath: combo or shower only. **Parking:** on-site. **Terms:** cancellation fee imposed, [ECP] meal plan available,

Motel

pets ($100 deposit). **Amenities:** video games (fee), high-speed Internet, voice mail, irons, hair dryers.
Some: CD players. **Pool(s):** small outdoor. **Leisure Activities:** exercise room. **Guest Services:** valet and
coin laundry, wireless Internet. **Business Services:** meeting rooms, business center. **Cards:** AX, CB, DC, DS, MC, VI.
(See color ad p 359)

SOME UNITS

FEE

---------- **WHERE TO DINE** ----------

BUTERA'S   Lunch: $10-$15   Dinner: $11-$23   Phone: 516/496-3633

Location: I-495, exit 44 (Syosset), 0.8 mi n on SR 135, then 0.9 mi ne. 7903 Jericho Tpke 11797. **Hours:** 11:30 am-4
& 5-10 pm, Fri-11 pm, Sat noon-4 & 5-11 pm, Sun 4 pm-9 pm. Closed: 3/23, 11/22, 12/25. **Features:** The

Italian

bustling trattoria-style restaurant offers a great selection of homemade pasta entrees, grilled chicken, veal
and fresh fish. The large open room is nicely appointed with contemporary stone wall accents, fieldstone
and hardwood floors and a stone fireplace. Each granite table is topped with a vase of fresh flowers. Patio seating and a
children's menu also are available. Casual dress; cocktails. **Parking:** on-site. **Cards:** AX, MC, VI.

YONKERS —*See New York p. 506.*

YORKVILLE pop. 2,675

---------- **WHERE TO DINE** ----------

SYMEON'S   Lunch: $5-$13   Dinner: $10-$20   Phone: 315/736-4074
Location: On SR 5A, 0.5 mi e of Sangertown Square Shopping Center. 4941 Commercial Dr 13495. **Hours:** 11 am-10

Greek

pm, Fri & Sat-11 pm, Sun noon-9 pm. Closed: 3/23, 11/22, 12/24, 12/25. **Features:** Greek artwork, posters
and pottery decorate the newly renovated, intimate dining rooms. Among well-prepared traditional dishes
are the specialty souvlaki, spanakopita and crisp, tasty salad. Casually uniformed servers are pleasant and
efficient. Casual dress; beer & wine only. **Parking:** on-site. **Cards:** AX, DS, MC, VI.

YOUNGSTOWN —*See Niagara Falls p. 528.*

⨀ *Offices*

Cities with main offices are listed in **BOLD TYPE** and toll-free member service numbers in *ITALIC TYPE*.
All are closed Saturdays, Sundays and holidays unless otherwise indicated.
The type of service provided is designated below the name of the city where the office is located:

✦ Auto travel services, including books/maps, marked maps and on-demand TripTik ® maps
● Auto travel services, including books/maps, marked maps, but no on-demand TripTik ® maps
■ Provides books/maps only. No marked maps or on-demand TripTik ® maps available
▲ Travel agency services

NATIONAL OFFICE: 1000 AAA DRIVE, HEATHROW, FLORIDA 32746-5063, (407) 444-7000

NEW YORK

ALBANY—AAA HUDSON VALLEY, 618 DELAWARE AVE, 12209. MON-FRI 9-5, THU 9-7, SAT 9-1. (518) 426-1000. ✦▲

AMSTERDAM—AAA NORTHWAY, 118 SANFORD FARMS, 12010. MON-FRI 9-5, TUE & THU 9-6. (518) 684-0064. ✦▲

BINGHAMTON—AAA SOUTHERN NEW YORK, 21 WASHINGTON ST, 13901. MON-FRI 8:30-5, MON & THU 8:30-6. (607) 722-7255. ✦▲

BROOKLYN—AAA NEW YORK, 2334 RALPH AVE, 11234. MON-FRI 8:45-5:30, SAT 9-5. (718) 224-2222. ✦▲

BUFFALO—AAA WESTERN AND CENTRAL NEW YORK, 100 INTERNATIONAL DR, 14221. MON-FRI 9:30-6, SAT 10-4. (716) 633-9860. ✦▲

BUFFALO—AAA WESTERN AND CENTRAL NEW YORK, 2658 DELAWARE AVE #300, 14216. MON-FRI 9-5:30, TUE 9-7, SAT 10-2. (716) 873-0111. ✦▲

CAMILLUS—AAA WESTERN AND CENTRAL NEW YORK, 5103 W GENESEE ST, 13031. MON-FRI 9-5:30, THU 9-7, SAT 9-1. (315) 487-2700. *(866) 432-9005.* ✦▲

CICERO—AAA WESTERN AND CENTRAL NEW YORK, 5663 E CIR DR STE 300, 13039. MON-FRI 9-5:30, TUE-THU 9-7, SAT 9-3. (315) 452-3282. ✦▲

COOPERSTOWN—AAA NEW YORK, 72 ELM ST, 13326. MON-FRI 8:30-5. (607) 547-2519. ✦▲

DUNKIRK—AAA WESTERN AND CENTRAL NEW YORK, 3968 VINEYARD DR, 14048. MON-FRI 9-5:30, THU 9-6:30, SAT 10-1. (716) 366-3599. ✦▲

ELMIRA HEIGHTS—AAA SOUTHERN NEW YORK, 99 W MCCANNS BLVD, 14903. MON-FRI 8:30-5, THU 8:30-6. (607) 734-5246. ✦

ENDICOTT—AAA SOUTHERN NEW YORK, 124 WASHINGTON AVE, 13760. MON-FRI 9-5, MON & THU 9-6. (607) 754-1060. ✦

GARDEN CITY—AAA NEW YORK , 1415 KELLUM PL, 11530. MON-FRI 8:45-5:30. (516) 746-7141.
[Administrative office only]

GARDEN CITY—AAA NEW YORK, 229 SEVENTH ST, 11530. MON-FRI 8:45-5:30, SAT 9-5. (516) 746-7141. ✦▲

HERKIMER—AAA NEW YORK, 246 N MAIN ST, 13350. MON-FRI 9-5. (315) 866-1830. ✦▲

HUDSON—AAA HUDSON VALLEY, 179 HEALY BLVD, 12534. MON-FRI 9-5, THU 9-7. (518) 828-4537. ✦▲

ITHACA—AAA WESTERN AND CENTRAL NEW YORK, 1284 DRYDEN RD, 14850. MON-FRI 8:30-5:30, SAT 9-1. (607) 257-2515. ▲

ITHACA—AAA WESTERN AND CENTRAL NEW YORK, 723 S MEADOW ST, 14850. MON-FRI 9-5, THU 9-5:30, SAT 9-1. (607) 273-6727. ●▲

JAMAICA—AAA NEW YORK, 186-06 HILLSIDE AVE, 11432. MON-FRI 8:45-5:30, SAT 9-5. (718) 224-2222. ✦▲

JAMESTOWN—AAA EAST CENTRAL, 111 W 5TH ST, 14701. MON-FRI 8:30-5. (716) 488-1981. ✦▲

LOCKPORT—AAA EAST CENTRAL, 7135 ROCHESTER RD, 14094. MON-FRI 9-5, THU 8-6:30. (716) 434-2865 ✦▲

NEW YORK—AAA NEW YORK, 1881 BROADWAY AT W62ND ST, 10023. MON-FRI 8:45-5:30, SAT 9-5. (212) 757-2000. ✦▲

NIAGARA FALLS—AAA WESTERN AND CENTRAL NEW YORK, 1595 MILITARY RD, 14304. MON-FRI 9-5:30, TUE 9-7, FRI 9-5, SAT 9:30-12:30. (716) 298-5651. ✦▲

OLEAN—AAA WESTERN AND CENTRAL NEW YORK, 1 BLUEBIRD SQ 175 N UNION, 14760. MON-FRI 9-5, SAT 9-1. (716) 372-3511. ●▲

ONEONTA—AAA NEW YORK, 195 ONEIDA ST, 13820. MON-FRI 9-5, SAT 9-12. (607) 432-4512. ✦▲

ORCHARD PARK—AAA WESTERN AND CENTRAL NEW YORK, 3364 SOUTHWESTERN BLVD, 14127. MON-FRI 9-5, TUE 9-7, THU 9-7, SAT 9-2. (716) 675-4900. ✦▲

PENFIELD—AAA WESTERN AND CENTRAL NEW YORK, 2156 PENFIELD RD, 14526. MON-FRI 9-5:30, TUE 9-7, THU 9-7, SAT 9-2. (585) 377-8500. *(800) 836-2582.* ✦▲

PITTSFORD—AAA WESTERN AND CENTRAL NEW YORK, 3240 MONROE AVE, 14618. MON-FRI 9-6, WED-THU 9-7, SAT 10-3. (585) 249-1390. ▲

PLATTSBURGH—AAA NORTHWAY, 20 BOOTH DR, 12901. MON-FRI 9-5, TUE & THU 9-6. (518) 563-3830. ✦▲

QUEENSBURY—AAA NORTHWAY, 345 BAY RD, 12804. MON-FRI 9-5, TUE & THU 9-6. (518) 792-0088. ✦▲

ROCHESTER—AAA WESTERN AND CENTRAL NEW YORK, 3160 W RIDGE RD, 14626. MON-FRI 9-5:30, MON & WED 9-7, SAT 9-2. (585) 227-9600. ✦▲

SARATOGA SPRINGS—AAA NORTHWAY, 26 WEST AVE, 12866. MON-FRI 9-5, TUE & THU 9-6. (518) 587-8449. ✦▲

SCARSDALE—AAA NEW YORK, 111 BROOK ST, 10583. MON-FRI 8:45-5:30, SAT 9-5. (914) 948-4600. ✦▲

SCHENECTADY—AAA NORTHWAY , 112 RAILROAD ST, 12305. MON-FRI 9-5, TUE & THU 9-6. (518) 374-4575.
[Administrative office only]

SCHENECTADY—AAA NORTHWAY, 1626 UNION ST, 12309. MON-FRI 9-5, TUE & THU 9-6. (518) 374-4575. ✦▲

SMITHTOWN—AAA NEW YORK, 729 SMITHTOWN BY-PASS, 11787. MON-FRI 8:45-5:30, SAT 9-5. (516) 746-7141. ✦▲

SYRACUSE—AAA WESTERN AND CENTRAL NEW YORK, 3175 E GENESEE ST, 13224. MON-FRI 9-5:30, THU 9-6:30, FRI 9-5, SAT 9-1. (315) 446-3134. ✦▲

TROY—AAA HUDSON VALLEY, 514 CONGRESS ST, 12180. MON-FRI 9-5, THU 9-7, SAT 9-1. (518) 426-1000. ✦▲

UTICA—AAA NEW YORK, 409 COURT ST, 13502. MON-FRI 8-6. (315) 797-5000. ✦▲

WATERTOWN—AAA WESTERN AND CENTRAL NEW YORK, 19482 US RT 11, 13601. MON-FRI 9-5:30, SAT 10-1. (315) 788-5250. *(800) 836-0532.* ✦▲

Metric Equivalents Chart

TEMPERATURE

To convert Fahrenheit to Celsius, subtract 32 from the Fahrenheit temperature, multiply by 5 and divide by 9.
To convert Celsius to Fahrenheit, multipy by 9, divide by 5 and add 32.

ACRES

1 acre = 0.4 hectare (ha)   1 hectare = 2.47 acres

MILES AND KILOMETRES

Note: A kilometre is approximately 5/8 or 0.6 of a mile.
To convert kilometres to miles multiply by 0.6.

Miles/Kilometres		Kilometres/Miles	
15	24.1	30	18.6
20	32.2	35	21.7
25	40.2	40	24.8
30	48.3	45	27.9
35	56.3	50	31.0
40	64.4	55	34.1
45	72.4	60	37.2
50	80.5	65	40.3
55	88.5	70	43.4
60	96.6	75	46.6
65	104.6	80	49.7
70	112.7	85	52.8
75	120.7	90	55.9
80	128.7	95	59.0
85	136.8	100	62.1
90	144.8	105	65.2
95	152.9	110	68.3
100	160.9	115	71.4

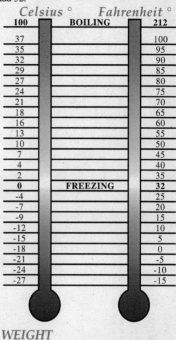

Celsius °		Fahrenheit °
100	BOILING	212
37		100
35		95
32		90
29		85
27		80
24		75
21		70
18		65
16		60
13		55
10		50
7		45
4		40
2		35
0	FREEZING	32
-4		25
-7		20
-9		15
-12		10
-15		5
-18		0
-21		-5
-24		-10
-27		-15

LINEAR MEASURE

Customary	Metric
1 inch = 2.54 centimetres	1 centimetre = 0.4 inches
1 foot = 30 centimetres	1 metre = 3.3 feet
1 yard = 0.91 metres	1 metre = 1.09 yards
1 mile = 1.6 kilometres	1 kilometre = .62 miles

WEIGHT

If You Know:	Multiply By:	To Find:
Ounces	28.000	Grams
Pounds	0.450	Kilograms
Grams	0.035	Ounces
Kilograms	2.200	Pounds

LIQUID MEASURE

Customary	Metric
1 fluid ounce = 30 millilitres	1 millilitre = .03 fluid ounces
1 cup = .24 litres	1 litre = 2.1 pints
1 pint = .47 litres	1 litre = 1.06 quarts
1 quart = .95 litres	1 litre = .26 gallons
1 gallon = 3.8 litres	

PRESSURE

Air pressure in automobile tires is expressed
in kilopascals. Multiply pound-force per
square inch (psi) by 6.89 to find kilopascals
(kPa).

24 psi = 165 kPa   28 psi = 193 kPa
26 psi = 179 kPa   30 psi = 207 kPa

GALLON AND LITRES

Gallons/Litres				Litres/Gallons			
5	19.0	12	45.6	10	2.6	40	10.4
6	22.8	14	53.2	15	3.9	50	13.0
7	26.6	16	60.8	20	5.2	60	15.6
8	30.4	18	68.4	25	6.5	70	18.2
9	34.2	20	76.0	30	7.8	80	20.8
10	38.0	25	95.0	35	9.1	90	23.4

658

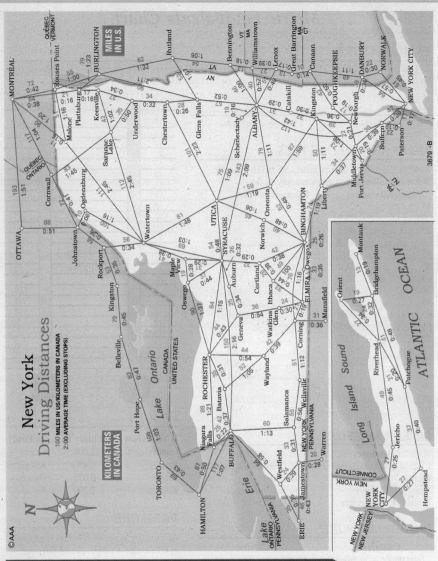

New York
Driving Distances
100 MILES IN US/KILOMETERS IN CANADA
2:00 AVERAGE TIME (EXCLUDING STOPS)

Border Information

FOR UNITED STATES RESIDENTS ENTERING CANADA

Native-born citizens of the United States:

- Passport not required (but is recommended)
- Proof of citizenship required (a birth certificate and photo ID)
- Proof of residence may be required

Naturalized citizens: naturalization certificate required

U.S. resident aliens: Alien Registration Receipt Card (Green Card) required

Single parents, grandparents or guardians traveling with a minor must show documentation of legal custody and provide proof of citizenship for each child (the minor's passport or a parent's passport that includes the child).

When a child is traveling with only 1 parent that parent should have a notarized letter of consent from the other parent or legal custody documents.

When a child is traveling alone or with an individual other than a parent the minor should have a notarized letter of consent with phone number(s) from both parents or a custody document.

Legal Issues: Persons with felony convictions, driving while intoxicated records or other offenses may be denied admittance into Canada. Contact the Canadian embassy or nearest consulate before travel.

Canadian Goods and Services Tax (GST):
- 7 percent GST levied on most items sold and most services rendered in Canada
- 15 percent Harmonized Sales Tax (HST) (7 percent GST and 8 percent provincial component) charged on most goods and services in Nova Scotia, New Brunswick and Newfoundland
- Apply for GST/HST rebate on items including short-term accommodations (less than 1 month in 1 location)
- Claim a rebate on a minimum of $200 of eligible purchases prior to taxes provided the goods are exported 60 days from purchase date

- GST/HST rebate not refundable on alcohol, food and beverages, tobacco, transportation, entertainment, automobile fuel and such services as dry cleaning
- Submit original receipts (amount must be at least $50 before tax)

Free GST brochures with rebate form available in Canada at land border and airport duty-free shops, tourist information centers, customs offices, hotels. Allow 4 to 6 weeks for claim processing. For information contact: Visitor Rebate Program, Summerside Tax Centre, Canada Revenue Agency, 275 Pope Road, Suite 104, Summerside, P.E., Canada C1N 6C6; 902-432-5608 outside Canada; 800-668-4748 in Canada.

Firearms: Canada has strict laws regarding the importing, exporting, possession, use, storage, display and transportation of firearms. These are federal laws that apply across the country.

Classes of Firearms:
- Non-restricted (most ordinary rifles and shotguns)
- Restricted (mainly handguns)
- Prohibited (full automatics, converted automatics, handguns with a barrel length of 105 m (≈4 inches) or less, and .25 or .32 caliber handguns, among others)

Certain handguns used in International Shooting Union sporting competition are classified as restricted even though they meet the prohibited handgun definition.

Yes: To bring a non-restricted or restricted firearm into Canada you must:
- Be 18 years of age or older
- Declare firearm(s) at first point of entry
- Get an Authorization to Transport (ATT) from a provincial or territorial Chief Firearms Officer before arriving at point of entry (Note: ATT not issued for hunting or self-protection purposes)

No: You may not bring into Canada a prohibited firearm or replica firearm, except replicas of firearms classified as antiques (a replica that looks exactly, or almost exactly, like a firearm but is not a firearm; it cannot discharge projectiles or discharges only harmless projectiles).

The Canada Border Services Agency is responsible for all customs procedures.

Yes:

- You may import non-restricted firearms for legitimate purposes: sporting or hunting; use in competitions; transit movement; or personal protection against wildlife in remote areas (customs officer must agree that circumstances warrant firearm possession)
- Register weapons with U.S. Customs before departure
- Upon return you must show proof that you had the weapon before departure
- Under certain circumstances individuals and businesses may import firearms

No: Non-residents may not import prohibited items.

Fees (in Canadian funds):

- Non-Resident Firearm Declaration – $50 covers all firearms listed on declaration
- Possession and acquisition license – $60 for non-restricted firearms; valid for 5 years
- Temporary Firearms Borrowing License (for non-residents) – $30; may renew once in a 12-month period at no extra cost; $30 thereafter (800-731-4000)
- Imported firearm registration fee – $25 per firearm registered in Canada

Prohibited: Any large capacity cartridge magazine (limited to 5 rounds for semiautomatic rifles or shotguns, 10 rounds for handguns), any device designed to stop the sound of a firearm, any knife with a blade opened by spring pressure (e.g., switchblade), martial arts weapons (e.g., shuriken (shooting stars), nunchaku sticks), mace, blowguns, hand-held compact crossbows and any other weapons declared prohibited by regulation.

Yes: Hunters may bring in, duty-free, 200 rounds of ammunition; competition participants 1,500 rounds. Must show valid license or declaration to purchase ammunition. If planning to hunt in multiple provinces or territories, you must obtain a hunting license from each one.
No: Firearms forbidden in many of Canada's national and provincial parks, game reserves and adjacent areas.

Parks and Hunting Regulation Information: Newfoundland and Labrador 800-563-6353 or 709-729-2830; Prince Edward Island 888-734-7529 or 902-629-2400; Nova Scotia 800-565-0000 ext 998 or 902-425-5781; New Brunswick 800-561-0123 or 506-789-4982; Quebec 800-363-7777 or 514-873-2015; Ontario 800-668-2746 or 416-314-0944; Manitoba 800-665-0040 or 204-945-3777; Saskatchewan 877-237-2273 or 306-787-2300; Alberta 800-661-8888 or 780-427-4321; British Columbia 800-663-6000 or 250-387-1642; Northwest Territories (Western NWT) 800-661-0788 or 867-873-4059; Nunavut (Eastern NWT) 800-491-7910 or 867-979-1261; Yukon 867-667-5340.

Note: Provinces and territories also have their own laws regulating the transportation of firearms through their areas, usually in connection with their hunting regulations. For further information on the entry of firearms, applying for a license or to obtain authorization to transport a firearm, contact: Canadian Firearms Centre at 800-731-4000.

Personal Baggage:

- Admissible into Canada on a temporary basis without payment of duty and taxes
- Customs may require a refundable security deposit at time of entry
- Deposits not normally required for health- or pleasure-related visits as long as all items are exported at trip's end

Personal baggage that may be taken into Canada on a duty- and tax-free basis includes clothing and personal items, sporting goods, automobiles, vessels, aircraft, snowmobiles, cameras, personal computers, food products and other items appropriate for the purpose and duration of the visit.

Tobacco products – Those meeting age requirements (18 years in Alberta, Manitoba, Northwest Territories and Nunavut, Saskatchewan, Quebec and Yukon Territory; 19 years in other provinces) may bring in 50 cigars, 200 cigarettes, 200 grams of tobacco and 200 tobacco sticks. **Alcohol** – Those meeting age requirements (18 years in Alberta, Manitoba and Quebec; 19 years in other provinces and territories) may bring in limited alcoholic beverages: 40 ounces (1.14 L) of liquor, 1.6 quarts (1.5 L) of wine or 9 quarts (8.6 L) of beer or ale (equivalent to 24 12-ounce bottles or cans).

- Generally, a minimum 24-hour stay is required to transport any liquor or tobacco into Canada

- Amounts exceeding the allowable quantities noted above are subject to federal duty and taxes, and provincial/territorial liquor fees
- Pay provincial fees at customs at the time of entry in all provinces and the Yukon Territory
- Illegal to bring more than the allowable alcohol quantity into the Northwest Territories and Nunavut

Articles purchased at Canadian duty-free shops are subject to U.S. Customs exemptions and restrictions; those purchased at U.S. duty-free shops before entering Canada are subject to duty if brought back into the United States.

Prescription Drugs: Persons requiring medication while visiting Canada are permitted to bring it for their own use. Clearly identify and carry in original packaging with a label listing the drug and its intended use. Have a copy of the prescription and prescribing doctor's phone number.

Gifts: Items not exceeding $60 (CAN) in value, excluding tobacco, alcoholic beverages and advertising matter, taken into or mailed to Canada are allowed free entry. Gifts valued at more than $60 are subject to regular duty and taxes on the excess amount.

Pets and Plants: You must have a certificate for a dog or cat age 3 months and older. It must clearly describe the animal, declare that the animal has been vaccinated against rabies within the past 36 months, and have a licensed veterinarian signature.

- Collar tags are not sufficient proof of immunization
- Be sure the vaccination does not expire while traveling in Canada
- The certificate is also required to bring the animal back into the United States

Exempt From These Rules: Assist dogs; healthy puppies and kittens under 3 months old with a health certificate, signed by a licensed veterinarian, indicating that the animal is too young to vaccinate.

Plants or plant material must be declared. For information, contact: Canadian Food Inspection Agency (CFIA), 59 Camelot Dr., Ottawa, OT K1A 0Y9; 613-225-2342.

Radio Communication Equipment

- Cell phone, PCS phone, citizens band (CB) or Family Radio Service radio allowed without prior registration
- Use of aircraft, marine or amateur radio allowed without prior authorization
- All other types of radio transmitting stations allowed with authorization letter from Industry Canada's Radiocommun-ication and Broadcasting Regulatory Branch

Special Permits: A CITIES (Convention on International Trade in Endangered Species) permit is required for any endangered species brought into Canada, including those kept as pets, and for any items made from them (e.g., coats, handbags, shoes). For information contact: Environment Canada, Canadian Wildlife Service at 819-997-1840.

An Export Permit may be required to take out of Canada objects more than 50 years old (e.g., fossils, archaeological artifacts, fine and decorative art, technological objects or books and archival material). Contact: Movable Cultural Property Program of Canadian Heritage, 15 Eddy St., 3rd Floor, Hull, Quebec, Canada K1A 0M5; 819-997-7761.

An Import Permit may be required for the importation of clothing, textiles, steel and certain agricultural products in excess of minimum quantities. For information contact: Department of Foreign Affairs and Int'l Trade, Export and Import Controls Bureau, Tower C, 4th Floor, LB Pearson Bldg, 125 Sussex Dr., Ottawa, OT K1A 0G2.

Vehicles

- Vehicles entering Canada for touring, including trailers not exceeding 8 feet 6 inches (2.6 m) in width are generally subject to quick and routine entry procedures.
- To leave or store a car, trailer or other goods in Canada while you leave the country you must pay import duty and taxes or present a valid permit. Canadian Customs officials issue permits at point of entry.
- You may not store a vacation trailer in Canada during the off-season.
- Vehicle registration cards required for Canadian travel.
- If driving a car other than your own, you must have written permission from the owner to use it.
- If driving a rented car, you must possess a copy of the contract.
- A valid U.S. driver's license is valid in Canada for time period specified by the individual provinces and territories.

- In all Canadian provinces and territories it is illegal to use radar detectors.
- Seat belts required for the driver and all passengers throughout Canada.

Headlights: Driving with vehicle headlights on for extended periods after dawn and before dusk is  a statutory requirement in provinces and territories.

- In Alberta, British Columbia, New Brunswick, Ontario and Prince Edward Island, lights must be turned on when light conditions restrict visibility to 500 feet (150 m).
- In Manitoba, lights must be turned on when light conditions restrict visibility to 200 feet (60 m).
- In Alberta, Yukon Territory, Northwest Territories and Nunavut, headlights must remain on at all times.
- Elsewhere in Canada, driving with headlights on during all hours of the day is advised.

FINANCIAL RESPONSIBILITY LAWS IN CANADA

When an accident involves death, injury or property damage, Canadian provinces and territories require evidence of financial responsibility. You may be asked to show this evidence at any time.

U.S. motorists should obtain from their own U.S. insurance companies a yellow Non-Resident Inter-Province Motor Vehicle Liability Insurance Card (accepted as evidence of financial responsibility throughout Canada). Those not carrying proper proof may be subject to a substantial fine (minimum $575). Fine varies in each province. If renting a vehicle, check with the rental car company.

The minimum liability insurance requirement is $200,000 in all provinces and territories except Quebec, which requires $50,000. Should the courts' judgments exceed these figures, motorists held accountable are responsible for paying the full amount.

If traveling in Quebec, discuss your collision, disability and bodily injury coverages with your insurance agent. Since Quebec's minimum requirement does not include bodily injury, coverage of $200,000 or more is recommended. Consider additional coverage (i.e., trip accident policy).

FOR UNITED STATES RESIDENTS RETURNING TO THE UNITED STATES

Everyone who seeks entry into the United States – whether foreign visitors, U.S. citizens, or U.S. lawful permanent residents – must be inspected at the point of entry. Random searches may be conducted by U.S. Customs and Border Protection agents.

U.S. Exemptions for a Stay in Canada No Less Than 48 hours

- You may bring back tax- and duty-free articles not exceeding $800 in retail value
- Any amount over the $800 exemption is subject to duty
- The exemption is allowed once every 30 days
- A family (related persons living in the same household) may combine its exemptions (a family of 6 is entitled to $4,800 worth of goods duty-free on 1 declaration, even if articles claimed by 1 member exceed that individual's $800 amount)
- Exemptions based on fair retail value (keep receipts of all purchases as proof of fair retail value)
- Exemptions apply to articles acquired only for personal or household use or as gifts, but not intended for sale
- The exemption may include 100 cigars, 200 cigarettes and 1 liter of liquor per person over age 21 (customs enforces state liquor laws)
- All articles claimed under this exemption must accompany you on your return

U.S. Exemptions for a Stay in Canada Less Than 48 hours

- You may bring back tax- and duty-free articles not exceeding $200 in retail value
- The exemption may include no more than 50 cigarettes, 10 cigars, 4 fluid ounces (150 milliliters) of alcoholic beverage or 150 milliliters of perfume containing alcohol
- A family may not combine purchases
- If purchases exceed the $200 exemption, you lose the exemption and all purchases become subject to duty
- All goods must be declared
- All articles claimed under this exemption must accompany you on your return

Gifts

- Gifts up to $100 fair retail value may be sent to friends or relatives in the United States provided no recipient receives more than 1 gift per day (need not be included in the $800 exemption)

- Gifts containing tobacco products, alcoholic beverages or perfume containing alcohol valued at more than $5 retail are excluded from this provision

- Write on outside of package the contents, retail value and "Unsolicited Gift"

Prohibited: Articles considered detrimental to the general welfare of the United States are prohibited entry: narcotics and dangerous drugs, drug paraphernalia, obscene articles and publications, seditious or treasonable matter, lottery tickets, hazardous items (fireworks, dangerous toys, toxic or poisonous substances) and switchblade knives. Any goods originating in the following countries are prohibited: Balkans, Burma, Cuba, Iran, Iraq, Liberia, Libya, North Korea, Sudan, Syria and Zimbabwe. Please note embargoes are not limited to these countries.

Restricted items include automobiles, biological materials (disease organisms and vectors for research), ceramic tableware, cultural treasures, firearms and ammunition, articles bearing marks or names copying or simulating trademarked articles or trade names (watches, cameras, perfumes), pirated copies of copyrighted articles (books, CDs, DVDs, audio- and video-tapes, computer programs), agricultural goods (plants and animal products) and pets, wildlife and fish.

You may bring into or take out of the United States an unlimited amount of money, however, if you transport more than $10,000 you must file a Form 4790 with U.S. Customs. Failure to comply can result in civil, criminal and/or forfeiture penalties. Monies include currency, traveler's checks, U.S. or foreign coins in circulation, money orders and negotiable instruments or investment securities in bearer form. For a currency reporting flier contact: U.S. Customs, P.O. Box 7407, Washington, D.C. 20044.

While some agricultural products of Canadian origin (fruits, some plants with phyto-sanitary certificates, meats, etc.) may be brought into the United States, many are restricted to prevent the introduction of plant and animal pests and diseases. All must be declared at the U.S. border. Write to APHIS, Dept. of Agriculture, 6505 Belcrest Rd., Hyattsville, MD 20782, for a free copy of *Traveler's Tips*. Write to U.S. Customs, P.O. Box 7407, Washington, D.C. 20044 for other

helpful leaflets: *Visiting the U.S.: Requirements for Non-Residents*, *Know Before You Go*, *Importing a Car*, and *Pets, Wildlife and U.S. Customs*.

FOR CANADA RESIDENTS ENTERING THE UNITED STATES

Native-born citizens of Canada:
- Passport not required (but is recommended)
- Proof of citizenship required (a birth certificate and photo ID)
- Proof of residence may be required

If traveling to the United States with a child, carry documentation proving your custodial rights. A person under age 18 traveling to the United States alone or with only 1 parent or another adult, must have certified documentation proving that the trip is permitted by both parents.

United States Customs permits Canadian residents to bring, free of duty, for personal use and not intended for sale: clothing, personal items and equipment appropriate to the trip, including 200 cigarettes, 50 cigars or 2 kilograms of tobacco, or proportionate amounts of each, and 1 liter of alcoholic beverage.

Visitors in the United States for at least 72 hours who have not claimed this exemption in the preceding 6 months may bring gifts totaling $100 (US) retail value. Perfume containing alcohol and valued at more than $5 retail, tobacco products and alcoholic beverages excluded from the gift provision.

Use of cell phones and General Radio Service Station (CB) is unrestricted.

FOR CANADA RESIDENTS RETURNING TO CANADA

The Canada Border Services Agency allows Canadian residents to bring, free of duty and taxes, goods valued up to $200 (CAN) any number of times a year, provided the visit to the United States is 48 hours or more and all goods accompany the purchaser (written declaration may be required).

You may claim a $50 (CAN) exemption on goods, excluding alcoholic beverages and tobacco products, if returning after an absence of 24 hours or more and are not using any other exemption. If bringing back more than $50 worth of goods, the regular duty and tax rate is levied on the entire value. This exemption may apply any number of times in a year.

If returning after 7 days or more in the United States (not counting departure day from Canada) you may claim up to a $750 (CAN) exemption on goods. Goods, other than alcohol and tobacco products, need not accompany you (written declaration may be required).

Permitted within the $200 and $750 exemptions: up to 50 cigars, 200 cigarettes, 200 tobacco sticks and 200 grams (6.4 oz) of tobacco, and up to 1.14 liters (40 oz) of liquor or 1.5 liters (1.6 qts) of wine or 8.5 liters (9 qts) of beer or ale (or its equivalent of 24 12-ounce bottles or cans). You must meet the minimum age requirement of the province or territory entered to claim alcohol or tobacco products.

Special Tariff: When exceeding the $200  or $750 exemption, a special rate of 7 percent combined duty and taxes is levied on the next $300 value in goods (except tobacco and alcohol) exceeding the maximum exemptible amounts, provided goods are of U.S origin. Regular duties apply on any additional amount. A 15 percent Harmonized Sales Tax (HST) (7 percent Goods and Services Tax (GST) and 8 percent provincial component) is charged on most goods and services supplied in Nova Scotia, New Brunswick and Newfoundland and Labrador. For information contact the Canada Border Services Agency before departing Canada. All extra goods must accompany you.

All exemptions are individual and may not be combined with those of other people. You may be asked to verify the length of your visit. Dated receipts normally constitute proof. Gifts (excluding alcoholic beverages, tobacco products and advertising matter) up to $60 (CAN) retail may be sent from abroad free of duty or taxes. For gifts valued at more than $60 (CAN), duty and taxes apply to amount exceeding $60. Gifts sent from abroad do not count against personal exemptions; gifts brought back must be included in exemptions.

NATIONAL PARKS ENTRANCE FEES

At Canada's national parks, the basic per person or per family entry fee gives visitors access to the park, scenic outlooks, picnic areas and a variety of facilities. Additional fees are charged for visitors who choose to use other recreational services such as campgrounds, special interpretation programs and golf courses.

To receive a free Parks Canada vacation planner, phone (888) 773-8888. Detailed information about the services, benefits, entry fees and discounts at all national parks and historic sites is available by calling the following numbers:

(800) 748-7275 for Alberta;

(902) 426-3436 for Atlantic provinces (Newfoundland and Labrador, New Brunswick, Nova Scotia and Prince Edward Island);

(604) 513-4777 for British Columbia;

(888)748-2928 for Manitoba;

(800) 748-7275 for Saskatchewan;

(800) 463-6769 for Québec;

(800) 661-0486 for Yukon Territory.

Points of Interest Index

Index Legend

NB...................national battlefield	NR.....................national river
NBP.............national battlefield park	NS.................national seashore
NC....................national cemetery	NWR............national wildlife refuge
NF......................national forest	PHP.........provincial historic(al) park
NHM..........national historic(al) monument	PHS.........provincial historic(al) site
NHP.............national historic(al) park	PP....................provincial park
NHS..............national historic(al) site	SF......................state forest
NL...................national lakeshore	SHM..........state historic(al) monument
NME...................national memorial	SHP.............state historic(al) park
NMO...................national monument	SHS..............state historic(al) site
NMP...............national military park	SME...................state memorial
NP......................national park	SP......................state park
NRA...............national recreation area	SRA...............state recreation area

 GEM: Points of Interest Offering a *Great Experience for Members*®

ARTS & CRAFTS

AUDITORIUMS

BATTLEFIELDS

BATTLE RE-ENACTMENTS

BEACHES

EXHIBITS & COLLECTIONS-AVIATION

EXHIBITS & COLLECTIONS-CIVIL WAR

EXHIBITS & COLLECTIONS-CLOCKS

EXHIBITS & COLLECTIONS-COINS

EXHIBITS & COLLECTIONS-DOLLS & TOYS

EXHIBITS & COLLECTIONS-INDIAN

EXHIBITS & COLLECTIONS-MUSIC

EXHIBITS & COLLECTIONS-RELIGIOUS ITEMS

EXHIBITS & COLLECTIONS-REVOLUTIONARY WAR

EXHIBITS & COLLECTIONS-SCIENCE

HALLS OF FAME

HISTORIC BUILDINGS & HOUSES

HISTORIC DOCUMENTS, MANUSCRIPTS & RARE BOOKS

HISTORIC SITES

INDIAN MOUNDS, REMAINS & RUINS

INDUSTRIAL TOURS

ISLANDS

MUSIC HALLS & OPERA HOUSES

MYTHICAL PERSONS & ANIMALS

NATIONALITIES & ETHNIC AREAS

NATURAL BRIDGES

NATURE CENTERS

NATURE TRAILS

PARKS, NATIONAL

PERFORMING ARTS ORGANIZATIONS

PIERS

PLANETARIUMS

RACETRACKS-AUTO

RACETRACKS-HORSE

RADIO & TV STATIONS

RELIGIOUS COLONIES

RESEARCH ORGANIZATIONS

RESTORED VILLAGES & SETTLEMENTS

ROCKS

SCENIC DRIVES

SCHOOLS

SCHOOLS-ACADEMIES

SCHOOLS-COLLEGES & UNIVERSITIES

SCHOOLS-INSTITUTES

SIGHTSEEING-AIRCRAFT RIDES & TOURS

SIGHTSEEING-HOT AIR BALLOON RIDES & TOURS

SIGHTSEEING TOURS

SIGHTSEEING TOURS-ARCHITECTURAL

SIGHTSEEING TOURS-BOATS

SIGHTSEEING TOURS-BUS & TROLLEY

SIGHTSEEING TOURS-HOUSE & GARDEN

SIGHTSEEING TOURS-RAFTING & CANOEING

SIGHTSEEING TOURS-TRAIN

SKI & SNOWBOARDING RESORTS & AREAS

THEATERS-DINNER SHOWS

THEATERS-PLAYS, DRAMAS & MUSICALS

TOWERS

TRAILS-SUMMER RECREATION

VISITOR CENTERS

VISITOR INFORMATION

WILDLIFE SANCTUARIES

WINERIES

ZOOLOGICAL PARKS & EXHIBITS

ZOOLOGICAL PARKS & EXHIBITS-CHILDREN'S ZOOS

🆂 *Attraction Admission Discount Index*

Bed & Breakfast Lodgings Index

Some bed and breakfasts listed below might have historical significance. Those properties are also referenced in the Historical index. The indication that continental [CP] or full breakfast [BP] is included in the room rate reflects whether a property is a Bed-and-Breakfast facility.

NEW YORK
ACCOMMODATIONS

ONTARIO
ACCOMMODATION

Country Inns Index

Some of the following country inns can also be considered as bed-and-breakfast operations. The indication that continental [CP] or full breakfast [BP] is included in the room rate reflects whether a property is a Bed-and-Breakfast facility.

NEW YORK
ACCOMMODATIONS

RESTAURANTS

Historical Lodgings & Restaurants Index

Some of the following historical lodgings can also be considered as bed-and-breakfast operations. The indication that continental [CP] or full breakfast [BP] is included in the room rate reflects whether a property is a Bed-and-Breakfast facility.

Resorts Index

Many establishments are located in resort areas; however, the following places have extensive on-premises recreational facilities:

Comprehensive City Index

Here is an alphabetical list of all cities appearing in this TourBook® guide. Cities are presented by state/province. Page numbers under the POI column indicate where points of interest text begins. Page numbers under the L&R column indicate where lodging and restaurant listings begin.

Comprehensive City Index (cont'd)

Comprehensive City Index (cont'd)

Comprehensive City Index (cont'd)

Comprehensive City Index (cont'd)

Travel Shopping Made Easy!

LUGGAGE • TRAVEL ACCESSORIES • BUSINESS CASES
DUFFELS & BACKPACKS

eTravel Store offers everything needed to make travel better — quality luggage, handy accessories, business cases, duffels, backpacks and more. All delivered right to your door, quality guaranteed.

Before your next trip, check out eTravel Store at participating club websites on aaa.com.

AAA TourBook® Guide Savings Section

At home and away, your AAA membership entitles you to exclusive savings.

Save every day of the year at thousands of participating AAA Show Your Card & Save® businesses — from hotels and car rental to movie theaters and attractions. Visit one of more than 1,000 club offices or AAA.com/save for national Show Your Card & Save offers or a complete list of savings by location.

Plus, enjoy special limited-time extras and savings at participating Show Your Card & Save lodgings, restaurants, and attractions with the following coupon offers for members.

With so many money-saving opportunities, it pays to be a AAA member!

Members Save With Our Partners

SAVINGS. SELECTION. SATISFACTION.—When contacting one of these lodging partners, you will be given AAA/CAA's best rates for your dates of stay. Your valid membership card must be presented at check-in. Select the chain you want and have your membership card available when making a reservation and checking in. Let the property know if you are dissatisfied with any part of your stay. If the matter cannot be resolved, you are entitled to recompense (see page 17).

Offer good at time of publication; chains and offers may change without notice. Lodging partners offering discounts to AAA/CAA members may vary in Mexico and the Caribbean.

| Visit | Over 1,000 AAA/CAA Offices | Click | AAA.com | Call | 866-AAA-SAVE |

Show Your Card & Save

Members Save With Our Partners

These National Show Your Card & Save® partners provide the listed member benefits. Admission tickets that offer greater discounts may be available for purchase at the local AAA/CAA club. A maximum of six tickets is available at the discount price at the gate. Visit AAA.com to discover all the great Show Your Card & Save® discounts in your area.

SeaWorld/Busch Gardens AAA.com/SeaWorld

- Save $5 on 1-day gate admission at SeaWorld, Busch Gardens, and Sesame Place
- Save $3 on 1-day admission at Water Country USA and Adventure Island

- Save 10% on select up-close dining. Reservations are required; visit Guest Relations for details AAA.com/BuschGardens

Six Flags Theme Parks

- 10% OFF Brunch with Bugs
- 10% OFF merchandise purchases of $15 or more at all Six Flags operated locations.

Universal Orlando AAA.com/Universal

- Save $4 on a 2-day/2-park pass at Universal Orlando's theme parks (savings apply to tickets purchased at the gate)
- Save 10% on select dining and souvenirs at both Universal Orlando theme parks and at select Universal CityWalk Orlando restaurants (excludes Emeril's)

Universal Studios Hollywood

- Save $3 on a 1-day Universal Studios Hollywood pass (savings applies to tickets purchased at the gate) AAA.com/Universal

- Save 10% on select dining and souvenirs at Universal Studios Hollywood and Universal CityWalk

Gray Line
AAA.com/GrayLine

- Save 10% on sightseeing tours of 1 day or less

Landry's Seafood House, The Crab House, Chart House, Muer Seafood Restaurants, Joe's Crab Shack and Aquarium and Downtown Aquarium Restaurants

- 10% discount on food and non-alcoholic beverages at all of the above restaurants.

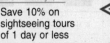

- 10% discount on novelty merchandise at Joe's Crab Shacks and Aquarium and Downtown Aquarium Restaurants.

Hard Rock Cafe

- Save 10% on food, beverage and merchandise at all U.S. and select Canadian and international locations

Restaurant Partner Savings applies to AAA/CAA members and up to five guests.

Tanger Outlet Centers www.tangeroutlet.com

- Save up to 20% on total purchase at select merchants with AAA/CAA coupon booklet
- Member BONUS: FREE $5 gift card for each additional Tanger Outlet Center visited after first within same calendar year
- Show membership card and register at the AAA customer service desk when you visit